Frommer's

FRUGAL TRAVELER'S GUIDES

Italy

FROM $50 A DAY

by Stephen Brewer,
Barbara Coeyman Hults &
Patricia Schultz

Macmillan • USA

ABOUT THE AUTHORS

Stephen Brewer has written many guidebooks and articles on Italy and spends most of his time traveling in Italy.

Barbara Coeyman Hults has commuted to Italy several times a year for many decades, and is the author of many guidebook and magazine articles on Rome and southern Italy. She lives in Manhattan when not in *bella Italia*.

Patricia Schultz is the author of numerous books and articles on travel in Italy. She is a contributor to *Condè Nast Traveler* and *Newsweek International*, and is a co-author of *Frommer's Europe from $50 a Day*.

MACMILLAN TRAVEL

A Simon & Schuster Macmillan Company
1633 Broadway
New York, NY 10019

Find us online at **http://www.mgr.com/travel**
or on America Online at Keyword: **Frommer's**

ISBN 0-02860916-6
ISSN 1091-9430

Editors: Alice Fellows, Reid Bramblett, Suzanne Roe
Production Editor: John Carroll
Digital Cartography by Roberta Stockwell and Ortelius Design
Design by Michele Laseau

SPECIAL SALES

Bulk purchases (10+ copies) of Frommer's and selected Macmillan travel guides are available to corporations, organizations, mail-order catalogs, institutions, and charities at special discounts, and can be customized to suit individual needs. For more information write to: Special Sales, Macmillan General Reference, 1633 Broadway, New York, NY 10019.

Manufactured in the United States of America

Contents

4   Settling into Rome   68

by Barbara Coeyman Hults

5   What to See & Do in Rome   109

by Barbara Coeyman Hults

List of Maps

INVITATION TO THE READER

In researching this book, we discovered many wonderful places—hotels, restaurants, shops, offbeat sights, and more. We're sure you'll find others. Please tell us about them, so we can share the information with your fellow travelers in upcoming editions. If you were disappointed with a recommendation, we'd love to know that, too. Please write to:

Frommer's Italy from $50 a Day, 1st Edition
Macmillan Travel
1633 Broadway
New York, NY 10019

AN ADDITIONAL NOTE

Please be advised that travel information is subject to change at any time—and this is especially true of prices. We therefore suggest that you write or call ahead for confirmation when making your travel plans. The authors, editors, and publisher cannot be held responsible for the experiences of readers while traveling. Your safety is important to us, however, so we encourage you to stay alert and be aware of your surroundings. Keep a close eye on cameras, purses, and wallets, all favorite targets of thieves and pickpockets.

SYMBOLS & ABBREVIATIONS

✪ Frommer's Favorites

Hotels, restaurants, and attractions you should not miss.

The following abbreviations are used for credit cards:

AE	American Express	EU	Eurocard
CB	Carte Blanche	JCB	Japan Credit Bank
DC	Diners Club	MC	MasterCard
DISC	Discover	V	Visa
ER	enRoute		

ABBREVIATIONS FOR LOCATIONS:

Borgo	B.	Riva	Rv.
Calle	C.	Ruga	R.
Campiello	Cplo.	Salizzada	Sz.
Campo	Cam.	Strada	S.
Corso	Cor.	Via	V.
Fondamenta	Fond.	Viale	Vle.
Largo	Lgo.	Vicola	Vc.
Piazza	Pz.	del/dei/d.	
Piazzale	Pzle.	delle	

Earthquakes Strike Assisi

In the fall of 1997, earthquakes and aftershocks rocked the heart of Umbria. In Assisi, Santa Chiara church and the Duomo were both damaged, but the Basilica of San Francesco was the worst hit. Frescoes by Cimabue and his followers were destroyed, and Giotto's *Life of St. Francis* frescoes were seriously damaged. Four people, including two Franciscan friars, were killed when part of the ceiling of the upper church collapsed. Restorations are underway, but the basilica's future remains uncertain. All hotels are open and functional in Assisi, however. For the latest details on the restoration of the basilica, call the Assisi tourist office at 075/812-534.

The Best of Italy

Italy is one of the most beautiful, diverse, and culturally rich countries in the world. The richness of its art treasures is legend, and is matched by the beauty of its countryside and the wonders of its cuisine. It can be bewildering to plan your trip with so many options vying for your attention. We've tried to make this task easier by pointing you in the direction of at least a few of its must-see treasures and its myriad experiences, although the choices we've made below only scratch the surface of Italy's offerings. You will soon find out for yourself that Italy is a land of enchanting discoveries, and whether this is your first trip to the peninsula or your fiftieth, you're bound to come away with your own personal *best-of* list.

1 The $50-a-Day Premise

Italy is a very expensive country, so you may wonder how to see and do everything without going flat broke. We've tried to help you out with insider advice on how to keep your basic living costs—a livable room and three meals a day—to as little as $50 a day. The assumption is that two adults traveling together will share the cost of a room. The costs of sightseeing, transportation, and entertainment are all extras, not included in this budget, but we provide tips on saving money on those things as well. And many of the best things are free, or almost free.

We've sought out affordable, even very affordable lodgings—family-run pensiones, hostels that are sometimes located in Renaissance palazzi, convent hotels that offer great rooms, and central locations for a song—and also suggested discount strategies for staying in more luxurious lodgings. And we've also included splurges—special places to stay or outstanding restaurants that you might not want to miss.

2 The Best Travel Experiences for Free— or Almost Free

Perhaps the best experiences of all are the cities themselves, and the enjoyment of the country's everyday life.

- **In Rome:** One of the greatest pleasures of being in Rome is just hanging out and watching the life around you. Good places to go

Italy

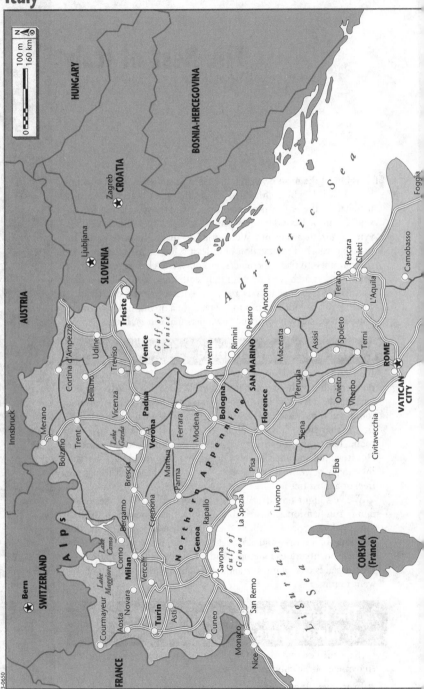

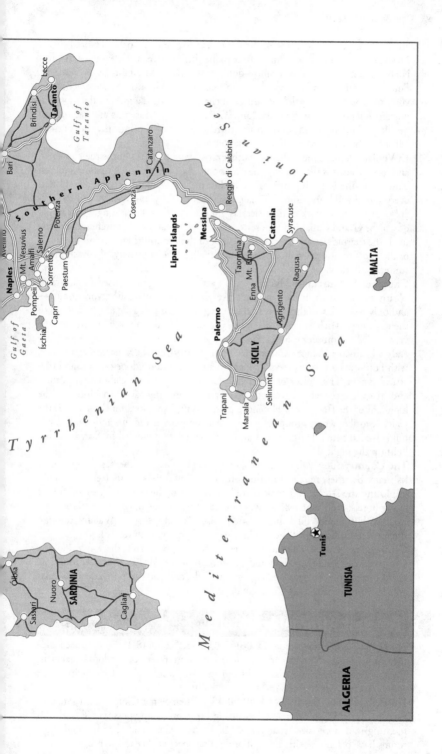

are the Campo de' Fiori, site of the flower market, and the ocher-colored Piazza Navona, one of the most beautiful of baroque sites. The must-see Fontana di Trevi is not the only fountain in Rome—don't miss the two fountains by Bernini, the Fountain of the Four Rivers and the Fountain of the Moor. In St. Peter's Basilica you can view Michelangelo's *Pietà* free of charge, or attend a mass in the most important religious site in Christendom. The Capitoline Museums are free the last Sunday of each month, and on the third Sunday of the month, the Vatican Museums have free admission (see chapter 5).

- **In Venice:** Perhaps more than any other city, Venice's best sight is the city itself, and its very heart is the magnificent Piazza San Marco, with its Campanile and Bell Tower and the imposing Byzantine Basilica di San Marco. Every hidden corner, every sound will bring home the realization that this city, ingeniously and remarkably built on a network of tiny islets, is unlike any other. For a song, you can sail down the Grand Canal (on vaporetto no. 1), past palazzi and churches, and draw up at the marble steps at the northwest foot of the Rialto Bridge, and in the shade of the city's most important bridge, watch the beehive of activity, all awash in the sunset's soft glow.

- **Churches & Museums:** Much of Italy's artistic heritage is housed in churches. Nearly every church in Italy in nearly every town contains major works of art—and only a very few of them have begun a trend of charging a small admission. For the most part, Michelangelos, Tiepolos, Giottos, and other masters are free for the viewing. Many museums have free days.

- **Italy's Festivals:** Venice's **Carnavale** (late February), can be a magical experience, with fantastic costumes everywhere and many free and outdoor musical and theatrical events. The **Palios** of Siena and Asti both begin with elaborate pageantry and historical reenactments, followed by their exciting races. In Florence, the highlight of the feast day of Florence's patron saint, San Giovanni (June 24), is the Calcio Storico, where groups of young men compete in a rough-and-tumble, no-holds-barred game that goes back to the Renaissance, followed by fireworks that light up the night sky.

- **The Countryside:** Walking in the countryside in Tuscany, the best way to enjoy its many beauties, reflected in the paintings of countless artists (see chapter 7). Exploring the streets and ancient wall of Ferrara by bicycle (bicycles are free at many hotels; see chapter 8). Driving or traveling by bus up the Great Dolomite Road with its wonderful scenic mountain vistas (see chapter 11). Walking through the untouched fishing villages of the Cinque Terre (see chapter 14).

- **Cruising the Lakes:** The Italian lakes are best enjoyed from the water, looking toward garden-clad shorelines and the curtain of the Alps in the background. A fleet of ferries ply the lakes and charge very little, and you can purchase a pass that entitles you to cruise Lake Como all day.

3 The Best Affordable Hotels

- **Hotel Bel Soggiorno** (Rome; ☎ 06/48-81-701, fax 06/48-15-755): Once inside the not-very-attractive entrance, you'll love its rooftop terrace overlooking ancient Roman sites and its airy high-ceilinged rooms, presided over by its with-it (*in gamba*) owner. See chapter 5.

- **Hotel Bolognese** (Rome; ☎ 06/49-00-45): When owner Giorgio Calderara isn't carefully watching his hotel and ensuring his guests' happiness, you'll find him painting in a closet-size studio. The hotel is very clean and cheerful, and three rooms have balconies with a neighborhood perspective. See chapter 4.

- **Hotel Venezia** (Rome; ☎ 06/44-57-101): In a unique 18th-century building, full of antiques and historical pieces in ample-sized rooms, this hotel in a quiet neighborhood not far from the train station is presided over by an exceedingly helpful staff, and serves a huge buffet breakfast that includes fruit from the owner's garden. Tell them you are a Frommer reader for a discount. See chapter 4.
- **Pontifical Irish College** (Rome; ☎ 06/70-45-46-78/9; fax 6/70-47-61-50): A bargain, especially for families, this hotel has simple but comfortable rooms, a swimming pool, squash and tennis courts, a lovely garden, and quiet from traffic, yet it's located between the Colosseum and St. John Lateran, convenient to sightseeing and to the Metro. See chapter 4.
- **Pensione Alessandra** (Florence; ☎ 055/28-34-38; fax 055/21-06-19): On a narrow cobblestone street, lined with medieval towers and early Renaissance palazzi, the antiquity of high ceilings and spacious rooms is appreciated, but so is the modernity of new bright bathrooms. Free air-conditioning can be requested. Signora Anna runs a lovely operation. See chapter 6.
- **Hotel Bellettini** (Florence; ☎ 055/21-35-61; fax 055/28-35-51): A stone plaque hanging in the breakfast salon tells us that there has been a hotel in this Renaissance palazzo since the 1600s. Handsome antique pieces, stained-glass windows, and hand-painted wood-coffered ceilings guarantee the distinctive air of this gem of a small hotel. See chapter 6.
- **Hotel Firenze** (Florence; ☎ 055/26-83-01; fax 055/21-23-70): The hotel is centrally located and very modernized, thanks to a multiple-year renovation completed in 1996. Clean, contemporary accommodations are in a historical palazzo located in a picturesque piazzetta snuggled between the Duomo and Piazza Signoria. See chapter 6.
- **Hotel Roma** (Bologna; ☎ 051/22-63-22; fax 051/23-99-09): The Roma is one of the most gracious hotels in town, with a great location only steps away from the Piazza Maggiore. The large guest rooms are full of old-fashioned comforts, roomy armchairs, and huge closets, and top-floor rooms have terraces. See chapter 8.
- **B&B Locanda Borgonuovo** (Ferrara; ☎ 0532/24-80-00): This elegant bed-and-breakfast near the Este palace has large and very stylish rooms filled with antiques and equipped with posh new baths. A hearty breakfast is served in the lovely rear garden, and bicycles and discount coupons for museums and nearby shops are available. See chapter 8.
- **Hotel Geremia** (Venice; ☎ 041/71-62-45; fax 52-42-342): Convenient to both the train station and strained budgets, this small, efficient, and seamlessly run hotel has recently been redone top to toe. The results are a sensitivity and attention to aesthetics that are a rarity in the one- and two-star hotel world. See chapter 9.
- **Hotel Bernardi-Semenzato** (Venice; ☎ 041/52-22-72-57; fax 52-22-424): Nestled between the resplendent Ca' d'Oro art gallery and the Rialto Bridge, everything inside this palazzo is bright and fresh, comfortably overseen by the young Pepoli family whose long-term plans may be an upgrade in category, so grab these rates while you can. See chapter 9.
- **Alloggi ai do Mori** (Venice; ☎ 041/52-04-817 or 52-89-293; fax 041/52-05-328): The ever-evolving, always improving hotel (one season bright new wall-paper, the next new ultrafirm orthopedic mattresses) sits just steps from the Piazza San Marco. From the top floors' sunny rooms, the Basilica di San Marco's Byzantine domes seem as if within reach. See chapter 9.
- **Locanda Fiorita** (Venice; ☎ 041/52-34-754; fax 041/52-28-043): Situated on its own hidden campiello just off the expansive Campo Santo Stefano—each postcard-perfect—the name of this inn refers to the secular wisteria vine whose late

spring blossoms drape this Venetian-red villa in lush purple buds. Two lucky rooms open onto private, tiny terraces that face the small piazza. See chapter 9.

- **Hotel Locanda Remedio** (Venice; ☎ 041/52-06-232; fax 041/52-10-485): Sunlight filters through the oversize leaded-glass windows of the ballroom-size breakfast room in this converted palazzo, 10 minutes away from Piazza San Marco. It's not the least expensive game in town, but the young, ambitious owner offers amenities otherwise found in hotels at twice this price. See chapter 9.
- **Hotel Menardi** (Cortina d'Ampezzo; ☎ 0436/24-00; fax 0436/86-21-83): This charming hostelry combines the luxury and service of a fine hotel with the home-like comfort of a mountain inn. The hotel looks out on forests and mountains, and offers half-board with an excellent cuisine. See chapter 11.
- **Doriagrande Hotel** (Milan; ☎ 02/66-96-696; fax 02/66-96-669): This luxury hotel offers a special price that applies to weekends (Friday and Saturday nights), most of August, and the Christmas/New Year holiday (check for exact dates before booking). Stylish, oversize guest rooms are exquisitely appointed, and the buffet breakfast is sumptuous. See chapter 12.

4 The Best Affordable Restaurants

The traditional Italian meal starts with an *antipasto* (appetizer), followed by a *primo piatto* (first course), usually a pasta dish or a soup. The *secondo piatto* (second course) is meat, fish, or chicken, and a vegetable side dish (*contorno*) usually accompanies it, followed by *frutta* (fruit) or a *dolce* (dessert). Most places expect their diners to take at least the *primo* and *secondo*, and the waiter will invariably "remind" you of this lest you "forget." *Pane e coperto* ("bread and cover charge"), ranging from 1,000L to 2,500L (65¢ to $1.55) per person, is an inexpensive but unavoidable menu item, a charge you'll have to pay at all restaurants. Also note that a tip (*servizio*) of 10% to 15% will automatically be added to your bill.

- **La Campana** (Rome; ☎ 06/68-67-820): Few can resist the simple, traditional grace of possibly Rome's oldest restaurant. A plain trattoria with a fine antipasto and fresh fish array, and with veal dishes a specialty, it's just the place for a lovely introduction to Rome. See chapter 4.
- **Le Maschere** (Rome; ☎ 06/68-79-494): Come to this restaurant to try Calabrese cuisine (virtually unknown in America). The atmosphere is festive, and at night it's romantic. On weekends there's music. See chapter 4.
- **Il Fontanone** (Rome; ☎ 06/58-17-312): A favorite just across the Ponte Sisto from the Campo dei Fiori area, where locals and tourists rub elbows happily. The owner, Pino, makes sure that everything is country-fresh. See chapter 4.
- **Trattoria Mario** (Rome; ☎ 06/58-03-809): In Trastevere, this charming place, decorated with the work of neighborhood artists, is an outstanding bargain. The *menu turistico* is full of variety, making it a visitors' favorite. See chapter 4.
- **Trattoria Le Mossacce** (Florence; ☎ 055/29-43-61): Don't be fooled by its bright, ordinary dining room—the food is anything but ordinary here. This is straightforward *cucina toscana*, deftly prepared and served in a lively and pleasant atmosphere. See chapter 6.
- **Trattoria Cibreo** (Florence; ☎ 055/23-41-100): The menu of this lesser-priced trattoria of the chef/owner comes from the creative kitchen of the premier ristorante next door. The ambience is rustic chic, the menu something of a revelation, inspired by traditional Tuscan recipes. See chapter 6.
- **Osteria alle Botteghe** (Venice; ☎ 041/52-28-181): Between the relaxed atmosphere, the wide selection of possibilities, the option of standing with a sandwich

at the bar with the neighborhood regulars, or sitting for a pizza or elaborate meal (less cheap) at a few back tables, this neighborhood tavern/pizzeria boasts another major advantage: It's easy to find. See chapter 9.

- **Vino Vino** (Venice; ☎ 041/52-37-027): By now this is everyone's favorite (after your first meal you'll see why), so come early or wait in line at Venice's best-stocked wine bar. With a short menu of simple, well-prepared food, you can style your own wine tasting by the glass, order up the day's delicious pasta, and take in the mixed crowd of hipsters and oldsters, tourists, and Venice's well-heeled, all sharing communal tables. See chapter 9.

- **A Le Do Spade** (Venice; ☎ 041/52-10-574): By the time Casanova took up his regular spot at the bar for his daily glass of wine (or two), this atmospheric wine bar had already been drawing a standing-room-only crowd for 300 years. You'll want to linger forever—and now you can, with a dozen or so tables and as many pastas and entrees. See chapter 9.

- **Pizzeria da Sandro** (Venice; ☎ 041/52-34-894): Everyone loves pizza, though not everyone north of Naples knows how to make a good one. Sandro has a dozen varieties to prove he's mastered the art—you might want to make a return trip to try out his pastas that are just as good. See chapter 9.

- **Da Giulio** (Lucca; ☎ 0583/55-948): Dazzled foreigners and discerning locals agree that this big, airy, and forever busy trattoria is one of Tuscany's undisputed stars. Save up your appetite and come for a full-blown Tuscan feast. See chapter 7.

- **Trattoria Da Bruno** (Milan; ☎ 02/73-00-29): It's well worth the trek out to this attractive, family-run place, just off the Corso Indipendenza, about a 15-minute walk east of the duomo. A fixed-price menu is usually offered, consisting of the freshest ingredients in the kitchen that day, at a price that rarely edges over the 20,000L ($13.15) mark. See chapter 12.

- **La Cantinetta** (Barolo; ☎ 0173/56-198): Two brothers, Maurilo and Paolo Chiappetto, do a fine job of introducing guests to the pleasures of the Piedmontese table in their cozy dining room grouped around an open hearth. The wonderful house wines come from the vines that run right up to the door of this delightful restaurant. See chapter 13.

- **C'era una Volta** (Turin; ☎ 011/65-04-589): The food is authentically Turinese and never seems to stop coming. A tasting menu is something of a splurge, but well worth it to experience the wonderfully prepared dishes in this unusual place. See chapter 13.

5 The Best Museums

A list of best museums can hardly scratch the surface of Italy's artistic and historic treasures. The ones below are, however, a short list of must-sees, famous throughout the world.

- **Musei Vaticani (Vatican Museums)** (The Vatican): This huge complex contains treasures accumulated by the popes from all over the globe. Most famous, of course, is the (not without controversy) restored Sistine Chapel of Michelangelo. The frescoes of Raphael and the *Belvedere Apollo* should not be missed. Greco-Roman antiquities, Renaissance art—the collections are endless. See chapter 5.

- **Museo Nazionale di Villa Giulia** (Rome): Mystery attaches itself to the Etruscans, the precursors of the ancient Romans. They left a legacy of bronze and marble sculpture, sarcophagi, and jewelry. The sophistication of their design is astonishing. See chapter 5.

- **Galleria degli Uffizi** (Florence): Where painting is concerned, this museum is Italy's crown jewel. Its collection is unsurpassed, and most of the important Renaissance masters are represented here, notably Botticelli's famous painting, *Allegory of Spring*. See chapter 6.
- **Bargello Palace and Museum** (Florence): The severely angular 12th-century exterior of the Bargello strongly expresses the raw power of the governing magistrate who built it. Its collection of sculpture and decorative accessories is outstanding. See chapter 6.
- **Pitti Palace** (Florence): The Pittis were the Medicis' major rivals, and they moved into this palazzo in 1560. Today, it houses a museum containing everything from paintings by Renaissance artists (Raphael and Titian) to works by modern artists, and Napoléon's bathtub. See chapter 6.
- **Galleria Nazionale dell'Umbria** (Perugia): On the uppermost floor of the Palazzo dei Priori, this collection of Tuscan and Umbrian painting includes works by Perugino, Piero della Francesco, Duccio, Fra Angelico, Benozzo Gozzoli, and others. See chapter 7.
- **Gallerie dell'Accademia** (Venice): This rich museum contains hundreds of paintings, many of them Venetian, executed between 1300 and 1790. Among the highlights here are works by Bellini, Giorgione, Carpaccio, and Titian. See chapter 9.
- **Pinacoteca di Brera** (Milan): Although Milan is usually thought of as a business city, it is an important art city as well. The Brera Picture Gallery, in a 17th-century palace, is especially rich in paintings from the schools of Lombardy and Venice. See chapter 12.
- **Museo Poldi-Pezzoli (Poldi-Pezzoli Museum)** (Milan): The art collection o the museum's namesake is the base for one of Italy's most influential museums. The collection includes Persian carpets, portraits by Cranach of Martin Luther and his wife, works by Botticelli and Bellini, and a collection of decorative art. See chapter 12.
- **Museo Archeologico Nazionale (National Archeological Museum)** (Naples): The region around Naples has been a rich source of archeological finds, and the museum contains one of the best collections in the world of Greco-Roman antiquities. Many artifacts excavated from Pompeii and Herculaneum are here, as well as the Renaissance collections of the Farnese family.

6 The Best Cathedrals

- **Basilica di San Pietro (St. Peter's Basilica)** (The Vatican): When the old Roman basilica of Constantine was in danger of collapsing, the Renaissance popes commissioned plans for the largest, most impressive cathedral that the world had ever seen. Amid the rich decor of gilt, marble, and mosaics are countless artworks, including Michelangelo's *Pietà*. An elevator ride up the tower to Michelangelo's dome provides breathtaking views of Rome. See chapter 5.
- **Il Duomo (Santa Maria del Fiore)** (Florence): With an exterior of pink, green, and white marble, and full of world-class art, it's one of the largest and most distinctive religious buildings in Italy. A view of its dome, designed by Brunelleschi using what was then a radical new technique, it dominates the city of Florence. Beside the cathedral is Giotto's Campanile, and the Baptistery with Ghiberti's famous bronze doors. See chapter 6.
- **St. Francis' Basilica** (Assisi): Consecrated in 1253, the cathedral dedicated to St. Francis is one of the highlights of Umbria and the site of many religious

pilgrimages. The interior was decorated by Cimabue and Giotto, who introduced a new kind of figurative realism in art. See chapter 7.

- **Basilica di San Vitale** (Ravenna): This ancient octagonal domed Byzantine church dates from the mid-6th century, and it is famous for its celebrated mosaics, in brilliant greens and golds, lit by translucent panels. In the apse, Christ is astride the world with saints and angels, with the Empress Theodora to his right and Emperor Justinian to the left. See chapter 8.

- **Basilica di San Marco** (Venice): The sumptuously Byzantine Basilica di San Marco, replete with five mosquelike bulbed domes and the famous *quadriga* of four bronze horses, honors St. Mark the Evangelist, Venice's patron saint, whose bones were stolen by two enterprising merchants and smuggled into Venice from Alexandria, Egypt. San Marco's cavernous interior is exquisitely gilded with Byzantine mosaics added over some seven centuries and covering every inch of the ceiling and pavements alike. The originals of the celebrated *quadriga* are now in the museum. The church's greatest treasure is the enamel- and jewel-encrusted golden altarpiece known as the Pala d'Oro. See chapter 9.

- **Il Duomo, Milan:** Begun in 1386, and finally completed in 1809 on orders of Napoléon, Il Duomo of Milan is an ornate and unusual building. Massed around a triangular gable bristling with 135 pointed and chiseled spires, it's both massive and airy at the same time. The interior is as severe as its exterior is ornate. One of the most remarkable buildings in Italy, it's often overlooked. See chapter 12.

7 The Best Ancient Sites

- **Ostia Antica** (Latium): During the height of the Roman Empire, Ostia ("mouth" in Latin) was the harbor town set at the point where the Tiber flowed into the sea. In the early 1900s archeologists excavated the ruins of hundreds of ancient buildings, many of which can be viewed. See chapter 5.

- **Il Foro Romano (Roman Forum)** (Rome): Two thousand years ago, most of the known world was directly affected by decisions made in the Roman Forum. Although you'll see only a rubble-strewn version of the site, it is still evocative of the great Roman center that once stood here. See chapter 5.

- **Il Palatino (The Palatine Hill)** (Rome): According to legend, this hillock was the site where Romulus and Remus (the orphaned infant twins who survived in the wild by suckling a she-wolf) eventually founded the city. Although it's one of the seven hills of ancient Rome, it's hard to distinguish it as such because of the urban congestion that rises all around it. See chapter 5.

- **Il Coliseo (The Coliseum)** (Rome): In this massive amphitheater, today amid a maze of modern traffic, the Coliseum was once the setting for gladiatorial contests and other games whose cruelty was a noted characteristic of the Roman Empire. All three of the ancient world's classical styles (Doric, Ionic, and Corinthian) are superimposed in tiers one above the other. See chapter 5.

- **Villa Adriana (Hadrian's Villa)** (near Tivoli): The massive and beautiful villa from A.D. 134 was excavated in the 1500s by the Renaissance popes. Its builder was the Emperor Hadrian, who wanted to incorporate the widespread wonders of his empire into one fantastic building site. See chapter 5.

- **Ercolano (Herculaneum)** (near Naples): Legend says that it was founded by Hercules. The historical facts tell us that it was buried under rivers of volcanic mud one fateful day in A.D. 79 after the eruption of Vesuvius. Hundreds of timbered structures that would otherwise have rotted over the course of time were thus preserved, giving us some of the best examples of houses to survive from the ancient world. See chapter 15.

- **Pompeii** (Campania): Once it was an opulent resort filled with 25,000 wealthy Romans. In A.D. 79, the same eruption that devastated Herculaneum (see above) buried Pompeii under at least 20 feet of volcanic ash. Since the 18th century when excavation began, the ruins and its treasures have been a renowned site throughout the world. See chapter 15.
- **Valle dei Templi (Valley of the Temples)** (Agrigento, Sicily): Although most of it lies in ruins, this is one of the most beautiful classical sites in Europe, especially in February and March when the almond trees surrounding it burst into pink blossoms. One of the site's five temples dates from as early as 520 B.C.; another—although never completed—ranks as one of the largest temples in the ancient world. See chapter 16.
- **Segesta** (near Trapani, Sicily): Even its site is impressive: a rocky outcropping surrounded on most sides by a jagged ravine. Built around 430 B.C. by the Greeks, Segesta's Doric colonnade is one of the most graceful in the ancient world. Segesta is stark, mysterious, and highly evocative of the ancient world. See chapter 16.
- **Selinunte** (near Castelvetrano, Sicily): Although its massive columns lie scattered on the ground, as if an earthquake had punished its builders, this is a favorite ancient ruin in Italy. Built by immigrants from Syracuse into an important trading port around 600 B.C., and a bitter rival of the neighboring city of Segesta (see above), Selinunte was destroyed around 400 B.C., and again in 250 B.C. by the Carthaginians. See chapter 16.

8   The Best Offbeat & Outdoor Experiences

- **Outdoors in the Parco Nazionale di Gran Paradiso** (Valle d'Aosta): One of Europe's largest tracts of unspoiled nature spreads across more than 1,400 square miles, covering valleys, mountain peaks, forests, and pasturelands. Ibex, chamoix, and other Alpine fauna roam wild, and humans can also roam these wilds via a vast network of trails, and can also kayak, ride horseback, and cross-country ski. The park office in Aosta provides all the information you need to enjoy this magnificent park (☎ 0165/44-126). See chapter 13.
- **Hiking along the Cinque Terre:** So named for the five villages that cling to cliffs plunging into the Mediterranean south of Genoa and north of La Spezia, this is one of the most scenic and blessedly undeveloped stretches of coastline in Western Europe. Centuries-old goat tracks link the five villages, providing splendid seaside walks amidst vineyards, olive groves, and forests. See chapter 14.
- **Touring the Abruzzi Massif:** A short drive southeast of Rome, amid the highest of the Apennine mountain range, this landlocked district boasts an odd, arid topography riddled with underground caverns, mountains, lakes, gullies, high plateaus, and fertile grazing fields. A circumnavigation of the Abruzzi Massif will take you through the most savage landscapes of the Parco Nazionale d'Abruzzo, with its bizarrely striated rock walls, clannish local families, and 155 square miles of mostly beech and maple forests.
- **Exploring the Campi Flegrei (Phlaegrean Fields):** Bubbling and steaming with geologic emissions, and rich in sites whose architecture was developed by the ancient Greeks and Romans, this is one of the weirdest places in Italy. The instability of the region means that its altitude above sea level changes by several inches at regular intervals.

One of the region's highlights is the Greek colony of Cuma (sometimes spelled Cumae), founded in the 8th century B.C. and believed to be the oldest archeological site in Italy. En route from Naples, you'll pass through the town of Pozzuoli, site of a massive ancient Roman amphitheater and hometown of Sophia Loren. Lago d'Averna, another crater lake you'll see en route, was believed by Cicero to be the entrance to the Underworld. See chapter 15.

- **A Driving Trip around the Gargano Promontory:** Set along the country's south-eastern coast, directly east of Naples, the Gargano Promontory projects like a spur from the "boot" of Italy (across from what used to be known as Yugoslavia). A region of limestone caves and relative poverty, it contains unspoiled scenery and such towns as Peschici, Vieste, Mattinata, and the region's spiritual centerpiece, Testa del Gargano, a rocky promontory at the region's easternmost tip, which juts out into the Adriatic Sea.
- **A Trip to the Lipari (Aeolian) Islands:** These islands were believed to be the home of Aeolus, the god of the winds. The island group evokes scenes of North Africa rather than Italy. The largest, most interesting islands are Vulcano and Stromboli. See chapter 16.

9 Money-Saving Tips

GETTING THE BEST DEAL ON ACCOMMODATIONS

- Take advantage of independent travel packages that include airfare and hotel accommodations, offered by airlines and touring companies.
- If you travel off-season, not only will hotel rates be reduced, but you will have more room to negotiate with hotel owners. Be sure to check what months are off-season for your destination. For example, in Venice and Rome, August is a reduced-rate month, while prices may be highest during carnival time in February in Venice, and at Easter in Rome. In Milan, avoid the periods when large trade-fairs occur.
- Always ask if a payment in cash or traveler's checks over credit cards can get you a discount.
- You might not be accustomed to the concept of a shared bathroom, but if it's off-season your room may be the only one using the hall facilities. Ask upon check in.

GETTING THE BEST DEAL ON DINING

- Take advantage of a casual eatery where you can order just one course without getting hostile looks.
- Try dining in a self-service pizzeria or a *rosticceria,* an Italian cafeteria. *Tavola calda* or "hot table" is Italian for takeout food.
- The cafe/bar is a great resource for inexpensive lunches. You can also buy the sandwiches (*tramezzine*) and have them wrapped to go (*portar via*).
- Some restaurants may accommodate a request for a *mezza porzione* or half portion of pasta at a discounted (though usually not half) price if you are ordering a second course.
- Try the local table wine or *vino della casa* instead of a finer bottled wine. Better yet, make do with *acqua minerale* and indulge in a leisurely after dinner drink at a cafe.
- Round off your dinner with dessert elsewhere: Order an ice cream to go at a neighborhood *gelateria* and stroll the city's sidestreets.

- Take advantage of tourist menus: The *menu turistico* or *menu del giorno* is an all-inclusive, fixed-price meal that usually ranges from 12,500L to 21,000L ($8.20 to $13.80) and usually consists of a pasta course, a main course, a vegetable side dish, bread, cover and service charges, and sometimes wine and dessert or fruit. The main disadvantage to this budget option is that you'll usually be offered only a very limited selection.
- Avoid buying a hotel breakfast if at all possible (unless, of course, it is included automatically in the price). Always expensive and often unsatisfying, they cannot compare with a visit to an Italian bar/cafe where you stand at the counter for a delicious cappuccino or espresso and a fresh *cornetto* (lightly glazed croissant), sometimes filled with fresh jam or cream, all for 3,000L to 4,000L ($1.95 to $2.65).
- Watch out for the difference between prices for standing up (*alla banca*/at the bar) and those for sitting at a table (*alla tavola*). You'll rarely see Italians sitting down to savor their cappuccino because sit-down prices on all items are at least twice those if you stand at the bar—three times as much in the most heavily touristed places. Sitting down means that you want to be served by the waiter. It's great for people-watching, but hard on the budget.

GETTING THE BEST DEAL ON SIGHTSEEING & TRANSPORTATION

- Look into the availability of a *biglietto multiplo* (multiple ticket) for bus/public transportation or *biglietto cumulativo* (cumulative ticket) for museums. But first check out their conditions and make sure they realistically meet your needs. If the city is small and you enjoy walking, you won't be using public transportation much at all or many of the museums included in the group ticket may be secondary museums that you have no time for.
- Take advantage of the free guided tours, led by English speaking volunteers, often offered at major attractions.
- Most Italian cities' *centro storico* are practically car-free, and perfect for walking, people-watching, and window-shopping.
- Check to see if any museums are offering a free day during your stay—for example, the Vatican has free admission on the third Sunday of the month.

Getting to Know Italy

2

by Stephen Brewer

Lord Byron called Italy his magnet; Robert Browning said Italy was engraved on his heart. Being poets, these fellows might have been given to hyperbole, but Italy does have a remarkably strong, and usually favorable, effect on most of us.

Part of the draw, of course, is Italy's cultural legacy—the country, after all, introduces travelers to many of the most remarkable achievements of ancient Rome and the Renaissance, two of the highest points of Western civilization. It is blessed with the endlessly varied and almost ridiculously seductive scenery of the azure sea, silvery olive groves, snow-capped–mountain variety that is bound to intoxicate. The cuisine only seems to get better from region to region, and in this country where enormous emphasis is placed on good food and hospitality, visitors are wholeheartedly encouraged to enjoy eating and drinking ("Mange!" "Bene!"). Most appealing of all, perhaps, quite simply Italians appear to place a high priority on enjoying life (that might mean strolling through town on the evening *passaggiata* or lingering over a glass of wine), and they seem determined to ensure their visitors do the same.

Yes, it's only fair to point out, Italy is not just a postcard: It has slumbered through dark centuries, and in the last half of this century alone has had umpteen governments and been riddled with political scandal. If you care to look, you'll find poverty, crime, some ugly urban development, and social injustice, just as there is in any other industrialized Western nation. It's just that Italy offsets these realities with more grace notes than most other places do, and in so doing rewards the traveler with a remarkable and enduring experience.

1 Regions in Brief

Italy is divided into 19 self-governing "regions," some of which trace their ancestry to the 11 regions ordained by Emperor Augustine in the 1st century B.C.

Piedmont Piedmont means "foot of the mountains," and the Alps are in sight from almost every parcel of Italy's northernmost province on the border of Switzerland and France. The flat plains of the Po River rise into rolling hills clad with orchards and vineyards. North of Turin—the historic, baroque capital of the region and, with its auto factories, a cornerstone of Italy's "economic miracle"—

the plains meet the Alps head-on in the Valle d'Aosta, with its craggy mountains, craggy mountain folks, and year-round skiing.

Liguria   Following the Ligurian Sea along a narrow coastal band backed by mountains, Liguria meets Tuscany to the south and France to the west. At the center of this rocky coast is Genoa, progenitor of navigators, the country's first port and still its most important—a fascinating city that greets visitors with a remarkable assemblage of Renaissance art and architecture. Some of Italy's most famous seaside retreats flank Genoa on either side: the Riviera di Levante (Rising Sun) stretches east past picturesque Portino and other resorts to the wild coasts and isolated villages of the Cinque Terre; the Riviera di Ponente (Setting Sun) comes to an end at its most famous resort, San Remo, next door to the French border.

Lombardy   Lombardy is Italy's richest province—its industrial, financial, and agricultural powerhouse. Beyond its factories and business cities, this prosperous region bordering Switzerland also runs the gamut of scenic diversity from legendary lakes backed by Alpine peaks to the fertile plains of the Po River. The region's capital, Milan, hotbed of high fashion, high finance, and avant-garde design, is a city of art and architecture as well, and the region's Renaissance past is much in evidence in Pavia, Cremona, Mantua, and the other cities of the Lombardian plains.

Trentino-Alto Adige   The mountains: The Dolomites, bordering Austria, cap the eastern stretches of the region with sharp pinnacles straight out of a fairy tale; the peaks of the Alps crown the western part of the region. The legendary resorts are here, foremost among them Cortina d'Ampezzo and Merano, as are cities that lie at the crossroads of the German-Italian worlds: Trento, famous for its 16th-century council, and Bolsano, more Nordic than Italian in its speech, dress, and architecture.

Venice and the Veneto   The Po River has created in the Veneto what is primarily one vast floodplain under the brow of the pre–Venetian Alps in the north and the Dolomites in the west. Agriculture in this region is intense, but what draws visitors to these flatlands are the treasures of Padua, the marvelous villas of Paladio, and—rising on pilings from a series of lagoons along the Adriatic coast—that year-round carnival, Venice.

Tuscany   Beautiful, magically-lit Tuscany, which produced artists the way Genoa turned out navigators. From the rolling vineyards arise one wonder after another: Florence, birthplace of the Renaissance, Siena, Pisa, and one art-filled town after the other.

Emilia-Romagna   Emilia-Romagna comprises two ancient lands: Emilia, named for the Roman road that bisects its plains and art cities, and Romagna, named for its prominence in the Roman Empire. History has left its mark here on some of Italy's most fascinating cities—Ravenna, last capital of the empire and later the stronghold of the Byzantines and the Visigoths; Ferrara, center of art and culture for much of the Renaissance; Parma, one of the most powerful duchies in Europe under the Farnese family; and Bologna, famous for its university since the Middle Ages.

Umbria and the Marches   St. Francis was born in Umbria, and perhaps his gentle nature derived from the region's serene hills and valleys that create a sun-blessed landscape similar to Tuscany. Aside from Perugia, Renaissance capital and bustling modern city, Umbrian towns—among them such art centers as Gubbio, Assisi, and Spoleto—are as mellow as the hills that surround them. The Marches borders the Adriatic and includes the ancient town of Urbino, present-day art center as befits the birthplace of Raphael, painting's most brilliant draftsman.

Latium   Latium and its major city, Rome, is very nearly the geographic center of Italy and, some say, the center of the Western world. This is the place where Western political, philosophical, and cultural traditions were finally defined, fought over, and solidified, and you can walk the streets of Rome and still feel this history all around you.

The Abruzzi and Molise   In eastern central Italy, flanking the Adriatic, this is the wild part of the country. Both regions share the grand and feral mountains of the Apennines and a severe climate. Wolves still roam the dark forests of Molise and chamoix are found in the Abruzzi National Park, also the country's last refuge for brown bears.

Campania   Welcome to the soft life: Campania has been a refuge for the world-weary for 2,000 years. Campania wraps around Naples, that chaotic but beautiful city often overlooked on the grand tour, and down along the Amalfi Coast with its neck-lace of comely villages catering to the visitor—Ravello, Sorrento, Positano. And just offshore lies the jewel of Capri. Pompeii, extraordinarily situated beneath Vesuvius, is an evocative reminder of civilizations past.

Calabria, Apulia & Basilicata   This is the very sole of Italy, the bottom of the boot. Apulia, running the length of the boot heel, puts the lie to the "poor south" reputation of southern Italy—10% of the world's supply of olive oil comes from here. The region's austerely beautiful scenery, whitewashed buildings, and serene beaches have recently begun attracting visitors in much larger numbers. The rocky scenery continues across Calabria and Basilicata.

Sardinia   Sardinia, an island nearly as large as Sicily, is 120 miles off Italy's south-central coast in the Tyrrhenian Sea. Until recently this was a quiet place of farmers and shepherds who spoke their own language, and many still do. The interior is rough and rocky and very scenic and very peaceful, while the island's legendary beaches attract sun-worshippers from around the world.

Sicily   A dry, mountainous triangle, and the Mediterranean's largest island, Sicily sits just a couple of miles off the tip of Italy's toe. The Apennines overlap the Atlas Mountains of North Africa here, accounting for that rough but theatrical interior and helping foster Mafia clans and codes of *omertà*. Sicily was coveted by invaders over several thousand years, and they left behind many wonderful sites, from Greek temples to Norman cathedrals, for us to gaze upon and wonder about.

2 Italy Past & Present

Dateline

- Prehistory Neanderthal man, and around 10,000 B.C., Cro-Magnon.
- **1200 B.C.** The Etruscans begin to filter in via Asia Minor.
- **800 B.C.** Greeks colonize the peninsula boot ("Magna Graecia").
- **753 B.C.** Romulus, says legend, founds Rome. In fact, Rome begins to develop from

continues

In its 3,000 years of history, Italy has endured emperors and kings, duchies and despots, fools and knaves, popes and presidents. Italy has been a definer of democracy, has fallen prey to dictators, and has sagged into anarchy. And Italy has not only survived it all, but has certainly known triumph as well.

A VERY LONG TIME AGO   Early arrivals may have come as long as a million years ago, when it was still possible to walk from Africa to Europe, and occupied caves around Isneria in Abruzzo. Cave findings indicate that Neanderthal man made a brief appearance on the peninsula, and Cro-Magnon, who clearly knew how to fish and domesticate animals, showed up about 18,000 years ago.

MAGNA GRAECIA   *Magna Graecia,* "Great Greece," describes Greek colonies begun in the 8th century B.C. along the foot of the peninsula. In Sicily, the Greeks had to contend with mighty Carthage. On the mainland they found easier going among the native peoples. The new towns, planned as carefully as any Levittown, were established from present-day Apulia northwest to Naples. The land along the coast had never been tilled and quickly turned out several bumper crops a year. Abundant timber and wool underpinned highly profitable trading. But these successful entrepreneurs also exported bad habits from the homeland: They fell to warring amongst themselves and by the 5th century B.C. Greece was no longer an influence in southern Italy. The best evidence of Magna Graecia exists in the Archeological Museum at Crotone, Calabria, and in the National Museum at Reggo di Calabria, on the very tip of the boot.

THE ETRUSCAN ENIGMA   So much is known and admired about the Etruscans, yet so little is understood. Even though researchers have deciphered the Etruscan alphabet, similar to the Greek, a Rosetta Stone to decode the vocabulary has not turned up, so language remains a major stumbling block to understanding this highly advanced culture.

The Etruscans were filtering into the Italian peninsula, probably from Asia Minor, as early as the 12th century B.C. Herodotus, the great Roman historian, said so, and modern-day researchers tend to bear him out. By the 8th century there was a clearly delineated Etruscan culture that reached a peak of power and wealth in the 6th century B.C. Savaged by the Gauls (we know them as Celts), the Etruscans began their slide into oblivion shortly thereafter, and by the 4th century B.C. were essentially gone from sight.

It is known that Etruia was a collection of city-states that cohesed along religious rather than political lines; key centers were such modern-day locations as Chiusi in Tuscany, Tarquinia north of Rome, Veio near Rome, and Perugia in Umbria. Etruscan artifacts can be seen at the Etruscan Museum in Chiusi and Volterra; the Etruscan Necropolis, Veio; and there is the grand Etruscan wall with gateways in Perugia.

The Etruscans were highly skilled artisans working not only iron but also in bronze, silver, and copper, as well as crafting elegant gold pieces. Etruscan potters threw handsome black vases with bas-relief figures using a sophisticated technique that is still

- a strategically located shepherd village.
- **700 B.C.** Etruscans rise in power, peak in the sixth century, and make Rome their capital.
- **509 B.C.** Republic of Rome is founded; power is shared by two consuls.
- **494–450 B.C.** Office of the tribune established to defend plebeian rights. The Twelve Tablets stating basic rights are carved, the foundation of Roman law.
- **300 B.C.** The Etruscans are defeated and disappear into veiled history.
- **279 B.C.** Romans now rule all of the Italian peninsula.
- **146 B.C.** Romans defeat Carthage and the Republic controls Sicily, North Africa, Spain, Sardinia, Greece, and Macedonia.
- **100 B.C.** Julius Caesar born.
- **60 B.C.** Caesar, Pompey, and Crassus share the first Triumvirate.
- **51 B.C.** Caesar triumphs over Gaul.
- **44 B.C.** March 15, Caesar assassinated, leaves all to his nephew and heir, Octavian.
- **27 B.C.** Octavian, now Augustus, is declared first emperor of the Roman Empire, beginning 200 years of peace and prosperity.
- **A.D. 29** Jesus is crucified in Judea.
- **64–100** Nero persecutes Christians; a succession of military commanders restore order; Trajan expands the empire.
- **200** The decline of the empire begins; the Goths invade from the north.
- **313** With the Edict of Milan, Constantine I declares Christianity the official religion of the state, establishes Constantinople as eastern capital.

continues

- **476** Collapse of the Roman Empire; the Dark Ages begin
- Late 6th century Lombards sweep through much of Italy.
- **600–675** Political control begins to adhere to the Church as Pope Gregory I brings some stability to the peninsula.
- **774–800** Charlemagne invades Italy, is crowned emperor by Pope Leo III. Italy dissolves into a series of small warring kingdoms.
- **962** Succeeding Charlemagne's empire, the Holy Roman Empire is founded as the temporal arm of the church's spiritual power.
- **11th-century** Normans conquer southern Italy, introduce feudalism there. The first Crusades are launched.
- **1350** The Black Death decimates Europe, reduces Italy's population by a third.
- **1450** City-states hold the power; Venice controls much of the eastern Mediterranean. The humanist movement heralds the rise of the individual. The art and philosophy of ancient Greece is rediscovered.
- **1500** Peak of the High Renaissance, its artists and poets financed by princes and merchant princes. Lorenzo il Magnifico in Florence is the patron of artists. Brunelleschi's dome caps the Duomo. Leonardo da Vinci completes *The Last Supper.*
- **1508** Michelangelo begins the Sistine Chapel ceiling.
- **1550** Carlos I of Spain is crowned Holy Roman Emperor as Charles V; he occupies nearly all of Italy. The second great decline begins.
- **18th-century** Italy's darkest hour: brigands control the

continues

not understood. And it was Etruscans who introduced that eventual favored vehicle of Ben-Hur, the chariot. Magnificent bronze portraits can be seen at the Conservatory Palace in Rome, and the Archaeology Museum in Florence. Their art derived essentially from Greece except, as one observer has noted, "that the underlying spirit retains a barbaric energy quite opposed to the Greek search for perfection in harmony."

THE RISE OF ROME   The Mother Wolf legend, in which that most accommodating lupine nurtures the twins, Romulus and Remus, giving them the strength to sit up and found Rome in 753 B.C., still persists in a way; reproductions of *La Lupa* are to be found in shops all over Italy.

However, Rome probably began as a collection of Sabine and Latin villages, ruled by kings, some of whom were Etruscans. In 509 B.C., the last one raped a favorite Roman daughter, who committed suicide. The infuriated Romans ejected him, if indeed, they didn't tear him asunder. Out of that civic outrage grew the Roman Republic. Rome and a united Italy lasted four centuries, then fell. Fifteen centuries would pass before Rome and Italy would recover.

There were two classes of people in the Roman Republic: the patricians, who controlled the government via two patrician consuls, and the plebeians, who included just about everybody else. There was constant conflict between these two groups as the plebeians fought for control over their daily lives and their destiny. Finally, the commoners were allowed to elect from their own ranks tribunes, high officials with real political power. Tribunes eventually became defenders of the people against mandates of the state. About 450 B.C., the commoners also won certain basic rights, carved onto wood tablets and known as the Twelve Tables. These became the basis for Roman law, which in later centuries coalesced into Western European law as we know it today (England not included).

A code of law, a citizen's voice in the government—genuine forerunners to democracy, and it may seem at first glance that the Roman Republic was democratic. Not so. The Republic began as a patrician aristocracy, and crashed as a senatorial oligarchy—probably inevitable in a government by the few.

Young and grasping Rome sent its military throughout the peninsula and by 279 B.C. the Romans ruled all of Italy. Rome's armies trampled

Grecian colonies, and even Carthage, Rome's magnificent enemy, led by Hannibal, was left with only a bitter taste in its mouth: Rome salted the growing fields of Carthage (present-day Tunisia). By 146 B.C., with Carthage finally ground down, Rome controlled not only all of Italy and Sicily, but North Africa, Spain, and Sardinia. Greece, along with Macedonia, was subjected. However, Rome's encounter with Greece transformed Roman culture.

Still, Rome wanted more, oddly enough. There was a side effect to all the military success: a severely weakened home front. With all the war booty pouring in, Rome ended taxation. So much grain poured in from North Africa that the Roman farmer couldn't find a market for his wheat and simply stopped growing it. While the Roman countryside suffered, the cities shrugged and danced in the streets. The booty had an additional price tag: corruption. The senators advanced their own lot rather than the provinces ostensibly in their care. The plebeian voice clamored for a bigger share. Slaves revolted several times. More reforms appeased the plebes while the slaves were put down with horrific barbarity. The one we remember best is the uprising led by Spartacus, courtesy of the Stanley Kubrick/Kirk Douglas movie.

HAIL CAESAR!   Julius Caesar had it both ways: he was born a patrician; he was also beloved by the plebeians. This duality certainly helped him pave the way for empire. Not to mention his amazing skills as orator, strategist, statesman, military commander, politician, and thinker. At the end of the century preceding Caesar's birth, about 102 B.C., the Republic, sped along by a corrupt Senate, was corroding itself into near-collapse. Caesar's initial ascent to power came when he shared the first Triumvirate in 60 B.C. with Pompey and Crassus. Caesar's final rise to sole Consul—dictator in fact—got him killed.

What endeared Caesar to the lowly crowd was his lifelong fight against the Senate. Before he was done, he forced many senators to flee Rome, introduced reform, and added Gaul (modern-day France) to the dying Republic. But on March 15, 44 B.C., that fatal Ides of March, at the age of 58, Julius Caesar, apparently fully aware of what lay in wait for him, strolled out to meet Brutus, Cassius, and other friends.

Caesar left everything to his nephew and heir, the 18-year-old Octavian. From the Senate, Octavian eventually received the title *Augustus,* and from the people, lifetime tribuneship. And so Octavian became Emperor Augustus, sole ruler of Rome and most of the Western world.

THE EMPIRE   Augustus's long reign ushered in *Pax Romana,* 200 years of Roman peace under Roman rule. The new emperor, who preferred being known as "First

countryside, the Austrians and Spanish everything else.

- **1784** The French Revolution sparks Italian nationalism.
- **1796–1814** Napoléon sweeps through Italy, installing friends and relatives as rulers.
- **1814** Napoléon's downfall at Waterloo.
- **1830** The rise of the *Risorgimento* and a renaissance of Italian literature and music.
- **1861** Italy is united under Victor Emmanuel II as the Kingdom of Italy.
- **Late 19th-century** mass emigration to America and other foreign shores, mostly from the south.
- **1918** Italy on Allied side during World War I, but becomes mired in postwar chaos.
- **1922** Mussolini marches on Rome and puts his Fascist Blackshirts in charge of the country.
- **1935** Mussolini defeats and annexes Ethiopia.
- **1939** Italy enters World War II on side of the Axis.
- **1943** Italy exits the war, Mussolini and mistress executed by vengeful partisans.
- **1946** A national referendum narrowly establishes the Republic of Italy.
- **1950–97** Fifty changes of government, yes, but also the "economic miracle" that has made Italy the world's fifth leading economy.

Citizen," reorganized the military and the provincial governments, and reinstituted constitutional rule. The famous Roman roads were extended even farther. He began postal, police, and fire services, increased commerce, aided the arts, and rebuilt Rome itself.

Succeeding emperors were not so virtuous. Vicious Caligula, henpecked Claudius I, and Nero, who in A.D. 64 persecuted the Christians of Rome with a viciousness easily equal to the earlier slave repressions, were among those that followed. Several of the military commanders who became emperors were exceptions to the tyrant mold. Late in the 1st century, Trajan expanded the empire's eastern boundaries and constructed great public works.

At this peak, Rome knew civilized amenities not to be enjoyed again in Europe until the 18th century. Police protection, fire fighting, libraries, sanitation, huge public baths such as the Caracalla by the Appian Way, even central heating and running water—if you could afford them.

The empire's decline began around A.D. 200. The Goths, Germanic tribes, were knocking hard at the door. Christianity played its part. The empire was split in two parts, west and east, when in 313, Constantine I embraced Christianity and moved the capital of the empire from Rome to Byzantium, later to be renamed Constantinople (modern-day Istanbul).

CURTAIN GOING DOWN: THE DARK AGES   In 476, the last emperor fell and the Roman Empire collapsed. It would be 1,500 years before Rome and Italy were once again united as capital and nation. As the 6th century opened, Italy was in chaos. Waves of barbarians from the north kept pouring in while provincial nobles engaged in petty bickering. The Goths ruled from Ravenna, until driven out by Constantinople. Rule by the Goths was followed by takeovers by strong warring factions. It was the Roman Catholic Church, beginning with Pope Gregory I late in the 6th century, that finally provided some stability. In the 7th century, the Church divided the population into four classes: clergy, nobility, soldiers, and the lowest class. In 731, Pope Gregory II renounced Rome's nominal dependence on Constantinople, and turned the Roman Catholic Church firmly toward Europe, completing the split between east and west.

During the Middle Ages, northern Italy became increasingly fragmented into a collection of city-states. The history of the southern half of the country was different, however, for in the 11th century the Normans defeated the papacy and invaded southern Italy. Once in place they applied the feudal system, which never took hold in northern Italy, with a death grip. There was a crippling fallout from the feudalism that dominated the southern part of the peninsula and stifled individual initiative; it accounts in large part for the social and economic differences between north and south that have continued well into the 20th century.

The Black Death, the plague that ravaged Europe, arrived in the mid-14th century and in Italy killed a third of the population. Even so, northern Italian cities were growing wealthy from the Crusades, Middle East trade, and banking, and they flexed their muscles in the vacuum of a strong central authority, especially the increasingly powerful Venetians. Some cities prospered in the south, too, but the Normans maintained tight control.

CURTAIN GOING UP: THE RENAISSANCE   The Renaissance peaked in the 15th century as northern cities bullied their way to city-state status. Even while warring constantly with each other as they tried to extend their territories, such ruling families as the Medici in Florence, the d'Este in Errara, and the Gonzaga in Milan grew incredibly rich and powerful, which was fine for them and their hometowns.

It didn't do much for a unified Italy, though, and the pattern of political fragmentation calcified, not to be chipped away for nearly 400 years. Machiavelli, almost alone, called for unification as Italy's only saving grace—a call unheeded until the mid-19th century.

The despots, oppressive or benevolent, who ruled what were supposed to be republics—Florence and Venice, Milan and Genoa—plus popes, princes, and merchant princes, collectively performed at least one very good action—they bankrolled the Renaissance, and for that we can all be grateful. But with no clear political authority or unified military, Italy was easy pickings and by mid-16th century Spain, courtesy of Carlos V, occupied nearly all of the country.

THE SECOND FALL   Between economic depression and foreign domination, Italy was hanging on the ropes from the mid-16th century until the end of the 18th century. The emphasis on world trade had shifted away from the Mediterranean. Spanish Bourbons controlled the duchies of the south, Austria those of the north. The Spaniards kept raising taxes, and farming declined, the birthrate sank, bandits were everywhere. The 18th century is viewed as Italy's nadir. Only Europe's eager ear for Italian music and eye for art and architecture kept the Italian profile haughty.

It was the French Revolution and the advent of Napoléon that lit Italy's fire, although it would be the mid-19th century before the *Risorgimento* and a new king could spread the flame.

THE SECOND RISE: THE 19TH CENTURY   Italians initially gave Napoléon an exultant *ciao* when he swept through the peninsula and swept out Italy's 18th-century political disasters, along with the Austrian army. But Napoléon, in the end, neither united Italy nor provided Italy with self-government. The nationalists, however, were fired up. The Risorgimento ("resurgence"), an odd amalgam of radicals, moderate liberals, and Roman Catholic conservatives, fought their way over 30 years to a constitutional monarchy. Giuseppe Mazzini provided the intellectual rigor for the movement, and Garibaldi and his Redshirts got the headlines. But it was the political genius of noble-born Camillo Cavour that engineered the result. In 1861, Vittorio Emanuele II, of the House of Savoy, became King of Italy.

FINALLY, A NATION UNITED   A united nation? Kind of. On paper, yes, but the old sectional differences continued. While there was rapid industrialization in the north, the south was still in a torpor in the late 19th century. Southerners flocked to the more industrialized north, antagonizing northerners in the process. It was then that the mass emigration to America from southern Italy began.

Italy entered World War I on the Allied side in exchange for territorial demands, and to vanquish that old foe, Austria. The Austrian-Hungarian Empire was indeed defeated, but at the Paris Peace Conference Italy got much less territory than had been promised, compounding the country's postwar chaos. And along came Benito Mussolini, promising to bring order out of chaos.

FASCISM REIGNS   Mussolini marched on Rome in 1922, forced the king to make him premier, and quickly repressed all other political factions. He put his Fascists in charge of the entire country: schools, the press, industry, labor. He instituted a vast public works program, most of which was a failure. Mussolini liked to see himself as a second Caesar, so he spent some time excavating—not always according to the most acceptable methods—the archeological remains of ancient Rome. The Great Depression of the 1930s made things worse and, to divert attention, Mussolini turned to foreign adventures, defeating and annexing Ethiopia in 1935. Mussolini put Italy into World War II on the side of the Nazis, but the Italian heart was not really in the war, and the Italians had little wish to pursue Hitler's anti-Semitic policies. In 1945, the Italian people rose against Mussolini and the Axis, the Fascists were disbanded, and Victor Emmanuel III, who had collaborated with the Fascists without much enthusiasm during the past two decades, appointed a new premier.

At the end of the war, Mussolini and his mistress were pictured in the world press hanging by their heels after being shot by partisans. Recent reports, however, raise the suspicion that the partisans, having accidentally shot the two, trussed up the two warm bodies hours after they were killed in order to appease a citizenry that had been promised a public execution.

DEMOCRACY AT LAST   After the war Italians voted to be, by a whisker, a republic and in 1948 a new republican constitution went into effect. Politically, though, some things don't change in Italy. The same old mistrust amongst factions continues, the cities are still paranoid about their individuality and their rights, and the division between north and south is as sharp as ever. In the modern era, there are three major parties representing left, center, and right, but because there are many other small parties, a vote of confidence is often difficult to achieve by the party nominally in power at the moment. As a result there have been more than 50 changes of government in the 50 years since the war. The Mafia has become a kind of shadow government, controlling a staggering number of politicians, national officials, even judges, and providing one scandal after another.

Economically, it's a different story. The "economic miracle" of the north somehow ignores political chaos to make Italy the world's fifth largest economy. Even the south, while continuing to lag far behind, is not in the desperate straits it once was.

The outsider looks and wonders how the place keeps going. The Italian just shrugs and rolls his eyes. Maybe he's right. They've only had 50 years' practice doing it this way. It's practically a brand-new, 3,000-year-old country.

3 Italy's Artistic Heritage

When you think of England, land of Shakespeare, Milton, Dickens, the first thought you have might be simply "words." For France, "style," maybe "taste." For Germany, ever probing inward, "philosophy." Italy? Opera fans aside, the first thought has to be the "eye." Italy has always been at the forefront of the visual arts. Our first response to the notion of art in Italy may be "the Renaissance," but Italy's artistic heritage actually began 2,500 years ago, and the beat goes on.

ARTS, ARTISTS & ARCHITECTS

ROME & THE ARTS   Today all, or almost all, design roads lead to Milan. In the beginning, though, all roads led from Athens. What the Greeks identified early on that captured the hearts and minds of so many others was classical rendering of form. To the ancients, "classic" or "classical" simply meant perfect—proportion, balance, harmony, form, demanded of all the arts. To the Greeks, man was the measure, an attitude lost in the Middle Ages, and not to be rediscovered until the dawn of the Renaissance.

Those early tourists to the Italian peninsula, the Etruscans, clearly borrowed from the Greeks in their buildings and in their sculpture. And the Romans, when early in the 6th century B.C. they began installing the Republic and kicking out all the foreigners, kept certain Greek innovations, some of which were pretty basic—such as how to put up a building so it wouldn't fall down. The first big idea was post-and-lintel construction—essentially, the weight-bearing frame, like a door. Later

Great Examples of Italian Art & Architecture

Architecture
- Coliseum, Rome, late 1st century A.D.; examples of Doric and Ionic columns
- Pantheon, Rome, 1st century B.C.—considered the most important Roman building
- Temple of Castor and Pollux in the Roman Forum, Corinthian columns, 1st century A.D.
- Basilica of Maxentius (or Constantine), 4th century A.D.; the Appian Way, Rome
- Baths of Caracalla, 3rd century A.D., Rome; enormous concrete structure
- Romanesque: Basilica of St. Ambrosio, Milan; 11th–12th century
- Romanesque: Cathedral at Pisa; 11th–12th century
- Renaissance: Palladio's Villa Rotunda, Vicenza, built around 1570; his work was a powerful influence in the spread of Italian architecture
- Renaissance: Farnese Palace, Rome; completed by Michelangelo, 1566
- Baroque: Bernini's Fountain of the Four Rivers, in the Piazza Navona, Rome
- Rococo: Fernando Fuga, Palazzo della Consulta, 1737, Rome

Paintings, frescoes & sculptures
- Roman: the Arch of Constantine, Rome; marble bas-relief, 1st century A.D.
- Roman: marble statue of Augustus as *Pontifex Maximus,* 1st century A.D.; National Museum, Rome
- Early Renaissance: Giotto, *The Lamentation,* fresco, 14th century, Arena Chapel, Padua
- Early Renaissance: Masaccio, *The Tribute Money,* 1427; Brancacci Chapel, Santa Maria del Carmine, Florence
- Early Renaissance: Botticelli, *The Birth of Venus,* about 1480; Uffizi Gallery, Florence
- High Renaissance: Leonardo da Vinci, *Adoration of the Magi,* panel, 1481; Uffizi Gallery, Florence
- High Renaissance: Raphael, *Pope Leo X and His Nephews Giuli de' Medici and Lugi de' Rossi,* 1518. Uffizi Gallery, Florence
- High Renaissance: Michelangelo, *Moses,* marble statue, 1513; Santo Pietro in Vincoli, Rome
- Post-Renaissance: Caravaggio, *The Calling of St. Matthew,* Contarelli Chapel, Santo Luigi dei Franseci, Rome
- Baroque: Pietro da Cortona, *Glorification of the Reign of Urban VIII,* ceiling fresco, about 1635; Palazzo Barberini, Rome
- Baroque: Bernini, *Throne of St. Peter,* bronze, marble, and stucco, 1657; St. Peter's, Rome

came adaptation of Greek columns for supporting buildings, Doric, Ionic, and Corinthian, with the Doric, being simplest and strongest, used on the ground floor.

The Roman persona was impelled to operate on a grand scale. Romans thrived on huge, complex problems for which they could produce organized, well-crafted solutions. And they were quick studies. By 509 B.C. they had built a great temple on Capitoline, highest of Rome's seven hills. Roman builders became inventive engineers, developing hoisting mechanisms and a specially trained workforce. They designed towns, built civic centers. They developed the *basilica*, a rectangle roofed and supported by columns along both sides of the interior with an apse at one or both ends. The earliest known basilica was built by Cato the Elder in 184 B.C. Basilicas were used for courts of justice, banking, and other commercial structures, and was a design repeated all over the Roman world, beginning around the 1st century A.D. A huge example is the Forum of Trajan in the Roman Forum, an enormous columned space.

"Marble" is what springs to mind vis à vis Roman architecture. But the Roman engineer could also do wonders with prosaic concrete. They used *pozzolana* from extensive beds at Pozzuoli, near Naples, for such palaces and huge domes, as the public baths of Caracalla, the Pantheon, and the Basilica of Maxentius. Concrete seating made possible such enormous theaters as the 6-acre, 45,000-seat Coliseum of Rome.

Painting got rather short shrift in the Roman world, being used primarily for decorative purposes. Bucolic *frescoes*, the technique of painting in wet plaster, adorned the walls of the wealthy in Rome and Pompeii. Sculpture, so much more useful for aggrandizing, is another story. A marble statue, solid, substantial, three-dimensional, lends validity to its owner. Regrettably, the Roman aesthetic was quite unadventurous. As the 1st century A.D. and the Roman Empire began, the Greeks yet again were called upon. The sculpture factories of Rome churned out endless clones of Grecian classics that had been around for generations. Bronze portraiture, a technique descended from the Etruscans, was polished to photographic perfection.

ROMANESQUE & BYZANTINE   When Pope Gregory the Great's strong hand brought some stability to Italy late in the 6th century, the rise of the Catholic Church created a demand for churches and cathedrals. The builders turned to the basilica and the resultant "romanesque" recalled the ancient building style of Rome. The word describes an architecture heavy and solid as opposed to the spires, misnamed "gothic," that would later thrust dramatically into the skies of France and Germany. The church front was usually quite plain, with a simple roofline. Doors got the decoration. The romanesque churches grew massive, but that creature of pagan Rome, the basilica, remained basic to their structure.

For an example of northern, or Tuscan, romanesque, you need only regard the cathedral at Pisa, with its columns set upon columns and against which the famous tower leans. In the south, the late 12th-century cathedral of Monreale near Palermo is practically a roll call of Sicily's conquerors, with its Byzantine mosaics and Norman copper doors with exquisite carvings by Bonnano Pisano.

THE RENAISSANCE   "Renaissance" to the participant at the time meant the rediscovery and renewal of classical Greek and Latin literature undertaken by the humanists in the 14th century in their revitalized interest in exploring man's capabilities. Along with this went a similar rediscovery of Greek art and form. To most of us since then, "Renaissance" has become a label for an era of explosion in science, exploration, politics, religion, and, most vividly, the arts.

Giotto, around 1300, charted a radical course change in Italian, indeed all, painting when he insisted on rendering the human figure and face with life and warmth in his frescoes in Padua's Scrovegni Chapel. It was probably an architect, Filippo Brunelleschi, about 1420, who first truly grasped "perspective," and provided artists with ground rules for creating the illusion of three dimensions on a flat surface. Brunelleschi built Florence's Pazzi Chapel and the Santa Maria degli Angeli and Santo Spirito Churches. Masaccio, who lived only until age 27, drew upon Brunelleschi's findings to produce the first sense of painted perspective in his Carmine frescoes.

The High Renaissance of the late 15th and early 16th centuries lasted for only about 25 years. It was driven and dominated by the triumvirate of Michelangelo,

Andrea Palladio

Order, balance, elegance, harmony with the landscape, and a human scale all come to mind when viewing the creations of the Andrea Palladio (1508–80). Palladio was working as a stonemason and sculptor when, at 30, he turned his hand to architecture, drawing his inspiration from the ancient buildings he studied on trips to Rome, and applying the principles of classical proportion to Renaissance ideals of grace, symmetry, and functionality. Vicenza, the little city near Venice where Palladio lived as a boy and where he returned in his prime, is graced with many Palladian palazzi and churches, as well as his Teatro Olympico; Palladio also designed the churches of San Giorgio Maggiore and Redentore in Venice. He is best known, though, for the villas he built on the flat plains of the Veneto for Venetian nobles yearning to escape the cramped city and enjoy open spaces. Nineteen of these villas still stand, including what may be the finest of them, La Rotunda, outside Vicenza. The design of this and his other villas—square, perfectly proportioned, and elegant yet functional—may well strike a note of familiarity with American and British visitors: Palladio influenced generations of architects who, knowing a good thing when they saw it, followed his lead when designing plantation houses in the American south and country estates in England.

Leonardo, and Raphael, as each tried to outdo the other (Michelangelo claiming the other two were stealing his ideas). Raphael, considered Western art's greatest draftsman, produced a body of work in his 37 short years that ignited European painters for generations to come. He contributed significantly as well to Roman architecture, most particularly to the ongoing construction of St. Peter's. Italian Renaissance architecture, in fact, was to spread throughout Europe. Leonardo da Vinci, master of all, painted very little in oils, but even so managed to originate such effects as the fine haze of *sfumato*, "a moisture-laden atmosphere that delicately veils . . . forms." Unfortunately, the best example of this effect, his fresco of *The Last Supper* in Milan, is sadly deteriorated.

Pope Julius both funded Michelangelo and drove him to despair. Michelangelo's artistic focus was on the human figure, and he devoutly believed that sculpture was the only true expression of that belief, as he showed in his 13-foot *David* in Florence. After completing the Sistine Chapel for the pope, Michelangelo avoided ceilings for the next 20 years.

The peculiar coincidence of circumstances of the High Renaissance in Italy—the combined force of available money, a philosophy that stated that certain artists had a God-granted genius, and, of course, the spectacular talents of those geniuses—were never to be repeated. Most of what followed for the next couple of hundred years were variations of the Renaissance themes. The late 16th-century *chiaroscuro* style of Caravaggio differed mainly in his insistence on working in a more realistic mode. His paintings reflect, with their renderings of the common man in dramatic contrasts of dark and light, his street-fighter personality.

By the mid-16th century, Spain under Carlos V occupied all of Italy. The Spanish laid the Inquisition on full bore and decreed that henceforth art was to serve the Church alone.

ON TO THE 20TH CENTURY   By the early 17th century, baroque (one definition says "baroque" is derived from the Italian word for "irregular, oversized pearl") influence was creeping in. Baroque architects, including Bernini and Maderno, who was contracted to complete St. Peter's at long last, were the pathfinders in European architecture for the next 150 years.

Except for a few rococo architectural designs—de Sancticis' Spanish Steps (1726), and Salvi's Trevi Fountain (1762)—the 18th to the 20th centuries were essentially one long decline in Italian painting, sculpture, and architecture. By the 19th century Italy had become a great teaching facility for eager students from all over the world to learn from the great masters, but Italy did not initiate. In the early 20th century, Italian futurism, in its brief life, directly influenced cubism. Painters Modigliani and Chirico drew international attention, Modigliani for his undulating, languorous figures. Giorgio de Chirico termed his work, "metaphysical painting," which was drawn on by early surrealists. In recent years, architect Pier Luigi Nervi has designed significant work, including his Exhibition Hall in Turin.

Today the Italian eye focuses, profitably for sure, on automobiles, clothes, graphics, and industrial design.

ITALY'S MUSIC

In the 14th century, Italy's music swept Europe, valued for the sweetness of its sound. Italy was an innovator in medieval music—St. Ambrose, Bishop of Milan in the 4th century, introduced the custom in the church of singing liturgical chants. In the 12th century, Guido Arezzo developed the basis of the musical notation that we use today. Blind Francesco Landini, whose work was much admired, introduced sophisticated, varied rhythms.

And in the mid-16th century, the first violin appeared. Stradivari, who learned his craft under the great master, Amati, achieved a perfection not yet improved upon.

Poets, who wanted a closer relationship between word and music, got their wish by the late 16th century. Music had been an incidental element in various entertainments until now, but a group in Florence wanted to adapt Greek drama, which they believed had been sung throughout, to a new kind of "musical drama." It came to be called "opera," a new form that caught on fast. The first great composer of opera was Monteverdi, who is enjoying a new popularity today. His *Orfeo* was performed in 1607 at Mantua. What Monteverdi could do best, as one observer puts it, was "translate human suffering into sound," lighting the way for succeeding generations of Italian composers.

Venice opened the first public opera house 30 years later. Venice's preeminent composer in the early 18th century was Antonio Vivaldi, who wrote more than 40 operas. And although he is known mainly for his instrumental music today, the prolific Scarlatti was also a composer of opera, turning out more than 100 in his exuberant, rococo style. It's possible that he played some of his music on one of Bartolomeo Cristofori's pianofortes—forerunner of the piano, it was first developed by Cristofori about 1709.

Italy has produced many fine composers of opera, but it is Verdi who is the unquestioned master, the one who rules alongside Mozart and Wagner. Giuseppe Verdi, son of an innkeeper, lived nearly the entire century and he had it all. He understood the dramatic form, he wrote exquisite melodies, and his musicianship was unsurpassed. He achieved success early on with his third opera, *Nabucco,* a huge hit, then turned out the ever-popular *Rigiletto, Il Trovatore, Un Ballo in Maschera,* and *Aïda.* His powers continued unchecked as he grew older, and beginning with *Don Carlo,* a change and deepening of his talent began. He wrote his great *Otello* at age 73, and when he was 80 years old he astonished the musical world with *Falstaff,* a masterpiece in opera-buffa form, unlike anything he had ever composed before.

The High Price of High Notes

The *castrato* performer in opera was hugely popular in the 17th and 18th centuries. Young boys with beautiful voices were castrated before their voices broke so they could retain their high soprano ranges, yet sing with all the lung power of an adult. The practice had begun a hundred years earlier by the Church, which wanted these voices for its choirs. It finally disappeared in the late 18th century. Today the castrato roles that appear in Monteverdi and Handel operas, and even in the early operas of Mozart, are usually assigned to women's voices.

Carlo Broschi Farinelli was considered the greatest of the castrati. He was the pop star of the 18th century. After achieving fame on the London stage and in France and Italy, Farinelli renounced public performing and, at 32, went to work exclusively for the king of Spain, Philip V. The job? Perform the same four songs, solely for Philip, night after night after night. Farinelli was paid amazing sums, and in 1759, at age 54, he called it a day and bought a castle near Bologna where he lived in retirement until his death 23 years later.

In the recent, probably apocryphal, film about his life, *Farinelli,* a soprano voice and a synthesizer were combined to create a computerized approximation of the castrato sound.

Opera buffa was Italy's most popular operatic form in the early 19th century, comic opera with more surface than depth in which, unlike grand opera, individual musical numbers alternate with spoken dialogue. Opera buffa had its origins in the wisecracking comedians who had long entertained at fairs. Rossini's charming *The Barber of Seville,* and Donizetti's *Daughter of the Regiment* are examples of the form.

Rossini and Donizetti were also significant contributors to grand opera in early and mid-century. Puccini came along a bit later. His lyrical *La Bohème, La Tosca,* and *Madama Butterfly* are continuing crowd-pleasers.

Well known to today's international audiences is Gian-Carlo Menotti, composer of *Amahl and the Night Visitors,* as founder of Spoleto's Festival of Two Worlds, the International Festival of Music, Drama, and Dance, which takes place annually in late June and early July.

4 Italy's Cuisine & Wine

For Italians, eating is not just something to do three times a day. Food is an essential ingredient of the Italian spirit, practically another art form in a place that knows a lot about art. Even when Italy was a poor nation it was said that poor Italians ate better than rich Germans or English or Americans.

What it comes down to is an appreciation of food and the pleasure of eating it. Italians pay careful attention to the basics in both shopping and preparation. They know, for instance, which region produces the best onions, which has the choice peppers or potatoes. If they're dining out, Italians expect the same care and pride they put into home cooking—and they get it. The result is that there are a lot of wonderful places to eat in Italy, from fancy places to plain places, from Via Veneto *ristorantes* to neighborhood *trattorias*.

Breakfast is treated lightly, and the cappuccino and croissant, maybe accompanied by some juice, at the corner bar is about as fancy as it gets. There are exceptions: many of the more luxurious hotels, tired of hearing guests grouse about the paltry morning offerings, have taken to serving sumptuous buffets like those offered north of the Alps, complete with ham, cheese, and eggs.

At the big meal of the day (be it lunch or dinner) portions on a plate may be smaller than visitors are accustomed to, but there will be more plates. The meal is usually divided into four courses preceded by an *antipasto* (appetizer), often a platter of *salumi* (cold cuts—that's salumi, not salami) and vegetables served either raw or prepared in oil or vinegar, or perhaps melon and prosciutto; followed by *primo* (first course), which could be soup, pasta, or risotto and might include some polenta; then *secondo* (entree), a wide range of meat, fish, seafood, or chicken, depending on which part of the country you are in; *contorno* (side dish), potato or vegetable or a salad (contorno is served sometimes with *and* sometimes after the entree); *dolce* (dessert) fruit or ice cream or *formaggio* (cheese). Of course, any meal is accompanied by wine, along with a bottle of mineral water (con or senza gas/fizzy or still), and followed by an espresso. (By the way, one sure way to alienate an Italian waiter is to order cappuccino after dinner—Italians don't go near the stuff any time after noon.) Espresso is often followed by grappa, a fiery digestivo made from what's left over during the wine making process. And on the subject of alcohol: though the full range of cocktails are available in bars and better restaurants, Italians don't often stray beyond wine or maybe a premeal beer.

A *ristorante* (restaurant) is usually a bit formal and often a bit expensive, and very often deservedly so. (It is a good idea to make reservations at most ristorantes. And note: Waiting tables is a respected profession in Italy, usually by males. Call him Signore and he'll respect you right back.) A *trattoria* is simpler, usually cheaper, can be just as good as a ristorante, often family-run, more relaxed and sociable (and Italians love to socialize over meals, even with strangers). Snacks, perhaps a small plate of pasta, can be found in wine bars. Unfortunately, McDonald's-type fast-food joints are becoming more common in Italian cities, and there's even McDonald's—but you're not in Italy for the Big Macs. And for the most part, though the kids like these places, Italian restaurants (and except for some Chinese places, you're not likely to find many eateries of other persuasions) remain firmly entrenched as a cornerstone of Italian life.

PASTA   Pasta is probably Italy's best-known export. It comes in two basic forms: *pastaciutta* (dried pasta), the kind most of us buy at the grocery store, and *pasta fresca* (fresh pasta), the kind that most self-respecting establishments in Italy, even those of the most humble ilk, will probably serve. The dried form goes into boiling water and is given flavor by sauces added after it's cooked. In fresh pasta, flavors are usually added before or during cooking.

Coffee All Day Long

Italians drink coffee all day long, but only a little at a time and often while standing in a bar—and a "bar" in Italy is a place that serves coffee. There is usually liquor available, too, but it's the caffeine that draws the customers.

There are four coffees that are most popular in Italy. The demitasse caffè is straight espresso, downed in one gulp. Cappuccino is espresso with an overlay of foamy steamed milk, usually sipped for breakfast with a croissant, and never as an after-dinner drink. Caffè macchiato is espresso with a wee drop of steamed milk, and caffè coretto is espresso boosted with a shot of liquor.

Pastaciutta comes in long strands including *spaghetti, linguini, trenette*; and in tubular *maccheroni* (macaroni) forms such as *penne* (smooth tubes) or *rigatoni* (fluted tubes), to name only a few. Pasta fresca is made in broad sheets, then cut into shapes used in lasagna and cannelloni, or into broad noodles for fettucine dishes. If you sense that this is not even a dent in the world of pasta, you're right: There are, it is said, more than 600 different pasta shapes in Italy.

ITALY'S REGIONAL CUISINES

Italy's present unification is only 50 years old, but the nation's "regions," within which there are provinces, have histories as independent locales stretching back 3,000 years. So each region had a long time to develop its own practices and guards them zealously. Likewise, each region has grown and developed its own wines and foods and generated its own ideas on how these foods should reach the table. So you can eat very, very well, in, say, Emilia-Romanga and do likewise but very, very differently in, say, Calabria.

Very generally speaking, northern cooking (Italy north of Rome) is fancier, pricier, more elaborate, has richer sauces, and ignores concerns about calories and costs; southern cooking is simpler, rougher, and cheaper. The north uses cream in its sauces, the south uses tomatoes; the north eats red meat, the south sticks to chicken, pork, and fish. The north uses butter, the south uses olive oil. The south (and all of Italy south of Milan) eats pasta, the northernmost regions sometime substitute it for risotto or polenta.

To sample the specialties of any region, fall back on that old standby: Ask. Cooks and waiters alike are usually happy to introduce foreigners to the particular pleasures of their table.

NORTHERN ITALY

PIEDMONT AND VALLE D'AOSTA   As befits these regions of cold winters, meat roasts and good, thick soups are served, often accompanied by thick slabs of polenta. Piedmont is the only place in Europe where strong-flavored white truffles are found (the lovely town of Alba is Italy's truffle center), and they're used in a favorite local dish, *fonduta*, a fonduelike cheese dip mixed with milk and eggs. Piedmont is also home to Gorgonzola cheese, white Asti Spumante wine (contrary to what most non-Italians think, there's a nonsparkling version, too), as well as several handsome reds.

LIGURIA   This is the homeland of the seafarers of Genoa, who brought back from the New World many cooking ingredients now taken for granted. What, for instance, would Italian cooking be without tomatoes, potatoes, or peppers? The sea-skirted region is also famous for its seafood, including a shell soup, *zuppa di datteri*, and for pesto, its basil-based pasta sauce. To the world of bread, Liguria has contributed focaccia, flat, delicious, often topped with herbs and, when eaten as a snack, with cheese and vegetables.

LOMBARDY   Like other northern places, Lombardy favors butter over olive oil for cooking and seems not to be overly concerned with cholesterol. A specialty is *ossobuco*, sliced veal sautéed with the bone and marrow, and served with a sauce, *gremalada*. A fine starter for any meal is the region's vegetable soup with rice and bacon, *minestrone alla milanese*, or a risotto made from arboreal rice that grows on the region's low-lying plains and is often served in place of pasta. *Panettone*, the region's most popular dessert, is a local version of fruit cake that arrived via Vienna practically unscathed, courtesy of Lombardy's 19th-century Austrian rulers. Remember, too, that

Lombardy is blessed with lakes—the Italian lakes, those romanticized bodies of water that supply lakeside restaurants with trout and perch, which are served sautéed and find their way into ravioli and other pasta dishes.

VENICE & THE VENETO   It made fame and fortune as the spice market of the world beginning in the 12th century, which may help account for the amazing ways local chefs dress up the scampi, crab, squid, and other creatures they pluck from the Adriatic. The Venetians also have raised that humble combination of liver and onions (*fegato alla veneziana*) to an irresistible level of haute cuisine, and done the same with rice and peas. Valpolicello (white) and Bardolino (red) wines are native to this region.

EMILIA-ROMAGNA   The region counts cheese and ham as its two top specialties, most notably *Parmegiano Regiano* (Parmesan cheese) and *prosciutto di Parma.* They appear on just about every menu: ham and melon is the ubiquitous appetizer here, and the rich cheese appears in and atop many dishes—often atop and in lasagna served with meat and tomato sauce (*alla bolognese*). Other pastas include *tagliatelli* and *tortellini,* often stuffed with pumpkin and squash and just about all of them topped in the creamy, buttery rich sauces for which the region is famous. Bologna, that wonderful old university city, is famous for its pork sausages, *salami,* and *mortadella,* as well as wonderful veal dishes.

TUSCANY   Here the Italian language, courtesy Dante, and Italian cooking, courtesy d'Medici, originated. *Bistecca alla florentine* is essentially a thick T-bone coated with olive oil, salt, and pepper and cooked very rare on a charcoal grill (in case you're longing for home). Another Florentine dish is *pollo alla diavolo,* chicken grilled and served with a ginger sauce. Tuscany is also famous for its beans, especially *fagioli* with oil, onions, and herb seasoning. And of course, Tuscany is one of Italy's most important wine producers, and red and white Chiantis are the perfect accompaniment to just about any meal.

UMBRIA & THE MARCHES   This mountainous region dishes up the kind of robust fare you would expect to find: *porchetta,* roasted suckling pig, trout, game birds, and wild boar, often accompanied by black truffles, mushrooms, and pungently seasoned with wild herbs. The popular Orvieto, white wine, is Umbrian, and the Marches produces another favorite, Verdicchio.

CENTRAL ITALY

LATIUM   It is, of course, dominated by Rome, and a list of the famous dishes of this city would certainly have to include *fettucine al burro,* or *alfredo,* not with a cream sauce as in America, but only butter, a whole lot of butter, and grated cheese; *saltimbocca,* thin slices of veal skewered to thin slices of *proscuitto* and sautéed in oil and Marsala wine; and *gnocchi alla romana,* pasta dumplings baked in butter and grated cheese. These hearty dishes are often accompanied by *carciofi alla romana,* artichokes cooked in oil and seasoned with wild mint. Frascati and Montefiascone are well-known white wines produced on the hillsides surrounding Rome.

THE ABRUZZI & MOLISE   These are mountainous regions that produce quite a lot of cheese, the most famous of which, *scamorza,* is molded into pear and egg shapes.

SOUTHERN ITALY

Americans, perhaps most foreigners, tend to think of "Italian food" as spaghetti and meatballs in a tomato sauce. That's native to southern cooking, which spread worldwide through the south's heavy emigration early in this century.

CAMPANIA Campania brings a lot to the table of world-renowned delights. Spaghetti began its long hike in Naples, and long ago the ill-fated residents of Pompeii chewed pizza. Fold the pizza crust to cover the topping and you have the region's other great contribution to fast food, *calzone*. Pasta comes with every sauce you can think of and probably a few you haven't. Try *alla vognole,* with shellfish, which could be clams, squid, or mussels, or settle for simpler fare like *pasta e fagoli,* pasta and beans. Naples is primarily a fish and seafood town, but a steak fillet topped with, of course, tomato sauce, *bistecca alla pizzaiola,* is very popular. *Mozzarella* and *provolone* are native cheeses. White Lacyrma Christi (Tears of Christ), and red Gragnano are local wines.

APULIA With Italy's longest coastline, Apulia has many kinds of fish and other seafood, all prepared wonderfully—as in the dishes that use oysters, lobster, mussels, and clams. Apulia also originated tasty *orcchiete* (little ears) pasta, often served with greens instead of a tomato sauce.

BASILICATA AND CALABRIA These regions serve what are essentially variations on the general theme of southern dishes, adding a few distinct dishes of their own. The regions' ginger-flavored *sopressato* sausage is hot stuff, true of much of the cooking in these southern climes. Lamb is a favorite dish here, as is game, such as wild boar and rabbit; *lepre alla cacciatora* is cooked in a sauce of oil, garlic, sage, rosemary, tomatoes, and the ever-popular ginger. *Spaghetti con lunache,* a spaghetti with a sauce made from snails, is a local specialty. This is also the land of the *aubergine* in many guises, the eggplant that the Greeks brought with them almost 3,000 years ago. For fish, try the spicy *trote arristo* (roast trout).

SICILY Sicily produces a bounty of citrus fruits, some of which go into one of the terrific Sicilian desserts, *cassata,* ice-cream cake with chocolate cream and candied fruits. That downfall of many a diet, *cannoli,* also originated in Sicily. The island's many cheeses, made mostly from goat's and sheep's milk, include *pecorino siciliano, formaggio al pepe, caciocavello,* and *Siciliano pepato,* a spiced cheese. For an entree try *farsumagru,* a stuffed veal dish. *Pasta ascuitta,* spaghetti with inkfish in its own inky juice is a Palermo specialty. Sicilian wines—and you will certainly encounter the sherrylike Marsala—generally lean to the sweet, with a high alcohol content.

SARDINIA The rough-and-tumble terrain is reflected in its fare. Many pigs graze on the island, and from them Sardinia makes wonderful hams, including *prosciuttos,* and sausages. Wild game and meat are island basics. *Vitella a s'idpìdu* is milk-fed veal roasted over charcoal. There's a great variety of fish and shellfish on menus along the coast. Meals tend to end with wonderful sweets, such as macaroons and *suspirus,* a concoction of crushed almonds, eggwhite, and sugar. The wine to accompany all that meat: try Oliena, a hearty red.

WINE

Italy happens to be ideal for growing grapes, having the right kind of terrain and the right amount of sun and rainfall. The Greeks recognized this nearly 3,000 years ago and transplanted vine cuttings from home to the south of present-day Italy (although it's possible the Etruscans slipped some vines onto the peninsula slightly ahead of the Greeks).

Today, Italy exports more wine to the rest of the world than any other country. There's plenty left at home to choose from—more than 2,000 different wines are produced in Italy. Over 30 years ago, the government brought order to this pleasant chaos by instituting Denominazione di Origine Controllata, or DOC, a system that is akin to the French Appellation Controlée and certifies a wine's quality and place of origin. The DOC stamp of approval ensures that a wine meets the fairly strict standards of the region in which it is grown—in short, that it is a decent bottle of wine. Some years later, a second category was ordained, Denominazione di Origine Controllata e Garantita, or DOCG, to denote wines of particularly high quality.

Very generally speaking, the wines of the north are drier and those of the south are sweeter and often quite a bit higher in alcohol volume, some as high as 20% (more sun equals more sugar). Each region has different growing conditions, so each has its own special wines. Piedmont is known for its heavy reds, including Barolo, Barbaresco, Barbera, and Grignolino, as well as sparkling white Asti Spumante; the Veneto, for Valpolicella and Bardolino reds and, among whites, Pinot Grigio and Soave; Emilia-Romagna, for white Albano and red Lambrusco. Chianti flows mightily in Tuscany, as does Brunello di Montalcino and Montepilciano; Montefiascone and Frascati, both whites, come from the vines that flourish on the hills around Rome; Ischia and Lacryma Christi have a delicate, somewhat sulfurous taste, due to the volcanic soil of Campania; Sicily is known for its sweet Marsala, an aperitif, as well as Corvo, Etna, and Lipari whites. Obviously, one of the pleasures of traveling in any of these regions is to sample these and other local wines close to the source.

Throughout Italy, and especially in Tuscany, you are also likely to encounter Vin Santo (sacred wine), made from grapes that are dried in the sun for a month or so before they are pressed. As a result, they yield a sweet wine that is not meant for drinking but for dunking biscotti, to provide a highly satisfying dessert. Grappa, made from the skins and other remnants at the bottom of the pressing barrel, is a fiery digestif.

5 Recommended Books

From the pens of natives and foreigners alike, Italy has inspired great literature, rich observations of its art, architecture, and history, and evocative writing on its food, wine, and other pleasures.

TRAVEL ACCOUNTS   Generations of travelers, among them some of Western civilization's most noted men and women of letters, have fallen under the spell of the peninsula. Still relevant are such classics as Goethe's *Italian Journey*, one of the most elegant travelogues ever written; Henry James's *Italian Hours*, full of youthful enthusiasm ("At last—for the first time—I live!"); D. H. Lawrence's *Etruscan Places* and *Twilight in Italy;* and John Ruskin's *The Stones of Venice*, required reading for anyone planning a visit to that city.

Jan Morris provides a marvelous 20th-century perspective in *The World of Venice*, which in turn is a fine companion piece to Mary McCarthy's *Venice Observed* (whose *The Stones of Florence* is equally worthy). Already classic are *A Traveler in Italy, A Traveler in Rome*, and *A Traveler in Southern Italy* by H. V. Morton, whose observations from the 1930s still ring ever so true, as do Norman Douglas's colorful accounts of travel through the south in the early days of this century, *Old Calabria*.

HISTORY   Werner Kerner's *The Etruscans* is a comprehensive and beautifully illustrated look at that civilization. Any history-minded traveler to Rome and Roman sights will want to tackle Edward Gibbons's *The History of the Decline and Fall of the Roman Empire* (also available in a Penguin abridged edition). Peter Gunn's *A Concise History of Italy* is as concise as this complex land allows a history to be, and Giuliano Procacci's *History of the Italian People* provides another fine overview.

If you are going to read one work on Italy's Renaissance brilliance, make it Jacob Burkhardt's highly readable *Civilization of the Renaissance in Italy*. The autobiographical *Life of Benvenuto Cellini* richly captures the social background of the Renaissance, and Castiglione's *The Book of the Courtier* is a fascinating account of life in a Renaissance Court.

Two works that are rich with insight into the fabric of everyday Italian life are *The Italians,* Luigi Barzini's overview of centuries of social culture, and Barbara Grizutti Harrison's *Italian Days,* a memoir of her quest for her roots, mixed with wry observations on the Italian way of life. Tim Parks, an Englishman who has settled outside Verona, is quickly becoming the favorite chronicler of late 20th-century Italian life with his *Italian Neighbors* and *An Italian Education.*

ART & ARCHITECTURE   *Roman Italy,* by T. W. Potter, is a comprehensive and heavily illustrated guide to Italy's vast archeological heritage. Giorgio Vasari's *Lives of the Artists* provides a veritable Who's Who of Renaissance art, with essays on Giotto, Brunelleschi, Mantegna, and others. Some of the most thorough and thoroughly enjoyable works on Italian painting are Bernard Berenson's *Italian Pictures of the Renaissance* and James Beck's *Italian Renaissance Painting.* For an equally knowledgeable—and remarkably entertaining and readable—overview of sculpture, consult John Pope-Hennessy's *Italian Gothic Sculpture, Italian Renaissance Sculpture,* and *Italian High Renaissance and Baroque Sculptures.* James Ackerman's *Palladio* is one the best works ever written on the architect, while Peter and Linda Murray's *The Architecture of the Italian Renaissance* provides a concise and all-encompassing look at some of the country's most important buildings.

LITERATURE   Dabbling in ancient Roman literature can be an insightful and downright juicy experience. For the most colorful accounts of the Empire, consider Livy's lively *Early History of Rome* and Petronius's *Satyricon,* about Rome under Nero, and Seutonius's *The Twelve Caesars.* Of recent vintage are *I, Claudius* and *Claudius, the God,* Robert Graves's enjoyable and informative fictional accounts of life in the Empire.

A brief perusal of other classics might include Giovanni Boccacio's *The Decameron,* the collection of 100 tales that capture the essence of 14th-century Italian life, and, of course, Dante's *The Divine Comedy* and Machiavelli's *The Prince.* Giuseppe Lampedusa's *The Leopard* is an exquisite novel evoking 19th-century Sicily, while a wealth of other literature captures aspects of Italy's turbulent 20th-century history. *Christ Stopped at Eboli,* by Carlo Levi, depicts the hardships of life in the south; *Bread and Wine* is Ignazio's Silone's hard-biting account of the his native Abruzzo. Giorgio Bassani's *Garden of the Finzi-Continis* is the story of Ferrara and the fate of its Jewish population during World War II, and Alberto Moravio's *Roman Tales* and *The Woman of Rome* are accounts of the dark side of one of the world's most fascinating and sensual cities. Travelers planning on visiting Il Vittorale, the home of the poet Gabriele D'Annunzio on Lago di Garda, might want to acquaint themselves with what is considered to his most lyrical work, *Halcyon.*

FOOD   Waverley Root's *The Food of Italy* is a mouth-watering, encyclopedic, and highly readable tribute to food and wine on the peninsula. Any cookbook by Marcella Hazen (*The Classic Italian Cookbook* and others) will inspire you to experiment with simple Italian cooking and is also simply a pleasure to read for a foretaste of the cuisine that awaits you. Burton Anderson's *Vino: The Wines and Wimemakers of Italy* and *Guide to Italian Wine* are thorough guides to the wines of each region. Marling's *Menu Master* is an indispensable little guide that translates typical Italian menus course by course and can be discretely brought to the table.

3

Planning a Trip to Italy

by Patricia Schultz

Every experienced traveler knows that an enjoyable, affordable trip begins way before boarding an aircraft. Study airline fare tables looking for special low-cost flights. Check out Italy's holiday calendar to see whether there are any upcoming holidays when hotel prices will rise by 15% to 20%.

This chapter is devoted to the where, when, and how of your trip—the advance-planning issues required to get it together and take it on the road.

1 Visitor Information & Entry Requirements

VISITOR INFORMATION

For information before you go, contact the **Italian National Tourist Office (Ente Nazionale Italiano per il Turismo, or ENIT).** In the United States branches are located in the following cities:

United States   630 Fifth Ave., Suite 1565, New York, NY 10111 (☎ **212/245-4822**); 401 N. Michigan Ave., Chicago, IL 60611 (☎ **312/644-0990**); 12400 Wilshire Blvd., Suite 550, Los Angeles, CA 90025 (☎ **310/820-0098**).

Canada   1 Place Ville Marie, suite 1914, Montréal, Québec H3B2C3 (☎ **514/866-7667**).

United Kingdom   1 Princes St., London W1R 8AY (☎ **0171/408-1254**).

You can also write directly (in English or Italian) to the provincial or local tourist boards of areas you plan to visit, but don't expect Swiss efficiency with a return response. These provincial tourist boards, **Ente Provinciale per il Turismo (E.P.T),** operate in the principal towns of the provinces. The local tourist boards, **Azienda Autonoma** *Soggiorno* or simply **Ufficio di Informazione,** operate in all places of tourist interest, and a list can be obtained from the Italian government tourist offices.

ENTRY REQUIREMENTS

United States, Canadian, Australian, and New Zealand citizens with a valid passport do not need a visa to enter Italy if they do not expect to stay more than 90 days and don't expect to work there. Those who want to stay longer can apply for a permit for an additional stay of 90 days, which as a rule is granted immediately. Applicants for such an extension should address themselves, with their passport, to the nearest police headquarters (*Questura*).

2 Money

There are no restrictions as to how much foreign currency you can bring into Italy, although if it is a substantial amount it is suggested that visitors declare the amount brought in so that, in case there's a question, they can prove to the Italian Customs office on leaving that the currency came from outside the country. Italian currency taken into or out of Italy may not exceed 200,000L in denominations of 50,000L or lower.

The basic unit of Italian currency is the lira (plural: lire). Coins are issued in denominations of 50L, 100L, 200L, and 500L (with 10s and 20s rarely found), and bills come in denominations of 1,000L, 2,000L, 5,000L, 10,000L, 50,000L, 100,000L, and 500,000L. Coins for 50L and 100L come in two sizes each, the newer ones both around the size of a dime (which cannot yet be used in any coin-accepting machines or public phones).

CURRENCY EXCHANGE   For the best exchange rate, go to a bank, not to a *cambio* (currency exchange), hotel, or shop. Currency and traveler's checks (for which you'll receive a better rate than cash) can be changed at the airport and some travel agencies, such as American Express and Thomas Cook. Note the rates and ask about commission fees; it can sometimes pay to shop around and ask the right questions.

Rarely will hotels in Italy accept a dollar-denominated check from your local home-town bank as a deposit sent in advance; if they do, they'll probably charge dearly for the conversion. In some cases they'll accept countersigned traveler's checks or a credit card (the latter more commonly done in the higher-grade hotels), but if you're pre-paying a deposit on hotel reservations, it's cheaper and easier to pay with a check drawn upon an Italian bank.

This can be arranged by a large commercial bank or by a currency specialist such as **Ruesch International,** 700 11th St. NW, Suite 400, Washington, DC 20001 (☎ **800/424-2923** or 202/408-1200). To place an order, call them and tell them the type and amount of the check you need. Ruesch will quote a U.S. dollar equivalent, adding a $2 service fee per check. After receiving your dollar-denominated personal check for the agreed-upon amount, Ruesch will mail you a lire-denominated bank draft, drawn at an Italian bank and payable to whichever party you specified. Ruesch maintains additional offices in New York, Los Angeles, Chicago, Atlanta, and Boston, although the Washington, D.C., office can supply the bank draft through phone orders.

ATM Networks   Plus and Visa networks of ATM or automated-teller machines can now be found throughout Italy's larger cities. There are over 13,000 Visa ATMs and more than 2,000 Plus ATMs throughout Italy, slowly taking hold in smaller towns as well.

If your bank card has been programmed with a PIN (Personal Identification Number), it is likely that you can use your card at ATMs abroad to withdraw money as a cash advance on your credit card. Before leaving, check to see if your PIN code must be reprogrammed for acceptable usage in Italy. Check with your home bank for affiliated Italian banks and possible locations of ATMs that accept Visa or Plus-marked cards.

The Italian Lira, the U.S. Dollar & the U.K. Pound

At this writing, US$1 = approximately 1,520 Italian lire, and this was the rate of exchange used to calculate the dollar values given throughout this book. The rate fluctuates from day to day, depending on a complicated series of economic and political factors, and might not be the same when you travel to Italy.

Likewise, the ratio of the British pound to the lira fluctuates constantly. At press time, £1 = approximately 2,380L, an exchange rate reflected in the table below.

Lire	U.S.$	U.K.£	Lire	U.S.$	U.K.£
50	0.03	0.02	20,000	13.16	8.40
100	0.07	0.04	25,000	16.45	10.50
300	0.20	0.13	30,000	19.74	12.60
500	0.33	0.21	35,000	23.03	14.70
700	0.46	0.29	40,000	26.32	16.80
1,000	0.66	0.42	45,000	29.61	18.90
1,500	0.99	0.63	50,000	32.89	21.00
2,000	1.32	0.84	100,000	65.79	42.00
3,000	1.97	1.26	125,000	82.27	52.50
4,000	2.63	1.68	150,000	98.68	63.00
5,000	3.29	2.10	200,000	131.58	84.00
7,500	4.93	3.15	250,000	164.47	105.00
10,000	6.58	4.20	500,000	328.95	210.00
15,000	9.87	6.30	1,000,000	657.89	420.00

American Express card-holders can use the ATM machines of Banco Popolare di Milano throughout Italy. Transaction fee is 2%, with a minimum charge of $2.50 and maximum of $20.00.

TRAVELER'S CHECKS   Traveler's checks are a safe method of carrying money, since in the event of theft, the value of your checks will be refunded if properly documented. Most large banks sell traveler's checks, charging fees that average between 1% and 2% of the value of the checks you buy. If your bank wants more than a 2% commission, it sometimes pays to call the traveler's check issuers directly for the address of outlets where this commission will cost less.

Issuers sometimes have agreements with groups to sell checks commission-free. For example, Automobile Association of America (AAA) clubs sell American Express checks in several currencies without commission.

American Express (☎ **800/221-7282** in the U.S. and Canada) is one of the largest and most immediately recognized issuers of traveler's checks. No commission is charged to holders of certain types of American Express credit cards.

Citicorp (☎ **800/645-6556** in the U.S. and Canada, or 813/623-1709, collect, from anywhere else in the world) issues their own checks. **Thomas Cook** (☎ **800/ 223-7373** in the U.S. and Canada; otherwise call 609/987-7300 collect from other parts of the world), issues MasterCard traveler's checks. **Interpayment Services** (☎ **800/732-1322** in the U.S. or Canada; call 44-17-33-31-89-49 collect from other parts of the world) sells Visa checks, which are issued by a consortium of member banks and the Thomas Cook organization.

What Things Cost in Rome	U.S. $
Taxi (central rail station to Piazza di Spagna)	8.55
Subway or public bus (to any destination)	1.00
Local telephone call	0.14
Double room at the Hassler (very expensive)	416.00
Double room at Hotel Romae (moderate)	92.10
Double room at Hotel Marini (inexpensive)	39.50
Continental breakfast (cappuccino and croissant at most cafes and bars)	3.00
Lunch for one at L'Insalata Ricca (inexpensive)	7.00
Dinner for one, without wine, at Relais Le Jardin (expensive)	75.00
Dinner for one, without wine, at Vecchia Roma (moderate)	25.00
Dinner for one, without wine, at Trattoria della Stampa (inexpensive)	12.00
Pint of beer	3.95
Glass of wine	2.00
Coca-Cola	1.50
Cup of coffee	1.30
Roll of color film, 36 exposures	6.50
Admission to the Vatican Museums and Gardens	8.30
Movie ticket	7.95

WIRE SERVICES   If you find yourself out of money, a new wire service provided by American Express can help you tap willing friends and family for emergency funds. Through **MoneyGram** from American Express, 6200 S. Québec St., P.O. Box 5118, Englewood, CO 80155 (☎ **800/926-9400**), money can be sent around the world in less than 10 minutes. Cash and credit cards (Visa, Discover, or MasterCard) are the only acceptable forms of payment (ironically, American Express cards are not accepted for this transaction). AMEX's fee for the service is $20 for the first $200; $30 up to $400, and with a sliding scale for larger sums. The beneficiary can pick up the transaction in US$ traveler's checks at any of the American Express offices in Milan, Florence, Rome, or Venice and must present a photo ID (such as a passport) to receive money.

3 When to Go

CLIMATE   It's warm all over Italy in summer, especially inland. The high temperatures (measured in Italy in degrees Celsius) begin in Rome in May, often lasting until some time in late September. Winters in the north of Italy are cold with rain and snow, and December and January are generally unpleasant unless you're skiing in Cortona. But in the south the weather is mild in the winter months, averaging in the high 40s or 50s Fahrenheit in winter.

For the most part, it's drier in Italy than in North America. High temperatures, therefore, don't seem as bad since the humidity is lower; exceptions are cities known for their humidity factor, such as Florence and Venice. In Rome, Naples, and the south, temperatures can stay in the 90s for days, but nights are most often comfortably cooler.

What Things Cost in Naples	U.S. $
Taxi from rail station to the port	8.50
Subway (to any destination)	0.90
Local telephone call	0.14
Double room at Grande Albergo Vesuvio (expensive)	268.80
Double room at Le Fonatane del Mare (moderate)	72.35
Double room at Hotel Casanova (inexpensive)	36.20
Continental breakfast (cappuccino and croissant)	2.50
Lunch for one at Brandi (historic pizzeria)	13.15
Lunch for one, without wine, at Mimi alla Ferrovia (moderate)	20.00
Dinner for one, without wine, at Vini e Cucina (inexpensive)	8.00
Dinner for one, without wine, at Dante e Beatrice (moderate)	14.80
Pint of beer	3.75
Glass of wine	1.60
Coca-Cola	1.50
Cappuccino	1.00
Roll of color film, 36 exposures	5.95
Admission to the Museo Archeologico Nazionale	7.70
Movie ticket	5.50

ITALY'S AVERAGE DAILY TEMPERATURE & MONTHLY RAINFALL

Florence

	Jan	Feb	Mar	Apr	May	June	July	Aug	Sept	Oct	Nov	Dec
Temp. (°F)	45	47	50	60	67	75	77	70	64	63	55	46
Rainfall"	3	3.3	3.7	2.7	2.2	1.4	1.4	2.7	3.2	4.9	3.8	2.9

Naples

	Jan	Feb	Mar	Apr	May	June	July	Aug	Sept	Oct	Nov	Dec
Temp. (°F)	50	54	58	63	70	78	83	85	75	66	60	52
Rainfall"	4.7	4	3	3.8	2.4	.8	.8	2.6	3.5	5.8	5.1	3.7

Rome

	Jan	Feb	Mar	Apr	May	June	July	Aug	Sept	Oct	Nov	Dec
Temp. (°F)	49	52	57	62	72	78	82	78	73	65	56	47
Rainfall"	2.3	1.5	2.9	3.0	2.8	2.9	1.5	1.9	2.8	2.6	3.0	2.1

HOLIDAYS   Offices and shops in Italy are closed on the following dates: January 1 (New Year's Day), Easter Monday, April 25 (Liberation Day), May 1 (Labor Day), August 15 (Assumption of the Virgin), November 1 (All Saints' Day), December 8 (Feast of the Immaculate Conception), December 25 (Christmas Day), and December 26 (Santo Stefano).

Closings are also observed in the following cities on feast days honoring their patron saints: Venice, April 25 (St. Mark); Florence, Genoa, and Turin, June 24 (St. John the Baptist); Rome, June 29 (Sts. Peter and Paul); Palermo, July 15 (Santa Rosalia); Naples, September 19 (St. Gennaro); Bologna, October 4 (St. Petronio);

Cagliari, October 30 (St. Saturnino); Trieste, November 3 (San Giusto); Bari, December 6 (St. Nicola); and Milan, December 7 (St. Ambrose).

In addition, try to avoid traveling to Italy in August, as this is when most Italians take their vacations and many shops and restaurants will be closed. Keep in mind that many of the less expensive hotels we list don't have air-conditioning, and nights can be intolerable.

ITALY CALENDAR OF EVENTS

For more information about these and other events, contact the various tourist offices throughout Italy. Dates often vary from year to year.

January
- **Carnival in Viareggio,** on the Tuscan coast. Fireworks, pageants, parades of papier-mâché floats, and a flower show. Popular with the kids and not as theatrical and culturally inclined as Venice's rendition. Dates vary; parades take place three consecutive weekends, culminating on Shrove Tuesday (February 24, 1998).
- **Epiphany Celebrations.** All cities, towns, and villages in Italy stage Roman Catholic Epiphany observances. One of the most festive celebrations is the Christmas/Epiphany Fair at Rome's Piazza Navona. From Christmas until January 6.
- **Festival of Italian Popular Song, San Remo (the Italian Riviera).** A three-day festival when major artists perform the latest Italian song releases. Late January.
- **Foire de Saint Ours, Aosta, Valle d'Aosta.** Observing a tradition that's existed for 10 centuries, artisans from the mountain valleys come together to display their wares—often made of wood, lace, wool, or wrought iron—created during the long winter months. Late January.

February
- ✪ **Carnival in Venice.** Venice's Carnevale evokes the final theatrical days of the Venetian Republic. Histrionic presentations, elaborate costumes, and music of all types in every piazza cap the festivities, culminating the last week prior to the beginning of Lent.

  Where: Throughout Venice. **When:** The week before Shrove Tuesday (Feb. 24, 1998). **How:** The balls are by invitation, but the cultural events, piazza performances, and fireworks are open to everyone. More information is available from the Venice Tourist Office, San Marco, Giardinetti Reali, Palazzetto Selva (☎ **041/52-26-356**).

April
- **Good Friday and Easter Week observances,** throughout Italy. Processions and age-old ceremonies—some from pagan days, some from the Middle Ages—are staged. The most colorful and evocative are in Trapanai and other towns throughout Sicily. Beginning on the Thursday or Friday before Easter Sunday, usually April.
- **Scoppio del Carro (Explosion of the Cart), in Florence.** An ancient observance: A cart laden with flowers and fireworks is drawn by three white oxen to the Duomo, where at noon mass a mechanical dove detonates it from the altar by means of a wire that passes through the Duomo's open doors. Easter Sunday.

May
- **Corso dei Ceri.** Every May 15, in this centuries-old ceremony, 1,000-pound wooden "candles" (ceri) are raced through the streets of this perfectly preserved medieval hill town in Umbria. Celebrating the feast day of St. Ubaldo, the town's patron saint, the candles are mounted by statues of the patron saints of the town's

medieval guilds, and are raced through the narrow streets of Gubbio and up a steep hill to the monastery.

⊕ **Maggio Musicale Fiorentino ("Musical May Florentine").** Italy's oldest and most prestigious festival takes place in Florence, the venue for opera, ballet performances, and concerts.
   Where: Teatro Comunale, V. Solferino 16; Teatro della Pergola, V. d. Pergola 18; and various other venues, including Piazza della Signoria and the courtyard of the Pitti Palace. **When:** Late April into early July. **How:** Schedule and ticket information available from Maggio Musicale Fiorentino/Teatro Comunale, V. Solferino 16, 50123 Firenze (☎ 055/27-791).

June

• **Venice's Biennale.** This is Europe's most prestigious—and controversial—International Exposition of Modern Art, taking place in odd-numbered years only from June until October. Over 50 nations take part, with art displayed in permanent pavilions in the Public Gardens and elsewhere about town. June to September.

• **L'Infiorata, Genzano, Lazio,** is a religious procession along streets carpeted with flowers in splendid designs, often copies of famous artworks. Details available from Azienda Autonoma di Soggiorno e Turismo dei Laghi e Castelli Romani, V. Risorgimento

• **San Ranieri e Gioco del Ponte, Pisa.** Pisa honors its own saint with candlelit parades followed the next day by eight-rower teams competing in 16th-century costumes. June 16 and 17. The Gioco del Ponte takes place the last Sunday of June, with teams taking part in a hotly contested tug-of-war on the Ponte di Mezzo that spans the Arno River.

⊕ **Festival dei Due Mondi.** Dating from 1958 (and with special performances already on the boards for 1998's 40th anniversary), this was the creation of Maestro Gian Carlo Menotti whose 85th birthday will be celebrated in 1997. International performers convene for three weeks of dance, drama, opera, concerts, and art exhibits; continues till mid-July.
   Where: Spoleto, an Umbrian hill town north of Rome. **When:** From last week in June to mid-July. **How:** Tickets and information available from Festival d. Due Mondi, V. Cesare Beccaria 18, 00196 Roma (☎ 06/32-10-288). For information in Spoleto, call the festival's office at either **0743/40-700** or 0743/44-097. Information is also available from the box office, c/o Teatro Nuovo, Piazza Belli, 06049 Spoleto, Italy (☎ **0743/22-03-65**).

July

⊕ **Il Palio.** Palio fever grips the Tuscan hill town of Siena for a wild and exciting horse race from the Middle Ages. Pageantry, costumes, and the celebrations of the victorious *contrada* mark the well-attended spectacle. It's a "no rules" event: Even a horse without a rider can win the race.
   Where: The Piazza del Campo at Siena. **When:** July 2 and August 16. **How:** Details available by writing Azienda di Promozione Turistica, Pz. d. Campo 56, 53100 Siena (☎ 0577/28-05-51). Tickets usually sell out by January.

• **Arena Outdoor Opera Season,** Verona. Brings culture buffs to the 20,000-seat Roman amphitheater. Season lasts from early July to mid-August for awesome productions of *Aïda* and others.

• **La Festa del Redentore (The Feast of the Redeemer),** in Venice. Marks the lifting of the plague in July of 1578, with fireworks, pilgrimages, and boating on the lagoon. Third Saturday and Sunday in July.

• **Festival Internazionale di Musica Antica,** Urbino. A cultural extravaganza, as international performers converge on Raphael's birthplace for 10 days in late July.

It's the most important Renaissance and baroque music festival in Italy, focusing on music written before 1750. Details available from Fondazione Italiana Per La Musica Antica C.P. 6159 I-00195 Roma (☎ **06/37-29-667** or 06/82-72-447).

August

○ **Venice International Film Festival.** Ranking after Cannes, this film festival at Venice brings together stars, directors, producers, and filmmakers from all over the world. Films are shown both day and night to an international jury as well as to the public.

   Where: Palazzo del Cinema, on the Lido and other venues. **When:** Late August to early September. **How:** Contact Venice Tourist Office, Giardinetti Reali, Palazzetto Selva, San Marco (☎ **041/52-26-356**), for exact dates.

September

• **Regata Storica,** on the Grand Canal in Venice. All seaworthy gondolas in Venice participate in the spectacular maritime procession down the Grand Canal that is followed by the much awaited race. First Sunday in September.

October

• **Sagra del Tartufo,** Alba, Piedmont. Honors the expensive truffle in Alba, the truffle capital of Italy, with contests, truffle-hound competitions, and tastings of this ugly but precious and delectable fungus. For details, contact the Azienda di Promozione Turistica, piazza Medford, 12051 Alba (☎ **0173/35-833**).

December

○ **Opera Season at La Scala.** The most famous opera house of them all.

   Where: Teatro alla Scala, Pz. d. Scala, Milan. **When:** The season opens on December 7, the feast day of Milan's patron St. Ambrogio, and runs into July. **How:** Although it's very difficult to get tickets, a few seats are sometimes available; ☎ **02/80-70-41** for information; 80-91-26 for reservations.

ROME CALENDAR OF EVENTS

January

• **Carnival,** in piazza Navona. Marks the last day of the children's market and lasts until dawn of the following day. Usually January 5.
• Festa di Sant'Agnese, at Sant'Agnese Fuori le Mura. An ancient ceremony in which two lambs are blessed and shorn. Their wool is then used later for palliums. Usually January 17.

March

• **Festa di Santa Francesca Romana,** at Piazzale del Colosseo near the Church of Santa Francesco Romana in the Roman Forum. A blessing of cars. Usually March 9.
• **Festa di San Giuseppe,** in the Trionfale Quarter, north of the Vatican. The heavily decorated statue of the saint is brought out at a fair with food stalls, concerts, and sporting events. Usually March 19.

April

• **Festa della Primavera.** The Spanish Steps are decked out with banks of flowers, and later orchestral and choral concerts are presented in Trinita dei Monti. Dates vary.
• **Holy Week.** The most notable procession is led by the pope, passing the Colosseum and the Roman Forum up to Palatine Hill. A torchlit parade caps the observance. Sometimes at the end of March, but often in April.

- **Easter Sunday,** Piazza di San Pietro. In an event broadcast around the world, the Pope gives his blessing from a balcony of St. Peter's.

May

- **International Horse Show,** at the Piazza di Siena in the Villa Borghese. Usually May 1–10, but dates can vary.

June

- **Son et Lumière,** at the Roman Forum and Tivoli. These areas are dramatically lit at night. Early June until the end of September.
- **Festa di San Pietro,** St. Peter's Basilica. The most significant Roman religious festival, observed with solemn rites in St. Peter's. Usually around June 29.

July

✪ **La Festa di Nolantri.** Trastevere, the most colorful quarter of Old Rome, becomes a gigantic outdoor restaurant, as tons of food and drink are consumed at tables lining the streets. Merrymakers and musicians provide the entertainment.

   Where: Trastevere. **When:** Mid-July. **How:** After reaching the quarter, find the first empty table and try to get a waiter. But guard your valuables. Details available from Ente Provinciale per il Turismo, V. Parigi 11, 00185 Roma (☎ **06/ 48-89-92-00**).

August

- **Festa delle Catene,** in the Church of San Pietro in Vincoli. The relics of St. Peter's captivity go on display. August 1.

September

- **Sagra dell'Uva,** a harvest festival in the Basilica of Maxentius in the Roman Forum. Musicians in ancient costumes entertain, and grapes are sold at reduced prices. Dates vary, usually early September.

December

- **Christmas Blessing of the Pope,** Piazza di San Pietro. Delivered at noon from a balcony of St. Peter's Basilica. It's broadcast around the world. December 25.

4 Outdoors in Italy

The Italian countryside has always been legendary for its beauty and architectural richness. Several companies specialize in introducing travelers to its wonders, usually through hill treks and mountain climbing. As a budget traveler, you may want to hike or bike on your own, making arrangements through local tourist offices. Listed below are some outdoor guided trips that are good value for the money.

CYCLING TOURS   Cycling tours are a good way to see Italy at your own pace. Some of the best are featured by the **Cyclists' Touring Club,** 69 Meadrow, Godalming, Surrey GU7 3HS (☎ **01483/41-72-17**). It charges £25 ($40) a year for adults and £12.50 ($20) for those 17 and under for membership, part of which includes information and suggested cycling routes through most European countries.

   For a guided one-day bike trip, see chapter 6 for information about **I Bike Italy** forays into the idyllic Tuscan countryside surrounding Florence. Bikes, a guide, a picnic lunch, and car transfer in and out of the city center are provided. Bike rentals in Lucca (Tuscany) can provide you with wheels to visit a number of the nearby Lucchesi country villas; see tourist office in Lucca.

HIKING IN THE ALPS   For serious trekkers, **Club Alpino Italiano,** 7 V. E. Fonseca Pimental, Milan 20127 (☎ **02/26-14-13-78**), publishes a guide *rifugi alpini* listing various huts available to hikers in the Italian Alps. The two-volume guide costs 95,000L ($60.80).

Waymark Holidays, 44 Windsor Rd., Slough Berkshire, England SL1 2EJ (☎ 01753/51-64-77), offers a walking tour along the Alta Via 4, the Italian "highway," which winds its way through the snow-encrusted peaks and lush green valleys of the Gran Paradiso National Park in northern Italy. The route is rigorous, but lets you experience unparalleled mountain vistas. The tour is 14 nights, with 2 consecutive nights spent in each hut to allow for exploration of individual peaks. The price is £675 ($1,080) including all meals and accommodations.

For a one-day guided or do-it-yourself walk in the area around San Gimignano in Tuscany, see chapter 7 for information about organized half- or full-day trips; San Gimignano's local tourist office has the details. Where the location lends itself to walking, many local tourist offices have detailed walking maps of the networks of hiking trails, popular itineraries particularly in the Dolomites. Umbria's hill town of Spoleto has a number of trails leading to hilltop retreats and historical monasteries; inquire at Spoleto's tourist office.

HORSEBACK RIDING IN TUSCANY   Some travelers prefer to visit Tuscany in a style popularized by everyone from the Etruscans to the soldiers and *condottieri* of the Renaissance: on horseback. One company that can help you combine a trek through the Italian countryside with equestrian panache is **Equitour,** P.O. Box 807, Dubois, WY 82513 (☎ 800/545-0019 in the U.S. and Canada). Established in 1983 from a base in northwestern Wyoming, this company markets highly organized horseback-riding holidays throughout the world. The tours are limited to four to seven participants and last for eight days, which usually includes six days of riding through the region around Siena. Only English tack is used. The tour traverses most of the breadth of Tuscany; nights are spent in a series of farmhouses and inns. The trek costs around $1,300 per person, double occupancy, and includes all meals and accommodations, horse rental, and guide fees.

5 Special Interest & Educational Travel

Note: The inclusion of an organization in this section is in no way to be interpreted as a guarantee. Information about the organization is presented only to point you toward possibilities for your own investigations.

CULTURAL EXCHANGE

Italy doesn't have an established "Meet the Italians" program, but cities and most towns have an official tourist office (called either Ente Provinciale per il Turismo or Azienda Autonoma di Soffiorno e Turismo) that might arrange for you to stay with or just meet an Italian family. Such arrangements are usually made for those staying for several weeks or more in an Italian city. Requests should be sent several months before your trip to Italy by writing to the official tourist office of the town.

The Friendship Force, 57 Forsyth St. NW, Suite 900, Atlanta, GA 30303 (☎ 404/522-9490), is a nonprofit organization existing to foster friendship among peoples around the world. Each participant is required to spend two weeks in the host country with one full week in the home of a family as a guest. Most volunteers spend the second week traveling in the host country.

Servas (an Esperanto word meaning "to serve"), 11 John St., Room 407, New York, NY 10038 (☎ 212/267-0252), is a nonprofit, nongovernmental, international, interfaith network of travelers and hosts whose goal is to help build world peace, goodwill, and understanding. They do this by providing opportunities for contacts among people of diverse cultures and communities worldwide through two-day home visits. Travelers pay a $55 annual fee, a $25 list deposit, fill out an application, and are interviewed for suitability. Hosts also are interviewed, make a voluntary contribution of $25, and are contacted by travelers who arrange for a two-night visit.

EDUCATIONAL TRAVEL

LEARNING THE LANGUAGE   Courses in Italian language, fine arts, history, literature, and Italian culture for foreign students are available at several centers throughout the Italian peninsula, with the best-recommended usually headquartered in what most Italians refer to as their nation's intellectual and cultural capital, Florence. You can write to any of the following addresses for information: **The British Institute of Florence,** Courses on Italian Language and Culture, Palazzo Lanfredini, Lungarno Guicciardini 9, 50125 Firenze (☎ **055/284031;** fax 055/289557); the **Centro di Lingua e Cultura Italiana per Stranieri,** Pz. Santo Spirito 4, 50134 Firenze (☎ **055/23-96-966;** fax 055/28-08-00); and the **Centro Linguistico Italiano Dante Alighieri,** V. de' Bardi 12, 50125 Firenze (☎ **055/2342984;** fax 055/2342766). The **Italian Cultural Institute** in New York (☎ **212/879-4242**) may also be able to provide information.

JUST FOR SENIORS   One of the most dynamic organizations for senior citizens is **Elderhostel,** 75 Federal St., Boston, MA 02110 (☎ **617/426-7788**), established in 1975. Elderhostel offers informal educational programs throughout Europe, most lasting for around three weeks. These represent good value, considering that airfare, hotel accommodations in student dormitories or modest inns, all meals, and tuition are included. Courses are especially focused in the liberal arts. Participants must be older than 55. Elderhostel's offerings in Italy include a historic and artistic overview of Sicily from headquarters in the fishing village of Mondello (near Palermo), and an introduction to the art and architecture of Umbria and Tuscany. Write the address above for Elderhostel's free catalog and a list of upcoming courses and destinations. Programs, of course, are subject to change.

6 Organized Tours, Package Tours & Tour Operators

With a good tour operator, you can know ahead of time just what your trip will cost—give or take a gratuity or two, or buying a souvenir. Best of all, when moving around a lot, you won't be bothered with having to arrange your own connections and transportation in places where language might be a problem, or looking after your own luggage, coping with reservations and payment at individual hotels, and facing other "nuts and bolts" requirements of travel in a foreign culture. Although several of the best-rated moderately priced tour companies are described below, check as well with a good travel agent for the latest offerings and advice.

By buying from a tour operator, you are tapping into their tremendous bulk buying power. They provide convenience, reliability, and expertise, and now offer the option of escorted and unhosted tours. But package tours are still not for everyone, and in the case of escorted trips, depend upon the dynamics of a bus full of strangers who may or may not get along swimmingly. Free time and serendipity to wander and explore are often at a premium. Some travelers may find the biggest compromise is the hotel factor. Most lodging is found in large modern facilities, not in the small and charming and characterful places in the centro storico.

One of the more moderate-priced package-tour operators for travel in Italy is **Italiatour,** a company of the Alitalia Group (☎ **800/845-3365** or 212/765-2183), which offers a wide variety of tours through all parts of the peninsula. The company appeals to the free-at-heart (i.e., clients who don't want any semblance of a tour), and specializes in tours for independent travelers who ride from one destination to another by train or rental car. In most cases, the company sells pre-reserved hotel accommodations which are usually less expensive than if you had reserved yourself. Their range of accommodations begins with three-star hotels which, when booked with their bulk volume discount, can account for a very attractive bottom line. Because of the company's close link with Alitalia, the prices quoted for air passage are sometimes among the most reasonable on the retail market. A best-selling loosely organized eight-night jaunt through the major art cities of Italy begins at $1,349 in low season, $1,489 in high season, and includes airfare, double occupancy in a three-star hotel, breakfasts, transfers between cities, and some city tours. Also attractive is their popular nine-day/seven-night "Treasures of Sicily" experience, beginning at $1,676 in low season and $1,866 in high season. Airfare, three-star hotel, all meals, all tours, and transfers between cities are included.

Also working with volume and affiliated with Alitalia—and therefore promising big-volume discounts—is the reputable **Central Holidays Tours (CHT)** (☎ **800/ 935-500**), which offers low and high season package tours that are escorted, hosted, or independent. Since 1972 they've been offering tours to Italy, with extensions to other Mediterranean countries.

However, you might get more attention by going with the small, established agencies who specialize in Italy and often come up with rates comparable to the big guys: **Maiellano/Travel Auto** (☎ **800/223-1616**) offers all-inclusive tours and/or car rental; both **Pino Welcome** (☎ **800/247-6578** or 212/682-5400) and **Penem** (☎ **800/628-1345** or 212/730-7675) offer a pick-and-choose menu of car rental, air, and hotel; **Auto Europe/Time & Tide** (☎ **800/472-8999** or 212/861-2500) specializes in discount car rental but successfully expanded into all aspects of travel.

7 Health & Insurance

STAYING HEALTHY   You will encounter few health problems traveling in Italy. The tap water is generally safe to drink (though complaints often have to do with what it tastes like, lacking our chemical makeup), the milk pasteurized, and health services good.

Bring along copies of your prescriptions that are written in the generic—not brand-name—form. If you need a doctor, your hotel can recommend one or you can contact your embassy or consulate. You can also obtain a list of English-speaking doctors before you leave from the **International Association for Medical Assistance to Travelers (IAMAT),** in the United States at 417 Center St., Lewiston, NY 14092 (☎ 716/754-4883); in Canada at 40 Regal Rd., Guelph, ON N1K 1B5 (☎ **519/ 836-0102**).

If you suffer from a chronic illness or special medical condition, consider purchasing a Medic Alert identification bracelet or necklace, which will immediately alert any doctor to your condition and will provide Medic Alert's 24-hour hotline phone number so that foreign doctors can obtain medical information on you. The initial membership is $35, and there's a $15 yearly fee. Contact the **Medic Alert Foundation,** 2323 Colorado Ave., Turlock, CA 95381-1009 (☎ **800/432-5378**).

INSURANCE   Before purchasing any additional insurance, check your homeowner's, automobile, and medical insurance policies, as well as the insurance provided by your credit card companies and auto and travel clubs. You may have adequate off-premises theft coverage or your credit card company may even provide cancellation coverage if your airline ticket is paid for with a credit card.

Remember, Medicare only covers U.S. citizens traveling in Mexico and Canada, not in Italy or other European countries. Also note that to submit any insurance claim you must always have thorough documentation, including all receipts, police reports, and medical records.

Travel Guard International, 1145 Clark St., Stevens Point, WI 54481 (☎ **800/ 826-1300**), features comprehensive insurance programs starting as low as $44. The program covers basically everything: trip cancellation and interruption, lost luggage, medical coverage abroad, emergency assistance, accidental death, and a 24-hour worldwide emergency hotline. A pre-existing medical conditions waiver is included.

Travel Insured International, Inc., P.O. Box 280568, East Hartford, CT 06128-0568 (☎ **800/243-3174** in the U.S., 203/528-7663 outside the U.S. between 7:45am and 7pm EST). Trip cancellation and emergency evacuation costs $5.50 for each $100 of coverage. Travel accident and illness insurance goes for $10 for 6 to 10 days, and $500 of insurance for lost, damage, or delayed luggage is $20 for 10 days. The insurance is underwritten by The Travelers.

Mutual of Omaha (Tele-Trip Co., Inc.), Mutual of Omaha Plaza, Omaha, NE 68175, offers cruise and tour insurance packages priced from $49 to $57 per person (or $98 to $114 per couple) for a tour valued at $1,000 with no time limitation on the trip. Included in the packages are travel-assistance services and financial protection against trip cancellation, trip interruption, flight and baggage delays, sickness, accident-related medical costs, accidental death and dismemberment, and medical evacuation coverages. Application for insurance can be made over the phone with a major credit card (☎ **800/228-9792**).

8 Tips for Travelers with Special Needs

FOR TRAVELERS WITH DISABILITIES   Before you go, there are several agencies that can provide advance-planning information. One is the **Travel Information Service,** MossRehab Hospital, 1200 W. Tabor Rd., Philadelphia, PA 19141, which provides information to telephone callers only: Call **215/456-9603** (voice) or 215/456-9602 (TDD).

You may also want to consider joining a tour for visitors with disabilities. Names and addresses of such tour operators and miscellaneous travel information can be obtained by writing to the **Society for the Advancement of Travel for the Handicapped,** 347 Fifth Ave., Suite 601, New York, NY 10016 (☎ **212/ 447-7248**). Annual membership dues are $45, or $25 for senior citizens and students. Send a stamped, self-addressed envelope.

FEDCAP Rehabilitation Services (formerly known as the Federation of the Handicapped), 154 W. 14th St., New York, NY 10011 (☎ **212/727-4200**), operates summer tours to Europe and elsewhere for its members. Membership costs $4 yearly.

You can also obtain a copy of "Air Transportation of Handicapped Persons," published by the U.S. Department of Transportation. For a free copy write for Free Advisory Circular No. AC12032, Distribution Unit, U.S. Department of Transportation, Publications Division, M-4332, Washington, DC 20590.

For the blind or visually impaired, the best source is the **American Foundation for the Blind,** 11 Penn Plaza, Suite 300, New York, NY 10001 (☎ **800/232-5463,** or 212/502-7600 for ordering information kits and supplies). It offers information on travel and the various requirements for the transport of and border formalities for seeing-eye dogs. It also issues identification cards to those who are legally blind.

FOR GAY & LESBIAN TRAVELERS Since 1861 Italy has had liberal legislation regarding homosexuality, but that doesn't mean it's always looked upon favorably in a Catholic country, especially in Sicily, although Taormina has long been a gay mecca. Homosexuality is much more accepted in the north than in the south. However, all major towns and cities have an active gay life, especially Florence, Milan, and Rome. Capri is the gay resort of Italy. Even more than Rome, Milan considers itself the "gay capital" of Italy, and is the headquarters of ARCI Gay, the country's leading gay organization, with branches throughout Italy.

To learn about gay and lesbian travel in Italy, you can secure publications or else join data-dispensing organizations before you go. Men can order *Spartacus,* the international gay guide ($32.95), or *Odysseus 1997, The International Gay Travel Planner,* a guide to international gay accommodations ($25). Both lesbians and gay men might want to pick up a copy of *Gay Travel A to Z* ($16), which specializes in general information, as well as listings of bars, hotels, restaurants, and places of interest for gay travelers throughout the world. These books and others are available from **Giovanni's Room,** 1145 Pine St., Philadelphia, PA 19107 (☎ **215/923-2960**).

Our World, 1104 North Nova Rd., Suite 251, Daytona Beach, FL 32117 (☎ **904/441-5367**), is a magazine devoted to options and bargains for gay and lesbian travel worldwide. It costs $35 for 10 issues. The upscale *Out and About,* 8 West 19th St., Suite 401, New York, NY 10011 (☎ **800/929-2268**), has been hailed for its "straight" reporting about gay travel. It profiles the best gay or gay-friendly hotels, gyms, clubs, and other places throughout the world. Its cost is $49 a year for 10 information-packed issues. Both publications are also available at most gay and lesbian bookstores.

The **International Gay Travel Association (IGTA),** P.O. Box 4974, Key West, FL 33041 (☎ **800/448-8550,** voice mailbox, or 305/292-0217), encourages gay and lesbian travel worldwide. With around 1,200 member travel agencies, it specializes in networking travelers with the appropriate gay-friendly service organizations or tour specialists. It offers a quarterly newsletter, marketing mailings, and a membership directory that is updated four times a year.

The following travel agencies specialize in gay and lesbian travel and offer frequent although erratically scheduled tours to Italy: **Yellowbrick Road Travel** (☎ 800/642-2488 or 312/561-1800); **Islanders/Kennedy Travel** (☎ 800/988-1181 or 212/242-3222); **Toto Tours** (☎ 800/565-1211 or 312/274-8686); **Advance-Damron Vacations** (☎ 800/695-0880 or 713/682-2650).

FOR SENIORS Many senior discounts are available, but note that some may require membership in a particular association.

For information before you go, obtain the free booklet "101 Tips for the Mature Traveler," from **Grand Circle Travel,** 347 Congress St., Boston, MA 02210 (☎ **800/221-2610** or 617/350-7500).

SAGA International Holidays, 222 Berkeley St., Boston, MA 02116 (☎ **800/343-0273**), runs all-inclusive tours for seniors, preferably for those 50 years old or older. Insurance is included in the net price of their tours.

AARP (American Association of Retired Persons) is the best organization in the United States for seniors. It offers discounts on car rentals and hotels. For more information, contact AARP at 601 E St. NW, Washington, DC 20049 (☎ **202/434-AARP**).

Information is also available from the **National Council of Senior Citizens,** 1331 F St. NW, Washington, DC 20004-1171 (☎ **202/347-8800**), which charges $12 per person or per couple, for which you receive a monthly newsletter, part of which is devoted to travel tips. Reduced discounts on hotel and auto rentals are available.

If you are 45 or older and need a companion to share your travel and leisure with, consider contacting **Golden Companions,** P.O. Box 5249, Reno, NV 89513 (☎ **702/324-2227**). Founded in 1987, this helpful service has found companions for hundreds of mature travelers from all over the United States and Canada. Members meet through a confidential mail network.

Mature Outlook, P.O. Box 10448, Des Moines, IA 50306 (☎ **800/336-6330**) is a travel organization for people over 50. Members are offered discounts at ITC-member hotels and a bimonthly magazine. The $14.95 annual membership fee entitles members to coupons for discounts at Sears & Roebuck Co., as well as savings on selected auto rentals and restaurants.

FOR FAMILIES   *Family Travel Times* is published quarterly by **TWYCH, Travel with Your Children,** and includes a weekly call-in service for subscribers. Subscriptions cost $40 a year and can be ordered by writing to TWYCH, 40 Fifth Ave., New York, NY 10011 (☎ **212/477-5524**).

Families Welcome!, 4711 Hope Valley Rd., Durham, NC 27707 (☎ **800/ 326-0724** or 919/489-2555), is a travel company specializing in worry-free vacations for families and can help with apartment rentals in Rome, Florence, and Venice.

FOR STUDENTS   **Council Travel** (a subsidiary of the Council on International Educational Exchange) is America's largest student, youth, and budget travel group, with more than 60 offices worldwide. The main office is at 205 E. 42nd St., New York, NY 10017 (☎ **212/822-2700**). International Student Identity Cards, issued to all bona fide students for $16, entitle holders to generous travel and other discounts. Discounted international and domestic air tickets are available. Eurail passes, YHA passes, weekend packages, and hostel/hotel accommodations are also bookable.

Real budget travelers should consider joining **Hostelling International/American Youth Hostels.** For information write Hostelling Information/American Youth Hostels, 733 15th St. NW, No. 840, Washington, DC 20005 (☎ **800/444-6111** or 202/783-6161). Membership costs $25 annually, but those under age 18 pay $10 and those over 54 pay $15.

9 Getting There

BY PLANE

The upheavals that shook the airline industry during the early 1990s have subsided a bit, but despite relative calm, the industry may still undergo some changes during the life of this edition. For last-minute conditions, including even a rundown on carriers flying into Italy, check with a travel agent or the individual airlines.

Alitalia (☎ **800/223-5730**) is, of course, the major Italian carrier, and offers the most extensive flight schedule. Alitalia flies nonstop to both Rome and Milan from a number of North American cities, including New York's JFK, Newark, Boston, Chicago, Miami, and Los Angeles. Schedules are carefully designed to facilitate easy transfers to all the major Italian cities. Unlike American carriers, Alitalia may add on a small leg to your flight, if your final destination is a secondary airport, for no extra cost. For example, on direct flights from New York to Milan, you may connect and fly on to Venice for the same rate. This does not apply to all fares. Alitalia participates in the frequent-flyer programs of other airlines, including Continental and USAir. All European airlines, including Alitalia, offer students or anyone ages 12 to 24 a youth fare of $1,008, which can be purchased only within 72 hours of departure; its primary advantage is that it is good for up to 12 months. Infants under 2 years fly for 10% of an adult fare and children under 12 fly for 75% of an adult fare.

Most of the U.S. airlines that service United States–Italy routes to Rome or Milan fly on a daily basis, and often with increased flight schedules during peak season. Major airlines flying to Italy are **American Airlines** (☎ 800/624-6262); **TWA** (☎ 800/221-2000); **United** (☎ 800/241-6522); and **Delta** (☎ 800/241-4141).

Canada's second largest airline, Calgary-based **Canadian Airlines International** (☎ 800/426-7000), flies every day of the week from Toronto to Rome.

Those interested in an attractive deal that combines a stopover of a few hours or a few days in a European city en route to Italy should consider one of the European carriers listed below. In order to encourage the public to choose a nondirect alternative, round-trip rates are often handsomely discounted by these airlines. By connecting in major European hubs, you may also be able to avoid Milan and Rome by flying into Italy's secondary international airports such as Venice, Pisa, Florence, Naples, or Palermo. **British Airways** (☎ 800/AIRWAYS) stops over in London; **Lufthansa** (☎ 800/645-3880) has a stopover in Frankfurt; **Air France** (☎ 800/237-2747) stops over in Paris, and **KLM** (☎ 800/374-7747) stops over in Amsterdam.

FINDING THE BEST FARE

APEX FARES   Most of the major airlines that fly to Rome charge approximately the same fare, but if a price war should break out over the Atlantic (and these are almost always brewing over the most popular routes), fares could change overnight, usually in the consumer's favor. Specific restrictions usually apply. January and February are low-season months when last-minute rates can be remarkably low.

Advance booking is usually the key to getting the lowest fare. You must be willing to make your travel plans and purchase your tickets as far ahead as possible: 21-day-advance-purchase APEX is seconded only by the 14-day-advance APEX, with a stay in Italy of 7 to 30 days. Moreover, since the number of seats allocated to low-cost "advance-purchase" fares is severely limited (sometimes to less than 25% of the capacity of a particular plane), it's often the early bird who gets the low-cost seat, although this may not always be the case. There is often a surcharge for flying on a weekend in either direction, and be aware that the peak season may have a "shoulder" season, comprising those weeks before and after the peak season, with only slightly better rates. Absolute freedom is given to those who buy a regular economy fare that has no restrictions and is naturally the most expensive item on the market.

High season on most airlines' routes to Rome usually stretches from June 1 until around September 6. This is the most expensive and most crowded time to travel. Shoulder season is from April through May, September 7 through October, and December 15 through 24. Low season is November 1 through December 14, and December 25 through March 31.

CONSOLIDATORS   Also called "bucket shops," consolidators act as clearing-houses for blocks of excess-inventory tickets that major international airline carriers discount to a wholesaler or consolidator. These are not charters, and the service is now available in peak periods as well as in the slow season. This is the factory-outlet approach to ticket shopping.

Tickets are sometimes—but not always—priced at up to 35% less than the full fare. Perhaps your reduced fare will be no more than 20% off the regular fare. Terms of payment can vary—say, anywhere from 45 days prior to departure to last-minute sales offered in a final attempt by an airline to fill an empty aircraft. Depending upon the consolidator, restrictions may apply: Inquire about the conditions involved in cancellations, refunds, and re-endorsing to another airline should your carrier delay or cancel. Ask if you can accrue frequent-flier miles. Paying by credit card should be your preference, if allowed, to guarantee further protection.

Since dealing with unknown bucket shops could be risky, it's wise to call the Better Business Bureau in your area to see if complaints have been filed against the company from which you plan to purchase a ticket.

One of the biggest U.S. consolidators is **Travac,** 989 Sixth Ave., New York, NY 10018 (☎ **800/TRAV-800** or 212/563-3303), which offers discounted seats throughout the United States to most cities in Europe on airlines that include TWA, United, and Delta. Another branch office is at 2601 E. Jefferson St., Orlando, FL 32803 (☎ **407/896-0014**).

In New York try **TFI Tours International,** 34 W. 32nd St., 12th Floor, New York, NY 10001 (☎ **800/745-8000** in the U.S., except for New York State ☎ 212/736-1140) This tour company offers services to 177 cities worldwide.

For the Middle West, explore the possibilities of **Travel Avenue,** 10 S. Riverside Plaza, Suite 1404, Chicago, IL 60606 (☎ **800/333-3335** in the U.S.), a national agency. Its tickets are often cheaper than those of most shops, and it charges the customer only a $25 fee on international tickets, rather than taking the usual $10 commission from an airline. Travel Avenue rebates most of that back to the customers—hence, the lower fares.

Another possibility is **TMI (Travel Management International),** 3617 Dupont Ave. S, Minneapolis, MN 55409 (☎ **800/245-3672**), which offers a wide variety of discounts, including youth fares, student fares, and access to other kinds of air-related discounts. **UniTravel,** 1177 North Warson Rd., St. Louis, MO 63132 (☎ **800/325-2222**) is your best choice for last-minute and short-notice flights to Europe.

The ultimate free-spirited traveler who is itinerary-flexible should contact **Airhitch** (2641 Broadway, 3rd floor, New York NY 10025 ☎ **800/326-2009** or 212/864-2000). Inform them of any five-day period during which you can fly to a general area of Europe (northern vs. southern); most passengers are booked within their first or second day. Typical one-way fares are: from the northeast U.S. to Europe, $169; midwest or southeast to Europe, $229; West Coast or northwest to Europe, $269.

CHARTER FLIGHTS   Strictly for reasons of economy (and never for convenience), some travelers are willing to accept the possible uncertainties of a charter flight to Italy.

In a strict sense, a charter flight occurs on an aircraft reserved months in advance for a one-time-only transit to some predetermined point. Before paying for a charter, check the restrictions involved. You'll pay a stiff penalty (or forfeit the ticket entirely) if you cancel or change dates. Charters are occasionally canceled when the plane doesn't fill up—an occurrence more frequent during low season. In some cases, the charter-ticket seller will offer you an insurance policy in case you must cancel (for hospitalization, death in the family, etc.).

There is no way to predict whether a proposed flight to Rome will cost less on a charter or less through a consolidator. You'll have to investigate at the time of your trip.

One very reliable charter-flight operator is **Council Charter,** run by the Council on International Educational Exchange, 205 E. 42nd St., 15th floor, New York, NY 10017 (☎ **800/2-COUNCIL** or 212/822-2800), which arranges charter flights using the reputable Tower Air. In high season, they can be substantially less expensive (up to $250 less round-trip) than those flights offered by Council Charter on regularly scheduled flights with European carriers such as Air France and Sabena.

Tower Air is also the charter company of choice for Travac (☎ **800/TRAV-800** in the U.S. or 212/563-3303), one of the biggest New York charter operators, and also a consolidator (see above). Tower rates are less expensive than those of regularly scheduled carriers (up to $100 less round-trip).

GOING AS A COURIER   This cost-cutting option is not for everyone. The free tickets of the past offered by courier services now cost a minimum of $150 round-trip from New York to Italy. If you go as a courier, you must be able to leave within one to two days' notice; otherwise, during peak season, you may be paying rates not much less than some consolidator's rates (sometimes topping $499 New York/Milan) as well as being locked into dates and restrictions imposed by the courier service. Couriers must waive their luggage allowance, which is utilized by the courier service to transport goods; couriers travel alone, so companions will have to make arrangements to meet; sometimes when the courier's representative meets you at the airport things go ultra-smoothly, sometimes they don't. Only the patient, flexible, light-packing, and adventurous of spirit should contact the following companies: **Halbart Express** (☎ **718/656-8189** from 10am to 3pm) or **Now Voyager,** 74 Varick St., Suite 307, New York NY 10013 (☎ **212/431-1616** from 10am to 6pm; at other times you'll get a recorded update of destinations and availabilities).

BY TRAIN

If you plan to travel a lot on the European and/or British railroads, you'll do well to secure the latest copy of the *Thomas Cook European Timetable of Railroads.* This comprehensive, 500-plus-page timetable documents all of Europe's mainline passenger rail services with detail and accuracy. It's available exclusively in North America from **Forsyth Travel Library,** P.O. Box 2975, Shawnee Mission, KS 66201 (☎ **800/FORSYTH**), at a cost of $27.95 (plus $4.50 shipping in the U.S. and $5.50 in Canada).

EURAILPASSES   One of Europe's greatest travel bargains, the **Eurailpass** permits unlimited first-class rail travel in any country in Western Europe (except the British Isles). Oddly, it does *not* include travel on the rail lines of Sardinia, which are organized independently of the rail lines of the rest of Italy. Passes may be purchased for 15 days to three months.

Here's how it works: The pass is sold only in North America. The pass costs $522 for 15 days, $678 for 21 days, $838 for one month, $1,148 for two months, and $1,468 for three months. Children under 4 travel free, providing they don't occupy a seat (otherwise, they are charged half-fare); children under 12 pay half-fare.

The advantages are tempting: No tickets; simply show the pass to the ticket collector, then settle back to enjoy the scenery. Seat reservations are required on some trains. Many of the trains have *couchettes* (sleeping cars), for which an additional fee is charged.

Obviously, the two- or three-month traveler gets the greatest economic advantage—with a 15-day pass, you'd have to spend a great deal of time on the train.

Eurailpass holders are entitled to considerable reductions on certain buses and ferries. You'll get a 20% reduction on second-class accommodations from certain companies operating ferries between Naples and Palermo, or for crossings to Sardinia and Malta.

Travel agents in all towns, and railway agents in such major cities as New York, Montréal, or Los Angeles sell these tickets. A Eurailpass is available at the North

American offices of CIT Travel Service, the French National Railroads, the German Federal Railroads, and the Swiss Federal Railways.

Eurail Saverpass is a money-saving ticket that offers discounted 15-day travel for groups of three or more people traveling together between April and September, or two people traveling together between October and March. The price of a Saverpass, valid all over Europe, good for first class only, is $452 for 15 days, $578 for 21 days, and $712 for one month.

Eurail Flexipass is valid in first class and offers the same privileges as the Eurailpass. However, it gives you a number of individual travel days that can be used over a much longer period. That makes it possible to stay in one city and yet not lose a single day of travel. There are two passes: 10 days of travel within two months for $616; and 15 days of travel within two months for $812.

If you're under 26, you can purchase a **Eurail Youthpass,** which entitles you to unlimited second-class travel wherever the Eurailpass is honored. The pass costs $418 for 15 consecutive days, $598 for one month, or $798 for two months. There's also a Eurail Youth Flexipass for travelers under 26. Two passes are available: 10 days of travel within two months for $438 and 15 days of travel within two months for $588.

EUROPASSES   Recently introduced by the folks who brought us Eurailpass, the **Europass** lets you travel in five Europass countries: Italy, France, Germany, Spain, and Switzerland. Start by choosing any three bordering Europass countries, and decide if you want a five-, six-, or seven-day pass of unlimited first-class train travel in two months; for two adults traveling together discounts apply. A five-day pass costs $237 for each of two adults, $316 traveling alone; six-day pass $268.50 for each of two adults, $358 traveling alone; seven-day pass $300 for each of two adults, $400 traveling alone. If you opt for an 8-, 9-, or 10-day pass you can extend your range of travel by adding a fourth country; 11- and 15-day passes will allow you to add the choice of a fifth associated country.

For travelers under 26, the **Europass Youth** allows unlimited second-class travel in any four of the associate countries. A five-day pass within a two-month period costs $210, a six-day pass within two months costs $239, a seven-day pass within two months costs $268, and so on. A 10-day ($384) to 15-day ($500) pass within a two-month period allows you to extend your travel range by adding a fifth country. All Europasses offer the option of "purchasing" an associate country, such as Austria, Benelux, Greece, or Portugal.

BY BUS

For daily departures to limited stops in cities in 11 European countries (including Venice, Florence, and Rome in Italy) and Great Britain, privately owned Eurobus leases a fleet of new air-conditioned Volvo buses (with double-deckers foreseen for 1997) and offers a convivial alternative to rail travel. A two-week pass for unlimited travel costs $150 for people under 27, $199 for those over 27; a one-month pass for those under 27 costs $219, for those over 27, $280; a two-month pass for those under 27 is $275, for those over 27, $350. Bus travel offers videos, game boards, on-board travel books, and a generally 20-something clientele who swap information. For information call **800/517-7778;** 355 Palermo Ave., Coral Gables, FL 33134.

BY CAR

If you're already on the Continent, or if you're based in London, you may want to drive to Italy. London to Rome is a distance of 1,124 miles via Calais/Bologna/Dunkirk, or 1,085 miles via Oostende/Zeebrugge, not counting Channel crossings, either by Hovercraft, ferry, or the Chunnel. Milan is some 400 miles closer to

Britain than Rome. Once you have arrived at one of the continental ports, you still face a 24-hour drive. Most drivers play it safe and budget three days for the journey.

Most of the roads from Western Europe leading into Italy are toll-free, with some notable exceptions. If you use the Swiss superhighway network, you'll have to purchase a special tax sticker at the frontier. You'll also pay to go through the St. Gotthard Tunnel into Italy. Crossings from France can be made through the Mont Blanc Tunnel, which also has a toll charge, or you can leave the French Riviera at Menton (France) and drive directly into Italy along the Italian Riviera in the direction of San Remo.

10 For British Travelers

CUSTOMS

If you are traveling in a European Union country, you can bring home as much wine, sprits, and cigarattes as you like. If you return home from a non–European Union country, the old rules for the duty-free shop still apply: You're allowed to bring home 200 cigarettes and two liters of table wine, plus one liter of spirits or two liters of fortified wine. You must declare any goods in excess of these allowances. For details, get in touch with **Her Majesty's Customs and Excise Office,** New King's Beam House, 22 Upper Ground, London, SE1 9PJ (☎ **0171/620-1313**) for more information.

TIPS FOR TRAVELERS WITH SPECIAL NEEDS

FOR TRAVELERS WITH DISABILITIES   **RADAR** (the Royal Association for Disability and Rehabilitation), Unit 12, City Forum, 250 City Rd., London ECIV 8AF (☎ **0171/250-3222**), publishes holiday "fact packs"—three in all—which sell for £2 each or £5 for a set of all three. The first one provides general information, including planning and booking a holiday, insurance, and finances. The second outlines transport and equipment, transportation available when going abroad, and equipment for rent. The third deals with specialized accommodations.

Another good resource is **Holiday Care Service,** 2nd Floor, Imperial Building, Victoria Road, Horley, Surrey RH6 7PZ (☎ **01293/77-45-35;** fax 01293/78-46-47), a national service organization that advises on accessible accommodations. Annual membership costs £25. Once someone is a member, he or she can receive a newsletter which includes information about hotels throughout Britain and Europe with access to a free reservations network for British hotels.

If you're flying around Europe, the airlines and ground staff will help you on and off planes, and reserve seats for you with sufficient legroom, but it is essential to arrange for this assistance in advance by contacting your airline.

Recent laws in Italy have compelled railway stations, airports, hotels, and most restaurants to follow a stricter set of regulations about wheelchair accessibility to rest rooms, ticket counters, etc. Many museums and other sightseeing attractions have conformed to these regulations. Alitalia, as Italy's most visible airline, has made a special effort to make its planes, public areas, rest rooms, and access ramps as wheelchair-friendly as possible.

FOR FAMILIES   The best deals for families are often package tours put together by some of the giants of the British travel industry. Foremost among these is **Thomsons Tour Operators** (☎ **0171/387-9321**), who offers dozens of air/land packages to Italy, where a designated number of airline seats are reserved for the free use of children under 18 who accompany their parents. To qualify, parents must book airfare and hotel accommodations lasting two weeks or more, as far in advance as possible. Savings for families with children can be substantial.

FOR STUDENTS   Campus Travel, 52 Grosvenor Gardens, London SW1W OAG (☎ 0171/730-3402), opposite Victoria Station, open seven days a week, is Britain's leading specialist in student and youth travel worldwide. It provides a comprehensive travel service specializing in low-cost rail, sea, and air fares, holiday breaks, and travel insurance, plus student discount cards.

The International Student Identity Card (ISIC) is an internationally recognized proof of student status that will entitle you to savings on flights, sightseeing, food, and accommodation. It sells for £5 and is well worth the cost. Always show your ISIC when booking a trip—you may not get a discount without it.

Youth hostels are the place to stay if you're a student or, in some cases, if you're traveling on an ultra-tight budget. You'll need an **International Youth Hostels Association** card, which you can purchase from either of London's youth hostel retail outlets, located near Covent Garden at 14 Southampton St., London WC23 7HY (☎ 0171/83-68-541), and at 52 Grosvenor Gardens, London SW1W OAG (☎ 0171/82-34-739; in the same building as Campus Travel). The outlets sell rucksacks, hiking boots, maps, and all the paraphernalia a camper, hiker, or shoestring traveler might need. To apply for a membership card, take both your passport and some passport-size photos of yourself, plus a membership fee of £9.30. For more information contact **Youth Hostels Association of England and Wales (YHA),** / 8 St. Stephen's Hill, St. Albans, Hertfordshire AL1 2DY (☎ 01727/85-52-15).

The Youth Hostel Association puts together a YHA Budget Accommodations Guide (Volumes 1 and 2), which lists the address, phone number, and admissions policy for every youth hostel in the world. (Volume 1 covers Europe and the Mediterranean; volume 2 covers the rest of the globe.) They cost £6.99 each and can be purchased at the retail outlets listed above. If ordering by mail, add 61p for postage within the U.K.

Many youth hostels fill up in the summer, so be sure to book ahead.

GETTING THERE

Because getting to Italy from the U.K is often expensive, savvy folks usually call a travel agent for a "deal." That could be in the form of a charter flight or some special air-travel promotion. These so-called deals—by land or air—are always available because of the great interest in Italy as a tourist destination.

BY PLANE   If a special air-travel promotion is not available or feasible at the time of your anticipated visit, then an APEX ticket might be the way to keep costs trimmed. These tickets must be reserved in advance. However, an APEX ticket offers a discount without the usual booking restrictions. You might also ask the airlines about a "Eurobudget ticket," which imposes restrictions or length-of-stay requirements.

British newspapers are always full of classified advertisements touting "slashed" fares to Italy. One good source is the magazine, *Time Out,* published in London. London's *Evening Standard* has a daily travel section, and the Sunday editions of almost any newspaper will run many ads. Although competition is fierce, one well-recommended company that consolidates bulk ticket purchases, and then passes the savings on to its consumers, is **Trailfinders** (☎ 0171/93-75-400 in London). It offers access to tickets on such carriers as SAS, British Airways, and KLM to Milan and Rome as well as Pisa, Florence, Venice, and other cities.

In London, there are many bucket shops around Victoria and Earls Court that offer cheap fares. Make sure that the company you deal with is a member of the IATA, ABTA, or ATOL. These umbrella organizations will help you out if anything goes wrong.

CEEFAX, a television information service included on many home and hotel TVs, runs details of package holidays and flights to Italy and beyond. Just switch to your CEEFAX channel and you'll find a menu of listings that includes travel information.

Make sure you understand the bottom line on any special deal you purchase—that is, ask if all surcharges, including airport taxes and other hidden costs are cited before committing yourself to purchase. Upon investigation, some of these "deals" are not as attractive as advertised. Also, make sure you understand what the penalties are if you're forced to cancel at the last minute.

Both British Airways (☎ **0181/89-74-000**) and Alitalia (☎ **0181/74-58-200**) have frequent flights from London's Heathrow Airport to Rome, Milan, Venice, Pisa, Florence, and Naples. Flying time from London to these cities is anywhere from two to three hours. BA also has one direct flight a day from Manchester to Rome.

BY TRAIN   Many different rail passes are available in the U.K. for travel in Europe. Stop in at the **International Rail Centre,** Victoria Station, London SW1V 1JZ (☎ **0171/83-46-744**). They can help you find the best option for the trip you're planning. Some of the most popular passes, including EuroYouth, is offered only to travelers under 26 years of age, entitling them to unlimited second-class travel in 26 European countries. Inter-Rail also offers special rates to those under 26 but is available to everyone.

Eurotrain "Explorer" tickets are another worthwhile option for travelers who can show proof that they are under age 26. They allow passengers to move in a leisurely fashion from London to Rome, with as many stopovers en route as their holders want, and a different route southbound (through Belgium, Luxembourg, and Switzerland) than the return route northbound (exclusively through France). All travel must be completed within two months of the date of departure. Such a ticket sells for £195 round-trip.

Even less expensive is the £165 round-trip rail ticket offered by Campus Travel (☎ **0171/730-3402;** see above) for direct London-to-Italy train travel for those under 26. No stopovers are allowed on the route through France and although the ferry crossing is included, there is no option for the Chunnel connection.

For Seniors   **Wasteels,** Victoria Station, adjacent to platform 2, London SW1V 1JY (☎ **0171/83-47-066**), will sell a Rail Europe Senior Pass to bona fide residents of the U.K. for £5. With it, a British resident more than 60 years of age can buy discounted rail tickets on many of the rail lines of Europe. To qualify, British residents must present a valid British Senior Citizen rail card, which is available for £16 at any BritRail office if proof of age and British residency is presented.

BY BUS   **Eurolines** is the leading operator of scheduled coach services across Europe. Its comprehensive network of services includes regular departures to destinations throughout Italy, including Turin, Milan, Bologna, Florence, and Rome; plus summer services to Verona, Vicenza, Padua, and Venice.

Eurolines' services to Italy depart from London's Victoria Coach Station and are operated by modern coach, with reclining seats and a choice of smoking or nonsmoking areas. Return tickets are valid for up to six months, and for added flexibility passengers may also leave their return date open. For information and reservations by credit card, call **01582/40-45-11** or 0171/73-08-235. Alternatively, passengers may book in person at Eurolines, 52 Grosvenor Gardens, Victoria, London SW1 (opposite Victoria Rail Station). A round-trip ticket from London to Rome using as direct a route as possible costs between £129 and £139, and from £87 one-way, depending on the season. Persons under 26 pay around £10 less each way. Departures in either direction are daily, and the trip takes around 37 hours each way.

Passengers can interrupt their journey, pending available space on subsequent legs of their trip, in Paris or Milan en route.

ORGANIZED TOURS The London headquarters of **IATA (International Association of Travel Agencies)** (☎ **0181/74-49-280**) can provide the names and addresses of tour operators who specialize in travel relating to your particular interest or destination in Italy.

TRAVEL INSURANCE

Most big travel agents offer their own insurance and will try to sell you their package when you book a holiday. Think before you sign. Britain's Consumers' Association recommends that you insist on seeing the policy and reading the fine print before buying travel insurance.

You should also shop around for better deals. You might contact **Columbus Travel Insurance Ltd.** (☎ **0171/375-0011** in London), or, for students, Campus Travel (☎ **0171/730-3402** in London). Columbus Travel will sell travel insurance only to people who have been official residents of Britain for at least a year.

11 Getting Around

BY PLANE

Italy's domestic air network on Alitalia is one of the largest and most complete in Europe. There are some 40 airports serviced regularly from Rome, and most flights take less than an hour. Fares vary, but some discounts are available. Tickets are discounted 50% for children 2 to 12 years old; for passengers 12 to 22 years old, there's a youth fare. And anyone can get a 30% reduction by taking domestic flights that depart at night. Prices are still astronomical for domestic flights and you are almost always better off taking a train, except for long-distance hauls (such as Palermo-Venice) where you'd rather spend the money than the time.

BY TRAIN

Trains provide a medium-priced means of transportation, even if you don't buy the Eurailpass/Europass or one of the special Italian Railway tickets (see below). As a rule of thumb, second-class travel regardless of the destination usually costs about two-thirds the price of an equivalent trip in first class, and with many trains the difference in quality is minimal. The relatively new InterCity trains (designated by IC on train schedules) are modern, air-conditioned trains that make limited stops; the supplement can be steep, but a second-class IC ticket will provide a first-class experience. Seat reservations are highly recommended during peak seasons and on weekends or holidays; they must be booked in advance. Minimal in cost, they are sometimes included in the cost of your ticket. Children ages 4 to 11 receive a discount of 50% off the adult fare, and children under 4 travel free with their parents.

Senior citizens get a break, too. Anyone 60 and over can purchase a Senior Citizen's Silver Card (Carta d'Argento) by presenting proof of age at any railway station. The card, which can only be purchased in Italy, allows a 20% discount off the price of any ticket between points on the Italian rail network. It's good for one year and costs 40,000L ($26.30). It's not valid on Friday, Saturday, or Sunday between late June and late August or anytime during Christmas week. The Italian railway system also offers a *cartaverde,* good for anyone under 26. Valid for one year, the card costs 40,000L ($26.30) and entitles a passenger to a 20% reduction off any state train fare. This pass can only be purchased in Italy.

An Italian Railpass (known within Italy as a BTLC Pass) allows non-Italian citizens to ride as much as they like on the entire rail network of Italy. Buy the pass in the United States, have it validated the first time you use it at any railway station in Italy, and ride as frequently as you like within the time validity of your pass. An 8-day pass costs $248 in first class and $168 in second class, a 15-day pass is $312 in first class and $208 in second, a 21-day pass runs $362 in first class and $242 in second, and a 30-day pass costs $436 in first class and $290 in second.

With the Italian Railpass and each of the other special passes, a supplement must be paid to ride on certain express trains. These are designated ETR-450 trains (also known as "Pendolino" trains). The rail systems of Sardinia are administered by a separate entity and are not included in the Railpass or any of the other passes mentioned.

Another option is the Italian Flexirail Card, which entitles holders to a predetermined number of days of travel on any rail line of Italy within a certain period of time. It's ideal for passengers who plan in advance to spend several days sightseeing before boarding a train for another city. A pass giving four possible travel days out of a block of one month costs $194 in first class and $132 in second class, a pass for eight travel days stretched over a one-month period costs $284 in first class and $184 in second, and a pass for 12 travel days within one month costs $356 in first class and $238 in second class.

In addition, the Kilometric Ticket is valid for two months' worth of travel on regular trains. (It can also be used on special trains if you pay a supplement.) The ticket is valid for 20 trips, providing that the total distance covered does not exceed 1,875 miles (3,000 kilometers). The price is $264 in first class, $156 in second.

In previous years, Italian Railway authorities have required that many of the above-mentioned passes be purchased outside of Europe. These rules have relaxed considerably in recent years, and at press time, some passes could be purchased within Italy. (Check with CIT, see below, before your departure, as this might change at any time.) The notable exception is the Italian Flexirail Card, which requires purchase in North America. You can purchase any of these passes from a travel agent or at **CIT Tours,** the official representative of Italian State Railway, with offices at 342 Madison Ave., New York, NY 10173 (☎ **800/248-8687** or 212/697-2100; fax 212/697-1394) and in Los Angeles (6033 West Century Blvd., Suite 980, Los Angeles, CA 90045; ☎ **800/248-7245** or 310/338-8616; fax 310/670-4269).

A warning: The dirty, overcrowded, and unreliable rail system with little regard for schedules has greatly improved over the last decade as Italy strives to meet the expectations and standards of the European Union. As you may have heard, strikes still occur, and you can never be perfectly sure when your train will reach its destination. A sense of humor (and a flexible itinerary) might be your best defense against aggravation and irritating delays. If anything, avoid overnight trains, where there have been a number of thefts across Europe—in the dead of night, robbers have been known to slip onto trains during scheduled stops, and travelers in a deep sleep awake to find their effects missing.

BY BUS

Italy has an extensive and intricate bus network, covering all regions of the country. But because rail travel is inexpensive, the bus is not the preferred method of travel.

SITA, V. Santa Caterina da Siena, in Florence (☎ **055/48-36-51**), and **ANAC,** Pz. Esquilino 29, in Rome (☎ **06/44-82-05-31**) are two companies that blanket the country with air-conditioned coaches.

Other companies operating buses are **Autostradale,** Pzle. Castello, in Milan (☎ **02/80-11-61**), which serves a large chunk of North Italy, and **Lazzi,** Pz. d.

Stazione 4–6, in Florence (☎ 055/21-51-54), which goes through Tuscany, including Siena and much of central Italy.

Where these nationwide services leave off, local bus companies operate in most regions, particularly in the hill sections and in the alpine regions where travel by rail is not possible. For more information about local services, refer to the "By Bus" sections, listed under "Getting There" in the various destinations.

BY CAR

Driving can be very expensive in Italy. However, there are several strategies that can be pursued to make renting a car more affordable, especially for a group of several people.

RULES & REGULATIONS   U.S. and Canadian drivers must carry an international driver's license when touring Italy or else obtain a declaration from the Automobile Club d'Italia (ACI) that entitles them to drive on Italian roads upon presentation of a valid U.S. or Canadian driver's license (with Italian translation). The declaration is available from any ACI frontier or provincial office. Several organizations, including AAA, can provide an Italian-language translation of a U.S. or Canadian driver's license. The possession of such a translation is intended to facilitate procedures with Italian police personnel, who don't necessarily understand English text. In practice, however, the translation is often not even looked at. But, if you're respecting the letter of the Italian law, it's necessary to have it.

Apply for an international driver's license at any **American Automobile Association (AAA)** branch. You must be at least 18 years old and have two two-by-two-inch photographs, a $10 fee, and a photocopy of your U.S. driver's license with an AAA application form. To find the AAA office nearest you, check the local telephone directory or contact AAA's national headquarters at 1000 AAA Dr., Heathrow, FL 32746-5063 (☎ 407/444-4300). Remember that an international driver's license is valid only if physically accompanied by your original driver's license. In Canada, you can get the address of the **Canadian Automobile Association** closest to you by calling its national office at **613/247-0117.**

The **Automobile Club d'Italia (ACI)** is the equivalent of the AAA. It has offices throughout Italy, including the head office, V. Marsala 8, 00185 Rome (☎ 06/49-98-23-89), open Monday to Saturday from 8am to 2pm. The 24-hour **Information and Assistance Center (CAT)** of the ACI is at V. Magenta 5, 00185 Roma (☎ 06/44-77). Both offices are located near the main railway station (Stazione Termini) in Rome.

RENTALS   Many of Italy's most charming landscapes lie far away from the railroad network. For that, and for sheer convenience, renting a car is usually the best way to explore the country. It is also the most expensive (Italy's rates have always been some of the highest in Europe) and is usually a consideration only for the budget traveler who is traveling with one or more companions to split the cost.

It is strongly recommended that you book the rental from the United States, where rates are invariably less expensive. If you decide to rent a car while in Italy, it's worth the call home to have a family member or friend book for you.

The legalities and contractual obligations of renting a car in Italy (where accident and theft rates are very high) are more complicated than in almost any other country in Europe. To rent a car in Italy, a driver must have nerves of steel, a sense of humor, a valid driver's license, a valid passport, and in most cases, be over age 25 (some accept 21). In all cases, payment and paperwork are simpler if you present a valid credit card with your completed rental contract (some companies won't even consider a non–credit card payment). If that isn't possible, you will almost certainly be required to pay a substantial deposit, sometimes in cash. Insurance on all vehicles is compulsory, although any reputable car-rental firm will arrange insurance in advance before you're even given the keys.

The three major car-rental companies in Italy are **Avis** (☎ **800/331-2112**), **Budget Rent A Car** (☎ **800/472-3325**), and **Hertz** (☎ **800/654-3001**). Another option is **Kemwel** (☎ **800/678-0678**). Although most frequently contacted for package deals and air travel, see any of the tour operators listed above under "Organized Tours, Package Tours & Tour Operators" who specialize in discounted car rental which can be purchased independently. You'll have to do your homework in this area, as the three major agencies listed above can either be far more or far less expensive than the tour operators, depending upon special promotions and seasonal rates being offered at the time. Never settle for the first figures quoted to you: Prices can vary greatly from agency to agency.

Rates for the least expensive vehicle (manual drive and no air-conditioning), vary from $290 to $450 for a week-long midsummer rental of a cramped but peppy Fiat Fiesta or Opel Corsa (although there's always a possiblity of a seasonal promotion). In some cases, slight discounts may be offered to members of the American Automobile Association (AAA) or the American Association of Retired Persons (AARP).

Each company offers a collision-damage waiver (CDW) that costs between $14 and $21 a day (depending on the value of the car). Some companies include CDWs in the prices they quote; others do not. In addition, because of the rising theft rate in Italy, all three of the major U.S.-based companies offer theft and break-in protection policies (Avis and Budget require it). For pickups at most airports in Italy, all three companies impose a 10% government tax. To avoid that charge, consider picking your car up at an inner-city location. There is also an unavoidable 19% government VAT tax (called IVA in Italy), although more and more companies are including this in the rates they quote. Automatic shift and air-conditioning will raise your rates, as will the option of picking up in one city and dropping off at another. Dropping off outside Italy is even more expensive: Make sure you ask all the right questions when calling around.

GASOLINE   Gasoline (known as *benzina*) is expensive in Italy, as are autostrade tolls. Carry enough cash if you're going to do extensive motoring. Filling the tank of a medium-size car with "super *benzina*," the octane rating appropriate for most of the cars you will be able to rent, will usually cost around 65,000L ($41.60) but will last you for days.

Gas stations (*distributori di benzina*) on autostrade are often open 24 hours a day, but on regular roads gas stations are rarely open on Sunday, may close between noon and 3pm for lunch, and shut down after 7pm. Others will have self-service machines accepting 10,000L bills/notes. Make sure the pump registers zero before an attendant starts refilling your tank. A popular scam, particularly in the south, is to fill your tank before resetting the meter so that you pay not only your bill but the charges run up by the previous motorist.

ROAD MAPS   The best touring maps are published by the Automobile Club d'Italia (ACI) and the Italian Touring Club, or you can purchase the maps of the Carta Automobilistica d'Italia, covering Italy in two maps on the scale of 1:800,000 (1cm = 8km). These two maps should fulfill the needs of most motorists. If you plan to explore one region of Italy in depth, then consider one of 15 regional maps (1:200,000; 1cm = 2km), published by Grande Carta Stradale d'Italia.

All maps mentioned above are sold at some autostrada gas stations, certain newsstands, and at all major bookstores, especially those with travel departments. Many travel bookstores in the United States also carry them. If U.S. outlets don't have these maps, they often offer Michelin's red map (no. 988) of Italy, which is on a scale of 1:1,000,000 (1cm = 10km). This map covers all of Italy in some detail.

BREAKDOWNS/ASSISTANCE   In case of car breakdown or for any tourist information, foreign motorists can call **116** (nationwide telephone service). For road information, itineraries, and all sorts of travel assistance, call **06/49-98-389** (ACI's information center). Both services operate 24 hours a day.

BY FERRY

With the exception of the ferry to Greece that departs from Brindisi on the Adriatic Coast, most ferries ply the waters off the western coast of Italy. Driving time from Naples to Sicily is cut considerably by taking one of the vessels operated by **Tirrenia Lines,** Molo Angioino, Stazione Marittima, in Naples (☎ **081/76-13-688**). Departures are daily at 8pm for the 11-hour trip to Palermo. Frequent ferry services and hydrofoils also depart from Naples for the offshore islands of Capri and Ischia and the Eolian Islands off the coast of Sicily. Farther north, from the Tuscan and Ligurian coastline, ferries leave for Corsica (France) and Sardinia, as well as Elba and other islands in the Tuscan archipelago.

HITCHHIKING

It is extremely risky to hitchhike anywhere in the world today and *Frommer's Italy* does not recommend it, although recognizing that hundreds of people will hitchhike regardless of the risks.

In Italy, it is illegal to hitch a ride on the autostrade, mainly because it's dangerous for a car to stop to take on a passenger. Savvy hitchhikers wait on the ramps leading up to the autostrade or take to the primary road systems instead. The less you're burdened with luggage and possessions, of course, the better your chances of getting a ride. Write your destination on a sign with large letters—it helps. Use the Italian name for a city, not the English one (Firenze instead of Florence, for example). Women should hitch in pairs, if at all, because sexual harassment—or worse—is commonly reported. One Italian male driver confided that he considered any woman hitching a ride "fair game," and such attitudes are prevalent. Young men traveling alone are also subject to propositions, and should take precautions. Don't let your baggage be stored in a locked trunk in case you should decide to make a hasty departure from the vehicle.

SUGGESTED ITINERARIES

If You Have 1 Week: From Rome to Venice

Days 1–3   Fly to Rome and spend most of the day recovering. View the floodlit Roman Forum at sunset from the balcony of the Campidoglio. Have an aperitivo in a cafe in the Piazza del Popolo, an alfresco dinner in the area of the Piazza Navona, and turn in early. Your second day, take in the Colosseum and Forum and stroll the old medieval neighborhood searching out the Pantheon and the Trevi Fountain. Spend the morning of your third day visiting the lively Campo dei Fiori marketplace, then head for the Vatican Museum (which includes the magnificently restored Sistine Chapel) and St. Peter's Basilica. Catch sunset over the seven hills of Rome from atop the Spanish Steps, then head off for your last dinner in the Eternal City.

Days 4–5   Transfer in the morning to Florence and soak up as much of this Renaissance city as time allows. Be ready for lines at the Uffizi Galleries or the Accademia to see Michelangelo's masterful David. No one has ever regretted the wait. Celebrate your stay with a great bistecca alla fiorentina in a characteristic trattoria.

Days 6–7   Transfer to Venice, where so many attractions await you that you'll promise yourself many more return visits. A ride on the no. 1 vaporetto down the Grand Canal could be the most luxurious cruise of your life—and for the cost of a water bus ticket!

If You Have Another Week: The Veneto, Lombardy & the Piedmont

Day 1   Leave Venice in the morning heading west for the attractions of nearby Padua (Padova). Visit Giotto's awe-inspiring Cappella degli Scrovegni and the Basilica di Sant' Antonio. Have lunch at one of the historical center's characteristic old wine bars and continue northwest to Vicenza for the night. See as many sights in the city of Andrea Palladio as you can before nightfall; even after dark, the city is beautifully illuminated.

Days 2–3   In the morning continue west to Verona, lovely medieval city of Romeo and Juliet. See such attractions as the 2,000-year-old Arena di Verona, the museum at the Castelvecchio, Il Duomo, and the Church of San Zeno Maggiore —maybe even Juliet's balcony. Explore the colorful Piazza delle Erbe marketplace, then sit with a cappuccino in the serene Piazza dei Signori at the historical Caffè Dante. If the summer opera season has arrived, do everything possible to experience the perfect accoustics in the ancient Roman amphitheater under the stars.

Day 4   Milan. You won't be able to see everything you want, but visit Leonardo's *Last Supper*—whose laborious renovation is close to completion—and visit the ultra-gothic Duomo. This is Europe's capital of design, fashion, style, and shopping, which means that window-shopping is also glorious.

Days 5–6   Bypass Genoa for Santa Margherita, next-door neighbor to the exclusive, postcard-perfect yachting enclave of Portofino. From Santa Margherita boats leave for day trips to the former fishing villages of Portofino and Cinque Terre that offer miles of walking paths along the coastline and excellent fresh seafood dinners on open waterfront terraces with views to match.

Day 7   For a final day of sightseeing visit the ancient seaport of Columbus's Genoa. Tour the regentrified area of the old harbor and visit the much talked-about acquarium.

If You Have 2 Weeks

One of the most interesting trips in Italy is along the Riviera, Italy's western coast, followed by an inland visit to Tuscany and Umbria.

Day 1   Begin at the Italian Riviera near the French border, heading first for an overnight stay in San Remo, capital of the Riviera. Visit its old city, its flower market (most famous in Italy), and drop in at its casino at night.

Day 2   Leave San Remo in the morning and drive along the coast, stopping at random at such towns as Albenga or Savona, and bypass Genoa for arrival in Santa Margherita late afternoon. Spend the two nights here, using your days for sightseeing nearby.

Day 3   Santa Margherita is a good base for visiting its expensive next-door neighbor Portofino, the most chic of the Ligurian port towns. Boats leave Santa Margherita for both Portofino and the Cinque Terre (see above). Spend your second night in Santa Margherita.

Day 4   Schedule your trip to be in Lucca in time for lunch at da Giulio's, one of Tuscany's best and most authentic trattorie. Rent bicycles in this traffic-free walled city to see some of its myriad churches, especially its cathedral, dating from 1060, and the church of San Michele in Foro. Stay in Lucca for the night, but pop over to nearby Pisa in the evening to view its Leaning Tower illuminated at night.

Days 5–6   Head southeast from Lucca or Pisa and plan to be in San Gimignano for lunch. Called the "Manhattan of Tuscany" because of the medieval towers that have survived the centuries, it is one of the most interesting of the hill towns of Italy. Continue southeast for the night, arriving after a brief half-hour drive through Chianti country in Siena. On Day 6, explore history-rich Siena, which means a compulsory visit to its hilltop Duomo and a sustaining cafe stop in the Piazza del Campo, one of Italy's great piazzas.

Day 7   From Siena head out in the morning to another hill town, Arezzo, to the east. See at least the newly restored frescoes of Piero della Francesca in St. Francis' Church and window-shop the handsome antiques stores that ring the lovely Piazza Grande. Continue southeast into Umbria to the ancient hilltop university city of Perugia for the night.

Day 8   You'll need most of the following day to see the attractions of Perugia, especially its Galleria Nazionale dell'Umbria, the world's greatest collection of Umbrian art. Don't miss the ritual of the late afternoon *passeggiata* along the timeless Corso Vannucci, winding up in the Piazza IV Novembre, the heart of Perugia. Sit on the steps of the Duomo, as students have for centuries, enjoying the 13th-century fountain and basking in the beauty of the square.

Day 9   From Perugia drive through the Umbrian countryside until you reach Assisi, hometown of St. Francis. This is one of the most popular destinations in Italy, and you'll want to spend at least a day and a night there; the town is most pleasant after the busloads leave. Enjoy dinner in a small family-run trattoria that will introduce you to the gastronomic wonders of the local, cherished truffle.

Day 10   Leave Assisi and head south to Spoleto for a morning visit and lunch at the informal and characterful *enoteca*. Stroll through the nearby Piazza Mercato before all the stalls and vendors pack up, or the expansive Piazza Duomo. After Spoleto, drive west to Orvieto to visit its famous gothic Duomo whose bold and colorful facade can be seen from a distance. Linger for a sampling of the local white wine and a late-afternoon snack, then head south for Rome.

Days 11–14   Explore the riches and architectural treasures of Rome, the Eternal City. See above.

If You Have Another 10 Days

Day 1   Rome to Naples is an easy two-hour ride by train or wheels. Even the non–archeologically minded should see Naples's Museo Archeologico Nazionale, arguably the best ancient Roman and Greek collection anywhere. In the city that gave the world pizza, spend an evening in a good pizzeria to see why simplicity is next to godliness.

Day 2   The next morning, catch the hydrofoil to Capri and spend the day walking the car-free footpaths past quietly magnificent homes and glimpses of dramatic views everywhere. When all the day-trippers go back to terra firma, the summer-villa owners come out. Have a simple dinner in a small family-run trattoria—fresh mozzarella and sweet tomato salad followed by homemade pasta. And a tart lemon-flavored gelato!

Days 3–4   From Capri take the hydrofoil to Sorrento and book a hotel for two nights there, or farther along the Amalfi Drive in Amalfi or, better yet, Positano. Spend the rest of the day enjoying one of these resorts and get to bed early so you'll be prepared for Pompeii. Either on your own or via an organized tour, make the traditional visit to the town that Vesuvius destroyed in A.D. 79, Pompeii.

Day 5   Archeology buffs can also take in Paestum to see the excavated site of this Roman town that dates back to 600 B.C.; others might spend the morning in the town of Ravello, perched high on a cliff, with flowering gardens, riveting views, ceramic shops, and cool breezes. Head back to Naples in the early evening to board a boat for Palermo, the capital of Sicily. If you don't have time for Sicily, you can break the tour here, returning to Rome for your flight back home. If you're going on to Sicily, you'll spend the night aboard the boat in a rented cabin, arriving in Palermo in the early hours of morning.

Day 6   Spend the day in Palermo, exploring its monuments and museums, especially the Church of Monreale in the hills. Don't miss the unique Vucciria market, more North African than Italian. Overnight in Palermo.

Day 7   Drive west from Palermo and arrive in the hilltop medieval town of Erice for lunch. However, don't linger too long in any place, as your major goal should be the ruins of Selinunte on the southern coast. Arrive in Agrigento for an overnight stop and drive around the illuminated "Valley of the Temples" at night.

Days 8   Spend the morning with a guide who will bring alive the history of the Valley of the Temples. Leave Agrigento and spend a leisurely day driving along the southeastern coast of Sicily. Arrive in Siracusa by the late afternoon and visit its Città Vecchia; dine in one of its waterfront restaurants.

Days 9–10   Visit Siracusa's famous ancient amphitheater before leaving for the drive north along the eastern coast of Sicily. Stop for two nights in the idyllic resort of Taormina, Sicily's most famous, and renowned throughout Europe. Visit its ancient amphitheater, one of the most dramatically sited, and enjoy an outdoor dinner in the small town. The following day, join an excursion to the nearby Mt. Etna, Europe's only active volcano, where the lava is still warm beneath your feet. Return to Taormina for dinner. Don't think about leaving Sicily without tasting a luscious canoli or shaved-ice lemon granita. You can leave Sicily from the nearby airport in Catania or drive back to Palermo.

FAST FACTS: Italy

American Express   Offices are found in Rome at Pz. d. Spagna 38 (☎ **06/ 67-641**), in Florence at V. Dante Alighieri (☎ **055/50-981**), in Venice at San Marco 1471 (☎ **041/52-00-844**), and in Milan at V. Brera 3 (☎ **02/72-85-571**).

Banks   Open Monday to Friday from 8:30am to 1 or 1:30pm, and 2 or 2:30 to 4pm; and are closed all day Saturday, Sunday, and national holidays. Hours change slightly from city to city.

Business Hours   Local business hours can vary greatly and change seasonally. Regular business hours are usually Monday to Friday from 9am (sometimes 9:30am) to 1pm and 3:30 (sometimes 4) to 7 or 7:30pm with Saturdays being half- or full days depending on the season or type of business in question. In July or August, some offices, stores, and businesses may not open in the afternoon until 4:30 or 5pm. An exaggerated siesta (*riposo*) closing is often observed in Rome, Naples, and most cities of southern Italy; however, in Milan and other northern and central cities the custom has been cut back considerably. Most shops are closed on Sunday, except for pastry stores/bars and certain barbershops that are open on Sunday morning. Some tourist-oriented stores now are permitted to stay open during high season.

Camera/Film   U.S.-brand film is available in Italy but it's expensive. Take in as much as Customs will allow if you plan to take a lot of pictures.

Currency   See "Money," earlier in this chapter.

Customs   Overseas visitors to Italy can bring along most items for personal use duty-free. This includes fishing tackle, a sporting gun and 200 cartridges, a pair of skis, two tennis rackets, a portable typewriter, a record player with 10 records, a tape recorder, a baby carriage, two ordinary hand cameras with 10 rolls of film, a movie camera with 10 rolls of film, a portable radio set (subject to a small license fee), and 400 cigarettes (two cartons) or a quantity of cigars or pipe tobacco not exceeding 500 grams (1.1 lb.). There are strict limits on importing alcoholic beverages. However, limits are much more liberal for alcohol bought tax-paid in other countries of the European Union.

Upon leaving Italy, U.S. citizens who have been outside the country for 48 hours or more are allowed to bring back $400 worth of merchandise duty-free—so long as they have claimed no similar exemption within the past 30 days. If you make purchases in Italy, it is important to keep your receipts.

Driving Rules   See "Getting Around," earlier in this chapter.

Drug Laws   Penalties are severe and could lead to either imprisonment or deportation. Selling drugs to minors is dealt with particularly harshly.

Drugstores   *Farmacia* take turns staying open at night and on Sunday. At every farmacia a list is posted of those that are open in off-hours.

Electricity   The electricity in Italy varies considerably. It's usually alternating current (AC), varying from 42 to 50 cycles. The voltage can be anywhere from 115 to 220. It is recommended that any visitor carrying electrical appliances obtain a transformer and an adapter plug. Check the exact local current with your hotel. Plugs have prongs that are round, not flat.

Embassies/Consulates   The Embassy of the **United States** is in Rome at V. Vittorio Veneto 121 (☎ **06/45-741**). U.S. consulates are in Florence at Lungarno Amerigo Vespucci 38 (☎ **055/23-98-276**); and in Milan at V. Principe Amadeo 2/10 (☎ **02/29-03-51**). These offices are open Monday to Friday from 8:30am to 4:30pm. There is also a consulate in Naples at Pz. d. Repubblica (☎ **081/58-38-111**), open Monday to Friday from 8am to noon. The consulate in Genoa is closed; however, there is an office of the U.S. Foreign Commercial Service, Pz. Portello 6 (☎ **010/54-38-77**), open Monday to Friday from 8:30am to 12:30pm.

Consulate and passport services for **Canada** are in Rome at V. Zara 30 (☎ **06/44-59-81**), open Monday to Friday from 10am to 12:30pm. The office of the United Kingdom is in Rome at V. XX Settembre 80A (☎ **06/48-25-441**), open Monday to Friday, from 9:15am to 1:30pm. The Consulate General's office in Naples is located at V. Francesco Crispi 122, I-80122, (☎ **081/66-35-11**), open Monday to Friday from 9am to 12:30pm and 2 to 4:30pm. In Milan, contact the office at V. San Paolo 7 (☎ **02/72-30-01**) Monday to Friday from 9:15am to 12:15pm and 2:30 to 4:30pm. The **Australian** Embassy is in Rome at V. Alessandria 215 (☎ **06/85-27-21**), open Monday to Thursday from 8:30am to noon and from 2 to 4pm, and on Friday from 8:30am to noon. The consular services for Australia are in Rome at Cor. Trieste 25 (☎ **06/85-22-721**), open Monday to Thursday from 8:30am to noon and 2 to 4pm, and on Friday from 9am to noon. For **New Zealand,** the office in Rome is at V. Zara 28 (☎ **06/44-02-928**), and hours are Monday to Friday from 8:30am to 12:45pm and 1:45 to 5pm. In case of emergency, embassies have a 24-hour referral service.

Emergencies   Dial **113** for an ambulance, police, or fire. In case of a breakdown on an Italian road, dial **116** at the nearest telephone box; the Automobile Club of Italy (ACI) will be notified to come to your aid.

Holidays   See "When to Go," earlier in this chapter.

Information   See "Information & Entry Requirements," earlier in this chapter, and specific cities for local information offices.

Legal Aid.   The consulate of your country is the place to turn, although offices cannot interfere in the Italian legal process. They can, however, inform you of your rights and provide a list of attorneys. You'll have to pay for the attorney out of your pocket, however, as there is no free legal assistance. If you're arrested for a drug offense, about all the consulate will do is notify a lawyer about your case and perhaps inform your family.

Liquor Laws   Wine with meals has been considered a normal part of family life for hundreds of years in Italy. Children are exposed to wine at an early age, and alcoholic consumption is not considered anything out of the ordinary. There is no legal drinking age for buying or ordering alcohol. There are no restrictions on the sale of wine or liquor in Italy.

Mail   At post offices, General Delivery service is available in Italy. Correspondence can be addressed c/o the post office by adding *Fermo Posta* to the name of the locality. You can pick up mail at the local central post office by showing your passport. In addition to the post offices, you can purchase stamps at little *tabacchi* (tobacco) stores throughout any city.

   Mail delivery in Italy is notoriously bad. Letters sent from New York, say, in November, are often delivered (if at all) the following year. If you're writing for hotel reservations, this can cause much confusion—visitors may arrive in Italy long before their hotel deposits do. Fax machines speed up the process tremendously.

Maps   See "Getting Around," earlier in this chapter. Also see certain map recommendations in the city listings for such cities as Rome, Florence, and Venice.

Newspapers/Magazines   In major cities, it is possible to find the *International Herald Tribune, USA Today, Time,* and *Newsweek,* as well as other English-language newspapers and magazines at hotels and news kiosks.

Pets   A veterinarian's certificate of good health is required for dogs and cats and should be obtained by owners before entering Italy. Dogs must be on a leash or muzzled at all times. Other animals must undergo examination at the border or port of entry. Certificates for parrots or other birds subject to psittacosis must state that the country of origin is free of disease. All documents must be certified first by a notary public, then by the nearest Italian consulate.

Police   Dial **113,** the all-purpose number for police emergency assistance in Italy.

Radio/TV   Most radio and television broadcasts are on RAI, the Italian state radio and television network. Occasionally, especially during the tourist season, the network will broadcast special programs in English. Announcements are made in the radio and TV guide sections of local newspapers. Vatican Radio also carries foreign-language religious news programs, often in English. Shortwave transistor radios pick up broadcasts from the BBC (British), Voice of America (United States), and CBC (Canadian). RAI television and private channels broadcast only in Italian. More expensive hotels often have TV sets in the bedrooms with cable subscriptions to the CNN news network.

Rest Rooms   All airport and railway stations have rest rooms, often with attendants, who expect to be tipped. Bars, nightclubs, restaurants, cafes, and all hotels have facilities; public toilets are found near many of the major sights.

Usually rest rooms are designated as W.C. (water closet) or "toilette" and marked as *donne* (women) or *uomini* (men). The most confusing designation is *signori* (gentlemen) and *signore* (ladies), so watch those final i's and e's!

Safety   Violent street muggings are uncommon in Italy, although these are increasing everywhere. The most usual menace, especially in large cities (particularly Rome) is the plague of pickpockets, and the roving gangs of gypsy children who virtually surround you, distract you, and in all the confusion, steal your purse or wallet. Never leave valuables in a car, and never travel with your car unlocked.

Taxes   As a member of the European Union, Italy imposes a tax on most goods and services which is already included in the price. It is a "value-added tax," called IVA in Italy. The tax affecting most visitors is that imposed at hotels, which, at approximately 9% in first- and second-class hotels, is usually incorporated into the bill.

If you make a purchase in Italy, and your bill at any one store totals 300,000L ($197.35), you are eligible for a tax rebate up to 19% (the IVA varies according to item). Ask the store for a formal receipt, and before leaving Italy, bring your receipt and purchase (the item must be available for inspection) to Italian Customs. The customs agent will stamp your receipt and give you further directions. The stamped receipt gets sent back to the store and your reimbursement will either be credited against your credit card or sent to you by check; either can take months. Be sure to allow enough time before you board your flight home.

Telegrams/Telephone/Telex/Fax   For telegrams, ITALCABLE operates services abroad, transmitting messages by cable or satellite. Both internal and foreign telegrams may be dictated over the phone (dial **186**).

A public telephone is always near at hand in Italy. Local calls cost 200L. You can use 100L, 200L, or 500L coins. Most phones, especially in the cities, accept a multiple-use phone card called a *carta telefonica,* which can be purchased at all *tabacchi* and bars in increments of 5,000L, 10,000L, or 20,000L. To use this card, insert it into the slot in the phone and then dial. A digital display will keep track of how many lire you use up during your call. The card is good until it runs out of lire, so don't forget to take it with you when you hang up.

Thanks to ITALCABLE, international calls to the United States and Canada can be dialed directly. Dial **00** (the international code from Italy), then the country code (1 for the United States and Canada), the area code, and the number you're calling. Calls dialed directly are billed on the basis of the call's duration only. A reduced rate is applied from 11pm to 8am Monday to Saturday and all day Sunday.

If you wish to make a collect call from a pay phone, simply deposit 200L (don't worry—you get it back when you are done), dial **170,** and an ITALCABLE operator will come on and will speak English. For calling-card calls, drop in the refundable 200L, then dial the appropriate number for your card's company to be connected with an operator in the U.S.: for AT&T, **172-1011;** for MCI, **172-1022;** and for Sprint, **172-1877.**

If you make a long-distance call from a public telephone, there is no surcharge. *However, hotels have been known to double or triple the cost of the call, so be duly warned.*

Chances are your hotel will send or receive a telex or fax for you. You can send a fax from the post office to any country in the world, with the exception of the United States. Look for stationery stores and Xerox copy centers who post "servizio fax" signs in their windows.

Television The RAI is the chief television network broadcasting in Italy, although its format is not as politically oriented as in the past. Every TV in the country receives RAI-1, RAI-2, and RAI-3. In addition, most Italians receive Canale 5, Rete 4, and Italia 1, which are controlled by media-magnate Silvio Berlusconi, as well as several other private stations.

Time In terms of standard time zones, Italy is six hours ahead of eastern standard time in the United States. Daylight saving time goes into effect in Italy each year from the last Sunday in March through the last Sunday in October.

Tipping This custom is practiced with flair in Italy—many people depend on tips to supplement their livelihoods. In hotels, the service charge is already added to a bill. In addition, it's customary to tip the chambermaid a minimum of 1,000L (65¢) per day and the bellhop or porter 2,000L ($1.30) per bag. If your concierge has helped to resolve a problem, procure a ticket to a sold-out concert, or find an overnight parking space, acknowledge his effort with 5,000L ($3.30) or more.

In restaurants, 15% is almost always added to your bill (*servizio inclus*). An additional tip for good service is expected in upscale eateries. It's customary in restaurants in Rome, Florence, Venice, and Milan to leave an additional 10%, which, combined with the assessed service charge, is a very high tip indeed. Washroom attendants expect at least 300 to 500L (20¢ to 30¢), more in nicer restaurants and hotels. Restaurants are required by law to give customers official receipts. Taxi drivers expect at least 15% of the fare from foreign customers, though Italians tip in frequently.

Tourist Offices See "Information & Entry Requirements," earlier in this chapter, and also specific city chapters.

VAT Value-added Tax is called IVA in Italy. See "Taxes," above.

Water It is generally safe to drink, though the taste may be different from what you're accustomed to. However, in the south of Italy, particularly the Naples region, it's best to stick to bottled water.

4 Settling into Rome

by Barbara Coeyman Hults

Rome is opera, grand and comic, soap and buffo. As majestic as the Empire and as nerve-wracking as a freeway at rush hour, Rome can be seductive, charming, sophisticated, infuriating, and slapstick in rapid succession. Federico Fellini seems still to be directing his city in its mondo bizzarro.

Classical antiquities, towering medieval structures, exuberant baroque churches, statues, and fountains mix with high-tech boutiques and artisan shops. Yet the more the Eternal City changes, it seems, the more it stays the same. The latest political scandals add to the confusion of Italy's future, especially now that the European Union is judging Italy's every move. As Rome begins to plan ahead for the Papal Jubilee Year 2000, when 60 million visitors from throughout the world are expected to visit the city and the Vatican, the government is much changed from only a few years ago, when corruption scandals were each day's headlines. "Everything's so clean now that no one knows how to do anything," an amused Roman says.

But Rome is still Rome—if more frenetic and noisy and traffic-clogged than ever (a *casino*, a real mess, taxi drivers always say). Yet the new floodlighting of buildings at night is spectacular, the streets are cleaner, the food is still wonderful, schoolchildren still wear long smocks, and families still feast away each Sunday.

Rome is a very expensive city in the usual sense, but lovers of art and antiquity will find that many of the best things are free. Even the Vatican Museums are free, if you can go on the last Sunday of the month. The Roman Forum and the Colosseum are not, to be sure, but, thanks to the Renaissance popes, Rome is a city where much of the best art was commissioned for churches and piazzas. The greatness of Michelangelo, Bernini, Borromini, Caravaggio, and so many others can be seen by simply entering a church or strolling through Piazza Navona. The Pantheon still charges no admission, and it is one of the most majestic buildings of the world, evoking awe even in the jaded traveler.

Discount books and passes that other countries have in abundance are less often seen in Italy, but always check with the tourist office (below) on arrival, to see if new passes have been issued. In general, keep your ID with you, and ask at museums whether student or senior discounts apply.

Northern Europeans and Americans, sometimes taught that minimal art or gothic art is the "best" art, may be shocked by the exuberant nature of the baroque. (And the baroque enjoys shocking, that's a certainty.) Yet those who fall in love with Rome fit into the city as easily as the swirls on a pillar. The grandeur of the city can best be seen on Sunday, when the cars have gone to grandma's for lunch. This is true during much of the month of August as well, when heat and the national vacation period (*ferragosto*) send Fiat and Vespa toward mountains or sea. The evening *passegiata*, or stroll, is made more pleasant by car-free streets such as the Via del Corso and Piazza di Spagna, where the whole city—especially the young people—link arms to stroll and enjoy people watching. At night, Piazza Navona is one of the most enchanted places on earth, when Bernini's fountain is floodlit at the center, and the lovely palazzi surrounding it offer glimpses of wealthy Roman life.

Take long walks and bicycle rides (on Sunday when the cars are away) to feel the enchantment that sunlight or even gray skies lend to ancient buildings in a fruit-basket blend of colors from lemon and peach to dark apricot, and to enjoy just watching the Romans go about living with a gusto all their own.

1   Arriving

BY PLANE   Most international flights land at Leonardo da Vinci Airport, also known as **Fiumicino** (☎ **06/65-951**), 18 miles from downtown Rome. Immediately after Passport Control (but before Customs) you'll see two tourist information desks to your left, one for Rome and the other for the rest of Italy. The Rome desk has a good map and some useful brochures; it's open Monday to Saturday from 8:30am to 7pm. When it's closed, maps are available from nearby racks. An adjacent bank changes money at reasonable rates; it's open daily from 7:30am to 11pm.

In the main arrivals hallway you'll find a luggage-storage office, open 24 hours, which charges 5,000L ($3.30) per bag per day.

There's a train station in the airport terminal. Express trains to Rome's Stazione Termini take about 30 minutes and cost 13,000L ($8.55) each way. Local trains are almost as frequent and cost 9,500L ($6.25) each way. But the local trains terminate at Ostiense, where you have to change to a subway (1,500L/$1) to Termini, a journey of about an hour with walking and stairs involved—not good for the heavy-laden.

The average price for a taxi ride to or from the airport is 70,000L ($45.10); taxis line up in front of the airport terminals. This fare includes luggage.

Charter flights sometimes land at the city's smaller **Ciampino Airport** (☎ **79-49-41**) Yellow ACOTRAL buses leave this airport every half an hour or so and deposit passengers at Cinecittà station, the last stop on Line A of the Metropolitana (subway). From there, take the subway to Rome's central rail station or beyond. Metro tickets cost 1,500L ($1).

BY TRAIN   Most Rome-bound trains arrive at the sprawling silver **Stazione Termini.** You'll almost certainly be approached by touts claiming to work for a tourist organization. These people really work for individual hotels and will say almost anything to sell you a room. It's best to ignore them.

The official tourist office (Ente Provinciale per il Turismo, or EPT) personnel staff a hard-to-find small window at the head of Track 3 (☎ **06/48-71-270**). It's usually open daily from 8:15am to 7:15pm. Here you can pick up a free map, as well as a brochure on museums and *Un Ospite a Roma,* the city's best free monthly tourist information booklet. This office also makes hotel reservations—use it if you've arrived without a reservation.

There's a branch of the Banca Nazionale delle Communicazioni between the entrance to Tracks 8 to 11 and 12 to 15. You can exchange currency here Monday to

Saturday from 8:30am to 7:30pm at the same or sometimes even better rates than banks charge elsewhere in the city.

In the station's massive outer hall is the **Informazioni Ferroviarie,** which answers questions about train times, to long lines of tourists usually, and nearby is a perpetually crowded long bank of ticket windows. Travel agents (*agenzie viaggi e turismo*) in Rome, some of which are located in Piazza Esedra nearby, sell train and some bus tickets as well, and may save you time waiting in line at the station.

The entrance to the Metropolitana, Rome's two-line subway system, is downstairs (marked by an illuminated red-and-white M). Many of the city's buses begin their journeys in Piazza dei Cinquecento, in front of the train station.

BY BUS   Bus travel is not well developed in Italy, except in parts of the South. If you do come to Rome by bus, you will probably arrive in Piazza della Repubblica, not far from the train station. There is a metro stop (Termini) here, and it is only a one-block walk to Piazza dei Cinquecento in front of Termini station; many bus lines begin and end here.

BY CAR   From the north the main access route is the toll road Autostrada A1. From the south take A2. All roads connect with Rome's ring road, the Grande Raccordo Anulare, which does indeed form a ring completely around the city. To reach the north of the city, take the northern exit off the ring road at Via Flaminia (uscita or exit 6). For the west or Vatican area and Trastevere, take uscita 1 onto the Via Aurelia. For Termini station (southeast), get off at uscita 19, which leads to Via Tuscolana.

Driving in Rome itself is not advisable (see "Getting Around" below). If you are arriving in Rome by car, the largest parking garage is near the Flaminia exit 6, in the Villa Borghese (underground).

2 Orientation

VISITOR INFORMATION

Rome's main **Ente Provinciale per il Turismo (EPT)** office at V. Parigi 5 (☎ 06/48-83-748), also distributes brochures, the supply of which varies with the season, and it offers a free hotel reservation service. The office is open Monday to Saturday, 8:15am to 7:15pm. To get there from the train station, exit through the front doors, cross the enormous bus lot called Piazza dei Cinquecento, look for the Grand Hotel, and turn right onto Via Parigi. One of Rome's best ideas in many years are the new information kiosks, found in three locations—one at Largo Goldoni, where Via Condotti meets the Via del Corso (☎ 06/68-75-027), one near the Colosseum at Largo Ricci, and one on Via Nazionale at the Palazzo delle Esposizioni. They are open Tuesday to Saturday from 10am to 6pm and Sunday from 10am to 1pm. They'll give you information on new happenings and practical information on opening hours and addresses. Their computers are on-line to their central office for questions they can't handle.

Enjoy Rome, V. Varese 39 (☎ 06/44-51-843; fax 06/44-50-734) was begun by a young couple (Fulvia and Pierluigi) with a very bright idea, and is the answer to many travelers' dreams. In their office near the station, they dispense information on just about everything in Rome. They also find hotel rooms at rock-bottom prices. Summer hours are Monday to Friday from 8:30am to 7pm, Saturday from 8:30am to 1:30pm. In winter they're open Monday to Friday from 8:30am to 1:30pm and 3:30 to 6pm, Saturday from 8:30am to 1:30pm.

CITY LAYOUT

FINDING YOUR WAY Although the winding streets in the center of Rome require a good map to find your way, the basic design of the city for touring purposes is pretty simple. The Tiber (Tevere) River comes into the city from the north, then makes a large S curve before straightening out again as it heads south. Most of the tourist's city lies on the east side of the Tiber, with only the Vatican and Trastevere (which means "across the Tiber") districts on the west.

Stazione Termini, the main railroad station which is almost everyone's first sight of Rome, is on **Piazza dei Cinquecento** and marks the eastern edge of the tourist's city. To the east of the station is the university district, to the southeast is the basilica of Santa Maria Maggiore, and off farther to the northwest is the languid curve and faded glamour of the **Via Veneto.** Almost connected to the Piazza dei Cinquecento (immediately to the station's northwest) is **Piazza della Repubblica,** where the broad, busy **Via Nazionale** begins. This road stretches down past the Quirinal palace to **Piazza Venezia,** which is about in the center of tourist's Rome.

Once you've located—and you will—the enormous, wedding cake–like Vittorio Emanuele monument here at Piazza Venezia, you're on your way. It stands, or rather expands, at one end of the Via del Corso. For an easy orientation to the city, first stand facing the monument. Around it to the left is **Via dei Fori Imperiali,** which skirts one edge of the Forum and leads eventually to the Colosseum. Around the monument to the right lies **Via Teatro di Marcello,** with the Capitoline Hill and its museums on the left, the Theater of Marcellus farther on to the right, and at the end of the road, on the left the Mouth of Truth and farther down, the Circus Maximus.

Now standing with your back to the monument, the wide boulevard **Corso Vittorio Emanuele II** goes off to your left, bisecting the large triangle of land formed by the first, outward bend of the Tiber River's S curve. Between Corso Vittorio and the river to its left lies the area around **Campo de' Fiori** and the **Piazza Farnese.** To the right of Corso Vittorio, in an area bounded by the top of the Tiber's S to the north and the **Via del Corso** to the west, is the triangular tangle of streets where you'll find Piazza Navona and the Pantheon. Where Corso Vittorio meets with the point of this Tiber bend, three bridges cross over the river into the **Borgo,** the area around Vatican City and St. Peter's.

Downriver on the Vatican side, beyond the Gianicolo hill, **Trastevere** lies tucked into the second, inward bend of the Tiber (and hence due south of, and across the river from, the Campo de' Fiori area).

Now, back at our landmark, the Vittorio Emanuele monument at Piazza Venezia, stand with your back to it again and look straight ahead toward the distant **Piazza del Popolo** at the opposite end of the Via del Corso. As you walk down the Corso, about one-third of the way down toward Piazza del Popolo, a left turn will take you into the Piazza Navona/Pantheon area, while a right on Via delle Muratte will lead to the Trevi Fountain. Two-thirds of the way down, a left will find you at Augustus's Mausoleum and the Ara Pacis, and a right will lead you through tony shopping streets, such as **Via Condotti,** to the Spanish Steps. At the end, of course, is Piazza del Popolo, the north gate to the city, and, rising to the northwest, Rome's main city park—the Borghese Gardens.

FINDING AN ADDRESS Street numbers in Rome are not assigned with any real consistency or order. In fact, order is considered boring in much of the Mediterranean, to the Northern traveler's frustration. Some numbers alternate even and odd on opposite sides of the street as in the United States, others start the numbering on

Rome Orientation

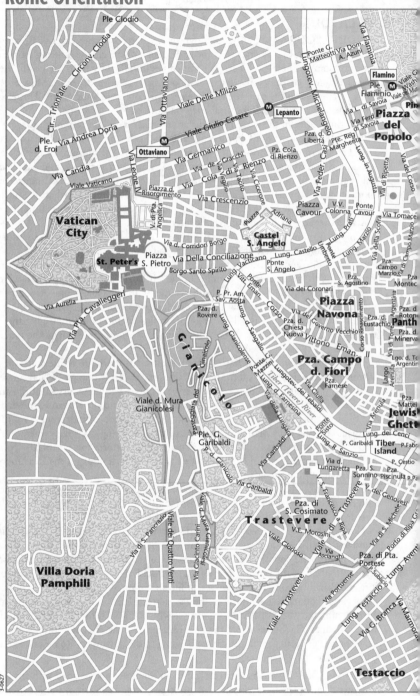

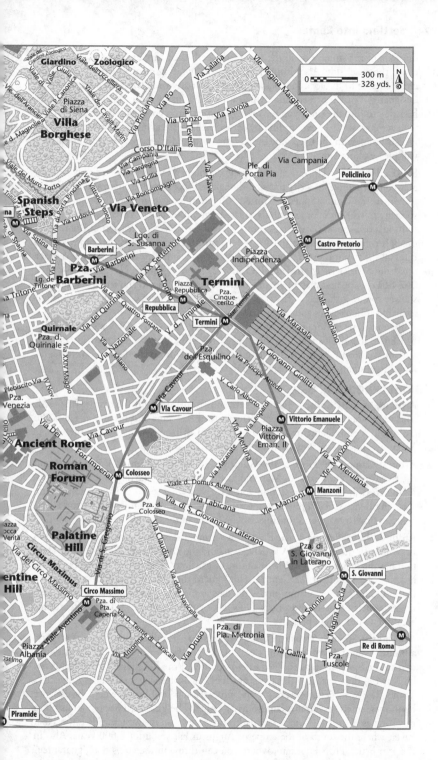

73

one side of the street, run all the way to the end, then turn around and come back down the other side. Also, Rome is full of tiny, winding medieval streets that often change name from block to block, and just about any wide point in the road can be designated a piazza or piazzetta, which usually has its own numbering system. The best way to find the street you're looking for is to buy a good map (see below) or ask your hotel to see their extraordinarily comprehensive street guide, *Tutta Città,* which is distributed with the telephone book. Once you find the page you need, ask if they will please photocopy it for you.

STREET MAPS   The free map of Rome distributed by the tourist office is remarkably comprehensive for a city this size, though its lack of an index makes street-finding tough. In the United States or United Kingdom, look in any bookstore, especially specialty travel stores, for the stiff, laminated *Streetwise Rome.* It costs only $5.95, folds to fit in a back pocket, and maps about 98% of the streets in the heart of Rome. Best of all, it comes with a street-finding index (*note:* the *Artwise Rome* version, which locates all the major museums and sights, doesn't have this index). You can also order one from **Streetwise Maps Inc.,** P.O. Box 2219, Amagansett, NY 11930 (☎ **516/ 267-8617**). The best map to get in Rome, listing every vicolo and largo, and bus and subway routes, is the yellow city plan produced by the Istituto Geografico de Agostini, available at bookstores and larger newsstands for 12,000L ($7.90).

If you will be in Rome long, or if you're driving, buy *StradaRoma 1997* (18,000L/ $11.85), a loose-leaf street atlas that makes street-finding easy. Major streets and bus and metro stops are listed on the current bus maps, available in bookstores or major newsstands. Even Romans have to use them.

NEIGHBORHOODS IN BRIEF

Around Ancient Rome   This is where most tourists spend their time. It spreads south and southeast from Piazza Venezia to the forums and reaches as far as the Colosseum, San Clemente, and San Giovanni in Laterano, as well as the Circus Maximus and San Pietro in Vincoli to the east.

Around Campo de' Fiori & the Ghetto   From Corso Vittorio Emanuele II and the river up to Via Teatro di Marcello in the east, this is one of Rome's most fascinating areas. In the Campo section you'll see a city that seems to have changed little since the Renaissance, and some of the Ghetto (where Roman Jewish trattorias and bakeries lure Romans and tourists) still has some of the old charm.

Around Piazza Navona & the Pantheon   Bounded on the south by Corso Vittorio Emanuele II, the east by the Via del Corso, and the north by Via Tomacelli, this section has the magic of old Rome in a more elegant way. The ancient Pantheon, at the heart of Old Rome, or the Centro, stands guard through the centuries over an area that is becoming more glamorous by the day, as the hotels and restaurants of the area upgrade their property and prices. Let's hope yuppification stops before all artisans are driven out by high prices.

Around the Spanish Steps & Piazza del Popolo   A rather wide-ranging category, admittedly, as it covers everything east of the Via del Corso, from the Trevi Fountain to the Spanish Steps to Piazza del Popolo and the Borghese Gardens, plus the bit between the Corso and the Tiber north of Via Tomacelli that includes Augustus's Tomb. The Spanish Steps section is the most stylish part of Rome, where the designer boutiques, smart restaurants, and tourists gather. The Piazza del Popolo looks up to the Borghese Gardens, Rome's city park, and close by on the western side is the Tiber River, where the tomb of the emperor Augustus has stood for 2,000 years. Also in the area is the Trevi Fountain, where you can throw in the coins that "guarantee" visitors a return to Rome.

Around Via Veneto & Piazza Barberini   The once chic Veneto is no longer even wild or trendy, but a renaissance is imminent, we hear. Piazza Barbarini shows off Bernini's exuberant sculpture as the Triton or Neptune fountain exults in its luck at being in Rome, and artistry is continued along Via Quattro Fontane, where the Borghese Museum holds sway. Farther down the hill, the Quirinale palace, presided over by Italy's famous tall, dark, and handsome palace guards, was once the king's residence, but now is the residence of the president of the republic. Many of the luxury hotels are located here, as well as the embassies.

Around Termini   The section around Termini station is making a comeback. South of the station, the beautiful Basilica of Santa Maria Maggiore is the star of an otherwise commercial neighborhood that is being slowly restored to the stately grace of the royal Savoy period of the 19th century. This area has the majority of budget hotels and restaurants with fixed-price menus printed in four languages. However, plans to close the large market at Piazza Vittorio and "upgrade" the neighborhood may mean that budget Rome is *via col vento* (gone with the wind). The northeast side of the station leads to the university area of San Lorenzo.

The Appian Way   Still one of the important roads that lead to Rome, the Via Appia is best known for the catacombs where Christians and other citizens were buried during the days of the empire.

The Aventine & South   The Aventine hill is a beautiful part of the south of Rome, a smart residential section where early Christian basilicas are fascinating places to visit. Some have Mithraic (an early Persian religion imported to Rome) remnants. Orange trees in flower and the annual rose show in May lend a gracious air to the hill. Testaccio, at the bottom of the hill and toward the Pyramid, is a former slaughterhouse district turned trendy, where young Romans and foreigners gather for its clubs at night. Many traditional good, inexpensive restaurants are surviving the new trends so far. Near this din, John Keats is buried in the Protestant cemetery.

Trastevere   The name means "across the Tevere" or the river Tiber. This is Rome's best-preserved neighborhood of medieval and Renaissance days, where life goes on as in a country town, unmindful of the expatriates who tend their expensive roof gardens and thank their lucky stars they're in Rome. The Villa Farnesina and Palazzo Corsini, both in Trastevere, have wonderful collections of painting and sculpture. The Gianicolo hill leads up to the private American Academy, where the Prix de Rome is awarded yearly, and the views over Rome from the hilltop promenade are exquisite.

Around Vatican City   Hotels and restaurants are not located, strictly speaking, within Vatican City, which occupies the area within its ancient walls only. The section between the Vatican and Castel Sant'Angelo is called the Borgo, and although its restaurants and souvenir shops cater to tourists, the neighborhood on Sunday morning could be in many a small Italian town, with families pushing baby carriages, everyone shopping for pastries for Sunday dinner, and men getting ready for the televised soccer match, especially if Rome or its region (state) of Lazio is playing.

GETTING AROUND

BY METRO   Most people walk or take the bus where they need to go, for Rome's Metropolitana (Metro) subway system is not very extensive—every time they try to dig a new tunnel, they run into ancient ruins and have to wait for the archeologists to pick over everything, then tell them which direction they have to veer off in before they can start again. There are only two lines, which cross at Stazione Termini. They connect most of the city's major hubs, but neither venture into the Piazza

Navona/Pantheon or the Campo de' Fiori areas, nor do they go anywhere near Trastevere.

Line A (red) is the most useful to the average tourist, traveling vaguely north-west (Ottaviano) to southeast (Anagnina). Along the way, it stops at the Vatican (Ottaviano), Piazza della Popolo (Flaminio), the Spanish Steps (Spagna), Via Veneto (Barberini), Piazza della Repubblica, Termini, and, after a few stops, the Basilica di San Gionvanni (San Giovanni), and eventually to Anagnina, where you can catch the bus to Ciampino airport. Line B (blue), meanwhile, runs northeast (Rebibbia), where you can catch a bus to Tivoli, to southwest (Laurentina). Running southwest from Termini, it stops first near San Pietro in Vincoli (Cavour), the Colosseum, the Circus Maximus, the Protestant Cemetery and Ostiense regional rail station (Piramide), the transfer station for the train to Ostia (Magliana), and E.U.R.

Tickets cost 1,500L ($1) each or 13,000L ($8.55) for 10 and can be purchased at tobacco shops (*tabacchi*), at many newsstands, and from machines in the stations. You can also buy a one-day pass, good on all buses and the Metro, for 6,000 ($3.95), or a one-week pass for 24,000L ($13.15). The Metro operates daily from 5:30am to 11:30pm.

BY BUS & TRAM   The city's buses are run by **ATAC** (☎ **06/46-951**). There are three major drawbacks to Rome's public bus and streetcar system—traffic, crowds, and petty thieves. Downtown congestion can be so bad that you're sometimes bet-ter off on foot. When navigating this sprawling city by bus, remember bus no. 64. This indispensable line, sometimes called "the pickpocket bus," begins right behind the ticket booth at the train station, travels along Via Nazionale, passes through Piazza Venezia, and continues across the heart of the Old City along Via Corso Vittorio Emanuele II, ending just off St. Peter's Square.

Bus 492 also makes the Termini-Vatican trip, on a longer route, by way of Piazza Barberini, Piazza Colonna, Piazza Venezia, Largo di Torre Argentina, and Piazza Navona; bus 492's western terminus is Piazza Risorgimento, about halfway between the entrances to St. Peter's and the Vatican Museums. Other key lines from the sta-tion include 27, which travels to the Colosseum, and 75 and 170, which cross the river into Trastevere. The 90 and 90/ both run from Piazza del Popolo along Via di Ripetta and Via del Corso south toward Piazza Venezia, Largo Argentina, and even-tually the Circus Maximus. The tiny electric 119 cuts across the heart of the Old City from the Pantheon area over to Piazza di Spagna before turning north to run to Piazza del Popolo. Night buses (which run after midnight to 6am) are denoted with an "N" at the beginning of their number and run on special routes.

You can buy bus tickets at a small gray-metal office in the corner of Piazza dei Cinquecento, in front of the Stazione Termini. It's open daily from 6am to 11:30pm. The adjacent bus information window is open daily from 7:30am to 7:30pm. Elec-tronic ticket dispensers have recently been introduced that seem to take only bills in mint condition. Tabacchi and newsstands—wherever the ATAC sign is displayed—also sell tickets. You cannot buy tickets on the bus, except on night buses. It is easiest is to buy 10 at a time—called a *carnet*—or a week's tourist pass for all lines (24,000L/$15.80). With a pass you can enter buses at the center instead of the back, often a help when buses are crowded (which is almost always). Everyone exits from the middle door.

Bus fare is 1,500L ($1); you must stamp your ticket in the red box at the back of the bus when you get on. A ticket is valid for 90 minutes from the time you stamp it, and you can get on any number of buses within that time (stamp the opposite end when you board your final bus). Inspectors have stepped up their patrolling of the buses, and they will fine you 50,000L to 100,000L ($32.90 to $65.80), which you must pay on the spot, if you don't have a stamped ticket (they've also become far less lenient toward the "I'm a tourist" excuse).

ON FOOT Rome is not a pedestrian's paradise. It's spread out and crowded with cars. Sidewalks are extremely narrow, if they exist at all. However, the heart of Old Rome, around the Spanish Steps and Piazza Navona, is a joy to wander through when cars are not in rush-hour mode, and more and more of these streets are being closed off to traffic every day as the big Jubilee Year 2000 approaches (although it seems, at times, that almost every Roman has a special permit to drive or double-park in these restricted areas). Try strolling from 1:30 until 3pm, when Romans are enjoying lunch. At rush hour, walking is almost always preferable to trying to cram yourself onto a city bus or subway along with commuters, although the hordes of Fiats choking the major roads, honking and roaring as they fight their way home through daily traffic jams of epic proportions, do create something of a hazard.

Almost every ambulatory Italian across the country turns out between 5pm and 7pm to promenade up and down the major street(s) in town, to see and be seen during the evening passegiata before dinner. In Rome, the main venues for strutting include the Via del Corso and Via Veneto.

BY TAXI Taxi fares begin at 7,500L ($4.95) for the first 3 kilometers and then click upward by 300L (20¢) every 250 yards. Suitcases are 500L (35¢). There's a 2,000L ($1.35) supplement for all rides between 10pm and 7am, a 5,000L ($3.30) add-on for travel on Sunday and holidays. If you order a taxi by telephone, the meter goes on when they receive the call, not when you begin riding. The airport ride is about 70,000L ($46.05).

Beware of unmetered cabs, which are illegal and unlicensed and charge sometimes exorbitant, uncontrolled rates. To call a legitimate taxi, dial **3570, 3875, 88177,** or **4994.** You can also find a cab at stands marked TAXI, or ask a hotel or coffee bar employee to call for you (give them 1,000L/65¢) for their trouble). Hailing a cab is rarely done, except late at night.

BY CAR Driving in Rome is not for anyone who wants to relax. Roman drivers speed, tailgate, and obey their own laws, which take time to learn. Streets change from one-way to the opposite daily, and even taxi drivers have a hard time figuring out which streets are going which way on which day. A map is no help. Car theft in Rome is higher than in Naples or Palermo.

Only cars with special permits may enter the historic center, and you cannot park in the center without a permit. Parking is rarely available, expensive, and cars cannot be left unattended. Many streets are pedestrian zones only, or at certain times of day. If you're driving, have someone stay in the car while you drop off your luggage, and then park in the garage at the Villa Borghese.

BY BICYCLE Traffic and crazy drivers make bicycling around Rome somewhat unnerving. But mountain biking in the historic center or up in the large Villa Borghese park are singular experiences. **I Bike Rome,** V. Veneto 156 (☎ **06/32-25-240**), rents bikes for 6,000L ($3.75) per hour, 15,000L ($9.85) per day, or 45,000L ($29.60) per week. They're open daily, year-round, from 8:30am to 8pm. Mopeds cost 30,000L ($19.75) for four hours, 45,000L ($29.60) per day.

You can also rent bikes from an outdoor dealer, immediately to your right as you exit the Spagna Metro stop. Prices there are 7,000L ($4.60) per hour or 25,000L ($16.45) per day. It's open daily, from 9am to midnight March through October, from 9am to 8pm the rest of the year. Both places require a document as deposit.

FAST FACTS: Rome

American Express   The American Express office at Pz. di Spagna 38 (☎ 06/67-641), exchanges traveler's checks (no fee) and is open Monday to Friday from 9am to 5:30pm and Saturday from 9am to 12:30pm. They also cash personal checks for AMEX card holders and operate an English-speaking travel agency open to all.

Banks   Standard bank hours are Monday to Friday from 8:30am to 1:30pm, then again from about 2:45 to 3:45pm; only a few banks are open Saturday, and then usually mornings only. There's a bank in the train station, between the entrance to Tracks 8 to 11 and Tracks 12 to 15, that usually exchanges currency Monday to Saturday from 8:30am to 7:30pm and Sunday from 8am to 2:15pm.

Bookstores   See "Shopping" in chapter 5.

Crime   See "Safety," below.

Business Hours   In summer, most businesses and shops are open Monday to Friday from 9am to 1pm and 4 to 8pm; on Saturday shops are only open in the morning. From mid-September through mid-June, most shops are open Tuesday to Saturday from 9am to 1pm and anywhere from 3:30 or 4:30 to 7:30pm; on Monday in winter, shops don't open until the afternoon. In Rome as throughout the rest of Italy, just about everything except restaurants is closed on Sunday. Most restaurants are required to close at least one day per week; the particular day varies from one trattoria to another (those in hotels often stay open all week). Most serve from noon to 3pm and 7:30 to 10:30pm.

Doctors/Dentists   For a list of English-speaking doctors and dentists, consult your embassy. At the private (and expensive) Salvator Mundi Hospital, Vle. Mura Gianicolensi 67 (☎ 06/58-60-41) or the Rome American Hospital (☎ 06/22-551) you're certain to find English-speaking doctors and staff.

Drugstores   Called *farmacia,* they are found in every neighborhood, recognized by the red cross in front. Many pharmacists speak English, especially in tourist areas. The daily papers list the rotating (*de turno*) Farmacia, open at night and weekends. Pharmacies also post a sign on their door, indicating the nearest one that is open. The one is the Termini station near Track 14 is open until 10pm.

Embassies/Consulates   The Embassy of the **United States,** V. Veneto 121 (☎ 06/46-741), is open Monday to Friday from 8:30am to 1pm and 2 to 5:30pm. Consular services are in the same building (the entrance is at the other end of the block) and are open the same hours. The Embassy of the **United Kingdom** is at V. XX Settembre 80a (☎ 06/48-25-441); the Embassy of **Canada** is at V. Zara 30 (☎ 06/44-03-028); the Embassy of **Australia** is at V. Alessandria 215 (☎ 06/85-27-21); and the Embassy of **New Zealand** is at V. Zara 28 (☎ 06/44-02-928)—they're all open Monday to Friday from approximately 9:30am to 12:30pm and 2 to 4pm. Call ahead to make certain.

Emergencies   Dial **113** in case of fire or in order to reach the police. The military-trained Carabinieri offer similar services (call **112**). For an ambulance, dial **5100.** For First Aid (Pronto Soccorso) dial **118.**

Holidays   For national holidays, see chapter 3, "When to Go." The city of Rome honors its patron saints, Peter and Paul, on June 29. Almost the entire city goes on vacation for the last two weeks of August, and most businesses, except restaurants and the like in heavily touristed areas, are closed.

Hospitals   See "Doctors/Dentists," above.

Information   See "Visitor Information," above.

Laundry   Onda Blu, near the station at V. Milazzo 8/a (☎ 06/44-41-665), is one of the few self-service laundries in Rome. It costs about 12,000L ($7.90) to wash and dry 6¹/₂ kilos (about 14¹/₂ pounds).

Lost & Found   Oggetti Rinvenuti is at V. Nicolò Bettoni 1 (☎ 06/58-16-040), at the Trastevere station, open Monday to Saturday from 9am to noon. At Termini there is one at Track 22. Don't expect anything to be there, alas.

Newspapers/Magazines   *Metropolitan* and *Wanted in Rome,* both in English, are good sources of news for the expatriate community. For daily entertainment sections, *Il Messaggero. La Repubblica,* or the Rome edition of *Corriere della Sera* are the best bets. On Thursdays, ask for the *supplemento*, which is a handy weekly entertainment guide.

Police   Dial **113** for the *polizia* (city police), or **112** for the military-trained *Carabinieri.*

Post Office   Rome's main post office, at Pz. San Silvestro 19, 00187 Roma, is located near Piazza di Spagna. For stamps (*francobolli*), visit windows 22 to 24, on the right side as you enter. You can also buy stamps at face value at almost all tobacconists.

Many Romans prefer to use the more efficient postal service at the Vatican. The three most accessible branches are (1) adjacent to the information office in Piazza San Pietro, to the left as you approach the church; (2) to the right of the right-hand colonnade on Piazza San Pietro (hidden behind souvenir stands); and (3) upstairs at the Vatican Museum entrance. They're open Monday to Friday from 8:30am to 7pm and Saturday from 8:30am to 6pm. Packages should be mailed from the Vatican as well, but inquire about package size before sending. Remember that the Vatican is in fact a separate country and, although the rates are the same, Italian stamps are not valid here and vice versa.

Safety   Violent street crime is uncommon in Rome. But watch out for pickpockets and thieving (usually gypsy) children. Pickpockets are clever, preying on unwary travelers, especially on buses and the Metropolitana. If you take the obvious precautions, however, you shouldn't have much trouble. The ubiquitous thieving children, on the other hand, are brash and bothersome and a real social problem. Routinely, bands of six or more unaccompanied children rove major tourist areas, wielding pieces of cardboard or a newspaper. They'll approach their target and begin babbling plaintively, waving or shoving the cardboard or newspaper into your face. Meanwhile, their free hand is rummaging through your pockets or purse. I've found that a modest challenge, rather than retreat, is the most effective defense. Yell back at them, stamp your foot, and invoke the name of the *polizia*—preferably before they actually reach you and begin their ploy. Of course, if you spot them before they spot you, do whatever you can to avoid these fearless, obnoxious criminals.

Telephone   The area code for Rome is 06. For more on how to use telephones in Italy, see "Fast Facts: Italy" in chapter 3.

NETWORKS & RESOURCES

FOR GAY MEN & LESBIANS   In Rome, the national organization is **ARCI-Gay,** V. delle Mille 23 (☎ 06/44-65-839), has all kinds of information. The **Archivio Massimo Consoli,** V. Einaudi 33 (☎ 06/93-54-75-67; fax 64-46-722) is an important gay organization, and publishes several magazines such as the *Roman Gay*

News, available on some newsstands. The **Coordinamento Lesbico Italiano** is at V. San Francesco de Sales 1A ☎ **06/68-64-201,** in Trastevere. The **Libreria Babele,** V. Paola 44 ☎ **06/68-76-628,** open Monday to Saturday from 9:30am to 7:30pm, sells lots of gay and lesbian books and maps.

FOR OUTREACH & RELIGIOUS SERVICES IN ENGLISH   For Catholics, Santa Susanna, on Via XX (Venti) Settembre 14 (☎ **06/48-27-510)** (American), and San Silvestro, at Piazza San Silvestro (☎ **67-97-775)** (British), conduct masses in English. For Anglicans, the Church of England at V. Babuino 153 (☎ **06/36-00-18-81)** and St. Paul within the Walls, V. Napoli 58 (☎ **06/48-83-339)** are very active churches. Each church also has outreach services, or information about organizations such as A.A. The synagogue or Tempio Maggiore is located at Lungotevere Cenci (☎ **06/68-75-051)** and the new mosque (Moschea) is at Monte Antenne (☎ **06/80-82-258)**. Also consult the booklet *A Guest in Rome,* provided at major hotels.

FOR SENIORS   Rome has discounts at some sights and museums, available if you show your passport. "Senior" minimum age varies from 60 to 65.

FOR STUDENTS   There are fewer students' associations active in Italy than in the United States. However, students can get discounts at some sights and museums. The Rome tourist office often has brochures directed toward student activities or discounts. Apart from that, the Spanish Steps, Piazza dela Rotunda (Pantheon), and Piazza Navona are where they hang out. The **Centro Turistico Studentesco e** (☎ **06/46-791)** provides information on studying in Italy.

FOR WOMEN   The women's bookstore, **Al Tempo Ritrovato,** in Piazza Farnese (☎ **06/68-80-37-49)**, is the source of information about local feminist activities. The **Virginia Woolf Center** at V. Lungara 1a (☎ **06/68-64-201)** in Trastevere is a women's center and general clearinghouse for information about women's issues.

3 Accommodations

Affordable hotels are usually what were formerly called *pensiones* and occupy one or two floors of a building. Most have undergone extensive renovations, but rooms vary, often enormously, in quality. Rome's prices are heading north, not south, and the number of budget accommodations is decreasing. Hotels that once had rooms without baths have installed tiny modular shower and toilet combos, thus upping their prices.

From January 10 to Palm Sunday is low season, when higher-class hotels reduce their rates. August, when Europeans seek the sea, sometimes sees dramatic rate reductions in luxury hotels.

Most of the budget pensiones are near the railroad station, an area that has improved enormously in the last year as Rome gets ready for the Papal Jubilee Year 2000. The area around Via Montebello (northwest of the station) now even has a kind of Left Bank bohemian charm, with outdoor markets and cafes. The opposite side of the station is also on the rise, with a goal of renovating the area entirely by the time of Jubilee Year 2000. The station-area hotels I've listed are all reasonably comfortable and of good value.

Some of the most attractive prices in tourist-quality hotels can be arranged before you leave through a tour operator like Central Holidays, 206 Central Ave., Jersey City, NJ 07307 (☎ **800-935-5000)**. For example, in off-season 1996, Central

Holidays offered a double at the Hotel Nizza (a tourist-class hotel) for $48 and a single for $42 per night, breakfast, tax, and tips included. Hotels closer to the center of town are priced at about double this.

Budget hotels can be booked ahead (by fax) through Enjoy Rome (☎ **06/ 44-51-843**; fax 44-50-734). If you must arrive without a reservation, try to arrive early; the best places fill up by around midday. You can walk to the Enjoy Rome office from the station.

CONVENTS, HOSTELS & OTHER OPTIONS
THE CONVENT HOTELS

With prices in Rome continuing to rise, convents that rent rooms are becoming the best bet for those who don't mind the curfew. Some are in wonderful locations, and all offer good value. They are booked up for months in advance by pilgrim groups around Easter. Single men and women or married couples are accepted. All faiths are welcomed.

○ **Convento Santa Francesca Romana.** V. d. Vascellari 61, 00153 Roma ☎ **06/ 58-12-125.** 42 rms, 9 with shower. Rates same with or without bath. 70,000L ($46.05) single; 67,000L ($44.05) double; 115,000L ($75.56) triple; 143,000L ($94) quadruple; 163,000L ($107.25) quintuple. Breakfast 5,000L ($3.30) extra. No credit cards. Bus: 170 to Vle. Trastevere. Cross viale, then walk through piazza to V. Buco at right, which becomes V. Salumi, which leads to V. Vascellari.

A lovely convent in Trastevere that is also used as a hotel, managed by a group of affable young men. The rooms are simple, but some have nice views of Trastevere street life. Some rooms have private baths, and there are very clean shower rooms on each floor. The inner courtyard is charming. It's a great location for those who want to see a Roman neighborhood at work and play. The convent was originally the home of the saint. Curfew is 11pm. Breakfast is offered, but you'd do better to go out to a cafe-bar.

Franciscan House of Hospitality. V. Nicolo V 35 (between Vle. Vaticano and V. Aurelia), 00165 Roma. ☎ **06/39-36-65-31.** 15 rms, none with bath. 45,000L ($29.60) per person, single or double, with breakfast. No credit cards at present. Bus: 46; get off 3 stops after the tunnel and walk up the stairs from V. Aurelia and turn left. With luggage a cab may be needed.

Just outside the Vatican walls, and with a lovely roof-terrace view of St. Peter's dome, this is a friendly, cheerful dwelling, run by American sisters from Syracuse, N.Y. It's up a flight of stairs from the Via Aurelia, just outside the Vatican walls. Reserve well in advance. No curfew.

Franciscan Sisters of the Atonement. V. Monte d. Gallo 105, 00165 Roma. ☎ **06/ 63-07-82.** 26 rms, all with bath. 66,000L ($43.40) per person with full board; 55,000L ($34.90) for rm with half-board; 38,000L ($25) per person for rm with breakfast. Bus: 34.

Beautiful surroundings in a pleasant neighborhood a short bus ride from the Vatican or you can walk down the hill to the Vatican (but the climb up is steep). Extremely well cared for with sparkling wood and flowers. Curfew is 11pm.

Istituto Lourdes. V. Sistina 113, 00187 Rome. ☎ **06/47-45-324.** 32 rms, 10 with bath. 45,000L ($29.60) per person without bath; 55,000L ($36.20) per person with bath. Rates include breakfast. No credit cards. Metro: Barbarini. Bus: 52, 56, 58, 119 to Lgo. Tritone.

In a great location on Via Sistina, near the Spanish Steps, this simple convent provides the basics at unbelievable prices for the area. Curfew is at 10:30pm, however, so it's not geared to nightlife.

Rome Accommodations

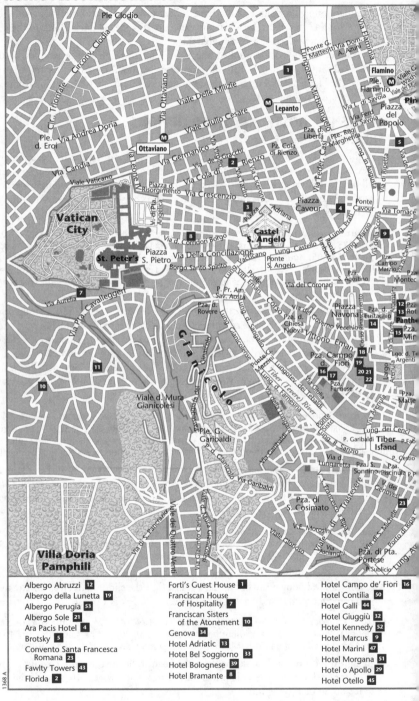

Albergo Abruzzi ▮12
Albergo della Lunetta ▮19
Albergo Perugia ▮53
Albergo Sole ▮21
Ara Pacis Hotel ▮4
Brotsky ▮5
Convento Santa Francesca Romana ▮23
Fawlty Towers ▮43
Florida ▮2

Forti's Guest House ▮1
Franciscan House of Hospitality ▮7
Franciscan Sisters of the Atonement ▮10
Genova ▮34
Hotel Adriatic ▮13
Hotel Bel Soggiorno ▮33
Hotel Bolognese ▮39
Hotel Bramante ▮8

Hotel Campo de' Fiori ▮16
Hotel Contilia ▮50
Hotel Galli ▮44
Hotel Giuggiù ▮32
Hotel Kennedy ▮52
Hotel Marcus ▮9
Hotel Marini ▮47
Hotel Morgana ▮51
Hotel o Apollo ▮29
Hotel Otello ▮45

Hotel Pensione Astoria Garden & Montagna **42**	Nord Nuova Roma **35**	Pensione Mimosa **15**
Hotel Pensione Parlamento **24**	Pensione Corallo **40**	Pensione Navona **14**
Hotel Piccolo **20**	Pensione Cortorillo **50**	Pensione Papà Germano **38**
Hotel Romae **46**	Pensione di Rienzo **50**	Pensione Primavera **18**
Hotel Smeraldo **22**	Pensione Elide **31**	Pensione Suisse **28**
Hotel Venezia **48**	Pensione Erdarelli **25**	Pontifical Irish College **54**
Istituto Lourdes **26**	Pensione Fiorella **6**	San Giorgio **49**
Massimo d' Azeglio **37**	Pensione Katty **41**	Santa Brigida **17**
Mediterraneo **36**	Pensione Lidia Venier **27**	Suore Teatine **11**
	Pensione Marvi **3**	YWCA **30**

🛈 Family-Friendly Places to Stay

Massimo d'Azeglio *(p.90)*   Rooms and baths are spacious, and kids are welcomed. It's near to the Metro and bus terminus.

Pontifical Irish College (summer only) *(p.84)*   The facilities are dormlike, but there are gardens, a swimming pool, and tennis courts, and it's near the Colosseum.

✪ Pontifical Irish College. V. d. Santissimi Quattro 1, 00184 Rome. ☎ **06/70-45-46-78.** Fax 06/70-47-61-50. 65 rms. Single without bath 60,000L ($45), single with bath 92,000L ($60.40); double without bath 115,000L ($75.65), double with bath 138,000L ($90.90); triple without bath 138,000L ($90.78), triple with bath 161,000L ($105.90); family rm (extra beds) 207,000L ($136.20). Children under 14 are charged half-price. Breakfast, pool, and courts (squash and tennis) included. No credit cards. Open June 29–Sept 15. Metro: San Giovanni. Bus: 85.

What a bargain. This V-shaped building looks out on garden views from most of the windows. Rooms are comfortable but dormitory-simple. Traffic sounds are but a memory. And yet, it's located between the Colosseum and St. John Lateran, convenient to sightseeing and to the Metro. Pilgrimage groups often come here, and daily mass is said, for those who wish to attend.

⑤ Santa Brigida. Pz. Farnese 96, 00186 Roma. ☎ **06/69-85-263.** 22 rms, all with bath. TEL. 110,000L ($72.35) single; 130,000L ($85.50) double. Rates include breakfast. Lunch or dinner 14,000L ($9.20). Bus: 54 or 64 to Palazzo d. Cancelleria.

The location is just about perfect, in the beautiful Piazza Farnese, just off Campo de' Fiori. They are often full, but telephone anyway (don't write). This was the home of St. Bridget, and she died here in 1373. It's not a dorm at all, but nicely furnished with antiques. The sisters have daily Mass and Vespers in the delightful chapel. At Christmas a wonderful crèche is set up.

Suore Teatine. Salita Monte d. Gallo 25, 00165 Roma. ☎ **06/63-74-084.** Fax 06/63-07-82. 40,000L ($26.30) per person for rm without board; 54,000L ($35.50) for rm with half-board; 64,000L ($42) rm with 3 meals. Bus: 34.

This convent is both away from it all but also just a short bus ride up the hill from the Vatican. It's in a little Roman neighborhood, apart from the bustle of the city. Curfew is 11pm. Parking is available.

HOSTELS & DORMS

Each summer a handful of Roman university dormitories are turned into unofficial youth hostels, charging ultra-low rates usually similar or identical to those at the Ostello Foro Italico. Their locations change just about every year, so you'll need to check with the tourist office when you arrive. Remember, however, that these locations, like the official IYHF hostel, are often distant from the central part of the city.

Ostello del Foro Italico. Vle. d. Olimpiadi 61, 00194 Roma. ☎ **06/32-36-267.** Fax 06/ 32-42-613. 350 beds. 20,000L ($13.15) per person per night; 32,000L ($21.05) half-board; 44,000L ($28.95) full-board. Room rates include continental breakfast and sheets. No credit cards. Metro: Ottaviano, then bus 32 to the 6th stop.

Unfortunately, the hostel is far from anything else in Rome, located out by the Olympic Stadium, about an hour's commute from the train station and slightly less from city center. And with few windows and no neighborhood charm, it rates as one of the less-appealing youth hostels. Rooms contain 6, 7, 12, or 20 beds. An International Youth Hostel Federation membership card is required, but you can buy it on the spot for 40,000L ($26.30). Despite its name, the youth hostel accepts travelers of any age. It's open from 7am to 9am and from 2pm until the 11pm curfew.

YWCA. V. Cesare Balbo 4, 001. Roma. ☎ **06/48-80-460** or 48-83-917. 29,000L ($19.10) per person, 40,000L ($26.30) per person half-board. Inexpensive meals are available in the garden or cafeteria. Metro: Termini.

Not far from Stazione Termini, the Y has many advantages—if you don't mind its midnight curfew and married-couples-only stipulation. The setting is attractive and it's a good price. Single men are also accepted,

NORTH OF TERMINI

The neighborhood on either side of the Stazione Termini has improved greatly in recent years and some streets are now quite attractive. The best-looking area is north and west of the station (ahead and to the right as you exit). Most budget hotels in this area occupy a floor or more of a building, and while the entryways are often drab, upstairs they can be charming—or at least clean and livable. If none of the hotels below are available, ask for the booklet *Roma con Poca Spesa (Budget Rome)* at one of the tourist offices listed above.

DOUBLES FOR LESS THAN 65,000 LIRE ($42.75)

☉ Hotel Bolognese. V. Palestro 15 (1st, 2nd, and 3rd floors), 00185 Roma. ☎ **06/49-00-45.** 21 rms, 3 suites. 40,000L ($26.30) single without bath, single with bath 50,000L ($32.90); double without bath, 65,000L ($42.75), double with bath 80,000L ($52.65); triple without bath 100,000L ($65.80), triples and suites with bath 130,000L ($85.50). No credit cards. Metro: Termini, Repubblica. (From Termini, walk along V. Marsala, which becomes V. Volturno; after 3 blocks, turn right on V. Montebello; the hotel is 4 blocks ahead past the corner of V. Palestro.) Bus: 3, 14, 27, 36, 36/, 38, 38/, 105, 170.

When owner Giorgio Calderara isn't carefully watching his hotel and ensuring his guests' happiness, you'll find him painting in a closet-size studio—in fact, all the canvases you see in the halls and rooms are his. The hotel has a lot of funny charm, and three rooms have balconies with a neighborhood perspective of wash on the line and such daily sights. It's very clean and cheerful.

Hotel Galli. V. Milazzo 20 (2nd floor) (100 yards from the station), 00185 Roma. ☎ **06/44-56-859.** 13 rms, 4 with bath. 45,000L ($29.50) single without bath; 58,000L ($38.15) double without bath, 70,000L ($46) double with bath; 90,000,000L ($59.20) triple without bath, 110,000L ($72.35) triple with bath. Breakfast 8,500L ($5.60) extra. No credit cards. Metro: Termini. (From Termini, turn right on V. Marsala, then left onto V. Milazzo.) Bus: 3, 14, 27, 36, 36/, 38, 38/, 105, 170.

They speak only enough English here to check you in, but the Galli is inexpensive in any language. The place has a familiar air, thanks to the owners' curios. Renovations within the last year have yielded new bathrooms and much-improved rooms. This is near the university area and convenient to all transport.

Hotel Marini. V. Palestro 35 (3rd floor), 00185 Roma. ☎ **06/44-40-058.** 10 rms, none with bath. 30,000L ($19.75) single, 60,000L ($39.50) double; 80,000L ($52.65) triple; 25,000L ($16.45) per person in shared rms. No credit cards. Metro: Termini. From Termini, head up V. Marghera to V. Palestro and turn left; the hotel is on the left after V. San Martino della Battaglia. Bus: 3, 14, 27, 36, 36/, 38, 38/, 105, 170.

The Marini's rooms are as Spartan as those at the Katty across the hall, but they're a bit brighter—meaning that the place feels less like a dormitory—and owner Antonia Marini is gracious and friendly. Likewise, the prices here are nearly identical to Katty's, and Antonia never puts more than three guests in a room. The building has no elevator.

Pensione Katty. V. Palestro 35 (3rd floor), 00185 Roma. ☎ **06/44-41-216.** 10 rms, 2 with bath. 65,000L ($42.75) double without bath; 85,000L ($55.90) double or triple with bath; 25,000L ($16.45) per person in shared rms. Refundable 2,000L ($1.25) key deposit required. No credit cards. To get here, see the directions for Hotel Marini, above.

Luigi and Maria Idda offer accommodations at bargain-basement rates—indeed, some of the lowest in Rome. This is a one-of-a-kind place, the last of a dying breed of pensione that rents by the bed rather than by the room. There are never more than three beds per room. Four blocks from the station, this hotel (no elevator) is just far enough away to be out of sight and earshot of the cacophony and seediness that blights the area. Reductions for students are sometimes made. It does not have the sparkling clean look that many of the others have, but it's okay in a pinch.

If the Katty is full, they'll send you to the nearby Pensione Lucy, V. Magenta 13 (☎ 06/44-51-740), with similar prices.

Pensione Papà Germano. V. Calatafimi 14A, 00185 Roma. ☎ **06/48-69-19.** 13 rms, 2 with bath. 35,000L ($23) single without bath; 60,000L ($39.50) double without bath, 70,000L ($46) double with bath; 75,000L ($49.35) triple without bath, 78,000L ($51.30) triple with bath; 23,000L ($15.15) per person in shared rms. 10% reduction Nov–Mar. AE, MC, V. Metro: Termini, Repubblica. Bus: 3, 14, 27, 36, 36/, 38, 38/, 105, 170. From Termini, walk along V. Marsala, which becomes V. Volturno; turn right onto V. Calatafimi, the hotel is ¹/₂ block ahead on your left.

Though he tops the list in just about every budget travel guide (they're framed like diplomas near his tiny reception desk), owner Gino insists that word of mouth keeps his pensione filled 365 days a year. In any case, this place truly is a budget standout, mostly because of Gino himself. Terminally happy, he loves his job, tirelessly offering help, advice, books, maps, and so on to even the one-day visitor. He keeps his 13 modern rooms spotless, despite the heavy traffic, and he's also one of the very few hoteliers left in Rome who rents by the bed, an important factor for solo travelers. He's just put hair dryers in all the rooms. Perhaps the one drawback is that because the place is so small, noise carries far—don't expect to sleep late. In the end, though, this pensione is worthy of all the accolades it gets. Gino also rents larger rooms by the bed. I recently saw a young Australian woman there who had just left her suitcase in the room and was off to see the sights, not knowing who might be in the room when she returned.

DOUBLES FOR LESS THAN 85,000 LIRE ($55.90)

Fawlty Towers. V. Magenta 39, 00185 Roma. ☎ **06/44-50-374.** 25 rms, 10 with shower. 65,000L ($42.75), single without bath; 75,000L ($49.35), double with shower, 90,000L ($59.20), double with bath. Triples or quads, 18,000L–25,000L ($11.85–$16.45) per person. No credit cards. Metro: Termini. Bus: 3, 14, 27, 36, 36/, 38, 38/, 105, 170. Turn right outside station into V. Marghera, then left into V. Magenta.

It's not in Cornwall, but it's as amusing as the John Cleese TV show it's named after. The offspring of the Enjoy Rome owners, this spot is fun and caters to a young (at heart, they say) crowd. There is a lounge with satellite TV, a rooftop terrace, and an international staff that keeps it all in good order. You can rent by the bed here, too, and they will store luggage.

Hotel Otello. V. Marghera 13 (4th floor), 00185 Roma. ☎ **06/49-03-83.** 6 rms, none with bath. 50,000L ($32.90) single; 70,000L ($46) double. No credit cards. Metro: Termini. Bus: 3, 14, 27, 36, 36/, 38, 38/, 105, 170. Just a few steps from Termini.

The Otello has exceptionally big, bright rooms for a location so close to the station. Its friendly proprietors understand only a bit of English but enough to make you feel at home.

Pensione Corallo. V. Palestro 44 (6th floor), 00185 Roma. ☎ **06/44-56-340.** 11 rms, 7 with bath. 60,000L ($39.45) single without bath, 70,000L ($46.05) single with bath; 73,000L ($48) double without bath, 87,000L ($57.25) double with bath; 101,000L ($66.45) triple without bath, 121,000L ($79.60) triple with bath. Breakfast 12,000L ($7.90). No credit cards. Metro: Termini. Bus: 3, 14, 27, 36, 36/, 38, 38/, 105, 170. From Termini, walk 4 blocks up V. Marghera, turn left onto V. Palestro, and the hotel is 3 blocks ahead.) Take the back elevator up to the fire-engine-red reception desk.

This is a classic family-run place, where the ever-professional and courteous Toni Cellestino or his wife is always on hand to make sure guests are properly cared for. This place has unusual charm, thanks to the proprietors and to the balcony with tables and flowers just off the sitting room, which has a bar for coffee and soda. Some of the rooms have balconies, and the views of Roman apartments with laundry on the line are fun.

A DOUBLE FOR LESS THAN 130,000 LIRE ($85.50)

✪ **Hotel Pensione Astoria Garden and Montagna.** V. Vittorio Bachelet 8, 00185 Roma. ☎ **06/44-69-908.** 32 rms, 20 with bath. TEL. 69,000L ($45.40) single without bath, 80,500L ($52.95) single with bath; 114,500L ($75.35) double without bath, 149,000L ($98) double with bath; 166,500L ($109.50) triple without bath, 218,000L ($143.40) triple with bath. Rates include continental breakfast. AE, CB, DC, MC, V. Bus: 16, 37, 136, 137. From Termini, walk up V. Marghera and go left on V. Varese for 3 blocks until it becomes V. Vittorio Bachelet.

Manager Signor Vannutelli runs this very pretty and dignified hotel for the Montagna family in good old-fashioned Roman style. Its spacious lobby leads on to a glass-enclosed veranda. Lots of well-polished wood and colorful floral bedspreads add an air of distinction. The rooms are modern, however, unlike the elegant old-fashioned lobby. Breakfast is served on the open veranda in the lovely back garden/courtyard during the warmer months.

WORTH A SPLURGE

✪ **Hotel Bel Soggiorno.** V. Torino 117, 00184 Roma, ☎ **06/48-81-701.** Fax 06/48-15-755. 17 rms. All with bath. MINIBAR TEL. 85,000L–112,000L ($55.90–$73.70) single; 115,000L–149,000L ($75.65–$98.00) double; 145,000L–195,000L ($95.40–$128.30) triple; 170,000L–220,000L ($111.85–$144.75) quadruple. Frommer readers receive a 10% discount. AE, MC, V. Metro: Repubblica. Bus: 57, 64, 65, 75.

Although the entrance is not very attractive and the closed tin-box elevator is not for claustrophobics—once inside, you'll love it. A rooftop terrace with lounge chairs and tables overlooks wonderful ancient Roman sites. Rooms are nicely decorated, high-ceilinged, and airy. The breakfast/dining room is attractive, with draperies and glass chandelier; it opens on a second terrace. The owner is *in gamba* (with-it). Half-pension also available.

Hotel Romae. V. Palestro 49, 00185 Roma. ☎ **06/44-63-554.** Fax 06/44-63-914; e-mail htlromae@mbox.vol.it. 20 rms, all with bath. TV TEL. 100,000L ($65.80) single; 140,000L ($92.10) double; 180,000L ($118.40) triple. Rates include continental breakfast; children under 6 free. Garage 30,000L ($20) per day. AE, MC, V. Metro: Termini. Bus: 27, 38, 64, 65, 613. From Termini, walk 4 blocks along V. Marghera, and turn left onto V. Palestro; the hotel is 3 blocks ahead on your left.

Though this hotel is just a bit above our budget, it represents one of Rome's best values. They're so progressive, they've even added an e-mail address. The friendly reception area contains a small espresso bar/lounge, and each sparkling-clean room has a bath, a direct-dial telephone, and even a hair dryer. All rooms are fresh and crisp, but those on the second floor are particularly recommendable. Owners Francesco and Lucy Boccaforno speak excellent English and have guaranteed these rates to Frommer's readers through 1997.

✪ Hotel Venezia. V. Varese 18, 00185 Roma. ☎ **06/44-57-101** or 06/44-63-687. Fax 06/ 49-57-687. 61 rms, all with bath. A/C MINIBAR TV TEL. 174,000L ($114.45) single; 242,000L ($150.20) double; 295,000L ($194.10) triple. Rates include buffet breakfast. AE, DC, MC, V. Metro: Termini. Bus: 27, 36, 38, 64, 65. From Termini, walk 3 blocks up V. Marghera to its intersection with V. Varese; the hotel is right there on the left.

Swiss expatriate Rosemarie Diletti and her daughter, Patrizia, have beautified this unique 18th-century building with their own personal touches. Antiques, rugs, and various historical pieces fill the ample-sized rooms. Several top-floor accommodations have sunny balconies, and all rooms have traditional Murano-glass chandeliers and hair dryers. The staff is both fluent in English and exceedingly helpful around the clock. And when the clock strikes breakfast, look forward to a huge buffet, which usually includes fruit from the owner's garden. The Venezia is close enough to the train station to be convenient and easily reached, but in a quiet neighborhood nonetheless. Tell them you are a Frommer reader when checking in for a further discount.

SOUTH OF TERMINI

In the area south of the station (to the left as you exit), the streets are wider, the traffic heavier, and the noise level higher than in the area north of Termini. There are scores of hotels here, but not all are good choices for budget-minded, safety-conscious travelers. This area is improving, however, and so I've included a few choices.

A DOUBLE FOR LESS THAN 65,000 LIRE ($42.75)

Hotel Giuggiù. V. d. Viminale 8 (2nd floor), 00184 Roma. ☎ **06/48-27-734.** 12 rms, 6 with bath. 62,500L ($41.12) single without bath; 65,000L ($42.80) double without bath, 95,000L ($62.50) double with bath. Continental breakfast 8,000L ($52.65). Rates include continental breakfast. No credit cards. Metro: Termini. Bus: 14, 27, 36, 64. From Termini, walk along left edge of the bus lot, turn left at Lgo. di Villa Peretti; hotel will be 2 blocks ahead on your left, across from the Hotel Columbia.

A neon sign sticks out over the slightly forbidding entrance, though once you're inside, friendly owner Mr. Chindamo will make you feel at home. This small pensione boasts 14-foot ceilings and medium-size rooms that show some wear. Still, the location is good, in a safe neighborhood a block from the Teatro dell'Opera. There is a midnight curfew.

DOUBLES FOR LESS THAN 85,000 LIRE ($55.90)

Hotel Kennedy. V. Filippo Turati 62,00185 Roma. ☎ **06/44-65-373.** Fax 06/44-64-17. 35 rms, all with bath. A/C TV TEL. 70,000L–99,000L ($46.05–$65.15) single; 85,000L–145,000L ($55.90–$95.40) double. Breakfast 10,000L. AE, MC, V. Metro: Termini. Bus: 3, 14, 26, 64, 65. Exit train station by Track 22, turn left, walk ¹/₂ block, and turn right onto V. Gioberti; V. Turati is the first left.

Younger travelers will find a home here and meet their counterparts. Breakfast even includes cornflakes, as well as a frothy cappuccino, and there's a small bar. The rooms are modern, colorful, and upbeat.

Pensione Cortorillo. V. Principe Amedeo 79a (5th floor), 00185 Roma. ☎ **06/44-66-934.** 7 rms. 50,000L ($32.90) single; 70,000L ($46.05) double; 107,000L ($70.40) triple. Discounts up to 30% during slow periods. Breakfast 10,000L ($6.60) extra. No credit cards. Metro: Termini. Bus: 14, 27, 36, 64, 170 to Termini. Exit the train station by Track 22, turn left, walk ¹/₂ block, turn right onto V. Gioberti (Bar Tavola Calda Etna is on the corner); after 2 blocks, turn left onto V. Principe Amedeo and, when you reach no. 79a, take stairs on the right side of the courtyard.

The warm and gracious Signora Iolanda Cortorillo has been running one of the least expensive hotels in the city for over 25 years. The rooms are spacious and clean, especially considering the price. All overlook the interior courtyard, which makes them feel peaceful despite the noisy neighborhood. All in all, this is an exceptional value. Another thing that hasn't changed in all these years: Signora Cortorillo still speaks hardly a word of English, though her daughter is almost always there to help. Also note that they prefer not to take reservations in summer.

Pensione di Rienzo. V. Principe Amedeo 79a (2nd floor), 00185 Roma. ☎ **06/44-67-131.** Fax 06/44-69-142. 20 rms, 6 with shower only. 40,500L–55,000L ($26.65–$36.20) single without shower, 50,000L–64,000L ($32.90–$42.10) single with shower; 50,000L–70,000L ($32.90–$46.05); double without shower, 70,000L–85,000L ($46.05–$55.90) double with shower; 100,000L ($65.80) triple without shower, 120,000L ($78.95) triple with shower. Discounts up to 30% during slow periods. No credit cards. See directions for Pensione Cortorillo above, in the same building.

Owner Balduino di Rienzo, with his wife and three daughters, hosts budget-minded travelers in what is certainly one of Rome's best rock-bottom-priced hotels. Indeed, when you inquire about his prices he's proud to say, "Little, very little." A shy, pleasant man, he speaks enough English to check you in and out, with his daughter often at hand for the big questions. His rooms are generally spacious and clean, with modern baths, and some have balconies over the courtyard.

DOUBLES FOR LESS THAN 100,000 LIRE ($65.80)

Hotel Contilia. V. Principe Amedeo 79, 00185 Roma. ☎ **06/44-66-942.** Fax 06/44-66-904. 40 rms, 35 with shower. TV TEL. 80,000L ($52.65) single with shower; 90,000L ($59.20) double without bath; 120,000L ($78.95) double with shower. Breakfast 15,000L ($9.90). No credit cards. Bus: 3, 14, 27, 65, 170. See directions for Pensione Cortorillo above, in the same building.

Each room has a TV and phone, which is the first plus. The second is the owner, who speaks English and is helpful. The place was recently redone entirely. They own other similar pensiones in the same building. Most rooms and halls are cheerful and some lobby areas have murals of Rome.

Hotel Morgana. V. Turati 33, 00185 Roma. ☎ **06/44-67-230.** Fax 06/44-69-142. 70 rms, 66 with bath. TV TEL. 109,000L ($71.70) single with bath; 95,500L ($62.80) double without bath, 177,000L ($116.45) double with bath; 217,000L ($142.75) triple with bath; 271,500L ($178.60) quad with bath. Rates include continental breakfast. AE, DC, MC, V. Metro: Termini. Bus: 3, 14, 27, 65, 170. Exit train station by Track 22, turn left, walk ¹/₂ block, and turn right onto V. Gioberti; V. Turati is the first left; the Morgana is on the left in the 1st block.

It's hard to say enough good things about brothers Mauro, Nicolà, and Roberto di Rienzo and their comfortable budget hotel. With spotless white walls, recessed lighting, and new baths, their ultramodern hotel is one of the best values in the city; some rooms even have brass beds. The brothers boast that they "won't rent a room they wouldn't sleep in themselves." Always extraordinarily professional, all three speak excellent English and one is always around to dispense information about the city. The all-you-can-eat breakfast is served in a spacious bright room. If you reserve ahead, their airport van will pick you up and deliver you to the hotel for free.

Pensione Elide. V. Firenze 50 (1st floor), 00184 Roma. ☎ **06/48-83-977** or 47-41-367. 14 rms, 4 with shower only, 5 with bath. TEL. 76,000L ($50) single without bath, 89,000L ($58.55) single with shower only; 101,000L ($66.45) double with shower only, 113,500L ($74.70) double with bath. Breakfast 10,000L ($6.60) extra. V. Metro: Repubblica. Bus: 57, 65, 75, 170, and 910 (also to Pz. d. Repubblica). From the Metro stop at Pz. d. Repubblica, turn into V. Nazionale; V. Firenze is the 2nd street on the right.

This remarkable place is operated by one of Rome's friendliest families—appropriately named the Romas. The floors and the new modern baths always sparkle, and the prices are surprisingly low. They even change the wallpaper and paint the ceilings every year, which is quite an undertaking for such a small and inexpensive place. Ask for Room 16 or 18; both have unusual carved and painted wooden ceilings. Everyone gets to enjoy the similarly decorated breakfast room. There's a 1:30am curfew.

WORTH A SPLURGE

There are times you may be looking above all else for a spacious room and modern facilities (especially heat, air-conditioning, or sound-proofing) and where the showers are large enough to turn around in. The Bettoja chain, whose hotels are listed below, is famous for good service. Owner Angelo Bettoja and his Georgia-born wife Jo have continued his family's fine hotel tradition. La Signora Jo has published several cookbooks, such as *Italian Cooking in the Grand Tradition* and *Southern Italian Cooking* (recipes from the noble families). The hotels are not inexpensive, but ask your travel agent what kind of package might be available. The Massimo d'Azeglio hotel has an excellent restaurant that looks as if Garibaldi just stopped by—it's smart, bright, and filled with Garibaldiana. Guests at all the Bettoja hotels can dine here on a meal plan; all hotels have bars and large public areas. They're all located near Termini, in what has become a good neighborhood again (and plans are under way to improve it still further). The hotels are in descending order of price.

Mediterraneo, V. Cavour 15, 00184 Rome (☎ **06/48-84-051;** fax 06/47-44-105) is the star of the group, and is truly luxurious. Doubles range from 325,000L to 435,000L ($213.80 to $286.20).

Massimo d'Azeglio, V. Cavour 18, 00184 Rome (☎/fax **06/48-27-386**) is old, solid, and traditional. Some of the old-fashioned bathrooms are enormous. Doubles cost from 285,000L to 385,000L ($187.50 to $240.15).

Genova, V. Cavour 33, 00184 Rome (☎ **06/47-69-51;** fax 06/48-27-580) is quite a beauty and a favorite with Italians. Doubles cost from 245,000L to 360,000L ($161.20 to $00,000).

San Giorgio, V. Amendola 61, 00184 Rome (☎ **06/48-27-341;** fax 06/48-83-191) is next to the Massimo d'Azeglio, joined by a passage to the Massimo's restaurant. Doubles are 340,000L ($223.70).

Nord Nuova Roma, V. Amendola 3, 00184 Rome (☎ **06/48-85-441;** fax 06/48-17-163), on a side street that needs improvement, is a bargain in that it charges three-star prices for a four-star (in amenities) hotel. Doubles range from 205,000L–275,000L ($134.50 to $180.92).

AROUND ANCIENT ROME
DOUBLES FOR LESS THAN 85,000 LIRE ($55.90)

Albergo Perugia. V. d. Colosseo 7, 00184 Roma. ☎ **06/67-97-200.** Fax 06/67-84-635. 11 rms, 5 with shower only, 1 with bath. TEL. 55,000L ($36.20) single without bath, 72,000L ($47.35) single with bath; 76,000L ($50.00) double without bath, 69,000L ($45.40) double with shower; 149,000L ($98) triple with shower. AE, MC, V. Metro: Colosseo. Bus: 11, 27, 81, 85, 87, 186. Turn right down the massive V. d. Fori Imperiali and right again onto the first small street, V. d. Tempio della Pace; make a 3rd right at the intersection with V. d. Colosseo; the hotel is just ahead on your left.

Location is everything for the fourth-floor Perugia. A short walk from the Colosseum in a quiet neighborhood, this budget place has spruced up considerably in the last year. All baths have windows, and rooms are airy. One top-floor room has a small terrace. There's no elevator and stairs are steep. The owners are nice and their prices are relatively low. Breakfast isn't available.

Hotel o Apollo. V. d. Serpenti 109, 00184 Roma. ☎ **06/48-85-889.** 11 rms, none with bath. 70,000L ($46) double, 80,000L (52.65) triple. Rates include breakfast. No credit cards.

Metro: Cavour. Bus: 64 from Termini to the Palazzo d. Esposizioni on V. Nazionale; then walk 2 blocks and turn left onto V. d. Serpenti; the hotel is 2 blocks down on your left.

The rooms are plain and aged, but clean, with some antique closets and desks; the area is respectable, across from the Bank of Italy in a characteristic Roman neighborhood. You'll especially enjoy leaving your hotel and seeing the Colosseum in the distance down the street. The management tries to be very helpful.

NEAR CAMPO DE' FIORI & THE GHETTO

The area surrounding Campo de' Fiori, Rome's best open-air vegetable and flower market, is atmospheric, historic, and well located. From here you can walk to the Pantheon, the Trevi Fountain, and even the Spanish Steps, as well as the Forum. Transport is nearby, as a main bus terminal is located at Largo Argentina.

A DOUBLE FOR LESS THAN 85,000 LIRE ($55.90)

Albergo della Lunetta. Pz. d. Paradiso 68, 00186 Roma. ☎ **06/68-61-080.** Fax 06/68-92-028. 37 rms, 18 with bath. TEL. 65,000L ($42.75) single without bath, 90.000L ($59.85) single with bath; 85,000L ($55.90) double without bath, 120,000L ($78.95) double with bath; 114,500L ($75.30) triple without bath, 155,000L ($102) triple with bath. No credit cards. Bus: 26, 44, 46, 66, 61, 64, 65, 70 to Lgo. di Torre Argentina. Continue in the direction the bus was going along Cor. V. Emanuele; after 3 blocks, turn left on V. Paradiso and the hotel is ¹/₂ block ahead.

A favorite of American students studying in Rome, the labyrinthine Lunetta is simply decorated, with fading floral wallpaper, and has small baths. Its best virtue is its location, near Campo de' Fiori and Piazza Navona. The Forum is within walking distance. Its student population means it's not always tranquil at night.

DOUBLES FOR LESS THAN 100,000 LIRE ($65.80)

Hotel Campo de' Fiori. V. d. Biscione 6, 00186 Roma. ☎ **06/68-80-68-65** or 68-74-886. Fax 06/68-76-003. 27 rms, 10 with bath. TEL. 100,000L ($65.80) double without bath, 115,000L ($75.65) double with shower only, 170,000L ($111.85) double with bath. Rates include continental breakfast. MC, V. Bus: 64 from Termini. Follow directions for Albergo della Lunetta above; Pz. Paradiso opens onto V. d. Biscione, which leads to Pz. del Biscione.

They've mastered the art of the unique at this hotel in the heart of the historic district. Each small room with bath is decorated in a different regional style, carried out in meticulous detail, with generous use of mirrors and occasionally gaudy details. The "rustic" room, for instance, feels uncannily like a Tuscan farmhouse. The rooms without bath have average furnishings, mini-chandeliers hanging over the beds, and floral wallpaper. Half a dozen rooms enjoy a view of the vibrant Campo de' Fiori, the open-air flower market, and all guests have access to the pocket-size roof garden with its view of St. Peter's. There's no elevator connecting the hotel's six stories, but the management has painted colorful floral scenes on the walls of the staircase. The management is gradually adding baths—and an individual style—to the rest of the rooms.

Hotel Piccolo. V. d. Chiavari 32, 00186 Roma. ☎ **06/68-80-25-60** or 68-92-330. 16 rms, 6 with shower only, 3 with bath. 74,500L ($49) single with shower only; 95,000L ($62.50) double without bath, 100,000L ($65.80) double with shower only, 109,000L ($71.70) double with bath. AE. Bus: 64 44, 46, 55, 60, 61, 62, 64, 65, 170 from Termini to Lgo. di Torre Argentina. Continue in the direction the bus was going along Corso V. Emanuele for 2 blocks and turn left onto V. d. Chiavari; the hotel is 3 blocks ahead on your right.

You enter this smartly modern hotel through a contemporary cast-iron gate that contrasts well with the small old-fashioned stone street in front. A marble-lined entrance leads up to the first-floor reception and to rooms that won't disappoint you. Some of the recently redecorated guest quarters are spacious, with spotless baths. Some baths are just stall shower/toilet units in a corner of the room. Floral bedspreads and ultramodern furniture give rooms a fresh look. The Piccolo is a shining star in one of Rome's top locations. Single rooms are much larger than in most hotels.

A DOUBLE FOR LESS THAN 130,000 LIRE ($85.50)

Albergo Sole. V. d. Biscione 76, 00186 Roma. ☎ **06/68-79-446.** Fax 06/68-93-787. 60 rms, 35 with bath. 75,000L ($49.35) single without bath, 100,000L ($65.80) single with bath; 105,000L ($69.10) double without bath, 130,000L–160,000L ($85.50–105.25) double with bath. No credit cards. Bus: 26, 44, 46, 55, 60, 61, 62, 64, 65, 170 from Termini. Follow directions for Albergo della Lunetta above; continue from Pz. Paradiso onto V. d. Biscione.

A longtime favorite of Rome cognoscenti, the Sole offers simple (if aging) rooms in what the owner says is the oldest hotel in Rome, dating from 1462! Of course, the area is even more ancient—the hotel is built above the remains of a Roman theater from 55 B.C. The attractive courtyard garden in back is the highlight of the place, and the antiques in the public area give the place a comfortable air.

Hotel Smeraldo. Vc. d. Chiodaroli 11, 00186 Roma. ☎ **06/68-75-929.** Fax 06/68-80-54-95. 35 rms, 30 with bath. A/C TV TEL. 95,000L ($62.50) single without bath or with shower only, 130,000L ($85.50) single with bath; 105,000L ($69) double without bath or with shower only, 126,000L ($78.75) double with bath; 140,000L ($92.10) triple without bath or with shower only, 166,500L ($109.55) triple with bath. Breakfast 15,000L ($9.85) extra. AE, MC, V. Bus: 26, 42, 44, 62, 64, 65, 170 from Termini to Lgo. di Torre Argentina. Turn south/left onto V. de Torre Argentina; take the 2nd right, V. d. S. Anna, and tiny Vc. d. Chiodaroli is just ahead on your left.

Success has not spoiled this hotel, but its location and (formerly) very low prices have drawn a steady stream of clients, so reserve ahead. It's a good value in a charming area of the historic center, just off Campo de' Fiori. This highly recommended choice features a modern reception area and granite floors. An elevator takes you to all four floors, where the rooms are simple but clean and redecoration is always going on. The baths are some of the shiniest I've seen in accommodations of this category. You're just a few steps from lots of good and inexpensive trattorias.

NEAR PIAZZA NAVONA & THE PANTHEON
DOUBLES FOR LESS THAN 100,000 LIRE ($65.80)

Albergo Abruzzi. Pz. d. Rotonda 69, 00186 Roma. ☎ **06/67-92-021.** 25 rms, none with bath. 60,000L–75,000L ($39.50–$49.35) single; 100,000L ($65.80) double. No credit cards. Bus 64, 44, 46, 55, 60, 61, 62, 64, 65, 170 from Termini (to Lgo. di Torre Argentina, then walk 4 blocks north along V. d. Cestari or V. T. Argentina; the hotel is in front of the Pantheon).

Unbelievably, this basic budget (though ever-increasing) hotel directly overlooks the Pantheon and the adjacent piazza. It's somewhat noisy, but you can't get more central than this. The hotel's four floors are filled with medium-size rooms, most with queen-size beds. The more expensive rooms have the piazza view, while the cheaper (and quieter) ones are in the rear.

Pensione Mimosa. V. Santa Chiara 61 (2nd floor), 00186 Roma. ☎ **06/68-80-17-53.** Fax 06/68-33-557. 12 rms, 5 with bath. 65,000L ($42.75) single without bath; 87,000L ($57.20) double without bath; 110,500L ($72.70) double with bath. Rates include continental breakfast. No credit cards. Bus: 64, 44, 46, 55, 60, 61, 62, 64, 65, 170 from Termini to Lgo. di Torre Argentina. Walk 2 blocks north on V. T. Argentina and turn left on V. S. Chiara; the hotel is on the left.

An aging place (the building is from the 1500s), the Mimosa is a wild mix of kitsch. It features an excellent location in the heart of Rome, and the owners are friendly and let guests use the living room and fridge, but abuse of privileges is not tolerated. The low rates and location make the place a favorite of American students spending a semester in Rome. Guests get copies of the front-door key so they can return at any hour. The owner's two sons speak English.

Pensione Primavera. Pz. San Pantaleo 3, 00186 Roma. ☎ **06/68-80-31-09.** 8 rms, 6 with shower. MINIBAR TV TEL. 100,000L ($65.80) double without bath, 130,000L ($85.50) double with bath. MC, V. Bus: 64 along Corso Vittorio to the intersection with the piazza, opposite the church of Sant'Andrea della Valle.

The location is right and the rooms are big enough for a Texan. Marble and tile are the decor and it's usually rather quiet, because rooms face an inner court. Clients may be French vacationers or Italian businessmen, as well as a stray Yank or two.

DOUBLES FOR LESS THAN 130,000 LIRE ($85.50)

Pensione Navona. V. d. Sediari 8, 00186 Roma. ☎ **06/68-64-203.** Fax 68-80-38-02. 22 rms, 10 with bath. 71,000L ($46.70) single with or without bath; 109,000L ($71.70) double with or without bath. Rates include continental breakfast. No credit cards. Bus: 64 from Termini or bus 44, 46, 55, 60, 61, 65, 70, 170 to Lgo. di Torre Argentina. Walk along Cor. V. Emanuele to Pz. S. Andrea della Valle and take a right onto Cor. Rinascimento; after 1 block turn right onto V. d. Sediari—the hotel is on your right.

Wrapped around an open courtyard, this pretty, first floor pensione is full of character. Recent renovations have made many of the rooms comfortable if not stylish. The hotel occupies a grand palace built in 1360 and holds architectural surprises at every turn. The baths are fully tiled, and the high ceilings lend an open, airy feel. The owners, the Australian-born Natale family, speak fluent English.

AROUND THE SPANISH STEPS & PIAZZA DEL POPOLO

The stylish streets around the Spanish Steps boast all the labels, from Armani to Valentino. This handful of hotels is in one of the wealthiest neighborhoods in town—and the prices certainly reflect that, but there are still a few hotels and trattorie that lure the frugal.

A DOUBLE FOR LESS THAN 85,000 LIRE ($55.90)

Pensione Fiorella. V. Babuino 196, 00187 Roma. ☎ **06/36-10-597.** 8 rms, none with bath. 55,000L ($36.20) single; 82,500L ($54.25) double. Rates include continental breakfast. No credit cards. Metro: Spagna. Bus: 119.

The orange-and-green tile floors of this delightfully simple little pensione are kept sparkling by Antonio and Caterina Albano. This is the sort of place that'll make you want to extend your stay just so you can be here. It's one of the nicest places in this price range in any part of town. Note that reservations are accepted only a day before checking in, and the doors are locked shut nightly at 1am. It can, however, get a bit noisy at night from the scooter traffic.

A DOUBLE FOR LESS THAN 100,000 LIRE ($65.80)

Pensione Suisse. V. Gregoriana 56, 00187 Roma ☎ **06/67-83-649.** Fax 06/67-91-256. 15 rms, 10 with bath. TEL. 80,000L ($52.65) single without bath, 100,000L ($65.80) single with bath; 90,000L–100,000L ($59.20–$65.80) double without bath, 85,000L–140,000L ($55.90–$92.10) double with bath. Rates include breakfast. MC, V for partial bill; some must be paid in cash. On a street that leads down from the top of the Spanish Steps.

This is a perennial favorite, so reserve ahead. The rooms are simple and attractive, some with antiques, some modern. It's on the 4th and 5th floors of an elevator building. The location is excellent, and if you are fortunate enough to land a top-floor room, you'll have a view of Roma. The terrace is lovely, and all is well maintained.

DOUBLES FOR LESS THAN 130,000 LIRE ($85.50)

Brotsky. V. d. Corso 509, 00186 Roma (3rd floor). ☎ **06/36-12-339.** 13 rms, all with bath. 72,000L ($45) single; 108,000L ($67.50) double; 149,000L ($93.15) triple. No credit cards.

Metro: Flaminio. Walk through the arch to Pz. del Popolo; V. d. Corso is the middle street fanning out at the opposite end of the square, and the hotel is 2 blocks up it. Bus: 119.

On one of Rome's main shopping streets and where the ancient Romans once held chariot races, the Brotsky can be quiet, as many rooms overlook an inner courtyard. Our recommendation is conditional this year, as the whole place is undergoing much-needed renovation, and prices will be renovated upward too. It's worth a call, however. The terrace upstairs affords fantastic views of town. Some rooms on the Corso have tiny balconies. Breakfast is not served (at last report) , but there are tables here for a picnic or relaxation. The place is often full, so try to reserve ahead.

Hotel Pensione Parlamento. V. delle Convertite 5, 00187 Roma. ☎/fax **06/69-92-10-00.** 23 rms, 18 with bath. TV TEL. 75,000L ($49.35) single without bath, 110,000L ($72.35) single with bath; 106,000L ($69.75) double with shower, 134,000L ($88.15) double with bath. Rates include breakfast. No credit cards. Metro: Spagna (exit onto Pz. di Spagna and walk down V. Condotti; turn left onto V. del Corso, then left onto V. delle Convertite). Bus: 119, 913 to Lgo. San Carlo al Corso.

Now much improved, this family-run budget hotel gets good marks for its lovely flowered rooftop terrace. Ask for a room overlooking it. Rooms 106 and 107 have balconies, and No. 92 is on the quieter courtyard. Number 108 has a nice view of San Silvestro's delicate bell tower. In addition to beds and bureaus, the guest rooms have safes, those with baths have hair dryers, and some rooms have balconies. The lounge is well equipped with magazines and newspapers. The pensione's biggest drawback is the 75-step climb up an elevatorless building. If you're hardy, however, you'll be rewarded with accommodations that are a particularly good value. Reserve in advance.

Pensione Erdarelli. V. Due Macelli 28, 00187 Roma. ☎ **06/67-91-265** or 67-84-010. Fax 06/679-07-05. 37 rms, 21 with bath. 79,000L ($52) single without bath, 98,000L ($64.50) single with bath; 126,000L ($82.90) double without bath, 137,500L ($90.45) double with bath; 158,500L ($104.25) triple without bath, 186,000L ($122.35) triple with bath. Rates include continental breakfast. Air-conditioning 20,000L ($13.15) per night extra. AE, MC, V. Bus: 119. Metro: Spagna. Turn left into Pz. di Spagna and head out the far end onto V. Due Macelli; the hotel's 2 blocks ahead on your right).

Operated by the Erdarelli family since 1935, this simple and somewhat dated pensione is perfectly situated—within walking distance of the Spanish Steps. Most rooms, on five floors, offer high ceilings and good views. The top-floor accommodations are smaller but come with private balconies. The view from Room 11 is particularly memorable, as it overlooks the baroque Church of Santa Andrea delle Frate.

Pensione Lidia Venier. V. Sistina 42, 00187 Roma. ☎ **06/67-91-744.** Fax 06/88-41-480, Attn: Lidia Venier. 30 rms, 10 with shower only, 10 with bath. 110,000L ($72.35) single without bath, 130,000L ($85.50) single with shower only, 109,000L ($71.70) single with bath; 130,000L ($85.50) double without bath, 150,000L ($98.70) double with shower only, 180,000L ($118.42) double with bath. Rates include continental breakfast. AE, DC, V. Bus: 119. Metro: Barberini. Walk up V. Sistina; the pensione is on the left just after V. Crispi.

You ascend an elegant winding marble staircase to the reception area, and from here you're dispatched to one of the clean, modern rooms—some even complete with frescoed ceilings. Breakfast is served in a room with painted ceilings and picnic tables with hard wooden benches. Despite the fine touches, the prices remain moderate. There's a 2am curfew.

WORTH A SPLURGE

Hotel Marcus. V. d. Clementino 94, 00186 Roma. ☎ **06/68-30-03-20.** Fax 06/68-32-567. 15 rms, all with bath. TV TEL. 110,000L ($72.35) single; 135,000L ($88.80) double; 160,000L ($105.25) triple. Breakfast included. AE, V. Bus: 119. Metro: Spagna. Turn right out of Pz. di Spagna onto V. Condotti; follow this street for 7 blocks—its name changes to V. Fontanella Borghese, then V. d. Clementino.

On a large street a few blocks from the Spanish Steps, the Marcus offers large, serviceable rooms. Salvatore, the owner, has managed this pleasant pensione for over 25 years. And even though the hotel's in the center of the hustle and bustle, the double windows he installed in all the rooms help cut out the noise. Some rooms have marble fireplaces (not working). Safes come with the room. That Italian habit of omitting a shower curtain is followed here, unfortunately. Air-conditioning is extra, 20,000L ($13.15) per day.

NEAR THE VATICAN

Hotels near the Vatican, across the river from the historic city center, are a good bet for quiet and a local charm often missing from lodgings in more bustling tourist areas.

DOUBLES FOR LESS THAN 85,000 LIRE ($55.90)

Florida. V. Cola di Rienzo 243, 00192 Roma. ☎ **06/32-41-872.** Fax 06/32-41-857. 9 rms, 7 with shower only. TEL. 60,000L–110,000L ($39.50–$72.35) single with shower; 80,000L–135,000L ($52.60–$88.80) double with shower. Breakfast 11,000L ($7.25). AE, MC, V. The metro stop Ottaviano or bus 81 along the V. d. Corso, which crosses the Tiber near Pz. d. Popolo.

Occupying two floors of a building on a busy thoroughfare, this is quite a find. Newly redecorated throughout, this pretty pensione boasts cheerful prints and sparkling baths with lots of goodies. The management aims to please and they usually do.

Forti's Guest House. V. Fornovo 7, 00192 Roma. ☎ **06/32-12-256.** Fax 06/32-12-222. 30 rms, 17 with bath. TEL. 70,000L ($46.05) single without bath, 80,000L ($52.65) single with shower; 99,000L ($65) double without bath, 125,000L ($82.25) double with shower. AE, MC, V. Metro: Lepanto.

Forti's Italian and American owners have made their spot a cherished one for American clients. They even prepare good meals family-style. Rooms are cheery and comfortable. The location is good, away from the center, yet a few blocks' walk to Piazza del Popolo. The very obliging proprietors make this a good stop for those uncomfortable with Rome's big-city brashness.

DOUBLES FOR LESS THAN 130,000 LIRE ($85.50)

Hotel Adriatic. V. Vitelleschi 25, 00193 Roma. ☎ **06/68-80-63-86.** Fax 06/68-93-552. 32 rms, 29 with shower only. TEL. 74,500L ($49) single without shower, 97,500L ($64.15) single with shower; 110,000L ($72.35) double without shower, 145,000L ($95.40) double with shower; 138,000L ($90.80) triple without shower, 182,000L ($119.70) triple with shower. AE, MC, V. Bus: 23, 34, 64 from Termini to Bgo. Sant' Angelo (near St. Peter's pass under the nearby portal; then continue 1 block along V. Porta Castello until you reach V. Vitelleschi, where you turn left.

Lanfranco Mencucci, his wife, and his son, Marino, take great pride in their hotel and see to it that their modern rooms and baths are kept clean and attractive. They also have a small terrace with fruit trees and a rose trellis.

Hotel Bramante. Vc. d. Palline 24, 00193 Roma. ☎ **06/65-40-426.** Fax 06/68-79-881. 20 rms, 17 with bath. 90,000L ($59) single with bath; 103,500L ($68) double without bath, 137,500L ($90.45) double with bath; 137,500L ($90.45) triple without bath; 218,500L ($143.75) quad with bath. Breakfast 12,000L ($7.90) extra. AE, DC, MC, V. Bus: 64 from Termini to the last stop, then walk behind the bus onto V. dei Corrodori; take a left on Vc. d. Palline and the hotel is on your left.

In a charming old building begun in the 14th century, this place is clean, comfortable, and about as close to the Vatican as you can get, even if the linoleum floors and tan wallpaper don't really match the old-Roman flavor of the neighborhood. The top floors have nice beamed ceilings. The ivy-covered breakfast terrace has a view of the Colonnato del Vaticano, the special escape wall connecting the Vatican with the Castel Sant'Angelo. Owner Giuliana Belli was actually born in this building.

Pensione Marvi. V. Pietro d. Valle 13, 00193 Roma. ☎/fax **06/68-80-26-21.** 7 rms, all with bath. TEL. 95,000L ($ 62.50) single; 135,,000L ($88.80) double; 175,000L ($102) triple. Rates include continental breakfast. No credit cards. Bus: 64, 492 from Termini to the 1st stop across the river, Castel Sant' Angelo (walk around the left of the castle to V. Alberico; V. Pietro della Valle runs between this corner and V. Crescenzio) or 34, 39, 990, which run along V. Crescenzio.

If you are looking for a wonderfully authentic Roman home stay, you'd do well to try this pensione on a quiet residential street. There's no sign outside, just a gold doorbell high up to the left of the building's big green door. No English is spoken here, but guests are welcomed with a warm smile in simple yet comfortable surroundings. It's one of Rome's best values. The breakfast is served in a pretty dining room.

WORTH A SPLURGE

Ara Pacis Hotel. V. Vittoria Colonna 11 (3rd floor), 00193 Roma. ☎ **06/32-04-446** or 32-04-447. Fax 06/32-11-325. 39 rms, 33 with bath. MINIBAR TV TEL. Summer 160,000L ($105.25) single; 250,000L ($164.50) double; 260,000L ($171.05) triple, 280,000L ($184.20) quadruple. Low season 130,000L ($85.50) single; 160,000L ($105.25) double; 250,000L ($164.50) triple; 250,000L ($164.50) quadruple. Breakfast included. AE, MC, V. Bus: 492, 910 from Termini (to the first stop across the river at Pz. Cavour, then walk back along V. Colonna toward the river), or 70, 913, 926, which run along V. Colonna.

This boutique hotel is a delightfully European-Roman kind of place. Think rich, dark, stained wood, and country prints. Wooden doors, shutters, and antique furniture fill the rooms and halls. And in almost all the large rooms you'll find inlaid wooden ceilings. This hotel has been open since the turn of the century, and the management has clearly worked hard to preserve its original character. Even the entrance is impressive and will make the weariest budget traveler feel like a returning emperor. Yet convenience is not lacking: Modern baths resembling ship-cabin facilities were recently installed in almost all rooms. Ask for one of the seven rooms with their own terraces. The breakfast room is charming, and the buffet is ample, and nicely presented. Look for the large bust of Minerva on the wall to the right as you step off the elevator.

4 Dining

Roman cooking is often overlooked by the food critics. It's simple cooking, wholesome yet inventive. Of course the city has restaurants serving food from most of Italy's regions, but to ignore the food of Rome and Lazio is to miss a very tasty opportunity. The vegetable dishes are memorable, especially *carcioffi all Giudea* (Jerusalem artichokes flattened and crisp-fried), *insalata verde* (simple salads of fresh local greens), or *fiori di zucchini* (crisp-fried zucchini flowers with a jolt of anchovy paste inside). For pasta, try *penne all'arrabbiata* (short, stubby pasta in a fiery tomato sauce with Pecorino cheese), *spaghetti alla carbonara* (in a rich sauce of diced pancetta bacon, whipped eggs, and grated Parmesan), *spaghetti all'amatriciana* (in a tomato sauce with pancetta, onion, and a touch of hot pepper *peperoncino*), and the famous *fettuccine Alfredo* (in a cream and Parmesan cheese sauce). Good Roman antipasti include *bruschetta* (grilled garlic-and-oil bread, with or without tomatoes) and *prosciutto e melone* (wedges of sweet cantaloupe draped with thinly sliced, salty prosciutto—a surprisingly tasty combination of sweet and salty); for soup, try *minestrone* (vegetable) or *stracciatella* (an egg-drop soup with Parmesan).

In spring, lamb is popular—especially *abbacchio al forno con patate* (roast baby lamb with potatoes), and in the fall, *porchetta* (pork roasted with wild fennel, rosemary, and garlic) is found everywhere, especially in the towns around Rome at fall festivals.

Ask your waiter for recommendations of typical local dishes, but keep in mind that some Roman delicacies are not to all tastes, especially when it comes to the second (meat) course. The more adventurous could try the very Roman *trippa* (cow intestines), *lumache* (snails), *coda alla vaccinara* (stewed oxtail), *fegato* (liver), *animelle alla griglia* (grilled calves' pancreas), or *pajata* (calf intestines with clotted mother's milk inside cooked in white wine, garlic, and hot peppers). Others may choose to stick to *involtini* (a veal roll with prosciutto, cheese, celery, and tomato sauce) or *saltimbocca* (literally "jump-in-the-mouth," a dish of veal, sage, and prosciutto cooked in white wine). For dessert (*dolce*), or *tiramisù* (a trifle of sweetened cheese custard and espresso-soaked ladyfingers dusted with cocoa) or a rich, chocolatey *tartufo* (ice-cream ball) should satisfy the sweetest tooth, or have fruit, as Italians prefer after a meal. Fruit salad, or *macedonia,* is rarely elaborate; *fragole* (strawberries) in season with sugar and lemon (the Italian way, with a drop of liqueur sometimes) are delicious.

In the listings below, prices are given for pasta and main courses only. Don't forget to add in charges for bread and cover, service, and other dishes, as well as wine and coffee, when calculating what you can actually expect to pay.

The restaurants below are a medley of those easy on tourists (self-service or English menus) and some typically Roman places for those comfortable in Italian-only spots. Traditional restaurants expect diners to order an antipasto and then a pasta *and* a second course. This presents a problem for American diners, who prefer one main dish. Many restaurants are content if you order only a pasta and salad with wine, especially at lunch, but you may see annoyance if you dine at a smart restaurant and want only a pasta. As the meal is an important event, tables are expected to be occupied for a long time.

AROUND ANCIENT ROME
MEALS FOR LESS THAN 12,000 LIRE ($7.90)
Snack Bar Venezia. V. Cavour 207. ☎ **06/48-45-40.** Pasta 6,000L–8,000L ($4.60–$5.25); meat courses 7,000L–11,000L ($4.60–$7.25). No credit cards. Mon–Sat 6am–11:30pm. Metro: Cavour (then walk down V. Cavour). Bus: 4, 9, 16, 27. CAFE/SNACKS.

Clean and modern, the Venezia serves up some tasty pasta from the back bar. Italians today also like *lo snack* at midday, as work hours in midtown rarely permit the long Mediterranean lunch. You can eat at a counter or at one of the few tables here. Tables cost slightly more.

MEALS FOR LESS THAN 19,000 LIRE ($12.50)
Trattoria Da Pasqualino. V. dei Santi Quattro 66 (a block from the Colosseum). ☎ **06/ 70-04-576.** Pasta courses 7,000L–11,000L ($4.60–$7.25); meat courses 9,000L–18,000L ($5.90–$11.85). AE, V. Tues–Sun, noon–3pm and 8pm–midnight. Metro: Colosseo (go around the left of the Colosseum and just before the piazza funnels into V. Labicana, turn right; then take the 2nd left). ROMAN.

The 100-year-old Da Pasqualino boasts a remarkable location. Yet despite its proximity to Rome's foremost arena, the prices here are remarkably reasonable and the ambience is very typical, with mostly Italians dining. Penne all'arrabbiata, with a fiery sauce, and saltimbocca are usually on the menu. Some Roman prints and a few flowers serve as decor.

Rome Dining

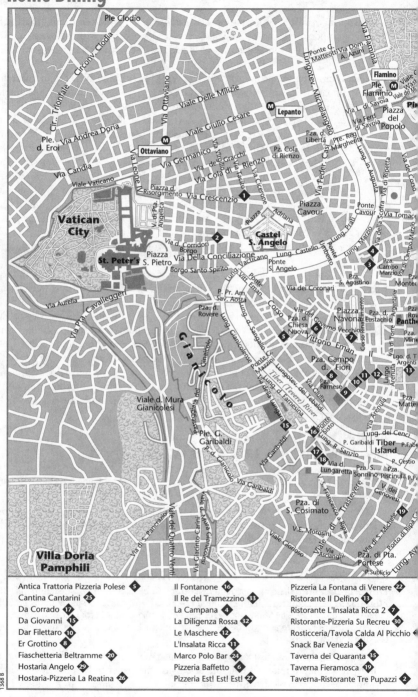

Antica Trattoria Pizzeria Polese
Cantina Cantarini
Da Corrado
Da Giovanni
Dar Filettaro
Er Grottino
Fiaschetteria Beltramme
Hostaria Angelo
Hostaria-Pizzeria La Reatina

Il Fontanone
Il Re del Tramezzino
La Campana
La Diligenza Rossa
Le Maschere
L'Insalata Ricca
Marco Polo Bar
Pizzeria Baffetto
Pizzeria Est! Est! Est!

Pizzeria La Fontana di Venere
Ristorante Il Delfino
Ristorante L'Insalata Ricca 2
Ristorante-Pizzeria Su Recreu
Rosticceria/Tavola Calda Al Picchio
Snack Bar Venezia
Taverna dei Quaranta
Taverna Fieramosca
Taverna-Ristorante Tre Pupazzi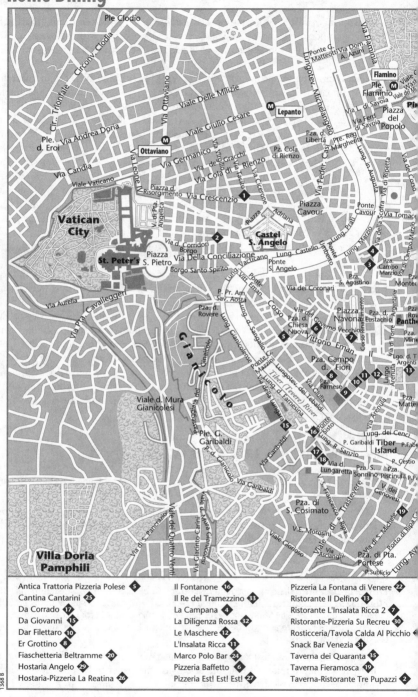

1368 B

Trattoria da Alfredo 28
Trattoria Da Luigi 5
Trattoria Da Pasqualino 34
Trattoria Da Sergio 9
Trattoria della Stampa 23
Trattoria Dino 1
Trattoria Mario 18
Vecchia Roma 14
Volpetti 3

WORTH A SPLURGE

Ristorante-Pizzeria Su Recreu. V. del Buon Consiglio 17. ☎ **06/67-94-918.** Pizza 11,000L–13,000L ($7.25–$8.55); pasta 10,000L–13,000L ($6.60–$8.55); meat courses 17,000L–20,000L ($11.20–$13.15). AE, DC, MC, V. Tues–Sun, noon–3pm and 7:30pm–1:30am. Bus: 16, 27. Metro: Cavour (then walk down V. Cavour and take the 3rd left onto V. d. Cardello; the pocket-size V. d. Buon Consiglio is immediately on your right). SARDINIAN.

The sign over the door, LOCALE TIPICO SARDO, means "typical Sardinian place." That tells it all about this popular restaurant with white stucco walls, closely packed tables, and Sardinian artifacts hanging from walls and ceiling. The food is outstanding, and the atmosphere lively. Popular dishes include risotto alla pescatore (a rice-and-seafood combination), pane frattau (very thin bread stuffed with tomato, cheese, and egg), linguine con bottarga (with fish roe), homemade ravioli stuffed with spinach and ricotta cheese, and fresh fish.

NEAR CAMPO DE' FIORI & THE GHETTO
MEALS FOR LESS THAN 12,000 LIRE ($7.90)

Dar Filettaro. Lgo. dei Librari 88. ☎ **06/69-64-018.** Cod fillet 5,000L ($3.15) each. No credit cards. Mon–Sat 11am–10pm. Bus: 44, 56, 60, 170 along V. Arenula to Pz. Cairoli (walk straight along V. Giubbonari to the largo). SALT COD.

A true local favorite near Campo de' Fiori, Dar Filettaro offers only one item: baccalà, deep-fried salt-cod fillets—a true Roman specialty. Just off Via de' Giubbonari, this charming old place is set in a piazza crowned by the lovely, always-closed church of Santa Barbara. The tiny spot is worth a look at least—old Roman places like this are disappearing fast.

MEALS FOR LESS THAN 19,000 LIRE ($12.50)

L'Insalata Ricca. Lgo. dei Chiavari 85. ☎ **06/68-80-36-56.** Pasta 7,000L–9,000L ($4.60–$5.65); meat courses 8,000L–13,000L ($5.25–$8.55); salads 6,000L–10,000L ($3.94–$6.55). AE. Thurs–Tues 12–3pm and 7–11:30pm. Bus: 64 from the train station to 1 stop after Lgo. di Torre Argentina; bus: 65, 70, 90, 170. SALADS/INTERNATIONAL.

Translated literally, this excellent budget trattoria's name means "the rich salad." The selection of second courses may be relatively limited, but you can always find at least ten salads, eight delicious first courses, and a handful of daily specials. You can save money by ordering just a pasta dish and salad, enough to satisfy the heartiest appetite for little more than 16,000L ($10.50). Indeed, the management boasts that their trattoria was created to provide a place where diners could order just one course or a salad. The menu is multilingual, and there's always a line for the excellent food served at this one-room restaurant.

Er Grottino. V. dei Baullari 25–27. ☎ **06/68-80-36.** Pizza 7,000L–9,000L ($4.60–$5.90); pasta 8,000L–9,000L ($5.25–$5.90); main courses 8,000L ($5.25) and up. No credit cards. Bus: 46, 64, 65 to the Palazzo Cancelleria, 2 stops beyond Lgo. Argentina, heading toward the Vatican. Walk through the Pz. d. Cancelleria into Campo dei Fiori. V. d. Baullari runs between the Campo and Piazza Farnese. ROMAN.

Near Campo de' Fiori, this little grotto has a good menu of Roman dishes. Penne all'amatriciana has a bacon touch to its tomato base; bistecca (grilled with olive oil with lemon and parsley) or spezzatino di pollo (chicken cutlets, browned and cooked, then simmered in sauce) could be a second course. Mushrooms (*funghi*) and sausages (*salsicce*) adorn the pizza. You might have a fresh green salad of puntarella, a flavorful green somewhat like arugula.

✪ **Le Maschere.** V. d. Monte della Farina 29. ☎ **06/68-79-494.** Pizza 9,500L–14,000L ($5.90–$7.90). Pasta 9,000L–13,000L ($5.90–$8.55). Meat courses 12,000L–22,000L

($7.90–$14.50). AE, MC, V. Tues–Sun 7pm–midnight. Bus: 46, 62, 64 to Lgo. di Torre Argentina. V. Barbieri links the largo with V. Monte d. Farina. CALABRIAN.

This restaurant looks like a Southern Italian festival, with folk art and wine jugs. For feasting, there's spicy salami, good vegetable sauces, such as broccoli or cauliflower, Pecorino and Cacciacavallo cheese, and an often merry atmosphere. It's a good place to try Calabrese dishes, which are virtually unknown in America. Try some Ciro, a fine Calabrian wine with an ancient history. It was drunk during the original Olympic Games, we hear. (Calabria once had important Greek settlements.) On weekends there is music, and a few tables are set outside in summer. A very good value.

Trattoria Da Sergio. Vc. delle Grotte 27. ☎ **06/65-46-669.** Pizza 7,000L–15,000L ($4.60–9.85); pasta 7,000L–14,000L ($4.60–$9.20); meat courses 9,000L–12,500L ($5.90–$8.20). No credit cards. Mon–Sat 12:30–3:30pm and 7:30pm–midnight. Bus: 46, 61, 64 to Lgo. Argentina. Go along the largo and down V. Arenula toward the river to Pz. Cairoli; turn right here onto V. dei Giubbonari and take the 5th left). PASTA/PIZZA.

For good home-cooking at moderate prices you'll enjoy Da Sergio, where every day a new pasta specialty emerges. The pizza and gnocchi are good, too. The simple interior includes hams hanging from the ceiling above a crowd of loyal locals.

NEAR PIAZZA NAVONA & THE PANTHEON
MEALS FOR LESS THAN 12,000 LIRE ($7.90)

Pizzeria Baffetto. V. d. Governo Vecchio 114 (at the corner with V. Sora). ☎ **06/68-61-617.** 6,000L–11,000L ($3.95–$7.25). No credit cards. Mon–Sat 6pm–1am. Closed 15 days in Aug. PIZZA.

If you want to see young Rome, stop here for a pizza. It's small, crowded, and the thin pizza and the calzone are delicious. In good weather the crowd spills out to a few streetside tables. If you're in a hurry or especially hungry, arrive to grab a table as soon as it opens, or prepare to stand in line. Pizzas blossom with myriad sauces, which shocks those who consider the Neapolitan original Margherita (tomato-mozzarella-basil) the only true pizza. But you might enjoy those with seasonal vegetables such as artichokes and even fiori di zucchini.

Volpetti. V. della Scrofa 31–32 (near the corner of V. d. Portoghese). ☎ **06/68-61-940.** Pasta courses 6,000L–7,000L ($3.95–$4.60); meat courses 6,000L–11,000L ($3.95–$7.25). No credit cards. Mon–Sat 7am–8:30pm. HOT FOODS DELI.

A stylish food store/rosticceria, Volpetti is best suited for a take-out meal, whether for a picnic or for a night when you want to crash early at the hotel. Fresh and varied food for a picnic is always available. You can have a snack at a counter. A vast array of country breads, salads, roasted chicken and pork, vegetables, lunch meats such as a fabulous mortadella with bits of pistachio nut cooked into the loaf, and cheeses from all over Italy—if you don't know the pleasure of Parmigiano Reggiano eaten with sweet pears, here's your chance.

MEALS FOR LESS THAN 19,000 LIRE ($12.50)

Ristorante Il Delfino. Cor. Vittorio Emanuele 67 (just past Lgo. Argentina). ☎ **06/68-64-053.** Pizza 8,000L–12,000L ($5.25–$7.90); pasta 6,000L–8,000L ($3.95–$5.25); meat courses 9,000L–12,000L ($5.90–$7.90); menu turistico 18,000L ($11.85). AE, DC, MC, V. Tues–Sun 8am–9pm. Bus: 46, 56, 60, 64 to Lgo. Argentina. PIZZA/FAST FOOD.

Rome's biggest self-service restaurant offers an exceptional selection of dishes, including pizza that's available all day (unlike in most pizzerias, where the ovens are fired up only for the dinner hour). It's a bright, cheery place, with polished green stone floors and piped-in pop music and less of a fast-food atmosphere than many of the newer self-services in town. It even offers an English/American-style breakfast of two eggs, bacon, toast, juice, and coffee for about 9,500L ($5.95). It's a good choice for those who want just a snack that they can point to, instead of a full restaurant meal.

Ristorante L'Insalata Ricca 2 and 3. Pz. Pasquino 72 (near Pz. Navona, at one end of V. Santa Maria dell' Anima). ☎ **06/68-80-78-81.** Reservations advised weekends. Pasta 6,000L–9,000L ($3.95–$5.90); meat courses 8,500L–15,000L ($5.60–$$9.85); salads 4,500L–8,000L ($2.95–$5.25). No credit cards. Tues–Sun 12:30–3pm and 7:15–11:30pm. Bus: 46, 62, 64 to Cor. Rinascimento. SALAD/INTERNATIONAL.

Once you eat here you'll discover why the owners opened a second and now a third place (V. d. Gazometro 62, ☎ **06/57-51-76**; Metro: Piramide) under the same name. The atmosphere is rustic (rare in Rome) with wood-beamed ceilings, copper pots and wine jugs dangling from the roof, and a hand-painted sign out front. Beside the salad, try the gnocchi alla gorgonzola or the whole-wheat pasta with tomatoes and fresh basil.

MEALS FOR LESS THAN 25,000 LIRE ($16.45)

Antica Trattoria Pizzeria Polese. Pz. Sforza Cesarini 40 (just off Cor. Vittorio Emanuele between Pz. di Chiesa Nuova and the Tiber). ☎ **06/68-61-709.** Reservations advised weekends. Pizza 7,000L–11,000L ($4.60–$7.25); pasta 8,000L–12,000L ($5.90–$7.90); meat courses 9,000–20,000L ($5.90–$12.50). AE, MC, V. Wed–Mon 12:15–3pm and 7–11pm. Bus: 46, 62, 64. ROMAN.

The large menu here changes regularly—the last time I visited they were featuring no fewer than 17 second-course selections. You can order such specialties as fettuccine alla Sforza (with a sauce of cream and mushrooms), fracostine di vitello alla fornata (veal in a white-wine sauce), or abbacchio al forno (roast lamb). The Polese remains busy year-round, with tables out on the piazza in summer and rustic old chandeliers over the tables inside. This is an excellent selection for the medium-price category, where you can expect to spend 22,000L to 33,000L ($13.75 to $20.65) for a plentiful, hearty, and delicious meal, including wine.

Trattoria Da Luigi. Pz. Sforza Cesarini 24. ☎ **06/68-65-946** or 06/68-80-54-63. Reservations advised weekends. Pasta 8,500L–10,500L ($5.60 –$6.90); meat courses 11,500L–17,000L ($7.60–$11.20). AE, V. Tues–Sun noon–3pm and 7pm–midnight. Bus: 46, 62, 64. ROMAN.

On the same square as the Polese (above), this well-established place is similarly priced and just about as popular. Also like its nearby competitor, it has outdoor tables in summer and red lampshades over the tables. It's darker and more romantic, though, and is tastefully decorated with the old theater posters and mirrors advertising various English liquors. Perhaps it's the latter that makes tourists and expatriates prefer this place, while more Italians can be found at the Polese. They don't seem to mind if you order only a pasta dish here; I especially recommend the penne alla vodka in a rich tomato-cream sauce.

WORTH A SPLURGE

Vecchia Roma. Pz. Campitelli 18 ☎ **06/68-64-604.** Reservations recommended. Meat courses 22,000L–25,000L ($14.50–$16.45). AE. Thurs–Tues 1–3:30pm and 8–11:30pm. Closed Aug 10–25. Bus: 95, 160 to V. Teatro di Marcello to the Teatro di Marcello. It's down the street from the Campidoglio. ROMAN.

This is a big splurge for a budget book but if you're feeling flush with lire, or want to celebrate, this is the spot. Many movie stars think so, too. Year after year Vecchia Roma lives up to its tradition of fine food served in a sophisticated setting, whether outside on the umbrella-shaded terrace on an ancient piazza with a baroque fountain, or in one of the little interior rooms, decorated in soft tones with frescoes that add to the restaurant's charm. In winter, their gnocchi or polenta specialties complement porcini mushrooms and meat. A summer salad menu is featured, with arugula and puntarelle, a Roman green, and pleases many who want to dine well without outgrowing their Hermès belts. Lamb with artichokes or grilled scampi with lemon are also excellent.

♦ La Campana. Vc. d. Campana 18, 00136 Rome. ☎ **06/68-67-820.** Pasta 8,000L–12,000L ($5.25–$7.90). Meat courses 9,000L–25,000L ($5.90–$16.44). AE, MC, V. Tues–Sun 12:30–3pm and 7:30–11pm. Closed Aug. ROMAN.

As sturdy as the Pantheon, La Campana continues on its own way year after year, as it has since it opened in the 15th century. A plain trattoria with prints of Rome on the walls, and a lovely antipasto and fresh fish array, it is the first place I think of when I want to introduce a new person to Rome. You will need an appetite here, though. Their first courses are tempting—carcioffi all Giudea (artichokes flattened and crisply deep fried) and fiori di zucchini are excellent here. They can be combined as a second course as well. Their soup vignarola is a delicious blend of fava beans, artichokes, and other vegetables—but it is a full meal for most diners. Veal dishes are also a specialty. They now have an English menu, but the restaurant never has a touristy ambience, even when tourists are there. At midday, Italian businesspeople dine here, and at night it's popular with journalists. There are few who aren't seduced by its simple traditional grace.

NEAR THE SPANISH STEPS & PIAZZA DEL POPOLO
MEALS FOR LESS THAN 19,000 LIRE ($12.50)

Rosticceria/Tavola Calda Al Picchio. V. d. Lavatore 39–40. ☎ **06/67-89-926.** Reservations not accepted. Menu turistico (with 6 options, all including wine) 18,000L–23,000L ($11.85–$15.15); pasta courses 4,500L–9,000L ($2.95–$5.95); meat courses 7,000L–12,000L ($4.60–$7.85). AE, MC. Tues–Sun noon–3:30pm and 6–10:30pm. Closed 2 weeks in Feb. Bus: 62, 85, 90 to Pz. di Trevi. Facing the fountain, take the road on your right. ROSTICCERIA/TAVOLA CALDA.

This restaurant around the corner from the Trevi Fountain is a bit more pleasant than its neighbors and can cater to your every whim, with six menu turistici. Its choices are advertised in six languages. The ambience is a bit unusual for Rome: tables under a long barrel vault more reminiscent of a Czechoslovakian beer hall than an Italian eatery. If you prefer, they also offer a self-service rosticceria with counter seating to the front of the restaurant. In summer, the air-conditioning is a lure.

Trattoria della Stampa. V. dei Maroniti 32 (a small street off Lgo. d. Tritone). ☎ **06/ 67-89-919.** Reservations recommended. Pasta 8,000L–10,000L ($5.25–$6.60); meat courses 8,000L–12,000L ($6.60–$7.90). No credit cards. Mon–Sat 12:30–3pm and 6:30 or 7–10 or 10:30pm. Metro: Barberini (then a short walk down V. Tritone to Lgo. Tritone, where V. Maroniti begins). Bus: 52, 53, 56 to Lgo. Tritone. ROMAN.

This is a typical place in the heart of Rome and a favorite of journalists (the name means "trattoria of the press"). The plain woodwork is decorated with onions, red peppers, and wine—all ingredients favored by owner Antonio Bucci, who presides over the kitchen. Linguine con vongole veraci (with clam sauce) is good, and if porchetta (roast baby pork) is on the menu (usually in fall), try it. Ask for the day's specials if your Italian can handle the answers.

Pizzeria La Fontana di Venere. Vc. dei Modelli 56 (just off Pz. di Trevi). ☎ **06/67-82-753.** Pizza and pasta 7,000L–10,000L ($4.60 –$6.60). MC. Mon–Sat 11:30am–2:30pm and 6pm–midnight. Bus: 56, 60, 85, 90. PIZZA/PASTA.

A traditional Roman kitchen, this small restaurant near the Trevi Fountain serves decent pizzas, along with very good lasagna, spaghetti, and the occasional risotto. Wine bottles and Roman memorabilia are the decor, and you won't be the only tourist, given the famous fountain.

MEALS FOR LESS THAN 25,000 LIRE ($16.45)

Fiaschetteria Beltramme. V. d. Croce 39. No phone. Reservations not accepted. Pasta courses 9,500L–13,000L ($5.95–8.15); meat courses 13,000L–24,000L ($8.15–$15). No credit cards. Mon–Sat noon–3pm and 7:45–10:30pm. Closed Aug. Metro: Pz. di Spagna. Bus: 81, 90 to Lgo. San Carlo al Cor. At the north end of Pz. d. Spagna. Reservations not accepted. ROMAN.

The sketches on the wall were done by artists who frequent this tiny one-room institution that's been serving Roman specialties for more than a century. In fact, it's so well known among the city's artists and intellectuals that there's neither a menu nor a sign (other than FIASCHETTERIA) out front identifying it as a place to eat. Owner Luciano Guerra points out that this is a "locale known to the national art authorities," though he doesn't say whether it's the food or the milieu—or the combination of the two—that attracts them. Meat dishes such as rabbit in wine sauce, fettuccine with a veal sauce, or other hearty fare are frequently on the menu.

NEAR TERMINI & VIA VENETO

Around the train station is certainly the best Roman neighborhood for budget dining, though neither the surroundings nor the food is particularly pleasant. Here are a few acceptable places.

MEALS FOR LESS THAN 12,000 LIRE ($7.90)

Marco Polo Bar. Lgo. Santa Susanna 108. ☎ **06/48-24-869.** Complete meal 14,000L–15,000L ($$9.20–$9.85). No credit cards. Mon–Sat noon–3pm and 6:30–10pm, Sun noon–3pm. Metro: Repubblica (then a 5-minute walk). Bus: 57, 65, 75. FAST FOOD.

A popular cafe/bar, the Marco Polo offers the lowest full-meal price around in a small self-service area beyond the cappuccino makers and pastry counters. The dining area is attractive for a self-service place, with dark-wood walls and private tables. Since you fetch the food yourself, you don't pay a service or cover charge. It's a good bet if you're tired of figuring out the intricacies of Italian ordering.

Pizzeria Est! Est! Est! V. Genova 32 (off V. Nazionale). ☎ **06/48-81-107.** 9,500L–11,500L ($5.95–$7.20), cover and service included. No credit cards. Tues–Sun 6–11:30pm. Closed 3 weeks in Aug. Metro: Repubblica. Bus: 57, 65, 75. PIZZA.

Open since the turn of the century, this is the oldest pizzeria in Rome. Is it the best? Only you can judge. The decor hasn't changed much in more than 90 years—diners still eat at wooden tables astride antique woodwork. Though it's not Rome's cheapest pizzeria, it's certainly the most storied and may, just may, be the best.

MEALS FOR LESS THAN 19,000 LIRE ($12.50)

Hostaria-Pizzeria La Reatina. V. San Martino d. Battaglia 17 (near intersection with V. Villafranca). ☎ **06/49-03-14.** Pizza 5,500L–9,500L ($3.60–$6.25); pasta courses 4,500L–7,000L ($2.50–$4.60); meat courses 7,000L–12,000L ($4.60–$7.90). No credit cards. Sun–Fri noon–3pm and 6:30–11:30pm. Closed 15 days in Aug. Metro: Termini. ROMAN.

There's no menu turistico here, but with the moderate à la carte prices you'll have no trouble filling up for less than you'd pay for a fixed-price dinner someplace else. A three-course meal here (without wine) shouldn't run more than 18,000L ($11.25). Don't expect much in the way of atmosphere—just hearty, inexpensive food and a satisfied local clientele. They serve pizza, but only in the evening. The service is not always the most attentive.

La Diligenza Rossa. V. Merulana 271 (near S. Maria Maggiore). ☎ **06/48-81-216.** Pasta courses 6,000L–8,000L ($3.90–$5.25); meat courses 10,500L–14,500L ($6.05–$9.21). MC, V. Tues–Sun 11am–11pm. Metro: Termini. Bus: 27, 36, 65, 105. ROMAN.

Outdoor Markets & Picnics

Most outdoor food markets are open from early morning (6 or 7am) to early afternoon (2pm or so). **Piazza Vittorio Emanuele,** near the train station, is Rome's principal open-air daily food market, where herbs and spices join the usual products. (Plans to renovate this area include a closing date for this popular market, which is apparently to be a gentrification casualty. However, it's still quite open now but watch your wallet.) There's another market in the area, on **Via Montebello,** covering a two-block stretch between Via Volturno and Via Goito. There's also a modest-size outdoor covered market, the **Mercato Rionale,** at V. Flaminia 60 (outside the gate of Piazza del Popolo and several blocks down Via Flaminia on the right), and the **Trionfale Market** (not to be confused with the nearby Trionfale flower market), north of the Vatican on Via Andrea Doria between Largo Trionfale and Piazzale d. Eroi. Plus there plenty of little shops in between where you can pick up meat, cheese, bread, fruit, and drinks. The market in **Campo de' Fiori** is especially characteristic and photogenic.

There are numerous storefronts behind the street vendors. Cold cuts are sold at the *salumeria*. To pick up cheese or yogurt, you'll have to find a *latteria*. Vegetables can usually be found at tiny hole-in-the-wall stands called *fruttivendoli*. For bread to put all that between, visit a *panetteria*. Wander into *pasticceria* to find dessert. And for a bottle of wine to wash it down, search out a *vini olii*. For a long time the closest thing Italy had to a grocery store was an *alimentari*. A few supermarket chains have opened up, such as G&S and the basements of Standa department stores, but they tend to be located in outlying residential neighborhoods, and are not nearly as fun (or fresh) as going to the little specialty shops or open-air markets.

The Villa Borghese, Rome's only downtown park, is the place to take your fixings for an imperial picnic. Some people like to pack their picnic into the Forum with them and dine with the ghosts of the emperors the Palatine Hill. Romans themselves sometimes head out onto the Via Appia Antica and spread a blanket by the roadside on Sunday afternoons.

Loosely translated as "The Red Coach Grill," La Diligenza Rossa offers an arm-long list of Italian specialties served in a comfortably downscale dining room. Seating is on bentwood chairs at plastic-covered wooden tables. Recommendable first courses include tortellini consommé and minestrone with rice and pasta. Next, try the chicken breast sautéed cacciatore or marsala-style or, better yet, order *saltimbocca* or osso buco. A variety of pizzas is also served, prepared in the restaurant's signature copper-top pizza oven. Air-conditioning and an English menu make this spot user-friendly in summer.

MEALS FOR LESS THAN 25,000 LIRE ($16.45)

Cantina Cantarini. Pz. Sallustio 12 (near intersection of V. XX Settembre and V. Piave, near Porta Pia) ☎ **06/48-55-28.** Pasta 8,000L–9,000L ($5.25–$5.95), meat and fish courses 9,000L–14,000L ($5.95–$9.20). No credit cards. Mon–Sat 12:30–3pm and 7:30–11pm. MARCHE REGION.

This is a bit away from the station, on a pleasant piazza with some of Rome's antiquities on view. Fish is featured from Thursday to Saturday nights, and reservations are suggested. Ask for specialties from the Marche (Mar–*kay*) region, too. It's not a tourist restaurant, and so refresh your Italian terms for the best dining.

Hostaria Angelo. V. Principe Amedeo 104 (between V. Gioberti and V. Cattaneo). ☎ **06/ 73-12-263.** Pasta courses 5,000L–8,000L ($3.15–$5.25); meat courses 8,500L–12,000L ($5.60– $7.50); menu turistico 23,000L ($14.40). AE, DC, MC, V. Thurs–Tues 11am–3pm and 6–11pm. Metro: Termini. Bus: 27, 36, 65, 613. ROMAN.

Angelo's atmosphere is pleasant enough, featuring checkered floors and wood paneling. Its clientele includes a good mix of Italians and tourists. Stick to the ample menu turistico, which includes a choice from among 10 second courses—otherwise you're likely to spend 24,000L ($15) or more.

Il Re del Tramezzino. V. Mecenate 18A. Off V. Merulana, behind station to the left. No phone. Pasta courses, 6,000L–8,000L ($3.95–$5.25). Second course 8,000L–12,000L ($5.25–$7.90). Lunch only. No credit cards. Mon–Sat 12:30–3pm. SANDWICHES.

At nonlunch hours it's open as a cafe-bar, but at lunch you will see the menu in the front window, and you can sit at the bar or outside tables. They have traditional dishes such as eggplant parmigiana, gnocchi, and (my favorite) penne all'amatriciana (short pasta tubes with a tomato sauce flavored with onion, garlic, hot peppers, and a touch of Italian bacon). Sandwiches and salads are also options. Get there early. English is "intermittent."

Trattoria da Alfredo. V. Principe Amedeo 126a. ☎ **06/44-64-298.** Pasta 5,000L–7,000L ($3.30–$4.60); meat courses 9,500L–12,000L ($5.95–$7.50); menu turistico 21,000L ($13.15) without wine, 24,000L ($15) with wine. AE, MC, V. Mon–Sat noon–3pm and 6:30–11pm. Metro: Termini. Bus: 27, 36, 65, 613. ROMAN.

A few steps beyond the Trattoria Angelo, with atmosphere and service a few notches below, Alfredo's is nonetheless a good choice. The menu turistico includes an unusually wide selection of main courses, including veal, chicken, liver, and fish. If you're waiting for a train and want a quick, easy-to-order meal, *eccola!*

IN TRASTEVERE

Trastevere is still an authentic Roman neighborhood, although the expatriate community can make it look less so. It's the artists' and writers' quarter of Rome, when they can afford it. "Everyone has his own favorite trattoria in Trastevere," so the Romans tell you. My favorite budget value is Mario's, but there are many others in this area just waiting to be discovered.

MEALS FOR LESS THAN 19,000 LIRE ($12.50)

Da Corrado. V. d. Pelliccia 39. ☎ **06/58-06-004.** Pasta 7,500L–9,500L ($4.95–$6.25); meat courses 9,500L–19,000L ($6.25–12.50). No credit cards. Tues–Sun noon–3pm and 7pm– midnight. ROMAN.

In the neighborhood known for its colorful restaurants, Da Corrado is kaleidoscopic. A quintessential working-class eatery, it serves excellent pastas, meats, and salads along with generous amounts of wine and spirits. The repartee is sometimes heated, often humorous, and always part of the fun. There's no menu, and the bill is usually toted up on your paper tablecloth. It's probably better saved for times when you feel confident in Italian, or are a good mime.

✪ **Trattoria Mario.** V. del Moro 53. ☎ **06/58-03-809.** Pasta courses 5,000L–8,000L ($3.30– $5.25); meat courses 8,000L–15,000L ($5.25–$9.90); menu turistico 17,000L ($11.20). AE, MC, V. Mon–Sat noon–4pm and 7pm–midnight. Closed 2nd half of Aug. Bus: 170, 181, 280 to Pz. Sonnino. Walk along V. Lungaretta to Pz. Santa Apollonia. V. Moro is to your right. TUSCAN.

The savior of struggling artists and other low-budget folk, this charming place, decorated with the work of neighborhood artists, has been operated by three generations of Mario's family and offers one of the better food values in Rome. The 17,000L ($11.20) menu turistico is the cheapest outside the train station area and full of variety, making it a big favorite of visitors. Finocchina is a tasty salami flavored with fennel seeds; Tuscan soups, such as ribollita, thick with vegetables, and a beef stracotta casserole are often on the menu. The à la carte menu is equally attractive to the budget and quite varied. Fresh game is reasonably priced here, too. You can walk back to Campo dei Fiori by continuing along Via dei Moro to Piazza Trilussa and cross the bridge. The Campo is ahead and to the left, about a 15-minute walk.

MEALS FOR LESS THAN 25,000 LIRE ($16.45)

✪ Il Fontanone. Pz. Trilussa 46. ☎ 06/58-17-312. Reservations advised. Pasta courses 7,000L–9,000L ($4.60–$5.90); meat courses 12,000L–16,000L ($7.90–$10.50). AE, MC, V. Wed–Mon 12:15–2:45pm and 7–11:15pm. Bus: 23, 65, 280 to Ponte Sisto.

A favorite just across the Ponte Sisto from the Campo dei Fiori area, where locals and tourists rub elbow happily, Il Fontanone is decorated country-style with dried herbs hanging from the ceiling and lots of hand-painted ceramics around the walls. The owner, Pino, makes sure that everything is country-fresh. The antipasto table is large and varied with vegetables from the garden. The pasta menu is extensive, but try the house special, fettuccine alla Fontanone, which combines fresh tuna with garlic, mushrooms, and tomatoes. Or have the Amatriciana sauce on a pasta—a classic tomato sauce with hot peppers and pancetta (Italian bacon). For *secondo*, try the abacchio al forno (roast lamb), osso buco, or chicken dishes. Tiramisù for dessert is essential.

Da Giovanni. V. d. Lungara 41 (near Ponte Sisto). No phone. Pasta courses 6,000L–8,000L ($3.95–$5.25). Main courses 6,000L–9,000L ($3.95–$5.90). No credit cards. Mon–Sat 12:30–3pm and 7:30–10pm. Closed Sun and Aug. Bus: 23, 65 to Ponte Sisto or 56, 60 to Pz. Sonnino. ROMAN.

This is one of the places that everyone wanted to keep out of the guidebooks. But now that tourists—if they can find it—come in occasionally, the atmosphere doesn't seem to have changed. It's a plain, worker's restaurant where you'll want to do as the locals do and order just a glass of red and some pasta. Nothing complex or yuppie. Dishes are mainly classics and very hearty. The waiter will rattle off to you in rapid Italian what's on for the evening, but you should be able to procure from him a written menu as well (not in English, though).

WORTH A SPLURGE

Taverna Fieramosca. Pz. de' Mercanti (across from Santa Cecilia in Trastevere). ☎ 06/58-90-289. Pizza 7,500L–17,000L ($4.70–$10.65); meat courses 9,000L–24,000L ($5.65–$15); vegetables 6,000L–8,000L ($3.75–$5). No credit cards. Mon–Sat 7pm–midnight. Closed 1 week in Aug. Bus 170 to the 1st stop across the river, Vle. Trastevere. Walk down V. d. Genovesi and turn right on V. Santa Cecilia to Pz. de' Mercanti. ITALIAN.

This delightful place bills itself as an authentic medieval taverna, and the decor tries to emphasize the theme—cannon hang from the ceiling, suits of armor stand at attention in the corner, and all eating is done at long wooden tables. They carry the theme to the extreme and don't serve any pasta, which came to Italy with Marco Polo toward the end of the Middle Ages. Indeed, the only modern intrusion is the eating utensils. This "medieval" mess hall enjoys a devout following of Romans and tourists alike. The menu here is a 24-by-36-inch souvenir poster, and during the evening guitar and accordion players add to the revelry. In summer, they place 200 seats on the piazza outside.

NEAR THE VATICAN
MEALS FOR LESS THAN 25,000 LIRE ($16.45)

Taverna-Ristorante Tre Pupazzi. V. Bgo. Pio 183 (at the corner of V. Tre Pupazzi). ☎ **06/68-68-371.** Pizza 8,500L–10,000L ($5.30–$6.25); pasta 8,500L–16,000L ($5.30–$10); meat courses 11,000L–21,000L ($6.90–$13.15); menu turistico 21,000L ($13.15). AE, MC, V. Mon–Sat noon–3:30pm and 7pm–midnight. Bus: 23 or 64 from Termini. ROMAN/ABRUZZESE.

This cozy and charming 17th-century-style taverna with a patio comes highly recommended from nearby hoteliers and many other Romans as well. Its 21,000L menu turistico is acceptable, considering the restaurant's delightful atmosphere and proximity to St. Peter's. The homemade agnolotti (meat-filled pasta) are good. It may be tourist-filled at lunchtime; at dinner or on Sunday afternoon locals may appear. Service can be slow, however.

Trattoria Dino. V. Tacito, 80. (off Castel Sant'Angelo). ☎ **06/36-10-305.** Pasta 8,000L ($5.25); meat courses 12,000L–15,000L ($7.90–$9.90). No credit cards. Mon–Sat lunch only 12:15–4pm. Metro: Lepanto. ROMAN.

Mamma is in the kitchen and creates good, hearty fare for this eight-table spot. It's decorated with dried herbs, braided garlic, and such. On a cold winter day you'll want the pasta e fagioli, a thick stewy pasta and bean classic. Each day a new menu is written and placed on the tables. No English is spoken. Carcioffi (artichokes) Roman-style, made with garlic and mint, marinated in oil; spaghetti with clam sauce; or saltimbocca alla Romana are light summer meals. An antipasto course and a pasta or main course will normally be acceptable, although Italians still have a second course of meat and fish, which most restaurants expect.

Taverna dei Quaranta. V. Claudia ☎ **06/70-00-550.** Pasta 8,000L–10,000L ($5.25–$6.60), meat courses 10,000L–16,000L ($6.60–$10.50). AE, MC, V. Mon–Sat noon–3pm and 8–11pm. Open Sun June–Sept, and open in Aug. Bus: 85, 87, 186. Metro: Colosseo. At the far side of the Colosseum, a half-moon turn from the Metro stop. ROMAN.

Tastefully decorated (Piranesi prints) in its three rooms (one above) and cool in its outside tree shade, this is an attractive and fun place to relax after visiting the beloved monster. Olives stuffed with meat, gnocchi with gorgonzola, a good Chianti (or beer on tap), and homemade desserts. Buon appetito.

Da Pommodoro. Pz. Sanniti (San Lorenzo area). ☎ **06/44-26-92.** Pasta 8,000L–14,000L ($5.25–$9.20). Meat dishes 9,000L–18,000L ($5.90–$11.85). Mon–Sat 12:30–3 and 7–11pm. Closed Aug. V. Bus: 11, 71, 415. ROMAN.

San Lorenzo, the student quarter where the university is located, has a wealth of trattorie, especially along Via Tiburtina. This one is just off that street, a small place run by Anna and Aldo. Bruschetta (country bread rubbed with garlic and oil and browned under the flame) is the prelude to game, brought from their village in the fall. Their own property is also the source for their olive oil, wine, salad, fruit, and vegetables.

What to See and Do in Rome

5

by Barbara Coeyman Hults

A word to the wise about sightseeing in Rome: Just about all the sights of significance, except the Vatican, the Colosseum, the Forum, and many churches, are closed Monday. During the rest of the week museums and attractions close by 2pm, and stop admitting visitors 30 to 60 minutes before that.

Check the English-language magazines *Metropolitan* and *Wanted in Rome* (at most newsstands) for special tours or other events. If your Italian is pretty good, buy the Rome daily paper, *Il Messaggero;* in the column at the back called *Appuntamenti,* tours of the lesser known places are advertised. Some charge 8,000L to 10,000L ($5.25 to $6.60), and others are *gratuita* (free). The same paper lists musical events, and many of the concerts held in churches are free—although a donation is gratefully received.

SUGGESTED ITINERARIES

If You Have 1 Day

Rome wasn't built in a day, so don't expect to see it all that quickly either. You'll just have to make the choice of combining two of the following themes and seeing both in a hurry: a historical tour that includes the Colosseum and Forum, a spiritual and artistic tour that includes St. Peter's and the Vatican area, or an architectural and cultural visit through the historical center's tangle of streets, encompassing the Spanish Steps, the Pantheon, Piazza Navona, and the Trevi Fountain, among other sites. Early risers will want to see the market come to life at Campo de' Fiori—take your camera. You'll see interesting bits of old Roman life, and you can walk to any of the sites mentioned above from there, or take a bus from nearby Largo Argentina.

If You Have 2 Days

Take one day and concentrate on either the Vatican/St. Peter's or the Forum/Colosseum, whichever interests you more. Take the other day and spend the morning at your second choice from the above and the afternoon and evening exploring the historical center.

If You Have 3 Days

What should you not miss once you've covered the Rome's best-known areas? The twin museums on the Capitoline Hill are

Rome Major & Outlying Attractions

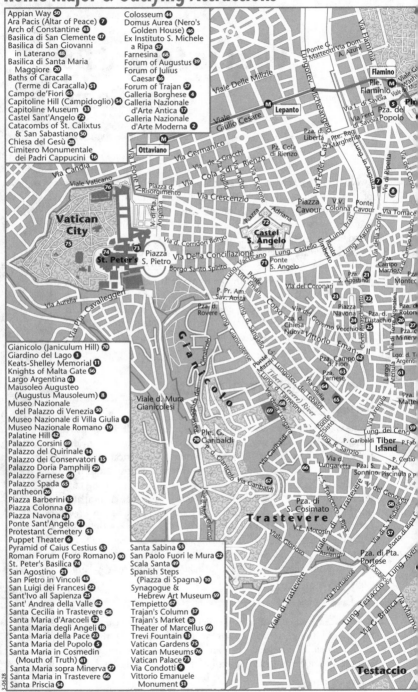

3-0628

something of a must-see, followed by the Etruscan Museum and the Galleria Borghese in the Villa Borghese park. If you'd prefer to wander through the neighborhoods (called *rione*), the streets around Campo de' Fiori are fascinating, especially the artisan shops.

If You Have 5 Days

There are so many places—Trastevere and its folklore museum, the Bocca della Verita, the tiny Byzantine jewel that is the basilica San Marco, and the lovely Franciscan Aracoeli church atop Capitoline Hill. Caravaggio lovers will want to visit Santa Maria del Popolo and San Luigi dei Francesi.

But if you've already managed to see all the Roman sights—a difficult task considering the capricious opening days and hours of most—leave the city to explore Tivoli or Ostia Antica.

1 St. Peter's & the Vatican

The Vatican is in fact a sovereign state of a few hundred citizens and is protected (theoretically) by its own militia, the curiously uniformed (some say based on designs by Michelangelo) Swiss guards.

There's a **Vatican Tourist Office** on the left side of St. Peter's Square as you face the basilica (☎ **06/69-88-44-66** or 69-88-48-66), open Monday to Saturday from 8:30am to 6:30pm. They'll sell you a map of the Vatican for 2,000L ($1.30), accept reservations for tours of the Vatican Gardens (see below), point you in the right direction for papal-audience tickets, and try to answer all your questions. A shuttle bus leaves from in front of this office for the entrance to the Vatican Museums daily every 30 minutes from 8:45am to 1:45pm in summer, 8:45am to 12:45pm in winter; the fare is 2,000L ($1.30). (Take it; it's a long walk, and you'll see the lovely gardens from the bus.) There is also a Vatican post office (superior to the Italian postal system) and rest rooms nearby.

✪ **St. Peter's Basilica.** Pz. San Pietro. ☎ **06/69-88-44-66.** Basilica, free; to climb the dome, 5,000L ($3.30) on foot, 6,000L ($3.95) with elevator halfway; Historical-Artistic Museum (Treasury), 3,000L ($2) Basilica, Apr–Sept, daily 7am–7pm; Oct–Feb, daily 7am–6pm. Dome, Mar–Sept, daily 8am–6pm; Oct–Feb, daily 8am–4:30pm. Grottoes, daily 7am–5pm. To see the necropolis where the tomb of St. Peter was found you must apply Mon–Sat 9am–12pm and 2–5pm to the office beneath Arco della Campana (Arch of the Bells) at the left of the basilica ☎ 6/69-88-53-18. The tour costs 10,000L ($6.60). Treasury, Apr–Sept daily 9am–6:30pm; Oct–Mar 9am–5:30pm. It may be difficult to get into the square and basilica on Wednesday mornings in summer if you don't have a ticket for the pope's weekly public audience (see below). Metro: Line A to Ottaviano. Bus: 23, 32, 41, 52, 62, 64, 492. (*Note:* The buses leave you closer than the Metro.) *Note:* A dress code for men and women prohibiting shorts, tank tops, and skirts above the knee is strictly enforced at all times in the church.

One of the glories of the Western world, **Piazza San Pietro,** or St. Peter's Square, is partly enclosed with a majestic colonnade designed by Bernini and topped by a gesticulating crowd of some 140 saints. Two fountains at the center add to the sound and sight of sparkling water and a never-ending flow of visitors from everywhere lends the excitement of a journey's end for millions of pilgrims each year.

The absolutely enormous St. Peter's Basilica is the second-largest church in the world (a pale imitation in the Ivory Coast recently became the largest) and the spiritual center for nearly a billion Catholics. Along the central aisle of the church, markers indicate the size of other major cathedrals in the world—St. Peter's dwarfs them by comparison. A traditional way to grasp its vast expanse is to stand next to one of the cherubs who adorn the holy water fonts near the entrance and measure your forearm next to a cherub foot.

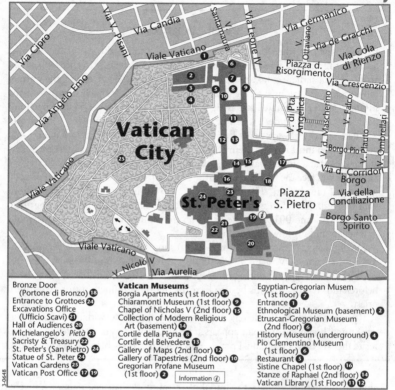

Although there has been a church on this site since the 4th century—as long as Christianity has been the official Roman religion—the present structure was not begun until the early 16th century and completed more than 100 years later. Immediately to the right as you enter is Michelangelo's magnificent *Pietà*—he sculpted four statues on this theme, but this first one was completed when he was only 25 years old. The sculpture is now protected by bulletproof glass after it was attacked by a madman in 1978.

St. Peter's is meant to be awe-inspiring, a church for processions and great celebrations. St. Peter's tomb lies beneath the altar, which is shaded by Bernini's captivating canopy called the Baldacchino.

Visitors can climb to the cupola of the dome for a terrific view of the Vatican complex and the rest of Rome. The entrance is at the far right end of the church as you enter. Be aware, though—there are still 330 steps *after* the elevator has taken you to the end of its line.

The **Treasury,** or Historical-Artistic Museum, is reached from the left nave of the basilica. Among its treasures is a ciborium (goblet for holding the Eucharist) by Donatello, adorned with angels on its sides. The monument of Pope Sixtus IV in bronze is a masterpiece of Pollaiolo (1493), elaborate with figures representing academic disciplines such as Mathematics and Grammar. Go up the tiny staircase to view it in its entirety. In Room V you'll see a candelabrum attributed to the celebrated silversmith Benvenuto Cellini.

To see the **Grottoes,** where many impressive tombs of the popes are found, go to the crossing marked by the Baldacchino, where steps lead downward. (The crypts and

Papal Audiences

Each Wednesday when the pope is in Rome, he speaks with the general public, usually at 11am (10am in summer; hour can change, so be sure to check when you arrive). Papal audiences take place outside in St. Peter's Square during the warmer months and in various interior rooms when it's cold or wet. During part of the summer, Mass is celebrated at Castelgandolfo, outside of Rome. Because Pope John Paul II travels a great deal, it can be difficult to see him, but it's worth the effort.

There are several ways to get free tickets to see the pope. Tickets are rarely "sold out," but you must request them at least a day in advance. You can reserve tickets at the Prefettura, up the stairs under the colonnade on the right side of St. Peter's Square as you face the basilica (where the ellipse meets the rectangular area directly in front of the church). The Prefettura is open Monday through Saturday from 9am to 1pm. The address for written inquiries is Prefettura della Casa Pontifica, Città del Vaticano 00120. In the letter, let them know for what week you would like tickets and for how many people.

Finally, you can also work through the Bishop's Office for United States Visitors to the Vatican, V. dell'Umiltà 30, 00187 Roma (☎ 06/67-89-184; fax 06/68-67-561), but only by writing before you arrive in Rome or calling at least a week beforehand. In any case, it's best to have a letter of introduction from your local priest.

If you can't make a Wednesday audience, you may catch up with the pope on Sunday promptly at noon, when he appears at his library window on St. Peter's Square to recite the Angelus, a traditional prayer, and issue his weekly blessing to the world.

---

altars of the basilica contain the burial places of more than 130 popes.) A lovely relief of the Virgin and Child marks the tomb of the much beloved Pope John XXIII, which is often covered with flowers.

The **necropolis,** below the grottoes, is reached (see above for entry applications) through the gate to the left of the piazza, past the Swiss guards. Stairs lead down into the pre-Constantine necropolis, where you can see many early Christian and pagan tombs from the 2nd and 3rd centuries; but the most important tomb is that of St. Peter himself. Tradition holds that the apostle Peter was martyred in Nero's circus and buried in a nearby cemetery. A shrine over St. Peter's grave was reported to be there during the 2nd century, and then Emperor Constantine, during the 4th century, leveled the previously hilly site of the cemetery and built a basilica in honor of the apostle. Present-day St. Peter's was built during the Renaissance to replace the older church. The elaborate Baldacchino was created in St. Peter's over the grave of the saint, considered to be there because of legends. Not until 1939, when workmen were preparing a tomb for Pius XI, did they uncover sections of the early church and beneath that, pagan, and farther down, Christian burial grounds. In 1960 a niche was seen to have a graffito scratched into the stone saying "Peter is here" in Latin. In this western section of the crypt there is an *iter,* or little street, for each of the families who have tombs there.

Mass is celebrated almost every hour on the hour from 7am to noon, and 5pm, seven days a week. The pontificale, or main Sunday mass, is celebrated at 10:30am. If you plan to attend, check at the Vatican information office first, as the many events that take place in the basilica can affect the timetables.

✪ **Vatican Museums & Gardens.** Vle. Vaticano. ☎ **06/69-88-33-33.** Admission 15,000L ($9.85), 10,000L ($6.60) with an International Student Identification Card, and free to children

3-foot-3 (1 meter) tall or under. Reserve in advance. July–Sept and Easter week Mon–Sat and last Sun of the month 8:45am–4pm; Oct–June (except Easter) Mon–Sat and last Sun of the month 9am–2pm. Closed Jan 6, Feb 11, Easter Mon, Ascension Day (Thurs before the 7th Sun after Easter), May 1, Corpus Christi (9th Sun after Easter, date varies with Easter), June 29, Aug 15, Nov 1, and Dec 8. Last admission 1 hour before closing. Bus: The main entrance is on Viale Vaticano, reached by Bus 49 from Piazza Cavour, which stops in front; Bus: 81 or Tram 19, which stop in Piazza Risorgimento, about a 5-minute walk away; or buses 64 or 492 from Termini. Metro: Ottaviano. The most convenient way to go from St. Peter's to the museums is to take the shuttle bus from outside the tourist office for 2,000L ($1.30). The schedule is printed at the stop. Buy your ticket on the bus.

The Vatican is home to a brilliant collection of artistic and historical treasures. The 4½ miles of corridors forming the Vatican Museums complex will take you through 15 outstanding museums, the breathtaking Raphael Rooms, and Fra Angelico's beautifully painted chapel, all culminating in the unparalleled Sistine Chapel. And that's just what's indoors. After you climb the spiral staircase, pay, and enter the museums, you'll find yourself at the edge of a small open-air garden where you will see a plaque describing four color-coded tours that you may follow (depending on the amount of time you can spend here and your interests). Also here are the rest rooms, a gift shop with slides and prints and books about the artists exhibited, and a snack bar. Before setting off on the tour of your choice, head to the right to enter the picture gallery.

In the **Pinacoteca** (picture gallery), look for the *Angel Musician,* part of a fresco by Melozzo da Forli. It's been reproduced widely in these days of angel fascination. The round painting of the *Virgin and Child* by Pinturicchio, Caravaggio's *Descent from the Cross,* and Guido Reni's fine *St. Jerome (San Girolamo)* are among the treasures here. Raphael's *Transfiguration,* often reproduced, was finished by followers of the maestro (he was working on it when he died). Nearby is his *Madonna di Foligno,* in which the Virgin and Child rest on a cloud of angels while Saint Francis and John the Baptist look on. The half-finished *Saint Jerome* by Leonardo da Vinci is one of his few works in Rome.

On the second floor of the museums, at the end of a series of long corridors hung with tapestries (some by the Raphael School), you'll find the **Raphael Rooms.** Commissioned by Pope Julius II in the 16th century, these salons are covered with frescoes that glorify the papacy.

The first room, the **Stanza dell'Incendio,** contains the grim *Incendio di Borgo* (Fire in the Borgo), depicting a 9th-century conflagration in the area between the Vatican and the river that was extinguished by the miraculous intervention of Pope Leo IV. It was mostly painted by Raphael's assistants to his designs, but many art historians attribute some of the figures to Raphael's brush itself. The master probably painted the surprised woman with a jug on her head to the right, and also possibly the Aeneas group on the left (a young man carrying a yellowed old man and accompanied by a child).

The second room, known as the **Stanza della Segnatura,** includes Raphael's famous *School of Athens.* This is one of the artist's best-known works, and it depicts philosophers from the ages, including Aristotle, Plato, and Socrates. Many of these figures are actually portraits of some of the greatest artists of the Renaissance, including Bramante (on the right as Euclid, bent over and balding as he draws on a chalkboard), Leonardo Da Vinci (as Plato, the bearded man in the center pointing heavenward), even Raphael himself (looking out at us from the lower right corner). While he was painting this masterpiece, Raphael stopped work to walk down the hall for the unveiling of Michelangelo's newly finished Sistine Chapel ceiling. He was so impressed that he returned to his *School of Athens* and added to his design a sulking Michelangelo (as Heraclitus) sitting on the steps. The other important fresco here is the *Disputation of the Sacrament.* There are two more portraits in this work. Towards the middle of the right half, half-hidden behind a golden-robed church dignitary, stands a dour-looking man in red with a laurel-leaf crown—the Tuscan poet Dante whose *Inferno* revolutionized Italian literature (he wrote in Tuscan vernacular rather than Latin) and became the basis for Italian language. Look also on the far left for a pious-looking man in black with just a wisp of white hair remaining—it's a portrait of the monastic painter Fra (Beato) Angelico, whose great work in Rome is just after these rooms (see below).

The third room, the **Stanza di Eliodoro,** painted by Raphael from 1510 to 1514, shows Pope Leo I negotiating with Attila the Hun to prevent him from sacking Rome (A.D. 452); the pope succeeded. At right, the Miracle of Bolsena depicts the origin (1264) of the feast of Corpus Christi (the Body and Blood of Christ), when a priest in the town of Bolsena, who had begun to doubt the miracle of the Real Presence of Christ in the Eucharist, saw blood darkening an altar cloth when he was consecrating the sacrament, revealing that it was indeed the Blood of Christ. The *Expulsion of Heliodorus* alludes to the Crusade of Pope Julius II against enemies of the Church. In the painting Raphael uses a Bible story (2 Maccabees) in which the king has Heliodorus confiscate the Temple's treasury; instead it is Heliodorus whom God punishes. "Hands off the Papal Treasury" was the message.

The **Sala di Constantino,** the final room, was actually painted by a student of Raphael. Notice that this less-skilled painter used black to signify shadowing, whereas the master employed varying shades of the same color.

Following the Raphael Rooms you'll come on the somber, contemplative, and more formal **Cappella di Beato Angelico** (1448–50), a small chapel painted by the Tuscan early Renaissance master (and devout monk) Fra Angelico. In fact, the scenes in his work look more like Florence and Tuscany than Rome, a testament to the artist's homesickness.

If you're interested in the Vatican's **Museum of Modern Religious Art,** visit this collection now, before descending to the Sistine Chapel—the Vatican traffic cops operate a one-way museum. The collection—55 rooms of painting and sculpture—was commissioned by Pope Paul VI, who feared that the religious artistic tradition was fading.

The Vatican Museum complex also includes an **Egyptian Museum,** with relics from the Roman conquest of that kingdom (Room 5 has some excellent statues of pharaohs), and an **Etruscan Museum,** on a par with the collection at Rome's Villa Giulia (see "More Attractions: Around the Spanish Steps and Piazza del Popolo" below). One star of the Etruscan Museum is in Room 5—the Tomb of the Regolini-Galassi (named for the discoverer). In Room 3 is another, the 5th-century B.C. statue *Mars of Todi* (the city where it was found), a bronze warrior influenced by the Greeks.

The **Pio-Clementine Museum** has an excellent collection dedicated to classical sculpture, including Roman copies of Greek works, that is not to be missed. The 1st-century B.C. *Belvedere Torso* became a model for art students, including Michelangelo. The *Laocoön,* struggling with his sons against two snakes, *Sleeping Ariadne, Augustus of Prima Porta,* the *Belvedere Apollo,* and many others are exceptional.

✪ **SISTINE CHAPEL (CAPELLA SISTINA)**   The Sistine Chapel, now almost completely restored (to the horror of some and admiration of others), contains some of the most powerful painting in history. Because Michelangelo was a sculptor, he saw the body differently from the artistic visions of his contemporaries (a glance at the wall paintings here done by fellow Renaissance masters demonstrates this clearly). Take binoculars.

The Sistine Chapel was, in fact, not built as a chapel at all, but was meant to be a vault—note its rectangular shape. It is here that the cardinals meet to elect each new pope. Pope Sixtus IV commissioned the frescoes that adorn its walls; the left wall shows the story of Moses, while the right side details the life of Jesus. Each of the works was painted by one of a group of early Renaissance masters including Perugino, Pinturicchio, Botticelli, Ghirlandaio, Roselli, and Signorelli. Each would be considered a masterpiece on its own, if they weren't literally overshadowed by the famous ceiling.

Sixtus IV's successor and nephew, Pope Julius II, still wasn't pleased with the look of the place, so he asked Michelangelo to connect the two walls by frescoing the ceiling—which at that time was the standard uniform darkish blue with bursts of gold stars. Lying on his back on scaffolding (alternating with standing for hours on end in a swayed-back crouch) in the damp chapel with paint dripping into his eyes painting frescoes was not was not what the Florentine sculptor wanted to be doing, but a commission by the pope couldn't be ignored. Luckily for the world, Michelangelo was too much of a perfectionist not to put his all into his work, even at tasks he didn't care for, and he proposed to Pope Julius that he paint a full cycle of frescoes rather than just the "decorations" the pope had originally asked for. At first Michelangelo worked with a group of assistants, as was the custom, but soon found he was not a good team player and fired all of them. On his own, it took four years of grumbling and complaining between brushstrokes before he finished the ceiling in 1512.

The scenes along the middle of the ceiling are taken from the Book of Genesis, and tell the story of creation (the first six panels) and the story of Noah (the last three panels, which were actually painted first and with the help of assistants). In thematic order, they are: *Separation of Light from Darkness; Creation of the Sun, Moon, and Planets; Separation of the Waters from the Land;* ✪ *Creation of Adam; Creation of Eve; Temptation and Expulsion from the Garden of Eden; Sacrifice of Noah; The Flood;* and *the Drunkeness of Noah.* These scenes are bracketed by false architecture, chubby cherubs, and 20 nude male figures reaching and stretching, twisting and turning their bodies to show off the straining muscles of the male physique—Michelangelo's favorite theme. As this chapel is vault-shaped, the ceiling itself is actually curved, and where the surface arcs down to become the walls, interrupted by pointed lunettes, Michelangelo ringed the ceiling frescoes with Old Testament prophets and ancient Sybils (sacred fortune-tellers of the classical age in whose cryptic prophecies the medieval and Renaissance Church liked to believe it found specific foretellings of the coming of Christ). The triangular lunettes contain less-impressive frescoes of the Ancestors of Christ, and the wider spandrels in each corner depict Old Testament scenes of salvation.

A lengthy and politically charged cleaning in the 1980s removed centuries of dirt and smoke from the paintings, although the merits of the restoration are still hotly debated (the techniques used and the amount of grime—and possibly paint—taken off are bones of contention among art historians; some even maintain that possible later additions, detailing, or shading by Michelangelo were lost in the cleaning).

The crowning glory of the room is the tremendously powerful *Last Judgment* (1535–41), painted by Michelangelo more than 20 years after he finished the ceiling. It was commissioned by Pope Paul III, who insisted it be painted above the altar (until that time, depictions of the Last Judgment had always been displayed above the church exit, for worshippers to contemplate as they left). Michelangelo carried on the medieval tradition of representing saints and martyrs holding the instruments of their martyrdom—St. Catherine carries a section of the wheel with which she was tortured and executed; St. Sebastian clutches some arrows. Look for St. Bartholomew, a little below and to the right of Jesus, holding his own skin and the knife with which he was flayed. The face on this skin is thought to be a self-portrait of sorts of

Michelangelo. Known throughout his life as a sulky, difficult character and most likely a manic-depressive, if the master was indeed painting himself here he shows us an almost terminally morose face. Michelangelo was getting old at the time (in his late sixties), Rome had been sacked by barbarians just a few years before, and both he and the city in general were undergoing religious crises—not to mention that Michelangelo was weary after years of butting his artistic head against the whims and directives of the Church and various popes who were his patrons.

In the lower right corner is a political practical joke of sorts—there is a figure portrayed as Midas in Hell, but it is in reality a portrait of Biagio di Cesena, Master of Ceremonies to the pope and a Vatican bigwig who protested violently against Michelangelo's painting shameless nudes here (although some of the figures were partially clothed or draped, the majority of the masses were originally naked). As the earlier Tuscan genius Dante had done to his political enemies in his poetic master-piece *Inferno*, Michelangelo put Cesena into his own vision of Hell, gave him jack-ass ears, and painted a serpent eternally biting off his testicles.

Twenty-three years and several popes later, the voices of prudery (in the form of Pope Pius IV) got their way and one of Michelangelo's former protégés, Daniele da Volterra, was protestingly brought in to paint pieces of cloth draped over the more objectionable bits of the nude figures. These loincloths stayed modestly in place until many were removed in the most recent and, of course, controversial cleaning that ended in 1994. Some critics of this restoration claim, among other things, that Michelangelo himself painted some of the clothes on after he was done and that too many were removed; others wanted all of the added draperies stripped from the work. It seems that the compromise, with the majority of figures staying clothed but a few bottoms uncovered, pleased nobody.

One thing is for certain, since the restorations of both the ceiling and the *Last Judgment,* Michelangelo's colors seem to pop off the wall in warm yellows, bright oranges, soft flesh-tones, and rich greens set against stark white or brilliant azure backgrounds. Many still prefer the dramatic, broodingly somber tones of the precleaning period. For all the controversy, the revelations provided by the cleanings have forced artists and art historians to reevaluate everything they thought about Michelangelo's color palette, technique, and painterly skills.

Michelangelo got the last word, by the way, over this continued "misuse" of him as a fresco painter when he'd rather be chipping away at his marble blocks. The dis-gruntled Tuscan master artist, after having created what was already acknowledged on the day of its unveiling as one of the greatest paintings the Western world had ever seen, signed his fresco cycle on the Sistine Chapel ceiling "Michelangelo, sculptor."

No photography of any kind is allowed, there are no guided tours (briefings are conducted in the halls and museum rooms preceding the chapel), and—ostensibly—no talking is permitted inside the Sistine Chapel.

THE VATICAN GARDENS   From the corridors of tapestries you'll doubtless see the lush Vatican Gardens. Guided tours of the Vatican City grounds are the only way to get in. From March through October, tours leave Monday, Tuesday, and Thurs-day through Saturday at 10 or 11am from the tourist information office on St. Peter's Square (see above); November through February, tours run only on Tuesday, Thurs-day, and Saturday. The tour costs 16,000L ($10.50) and lasts two hours. You'll also see the Vatican radio station (outside only) and many places important in Vatican history. You will also enjoy the great dome of St. Peter's from the back, positioned as Michelangelo intended for the front of St. Peter's, without the wide facade, eas-ily visible and harmonious. Reservations required; reserve several days in advance. For information call **06/69-88-44-66** or 84-866.

In case you want to see the world.

At American Express, we're here to make your journey a smooth one. So we have over 1,700 travel service locations in over 120 countries ready to help. What else would you expect from the world's largest travel agency?

do more

Travel

http://www.americanexpress.com/travel

In case you want to be welcomed there.

We're here to see that you're always welcomed at establishments everywhere. That's why millions of people carry the American Express® Card — for peace of mind, confidence, and security, around the world or just around the corner.

do more

Cards

In case you're running low.

We're here to help with more than 118,000 Express Cash locations around the world. In order to enroll, just call American Express before you start your vacation.

do more

Express Cash

And just in case.

We're here with American Express® Travelers Cheques and Cheques *for Two*® They're the safest way to carry money on your vacation and the surest way to get a refund, practically anywhere, anytime.

Another way we help you...

do more

**Travelers
Cheques**

2 Ancient Rome

⊙ **The Roman Forum and Palatine Hill.** V. d. Fori Imperiali. ☎ **06/69-90-110.** Admission 12,000L ($7.90). Apr–Sept Mon–Sat 9–6, Sun 9–1; Oct–Mar Mon–Sat 9–3, Sun 9–1. Closed Jan 1 and May 1. Bus: 27, 85, 718, 719. The entrances are in back of the left side of the Monument to Vittorio Emanuele in Piazza Venezia, and near the Arch of Titus (at the Colosseum end). Metro: Colosseo.

The Roman Forum (Foro Romano), in noble ruins, evokes the centuries when Rome ruled the world. Remember that the Forum stays open during the long Roman lunch, when most things are closed, but also that the Forum has no roof and the lunch hour in Rome during the summer may not be the best time to be baking out under the hot August sun. For a more complete walking tour of the Forum and Palatine Hill that will help you make sense out of the vast archeological area and explain the details of every sight along the way, see the "Roman Forum " walking tour, below.

Long the seat of commerce, government, and religion, the Forum drew all of Rome to its porticoes to discuss the business of state and to check out the farmers and merchants hawking their wares. Temples to Vesta, Janus, and Saturn drew the faithful. The Arch of Septimius Severus (emperor A.D. 193–211) was erected in appreciation of his extending the empire as far as Mesopotamia. (His son Caracalla murdered his brother Geta in order to become emperor.) At the far end, the Arch of Titus celebrated the sack of Jerusalem by the emperor Titus, and you can see the sacred objects, among them a menorah, being brought back to Rome as spoils of war. Beyond and outside the Forum stands the largest and best preserved of all, the Arch of Constantine (see under "Colosseum" below). Its reliefs are often very well done, and depict the emperor doing brave deeds, of course.

The basilicas were not originally churches but rather places to conduct legal and business transactions. They were often monumental in size, as the basilicas of Emilia and of Maxentius (begun in 308 but completed during the reign of Constantine) show. Temples to Roman gods abound, but the most famous is that of the Vesta, where Vestal virgins lived and tended the flame; if it went out, the lax maiden would join it in oblivion. It was an honor to be a Vestal, but not everyone fought for it.

Above the Forum, accessible from stairs near the Arch of Titus, is the Palatine Hill. Rome was built on seven hills, beginning with this one. The tall umbrella pines here bring to mind Respighi's orchestral suite *The Pines of Rome.* The Farnese gardens are lovely in the spring, and beyond them you'll see signs to descend to Livia's villa, where bright frescoes still adorn the walls where she and the emperor Augustus were regally ensconced. Farther along stand the circular huts of the Iron Age village on this site, where Romulus and Remus supposedly lived. These legendary founders of Rome may be more fact than fiction, for archeologists have dated the area at the mid-8th century B.C., when the twins were said to have lived.

From the far end of the Palatine, look across to the oval that was the Circo Massimo (Circus Maximus). Although today it's just a grassy field and jogging track, it once felt the wheels of Ben-Hur's chariot.

The main entrance to the Forum is on Via dei Fori Imperiali, a huge boulevard created by World War II dictator Benito Mussolini as a place to hold military parades. Another entrance to the Palatine Hill and Forum is down Via di San Gregorio from the Colosseum, to the left of the Colosseum as you exit. If you're in a hurry and would prefer to see only the Forum, you can make a quick getaway behind the Arch of Titus, the closest exit to the Colosseum.

The Colosseum. V. d. Fori Imperiali. ☎ **06/70-04-261.** Colosseum, street level of interior, free; upper levels, 8,000L ($5.25). Apr–Sept Mon–Tues and Thurs–Sat 9am–6pm (June–Aug until

7pm), Wed and Sun 9am–1pm; Oct–Mar Wed and Sun 9am–3pm. Bus: 11, 13, 15, 27, 30, 85, 87, 118, 186, 673; Metro: Colosseo.

Every major city has at least one icon that symbolizes it: the Eiffel Tower in Paris, Big Ben in London, and the Colosseum (Colosseo) in Rome. It's most impressive from the outside, a mammoth remnant of the golden age of the Roman Empire. Completed in the 1st century A.D., it was in this 50,000-seat stadium that gladiators fought each other or wild beasts, and Christians were most likely *not* thrown to the lions—certainly persecuted under several Imperial regimes, some Christian prisoners may have indeed been sent to fight in the gladiator ring, and this would sometimes involve battles against wild beasts, but "throwing them to the lions" was not some sort of official Roman sport. Any defeated gladiator, Christian, slave, or otherwise, feared the moment when the emperor would ask the crowd whether to spare his life. A yes brought a thumbs-up sign; a no was thumbs-down.

Much of the destruction to the Colosseum's interior came from a series of earthquakes and the natural disintegration of the cement seats, but its ruined state is also due to its being used for centuries as a quarry for other Roman construction projects, such as building the Palazzo di Venezia and Palazzo Barberini as well as parts of St. Peter's (much of Rome was regularly rearranged that way). The original floor of the structure is also gone, revealing the labyrinthine underground network where prisoners, lions, and general provisions were kept.

To clamber up to the higher levels, go to the stairway just to the left as you face the main entrance. In recent years various of the three upper levels have been closed for reconstruction and reinforcement in a major restoration project to prepare for Jubilee Year 2000. Nightlights inside the arches give the structure a new mystery, making it impressive from far off in the glow of its three tiers of open arches.

Just outside the Colosseum, between the Colosseum and the Forum, stands the Arch of Constantine, the largest and best preserved of classical antiquities, erected in A.D. 315 to commemorate the emperor's victory over Maxentius in 312. During the Middle Ages it was incorporated into a fortress, and it was most recently and splendidly restored between 1981 and 1988. Along the top of the side facing the Colosseum is an excellent frieze of the triumph of Marcus Aurelius (174). Constantine is shown over each of the side arches. The top of the opposite side also has friezes of Aurelius.

Directly opposite (through the Colosseum) from the Arch of Constantine stands the Domus Aurea of Nero, which cannot be visited. Nero's "Golden House" was typical of the despicable emperor in its extreme luxury. "Good, now at last I can live like a human being," was his comment when the house was finished. Suetonius, the Roman historian born in A.D. 69, had this to say: "The entrance hall was large enough to contain a statue of himself [Nero] 120 feet high; and the pillared arcade ran for a whole mile. An enormous pool, like the sea, was surrounded by buildings made to resemble cities, and by a landscape garden consisting of ploughed fields, vineyards, pastures, and woodlands—where every variety of domestic and wild animal roamed about." (Could he have inspired Michael Jackson?)

The Imperial Forums. V. d. Fori Imperiali. Bus: 27, 85, 87, 186. Metro: Colosseo.

If you walk away from the Colosseum up Via dei Fori Imperiali and then fork right onto Via Alessandrina, you'll find Augustus's Forum on the right side and Trajan's Forum farther down on the left. (Both are across the Via dei Fori Imperiale from the Roman Forum.) Neither of these is open to the public, except by a guided tour (buy tickets at the entrance at V. IV Novembre 94). Admission to Trajan's Market, just beyond Augustus's Forum on your right, is 3,750L ($2.50) (free for EU members under 18 or over 60), but you can see the basic structure from the sidewalk above.

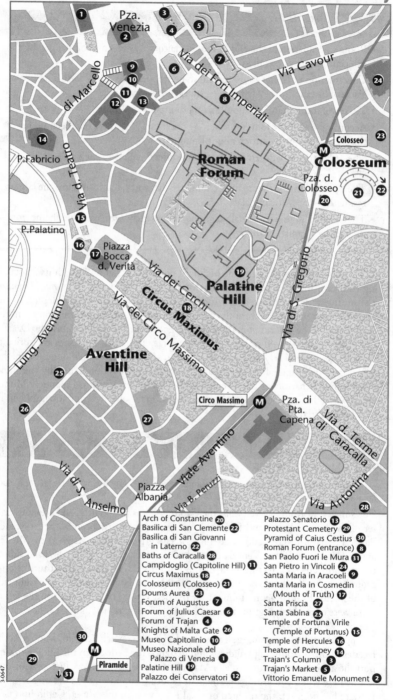

Ancient Rome & Attractions Nearby

Pza. Venezia

Via dei Fori Imperiali

Via Cavour

Roman Forum

Colosseo

M

Colosseum

Pza. d. Colosseo

P.Fabricio

di Marcello

Via d. Teatro

P.Palatino

Piazza Bocca d. Verità

Via dei Cerchi

Palatine Hill

Via di S. Gregorio

Circus Maximus

Via dei Circo Massimo

Aventine Hill

Lung. Aventino

Circo Massimo

M

Pza. di Pta. Capena

Via d. Terme di Caracalla

Viale Aventino

Piazza Albania

Via B. Peruzzi

Via Antonina

Via di S. Anselmo

M

Piramide

3-0647

Arch of Constantine 20	Palazzo Senatorio 13
Basilica di San Clemente 22	Protestant Cemetery 29
Basilica di San Giovanni in Laterno 22	Pyramid of Caius Cestius 30
Baths of Caracalla 28	Roman Forum (entrance) 8
Campidoglio (Capitoline Hill) 11	San Paolo Fuori le Mura 31
Circus Maximus 18	San Pietro in Vincoli 24
Colosseum (Colosseo) 21	Santa Maria in Aracoeli 9
Doums Aurea 23	Santa Maria in Cosmedin (Mouth of Truth) 17
Forum of Augustus 7	Santa Priscia 27
Forum of Julius Caesar 6	Santa Sabina 25
Forum of Trajan 4	Temple of Fortuna Virile (Temple of Portunus) 15
Knights of Malta Gate 26	Temple of Hercules 16
Museo Capitolinio 10	Theater of Pompey 14
Museo Nazionale del Palazzo di Venezia 1	Trajan's Column 3
Palatine Hill 19	Trajan's Market 5
Palazzo dei Conservatori 12	Vittorio Emanuele Monument 2

121

> ## ❓ Did You Know?
>
> - Rome's population at the end of the 1st century was one million people; by the 6th century it was less than 50,000.
> - Construction of Rome's subway had to be stopped frequently so that archeologists could examine newly found vestiges of the city's past.
> - There are more than 300 monumental fountains in Rome.
> - According to author John Gunther, by the mid-1960s there had been no fewer than 230,000 books written about Rome.
> - The 1985 treaty between Italy and the Vatican ended Rome's title of "sacred city."
> - The Vatican may be the smallest country in the world, but it contains the largest residence—the Vatican Palace.
> - The Spanish Steps were actually a gift of the French but received their name from the nearby Spanish Embassy.

Trajan's Forum is certainly the highlight of this imperial walk, with its 25 standing columns, including the intricately carved Trajan's Column (*Colonna Traiano*), a stunning series of bas-reliefs winding up a monumental pillar, depicting the emperor's military career, from the crossing of the Danube (at bottom) on up to the deportation of the Dacian population, which ended the campaign against the Dacians (A.D. 101–3 and 107–8) in what is contemporary Romania. His ashes are buried at the base. It's worth carrying your binoculars to see, especially when floodlit at night.

Via dei Fori Imperiali ends at Piazza Venezia, which is dominated by the stark-white winged chariots of the ostentatious 19th-century Vittorio Emanuele Monument, where Italian soldiers keep watch over the grave of Italy's unknown soldier, lit by an eternal flame.

3 More Attractions

NEAR ANCIENT ROME

Campidoglio (Capitoline Hill). Pz. del Campidoglio. Bus: Any bus to Piazza Venezia, such as 26, 44, 46, 56, 57, 60, 62, 64, 65, 70, 75, 81, and others.

The smallest of Rome's seven hills, the Capitoline was the political and religious center of the imperial city, and for many centuries since it has been home to Rome's Palazzo Senatorio (city hall). The hill's sweeping front steps, designed by Michelangelo, lead from Piazza Venezia up to this majestic plateau, while the back side of the summit enjoys a terrific view of the Forum below—especially beautiful on a moonlit night. Walk up the gently graded steps that begin around to the right side of the Victor Emmanuel monument for the best view. The steep steps to the left of these were created for pilgrims to ascend on their knees to the Church of the Aracoeli (see below) at the top.

The Campidoglio square itself was also designed by Michelangelo, who redid the facades of the surrounding buildings and designed the pedestal in the middle to support the ancient equestrian statue of Marcus Aurelius (a replica of which may or may not be here when you visit—a permanent replica is supposed to be set up soon, but no date has been set; the restored original is on view in the Museo Capitolino next door). This statue originally sat atop the Marcus Aurelius column (now in Piazza di Colonna)—which explains its odd perspective, as it was meant to sit more than

130 feet above the observer—and was saved from being melted down in Christian antipagan purges throughout the Middle Ages because it was thought to be a statue of Constantine, the 2nd-century Roman emperor who converted to Christianity. Statues in Rome were moved around as often and as easily as furniture.

Note that the piazza is not square, but rather it widens as it heads from the steps to the palace opposite, and that the ground slopes gently toward the center and the pedestal from all directions. Sharing this tiny square are the Palazzo dei Conservatori, on the right as you reach the top, and the Museo Capitolino, opposite, both containing many celebrated ancient works as well as a Renaissance and baroque painting collection (see below).

Museo dei Conservatori and Museo Capitolino. Pz. del Campidoglio. ☎ **06/67-10-20-71.** Admission for both 10,000L ($6.25); free the last Sun in each month. May–Sept Tues 9am–1:30pm and 5–8pm, Wed–Fri 9am–1:30pm, Sat 9am–1:30pm and 8–11pm, Sun 9am–1pm; Oct–Apr Tues and Sat 9am–1pm and 5–8pm, Wed–Fri and Sun 9am–1:30pm. Bus: 46, 89, 92, 94, 716.

Flanking the Campidoglio square atop the Capitoline Hill (see above) are the Palazzo dei Conservatori, on the right as you reach the top, and the Museo Capitolino, opposite.

In the courtyard of the Capitoline Museum reclines the *Marforio,* a 2nd-century Roman river god that was once one of Rome's famous talking statues, carrying on conversations with the Pasqino statue across town. These "conversations" took the form of plaques hung around the statues' neck containing pithy observations by local pundits deriding the grossest church or state mismanagement of the moment, whether it be aristocratic scandal or papal blunder (sort of the satirical editorial cartoons of the times). Inside, you'll want to see the busts of the philosophers and poets, and also those of the Caesars, as well as the *Dying Gaul* (a Roman copy of a bronze 3rd-century B.C. Greek original), the *Capitoline Venus,* and some fine mosaics from Hadrian's villa.

In the courtyard of the Palazzo dei Conservatori the enormous head (8'6" high), hands, foot, kneecap, and other body parts of the colossal statue of Constantine line the walls. The statue originally looked down from a seat in the Basilica of Maxentius in the Forum (most likely, these pieces were always the only bits made of marble, the rest of the figure being draped in robes carved out of much more economical wood). Inside the museums, you'll find several ancient treasures, including the 1st-century B.C. bronze *Spinario* (Boy with a Thorn), and the 5th-century B.C. bronze *Capitoline Wolf,* symbol of the ancient Roman Republic and still the icon of the Eternal City. The foundling twins Romulus and Remus suckling underneath, whom legend holds were to go on and found Rome, were 16th-century additions. The Pinacoteca contains some very fine paintings, including works by Titian, Guido Reni, Van Dyck, and Valazquez, and two Caravaggios: the *Gypsy Fortune Teller* and, hidden in a hall lined with display cases of expensive trinkets and baubles, his rather shockingly young and suggestive *St. John the Baptist,* the antithesis of the Gospel John.

Santa Maria in Aracoeli. Capitoline Hill, between Victor Emmanuel monument and Capitoline Museums. ☎ **06/67-98-155.** Free admission. Daily 7am–noon and 4–7pm. Bus: 46, 89, 92, 94, or 95.

Santa Maria in Aracoeli is a delight. It's popular with the Romans because it houses the curious Santo Bambino, a bejeweled figure of the Christ Child. Reference to this figure has appeared in books ever since the 17th century. Although the statue is not a work of art, legends have been abundant about its mystical properties. It was carved by angels out of wood from the Garden of Gethsemane, some say. In any case, the Bambino has been rushed to bedsides of the ailing throughout Rome for many years, and in less secular ages traffic has been stopped to let it pass, clutched in the arms of the officiating priest. Now it occupies an altar of honor in the church, and at Christmas schoolchildren line up to read poems they've written to the Holy Child (or rather to a copy, as a thief stole the Bambino a few years ago).

Apart from the Bambino, this Franciscan church has many charms, among them its spacious, dimly lit interior on a hillside, making it cool on the hottest of days. You'll need the coolness after ascending the 1,224 steep marble stairs in front, on your knees if you want to do it correctly. Of course, some do cheat and ascend the wide, deep steps of the Cordonata that leads to the Capitoline Museums.

The church was built over the temple of Juno Moneta, the Roman mint, from which we get the word "money." The emperor Augustus also had a palace here. The story told is that Augustus summoned the Tiburtine Sibyl to consult her about his accepting divine status when the Roman Senate wanted to make him a god. Within her prophecy was the phrase "from the sun will descend the king of future centuries." While she was speaking the emperor saw the Virgin holding the Child (before the birth of Christ), voices cried out: "This is the Virgin who will receive in her arms the Savior of the world; this is the altar of the Son of God." And so Augustus built the Ara Coeli, "the altar of the son of God."

An earlier church was erected here in 1285, and subsequent restorations, until 1689, have enlarged the interior. The most important work of art is the series of frescoes in the first chapel to the right of the right nave, the 15th-century project of Pinturicchio. They are radiant, after you've invested some coins in the light box.

San Pietro in Vincoli (Saint Peter in Chains). Pz. di San Pietro in Vincoli 4a. ☎ 06/
48-82-865. Free admission. Daily 7am–12:30pm and 3:30–6pm. Metro: Cavour (cross V.
Giovanni Lanza and turn right to walk down V. Cavour until you reach a long set of stairs on
your left that disappear under an arch; these lead to the church) or Colosseo (walk up to Lgo.
Polveriera and go left on V. Eudossiana to the church).

Although in suspiciously good shape for a set of 2,000-year-old iron rings, the chains that supposedly once held St. Peter are kept behind glass under the high altar of this church. The chief attraction is not the chains, however, but rather Michelangelo's fabulous statue of *Moses*, complete with a marvelously carved waist-length beard (to the right as you face the altar). The horns sprouting out of this head were consciously kept, as in medieval representations. They derive from a mistranslation of the Hebrew word for "rays of light," which is the way ancient texts describe his head, which meant it was ringed with a halo. In the ancient world a horned head often symbolized divinity, honor, and power, and he may also have kept them for that reason.

The figure is at the center of the tomb of Julius II, and presents the pope's qualities of strength and leadership. The figures at either side are of Rachel and Leah, representing the Active and the Contemplative life; they are the last statues the artist ever finished.

Basilica di San Clemente. Pz. di San Clemente, V. San Giovanni in Laterano. ☎ 06/
73-15-723. Main church, free; excavations, 3,000L ($1.90). Mon–Sat 9am–noon and 3:30–
6pm, Sun 10am–noon and 3:30–6pm. Metro: Colosseo (then a long 1 block up V. Labicana).

While so much of Rome is glorious and monumental, a visit to the several layers of San Clemente will give you a feeling of what it was like to be an early Christian in Rome. Beneath this plain 12th-century structure are the remains of two earlier structures, dating from the 4th and 1st centuries A.D., respectively. At the bottom you'll also see fascinating sculpture from the ancient temple of Mithras that was once on the site. Mithras was a Persian god born of a rock, who killed, at Apollo's order, the bull that symbolized fertility. During the struggle a scorpion was helping him and he spilled part of the bull's precious blood, from which the world and its creatures were created, thus introducing evil into the world.

The chapel immediately to your right as you enter the church contains frescoes of the life of St. Catherine, painted in the 1420s by Masolino, possibly with the help of his even more talented student Masaccio, both masters of the early Florentine Renaissance. Part of the cycle is now being restored.

The medieval Triumph of the Cross mosaic in the apse of the church is particularly noteworthy, as are the two intact and well-preserved 11th-century frescoes: one, scenes from the legend of St. Alexis, and the other, St. Clement celebrating mass. When soldiers came for him they were blinded by God and carried off a pillar, thinking they had St. Clement in tow, as the fresco depicts. San Clemente has a good gift shop with inexpensive prints for sale.

Basilica di San Giovanni in Laterano (Saint John in Lateran). Pz. San Giovanni in Laterano 4. ☎ **06/69-88-64-33.** Free admission. Daily 7am–6pm. Metro: San Giovanni (then walk through the portal in the Roman wall).

One of Rome's major basilicas, San Giovanni is the city of Rome's own cathedral (St. Peter's is part of Vatican City, technically a separate country), where the pope, as Bishop of Rome, comes to celebrate mass on certain holidays. Indeed, the crimson building to the right as you face the church was the papal residence from the 4th through much of the 14th century.

Much of the original 4th-century church has been slowly destroyed by various fires, earthquakes, barbarian sacks, and declines of papal fortunes (and desire) for its maintenance. It was completely remodeled in the 17th century by Borromini (the interior) and in the 18th century by Alessandro Galilei (the facade). To reinforce the building's structure, Borromini filled in the spaces between each set of two columns to create wide piers with niches on both sides. Look for the remnants of a fresco of *Boniface VIII's Jubilee* on the back of the second pier on your right as you enter; the work has only recently been rediscovered and is now attributed to the revolutionary early Renaissance master Giotto. The adjoining baptistry's octagonal form became the prototype for baptistries in Italy. The cloisters have some lovely 13th-century Cosmatesque work on the columns. A terrorist bomb exploded here in 1993, damaging part of the facade and some frescoes. Restoration is not yet complete.

Santuario Scala Santa. Pz. San Giovanni in Laterano. ☎ **06/75-94-619.** Free admission. Daily 6:15am–12:30pm and 3–7pm. Metro: San Giovanni (across the street from San Giovanni above).

The building off to the left and across the street as you exit the Basilica of San Giovanni in Laterano houses the Holy Stairs (Scala Santa), the original 28 marble steps brought from Pontius Pilate's villa—now covered with wood for preservation—that Christ is said to have climbed on the day he was condemned to death. According to a medieval tradition they were brought from Jerusalem to Rome by Constantine's mother, St. Helen, in 326, and the stairs have been in their present location since 1589 (St. Helen was a prodigious relic hound and also brought back large chunks of the True Cross, one of which she kept in her palace nearby, which was later converted into the church Santa Croce in Gerusalemme, just a few blocks away down Viale C. Felice). Today pilgrims from all over the world come here to climb the steps on their knees. This is one of the holiest sites in Christendom; please show respect for those worshiping here and refrain from talking or taking pictures.

Santa Maria in Cosmedin. Pz. d. Bocca della Verità 18. ☎ **06/67-81-419.** Free admission. Porch, daily 9am–5pm; church, daily 9am–1pm and 2:30–6pm. Bus 15, 23, 57, 95, or 716.

This church is better known for its porch, where the famous Bocca della Verità, or Mouth of Truth, is found, This enormous stone face with an open mouth is the place for lovers to swear their fidelity to each other by placing a hand in the mouth. If one partner should lie, he or she would withdraw a bitten hand. Tour buses come in droves and you may need to work your way past gobs of camera-clickers eager to be photographed with their hand in the Bocca.

The church was built on the ruins of temples devoted to Hercules and to Ceres, the earth goddess. The original church was transformed by Pope Hadrian I in the 8th century, and consigned to Greeks who had sought refuge from persecution in Constantinople. Even today the Byzantine mass is celebrated here on Sunday. "Cosmedin" is a Greek word for ornament.

The Choir, or scuola cantorum, is in the central nave, decorated by the Cosmati family, whose marble floors are one of Rome's joys. At right, the base of the Paschal candle's tall, twisting holder is supported by a lion. Outside the church, the slender seven-story bell tower is delightful, despite poor restoration. The gift shop sells miniatures of the Bocca della Verità and postcards.

Santa Sabina and Santa Prisca. V. Santa Sabina and V. Santa Prisca. Both churches, 6am–12:30pm and 3:30–7pm. Bus: 94, or walk up the Aventine hill from the Circus Maximus to Santa Sabina, and then along the street called Clivo dei Pubblici to Santa Prisca through the lovely Parco Savello.

These lovely early Christian churches on the Aventine Hill evoke a simple Christian worship. The Parco Savello, just before you reach the Santa Sabina, is a charming public garden filled with orange trees that looks out toward the dome of St. Peter's. Santa Sabina has the clean, beautiful lines of the early Christian basilica. It was built during the 5th century on the site of the house of martyred Saint Sabina, who had been converted by her Greek slave. The 24 fluted columns came from a temple, probably to Juno, that stood on the site. Restorations and alterations through the centuries have not diminished the impact of the church's simplicity. Twenty-four Corinthian columns, intricate mosaics, clerestory windows, and frescoes add to the splendor. The main door (go outside onto the porch) is a wonder, made in the 5th century out of cypress wood and decorated with biblical scenes and animals and flowers. The scene of the Crucifixion, behind glass, is one of the earliest in existence.

Saint Prisca, like Saint Sabina, was an early convert to Christianity. The church bearing her names was erected over the dwelling where she and her husband Aquila had "a church that meets in their house," according to St. Paul (I Corinthians:15) She was decapitated during the reign of the emperor Claudius.

At the church of Santa Prisca was discovered a richly decorated temple of Mithras (a pre-Christian cult), which you might see if you can find the sacristan. If you are disappointed here, go to San Clemente (above) to see a fascinating Mithraic temple. *Note:* This is a wealthy part of town, and there are thieves on the prowl to pick-pockets, so pay attention to your belongings.

Terme di Caracalla (Baths of Caracalla). V. d. Terme di Caracalla 52. ☎ **06/57-58-302.** Admission 8,000L ($5.25), children under 12 and EU citizens under 18 or over 60 free. Apr–Sept Tues–Sat 9am–6pm, Sun–Mon 9am–1pm; Oct–Mar Tues–Sat 9am–3pm, Sun–Mon 9am–1pm. Bus: 90 or 93.

You may have already seen these Roman baths on television during the first "Three Tenors"—Pavarotti, Carreras, and Domingo—concert. In its Roman heyday these enormous and attractive baths could accommodate up to 1,600 guests. They were begun in A.D. 212 by Emperor Caracalla, and opened in 221. Many of the statues of athletes now on display in the Vatican Museums, as well as the torso Belvedere, originally decorated the sumptuous baths, which were also places to read and enjoy art. They lasted for about 300 years, until the Goths destroyed them. Now opera is staged here in the summer, despite constant threats of closure because of damage to the structure. If it's open for summer opera, go. The setting is superb. For information about tickets, see "Rome After Dark."

AROUND CAMPO DE' FIORI & THE GHETTO

Campo de' Fiori. Follow V. d. Baullari from Cor. Vittorio Emanuele II. Market, Mon–Sat 7am–1:30pm. Bus: 64 from Termini to Museo di Roma, then walk.

Nestled between Corso Vittorio and the Tiber River, Campo de'Fiori is a wonderful jumble of umbrella-topped stalls bursting with flowers and vegetables, meats and cheeses, and even T-shirts, hosiery, and luggage. The market takes place each morning except Sunday, and neighbors fill shopping bags with all the very freshest treats of Lazio (Rome's region, similar to a U.S. state). Carciofi (artichokes), piselli (peas), peperoni, zucchine, funghi (mushrooms), pomodori (tomatoes), and a wealth of the greens Romans love—such as *puntarelle*, which has a sharp bite. Only seasonal foods are found here, nothing from greenhouses or freezers. Buy some bread at one of the bakeries on the square (in back of the flower mart) and choose a picnic here. The backdrop here is neighborhood Rome at its medieval and Renaissance best. The somber statue is that of Giordano Bruno, the philosopher who was burned here as a heretic in 1600. The streets that lead into the Campo are named for the artisans who had shops here: Baullari for trunk makers (bauli), Cappetelli for hat makers, Giubbonari for tailors and furriers, and Chiavari for key makers.

Church of Sant'Andrea della Valle. Cor. Vittorio at V. d. Chiavari. Mon–Sun 7:30am–noon and 4:30–7:30pm.

Opera lovers will feel immediately at home upon entering this church, for it is here that the first scene of *Tosca* takes place. The film version shot in Rome, designed by Franco Zefferelli, was actually filmed inside. It is a dramatic church, spatially, thanks in part to the design of Carlo Maderno, assisted by a very young Francesco Borromini, working on his first Roman project. One of Rome's largest churches, it was begun in 1591 but not finished and consecrated until 1650. The facade, which was added from 1656 to 1665, has been recently restored to show the harmony of its design by Carlo Rainaldi and Carlo Fontana. The one chord of disharmony is the solitary angel on the left, who has no angelic partner on the right. The story goes that Pope Alexander VII criticized the angel, so enraging the sculptor, Ercole Ferrata, that he left in anger. (Another source says the sculptor wanted more money than the pope deemed adequate.) In the apse are frescoes by Domenichino, telling the story of St. Andrea by Mattia Preti, depicting his crucifixion, martyrdom, and burial. One of the most impressive works in this richly decorated church is *The Glory of Paradise*, painted by Lanfranco (1625).

Area Sacra of Largo di Torre Argentina. At Cor. Vittorio Emanuele II.

Largo Argentina is best known as a major bus stop, but actually there are important ruins to be seen here by simply looking over a wall. Pompey's Theater and Curia (where Julius Caesar was assassinated) stood here in the 1st century B.C. Nero held dazzling water parties in the pool near the Baths of Agrippa. What we can see today are the ruins of four temples ranging from the 4th century B.C. to the 1st century A.D. Today the temple area is home to cats who enjoy frequent offerings from passersby.

Chiesa del Gesù. Cor. Vittorio at Pz. Gesù. ☎ **06/67-86-341.** Apr–Sept daily 6am–12:30pm and 4–7pm; off-season daily 6am–12:30pm and 4:30–7:15pm. Bus: 44, 46, 56, 60, 62, 64, 65, 70, 81, or 90.

St. Ignatius Loyola, founder of the Jesuit order, officially the Society of Jesus (Gesù), reposes amid gold and silver and colored marble within this elaborate church, which was built through the coffers of Cardinal Alessandro Farnese, and created by Jesuits, under the guidance of Vignola.

The facade by Giacomo della Porta, now being restored, was built from 1571 to 1577. The opulent baroque interior is covered with frescoes by Gaulli. On the vault of the nave, *The Triumph of the Name of Jesus* is a brilliant creation made to appear in the 7th-century's version of 3-D—you almost expect the damned to fall down on you. The saint's tomb is the work of Andrea Pozzo.

AROUND PIAZZA NAVONA & THE PANTHEON

Piazza Navona is a spectacular oblong surrounded by Renaissance palaces and churches. It's the place to have a cup of coffee and contemplate your good fortune at being in a city as beautiful as Rome. The piazza's form dates back to the 1st century A.D., when the emperor Domitian created a stadium to accommodate some 30,000 people. The fountain water is the Acqua Vergina, from an ancient spring. Of the three fountains, the central one, the **Fountain of the Rivers,** a work of Gian Lorenzo Bernini, is the prize. The noble Pamphilj family (Pope Innocent X was a Pamphilj) had hired Bernini's rival Borromini to design their palace and part of the church at the center of the west side of the piazza. The Pope Innocent wanted an Egyptian obelisk, like the one that lay in pieces on the Appian Way, to be re-created here, and a contest was held to choose the sculptor. When the pope saw Bernini's model he was ecstatic, and so the Fountain of the Rivers was built in 1651. The Nile, Danube, Plata, and Ganges are each represented with animals and vegetation of their location. Its "exuberant stagecraft," as Bernini historian Howard Hibbard calls it, rivals even the piazza.

The church behind it, **St. Agnese in Agone** (from which the word Navona comes), dates from 1123, when St. Agnes was martyred on this spot. The present church was begun in 1652 under Borromini's direction.

Every year from Christmastime until Epiphany (January 6), the piazza becomes an outdoor fair, with a crèche, tables selling ornaments and varied junk, and of course sweets. At other times it still seems festive, with artists displaying their works, families watching a child try out a tricycle, diners at the piazza restaurants, lovers entangled in baroque spirals, and ice-cream cones at almost every mouth.

San Luigi dei Francesi. Pz. San Luigi d. Francesi, at north end of V. d. Dogana Vecchia. ☎ **06/68-33-818.** Daily 8am–12:30pm and Fri–Wed 3:30–7:30. Bus: 70, 81, 97, or 186.

This French national church was built during the 16th century by Domenico Fontana. The frescoes by Domenichino (second chapel at right) of *The Life of Saint Cecilia* (1617) are done in an exquisite classical style. The far left side chapel contains three works of Caravaggio painted about 1597, when the artist had reached full maturity: *St. Matthew and the Angel; The Calling of St. Matthew,* and *The Martyrdom of St. Matthew. The Calling of St. Matthew* introduced a narrative form into Roman painting and in all these his dramatic use of light and shade has a strong impact. (Take 200L coins to turn on the lights.)

Sant'Agostino. Pz. Sant'Agostino, off V. d. Scrofa and north end of Pz. Navona. ☎ **06/68-80-19-62.** Free admission. Daily 7:45am–noon and 4:30 to 7:30pm. Bus: 81, 90, or 90B.

Expectant mothers come here to pray to the *Madonna del Parto* (Birth), and gifts to the Virgin are displayed around the painting, which Sansovino painted in 1521. The church was built during the 15th century and expanded later. Vanvitelli transformed the interior (1756–61). Caravaggio's *Madonna of Loreto,* in the first alter on the left

Attractions Near Campo de' Fiori & Piazza Navona

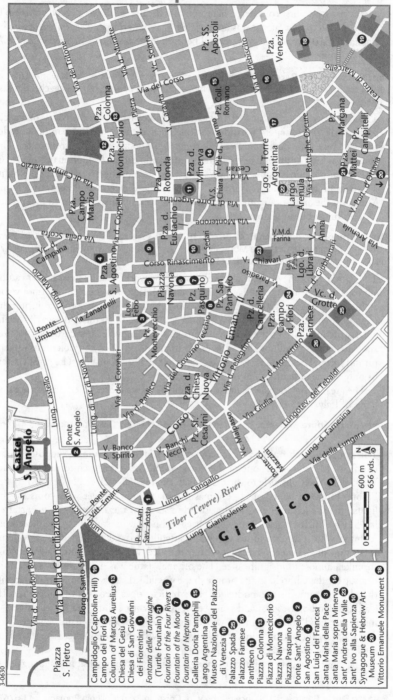

Campidoglio (Capitoline Hill) **19**
Campo dei Fiori **24**
Column of Marcus Aurelius **13**
Chiesa del Gesù **17**
Chiesa di San Giovanni
  dei Fiorentini **1**
Fontana delle Tartarughe
  (Turtle Fountain) **21**
Fountain of the Four Rivers **6**
Fountain of the Moor **7**
Fountain of Neptune **5**
Galleria Doria Pamphilj **15**
Largo Argentina **22**
Museo Nazionale del Palazzo
  di Venezia **16**
Palazzo Spada **25**
Palazzo Farnese **26**
Pantheon **11**
Piazza Colonna **13**
Piazza di Montecitorio **12**
Piazza Navona **6**
Piazza Pasquino **8**
Ponte Sant' Angelo **2**
San Agostino **9**
San Luigi dei Francesi **9**
Santa Maria della Pace **4**
Santa Maria sopra Minerva **14**
Sant' Andrea della Valle **23**
Sant' Ivo alla Sapienza **10**
Synagogue & Hebrew Art
  Museum **20**
Vittorio Emanuele Monument **18**

as you enter, was first considered inappropriate because of the scruffy look of the pilgrims to Loreto, but later it was appreciated as a masterpiece. *The Prophet Isaiah* by Raphael (1510) is another treasure, and beneath it is Sansovino's *Madonna and Child with St. Anne.*

Santa Maria della Pace. V. di Tor Millina, off northwest corner of Pz. Navona. Enter at Vc. d. Pace 5. ☎ **06/68-80-19-62.** Closed for restoration at present, but double-check in case it opens.

The harmony of the facade of this church makes its name, St. Mary of Peace, particularly appropriate. Pietro de Cortona created this masterful baroque facade, preceded by a semicircular porch that integrated the design with its surroundings. The church was built at the end of the 15th century and restored by Cortona about 1656. The treasure inside is Raphael's *Sibyls,* above the arch of the first chapel at the right. The adjoining Cesi Chapel is lovely, especially the Renaissance designs of Simone Mosca on the arch; Bramante designed the cloisters, his first work in Rome. Again, proportion and beauty are united.

The Pantheon. Pz. d. Rotonda. ☎ **06/68-30-02-30.** Free admission. July–Sept daily 9am–6pm (light permitting); Oct–June Mon–Sat 9am–4:30pm, Sun 9am–1pm. Bus 64, 170, or 175 to Lgo. Argentina, then walk up V. d. Cestari.

The Pantheon is one of the finest buildings in the world, and its sheer power can be admired in every light, from dawn to moonlight. Inside, it's a marvel of harmony and architectural ingenuity. The original building, built by Marcus Agrippa during the reign of Augustus Caesar (around 27 B.C.) as a temple to all the gods, was a rectangular structure. All but the front columns and portico were later destroyed by fire, and when it was rebuilt by the emperor Hadrian (A.D. 118–25), it took on its present rotund form. The dome's 142-feet diameter is equal to its height. The open center, its only source of light, is almost 30 feet across.

The great artists Raphael Sanzio and Annibale Carracci are buried here, as are two kings of Italy.

Santa Maria Sopra Minerva. Pz. Minerva. ☎ **06/67-93-926.** Daily 7am–noon and 4–7pm. Bus: 119.

This church is a chronology of Italian art. Built on ancient ruins—supposedly of a temple to Minerva—it is one of the rare examples of gothic architecture in Rome. Walk along the right aisle to the Cappella Carafa (1488–92), richly frescoed by Fra Filippo Lippi, in honor of St. Thomas Aquinas. (Don't forget your coins for the lights.) To the left of the main altar stands a statue of the *Resurrected Christ* started in 1521 by Michelangelo (it may have been finished by his students). The Florentine sculptor, who according to his notebooks attended mass daily, dared to carve Jesus at the time of Resurrection as a powerfully muscled, very human figure—with a cross shrunken almost to insignificance. The original statue was nude, which was far too realistic for the Church, so the bronze drape was added. A pantheon in its own right, the church contains the bodies of the Medici Popes Leo X and Clement VII, Cardinal Bembo, the great and saintly early-Renaissance painter Fra Angelico, and—minus her head and one finger, which are in her hometown—Saint Catherine of Siena, one of the patron saints of Italy (you can visit the rooms where she stayed, to the left of the main altar).

The whimsical baby elephant carrying a small Egyptian obelisk in the piazza outside the church was designed by Bernini.

Palazzo Doria Pamphilj. Entrance off the V. d. Corso, in Pz. d. Collegio Romano. ☎ **06/67-94-365.** Fri–Tues 10am–1pm. Admission 10,000L ($6.60), 5,000L ($3.30) for apartment tour.

The Principessa Doria, last of the line, still lives in the 17th-century family palace, a rarity in these hard times for the nobility. Bramante designed part of the gracious courtyard. The art gallery is one of the finest private collections, and highlights Caravaggio's *Rest on the Flight into Egypt* and Valesquez's *Portrait of Innocent X*. Among the celebrated artists represented are Tintoretto, Titian, Brueghel, Paris Bourdon, Parmigiano, and Veronese. In the apartments, which provide a rare view of Renaissance life in Rome, you'll find, in the Salone Verde, an *Annunciation* by Fra Filippo Lippi.

NEAR THE SPANISH STEPS & PIAZZA DEL POPOLO

Fontana di Trevi (Trevi Fountain). Pz. d. Trevi. Metro: Pz. Barberini.

This dazzling fountain owes much of its superstar celebrity to the film *Three Coins in the Fountain,* although its recently cleaned charms shouldn't need Hollywood as press agent. H.V. Morton, who combines awe and amused affection in his *A Traveller in Rome,* says "The idea of transporting a rocky landscape gushing with waterfalls, with Neptune and his steeds in violent action, upon the sedate and formal façade of a Renaissance palace is itself such a startling improbability that one stands amazed. It is the singular charm of Rome that, turning a corner, one comes suddenly face to face with something beautiful and unexpected that was placed there centuries ago, apparently in the most casual fashion." The Trevi's water comes from the Acqua Vergine, the aqueduct built by Agrioppa in 19 B.C., and reopened after many clogged centuries in 1453. Nicola Salvi worked on an idea for the fountain, based on Bernini's use of water with sculpture, from 1732 to 1751. It was finished after his death in 1762. Turning your back to the fountain and tossing in a coin guarantees your return to Rome, it's said. It's worked for many of us year after year. Go in early morning and late at night to see the two moods of the fountain and because tourist crowds can be oppressive during the day.

Piazza Colonna. Along the V. d. Corso.

The column that gives its name to the piazza is the splendidly restored column of Marcus Aurelius, with a scroll of his victories reaching to the top (83 feet tall). The emperor is depicted as victorious, but with fatigue and age showing. St. Paul looks out over the piazza from the top. This part of Rome, a section of the ancient Campo Marzio, or Field of Mars, is the governmental center of the city. The Palazzo Chigi that flanks the north side is now the seat of the prime minister. The Chamber of Deputies meet in the adjoining piazza, Montecitorio, where police and press are ubiquitous if the council is meeting.

Spanish Steps (Piazza di Spagna).

The Piazza di Spagna and the Spanish Steps are best appreciated on a spring morning before the crowds fill the stairs. It is then that you can enjoy the steps' graceful curve, in three tiers that represent the Trinity, leading to the Church of Trinita dei Monti, built by the kings of France, at the top. Walk up the Via Condotti from the Via del Corso for the maximum visual effect. From the church's balustrade, the view over Rome to St. Peter's is a delight. In spring and summer the steps are pink and red with tubs of azaleas, which have endured the winter patiently in the hothouses of the Villa Cielimontana. The piazza gets its name from the Spanish Embassy on the other side of the piazza. During the 19th century, artists' models lined up on the steps awaiting an artist to hire them. The house/museum on the south side of the square was the home of John Keats and where he died. The horizontal fountain at the foot of the steps was cleverly designed by the elder Bernini to obscure the low water pressure. The piazza was the center of "foreigners' Rome," and people of note

The Lure of Rome

Rome was an enchantment to English writers, painters, and poets of the 19th century. Lord Byron's *Childe Harold's Pilgrimage* was one of the first poems to wax romantic about the Colosseum: But when the rising moon begins to climb / Its topmost arch, and gently pauses there. / Heroes have trod this spot—'tis on their dust ye tread. Nathaniel Hawthorne's *Marble Faun* was equally seductive.

Byron's friend John Keats lived and died next to the Spanish Steps. His house is open to visitors and poignant memories fill the rooms of the tragic young poet (Pz. di Spagna 26, ☎ 06/67-84-235. Admission 5,000L/$3.25). Tiny volumes of his verse are sold here. Keats is buried in the Protestant Cemetery near Testaccio (V. Caio Cestio 6, ☎ 06/57-41-900), where the epitaph he composed for himself reads, inappropriately as it turned out, "Here lies one whose name was writ on water."

On the other side of the Spanish Steps, Babbington's Tea Rooms (☎ 06/67-86-027) offer tea and crumpets at prices that would start a new Boston Tea Party. But it's a genteel place in which to relax, and you can stay at your table long enough to write an ode.

from Hans Christian Andersen and Byron to Stendahl and Wagner lived in the area and frequented the Caffe Greco at V. Condotti 86, which looks almost as it did at its opening in 1760.

Via Condotti and much of this area comprise Rome's chic quarter, where the Armani and Fendi boutiques keep a well-groomed eye on Krizia and Valentino, and the click of gold credit cards is heard at jewelers like Bulgari and shoeshops like Ferragamo and Bottega Veneta.

Mausoleum of Augustus. V. Ripetta and V. Ara Pacis. Bus: 81, 90, or 90B.

This vast mound does not seem a fitting memorial to this most august of emperors, but it once was flanked with cypress trees (Italian cemetery tree) and a statue of the emperor. The interior, where the urns were kept, is scheduled for opening this year to the public. Check when you visit the Ara Pacis.

Ara Pacis Augustae (Altar of Peace). V. Ripetta and V. Ara Pacis. ☎ **06/71-92-071.** Admission 4,000L ($2.65). Apr–Sept Tues, Wed, and Fri–Sun 9am–1:30pm, Tues and Sat 4–7pm; Oct–Mar Tues, Wed, and Fri–Sun 9am–1:30pm. Bus: 81, 90, or 90B.

This stunningly beautiful monument was completed in 9 B.C. to commemorate the peace that reigned in the empire under Emperor Augustus. It was reassembled from fragments discovered during the 16th century, and its original site on the Via del Corso was excavated after 1938. The Altar of Peace consists of a marble screen surrounding an altar raised on a dais of steps. The side of the screen facing the mausoleum is brilliantly decorated with figures of Augustus and his family depicted in graceful procession. Note the classical elements of acanthus leaves and swans with outstretched wings. The scenes on the west (river) side of the screen of Aeneas sacrificing the white sow (right panel) and on the east side of Tellus the Earth Goddess are superb.

Piazza del Popolo. Metro: Flaminio; Bus: 90, 90B, 95, 490, 495, and 926 (or trams 119 and 225) to Pzle. Flaminio, then through city gate.

Through the ages, everyone knew that all roads led to Rome, and this northern gate was where those who had made it somehow over the Alps to the Eternal City finally

Attractions Near The Spanish Steps & Piazza del Popolo

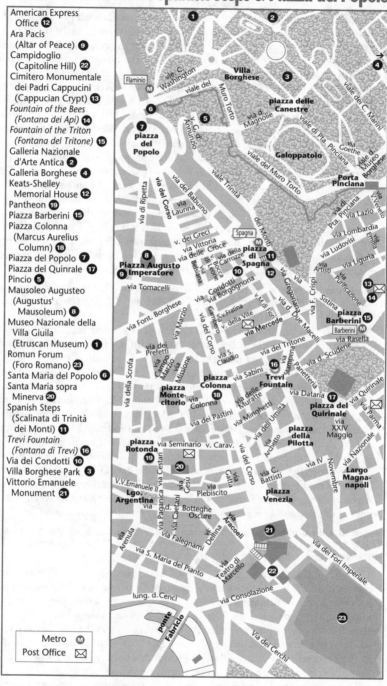

Metro Ⓜ
Post Office ✉

3-0632

133

entered the majestic gate. It was once called the Porta Flaminia, for the road that ended at the gate. Today the piazza is a place to stroll—thanks to the recent pedestrian zone established on part of the piazza, although the ever-present Vespas make sure it stays noisy—and a place to enjoy a coffee at Dal Bolognese, a prime place for celebrity-spotting. If you go early in the day you'll have an exceptional view of the proportions of the piazza from the Porta, the first view travelers often had of Rome. At the center of the piazza is an Egyptian obelisk, the second oldest in Rome (the first is at St. John Lateran), dating from the middle of the 14th century B.C. The twin churches you'll see opposite the Porta are Santa Maria de Montesanto (April through June Monday to Friday 5 to 8pm; November through March 4 to 7pm) and Santa Maria dei Miracoli (Monday to Saturday 6am to 1pm and 5 to 7:30pm, Sunday 8am to 1pm and 5 to 7:30pm). Bernini and Carlo Fontana were the architects of the former, which opened in 1679. The latter, also a work of Fontana and of Carlo Rainaldi, opened two years later; its name is linked to a miracle performed by the Madonna in saving a baby thought drowned in the Tiber nearby. An earlier miracle had influenced the design of this piazza. Legend has it that Pope Pasquale II dreamed (in 1099) that the Madonna wanted him to erect a church here, to ward off the pagan spirits around Augustus's Mausoleum (Augustus was considered an emperor god). Santa Maria del Popolo (of the people) (below) was the result.

Santa Maria del Popolo. Pz. del Popolo. ☎ **06/36-11-04-87.** Daily 7am–12:30pm and 4–7:30pm. Metro: Flaminio; Bus: 90, 90B, 95, 490, 495, and 926 (or trams 119 and 225) to Pzle. Flaminio, then through city gate.

Work began on the present church as Columbus was setting sail for the Indies in 1492. Some years later both Bramante and Bernini put their expert hands to the project. The first chapel on the right is marked with the coat of arms of the Della Rovere family—an oak tree with initials S.D. for Soli Deo (only God)—and decorated with frescoes of the life of Saint Gerolamo by Pinturicchio. The tombs of Cardinale Cristoforo Della Rovere (1507) and Cardinal Ascanio Sforza (1505), masterpieces of Sansovino, are at the left. In the left transept an altarpiece by Annibale Carracci of the Assumption (1601) leads the way to two famous and stirring paintings by Caravaggio, *The Conversion of Saint Paul* and *The Crucifixion of Saint Peter* (1601–2). The dramatic light, the strong diagonals, and the extreme realism of these paintings keep this chapel filled with admirers (who have 200L pieces for the light).

Also on the left, the Chigi Chapel was designed by Raphael for the wealthy banker Aagostino Chigi (pronounced *Kee*–Gee). Bernini's *Habbakuk and the Angel* is at the right of the altar and Lorenzetti's *Jonah Emerging from the Whale* is at the left.

Museo di Villa Giulia (Etruscan Museum). Pzle. di Villa Giulia 9 (off Vle. d. Belle Arti). ☎ **06/32-01-951.** Admission 8,000L ($5.25). Tues–Sat 9am–7:30pm, Sun 9am–1pm. Bus: 910. Metro: Flaminio, then a 30-minute walk or take bus 48.

This fine museum happens to be in a lovely villa at one end of the Villa Borghese, Rome's main urban park. Some of the finest Etruscan statues in Italy are here, and it's a wonderful opportunity to touch the lives of these mysterious people who lived in central Italy since before the Romans arrived. Although no one knows where they came from originally (they arrived in Italy sometime around the 10th century B.C.), scholars agree that they brought with them a highly developed culture, as evidenced by their exceptionally advanced art and sculpture. They're believed to have ruled Rome itself for a century or more beginning in the 7th century B.C.

The museum, packed with archeological treasures, offers a window into their still poorly understood civilization, mostly in the form of pottery (downstairs), through there's also a fine collection of bronze implements (upstairs), plus several outstanding larger sculpted pieces. The highlights of the first floor include the two figures of Apollo in Room 7, and the *Sarcofago degli Sposi* in Room 9, a remarkably well preserved sarcophagus with a half-reclining married couple on top. The naturalness of Etruscan sculpture and their facial expressions make it one of the most accessible of art forms. Among the most impressive pieces upstairs is a 2-foot-tall bronze figure in Room 15, *Veiovis di Monterazzano* from the 1st century A.D., found near Viterbo in 1955, and an Etruscan chariot in Room 18.

Galleria Borghese. Pz. Scipione Borghese ☎ **06/85-48-577.** Admission 4,000L ($2.50). Tues–Sat 9am–7pm, Sun 9am–1pm. Bus: 910 (from Termini) or 56 (from Pz. Venezia), to the park entrance closest to the museum. To get here from the Villa Giulia, walk around behind the museum along V. d. Belle Arti, past the Modern Art Museum on your left, and straight into the heart of the park on V. d. Villa Giulia; when you get to the top of the hill, you'll see a path branching off to the left and sign directing you to the Galleria Borghese. The building is being restored and may look closed, but look for the "Entrata" in the scaffolding.

At the opposite end of the Villa Borghese park from the Etruscan Museum is the Galleria Borghese, with an excellent collection of both paintings and sculpture. The first floor is home to Bernini's moving *Rape of Persephone,* as well as his *Apollo and Daphne* and his *David,* the face of which is thought by many to be a self-portrait. Compare Bernini's baroque *David* with Michelangelo's earlier, and much more famous, Renaissance one in Florence: Michelangelo chose to capture David in the moment of contemplation, feeling the weight of the task (slaying Goliath) he was about to attempt; Bernini shows David in the moment of action, fierce determination scowling his face as his whole body twists and swings his arm to release the deadly stone. The sculpture of Daphne again shows Bernini's genius for capturing a precise moment of action as we see Daphne, fleeing from the lustful Apollo, beginning to sprout leaves as she turns into a tree (in Greek myth this was a perfectly respectable and not terribly tragic way at all to escape from the unwelcome advances of a god). Canova's erotic, half-nude sculpture of Princess Pauline Borghese (Napoléon Bonaparte's sister) was a scandal in its time.

The picture collection, which was once displayed on the second floor (it has languished under a protracted restoration for several years now), is at present housed across the river in Trastevere in the former monastery of San Michele at V. d. San Michele a Ripa 22 (☎ **06/58-16-732).** Make sure you hang onto your ticket so you can get in for free when you visit that part of the city. Among the notable works there are Raphael's *Descent from the Cross,* three Caravaggios, and paintings by Titian, Botticelli, Del Sarto, and Rubens, and Bernini's painted self-portrait.

AROUND VIA VENETO & PIAZZA BARBERINI

Via Veneto. Metro: Barberini.

The shady, curvaceous Via Veneto, once the haunt of movie stars, gossip columnists, paparazzi, pimps, prostitutes, and transvestites, now sees only the last four groups. Movie stars do indeed emerge from the Excelsior Hotel near the top of the Via Veneto, but they are swirled away in limos to more congenial surroundings. Signs of new life, however, have been appearing, and soon a new glamour may take over. Sidewalk cafes such as the world-famous Caffè de Paris, across from the Excelsior, will happily welcome the change.

Piazza Barberini. Metro: Barberini.

The Barberini bees (the symbol on that noble family's coat of arms) buzz all over Rome, but, at the corner of the Via Veneto, they have their own fountain, designed by Bernini and called the Fontana delle Api (of the Bees). Bernini's talent, however, is used much more emphatically in the center of the piazza, where his wonderful Triton, or Neptune, exults in being a Roman fountain. Art historian Howard Hibbard in his book on Bernini sums up my own feeling: "There are other distinguished fountains in Rome, but for anyone who has stood in the Piazza Barberini and watched the virile sea god blow the glistening stream high from his wreathed horn, Bernini's Triton will always be *the* fountain." Four dolphins hold up a massive conch shell with their tails (which are entwined with the bees coat of arms of the Barberini Pope Urban VIII), and from the shell the sea god emerges. Bernini paid careful attention to the water here, and the jet rising high in the air, splashing down over Neptune's muscular back to the pool below makes the fountain, in Hibbard's estimation, "one of the most sublime creations in all art."

Cimitero Monumentale dei Padri Cappucini. V. Veneto 27. Admission 2,000L ($1.30). Summer daily 9am–noon and 3–6:30pm; winter daily 9am–noon and 3–6pm. Metro: Barberini (walk up the right side of V. Veneto and take the right-hand stairs of the Chiesa Immacolata Concezione to the first landing).

This is perhaps the most unusual sight in the city: Every inch of the crypt's walls and ceilings is adorned with mosaics of sorts made from the skeletal remains of 4,000 Capuchin friars who died between 1528 and 1870. It's of no special religious significance; their sign of explanation reads simply that these bones "speak eloquently to the visitors about the drama of a life which is passing" and urges prayer and meditation." This is a grisly, haunting, unapologetically weird, and thus rather popular attraction.

Palazzo Barberini: Galleria Nazionale di Arte Antica. V. d. Quattro Fontane 13 (off Pz. Barberini) ☎ **06/48-14-430.** Admission to galleries and apartment 6,000L ($3.95). Tues–Sat 9am–7pm; Sun 9am–12:30pm.

The facade of the Palazzo is being restored, but the painting collection, which extends from the 12th to the 18th century, is on view, including Raphael's *La Fornarina*. Mystery has always surrounded this painting. Is she really the mistress/baker's daughter Raphael adored? He seems to have been enchanted with her, in any case. Filippo Lippi's *Madonna and Child* enjoys a loftier plane. Two Caravaggios are excellent: *Judith Beheading Holofernes* and *Narcissus* about to metamorphose with the stress of vanity. In the grand salon, newly reopened, Pietro da Cortona's *Triumph of Divine Providence* shows Divine Providence receiving a starry crown from Immortality. Those garlands of bees soaring to immortality are of course from the Barberini hive. The Corsini Museum in Trastevere (see below) also is called the Galleria Nazionale di Arte Antica, for some odd reason.

Quattro Fontane. V. Quattro Fontane at V. d. Quirinale. Metro: Barberini.

From this crossroads you'll have a good view of the obelisk and marble horses of the presidential residence, the Quirinale Palace (not open to the public). The figures in the fountains, one on each corner, represent the rivers Tiber and Aniene plus Fidelity and Strength.

Santa Maria della Vittoria. V. XX (Venti) Settembre 17 ☎ **06/48-26-190.** Daily 7am–noon and 4:30–6:30pm. Dress code enforced here: no bare legs, arms, back. Metro: Repubblica.

Quiet and cool on the hottest days of summer, this dimly lit church houses Bernini's *Ecstasy of St. Teresa* (1652), in which the mystical Spanish saint is seen in a state of divine bliss as her heart is pierced with love for Christ. Bernini often said it was the best thing he had ever done. Heavenly light seems to flood the chapel around the figures. Cardinals of the Cornaro family are seen talking and gesturing at either side in

Attractions Near Termini & Via Veneto

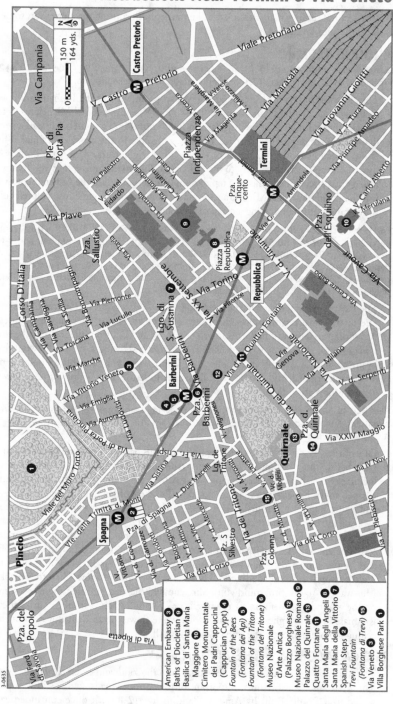

American Embassy 3
Baths of Diocletian 9
Basilica di Santa Maria
Maggiore 10
Cimitero Monumentale
dei Padri Cappucini
(Cappucian Crypt) 4
Fountain of the Bees
(Fontana dei Api) 5
Fountain of the Triton
(Fontana del Tritone) 6
Museo Nazionale
d'Arte Antica
(Palazzo Borghese) 12
Museo Nazionale Romano 9
Palazzo del Quirinale 13
Quattro Fontane 11
Santa Maria degli Angeli 8
Santa Maria della Vittorio 7
Spanish Steps 2
Trevi Fountain
(Fontana di Trevi) 15
Via Veneto 3
Villa Borghese Park 1

137

architectural settings that stretch back like transepts. Surprising the viewer was something Bernini loved.

AROUND TERMINI

Santa Maria degli Angeli (Saint Mary of the Angels). V. Cernaia 9. ☎ **06/48-80-812.** Free admission. Daily 7:30am–12:30pm and 4–6:30pm. Metro: Repubblica.

The church is more valuable as an idea of the scope and luxury of a Roman bath than as an example of church architecture. Pope Pius IV commissioned Michelangelo to convert the central hall of the frigidarium (cold room) into a church. He had a very light hand here, and left the space as near as possible to the classical original. The church occupies only about half of the original frigidarium. The main door was moved during the 18th century to the calidarium (hot room). From here you'll move into a great circular hall, once the tepidarium (warm room) into the vast transept that was the frigidarium and Michelangelo's nave. Eight of the original rose-colored columns can be seen supporting a classical entablature.

Museo Nazionale Romano delle Terme (National Roman Museum). Pz. della Repubblica. ☎ **06/48-80-530.** Admission 12,000L ($7.90); EU citizens over 60 or under 18 free. Tues–Sat 9am–1:30pm, Sun 9am–12:30pm. During July also 5–7pm. Metro: Pz. d. Repubblica. (At present some of the sculpture from the Baths of Diocletian and other imperial baths is exhibited on V. Romita between V. Parigi and V. Cernaia, near the Church of Santa Maria degli Angeli. Free admission. Daily 10:30am–1pm and 3–6pm.)

The most important object in the collection is the Ludovisi throne (5th century B.C.), one of the most beautiful Greek originals found in Rome. The radiant goddess Aphrodite stretches out her arms to attendants as she rises from the foam of the sea. Look also for the *Discobolus* and *Daughter of Niobe,* showing a girl fatally wounded by arrows shot by Artemis and Apollo. The *Venus of Cyrene* is probably a Roman copy of a Greek original, and the *Boxer* is the work of Nestor, who sculpted the *Belvedere Torso* in the Vatican Museums.

Basilica di Santa Maria Maggiore. Pz. Santa Maria Maggiore. ☎ **06/48-31-95.** Free admission. Summer, daily 7am–8pm; winter, daily 7am–7pm. Metro: Termini. From Termini, it's a short walk down V. Cavour.

One of the seven pilgrimage churches in Rome, this basilica houses relics of the Holy Crib below the altar and a 5th-century triumphal arch above. Its other features include two richly decorated chapels just before the altar—the right one (Sistine Chapel) in the Renaissance style, the left one (Borghese or Pauline Chapel) baroque—and a stunning 13th-century mosaic in the apse. The coffered ceiling was decorated by Giuliano da Sangallo with what is said to be the first gold brought back from the Americas by Columbus (a gift from the Spanish king Ferdinand to Pope Alexander VI). The church's legendary origin lies in a joint dream of Pope Liberius (352–66) and a rich Roman patrician named John, in which the Virgin Mary told them to build a church on the Esquiline Hill where they would find snow when they awoke (this was on August 5th, mind you). Sure enough, the next morning there was snow on the ground neatly outlining the basilica to be built. Each year on August 5 there is a mass in the Borghese chapel in which white flower petals drift down from the ceiling to commemorate the miraculous snowfall.

THE CATACOMBS & THE APPIAN WAY

The Appian Way, which approaches Rome from the south and enters the city at Porta San Sebastiano, was the most important of the consular roads, and is still well preserved near Rome. Built by Appius Claudius in 312 B.C., it once continued east through Italy to Brindisi in Puglia, the gateway to Greece and the Mediterranean. It was once lined with the tombs of Rome's rich and famous, who saw no reason to let death put an end to their luxury. It is famous today for the catacombs, miles of underground tombs for Rome's less fortunate. Cemeteries were required by law to be outside the city living areas, and so the dead were buried on the roads that led to the city, in layers cut in the soft tufa stone. All burial places were protected by law, and so the catacombs were free from thieves. An elaborate series of galleries, rooms, and corridors developed, occupying hundred of miles around the city's perimeter. Some of the martyred saints were buried there, and the bones of St. Peter and St. Paul were kept there for protection (see below). Many were decorated with frescoes, and early Christian symbols such as the fish can be seen. Eucharistic celebrations were held at the tombs of martyrs during the 4th century. They were never places where Christians lived. The catacombs were no longer used after the Goth invasions of the 5th century.

Catacombs of St. Sebastian (Catacombe di San Sebastiano). V. Appia Antica 136 ☎ **06/78-87-035.** Admission 8,000L ($5.25), under 10 free. Wed–Mon 8am–noon and 2:30–5:30pm. Bus: 118 from San Giovanni Laterano..

During the 4th century the bones of St. Peter and St. Paul were brought here for safe-keeping, and 8th-century Christian frescoes can be seen. In the crypt of St. Sebastian is a bust of the saint by Bernini.

Catacombs of St. Callixtus (Catacombe di San Callisto). V. Appia Antica 110 ☎ **06/51-36-725.** Admission 8,000L ($5.25). Thurs–Tues 8am–noon and 2:30–5pm. Bus: 118 from San Giovanni Laterano.

The Catacombs of San Callixtus extend over several miles of galleries on four levels. During the 3rd century, Pope Calixtus (who had been in charge of them before becoming pope) extended them, making them the official burying place for the popes. St. Damasus (A.D. 336–84) had the Papal Crypt built to honor the martyred popes buried there. (Bones of saints and martyrs were long removed to church reliquaries.) St. Cecilia was buried in the adjoining crypt, before being removed to her church in Trastevere. Some of the earliest frescoes (2nd century) are of the fish, symbol of the Eucharist.

TESTACCIO & SOUTH

Pyramid of Caius Cestius. V. Ostiense at Porta San Paolo. Metro: Piramide. Bus: 30.

Gaius Cestius was a Roman tribune who was responsible for sacred banquets. This pyramid, his tomb, was built at the end of the 1st century B.C., in less than 330 days, according to Cestius's will.

Protestant Cemetery. V. Caio Cestio. Donations accepted. Apr–Sept 9am–6pm, Oct–Mar 9am–5pm. Closed Mondays. Metro: Porta San Paola. Bus: 13, 27, 30b, 57, or 318. Ring bell for admission at number 6.

The lure of Rome for foreigners, especially English, is evident in this little cemetery where John Keats is buried, with the epitaph "here lies one whose name was writ on water." Keats's friend, the painter Joseph Severn, Goethe's son, and the ashes of Percy Bysshe Shelley, are also in residence in this peaceful garden.

San Paulo Fuori le Mura (St. Paul Outside the Walls). V. Ostiense 186. ☎ **06/54-10-341.** Daily 7am–6:30pm. Metro: San Paolo.

On July 15, 1823, a brazier fire left by a workman almost entirely destroyed this church, after its having survived earthquakes and sacking by the Saracens. The entire world contributed to its rebuilding. Alabaster columns came from Egypt, Czar Nicholas I of Russia sent malachite and lapis lazuli, and 30 years later the new St. Paul's "Outside the Walls" was born. The original church, almost faithfully reproduced here but without the mystery of other ancient churches, had been founded by Constantine on the site of St. Paul's martyrdom. Pilgrims came by the thousands. The splendid gothic marble canopy is signed by the sculptor Arnolfo di Cambio (1285). At the right of the altar, the Pascal (Easter) candlestick is a splendid oddity with animals at the base. Some of the mosaics in the apse were preserved from the original church. Looking down the nave at 80 tall granite columns, reflected in the marble floor, one has more than a hint of its former majesty. The Benedictine cloisters glitter with twisted columns of green, red, and gold mosaics.

TRASTEVERE

Piazza Santa Maria in Trastevere. Bus: 26, 44, 56, 60, 75, 170, 280 to Pz. Sonnino (walk down V. Lungaretta to the piazza), or 23 or 65 to Pz. Trilussa (walk down Vc. d. Cinque).

This piazza is really the center of Trastevere life. Kids play soccer against one wall, Italian youth and American expatriates strum guitars and chatter sitting around the fountain, neighborhood women stop to exchange the latest *pettegolezzo* (gossip), and tourists sit at expensive outdoor cafe tables and sip cappuccino.

The fountain at the center was recycled from an ancient Roman basin by Fontana. The facade of the church of Santa Maria is one of the gems of Rome, especially because of its mosaics, which sparkle in the sunlight and glow from floodlights after dark.

Basilica of Santa Maria in Trastevere. Pz. Santa Maria. ☎ **06/58-14-802.** Daily 7:30am–12:30pm and 4–7pm. Bus: 56, 60, 75, 170, or 710 to Vle. Trastevere.

This ancient church (founded A.D. 38), the first devoted to the Virgin Mary, is enchanting at all hours of the day, and at night the gold of the frescoes on the facade sparkles in the light of the piazza. Pope Julius I, in the 4th century, had it restructured as a basilica, and remodeling has occurred in subsequent centuries. The 12th-century facade, rebuilt by Pope Innocent II, whose family was from Trastevere, glistens with the 13th-century mosaic of the Virgin Enthroned. The portico, with older reliefs and sarcophagi, is an 18th-century work of Fontana. The nave inside is graced with 22 massive columns of granite. The rich gilded ceiling was decorated by Domenichino in 1617, who painted the picture of the Assumption in the center. In the semi-dome, the 12th-century Madonna, seated on the throne with Christ, is the earliest known depiction of that scene and is remarkable for the majestic portrayal of Christ's face and the ethereal beauty of the Virgin. The prophets hold caged birds, symbolizing Christ as prisoner for the sufferings of the world.

Below these mosaics is a series of panels by Pietro Cavallini.

Santa Cecilia in Trastevere. Pz. Santa Cecilia ☎ **06/58-99-289.** Admission to frescoes free, but donation expected; admission to excavations below church 12,000L ($7.90). Main church daily 10am–noon and 4–6pm; Cavellini frescoes Tues and Fri 10–11am. Bus: 56, 60, 75 to Pz. Sonnino, or 710 to Vle. Trastevere.

As you near the church you'll find yourself in a true old Roman neighborhood, which gentrification has made a rarity. The church was built over the house of the saint and her husband Saint Valerian, which had been preserved since her martyrdom under Marcus Aurelius (3rd century).

The lovely garden and church that we see today was rebuilt by Pope Paschal I in the 9th century; the bell tower was added during the 12th century. Inside, the ciborium on the main altar is a fine work by Arnolfo di Cambio (1293), but it is the celebrated statue of the saint by Stefano Maderno (1600) that is engrossing. According to tradition, when her tomb was opened in 1599, she was found in this position, with the sword marks on her neck clearly visible.

Attractions in Trastevere

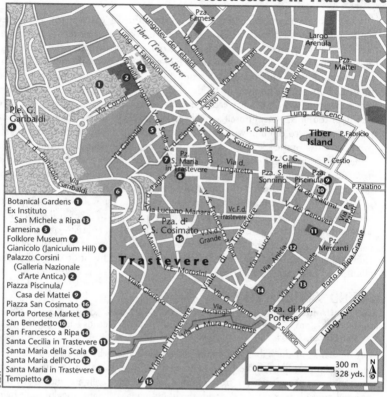

Botanical Gardens ❶
Ex Instituto
  San Michele a Ripa ❸
Farnesina ❸
Folklore Museum ❼
Gianicolo (Janiculum Hill) ❹
Palazzo Corsini
  (Galleria Nazionale
  d'Arte Antica) ❷
Piazza Piscinula/
  Casa dei Mattei ❾
Piazza San Cosimato ⓰
Porta Portese Market ⓯
San Benedetto ⓾
San Francesco a Ripa ⓮
Santa Cecilia in Trastevere ⑪
Santa Maria della Scala ❺
Santa Maria dell'Orto ⑫
Santa Maria in Trastevere ❽
Tempietto ❻

The church also contains a difficult-to-visit fresco by Cavallini in its inner sanctums, and for a small fee you can descend under the church to inspect the ruins of some Roman houses as well as peer through a gate at the highly stuccoed grotto underneath the altar.

Palazzo Corsini (Museo Nazionale dell'Arte Antica). V. d. Lungara 10. ☎ **06/68-80-23-23.** Admission 8,000L ($5.25). Tues–Fri 9am–7pm, Sat–Sun 9am–pm. Bus: 23, 41, 65, 280.

Before Cardinal Corsini took up residence here in the structure completely rebuilt by Fuga in 1736, the palace belonged to the Riario family, who played host to Michelangelo, Bramante, Erasmus, and Queen Cristina of Sweden. Among its treasures are works by Van Dyck and Rubens, one of Caravaggio's paintings of *Saint John the Baptist,* and Poussin's *Triumph of Ovid.*

Villa Farnesina. V. d. Lungara 230. ☎ **06/65-40-565.** Free admission. Mon–Sat 9am–1pm. Bus: 23, 65, 280 to La Farnesina.

This magical Renaissance palace (1508–11) was built by Baldassare Peruzzi for banking mogul Agostino Chigi. It was here that Chigi threw his lavish parties and displayed the opulent wealth that being the papacy's personal financier gained him. At one such party, the guests were served their meal on elaborate gold and silver plates, which were then tossed out of the windows into the nearby Tiber after each course (successful bankers, however, don't become rich through such folly—Chigi had underwater nets stretched across the river and after dinner the servants fished out the costly dinnerware).

Chigi commissioned some of the finer artists of the day (particularly fellow Siena natives) to decorate his palace. One of the few non-Sienese painters to be called in was Raphael, who drew up the cartoons for a ceiling cycle depicting the Greek myth of Cupid and Psyche. (He left the actual job of painting most of them to his students, the master himself being otherwise occupied with the daughter of the baker, the famous La Fornarina, who lived down the street at V. d. Santa Dorotea 20.) The current restoration project of the frescoes may be over by the time you visit. In another first-floor room, Raphael himself actually picked up his brushes to paint the *Galatea,* riding a pug-nosed dolphin with three mischievous cupids aiming their arrows from overhead. Most of the rest of the frescoes in this room were painted by Michelangelo's student, Sebastiano del Piombo, with the exception of Chigi's personal horoscope that decorates the ceiling and the huge charcoal head sketched in one of the lunettes, both of which are now attributed to Peruzzi, the palace's architect.

Upstairs you'll find more Peruzzi frescoes, this time the walls of a salon painted with more mythological stories and several quite masterful trompe l'oeil scenes of the surrounding neighborhoods—as they looked in the 1510s, at least—and a bedroom painted with *The Marriage of Alexander the Great and Roxanne* by Il Sodoma, who enlisted painted chubby cherubs to help the emperor and his bride ease out of their clothes and into their nuptial bed.

AROUND VATICAN CITY

Castel Sant'Angelo. Lungotevere Castello. ☎ **06/68-75-036.** Admission 8,000L ($5.25). Mon–Sat 9am–2pm, Sun 9am–noon. Closed 2nd and 4th Wed of each month. Metro: Ottaviano. Bus 23, 34, 64, 280.

On the banks of the Tiber and connected to the Vatican by a wall that includes a secret escape tunnel for the pope (as a medieval and Renaissance city-state, the Vatican was as prone to attack from political enemies and foreign armies as any other regional power was at the time) stands the imposing Castel Sant'Angelo. Built by the emperor Hadrian in A.D. 139 as his mausoleum, it has subsequently served many purposes, as a fortress, a prison (artist and famed autobiographer Benvenuto Cellini languished in its dungeons, as did the notorious Cenci family), and, most notably, a papal refuge. Highlights of the fortress include the weapons and uniform exhibits, the Pauline Hall, the Perseus Room, and the Library. Its look of storybook drama will enthrall travelers of all ages. At the top you'll find panoramic views of Rome and an impressive statue of St. Michael the Archangel. It was from here that the character Tosca hurls to her death at the end of Puccini's opera.

Ten angels, each carrying a symbol of Christ's Passion, grace the expanse of the Ponte Sant'Angelo that spans the Tiber from the castle's base. It's free of traffic, but not of traffickers. Sellers of various goods—T-shirts, sunglasses, or artwork—lay them out along the bridge.

4　Parks & Gardens

Rome is a city of stone, not of green. Nonetheless, those who need a fix of fresh air should venture into the **park of the Villa Borghese,** located on the north side of the Old City. You'll find some of the best views over Rome from the edge of the park (in the part above the Piazza del Popolo called the Pincio), as well as countless hills and trees and a duck pond. The park is best approached from the Spagna or Flaminio Metro stations, on the south and west sides, or by taking bus no. 910 from the station, or bus no. 56 from Piazza Barberini or Piazza Venezia, to the east side of the green lands. Bicycling, tennis, horseback riding, and jogging are popular sports here (see "Outdoor Activities & Catching a Soccer Match" for more information). The park is also home to three of Rome's museums, the Galleria Borghese and Villa Giulia (see listings under "More Attractions: Around the Spanish Steps & Piazza del Popolo," above) and the rather unimpressive Municipal Gallery of Modern Art (☎ 06/32-24-154); admission 8,000L ($5.25).

On the **Aventine Hill,** south of the Circus Maximus, May ushers in a brilliant display of roses. At other times the Aventine orange trees alongside the church of Santa Sabina are lovely in season. (Pz. Pietro d'Illiria 1; Bus: 94.)

The **Janiculum (Gianicolo)** is one of Rome's hills, set above Trastevere, and from it is one of Rome's spectacular views. Bus 41 will give you a good tour of the park, and you can stroll along the belvedere where the view is best. At this belvedere you'll also find the church of San Pietro in Montorio, believed to be on the spot where St. Peter was crucified upside down. Inside the church's gates is the elegant little tempietto, or little temple, of Bramante. Franciscan sculptor Padre Martini's studio adjoins the church (he died in 1996); ask if you can see his refreshingly vigorous works of religious art. To the right of the fountain, take the Vailae Aldo Fabrizi to the Passegiata del Gianicolo, where you may see lovers in positions the Kama Sutra authors might marvel at. (Most are fully clothed, by day at least.) You'll also see a fine statue of Garibaldi, Italy's George Washington, the general who united the country in 1870. ROME OR DEATH reads the inscription beneath the statue. Farther along is another wonderful equestrian statue, this of his courageous wife Anita, who lies buried beneath the statue.

5 Especially for Kids

Many parents find that their kids are happy doing most of the same things they do, unless they are teenagers, who are satisfied only with a mall and hanging out with their own kind. Younger children can enjoy the dark and mysterious churches, full of candles and odd saints. Giving them a game to play, such as who can count the most angels or who can pick out the weirdest or scariest scene may help, if the reward for the winner and consolation for the loser is good enough.

Kids will like Castel Sant'Angelo (see above), where the castle, dungeon, and medieval armor are fascinating; exploring the Catacombs; Villa Borghese (see above), for bicycling (some rental bikes have baby seats), rowboats, or paddle-boats, or amusements at the Pincio section of the park (model trains are sometimes there to take you around the park); the Colosseum (tell them tales of gladiators first); Piazza Navona, where they can feed the pigeons; and the view from the dome of St. Peter's, if parents can handle it.

Luna Park. V. d. Tre Fontane, EUR. ☎ 06/59-25-933. Free admission; rides cost about 3,000L ($2) each. Mon–Sat 5pm–midnight. Metro: San Paolo. Bus: 707 from San Paolo fuori le Mura to the area.

Not Disneyland, but more like the neighborhood fair, with a Ferris wheel and pretty scary rides. Anyway, you can watch Italian parents with their kids.

Changing of the Guard at the Quirinale Palace. 4pm daily. Metro: Barberini.

It's not as elaborate as Buckingham Palace by any means, but those tall, elegant guardsmen are inspiring.

Museo dell Civiltà Romanà. Pz. Giovanni Agnelli. ☎ 06/54-48-993. Admission 5,000L ($3.30). Mon–Sat 9am–1:30pm, Sun 9am–1pm. Metro: Linea B to EUR Marconi.

Scale models of Rome and close-up models of Trajan's Column will interest the whole family.

WALKING TOUR
The Roman Forum

Start: Piazza del Campidoglio.
Finish: Arch of Titus.
Time: 3 hours.
Best Time: 8:30am (Forum opens at 9am), especially in the summer.
Worst Times: When tour groups arrive en masse.

Tip: Buy the loose-leaf book on sale at the Forum called *Rome Past and Present.* It has overleaf reconstructions of the monuments to give you a better idea of how things were, given that you'll see only fragments of the past here.

1. From the beautiful **Piazza del Campidoglio,** located behind the Vittorio Emanuele Monument, take the street to the left of the Palazzo Senatorio, Via San Pietro in Carcere, to the stairs that lead down to the Church of Saints Luke and Martin. Opposite the church, a portico leads to the Carcere Mamertino (Mamartine Prison). It's open daily from 9am to noon and 2 to 5pm; a donation is expected.

   Beneath the Church of St. Joseph of the Carpenters is a jail that predates Jesus by 40 years. The dank prison has steps that lead to a circular Rome in which prisoners of state were strangled and thrown into the sewer below. Vercingetorix, leader of the Gauls, whom Julius Caesar defeated in 52 B.C., met his end here. According to legend, St. Peter was imprisoned here, but a spring bubbled up, allowing him to baptize the astounded guards, who let him walk past them to freedom.

   From here, walk out to the Via dei Fori Imperiale, turn right, and then right again at the entrance to the Forum. Turning to the right when inside, you'll see the flat surface and truncated columns of the

2. **Basilica Aemilia,** the oldest remaining basilica in the Forum, built by the censor Aemilia Lepidus in 179 B.C. Like many basilicas, it was used mainly for legal and commercial activities. The interior was divided into four aisles; the facade was formed by two superimposed arcades fronted by a flight of steps and several shops. Sharp eyes may pick up some round green stains in the pavement made by copper coins during a fire.

   Continuing right,

3. **The Curia,** once seat of the Roman Senate, stands at the foot of the Capitoline Hill. The present building, begun by Caesar and inaugurated by Augustus in 29 B.C., was built over the ruins of the ancient Curia Hostilia, and some of the older pavement can be seen. The very utilitarian exterior reflects the Republican-age taste in architecture.

   Across from the Curia, the triple

4. **Arch of Septimius Severus** was built in A.D. 203 to commemorate Rome's victories over the Parthians. The long dedication to the emperor and his son, the mass-murderer Caracalla, was "edited" by Caracalla to remove his brother Geta's name, after Caracalla killed him.

   Left of the arch is the platform of the

5. **Rostra,** from which magistrates harangued the people. Mark Antony read Caesar's will from here. Suetonius, the 1st-century A.D. Roman historian with a flair for the dramatic, says "[Caesar's friends raised] a gilded shrine on the Rostra resembling that of Mother Venus. In it they set an ivory couch, spread with purple and gold cloth, and from a pillar at its head hung the gown in which he had been murdered." (See Suetonius's *The Twelve Caesars* for fascinating tales of the emperors;

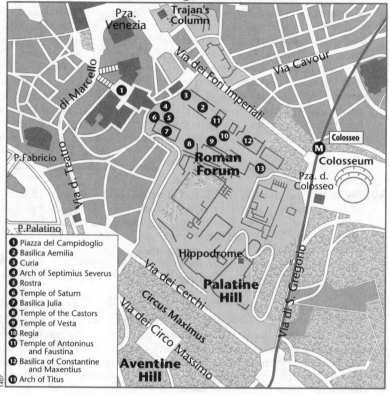

1. Piazza del Campidoglio
2. Basilica Aemilia
3. Curia
4. Arch of Septimius Severus
5. Rostra
6. Temple of Saturn
7. Basilica Julia
8. Temple of the Castors
9. Temple of Vesta
10. Regia
11. Temple of Antoninus and Faustina
12. Basilica of Constantine and Maxentius
13. Arch of Titus

Shakespeare's *Julius Caesar* is an almost faithful docudrama, with the added brilliance of the bard.)

Slightly in back and to the left are the eight surviving columns of the

6. Temple of Saturn (498 B.C.). The god Saturn was popular, and was celebrated with feasting and fairs in the December festival of the Saturnalia.

In front of the Rostra, to the far left, the

7. Basilica Julia was begun by Julius Caesar in 54 B.C. and completed by Augustus. It was used primarily as a law court, but it also contained gaming tables—an interesting combination. The body of the murdered Julius Caesar was brought here to be cremated.

In front of the basilica, looking away from the Capitoline Hill, three graceful Corinthian columns mark the

8. Temple of Castor and Pollux. These mythical twins are usually pictured on horseback, as you may have noted at the top of the steps at the piazza of the Capitoline Hill. Their temple is one of the earliest sacred areas of the Forum (496 B.C.), but it was rebuilt several times. The columns date from the last rebuilding, about the 1st century B.C. During a battle against the Tarquin kings, the Roman dictator promised to build a temple to these patrons of horsemanship if Rome was victorious. Some accounts say that the twins appeared on the battlefield. At any rate, they got their temple.

The semicircle of the temple ahead marks the beginning of one of the Forum's most intriguing areas,

9. Temple of Vesta and the House of the Vestal Virgins. The oldest remains of this temple date back to the 7th century B.C., ancient even for Rome. The goddess of the family was revered to the extent that the six virgins assigned to keep her sacred flame burning were buried alive if the flame died on their watch. The present building is a recent (20th-century) reconstruction in which original fragments were used and the round shape of the original wooden structure was preserved. The House of the Vestal Virgins, in front of the temple, has a lovely garden, once graced with ponds of water lilies. Today, some of the statues of the virgins (one virgin who became a Christian had her name removed) and a mill and an oven can be seen. The house had at least three stories, as a staircase leads upward from the second floor.

The area across from the Vestal temple, at about the center of the Forum, is called the

10. Regia, once the residence of the king (7th century B.C.). Primitive circular huts, similar to those you'll see later on the adjoining Palatine Hill, were uncovered here, dating from near the period when Rome began, which, according to legend, was when the twins Romulus and Remus were found (753 B.C.).

The "street" on the far side is the end of the Via Sacra, the processional route used by emperors after victory on their way to make sacrifices to Jupiter on the Capitoline Hill. It's Rome's oldest street.

Across the Via Sacra stands the

11. Temple of Antoninus and Faustina. When the emperor Antoninus's wife Faustina died in A.D. 141, he decided to deify her (then a Roman custom). The front colonnade of 10 columns is well preserved, and part of the temple's marble freize, with griffins and candelabra, is almost intact. An oddity here is the baroque facade, in back, of the church of San Lorenzo in Miranda, erected where Saint Lawrence was condemned to death. The current 17th-century church is closed to the public.

Heading to the right along the Via Sacra, another church (Sts. Cosma and Damian) has, embedded in its facade, the round structure with columns called the Temple of Romulus, son of the emperor Maxentius, who died in A.D. 307.

Next to the right is the enormous

12. Basilica of Constantine and Maxentius. The two men honored here would never have linked their names this way, since Constantine killed Maxentius in the battle at the Milvian Bridge (above Piazza del Popolo on the Tiber). The structure, one of the most significant examples of Roman architecture in existence, inspired Michelangelo, who sketched it often. A harmonious blend of columns and arches and many colors, the basilica was arranged to draw the visitor to the massive statue of Constantine at its far end. Parts of this or a similar statue can be seen in the Capitoline museum.

The final stop on the tour is the

13. Arch of Titus, erected under Domitian in A.D. 81 in honor of the victories of Titus and Vespasian against the Hebrews. The spoils of Jerusalem, such as the altar of Solomon's temple and a golden seven-candle menorah, are depicted inside the arch.

WALKING TOUR
A Tour of the Renaissance Center

Start: Fontana di Trevi (Trevi Fountain).
Finish: Piazza Farnese.
Time: 2 hours.

Best Time: To see the architecture without cars and Vespas at your heels, go on Sunday morning, or between 1:30 and 4:30pm (during *riposo*), or in August. Then repeat the trip at night, after 9pm, to see *Roma Illuminata*.

This is the most exciting part of the city, apart from the ancient archeological sites. Each corner you turn seems to lead into another world. Wear comfortable flat shoes and take lots of 200L coins to turn on the lights in some church chapels. For complete write-ups of most of the major sights on this walking tour, see the sections "More Attractions: Around Piazza Navona & the Pantheon" and "More Attractions: Around Campo de' Fiori & the Ghetto," above.

1. Fontana di Trevi. This sparkling fountain is especially exciting because it is tucked away in a tiny piazza on the back wall of a palace (rent *La Dolce Vita* for a preview). It is beautiful any time of the day or night. Since its completion in 1650, the fountain has drawn Romans and tourists alike. Turn your back and throw a coin over your shoulder to ensure your return to the Eternal City.

   With your back to the fountain, take a right out of the piazza onto Via delle Muratte. Cross the Via del Corso and turn right down it to reach the exquisite column at

2. Piazza Colonna. This column commemorates the victories of Marcus Aurelius over Germanic tribes in A.D. 196, and used to support the gilded bronze statue of the emperor that is now housed in the Museo Capitolino on the Capitoline Hill (see above).

   This area is Rome's political capital, and many of the suits you see rushing around work for the government. Walk past the column but turn left before the piazza ends, crossing Piazza Colonna and exiting by the far corner. You'll enter

3. Piazza di Montecitorio. The palazzo to your right is where the Chamber of Deputies meets. (Thus the preponderance of police and journalists.) The 17th-century palace begun by Bernini is unusual in that its far side was done in a different style (Art Nouveau), the work of Ernesto Basile in 1918. The 6th-century B.C. obelisk on the piazza was transported from Heliopolis to Rome in 10 B.C.

   With your back to the palace, walk straight ahead into Via Guglia. Turn right after one block into Via dei Pastini. In a few minutes you'll see

4. The Pantheon, one of Rome's most venerated monuments. Stop in to see its "heavenly dome," open to the elements (for details, see the listing under "Ancient Rome," above).

   ☕ **TAKE A BREAK**   The piazza in front of the Pantheon is quite a beauty, and you might want to stop for an expensive coffee in one of the cafes. A grocery (*alimentari*) in the piazza sells soft drinks at less-usurious prices, but you'll have to share the base of the piazza's fountain with entangled teenage lovers.

   Head around to the left of the Pantheon, where you'll find Piazza della Minerva and

5. The Church of Santa Maria sopra Minerva, one of the few examples of gothic architecture in Rome and final resting place for two popes, a cardinal, Italy's patron Saint Catherine, and the monkish painter Fra Angelico (see full review under "More Attractions: Around Piazza. Navona & the Pantheon," above).

   Take a quick detour outside the church, along its right side, and you'll see, about a block away, on the right, an enormous marble foot, casually placed here, on the aptly named Via Pie' di Marmo (Marble Foot Street). Return to Piazza della Minerva and walk along the back of the Pantheon on Via della Palombella. When you see the stag's head above a church, to the left, you'll have found

6. Piazza Sant'Eustachio. The church on this square was named for Saint Eustachio, converted when he saw Jesus' face in the face of a stag he was about to kill.

☕ **TAKE A BREAK**   Across from the church (you've already smelled the coffee) is one of the best cafes in the world for cappuccino: Caffè Sant'Eustachio at no. 82 on the piazza.

Across the piazza you'll see Via Stadarari. Follow it until you come to a two-lane street, Corso Rinascimento. Take a left, and in the first building on your left you'll see the entrance to the courtyard of

7. Sant'Ivo alla Sapienza. From the courtyard you can look up to the spectacular curving and counter-curving facade and swirling belltower of this church, one of baroque master architect Borromini's most innovative works.

Now retrace your steps past Via Stadarari and pass the Palazzo Madama (where the Senate meets). Take the next right for one block to the church of

8. San Luigi dei Francesi, where the chapel to the left of the altar filled with Caravaggios will delight you (you'll need to bring change to operate the light box in this gloomy church).

Retrace your steps to Palazzo Madama and cross Corso Rinascimento. Walk straight ahead until you see the very large oval filled with fountains that is

9. Piazza Navona. Pure theater from morning till night, this gorgeous piazza is the place to relax and have an expensive meal, or at least a drink. Or buy an ice cream and wander about, enjoying especially the central *Fountain of the Rivers* by Bernini and the elegant apartments that line the piazza.

When you're ready to leave the artists and tourists and pigeons, retrace your steps to Corso Rinascimento and turn right until you see a newly restored church across the street

10. Sant'Andrea della Valle. *Tosca* fans will want to walk inside, for this is where the first act of the opera is set.

Walk around the right side of the church around to the back and take the first right, which will lead to Piazza Biscione, which in turn opens onto the wonderful

11. Campo de' Fiori. If you reach here before noon and it's not Sunday you can enjoy an exuberant outdoor market presided over by a striking statue of Giordano Bruno, an intellectual and victim of the Inquisition. This campo evokes Renaissance and medieval Rome as no other can.

☕ **TAKE A BREAK**   Buy rolls (*panini*) at the bakery (*panetteri'a*) Il Fornaio in back of the flower market and then some cheese or meat at the opposite side of the piazza at the shop marked ALIMENTARI (grocery store). Fresh fruits from the stalls can be washed at the water fountains.

Exit the opposite corner of the piazza from where you came in onto Via dei Baullari and walk one block until you see the fountain at

12. Piazza Farnese. This elegant piazza is crowned by the Palazzo Farnese, now the French embassy and rarely open to visitors for security reasons. Its Renaissance facade is partly the work of Michelangelo, and it served as a model for many later palaces. You can have lunch here in an outdoor restaurant or just sit at the fountain and be glad Rome exists.

Walking Tour—A Tour of the Renaissance Center

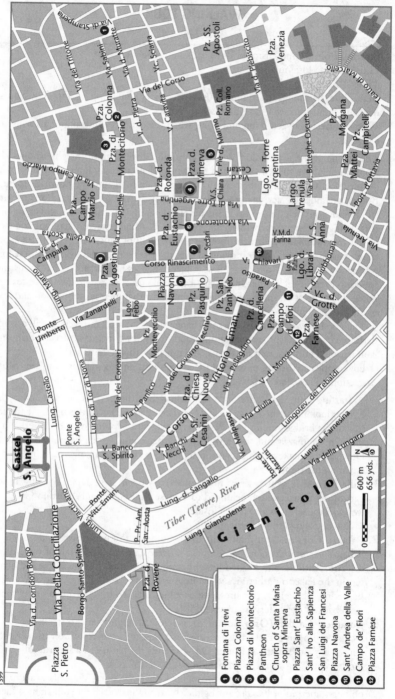

Castel S. Angelo

Piazza S. Pietro

Tiber (Tevere) River

Gianicolo

600 m
656 yds.

1 Fontana di Trevi
2 Piazza Colonna
3 Piazza di Montecitorio
4 Pantheon
5 Church of Santa Maria sopra Minerva
6 Piazza Sant' Eustachio
7 Sant' Ivo alla Sapienza
8 San Luigi dei Francesi
9 Piazza Navona
10 Sant' Andrea della Valle
11 Campo de' Fiori
12 Piazza Farnese

WALKING TOUR
Trastevere

Starting Point: Ponte Sisto (bridge near Campo de' Fiori).
Finish: Piazza Piscinula.
Time: 1 hour.
Best Time: Morning, to see museums, especially late morning on Tuesday, Thursday, and Sunday to see Cavallini fresco in Santa Cecilia.
Worst Times: Between noon and 4pm, when the churches and some museums are closed.

This is one of the most colorful, most culturally distinct rioni (neighborhoods) in Rome. They have their own version of Roman dialect (made famous by the 19th-century poet G. G. Belli), their own take on Roman food, and their own sharpened Roman attitude. In fact, many people claim that the last of the "real Romans" are still holding out here, holed up in medieval palazzi plying their trades and eking out their livings as the area slowly becomes gentrified. Another factor changing the face of this most Roman of Roman rioni is the onslaught of American and British expatriates who have been slowly moving in over the last two decades. Most of these foreigners, however, tend to try their best to blend in, dressing and acting like locals and speaking even to each other in Italian. But while these ex-pats may not be readily noticeable to most outsiders, the Trasteverini know that their neighborhood and way of life are changing forever.

The good news is that this doesn't change the fact that Trastevere is still a wonderfully characterful place, a neighborhood of winding medieval streets, dripping laundry, old churches, rich museums, and excellent tiny restaurants.

For complete write-ups of most of the major sights on this walking tour, see "More Attractions: Trastevere," above.

Starting from the Ponte Sisto just below the Campo de' Fiori area, cross the bridge, looking at the lovely view of St. Peter's dome far to the right. At the far side of the bridge you'll reach Piazza Trilussa, with a fountain at its center. Walk through the piazza and take a right at Via Benedetta, which becomes Via Santa Dorotea, then take a right to go through the gate onto Via Lungara. A little ways down on the right is the

1. **Villa Farnesina,** which seems to be only rarely open these days. But you can see part of the palace, which belonged to Sienese banking mogul Agostino Chigi, as well as Raphael's *Galatea* fresco inside.

   Directly across the street is the

2. **Palazzo Corsini.** You may want to see some of the paintings inside, such as Ribera's *Venus and Adonis* or Carracci's *Rebecca at the Well.* Half of the Museo dell'Arte Antica is also located here (the other half is still housed in the old quarters in the Palazzo Barberini, see "More Attractions: Around Via Veneto & Piazza Barberini," above). Its treasures include a Fra Angelico triptych and a Caravaggio.

   In back of the gallery is a wonderful

3. **Botanical Garden (Orto Botanico),** where you might want to stroll in relative seclusion. Its tan gravel paths and trees are kept in better condition usually than almost any other part of Rome. On weekends the garden is a favorite of young mothers pushing strollers. Admission is 4,000L ($2.65).

   Return to Via Lungara and turn right. Keep right along Via della Scala to the oblong trapezoid of Piazza Sant'Egidio. Next to the church on your right is the:

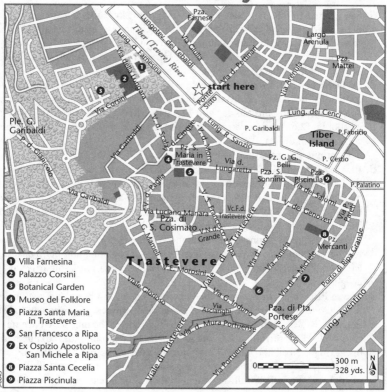

Legend:
1. Villa Farnesina
2. Palazzo Corsini
3. Botanical Garden
4. Museo del Folklore
5. Piazza Santa Maria in Trastevere
6. San Francesco a Ripa
7. Ex Ospizio Apostolico San Michele a Ripa
8. Piazza Santa Cecelia
9. Piazza Piscinula

4. Museo del Folklore. Inside are wonderful memorabilia and dioramas of old Roman life (☎ **06/58-16-563**). Admission is 3,750L ($2.45). It's open Tuesday and Thursday evenings, also, if you want to come back.

Out the other end of the piazza, turn left and you'll soon be in:

5. Piazza Santa Maria in Trastevere. This piazza, the heart of Trastevere, is lively almost any time of day or night. Its a good place to sit and relax on the steps of the fountain, wander into the church to gaze at the Cosmatesque floor and mosaicked apse, or shell out the extra lire to sit at an outside table at one of the bars lining the square and watch Trastevere life go by.

Exit the piazza by the far right corner and follow San Francesco a Ripa, where pizza-by-the-slice places and pastry shops will tempt you.

☕ **TAKE A BREAK** **The Pizzerio Ivo,** Via di San Francesco a Ripa 158 (☎ **06/58-17-082**), is apt to be crowded, but worth some line time. Full pizzas cost from 9,500L (6.30) to 13,000L ($8.55). Slices, or "piazza a taglio" (pronounced *ta*-lio) cost 1,500L ($1) *l'etto* (each piece). Daily 1:30 to 3:30pm and 6pm to 2am. Closed August.

Cross the major boulevard, Viale Trastevere, and continue straight on San Francesco a Ripa to Piazza San Francesco d'Assisi and the church of

6. **San Francesco a Ripa,** which has a brilliant statue by baroque master Bernini of the *Ecstasy of Beata Ludovica Albertoni* (1674) in the last chapel on the left. Her "ecstasy" is supposedly celestial, but we'll let you be the judge.

    From here, follow Via Porta Portese for a block and turn left into Via San Michele a Ripa, where to your right you'll see

7. **Ex Ospizio Apostolico San Michele a Ripa** at no. 22, a rather plain building containing the transplanted Galleria Borghese collection of paintings. It's open till 7pm every evening but Sunday and Monday, when it closes at 1pm. Admission is 4,000L ($2.65), but if you have a ticket stub from the Galleria Borghese itself, you can get in on that.

    Continue along Via an Michele a Ripa to

8. **Piazza Santa Cecilia,** and the church of that name, where a remarkable statue of the martyred saint, in the position in which she was found, beheaded, is under the main altar. This church also houses the remains of Cavallini's 1293 *Last Judgment* fresco, the naturalism and humanity of which anticipates the Renaissance. In the late afternoon, you can sometimes hear vespers being chanted.

    Turn left upon exiting the church and continue on Via Santa Cecilia, which changes its name to Via Vascellari after one block and, after another block, turn left onto Via dei Salumi, then right onto Via Scarpetta until you arrive at the delightful

9. **Piazza Piscinula.** The fragile-looking tower belongs to San Benedetto, the smallest romanesque church in Rome. Go in to see the Cosmatesque pavement and the fresco of St. Benedict, Christianity's first official monk (he may have once stayed for a while in the tiny cell off a room to the left of the entrance). If the church isn't open, ring the bell and watch for a little old lady to pop her head out of a window above. Say "San Benedetto" a few times and be sure to seem like a pious pilgrim and she will gleefully let you in to show you the church's few treasures.

    To the right of the piazza you'll see the river again. You're near the Ponte Cestio to Tiber Island and the Ponte Palatino across to the Piazza della Bocca della Verità area. If you want to grab a bus, head out of the left (narrow end) of the piazza and up Via della Lungaretta to Piazza Sonnino and an assortment of bus choices.

6 Organized Tours

American Express (see entry under "Fast Facts: Rome" in chapter 4) and Carrani Tours (see below) offer traditional tours of the city. On foot, try **Secret Walks,** Vle. Medaglie d'Oro 127 (☎ **06/39-72-87-28**). They offer a wide variety of themed walks, bike tours, and other walks. If your Italian is reasonably good, read *Il Messaggero,* a Rome daily paper, for listings of special tours. Two Anglo-American papers, *Wanted in Rome* and *Metropolitan,* also list English tours periodically—as well as much more of interest to the English-speaking community.

BUS TOURS   For the standard bus tour of the Forum, Colosseum, and several of the cathedrals, try **Carrani Tours,** Via Vittorio Emanuele Orlando 95 (☎ **06/ 48-80-510** or 47-42-501). They've been in business since 1927—about as long as buses have roamed the Roman roads. Most of their 20 tour options (which include the Villa d'Este and the Castelli Romani, towns outside the city) range in price from to 40,000L to 60,000L ($26.30 to $39.50). Some include lunch. You can pick up their brochure in just about every hotel and pensione in Rome, or at their headquarters a block up from Piazza della Repubblica. Note that they'll usually come and pick you up at your hotel.

Less expensive is the tour provided by **ATAC,** Rome's bus line. The once-daily tours on bus 110 leave from Piazza dei Cinquecento, near the railroad station, at 2:30pm in winter and 3:30pm in summer. The tour lasts three hours, and costs 15,000L ($9.85). Buy tickets at the ATAC information booth on the piazza. To double-check that the tour departure time has not changed, call ATAC at **06/46-951.**

7 Outdoor Activities & Catching a Soccer Match

OUTDOOR ACTIVITIES

BIKING Sunday mornings and weekdays between 1pm and 3pm are the best hours for biking on the city streets, when the cars have gone away or home to lunch. You can also rent bikes and pedal through the Villa Borghese, but keep off the main park thoroughfares; cars are king there, too. **I Bike Rome,** located in the Villa Borghese's underground parking lot—the entrance is near the top of the Veneto at Via San Paulo de Brasile, rents bikes for 5,000L ($3.30) per hour, or 13,000L ($8.55) per day. Mopeds are 30,000L ($19.75) for four hours, or 45,000L ($29.60) per day. Open daily from 9am to 8pm. Bikes are also often rented at the Piazza di Spagna entrance of the Metro. Other places in Rome have rentals as well, including **Bicimania** (Piazza Sonnino; ☎ **06/78-07-755**), in Trastevere, which rents five-speeders for 5,000L ($3.30); open daily from 9am to 12:30am. **Enjoy Rome,** located near the train station at Via Varese 39 (☎ **06/44-51-84-30**) can put you in touch with other rental locations.

BOWLING Italians flock to the lanes at the air-conditioned **Bowling Roma,** Vle. Regina Margherita 181 (☎ **06/85-51-184**), located past the Porta Pia off Via Nomentana (take bus 36, 37, 60, or 62). It's open Monday through Saturday from 10am to 11:30pm, and Sunday from 5pm to midnight.

FITNESS CENTERS The jock and spa set meet at the **Roman Sport Center,** Via del Galappatoio 33 (☎ **06/36-14-358**), in Villa Borghese, for squash and sauna, plus a weight room and swimming pool. A day's use of the facilities costs 25,000L ($16.45).

HORSEBACK RIDING The Villa Borghese is the place. Two riding clubs that can get you set up in the saddle are the **Associazione Sportiva Villa Borghese,** Via del Galoppatoio 23 (☎ **06/36-06-797**) and the Societa Ippica Romana, V. Monte d. Farnesina 18 (☎ **06/32-40-592**).

JOGGING For the fleet of foot, the Villa Borghese is again the best place, but it's fun to jog along the river when traffic is not blowing smoke and horns, that is, Sunday morning. The Villa Ada, off Via Salaria in the northeast region of the city, is another option, as is the Circo Massimo—but watch those chariots! You saw *Ben-Hur.* The Villa Doria Pamphilj on the Janiculum is still another possibility.

SWIMMING Pools are found at the **Roman Sport Center** (see above) and the **Associazione Sportiva Augustea,** Via Luciani 57 (☎ **06/23-23-51-12**), north of Villa Borghese (bus 926 from Piazza del Popolo. The latter charges 7,000L for a day's swimming privileges. The **Piscina della Rosa** at Vle. America 20 (☎ **06/59-26-717**) is in the suburban area EUR (take Metro line B to EUR-Palasport). A full day costs 15,000L ($9.85) or after 2pm 13,000L ($8.55). Take a bathing cap. It's open from June through September from 9am to 7pm. Ask also at your hotel or the tourist office for the *piscina pubblica* (public pools) in your area.

TENNIS Italians have taken to tennis and the opportunities to play have increased. The Associazione Sportiva Augustea (see above) has tennis courts available at 14,000L

($92.10) for singles and 18,000L ($11.85) for doubles. It's open Monday to Saturday from 9:30am to 12:30pm and 3:30 to 7pm, Sunday from 9:30am to 12:30pm and from 3:30 to 5pm.

SOCCER

Soccer, calcio (*cal*-cho) in Italian, is a national pastime. Romans cheer both Roma and Lazio, the city's two intensely competitive teams. Just yelling *Forza!* (Go!) now and then should get you through without cheering on the wrong team. Italian fans are loud and enthusiastic but violence is rarely a problem unless the Brits (of all people) are in town. Those non-Latin tempers worry Italian security each time they play. Matches are held on Sunday afternoons in the Stadio Olimpico, Foro Italico dei Gladiatori (☎ **06/36-851**). Thousands of tickets, ranging in price from 20,000L to 50,000L ($13.15 to $32.90), are sold during the two or three hours before each game. The players usually take a break during June, July, and August.

To truly appreciate the hold soccer has over the Roman populace, stroll the streets of Trastevere any Sunday when a big match is being played and listen to sounds of agony or ecstasy coming from the coffee bars.

8 Shopping

THE SHOPPING SCENE

The streets around **Piazza di Spagna** are the most fashionable addresses in Rome. Along the streets to the west of the square, particularly Via Condotti, you'll find all the best Italian and international names in clothing and footwear. Needless to say, prices in this high-rent neighborhood are stratospheric. However, if you still want to buy that Armani, come in January when the prices are a fraction of those in the United States—not that this fraction means inexpensive, but it often means a very good value.

One of Rome's most popular—and most popularly priced—shopping areas is **Via Cola di Rienzo** near the Vatican, running from Piazza del Risorgimento to the Ponte Margherita (near Piazza del Popolo). Here you'll find souvenir shops, as well as pharmacies, supermarkets, boutiques, and small department stores, all with prices considerably more moderate than those across the river. This is where the average middle-income Roman comes to shop. To get here, take the Metro to Lepanto or Ottaviano.

Via Nazionale and **Via del Corso** are also fine areas for window-shoppers (and those with fewer lire to spend, too). Here you'll find many of Rome's department stores.

Finally, **Old Rome,** particularly north of Piazza Venezia and between Piazza Navona and the Trevi Fountain, is the place to wander for handicrafts and one-of-a-kind shops and boutiques. The antiques dealers line **Via dei Coronari,** which runs from near the north end of Piazza Navona to near the Ponte Sant'Angelo.

Do remember that Roman stores, for the most part, close for a long lunch during the week and are closed all day Sunday and on Monday mornings. Hours are usually from 9:30am to 1pm and from 4 to 7 or 7:30pm. Food stores usually close Thursday afternoon.

SHOPPING A TO Z
ANTIQUES

Real antiques at budget prices are as rare in Rome as they are anywhere. But if you're a browser, the Via dei Coronari is expensive Rome's antiques center. Unless you appear affluent, don't expect help from store owners.

March is Antiques month in Rome. Consult the tourist office's publication *WHERE Rome* for information. If you want to check out the antiques at the **Porta Portese Flea Market,** get there early Sunday morning (it's open from 7am to 2pm), because it's impossible to even move about when the crowds arrive after 11. To reach the market, take bus 13, 27, or 30 to Porta Portese, or follow Via Francesco a Ripa from Trastevere to Piazza San Francesco d'Assisi, where the antique-furnishing section begins. (Old books, prints, and small objects are found throughout the market, however.) Piazza della Fontanella Borghese has a daily mart of books and prints.

ART

Paintings can be purchased from artists at Piazza Navona, although the quality varies. Old prints of Roman scenes can be found at **Tanca,** Salita dei Crescenzi 10, near the Pantheon, and at **Alinari,** V. Aliberti 16/a, off Via Babuino. **Aldo di Castro,** V. Babuino 71, has an enormous collection of antique prints, starting at about $30.

BOOKS

Economy Book and Video Center. V. Torino 136. ☎ **06/47-46-877.**

This is a large store offering nonfiction and fiction and children's books and games in English, as well as birthday cards and other things useful to expatriates, including video rental.

Corner Bookshop. V. del Moro 48. ☎ **06/58-36-942.**

This is a friendly neighborhood bookstore in Trastevere with English-language books.

DEPARTMENT STORES & SHOPPING MALLS

Department Stores

Coin. Pzle. Appio 15. ☎ **06/70-80-020.** Also in Shopping Mall Cinecitta Due, Piazza di Cinecittà, Viale Palmiro Togliatti, ☎ 06/72-20-902.

Coin is a full department store with reasonable, not bargain prices.

La Rinascente. Pz. Colonna, V. del Corso 189. ☎ **06/67-97-691.**

Few bargains are to be found here, but it's still a handy place for shopping, especially during the long Roman lunch hour. Open Monday from 2 to 7:30pm, Tuesday to Saturday from 9:30am to 7:30pm.

Standa. Cor. Francia 124. ☎ **06/33-38-719.** Also at Cor. Trieste 200 and V. Cola di Rienzo 173.

Standa is a good place to find hair spray, toothbrushes, and such on the racks, without having to negotiate in Italian. Clothes are not particularly good quality, but for an emergency sweater, it will do. The children's department sells toys. Many Standa branches have full supermarkets.

Upim. Pz. Santa Maria Maggiore. ☎ **06/73-66-58.** Also at V. d. Tritone 172.

This is the least impressive of the Rome department stores, but it's a good place to replace your lost toothbrush or find a notebook in which to record your Roman adventures.

Shopping Malls

Two shopping malls accessible by Metro should satisfy those in the throes of mall-withdrawal, especially teenagers.

Cinecitta Due. V. Palmiro Togliatti 2, ☎ 06/72-20-902 is near the Cinecittà Metro stop (on Line A). The first mall to open in Rome, it boasts more than 100 shops, including coffee bars and restaurants. It's open from 9:30am to 8pm.

I Granai, V. Laurentina, in the EUR area (☎ 06/51-95-58-90), is even larger, with more than 120 shops, bars, and restaurants. It's open from 10am to 8pm. Laurantina is the Metro stop.

Discount Shopping

Rome's true bargains (if you can call them that) occur in January and August in the Via Condotti area when Armani, Max Mara, and the rest of the glamorous high-fashion shops have their wonderful sales. But even on sale, prices are still very high for these smart lines.

At the other end of the spectrum, **Porta Portese** (see "Markets" below) has racks of clothes at fairly good prices, and you may strike a bargain, although the quality won't be terrific. The **Via Sannio market** near San Giovanni in Laterano can have also good bargains (open Monday to Friday from 10am to 1pm, and Saturday from 10am to 6pm. Designer shoes appear at the Testaccio market.

Fashion

For Men   The department stores and markets listed above are your best bets. For neckties, the **Cravatterie Nazionale,** V. Virroria 62 off Via Babuino (☎ 06/69-92-21-43) has an excellent selection, suitable for all elegant restaurants or job interviews. **Versus Uomo,** V. Borgognona 34 (☎ 06/67-84-193) has stylish clothes for young men and a multilingual staff.

For Women   Boutiques along Via Giubbonari, off Campo de' Fiori, have relatively inexpensive shops for clothing, lingerie, and shoes. The section around Via Nazionale and Via Cola di Rienzo (Metro: Ottaviano) have reasonably priced shops. The medium-priced lines in Italy are not as inexpensive as similar-quality clothes in the United States. Boutiques selling women's clothing abound in Rome, and are found all along the Via del Tritone, Via del Corso, and around the Fontana di Trevi. Teenagers and those out for shocking styles can probably find something along the Via del Corso. Apart from the main department stores, the mall at Cinecittà (see above) has more than 100 shops, many of which cater to women.

For Children

Apart from Standa and Upim, there are few inexpensive places for children's clothing.

Baby House. V. Cola Di Rienzo 117. ☎ **06/32-14-291.**

Designer clothes and some (not-much) less-expensive goodies fill this popular store.

Mettemi Giù. V. Due Macelli 59. ☎ **06/67-89-761.**

This is a bit lower in price than the former and worth a look. It's near the Trevi Fountain.

Chicco. V. della Penna 16.

Located near Piazza del Popolo, this is a major Italian baby store, with everything from rattles to cribs.

Food

The morning food markets at **Campo de' Fiori; Piazza Vittorio Emanuele,** near Santa Maria Maggiore (which is scheduled to be closed soon); **Via Milazzo,** not far from the train station; **Piazza Testaccio;** and the **Mercato Trionfale,** north of the Vatican, are all good bets for fresh fruits, vegetables, and cheese.

Jewelry

The Porta Portese market has many jewelry stalls. The area around Campo dei Fiori near the Ponte Sisto is a center for handmade and other gold objects.

The **Museum Shop,** V. Nazionale 185 and V. d. Consulta 67, sells reproductions of jewelry, as well as other objects, from museum collections worldwide.

If you win the lottery while abroad, **Bulgari,** at V. Condotti 10, will be happy to sparkle you. It's Italy's Tiffany.

LEATHER

Apart from the high-quality merchandise you'll find in the Via Condotti area, you may be disappointed in the average quality of lower-priced leather goods in Rome. The Via del Corso has many leather stores, such as **Merola** at no. 14 (for gloves), **Charles al Corso** at no. 109, **Mishelle** at nos. 483 and 526, and **Shoeshop** at nos. 147 and 378. More stores can be found on Via Nazionale, including another branch of Shoeshop at no. 252. Via Cola di Rienzo is another good bet; here you'll find another Shoeshop at no. 146 (there's yet another branch at V. Tritone 59) and Trancanelli at no. 84. The Fontana di Trevi area and Via dei Giubbonari, off Campo de' Fiori, are also areas for leather shopping.

LINGERIE

For inexpensive lingerie, Via Giubbonari is one of the best streets (between Via Arenula and Campo dei Fiori); check out **AR.TE** at no. 39. Via Cola di Rienzo also has several lingerie shops, including **Marnetto** at no. 73 and **Casa del Corredo** at no. 256. **Mondini** at Vle. di Trastevere 249 and **Rea** at V. Tritone 207 have good values.

MARKETS

Every Sunday you can find everything from a 17th-century candelabra and antique door knockers to 5,000L ($3.30) cassette tapes and 20,000L ($13.15) shoes at the seemingly endless **flea market at Porta Portese** in Trastevere. Countless vendors and just plain folks set up shop here each Sunday from roughly 7 or 8am to about 1 or 2pm. Most of the wares (mostly clothes) are pretty chintzy and of little interest to the tourist, but the market is a sight in and of itself. You'll see precious few tourists and thousands of Romans—still, watch out for pickpockets.

To reach the market, take bus 27 from the train station and downtown; get off at the second stop after the river, on Via Ettore Rolli, just past the corner of Via Panfilo Castaldi. The market, the size of which varies with the meteorological and economic climate, stretches at least to Via Pietro Ripari and Piazza Ippolito Nievo, which is on the 170 bus line.

The best of the many markets specializing in flowers and produce in Rome is on **Campo de' Fiori.** The small but colorful market, crammed with fresh fruit and vegetables, is open Monday to Saturday from 7 or 8am to about 1 or 2pm. In spring and fall look for untrimmed artichokes on long stalks. Autumn brings Muscat grapes and porcini mushrooms.

A handful of pushcarts offering used books, etchings, lithographs, art reproductions, antique jewelry, and other odds and ends and one-of-a-kind items sets up Monday to Saturday from 9am until about 6pm (4:30pm in winter) at Piazza Borghese, near Ponte Cavour. To find them, walk out Via Condotti from Piazza di Spagna and continue for 2½ blocks past Via del Corso on Via della Fontanella Borghese.

Piazza Vittorio Emanuele, south of Stazione Termini, is the site of Rome's biggest daily open-air food market, open Monday to Saturday roughly from 8am to 2pm.

RELIGIOUS ART

The Via della Conciliazione, near St. Peter's, has several shops where you can find religious art and icons. Piazza Minerva and Via Cestari have exquisite shops, such as

Guadenzi, Piazza della Minerva 69A (☎ **06/67-90-431**), for crosses, Della Robbia–style plaques, holy water fonts, and statues.

SOUVENIRS

Souvenirs, of various quality, abound in Rome. The **Vatican Museum shops** sell good prints of paintings found in their collection. Chocoholics may want something handmade from the charming **Moriondo & Gariglio,** up the hill from the Trevi Fountain at V. della Pilotta 2. Liqueur, honey, and other such products from the monasteries can be found at **Ai Monasteri,** Pz. Cinque Lun 2, off Piazza Navona. Tapes (audio) are found literally everywhere, featuring everything from Palestrina to the Macarena. Religious items can be found in the Vatican and the area near the Pantheon (see above).

Terrecotte Persiane, located in a courtyard of V. Napoli 92, has a good mix of terracotta objects, from tiles to masks and planters and jardinieres.

WINE & LIQUORS

Trimani's, at V. Goito 20, has been in operation since 1821 and knows everything there is to know about wines and spirits.

9 Rome After Dark

Un Ospite a Roma, a free magazine available from the concierge desks of top hotels, is full of current information on what's happening around town. *Trova Roma,* a weekly listings magazine inserted in the Thursday edition of *La Repubblica* newspaper is indispensable for its coverage of films, music, art, opera, dance, and the like. Most newsstands stock extra free copies of *Trova Roma* in case you weren't able to pick it up on Thursday. The mini-magazine *Metropolitan* (in English) has good listings of jazz, rock, and such, and is an interesting look at expatriate Rome. The daily paper *Il Messaggero* also lists current cultural news, especially in its Thursday magazine supplement, called *Metro.* (*Note:* The supplements are separate small booklets. If the newsstand dealer doesn't give one to you, ask for it. They often don't think foreigners want it, as it's in Italian, but the listings are clear to English-speakers.)

THE PERFORMING ARTS
CLASSICAL MUSIC

Check the Thursday supplements *Trova Roma* and *Metro* (see above) as well as *Metropolitan,* the Rome magazine in English, for up-to-date performance listings.

Performances of both chamber music and symphonic music are often given by the notable **Accademia Nazionale di Santa Cecilia,** V. d. Conciliazione 4 (☎ **06/ 67-80-742**). In the summer, performances are held at Piazza di Villa Giulia, site of the Etruscan Museum. Tickets cost from 15,000L to 30,000L ($9.85 to $19.75).

On Saturdays at 9pm, head for the Castel Sant'Angelo, Lungotevere Castello 50, where, amid the brooding charm of the castle, you can enjoy beautiful music sponsored by the **Amici di Castel Sant'Angelo** (☎ **06/85-46-192**). Tickets are 15,000L ($9.85).

Musical events are also often presented by the **Accademia Filarmonica Romana** (☎ **06/32-01-752**) and the **Associazione Musicale Claudio Monteverdi** (☎ **06/ 48-14-800**). A.GI.MUS. presents exceptional offerings at the Public Hall of the Papal Institute for Holy Music, Pz. Sant'Agostino 20 (☎ **06/36-00-19-02**). In addition, check the daily papers for free church concerts, especially near Christmas or Easter.

OPERA & BALLET

The opera season at Rome's historic opera house, **Teatro dell'Opera,** Piazza Gigli (☎ 06/481-7003), runs from around December through June. The box office is open Monday to Saturday from 9am to 5pm, and Sunday from 9am to 1pm; tickets range from 16,000L to 250,000L ($10.50 to $164.50). Ask about student discounts. Ballet performances are also given at the opera house.

Open-air **opera and ballet at the Terme di Caracalla** (Baths of Caracalla), Via delle Terme di Caracalla, are among the great summer events of Italy, in an atmospheric setting amid the ruins of this one-time Roman spa. Usually two operas and a ballet are put on here each summer, with shows three or four times a week in July and August. The production of *Aïda* is particularly spectacular. Tickets, which can be purchased at the Teatro dell'Operara (see below), cost 25,000L to 65,000L ($15.65 to $40.65) for the opera or 20,000L to 50,000L ($12.50 to $31.25) for the ballet.

THE CLUB & MUSIC SCENE
NIGHTCLUBS & DISCOS

One thing Romans who aren't millionaires don't do is dance much, since it can be prohibitively expensive: Expect to spend 40,000L to 50,000L ($25 to $31.25) just for entrance and a few drinks. Good clubs at press time were **Billow,** V. Campania 37 (☎ 06/482-18-90), and **Promozione Incontro,** V. dell'Imbrecciato 263 (☎ 06/55-28-68-00). The entrance to the latter is hidden on Via della Magliana. Check *Metropolitan,* the English-language biweekly, for the latest.

Testaccio, the trendy neighborhood, is the setting for the sophisticated **Spago,** V. de Monte Testaccio (☎ 06/57-44-999).

Jackie O, V. Boncompagni 11, off the Via Veneto (☎ 06/48-85-754), is back, and **Gilda,** V. Mario dei Fiori 97, near the Spanish Steps (☎ 06/67-84-838), is going strong—stylish dancers and celebs are found at both. In summer it's **Gilda on the Beach** at Fregene, near Rome; open Tuesday to Saturday from 11pm to 4am.

JAZZ

Rome also sports a fair variety of small jazz clubs with frequent performances of local musicians (you'll find most of them listed in the entertainment sections of Italian newspapers).

One favorite is the **St. Louis Music City,** V. del Cardello 13a (☎ 06/47-45-076). A long, cavernous club with a jazz stage at one end, this place also has a restaurant area and a pool table off to the side. Entrance is free, but you must become a club member first, a formality which will set you back 10,000L ($6.25). Happily, club owner Mario Ciampa has traditionally offered a 50% discount on membership to bearers of this book. It's still not cheap, however. If you sit at one of the tables near the stage, expect to pay 5,000L to 10,000L ($3.30 to $6.55) per drink. There's live music almost every night from 10:30pm or so. Via del Cardello is halfway between the Colosseum and Via Cavour. Closed Sunday.

Big Mama in Trastevere at Vc. San Francesco a Ripa 18 (☎ 06/58-12-551) has a good selection of sounds from jazz to R&B. There's a weekend cover of 20,000L ($13.15). Open October through June daily from 9pm to 1am; sometimes closed Sundays—call ahead first.

LATIN SOUNDS

A long-time favorite is the tiny **Yes, Brazil,** V. San Francesco a Ripa 103 (☎ 06/58-16-267). Crowded and palmy with good tropical drinks. Open Monday to Saturday from 8pm to 2:30am. No cover. See also Caffe Latino, below.

GAY AND LESBIAN CLUBS

Clubs move in and out of fashion rapidly, but here are a few current popular spots:

L'Alibi. V. Monte di Testaccio 18 ☎ **06/574-3448.** Cover 20,000L ($13.15) Wed, Fri–Sun. Metro: Piramide. Bus: 20N and 30N.

Mostly men, but some women, the less conventional the better. It's a large, attractive building of three levels and a roof terrace, making it a summer playground. Open Tuesday to Sunday from 11pm to 5am.

Hangar. V. in Selci 69 ☎ **06/48-81-397.** No cover. Metro: Colosseo.

Claudius's insane wife Messalina once lived at this location. Now an American (John) is the friendly proprietor. It's very popular and often packed. Men are in the majority. Women are welcome, except on Monday, which is Movie Night. Open Wednesday to Monday from 10:30pm to 2am; closed 2 weeks in August.

Radio Londra. V. di Monte Testaccio 67 ☎ **06/57-50-04.** No cover. Metro: Piramide.

Down the street from Alibi, this club is popular with nongays as well, especially in summer when the outdoor terrace is open. Open daily from 11:30 to 4am. A drink will set you back 15,000L ($9.85), and a tap beer 6,000L ($3.95).

Joli Coeur. V. Sirte 5, east of Villa Ada. ☎ **06/83-93-523.** Cover 15,000L ($9.95), includes one drink.

This is Rome's most popular lesbian bar, although it's a bit out of the way. A cab is the safest way to get around at night in this area, which isn't the best. An international group of women meet here, keeping it a popular spot.

CAFES & GELATERIE

When in Rome, do as the Romans do: Enjoy a leisurely dinner at some hidden-away trattoria's outdoor tables or while away the night at a cafe in a peaceful neighborhood.

NEAR THE PANTHEON   The outdoor cafes on the pedestrians-only Piazza della Rotonda, in the shadow of the Pantheon, are perhaps the best places to be on warm summer nights. Cappuccino prices are a steep 4,000L ($2.50).

Some locals prefer the ice cream at **Giolitti,** V. Uffici del Vicario 40 (☎ 06/67-94-206), a fancy cafe sporting a turn-of-the-century look with marble floors and hanging chandeliers, but no outdoor tables. It's open Tuesday to Sunday from 7am to 2am.

AROUND PIAZZA NAVONA   The long, oval Piazza Navona, with the splendidly baroque fountain in the center, is also popular at night. The famous **Gelateria Tre Scalini,** Pz. Navona 28, is the headline hangout on this square. Its most noteworthy dessert is tartufo, the ice-cream confection by which all other ice-cream confections in this gelato-rich country are judged. This homemade delicacy is the richest configuration of chocolate you can imagine, a mound of bittersweet chocolate chips held together by a smidgen of chocolate ice cream crowned with whipped cream. Open in summer, Thursday to Tuesday from 8am to 1:30am; in winter, Thursday to Tuesday from 8am to 1am.

AROUND THE PIAZZA DI SPAGNA   The Spanish Steps on Piazza di Spagna are almost a sight in and of themselves. There are no cafes actually on the staircase, but on warm summer nights the place is buzzing with the sounds of (mostly) young people from all over the world just sitting around, hanging out, and generally having a good time. Of the cafes near the Spanish Steps, the **Antico Caffè Greco,** V. Condotti 86, is the standout, being the oldest in Rome. It offers that Renaissance look at tourist prices and is open Monday to Saturday from 8am to 8:40pm.

NEAR THE FONTANA DI TREVI   **Cafe Gelateria Fontana di Trevi,** Pz. Fontana di Trevi 9, is the most popular of the several *gelaterie* (ice-cream shops) ringing the piazza. Try their cornetto, a chocolate-covered croissant stuffed with whipped cream, chocolate cream, or custard. Small pizzas and sandwiches are also sold here. In summer it's open daily from 7am to 2am; in winter, Thursday to Tuesday from 7am to midnight.

PUBS & BARS

Several of Rome's favorite watering holes are along Via del Governo Vecchio, a charming (but watch your wallet; pickpockets find it charming, too) narrow backstreet near Piazza Navona. Cafes here move in and out of favor quickly, so it's best to stroll along the street until you see an interesting one. The **Caffe del Pace** has been a favorite for many years at V. della Pace 3 (☎ 06/68-61-216), off Piazza Navona.

For a budget drink, you can't do better than **Vineria Reggio,** Campo de' Fiori 15 (☎ 06/65-43-268), a small wine store/bar that specializes in small glasses of prosecco (sparkling wine) for only 1,500L to 2,000L ($1 to $1.30). Quintessentially Roman, Reggio's patrons either stand along the long bar or sit on adjacent wooden benches. It's open Monday to Saturday from 9:30am to 1pm and 5pm to 1am.

Ireland is enjoying a renaissance in Rome, with Irish pubs popping up all over. **Flann O'Brien,** the famous Irish satirist who enlivened the *Irish Times* has a good bar named for him at V. Napoli 29 ☎ 488-0418. Although it's run by Italians, it has the look and feel of an Irish pub and attracts an international crowd. **Fiddler's Elbow** has lasted many a year at V. dell'Olmata 43, near Santa Maria Maggiore (☎ 06/48-72-110). Open 5pm till midnight, it's a pub where singing is the thing (not an Italian custom). **Guinness Pub** (V. Muzio Clemente 12, ☎ 06/32-18-42-40) has less Irish an air usually, but it serves up that frothy brew nicely to cool customers. Live music downstairs. It's near the Ponte Cavour across the Tiber.

Beer drinkers may also find a safe haven at the **Birreria Santi Apostoli,** Pz. Santi Apostoli 52 (☎ 06/48-72-110). They serve many kinds of beer and food until 2am.

Young Rome heads toward Testaccio at night for disco dancing at crazy **Radio Londra,** V. di Monte Testaccio 18 (☎ 06/57-43-448); slightly older sibs go to the **Caffe Latino,** V. di Monte Testaccio 96 (☎ 06/57-44-020), to hear jazz and watch the video.

10   Side Trips from Rome

TIVOLI

GETTING THERE   The easiest way to Tivoli, which is 23 miles outside of Rome, is to take the Metro to Rebibbia (1,500L/$1), then take the COTRAL bus, which you can catch at the station, to Tivoli. Generally, buses depart every half-hour from 5am to midnight for the one-hour trip.

WHAT TO SEE & DO

✪ **Villa d'Este.** Piazza Trento, Vle. d. Centro Fontane. (☎ **0774/22-070**). Admission 8,000L ($5.25). May 1–Aug 31, 9am–6:45pm; Sept–Apr 9am–1 hour before sunset. Bus stops near entrance (see "Getting There," above). Wear nonskid shoes, as the paths are often wet.

This delightful tiered water park, built by Cardinal d'Este in the 16th century, is the more interesting of the two villas here. Amazingly enough, the villa's 500 fountains, conduits, and waterfalls operate entirely by gravity—quite an engineering feat.

Go when the waters are running, if possible. (Call ahead or check with the tourist office.) H. V. Morton described it as "an extravaganza of falling water; of rising water; of water thundering up into snowy Alps under tremendous pressure; or water whispering and tinkling as it finds its way through moss and fern; of water lazily curving from the mouths of urns, and even, in some surely Freudian moment, from the breasts of sphinxes."

✪ **Villa Adriana (Hadrian's Villa).** V. di Villa Adriana. ☎ **0774/53-02-03.** Admission 8,000L ($5.25). May–Aug 9am–7:30pm, Sept–Apr 9am–dusk. Bus: 4 from Tivoli

On this, one of the greatest estates ever erected, the emperor Hadrian amassed a collection of replicas of all the beautiful places he had seen in the world. It was begun about the year A.D. 126, as a place for Hadrian to retire amid peaceful pomp and devote himself to the arts. Stop at the museum near the entrance—if it's open, the hours are irregular—where scale models help to put the complex into perspective. Hadrian assembled all the necessities of rich Roman life, baths, stadium, temples (the temple to the Egyptian god Serapis drew devotees from all over the world to consult its oracle and invoke favors), swimming pools, and a theater. At the Canopus, a group of caryatids were placed so that they were reflected in the pool. A lover of Greek philosophy, he re-created the Vale of Tempe (at right of the Temple of Venus) from northern Greece in Thessaly, where the goddess Diana was said to hunt. Much of the villa was destroyed by barbarians through the century, but during the Renaissance Pope Alexander VI began excavations and restorations continue until the present.

WHERE TO DINE

Le Cinque Statue. Lgo. Sant'Angelo 1. ☎ **0774/20-366.** Reservations recommended. Main courses 10,000L–25,000L ($6.60–$16.45). AE, MC, V. Sat–Thurs 12:30–3pm and 7:30–10pm. Closed Aug 15–Sept 9. Transportation: The ACOTRAL bus from Rome stops nearby.

This restaurant takes its name from the quintet of old carved statues, including Apollo Belvedere and gladiators, that are part of its decoration. The restaurant is run by a hard-working Italian family who serve an unpretentious cuisine, accompanied by the wines of the hill towns of Rome. Try the rigatoni with fresh herbs or tripe fried Roman style. All pasta is freshly made on the premises. There is also an array of ice creams and fruits.

OSTIA ANTICA

GETTING THERE   From Rome, take Metro B to Magliana, then take the Lido train (probably just across the platform) for Ostia Antica. From the station in Ostia Antica, take the bridge across the highway to the excavations. You can return to the train later and go out to the beach (Lido di Ostia).

WHAT TO SEE & DO

Ostia Antica. Vle. d. Romagnoli 717. ☎ **06/565-0022.** Admission 8,000L ($5.25). Apr–Sept 9am–6pm, Oct–Mar 9am–5pm. Metro: Ostia Antica (Line B). Get a map of the site at the ticket office.

Side Trips From Rome

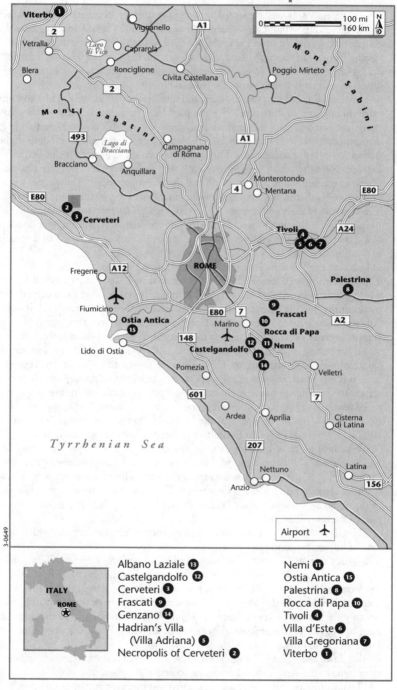

Location	Number
Albano Laziale	13
Castelgandolfo	12
Cerveteri	3
Frascati	9
Genzano	14
Hadrian's Villa (Villa Adriana)	5
Necropolis of Cerveteri	2
Nemi	11
Ostia Antica	15
Palestrina	8
Rocca di Papa	10
Tivoli	4
Villa d'Este	6
Villa Gregoriana	7
Viterbo	1

163

A vast, astonishingly well preserved ancient Roman city, once the port of Rome, in a pastoral setting without any nearby sign of modernity, Ostia Antica captures the essence of Imperial Rome in the middle of the 2nd century A.D. It's especially worth visiting if you won't have a chance to go to Pompeii, for here you'll see such dazzling details of Roman architecture as mosaic floors, marble walls, a few wall paintings—details by and large missing from the Roman Forum.

The site is divided into five districts, and into blocks that include public and private buildings. From the ticket office and past the Porta Romana you'll see the main street, the Decumanus Massimo, which leads to the sea. It's about 37 feet wide to accommodate two-way cart traffic. To the left is a burial ground. The Tomb of the Arches has colorful decorations. The large structure ahead at right is the Terme, or Baths, of Neptune, which were begun in A.D. 133 at the expense of emperor Hadrian. Climb to the landing to see the rooms and the Neptune mosaic. The Via dei Vigili, just before the baths, has remnants of the mosaics of the provinces and the winds. The Caserma of the Vigili (Firemen's Barracks) lodged firemen from Rome assigned to this garrison to tend fire and keep watch on the harbor. The large interior court had a chapel for the worship of the emperor and his family, preceded by a mosaic of a sacrificial scene.

Leave on the Via della Palestra and turn left onto picturesque Via della Fontana. The 1st-century A.D. teatro (theater) was restored in 1940, but its original layout, which accommodated 3,000 spectators, is intact. It was flooded for mock aquatic battles during the late empire. Three theatrical masks can be seen reproduced in stone. Behind the stage is the Piazzale of the Corporations, which were associations of magistrates, artisans, or workers similar to the later guilds. Some of the finest mosaics are found here, many with maritime themes, such as the lighthouse at Portus with cargo-laden ships entering the harbor. The Tiber once flowed near this square. Insignias such as the elephant referred to shipowners' associations from throughout the Mediterranean. This square may have been used as a private clubhouse for members, who could have pre- and posttheater refreshments here. At the southwest angle is a plaster cast of an altar (the original is at the Museo Nazionale Romano in Rome) decorated with scenes of the twins Romulus and Remus, Rome's legendary founders.

In the next block of buildings, the Mithraeum of the Seven Spheres is relatively well preserved. The Persian god Mithras, a sun god, had a large following in Rome, imported by merchants and sailors from the east. The niche contains a typical Mithraic scene in which a bull is slaughtered. The floor mosaic shows representations of the Seven Spheres, or Celestial Gates, through which souls of the initiated would pass to the upper heaven.

The Grand Horres, or flour mills, still have their original millstones, which donkeys or horses turned to grind flour.

Go back to the Decumanus Massimo, and you'll find the Thermopolium, which is the second structure down. This was a 3rd-century osteria (pub). A fresco shows the food and beverages sold. In back, follow the Via dei Depinti to the Insula dei Depinti. Buildings in this and many other sections of Ostia were apartment blocks, which were limited by law in height to about 70 feet, although in Rome they had risen to five stories (the amount of steps one could walk). In the Giove e Ganimede house you'll find frescoes, a garden, and mosaics.

Also down the Via dei Depinti is the museum, which is open mornings and contains some of the sculpture and terracotta objects that were found in the town.

The Capitolium (back on the Decumanus) was the most important temple, and across the Decumanus from it are the baths (*termi*). Farther along on this side of the Decumanus is the basilica—which was once two stories high—a meeting place for merchants and businesspeople. The Round Temple was a pantheon for the emperor gods.

Across the Decumanus again, take the right fork, Via della Foce. (The Decumanus continues to the left.) The first street to the right, Via del Tempio di Ercole, leads to the House of Cupid and Psyche, a 4th-century house with an ornate nymphaeum, or decorated fountain or pool, here set in a garden court. The sculptures of Cupid and Psyche found here are now on display in the museum. Cross Via della Foce to Via della Calcara and the baths (*termi*) of the Sette Sapienti, or Seven Wise Men, where an osteria has a satirical stucco painting about the bodily functions of the Seven. (Humor was always broad in Rome.) The second floor has a belvedere, or porch, with a view. Continue through the lovely cortile with two orders of arcades.

From here you can see the Cardo degli Aurighi. Turn left and then right on Via delle Volte Depinte to, at left, the Insula delle Muse, one of the most richly appointed, which houses the splendid painting of *Apollo and the Nine Muses.* Farther down this street is the house of the Dioscuri, with an excellent mosaic of the *Birth of Venus.*

Obviously there is still much to see and we have chosen only the highlights. This beautiful site should keep you occupied for hours.

ETRUSCAN CITIES: CERVETRI & TARQUINIA
CERVETRI

GETTING THERE   From Rome take Metro line A to Lepanto. From Lepanto, a COTRAL bus to Cerveteri leaves the station every half hour. The trip takes about an hour and costs 3,900L ($2.55). There's a small **tourist office** across from the bus stop at Caere Viaggi, Pz. Moro 17 (☎ **06/99-42-86-90**); check whether a bus is running to the necropolis, or else it's a 2-mile walk.

What to See & Do
Cerveteri was founded by Etruscans in the 8th century B.C. The main attractions are the *tumulae,* tombs that are great mounds of earth with stone bases. Rome museums (Vatican and Villa Giulia) have collections taken from them. The main necropolis (city of the dead) area is called **Banditacccia** (☎ **06/99-50-003**). It's open May through September, Tuesday to Sunday from 9am to 7pm; October through April, Tuesday to Saturday from 9am to 4pm, Sunday from 11am to 4pm. The tombs were designed to resemble Etruscan houses, with small rooms outside the main one, for servants. A flashlight will come in handy. Only about 50 of the estimated 5,000 tombs have been excavated thus far. The Tomba dei Relievi, or Tomb of the Reliefs, is elaborately decorated with sculpture and reliefs. The Tomb of the Alcove has a matrimonial bed carved out.

Where to Dine
Da Fiore. Near Procoio di Ceri (near the site). ☎ **06/99-20-42-50.** Thurs–Tues 12:30–3pm and 7:30–10pm. Main courses 7,000L–18,000L ($4.60–$11.85). No credit cards.

This is a simple local trattoria in the country. Relax here with bruschetta, country bread toasted with olive oil and garlic, from their wood-fired oven, and a glass of wine before enjoying a pasta with mushrooms or sausages.

TARQUINIA

GETTING THERE   From Termini in Rome, it's a one-hour train trip (take the train headed for Grosseto) to Tarquinia. The round-trip fare is 15,000L ($9.85).
Caveat: Take an early train or you'll arrive when they close for lunch.

What to See & Do

If you only have time to see either Cerveteri or Tarquinia, not both, Cerveteri is the choice. However, Tarquinia—the Etruscan site and museum, not the town—has its fine points. Tarquinia may have been inhabited as early as the 12th century B.C. It was the home of the Tarquin kings who ruled Rome long before the republic was born.

The **tourist office** here is better equipped than that of Cerveteri. It's at the Barriera San Giusto, just outside the main entrance to the town (☎ 06/85-63-84). It's open Monday to Saturday from 8am to 2pm and 4 to 7pm.

The **Tarauinia National Museum** (☎ 06/85-60-36) is in the adjoining Piazza Cavour; it's open Tuesday to Sunday from 9am to 7pm during the summer, and from 9am to 2pm in winter. Ask if there are guided evening tours. Admission (including the tombs) is 8,000L ($5.25).

Many of the most important Tarquinian families are represented in the museum with portraits on their tombs. The terracotta horses on the second floor were probably part of a temple frieze. Funeral urns, pottery, and jewelry complete the collection.

The **tombs** can be reached by a bus that stops near the tourist office, or it's about a 15-minute walk from the museum. From the Via della Croce, you'll see small houses with stairways going down into underground rooms. These underground chambers are works of art, bright with paintings that make Etruscan life seem contemporary. Only a few are open on any given day because of their perishable state.

Where to Dine

Tarquinia's Lido, which is a not-always-well-kept beach, can be reached by bus from the tourist office. Several restaurants are there offering meals at varying prices. For a splurge, go to **Velca Mare,** V. degli Argonauti 1 (☎ 0761/86-40-44), open Tuesday to Sunday from 12:30 to 3pm and 7 to 11pm. Main courses cost from 10,000L to 25,000L ($6.60 to $16.45), and a taste menu (degustazione) is 65,000L ($42.75). Soup with shrimp and mussels or sole in orange cream with basil and nutmeg may be on the menu. It's a well-cared-for place, with fresh flowers on the table.

VITERBO

GETTING THERE   Take Metro Line A to Flaminio. From there, follow the signs to Roma Nord Station and take the 15-minute train trip to **Saxa Rupra Station** ☎ 06/33-28-333, where you board a COTRAL bus for the 1¹/₂-hour trip to Viterbo. A combined bus and train ticket costs 11,500L ($7.55) round-trip. The last bus to Rome leaves Viterbo at 7pm.

VISITOR INFORMATION   The **tourist office** is on Pz. dei Caduti 16 (☎ 06/34-63-63), near the center of town.

WHAT TO SEE & DO

Viterbo is the most historic city in northern Lazio, and during the 13th century it was a papal residence. Viterbo has lots of medieval charm, but it can be unattractive as well. It's often filled with young draftees into Italy's armed forces, who are on their own for the first time, although they tend to behave pretty well given their circumstances.

The best way to see the town is to take a walking tour. Piazza del Plebiscito is about the center of town, circled by 15th- and 16th-century governmental buildings. The **Quartiere Pellegrino** is the most interesting section, a collection of hilly streets that make up the well-preserved 12th-century Medieval Quarter. Piazza San Pelligrino is considered the most comprehensive medieval piazza in Italy. Lined with art galleries and antiques shops, it's a great place to stroll.

The **Papal Palace,** built from 257 to 1266, housed a papal conclave that seemed endless, until the citizens removed the roof and started throwing stones in. You can still see where they landed as the cardinals dove for cover. Along Via San Lorenzo, have a look at the **Palazzo Chigi,** with a lovely court and loggia. The **Duomo** in Piazza San Lorenzo contains a *Holy Family* in the right aisle and *St. Lawrence in Glory* in the presbytery, both by the baroque artist Giovanni Romanelli. *Christ the Redeemer and Four Saints* by Girolamo da Cremona (1472) is in the left aisle.

The **Museo Civico,** in Piazza Crispi, is housed in the convent of the church of Santa Maria della Verità, where Sebastiano del Piombo's *Pietà* is the city's finest painting. It's based on a lost drawing by Michelangelo of 1512. The powerful forms recall Michelangelo and the colors reflect del Piombo's Venetian background. The 14th-century *Madonna* by Vitale da Bologna is another treasure.

In the nearby suburb of Bagnaia, the **Villa Lante** (☎ **0761/28-80-08**), is a lush Renaissance treasure. The buildings are not open to the public, but the flowers and fountains are worth the trip alone. Buses for the villa leave every half hour from Piazza dei Martiri. The trip takes just 15 minutes, and the fare is 1,500L ($1). The villa is open Tuesday to Sunday from 9am to 7:30pm during the summer, and from September through April from 9am to 5pm. Tours of the inner garden are offered every half-hour (4,000L/$2.65).

WHERE TO DINE

An alternative to the restaurant listed below is to buy sandwich material at the **Salumeria Cencioni** at V. Cairoli 18, where salamis, cold meats, and local cheeses are the specialty. The **Gran Caffe Schenardi** in Corso Italia 11 is a traditional coffeehouse in which to have a cappuccino in style.

La Torre. V. d. Torre 5 ☎ **0761/22-64-677.** Main courses 9,000L–15,000L ($5.92–$9.85). AE, MC, V. Mon–Sat 12:30–3pm and 7–10:30pm. Closed Aug.

In fast-food Viterbo, this enoteca (wine bar with food) is a find. Omelettes with herbs or goat cheese; agnolotti (pasta) filled with duck, rabbit, chestnuts, or artichokes; fiori di zucca (pumpkin flowers) stuffed with rabbit; and for dessert creamy *panna cotta* or sometimes a torrone mousse with hazelnut cream.

FRASCATI & THE CASTELLI ROMANI

The Castelli Romani are actually towns in the Alban hills southeast of Rome, where Romans like to wander about on Sundays, usually tasting the wines of the area and porchetta (roast pork) or whatever the local fairs are selling. The towns are most beautiful in October and November, when the grapes are being harvested (vendemmia), the air is cool, and the leaves have turned—although the wine festivals can get a bit raucous.

GETTING THERE   All of the towns discussed below can be reached from Rome by taking the Metro (Line A) to the Subaugusta station and then catching a COTRAL bus from there. Buses leave about every 20 minutes from 5:30am to 10:30pm, and the fare is 2,000L ($1.30).

FRASCATI

Frascati is the closest hill town and has great views of Rome. The **tourist office** in the Piazza Marconi, where the bus stops, has lots of information ☎ **06/942-0331.**

The **Villa Aldobrandini** has lovely gardens (3,000L/$1.95). Unfortunately the property is in poor shape, but you can, as you take in the fountains by Bernini and Fontanta, imagine the gracious parties that were once hosted here.

Piazza del Mercato has a morning market where you can buy snacks to take with you to the wine bars (cantine) in the neighborhood, such as **Cantina Farina** at V. Cavour 20. A quieter, more ambitious, and very good restaurant is the **Pizzeria/ Birreria Pinocchio,** Pz. d. Mercato 20, where grilled shrimp and cannelloni ai quatro formaggi (pasta stuffed with four cheeses) are on the reasonably priced menu.

CASTELLI ROMANI

Near Lago Albano, the towns of Castelgandolfo, Albano Laziale, Genzano, Nemi, and Rocca di Papa and Marino are interconnected by COTRAL bus.

Castelgandolfo is famous for the papal palace, where the pope gives his Wednesday audience in the summer when he is in residence.

Albano Laziale has wonderful oak trees and paths for walking in the Villa Comunale.

Genzano has a famous flower festival when the streets are literally totally covered with flowers laid out in decorative patterns. The festival is held on the Sunday after Corpus Christi (nine Sundays after Easter).

In late June and early July, **Nemi's** prized little strawberries brighten every bowl in town at the town's Festival of Strawberries (Fragolini), which lasts a few weeks

Rocca di Papa has winding steep streets with good views of Lazio as far as the coast. It's the highest of the towns. The trip here in the fall is especially beautiful, as the trees in this area are particularly colorful.

Where to Dine

In Castelgandolfo, the **Antico Ristorante Paganelli,** Pz. Gramsci 4 (☎ **06/ 93-60-000**), makes a good Amatriciana sauce (tomato with bits of bacon, cream, and spices) and roast boar or roast pork. (Closed Tuesday.)

La Foresta, Via dei Laghi (☎ **06/94-91-67**), a picturesque restaurant by the lake in the forest. A cab from Rocca di Papa should be 15,000L ($10), but check first. Menu items include the appropriate mushrooms (*funghi*) and game (*caccia*); for dessert try the zuppone al caffé, which is something like a tiramisù. Closed Tuesday.

PALESTRINA

GETTING THERE   Buses leave every 30 to 45 minutes during the day from Rome; departures are from Via Castro Pretorio (take the Metro to the stop at Castro Pretorio to catch the bus). It takes about an hour to reach Palestrina.

WHAT TO SEE & DO

Built on the site of Praeneste, an Etruscan settlement and then a resort for pampered Romans, Palestrina was the site of the Roman Temple of Fortune, which is dramatically stepped in terraces up the hill like the present town. Native son Pier Luigi da Palestrina is called the father of poluphonic harmony. Visit the museum in the **Colonna-Barberini Palace** (☎ **06/95-58-100**), high on a hill overlooking the valley. The 1st-century Nile mosaic depicts the flooding of the Nile with scenes of Egyptian life. It was taken from the temple. The terrace outside the museum has a fine view of the countryside.

A DAY OF HILL WALKING AT SUBIACO

Subiaco, St. Benedict's retreat, is a lovely spot with breathtaking views. From **Santa Scolastica** (☎ **0774/85-525**), a monastery he built with his sister, you can take tours led by monks through the complex of three cloisters. From here take the dramatically beautiful path about a third of a mile to the **Convento di San Benedetto** (☎ 0774/85-039). It was founded on the Sacro Speco, the grotto where St. Benedict prayed. A statue of the saint is in the grotto, the work of a student of Bernini. Inside the church, you can see the Chapel of the Madonna and the Chapel of St. Gregory, where you'll find the 14th-century *Triumph of Death* frescoes in the former and a delicate Pietà in the latter. The Grotto dei Pastori, on the lowest level, is the place where St. Benedict taught catechism to the local shepherds. The upper church has a fresco series of scenes of Crucifixion and Resurrection. A shop sells a potion the monks brew. Admission to the complex is free, and it's open daily from 9am to 12:30pm and 3 to 6pm. A bus from Rome's Rebibbia Metro station leaves hourly—less often on Sundays—for the two-hour trip. You can also come here from Tivoli. Try to avoid rush hours each way.

6 Florence

by Patricia Schultz

Five hundred years ago, Florence was the heart and nerve center of European culture and life. It was here from the 14th through the 16th century that many of the most important developments in art, science, literature, and architecture took place. Florence was considered one of the richest and most beautiful cities in western civilization, and today it remains to be seen and experienced by today's awe-struck visitors much as it was then.

Florence is no longer the axis around which the cultural world revolves, but the taste, elegance, and aesthetic sensibility that marked the Renaissance are still alive and well. Today the city boasts Europe's richest concentration of artistic wealth, a great deal of which can be seen or sensed without even entering any of its myriad world-class museums. Elegant young Florentines hurry down the narrow cobblestone streets, across the spacious stone-paved piazzas, and past the great august palazzi with the same confidence and pride as their forebears.

Europe's cultural revolution was financed in large part by the Medicis (and those who flourished under their commercial success), Florence's powerful ruling family throughout much of the Renaissance. They came to power as shrewd bankers and used their unprecedented acumen and wealth to foster artistic and intellectual genius. The city is filled with this heritage: Fully half a dozen principal museums, as well as myriad churches and palazzi, house major paintings and sculpture of that golden period when Florence was, as D. H. Lawrence described it, "Man's perfect center of the Universe."

However, it's not only sights and history that make Florence a special place for visitors. The nuts and bolts of where you stay and what you eat will make this city special in- and off-season. Many of the budget hotels I've listed are housed in imposing palazzi that date to the time of the Medicis and Michelangelo and his peers. You may find yourself sleeping beneath a ceiling decorated with colorful frescoes whose origins reach back into the centuries, or sampling a glass of Chianti in the cantina of a palazzo built before the locally born Giovanni Verrazzano set eyes on New York Harbor. The rustic though delicious cuisine of this region, *la cucina toscana,* from the heart of the nation's wine- and olive-producing farmland, is one of the finest in Italy.

1 Orientation

ARRIVING

BY PLANE   Alitalia, British Air, Lufthansa, and many other European airlines service Florence's newly expanded **Amerigo Vespucci Airport** (☎ 055/37-34-98) (also called **Peretola** after the zone in which it's located), although to date there are no direct flights from the United States. The regularly scheduled city bus no. 62 connects the airport with the Piazza Stazione in downtown Florence, making the journey in about 30 minutes, and costs 1,400L (90¢) each way. Slightly more expensive but without the local stops is the hourly SITA bus to and from downtown's **bus station** on V. Santa Caterina 15r (☎ 21-47-21) behind the train station, costing 6,000L ($3.95). Metered taxis line up outside the airport's arrival terminal and charge about 25,000L ($15.65) to most hotels in the city center.

A greater number of flights from the United States connect in European cities such as London, Paris, and Frankfort for Pisa's **Galileo Galilei Airport** (☎ 050/50-07-07). A frequent one-hour train service to Florence S.M.N. train station costs 9,200L ($6.05). When departing from the Pisa airport, you can check in your baggage for all flights and receive your boarding pass at the **Air Terminal** on track 5 in Florence's train station.

BY TRAIN   Most Florence-bound trains roll into the **Stazione Santa Maria Novella** (☎ 055/28-87-65), which you'll often see abbreviated as "S.M.N." The station is on the western edge of the city's compact *centro storico* or historical center, a leisurely 10-minute walk from the Duomo and 15 minutes from Piazza della Signoria and the Uffizi Galleries.

With your back to the tracks, you'll find an **Ufficio Turismo** information and hotel accommodations service office (☎ 055/28-28-93) toward the station's left exit. It's open April through October, Monday to Saturday from 9am to 9pm and Sunday from 10:30am to 6:25pm; November through March, the office closes at 8pm. The train information office is near the opposite exit to your right. Walk straight through the large glass doors into the outer hall for tickets at the *biglietteria* and a bank that changes money Monday to Saturday from 8:20am to 7:20pm. Adjacent to track 16 is an Albergo Diurno, or day hotel, where you can wash up or take a shower after a long train ride. There's also a 24-hour **luggage depot** at the head of track 16 (☎ 055/21-23-19) where you can drop your bags while you search for a hotel. It charges 2,000L ($1.25) per piece.

Some trains stop at the outlying **Stazione Campo di Marte** or **Stazione Rifredi,** which can be inconvenient and is worth avoiding. Although there's 24-hour bus service between these satellite stations and the principal S.M.N. station, departures are not always frequent and taxi service is erratic and expensive.

BY CAR   Driving to Florence is easy; the problems begin once you arrive. Almost all automobiles are banned from the city's centro storico—only those with special permits are allowed in. You will most likely be stopped at some point by the traffic police who will assume from your rental plates that you're a tourist heading to your hotel. Have the name and address of your hotel ready and they'll wave you through. You can drop off baggage at your hotel (the hotel staff will give you a sign for your car advising traffic police that you are unloading), then you must relocate to a parking lot.

VISITOR INFORMATION

The main train station's Ufficio Turismo (I.T.A.) information and accommodations service office (see above) distributes fairly good free city maps, answers simple questions, and makes hotel reservations for a 3,000L to 10,000L ($1.95 to $6.60) fee (depending on the category of hotel). Especially during the crowded summer months, however, travelers arriving by train may wish to bypass this office and walk a few steps farther to a second municipal office just outside the station. With your back to the tracks, take the left exit, cross onto the concrete median, and turn right; the office will be about 100 feet ahead. This **alternative information center** (☎ 055/ 21-22-45) distributes a wider variety of government tourist publications, including *Firenze Oggi (Florence Today)*, a helpful 2,000L ($1.30) bimonthly. It's usually open daily from 8am to 7:30pm.

The city's largest **A.P.T. tourist office** is the V. Cavour 1r (☎ 055/29-08-32 or fax 29-08-33), about three blocks north of the Duomo. This office is less harried than the busy station offices, offers lots of literature, and boasts a helpful staff. The office is usually open Monday through Saturday from 8am to 7:00pm in the summer, 8am to 2pm in the winter. A more conveniently located tourist office is just off the Piazza Signoria at Chiasso Baroncelli 17r (☎ 055/23-02-124). It has all general information, including up-to-the-minute info on museum hours, concert schedules, and a list of *affittacamere*, or boarding-house situations, usually available by the week.

The bilingual *Concierge Information* magazine, available free from the concierge desks of top hotels, contains a monthly calendar of events, as well as information on museums, sights, and attractions. *Firenze Spettacolo*, a 2,700L ($1.75) Italian-language monthly sold at most city newsstands, lists the latest in nightlife, arts, and entertainment.

CITY LAYOUT

Florence is a compact city that's best negotiated on foot. No two sights are more than a 20- or 25-minute walk apart, and all the hotels and restaurants listed in this chapter are located in the downtown area.

The city's relatively small, beautiful, and touristy Centro Storico (Historic Center) is loosely bounded by the S.M.N. Train Station to the northwest, Piazza della S.S. Annunziata to the northeast, Piazza Santa Croce to the east, and the Arno River to the south. South of the river is the Oltrarno (literally meaning "on the other side of the Arno"), generally considered an adjunct to the centro storico.

Piazza del Duomo, dominated by Florence's magnificent cathedral and ancillary baptistry, is at the geographic center of the tourist's city. During your stay, you'll inevitably walk along many of the streets radiating from this imposing square, the nucleus of the city.

Borgo San Lorenzo, a narrow street running north from the Baptistery, is best known for the excellent outdoor market at its far end; it sells everything from marbleized paper-wrapped pencils and boxes to leather bags and jackets. It borders the train station neighborhood, home to a cluster of the city's cheapest hotels.

Via Calzaiuoli, Florence's most popular pedestrian thoroughfare and shopping street, runs south from the Duomo, connecting the church with the romantic, statue-filled **Piazza della Signoria.** West and parallel to this is **Via Roma,** which becomes **Via Por Santa Maria,** more excellent pedestrian shopping territory. Midway between the two is the **Piazza della Repubblica,** a busy shop- and cafe-ringed square surrounded by expensive shopping streets. Farther west still, and you're on **Via Tornabuoni**, the designer-lined Fifth Avenue of Florence.

Exit the Piazza della Signoria by the Via Vacchereccia, then turn left for two blocks to the **Ponte Vecchio (Old Bridge),** the Arno's oldest and most famous span. Topped with dozens of tiny gold and jewelry shops, the bridge crosses over to the **Oltrarno** area, a section of artisans and shopkeepers that's best known for the Pitti Palace, just a few blocks past the bridge and the green Boboli Gardens behind it, and the lovely Piazza Santo Spirito west of that.

Confused? Climb the 414 steps to the top of Giotto's Campanile (Bell Tower) that flanks the Duomo and you'll be rewarded with a beautiful eagle's-nest view of Florence that will help you navigate your way around. For a sunset memory that will stay with you for life, view Florence from afar at the Piazzale Michelangiolo.

Finding an Address   Traditionally, two systems of street numbering have been used here: black (*nero*) and red (*rosso*). Black numbers are used for residential and office buildings, including hotels, while red numbers are used to identify all commercial enterprises, including restaurants and stores. Florence is the only city to use this system and as of mid-1996 a regulation was passed to eliminate all red numbers and renumber in black. However, this is being protested by merchants who want to keep their red numbers—the situation is at the moment in a state of impasse, which may or may not be resolved in 1997. In this chapter, red-numbered addresses are indicated by a lowercase "r" following the number. The addresses used in this chapter do not reflect any future change.

GETTING AROUND

BY BUS   You'll rarely need to take advantage of Florence's efficient A.T.A.F. bus system, since the city is so wonderfully compact. Bus tickets cost 1,400L (90¢) and must be purchased before you board. A four-pack of tickets (*biglietto multiplo*) will run 5,400L ($3.55), while a 24-hour pass costs 5,000L ($3.25). Tickets are sold at the **A.T.A.F. booth** at the head of track 14 in the train station (☎ **055/58-05-28**) and at tobacco shops (tabacchi), bars, and most newsstands. Once on board, validate your ticket in the box near the rear door or you could be fined (60,000L, or $39.50!).

If you intend to use the bus system, the first thing you should do is pick up a bus map at any of the tourist offices. Since most of the historical center is *zona blu* with limited traffic, buses make runs on principal streets only, leaving the rest of the city as a more enjoyable area in which to stroll.

BY TAXI   Cabs cannot be hailed, but can be found at taxi ranks in or near principal piazzas, or called to your restaurant or hotel by dialing **4242, 4798,** or **4390.** Taxis charge 1,350L (90¢) per kilometer, but there's a minimum fare of 6,000L ($3.95) and most hops around the city average about 10,000L ($6.60); don't forget to include a 10% tip.

BY BICYCLE   Despite the relatively traffic-free historical center, the alternative of biking has never really caught on. Permanent shops such as **Ciao & Basta** on Costa dei Magnoli 24 (☎ **055/29-62-30**) rent bikes by the hour and day, while the city sets up temporary sites about town during summer months (look in front of the Biblioteca Nazionale south of the Piazza Santa Croce on the Arno River).

ON FOOT   With its medieval and 15th-century palazzi lining cobblestone streets that are even older, Florence is one of the most delightful cities in Europe to explore on foot. Florence is very compact. A leisurely walk will take you from one end of the tourist area to the other—from the train station to Piazza Santa Croce—in about 40 minutes, or perhaps five hours if you give in to window-shopping. The free map handed out by the tourist office lacks a street index, but may be all you need. The best full map of the city is the yellow-jacketed map by Studio F.M.B. Bologna, available at most newsstands for 7,000L ($4.60).

BY CAR Florence's historic center, where most hotels are located, is strictly off-limits to all vehicular traffic, except that of local residents. Standard rates for parking near the center are 1,500L to 4,000L ($1 to $2.65) per hour; some lots offer a daily rate of 25,000L ($16.45). The garage most convenient to the historic center is the Europa, at Bgo. Ognissanti 96, next to Avis; it's open daily from 6am to 2am. The International Garage, at V. Palazzuolo 29, just west of Va Porcellana, is only a few blocks away. Special rates may be available through some hotels or at some lots.

FAST FACTS: Florence

American Express A new, recently opened office is east of the Piazza della Repubblica at V. Dante Alighieri 22r (☎ 055/50-981) while the original office still operates at V. Guicciardini 49r (☎ 055/28-87-51), the street that leads to the Palazzo Pitti. Both exchange traveler's checks without a fee and are open Monday to Friday from 9am to 5:30pm; the Via Dante location is also open Saturday from 9am to 12:30pm.

Babysitting There is no official organization, but ask at your hotel and give advance notice.

Bookstores The **BM Libreria Book Shop,** Bgo. Ognissanti 4r (☎ 055/29-45-75), is the best place in town for books in English. The best travel bookstore in town is **Libreria Il Viaggio**, Bgo. degli Albizi 41r (☎ 055/24-04-89). For more bookstores, see section 5, "Shopping."

Business Hours In summer, most **businesses and shops** are open Monday to Friday from 9am to 1pm and 4 to 8pm; on Saturday, most shops are open in the morning only. From mid-September through mid-June, most shops are open Tuesday to Saturday from 9am to 1pm and 3:30 to 7:30pm; on Monday during winter, shops don't open until the afternoon. The exception to this winter rule are alimentari (small grocery stores), which are open on Monday morning in low season but closed Wednesday afternoon. In Florence, as throughout Italy, just about everything is closed on Sunday except touristy shops in the center of town with special permits. Restaurants are required to close at least one day per week (known as their *giorno di riposo*), though the particular day varies from one trattoria to another. Many serve lunch on Sunday but close for Sunday dinner.

Climate The city's position in the Arno Valley, guarantees still, humid summers where mid-July through mid-August can be unbearable with temperatures in the high 90s. May and September are the nicest months to visit, with weather in the 60s, but huge crowds to dampen your spirits. October is cooler, in the 50s, but can be very wet. January and February are the coldest with days in the 30s to 40s, but with regular rainfall. You'll never wait in line at the Uffizi, however.

Consulates The Consulate of the **United States** is at Lungarnoamerigo Vespucci 38 (☎ 055/23-98-276), near its intersection with Via Palestro; it's open Monday to Friday from 9am to noon and 2 to 4pm. The Consulate of the **United Kingdom** is at Lungarno Corsini 2 (☎ 055/28-41-33), near Piazza Santa Trinita; it's open Monday to Friday from 9:30am to 12:30pm and 2:30 to 4:30pm.

Crime Petty thefts are performed deftly and swiftly by Florence's gypsy (zingari) population, despite the efforts of plainclothes police. They show up in small groups at the most touristed spots, and will jostle or distract you while relieving you of your valuables. Nongypsy incidents are known to happen at the crowded markets or on public buses.

Currency Exchange   Standard bank hours are Monday to Friday from 8:20am to 1:20pm and 2:45 to 3:45pm; only a few banks are open on Saturday. There is an ATM at the train station. Look for privately owned cambios around town; their rates are often good but the fine print confesses they charge 3 to 6% commission. The state railway will change money at any hour at window 19.

Dentists/Doctors   For a list of English-speaking dentists or doctors, ask at the American or British Consulate or at the American Express office. Visitors in need of emergency medical care can call Volunteer Hospital Interpreters (☎ 055/ 23-44-567) day or night. The interpreters are always on call and offer their services free of charge.

Drugstores   Two addresses offering 24-hour schedules are the Farmacia Communale, at the head of track 16 in the train station (☎ 055/21-67-61) and Molteni on V. Calzaiuoli 7r just north of the Piazza Signoria (☎ 055/21-54-72).

Emergencies   As throughout Italy, dial **113** for the police. Some Italians recommend the military-trained *Carabinieri* (call **112**), whom they consider a better police force. To report a fire, dial **115.** For an ambulance, dial **118** or **055/21-22-22.**

Fax   Fax service is available from the post office (see "Mail," below) to almost every destination with the exception of the United States. Ask your hotel if they can provide the service, or look for stationery and office supply stores with "servizio fax" posted in their windows.

Holidays   See chapter 2 for details. Florence's patron saint, San Giovanni (John the Baptist), is honored on June 24.

Laundry/Dry Cleaning   North of the Duomo is one of four modern, self-service locations of the American-owned Wash & Dry, V. d. Servi 105r (☎ 055/ 29-15-04 for other locations or ask your hotel). They charge about 12,000L ($7.90) for a wash and dry and are open daily from 8am to 10pm. Slightly less expensive at 9,000L ($5.90) is the self-service Launderette at V. Guelfa 55r between the train station and the Duomo; daily 8am to 10pm.

Lost & Found   All objects handed over to the police and railroad officials wind up at Oggetti Smarriti (Lost Property), V. Circondaria 19 (☎ 055/36-79-43), in the area behind the train station. For objects left in taxi cabs, call the Vigili Urbani (☎ 28-49-26).

Mail   Florence's **main post office** is on Via Pellicceria, off the southwest corner of Piazza della Repubblica. Purchase stamps (francobolli) at windows 21 and 22. Letters sent "Fermo Posta" (Italian for General Delivery) or *Poste Restante* can be picked up at windows 23 and 24. The post office is open Monday through Friday from 8:15am to 7pm and Saturday from 8:15am to 12:30pm.

All packages heavier than 1 kilo (2¼ lb.) must be properly wrapped and brought around to the **parcel office** at the back of the building (enter at V. d. Sassetti 4, also known as Piazza Davanzati). If you're uncertain about Italy's complex parcel-post standards, take your shipment to **Oli-ca,** Bgo. SS. Apostoli 27r (☎ 055/ 23-96-917), off Via Por Santa Maria and south of the post office, where they'll box and wrap your shipment for 4,500L to 15,000L ($2.95 to $9.85) according to size (they follow regular store hours).

Rest Rooms　There are public rest rooms at the train station, on the ground floor of the Palazzo Vecchio, and in all museums. The cost of a coffee or mineral water will give you access to any bar's facilities, which are reserved for the use of patrons only.

Shoe Repair　East of the Duomo, the one-man show at Heel Express, at V. Oriuolo 29r (no phone), repairs while-you-wait.

Student Networks & Resources　Florence's university is between the Mercato Centrale and Piazza San Marco, the latter being the center of student activity in Florence. The mensa, or cafeteria, where students congregate at mealtimes is at V. San Gallo 25a. There's a sizable community of American students in Florence enrolled in over 32 study-abroad programs.

The **Centro Turistico Studentesco (C.T.S.)**, at V. dei Ginori 25r (☎ **055/ 28-95-70**), across from the Medici-Riccardi Palace near the San Lorenzo Market, is the best budget travel agent in Florence, selling reduced-price train, air, and ferry tickets and will book all-category discounted hotel accommodations in Italy and abroad. This agency specializes in youth and student fares but is helpful to thrifty travelers of all ages. Note that the staff doesn't make train reservations and doesn't accept credit or charge cards. It's open Monday through Friday from 9:00am to 1pm and 2:30 to 6pm and Saturday from 9:00am to noon.

Also worth checking out is **S.T.S.** (**The Youth and Student Travel Service**) at V. Zannetti 18r (just off Via Cerretani, ☎ **055/28-41-83**), which offers many of the same services but accepts credit cards.

Taxis　There are taxi ranks in or near all the major piazzas. Or call a taxi at **4242, 4390,** or **4798.** Taxis are metered and there are supplements for Sunday and night-time travel and luggage.

Telephone　The telephone area code for Florence is 055.

2 Accommodations

During the peak summer months it's important to arrive early, as many hotels fill up for the next night even before all their guests from the previous evening have checked out. If you have trouble with or are intimidated by the language barrier, try the **room-finding office** in the train station, near track 16 (see "Arriving," earlier in this chapter). Peak season is generally considered mid-March through mid-July, September through early November, and December 23 through January 6.

HOSTELS

In addition to the inexpensive multibed accommodations at the Archi Rossi (see Albergo Mia Cara, below), look to the following hostels for cheap dorm-style rooms.

Ostello Santa Monaca. V. Santa Monaca 6 (off Pz. d. Carmine), 50125 Firenze. ☎ **055/ 26-83-38** or 23-96-704. Fax 055/28-01-95. 111 beds in 13 rms. 20,000L ($13.15) per person, sheets included. No credit cards. From the train station, walk around to Pz. Santa Maria Novella; go along V. d. Fossi, which begins at the far left corner of the piazza, until that street ends on the banks of the Arno; cross the Ponte alla Carraia (bridge) to the Oltrarno and walk along V. de' Serragli; V. Santa Monaca will be the third right (about a 15-minute walk). Otherwise catch bus no. 36 or 37 and get off at 2nd stop after bridge.

Much more convenient if not as clean as the remote IYHF youth hostel (below), this privately run hostel is a lively gathering spot for travelers from all over the world, as well as a great place to trade budget tips and meet travel companions. The rooms are closed from 9:30am to 2pm, and the building itself is locked up from 1 to 2pm. You can register from 9:30am until 1pm and from 2pm until midnight. There's an air-tight 12:30am curfew, and the doors aren't reopened until 6:30am. Breakfast is not available; the hostel has arrangements at a nearby trattoria for fixed-price meals. Reservations accepted by fax for singles and groups. Note that some readers have reported thefts here.

Ostello Villa Camerata. Vle. Augusto Righi 2/4, 50137 Firenze. ☎ **055/60-14-51.** Fax 055/61-03-00. 322 beds. 23,000L ($15.15) per person. Rates include continental breakfast and sheets. Dinner 13,000L ($8.55) extra. No credit cards. Bus: 17B to the end (capolinea) of the route or 17A; then a half-mile walk.

Florence's beautiful IYHF youth hostel is housed in a mammoth 15th-century villa surrounded by a large park and garden north of Florence. The morning views from this hilltop location are fantastic. The hostel is almost a community unto itself, with movies in English every evening, a bar, and a budget restaurant serving dinner only. The hostel accepts IYHF members only, but you can buy a card (valid for a year) on the premises for 30,000L ($19.75) or become a member for the night for 5,000L ($3.30). In summer, arrive by 1pm, when the reception opens, in order to secure a bed; this popular, peaceful, and dirt-cheap hostel fills quickly. Curfew is 11:30pm year-round, and dinner is served from 6:30 to 8pm among the most comfortable, least institutional hostels in Europe; this is one of the few with baths in some rooms (four to eight beds per room). A maximum stay of three days is usually enforced.

NEAR THE TRAIN STATION

Being within easy striking distance from the train station explains the proliferation of cheap hotels in this general area, particularly Via Fiume and Via Faenza; some buildings house as many as six pensiones. Exit the train station near the 24-hour pharmacy and turn right towards the Via Nazionale where you take a left. Via Faenza is the second left (Via Fiume is the first left) off Via Nazionale. This is the bustling area of the sprawling open-air Mercato San Lorenzo and is generally safe.

DOUBLES FOR LESS THAN 75,000 LIRE ($49.35)

Albergo Azzi. V. Faenza 56 (1st floor), 50123 Firenze. ☎ **055/21-38-06.** Fax 055/21-38-06. 12 rms, 3 with bath. 42,000L ($27.65) single without bath; 65,000L ($42.75) double without bath, 75,000L ($49.35) double with bath; 90,000L ($59.20) triple without bath; 100,000L ($65.80) quad without bath. Rates include breakfast in high season only; low season optional at 5,000L ($3.30) per person. Rates discounted approximately 15% low season. AE, D, MC, V.

Sandro and Valentino, the new owners of this pensione, also known as the Locanda degli Artisti (the Artists' Inn), are themselves musicians and are slowly creating a home away from home for traveling artists, artists manqué, and student types. Not for the fastidious or fussy, this venerable place exudes a relaxed bohemian feel—not all doors hang straight, not all bedspreads match. A little down at the heels, the young owners are slowly bringing it around. In the meantime, the lovely open terrace with a view where breakfast is served in warm weather will disappoint no one. The Albergo Anna (eight rooms, four without bath) is located in the same building: same management, same phone, similar rates.

Albergo Merlini. V. Faenza 56 (3rd floor), 50123 Firenze. ☎ **055/21-28-48.** Fax 055/28-39-39. 10 rms, 2 with bath. 50,000L ($32.90) single without bath; 70,000L ($46.05) double without bath, 85,000L ($55.90) double with bath; 90,000L ($5920) triple without bath, 96,000L ($63.15) triple with bath. Breakfast 9,000L ($5.90) extra. Off-season rates approximately 15% less. No credit cards.

Family-run (with the English-speaking Signora Mary at the helm for more than 40 years) and cozy, this small place is proudly appointed with wooden-carved antique

Florence Accommodations

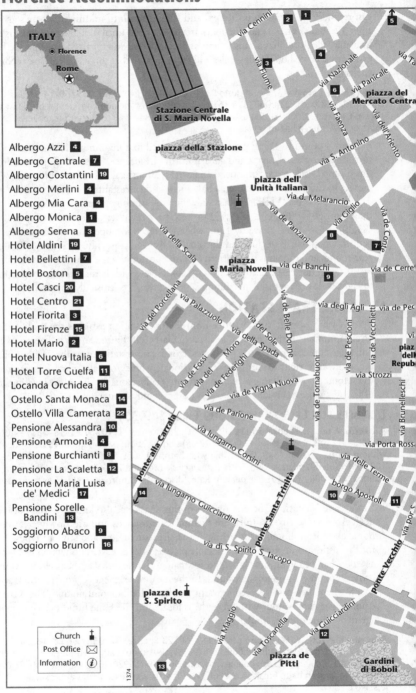

Albergo Azzi **4**
Albergo Centrale **7**
Albergo Costantini **19**
Albergo Merlini **4**
Albergo Mia Cara **4**
Albergo Monica **1**
Albergo Serena **3**
Hotel Aldini **19**
Hotel Bellettini **7**
Hotel Boston **5**
Hotel Casci **20**
Hotel Centro **21**
Hotel Fiorita **3**
Hotel Firenze **15**
Hotel Mario **2**
Hotel Nuova Italia **6**
Hotel Torre Guelfa **11**
Locanda Orchidea **18**
Ostello Santa Monaca **14**
Ostello Villa Camerata **22**
Pensione Alessandra **10**
Pensione Armonia **4**
Pensione Burchianti **8**
Pensione La Scaletta **12**
Pensione Maria Luisa
   de' Medici **17**
Pensione Sorelle
   Bandini **13**
Soggiorno Abaco **9**
Soggiorno Brunori **16**

Church ✝
Post Office ✉
Information ⓘ

178

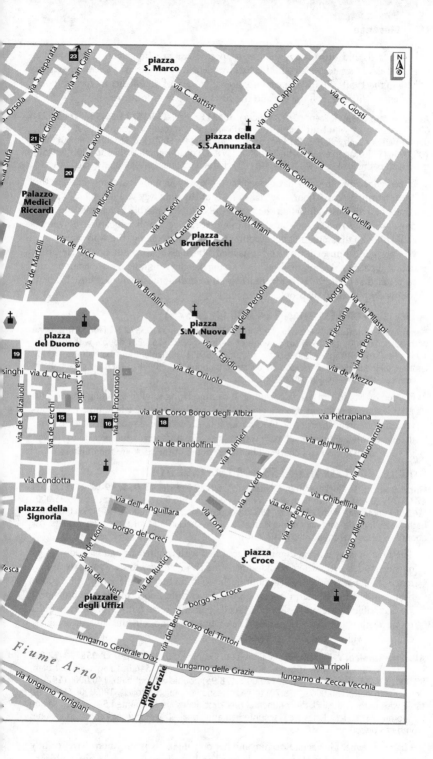

headboards and furnishings that set it apart. Breakfast (optional) is served on a glassed-in terrace decorated with frescoes by talented American art students who lived here in the 1950s. Enjoy your cappuccino with a view of the Medici Chapel's cupola, Florence's different bell towers, and the city's terra-cotta roofscape.

Albergo Mia Cara. V. Faenza 58 (2nd floor), 50123 Firenze. ☎ **055/21-60-53.** Fax 055/23-02-601. 22 rms, 9 with bath. Single with and without bath (call for rates); 70,000L ($46.05) double without bath, 80,000L ($52.65) double with bath; 94,500L ($62.15) triple without bath, 108,000L ($71.05) triple with bath; 119,000L ($78.30) quad without bath, 136,000L ($89.50) quad with bath. Breakfast 7,000L ($4.40) extra. Rates discounted off-season. No credit cards.

In Florence you can easily pay quite a bit more and get a lot less than you do at the Noto family's second-floor, one-star hotel (but the only way you'll pay less is at the family's Archi Rossi Hostel on the ground floor). New marble pavements and windows, spacious rooms, renovated plumbing, attractive iron headboards—now if we could only up the wattage of light fixtures for nighttime reading. But who cares, when you get good housekeeping and a needed Stairmaster workout in this elevator-deprived palazzo. Angela, the English-speaking daughter running both operations, can be reached at 055/29-08-04 for information regarding the downstairs hostel, where rooms sleep three to six people.

A DOUBLE FOR LESS THAN 114,000 LIRE ($75)

Pensione Armonia. V. Faenza 56 (1st floor), 50123 Firenze. ☎ **055/21-11-46.** 7 rms, none with bath. 50,000L ($32.90) single without bath; 90,000L ($59.20) double without bath; 105,000L ($69.10) triple without bath; 140,000L ($92.10) quad without bath. Rates include continental breakfast in high season; in low season, optional at 5,000L ($3.30) per person. Rates discounted 30% low season. No credit cards.

Owned by Mario and Marzia, a young, accommodating English-speaking brother and sister act, this small pensione is a reliable two-star–hotel choice when those more conveniently located closer to the Duomo are full. An occasional touch sets it apart from the pack: Some whitewashed, tiled rooms have nice bedspreads and breakfast is served in your room at no extra charge. The three rooms in the back are the quietest.

DOUBLES FOR LESS THAN 150,000 LIRE ($98.70)

Hotel Boston. V. Guelfa 68 (off V. Nazionale), 50129 Firenze. ☎ **055/49-67-47.** Fax 055/47-09-34. 20 rms, 14 with bath. A/C TEL TV. 70,000L ($46.05) single without bath, 95,000L ($62.50) single with bath; 150,000L ($98.70) double with bath; 200,000L ($131.60) triple with bath. Rates include continental breakfast. These are special rates for Frommer's readers. Ask about low-season discounts. No credit cards.

The Boston is a peaceful, dignified place filled with original art and blessed with an outside shaded patio where breakfast becomes an idyllic way to start your day in Florence. The first two floors were built in the 17th century and have exposed wooden beams and plenty of charm (rooms on the newer third floor, equally recommended, are accessible by elevator). The Via Guelfa gets moderate traffic, so ask for a quiet room overlooking the back patio garden whose only noise is the clink of breakfast china that will serve as your wake-up call.

Albergo Monica. V. Faenza 66B (1st floor; at V. Cennini), 50123 Firenze. ☎ **055/28-17-06.** Fax 055/28-38-04. 16 rms, 10 with bath. TEL TV A/C. 70,000L ($46.05) single without bath, 80,000L ($52.65) single with bath; 120,000L (78.95) double without bath, 140,000L ($92.10) double with bath; 150,000L ($98.70) triple with shower only (no toilet), 180,000L ($118.40) triple with bath. Rates include continental breakfast. Rates are discounted 5% in high season for Frommer's readers. Rates are discounted an additional 40% in low-season, which includes Frommer's discount. AE, MC, V.

Gracious owner Giovanna Rocchini and her polylingual assistant Rhuna have recently supervised the facelift of their already fine hotel, resulting in a bright, airy ambience and newly redone bathrooms. Their prices have increased but so have the amenities they now offer, and it is only their train-station location that keeps these prices subdued compared to competitors nearer the Duomo. Highlights include terracotta floors, the occasional exposed-brick archway redolent of other times, the bar area's marble-topped cafe tables, and a wonderful open-air, terrazza where breakfast is conducted the minute the weather turns warm. The quietest rooms are in the back, and if you're lucky, yours will have an antique wrought-iron bed.

✪ **Hotel Nuova Italia.** V. Faenza 26 (off the V. Nazionale; around the corner from the San Lorenzo Market), 50123 Firenze. ☎ **055/26-84-30** or 28-75-08. Fax 055/21-09-41. 20 rms, all with bath. TEL. 100,000L ($65.80) single; 150,000L ($98.70) double; 200,000L ($131.60) triple; 240,000L ($157.90) quad. Rates include breakfast. These are special rates for Frommer's readers. Ask about low-season rates. AE, MC, V.

This top-notch hotel is carefully watched over by English-speaking Luciano and Eileen Viti and their daughter, Daniela. Eileen met Luciano more than 30 years ago, when she stayed at his family's hotel on the recommendation of *Europe on $5 a Day*. Today the couple is especially welcoming to our readers (this is also an ideal selection for traveling families), who can expect to be treated like visiting royalty. The improvement of their already lovely hotel is a work in progress: One season triple-paned soundproof windows and rarely found mosquito screens were installed, the next season bathrooms were all retiled (air-conditioning is expected to be installed by 1977; ask when booking). The family's love of art is manifested in the framed posters and paintings found everywhere, and Eileen is a better source of information about local art exhibits than the Board of Tourism. The location of the very good Trattoria Antichi Cancelli directly across the street couldn't be any more convenient; the *menu turistico* is 17,000L ($11.20).

A DOUBLE FOR 200,000 LIRE ($131.45)

Hotel Mario. V. Faenza 89 (1st floor; near V. Cennini), 50123 Firenze. ☎ **055/21-68-01.** Fax 055/21-20-39. 16 rms, all with bath. A/C TEL TV. 160,000L ($105.25) single; 200,000L ($131.60) double; 240,000L ($157.90) triple. Rates discounted approximately 40% in low season. Rates include continental breakfast. AE, DC, MC, V.

In a traditional Old Florentine atmosphere, owner Mario Noce and his family run a first-rate ship that has been a long-enduring favorite with our readers. Your room may have a wrought-iron headboard and a massive reproduction antique armoire, and look out onto a peaceful garden. Included are rare amenities such as CNN, hair dryers, and air-conditioning at no extra charge. You could stay in a grand hotel for thrice this price and not have fresh flowers and fruit that appear daily in your room, compliments of Mario. The beamed ceilings in the common areas date from the 17th century, though the building became a hotel only in 1872.

BETWEEN THE TRAIN STATION & THE DUOMO
DOUBLES FOR LESS THAN 114,000 LIRE ($75)

✪ **Albergo Centrale.** V. d. Conti 3 (2nd floor; off V. Cerretani), 50123 Firenze. ☎ **055/ 21-57-61.** Fax 21-51-216. 18 rms, 15 with bath. TEL TV. 93,000L ($61.20) single with bath; 114,000L ($75.00) double without bath, 142,000L ($93.40) double with bath; 150,000L ($98.70) triple without bath, 185,000L ($121.70) triple with bath. Continental buffet breakfast included. These are special rates for Frommer's readers. Rates further discounted low season Jan 10–Mar 10 and Aug. AE, DISC, MC, V.

If you are as sensitive to detail and attention as I am, you'll greatly appreciate the Centrale's bright, spacious rooms freshly painted in soothing pastel shades and outfitted with matching antique armoires and headboards. You'll notice the chenille bedspreads and tasteful choice of floral wallpaper, the attentive housekeeping and the thoughtful touch of white lace doilies or dried-flower arrangements. The presence of Normandy-born manager Marie-Thérèse Blot is everywhere in this welcoming and comfortable pensione housed in the former 14th-century patrician residence known as the Palazzo Malaspina, many of whose rooms overlook the Medici Chapels. A perfect choice for families; off-season travelers who stay for a minimum of four nights only pay for three. And not to mention one of the most ample buffet breakfasts in town at this price.

✪ **Pensione Burchianti.** V. d. Giglio 6 (off V. Panzani), 50123 Firenze. ☎/fax **055/ 21-27-96.** 11 rms with shower only, 6 with complete bath. 50,000L ($32.90) single without bath, 70,000L ($46.05) single with bath; 100,000L ($65.80) double without bath, 120,000L ($78.95) double with bath; 120,000L ($78.95) triple without bath, 160,000L ($105.25) triple with bath. Rates include continental breakfast; not mandatory (deduct 5,000L/$3.30/from room rate). Ask about low season discounts. No credit cards.

Fraught with history and redolent of a grand lifestyle past, this is a most unusual find for lovers of high drama and low prices. Established in the late 19th century by the Burchianti sisters (the last of whom died in 1973) in the noble 16th-century Salimbeni palazzo, this once renowned pensione hosted royal and VIP guests (you might wind up in Benito Mussolini's room) during its golden days. Most of that same historical grandeur is still intact throughout—leaded and stained-glass windows and doors, beautifully frescoed walls and ceilings, hand-painted wooden coffered ceilings, and here and there remnants of valuable antique furniture left behind by the former owners (steer clear of the two rooms as painstakingly plain as the others are theatrical). Prohibitive costs forbid a much deserved restoration, but if you love such nostalgic threadbare romance, you'll be in heaven here. Imaginative plumbing results in the eyesore addition of prefabricated shower stalls insensitively stuck in corners and sinks bolted directly onto precious 19th-century frescoed walls. A pretty sun-filled salon and handsome breakfast room seems pulled out of an E. M. Forster movie.

Soggiorno Abaco. V. d. Banchi 1 (2nd floor; where V. Panzani intersects with V. Tornabuoni), 50123 Firenze. ☎/fax **055/23-81-919.** 7 rms, 3 with bath. TEL TV. 55,000L ($36.20) single without bath, 60,000L ($39.50) single with bath; 85,000L ($55.90) double without bath, 110,000L ($72.35) double with bath; 100,000L ($65.80) triple without bath; 130,000L ($85.50) triple with bath; 120,000L ($78.95) quad without bath, 150,000L ($98.70) quad with bath. Breakfast 8,000L ($5.25) per person extra. These are special rates for Frommer's readers. Rates discounted 10–20% in low season. MC, V.

Although upscale shoppers will appreciate this location at the foot of the tony Via Tornabuoni, Florence's Fifth Avenue, the small and homey Abaco offers a relaxed and laid-back atmosphere better suited to students and student-types who won't notice the three-story walk up. Young English-speaking Bruno has put in a washer and dryer for the use of guests (5,000L/$3.30), makes sure the breakfast croissants are fresh, and is a walking resource for nighttime entertainment and music venues (having worked at most of them himself) for those looking to do the town.

DOUBLES FOR LESS THAN 150,000 LIRE ($98.70)

✪ **Hotel Bellettini.** V. de' Conti 7 (off V. d. Cerretani), 50123 Firenze. ☎ **055/21-35-61.** Fax 055/28-35-51. TEL TV A/C. 27 rms, 23 with bath. 85,000L ($55.90) single without bath, 98,000L ($64.50) single with bath; 130,000L ($85.50) double without bath, 160,000L ($105.25) double with bath; 216,000L ($142.10) triple with bath; 272,000L ($178.95) quad with bath. Rates include breakfast. AE, DC, MC, V.

A *pietra serena* stone plaque hangs in the wooden-beamed breakfast salon stating that there has been a hotel in this Renaissance palazzo since the 1600s. Two young sisters, Gina and Marzia, third-generation hoteliers, arrived in 1993 to carry on the

AT&T Direct℠ Service

How to call internationally from overseas:

1. Just dial the AT&T Access Number for the country you are calling from.
2. Dial the phone number you're calling.
3. Dial the calling card number listed above your name.

AT&T Access Numbers

Argentina ✶	001-800-200-1111	Costa Rica ■	0-800-0-114-114
Australia	1800-881-011	Czech Rep. ▲	00-42-000-101
Austria ● ○	022-903-011	Ecuador ● ▲	999-119
Bahamas	1-800-872-2881	Egypt ● (Cairo)‡	510-0200
Belgium ●	0-800-100-10	France	0-800-99-0011
Brazil	000-8010	Germany	0130-0010
Canada ■	1-800-225-5288	Greece ●	00-800-1311
China, PRC ▲	10811	Guam	018-872
Colombia	980-11-0010	Guatemala ○	190

AT&T Direct℠ Service

How to call internationally from overseas:

1. Just dial the AT&T Access Number for the country you are calling from.
2. Dial the phone number you're calling.
3. Dial the calling card number listed above your name.

AT&T Access Numbers

Argentina ✶	001-800-200-1111	Costa Rica ■	0-800-0-114-114
Australia	1800-881-011	Czech Rep. ▲	00-42-000-101
Austria ● ○	022-903-011	Ecuador ● ▲	999-119
Bahamas	1-800-872-2881	Egypt ● (Cairo)‡	510-0200
Belgium ●	0-800-100-10	France	0-800-99-0011
Brazil	000-8010	Germany	0130-0010
Canada ■	1-800-225-5288	Greece ●	00-800-1311
China, PRC ▲	10811	Guam	018-872
Colombia	980-11-0010	Guatemala ○	190

AT&T Access Numbers

Country	Number	Country	Number
Honduras ■	123	Panama ●■	109
Hong Kong	800-1111	Philippines ●■	105-11
Ireland	1-800-550-000	Saudi Arabia◇	1-800-10
Israel	177-100-2727	Singapore	800-0111-111
Italy●	172-1011	Spain◇	900-99-00-11
Jamaica□	872	Sweden	020-795-611
Japan●▲	0039-111	Switzerland●	0-800-550011
Japan●	0066-55-111	Taiwan●	0080-10288-0
Korea, Republic●	00-911	Thailand✕	0019-991-1111
Mexico▽	95-800-462-4240	U.K.●	0800-89-0011
Netherlands●	06-022-9111	U Arab Emirates●	800-121
New Zealand	000-911	Venezuela●	800-11-120

● Bold-faced countries permit country-to-country calling outside the U.S.
■ Public phones require coin or card deposit.
□ Country-to-country calls can only be placed to this country.
◇ Calling available to most countries
✕ Not available from public phones.
◆ Dial "02" first, outside of Cairo.
▲ May not be available from every phone/pay phone.
○ Public phones require local coin payment through the call duration.
▽ When calling from public phones, use phones marked "Ladatel."
◁ Calling card calls available from select hotels.

For a wallet card listing over 140 AT&T Access Numbers, dial the number for the country you're calling from, and ask the operator for customer service. In the U.S., call 1 800 331-1140, ext 704.

©1996 AT&T

AT&T Access Numbers

Country	Number	Country	Number
Honduras ■	123	Panama ●■	109
Hong Kong	800-1111	Philippines ●■	105-11
Ireland	1-800-550-000	Saudi Arabia◇	1-800-10
Israel	177-100-2727	Singapore	800-0111-111
Italy●	172-1011	Spain◇	900-99-00-11
Jamaica□	872	Sweden	020-795-611
Japan●▲	0039-111	Switzerland●	0-800-550011
Japan●	0066-55-111	Taiwan●	0080-10288-0
Korea, Republic●	00-911	Thailand✕	0019-991-1111
Mexico▽	95-800-462-4240	U.K.●	0800-89-0011
Netherlands●	06-022-9111	U Arab Emirates●	800-121
New Zealand	000-911	Venezuela●	800-11-120

● Bold-faced countries permit country-to-country calling outside the U.S.
■ Public phones require coin or card deposit.
□ Country-to-country calls can only be placed to this country.
◇ Calling available to most countries
✕ Not available from public phones.
◆ Dial "02" first, outside of Cairo.
▲ May not be available from every phone/pay phone.
○ Public phones require local coin payment through the call duration.
▽ When calling from public phones, use phones marked "Ladatel."
◁ Calling card calls available from select hotels.

For a wallet card listing over 140 AT&T Access Numbers, dial the number for the country you're calling from, and ask the operator for customer service. In the U.S., call 1 800 331-1140, ext 704.

©1996 AT&T

I love 0-800-99-0011 in the springtime.

All you need for the fastest, clearest connections home.

Every country has its own AT&T Access Number which makes calling from France and other countries really easy. Just dial the AT&T Access Number for the country you're calling from and we'll take it from there. And be sure to charge your calls on your AT&T Calling Card. It'll help you avoid outrageous phone charges on your hotel bill and save you up to 60%.* 0-800-99-0011 is a great place to visit any time of year, especially if you've got these two cards. So please take the attached wallet card of worldwide AT&T Access Numbers.

AT&T

building's legend of hospitality in this gem of a small hotel. Terracotta tiles, chenille bedspreads, and wrought-iron beds decorate most rooms, but it's the mix of handsome antique pieces found throughout the two-floor hotel (a polychrome Venetian sideboard, 18th-century armoires) as well as the palazzo's architectural elements (stained-glass windows, hand-painted wood-coffered ceilings) that guarantee its distinctive air. Room no. 44 even offers a small balcony which, when blooming with jasmine and geraniums by late spring, makes it second-best only to room no. 45, with its view of the Medici Chapels, Florence's terracotta rooftops, and the Duomo's cupola. Breakfast is a big affair here, with the unusual appearance of fresh fruit, sliced ham, homemade breads, and sweets and baked goods, among other things, displayed in self-service buffet style.

🟢 **Hotel Casci.** V. Cavour 13 (between V. de'Gori and V. Guelfa), 50129 Firenze. ☎ **055/21-16-86.** Fax 055/23-96-461. 25 rms with bath. TEL TV. 100,000L ($65.80) single; 150,000L ($98.70) double; 200,000L ($131.60) triple; 250,000L ($164.50) quad. Rates include continental breakfast. Rates discounted 20–30% during low season. AE, DC, MC, V.

The arrival of the Lombardi family has slowly transformed this former pensione from student crash pad into a comfortable and attractive hotel that aims to please—and effortlessly so—an older and more discerning guest. Firm mattresses are draped in bedspreads of paisley or floral designs, with green-stained wooden headboards matching freestanding armoires. Signora Lombardi is a stickler for cleanliness and it's obvious: Most bathrooms are brand-new and literally gleam. Rooms overlooking the busy Via Cavour that heads north out of Piazza Duomo have double-paned windows to ensure quietness, but ask for a room overlooking the inner courtyard's four-story magnolia tree to be safe. A large breakfast buffet is served in a spacious frescoed room, one of the many throwbacks to the past century when this building was the home and property of Gioacchino Rossini.

Hotel Centro. V. Ginori 17 (off Pza. San Lorenzo), 50123 Firenze. ☎ **055/23-02-901.** Fax 055/23-02-902. 16 rms, 12 with bath. TV TEL. 85,000L ($55.90) single without bath, 105,000L ($69.05) single with bath; 105,000L ($69.05) double without bath, 140,000L ($92.10) double with bath; 180,000L ($118.40) triple with bath; 220,000L ($144.75) quad with bath. Rates discounted approximately 20% in low season. Rates include continental breakfast. AE, MC, V.

Just one block north of the sprawling outdoor Mercato San Lorenzo, this new hotel is housed in an old Florentine palazzo that was the preferred home of the Renaissance master painter Raphael. There is precious little he would recognize in this contemporary and bright hostelry whose ample-sized rooms are outfitted in pastel-colored bedspreads and blond-wood furnishings. Bathrooms are new, tiled in white and clean as a whistle. If you're looking for a cozy, old-world ambience, you better keep looking. The renovations that created this pleasant environment were orchestrated by Andrea and Sandra Vendali, the new owners. Rates for a stay exceeding three nights are discounted 10%.

NEAR THE DUOMO
DOUBLES FOR LESS THAN 75,000 LIRE ($49.35)

🟢 **Albergo Costantini.** V. Calzaiuoli 13 (2nd floor), 50122 Firenze. ☎ **055/21-39-95;** ☎/fax 055/21-51-28. 14 rms, 8 with bath. TEL. 56,000L ($36.85) single without bath, 75,000L ($49.35) single with bath; 76,000L ($50.00) double without bath, 100,000L ($65.80) double with bath; 135,000L ($88.80) triple with bath; 170,000L ($111.85) quad with bath. Breakfast 15,000L ($9.85) per person extra. AE, V.

Little is left of the two 13th-century towers long ago joined together to create this palazzo just south of the Piazza Duomo. Upon arrival, inquire about the availability of six spacious rooms with a view of Giotto's slender Campanile (bell tower) and the tricolored Duomo that seem within reach. Recent retiling, matching bedspreads, and the impeccable housekeeping of owner Anna Mollica makes this an excellent choice for those who find the proximity of the Campanile's frequent bells glorious and not annoying. Breakfast is expensive though substantial, and tastes better underneath period frescoes that can also be found in two of the guest rooms. The recently renovated Hotel Aldini (see below) is located just above the more Spartan Costantini.

✪ **Locanda Orchidea.** Bgo. d. Albizi 11 (1st floor), 50122 Firenze. ☎/fax **055/24-80-346.** 7 rms without bath. 45,000L ($29.60) single without shower; 68,000L ($44.75) double without shower; 102,000L ($67.10) triple without bath. Breakfast not available. No credit cards. Closed Dec 24–26 and 1 week in Feb.

The elegant and friendly proprietor, Maria Rosa Cook, will happily recount for you in perfect English the history of this 13th-century palazzo, located midway between the Duomo and the Bargello Museum, where Dante's wife was born. With just seven rooms thoughtfully decorated with floral bedspreads and white lace touches, you'll feel like a guest in her home, and women traveling alone feel particularly comfortable here. The rooms overlooking a lovely garden and a magnificent wisteria vine (bloom forecast: mid-May) are the best beds in the house, with especially large windows that let in lots of sunlight. Signora Cook and Miranda, her take-charge daughter, run a serious operation and discourage partying hostel-escapees attracted by these exceptional prices.

Soggiorno Brunori. V. d. Proconsolo 5 (2nd floor; south of Pz. Duomo), 50122 Firenze. ☎ **055/28-96-48.** 9 rms, 1 with bath. 76,000L ($50.00) double without bath, 84,000L ($55.25) double with bath; 90,000L ($59.21) triple without bath, 115,000L ($75.65) triple with bath; 113,000L ($74.35) quad without bath, 143,000L ($94.10) quad with bath. Breakfast 9,000L ($5.90) extra. No credit cards. Closed for 1 month between Jan and Feb.

The rooms here are clean but a bit tired from the wear and tear of countless backpackers. But the prices are among the lowest around and things are brightened up considerably by the two young English-speaking owners, Leonardo and Giovanni, who are exceptionally friendly and full of helpful hints. They'll sell you stamps, help you decipher the train schedules they keep on hand, and offer you a city map at check-in. Their unusually spacious rooms make this a fine selection for backpacking groups. This is a casual place to kick back, with bare-bones amenities that may not appeal to the après-college crowd. For example, each of the two communal baths is shared by four rooms. You may want to ask for one of the two rooms away from the noisy street that runs south from the Piazza Duomo past the nearby Bargello museum to the river. There's a 12:30am curfew.

DOUBLES FOR LESS THAN 114,000 LIRE ($75)

Albergo Serena. V. Fiume 20 (2nd floor), 50123 Firenze. ☎ **055/21-36-43.** 7 rms, 3 with bath. TEL. 95,000L ($62.50) double without bath, 110,000L ($72.35) double with bath; 128,000L ($84.20) triple without bath, 148,500L ($97.70) triple with bath. Rates include continental breakfast. Ask about low-season discounts. MC, V.

Family-run with pride by the Bigazzi family, this unpretentious one-star place comes through with pleasant surprises: some brand-new and nicely tiled bathrooms, molded ceilings, and turn-of-the-century stained-glass French doors. Rooms are airy and bright and kept clean as a whistle by the owner's wife. A dignified choice for those looking for a comfortable place to hang their hat near the train station. If this place is full, try the smaller and even less expensive Otello Tourist House upstairs on the third floor next to the Hotel Fiorita. It has just four simple but lovely rooms, two with bath, at rates even less than the Serena (☎ and fax 055/23-96-159) and is run by the gracious owners, English-speaking Anna and her husband Otello.

Hotel Fiorita. V. Fiume 20 (3rd floor), 50123 Firenze. ☎ **055/28-31-89.** Fax 055/28-36-93. 13 rms, 6 with bath. A/C TEL TV MINIBAR only in rooms with bath. 85,000L ($55.90) single without bath; 110,000L ($72.35) double without bath, 150,000L ($98.70) double with bath; 156,000L ($102.65) triple without bath, 210,000L ($138.15) triple with bath; 260,000L ($171.05) quad with bath. Rates include continental breakfast; not mandatory (deduct 7,000L or $4.60 from room rate). Low-season discount 25%. MC, V.

The friendly Maselli family has recently gussied up their one-star establishment to meet two-star standards, but despite the addition of welcomed amenities (the air-conditioning is a summertime blessing, although at a daily 20,000L/$13.15 supplement per room), things are still a little old around the edges. Rooms are unimaginatively decorated, but a venerable charm can be found in the original, stained-glass doors and windows that hint of the palazzo's late 19th-century origins and a sunny breakfast room.

DOUBLES FOR LESS THAN 200,000 LIRE ($131.50)

Hotel Aldini. V. Calzaiuoli 13 (south of Pz. Duomo), 50122 Firenze. ☎ **055/21-47-52.** Fax 055/29-16-21. TEL TV A/C. 14 rms with bath. 120,000L ($78.95) single; 180,000L ($118.40) double; 240,000L ($157.90) triple; 270,000L ($177.65) quad. Rates include continental breakfast. Ask about low-season rates. MC, V.

What better location for your hotel than in the shadow of the magnificent Duomo and its slender 14th-century campanile designed by Giotto? The same convenience can be found at the Hotel Costantini downstairs, where prices are lower, but then again so are their standards of amenities and decor. This is a handsome place with rich terracotta floors covered by Persian runners and large rooms whose fresh floral bedspreads and spacious bathrooms reflect a recent renovation. The clip-clop of horse-drawn carriages and the chatter of late-night strollers from the heart of Florence's pedestrian area drift in the windows of the front rooms privileged with a partial view of the Duomo. For comfort and location, location, location, Aldini is a find.

✪ **Hotel Torre Guelfa.** Bgo. S.S. Apostoli 8 (between V. Tornabuoni and V. Por Santa Maria), 50123 Firenze. 11 rms with bath. A/C MINIBAR TEL TV. 120,000L ($78.95) single; 180,000L ($118.40) double; 240,000L ($157.90) triple; 300,000L ($197.35) quad. Rates include continental breakfast. Ask about low-season discounts. AE, V.

To experience the breathtaking 360° view from this new hotel's medieval tower (hence the hotel's name) indubitably justifies these budget-testing prices. The tallest privately owned tower in Florence's centro storico, its riveting view is only one reason to stay in this tastefully renovated landmark hotel before it applies for three-star category and raises its rates completely out of your sphere.

You'll want to linger in your canopied iron bed, your room made even more inviting by warm-colored walls and rich paisley carpeting (for a view similar to the tower's, ask for room no. 15 with a huge, private terrace). But follow the wafting strains of classical music to the salon, whose vaulted ceilings and lofty proportions hark back to the palazzo's 14th-century origins. Less expensive rooms without baths are expected to be gone by 1997, but double-check when booking: They are about 30% less.

BETWEEN IL DUOMO & THE ARNO RIVER
DOUBLES FOR LESS THAN 114,000 LIRE ($75)

✪ **Hotel Firenze.** Pz. Donati 4 (on the V. d. Corso, off V. Calzaiuoli), 50122 Firenze. ☎ **055/26-83-01** or 21-42-03. Fax 055/21-23-70. 61 rms with bath. TEL TV. 65,000L ($42.75) single with bath; 91,000L ($59.85) double with bath; 120,000L ($78.95) triple with bath; 150,000L ($98.70) quad with bath. Rates include continental breakfast. Ask about low-season rates. No credit cards.

For years this perfectly located hotel was a favorite student's choice, but a multiple-year renovation scheduled to be completed by 1997 has transformed it into a shining two-star establishment with little impact on its consistently low rates—some of the most attractive in town (for even lower rates, ask if there are any unrenovated bathless rooms left). Sitting on its own little piazza in the middle of the centro storico's pedestrian zone of shops and landmark buildings, the hotel is actually two adjoining historical palazzi now boasting brightly tiled, sunlit guest rooms and the best bathrooms in this price range in town.

Pensione Alessandra. Bgo. S.S. Apostoli 17 (between V. Tornabuoni and V. Por Santa Maria), 50123 Firenze. ☎ **055/28-34-38.** Fax 055/21-06-19. 25 rms, 17 with bath. A/C (in some rooms) TEL TV. 80,000L ($52.65) single without bath, 100,000L ($65.80) single with bath; 110,000L ($72.35) double without bath, 160,000L ($105.25) double with bath; 150,000L ($98.70) triple without bath, 215,000L ($141.45) triple with bath; 180,000L ($118.40) quad without bath, 250,000L ($164.50) quad with bath. Rates include continental breakfast. Ask about low-season rates. AE, MC, V.

This special pensione is located between two principal shopping streets on a narrow cobblestone street, lined with medieval towers and early Renaissance palazzi and running parallel to the Arno River. Street-level, etched-glass doors hint of the architectural and historical significance of the Alessandra's palazzo nobile, designed in 1507 by Baccio d'Angnolo, a pupil of Michelangelo. The antiquity of high ceilings and spacious rooms is appreciated, but so is the modernity of new bright bathrooms. This is a good spot to opt for a room without a bath, since only seven rooms share four large, communal baths. Good housekeeping and the simplicity of tasteful floral bedspreads and sheer white curtains are much welcome, as is the free-of-charge air-conditioning—but request it upon reserving, as not all rooms are equipped. Signora Anna runs a lovely operation.

Pensione Maria Luisa de' Medici. V. d. Corso 1 (2nd floor; between V. Calzaiuoli and V. Proconsolo), 50122 Firenze. ☎ **055/28-00-48.** 9 rms, 2 with bath. 93,000L ($61.20) double without bath, 114,000L ($75.00) double with bath; 129,000L ($84.85) triple without bath, 158,000L ($103.95) triple with bath; 165,000L ($108.55) quad without bath, 201,000L ($132.25) quad with bath. Rates include breakfast. No credit cards.

Named after the very last Medici princess, this pensione located around the corner from Dante's house is one of Florence's more eclectic and unusual places to sleep. Rooms are named after the different members of the Medici clan whose portraits grace their walls. The owner, Dr. Angelo Sordi—physician, collector, history and design buff—has furnished each of the nine huge rooms with 1960s avant-garde Italian furniture—an unexpected collection that contrasts (purists might find it jarring) with a veritable treasure trove of museum-quality baroque paintings and sculptures displayed in the main foyer that are more compatible with the 17th-century palazzo. With enormous rooms sleeping up to five people, the Maria Luisa is a good choice for traveling families, who will also relish the breakfast served in the room (there is no breakfast room) by Dr. Angelo or his Welsh partner Evelyn Morris. Sustained by eggs, cereal, and juice, you shouldn't mind the three-story walk up or down.

IN THE OLTRARNO
DOUBLES FOR LESS THAN 150,000 LIRE ($98.70)

✪ **Pensione La Scaletta.** V. Guicciardini 13 (2nd floor, near Pz. Pitti), 50125 Firenze. ☎ **055/ 28-30-28** or 21-42-55. Fax 055/28-95-62. 12 rms, 11 with bath. TEL. 65,000L ($42.75) single without bath, 85,000L ($55.90) single with bath; 110,000L ($72.35) double without bath, 140,000L ($92.10) double with bath; 175,000L ($115.15) triple with bath; 210,000L ($138.15) quad with bath. Rates include continental breakfast. Ask about low-season rates. 10% discount for Frommer's readers who pay in cash. MC, V.

Bring your travel journal, order an iced tea, and head for this pensione's two-tiered, umbrellaed terrace at sunset—then try to put down in words the stunning 360° panorama that surrounds you. Overlooking the stalwart Pitti Palace and housed in one of only two historical palazzi on this street to survive World War II, the comfortable top-floor pensione is efficiently run by owners Barbara Barbieri and her enthusiastic son Manfredo. Rooms are clean, spacious, and vary greatly in decor. Those that front the very busy Via Giucciardini have double-paned windows to cut the noise, but the ones in back overlook the verdant Boboli Gardens that fan up the hill. Young Manfredo himself whips up a fixed-price dinner of 20,000L ($13.15) upon request. He peruses the daily marketplace before creating the menu that includes antipasto, pasta, a meat-based entree, vegetable, and sweet; repair afterward to the terrace for your après-dinner *vin santo*.

Pensione Sorelle Bandini. Pz. S. Spirito 9, 50125 Firenze. ☎ **055/21-53-08.** Fax 055/28-27-61. 14 rms, 5 with bath. TEL. 125,000L ($82.23) double without bath, 155,000L ($102.00) double with bath; 173,000L ($113.80) triple without bath, 214,000L ($140.80) triple with bath. Inquire about single and quad rates and availability. Rates include continental breakfast. No credit cards (personal checks from U.S. banks accepted).

You'll know this is your best shot at time travel as you stand, humbled, before the massive Renaissance palazzo in Piazza Santo Spirito, one of Florence's most authentic squares. If you step back, on the top floor you can see the massive open-air loggia that wraps around the landmark building: This is your chance to live like the noble families of yore. With 15-foot ceilings, the 10-foot windows and over-sized pieces of antique furniture are proportionately appropriate. But upon closer inspection, you'll see that the resident cats have left their mark on common-area sofas, and everything seems just a little ramshackle, musty, and uneven. But that seems to be the point—or so the return guests will have you believe, judging from the students, older folks, and families who love the huge lofty-ceilinged rooms (room no. 9 sleeps five and offers a view of the Duomo from its bathroom window) and hallways dripping with history. And don't forget that monumental terrace where Mimmo, the English-speaking manager, oversees breakfast and encourages brown-bag lunches and the chance to relax and drink in the view.

3 Dining

Judging from the innate elegance of the Florentine people and the tony stores from which they fill their wardrobes, you'd never think the local cuisine would be so rustic and simple. In true Tuscan style, when they tell you theirs is the best and most genuine, you're best off believing them.

Almost all of the eating establishments that follow specialize the poor man's *cucina povera,* based on the region's agricultural role in history. Slabs of crusty bread are used for *crostini,* spread with chicken-liver pâte as the favorite Florentine antipasto. Hearty Tuscan peasant soups often take the place of pasta, especially *ribollita,* a rich soup of twice-boiled cabbage, beans, and bread, or *pappa al pomodoro* a similarly thick soup made from tomatoes and drizzled with olive oil. Look for *pasta fatta in casa* (the homemade pasta of the day), or the typically Tuscan *pappardelle,* thick flat noodles often covered with a simple tomato sauce. Your *contorno* or side dish of vegetables will likely be the classic *fagioli all' uccelletto,* humble pinto beans smothered in a sauce of tomatoes, rosemary, and sage (or simply dressed with virgin olive oil from the surrounding hills). Rustic grilled meats are a specialty, the jewel in the culinary crown being *bistecca alla fiorentina,* an inch- (or more) thick charcoal-broiled steak on the bone: It is usually the most expensive item on any menu (meat eaters should seriously

Florence Dining

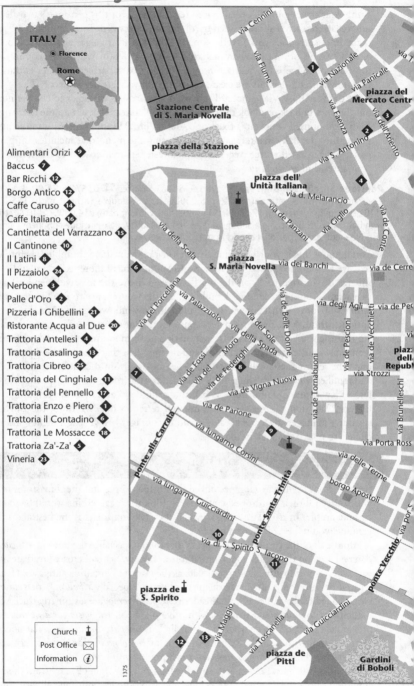

Alimentari Orizi 9
Baccus 7
Bar Ricchi 12
Borgo Antico 12
Caffe Caruso 14
Caffe Italiano 16
Cantinetta del Varrazzano 15
Il Cantinone 10
Il Latini 8
Il Pizzaiolo 24
Nerbone 3
Palle d'Oro 2
Pizzeria I Ghibellini 21
Ristorante Acqua al Due 20
Trattoria Antellesi 4
Trattoria Casalinga 13
Trattoria Cibreo 25
Trattoria del Cinghiale 11
Trattoria del Pennello 17
Trattoria Enzo e Piero 1
Trattoria il Contadino 6
Trattoria Le Mossacce 18
Trattoria Za'-Za' 5
Vineria 23

ITALY
● Florence
Rome ★

Church †
Post Office ☒
Information ⓘ

1375

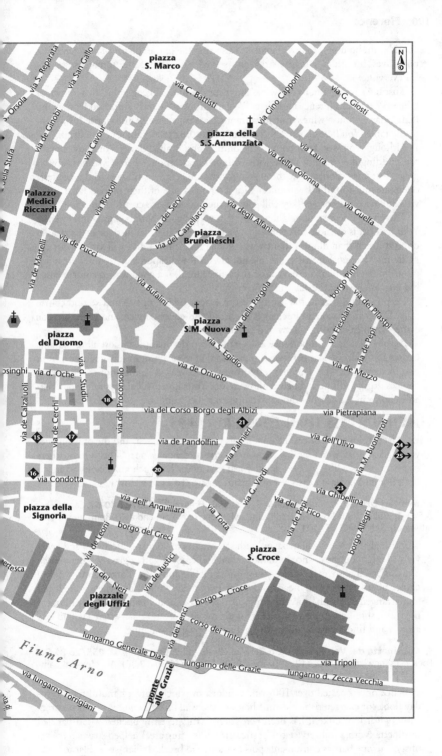

consider the splurge). Many Florentines also sing the praises of *trippa alla fiorentina,* but calves' intestines, cut into strips and served with onions and tomatoes, are not for everyone.

Tuscany's most famous red wines are from the limited geographic area known as Chianti between Florence and Siena. You might be pleasantly surprised by the vino della casa, or house wine, your restaurant's least expensive. A full bottle is brought to the table: You'll be charged al consumo, according to the amount you drink.

Although you won't swoon over the unfussy and limited desserts on most menus, the puddinglike tiramisù made with whipped mascarpone cheese is almost always great. But after dinner walk through the city's quiet streets till you find a gelateria open late and round off your meal with a scoop of one of their myriad favors. Flavors like riso (rice) or whiskey will convert diehard non–ice-cream lovers.

There's no one dish or neighborhood that equals good budget dining in Florence. Your best bet is to choose an eatery that will allow you to order just one course (easier done at lunch than dinner) though whether a modest pasta dish will satisfy your appetite may be another matter. While not always the cheapest way to dine, the ubiquitous menu turistico (a three-course fixed-price meal) is a good way to contain costs, but check out what the day's menu consists of.

Keep in mind that in the listings below, prices are for a pasta and second course only. Don't forget to add in charges for bread and cover, service, and vegetable side dishes when calculating what you'd expect to pay.

Despite Florence's importance as a Grand Tour destination, almost all restaurants (stores and offices) close per ferie (for vacation) at some point in July or August from two to six weeks. The date may vary from year to year, so call any of the following choices during this period before showing up: Your hotel will always know of a reliable choice in the neighborhood. No one ever goes hungry.

LUNCH FOR LESS THAN 7,500 LIRE ($4.95)

Let's face it, for these prices the only meals you'll get are lunch, and the only lunches you'll get will be *panini* sandwiches—fresh, crusty, delicious ones. This is Italy, where every morsel is edible art and you'll swear you never had such a delicious $5 lunch back home. Maybe it's the glass of Chianti classico to wash it down.

Alimentari Orizi. V. Parione 19r (off V. Tornabuoni), Firenze. ☎ **055/21-40-67.** Sandwiches 3,500–4,000L ($2.30–2.65). No credit cards. Mon–Sat 9am–2pm and 4:40–8pm. Closed Wed afternoon. SANDWICHES/DELI

Surprisingly few spots will make up fresh sandwiches to your specifications, and fewer yet will offer you the chance to pull up a seat and enjoy it with a glass of wine. Search out this small alimentari (grocery store) just off the tony Via Tornabuoni, where a choice of crusty rolls and breads and a variety of quality meats and cheeses are sliced and arranged according to your whim. There's a bar and a half-dozen stools, but if the sun is shining you might consider asking for your creation *da portare via* ("to take away") and find a piazza bench-with-a-view for people watching.

✪ **Cantinetta del Verrazzano.** V. d. Tavolini 18/20r (off V. Calzaiuoli). ☎ **055/26-85-90.** Focaccia sandwiches 3,500L ($2.30); wine 2,000L–3,500L ($1.30–$2.30). AE. Mon–Sat 8am–8pm. WINE BAR.

Florence once boasted over 100 wine vendors, of which only a handful remain today (look for characteristic old-time holes-in-the-wall billed as *vinaio* or *fiaschetteria*). Although it looks like it has been here forever, this recently opened wood-paneled cantinetta (with a full-service bar/pasticceria and seating area) helped spawn a revival of stylish wine bars as convenient spots for fast-food breaks Italian-style. Flat focaccia bread, plain or studded with peas, rosemary, onions, or olives, is fresh from the wood-burning oven in the back; buy it hot by the slice or farcite ("filled" with prosciutto, rugola, cheese, tuna, etc., as sandwiches). Verrazzano is the location of the owners' *fattoria* farm (the same town that gave us Giovanni da Verrazzano, the first European explorer to sight New York harbor) that supplies the wine bar with most of its products. Try a glass of any of their full-bodied Chianti wines to make this the perfect Tuscan respite.

EAST OF THE TRAIN STATION
MEALS FOR LESS THAN 15,800 LIRE ($10.40)

Nerbone. In the Mercato Centrale, entrance on V. dell'Ariento, stand no. 292 (ground floor). Sandwiches 4,000L ($2.65); pasta and soup 6,000L ($3.95); meat dishes 7,000L ($4.60). No credit cards. Mon–Sat 7am–2pm. ITALIAN.

One of the best basic eateries in Florence for those seeking good food and local color, this simple red-and-green food stand inside Florence's covered turn-of-the-century meat-and-produce marketplace is best described as a hole-in-the-wall minus the wall. Packed with market-goers and local working-class types who stand around the marble bar eating, drinking, and discussing soccer scores and politics, Nerbone offers only four small tables next to an adjacent meat counter. Daily specials include a limited choice of pastas such as penne or rotelli, soups, huge plates of cooked potatoes and other vegetables, and fresh, fresh sandwiches. Service is swift, and wine and beer are sold by the glass. If at first you can't find Nerbone, just ask.

MEALS FOR LESS THAN 22,000 LIRE ($14.45)

Palle d'Oro. V. Sant'Antonio 43–45r (in the Mercato San Lorenzo area). ☎ 055/28-83-83. Primi 7,000L–8,000L ($4.60–$5.25); main courses 8,000L–19,000L ($5.25–$12.50). AE, D, V. Mon–Sat 12:30–2:30pm and 7:30–10:30pm. ITALIAN.

This neighborhood trattoria is ever full of the market's vendors and shoppers, most of whom crowd the front area where a number of pastas, soups, and vegetable side dishes are available for a quick lunch standing at the bar. The prices aren't much lower than those quoted above for table service in the less-crowded back area, but here you're not expected to order a full and leisurely meal. Wherever you wind up, make sure you look for the house specialty, penne della casa, pasta made with porcini mushrooms, prosciutto, and veal. For a cholesterol boost with a kick, try the homemade gnocchi alla gorgonzola.

Trattoria Enzo e Piero. V. Faenza 105r (off V. Nazionale). ☎ 055/21-49-01. Pasta courses 8,000L–9,000L ($5.25–$5.90); meat courses 9,000L–10,000L ($5.90–$6.60); from the grill 11,000L–18,000L ($7.25–$11.85); menu turistico 18,000L ($11.85). AE, DC, MC, V. Mon–Sat noon–3pm and 7–10pm. ITALIAN.

This is a pleasant spot with helpful service that is filled during lunch with the salespeople from nearby shops (always a good sign) and in the evening with an international mix from the numerous small hotels in this area. The menu is in Italian and English, and most of the waiters speak English and will be happy to help you make your selections. Unpretentious Tuscan food shows up on the menu in the selections of pastas and traditionally grilled meats: Ask your waiter for guidance and changing specialties.

✪ **Trattoria Zà-Zà.** Pz. Mercato Centrale 26r. ☎ 055/21-54-11. Primi courses 7,000L–11,000L ($4.60–$7.25); meat courses 13,000L–15,000L ($8.55–$9.85); menu turistico 20,000L ($13.15). AE, DC, MC, V. Mon–Sat noon–2:30pm and 7–10pm. Closed Aug. ITALIAN.

The walls are lined with Chianti bottles and photographs of old movie stars and not-so-famous patrons, the long wooden tables with an eclectic mix of tourists and local workers. Convenient to the open-air San Lorenzo market—and forever crowded—this typical Florentine eatery serves such long-enduring Tuscan favorites as ribollita and crostini caldi misti at reasonable prices. This is also a reliably good spot to try the fabled bistecca fiorentina without losing your shirt (the menu usually quotes price per ounce, so consult your waiter: The average steak costs approximately 30,000L/ $19.75). Zà-Zà has a serious competitor in Mario, directly around the corner on V. Rosina 2 (also closed Sunday), whose simple trattoria decor, good food, and slightly less expensive prices make it a great alternative choice; it's open, unfortunately, for lunch only.

WORTH A SPLURGE

il Latini. V. Palchetti 6r (off V. Vigna Nuova). ☎ **055/21-09-16.** Primi courses 8,000L–10,000L ($5.25–$6.55); meat courses 15,000L–20,000L ($9.85–$13.15); fixed-price meal 50,000L ($32.90). AE, MC, V. Tues–Sun noon–3pm and 7:30–10:30pm. Closed July 20–Aug 10. ITALIAN.

Family patriarch Narcisio Latini and his sons, Giovanni and Torello, operate one of the busiest tavern-like trattorias in town. There's always a line waiting for a cramped seat at one of the long wooden tables (this is an even longer affair if you haven't reserved) in one of many rooms. But the raucous, delicious Tuscan adventure is worth the wait. Papa Latini watches over the operation with an eagle eye, shouting commands, talking to four people at once, placing phone orders to the Latini family farm 20 miles away (where the wine, oil, and most of the food are produced), and never losing control over the wonderful chaos.

There is a written menu—though you probably won't see one: One of the brothers will explain the selection in a working version of English. Gargantuan eaters should indulge in the *menu completo*—a hearty, meaty feast for 50,000L ($32.90) that begins with an antipasto of prosciutto crudo (ham) and homemade sausage, followed by a pasta or soup, a main course such as the misto di carne alla griglia (assortment of mixed grilled meats), a fresh vegetable in season, gelato, and biscotti di Prato (hard almond cookies). Oh, and all the wine and mineral water you can drink, which may explain why at least one table usually breaks out into song and diners linger on forever. More restrained appetites and wallets should just order à la carte.

✪ **Trattoria Antellesi.** V. Faenza 9r (near Medici Chapels and the Mercato San Lorenzo). ☎ **055/21-69-90.** Primi 8,000L–12,000L ($5.25–$7.90); main courses 15,000L–24,000L ($9.85–$15.80). AE, D, MC, V. Mon—Sat noon–2:30pm and 7–10:30pm.

This is a rustic and welcoming spot in a converted Renaissance palazzo almost within reach of the Medici Chapels. The young Florentine-Arizona combination of chef Enrico and manager/sommelier Janice Verrecchia guarantees a lovely Tuscan experience of wonderfully authentic dishes accompanied by a well thought out wine list. Knowledgeable, capable, and never without a smile, Janice will talk you through a memorable dinner that should start with their signature antipasto of Pecorino cheese and pears. Then onto small, light crepes stuffed with ricotta cheese and spinach then baked (crespelle alla fiorentina) or spaghetti alla Chiantigiana with Chianti-marinated beef cooked in a tomato sauce. This is the spot to try the Tuscan cuisine's crown jewel: the bistecca alla fiorentina and, while you're at it, some of the cantina's excellent moderately priced red wines (21,000L to 24,000L / $13.80 to $15.80).

BETWEEN THE TRAIN STATION & THE ARNO
MEALS FOR LESS THAN 15,800 LIRE ($10.40)

Baccus. Bgo. Ognissanti 45r (near Pz. Ognissanti). ☎ **055/28-37-14.** Pasta dishes 10,000L–13,000L ($6.60–$8.55); pizza 7,000L–13,000L ($4.60–$8.55). AE, MC, V. Tues–Sun 11am–3pm and 7pm–midnight. ITALIAN.

It is not always easy to appease an urge for a simple plate of pasta in Italy without feeling pressed to indulge in the whole nine yards of a full dinner. Pasta is precisely what this place promotes. Order one as an entree with a salad and be on your way. With 20 to choose from (with English translations), it may not be such a fast deal, but take your time: The kitchen stays open till midnight. Stick with the simple choices, as is true of Italian cuisine in general, and you'll be happy. Or consider the alternative of pizza: There are also 20 to pick from.

Trattoria il Contadino. V. Palazzuolo 69r (between V. de' Canacci and V. dell'Albero). ☎ **055/23-82-673.** Menu turistico (dinner) 15,000L ($9.85); (lunch) 14,000L ($9.20). No credit cards. Mon–Sat 11am–3pm and 7pm–midnight. ITALIAN.

The menu turistico is the only game in town at this simple trattoria. Consisting of a pasta, an entree, a side dish of a fresh vegetable, mineral water, and wine, it seems to meet with everyone's approval, judging by the two-room turnout at this simple place with red-and-white-checkered tablecloths. Unless you come early, expect to wait with a cadre of hungry backpackers and soldiers away from home, all looking for a home-cooked meal.

SOUTH OF THE PIAZZA DEL DUOMO
MEALS FOR LESS THAN 15,000 LIRE ($9.85)
Caffe Caruso. V. Lambertesca 16r (off V. Por Santa Maria), Firenze. ☎ **055/28-19-40.** Pasta 6,000L–8,000L ($3.95–$5.25), meat entrees 6,000L–8,000L ($3.95–$5.95). No credit cards. Mon–Sat 8am–8pm. ITALIAN.

On a quiet side street in the very heart of town (the first right off Via Por Santa Maria when coming from the Ponte Vecchio), this family-run caffe(teria) offers a surprisingly varied and well-prepared selection of inexpensive hot dishes in a bright, airy setting with lots of seating—I could eat lunch here every day. It's busy with the local salespeople during lunch, but continuous hours promise less commotion if your appetite is flexible. With four or five pastas and over a dozen vegetable side dishes to pick from, this is a recommended destination for light (or not) eaters and vegetarians. Most of it is on display and self-service keeps prices rock-bottom for this area of town. Keep this place in mind for an inexpensive breakfast or coffee break, or just an afternoon beer that promises a quiet table for postcard scribbling.

Caffe Italiano. V. Condotta 56r (off V. Calzaiuoli). ☎ **055/29-10-82.** Appetizers 6,000L ($3.95); main courses 9,000L ($5.90). No credit cards. Daily 12:30–3pm and 8–10pm (bar open 8am–1am nonstop). ITALIAN.

Umberto Montano, the young, entrepreneurial owner of this handsome cafe (whose restaurant Alle Murate and its less expensive sidekick Vineria is one of the city's best; see below), has created an inviting turn-of-the-century ambiance near the center's Piazza della Signoria and offers a simple and delicious lunch at reasonable rates to standing-room-only crowds (come early!). Delicate but full-flavored soups and an unusual variety of mousse-like soufflés of parmesan or broccoli might be today's choice of primi (first course). A light dinner has since been added, though with a choice of first courses only. All the more room for dessert. Don't miss them: Made on the premises by a talented pastry chef, they go perfectly with the cafe's exclusive blend of coffee from Africa.

MEALS FOR LESS THAN 22,000 LIRE ($14.45)
Trattoria del Pennello. V. Dante Alighieri 4r (between V. dei Cerchi and V. d. Proconsolo). ☎ **055/23-94-848.** Pasta courses 9,000L ($5.90); meat courses 15,000L–18,000L ($9.85–$11.90). AE, V. Tues–Sat noon–3pm and 7pm–midnight, Sun noon–3pm. Closed Aug. ITALIAN.

Though his house was just around the corner, Dante never dined here. That was his loss. Often referred to as "da Dante" (Dante's) nonetheless, this is an attractive restaurant with a bright interior and unassuming plain white curtains. The specialty here is a wide array of two dozen delicious antipasti (appetizers) on display. Prices vary with quantity and dish, but expect to spend about 10,000L ($6.55) for a healthy sampling. Continue your sampling and order the tris di primi a piacere, your choice of any three pastas for a minimum of two people (20,000L/$13.15 per person). More contained appetites might be just as happy with a simple pasta and perfectly prepared grilled chop for approximately the same cost.

Trattoria Le Mossacce. V. d. Proconsolo 55r (1 block south of the Duomo). ☎ **055/29-43-61.** Pasta courses 7,000L–8,000L ($4.60–$5.25); meat courses 9,000L–11,000L ($5.90–$7.25); menu turistico 24,000L ($15.75). AE, MC, V. Mon–Fri noon–2:30pm and 7–9:30pm. ITALIAN.

Don't be fooled by its narrow doorway or bright ordinary dining room. The food is anything but ordinary here. This is straightforward *cucina toscana*, deftly prepared and served in a lively and pleasant atmosphere. Long-enduring favorites on the menu are the thick ribollita (literally "twice boiled") soup or any of the daily changing pastas (one day made with a sauce of tomato and melanzane or eggplant, another with the slightly spicy Amatriciana sauce). If the thought of a thick slab of steak is your idea of heaven, indulge here in the bistecca alla fiorentina, perfectly grilled and a splurge worth considering at approximately 20,000L ($13.15).

EAST OF VIA PROCONSOLO

This main street runs north/south from the east side of Piazza del Duomo past the Bargello Museum and, changing names, eventually finishes at the Arno River. To its east of this thoroughfare is the Piazza Santa Croce neighborhood.

MEALS FOR LESS THAN 15,000 LIRE ($9.85)

Pizzeria I Ghibellini. Pza. San Pier Maggiore 8–10r (at the end of Bgo. degli Albizi east from V. d. Proconsolo). ☎ **055/21-44-24.** Pizza 5,500L–10,000L ($3.60–$6.60); pasta courses 5,500L–8,000L ($3.60–$5.25); meat courses 7,500L–20,000L ($4.90–$13.15). AE, DC, MC, V. Thurs–Tues noon–4pm and 7pm–12:30am. ITALIAN.

With its exposed brick walls and ceilings and curved archways inside and its white umbrellaed tables in the quiet, picturesque piazzetta outside, I Ghibellini is a good bet year-round. Pizza is the draw and there's a long list of possibilities to make your choice difficult: Go with the house specialty, pizza alla Ghibellini (prosciutto, mascarpone cheese, and pork sausage). The rest of the menu holds its own and deserves more merit, especially some of the pastas such as the penne alla boccalona, whose tomato sauce with garlic and a pinch of hot pepper is just spicy enough. Long hours and air-conditioning only enhance this spot's popularity.

✪ **Ristorante Acqua al Due.** V. d. Vigna Vecchia 40r (at V. dell' Acqua, behind the Bargello). ☎ **055/28-41-70.** Reservations required. Pasta courses 8,000L–10,000L ($5.25–$6.60); meat courses 10,000L–20,000L ($6.60–$13.15); assaggio 11,000L ($7.25) for pasta, 8,500L ($5.60) for dessert. AE, V. Sat–Sun 12:30–3pm and 7:30pm–1am; Tues–Sat dinner only. ITALIAN.

Italy, of course, is world-famous for its pasta, and this is the perfect place to sample as much as you can at one sitting without breaking the bank or bursting your seams. The specialty of the house is the *assaggio di primi*, a sampling of five different types of pasta (with an occasional risotto alternative) in various sauces. These are not five full-size portions, but don't expect to have room (or feel obligated to find it) for an entree afterward either. There are also assaggi of salads (insalate) and sweets (dolci).

There's no English menu, but all the waiters speak English since half the crowd (and there is always a crowd) is from foreign shores. If you don't have a reservation, come back when you do (the newly instated weekend lunches are less busy). Low prices make this comfortable restaurant especially popular with an under-30 international crowd, while good quality guarantees a prevalent Florentine demographic who are fussy about their pasta sources.

MEALS FOR LESS THAN 22,000 LIRE ($14.45)

✪ **Il Pizzaiolo.** V. de' Macci 113r (near Mercato Sant'Ambrogio), Firenze. ☎ 055/24-11-71. Reservations suggested. Pizza 7,000L–12,000L ($4.60–$7.90); primi 8,500L–10,000L ($5.60–$6.60); main courses 9,000L–12,000L ($5.90–$7.90). No credit cards. Mon–Sat 7pm–midnight. PIZZERIA/TRATTORIA.

There's a full menu here but I've never seen anyone order anything other than pizza. And the ever-present crowd waiting out on the sidewalk is confirmation that this new pizzeria guarantees the best pizza in town. Italy remains proudly and adamantly regionalistic about its food: No one prepares risotto like the Milanesi, and don't even think of eating pesto outside of Liguria. Pizza? You're looking for trouble unless your roots are in the south, home of this simple poor man's food. And so Florence was elated to welcome Carmine, who headed north after 30 years in Naples perfecting his art, bringing with him his expertise and such integral ingredients as garlic and oregano. The simple pizza margherita (fresh tomato, mozzarella, and oregano) is perfection, as is the more endowed pizza pazza, a "crazy pizza" decorated with fresh tomato, artichokes, olives, mushrooms, and oregano.

Trattoria Cibreo. V. Andrea d. Verrocchio 4r (near the Mercato Sant'Ambrogio). ☎ **055/ 23-41-100.** Primi 7,000L ($4.60); entrees 13,000L ($8.55). No credit cards. Tues–Sat 1–2:30pm and 7:30–11pm. TUSCAN.

This is the casual, lesser-priced trattoria of chef/owner Fabio Picchi and his wife Benedetta; its limited menu comes from the same creative kitchen that put their premier 50-seat ristorante next door on the map, now considered one of Italy's best (peak at the menu for a future splurge). The ambiance is rustic chic, the menu something of a revelation: Picchi takes his inspiration from traditional Tuscan recipes now quasi-extinct, but the first thing you'll notice is the absence of pasta (apparently a more recent addition). After you taste the velvety yellow bell pepper soup, you won't care much. Stuffed roast duck demands the same admiration. Desserts, such as the bitter chocolate tart, are made to perfection by Fabio's wife, Benedetta. To complete the Cibreo experience, enjoy your after-dinner espresso at the handsome Caffe Cibreo across the way.

Vineria (alle Murate). V. Ghibellina 52r (east of V. Proconsolo). ☎ **055/24-06-18.** Reservations suggested. Fixed-price menu a prezzo fisso 35,000L ($23.00). No credit cards. Dinner only Tues–Sun 7–11pm. ITALIAN.

This is the less expensive, casual alcove of Umberto Montano's celebrated restaurant you'll see on your right as you enter. "Vineria" refers to the leading role carefully selected wines will play in the course of your evening: There are five to seven Tuscan and Italian wines to choose from and a charming English-speaking waiter or waitress to enlighten you about their attributes. A pared-down, slightly simplified menu from Alle Murate's kitchen will give you a better understanding of the restaurant's fame as one of the city's best venues for contemporary Italian cuisine, regardless of where you sit. Choose from three delicious first courses, one fish-, meat-, or vegetable-based entree, and two remarkable desserts. The Vineria is an excellent choice for wine appasionati interested in Florence's young front-runners in nontraditional and rather un-Tuscan food.

IN THE OLTRARNO

Head south over the Ponte Vecchio for the "Left Bank" of Florence. Rents and prices are catching up with the north or Duomo side of the river, but the atmosphere here is still one of artisan shops and casual eateries with a more palpable neighborhood feel.

MEALS FOR LESS THAN 15,000 LIRE ($9.85)

Bar Ricchi. Pz. Santo Spirito 9r. ☎ **055/21-58-64.** Primi 6,000L ($3.95); main courses 8,000L ($5.25). V, AE. Mon–Sat 12–2:30pm. Bar open winter 7am–8:30pm. Summer 7am–1am. ITALIAN.

This much-beloved bar (especially so when spring arrives and tables appear outside in one of Florence's great piazzas) has a great inexpensive menu for lunch—if only they'd repeat the performance for dinner. Four or five pastas are made up "espresso" upon order and, as an alternative to the usual entrees (such as arrista, a thick slice of roast pork roasted with rosemary, or roast chicken), peruse the different "super salads" (8,000L/$5.25), a brief nod to foreign influence. A table in the shady piazza (one of few green piazzas in Florence) is ringside, but don't leave without taking a look at the cozy inside room whose walls are covered with 350 framed designs from a 1980 contest to design the unfinished facade of Brunelleschi's Church of Santo Spirito.

Il Cantinone. V. Santo Spirito 6r (off Pz. Santa Trinita). ☎ **055/21-88-98.** Crostoni 6,000L–7,000L ($3.95–$4.60); primi 6,000L–8,000L ($3.95–$5.25). No credit cards. Tues–Sun. 12:30–2:30pm and 7:30–10:30pm. WINE BAR.

Appropriately set in the brick-vaulted cantina or wine cellar of a 16th-century palazzo, this well-known wine bar promises "a pinch of country Tuscan cooking, by candle-light, in the heart of Florence." You might consider it more jovial than romantic on nights when the wine gets flowing—and a fine selection of Chianti's best there is to pick from; there are five or six red wines available by the glass, but don't overlook a liter of the good house wine, a bargain at 13,000L ($8.55). Order a number of different appetizers and first courses and you'll understand why they call Tuscany's peasant food the food of kings. "Crostoni" are large slabs of home-baked bread covered with either prosciutto, funghi (mushrooms), tomatoes, or salsiccia sausage. Primi courses might be a hearty pappa al pomodoro or ribollita soup, with a pasta of the day. Delicious, basic fare to accompany a quintessentially Florentine evening.

Trattoria Casalinga. V. Michelozzi 9r (between V. Maggio and Pz. Santo Spirito). ☎ **055/218-624.** Primi 4,800L–6,300L ($3.15–$4.15); main courses 7,000L–13,000L ($4.60–$8.55). No credit cards. Mon–Sat 12:30–2:30pm and 7:30–10:30pm. ITALIAN.

"Casalinga" refers to the home cooking that keeps this recently expanded, unpretentious place always full. Along with the larger seating capacity came the frayed nerves of the help and a sometimes erratic performance from the kitchen. Or so I've heard, but I've never experienced anything but a smile and a good meal in one of my favorite neighborhoods in Florence. The menu is straightforward Tuscan—try the hearty ribollita, or the less easily found ravioli al sugo di coniglio in a rabbit-flavored sauce. You're just a one-block walk east of Piazza Santo Spirito, so save your caffe or dessert for one of the indoor/outdoor bars there in one of Florence's most frequented after-dinner rendezvous spots.

MEALS FOR LESS THAN 22,000 LIRE ($14.45)

Borgo Antico. Pz. Santo Spirito 6r. ☎ **055/21-04-37.** Pizza 10,000L ($6.60); primi 10,000L ($6.60); main courses 15,000L–18,000L ($9.85–$11.85). AE, MC, V. Tues–Sun 12:30–2:30pm and 7:30–11pm. ITALIAN.

A Moveable Feast

One way to have a delicious and inexpensive meal is to pick up your own food. Doing your own food shopping in Italy is an interesting experience. To buy cold cuts, you'll have to look for a *salumeria*. To pick up cheese or yogurt, you'll have to find a *latteria*. Vegetables and fruit can be found at a produce stand called *orto e vedura* or at an *alimentari,* the closest thing Italy has to a grocery store. For bread to put all that between, visit a *forno* or *panetteria.* Wander into a *pasticceria* to find dessert. And for a bottle of wine to wash it down, search out a shop selling *vino e olio.* Via dei Neri, which begins at Via de' Benci near Piazza Santa Croce and stretches over toward Piazza della Signoria, is lined with small specialty food shops and is a good area for purchasing food for an outing.

If you prefer to find all you need under one roof, visit the colorful **Mercato Centrale,** Florence's block-long two-story central marketplace, at V. dell' Ariento 12, in the midst of the open-air San Lorenzo market.

Or if you're just as happy to have someone else make up your sandwiches for you, seek out **Forno Sartoni** on V. dei Cerchi 34r directly behind the large Coin department store on Via Calzaiuoli. This is something of an institution—the crowd in the back is waiting for fresh pizza straight out of the oven, sold by the slice and weighed by the ounce (the average slice costs 2,500L /$1.65). They also make up fresh sandwiches for approximately 3,500L ($2.30) on freshly baked focaccia bread. **Alimentari Orizi,** on V. Parione 19r off Via Tornabuoni, will also make up fresh sandwiches according to your specifications. Ask for it "da portare via" (to go).

The **Boboli Gardens,** on the opposite side of the river Arno, is without a doubt the best picnic spot in town. A grand amphitheater behind the Palazzo provides historical seating, but it's worth the hike to the top to the Forte Belvedere for the breathtaking view (and hence the fortress's name). If you'd just as soon pull up a park bench in the centro storico, a number of the city's most beautiful piazzas have stone benches and open spaces: Piazza Santa Croce comes to mind for its proximity to Vivoli's for a postlunch gelato. Piazza Santa Maria Novella offers stone benches and the only plots of grass in any of the city's squares. Piazza Santissima Annunziata is a wide Renaissance square with inviting steps for sun-basking on its west side, and for convenience, you can't beat the central Piazza della Repubblica and its new circular planters-cum-seats. If Florence's summer heat has set in, look for the shady Piazza Massimo d'Azeglio, east of the Accademia near the Synagogue, and the lovely Piazza Santo Spirito in the Oltrarno.

In the spirit of the Oltrarno's "left bank" atmosphere and Santo Spirito, its favorite piazza, the Borgo Antico, is a relaxed eating spot where you can order as little or as much as you want, and enjoy it in the interesting company of a mixed bag of tourists and Florentines. The scene inside is always buzzing, where an open kitchen and wood-burning pizza oven provide a show, but from April to September tables are set up outside where the million-dollar view of Brunelleschi's church is free of charge. There are a dozen great pizzas to pick from and a number of combination "super salads," with mostly un-Italian ingredients such as corn, hearts of palm, and shrimp. Specialties of the day get equally creative (as in "expensive"), but you'll want to come here for the pizza-with-a-view.

Trattoria del Cinghiale. Bgo. San Jacopo 43r (off Pz. Santa Trinita). ☎ **055/21-57-06.** Primi 6,000L–8,500L ($3.95–$5.60); main courses 13,000L–19,000L ($8.55–$12.50). No credit cards. Wed–Sun noon–3pm and 7–10:30pm. ITALIAN.

Set in a medieval tower, this friendly trattoria is dedicated to the cinghiale, the wild boar so ubiquitous in the Tuscan hills and traditional cuisine. Its presence is felt strongly during the autumn game season, but you'll usually see year-round dishes here such as pasta with a cinghiale sauce or a wild boar sausage (salsiccia) antipasto to satisfy your curiosity if not your palate. But much of the menu is cinghiale-free, such as the delicious strozzapreti (literally "priest stranglers"—don't ask), a baked pasta made with ricotta cheese and spinach. Things are relaxed here during lunch, where the owners have even added an insalata dello chef (chef's salad), a concession to the light eating habits of American customers.

FOR GELATO (ICE CREAM)

There are innumerable gelato sources around town. The following four are not only considered the best, they also have the largest selections, and are all centrally located. Ask for a cone (cono) or cup (coppa) ranging from 3,000L to 7,000L ($2.00 to $4.60)—point and ask for as many flavors as can be squeezed in.

Festival del Gelato. V. d. Corso 75r (just off V. Calzaiuoli). ☎ **055/23-94-386.** From 3,000L ($2.00) for a small dish or cone. No credit cards. Summer, Tues–Sun 8am–1am; winter, Tues–Sun 11am–1am. ITALIAN GELATO.

Of all the gelaterias in Florence, Festival del Gelato has been the only serious contender to the premier Vivoli (see below). Offering about 50 flavors along with pounding pop music and blinding neon, the gelateria is as much a scene as a substance.

Gelateria delle Carrozze. Pz. d. Pesce 3–5r (immediately northeast of the Ponte Vecchio). ☎ **055/23-96-810.** From 3,000L ($2.00) for a small dish or cone. No credit cards. Thurs–Tues 9am–midnight.

The major advantage of this always crowded parlor is its can't-miss location at the foot of the Ponte Vecchio (Old Bridge)—if you're coming off the Ponte Vecchio and about to head toward the Duomo, it is just to your right on a small alleyway that forks off the main street. It's just as wonderfully delicious as all of the above, maybe easier to find, and has quite a few tables inside for those who prefer to sit while savoring the moment.

Perche No!. V. d. Tavolini 19r (just off V. Calzaiuoli). ☎ **055/23-98-969.** From 3,000L ($2.00) for a small dish or cone. No credit cards. Wed–Mon 8am–12:30am. ITALIAN GELATO.

This fine gelateria is called "Why Not!"—a good question indeed. Both this location and Festival del Gelato are popular locations between the Piazza Signoria and Piazza Duomo, off the pedestrian Via Calzaiuoli.

✪ **Vivoli.** V. Isole d. Stinche 74 (1 block west of Pz. Santa Croce). ☎ **055/23-92-334.** From 3,000L ($2.00) for a small dish or cone. No credit cards. Tues–Sun 9am–1am. Closed Aug and Jan to early Feb. ITALIAN GELATO.

Vivoli is world-famous, but recent taste tests have detractors wondering if it's now relying a bit too heavily on its reputation. Exactly how renowned is this brightly lit gelateria? Taped to the wall is a postcard bearing only "Vivoli, Europa" for the address, yet it was successfully delivered to this world capital of ice cream.

4 Attractions

Seeing all of Florence in a short time requires organization. It's not just that there's so much to see in this great city; it's also that establishments close for long lunch breaks and many museums close for the day at 2pm or sooner (remember that the last entrance is at least 30 minutes, sometimes 45 to 60 minutes, before closing). Most museums are closed on Monday. The first thing you should do is stop by the tourist office for an up-to-the-minute listing of museum hours. Churches and the markets are good alternatives for afternoon touring time, since they usually remain open until 7pm.

SUGGESTED ITINERARIES

If You Have 1 Day

There's so much to see in Florence, each attraction as historically significant and aesthetically captivating as the next. The best approach is to choose sites from our Top Attractions, according to your personal interests.

Except in the dead of winter there are almost always lines at the Uffizi. Regardless, begin your day here, as this is Italy's most significant picture gallery and the most important art museum in Europe after the Louvre in Paris. You'd have to race at breakneck speed through the museum's 45 rooms to see everything, so I suggest that you choose a particular period or painter—perhaps the High Renaissance— the museum is organized accordingly. Unless your head is swimming, try to visit the Accademia (more lines!) as well, where there are several pieces by Michelangelo, one of which is his legendary *David,* considered one of the great sculptures of all times.

Lunch on Piazza della Signoria in the shadow of the Palazzo Vecchio and its many statues is expensive (try instead the casual but stylish Cantinetta dei Verrazzano or Caffe Italiano), but for a memorable break from sightseeing, splurge on an outdoor iced tea at the historical Caffe Rivoire. Find time after lunch to visit the Duomo and Baptistery which remain open till late afternoon.

For a quick shot at shopping—as much for the color and experience as for actual buying—head north from the Duomo to the sprawling open-air Mercato San Lorenzo, open until 7pm; take advantage of the bargains on leather goods and wool sweaters and scarves in particular.

Finally, try not to miss an opportunity to make dinner a memorable Tuscan experience at any one of the restaurants I've recommended (see "Dining," earlier in this chapter).

If You Have 2 Days

The above one-day schedule is quite busy: Spread its wealth over two days while incorporating some of the following.

Divide the wonders of the Uffizi collection into the East and West galleries, spending part of each of your two days there at a more leisurely pace. There's so much to see and savor that you could return a dozen times. And if it's still early and you're anxious to continue your exploration of Renaissance art—this time with sculpture— remember that the nearby Bargello is one of the many museums closing at 2pm.

Many museums are housed in the Pitti Palace across the Ponte Vecchio in the Oltrarno neighborhood, but first visit its Galleria Palatina and its collection of masterworks by Raphael. A picnic lunch is preferable, but even a stroll through the Boboli Gardens behind the Pitti Palace is a lovely way to recharge your batteries while taking in the views that have captivated tourists for centuries. If it's not too late, return to the Duomo and consider a Stairmaster workout to the gods, and climb to the top of Brunelleschi's dome or the only slightly less strenuous hike to the top of Giotto's bell tower for an eagle's-nest view of the city and surrounding hills.

After that, you deserve a marvelous dinner highlighted by the Tuscan menu's bistecca alla fiorentina and an outdoor drink at any of the bars in the lively Piazza Santo Spirito.

Florence Attractions

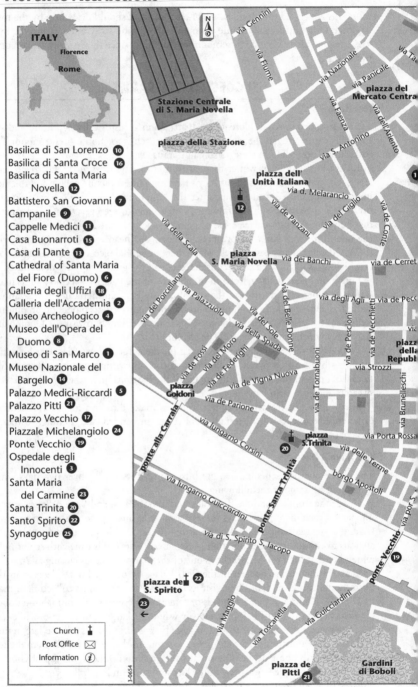

Basilica di San Lorenzo ⑩
Basilica di Santa Croce ⑯
Basilica di Santa Maria
  Novella ⑫
Battistero San Giovanni ⑦
Campanile ⑨
Cappelle Medici ⑪
Casa Buonarroti ⑮
Casa di Dante ⑬
Cathedral of Santa Maria
  del Fiore (Duomo) ⑥
Galleria degli Uffizi ⑱
Galleria dell'Accademia ②
Museo Archeologico ④
Museo dell'Opera del
  Duomo ⑧
Museo di San Marco ①
Museo Nazionale del
  Bargello ⑭
Palazzo Medici-Riccardi ⑤
Palazzo Pitti ㉑
Palazzo Vecchio ⑰
Piazzale Michelangiolo ㉔
Ponte Vecchio ⑲
Ospedale degli
  Innocenti ③
Santa Maria
  del Carmine ㉓
Santa Trinita ⑳
Santo Spirito ㉒
Synagogue ㉕

Church ✝
Post Office ✉
Information ⓘ

3-0654

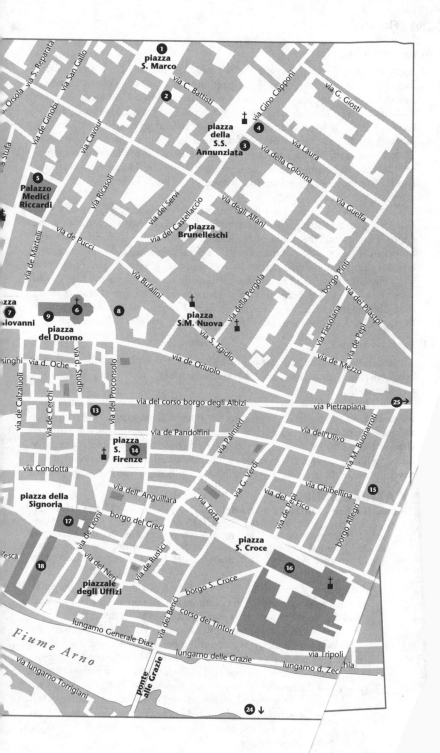

piazza
S. Marco ❶

via C. Battisti

❷

via G. Giosti

via Gino Capponi

piazza
della
S.S.
Annunziata ❸

✝
❹

via Laura

via della Colonna

❺
Palazzo
Medici
Riccardi

via S. Reparata
via Reparata

via San Gallo

via de Ginobi

via Cavour

via Ricasoli

via dei Servi

via del Castellaccio

via degli Alfani

via Guelfa

via de Martelli

via de Pucci

piazza
Brunelleschi

via Bufalini

via della Pergola

borgo Pinti

via dei Plastpi

piazza
S.M. Nuova ✝
■

via S. Egidio

via Fiesolana

via de Pepi

zza
S.
iovanni ❼

✝
❻

❾ ❽

piazza
del Duomo

via de Oriuolo

via de Mezzo

singhi

via d. Oche

via d. Studio

via del Proconsolo

via de Calzaiuoli

via de Cerchi

via del corso borgo degli Albizi

via Pietrapiana

25→

❶❸

via de Pandolfini

via dell'Ulivo

via M. Buonarroti

piazza
S.
Firenze ❶❹
✝

via Condotta

via dell' Anguillara

via Palmieri

via G. Verdi

via del Pepi

via Ghibellina

❶❺

piazza della
Signoria

❶❼

borgo del Greci

via de Leoni

Via Torta

via del Fico

piazza
S. Croce

borgo Allegri

'esca

❶❽

via del Neri

via de Rustici

❶❻

✝
■

piazzale
degli Uffizi

borgo S. Croce

via del Benci

corso dei Tintori

Fiume Arno

lungarno Generale Diaz

lungarno delle Grazie

via Tripoli

lungarno d. Zec hia

via lungarno Torrigiani

ponte
alle Grazie

❷❹ ↓

201

If You Have 3 Days

Approach all of the above suggestions at a more civilized and human pace, inter-spersed with a casual stroll through the centro storico's store-lined pedestrian streets and a look-see at the goods sold at the covered Mercato Nuovo, a miniature version of the much larger Mercato San Lorenzo. While you're in the neighborhood, visit the Palazzo Vecchio in the Piazza Signora, whose upstairs salons merit a visit. Then en-gage in a window-shopping look-see of the Ponte Vecchio and the dazzling wares of its dozens of small gold and jewelry stores. If you find that you're swooning less to the splendor and magnitude of the Renaissance, visit the Medici Chapels in the Basilica San Lorenzo, Michelangelo's homage to the Medici rulers and his lifelong patrons.

The treasures of Florence's half-dozen important churches can easily consume your third day (lines are usually not a problem): Fra Angelico's frescoes at San Marco, the Giotto frescoes and the tombs of Michelangelo and Galileo at Santa Croce, the Brunelleschi fresco cycle and the Spanish Chapel at Santa Maria Novella, the revo-lutionary early Renaissance frescoes of the Brancacci Chapel in Santa Maria del Carmine, and the gothic Orsanmichele will easily combine for a splendid day of sightseeing in Florence. Map out your preferences, and remember that all churches close during lunch hour. Don't forget that Santa Croce is but two steps away from the legendary Vivoli gelateria, and Orsanmichele is an easy hop to Perche No!

If You Have 5 Days

Some visitors have fallen so deeply in love with Florence that on their fifth day they've been seen sitting at a cafe searching the classified ads of *Il Pulce* looking for a job and an apartment.

If you have a full five days, I suggest that you stretch out the hectic itineraries sketched above. On the fourth or fifth, get out of town. Siena, Lucca, San Gimignano, and even nearby Fiesole are all lovely towns that can easily be reached on a day trip (see chapter 14 for detailed information about these destinations). Or consider a one-day ing or biking trip into the surrounding hills (see "Organized Tours," below). You'll r run out of things to do. A week's stay would be better. A lifetime would be nice.

ATTRACTIONS

Cao (Cathedral of Santa Maria del Fiore). Pz. d. Duomo. ☎ **055/21-32-29.** Fri free; cupola ascent, 8,000L ($5.25); excavations, 3,000L ($2.00). Summer: Mon–excan, Sat 8:30am–5pm, Sun 1–5pm (open Sun morning for services only; cupola and Sun closed Sun); Winter: Mon–Fri 10am–7pm, Sat 9:30am–5pm, Sun 1–5pm (open cupola for services only; cupola and excavations closed Sun). Last entrance to ascend the tes before closing.

The just as d dome of Florence's magnificent Duomo dominates the skyline today in 1434 hen it was constructed five centuries ago. At the time it was completed structure the largest unsupported dome in the world, intended to dwarf the si puo" (a ient Greece and Rome. In Renaissance style, to be "il piu bello che feat and wa iful as possible), it was and still is considered a major architectural took 14 year high point of architect Filippo Brunelleschi's illustrious career—it marble exteric mplete. The cathedral's colorful white-, red-, and green-patterned "modern" facad the color of the Italian flag) comes from Tuscan quarries. This Florence became lacing the original, was only added in the late 19th century when interesting contra capital of the newly united Italy. The tricolored mosaic is an azzi throughout the rather somber, sienna-colored medieval and fortresslike rest of the city.

Though much of the church's interior decoration has been moved to the Museo dell'Opera del Duomo (see below), the cathedral still boasts three stained-glass windows on the entrance wall by Lorenzo Ghiberti (sculptor of the famous Baptistery doors) next to Paolo Uccello's giant clock using the heads of four prophets. In late 1995, an extensive and elaborate restoration was finally completed on the colorful 16th-century frescoes covering the inside of the cupola and depicting the Last Judgment. They were begun by Giorgio Vasari and finished by Federico Zuccari. When the restorers began their work, they discovered an ugly surprise: A good portion of the work was executed not in "true fresco" but in tempera, which is much more delicate.

Brunelleschi's cupola was built double-walled and is strong enough to withstand the thousands of athletic tourists who climb the spiraling, dizzying 463 steps leading to the summit for its spectacular view of Florence.

Beneath the Duomo's floor is the crypt (look for the Scavi della Cripta di Santa Reparata), the ruins of the romanesque Santa Reparata Cathedral, believed to have been founded in the 5th century on this site; it was continuously enlarged until it was done away with in 1296 to accommodate the present structure. Brunelleschi's tomb is appropriately located here. The entrance to the excavations is through a stairway near the front of the cathedral, to the right as you enter.

Note that free guided visits of the Duomo by English-speaking volunteers were offered in 1996 every day except Sunday from 10am to noon and 3 to 5pm. Ask if these are still available.

✪ Battistero di San Giovanni (Baptistery). Pz. d. Duomo. ☎ 055/23-02-885. Admission (expected for 1997) 3,000L–5,000L ($2.00–$3.30). Mon–Sat 1:00–5pm, Sun 9am–12:30pm.

In front of the Duomo is Florence's octagonal Baptistery, dedicated to the city's patron saint, San Giovanni or John the Baptist. The highlight of the romanesque Baptistery, constructed in the 11th and 12th centuries and considered one of Florence's oldest buildings, is Lorenzo Ghiberti's bronze exterior doors known as the *Gates of Paradise*, on the side facing the Duomo (east). Ten bronze panels depict various scenes from the Old Testament, including Adam and Eve in creation, in stunning three-dimensional relief. Ghiberti labored over his masterpiece from 1425 to 1452, dying three years later. The originals can be viewed in the Museo dell'Opera del Duomo (see below); those exposed here are convincing replicas.

The doors at the north side of the Baptistery were Ghiberti's "warm-up" to the Gates and the work that won him, at the age of 23, the commission for the eastern doors. The doors on the south side, through which you enter, are by Andrea Pisano. They are the oldest doors, completed in 1336, and depict the life of St. John.

The vault of the Baptistery is decorated with magnificent gilded mosaics dating to the 1200s dominated by a figure of Christ.

✪ Campanile di Giotto (Giotto's Bell Tower). Pz. d. Duomo. ☎ 055/23-02-885. Admission 8,000L ($5.25). Mar–Oct, daily 9am–6:50pm; Nov–Feb, daily 9am–4:20pm; last entrance 40 minutes before closing.

Giotto spent the last three years of his life designing the Duomo's "Tuscanized gothic" campanile, or bell tower, and so it's often referred to simply as Giotto's Tower. Clad in the same three colors as the cathedral, it is 20 feet shorter than the dome. The bas-reliefs decorating its slender exterior are copies of works by Andrea Pisano, Francesco Talenti, Luca della Robbia, and Arnoldi (the originals are in the Duomo Museum). The view from the top of Giotto's Tower is about equal to that from the Duomo; there are, however, a mere 414 steps here (as opposed to the Duomo's 463). There are fewer crowds on this rooftop, but you won't get the chance to get up close and personal with Brunelleschi's architectural masterpiece here.

✪ **Galleria degli Uffizi (Uffizi Galleries).** Pzle. degli Uffizi 6 (south of the Palazzo Vecchio and the Pz. Signoria). ☎ **055/23-885.** Admission 12,000L ($7.90). Tues–Sat 9am–7pm, Sun 9am–2pm; the ticket office closes 45 minutes before the museum (also see below).

The Uffizi is one of the most important art museums in the world and should be the first stop in Florence for anyone interested in the rich artistic heritage of the Renaissance. Six centuries of artistic development are housed in this impressive Renaissance palazzo, commissioned by Duke Cosimo de' Medici in 1560 and initiated by Giorgio Vasari to house the Duchy of Tuscany's administrative offices (in fact, *uffizi* means "offices"). The art collection, whose strong point is Florentine Renaissance, but includes major works by Flemish and Venetian masters, was amassed by the Medici and bequeathed to the people of Florence in 1737 by Anna Maria Ludovica, the last of the Medici line.

The gallery consists of 45 rooms where paintings are nicely grouped into schools in chronological order, from the 13th to the 18th century (don't overlook the details of the building itself, whose frescoed ceilings and tapestried corridors are overshadowed by the wealth of paintings). Vasari's monumental staircase leads upstairs to the superb collection that begins in room 2 in the east wing, with Giotto's early 14th-century *Madonna,* considered by most scholars the first painting to make the transition from Byzantine to Renaissance style. Look for the differences between Giotto's work and his teacher Cimabue's *Madonna in Maestà* on the opposite wall. Some of the museum's best-known and most visited rooms are dedicated to 15th-century Florentine painting, the eve of the Renaissance or the "First Renaissance." In Room 7 are major works by Paolo Uccello, Masaccio, Fra Angelico, and Piero della Francesca. As you proceed, look for the elegant Madonnas of Filippo Lippi and Pollaiolo's delightful little panels.

For many (and judging from the crowds), the Botticelli Rooms (rooms 10 to 14) are the undisputed highlight of a museum whose every niche is hung with extraordinary art. Arguably the most stunning are the restored *Primavera (The Allegory of Springtime)* whose three graces form the painting's principal focus and *The Birth of Venus* (commonly referred to as "Venus on the Half-Shell." Botticelli's *Adoration of the Magi* is interesting for the portraits he incorporated of his Medici sponsors, and his self-portrait, on the far right-hand side. Other notable works include Leonardo da Vinci's unfinished *Adorazione dei Magi* and his famous *Annunciation* in room 15.

Since the May 1993 bombing that damaged 200 works (37 of them seriously), the museum has staged an amazing recovery. Only four of those damaged were considered superior examples from the Italian Renaissance; two were destroyed beyond repair. Restorators, many of whom had recently spent decades working to undo the devastating effects of the 1966 floods, have again been working around the clock to repair damage from this more recent disaster. There has been some temporary relocation of paintings that may conflict with the original layout listed above while final repairs to the structural damage of the building itself are completed.

Note that in 1996 an experimental program of advance reservation tickets to the Uffizi was offered, saving visitors hours of waiting in line. Check with the tourist office off the Piazza della Signoria at Chiasso Baroncelli 17r (☎ **055/23-02-124**) to see if this is still in effect when you visit.

○ **Galleria dell'Accademia (Academy Museum).** V. Ricasoli 60 (between Pz. d. Duomo and Pz. San Marco). ☎ **055/23-885.** Admission 12,000L ($7.90). Tues–Sat 9am–7pm, Sun 9am–2pm; last entrance 30 minutes before closing.

Nowhere else in Europe do so many wait in line for so long to see so little. The wait can be up to an hour, so try getting there before the museum opens in the morning or around midday. The Accademia is home to Michelangelo's *David* (1501–4), generally considered his greatest work. Most remarkable is the fact that Michelangelo was just 29 years old and had only recently been recognized for his promising talents. Sculpted from a used, 17-foot column of white Carrara marble that had been discarded and abandoned, the *David* looms in stark perfection beneath the rotunda of the main room built exclusively for its display in 1873 when it was moved here from the Piazza Signoria (a copy now stands in its place while a second copy lords over the Piazzale Michelangiolo). From its very beginning nicknamed "Il Gigante," or the Giant, the colossal statue has been protected by a high transparent Plexiglas shield since the 1991 attack that damaged its left foot (it was immediately and undetectably repaired). The museum houses several other Michelangelos, including four never-finished *Prisoners* (or *Slaves*) struggling to free themselves, originally commissioned for the tomb of Julius II—Michelangelo believed he could sense their very presence within the stone, and he worked to release their forms from within. The *Palestrina Pietà* is also here (another *Pietà* is displayed in the Museo dell'Opera del Duomo). A number of 15th- to 16th-century Florentine artists are represented here, though overshadowed by the presence of the Giant. Search out the *Madonna del Mare (Madonna of the Sea)*, attributed to Botticelli.

Piazza della Signoria, Palazzo Vecchio & Orcagna's Loggia. Pz. d. Signoria. ☎ **055/ 27-681.** Palazzo Vecchio (Appartamenti Monumentali): 8,000L ($5.25) Mon–Fri, free Sun. Mon–Wed, Fri–Sat 9am–7pm, Sun 8am–1pm. Closed Thurs.

In Italy, all roads lead to Rome, but in Florence all roads lead to the spacious, elegant **Piazza della Signoria**—the cultural, political, and social heart of the city since the 14th century.

The square is dominated by the imposing rough-hewn fortress architecture of the late 13th-century **Palazzo Vecchio** (the Old Palace). Its severe gothic style, complete with crenellations and battlements, is highlighted by a campanile that was a supreme feat of engineering in its day. It served as Florence's city hall for many years (a role it fulfills again today) and then was home to Duke Cosimo de' Medici (that's Giambologna's bronze statue of him on horseback anchoring the middle of the piazza). He lived here for 10 years beginning in 1540, when much of the interior was remodeled to the elegant Renaissance style you see today, before moving to the Palazzo Pitti. You'll enter through the stunning main courtyard of the palazzo, with its intricately carved columns and extraordinarily colorful 16th-century frescoes by Vasari; the central focus is the Putto Fountain, a copy of Verrochchio's original, which is displayed upstairs.

The highlight of the interior is the first-floor massive Salone dei Cinquecento (Hall of the Five Hundred) whose rich frescoes by Vassari depicted Florence's history; formerly the city's council chambers, it is still used for government and civic functions. The statue *The Genius of Victory* is by Michelangelo. Upstairs, the richly decorated and frescoed salons, such as the private quarters of Cosimo's wife, Eleanora of Toledo, offer an intriguing glimpse into how the ruling class of Renaissance Florence lived.

A small disk in the ground in front of Ammanati's enormous Neptune fountain (1576) marks the spot where Savonarola, reformer and religious fundamentalist, was

Renaissance Men: Florence's Artistic Geniuses

The Florentine Renaissance was a time that recognized and nurtured artistic genius in whomever it showed, and the era's legends came from all walks of life.

Giotto di Bondone (1266–1337)   Giotto was born a shepherd boy. The renowned artist Cimabue discovered Giotto one day sitting by his herd, scratching a sketch of one of the sheep with a pointed rock on a stone slab. Cimabue took the lad into his studio, and it wasn't long before the student's mastery eclipsed that of his teacher. Although other artists had begun introducing naturalistic elements into the highly stylized medieval forms, Giotto exploded convention and plunged painting into a humanism that would quickly become the earmark of the Renaissance. While he lacked a good grasp of perspective or a sense of photographic realism—neither concept had yet been invented—he painted his biblical characters in a way that had never been seen before. His figures have bulk under their clothes, they have weight, they each have distinct faces and personalities—they are, in a word, individuals, caught almost as if in private moments—the people laugh, sleep, fidget, preach, move, cry, and even sit with their backs turned to us. Giotto became so famous in his lifetime he was kept traveling the length of Italy to ply his craft. Although Giotto's most famous fresco cycles are in Assisi and Padova, Florence is home to many works, including his *Maestà* in the Uffizi and the Peruzzi and Bardi Chapels in Santa Croce.

Filippo Brunelleschi (1377–1446)   A diminutive man whose ego was as enormous as his talent, Brunelleschi managed, in his arrogant, quixotic, suspicious, and brilliant way literally to invent Renaissance architecture. Having been beaten by Ghiberti in the famous contest to cast the Baptistery Doors, Brunelleschi resolved he'd rather be the top architect than second-best sculptor. Apart from creating the serene churches of San Lorenzo and Santo Spirito and the elegant Ospedale degli Innocenti, his greatest achievement by far was erecting the Dome over Florence's cathedral.

The Duomo, the largest church in the world, had already been built, but nobody had been able to figure out how to cover the daunting space over its center— no one was sure whether they could create a dome that would hold up under its own weight. Our irascible young architect Filippo kept insisting he had the answer, only he wouldn't share it, fearful that others would use his ideas and get the job away from him. In several committee meetings, he became so heated that he had to be bodily carried out. Finally he came into a meeting bearing an egg and issued a challenge: He bet that none of the learned architects and councilmen in the room could make an egg stand on its end. A marble slab was brought in for the balancing act, but, try as they might, the others couldn't get the egg to stay vertical. Brunelleschi took the egg in his hand, and with one quick movement slammed it down on the marble, smashing its end—but leaving it standing. The others protested that they, too, could have easily done that, to which Brunelleschi replied that they would say the same thing if he showed them his plans for the dome. Eventually, he was granted the commission, and revealed his ingenious plan—he built the dome in two shells, the inner one thicker than the outer one, both shells thinning as they neared the top, thus leaving the center hollow and removing a good deal of the weight. He also planned to construct the dome of giant vaults with ribs crossing over them, each of the stones making up the actual fabric of the dome dovetailed. In this way, the walls of the dome would support themselves as they were erected.

Brunelleschi was even far-sighted enough to build in drainage systems for the rain and iron hooks to support interior scaffolding for future cleaning or repair.

His finished work speaks for itself, rearing its orangey-russet bulk eternally over the city's skyline—Florentines will proudly claim that they have lived their whole lives within sight of the dome. For his achievement, Brunelleschi was accorded a singular honor: He is one of the very few people buried in Florence's cathedral, under his own ingenious and revolutionary dome.

Lorenzo Ghiberti (1378–1455)   In choosing a date to mark the beginning of the Renaissance, art historians often seize upon 1401, when 22-year-old Ghiberti, competing against the likes of Donatello and Brunelleschi, won the commission to cast the South Doors of Florence's Baptistry. He spent the next 21 years casting 28 bronze panels and building his doors. The result was so impressive, he was asked to do the East Doors as well. Twenty-eight years later, just before his death, Ghiberti finished 10 dramatic, lifelike scenes from the Old Testament and mounted the gilded bronze panels on the East Doors of the Baptistery. Years later, Michelangelo was standing before these doors, and somebody asked him what he thought. His response sums up Ghiberti's life accomplishment as no art historian ever could: "They are so beautiful that they would grace the entrance to Paradise."

Donatello (Donato de' Bardi; 1386–1466)   One of the greatest sculptors of the Renaissance, Donatello perfected the use of perspective in bas-relief and cast the first freestanding nude statue since antiquity (the erotic and androgynous bronze *David* in the Bargello). A true Tuscan eccentric, he was as spare, humble, and giving in his personal life as he was driven and devoted to his art and his patron, Cosimo de' Medici. Always striving for a marriage of classical grace with studied naturalism, Donatello was one of the first sculptors to infuse his works with a real sense of life. While carving the highly idiosyncratic *Lo Zuccone* (in the Museo dell'Opera dell Duomo), he could be heard muttering to his creation "Speak, damn you, speak!"

Donatello never lacked for commissions, and he was known to keep the money from his considerable income hung from the rafters of his studio in a basket, to which any one of his students or friends could help themselves. Before Cosimo de' Medici died, he told his son Piero to look after the aging sculptor and make sure Donatello never wanted for money, so Piero gave him a small farm to create an income for him. Years later, as Donatello himself lay on his deathbed, he refused to leave this farm to his greedy relations; he told them it seemed only right to leave the farm to the peasant who had always worked it. Donatello was buried in San Lorenzo, at his request, close to the tomb of his great friend and benefactor, Cosimo.

Fra (Beato) Angelico (Giovanni da Fiesole; 1400–55)   A monk of the Order of Friars Preachers, Fra Angelico was an extremely devout man, displaying his love of Christ and his church through his paintings and illuminated manuscripts. One of his most famous works is the cycle of frescoes in his adopted convent of San Marco in Florence. His renowned *Annunciation* is at the top of the stairs that lead to the monk's cells. Fra Angelico also painted the cells themselves with simple works to aid meditations. One of these almost anticipates surrealism—a *Flagellation* scene where disembodied hands strike at Christ's face and a rod descends upon him from the blue background. A small, saintly man, Angelico was kind and religiously observant almost to the point of simpleness. Angelico never retouched his works,

continues

believing that the hand of God moved him and his talents. When he picked up his brushes he uttered a prayer, and it is said that whenever he painted a Crucifixion, tears would stream down his face.

Fra Filippo Lippi (1406–69)   Filippo's parents died during his infancy, and he was brought up in a Carmelite monastery but, even though he took orders, monastic life never quite appealed to him. Having discovered his talent for painting at an early age, Fra Filippo spent his time womanizing, occasionally painting to support his carousing. Cosimo de' Medici once got so fed up with his procrastination that he locked Filippo in his room and told him he couldn't come out until the commission was finished. Filippo availed himself of scissors and the bedsheets and made the clichéd escape out the window to embark on a multiday binge. Cosimo eventually gave up—it was easier to indulge the painter than to lock him up. While painting an altarpiece for a convent in nearby Prato, Filippo seduced a pretty young novice there named Lucrezia. He stole her away from the nuns, and eventually had a son by her (Filippino, who also became a famous painter). Although Filippo used Lucrezia as a model for his Madonnas and remained with her for the rest of his life, he continued to womanize. When the pope offered to release him from his old vows and allow him to marry, Filippo refused—marriage would have cramped his style. To judge his worth as an artist, visit his *Annunciation* in San Lorenzo, the *Pitti Tondo* in the Pitti Palace, and his *Coronation* in the Uffizi, hung near the paintings of his star pupil, Botticelli.

Sandro Botticelli (1444–1510)   Though he later turned to religious works, Botticelli's early career glorified pagan mythology. The two most famous of these paintings, of course, are *The Birth of Venus* and *Allegory of Spring*, both hanging in the Botticelli Room of the Uffizi. His tall, languorous women with lithe necks and sinuous bodies draped in intricately pleated dresses almost look forward to the later Mannerist movement. Botticelli squandered his money so rapidly he had to keep moving from commission to commission to stay solvent. Lorenzo de' Medici gave him work and money just to keep him out of the poorhouse. He was also quite the practical joker, playing tricks on his pupils such as altering their paintings when they left the room and having everyone in the room pretend there hadn't been any change (he even got potential buyers in on the gags).

Leonardo da Vinci (1452–1519)   A genius by anyone's count, and the prime example of the Renaissance Man, Leonardo dabbled in a bit of everything. His inventions (on paper, mostly) were so revolutionary that most of them were brushed off as fantastical by his contemporaries and few were built until recent times, by experimenters who wanted to find out whether they would work. They did. He drew plans for parachutes, innumerable machine guns, siege weapons, water pumps—even several versions of a helicopter! He was also fascinated by living beings. He left us reams of paper with detailed anatomical sketches of humans, horses, and other animals, including all three in various stages of dissection.

Leonardo was also always trying new methods, materials, and mixtures in his painting, and this penchant for constant experimentation had an unfortunate effect on his work. He did not try out his experiments first—he used his trial techniques on commissions, and often the odd mixtures proved faulty. The *Last Supper* in Milan started deteriorating almost as soon as he finished it. Once, when a giant fresco he was painting in the main hall of the Palazzo Vecchio wasn't drying fast enough, he brought in heaters to try and hurry the process along. However, he had used wax in the pigment mixtures and, as others watched in horror, the fresco melted and ran down the walls to the floor. Many of his works remain unfinished, for he would get sidetracked by his experiments or take so long procrastinating and pondering what he planned to do that the commission would be dropped.

Little of his work remains in Florence today. His most famous works are, of course, in the Louvre. The Uffizi houses the best work of his in town, including his *Annunciation* and two unfinished works, *Adoration of the Magi* and *Baptism*.

Michelangelo Buonarroti (1475–1564)   Irascible, moody, and manic-depressive, Michelangelo was quite simply one of the greatest artists of all time. He grew up on the family farm at Settignano, just outside Florence, and was wet-nursed by the wife of a local stonecutter—he used to joke that he sucked his skill with the hammer and chisel along with the milk. He was apprenticed early to the fresco studio of Ghirlandaio who, while watching the young apprentice sketching, remarked in shock, "This boy knows more about it than I do." After just one year at the fresco studio, Michelangelo was recruited by Lorenzo de' Medici to become part of his new school for sculptors.

Michelangelo learned quickly. After his success at the age of 19 with the *Pietà* sculpture in Rome, Michelangelo was given the opportunity by the city council to carve an enormous block of marble that a previous sculptor had declared unworkable. To represent his city, and with a touch of irony, Michelangelo decided to carve a Goliath-size *David*, working on it behind shuttered scaffolding so that few saw it until the unveiling. When Soderini, the head of the city council came to see it, he remarked that the nose looked a tad too large. Michelangelo climbed up to the head (out of view), grabbed up a handful of leftover plaster dust and, while tapping his hammer lightly against his chisel, let the dust sprinkle down gradually as if he were actually carving. "Much better," remarked Soderini when Michelangelo climbed down again. "Now you've really brought it to life." The *David* was wheeled down to pose in front of the civic palace, where its arm was broken off during an anti-Medici riot several years later. The original is now in the Accademia gallery.

Michelangelo spent the rest of his long life on two long-running, onerous, and oft-interrupted commissions to design and carve a tomb for Pope Julius II and to fresco the Sistine Chapel in Rome. The unfinished *Slaves* (or *Prisoners*) in the Accademia were originally intended for the Julius Tomb. Each in various partially finished stages, these statues are invaluable for the insights they give into how Michelangelo went about carving his sculptures. He always said that the art of sculpture consisted of knowing what finished work lay dormant in the marble—the artist's job was merely to chip away all the superfluous stone that was hiding it. During the downtime when he was kept, for various reasons, from working on the Sistine or the Tomb, he made many smaller pieces, wrote sonnets, built unusual and successful defenses for San Miniato during a siege of Florence, and, as he grew old, explored architecture and created the dome of St. Peter's in Rome.

The later *Pietà* in the Museo dell'Opera dell Duomo, the Medici tombs in San Lorenzo, the early pieces in the Casa Buonarroti, and the *Baccus* and *Bust of Brutus* in the Bargello finish off Michelangelo's sculpture in Florence. For a hint at the painting skills he plied on the Sistine Chapel in Rome, head for the *Doni Tondo* in the Uffizi, and for the Laurentian Library to see his architecture. Michelangelo died in his studio in Rome, after what was probably a stroke, at the age of 89. His body was sneaked back to Florence and buried in Santa Croce.

—Reid Bramblett

burned at the stake for heresy in 1498. Flanking the life-size copy of Michelangelo's *David* are copies of Donatello's *Judith and Holofernes* and the *Marzocco*, heraldic lion of Florence. On the south side of the Piazza Signoria is the 14th-century **Loggia dei Lanzi,** Florence's captivating outdoor sculpture gallery. It's been undergoing restoration for years, but much of the scaffolding is down and a copy of Cellini's *Perseus* and Giambologna's *Rape of the Sabine Women* and *Hercules Slaying the Centaur* can be seen.

✪ **Museo Nazionale del Bargello (Bargello Museum).** V. d. Proconsolo 4 (at V. Ghibellina, near the Uffizi). ☎ 055/23-885. Admission 8,000L ($5.25). Tues–Sun 9am–2pm.

If a visit to the Accademia has whetted your appetite for more fine Renaissance sculpture, then you'll be interested in the national museum's outstanding collection. This stark 13th-century building originated as the city's town hall and later served as the city's jail in Renaissance times. In the middle of the majestic courtyard is a tank where prisoners were once tortured and executed; some hangings took place out the windows for public viewing. Today Il Bargello, named for the police chief or Constable (Bargello) who ruled from here, houses three stories of treasures by Florentine Renaissance sculptors and a collection of Mannerist bronzes.

On the ground floor begin with a visit to Michelangelo's room, including another *David,* originally called *Apollo* and sculpted 30 years after the original; the *Pitti Tondo,* depicting the Madonna teaching Jesus and San Giovanni to read; and *Brutus.* Take a look at his *Bacchus*—it was the young artist's first major work when he was 22 (1497), and effortlessly captures in marble the Roman god's drunken posture. Among the other important sculptures here are Ammanati's *Leda and the Swan,* Giambologna's significant *Winged Mercury,* and several of Donatello's works, including his famous bronze *David,* the first nude statue by an Italian artist since classical times. In another room are the two original bronze plaques by Brunelleschi and Ghiberti that were made for the competition to decide who should sculpt the second set of doors for the Bapistery—of course, Ghiberti's won.

✪ **Palazzo Pitti (Pitti Palace).** Pz. Pitti (south of the Ponte Vecchio in the Oltrarno, at end of V. Giucciardini). ☎ **055/21-34-40.** Galleria Palatina, 12,000L ($7.90); Galleria d'Arte Moderna (Modern Art Gallery), 4,000L ($2.65); Museo degli Argenti (Silver Museum), 8,000L ($5.25). Tues–Sun Palatina and Monumental Apartments 9am–7pm, all others 9am–2pm; last entrance 45 minutes before closing. Call to confirm hours.

It's ironic that this rugged golden palazzo, begun in 1458 for the wealthy textile merchant and banker, Luca Pitti, in an attempt to keep up with the Medici was bought by their descendants in 1549, and used as their official residence as rulers of Florence. The Medici tripled its size, elaborately embellished it, and graced it with the Boboli Gardens that still fan up the hill behind it, once the quarry from which the palazzo's *pietra dura* was taken. Today it is home to seven museums.

The **Galleria Palatina (Palatine Gallery),** on the first floor (☎ 055/21-03-23), is the star attraction, home to one of the finest collections of Italian Renaissance and baroque masters after the Uffizi's. In addition to outstanding Raphaels displayed here, including the prized and much beloved *Madonna of the Chair* and the veiled *La Fornarina* (his baker's daughter and mistress), the museum's treasures include a large collection of works by Andrea del Sarto; Fra Bartolomeo's beautiful *Descent from the Cross* and *San Marco;* some superb works by Rubens, including *The Four Philosophers;* canvases by Tintoretto and Veronese; and some stunning portraits by Titian, including *Pope Julius II, The Man with the Gray Eyes,* and *The Music Concert.* Also represented are Caravaggio, Pontormo, Van Dyck, and Botticelli.

The restored **Appartamenti Monumentali (Royal or Monumental Apartments)** (☎ 055/21-03-23) are ornate, gilded, and chandeliered, with portraits, tapestries, and furnishings from the days of the Medici, and later the Dukes of Lorraine. Upstairs, the **Galleria d'Arte Moderna** (☎ 055/28-70-96) houses an interesting array of 19th-century Italian impressionists (known as the *machaioli* school) and early 20th-century art. Visit the **Museo degli Argenti (Silver Museum),** on the ground floor (☎ 055/21-25-57), for a look at 16 rooms filled with the priceless, private treasure of the Medici family. Other small museums here that open and close without notice are the **Museo della Porcellana** (Porcelain), the **Coach and Carriage Museum,** and the **Galleria del Costume.**

✪ **Basilica di San Lorenzo and the Cappelle Medicee (Medici Chapels).** Pz. Madonna (at the end of Bgo. San Lorenzo, north of the Duomo). ☎ 055/23-885. San Lorenzo and the Biblioteca Laurenziana, free; Medici Chapels, 10,000L ($6.60). Basilica, daily 8am–noon and 3:30–5:30pm; Biblioteca Laurenziana Mon–Sat 9am–1pm; Medici Chapels, Tues–Sun 9am–2pm.

The San Lorenzo Basilica (whose facade was never finished) was the Medici family's parish church as well as the final resting place for most of the clan. The key feature of the main part of the church is the **Biblioteca Laurenziana,** a stunning bit of architecture by Michelangelo containing one of the largest and most valuable collections of manuscripts and codices in the world, amassed by the Medici. An elaborate stone staircase designed by Michelangelo leads to it from the cloister.

San Lorenzo is best known, however, for the **Medici Chapels.** These can only be entered by going around to the back of the church; you must pass through the Cappella dei Principi (Chapel of the Princes), added on in 1604 but not finished until 1962. The reason for your visit is the New Sacristy, which contains the Michelangelo-designed tombs for the powerful Lorenzo de' Medici (with statues of female *Dawn* and male *Dusk*), and Giuliano de' Medici (with statues of female *Night* and male *Day*), considered some of Michelangelo's greatest work (1521–34). The Old Sacristy, designed by Brunelleschi and decorated by Donatello, contains several important works, including a sarcophagus by Verrocchio. A large number of charcoal sketches, confirmed to be doodles by Michelangelo himself, were discovered by sheer chance in the 1980s in a room beneath the sacristy, now open to the public.

Museo di San Marco. Pz. San Marco 1 (north of the Duomo on V. Cavour). ☎ 055/23-88-608. Admission 8,000L ($5.25). Tues–Sun 9am–2pm; the ticket office closes 30 minutes before the museum.

Originally built in the 13th century, then enlarged and rebuilt by Michelozzo as a Dominican monastery in 1437, this small museum is a monument to the devotional work of Florentine-born friar/painter Fra Angelico, one of the great masters of the 15th-century Renaissance. Directly to your right upon entering is a room containing the largest collection of his movable paintings in Florence. The chapter room nearby is home to Fra Angelico's large and impressive *Crucifixion* fresco. On the ground floor visit the Refectory, dedicated to the work of Ghirlandaio (under whom a young Michelangelo apprenticed), particularly his *Cenacolo* or *Last Supper*. At the top of the stairs leading to the monks' cells on the second floor is Fra Angelico's stunning and beautiful masterpiece, *The Annunciation*. Each of the cells on this floor is decorated with a fresco from the life of Christ, painted either by Fra Angelico or by one of his assistants under the master's direction and intended to aid in contemplation and prayer.

At the end of the corridor is the cell of Girolamo Savonarola, which includes a stark portrait of the monastery's former prior by his convert and student, Fra Bartolomeo, as well as his sleeping chamber, notebook, and rosary, and remnants of the clothes worn at his execution. A reformer who crusaded against political and religious corruption, he led a revolt in 1494 that expelled the Medicis, and Florence was set up as a republic. Also a fundamentalist and fanatic, he inspired the people to participate in bonfires of their vanities (including the burning of priceless artwork and hand-illuminated books). His denunciations against the pope eventually led to his excommunication, arrest, and trial; he was burnt for heresy in Piazza Signoria in 1498.

MORE ATTRACTIONS
MUSEUMS

Museo dell'Opera del Duomo (Cathedral Museum). Pz. d. Duomo 29. ☎ **055/ 23-98-796.** Admission 8,000L ($5.25) Mar–Oct, Mon–Sat 9am–7:30pm; Nov–Feb, Mon–Sat 9am–5:20pm; last entrance 60 minutes before closing.

Opened to the public in 1891 and ever since overlooked, this quiet, airy museum behind the cathedral contains much of the art and furnishings that once embellished both the interior and exterior of the Duomo. A bust of Brunelleschi at the entrance is a nod to the man who gave us the Duomo's magnificent cupola, and over the door hang two glazed della Robbia terracottas. In the second inner room to your left you'll find sculptures from the cathedral's old gothic facade (destroyed in 1587), including work by the original architect, Arnolfo di Cambio (1245–1302). Also here are a number of statues, the most noteworthy being a weatherworn but noble *St. John* by Donatello and Nanni di Banco's intriguing *San Luca.*

The highlight of the center room upstairs is the enchanting twin white marble choirs or *cantorie* dating to the 1430s by Donatello and Luca della Robbia that face each other, as well as two statues by Donatello: his celebrated *Magdalene* (originally in the Baptistery) and *Zuccone* (from Giotto's bell tower). In the next room, the Sala delle Formelle (Room of the Panels) are the original bas-reliefs that decorated the first two stories of the campanile's exterior. One of the museum's most important displays is four of the original bronze panels from Ghiberti's *Gates of Paradise* door of the Baptistery (the other six are soon to appear following restoration). A major attraction to the museum is Michelangelo's last, and unfinished, *Pietà.* Originally intended for his own tomb, and done when the sculptor was 80 and partially blind, it is said that Nicodemus, holding Christ, is a self-portrait. A 14th- to 15th-century silver-gilt altarpiece with scenes from the life of St. John, another priceless masterpiece, can be found in the last room on the second floor.

Museo della Casa Buonarroti. V. Ghibellina 70 (5 blocks east of the Bargello). ☎ **055/ 24-17-52.** Admission 8,000L ($5.25). Wed–Mon 9:30am–1:30pm. From Pz. Santa Croce, you'll find Casa Buonarroti at the top of V. d. Pinzochere, 2 blocks north of the piazza.

This graceful house, which Michelangelo bought late in life for his nephew, was turned into a museum by his heirs. Today it houses two of the master's most important early works, *Madonna alla Scala (Madonna on the Stairs)* and *Battaglia dei Centauri (Battle of the Centaurs),* both sculpted in his teenage years when he was still working in relief. The museum also houses a sizable collection of his drawings and scale models, and is used for temporary exhibitions.

CHURCHES

Basilica di Santa Croce and the Cappella Pazzi. Pz. Santa Croce. ☎ **055/24-46-19.** Admission to Pazzi Chapel 3,000L ($1.90). Basilica, daily 8am–12:30pm and 3–6:30pm. Pazzi Chapel, Mar–Sept, Thurs–Tues 10am–12:30pm and 2:30–6:30pm; Oct–Feb, Thurs–Tues 10am–12:30pm and 3–5pm.

Begun in 1294 by Arnolfo di Cambio, original architect of the Duomo, the cavernous Church of Santa Croce is the largest Franciscan church in the world. The humble presence of St. Francis is best felt in the two chapels located to the right of the main altar; entirely covered with faded early 14th-century frescoes by Giotto and his gifted student Taddeo Gaddi, they depict the life of the saint. To the left of the main altar is a wooden crucifix by Donatello, whose portrayal of Christ was considered too provincial by early 15th-century standards.

Santa Croce is also the final resting place for many of the most renowned Renaissance figures: the Pantheon of Florence. Michelangelo's tomb, designed by Vasari, is the first on the right as you enter; the three allegorical figures represent Painting, Architecture, and Sculpture. Dante's empty tomb is right next to him (he was exiled from Florence in 1302 for political reasons and died in Ravenna in 1321), while Machiavelli rests in the fourth. Galileo and Rossini, among others, were also laid to rest here.

The entrance to the tranquil Pazzi Chapel (marked "Museo dell'Opera di Santa Croce") is to the left as you leave the church. Commissioned in 1443 by Andrea de' Pazzi, a key rival of the Medici family, and designed by Filippo Brunelleschi, the chapel is a significant example of early Renaissance architecture. Serving as the church's museum, it houses many works from the 13th through the 17th century, highlighted by one of Cimabue's finest works, the *Crucifixion,* which suffered serious damage in a 1966 flood. Completely submerged when floodwaters rose to three feet within the church and five feet within the museum, it has now been restored and is displayed on an electric cable that will lift it out of reach of future harm.

Basilica di Santa Maria Novella. Pz. Santa Maria Novella (just south of the train station). ☎ **055/28-21-87.** Basilica, free; Cappella degli Spagnoli (Spanish Chapel), 5,000L ($3.30). Basilica, Mon–Fri 7–12:30am and 3:30–6:30pm, Sat 7–11:30am and 3:30–5pm, Sun 3:30–5pm; Cappella degli Spagnoli (Spanish Chapel), Mon–Thurs and Sat 9am–2pm, Sun 8am–1pm.

Begun in 1246 and completed in 1360 (with a green-and-white marble facade added in the 15th century), this cavernous gothic church was built to accommodate the masses who would come to hear the word of God as preached by the Dominicans. To educate the illiterate, they filled it with cycles of frescoes that are today considered some of the most important art in Florence, a claim not to be taken lightly. In the **Cappella Maggiore** (Main Chapel or chancel) directly behind the main altar, Ghirlandaio created a fresco cycle supposedly depicting the lives of the Virgin and St. John the Baptist, when in fact what we see is a dazzling illustration of daily life in the golden days of Renaissance Florence. To the right of this in the Cappella Filippo Strozzi are frescoes by Filippino Lippo, while to the left of the Cappella Maggiore is a 15th-century crucifix by Brunelleschi, his only work in wood. In the left aisle near the main entrance is an early 15th-century painting of *The Trinity* by Masaccio, revolutionary for its perspective.

If you're not yet frescoed out, exit the church and turn right to visit the **Chiostro Verde** (Green Cloister) and its Cappellone degli Spagnoli (Spanish Chapel), whose important and captivating series of early Renaissance frescoes (recently restored) by Andrea de Bonaiuto illustrate the history of the Dominican church. The chapel got its name from the nostalgic Eleanora de Toledo, wife of Cosimo de' Medici, who permitted her fellow Spaniards to be buried here. The Green Cloister, on the other hand, took its name from the prevalent green tinge of Paolo Uccello's 15th-century fresco cycle, which, unfortunately, was heavily damaged in the 1966 floods.

Chiesa di Orsanmichele. V. de' Calzaiuoli (north of Piazza Signoria). Free admission. Daily 8am–noon and 3–6:30pm.

The 14th-century boxlike church is the last remnant of ornate gothic architecture in Florence and was originally built as a covered market with an upstairs granary. The downstairs was eventually converted to an oratory, the open archways bricked up, and the outside decorated by donations from the city's powerful and wealthy *arti* or guilds, such as the tanners, silk weavers, bankers, furriers, goldsmiths, etc.; their patron saints fill the 14 niches surrounding the exterior of the church (note Ghiberti's *St. John* and Verrocchio's *St. Thomas* on the front facade). They virtually comprise a history of Florentine sculpture from the 14th through the 16th century (though almost all of them have been relocated to indoor museums and replaced with copies). Inside—among the vaulted gothic arches, stained-glass windows, and 500-year-old frescoes—is the colorful, encrusted 14th-century gothic tabernacle by Andrea Orcagna and a *Madonna and Child*, from the same period, by Bernardo Daddi. The name Orsanmichele is a corruption of Orto di San Michele, St. Michael's Garden, which occupied this site well before the granary was built.

Church of Santa Maria del Carmine and the Cappella Bancacci. Pz. Santa Maria d. Carmine (west of Pz. Santo Spirito and the Palazzo Pitti in the Oltrarno). ☎ 055/23-82-195. Admission to Cappella Brancacci 5,000L ($3.30). Mon, Wed–Sat 10am–5pm, Sun 1–5pm.

This baroque church dates from the 18th century when a fire ravaged the original 13th-century structure built for the Carmelite nuns; smoke damage was major but the fire left the Brancacci Chapel miraculously intact. This was a miracle indeed, as the frescoes begun by Masolino in 1425 and continued by his young and brilliant student Masaccio (who quickly outshone his maestro) are considered seminally crucial to the development of Renaissance painting. The frescoes have recently and painstakingly been restored, showing more clearly than ever the painters' unprecedented expression of emotion as well as their pioneering use of perspective and chiaroscuro. The *Expulsion of Adam and Eve* (extreme upper-left-hand corner) best illustrates emotions of anguish and shame hitherto unknown in painting, while *The Tribute Money* is a significant study in perspective. The bulk of the frescoes depict the *Life of St. Peter* (who appears in a golden-orange mantle). The lower panels were finished by Filippino Lippi (son of the great painter Filippo Lippi) in 1480, 50 years after the very premature death of Masaccio at 27.

A PALAZZO

Palazzo Medici-Riccardi. V. Cavour 1 (north of the Pz. Duomo). ☎ 055/27-60-340. Free admission. Cappella d. Magi 6,000L ($3.95). Mon–Tues and Thurs–Sat 9am–1pm and 3–6pm, Sun 9am–1pm.

Built for Cosimo the Elder, one of the early Medici rulers, by Brunelleschi's student Michelozzo, this austere palazzo became the Palazzo Medici from 1460 to 1540 (before Cosimo I moved to the Palazzo Vecchio and eventually the Palazzo Pitti) and became the prototype for subsequent residences of the nobility. Only two rooms are open to the public, but they make your trip worth while. The Chapel of the Magi takes its name from the magnificent frescoes by Benozzo Gozzoli, who worked several members of the Medici family as well as his master, Fra Angelico, and himself (look for a child on the far left wearing a red hat inscribed "Opus Benotii") into his beautiful depictions of the Wise Men's journey through the Tuscan countryside. Across the courtyard and upstairs is an elaborate 17th-century baroque gallery commissioned by the subsequent owners, the Riccardi; amidst the gilt and stucco are Luca Giordano's frescoes, masterfully illustrating the Apotheosis of the Medici dynasty. The palazzo now houses government offices, though parts of it are frequently used for temporary and traveling exhibitions.

THE BOBOLI GARDENS

The expansive Giardini Boboli (☎ 055/21-33-70) begin behind the Pitti Palace and fan upward to the star-shaped Fortezza Belvedere (☎ 055/234-24-25), which crowns the hill. Enter the gardens via the rear exit to the Pitti Palace or the entrance to the left facing the palace. The green gardens, particularly beautiful in the spring, were originally laid out in the 16th century by the great landscape artist Tribolo. They are filled with graveled walkways, grottoes, and antique and Renaissance statuary and are the best spot in Florence for a picnic lunch. The view from the fortress is stunning, but there's not much to see inside unless there's a special exhibition; ask at the tourist office or look for posters around town.

The Boboli Gardens are open daily from 9am to dusk; fortress hours vary with exhibitions. Admission to the gardens is 5,000L ($3.30); admission to fortress grounds is free, but exhibition admission varies.

ESPECIALLY FOR KIDS

Perhaps Florence's biggest plus for travelers with children is its accessibility and compact layout in relatively traffic-free streets. Much of your visit will be spent strolling the streets of a city that is, in fact, one big open-air museum. Young legs that can sustain a 400-plus step workout should head up to either Brunelleschi's dome or the top of Giotto's campanile for an awesome view of the city. Batteries can be recharged during picnic lunches in the green Boboli Gardens or, higher yet, on the grounds of the Forte Belvedere above. Kids will enjoy a leisurely (albeit expensive) horse-drawn cab ride through the cobblestone streets of the centro storico (establish your price before taking off). Carriages gather in the Piazza Signoria. If you're visiting in June, try to catch one of the four processions and games of the Calcio in Costume (see "Special Events," below) with their historical costumes. The Florentine substitute for incentive is a guaranteed pleaser regardless of age or background—don't miss tasting your way through the many excellent gelaterie, *or* ice-cream parlors, whose variety (they can squeeze four or five flavors into some of those cups!) and quality makes Baskin-Robbins look ho-hum.

SPECIAL-INTEREST SIGHTSEEING
FOR JEWISH HERITAGE

Florence's 19th-century green copper–domed **Tempio Israelitico** or **Jewish synagogue,** is an excellent and delightful, if incongruous, example of neo-Moorish architecture (V. Farini 4, ☎ 055/24-52-52). The synagogue's caretake gives an interesting talk on the synagogue's history. Call to verify the synagogue's hours, Monday to Thursday from 11am to 1pm and 2 to 5pm and Friday and Sunday from 10am to 1pm. Admission is 5,000L ($3.30). The synagogue is at the intersection of via Farini and via Pilastri.

FOR LITERARY ENTHUSIASTS

Literary enthusiasts will enjoy a pilgrimage to the **Casa Guidi,** the home of Elizabeth Barrett and Robert Browning. The famous couple came to the Casa Guidi in 1846 and remained until 1861, when Barrett passed away. Their home was the center of the Anglo-Florentine community, where they hosted Nathaniel Hawthorne, Margaret Fuller, and other great English and American figures. For the record, Guidi was the family that owned the palazzo in the days of the Medicis. This notable place, which is always staffed by American or British expatriates, is open Monday to Friday from 3 to 6pm, and at other times by appointment; verify the winter hours. Admission is free. The house is on Pz. San Felice 8 (☎ 055/28-43-93), in the Oltrarno. Piazza San Felice is at the intersection of Via Romana, Via Mazzetta, and Via Maggio, opposite the Pitti Palace.

Those whose interests reach back even further in time might want to visit the **Casa di Dante (Dante's House)**, V. S. Margherita 1 west of Via Proconsolo (☎ 055/21-94-16). Just opened in late 1994, it is a three-story building constructed next door to the alleged site of poet Dante Alighieri's Florence home (now used as gallery space). The first floor depicts Florence in the late 13th century, and contains a scale model of the Battle of Campaldino, along with reproductions of medieval armor. The second floor has exhibits relating to Dante's wanderings around Verona, Bologna, and Ravenna, and the third floor contains reproductions of famous works of art relating to the poet's compositions. It's worth a look, especially the surrounding neighborhood, which retains much of its medieval character: Just north on Via Margherita is the small 11th-century church where Dante is said to have first laid eyes on his beloved Beatrice. Admission is 5,000L ($3.30) for adults. It's open in summer, Wednesday to Monday from 10am to 6pm; in winter, Monday and Wednesday to Saturday from 10am to 6pm and Sunday from 10am to 2pm.

FOR SCIENCE BUFFS

While Florence is best known and most often visited for its legacy of art and architecture, the collection of its **Museo di Storia della Scienza (History of Science Museum)**, Pz. d. Giudici 1, just east of the Uffizi Galleries (☎ **055/29-34-93**), on the river behind the Uffizi, is interesting and worth a visit for those with a special interest in the roots of technology. Its halls are filled with 16th- and 17th-century clocks, microscopes, telescopes, surveying instruments, and models of the solar system—all lovely as works of art in addition to their historical and scientific value. Most interesting are the original instruments of the Pisa-born scientist Galileo Galilei (1564–1642), a collection of Giovanni Alessandro Brambilla's surgical instruments, and a map of the world dating to 1554 by Lopo Homen. The museum is open Monday to Saturday from 9:30am to 1pm; in the summer on Monday, Wednesday, and Friday it's also open from 2 to 5pm. Admission is 10,000L ($6.60).

SPECIAL & FREE EVENTS

The **Maggio Musicale,** or "Musical May," is Italy's oldest music festival and one of Europe's most prestigious. Events take place at various indoor and outdoor locations throughout Florence, including Piazza della Signoria and the courtyard of the Pitti Palace. Maestro Zubin Mehta is the honorary director, often conducting Florence's own Maggio Musicale Orchestra, and guest conductors and orchestras appear throughout the festival, which, despite its moniker, runs from late April into early July. For schedules and ticket information, inquire at one of the tourist offices.

From June to August, the Roman theater in nearby Fiesole comes alive with dance, music, and theater for the **Estate Fiesolana,** or "Summer in Fiesole." A.T.A.F. bus no. 7 travels to Fiesole from the train station and Piazza del Duomo.

The highlight of June 24, the feast day of Florence's patron saint, San Giovanni (St. John the Baptist), is the **Calcio Storico,** a rough-and-tumble no-holds-barred game, a cross between rugby, soccer, and wrestling, played with a ball and few (if any) rules (its origins go back to the Renaissance, though many argue that its roots are medieval, or even reach back to ancient Roman). Teams representing the four original parishes of Florence, identified by their colors and clad in 16th-century costume, square off against one another in consecutive playoffs in the dirt-covered piazza Santa Croce, compete vigorously for that year's bragging rights and the prize, a cow. The final *partita* is most worth seeing (it often falls on June 24th itself). Later on, fireworks light up the night sky, best viewed from along the north banks of the Arno River east of the Ponte Vecchio. See the tourist office for ticket information about numbered seats in the bleachers lining the piazza. No tickets are needed to view the equally dazzling procession in full historical regalia that wends its way through the cobblestone streets and piazzas of Florence prior to each match.

The month of July sees the annual **Florence Dance Festival** held in the beautiful amphitheater in the Cascine Park. A wide range of dance is performed, varying from classic to modern, with an emphasis on the latter. Again, check with the tourist office for details.

It's pretty much guaranteed that you won't be able to afford anything at the bi-annual **International Antiques Show** held mid-September for two weeks in uneven years only. Celebrating its 20th edition in 1997, more than 100 internationally noted dealers bring their choicest and most exquisite pieces to this well-known show, where the crowd is as interesting as the wares. It is not unlike visiting the royal apartments at the Palazzo Pitti, but imagine every piece with a price tag. The historically potent setting of the massive Renaissance Palazzo Strozzi could not be more appropriate, but check for a possible change of venue. Two to three weeks beginning mid-September, admission is 12,000L ($7.90). For information see the tourist information office.

ORGANIZED TOURS & WALKING TOURS

Florence's historical center is so conveniently compact (though chockablock with sites) that walking along its palazzo- and store-lined streets is a true pleasure. Florence is one big open-air museum that warrants a thorough and leisurely walk-through.

A bus tour is not really the most enjoyable way to see this wonderful city, unless you have some difficulty with walking. However, **C.I.T.,** at the corner of Piazza della Stazione and Piazza dell'Unità Italiana (☎ **055/21-09-64**), offers two separate half-day bus tours of the city, including visits to the Uffizi Galleries, the Medici Chapels, and the breathtaking Piazzale Michelangiolo overlooking the city. Each tour costs 48,000L ($31.60). C.I.T. is also the place to inquire about organized tours to the Chianti region and other cities and small towns in Tuscany. It's open Monday to Friday from 8:30am to 12:30pm and 3 to 6:30pm, and Saturday from 8:30am to noon. You can book the same tours through American Express (See "Fast Facts," above) and many other travel agencies throughout town.

If you'd love to spend a day walking or biking in the surrounding countryside, and are willing to splurge a bit, organized **Country Walks in Tuscany,** year-round, as well as one-day bike rides can be booked from March through November with **I Bike Italy;** call **055/23-42-371** (weekends call cellular no. **0368/45-91-23**). Guided walks are 65,000L ($42.75) and guided bike-rides (21-speed bikes supplied) are 75,000L ($49.35); shuttle to outskirts of town and hearty picnic lunch included in both. It might stretch your budget, but unless you plan to travel in Tuscany (see chapter 14), you should try to get a glimpse of the incomparable Tuscan countryside that has inspired Florence's master artists for centuries.

5 Shopping

In terms of good-value shopping, Florence is easy to categorize: It's paradise. This one-time capitalist capital, where modern banking and commerce first flourished, has something for every taste and price range. Whether you can afford little more than a bargain-priced wool sweater in the open-air market or are interested in investing in a butter-soft leather jacket that will burst your budget, Florence is for you. With a history of commercial and mercantile trade behind them, Florentine merchants are not the born negotiators of the south, and few will encourage bartering.

All stores follow the same general business hours; see "Fast Facts," above.

BEST BUYS   "Alta moda" fashion in Florence is alive and well and living on **Via Tornabuoni** and its elegant off-shoot **Via della Vigna Nuova,** where some of the high priests of Italian and international design and fashion share space with the occasional bank (which you may have to rob in order to afford any of their goods). But it makes for great window-shopping.

Between the Duomo and the river are the pedestrian-only **Via Roma** (which becomes **Via Por Santa Maria** before reaching the Ponte Vecchio) and the parallel **Via Calzaiuoli;** lined with fashionable jewelry and clothing stores (and the city's largest department store, Coin), they are the city's main shopping streets. Stores here are only slightly less high fashion and less high priced than those on the gilded via Tornabuoni. A gelato stop is a guaranteed spirit-lifter.

Via del Corso and its extension east of Via del Proconsolo, **Borgo degli Albizi,** is another recommended shopping street, boasting historical palazzi as well as less pretentious and more approachable boutiques.

Unless you have a Medici-size fortune and hope to leave with a Renaissance trinket, window-shop the stores with museum-quality antiques on **borgo Ognissanti** near the Arno and the perpendicular **Via dei Fossi. Lungarno Corsini** and **Lungarno Acciaiuoli** run along the river, where you'll find merchants offering fine paintings and sculpture, objets d'art, and antiques. But perhaps the most impressive antique row is **Via Maggio** on the Oltrarno and, to a lesser degree, its perpendicular offshoot, the **Via Santo Spirito.**

Leather is perhaps what Florence is most famous for. Many travelers are happily, albeit mistakenly, convinced that they can buy a leather coat for a song. For quality and selection, no European city can hold a candle to Florentine quality, but prices are higher than all those rumors you heard quoting dirt-cheap prices not seen since the 1970s. Expect to spend $200 to $300 for a leather jacket with moderate workmanship, detail, and skin quality. The shops around **Piazza Santa Croce** are the best places for leather and are not much more expensive than the pushcarts at the San Lorenzo Market. Leather apparel may be beyond your budget, but consider the possibilities of small leather goods, from wallets and eyeglass cases to fashion accessories such as shoes, belts, and bags.

Florence has been known for its gold for centuries, and jewelry shops of all price levels still abound. Dozens of exclusive gold stores line both sides of the pedestrian **Ponte Vecchio,** the only bridge in Florence that escaped destruction in World War II. Gold is almost always 18 karat (ask them to point out the teensy stamp), beautifully machine-crafted and, though not a bargain, reasonably priced—think instant heirlooms.

MARKETS   There's nothing in Italy, and indeed perhaps nothing in Europe, to compare with Florence's bustling, sprawling, open-air **Mercato San Lorenzo.** Hundreds of awninged pushcarts crowd together along the streets around the San Lorenzo Church and the Mercato Centrale, offering countless varieties of hand-knit wool and mohair sweaters, leather jackets, handbags, wallets, and gloves—not to mention the standard array of souvenir T-shirts and sweatshirts, wool and silk scarves, and other souvenirs.

The market stretches for blocks between Piazza San Lorenzo behind the Medici Chapel to Via Nazionale, along Via Canto de' Nelli and Via dell' Ariento, with stalls also set up along various side streets in between. The market operates daily from 9am to 7pm from mid-March through October (closed Sunday and Monday the rest of the year). Many vendors accept credit and charge cards.

Much smaller, but still worth a look, is the outdoor **Mercato del Porcellino,** once known as the Straw Market and today more commonly known as the **Mercato Nuovo** or New Market, where a couple of dozen pushcarts crowd together beneath an arcade two blocks south of the Piazza della Repubblica. Vendors here offer mostly handbags, scarves, embroidered tablecloths, and souvenirs. The market is named for the bronze boar (porcellino) on the river side of the arcade, whose snout has been worn smooth by the countless Florentines who have touched it for good luck. Hours here are generally 9am to 6pm, daily from mid-March through November 3 and Tuesday to Saturday the rest of the year.

Mercato delle Pulci in the small Piazza Ciompi (follow the Via Oriuolo east out of Piazza Duomo) is Florence's rather unimpressive, permanent flea market that doubles in size the last Sunday of every month when a look-see can be fun. Serious flea-market goers should check out Tuscany's major flea market held in Arezzo (accessible by bus or train in one hour) the first weekend of every month. Tuesday to Saturday 8:30am to 1pm and 3:30 to 7pm. Also last Sunday of every month.

SHOPPING A TO Z
BOOKSTORES

The **BM Libreria Book Shop,** Bgo. Ognissanti 4r (☎ 055/29-45-75), at Piazza Goldoni west of Via Tornabuoni, is the best place in town for top-quality American and British books from both large and small publishing houses. East of the Duomo is **Paperback Exchange,** V. Fiesolana 31r (☎ 055/24-78-154), with a large selection of new and used titles as well as the chance to trade in your used books.

The oldest and most beautiful bookstore in town, **Libreria Internazionale Seeber,** V. Tornabuoni 68r (☎ 055/21-56-97), sells a quality collection of guidebooks, novels, and Italian art, history, cuisine, and antiques books, a good number of them in English.

Florence's biggest and one of its newest bookstores is the **Libreria Feltrinelli,** V. Cerretani 30/32r (☎ 055/23-82-652). It sells everything imaginable with a foreign language division. The best travel bookstore in town.

Libreria Il Viaggio, Bgo. degli Albizi 41r (☎ 055/24-04-89), sells guides and maps for every imaginable destination, including Florence and all of Italy.

CERAMICS
Sbigoli. V. Sant'Egidio 4r. ☎ 055/24-79-713.

Lovely hand-painted Tuscan ceramics, particularly 16th- to 17th-century reproductions, are the specialty of this store east of the Duomo. Products of skilled craftsmanship are never cheap, but here you'll find colorful terracotta mugs, ashtrays, and other small items that are easy to carry and reasonable in price.

DEPARTMENT STORES
Standa, V. dei Panzani 31r (☎ 055/23-98-963), and **Upim,** Pz. della Repubblica 1r (☎ 055/21-69-24), are two well-located mid- to low-end department stores where you can come up with some surprising finds in accessories, household goods, and miscellaneous items. Clothes are classic and either poor quality or nice quality, but expensive. Also a good spot to pick up toiletries on the ground floor.

Coin, V. dei Calzaiuoli 56r (☎ 055/28-05-31), is as close to Macy's as you'll get in Florence: four floors of made-in-Italy apparel and accessories for men, women, and children. There are moderately priced items mixed in with the high-end merchandise, and it all makes for enjoyable browsing even for those not buying. Check out the sales amid the January and July crowds.

DESIGN ITEMS
Vice Versa. V. Ricasoli 53r. ☎ 055/23-98-281.

On your way to or from a visit to see *David* at the Accademia, stop by this design emporium that showcases the most interesting items from the creative studios of

Milan. Much of this looks like it belongs in the Museum of Modern Art, with a number of small items that embody the latest in Italian design and make great souvenirs for yourself or design-conscious friends. Bottle openers, key rings, ashtrays, pens, and hot plates all cost under 20,000L to 25,000L ($13.15 to $16.45).

HERBS & SPICES

Erboristeria Palazzo Vecchio. V. Vacchereccia 9r. ☎ **055/239-6055.**

Just a palazzo or two removed from the Piazza Signoria is this tiny, old-world herbal store whose traditions and origins (and some of its recipes and formulas) go back centuries. There are natural pomades and elixirs for everything from dandruff to the blues, but you'll be most interested in the nicely packaged scented soaps, room scents, essences, candles, and sachets that will permeate your entire suitcase by the time you reach home. Packaged seasonings and spices used in the *cucina italiana* make nice gifts for Italophile friends.

GOLD

C.O.I. V. Por Santa Maria 8r, second floor. ☎ **055/28-39-70.**

There's no such thing as cheap Italian gold: The weight per gram is government-regulated. What you're guaranteed at this second-floor gold market is quality. There's an enormous selection of beautiful 18k jewelry, each piece carefully weighed before you, and a professional and patient English-speaking sales staff. Have some idea of what you want: a chain, hoop earrings, a child's bracelet, or a wedding band, and the sales help will return from the vault with rolls of every variation imaginable. (However, gold jewelry with precious and semiprecious stones is limited in selection.) The volume keeps prices down; the remarkable variety keeps customers coming back.

PAPER GOODS

Il Torchio. V. de' Bardi 17. ☎ **055/23-42-862.**

Marbleized paper and the myriad items it covers (agendas, albums, boxes, diaries, pencils, and pencil holders) is a centuries-old craft that has experienced a popular resurgence—few are the stores nowadays that *don't* carry a selection. But this store, whose name translates as "The Press," takes pride in the quality of its hand-printed papers and the carefully crafted items they cover. Its easy-to-reach Oltrarno location east of the Ponte Vecchio keeps prices lower than those in the high-rent Duomo neighborhood.

SHOES

Eusebio. V. del Corso 1. ☎ **055/29-29-17.**

This is the cheapest shoe store in town, with large rooms where self-service is not only possible but required. Men's and women's shoes are arranged according to size, with styles ranging from out-of-date to the up-to-date, priced from 29,000L to 39,000L ($19.05 to $25.65). These are no Ferragamos, but some of the knock-off fashions at throw-away prices are snatched up by Florence's well-heeled.

6 Florence After Dark

The best source for entertainment and happenings is the Italian-language monthly *Firenze Spettacolo* (2,700L/$1.80), offering comprehensive listings of dance, theater, and music events in the city. The magazine is available at most newsstands.

THE PERFORMING ARTS

One of Italy's busiest stages, Florence's principal contemporary theater—**Teatro Comunale,** Cor. Italia 16 (☎ **055/21-08-04** or 21-11-58)—offers everything from symphonies to ballet to plays, opera, and music concerts. The large main theater has orchestra rows topped by horseshoe-shaped first and second galleries. The smaller **Piccolo Teatro** is rectangular, offering good sightlines from most any seat. Tickets begin at 15,000 to 45,000L ($9.85 to $29.60), depending on the production.

The excellent, centrally located and recently renovated **Teatro Verdi,** V. Ghibellina 101 (☎ **055/21-23-20**), schedules regular dance and classical music events, often top-name foreign performers, troupes, and orchestras, and the occasional European pop star. Tickets vary greatly according to concert schedule; expect to pay approximately 10,000 to 35,000L ($6.60 to $23.00).

Stop by the tourist office for a list of the season's concerts that take place in the city's churches and theaters. For the important music festivals, **Maggio Musicale** and the **Estate Fiesolana,** see "Special & Free Events," above.

CLUBS & DISCOS

Nightlife is not Florence's strongest suit, but it has improved considerably over the last few years.

Chiodo Fisso. V. Dante Alighieri 16r (between V. d. Calzaiuoli and V. d. Proconsolo, just west of the new American Express building). ☎ **055/23-81-290.**

A self-proclaimed "guitar club," this cozy and intimate wine cavern is about the only place to listen to live acoustic and folk music in Florence. There's no admission charge but relatively steep drink prices. There are small plates of finger foods and Chianti, the only wine served: A bottle will set you back 25,000L ($16.45); a mini-carafe (basically, two glasses), 6,000L ($3.95). Open daily from 9pm to 3am; closed two weeks in August.

Fiddler's Elbow. Pz. Santa Maria Novella 7r (about 3 blocks from the train station). ☎ **055/21-50-56.**

This Irish-style pub is always abuzz with young international travelers and assorted locals. It's one of the few places in town where you can get an authentic pint of Guinness on tap for 7,000L ($4.60). Open Thursday to Tuesday from 4:00pm to midnight.

Full-Up. V. d. Vigna Vecchia 25r. ☎ **055/29-30-06.** Cover (includes 1 drink) 15,000L–25,000L ($9.85–$16.45).

Located in the city center, near Santa Croce, this long-enduring and upscale (no grunge attire here) disco/piano bar is one of the top (though more restrained) dance spaces in Florence with some of the best-known DJs. There are plenty of theme evenings (revival, samba, punk), so call to find out what's on. Open Wednesday to Monday from 9pm to 3am.

Space Electronic Disco. V. Palazzuolo 37. ☎ **055/29-30-82.** Cover 20,000L ($13.15), which includes the first drink; there's a 5,000L ($3.30) discount for bearers of this book.

Students and teenage revelers will find a balanced combination of tourists and Italians at this wildly decorated disco/karaoke bar. Its motley collection of artifacts and electronics includes two enormous carnival faces plucked right from an American boardwalk, an open parachute that hangs from the ceiling, an imitation space capsule that sails back and forth across the dance floor, and of course the requisite video screens and lasers. Draft beer costs 6,000L ($3.95); mixed drinks, 8,000L ($5.25). From 9:30pm to 1:30am (closed Monday off-season).

Tabasco. Pz. Santa Cecilia 3. ☎ **055/21-30-00.** Cover free–15,000L ($9.85).

Florence's oldest gay dance club is open to both men and women of a 20-something demographic within stone's throw of Piazza Signoria and Michelangelo's *David,* god of anatomical perfection. The dance floor is downstairs, while a small video room and piano bar is up top. There are occasional cabaret shows and karaoke. Open Thursday to Tuesday from 9pm to 3am. For an older, male gay crowd only, try Crisco, V. San Egidio 43r (☎ 055/24-80-580).

Zut. V. il Prato 58r, Parco d. Cascine. ☎ **0330/28-37-49.** Cover: Free–15,000L ($9.40).

One of the best new dance clubs, Zut offers something different each night of the week. Sometimes it's hip-hop, sometimes it's techno, often it's acid jazz. The club can hold about 500 people, and often does. Since it's located near Cascine Park (a cab ride from the city center), tourism is minimized. Open Tuesday to Saturday from 10pm to 3 or 4am.

Two other popular cavern-size discos with a young American/Florentine crowd in the Piazzale della Cascine, bordering Cascine Park, are **Meccanò** (☎ **055/ 33-13-371**) and **Central Park** (☎ 055/33-34-88); in the summer they offer indoor/ outdoor dance floors with a wide range of music possibilities.

CAFE & BAR SOCIETY

While the above are most frequented by the members of the dozens of American university programs in Florence, and the golden Florentine boys looking for a socially inclined semester themselves, the following cafes are more enjoyable, less ear-taxing environments in which to while away a nocturnal hour or two. For the more historical cafes, check out the Piazza della Repubblica, particularly **Gilli's,** or the turn-of-the-century **Caffe Rivoire** in Piazza della Signoria.

Cabiria Cafe. Pz. S. Spirito 4r. ☎ **055/21-57-32.**

Piazza San Spirito, hiding behind a tangle of back streets, just blocks from the Pitti Palace, is the locals' most loved piazza. Once a haven for drug abusers, the square has cleaned up its act, but still has enough edginess to be an authentic hangout for the "alternative" crowd. There's some seating area inside but outdoor tables overlook the dramatic San Spirito Church. There's a variety of reasonably-priced fresh dishes daylong (approximately 5,000L/$3.30 each), but this place bustles with young trendies who come to hang out before and after dinner hours. Wednesday to Monday 8am to 1am (Friday and Saturday till 2am).

Caffe degli Artisti/Art Bar. V. d. Moro 4r. ☎ **055/28-76-61.**

Also known as Caffe del Moro because of its street location (north of Ponte alla Carraia), this longtime favorite is a watering hole worth searching out. An interesting crowd comes to mingle and talk (though music can get loud) and sample the long list of "cocktails" and mixed drinks (well, maybe it's the people who get loud), uncommon in this wine-imbibing society. The atmosphere is upscale and a downstairs room with wooden tables attracts groups of friends who linger for hours. It's open Monday to Saturday from 10pm to 1am, sometimes later.

Caffé Cibreo. V. Andrea d. Verrochio 5r. ☎ **055/23-45-853.**

From the clever and entrepreneurial Midas who gave Florence the restaurant and trattoria Cibreo, this handsome bar across the street first became known for its informal and inexpensive lunch and dinner menus, many of whose dishes came from the acclaimed kitchen across the way (dinner served from 7:30 until midnight). But this is also a lovely and quiet spot for an attractive, older crowd who take their hot chocolate, tea blends, or coffee roasts seriously or who want to people watch before or after dining at the Trattoria Cibreo or the popular Il Pizzaiolo, also across the street (see "Dining," above).

7 Day Trips to Pisa & Fiesole

FIESOLE   Situated five miles to the north of town on a hill rising above Florence, Fiesole is an important archeological site, once a pre-Roman Etruscan settlement, and later a Roman town. It's a popular excursion, so you may find yourself surrounded by tourists. The town can be reached in 30 minutes by taking municipal bus no. 7 from the Piazza Stazione or Piazza San Marco to the end of the line. Most sites are open in winter, Wednesday to Monday from 9am to 6pm; and in summer, Wednesday to Monday from 9am to 7pm.

Fiesole contains vast 2,000-year-old Etruscan and Roman ruins, including a large, restored amphitheater (☎ **055/5-94-77**), which is used for the annual Estate Fiesolana festival. The skeletal remains of the baths can also been seen. Next to it is the **Museo Civico** or the Museo Faesulanum, which contains many interesting finds from the excavations.

The town center surrounds a large square dedicated to the sculptor Mino da Fiesole (around 1430–84). Fronting the square is the romanesque **Cattedrale di San Romolo,** dating from 1000, and much altered during the Renaissance. The Salutati Chapel contains important sculptures by Mino da Fiesole. Also on the piazza is the 17th-century **Bishop's Palace** (☎ **055/5-92-42**), and the **St. Maria Primerana Church** (☎ **055/59-400**).

No one leaves without a look at the splendid panorama of Florence and the countryside below it, but first you'll have to hike up the steep Via di San Francesco—go west (left) out of the main square—to the **Convent of San Francesco.** You can visit the Franciscan church, built in the gothic style in the early 1400s. Inside are a number of paintings by Florentine artists. In the basement is an ethnological museum containing artifacts from China as well as a Etruscan-Roman collection.

Restaurants, bars, and cafes are abundant, but principally work as tourist traps. Sip a Campari or order a gelato, but don't plan on eating here.

PISA   The truth is that unless you are determined to see for yourself that the **Leaning Tower of Pisa** does in fact lean, you may be disappointed by the fact that Pisa is not a quaint little town but rather a large and busy city. However, it is blessed with the magnificent **Campo dei Miracoli.** The tower itself has been closed to the public since 1990, but it is fascinating to see from a perspective and at any angle. It was built as the free-standing bell tower to the adjacent **Duomo,** begun in 1063, whose **Battistero** completes the trio of remarkable structures in the piazza. Pisa is just one hour west of Florence by frequent trains; the round-trip costs 18,000L ($11.85).

7

Tuscany and Umbria

by Patricia Schultz

Tuscany and Umbria share much of the same cultural and artistic heritage, a history that dates to the pre-Roman Etruscans, cuisine, and to some degree a similarity in landscape. However, it behooves you never to mention these two regions in the same breath to a Tuscan or Umbrian. Like two first cousins, Tuscany and Umbria are just as often fiercely individualistic in characteristics and traditions they have preserved and nurtured over the centuries.

Italians are rarely modest about their unabashed love for the region they call home. But nowhere is this emotion-packed loyalty of *provincia* so deservedly heartfelt as in Tuscany, one of the country's most visited rural destinations. Richly endowed with a wide variety of topography, from the Apennine Mountains in the northwestern corner to the open rolling plains of the Maremma area in the south, Tuscany is also endowed with a coastal riviera (admittedly less alluring than Liguria's but with the benefit of wide sandy beaches) and a number of idyllic islands in the Ligurian Sea of which Elba, Napoléon's exile retreat, is the largest and most renowned.

Almost three-quarters of Tuscany is comprised of gentle hills, terraced by man over time to prevent erosion while providing more room for crops. It is not hard for the average visitor to recapture the magical beauty of a Merchant-Ivory movie: Hollywood would never think of filming on location elsewhere. Tuscans are only half-joking when they tell you that God may be responsible for the beauty that is Tuscany's, but Michelangelo drew up the plans.

The Umbrian cities featured in this chapter have not changed much since the Middle Ages, but you will never mistake them for museum cities: they are very much alive, fueled by their cultural interests and thriving economies only partially sustained by tourism. Two of Italy's most important summer festivals take place here, the Umbrian Jazz Festival in Perugia and Spoleto's Festival of Two Worlds.

FINDING AN AFFORDABLE PLACE TO STAY   Most of the tourist offices in the towns and cities can supply you with lists of *affittacamere,* or bed-and-breakfast accommodations that often offer the best deal in town. In many places there is also the possibility of *agriturismo* accommodations in the countryside that range from the very basic to working farms with swimming and horseback riding.

Tuscany & Umbria

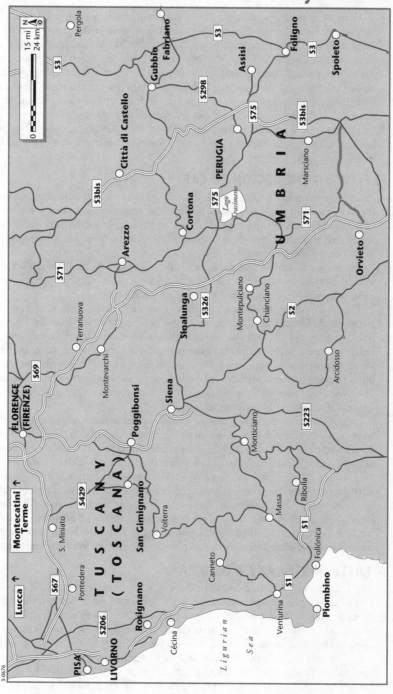

225

As regional prices go, these small cities and towns can be quite moderate, but they've seen their share of tourism. Don't expect any giveaway bargains, but rest assured rates are a fraction of Rome's and Florence's for hotels that are often superior in charm and amenities. Towns that rely on tourism (such as San Gimignano and Assisi) pretty much close up shop in January and February. Easter through June is usually busy, with the heat arriving in July and things coming to a standstill in August (look for off-season discounts but watch out for sleepless, un–air-conditioned nights). You'll need to book in advance for September and October, everyone's favorite time to tool around the back roads of these wine-producing regions. November can be rainy and cold and except for the Christmas holidays, December is a dead month.

EXPLORING THE REGION BY CAR

From Florence, head due west towards the coast and Pisa for a quick look at the Leaning Tower and associated sights, then backtrack to spend the night in the lovely town of Lucca. This wealthy and lively town is a delightful glimpse into a perfectly preserved medieval city (minus the hill; this area of Tuscany is quite flat) swathed within magnificent Renaissance walls.

For the beach-inclined, Lucca is an easy half-hour drive from the popular Viareggio seaside resort or the tonier Forte dei Marmi, where you can rent chairs and umbrellas on wide sandy beaches flanked by cool pine forests.

Then head south of Florence. San Gimignano and Siena are excellent bases for exploring the Chianti wine region, one of the loveliest corners of Tuscany. Spend a few days here and discover the environs' romanesque churches, Etruscan tombs, walled cities, and wine-producing estates that welcome you to come, taste, and stay for dinner. Aimlessly meandering the countryside's backwater roads requires a car, but if you do your homework, you can rely upon public transport to get you to and from towns and sites farther afield (like the alabaster-producing town of Volterra or Montalcino, home of Brunello wine).

From Siena, head southeast across the Umbria border to the hilltop city of Perugia, whose cultural events, hotels, historical cafes, restaurants, and rich university atmosphere warrant a few days. From here you can branch out to visit Umbria's hill towns of Assisi and Spoleto, but in Assisi you'll want to spend a full afternoon walking to St. Francis's rural retreat, returning to the town's center when it is at its loveliest—after the tour buses leave in the late afternoon and you can have your pick of small family-run restaurants. Spoleto is also an easy train ride from Perugia—even from Rome—but ideally you should stay a while at each of these towns. Some may be lacking in major museum collections or awe-evoking architecture, but sometimes the smallest towns and the laziest afternoons provide you with the most vivid memories.

A TASTE OF TUSCANY & UMBRIA

The Tuscan and Umbrian *cucina* draws heavily from the grains, beans, and ingredients of the farmer's simple pantry and the woods and forests that cover its hills. Nouvelle cuisine it's not. Rustic sausage antipasti (salsicce), and game (cacciagione) and grilled or roasted meats are the highlight of every meal—the *bistecca alla fiorentina* being the fabled albeit expensive entree you'll want to try at least once. The unquestioned prominence of olive oil makes an appearance from the groves of Lucca and Spoleto, the Tuscan and Umbrian suppliers of Europe's best *olio di oliva*. Renowned red and white Chianti wines from the area between Florence and Siena, and distinctive Orvieto whites make this area an oenophile's dream—and you most likely won't be disappointed with the humble vino della casa (house wine). Umbria's touted claim to gastronomic fame is the underground tartufo (truffle) from Norcia. Preciously grated over pastas and pizza, it is expensive but its acquired taste is considered sublime by gourmand palates. This is the place to try it: not only for the local expertise and abundance but for the moderate prices (moderate when compared to over-the-top American ones).

1 Lucca

72km (45 miles) W of Florence; 21km (13 miles) E of Pisa; 336km (209 miles) N of Rome; 96km (60 miles) NW of San Gimignano

You will hear first about—and remember always—the great walls of this unspoiled Tuscan town. Brick ramparts built in the 16th and 17th centuries encircle this elegant and graceful city in their Renaissance swathe. Although it has a population of 90,000, only a marginal percentage lives within the walls where a small-town atmosphere prevails. The city preserves much of its tangible past: Streets are lined with medieval towered palazzi redolent of Lucca's wealth in past centuries. A sophisticated silk and textile trade reinterpreting the luxurious silks that arrived from the Orient made this small town famous throughout Europe in the Middle Ages and early Renaissance. But its wealth and power slowly dissipated and, having tenaciously kept its independence from Pisa and Florence for so many centuries, it finally fell to Napoléon, who handed it over to his sister Elisa Baciocchi in 1805.

Today's quiet streets—where 25,000 workers once kept 3,000 hand-looms operating—open onto small squares, each anchored by a marble-faced church built during the city's golden heyday. Lucca is said to have one of the largest concentrations of churches per capita, though many of them today are permanently closed or open erratic, limited hours. Medieval highlights are the Duomo and the elaborate San Michele, both exquisite examples of Pisan-Lucchese architecture.

Proximity to Pisa airport makes this an excellent first or last stop in Tuscany, recommended more than the less charming city of Pisa itself, despite its legendary leaning tower. The lack of traffic enhances the city's low-profile, unhurried air where monied matriarchs, whose noble family histories have survived the centuries, do their daily shopping around town on battered bicycles. Although tourism has grown, it is still a secondary consideration—most tourists bypass Lucca on their way from Florence to Pisa. The hotel situation does not bode well for the budget traveler, but once you find a place to settle down, the general lack of mass tourism is the city's, and your, greatest blessing.

ESSENTIALS

GETTING THERE   By Train   Trains from Florence are not frequent and rarely direct; bus transportation is, by comparison, a breeze and more recommended. Trains to Pisa take approximately 30 minutes and some go the extra 10 minutes directly to Pisa's airport.

Lucca's station (☎ 0583/47-013) is south of the city walls, but is an easy walk only if you're unencumbered with luggage (there's bus and taxi service into the center of town).

By Bus   LAZZI buses (☎ 0583/58-48-76) connect Lucca with Florence and other principle cities (including Pisa airport, 1½ hours) while **CLAP** (☎ 0583/58-78-97) services most outlying Tuscan towns. Quasi-hourly LAZZI buses leave from Florence to Lucca from 6am to 8pm Monday to Saturday (every two hours Sundays), and cost

8,600L ($5.65) each way for the 1¹/₄-hour ride (avoid the lengthy route of local buses). The buses let you off on the west side of town within the walls, just across the piazza from the tourist office.

By Car   You'll have to leave your car in a parking facility (the largest, in Piazza Napoléon, fills up fast), as almost all of Lucca is closed to traffic. The effortless Autostrada del Sole (A11, direction west) connects Florence to Lucca, continuing onto Pisa and "direzione mare" (the seaside resorts of Viareggio and Forte dei Marmi). While a car enables you to explore the idyllic countryside outside Lucca, getting here to and from Florence or Pisa and visiting the town itself is more easily done by public transportation and on foot.

By Plane   Many flights from the United States connect in European cities such as London, Paris, and Frankfurt for Pisa's international **Galileo Galilei Airport** (☎ **050/50-07-07**), an easy 20- to 30-minute bus ride from Lucca. Florence's newly expanded **Amerigo Vespucci Airport** (☎ **055/37-34-98**) is another option, but more inconvenient if your first stop is Lucca. In Florence, take the city bus from the airport to the central bus station and change for a LAZZI bus to Lucca (see "By Bus," below).

VISITOR INFORMATION   **Tourist Information,** Vecchia Porta San Donato at Piazzale Verdi, ☎/fax **0583/41-96-89.** Open summer 9am to 7pm, winter 9:30am to 4:30pm.

CITY LAYOUT   Lucca is an easy place to get your bearings. The historical center is entirely contained within its 16th-century walls; the modern city outside them holds little of interest to the visitor. Piazza San Michele has been the center of town since Roman times, and a climb to the top of the tower of the Palazzo Giunigi will give you an awesome view of the city and the mountains beyond.

GETTING AROUND   There's nothing of interest that you can't easily cover by foot. Lucca is not a hill town; in fact it's rather flat. This, plus the fact that it is virtually devoid of car traffic, makes it perfect for bike touring. You can rent one from outside the tourist office in Piazzale Verdi (April through October) at 2,500L ($1.65) for the first hour, 1,500L ($1.00) for each consecutive hour, with a full-day rate of 20,000L ($13.15). Tandem bikes are 4,000L ($2.65) for the first hour and 2,000L ($1.30) for each hour after that. Bikes are also a great way to experience the tree-lined promenade atop the Renaissance walls that encircle the city.

WHAT TO SEE & DO

✪ **Duomo (Cattedrale di San Martino).** Pz. San Martino. Admission to church free; sacristy 2,000L ($1.30). Summer, daily 7am–12:30pm and 3–7pm. Winter, daily 7am–noon and 5–6pm.

Started in 1060 and completed two centuries later, the Duomo has a much admired asymmetrical facade (due to the preexisting bell tower from a former building on this site) of slender decorated columns and early 13th-century Pisan bas-reliefs. The main protagonist of the church's interior is the robed figure of Jesus on the cross: The hauntingly beautiful Volto Santo (the Holy Face) is enshrined in its own elaborate 15th-century marble chapel by Luccan sculptor Matteo Civitali. The *volto* is said to be carved by Nicodemus, a fervent follower of Christ who helped lower him from the cross, and is therefore believed to be a true image of Jesus (art historians attribute the work to a much later date). It was miraculously transported across the Mediterranean and washed up on Tuscany's shores; the bishop of Lucca transported it to Lucca in 782. Every September 13 the whole town turns out to carry the venerated statue through the streets in a candlelight procession.

Olio Di Oliva: Fruit & Frond of Peace

Since time immemorial, the olive and grape have been elements of the Italian and the Mediterranean cuisine. Recent studies now confirm that not only is the plump olive heaven to the palate but—good news!—also good for one's health, thus cementing its place in a growing culinary trend in food preparation worldwide.

The olive can be traced back at least as far as 1600 B.C. The ancient Romans crowned their heroes with wreaths of olive fronds; an olive branch was the quintessential offering of peace. Sacred, revered, and ubiquitous, the olive would spread to the far-flung corners of the Roman Empire. By the 18th century it had become one of Italy's principal export products, and by the 19th century, 67 out of 97 provinces in a newly united Italy boasted hills covered with olive trees. It would be hard to imagine the lovely Tuscan and Umbrian countryside without the noble silver-blue trees, often with scuplturelike gnarled trunks that testify to the many centuries some trees can survive. An essential component of local, rustic cuisines, the mark of a solid, serious trattoria is often the deep green intensity of the label-free bottle of olive oil brought to the table—not just a bottle set aside for the local regulars, but for any patron ready to revel in its distinctive taste.

The olive-growing pockets of Tuscany's Chiantigiana and Lucchesia areas are best known for their world-class olive oil. But their unrivaled positions as the best in the Italian market have recently come up against some unprecedentedly intense competition. The prestigious olive-oil fair held yearly in Spoleto (Umbria) has showed Tuscan oils competing with Umbrian oils and with those from central Italian regions and Puglia in the medium category, as determined by their "fruity" quality. The oils of northern Lombardia around the Lake District and coastal Liguria rank as the best in the lightest of categories, while the sun-drenched islands of Sardinia and Sicily unsurprisingly capture the category of oils with the most intense fruitiness of all. Each kind is favored by professional chefs and discerning palates for use in different preparations—frying, marinating, in soups or on cold salads, for fish and meats. Often it comes down to a question of personal preference.

Prices for this green elixir reflect the limited production and often hand-harvested procedure associated with many of the well-known labels, labels that carry a designation and cache not unlike that of Tuscany's better vineyards. The best oil is unquestionably extra-virgin, made in a cold first pressing that produces minimum acidity of about 1%; its color is the deepest, its taste—the most pronounced—is not for everyone. Virgin olive oil is slightly less expensive, with an acidity between 1% and 2%. Those that are merely bottled and sold as olio di oliva may be mixed with oils imported from Spain or Greece, and are usually what wind up on the world's supermarket shelves, touted as "Italian Olive Oil." Maybe, but just barely.

Competing for historical importance is the recently restored tomb of Ilaria del Carretto, now located in the sacristy along with important frescoes by Ghirlandaio. Sculpted with her beloved dog at her feet by Jacopo della Quercia (1408) who breathed softness into the silklike folds of her dress, Ilaria was the wife of a young lord of Lucca and is a much beloved figure in local history. Look into the first chapel on the left for a painting by Bronzino, and the third chapel on the right for one by Tintoretto. You can visit the Museo della Cattedrale (cathedral museum), directly across the street, on a joint 7,000L ($4.60) ticket together with the Chiesa di San Giovanni.

Inaugurated in 1992, the small Cathedral Museum displays choice pieces of religious art such as paintings, silver chalices and reliquaries, and wooden and marble statuary, all from the Duomo's original collection. Although the restoration was severe, there is still much left to admire in the museum space created by joining a 13th-century tower, a 14th-century palazzo, and an adjacent 16th-century church. The Chiesa di San Giovanni and its baptistery, recently reopened after years of work where stratum upon stratum of archeological foundations was unearthed, provides a one-stop look into the cathedral's and city's distant past. The deepest and lowest level you can visit is the original Roman foundation that dates to the 1st century B.C., the latest is the foundation of the church's most recent reincarnation from the late Middle Ages.

✪ **Chiesa di San Michele in Foro (Church of St. Michael in the Forum).** Foro di San Michele. Free admission. Daily 7:30am–12:30pm and 3–6pm.

San Michele is considered the social, if not the religious, center of town (and the original site of the Roman Forum, hence its name). Of the dozens of churches that populate this small city, it is second only to the Duomo in importance. Begun in 1143, it is dedicated to the winged Archangel Michael who crowns its lofty facade, and is a wonderful example of the elaborate Pisan-Lucchese architecture influenced by the cathedral in nearby Pisa. The exquisite romanesque facade is composed of four tiers of patterned pillars of every variety, size, and thickness; the ornate facade soars considerably higher than the church itself. Things are decidedly less exuberant inside since money ran out after completion of the facade's extravaganza, but there is a painting of several saints by Filippino Lippi in the left transept and a glazed terracotta bas-relief by Andrea della Robbia. Take a minute to stroll past the buildings that line the piazza; some of them date back to the 13th century.

Pinacoteca Nazionale e Museo di Palazzo Mansi (National Picture Gallery). V. Galli Tassi 43. ☎ **0593/55-570.** Admission 8,000L ($5.25). Tues–Sat 9am–7pm; Sun 9am–2pm. From Pz. San Michele: down V. S. Paolino, right on V. G. Tassi.

This small-scale museum is both impressive and appropriate for a city of this size and historical background. This was the town dwelling of the Mansi, a wealthy local family who still live in the family country villa outside of town. The palazzo is now used as a picture gallery for works by Guido Reni, Bronzino, Pontormo, and others. Don't leave without seeing the *Camera degli Sposi* (Bridal Chamber), an elaborate 17th-century Versailles-like alcove of decorative gold leaf, putti, and columns, where trembling Mansi brides awaited their conjugal duties amidst the sumptuous Luccan silks and heavy brocades.

Anfiteatro Romano (Roman Amphitheater). Between V. Fillungo and V. Mordini.

The aerial photograph of Lucca's amphitheater on local postcards is remarkable, showing the perfect elliptical shape of the ancient theater built here in the second century A.D.; the buildings from varying eras you see today were built on its ancient foundations, and many incorporated its arches into their walls. The most recent structures date to the 19th century when Napoléon's sister, Elisa, as city governor attempted to clean up the medieval jumble. The amphitheater, which once could seat 10,000, testifies to Lucca's early importance as a Roman city; the city's neat grid pattern of streets further reflects its origin as a Roman outpost.

Le Mura (the Walls).

Succumb to the leisurely pace of this human-scale city, and stroll or bike the shady 4-km path atop its perfectly intact walls. Join the local *Lucchesi* as they jog along or push grandchildren in strollers, enjoying a view of the city's architecture within the

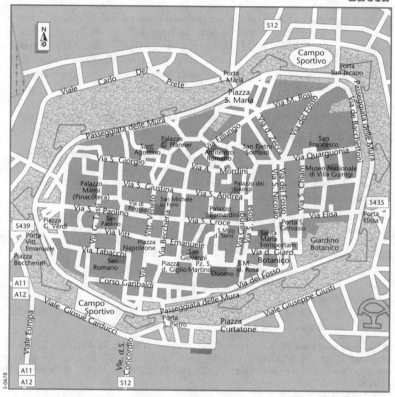

walls and the lovely countryside that unfolds outside. These are the city's third set of walls, an enormous feat of engineering and considered the best-preserved of Renaissance defense ramparts in Europe. They were begun in the 16th century long after centuries of feuds and strife, apparently from the belief that good fences make good neighbors. They replaced the crumbling medieval ramparts, and measure 115 feet at the base and 40 feet high. The emerald-green lawns that stretch out beyond them were not planted until the last century. You can access the tree-lined promenade at any of the 10 bastions, such as behind the tourist office in Piazzale Verdi (which is where, during the summer, you can rent a bike; see "Getting Around," above).

Antico Caffè di Simo. V. Fillungo 58. ☎ **0583/46-234.** Tues–Sun 8am–8pm.

Conclude an early evening *passeggiata* (stroll) along the centuries-old storefronts of Via Fillungo in the company of what will seem like Lucca's entire population, then stop for your *aperitivo* or gelato at this historical cafe. This was a preferred watering hole of Lucca-born opera composer Giacomo Puccini, who loved to linger in the old-world ambience of marble, brass, and antique mirrors. There's a piano bar with occasional jazz evenings during winter months.

SPECIAL EVENTS

Hundreds of antique vendors converge upon the area around Piazza Antelminelli and Piazza Giusto the third Sunday of every month. Reserve (in advance) at Da Giulio's for Sunday lunch before or after to complete the Luccan experience. The opera season takes place at the **Teatro Comunale del Giglio** (Pz. d. Giglio) in September or October, and usually features at least one opera by local son Puccini. For ticket information, call **0583/44-21-03**, or fax 0583/49-03-17. The annual **Settembre Lucchese** fills the month of September with a lively combination of music, dance, and celebrations. The highlight is the **Volto Santo** feast day on September 13 (see the Duomo under "What to See and Do," above). Ask Tourist Information for a schedule of events. Summer musical events are sometimes scheduled in the gardens of the historical villas in the surrounding countryside; ask at the tourist office.

WHERE TO STAY

The hotel situation in Lucca continues to be disheartening. Most of the one- and two-star hotels are in the newer, less interesting section of town outside the walls. In high season, be sure to make a hotel reservation in advance, or you may have to stay in Florence, nearby Pisa, or one of the seaside resorts.

Hotel Diana. V. d. Molinetto 11, 55100 Lucca. ☎ **0583/49-22-02.** Fax 0583/47-795. 9 rms, 7 with bath. TEL TV. 48,000L ($31.60) single without bath, 65,000L ($42.75) single with bath; 78,000L ($51.30) double without bath, 95,000L ($62.50) double with bath; 128,000L ($84.20) triple with bath. Breakfast (optional) 4,000L ($2.65) per person. AE, DC, MC, V. Off Pz. Duomo.

This is one of the nicest of the town's two-star hotels and, at just one block west of the Duomo, has the best location. A 16th-century palazzo houses contemporary rooms with appreciated amenities such as telephones, color TV, hair dryers, and cool marble floors. Quiet rooms overlook a next-door neighbor's garden. Breakfast is served in your room—not a bad way to start a relaxing day.

✪ **Piccolo Hotel Puccini.** V. di Poggio 9, 55100 Lucca. ☎ **0583/55-421.** Fax 0583/53-487. 14 rms with bath. TEL TV. 85,000L ($55.90) single; 120,000L ($78.95) double. Ask about off-season discounts. Breakfast optional at 12,000L ($7.90) per person. AE, MC, V. Parking can be arranged.

If you're planning a stay in Giacomo Puccini's hometown, an enviable location would be this charming three-star hotel in a 15th-century palazzo that sits just in front of the building where the great composer was born. Some of the hotel rooms overlook the small piazza and its bronze statue of Puccini that borders the far side. Paolo and Raffaella, the young and enthusiastic couple who have just taken over the management, have lightened and brightened up the place with a new marble-tiled lobby, fresh curtains in the guest rooms, flower arrangements in the public areas, and their extremely helpful and friendly presence throughout. A perfect choice for those who appreciate tasteful attention and discrete professionalism. You can get a less expensive breakfast two steps away in Piazza San Michele, one of Lucca's loveliest squares.

Hotel La Luna. V. Fillungo (in Cor. Compagni) 12, 55100 Lucca. ☎ **0583/49-36-34.** Fax 0583/49-00-21. 27 rms with bath. TEL TV. 85,000L ($55.90) single; 120,000L ($78.95) double; suites 150,000L–170,000L ($98.70–$111.85). Breakfast buffet extra 15,000L ($9.85) per person. AE, DC, MC, V. Closed Jan 7–31. Limited parking (reserve in advance; 15,000L / $9.85 a day).

Set off in a small courtyard a block from the amphitheater and quietly functioning as a hotel for more than two centuries, this efficient choice may have a little less charm than the small Piccolo Puccini but offers better availability during the high season. Rooms are well thought out and decorated in a fresh and contemporary vein—although those who splurge on the suites will find more spacious and characteristic quarters with turn-of-the-century ceiling frescoes, original fireplaces, and large sitting areas. Some rooms have air-conditioning. Late risers with big appetites can tuck into the well-supplied breakfast buffet table and later skip lunch without feeling it—though that would be a shame. A convenient alternative is the lobby bar, where a coffee and croissant keep breakfast costs more contained.

Universo. Pza. del Giglio 1, 55100 Lucca. ☎ **0583/49-36-78.** Fax 0583/95-48-54. 60 rms with bath. MINIBAR TEL TV. 120,000L ($78.95) single; 160,000L ($105.25) double; 185,000L ($121.70). Breakfast 16,000L ($10.50) per person extra. V. Parking available.

This hotel-with-an-attitude aspires to be the grandest of Lucca's limited hotel roster; a gradual renovation of all guest rooms is resuscitating some of their former 19th-century charm. Ask for any of the refurbished rooms with a view of the small Piazza del Giglio and the town theater. They vary greatly in decor from contemporary to period, with chintz or damask bedspreads and the occasional added treats of molded ceilings, antiques, and hand-painted tiles in the bathrooms. Some rooms are air-conditioned. If you've biked around town and are too tired to make it to Giulio's, check out the fixed-price menu in the hotel's well-known restaurant: there are five first courses and as many entrees to choose from for 25,000L ($16.45).

WHERE TO DINE

Da Guido. V. C. Battisti 28 (at V. degli Angeli near Pza. Sant'Agostino), Lucca. ☎ **0583/47-219.** First courses 4,000L–5,000L ($2.65–$3.30); entrees 7,000L ($4.60). 3-course menu turistico 17,000L ($11.20). AE. Mon–Sat 12:30–2:30pm and 7:00–11:00pm. TUSCAN.

The amiable proprietor Guido welcomes hometown cronies and hungry out-of-towners with the same warm smile and filling meals that keep 'em all happy. The bar in the front and the TV locked into the sports channel create a laid-back atmosphere that will make you want to linger; the fresh tortellini made on the premises and the simplicity of roast rabbit (coniglio) or veal (vitello) will wipe out any conflicting inclinations to do otherwise. This is a cut below the price- and quality-level of Giulio's (see below), but you're guaranteed of a good home-cooked meal here in a no-frills, family-run trattoria.

Da Leo. V. Tegrimi 1 (off Pz. San Michele), Lucca. ☎ **0583/49-22-36.** First courses 6,000L–7,000L ($3.95–$4.60); 2nd courses 10,000L–13,000L ($6.60–$8.55). No credit cards. Mon–Sat noon–2:30pm and 7:30–10:30pm; open for lunch the 3rd Sun of every month for Antique Fair. TUSCAN.

There's no menu here but the good-natured waiters by now are used to dealing with foreigners who have discovered one of the best and most authentic *Lucchese* eating spots in town. This is not as much a bare-bones tavern as Guido's, but not quite as polished an operation as the well-regarded Giulio's. Its location, two steps from the central Piazza San Michele, draws strolling tourists who happen by, lured into the cozy peach-colored rooms by the aroma of roasting meats and the scent of rosemary. The ubiquitous *farro* soup made from elmer (a kind of barley) should be followed by the simple but delicious pollo fritto con patate arroste (fried chicken with roast potatoes) for a meal that will have you promising your waiter to return tomorrow.

✪ **Da Giulio.** V. d. Conce 45 (north of Pza. San Donato), Lucca. ☎ **0583/55-948.** Reservations suggested. 1st courses 8,000L ($5.25); entrees 12,500L–15,000L ($8.20–$9.85). AE, DC, MC, V. Tues–Sat 12:30–2:30pm and 7–11pm, open for lunch the third Sun of each month for Antique Fair. TUSCAN.

Dazzled foreigners and discerning locals agree that this big, airy, and forever busy trattoria is one of Tuscany's undisputed stars. Although casual, this is not the place to occupy a much-coveted table for just a pasta and salad. Save up your appetite and come for a full-blown Tuscan feast, trying all of Giulio's traditional rustic specialties. Begin with the thick *farro* soup made with a local barleylike grain or the fresh *maccheroni tortellati* pasta stuffed with fresh ricotta and spinach, both made to perfection. Perfect also are the grilled and roast meats such as an *arrosti misti* of beef and turkey or *pollo al mattone,* chicken flattened and roasted under the weight of heated bricks. Waiters know not to recommend certain local favorites to non-Italian diners, unless you look like the tartara di cavallo (horsemeat tartar) type.

SIDE TRIPS FROM LUCCA

Surrounding Lucca is the fertile Lucchesia corner of Tuscany, one of Italy's richest agricultural areas renowned worldwide for its deep green virgin olive oil and other produce. The remote hills and valleys of the **Garfignana Mountains** provide networks of lovely hiking trails, and the nearby marble quarries of **Carrara**—already famous when frequented by the Florentine sculptor Michelangelo—are an easy excursion. A number of villas of historical importance are within biking distance, notably the **Villa Reale** in Marlia and the **Villa Torrigiani** in Camigliano (visit the tourist board for a map). Lucca is also convenient to **Pisa,** where you can spend half a day seeing the famous tower and its Duomo and baptistery (see "Day Trips to Pisa and Fiesole" in chapter 6 for details). On the coast to the northwest (follow signs that say DIREZIONE MARE to the A12 north) lie the seaside resort towns of Viareggio and the tonier and more picturesque Forte dei Marmi.

2 San Gimignano

57km (35 miles) SW of Florence; 65km (40 miles) SE of Lucca; 42km (26 miles) NW of Siena; 100km (62 miles) SE of Lucca

Once you have seen the delightful hill town of "San Gimignano delle Belle Torri," San Gimignano of the Beautiful Towers, you'll understand its timeless popularity as a must-do tourist destination; hence the endless busloads of wilted travelers who pack the town during the day. But slip into a cool back alleyway and escape the herds of day trippers who "do" the town in an hour; stay into the evening for a lovely dinner when the town reverts to its timeless character and you have the place to yourself. You'll discover the magic and views captured by the film *Where Angels Fear to Tread,* an adaptation of the novel by E. M. Forster filmed here, though based on a town he calls "Monteriano."

San Gimignano has arrested the traveler's imagination as the quintessential Tuscan hill town for centuries. Its stunning skyline bristles with medieval towers (there remain 14 of an estimated 70) whose construction dates back to the 12th and 13th centuries when they were built as much for defense purposes as for the prestige of outdoing the neighbors. Located on the ancient Francigena road that transported medieval trade and pilgrims from northern Europe to Rome, San Gimignano was considered quite the wealthy agricultural town in its 14th-century heyday and could therefore afford handsome palazzi and impressive frescoed churches.

ESSENTIALS

GETTING THERE   By Train   There is no train station in San Gimignano; the nearest is in Poggibonsi, where you'll need to connect to bus service (20 minutes). If you're traveling from Florence, bus service is more convenient, although not direct.

By Bus   All TRA.IN buses (☎ **0577/20-41-11**) that run between San Gimignano and both Florence or Siena change in the small Poggibonsi bus station. One-way bus fare from Florence to San Gimignano is 9,500L ($6.25); from Siena to San Gimignano is 7,900L ($5.20). The trip from Florence to Poggibonsi takes about an hour, from Siena to Poggibonsi about 45 minutes. Count on a layover in Poggibonsi of anywhere from 10 minutes to an hour before you can catch a connection for the remaining 10- to 20-minute ride to San Gimignano.

The bus station for San Gimignano is a covered stop with a posted schedule immediately outside the city walls, southwest of the Porta San Giovanni on the Piazza Montemaggio (you can also get a bus schedule from the tourist office).

By Car   If you're coming from Lucca, it's a 1¹/₂-hour drive (110km). It's most direct to backtrack to Florence on the A11 autostrada, then head south on the Superstrada del Palio Firenze-Siena. Exit at Poggibonsi and follow signs for S324 to San Gimignano. A slightly longer alternative that avoids the superhighways is to leave Lucca on the autostrada southwest for Pisa Aeroporto. Head east, in the direction of Ponte a Elsa, where you turn south for Certaldo. From here follow the signs to San Gimignano.

San Gimignano is entirely closed to traffic within the walls (except to drop off luggage at your hotel), so you'll need to park in any one of a number of small parking areas along the road that follows the outer rim of the walls.

By Plane   San Gimignano is roughly equidistant to Pisa and Florence's airports (see Florence chapter).

VISITOR INFORMATION   Associazione Pro Loco is the local name for the tourist office, located in Pz. Duomo 1. Summer hours are 9am to 1pm and 3 to 7pm (daily). Winter hours (November 1 through February 28) are 9am to 1pm and 2 to 6pm (daily).

CITY LAYOUT   The principle entrance points from outside the walls are Porta San Matteo in the northwest, and the more popular Porta di San Giovanni in the south, where most bus routes end. Anchored by a 13th-century cisterna or well, the central Piazza della Cisterna is lined with herringbone bricks and interlocks with the more austere Piazza Duomo just north of it. All roads radiate out from these squares, the most important being Via San Giovanni to the south and the slightly less commercial Via San Matteo north of Piazza della Cisterna. The Via del Castello runs east out of the piazza. Any of the cobblestoned back streets offer the chance to escape the San Gimignano/Siena package tours. You can walk across town in 15 minutes or take the whole day. The entire town is encircled by its medieval ramparts, beyond which a smattering of newer construction has taken place.

GETTING AROUND   The town's position atop one of the valley's many hills means gentle inclines in the streets leading to and from the main square. You'll have to get around by foot, as traffic is rigidly restricted within the walls.

WHAT TO SEE & DO

The *biglietto comulativo* (joint ticket) is no great deal at 16,000L ($10.50) and only offers savings to those with the time and inclination to see all the museums included: Museo Civico, Torre Grossa, Museo d'Arte Sacra/Museo Etrusco, Capella di Santa Finta (in the Duomo). Unfortunately, it does not include the privately owned Museum of Medieval Criminology.

✪ **Museo Civico (Civic Museum) and the Torre Grossa (tower)**. Palazzo d. Popolo, Pz. d. Duomo 1. ☎ **0577/94-03-40.** Admission: Museo and Tower each 7,000L ($4.60). Summer, Wed–Sun 9:30am–7:30pm, Winter, 9:30am–6pm.

Labor to the top of the Palazzo's 117-foot Torre Grossa, the highest of San Gimignano's towers, and you'll feel like you're on top of a flagpole with heart-stopping views of the town, its towers, and the Val d'Elsa beyond. Once you've gotten that out of your system, backtrack to see some of the museum's collection, housed in the perfectly preserved 14th-century Palazzo del Popolo or Comune (town hall).

The first floor's frescoed Sala di Dante is the spot where the poet Dante, as ambassador from pro-pope (Guelph) Florence, came to pro-emperor (Ghibelline) San Gimignano in the year 1300 to plead for unity. Here you'll find the town's masterpiece, the *Maestà (Enthroned Madonna)* by Sienese painter Lippo Mimmi (1317). The pinacoteca (picture gallery) on the second floor is composed mostly of 12th- to 15th-century paintings from the Sienese school, with highlights by Gozzoli, Pinturicchio, Filippino Lippi, and a painting of San Gimignano himself, holding the town in his lap, by Taddeo di Bartolo.

If you've purchased a joint ticket, spend a few minutes in the small **Museo d'Arte Sacra, Museo Etrusco** to the left of the Duomo (enter from the Piazza Pecori) for its medieval tombstones, wooden sculptures, and Etruscan artifacts. It is open April through September noon to 3pm and 6 to 7:30pm, from October through March 12:30 to 3pm only. Without the joint ticket, admission is 7000L ($4.60).

⭕ **Duomo (also called the Collegiata).** Pz. Duomo. Admission to Duomo free; 3,000L ($2.00) for Cappella di Santa Fina. Summer, daily 9:30am–12:30pm and 3–6:00pm; Winter, daily 9:30am–12:30pm and 3–5:30pm.

Because there is no longer a bishop of San Gimignano, the Duomo (cathedral) has been demoted to a Collegiata (though forever a "Duomo" in the locals' eyes) and is a prime example of not judging a 12th-century church by its facade. Never finished on the outside, its interior is heavily frescoed with scenes from the Bible, testimony to the city's prosperity in centuries past. On the north wall are scenes from the Old Testament, on the south wall, scenes from the life of Christ. On the back wall are scenes from the Last Judgment, attributed to Lippo Memmi. The Cappella di Santa Fina in the southwest corner of the Duomo is worth a visit for the important frescoes by Ghirlandaio (1475) recounting the life of a young local girl named Fina. She spent her 15 short years in prayer and is the patron saint of San Gimignano. Another of Ghirlandaio's works, *The Annunciation,* graces a courtyard adjacent to the Baptistery.

If you're not all frescoed out, visit the 13th-century church of Sant'Agostino (free admission) in the north end of town (Piazza Sant'Agostino). Its simple romanesque contrasts with its rococo interior. The interior's highlight is the simple choir entirely covered by a cycle of frescoes showing the life of St. Augustine by Benozzo Gozzoli, a master 15th-century painter.

Museo di Criminologia Medioevale (Museum of Medieval Criminology). V. d. Castello 1. ☎ **0577/94-22-43.** Admission 8,000L ($5.25). Summer hours (daily) 10:00am–1pm and 2–6:30pm. Winter hours Sat and Sun 11:00am–1:00pm and 2–6:00pm. Dec 21–Jan 7 open daily.

Is it karmic happenstance or a quirk of history that this peculiar museum of medieval torture is housed in the 13th-century Palazzo del Diavolo (The Devil's Palace)? Inarguably one of Tuscany's more unusual sights, this surprisingly expansive collection contains over 100 instruments of torture. Most of them are original pieces, and all of are thoughtfully and impressively displayed and explained in both Italian and English. This is good, because items such as knuckle- and skull-crushers, and iron gags to stifle screams are not always immediately recognizable to the innocent. It's worth the admission just to see the cast-iron chastity belts. As unsettling as some of the original prints depicting the atrocities of the 15th-century Inquisition are many of the item descriptions, such as that accompanying the garrote—a punishment used in Spain until 1975 and still used in South America today.

WINE TASTING IN CHIANTI'S BACKYARD

A stroll up Via San Giovanni will impress you with the number of wine shops whose windows are stocked floor-to-ceiling with the fruits of the Chianti vineyards. The gently rolling hills of Tuscany supply Italy's finest red wines, while San Gimignano itself is known for *vernaccia,* a distinctive white wine. The curious and the *appassionati* should make a beeline for **Da Gustavo** (☎ 0577/94-00-57, V. San Matteo 29; summer, daily 8am to midnight; winter, Saturday to Thursday 8am to 8pm), a small, old-time wine bar where you can orchestrate an informal wine tasting from over 20 types of Tuscan and Italian white and red wines by the glass (3,000L to 5,000L ($2.00 to $3.30) per glass). There's no place to sit, but there are fresh, delicious panini sandwiches made to order using the region's top-quality cheeses and salamis.

A more expensive alternative-with-a-view is the lovely, sit-down **Bar Enoteca il Castello** (☎ 0577/94-08-78, V. d. Castello 20; Thursday to Tuesday 9am to 11:30pm) where you can stop by for a glass of wine, perhaps a plate of crusty bread and Tuscan salami, and a memorable view of the hills in the soft, late afternoon light. They also serve full meals.

GUIDED WALKS IN GOD'S COUNTRY

For those blessed with the opportunity of spending more than a rushed afternoon in San Gimignano, stop by the tourist office to inquire about their guided excursions into the countryside, scheduled to be repeated again in 1997. Gentle walks through the nearby hills include visits to an Etruscan necropolis, abandoned medieval castles, churches dating back to the 1100s, and even a tipple or two at wine-producing estates. Bilingual guides take small groups for half-day (10,000L/$6.60) or full-day (20,000L/$13.15) excursions that technically must be booked a minimum of two days in advance, though last-minute queries are welcomed. Call the **tourist office** at 0577/94-00-08, fax 0577/94-09-03. For self-guided tours, pass by the office in Piazza Duomo to pick up a map of designated walking paths in the area.

SPECIAL EVENTS

San Gimignano has two patron saints, San Gimignano himself (a 4th-century bishop from Modena), whose feast day is celebrated January 31, and Santa Fina (who died in 1253 at the age of 15), whose feast day is on March 12. Both are celebrated with a High Mass in the Duomo and an all-day outdoor fair in the main square. San Gimignano also boasts one of Tuscany's more animated *carnevales,* held each of the four Sundays prior to Ash Wednesday. The third weekend of June is the **Fiera delle Messi,** when the town effortlessly resuscitates its medieval character during a weekend of outdoor markets, musical and theatrical events, and a jousting tournament of knights on horseback, all in medieval costume. From mid-June throughout August is the dance and music festival, **Estate Sangimignese,** when you can look for art exhibits, outdoor classical concerts, alfresco opera, or ballet in the Piazza della Cisterna. See the tourist office for a schedule. Santa Fina shows up again for the first Sunday of August's **Festa di Ringraziamento;** the next day (Monday) a large fair takes place in the main square.

WHERE TO STAY

Ask the tourist office or the **Agenzia Munditravel,** V. San Matteo 74 (☎ 0577/94-08-27 or fax 0577/94-08-88) for a list of bed-and-breakfast or farm accommodations.

Ostello della Gioventù (Youth Hostel). V. d. Fonti 1, 53037 San Gimignano. ☎ 0577/94-19-91. Fax 055/80-50-104. 75 beds total in 9 rms: 5 large dormitories, 4 private rms for

2–4 people (depending on demand). No Youth Hostel membership needed. 19,000L ($12.50) per person dormitory; 21,000L ($13.80) per person in room. Maximum 6 nights. Breakfast extra at 5,000L ($3.30) per person. Closed Nov 1–Mar 1. No credit cards.

This former grade school has reincarnated as a youth hostel popular with shoestring-budget travelers. The alternative to sleeping in any of the five large male or female dormitory rooms is the unusual option of four smaller rooms that accommodate 2 to 4, though with rates only marginally less than *affittacamere* (bed-and-breakfast) you might prefer that over this youth hostel (see above). This hostel even accepts faxed reservation requests, and some rooms have lovely views. When the kitchen is cooking meals for groups, individual guests are welcome to eat for 14,000L ($9.20). Located within the town's ring of walls, it's just a five-minute walk to the central square.

Hotel Bel Soggiorno. V. San Giovanni 91, 53037 San Gimignano. ☎/fax **0577/94-03-75.** A/C TEL TV. 21 rms with bath. 90,000L ($59.20) single; 110,000L ($72.35) double; 160,000L ($105.25) triple. Breakfast extra at 10,000L ($6.60) per person. AE, V. Often closed a few weeks in Jan or Feb.

Located close to the San Giovanni city gate, and a gentle five-minute walk uphill to the main square, this well-known hostelry gets two thumbs up—one for the simply decorated rooms with large patios that command awesome views of the rolling hills of Tuscany's Val d'Elsa (add 10,000L/$6.60 to a double rate for the view), and one for the acclaimed restaurant downstairs (see "Where to Dine," below). Half of the hotel's rooms are blessed with the priceless view, but only three share the large terracotta patio. If you have access to wheels and long for a more rural environment, ask at the desk about their country property, the Hotel Le Pescille, a nearby converted farmhouse/hotel with 50 rooms, boasting a lovely setting three miles out of town, with pool, tennis, and an excellent restaurant at very reasonable rates comparable to those quoted above (☎ and fax 0577/94-01-86).

✪ **Hotel La Cisterna.** Pza. d. Cisterna 23, 53037 San Gimignano. ☎ **0577/94-03-28.** Fax 0577/94-20-80. TEL TV. 50 rms with bath. 80,000L ($52.65); 100,000L–135,000L ($65.80–$88.80) doubles without and with views. Buffet breakfast 13,000L ($8.55) per person extra. AE, DC, MC, V. Closed Jan 7 to Mar 8. Parking available.

The town's nicest hotel is housed in one of the imposing palazzi flanking the central Piazza della Cisterna. Like the Bel Soggiorno, the hotel includes one of San Gimignano's better restaurants, Le Terrazze, which keeps the public areas busy during lunch hours. But repair upstairs to the serenity of your large room, many of which have balconies whose views are spellbinding. If Tuscany's hill towns are lovely to view from a distance, they are even more wonderful for the vantage points they offer and panoramas from windows such as these. If you saw the film *Where Angels Fear to Tread* (1991), you'll recognize that some parts were filmed here.

Hotel Leon Bianco. Pz. d. Cisterna 8, 53037 San Gimignano. ☎ **0577/94-12-94.** Fax 0577/94-21-23. A/C TEL TV. 20 rms with bath. 75,000L ($49.35) single; 115,000L–135,000L ($75.65–$88.80) doubles; 165,000L ($108.55) triple. Buffet breakfast extra 11,000L ($7.25) per person. AE, V. Closed Nov 15–Dec 12 and Jan 15–Feb 15. Next-door parking available for 19,000L ($12.50) per day.

Located directly across the main piazza from La Cisterna, this smaller hotel is housed in a beautifully restored medieval palazzo. The central part of the hotel is housed in a 12th-century patrician home that was eventually expanded in the next century with the addition of a medieval tower on either side, parts of which are incorporated into the hotel. Modernized rooms are historically offset with exposed brick walls, vaulted ceilings, archways, and terracotta floors and are priced according to size and view: Five overlook the main piazza, nine have views of the countryside, and all others overlook an enclosed courtyard. The brick courtyard is the lovely setting for breakfast from May through September.

WHERE TO DINE

Bars about town offer indoor/outdoor tables for snacks of *panini* sandwiches or *pizza al taglio* (by the slice). For the latter, try **Lo Sfizzio** (V. San Giovanni 110) or **Del Diavolo** (in Pz. d. Cisterna), both centrally located and offering a variety of pizzas at 2,500L ($1.65) a slice. When lunch is just an excuse to sample the region's wine selection, see "Wine Tasting," above in "What to See and Do."

Trattoria Chiribiri. Pz. d. Madonna (off V. San Giovanni near Porta San Giovanni). ☎ 0577/94-19-48. 1st courses 8,000L–10,000L ($5.25–$6.60); entrees 10,000L–12,000L ($6.60–$7.90). No credit cards. Thurs–Tues noon–10pm. TUSCAN.

If you arrive at the perfect moment, the bells of the tiny Chiesa della Madonna will be pealing your arrival. Situated off the principle pedestrian Via San Giovanni on a small piazzetta it shares with the church is this cozy little trattoria with just 10 tables and a young and friendly staff. Its highly unusual "no-stop" hours afford you the chance to procure one of those coveted tables if you come before or after the crush of conventional dining hours, when you can get away with a simple plate of homemade pasta and salad. But with such reasonable prices and impressive talent in the kitchen, this is also the right spot to indulge in a multicourse meal of the unpretentious *cucina toscana* and discover the delights of the region's poor-man's cuisine.

Le Vecchie Mura. V. Piandornella 15 (1st right off V. San Giovanni coming from Porta San Giovanni). ☎ 0577/94-02-70. 1st courses 9,000L ($5.90); meat entrees 11,000L–14,000L ($7.25–$9.20). AE, DC, V. Wed–Mon 12:30–2:30pm and 7:30–10:30pm. TUSCAN.

The first thing you must do is see if either of the two comfortable bedrooms-with-bath upstairs are available (60,000L/$39.45 for a double). If not, you can effortlessly console yourself with a marvelous meal downstairs in the cool, brick-vaulted trattoria in what once served as a patrician family's stables in the 1700s. The thick *ribollita* cabbage-based soup and homemade *tagliatelle al cinghiale* (pasta with wild-boar sauce) are deservedly the house specialties. The regional specialty of wild boar shows up again as a favorite entree, marinated in the local Vernaccia white wine then grilled. Scheduled to be ready in 1997 is a small alfresco terrace directly across the narrow graveled road, whose gorgeous views out over the ancient city walls may make concentrating on your meal difficult.

✪ Ristorante Bel Soggiorno. V. San Giovanni 41 (near Porta San Giovanni). ☎ 0577/94-31-49. Reservations suggested. Antipasti and 1st courses 10,000L–13,000L ($6.60–$8.55); meat entrees 14,000L–19,000L ($9.20–$12.50); menu turistico, minimum 30,000L ($19.75). AE, V. Tues–Sun 12:30–2:30pm and 7:00–10:30pm. TUSCAN.

A nice mix of delighted tourists and Tuscan bigwigs fill this rustic and spacious restaurant whose menu shares the spotlight with the glorious countryside framed by oversized windows. Patrons who work in the area's wine industry entertain their important buyers here, assured of the *bella figura* they'll make with a meal that is both casual but of the utmost Tuscan quality. Many of the kitchen's limited-production ingredients are from the owners' private estate: olive oil, honey, grappa, and wines labeled AZIENDA AGRICOLA PESCILLE. Thick-crusted bread and wide *pappardelle* noodles are made fresh daily—try the latter traditionally prepared with a tomato-based sauce flavored with either hare (*alla lepre*) or wild boar (*al cinghiale*). The specialty of meats simply prepared on the grill is ultra-Tuscan; ultra-delicious is the homemade *crostata di ficchi* dessert, a delicate fig tart made with the family estate's bounty. Want to stay forever? Guest rooms are available just upstairs; see "Where to Stay," above.

3 Siena

34km (21 miles) S of Florence, 42km (26 miles) SE of San Gimignano, 230km (143 miles) SW of Rome, 107km (66 miles) NW of Perugia

Siena "the Beloved" is often bypassed on the mad rush of tourists traveling the Rome–Florence autostrada. Others allot it minimum time to revel in its perfectly preserved medieval charm. You will see nothing of the baroque so prevalent in Rome nor the Renaissance character of nearby Florence. Founded by the Etruscans and colonized by ancient Rome, Siena flourished as a republic in the Middle Ages from wool trade and early, sophisticated banking. It was considered one of the major cities of Europe and became a principal center of art as well. The Piazza del Campo, the city's imposing palazzi, Duomo, and churches that you see today were the result of a building boom that flourished in those years. But prosperity was aborted after devastating and recurring bouts with the bubonic plague beginning in 1348 that diminished the city's population from 100,000 to 30,000.

Forever locking horns over the centuries with its powerful neighbor Florence, and never having fully stabilized after its brush with the Black Death, it finally succumbed to Florence after an 18-month siege in 1554–55, and was reduced to a small provincial town of little consequence. Siena seems frozen in time even today, one of the country's best preserved medieval cities. Because of its golden days of full coffers, it boasts one of the most beautiful duomos, town halls, and main squares in all of Italy.

The Monte dei Paschi Bank in the postcard-perfect Piazza Salimbeni was founded in 1472; it is Europe's oldest bank and still one of Italy's most solvent. But while Siena's architectural expansion may have never progressed beyond the early years of the Renaissance, Siena today is still a very vital city, as you can witness during the early evening *passeggiata* hour when the city's folk take to strolling the Via di Città and the Banchi di Sotto and Banchi di Sopra. Proud, handsome, fashionably turned out, and more welcoming than the reserved Florentines, the Sienese people will make your stay here a memorable one.

ESSENTIALS

GETTING THERE   By Train   Arriving by train is less convenient than by bus for three reasons: Siena is not on a principal line, so you must often change and wait somewhere; departures are not as frequent as the bus; the **train station** (☎ 0577/28-01-15) is located 2km outside of town. Florence/Siena one-way is 9,800L ($6.45). From the train station, buses (1,200L/75¢) will bring you as far as Piazza Matteotti.

By Bus   SITA buses leave Florence for Siena about every 30 minutes from the station at V. Santa Caterina da Siena 15r (☎ 055/48-36-51), located near the train station. The 75-minute journey follows a lovely route for the most part and costs about 10,000L ($6.60) each way; avoid local stops by taking the *corsa rapida*, a 70-minute trip costing 10,500L ($6.90). **TRA.IN/SITA** buses will leave you off in Piazza San Domenico (☎ 0577/20-42-45), an easy 15-minute walk from the Piazza del Campo.

By Car   From Florence take the Florence–Siena autostrada or, alternatively, the S222 (the Chiantigiana), which takes a more winding, panoramic route through the Chianti countryside (see "Side Trips," below). The entire historical center of Siena is closed tight to traffic. The majority of car parks are located around the stadium, the Fortezza Medicea, and Piazza San Domenico in the northwest area of town. Some of the hotels listed will provide more convenient parking within a few blocks of their property; ask when reserving a room. You may not be able to use your car while in Siena, but it is invaluable to have if you plan to explore Chianti's wine estates and small towns.

If you're coming from San Gimignano, follow the signs for Poggibonsi. Avoid picking up the autostrada, but instead follow the signs for the secondary "panoramic" road to Staggia, Monteriggioni, Badesse, Uopini, and Siena.

By Plane   Florence's **Amerigo Vespucci Airport** (☎ **055/37-34-98**) is the nearest (see "Getting There" in the Florence chapter). Slightly less convenient is Pisa's international **Galileo Galilei Airport** (☎ **050/50-07-07**), 106km northwest of Siena.

VISITOR INFORMATION   The **A.P.T. (Azienda di Promozione Turismo)** for tourist information is located in the Piazza del Campo 56 (☎ **0577/28-05-51**), open in summer Monday to Saturday from 8:30am to 7:30pm, in winter Monday to Friday 8:30am to 1pm and 3:30 to 6:30pm and Saturday 8:30am to 1pm only. (*Note:* There is a possibility they will relocate in 1997.) A second location on V. d. Città 43 (☎ **0577/42-209**) is primarily administrative and has much less information, with the exception of a listing of *affittacamere* (rooms for rent).

CITY LAYOUT   The city is laid out around the fan-shaped **Piazza il Campo** (or simply "il Campo")—some fascinated visitors never make it beyond the outdoor cafe tables that ring this unique piazza. Its principal palazzo-lined streets are also the address for the most interesting stores and bars: **Via di Città** (which will lead you from the Campo to the Duomo) and **Banchi di Sotto.** Perpendicular to the latter is Banchi di Sopra. The best vantage point to see it all is from atop the *Torre del Mangia* next to the Palazzo Comunale in the Campo; it's worth the 505 steps.

GETTING AROUND   Siena is built on three hills. Some of the alleyways can be so steep they turn into steps. The only way to see the town is by foot and how much you'll discover depends on your tolerance. It is extremely easy to lose the crowds around il Campo, the Palazzo Pubblico, and the Duomo. Even in the heat of the summer months, the narrow streets are shaded and cool, but the hills don't go away.

WHAT TO SEE & DO

○ **Piazza del Campo and the Palazzo Pubblico (Museo Civico).** Pz. d. Campo. ☎ **0577/29-22-63.** Admission to Torre del Mangia 5,000L ($3.30); Museo Civico 6,000L ($3.95). Torre, daily 10am–dusk. Museo (within Palazzo Pubblico) Apr–Oct Mon–Sat 9am–6:45pm, Sun 9am–12:45pm; Nov–Mar daily 9am–12:45pm.

You will see posters and postcards with aerial shots of the unusually-shaped Piazza il Campo (also called il Campo) though they don't prepare you for its size or beauty. All roads and events, all visitors and residents seem to gravitate toward it; you can catch a glimpse of its sunlit expanse from a dozen narrow alleys that lead down to it. Built at the point where the city's three hills converge, it is divided into nine marble-trimmed strips representing the city's ancient Government of Nine and is also said to imitate the folds in the cloak of the Virgin Mary. It has always been the city's center stage and is today lined with 13th- and 14th-century palazzi and their ground-floor cafes. At its highest point is the piazza's famous Fonte Gaia, dedicated to the ancient mythological goddess of the seas. It is a copy of the original early 15th-century fountain by Jacopo della Quercia and is fed by a 15-mile aqueduct that has supplied the city with fresh water since the 14th century.

Directly opposite it and taking up the entire southside of the piazza is the Palazzo Pubblico with its sky-scraping 320-foot bell tower, the Torre del Mangia. A stunning and perfectly preserved symbol of civic pride, and still the site of the Town Hall, the

Palazzo Pubblico was built between 1288–1309 and was expanded in the 17th century. The adjacent brick tower crowned with marble, the highest in Italy after Cremona, was added to punctuate its significance. The tower is named after its indolent glutton of a bellringer, who was nicknamed "mangiagaudagni" (literally profiteater). Its bells were used to announce the opening and closing of the city gates, threat of attack, and special events such as the arrival of a pope. Its 505 steps will provide you with vertigo-inducing views over il Campo, the hills of Siena, and the Tuscan countryside that spreads out beyond where the modern city has spread beyond the city walls. At the base of the tower is the Cappella di Piazza built in 1348, erected by the grateful Sienese people in thanksgiving for the passing of the Black Death earlier that year.

Within the Palazzo Pubblico and gathered in the Museo Civico are some of the Sienese school of art's most significant works. One of the two important rooms is the Sala del Mappamondo (the Globe Room) frescoed in 1315 with two important works by the prominent local artist Simone Martini, a student of Duccio. The *Maestà (Madonna Enthroned)*, the town's patron saint, and on the opposite wall *Guidoriccio da Folignano*, a condottiere of the time in full battle regalia, were both meant to protect the city from harm. The next room, the Sala di Pace (Hall of Peace), contains the two famous allegorical frescoes by Pietro and Ambrogio Lorenzetti *The Effect of Good and Bad Government on Town and Country* (1337–39). You won't have a hard time determining which is which. They are some of the most important secular artworks handed down from the Middle Ages.

✪ **Duomo.** Pz. Duomo. Admission free to Duomo; 2,000L ($1.30) to Libreria Piccolomini; 3,000L ($2.00) to Baptistery; 5,000L ($3.30) to Museo dell'Opera. Summer daily 7:30am–7:30pm; winter daily 7:30am–1:30pm and 2:30–5pm.

Begun in 1196, this black-and-white marble striped cathedral dedicated to the Virgin Mary of the Assumption sits atop Siena's highest hill, and is one of the most beautiful and ambitious medieval churches in Italy. Much of what you see today was completed within the 13th century. The unfinished, freestanding construction to the right of the Duomo is what the Sienese call the *Facciatone* (Big Facade). Begun in 1339 (when Siena was reaching its medieval zenith and in response to Florence's construction of its own Duomo), plans were launched to build an even greater duomo that would incorporate the extant structure as the transept and thus become Christendom's largest church outside of Rome. Work was abandoned forever when money ran short and the bubonic plague of 1348 altered local history.

Local attention turned back to the original church, whose zebra-striped bands borrowed from Pisan-Lucchese architecture are reflected in the interior. Entry can be visually startling, with your focus soon being drawn to the priceless pavement mosaics, 56 masterful panels completed between the mid-14th through 16th centuries, with some finished as late as the 19th century. They are partially roped off and many are covered for protection, but all are uncovered for a few weeks around the August 15 feast day of the Assumption.

Located beneath the central vault is the octagonal pulpit, whose famous upper panels depicting the life of Christ were carved by master sculptor Nicola Pisano in the 13th century. It is considered his masterpiece, even greater than his then-recent work in Pisa's baptistery, and is one of the Duomo's most important artistic treasures. Within the Duomo at an entrance in the north (left) aisle is the lavish Libreria Piccolomini, built in the late 15th century by Francesco Piccolomini (the future Pius III) to house the important illuminated book collection of his uncle Pius II, both from an important local family. The elder pontiff's life is the subject of 10

Siena

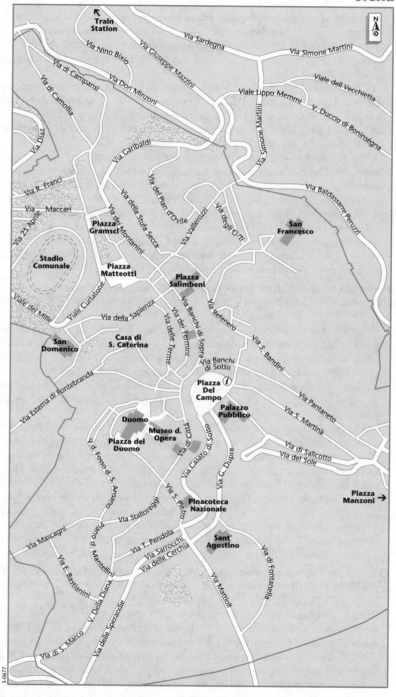

brilliantly colored frescoes, together the acknowledged masterpiece of Umbrian artist Pinturicchio, while a Roman statue of the *Three Graces* stands in the center. The late 15th-century Piccolomini altar is adorned with four statues attributed to a very young Michelangelo; although commissioned to do 15, he left early for Florence to create his *David*.

Unfortunately, few people visit the Baptistery of St. John, due to its separate entrance and obscure placement below the Duomo in the rear, a location meant to shore up the hilltop foundation. Its focal point is the 15th-century hexagonal baptismal font by Jacopo della Quercia, adorned with gilded bronze bas-reliefs panels by Donatello and Ghiberti.

The Museo dell'Opera, located in the area of the above-mentioned *Facciatone* adjoining the Duomo, houses all of the sculpture and artwork that formerly graced the cathedral. Most interesting is the first-floor statuary originally meant for the facade by Giovanni Pisano (who helped his father with the completion of the pulpit inside the church) with a single, important contribution by Donatello. Upstairs is the *Maestà* (*Madonna Enthroned*, 1311) the museum's most celebrated work; it is a complex work by Duccio di Buoninsegna, a student of Cimabue and a native son of Siena. Follow signs for access to the top of the Facciatone for an inspiring view over Siena, perhaps even better than the view from the Torre di Mangia.

Pinacoteca Nazionale (National Picture Gallery). Palazzo Buonsignori, V. San Pietro 29. Admission 8,000L ($5.25). Summer Tues–Sat 9am–7pm, Sun 8am–6pm; winter 8:30am–1:30pm and 2:30–4pm, Sun 8am–1pm.

If you have visited the Duomo Museum or the Museo Civico in the Palazzo Pubblico you will recognize some of the names and styles of the Sienese school of painters, whose works are displayed here in the Palazzo Buonsignori, a typical 14th-century construction redolent of the city's golden period of wealth and power. Though it cannot hold a candle to what was transpiring simultaneously in nearby Florence, art lovers will find this sliver of local art history fascinating, following its evolution from the 13th to the late 15th century.

The ground floor is usually bypassed on the way to the second floor's principal treasures, highlighted by the works of Duccio di Buoninsegna, simply known as Duccio. He was considered the last great painter of antiquity and the most acclaimed of Siena's movement; artistic advancements in composition, perspective, and expression can be followed in his work. His student Simone Martini is also represented, as are the Lorenzetti brothers, Pietro and Ambrogio. The predictable use of gold hangs on longer in the Sienese school than the Florentine, perhaps a preference of the patrons who commissioned these paintings to have their works shine in the gloomy medieval chapels. Florence was already onto more advanced developments, while Siena was slow to break with its religious compositions.

✪ **Enoteca Italica Permanente.** Fortezza Medicea (beyond Stadium, NW corner of town). ☎ **0577/28-84-97.** Free admission. Glass of wine 2,500L–5,500L ($1.65–$3.60). Summer daily noon–1am; winter daily noon–12:30am.

There could be no better setting to showcase Italy's timeless wine culture, making this a unique and obligatory destination for both serious connoisseurs and casual oenophiles alike. Set within the massive military fortress built by Cosimo dei Medici in 1560 after Siena had fallen to Florence, this wine-tasting bar provides a wide selection of wines to be enjoyed both inside and out, where tables are set up on the terrace. It's most popular in the late afternoon or early evening when local wine devotees and a young crowd drop in for an *aperitivo,* choosing from dozens of wines sold by the glass (wines can also be purchased by the bottle). The emphasis is on Tuscan

The Palio

To understand something of the hysteria and excitement that surrounds the twice-yearly bareback horse race that takes place in the earth-covered Piazza del Campo, it is essential to know something of the city's division into 17 contrade (wards), only 10 of which are assigned by lottery as contestants in the race. The division of the contrade (each with its own name, church, museum, social center, flag, colors, and coat of arms, and centuries-old gripes whose foundations have been lost in time) goes back to the 12th century, the running of the race in homage to the Virgin Mary. The bareback jockeys are rarely Sienese or even Tuscan. Nor are they trustworthy or ethical, and last-minute pacts and bribes are a commonplace—though highly secretive they occur between contrade and, sometimes unbeknownst even to the contrade, between the mercenary jockeys. And yet, in this treacherous, freewheeling three-lap race with (padded) death-defying corners, a horse without a rider is qualified to win. The prize? A banner of cloth painted with the image of the Virgin Mary and official bragging rights for the year.

If the point of all this escapes you, let it be known that non-Sienese Italians come from afar to experience the emotion-packed days leading up to the race, as this spectacular historical feast day is unlike any other folkloric feast in Italy, quite possibly in the world. The motivation for the annual re-creation of the pomp and pageantry of Siena's medieval past is not motivated by tourism dollars, but by a very authentic emotional pride in the city and its history. Being born and baptized into a particular contrada is a sacred thing—the contrade are the mosaic that held the city together in the past through plague and siege, and they represent a continuity and cohesion that has survived undiminished. Allegiance to one's contrada is part of local identity, and until recently, marrying outside one's contrada was a reason for ostracism. The fanatical intensity of the days before and during the Palio comes as something of a shock to outsiders, Italians and foreigners alike.

As fascinating as those 90 hair-raising demented seconds thrice around the earth-covered square is the *corteo storico* (procession in historical costume). Don't miss this event, even if it means spending hours under the Tuscan sun standing in the square (you'll make dozens of fast friendships). It is a memory you will never forget.

wines—many made in Siena's backyard—but this *enoteca* is a national concern owned and operated by the government to support the Italian wine tradition, so its 750-label collection is representative of the country's various regions.

SPECIAL EVENTS

Though travel material would have you believe otherwise, there is more to see here than just the twice-annual Palio horse race.

A two-week **Antiques Fair** takes place in February of even years. A **Wine Week (Settimana dei Vini)** takes place the first week of June at the Enoteca Nazionale. The **Settimana Musicale Sienese,** a noteworthy classical musical festival, takes place in July and August, attracting world-class names and culminating in the first week of August. Contact the tourist office for a schedule or call the Accademia Musicale Chigiana (☎ 0577/46-152), the city's prestigious music conservatory that organizes it.

Foremost of the year's events is the legendary ✪ **Palio,** held July 2 (7:30pm) and August 16 (7:00pm). Tickets in the bleachers are exorbitant, usually costing at least 200,000L ($131.60) and can only be purchased directly from the piazza's

30-some-odd stores and cafes who own the rights for ticket sales in the bleachers put up outside their businesses. Some of them have faxes; a list of names and contacts can be had from the tourist office. Tickets for either of the two Palios usually are sold out by January (and hotels by February); a last-minute appeal directly to a store or cafe owner might turn up a cancellation. The alternative is to join the crowd, estimated anywhere from 50,000 to 100,000 strong, that stands in the inner piazza (the later in the day you show up, the farther from the outer rail you'll find free space); remember this all happens during the peak summer heat, vision is limited, and emotions run high. But hey, it's free. A remarkable procession, the **corteo storico,** unfolds where each of the 17 contrade (with names like Giraffe, She-Wolf, Wave, and Tower; see box) are represented by dozens of pages, drummers, and banner-bearers dressed in the contrada's colors and elaborate historical costumes. A highlight of the parade is the synchronized flag-throwing that Sienese youths practice yearlong from their earliest days.

You can also attend two *prove,* or trial races, run the night before each Palio, though these tickets are also hard to come by (the trial races held two nights before the race offer the best chance to find tickets). If the crowd scene is too insane and the bleacher seats too expensive—and you're not related to the mayor—seek out any of the contrada's neighborhoods the evening before or, much better yet, the winning contrada's neighborhood the evening after the Palio for guaranteed celebration that will go on well into the next day, if not much of the subsequent week.

WHERE TO STAY

There are no youth hostels directly in town; ask at the tourist information office about the two located a few miles outside of town. If all the hotels listed below are full, try the English-speaking **Prenotazioni Alberghiere** (hotel reservations) stand (☎ 0577/ 28-80-84) in the Piazza San Domenico—convenient for those arriving by bus— where you'll pay 4,000L to 8,000L ($2.65 to $5.25) per reservation according to the category of hotel. Hours in summer are Monday to Saturday 9am to 8pm; winter Monday to Saturday 9am to 7pm.

Albergo Tre Donzelle. V. d. Donzelle 5 (off Banchi di Sotto), 53100 Siena. ☎ **0577/ 28-03-58.** Fax 0577/22-39-33. 27 rms, 5 with bath. 38,000L ($25.00) single without bath; 62,000L ($40.80) double without bath, 78,000L ($51.30) double with bath; 84,000L ($55.25) triple without bath, 105,000L ($69.10) triple with bath. No credit cards.

Though worn with wear, this is a favorite budget choice in a very good location. Located on a quiet side street close to the central piazza, this medium-size hotel offers basic amenities and plain rooms with decent bathrooms. English-speaking Valentina (wo)mans the front desk and will help with questions, but don't expect this to be your most memorable stay in Tuscany.

✪ **Hotel Piccolo Etruria.** V. Donzelle 3 (off Banco di Sotto), 53100 Siena. ☎ **0577/ 28-80-88.** Fax 0577/28-84-61. 13 rms with bath. TEL TV. 62,000L ($40.80) single; 95,000L ($62.50) double; 129,000L ($84.85) triple. Breakfast 6,000L ($3.95) per person. Ask about low-season rates. AE, DC, MC, V. Nearby parking 10,000L–15,000L ($6.60–$9.85) per day.

This recently refurbished hotel is lovely enough to be your base in Tuscany—it's too great a find to be used as a one-night stop. The proud Fattorini family oversaw every painstaking detail in its recent renovation, and the taste and quality level is something one usually finds in hotels thrice the cost. Rooms are simple but tasteful and charming, the use of terracotta pavements and blond oak wood ubiquitous, and housekeeping impeccable. Rooms are divided between the main building and a *dipendenza* directly across the narrow, traffic-free street; some guests prefer the privacy of the latter, others seek out the friendly presence of the Fattorini family in the former. The many appreciated touches include fresh floral bedspreads, sheer ultra-white curtains, and hair dryers in the brand-new, white-tiled bathrooms. In high season book well in advance—this secret is out.

Albergo Cannon d'Oro. V. Montanini 28 (near Pz. Matteotti), 53100 Siena. ☎ **0577/44-321.** Fax 0577/28-08-68. 30 rms with bath. TEL. 80,000L ($52.65) single; 100,000L ($65.80) double; 135,000L ($88.80) triple. Breakfast 9,000L ($5.90) per person. Rates discounted in low season. AE, MC, V.

The popular street Banchi di Sopra originates at the main square, il Campo, and ascends a few ancient, store-lined blocks before becoming Via Montanini—the convenient location of the Cannon d'Oro. Rooms here are a grab-bag of color schemes and decor, where a piecemeal job of sprucing up the place is slowly happening over the years. If your room is a disappointment and the hotel isn't full, ask for a renovated room at the same rate and you might find new bathrooms, beds with wrought-iron headboards, and firm mattresses. If not, content yourself with what is considered standard two-star decor and a helpful, English-speaking concierge.

Hotel La Toscana. V. C. Angiolieri 12 (between Banchi di Sotto and Banchi di Sopra), 53100 Siena. ☎ **0577/46-097.** Fax 0577/27-06-34. 42 rms, 22 with bath. TEL TV. 53,000L ($34.85) single without bath, 80,000L ($52.65) single with bath; 80,000L ($52.65) double without bath, 120,000L ($78.95) double with bath; 108,000L ($71.05) triple without bath, 160,000L ($105.25) triple with bath. Breakfast 10,000L ($6.60) per person. Special winter discounts that include breakfast available with 2-night minimum. AE, DC, MC, V. Nearby parking 12,000L ($7.90) per day.

The Mazzini family has been running this old-world hotel in the very heart of historic Siena since 1894. Unremarkable guest rooms in a remarkable palazzo built in 1248 are the draw for history buffs who like the 1960s bathrooms and plain, pensionelike furnishings just fine. The tradeoff is the character and charm of the common areas that begin with the entrance's oversized etched-glass doors and ends with the vaulted, frescoed TV room located in the seventh-floor tower. With the management's okay, walk up the last two floors to the tower's summit for an eagle's-nest view and the ultimate photo op.

✪ Hotel Chiusarelli. V. Curtatone 15 (near Pz. San Domenico), 53100 Siena. ☎ **0577/28-05-62.** Fax 0577/27-11-77. 50 rms with bath. TEL TV. 82,000L ($53.95) single; 120,000L ($78.95) double; 162,000L ($106.60) triple. Breakfast 12,000L (($7.90) per person. AE, MC, V.

Two regal palms (not entirely surprising flora for Tuscany) stand guard before the columned facade of this stately 19th-century villa-turned-hotel. On the outskirts of the historical center, it's an easy two-block walk from the bus station for those with light luggage, and yet also an easy walk uphill to the central piazza. This is one of the larger hotels we're listing, so availability is slightly better here during prime months. Plain, modernized rooms are prettied up with rose chenille or flowered bedspreads—light sleepers should request a room overlooking the green stadium behind, not terribly picturesque but quieter than those on the trafficked via Curatone. This is a "proper" hotel replete with bar, breakfast terrace, brick-vaulted restaurant, and, alas, tour groups that come and go—a good buy nonetheless. Ask about low-season discounts.

WHERE TO DINE

Pizzeria da Carlo e Franca. V. di Pantaneto 138 (near V. dei Pispini). ☎ **0577/22-04-85.** Pizza 5,500L–6,500L ($3.60–$4.25). Thurs–Tues noon–3pm and 5pm–midnight. No credit cards. PIZZERIA.

It's always crowded here—the pizza's too good and the prices too moderate to expect otherwise. Plain wooden tables with paper placemats can't accommodate the lines, so the more impatient patrons know to grab a *pizza al taglio* (by the slice) and eat it on the run. But if you come a little early you can sit, order an appetizer of *bruschetta* (small slabs of toasted bread brushed with garlic and drizzled with olive oil) and peruse at leisure the 30 different types of pizza and calzone. Most ultimately opt for the house specialty: *pizza alla boscaiola* with tomatoes, sausage, mushrooms, mozzarella, and garlic.

Da Roberto. V. Calzoleria 26 (near Pz. Salimbeni). ☎ **0577/28-50-80.** Pizza 5,000L–10,000L ($3.30–$6.60); primi 8,500L ($5.60); entrees 8,000L–10,000L ($5.25–$6.60). Four-course menu turistico 22,000L ($14.45). No credit cards. Wed–Mon 12:30–2:30pm and 7:30–11:30pm. TUSCAN/PIZZERIA.

The delicious pizza indubitably overshadows the full restaurant menu here. But during my last visit I broke away from my love story with Roberto's special pizza alla fattoressa (smothered with tomato, mozzarella, and thinly-sliced potatoes sprinkled with fresh rosemary) long enough to order from the other half of the menu. Homemade pici alla pettitosa, a hard-to-find spaghettilike pasta homemade here with a faintly spicy tomato sauce, followed by cosce di maiale, roast leg of pork fragrant with rosemary was my brave order. The most demanding Sienese diner would have been won over: This was *cucina toscana* as you can only hope to find at these prices. But I'm still going back for the pizza—maybe its the wood-burning oven.

✪ Antica Trattoria Papei. Pz. del Mercato 6 (southeast of Pz. del Campo), Siena. ☎ **0577/28-08-94.** Primi 8,000L–10,000L ($5.25–$6.60); entrees 10,000L–15,000L ($6.60–$9.85). MC, V. Tues–Sun noon–2:30 and 7–10:30pm. TUSCAN.

It's rather ambitious, in a city whose origins go back to the ancient Roman Empire, for a restaurant to call itself the "Old Trattoria" when its been around for a mere 50 years. But three generations of the proud Papei family have put this wonderful restaurant on the map from day one—where it intends to stay for the next half century. You'll understand why its future is secure when the homemade papparedelle alla cinghiale (flat noodles in a wild-boar–flavored tomato sauce) arrive at your outdoor table in one of the city's oldest and most popular piazzas. The quintessential Tuscan theme continues with coniglio all'arrabiata, rabbit marinated in white wine then simmered with sage and a pinch of hot pepper. Too gamy? Homemade pici, a fat spaghetti made from flour and water and simply prepared here with a full-flavored fresh tomato sauce is one of myriad possibilities for the non–hunters and gatherers among us.

SIDE TRIPS FROM SIENA

If you have access to wheels, equip yourself with a map of *Siena provincia* supplied by the tourist office and take to the hills. The **fabled Chianti region** stretches between here and Florence along the S222, where you'll want to make stops in the small towns within a half-hour's drive that are its focal points: Radda in Chianti, Castellina in Chianti, and Greve in Chianti, a small town with an irregular street plan and ancient marketplace that's worth poking around by foot. The adjacent village of Montefioralle has a medieval castle and the ornately decorated Church of San Stefano.

Along the way look for the signs DEGUSTAZIONE or VENDITÀ DIRETTA, advising that these are wine operations that offer tastings and sales direct to the public. The signs AZIENDA AGRICOLA or FATTORIA indicate the wine producing operations—some multimillion-dollar affairs, others family-run.

By car you can also take-in the nearby **Monteriggioni,** sitting atop a hill within perfectly preserved 13th-century walls or, farther afield, the wine-producing towns of southern Tuscany: Montalcino (home of the famous Brunello wine), Montepulciano, and the Renaissance jewel of Pienza, where film director Franco Zefferelli found all in place to film his *Romeo and Juliet.*

Due east of Siena is **Arezzo,** worth a day trip for its medieval *centro storico* and frescoes by Piero della Francesca and—if you can time it right—the sprawling antiques fair the first weekend of every month. Arezzo is transported back to the Dark Ages with its much-felt historical Jousting Tournament held the last Sunday in August and the first Sunday in September; even if you can't get tickets (contact the local **tourist office** at ☎ **575/37-76-78;** fax 575/20-839), go for the elaborate procession that wends through the narrow cobblestone streets beforehand—the colorful costumes and authentic armor (on knights and horses alike) are the result of archival research and Tuscan-born Zefferelli's artistic involvement.

4 Perugia

80km (50 miles) SE of Arezzo, 188km (117 miles) NE of Rome, 154km (96 miles) SE of Florence, 26km (16 miles) NW of Assisi

From Tuscany's Siena, we cross over into the region of Umbria and its commercial and economic capital. Perugia, principally known today for its celebrated university and as home to Biuttoni and Perugina chocolate, is a good home base for car-less travelers who would like to visit Umbria's small towns such as Assisi and Spoleto.

The easternmost satellite of the 12 Etruscan League cities, Perugia's strategic position would later make it a Roman stronghold beginning in the 3rd century B.C. and lasting for eight centuries. But Perugia would assert itself as a strong and progressive city, an independent *comune* with the griffin as its emblem; trade and the arts flourished, and the university was established in 1270. This was Perugia's heyday and much civic architecture was constructed upon the Roman foundations, which were, in turn, built upon the Etruscan foundations. You can peel away the epochs and follow the story of Perugia's legendary past; the griffin can still be sighted around town.

If everyone you see seems to be 21 (and playing hooky), it's because, in addition to the ancient state university, which is one of Italy's largest, there is a second university for foreigners only, with more than 5,000 students representing more than 111 countries. This explains the proliferation of concerts, pizzerias, and music stores and lends an air of energy and vitality that is all but absent in many of Italy's provincial or historical cities.

ESSENTIALS

GETTING THERE   By Train   Most trains from Rome connect in Foligno for a 3-hour trip total if you make an immediate connection (the wait can sometimes stretch to a full hour, though). There are occasional direct trains that take three hours, and direct IC trains that make the trip in about $2^{1}/_{2}$ hours. All trains cost 17,000L ($11.20), but the IC direct requires an additional 10,000L ($6.57) supplement. There are occasional direct trains from Florence, though most connect in Terontola. Direct trains take 2 hours, direct IC $1^{1}/_{4}$ hours, and trains that stop in Terontola 2 hours minimum (if the connection is immediate). All train cost 13,000L ($8.55), but the IC direct requires an 8,200L ($5.40) supplement.

Perugia's **train station** (☎ 075/50-01-091) is inconveniently located far below the town's center in Piazza Vittorio Veneto. Take bus 20, 26, 27, 28, or 29 to Piazza Italia, which is as far as they can go into the *centro storico.*

By Bus   There is one bus daily servicing Perugia from downtown Rome ($2^{1}/_{2}$ hours; 19,000L/$12.50 one-way), and another from Rome's airport ($3^{1}/_{4}$ hours; 27,000L/

$17.75 one-way). The two-hour trip from Florence costs 19,000L ($12.50) one-way. Call **SULGA** (☎ **075/50-09-641**) for information.

By Car   From Florence or Rome use the Austostrada del Sole A1 as far as the junction for Perugia, then head due east. From Siena, take the scenic S73 which will connect with the autostrada east to Perugia. Cars are not allowed within Perugia's *centro storico* and you will need to request a pass from the traffic police to drop your luggage off at the hotel before returning your car to a pay parking lot on the outskirts.

VISITOR INFORMATION   The **A.P.T. (Azienda Promozione Turistica)** or **tourist information office** is located in the very central Piazza IV Novembre, Logge della Cattedrale (behind the Cathedral), ☎ **075/57-36-458.** It is open daily 9am to noon and 3 to 7:30pm; closed Sunday afternoons. For years they have been hoping to move to a permanent location somewhere within the immediate area, so check upon arrival. Pick up a copy of *Perugia, What When and Where* to find out what's going on around town and details on upcoming events.

CITY LAYOUT   The main artery and pedestrian thoroughfare is **Corso Vannucci,** Perugia's medieval Main Street. It is anchored on the north by **Fontana Maggiore,** the city's social hub, with the Duomo just beyond it and on the south by the adjacent **piazzas della Repubblica** and **Italia,** home to the shaded Giardini Carducci park, with benches and a beautiful view over the Tiber Valley. Beneath the gardens are the foundations of the 16th-century *Rocca Paolina* fortress and the *scala mobile* network of escalators that bring you down through the ruins of the fortress to the town's lower level and bus station at Piazza Partigiani. Corso Vannucci, lined with historical cafes, bars, and the city's best stores, is the city's highest point; narrow, vaulted streets branching off west and east invariably lead down, often with steps built into them.

GETTING AROUND   With this medieval hill town's steep streets made of steps and the broad expanse of Corso Vanucci closed to traffic, the use of a car anywhere is impractical. Put on your walking shoes and wander through the city's medieval back streets, narrow, cobblestoned, vaulted, and sheltered from the summer sun.

WHAT TO SEE & DO
Corso Vannucci.

If ever there was a venue to see and be seen, the Corso Vannucci, the city's north-south pedestrian strip, is it. Small clumps of the young and beautiful stand here and there, tables are set up to collect signatures supporting human rights, local politicians, or the cause-of-the-moment, matrons with their dogs, pensioners with their cronies discussing soccer and union dues increases, cafe tables set out to capture the sun (or shade)—and that's just on an a slow moment. When it's the bewitching hour of the *passeggiata* (the evening promenade around 5 or 6pm), the entire ambulatory Perugian population seems to turn up. It's time to take some fresh air, window-shop, stop for an aperitivo in a unique theatrical backdrop that has one imagining the costumes and pageantry of the *passeggiata* in the days of the Middle Ages when Perugia was already alive with university students in the late 1200s.

✪ The Fontana Maggiore (Pz. IV Novembre). Piazza IV Novembre.

Perugia grew wealthy with grand monuments that still stand testimony today of its medieval sway—the Fontana Maggiore, the Palazzo dei Priori, the Palazzo del Cambio—perfectly preserved medieval architecture that sets Perugia apart from Italy's less-embellished cities and towns. The Fontana Maggiore (The Great Fountain), is the centerpiece of the wonderfully picturesque Piazza IV Novembre, if not all of

Perugia. The fountain has just resurfaced from an elaborate renovation finished in 1996 that has it once again appear as the city's greatest artistic treasure that it was meant to be. Designed and engineered in 1278 by a local monk and architect, Fra Bevignate, to commemorate the completion of the town's aqueduct, it was then decorated with a lower tier of 50 bas-relief panels sculpted by Nicolò Pisano, his last major work. They depict everything from Aesop's Fables and signs of the Zodiac to episodes from Genesis and the origin of ancient Rome. The upper tier of 24 statuettes and panels is attributed to Nicolò's son, Giovanni. The plain-faced cathedral to the north of the fountain was built after the fountain's completion. It was begun in 1347 and its external walls have been left in their uncompleted state. There are a number of 15th- and 16th-century paintings decorating the baroque interior, but the most curious item on display is the alleged wedding band of the Virgin Mary, displayed (though hidden within 15 boxes that graduate in size) in the Cappella del Sant'Anello, the first chapel on the left.

✪ **Palazzo dei Priori & the Galleria Nazionale dell'Umbria (National Gallery).** Cor. Vannucci 19 (at Pz. IV Novembre), Perugia. ☎ **075/57-41-247.** Admission 8,000L ($5.25). Mon–Sat 9am–9pm; Sun 9am–1pm. Closed the first Mon of every month.

The bulk of the impressive Palazzo dei Priori (the Priors' Palace) lines the west side of the Corso Vannucci, but its oldest facade presides over the Piazza IV Novembre. Dating to the 13th century, the facade is distinguished by a grand staircase, and a 13th-century griffin and Guelph lion who hold the massive, ancient chains that were once used to close the streets of Siena, stolen from the town by Perugia in the 14th century. It is crowned by a row of bristling crenellations above rows of gothic windows. Used as the town hall for hundreds of years, the Palazzo dei Priori is one of the greatest extant examples of secular architecture from its period.

Its fourth floor houses the region's most important museum of Umbrian art, the Galleria Nazionale dell'Umbria, which has just undergone an extensive refurbishment and reorganization that once again secures its former status as one of Italy's richest art collections. The gallery is a showcase of Umbrian art that traces its chronology from the 13th to the 18th centuries and the schools that influenced it. Rooms dedicated to Tuscan masters include works by Duccio, Fra Angelico, and Piero della Francesca that just about steal the show. But a dozen or so paintings by Pietro Vannucci (called Perugino), native son and Umbrian master artist, are the museum's treasure, particularly his *Pietà* and the *Adoration of the Magi* from the late 15th century. Known for his landscapes and as the teacher of Raphael, he is regarded as one of the principal figures of the Italian Renaissance. Others may contend that the gentle landscapes and deep colors of Pinturicchio, Perugino's student, occasional collaborator and the one responsible for the Piccolomini Library in Siena's Duomo, demand their fair share of attention.

It's worth a visit next door to the 15th-century Collegio del Cambio for Perugino's vibrant frescoes alone, considered to be his masterpiece. Both Pinturicchio and Raphael were said to have collaborated with him (within the Palazzo dei Priori; admission is 6,000L ($3.95).

SPECIAL EVENTS

Undoubtedly the highlight of Perugia's yearly events is the important **Umbria Jazz,** Italy's foremost jazz event, which takes place over a 10-day period in early or mid-July (names like Wynton Marsalis and Herbie Hancock almost always stay at Hotel La Rosetta). World names are guaranteed to participate and some of the less-known names perform for free; for ticket sales see either tourist information or call **075/57-32-432,** or fax 075/57-22-656. A more dispersed **Jazz Fest** is held throughout

Umbria February through April; contact the tourist information office. The **Sagra Musicale Umbra (Umbrian Festival of Sacred Music)** has been held the last two weeks of September since 1937. It attracts such major maestros as Van Karajan and Riccardo Muti (☎ **075/57-21-374,** or fax 075/57-27-614 for information). For 10 days at the end of October and the beginning of November a large **international antiques fair** is held in the Rocca Paolina (☎ **075/57-31-322**).

WHERE TO STAY

Agriturist Umbria (☎ **075/32-028;** fax 075/32-028) is an independent agency that can book for you at any of 30 Umbrian farms that rent rooms of varying costs. The tourist office can supply a list of half a dozen religious institutions that offer inexpensive lodgings as well as give information about the city's youth hostel (☎/fax **75/57-22-80**). **Promhotel Umbria** is a local travel agency that can book for you at over 80 hotels in Perugia and throughout Umbria (☎ **075/50-02-788;** fax 075/50-02-789; toll-free within Italy 0678/62-033).

Hotel Umbria. V. Boncambi 37 (west off Cor. Vannucci), 06123 Perugia. ☎ **075/57-21-203.** Fax 075/57-21-203. 18 rms with bath. TEL TV (some). 60,000L ($39.50) single; 80,000L ($52.65) double; 120,000L ($87.95) triple. Breakfast 7,000L ($4.60) per person. No credit cards.

As of a recent visit, this small hotel popular with students is acceptable enough, especially for its convenient location just off the main store-lined Corso Vannucci (it's a steep, step-lined hike up). That's the bad news; the good news is that a general face-lift promised to freshen up all rooms and include private baths is scheduled for completion in 1997. If the work is not done, make sure you ask for one of the rooms that has been finished.

Hotel Priori. V. dei Priori (west off the Cor. Vannucci), 06123 Perugia. ☎ **075/57-23-378.** Fax 075/57-23-213. 51 rms with bath. TEL TV. 85,000L ($55.90) single; 120,000L ($78.95) double; 160,000L ($105.25) triple; 185,000L ($121.70) quadruple. Breakfast included. Ask about off-season discounts. No credit cards.

Centrally positioned three short blocks down the principal Via dei Priori and directly behind the Palazzo dei Priori, this modernized hotel still enjoys the fruits of a 1995 renovation. Half the spacious rooms with terracotta floors overlook the Chiesa di San Filippo Neri, the lucky ones overlook the hotel terrace and the valley beyond. The terrace is surprisingly spacious, given the typical hill-town problems of limited space, and guests are welcome to use it at any time of the day. At least begin your day here when weather permits, when breakfast is served beneath white canvas umbrellas and yours is the terracotta roofscape and gentle countryside that inspired Umbria's painters. TVs are available upon request for 5,000L ($3.30) a day.

✪ **Palace Hotel Bellavista.** Pz. Italia 12 (at southern end of Cor. Vannucci), 06100 Perugia. ☎ **075/57-20-741.** Fax 075/57-29-092. 75 rms with bath. MINIBAR TEL TV. 90,000L ($59.20); 130,000L ($85.50) double; 160,000L ($105.25) triple. These rates reflect special discounts for Frommer's readers. Breakfast 4,500L ($2.95) continental, 15,000L ($9.85) buffet per person. AE, DC, MC, V.

For the hilltop location-with-a-view, amenities, smiling service, and value for your money, this could easily be the best hotel in Umbria. Sharing a noble 16th-century palazzo with the five-star, and three times as expensive, Bruffani Hotel just next door (of which it was once a part), this gracious old-world hotel still has grand public areas redolent of yesteryear. Intricate parquet, soaring ceilings, and wrought-iron banisters around a wide open staircase maintain the lobby's historical ambience, while the guest rooms upstairs are decidedly more contemporary. Spacious and quiet, all the rooms are lovely, but ask for one of those recently renovated with a new bath, cool beige tiles, and deluxe views. The top floor has a huge alfresco terrace blessed with that same rolling view: guests are welcome to linger for drinks, postcard inspiration, or sunbathing. I'm always tempted to set up camp here and use Perugia as my base for forays into the country.

⊙ **Hotel Fortuna Perugia.** V. Bonazzi 19 (west of Pz. Italia), 06123, Perugia. ☎ **075/57-22-845.** Fax 075/57-35-040. 34 rms with bath. TEL TV MINIBAR. 125,000L ($82.25) single; 145,000L ($95.40) double. Rates reflect special discounts for Frommer's readers. Breakfast extra at 12,000L ($7.90) per person. AE, DC, V.

The Fortuna is particularly recommended for its four-star accommodations at three-star rates (it went "down-market" and switched categories in 1996). Beveled and leaded glass doors welcome you to this charming hotel where thoughtful service and details such as silk- and dried-flower arrangements and white-lace doilies hint more of a provincial inn. That same cozy charm continues in the guest rooms where a contemporary character prevails despite the floral bedspreads and upholstery and matching blonde-wood headboards and tables. Rooms have views south over the historical center or north over the Umbrian Valley and a fifth-floor roof-garden/terrace with stunning views. Breakfast is served here in warm weather which helps explain its cost: This is a million-dollar view.

WHERE TO DINE

In addition to the restaurants below, try **Caffè Sandri, Caffè Ferrari,** or **Caffè del Cambio,** all bar/cafes on or near the Corso Vannucci, for a light lunch.

Pizzeria Il Cantinone. V. Ritorta 6 (W of the Fontana Maggiore), Perugia. ☎ **075/57-34-430.** Pizza 7,000L–8,000L ($4.60–$5.25); first courses 7,000L–12,000L ($4.60–$7.90). AE. Wed–Mon noon–3pm and 7pm–midnight. PIZZERIA/UMBRIAN.

If you're in search of something casual and inexpensive in the area of Corso Vannucci or Piazza IV Novembre, wander down the narrow street west of the Fontana Maggiore and, where the pedestrian traffic flows right onto Via Ulisse Rocchi, look to the left instead, where you'll find this popular pizzeria. Despite its central location, prices are kept moderate while the lure of their pizzas keeps the place full. There's a full menu of local specialties as well, though the steady patrons are pizza devotees who return for the pizza alla gorgonzola e funghi (made with heady gorgonzola cheese and mushrooms) or any one of the dozens of others.

Da Peppone. V. Baldeschi 4 (NW of Pz. IV Novembre, off V. Ulisse Rocchi), Perugia. ☎ **075/57-20-218.** Pizzas 7,000L–10,000L ($4.60–$6.60); 1st courses 8,000L–10,000L ($5.25–$6.60); entrees 15,000L–20,000L ($9.86–$13.15). AE, MC, V. Mon, Tues, Thurs–Sun. 12:30–2:30pm and 7:30–11:00pm. PIZZERIA/UMBRIAN.

This small, family-run eatery is more upscale than the town's usual pizzerias that overflow with the student population. Spotless green-and-white tablecloths and tasteful place settings give it the proud air of a "ristorante," yet patrons are welcome to sit for a simple pizza (or not so simple: try one with the local specialty of tartufo, truffles). Yes, the pizza is wonderful but the home-cooking usually wins out: Sample the house specialty of tortellini al tartufo, homemade daily on the premises, to see why.

⊙ **Ristorante Vecchia Perusia.** V. Ulisse Rocchi 9 (NW of Pz. IV Novembre), Perugia. ☎ **075/57-25-900.** 1st courses 7,000L–9,000L ($4.60–$5.90); entrees 9,000L–12,000L ($5.90–$7.90). No credit cards. Wed–Mon 12:30–2:30 and 7:00–11:00pm. UMBRIAN.

There are just 10 tables in this small, homey trattoria where the aroma from the open kitchen is enough to have you order one of everything. If you don't have an Umbrian grandmother, come here for the genuine *cucina umbra* that you've been missing.

Every day a new "pasta fresca" appears (look out for *tagliatelle con porcini freschi,* made with fresh mushrooms), but happy habitués all seem to go with the crepe alla perusia: homemade crepes spread with four cheeses and ham, then rolled, smothered with a mushroom-and-cream sauce, and baked. There's the menu's traditional Umbrian game (faraona, pheasant; coniglio, rabbit) to choose from, or the simplicity of a pork or veal chop simply prepared on the grill.

Da Giancarlo. V. dei Priori 36 (W of Cor. Vannucci and Palazzo Priori), Perugia. ☎ **075/ 57-24-314.** 1st courses 10,000L ($6.60); entrees 14,000L–22,000L ($9.20–$14.50). AE, V. Mon–Thurs, Sat, Sun 12:30–2:30pm and 7:30–11:00 pm. UMBRIAN.

This is the classiest of our suggestions, and the easiest to go over the top with expensive truffle-sprinkled dishes (the *spaghetti al tartufo* is pretty remarkable; it should be for $18.40). But a dinner here can be a splurge in terms of quality with a surprisingly contained check at the end of the evening, given a little caution and restraint. Easy to find, yet filled mostly with Perugians and not tourists, this brick-vaulted restaurant has a cool, contemporary air despite its 16th-century palazzo setting. Try the daily homemade pasta and the vitello al forno (roast veal) accompanied by a local *vino umbro,* and pay no more than $25.00 per person, soup to nuts.

SIDE TRIPS FROM PERUGIA

This is the countryside that gives us Orvieto's distinctive white wine and the region's unrivaled contribution to the gourmet world: truffles. Visit **Gubbio** (1 hour northeast of Perugia; take the S298), hyped as the Umbrian Siena, though I find it more like an Umbrian San Gimignano minus the towers. Ten miles to Perugia's southeast lies the small town of **Torgiano,** whose wine museum is one of the most respected in the country, and farther south the tiny town of **Deruta** (take the S3bis), known since the Middle Ages as a ceramic center. The smaller towns of Umbria are serviced by frequent buses (call **075/57-31-707** for information); trip times and one-way prices are as follows: Gubbio (70 min., 7,400L/$4.85); Todi (75 minutes., 9,200L/ $6.05); Torgiano (20 minutes, 3,200L/$2.10). Almost all buses leave from the Piazza dei Partigiana, down the scala mobile (escalator) from Piazza Italia.

5 Assisi

26km (16 miles) SE of Perugia, 48km (30 miles) N of Spoleto

More than 700 years—and countless hundreds of millions of pilgrims and tourists— have passed since St. Francis lived and died here in this small hill town that sits on the wooded slopes of Mount Subasio. And despite the mania of stores and shops that sell St. Francis everything—from ashtrays and pot holders to embroidered towels and rosary-beads—the spirit of the young barefoot monk who forsook these very material goods to preach poverty, chastity, and obedience lives on. His spirit may seem diminished at times when crowds and heat reach their peaks, but it is easy to find it again, in a quiet moment at the saint's crypt below the Lower Basilica or during a delightful walk to the shaded serenity of the hermitage outside the city's medieval walls. The universality of his humanity and love for nature transcends all nationalities and religions. If the Church had to create a figure that would endure the millennium and be so embraced by so many, they could not have outdone this disarmingly simple character who lived to love God.

Born in 1182 to a local family of textile merchants, Francis renounced his social status and youthful carousing only after a number of apparitions and visions. He traveled on foot through Italy, Spain, and Egypt, a revolutionary spirit who took the

Roman Catholic Church back to the basics when the papacy was rotten with corruption. Dante compared him to John the Baptist; his fame grew beyond the confines of Umbria and even Italy. Within 15 years there was a growing community of 5,000 Franciscans who followed his barefoot asceticism. His friendship with the lovely Clare (*Chiara*), a local girl of a noble and wealthy family who followed him, created the female Order of the Poor Clares; together they pushed this sleepy Umbrian town unto the Church's center stage, where it has remained ever since.

St. Francis's spirit somehow survives the unashamed commercialization of the town. Young groups of Italian and European students who come for seminars, and pilgrims from the earth's four corners who come to pay homage to Italy's patron saint, find in these narrow back streets something of the town as it was in the saint's own time. As a former Roman stronghold, Assisi reached its medieval zenith in the years surrounding the lives of Francis and Clare. Much of what you see today is true to its 13th-century origins, and the city, with its patrician palazzi made of a pink-tinged stone, is handsomely preserved. Atheists, agnostics, and devouts alike visit this pilgrimage site; accommodations are very good and the restaurants serving Umbrian specialties even better.

ESSENTIALS

GETTING THERE   By Train   Like rail travel to all hill towns, the inconvenience is in connecting to bus service to bring you hilltop. Buses run every 20 to 30 minutes, and almost all that stop in front of the small Assisi train station near Santa Maria degli Angeli are headed up to Piazza Matteotti, your ultimate destination. Trains from Perugia are frequent (every 30 minutes, 3,500L/$2.30 one-way). Trains from Florence connect in Terontola 20,000L/$13.15 one-way); from Rome, you transfer in Foligno (18,000L/$11.85 one-way).

By Bus   Most buses leave Assisi from Piazza Matteotti, northeast of Piazza del Comune. Frequent buses service Perugia (1 hour, 5,000L/$3.30). There is one bus daily to Rome (3 hours, 30,000L/$19.75) and two daily to Florence (2¹/₂ hours, 25,000L/$16.45).

By Car   It's only half an hour by car from Perugia, heading southeast on S3; at the junction of Route 147 follow signs east for Assisi. The entire historical center is closed to traffic, but traffic police will let you drop off your bags at a hotel; check with hotel for special agreements they may have with nearest municipal parking lot.

VISITOR INFORMATION   The **A.P.T. (Azienda Promozione Turistica)** or **tourist information office** (☎ **075/81-25-34,** fax 075/81-37-27) is in the main square, Pz. Comune 12. Hours are Monday to Friday 8am to 2pm and 3:30 to 6:30pm; Saturday 9am to 1pm and 3:30 to 6:30pm.

CITY LAYOUT   The city is long and narrow, running west to east, and even the farthest sites such as the Convent of San Damiamo and the Eremo delle Carceri can be reached by foot for those in good shape (you can taxi it back). The Basilica di San Francesco is at the westernmost end, while the center of town is the main square, Piazza del Comune. Northeast of this is Piazza Rufini, site of the Duomo, and— beyond this—the Piazza San Matteotti, last stop for all buses. Pick up a map from the Tourist Office upon your arrival.

GETTING AROUND   Your feet are all you need to get you around. Unlike some other small hill towns, taxis are on standby about town, but can only be found at a few designated places (the Basilica di San Francesco, Piazza del Comune).

WHAT TO SEE & DO

✪ **Basilica di San Francesco (St. Francis' Basilica).** Pz. di San Francesco. ☎ **075/81-90-01.** Admission to basilica free. Apr–Oct, daily dawn–dusk. Sun morning visits allowed only for those attending services. Nov–Mar, daily 6:30am–noon and 2–6pm. Basilica Treasury (Tesoro della Basilica) and the Perkins Collection (Collezione Perkins) 3,000L ($2.00), open Apr–Oct 9:30am–noon and 2–6pm; closed in winter.

The upper and lower basilica of St. Francis is the first thing you see upon approaching this pink-hued hill town: Shored up and extending from the western end of town, it was a medieval architectural feat and is still considered one of the engineering marvels of that period. If you haven't pinpointed what it is that bothers you, it most likely is what has bothered the Franciscan religious community for centuries: The commanding figure cut by the imposing two-tiered basilica has little if nothing to do with the vows of poverty and humility and stark asceticism that were the very tenets of St. Francis's back-to-basics life. While this may hardly be the lavish display of extravagance one tries to come to terms with at the Vatican, it is nevertheless disheartening to know that Fra Elias of Cortona, one of Francis's earliest disciples and the controversial monk who would be firmly in control in the years following Francis's death in 1226, cashed in on the saint's popularity by selling indulgences across Europe; his fund-raising resulted in this impious monument to wealth, a point of pilgrimage that would become second to Rome alone.

To follow the chronology of this immense shrine, visit the **Lower Basilica** (1228–30) first, reached by the entrance in Piazza Inferiore. Low, dark, and mystical—if you are lucky enough to find a moment of calm in between the arrival of fender-to-fender tour buses—the lower church is almost entirely covered with frescoes by the greatest painters of the 13th and 14th centuries. The Cappella di San Martino (first chapel on the left), dedicated to St. Martin of Tours, the father of monasticism in 4th-century A.D. France, is covered with frescoes by Simone Martini of Siena and date to the early 14th century. The earliest and one of the most prominent artists to work in the church was Cimabue (1240–1302) whose frescoes in the south transept are some of the most important here. His faded but masterful *Madonna, Child and Angels* includes St. Francis looking on, a depiction of him that you will see duplicated endless times around town. Across the transept is a cycle of frescoes that surround the *Deposition of the Cross*, considered to be one of the masterpieces of the Tuscan painter Pietro Lorenzetti, a contemporary of Simone. But the frescoes creating one of art history's greatest controversies are those attributed to Cimabue's student, Giotto. At the turn of this century, most art historians had decided that nameless followers or apprentices of Giotto had covered much of the Upper and Lower Basilica with cycles of frescoes that broke with the static icons of the Byzantine School. The 1995 completion of the renovation of the Cappella della Maddalena or Chapel of St. Mary Magdalen (the third and final one to the right of the nave), provided the confirmation of Giotto's authorship (1307) in the eyes of many Italian scholars.

From the Lower Basilica you can reach the **Crypt,** where the saint's body was not discovered until 1818; a new and typically simple stone tomb was built early this century. Four of his closest followers are buried together with St. Francis. From the Lower Basilica (behind the main altar) you can also reach the **Treasury** and **Perkins Collection.** The former contains the likes of chalices and silver objects, but also the original gray sackcloth (the brown tunic was adopted much later) worn by St. Francis. The Perkins Collection is a small but rich collection bequeathed by an American philanthropist with some surprisingly important Tuscan Renaissance artworks by Fra Angelico, Luca Signorelli, and Masolino.

From the south transept of the Lower Basilica take the stairs to the **Upper Basilica** (1230–53), built upon the romanesque framework of the lower church. Where the lower spaces encouraged contemplation and meditation, the upper reaches of the airy, gothic basilica are another experience entirely: Tall, bathed in light, it was created, it would seem, as the blank canvas on which Giotto was to create the masterpiece frescoes depicting the life of St. Francis (1296–1304). Twenty-eight scenes (the last four not attributed to Giotto) unfold left to right beginning in the transept; one of the most recognizable panels is the *Sermon to the Birds,* underlining the saint's tenet that all nature is the reflection of God. In many of the narrations you will see medieval Assisi illustrated much as you see it now, starting with the very first panel's *Homage in Piazza del Comune.*

Giotto was believed to be just 29 when he began this cycle of frescoes, already a longtime lay follower of St. Francis. He seemed to particularly embrace the message of St. Francis, whose love of man and warmth of expression is reflected in Giotto's radical break from the lifeless images of the Byzantines' icons. The single undivided nave was meant to accommodate the masses while Giotto's extensive pictorial narrations were meant to educate them about Assisi's native son while attempting to express his love for nature and humanity. Francis broke with the traditional excesses of the medieval papacy as Giotto would revolutionize the art world with his break from the lifeless Byzantine order.

Other highlights of the Upper Basilica is the 15th-century choir, made of 105 inlaid stalls. The choir's central "throne" was reserved for the pope, the only papal throne outside of St. Peter's. Located behind and above in the left transept is a cycle of badly damaged cycles by Cimabue dominated by his dramatic *Crucifixion.*

Eremo delle Carceri (Prisons' Hermitage). V. Eremo d. Carceri. No phone. Donations appreciated. 8am–dusk. About 2¹/₂ miles outside town.

St. Francis and his followers spiritually "imprisoned" themselves in prayer at this rural retreat on the wooded slope of Monte Subasio. They lived in tiny carceri or cells naturally carved out of the stone centuries before the extant friary was built. A time-worn holm oak, thought to be at least 1,000 years old, still stands supported by metal bars near the saint's cave where he meditated and prayed. The gnarled tree is said to have shaded Francis and the birds that gathered to listen to his sermons; they once flew off in the four cardinal directions, symbolizing how the Franciscans would one day leave Assisi to bring the word of Francis to all corners of the world.

Leave behind the crowds in the basilica and the town's tacky tourist shops; it's an easy one-hour walk from the Porta Cappuccini (leaving from the Rocca Minore is not recommended as the pathway is not as clearly marked) on a paved road past cypresses and with wide-open views used by both pedestrians and cars (taxis should charge 20,000L to 25,000L/$13.15 to $16.45 one-way). A handful of friars still live at the retreat established by St. Bernardino in the 15th century and act as guides; a donation of any size is appreciated—the friars live by alms alone. A visit here better conveys the spirit and serenity of St. Francis than the cavernous basilica built by his followers.

Basilica di Santa Chiara. Pz. di Santa Chiara (SW of Pz. d. Comune). Free admission. 7am–noon and 2pm–dusk.

St. Clare died in the Convent of San Damiano on August 12, 1253; just 12 years later this pink-and-white basilica was dedicated to her and became the home of the Poor Clares. The interior is Spartan, thanks to the 17th-century obliteration of elaborate frescoes that were whitewashed over by orders of a German bishop who attempted to discourage tourism and the temptations it would supply the nuns. The small, adjacent Church of San Giorgio predates the basilica; it was the site of Francis's early schooling and where his remains awaited the completion of the Basilica of St. Francis upon his death. Today it houses the 12th-century Crucifix of San Damiano that spoke to him in 1209, informing him of his calling. The chapel also contains the remains of St. Clare. The Basilica's terrace offers lovely views of the surrounding countryside.

Convento di San Damiano. 1 1/2 miles from Porta Nuova. No phone. Free admission. 8am–noon and 2pm–dusk. Transportation by foot, car, or taxi.

Standing alone amid the olive groves and wildflowers, amid the serenity of the Spoleto Valley, this spot easily evokes the time and atmosphere of a young Francis who came here (the church dates to the 11th century) to escape the wrath of his father. It was in this church in 1209 that a wooden crucifix told a 27-year-old Francis to "repair the Church," referring to the decadent papacy and corrupt monastic orders (the crucifix is now housed in the Basilica of St. Clare). Francis took the orders literally, however, and sold his father's textile stock and offered the money to San Damian's priest, who threw the money pouch back at him. In 1210, he would find the approval of Pope Innocent III to create his own order of mendicant monks and, in 1212, a second order for women. St. Clare would later live here at San Damiano, though her Order of Poor Clares would move up to the newly constructed Basilica of St. Clare upon her death; you can visit the 13th-century convent's dormitory where a cross marks the spot of the saint's death. The cloisters and refectory still have the original tables and benches where the nuns shared their Spartan meals. St. Francis visited just once during Clare's stay here and is said to have composed his famous *Canticle of the Creatures.*

From the Piazza Santa Chiara or the Church of Santa Chiara, take Via Borgo Aretino and at Porta Nuova (the eastern gate to the city) take a right and head south down a steep road to the Convent of San Damiano following the signs. It's 20 to 30 minutes downhill; a road for vehicle traffic runs parallel to a pedestrian road. Taxis who have dropped passengers off are usually lingering about to take you back uphill for 20,000L to 25,000L ($13.15 to $16.45) one-way.

SPECIAL EVENTS

The **Settimana Santa (Holy Week)** that precedes Easter is understandably commemorated in this site of religious pilgrimage with numerous processions between churches, including evocative nighttime processions by torchlight. The feast day of the **Calendimaggio** is the year's largest event and is celebrated during a 3-day period the first week of May (starting the first Thursday after May 1) when the entire town is thrown back to its medieval glory. Reenacting the rivalry between two ancient factions of town, there are competitions of concerts, crossbows, and flag-throwing, to name a few, and the entire town turns out in elaborate medieval costume, invoking the days of St. Francis. Oddly, San Rufino and not St. Francis is the patron saint of Assisi, and his **feast day** is celebrated August 11 with a procession and crossbow contest in medieval costume. October 3 and 4 commemorate the **Death of St. Francis** (1226) who, as patron saint of the country, is duly honored with great pageantry.

WHERE TO STAY

If you've arrived during high season and need help finding a room, call the **Consorzio Albergatori,** Viale Marconi (☎/fax **075/81-35-99**), a kind of clearinghouse for local hotels that will help you stick to your budget by booking a hotel category you request; a fee is determined by daily rate.

Unless it's all the same to you, make sure you insist on being in the historical center of town and not the satellite of Santa Maria degli Angeli (which always tries to pass itself off as *Assisi centro* to unwitting tourists) down near the train station or, worse yet, the town of Bastia where tour buses usually put up their groups.

SMALL TWO-STAR DELIGHTS   A number of small hotels in the historical center of town offer limited accommodations only slightly more expensive than the religious institutions. With an average of seven rooms-with-baths at approximately 85,000L to 100,000L ($55.92 to $65.80) each, they fill up fast and are often closed in the winter months. Try the following: **Hotel La Fortezza,** Vc. d. Fortezza 19b (☎/fax **075/81-24-18;** see "Where to Dine" below); **Hotel Lieto Soggiorno,** V. A. Fortini (☎ **075/81-61-91**); **Hotel Palotta,** V. San Rufino 6 (☎/fax **075/ 81-23-07**); **Hotel Properzio,** V. San Francesco 38 (☎ **075/81-31-88;** fax 075/ 81-52-01).

RELIGIOUS INSTITUTIONS

The tourist information office has a list of *Case Religiose di Ospitalità*, some 20 local religious convents, monasteries, and religious-run hostelries that offer accommodations; a double with bath ranges from 50,000L to 80,000L ($32.90 to $52.65) and many close for the low season mid-November through mid-March. The following is the only American religious order, though almost all others are English-speaking to some degree.

Sisters of the Atonement (Suore dell'Atonement). V. Galeazzo Alessi 10 (NE of the Pz. d. Comune), 06081 Assisi. ☎ **075/81-25-42.** Fax 075/81-25-42. 20 rms with bath. 40,000L ($26.30) single; 70,000L ($46.05) double; 105,000L ($69.10) triple. Breakfast included. No credit cards. Closed mid-Nov to mid-Mar. Parking available on grounds (donation welcomed).

The gracious, ever-smiling Sisters of the Atonement welcome you into their inn, whose foundations go back to the medieval times of St. Francis and St. Clare. The American sisters offer simple spotless rooms and a terrace and graveled patio whose valley views can prove as calming as a visit to their small chapel. Reserve a 1pm lunch family-style (20,000L/$13.15) where pilgrims and travelers share tables and exchange travel anecdotes. A two-night minimum is required, and a one-night deposit (personal U.S. checks accepted) by mail is requested to hold your room.

HOTELS

✪ **Hotel Sole.** Cor. Mazzini 35 (2 blocks E of Pz. d. Comune), 06081 Assisi. ☎ **075/81-23-73.** Fax 075/81-37-06. 35 rms with bath. TEL TV. 80,000L ($52.65) single; 95,000L ($62.50) double; 123,000L ($80.90) triple. Breakfast 10,000L ($6.60) per person. Ask about low-season rates in winter and July. AE, DC, MC, V. Nearby parking 10,000L ($6.60) per day.

This is one of the loveliest family-run hotels for these prices that I have seen in Umbria. Its excellent location is enhanced by the charm of the freshly redone rooms on the top two floors and those across the street in the annex (even those not yet refurbished are nice enough). There's an elevator in the annex, though not in the principal building, yet I prefer the latter whose spacious rooms have been done with more charm and antique (and antique-inspired) wrought-iron painted beds and thoughtfully chosen framed prints. Beige chenille bedspreads and light terracotta tiles keep things cool while exposed stone walls and wide marble staircases hint of the building's antiquity. The family's restaurant, Hostaria Ceppo della Catena, is set in a series of stone-vaulted rooms in a 15th-century palazzo adjacent to the restaurant, where half-board can be arranged (80,000L/$52.65 per person, double-occupancy basis). Consider at least one meal here of local Umbrian cooking: first courses run 8,000L to 10,000L ($5.25 to $6.60); entrees 9,000L to 16,000L ($5.90 to $10.50).

Hotel Umbra. V. degli Archi 6 (off SW corner of Pz. d. Comune), 06081 Assisi. ☎ **075/81-22-40.** Fax 075/81-36-53. 25 rms with bath. A/C MINIBAR TEL TV. 100,000L ($65.80) single; 140,000L ($92.10); 170,000L ($111.85) triple. Buffet breakfast 15,000L ($9.86) per person. AE, DC, MC, V. Closed mid-Jan–Feb. Nearby parking 15,000L ($9.86) a day.

The majority of this three-star hotel dates back to the 15th century, but the basement's laundry and kitchen area boast ancient Roman foundations. Three generations of a local family have proudly run this excellently situated hotel, known for its well-respected alfresco restaurant (fixed-price 35,000L/$23); patrons dine in a shaded garden patio where birdsong easily reminds you that St. Francis was born just blocks away. When booking, ask for one of the rooms that overlook the Umbrian Valley. Most rooms are highlighted with 18th- and 19th-century antiques; all are scheduled to have air-conditioning soon.

Hotel dei Priori. Cor. Mazzini 15 (1 block E of the Pz. d. Comune), 06081 Assisi. ☎ **075/81-22-37.** Fax 075/81-68-04. 4 rms with bath. A/C TEL TV. 115,000L ($75.65) single; 168,000L ($110.50) double; 218,000L ($143.42) triple; 258,000L ($169.73) quadruple. Breakfast included. AE, DC, MC, V. Closed Nov. 20–Mar 15. Parking nearby 10,000L ($6.60).

A stay in this seigniorial 16th-century palazzo of grand proportions and stained-glass windows will bring you back in time when local families made their fortunes in trade and textiles and lived like royalty, as can you—for a price. Royal rates are something this book avoids, but I find the lovely rooms in this hotel housed in a landmark building to be reasonable, particularly if you can wrangle one of the few rooms (no. 201 or no. 202) with 19th-century frescoed ceilings. Persian runners and valuable antiques and handsome prints decorate both the public rooms and guest rooms. This is the type of character and history you would never be able to afford in a similar hotel in Rome or Florence. Ask for off-season discounts (including July).

Hotel Giotto. V. Fontebella 41 (just E of Pz. San Francesco), 06082 Assisi. ☎ **075/81-22-09.** Fax 075/81-64-79. 70 rms with bath. MINIBAR TEL TV. 130,000L ($85.52) single; 180,000L ($118.40) double. Rates include special discount for Frommer's readers. Breakfast included. AE, DC, MC, V. Parking available on grounds.

This large hotel, located in the western part of town not far from St. Francis Basilica, has five floors built into the side of the hill with wonderful views from almost all of its rooms. If you ask when booking, the staff will do their best to hold one of the five rooms that share a large terracotta terrace. A wonderful outdoor breakfast terrace comes equipped with the same expansive view that includes the romanesque church of San Pietro below. The rooms are nice in an old-fashioned kind of way, with brass headboards and bathrooms that will soon need a face-lift but are fine for the moment. The hotel had a four-star (first-class) rating until 1966, when it went down-market, but gracious aspects of its public areas—open landings of patterned gray-and-white marble tiles, wrought-iron handrails, and Persian runners on the wide marble steps—are reminiscent of its recent status. The view still remains, and it is a four-star beauty.

WHERE TO DINE

Pizzeria Duomo. V. Porta Perlici 11 (N of Pz. San Rufino), Assisi. ☎ **075/81-63-26.** Pizza 5,000L–9,000L ($3.30–$5.90); pastas 8,000L–9,000L ($5.25–$5.90). AE, DC, MC, V. Daily noon–2pm and 5pm–midnight; closed Wed in winter. PIZZERIA.

Just barely beyond the Piazza Comune–Piazza San Rufino route enough to discourage the masses, this is a casual and reliable place frequented by locals. With three spacious rooms in medieval surroundings and the modern-day luxury of air-conditioning, you can always find a cool respite here despite the wood-burning oven, which produces a stream of delicious, bubbling pizzas. There are more than 30 to pick from, but it looks like the simple *pizza alla margherita* (with tomato, oregano, and mozzarella) and the *pizza con funghi porcini* (with fresh porcini mushrooms) contend for first place. The region's famous Norcia truffles show up on the *pizza al tartufo*, a delicious "white pizza" (no tomato sauce) of mozzarella and black truffles. Pastas, fresh vegetables, and salads are also available, and carbohydrate lovers whose idea of heaven is a pizza, some pasta, and a beer will be most happy here.

Trattoria Pozzo della Mensa. V. Pozzo d. Mensa 11 (off V. San Rufino), Assisi. ☎ **075/ 81-62-47.** Pastas 8,500L–16,000L ($5.60–$10.50); entrees 8,000L–20,000L ($5.25– $13.15). AE, DC, V. Daily noon–2:30pm and 7–9:30pm. Closed Wed in winter and 3 weeks late January/early February. UMBRIAN.

On a hidden alleyway off the street that connects Piazza Comune and Piazza San Rufino is this bustling spot where you can have a delicious Umbrian meal inexpensively—if you don't surrender to the temptation of tartufo-flavored dishes. On the other hand, even the prices for truffle dishes are very reasonable, so if you want to see what all the fuss is about, sample the homemade *strengozzi al tartufo*, a typical Umbrian pasta, or ravioli al tartufo, filled with cheese—both are flavored with the potent black tubular that put Umbria on the culinary map. Among the entrees are regional specialties such as coniglio (rabbit) and agnello (lamb) or, if your first course has you hooked, the specialty tornedo del Pozzo, a tender beef fillet marinated in red wine and flavored with, you guessed it, black truffles.

✪ **La Fortezza.** V. d. Fortezza 2b (north of Pz. Comune), Assisi. ☎ **075/81-24-18.** Pastas 10,000L–15,000L ($6.60–$9.85); entrees 11,000L–18,000L ($7.25–$11.85). AE, DC, MC, V. Mon–Wed, Fri–Sun 12:30–2:30pm and 7:00–10:30pm. Closed in Feb. UMBRIAN.

Up a stepped alleyway across from the Tourist Information Office and considered by many to be the best place in town, this lovely and very centrally located restaurant has been family-run for 35 years and is prized for its high quality and very reasonable prices. An exposed ancient Roman wall to the right of the restaurant's entrance immediately establishes the antiquity of this handsomely refurbished palazzo with brick-vaulted ceilings, the rest of which dates to the 13th century. The delicious homemade pastas are prepared with sauces that follow the season's fresh offerings, while the roster of meats skewered or roasted on the grill (alla brace) range from veal and lamb to duck. The ubiquitous tartufo nero (black truffle) is available here, yet contained prices can guarantee you one of your most enjoyable meals in Umbria for approximately 30,000L ($19.75)—house wine included! La Fortezza also rents seven rooms upstairs; see "Small Two-Star Delights" above.

6 Spoleto

129km (80 miles) N of Rome, 209km (130 miles) S of Florence, 48km (30 miles) SE of Assisi, 64km (40 miles) SE of Perugia

The Festival of the Two Worlds put Spoleto back on the map after centuries of historical obscurity. However, it was the obscurity that is responsible for the town's untouched medieval preservation that makes it worth visiting, even when the world-class arts festival is not turning it on its ear. Established by Italian-American composer Gian Carlo Menotti in 1957, the celebrated arts festival brings together performers from all over the world for three weeks of dance, concerts, art, and drama known for their diversity and quality.

Much is made of the city's Roman past. As Spoletium, it was one of the empire's most important outposts. On the well-trafficked axis linking Rome and Ravenna it flourished for centuries, becoming the important Lombard Duchy of Spoleto from the 6th to the 8th centuries. The arrival of the emperor Barbarossa in 1155 saw widespread destruction, after which the city only partially recovered before falling into the hands of the Church. The 15th-century Pope Alexander VI presented the town to his teenage daughter and appointed her governor. And that was pretty much the cap on excitement until Maestro Menotti arrived in 1957.

ESSENTIALS

GETTING THERE   By Train   Spoleto is on the popular Rome/Ancona line; to/ from Rome is 1 hour, 40 minutes (12,500L/$8.25 one-way). There are numerous trains to/from Assisi, $^1/_2$ hour (3,500L/$2.30); these trains continue onto Perugia, 1 hour (5,600L/$3.70). Public buses run from the train station in the Lower Town to the Upper Town's Piazza della Libertà. The tourist office has schedules posted.

By Bus   There are two buses daily to/from Perugia (1$^1/_2$-hour trip; 5,600L/$3.60) and one bus daily to/from Rome (1 hour, 50 minute trip; 6,500L/$4.25). The tourist information office has schedules posted.

By Car   From Perugia or Assisi, head south on S3 to Spoleto, an easy 30-minute drive from Assisi. Once you arrive in Spoleto, it is best to leave your car parked in the Upper Town, preferably at your hotel or close to it. Ask about parking arrangements when making your reservations.

VISITOR INFORMATION   The tourist information office or Azienda di Promozione Turistica (A.P.T.) is located in the central Pz. d. Libertà 7 (☎ **0743/ 22-03-11;** fax 0743/46-241). Summer hours are Monday to Friday, 9am to 1pm and 4:30 to 7:30pm, Saturday to Sunday 10am to 1pm and 4:30 to 7:30pm (all hours are slightly extended during the Festival of Two Worlds); winter hours run Monday to Friday, 9am to 1pm and 3:30 to 6:30pm, Saturday 10am to 1pm and 3:30 to 6:30pm, and Sunday 10am to 1pm (closed Sundays in January and February).

STROLLING AROUND SPOLETO

With the exception of the Duomo, there is no plethora of must-see sites like those that fill the itineraries of visits to other hill towns. Yet a visit here can be every bit as enjoyable, if only for a walk through town, one that illustrates the antiquity of a city that is still very much alive, and that does not live for tourism's sake alone.

Begin your walk at the **A.P.T. office** Piazza della Libertà, which will supply you with a map and any other information you might need. Just west of here is the ancient **Teatro Romano** that dates back to the 1st century A.D., when Spoleto was a thriving Roman city. It has recently been restored and is a popular venue for festival performances.

From the Piazza della Libertà, take a right on Via Brignone and a left on Via Arco di Druso, which leads into the **Piazza del Mercato,** a window to centuries past. A daily produce and flower market takes over the ancient square, originally the site of the ancient Roman Forum, in organized chaos every morning except Sunday. The second Sunday of every month a Mercato delle Briciole takes place, where merchants hawk collectibles and choice antiques together with the undesirable. Stores around its periphery sell the gourmet products of Umbria, including the prized black truffles from nearby Norcia. Outdoor cafes such as the **Bar Primavera** (excellent gelato) set up tables outside as alfresco command posts for taking in the piazza life. Explore the vaulted alleyways and hidden corners just off the piazza, or follow the characteristic Via dei Duchi north out of the Piazza del Mercato to window-shop on one of the city's most pleasant streets. At its end, turn left onto Via del Mercato or right onto Via Fontesecca for more streets evocative of the city's medieval past, now inhabited by tasteful shops, antique stores, and boutiques.

It's a short walk east to the **Duomo,** a 12th-century building (on the site of a 7th-century church) whose lovely facade is graced by five rose windows and crowned with a mosaic by Solsterno (1207). The most illustrious (and recently restored) pictorial masterpiece of the city is found in the domed apse, the last works done by the Florentine painter Filippo Lippo (1467–69). From left to right they are the *Annunciation,* the *Passage of the Virgin Mary,* and the *Nativity;* the *Coronation* fills the space above. In the scene of the Virgin's death you'll find self-portraits of the painter and his son Filippino to the right. Filippino also designed his father's tomb found in the right transept; the body mysteriously disappeared two centuries later. The Duomo is open from 8am to 1pm and 3 to 6:30pm (closing at 5:30pm in winter). Down the steps on the west side of the Piazza Duomo are the shaded, hanging gardens of the **Piazza della Signoria,** whose benches and postcard views of the valley make this the city's most idyllic picnic spot (buy your provisions at the open-air market before vendors pack up at 1pm).

The decade-long renovation of the towered and crenellated papal **Rocca fortress** is rumored to be near completion. It was recently used as a prison, most recently having housed Pope John Paul II's would-be assassin Ali Agha for a brief period. Take a walk up, if only for the town's best views and a visit to the 14th-century **Ponte delle Torri.** Initially begun upon the foundation of an ancient Roman aqueduct, it was later incorporated into the city's defenses. Its 10 gothic arches span a 760-foot-wide chasm 240 feet above a torrent. A favorite summertime hike is to the rural retreat and **monastery of Monteluco,** once favored by St. Francis. If the footbridge is closed, as it often is, you can catch a bus from Piazza della Libertà (2,600L/$1.70) for the 5-mile ride. The tourist office can supply you with maps of walking paths to Monteluco and other sites of interest in the immediate countryside.

✪ THE FESTIVAL OF TWO WORLDS

For three weeks every year beginning in the last week of June, Spoleto turns its attention to the Festival of Two Worlds, an American-Italian collaboration that celebrates its 40th anniversary in 1997. World-class symphonies and music ensembles, dance and drama troupes come from all over the world, culminating in the final evening's SRO symphonic performance in the Piazza del Duomo. There are often 5 to 10 events happening daily at different indoor/outdoor venues about town. Tickets go on sale mid-April from the **Teatro Nuovo** (☎ **0743/40-265**), although this is problematic since they aren't yet accepting credit cards. "Fringe" and "alternative" performances are finding their way into the program to resuscitate some of the cutting-edge energy of the festival's early years, and tickets can often be found at the last moment. For a general program contact, and instructions for ticket purchase after mid-April, contact: **Associazione Festival dei Due Mondi,** V. Cesare Beccaria 18, Rome 00196 (☎ **06/32-10-288;** fax 0743/32-00-747).

WHERE TO STAY

Rates are usually discounted November through March (low season). If you plan to visit during the festival, book two to three months in advance (last-minute cancellations are rare); you might also consider commuting by car or bus from Perugia or the neighboring towns. Note that prices during the three-week festival may be higher than those quoted below: Hoteliers charge whatever they believe the demand will support.

Albergo dell'Angelo. V. Arco di Druso 25 (off Pz. d. Mercato), 06049 Spoleto. ☎ **0743/ 22-23-85.** Fax 0743/22-16-95. 7 rms with bath. TEL TV. 90,000L ($59.20) double; 117,000L ($76.80) triple. Breakfast not available. Prices discounted 25% low season. V.

Receiving travelers since the 15th century, Spoleto's oldest hotel is located in one of the city's most colorful corners just south of the market square. You might be sleeping in Goethe's room or next door to Rossini's; they undoubtedly appreciated the columns and stained-glass windows that tell of the palazzo's eventful history. The current owner moonlights as an antiques dealer who dabbles with Sotheby's in London, but some of his best 19th-century pieces have stayed behind to decorate the guest rooms: hand-painted wrought-iron beds and massive carved armoire and headboard sets. Guests will like the old-world character of this pensionelike hostelry while projected plans to redo all bathrooms should bring standards more up-to-date. Those who see nothing romantic about the terracotta tiles worn by 500 years of traffic will fare better at the bright and newly fitted rooms at Hotel il Panciolle.

Hotel Aurora. V. Apollinare 3 (on Pz. d. Libertà), 06049 Spoleto. ☎ **0743/22-03-15.** Fax 0743/22-18-85. 15 rms with bath. TEL TV MINIBAR. 80,000L ($52.65) single; 100,000L ($65.80) double; 130,000L ($85.50) triple. Breakfast 8,000L ($5.25) per person. Prices discounted 20%–25% off-season. AE, DC, MC, V.

Directly off the principal Piazza della Libertà in a small courtyard that ensures a central location but quiet nights, this popular hotel is especially recommended if you can procure one of the five renovated guest rooms—ask when booking. Rather stylish for these rates, the new rooms boast a warm, coordinated decor of wall-to-wall carpeting, discreetly patterned wallpaper, and rich, heavy curtains of deep mauve. The other rooms—with bathrooms that hark back to the 1970s—have been kept up but are due for a facelift. The hotel's Ristorante Apollinare is one of the city's more upscale dining spots with a menu offering regional Umbrian specialties prepared with a light, and at times creative, hand. The special menu of 30,000L ($19.75) per person for hotel guests comes recommended for those preferring a less casual—and highly convenient—alternative to the restaurants listed below.

Hotel Charleston. Pz. Collicola 10 (NW of Pz. d. Libertà), 06049 Spoleto. ☎ **0743/22-00-52.** Fax 0743/22-20-10. MINIBAR TV TEL . 18 rms with bath. 107,000L ($70.40) single; 149,000L ($98.02) double; 190,000L ($125.00) triple. Breakfast included. AE, DC, MC, V. Garage parking 15,000L ($9.85) per night.

Much of the hotel's centuries-old character survived a recent renovation with open fireplaces, chestnut-beamed ceilings, and terracotta pavements admirably intact. Within such a historical context, the mix of contemporary furnishings and artwork is a seamless and tasteful one. Despite its small size, the Charleston is run with an efficient air, offers amenities such as a sauna, and organizes open-air art exhibitions in the small piazza in front, as well as walking tours and bicycle outings in the immediate area.

✪ **Hotel Nuovo Clitunno.** Pz. Sordini 6 (just W of Pz. d. Libertà), 06049 Spoleto. ☎ **0743/22-33-40.** Fax 0743/22-26-63. 38 rms with bath. TEL TV. 85,000L ($55.90) single; 130,000L ($85.50) double; 160,000L ($105.25) triple. Buffet breakfast included. Rates discounted off-season. AE, DC, MC, V. Closed Feb. Free parking available.

Little is left that recalls this 19th-century palazzo's past incarnation as a firehouse. The Tomassoni family's welcome augments the comfort and warmth of the public area's fireplace, beamed ceilings, and gold-plastered walls. To accommodate disparate tastes, the guest rooms have recently been refitted in two distinct styles. Request "Old Style" and you'll have reserved one of 10 lovely rooms with terracotta floors, antique iron beds, armoires, and rough-hewn ceiling beams. The majority of rooms are decorated in a "standard" style, with stylish contemporary furnishings in warm, pastel colors. All have new bathrooms but only 15 of the standard-style rooms offer a handsome view over the Vale Spoletino. Not all rooms have air-conditioning; it is available at no extra cost, but should be requested when booking. Be assured that the Tomassoni try to accommodate wherever possible—and then some.

Hotel il Panciolle. V. d, Duomo 3–5 (2 blocks W of the Pz. d. Signoria), 06049 Spoleto. ☎ **0743/45-677.** 7 rms with bath. TEL. 55,000L ($36.20) single; 80,000L ($52.65) double; 100,000L ($65.80) triple. Breakfast 7,500L ($4.95) per person. Rates discounted 20%–25% low season. AE, V.

You can't beat this inexpensive family-run place for new, clean, and nicely decorated accommodations so close to the Duomo. Newly painted white walls offset the guest rooms' matching sets of oak headboard, armoire, and bedside table—proof that careful attention went into the decoration of these seven simple rooms. Chenille bedspreads and light terracotta floors keep everything looking fresh and looked-after; bathrooms are smallish but were recently redone and are as nice as you could hope for at these rates. In warm weather breakfast can be enjoyed on the restaurant's flagstone terrace, also a pleasant setting for dinner (see "Where to Dine," below).

WHERE TO DINE

✪ **Enoteca Provinciale.** V. A. Saffi 7 (between Pz. d. Duomo and Pz. d. Mercato), Spoleto. ☎ **0743/22-04-84.** Antipasti 2,000L–6,000L ($1.30–$3.95); pastas and omelets 6,500L–11,000L ($4.25–$7.25); soups 6,000L ($3.95). Wines and liqueurs by the glass 2,500L–4,000L ($1.65–$2.65). AE, DC, MC, V. Summer daily 10am–midnight; winter daily 10am–8:30pm. UMBRIAN.

Make at least one of your lunches, light dinners, or snacks in this medieval tower where casual meals are accompanied by self-organized wine tastings. Meals consist of the region's simplest—and in this case the most delicious—offerings: The toasted *bruschetta all'olio di Spoleto* showcases the local olive oil; homemade *strangozzi al tartufo* pasta is just an excuse to revel in its unrivaled truffle sauce; *polenta alla spoletina* is made with a barleylike flour (not the usual cornmeal) and heaped with sausage and lentils. Did I mention that the focus here was the wine? You can order more than 30 red and white Umbrian wines by the glass, but toast the night with the very unusual *amaro di tartufo*, a bitter made from the ubiquitous truffle. Eat and drink as little or as much as you want; the atmosphere is relaxed and jovial and you'll be welcomed into the fold the longer you stay and the more you imbibe.

Trattoria del Festival. V. Brignone 8 (N and E of the Pz. d. Libertà), Spoleto. ☎ **0743/22-09-93.** Primi 7,000L–10,000L ($4.60–$6.60); entrees 12,000L–14,000L ($7.90–$9.20); pizza 6,000L–10,000L ($3.95–$6.60); menu turistico 23,000L ($15.15). MC, V. Mon–Thurs and Sat–Sun 12:30–2:30pm and 7:30–10:30pm. UMBRIAN.

Don't be put off by the menu written in four languages; this place caters primarily to locals—always a good sign. Linen tablecloths and contemporary chairs belie its reputation as one of the town's best pizzerias (including their signature pizza con tartufo with truffles). The menu turistico here is particularly appealing, starting with simple bruschetta drizzled with the local olive oil, and including a pasta, meat entree, and fresh vegetable. Meals can be ordered à la carte from a full trattoria menu with an emphasis on regional specialties of pastas and grilled meats.

Pizzeria Arco di Druso. V. Arco di Druso 25 (off Pz. d. Mercato), Spoleto. ☎ **0743/22-16-95.** Primi 7,000L–12,000L ($4.60–$7.90); entrees 10,000L–20,000L ($6.60–$13.15); pizzas 7,000L–13,000L ($4.60–$8.55). Menu turistico 25,000L ($16.45). MC, V. Tues–Sun 12:30–2:30pm and 7:00–11:00pm. PIZZERIA.

With a location practically within the daily market, there's little doubt that what winds up on your plate was a farmer's freshly-picked special this morning. Still known as All'Angelo, a recent change of management has left this popular spot's reputation as a favorite pizzeria secure: The wood-burning stove turns out a stellar *pizza al tartufo* and *pizza con funghi porcini* with mushrooms. Ceilings alternate between vaulted brick and exposed wooden beams, redolent of the palazzo's origins in the 1400s as horse stables. Humans now chow down in two busy rooms with murals and pink linen tablecloths, a fancy setting for such simple offerings as the delicious *polenta con funghi porcini*. Any of the season's changing pastas are good; ask which is the day's *pasta fatta a casa* or homemade specialty.

Il Panciolle. V. d. Duomo 3–5 (W of Pz. d. Signoria), Spoleto. ☎ **0743/45-598.** Reservations suggested. Primi 9,000L ($5.90); entrees 10,000L–16,000L ($6.60–$7.90). AE, V. Thurs–Tues 12:30–2:30pm and 7:30–10:30pm. UMBRIAN.

This family-run restaurant, popular with performers during the festival, offers two wonderfully distinctive eating experiences: a wintertime evening in the cantina's stone-walled room with beamed ceilings and an open fireplace, where the aroma of roasting meat teases your appetite before you're even seated; and in the warm weather a dinner on the open flagstoned terrace, shaded by a huge pine and enhanced by an open view of the Spoleto Valley. What remains invariable is the *cucina umbra casalinga*, the home-cooking Umbria-style that is the kitchen's specialty. Homemade *strangozzi* pasta can be enjoyed simply prepared with *aglio e olio* (garlic and olive oil) or dressed up royally with *funghi e tartufi* (truffles and mushrooms). The meats *alla brace* (grilled over an open fire) are delicious, but also sample the grilled mozzarella or *scamorza alla brace*, a peasant's dish you could serve to a king. For the restaurant's charming rooms, see "Where to Stay," above.

✪ **La Barcaccia.** Pz. Fratelli Bandiera (N of Pz. d. Mercato), Spoleto. ☎ **0743/22-11-71.** Reservations suggested. Primi 8,000L–10,000L ($5.25–$6.60); entrees 16,000L ($10.50). Menu turistico 25,000L ($16.45). AE, DC, MC, V. Wed–Mon 12:30–2:30pm and 7:30–11:00pm. UMBRIAN.

This is one of Spoleto's finer restaurants, where you can have a modestly priced dinner if you resist, alas, the allure of its otherwise highly recommended truffle dishes. A safe way to dine is with the well-priced menu turistico that includes a choice of truffle-free pasta, a meat entree, fresh vegetable, fruit, and service—everything except a glass of the local Umbrian vintage. A covered terrace extends the length of the restaurant in front, though the small piazza's use as a parking lot does little to romanticize the view. Truffle-deprived and -innocent diners should employ the *carpe diem* approach to dining in Umbria and try any of the truffle-sprinkled first courses: risotto, tagliatelle, and strangozzi dishes all cost a reasonable 18,000L ($11.85). An entree of mixed roast meats (*grigliata alla brace*) is the house's deservedly promoted specialty.

A SIDE TRIP TO ORVIETO

Whether you're heading on south to Rome or north to Florence, a side trip to Orvieto (25 miles; take the S418 to the S3bis north. Just past Todi, get on the S448 west to Orvieto) is definitely worth your while.

Situated atop a high, flat table of tufa stone, this city's main draw is its 13th-century **Duomo,** one of Italy's treasures. It is noted for its breathtaking facade and contains one of the greatest fresco cycles of the Renaissance in the Chapel of San Brizio, recently reopened after a lengthy period of restoration. The cycle, begun by Fra Angelico and completed by Luca Signorelli, depicts in vivid detail the Last Judgment. Admission to the chapel is 3,000L ($2) with tickets available at the tourist office; it's open daily from 10am to 12:45pm and 2:30pm until sunset.

Orvieto's white wines are also renowned, making lunch here an even better reason to stop. **Al San Francesco,** V. B. Cerretti 10, is a cafeteria-style restaurant off Via Maitani near the Duomo. For a splurge, try **La Palomba,** V. C. Manente 16, first left under arch at Pz. Repubblica (☎ 0763/43-395).

Bologna & Emilia-Romagna

by Stephen Brewer

Emilia-Romagna comprises two ancient lands: Emilia, named for the Roman road that bisects its plains and art cities, and Romagna, named for its prominence in the Roman Empire. History has left its mark here on some of Italy's most beautiful cities—Ravenna, last capital of the empire and later the stronghold of the Byzantines and the Visigoths; Ferrara, center of art and culture for much of the Renaissance; Parma, one of the most powerful duchies in Europe under the Farnese family, and Bologna, famous for its university since the Middle Ages.

With such a collection of exquisite cities at hand, the pleasures of the region are primarily urban. No small part of the delight of visiting these cities is to partake of the bounty of the rich farmland that lies between them and comes to the tables of the region's simple but excellent restaurants—prosciutto, Parmigiano cheese, fruits and vegetables, salamis, the cream and butter used in the rich sauces that top tortellini and other pastas, and from the nearby Adriatic, a rich selection of seafood.

North Americans often speed through Emilia-Romagna on high-speed trains and autostradas en route to and from Florence, Milan, Venice, or Rome. Not only are they bypassing some of Italy's finest art and architecture, but also the opportunity to experience a way of life that has been largely unaffected by those two great demons of the 20th century, mass tourism and massive industrialization.

EXPLORING THE REGION

A car is unnecessary in Emilia-Romagna, given the proximity of its cities to one another and their excellent rail connections. You can base yourself centrally in Bologna and from there explore the entire region with ease. But that means forgoing the pleasure of spending leisurely hours in smaller, easy-going places. The following tour includes short stays in each of the major cities.

On your first day, arrive in Bologna, easily reached by train from Rome, Milan, Venice, or Florence. Spend the day exploring the neighborhoods and sights of the central city. The place to begin is the Piazza Maggiore and the Duomo, and from there, walk to the Due Torri and through the medieval streets into the university quarter. After dinner at a trattoria, take a look at the brilliantly illuminated Fontana Nettuno before dropping into an osteria for a glass of wine.

Spend the morning of the second day at the Pinacoteca Nazionale, then visit some of the city's churches and other museums. Take a late afternoon train to Ferrara (about 45 minutes by train) and enjoy a meal and an evening stroll through the romantic brick streets of the quiet city.

Spend day 3 exploring the sights of this walkable city, leaving time for a bicycle ride along the city walls. You may choose to spend another night, just for the pleasure of enjoying the calm of the palaces and gardens and the nighttime views of the illuminated Castello d'Este.

On day 4 arrive in Ravenna, only a little more than an hour from Ferrara by train, in the morning, and spend the day viewing the mosaics and other sights. If you have enough time here, make the short trip to the Adriatic beaches by bus.

On the fifth day, arrive in Parma, about two hours by train from Ravenna (the trip may require a change in Bologna or Ferrara). Spend the afternoon and next day exploring the sights and enjoying the street life of this sophisticated city. If the opera is in season, try to snare tickets for a performance at the Teatro Regio. You may also want to make the trip by bus to one of the surrounding castles or to the towns of Colorno or Busetto.

1 Bologna

105km (63 miles) N of Florence, 210km (126 miles) SE of Milan, 210km (126 miles) S of Venice, 380km (220 miles) N of Rome

Bologna is known the world over as the home of the oldest university in Europe, and this venerable institution accounts for much of what you'll see of the city's past and present. By the 13th century, scholastics had begun descending upon the city in droves, and the city took shape to accommodate them. The city's famous loggias, 21 miles in length, covered sidewalks gave them the opportunity to stroll and discourse in any kind of weather; palazzos and churches were built by the burgeoning community, and artists came from throughout Italy to decorate them. These treasures remain, amid a handsome cityscape of ocher-colored buildings, loggia-covered sidewalks, red-tile rooftops, and the occasional tower constructed by powerful medieval families to display their wealth and power. And the students remain a vibrant presence, giving Bologna a youthful exuberance.

ESSENTIALS

GETTING THERE   By Plane   European flights land at Aeroporto G. Marconi, connected to the train station by bus.

By Train   Trains arrive from Florence ($1^1/_2$ hours away) about every half hour, and from Rome ($3^1/_2$ hours away), Milan (3 hours away) and Venice ($2^1/_2$ hours away) almost hourly. Luggage storage is available at the station.

By Car   Bologna lies directly on the A1 autostrada, which runs up the center of the peninsula and connects Rome and Milan.

VISITOR INFORMATION   The main **APT tourist office** is in the Palazzo Communale, on Piazza Maggiore (☎ **051/24-65-41**); open Monday to Saturday from 9am to 7pm, Sunday from 9am to 1pm. The English-speaking staff is extremely helpful and dispenses a library's worth of information on the city. The branch office in the train station will book rooms; they are open Monday to Saturday from 9am to 12:30pm and 2:30 to 6:30pm. The APT has also installed terminals all around the

100 mi
160 km

Porto Garibaldi
Marina di Ravenna
Ravenna
S16
S71
S67
S309
Comacchio
Migliarino
S309
Baghacavallo
Alfonsine
Lugo
A14
Faenza
Copparo
Portomaggiore
Argenta
Imola
S9
Ferrara
S16
Medicina
A14
Bondeno
Malalbergo
Budrio
Finale Emilia
Altedo
A13
S64
Bologna
Cento
Pianoro
Crevalcore
S. Giovanni in Persiceto
Casalecchio di Reno
S65
Mirandola
Modena
S64
Sasso Marconi
Novi di Modena
S9
Carpi
Vignola
Pavullo nel Frignano
Cavezzo
Sassuolo
A1
S12
Reggiolo
Formigine
Scandiano
Luzzara
A22
Maranello
Carpineti
Guastalla
Novellara
A1
Sabbioneta
S63
Reggio nell'Emilia
S63
Villa Minozzo
Casalmaggiore
S9
Casina
Colorno
Montecchio
Castelnovo ne' Monti
S343
Parma
S. Polo d'Enza

Bologna 4
Ferrara 3
Modena 2
Parma 1
Ravenna 5

ITALY
ROME
Emilia-Romagna

3-0679

269

city that display tourist information in English; look for the machines marked TUTTO BOLOGNA. The telephone area code for Bologna is 051.

WHAT TO SEE & DO
CHURCHES & MUSEUMS

Basilica di San Petronio. Pz. Maggiore. ☎ **051/23-14-15.** Daily 7am–noon and 3:30pm–7:30pm.

Massive as this church is, it's not nearly as big as its 14th-century builders intended it to be. Rome got wind of the Bolognese scheme to build a church bigger than Saint Peter's and cut off the funds. Even so, what's here is mighty impressive, and beyond the doorway, carved by Jacopo della Quercia, lies a cavernous interior richly decorated with frescoes by Giovanni di Modena and containing, embedded in the floor, an enchanting curiosity—Italy's largest sundial.

Basilica di Santo Stefano. V. Santa Stefano 24. Daily 9am–noon and 3:30–6pm.

This remarkable assemblage of hallowed buildings incorporates four churches, dating from the 4th to the 13th centuries. San Petronio, Bologna's patron saint, lies in the most charming church in the group, the 12th-century Chiesa del San Sepolcro, modeled after the church of the Holy Sepulchre in Jerusalem. According to legend, the basin in the courtyard is the one in which Pontius Pilate absolved himself after condemning Christ to death (in truth, it's a Lombard piece from the 7th century). The oldest church here is the 8th-century Santi Vitale e Agricola, incorporating fragments of a Roman temple.

Chiesa di San Domenico. Pz. San Domenico 13. ☎ **051/64-00-411.** Daily 7am–8pm.

Here, in the sixth chapel on the right, is one of the great treasures of Bologna, the beautifully crafted tomb of St. Dominic. These saints and angels are a joint effort of Michelangelo, Pisano, and, most notably, Nicolo di Bari, who was so proud of his work on the cover of the tomb (arca) that he dropped his last name and is better known as Nicolo dell' Arca. A plan near the entrance to the chapel tells you who carved what, and an English-speaking guide will give you a highly informative earful about the tomb and the saint, who founded the Dominican order and died in Bologna in 1221.

Chiesa di San Giacomo Maggiore. Pz. Rossini. ☎ **051/22-59-70.** Daily 8am–noon and 3:30pm–6pm.

The masterpiece in this 13th-century church, which took on its gothic appearance in subsequent centuries, is the chapel cum burial chamber of the Bentivoglio family. The frescoes they commissioned from Lorenzo Costa depict life in a Renaissance court, an apt decoration for Bologna's most influential (and tyrannical) clan. An underground passage connects the chapel to the spot, now occupied by the Teatro Communale, where the family's palazzo stood until it was razed by an angry mob in the 16th century. Bologna, these days the stronghold of the Italian Communist Party, has always been indomitable in spirit.

Due Torri. Pz. Porte Ravegna. Torre degli Asinelli, admission 3,000L ($2). Daily 9am–6pm.

Of the more than 200 towers that once rose above Bologna—built by noble families as symbols of their wealth and prestige—only these and a scant scattering of others still stand, but barely—the 165-feet-tall Torre Garisenda tilts a precarious 10 feet off the perpendicular; 320-feet-tall Torre degli Asinelli leans $7^1/_2$ feet. A climb up the 500 steps of the Torre degli Asinelli rewards you with a stunning view of Bologna's red-tile rooftops and the surrounding hills. At the base of the towers, the seven main streets of medieval Bologna spread out from Piazza Porta Ravegna.

Bologna

Basilica di San Petronio ⑥
Basilica di San Domenico ⑨
Chiesa di San
   Giacomo Maggiore ②
Fontana del Nettuno ⑤
Museo Civico Archeologico ⑦

Museo Civico Medioevale
   e del Rinascimento ⑩
Palazzo Comunale ④
Pinacoteca Nazionale
   di Bologna ①
Santo Stefano ⑧
Due Torri ③

Museo Civico Archeologico. V. dell'Archiginnasio, 2. ☎ **051/23-38-49.** Admission 5,000L ($3.30). Tues–Fri, 9am–2pm, Sat 9am–1pm and 3:30–7pm, Sun 3:30–7pm. Closed Mon.

The Etruscan and Roman finds from the surrounding region comprise just part of this stunning collection. The museum also houses many fine Egyptian antiquities, including a portion of the Book of the Dead and bas-reliefs from the tomb of Horemheb.

Museo Civico Medioevale e del Rinascimento. V. Manzoni 4. ☎ **051/22-89-12.** Admission 5,000L ($3.30), students 2,500L ($1.64). Mon and Wed–Fri 9am–2pm, Sat and Sun 9am–1pm and 3:30pm–7pm. Closed Tues.

Though a Roman wall runs through the courtyard, the collection is determinedly devoted to depicting life in medieval Bologna. The city then revolved around its university, and the most enchanting treasures among the ceramics and other objects are the sepulchers of professors, surrounded for eternity by carvings of dozing and mocking students.

Pinacoteca Nazionale. V. d. Belle Arti 56. ☎ **051/24-32-22.** Admission 8,000L ($5.25), Tues–Sat 9am–2pm, Sun 9am–1pm.

An amble through this stunning collection, one of Italy's finest, presents a marvelous survey of Bolognese painting, with works by Guido Reni, Ludovico Carracci, and just about every other native painter of note from the gothic to the baroque. Other schools are well represented here, too, and the well-lit galleries are hung with works by Giotto, Parmigianino, Perugino, and, the most famous picture here, Raphael's *Santa Cecilia*.

HISTORIC AREAS

Piazza Maggiore and Fontana del Nettuno

Bologna's central square and heart of the city is flanked by the city's finest buildings: the medieval **Palazzo di Rei Enzo,** named for Enzo, king of Sardinia, who died here in 1272 after languishing in captivity for 23 years until his death; the romanesque **Palazzo del Podesta;** and the **Palazzo Communale,** seat of the local government. The square is dominated, though, by a relative newcomer: an immodestly virile, 16th-century bronze statue of Neptune, who presides over an ornate fountain inhabited by sensual sirens.

Zona Universita (University District)

Bologna's university is Europe's oldest, rooted in a Roman law school dating from A.D. 425 and officially founded in the 10th century. By the 13th century, more than 10,000 students from all over Europe were descending upon this center of learning, and their scholarly numbers have included Thomas à Becket, Copernicus, Dante, Petrarch, and, much more recently, Federico Fellini. Always forward-thinking, even in the unenlightened Middle Ages the university employed female professors, and the political leanings of today's student body are displayed in leftist slogans that emblazon the 15th- to 19th-century buildings.

You may visit one of the old buildings, the **Palazzo di Archiginnasio,** near the university district, south of Piazza Maggiore, just behind the duomo at Piazza Galvani 1. This large, baroque palazzo houses an anatomical theater where ancient wooden benches surround a much-used marble slab and eerily humanlike pillars support the lectern. It's open Monday to Friday from 8:30am to 1:45pm, and on Saturday from 8:30am to 12:45pm.

WHERE TO STAY

A HOSTEL

Ostello Di San Sisto. V. Viadagola 5, Localita San Sisto. 6km (3.5 miles) from the center of town. ☎ /fax **051/50-18-10.** 30 beds. 17,000L ($11.20) per person. Rates include breakfast. No credit cards. Bus: 93, 20B, or 301 from V. d. Mille, 3 blocks south of the train station; last bus at 8:30pm; ask the driver where to get off.

It's out of the way, but you might find that the grassy grounds and nice, clean rooms and shower facilities in a villa make the trip out here worth it. There's an 11:30pm curfew and a lockout from 9am to 5pm (you cannot leave your bags). You should also ask at the tourist office about the **Due Torri,** a larger hostel that's much better located right in town—it's been closed but is due to reopen.

DOUBLES FOR LESS THAN 85,000 LIRE ($55.90)

Albergo Apollo. V. Drapperie 5, 40124 Bologna. ☎ **051/22-39-55.** Fax 051/23-87-32. 14 rms, 10 with bath or shower. TEL. 46,000L ($30.25) single without bath; 75,000L ($49.35) double without bath; 98,000L ($64.45) double with bath; 135,000L ($88.80) triple with bath. AE, MC, V.

The location's great, especially if you like to eat—you have to pick your way through the stalls of one of Bologna's outdoor food markets to make your way to the door of this homey establishment on the upper floors of an old apartment house. Rooms are really basic but big and clean, and many of the doubles have baths.

Albergo Panorama. V. Livraghi 1, 40121 Bologna. ☎ **051/22-18-02.** Fax 051/26-63-60. 9 rms, 3 with bath or shower. 55,000L ($36.20) single; 80,000L ($52.65) double; 105,000L ($69.05) triple; 125,000L ($82.25) quadruple; 135,000L ($88.80) quintuple. No credit cards.

You may choose to stay in this charming old-fashioned pensione near the Palazzo Cummunale even if your budget allows for more luxurious digs. Only a few rooms have baths, but they're big, bright, and kept spanking clean by the friendly mother-daughter team who runs the place. Many rooms overlook a lovely courtyard, and some sleep four and five dormitory-style.

DOUBLES FOR LESS THAN 120,000 LIRE ($78.95)

Albergo Centrale. V. d. Zecca 2, 40121 Bologna. ☎ 051/22-51-14. Fax 051/23-51-62. 20 rms, 17 with bath or shower. TEL TV. 70,000L ($46.05) single without bath, 90,000L ($59.20) single with bath; 115,000L ($75.65) double with bath; 150,000L ($98.70) triple with bath; 185,000L ($121.70) quadruple with bath. AE, MC, V.

You're not going to sleep much closer to the Piazza Maggiore for the price. This snappy pensione, on two floors of an old apartment house, is not without its charms, either. There's an elegant little bar area and simple, tile-floored rooms with some nice views over the centro storico. Several of the rooms have three and four beds, making this a good stopover for travelers with kids in tow, and some are air-conditioned, a real blessing in the Bolognese summer.

Albergo Rossini. V. Bibiena 11, 40121 Bologna. ☎ 051/23-77-16. Fax 051/26-80-35. 19 rms, 12 with bath or shower. TEL. 60,000L ($39.45) single without bath, 80,000L ($52.65) single with bath; 115,000L ($75.60) double with bath. AE, MC, V.

In the heart of the university district, the plain rooms here are usually filled with visiting academics, Which may explain why every room has a big desk, and reading lights over the beds—a rarity in Italian hotels. The bar in the lobby is a fun place to sit around sipping a glass of Chianti and listening to some intellectual chatter.

DOUBLES FOR LESS THAN 165,000 LIRE ($108.55)

Hotel Holiday. V. Bertiera 13, 40123 Bologna. ☎ 051/23-53-26. Fax 051/23-53-26. 36 rms, all with bath or shower. A/C MINIBAR TEL TV. 110,000L ($72.30) single, 150,000L ($98.70) double, 215,000L ($141.45) triple. Rates include breakfast. AE, MC, V.

Though this recently renovated hotel is a little short on character—in fact, the white-tiled lobby and bar area are so antiseptic they resemble a hospital—it offers a lot of comfort for the price. The quiet rooms are attractively done up with sleek built-in cabinetry and soothing pastel fabrics, and equipped with air-conditioning, minibars, and TVs—making this a good place to chill out after a day of doing the sights.

✪ **Hotel Roma.** V. D'Azeglio 9, 40123 Bologna. ☎ 051/22-63-22. Fax 051/23-99-09. 86 rms, all with bath or shower. A/C TEL TV. 110,000L ($72.35) single; 160,000L ($105.25) double. AE, MC, V.

Though it's been eclipsed in stature by some of Bologna's glossier establishments, the Roma is still one of the most gracious hotels in town, with a great location only steps away from the Piazza Maggiore. The large guest rooms have a lot of old-fashioned comforts, such as roomy armchairs and huge closets, and they are very fairly priced for what they offer in the way of amenities and attractiveness. Try to nab one of the rooms on the top floor with a terrace; they don't cost extra.

CAMPING

Campeggio Città di Bologna. V. Romita 12/4A, 40127 Bologna. ☎ 051/32-50-16. Fax 051/32-53-18. 150 tent sites, 48 bungalows. Tent sites: depending on month, 5,500L–7,000L ($3.60–$4.60) per person, 11,000L–13,000L ($7.25–$8.55) for tent. Bungalows: 110,000L ($72.75) for 2 persons, 15,000L ($9.85) each additional person (it's best to reserve these). May–Oct (call ahead or ask the tourist office to verify dates; they vary a lot). Bus: 11, 25, 30 from train station; ask the driver where to get off.

The Comune of Bologna has recently opened this campground to accommodate summertime visitors. The facilities are spanking fresh and include a Laundromat, a restaurant bar, and a grocery store, and sites are surrounded by trees and a lot of open, grassy space. The bungalows have bathrooms, kitchens, TV, and telephone, and sleep three to four, in one double bed and a fold-out couch.

WHERE TO DINE

It's not called Bologna the Fat for nothing. Chubby tortellinis are filled with cheese and meat and topped with cream sauces, and heaping platters of grilled meats are served without a care for cholesterol. Get the idea? You can eat very well in Bologna, and not spend a fortune doing so.

MEALS FOR LESS THAN 15,000 LIRE ($9.85)

Bar-Pizzeria-Ristorante-Self Service-Taverna La Mama. V. Zamboni 16. ☎ 051/ 22-08-18. Antipasto and pasta, from 5,000L ($3.30), main courses 7,000L–12,000L ($4.60–$7.90), pizzas from 6,000L ($3.95). No credit cards. Mon–Sat, noon–2:30pm and 7pm–10pm. Closed Sun. CAFETERIA/PIZZERIA.

The long-winded name says it all. Heck, there's even karaoke some nights. You dish up your own plates of homemade lasagna, spaghetti Bolognese, and pollo cacciatore from a cafeteria-style line, or place your pizza order with one of the guys wandering around the room with pies trying to figure out who ordered what.

L'Osteria il Cantinone. V. d. Pratello 56/A. ☎ 051/55-223. Antipasto and pasta, from 5,000L ($3.30), main courses 7,000L–12,000L ($4.60–$7.90). No credit cards. Thurs–Tues, 8am–1:30am; closed Wed. BOLOGNESE.

One of the oldest and best eateries on this animated street is noisy, convivial, and decidedly bohemian. You'll share a seat at one of the long tables with characters young and old, many of whom look like they close the place down every night—which is well into the wee hours, making this a good late-night spot. You can get by with ordering just some crostini and a glass of wine from the house vineyards for a light, casual meal, but the pasta dishes are too good to pass up.

MEALS FOR LESS THAN 20,000 LIRE ($13.15)

Trattoria Belfiore. V. Marsala 11a. ☎ 051/22-66-41. Antipasto and pasta, from 7,000L ($4.60); main courses, 10,000L–18,000L ($6.60–$11.85). AE, MC, V. Mon–Wed and Fri–Sun, and 7:30pm–10:30pm. Closed Thurs. BOLOGNESE.

A series of plain high-ceiling rooms is usually filled with noisy students and businesspeople chattering away on their cellulars as overworked waiters run back and forth from the kitchen. This is not the place for a romantic conversation or a foray into fancy fare, but if you stick to pizza or pasta you can't go wrong.

Trattoria Danio. V. San Felice 50. ☎ 051/55-52-02. Antipasto and pasta, from 7,000L ($4.60); main courses, 8,000L–15,000L ($5.25–$9.85). AE, MC, V. Mon–Sat, noon–2:30pm and 7:30pm–10pm. Closed Sun. BOLOGNESE.

Your walk to this simple tiled room (from the Piazza Maggiore, follow the Via Ugo Bassi its length to Via San Felice) will be rewarded with heaping bowls of tortellini Bolognese and some homey chicken and pork dishes. The menu turistico (pasta, main course, and glass of wine) is a great deal at 17,000L ($11.20).

MEALS FOR LESS THAN 30,000 LIRE ($19.75)

Ristorante al Montegrappa da Nello. V. Montegrappa 2. ☎ 051/23-63-31. Antipasto and pasta, from 10,000L ($6.60), main courses 15,000L–30,000L ($9.85–$19.75). AE, MC, V. Tues–Sun, noon–3pm and 7:30pm–11:30pm; closed Mon and Aug. BOLOGNESE.

You can sit outside on an all-weather covered terrace, but just watching the whirl in the clamorous, cavernous rooms downstairs is part of the experience here. And while you can get by with a simple and relatively inexpensive meal here, you'll probably

---

A Moveable Feast

At **Enoteca Italiana,** V. Marsala 2/B (☎ **051/23-59-89**), an inviting and aromatic shop-cum-wine bar on a side street just north of Piazza Maggiore, you can stand at the bar and sip on a local wine while enjoying a sandwich. For a moveable feast, you can also stock up on a wide selection of ham, salamis, and cheese at the deli counter, and enjoy a picnic near the gurgles of the Neptune fountain. It's open daily from 10:30am to 3pm and 6 to 9:30pm.

On a stroll through the **Pescherie Vecchie,** the city's market area near the Due Torri, you can assemble a meal. Along the Via Drapperie and adjoining streets, salumerias, cheese shops, bakeries, and vegetable markets are heaped high with attractive displays. The stalls of Bologna's other food market, the **Mercato delle Erbe,** V. Ugo Bassi 2, are open Monday to Wednesday and Friday and Saturday, 7:15am to 1pm, and Monday to Wednesday from 5 to 7pm.

---

want to spend the extra lire and sample this fine and unusual fare without fiscal constraint. Truffles and fungi porcini are the specialties of the house, and they appear in salads, atop rich pastas, and accompanying grilled meats, which range into wild boar and venison in season. There's a menu, but since the chef only prepares what's fresh at the market that day, it's best just to let the waiters tell you what they're serving.

Trattoria Anna Maria. V. Belle Arti 17/A. ☎ **051/26-68-94.** Antipasto and pasta, from 8,000L ($5.25), main courses 10,000L–20,000L ($6.60–$13.15). AE, MC, V. Tues–Sun, noon–2:30pm and 7:30pm–11:30pm. Closed Mon. EMILIA-ROMANGNOLA.

Anna Maria, the super-animated proprietor, serves some of the finest trattoria food in Bologna in a big room adorned with old photos of opera stars. All of the pasta is freshly made and appears in some unusual variations, such as quadrettini, four different shapes of ricotta-stuffed pasta floating in chicken broth. You'll probably be tempted to go all the way and follow a pasta dish with a grilled pork chop, platter of tripe, or one of the other downhome-style second courses.

Trattoria-Pizzeria Belle Arte. V. Belle Arti 14. ☎ **051/22-55-81.** Antipasto and pasta, from 10,000L ($6.60); main courses, from 15,000L–25,000L ($9.85–$16.45). AE, MC, V. Mon–Tues and Thurs–Sun, noon–2:30pm and 7pm–11:30pm. Closed Wed and part of Jan and Aug. PIZZERIA/ITALIAN.

The only drawback to this attractive restaurant near the university and museum is its popularity. Even on weeknights you may have to wait to get a table in the handsome brick- and panel-walled dining room, but once the tortellini alla panna or taglietta con fungi porcini start arriving at the table you'll be glad you came. The kitchen specializes in seafood but prepares many meat dishes as well and bakes a stupendous selection of pizzas in a wood-burning oven.

BOLOGNA AFTER DARK
THE PERFORMING ARTS

The **Teatro Communale,** V. Largo Respighi 1 (☎ **051/52-99-99**), hosts Bologna's lively opera, orchestra, and ballet seasons.

If you're in town in July and August, you can spend your evenings at the jazz concerts and other free events that are part of the **Bologna Sogna festival.** Ask the tourist office for details.

BARS & CLUBS

Given its young and restless student population, Bologna stays up later than most Italian cities. The Via del Pratello and, near the university, Via Zamboni and Via delle Belle Arte and their surrounding areas are the usual haunts of night owls. You can usually find a place for a drink, shot of espresso, or a light meal as late as 2am.

Cassero. Pz. Porta Saragozza 2. ☎ **051/64-46-902.** Daily 9:30pm–2:30pm.

Bologna's most popular gay bar caters mostly to men, with a noisy clublike atmosphere and floor shows.

Irish Times Pub. V. Paradiso 1. ☎ **051/26-16-48.** Tues–Sun, 7pm–2am.

There's Guinness and Harp on tap and an attendant Anglophone following, accompanied by a well-heeled young Italian crowd.

Piccolo Bar. Pz. Giuseppe Verdi 4. ☎ **051/22-71-47.** Daily 8:30am–3:30am.

This is the closest Bologna comes to a counterculture bar, though it's pretty tame compared to what you'd find in London or New York. Most of the purple-haired youths who hang out here all the day long are cutting classes from the nearby university.

2 Ferrara

45km (27 miles) N of Bologna, 110km (66 miles) S of Venice, 250km (150 miles) SE of Milan, 425km (250 miles) N of Rome

One family, the Estes, accounts for much of what you will find in this enchanting city on the plains of Romagna. From 1200 to 1600, the Estes ruled and ranted from their imposing palazzo-cum-fortress that is still the centerpiece of the city. They endowed the city with palaces, gardens, and avenues, as well as intrigues, including those of their most famous duchess, Lucrezia Borgia. After the Estes left (when Rome refused to recognize the last heir of the clan as duke) Ferrara fell victim to neglect and finally, during World War II, to bombs. Much of the Renaissance city remains and has been restored; in fact, this city of rose-colored brick is one of the most beautiful in Italy, and shrouded in a gentle mist from the surrounding plains as it often is, one of the most romantic.

ESSENTIALS

GETTING THERE   By Train   Trains arrive from Bologna (30 to 45 minutes away, depending on service) about every half hour, and from Venice (about two hours) and Ravenna (one hour) about every hour. The train station is a 15-minute walk from the center; you can rent a bike from the lot just to the left as you leave the main entrance. Luggage storage is available.

By Car   Ferrara is 45km (27 miles) north of Bologna on A13 and 85km (51 miles) south of Padua

VISITOR INFORMATION   The extremely helpful **tourist office** is in the center, at Cor. Giovecca 21 (☎ **053/20-93-70**). They even rent bikes. They're open Monday to Saturday from 8:30am to 7pm and Sunday from 2:30pm to 5:30pm. The telephone area code for Ferrara is 053.

WHAT TO SEE & DO

Casa Romei. V. Praisolo and V. Savonarola. ☎ **0532/24-03-41.** Admission 4,000L ($2.65). Tues–Sun, 8:30am–2pm. Closed Mon.

The most famous resident of this airy villa, built by a 15th-century merchant, was Lucrezia Borgia, who retreated here from the rigors and intrigues of court life at the castello. (Wife of Duke Alfonso I D'Este, her reputation for murders, poisonings, and intrigues has been shown by history to be largely unwarranted.) The lovely rooms, connected by loggias that wrap around two peaceful courtyards, are filled with frescoes and statues rescued from Ferrara's deconsecrated churches and convents.

Castello Estense. V. Cavour and Cor. Ercole I d'Este. ☎ **0532/29-92-79.** Admission 6,000L ($3.95). Tues–Sun, 9:30am–5:30pm. Closed Mon.

This imposing, moat-encircled castle dominates the city center and much of the city's Renaissance history. It was here in 1435 that Nicolo III d'Este, with a contrivance of window mirrors, caught his young wife Parisina Maletesta *in flagrante delicto* with his son Ugo and had them beheaded in the dank dungeons below. Robert Browning recounted the deed in his poem "My Last Duchess," and today's visitors clamber down a dark staircase to visit the damp cells where the lovers and others who fell out of favor with the Este clan once languished. Not to be overlooked is the fact that the Estes also made Ferrara a center of art and learning. Their enlightenment is revealed in the salons above, where the Sala dell'Aurora and Sala dei Giochi (Game Room) are festooned with stunning frescoes, and the orangerie continues to bloom as it did when Lucrezia Borgia entertained poets and artists beneath the fragrant bowers.

Cimtero di Certosa and Cimitero Erbacio (Jewish Cemetery). Both near the walls off the Cor. Porta Mare. Certosa: daily 8am–8pm; Cimitero Erbacio: Apr–Sept, daily 8am–6:30pm, and Oct–Mar, daily 9am–4:30pm.

The centerpiece of the Certosa is the Church of San Cristoforo, a graceful sweep of a building by architect Biagio Rossetti. The Jewish cemetery, with its ancient tumble of overgrown tombstones, is the most haunting place in town. A monument to the Ferrarese murdered at Auschwitz is a reminder of the fate of the city's once sizable Jewish community, whose last days are recounted in the film, *Garden of the Finzi-Continis,* evocatively set in the gardens and palaces of Ferrara and required viewing for anyone planning to visit the city.

Bicycling on the Medieval Walls

The preferred mode of transportation in Ferrara is pedal-powered; beware of octogenarian cyclists whizzing by you with shopping bags flapping in the wind. Ferrara's medieval walls, massive enough to be topped by trees and lawns, encircle the city with an aerie of greenery, and the wide paths are ideal for bicycling and provide wonderful views of the city and surrounding farmland.

Many hotels offer guests free use of bicycles, or you can rent them from the tourist office on Corso Giovecca and from the large lot outside the train station for about 3,000L ($2) an hour or 20,000L ($13.15) for a day.

Buy your picnic on the Via Cortevecchia (here's a dare: Try to walk down this street without eating anything). This narrow brick street near the cathedral is where locals come to food-shop and it is lined with salumerias, cheese shops, and bakeries. The nearby Mercato Communale, at the corner of Via Santo Stefano and Via del Mercato, is crowded with food stalls and open until 1pm Monday to Saturday, and 3:30 to 7:30pm on Friday. At Negozio Moccia, V. degli Spadari 9, you can indulge in a chunk of pampeteto, Ferrara's hallmark chocolate-covered fruit cake.

Duomo. Cor. Liberta and Pz. Cattedrale. ☎ **0532/20-74-49.** Church Mon–Sat, 7:30–noon and 3pm–6:30pm, Sun 7:30pm–1pm and 4–7:30pm. Museum (donation requested) Mon–Sat, 10am–noon and 3pm–5pm.

With its pink-marble facade emblazoned with layers of arches and a fearsome depiction of the Last Judgment, this handsome 12th-century structure reflects a heady mix of the gothic and the romanesque. To see the paintings, sculptures, and other works that noble families have commissioned for the cathedral over the centuries, climb the stairs to the Museo della Cattedrale; the pride of the collection are the panels by Cosme Tura. The Loggia of the Merchants, flanking one side of the church, is still the scene of active secular trade, as it has been since the 18th century, and the surrounding streets and piazzas are filled with lively cafes.

Palazzo dei Diamanti. Cor. Ercole I D'Este 21. ☎ **0532/20-58-44.** Admission 8,000L ($5.25). Tues–Sat 9am–2pm, Sun 9am–1pm.

No problem figuring out where this palazzo gets its name: 9,000 pointed marble blocks cover the facade with enticing glitter. Less interesting are the collections in the **Pinacoteca Nazionale,** housed within—while containing some notable works by Cosme Tura and other painters of the Ferrara school, as well as Carpaccio's *Passing of the Virgin,* they are not as stellar as the works to be seen elsewhere in town. The ground-floor galleries often house temporary exhibitions and charge separate admission.

Palazzo Ludovico il Moro. V. XX Settembre. Admission 4,000L ($2.65). Closed for restoration.

The museum is due to reopen "soon"; in the meantime, many of the treasures are on display in an adjoining church.

Ludovico il Moro, duke of Milan who married Beatrice D'Este, commissioned this lovely little palazzo as a place to retire from his courtly duties. Beatrice died young and the duke spent his last years as a prisoner of the French, but their 15th-century palace, built around a lovely rose garden, contains their furniture and paintings and also houses the fascinating collections of the **Museo Archeologico.** The bulk of the treasures are Etruscan and Greek finds unearthed near Ferrara at Spina.

Palazzina di Marfissa d'Este. Cor. d. Giovecca 170. Admission 3,000L ($2), free 2nd Sun and Mon of each month. Daily 9am–noon and 2pm–5pm.

A recent restoration has returned the 16th-century home of this ardent patron of the arts to its former splendor. Period furniture and ceiling frescoes bespeak the heyday of the Este dynasty, and the little theater in the garden is a reminder that drama, on stage as well as off, was one of the family's great passions.

Palazzo Massari. Cor. Porto Mare 9. Admission 8,000L ($5.25) adults, 5,000L ($3.30) students. Daily 9:30am–1pm and 3:30–7pm.

The complex of museums housed in this exquisite palace contain some real treasures, most notably the works of Giorgio de Chirico and other 20th-century painters in the **Museo Documentario della Metafisica.** Also here are the **Museo Giovanni Boldini,** with works by the 19th-century Italian painter, and the **Museo Civico d'Arte Moderna,** largely devoted to works by contemporary regional artists.

Palazzo Schifanoia. V. Scandiana 23. ☎ **0532/64-178.** Admission 6,000L ($3.95) adults, 3,000L ($2) seniors, students free. Daily 9am–7pm.

Borso D'Este, who made Ferrara one of the Renaissance's leading centers of art, commissioned the best-known frescoes here from Francesco del Cossa. Not only does the fresco cycle's depiction of the months constitute a giant Renaissance wall calendar, but its scenes of 15th-century courtly life and leisure give us an evocative portrayal of life among the Este clan.

WHERE TO STAY
DOUBLES FOR LESS THAN 66,000 LIRE ($43.40)

Casa degli Artisti. V. Vittoria 66, 44100 Ferrara. ☎ **0532/76-10-38**. 27 rms, 5 with bath. 26,000L ($17.10) single without bath; 45,000L ($29.60) double without bath, 65,000L ($42.75) with bath. No credit cards.

It's more utilitarian than artistic, but the simple rooms, furnished in heavy 1950s-era pieces, are big, bright, and clean (and don't worry—the menacing-looking dog in the lobby doesn't bite). Guests have use of kitchen facilities at the end of the hallway on each floor, and there's a nice terrace on the roof.

Hotel Nazionale. Cor. Porto Reno 32, 44100 Ferrara. ☎/fax **0532/20-96-04**. 18 rms, 12 with bath. 38,000L ($25.00) single without bath, 50,000L ($32.90) single with bath; 85,000L ($55.90) double with bath. AE, MC, V.

There are Technicolor photos of puppies and kittens on the walls and garish green tiles on the floor, but if you don't mind the lack of glamour, the location near the center of town is great. Most of the rooms, decorated in basic hotel-modern style, have private baths, and the English-speaking manager is really friendly. It's best to reserve in advance.

Hotel Santo Stefano. V. Boccacanale d. San Stefano 21, 44100 Ferrara. ☎ **0532/20-69-24**. Fax 0532/21-02-61. 27 rms, 3 with full bath, 8 with shower. 40,00L ($26.30) single without shower or bath; 65,000L ($42.75) double without bath or with shower, 85,000L ($55.90) double with bath. MC, V.

Though it's nothing to write home about, this spotless little hotel is much better maintained than most budget places. Singles and doubles alike are very large and tidily furnished. Though the Este palace and cathedral are only a short stroll away, the location on a quiet side street ensures a peaceful night's sleep.

DOUBLES FOR LESS THAN 135,000 LIRE ($88.80)

✪ **B&B Locanda Borgonuovo.** V. Cairoli 29, 44100 Ferrara. ☎ **0532/24-80-00**. 4 rms, all with bath. A/C MINIBAR TEL TV. 85,000L ($55.90) single, 130,000L–140,000L ($85.55–$92.10) double. Rates include breakfast. AE, MC, V.

This elegant bed-and-breakfast near the Este palace is one of the best hostelries in town. Signora Adele has spruced up an old apartment, which once housed her father's law offices, and puts up her guests in large and very stylish rooms filled with antiques and equipped with posh new baths (one big double also has a kitchenette). She also provides a hearty breakfast (served in the lovely rear garden, weather permitting), bicycles, discount coupons for museums and nearby shops, and plenty of advice on how to enjoy her native Ferrara. Book well in advance, since signora's rooms and hospitality are much in demand; fortunately, she's planning to expand her domain to five or six more rooms in a house down the street.

WORTH A SPLURGE

✪ **Ripagrande Hotel.** V. Ripagrande 21, 44100 Ferrara. ☎ **0532/76-52-50**. Fax 0532/76-43-77. 40 rms and suites. A/C MINIBAR TEL TV. From 230,000L ($151.30), single and double; 320,000L ($210.55) suites. Rates include breakfast. AE, MC, V.

With its brick-walled, vaulted public rooms and lovely rear garden, this converted Renaissance palazzo near the center of town is one of those enchanting places where you'll be tempted to throw caution to the winds and just hand over the credit card. Go for it. The guest rooms are large and distinctive. Many are trilevel, with a bath and dressing room connected by a short staircase to a sitting room, and with a loftlike bedroom above; top-floor rooms open onto large terraces overlooking red-tile rooftops. The price of a room—all of which are nicely decorated with a mix of stylish contemporary pieces and reproduction antiques—includes a buffet breakfast, use of bicycles, and gracious service.

WHERE TO DINE
MEALS FOR LESS THAN 12,000 LIRE ($7.90)

Trattoria da Giacomino. V. Garibaldi 135. ☎ **0532/20-56-44.** Antipasto and pasta from 6.000L ($3.95), main courses 8,000L–15,000L ($5.25–$9.85). Tues–Sun, noon–2pm and 5:30pm–10pm. Closed Mon and Aug. FERRARESE.

If a native Ferrarese were to take you out to dinner, it might well be to this boisterous trattoria that's always filled to the rafters with students, business folks, families, and tourists. It's the sort of casual, anything-goes place where they won't look askance at you if you order only a plate of salami or a heaping bowl of homemade gnocchi or cappelletti (a triangular ravioli) and a salad for an easygoing dinner.

Orsucci dal 1949 Pizzeria. V. Garibaldi 76. ☎ **0532/20-53-91.** Pizza from 8,000L ($5.25). Daily noon–11:00pm. No credit cards. PIZZA.

One of the newer entries on Ferrara's casual dining scene, this charming, beamed-ceiling room has a cozy bar up front and a pretty dining area in the rear with large windows opening to a courtyard. The focal point is the wood-burning oven, from which a delicious array of individual-size pizzas emerge, served with frosty glasses of beer and salads; pasta dishes and sandwiches are also available.

MEALS FOR LESS THAN 25,000 LIRE ($16.45)

Ristorante/Pizzeria Buca San Domenico. Pz. Sacrati 26b. ☎ **0532/20-91-52.** Pizza, from 8,000L ($5.25); pasta and antipasto, from 8,000L ($5.25); main courses 10,000L–16,000L ($6.60–$10.50). AE, MC, V. Tues–Sun noon–2:30pm and 7:30pm–11:00pm. Closed Mon and Aug. PIZZA/PASTA.

This local institution is almost always booked solid on weekend nights. The main dining room is cozy and rustic, with wooden booths and the fragrant odor of baking pizzas and wood smoke wafting from the large ovens in the rear. (Lone diners should be warned, though, that they are likely to be shunted off to a modern, garishly-lit room to the side.) You can dine very well and inexpensively here are on what is considered to be the best pizza in town, or venture into the full menu of reasonably-priced homemade soups, pastas, and meat dishes.

Ristorante Grotta Azzurra. Pz. Sacrati 43. ☎ **0532/20-91-52.** Antipasto and pasta from 8,000L ($5.25), main courses 13,000L–25,000L ($8.55–$16.45). AE, MC, V. Mon–Tues and Thurs–Sun, 12:30pm–2:30pm and 7:30pm–9:30pm. Closed Wed and part of Aug and Jan. SEAFOOD/FERRARESE.

The name evokes easygoing southern climes, but the pink dining room glowing beneath crystal chandeliers is anything but casual. The bow-tied serving staff is friendly, though, and supervised by burly, outgoing manager Giovanni who sits behind a desk at one end of the dining room chomping on a cigar. Tables are usually filled with a devoted and animated local clientele who come here to enjoy a menu that, true to the restaurant's name, leans toward seafood, including a wonderful platter of grilled Adriatic fish; it also strays into excellent pastas, a good number of meat dishes, and local specialties, including salama da sugo, a round sausage that looks like a matzo ball and is served in a broth of its own juices.

FERRARA AFTER DARK

Ferrara has a lively university community and a good many beer halls and enotecas to accommodate a young clientele wishing to drown their sorrows in a glass. In addition to the places below, the cafes around the Este palace are usually jammed with a wide range of creatures of the night.

Bierfilz. Pz. Sacrati 32, ☎ **0532/20-97-25.** Open until midnight on weekends. Closed Wed.

The liveliest beer hall in town occupies two floors that seem to be perpetually dim, smoky, and crowded. You may also want to dip into the offerings of panini and snack fare, or make an evening meal out of one the pasta dishes. Sandwiches begin at about 5,000L ($3.30), pasta at 7,000L ($4.60); no credit cards.

Osteria Al Brindisi. V. d. Adelardi 9/B. ☎ **0532/20-91-42.** Open Tues–Sun, 8:30am–8:30pm weekdays, until midnight weekends. Closed Mon.

What claims to be the oldest wine bar in the world (since 1435) serves a staggering selections of wines by the glass, and so you won't be staggering, too, a fine selection of fortifying panini. Wine costs from about 2,000L ($1.30) a glass; sandwiches, from about 4,000L ($2.65); no credit cards.

3 Ravenna

75km (45 miles) SE of Bologna, 75km (45 miles) SE of Ferrara, 135km (81 miles) NE of Florence

Few cities in Europe are so firmly entrenched in so distant a past. The last days of ancient Western Civilization waned in this flat little city on the edge of the marshes that creep inland from the Adriatic. Though Ravenna has been an off-the-beaten-track backwater since the 6th century, it continues to dazzle its visitors with its mosaics and other artistic vestiges of the Romans, the Byzantines, and the Visigoths. Aside from its horde of treasures, Ravenna is also a fine place to pass the time in sun-drenched piazzas and pleasant cafes.

ESSENTIALS

GETTING THERE   By Train   Twelve trains a day from Ferrara (about an hour away) and eight trains a day from Bologna (1½ hours away). The train station is about a 10-minute-walk from the center; you can rent a bike from the lot near the front of the station. Luggage storage is available.

By Car   Ravenna is 75km (45 miles) southeast of Bologna on A14 and A13 and 75km (45 miles) southeast of Ferarra on S309.

VISITOR INFORMATION   The **tourist office,** an essential stop for the maps that will guide you to the mosaics, is just off the Pz. Popolo at V. Salara 8; ☎ **0544/ 36-494;** open Monday to Saturday from 8:45am to 1:45pm and 3pm to 6pm, Sunday from 9am to 12:40pm and 3pm to 6pm. The telephone area code for Ravenna is 0544.

WHAT TO SEE & DO

Basilica di Sant'Apollinare Nuovo. V. Carducci. Admission 4,000L ($2.65). Apr–Sept, daily 9am–noon; Oct–Mar, daily 9am–4:30pm.

The famous mosaics in this 6th-century church are clearly delineated by gender. On one side of the church, the side traditionally reserved for women, a procession of 22 crown-carrying virgins make their way toward the Madonna; on the other side, the men's side, 26 male martyrs march toward Christ.

Basilica di San Vitale. V. San Vitale, 17. Admission 4,000L ($2.65), includes admission to mausoleum of Gallo Placidia. Apr–Sept, daily 9am–7pm; Oct–Mar, daily 9am–4:30pm.

Ravenna's most dazzling display of mosaics adorn the dome of this 6th-century octagonal basilica that is not by accident exotically Byzantine in its design—the emperor Justinian commissioned the church to impose the power of Byzantine Christianity over Ravenna. The emperor and his court appear in splendidly detailed mosaics on one side of the church; Theodora, his empress (a courtesan born into the circus whose

---

A Day at the Beach

Just 20 minutes from Ravenna by bus, the Adriatic washes up to white sand beaches backed by pine forests. Well, it's not all that paradisiacal: the strands are lined with beach clubs and gelato shops and are usually packed sardine-style in the summer. But a trip out here can be a refreshing respite from the rigors of gazing at mosaics. From Piazza Farini in front of the train station, hop onto Bus 70 to Punta Marina and Marina di Ravenna or Bus 70 to Punta Marina and Lido Adriano. Tickets are 1,700L ($1.10) each way and can be purchased at tabacchi and newsstands.

---

ambition, intelligence, and beauty brought her to these lofty heights) and her ladies-in-waiting appear on the other; and above and between them looms Christ.

Battistero Neoniao. V. Battistero. Admission 4,000L ($2.63). Apr–Sept, daily 9am–7pm; Oct–Mar, daily 9:30am–4:30pm.

Fittingly, the mosaics on the dome of this little 4th-century structure behind the Duomo depict the baptism of Christ by John the Baptist.

While you're in the area, visit the nearby **Museo Arcivescovile** for a look at the ivory throne of Emperor Maximilian, and the even more dazzling mosaics that adorn the chapel of the bishops.

Mausoleum of Gallo Placidia. V. San Vitale, behind the Basilica di San Vitale. Admission 4,000L ($2.65), includes admission to Basilica of San Vitale. Apr–Sept, daily 9am–7pm; Oct–Mar, daily 9am–4:30pm.

Perhaps the most striking of all Ravenna's monuments is this small and simple tomb of Galla Placidia. The life of this early Christian was not without drama. She was the sister of Honorius, last emperor of Rome and wife of Ataulf, king of the Visigoths. Upon his death she became regent to her six-year-old son, Valentinian III, and, in effect, ruler of the Western world. Though the three sarcophagi beneath a canopy of blue and gold mosaics are meant to contain Galla Placidia's remains and those of her son and husband, it is more likely that she lies unadorned in Rome, where she died in A.D. 450. Nonetheless, these glittering scenes of Christian salvation pay moving tribute to one of early history's most powerful women.

Sant'Apollinare in Classe. V. Romeo Sud, Classe. Free admission. Daily 8am–noon and 2pm–6pm. Bus: 4 or 44 from Pz. Farini in front of the train station.

This long and high early Christian basilica has loomed amid the pine woods near the old Roman port, long ago silted up, since the 6th century. The plain exterior belies the splendor that lies within, a wondrous display of lustrous gold mosaics (made so by the application of gold leaf) that depict the transfiguration of Christ on Mount Tabor. The other dominating figure depicted here, flanked by lambs, is St. Apollinare, the bishop of Ravenna to whom the basilica is dedicated.

Tomba di Dante. V. Dante Alighieri. Basilica and tomb free, museum 4,000L ($2.65). Daily 8am–7pm.

In exile from Florence, the poet made Ravenna his home, and it was here that he died in 1321. Despite efforts by the Florentines to reclaim their famous son's remains, he resides here for eternity, next to the Basilica di San Franceso, beneath an inscription, "Here in this corner lies Dante, exiled from his native land, born to Florence, an unloving mother." To pay further tribute to the poet, step into the adjoining **Museo Dantesco** for a look at some Dante memorabilia, including a manuscript of the *Divine Comedy*.

WHERE TO STAY
DOUBLES FOR LESS THAN 65,000 LIRE ($42.75)

Albergo Al Giaciglio. V. R Brancaleone 42, 48100 Ravenna. ☎ **0544/39-403.** 16 rms, 9 with bath or shower. 30,000L ($19.75) single without bath, 35,000L ($23.05) single with bath; 43,000L ($28.30) double without bath, 55,000L ($36.20) double with bath; 75,000L ($49.35) triple without bath, 85,000L ($55.95) triple with bath. AE, MC, V.

If no one's around when you come into this hotel/restaurant near the station, just poke your head into the kitchen of the downstairs restaurant—where you should also plan to eat even if you don't stay here (see below). The rooms upstairs are no-frills but real homey in a mismatched-furniture kind of way, and the place is usually filled with friendly chatter from the family that runs it.

Albergo Ravenna. V. Maroncelli 12, 48100 Ravenna. ☎ **0544/21-22-04.** Fax 0544/21-20-77. 25 rms, 18 with bath or shower. 38,000L ($25.00) single without bath, 50,000L ($32.90) single with bath; 60,000L ($39.45) double without bath, 75,000L ($49.35) double with bath. No credit cards.

Right across from the train station, this small hotel is only a 10-minute walk to the sights in the town center. The rooms are crisp and clean, and a lot more attractive than you'd expect to find in a one-star hotel. They're so well-priced that you'll probably be able to splurge for one with a private bath.

DOUBLES FOR LESS THAN 115,000 LIRE ($75.65)

Hotel Argentario. V. di Roma 45, 48100 Ravenna. ☎ **0544/35-555.** Fax 0544/35-147. 28 rms, all with bath or shower. A/C MINIBAR TEL TV. 60,000L ($39.45) single; 90,000L ($59.20) double. AE, MC, V.

You might do a double take when you see the rooms here: With Early American–style furnishings and flowery quilts on the beds, they seem a lot more like the accommodations you'd expect to find in a New England bed-and-breakfast than in Ravenna. Some are even paneled in cozy pine and tucked under the eaves. All enjoy a quiet location on a side street only five minutes from the town center.

Hotel Centrale Byron. V. IV Novembre 14, 48100 Ravenna. ☎ **0544/21-22-25.** Fax 0544/34-114. 57 rms, all with bath or shower. A/C MINIBAR TEL TV. From 80,000L ($52.65) single, 114,000L ($75) double. AE, MC, V.

True to its name, this recently renovated hotel couldn't be more central, right off the Piazza del Popolo. The second part of the name is a tribute to Lord Byron, who shared a nearby palazzo with his mistress and her husband. Despite these colorful associations, the ultramodern lobby and sleek guest rooms lack character, but have all the comforts the largely business clientele expect here.

CAMPING

Rivaverde. Vle. d. Nazione 301, Marina di Ravenna. ☎ **0544/53-04-91.** 12,000L ($7.90) per site, 6,000L ($3.95) a person. No credit cards. Open Apr 25–Sept 12. Bus: 70 runs twice hourly until 7:30pm from Pz. Farnese in front of Ravenna's train station (about 20 minutes).

The best campground in the vicinity is an alternative in the summer, when Ravenna's hotel are often completely filled. You might find yourself sleeping closer than you care next to boisterous outdoor types of all nationalities, but the surrounding pine forests are pretty and the beach is right across the road. The tourist office in Ravenna can provide you with a list of other campgrounds in the area.

WHERE TO DINE
MEALS FOR LESS THAN 15,000 LIRE ($9.85)

Ca de Ven. V. C. Ricci 24. ☎ **0544/30-163.** Antipasto and pasta from 2,000L ($1.30), main courses 8,000L–12,000L ($5.25–$7.90). AE, MC, V. Tues–Sun 11am–2pm and 6pm–10:30pm. Closed Mon. RAVENNESE.

The most atmospheric restaurant in Ravenna is tucked away in an ancient wine cellar next to Dante's tomb. Piadine, the local flat bread, is topped with cheeses and vegetables here, or served plain as a perfect accompaniment to a light meal of cheese and assorted salamis, and you can wash it all down with a glass of Trebbiano from local vineyards.

Mensa il Duomo Self-Service. V. Oberdan 8. ☎ **0544/21-36-88.** Antipasto and pasta from 3,000L ($1.95), main courses 6,000L–12,000L ($3.95–$7.90). No credit cards. Daily noon–2:30pm and 7pm–10:30pm. CAFETERIA.

It's just a cafeteria, as you can probably surmise from the name, but you don't come to this bright, busy eatery near the Duomo for the atmosphere. You can get a heaping bowl of pasta for less than 4,000L ($2.65), or go all the way for a full meal.

MEALS FOR LESS THAN 20,000 LIRE ($13.15)

Ristorante Al Giaciglio. V. Rocca Brancaleone 42. ☎ **0544/39-403.** Antipasto and pasta from 6,000L ($3.95), main courses 8,000L–15,000L ($5.25–$9.85); pizza, from 6,000L ($3.95). All major credit cards. Daily noon–2:30pm and 7pm–10:30pm. PIZZERIA/PASTA.

The food is as no-nonsense as the decor, and you can feast regally on big bowls of pasta e fagiole or spaghetti Bolognese. When the family who owns this restaurant and hotel fires up the pizza oven in the evenings, an appreciative crowd of locals packs the place to enjoy what is considered to be the best pie in town.

Ristorante Renato-Guidarello. V. Mentana 33. ☎ **0544/21-36-84.** Antipasto and pasta from 6,000L ($3.95), main courses 8,000L–15,000L ($5.25–$9.85). AE, MC, V. Daily noon–2:30pm and 7pm–9pm. ITALIAN.

The cavernous rooms seem to extend forever, and even at that there never seem to be enough tables to accommodate locals and tourists alike who come here to enjoy pizzas and hearty trattoria fare. Given the proximity of the Adriatic, daily specials often include fresh fish. If there's not a table to be had, try **Ristorante Renato Galleria** around the corner at V. R. Gessi 9—same management, same food, same prices, same boisterous atmosphere, same hours, but closed Sunday.

4 Parma

95km (57 miles) NW of Bologna, 122km (75 miles) SE of Milan

Its hams and cheeses are justly famous, as they have been since Roman times, but the pleasures of this exquisite little city extend far beyond the gastronomic. The Farneses, who made their duchy one of the art centers of the Renaissance, were succeeded by Marie-Louise, a Hapsburg and wife of Emperor Napoléon. Her interest in everything cultural ensured that Parma never languished as a once-glorious backwater, as was the case with nearby Ferrara and Ravenna. As a result, today's residents of Parma live in one of Italy's most prosperous cities and are surrounded by palaces, churches, and artworks—all of which, of course, can also be enjoyed by travelers who choose to spend some time here.

ESSENTIALS

GETTING THERE   By Train   Trains every half-hour from Bologna (about an hour) and every hour from Milan (1½ hours) and Rome (6 hours). Seven direct trains a day from Florence (about 3 hours). The train station is about a 20-minute walk from the center. Luggage storage is available.

By Car   Take the A1 from Bologna or Milan to reach Parma.

VISITOR INFORMATION   The **tourist office,** Pz. d. Duomo 5 (☎ **0521/23-47-35**) is open Monday to Friday from 9am to 12:30pm and 3 to 5pm, Saturday from 9am to 12:30pm. The telephone area code for Parma is 0521.

SPECIAL EVENTS   The city's annual Parmigiano festival takes place in August. You can tour the factories of the **Consortio di Parmigiano** (V. Gramsci 26a) and **Consortio di Prosciutto** (V. Dell'Arpa 8b). The tourist office can provide further details, along with a schedule of events slated for the festival.

WHAT TO SEE & DO

✪ **Batissero.** Pz. Duomo. ☎ **0521/23-58-86.** Admission 4,000L ($2.65) adults, 1,000L (65¢) students. 9am–12:30 and 3pm–6pm.

Obviously, the 12th-century architects of the baptistry knew how to put on a good show. Their stunning octagon is clad in pink marble and festooned with reliefs by Antelami. Inside, frescoes depict the lives of the apostles in a stunning display of visual storytelling and color.

Camera di San Paolo. V. Melloni 3 (just off Pz. Pilotta). Donation requested. Daily 9am–7:30pm.

The abbess of this convent commissioned Corregio to decorate her dining room, and he rose to the occasion with magnificent, highly-colored trompe l'oeil re-creations of mythological scenes.

Chiesa di San Giovanni Evangelista. Pzle. San Giovanni (just behind the Duomo). Church free, pharmacy 4,000L ($2.65). 6:30am–noon and 3:30pm–8:00pm.

Behind the baroque facade are works by Corregio, including his depiction of the saint for whom the church is named, and Parma's other famous painter, Parmagianino. Off one of the cloisters in the adjoining monastery is the pharmacy from which the good monks supplied Parma with potions and poultices for nearly 600 years, up until the late 19th century. An array of medieval-looking mortars and jars continue to line the shelves.

Duomo. Pz. d. Duomo. ☎ **0521/23-58-86.** 9am–noon and 3pm–7pm.

In this 12th-century structure, all eyes are lifted to celestial realms: Corregio's dramatic *Assumption of the Virgin* adorning the cupola. The Virgin and her entourage of *putti* seem to be floating right through the roof into an Easter egg–blue heaven. Even before Corregio added his crowning embellishment, the Duomo shone with romanesque sculpture, most notably Benedetto Antelami's bas-reliefs in the right transept.

Palazzo della Pilotta and Galleria Nazionale. Pz. d. Palce. ☎ **0521/23-33-09.** Admission 12,000L ($7.90), includes admission to Teatro Farnese. Daily 9am–1:45pm. Teatro Farnese only, 5,000L ($3.30). Daily 9am–7:30pm.

This massive and grim-looking complex, which the Farneses put up near the banks of the river Parma in 1603, would be an empty shell if it weren't for Marie-Louise, the Hapsburg wife of Emperor Napoléon and niece of Marie-Antoinette, who ruled the duchy in the early 19th century. Marie-Louise shared her aunt's passion for art, and under her guidance paintings from throughout her domain were brought here to fill the rooms the Farneses had left empty when Isabella Farnese assumed the throne of Spain in the 18th century, and the clan got out of town for good. Though Allied bombings came close to flattening the palace, much of it has been restored. Visitors first enter the **Teatro Farnese,** a wooden jewel box of a theater modeled after the Paladian theater in Vincenza (see chapter 10), and then walk along a series of modern metal walkways through salons hung with works by Corregio, Parmigiano, El Greco, and Leonardo da Vinci.

PARKS & GARDENS

The gravel paths, wide lawns, and splashing fountains of the Parco Ducale, another Farnese creation across the river from the Palazzo Pilotta, provide a nice retreat from Parma's busier quarters. Great for a picnic, but don't even think of pitching a tent. Open May through August daily from 6am to midnight; September through April, daily from 7am to 6pm.

WHERE TO STAY
A HOSTEL

Ostello Citadella. V. Passo Buole (in the Citadella), 43100 Parma. ☎ **0521/96-14-34.** IH card required. 3-day maximum stay (11pm curfew). 15,000L ($9.85) a person. No credit cards. Open May–Sept. Bus: 9 from the station, 2 or 6 from Pz. Garibaldi (about 15 minutes south of the center); ask the driver where to get off.

The six-bedded rooms occupying part of Parma's 16th-century citadel complex haven't been spruced up much since they were used as prison cells, but there's plenty of hot water and the surroundings are sure interesting. From April through October, you can also camp on the grounds for 6,500L ($4.30) per tent, 8,000L ($5.25) per person.

DOUBLES FOR LESS THAN 70,000 LIRE ($46.05)

Locanda Lazzaro. Bgo. XX Marzo 14, 43100 Parma. ☎ **0521/20-89-44.** 8 rms, 4 with bath. 42,000L ($27.65) single, 65,000L ($42.75) double. AE, V.

The main business here is the lively ground-floor restaurant (see below), but the eight rooms upstairs are terrific and a real bargain. With their tall windows and high-beamed ceilings they have an awful lot of character, and they are cozily furnished with old armoires and cane chairs. In some you'll have to use a bath down the hall, but you'll probably only be sharing it with one other room. There's no sign indicating the hotel entrance, so go into the restaurant and ask about the rooms; don't show up without a reservation on Sunday because the restaurant, and hence the informal check-in system, is closed up tight.

Albergo Moderno. V. A. Cecchi 4, 43100 Parma. ☎ **0521/77-26-47.** 46 rms, 37 with bath or shower. 44,000L ($28.95) single without bath, 57,000L ($37.50) single with bath; 63,000L ($41.45) double without bath, 89,000L ($58.55) double with bath. No credit cards.

Pretty bleak, with dingy, graying wallpaper and broken-down 1950s-style furniture— but not bad for a short stopover, since the rates are some of the lowest in town and the train station is just down the block. The folks at the desk tend to wander off; if no one's there, just hang out at the bar on the corner until someone shows up to check you in.

DOUBLES FOR LESS THAN 120,000 LIRE ($78.95)

Albergo Brenta. V. G.B. Borghesi 12, 43100 Parma. ☎ **0521/20-80-93.** 28 rms, all with bath. TEL. 70,000L ($46.05) single; 110,000L ($72.35) double. Continental breakfast 8,000L ($5.25). AE, MC, V.

One of the best hotels near the train station, this is a perfectly decent fallback if the more atmospheric places in town are full. As you'll be able to glean from the dark-paneled lobby, the surroundings are a bit glum, but the rooms are big and quite up-to-date, with functional modern furniture and new baths. One convenience the hotel doesn't have is an elevator.

Hotel Button. Bgo. Salina 7, 43100 Parma. ☎ **0521/20-80-39.** Fax 0521/23-87-83. 41 rms, all with bath. TEL TV. 90,000L ($59.20) single, 115,000L ($75.65) double.

Just off the Piazza Garibaldi, the location is great (and surprisingly serene since the surrounding warren of little streets and squares don't see much traffic). The rooms are large and serviceable though a little somber, with dark floral wallpaper and Spartan modern furnishings. The Cortesis, who run the place, are most accommodating, and you are always welcome to join them in the lobby lounge to watch a soccer match.

DOUBLES FOR LESS THAN 140,000 LIRE ($92.10)

Hotel Torino. V. A. Mazza 7, 43100 Parma. ☎ **0521/28-10-46.** Fax 0521/23-07-25. 33 rms, all with bath. TEL TV. 92,000L ($60.55) single, 139,000L ($91.45) double. AE, MC, V. Free parking in attached garage.

Maybe the most hospitable place in town, with a great location in the pedestrian zone near the Duomo, run by a charming and elegant proprietress who takes great pride in her hotel. There are fresh-cut flowers and a collection of antique porcelains in the pretty lobby, and the natty, homey rooms are adorned with dramatic reproductions of Corregio frescoes and have sparkling modern baths.

WHERE TO DINE

One of the great pleasures of being in Parma is dipping into the wonderful cholesterol-boosting local bounty, most notably ham (prosciutto di Parma) and cheese (Parmigiano Reggiano). The favored pasta in these parts is taglietelli and tortellini, often stuffed with pumpkin or squash, and they come to the table with some wonderfully creative sauces. Be prepared: Filetto di cavallo (yes, as in Trigger) shows up on menus all around town; horse meat doesn't taste a bit like chicken, and has a distinctive, delicate, sweet flavor all its own. Whatever your tastes, the restaurants below provide a memorable dining experience at reasonable prices.

MEALS FOR LESS THAN 10,000 LIRE ($6.60)

Pizzeria La Duchessa. Pz. Garibaldi 1. ☎ **0521/23-59-62.** Pasta, about 9,000L ($5.90); pizza from about 7,000L ($4.60), main courses 10,000L–15,00L ($6.60–$9.85). MC, V. Tues–Sun, 10:30am–2:30pm and 7pm–1am. Closed Mon. PIZZA/PASTA.

The most popular pizzeria in Parma is open late and almost always crowded. You'll probably have to wait for a table, especially if you want one outdoors, but there's a lot of activity to watch in the piazza while you're cooling your heels. Although you can eat a full meal here, you're best off with the exquisite pizzas and meal-in-themselves plates of pasta, washed down with a carafe of Lambrusco.

MEALS FOR LESS THAN 20,000 LIRE ($13.15)

Gallo d'Oro. Bgo. d. Salina 3. ☎ **0521/20-88-46.** Antipasto and pasta from 8,000L ($5.25), main courses 10,000L–20,000L ($6.60–$13.15). AE, MC, V. Wed–Mon, 11:30am–3:30pm and 7:00pm–midnight. Closed Tues. PARMIGIANA.

Diners are wedged in among an odd assortment of antique toys, movie posters, and casks of the wonderful house Lambrusco in this lively, yellow-walled trattoria near Piazza Garibaldi. The kitchen keeps longer hours than most places in town, and the huge platters of prosciutto di Parma and assorted salamis make a satisfying late-night supper; the homemade tortellini stuffed with pumpkin is sublime.

Ristorante Lazzaro. V. XX Marzo 14. ☎ **0521/20-89-44.** Antipasto and pasta from 8,000L ($5.25), main courses 10,000L–20,000L ($6.60–$13.15). AE, V. Mon–Sat, 11:30am–3:30pm; also, Fri– Sat, 7:30pm–10:30pm. Closed Sun. PARMIGIANA.

This white-walled, boisterous trattoria caters to a local and mostly male business clientele. The menu tends toward meat dishes, such as tripe, lamb, and horse meat,

Cheese & Picnic Food

The **food market** in Piazza Ghaia, near the Palazzo della Pilotta, is the place to stock up on fresh fruits, cheeses, ham, bread, and all the other fixings for an outdoor meal. It's open Monday to Saturday from 7am to 1pm, and Saturday afternoons. You should also sniff out **Salumeria Specialita di Parma,** S. Farini 9C, for a huge selection of meats, and **Formaggio Del Re,** V. Garibaldi 46E, which is piled ceiling-high with huge wheels of Parmigiano.

though the homemade pastas are wonderful, too, and are served in copious portions that constitute a meal in themselves.

Trattoria Madonna. V. G.B. Borghesi 3. ☎ **0521/33-126.** Pasta, about 7,000L ($4.60); main courses, 10,000L–18,000L ($6.60–$11.85). No credit cards. Daily, noon to 2:30pm and 6:30–10:30pm. PARMIGIANA.

There's no menu, and the few tables would be right in the kitchen if the tiny room weren't divided by a low counter where folks from the neighborhood pick up food to take home. The woman who cooks and owns the place will come out and tell you what's she's making and invite you to come into the kitchen for a look. Often, there's a wonderful lasagna in the oven and a thick rabbit stew bubbling away on the stove.

MEALS FOR LESS THAN 30,000 LIRE ($19.75)

Croce di Malta. Bgo. Palmia 8. ☎ **0521/23-56-43.** Reservations recommended. Antipasto and pasta from 12,000L ($7.90), main courses 15,000L–25,000L ($9.85–$16.45). MC, V. Mon–Sat, 11:30am–3:00pm and 7:30–10:30pm. Closed Sun. PARMIGIANA.

Weather permitting, the place to sit here is on the pretty terrace in front, facing the church. Inside this former convent, and later an inn, the turn-of-the-century decor is a bit stuffy and out of sync with the friendly, informal service and homestyle fare that comes out of the kitchen. This is a fine place to indulge in such forbidden pleasures as a huge platter of assorted salamis followed by steak tartare or tripe.

TEA & PASTRY

Pasticerria Torino, V. Garibaldi 61, is a good source for Parma violets, a prissy delicacy of violets coated in sugar that you've probably encountered affixed to wedding cakes (they make a great gift for pastry-chef friends back home). In this elegant shop-cum-coffeehouse, you can enjoy them plain or topping an assortment of cakes and tarts.

Miss Pym Sala de Te, Bgo. Parmigiano 5/B, is a refuge for footsore shoppers laden with bags from the chic shops between Piazza Garibaldi and the Duomo. Not too surprisingly, British tourists also drop in around 4pm to sample the big assortment of teas and sweets.

PARMA AFTER DARK

THE PERFORMING ARTS   Parma's opera house, the **Teatro di Regio,** is not too far down the scale of high regard from Milan's La Scala. After all, Verdi was born nearby (see below) and Arturo Toscanini, who often conducted at the theater, is a native son. Tickets can be hard to come by, since they're swallowed up for the |entire October though March season well in advance by opera buffs from all over Emilia-Romagna. However, the tourist office sometimes sells standing-room tickets, and you should also check out the box office (☎ **0521/21-86-87**) on Via Garibaldi for last-minute cancellations.

CAFES & BARS   Parma does not have a lively nightlife. The prime night spots are the outdoor cafes in Piazza Garibaldi.

If the opera's not in season, and you don't want to sit in a cafe, you can spend an intoxicating evening working your way through the long list of local wines, about 2,000L ($1.30) a glass at **Enoteca Fontana,** Via Farina 24/a. To fortify yourself between vintages you can get a sandwich or plate of ham for about 4,000L ($2.65). It's open daily from noon to 10pm.

DAY TRIPS FROM PARMA

TORRECHIARA   The fertile plains that surround Parma are dotted with castles. One of the most dramatic is the 15th-century Farnese fortress of Torerechiara, near the village of Langhirano, whose gloomy, massive walls and crenellated towers top a bluff above the river Parma. Aside from the thrill of stepping back in time, the main attraction here is the room adorned with frescoes and wall tiles by Benedetto Bembo. You can top off your outing with a pizza at **Taverna del Castello,** housed in what were once the castle dungeons; a table on the terrace comes with a view over the valley below.

The castle is 11 miles south of Parma. A bus makes the 40-minute trip hourly (5,000L/$3.30), but be sure to check the time of the last return bus (usually about 5:30pm). Tell the driver where you want to get off. For information you can call **0521/35-52-55;** admission is 5,000L ($3.30), and the castle is open Tuesday to Saturday from 9am to 1pm, and Sunday from 9am to 1pm and 3 to 7pm.

BUSSETO   All of Busseto seems to be a shrine to the beloved composer Giuseppe Verdi, who was born nearby in the little village of Roncole Verdi; the home of his youth is now a museum. The composer returned to the region in 1849 and built, just outside Busseto, the **Villa Verdi di Sant'Agata.** He shared his retreat with a companion, the soprano Giuseppina Strepponi, who later (and after much local gossip) became his wife. Their villa is filled with the couple's mementos and, most touchingly, houses a reconstruction of the hotel room in Milan where the composer died. The villa is open April through October daily from 9 to 11:40am and 3 to 6:40pm; it's closed Monday and from November through March. Admission is 5,000L ($3.30).

Shops all over town sell Verdiana—scores, recordings, prints, postcards, and just about all manner of objects, many of them quite tacky, upon which the composer's visage can be imprinted. If you're lucky, you may stumble into town on one of the rare occasions when a Verdi work is being performed in the **Teatro Verdi,** a little opera house in the castle.

Busseto is about 18 miles northwest of Parma via route S9, or, really speedily, via the autostrada A15 from Parma to Soragana and from there a few miles farther northwest to Busseto. There are buses every half hour from Parma.

9 Venice

by Patricia Schultz

Certainly, the tourists are inescapable. And prices can be double what they are anywhere else in Italy. But this, after all, is Venice. Visitors flock here for a very good reason—Venice is unique, it is magical, and it is worth every lira. Underneath the bizarre beauty and sometimes-stifling tourism, Venice is a living, breathing city that seems almost too exquisite to be genuine, to fragile to survive the never-ending stream of tourism that began over 1,000 years ago.

Venice was at the crossroads of the Byzantine and Roman worlds for centuries, a fact that lends to its unique heritage of art, architecture, and culture. And although traders and merchants no longer pass through "La Serenissima" as they once did, it nonetheless continues to find itself a crossroads: an intersection in time between the uncontested period of maritime power that built it and the modern world that keeps it ever-so-gingerly afloat.

SPECIAL VENICE DISCOUNTS Anyone between 16 and 29 is eligible for a **Rolling Venice pass,** entitling the holder to discounts in museums, restaurants, stores, language courses, hotels, and bars across the city. Valid for one year, it costs 5,000L ($3.30) and can be picked up at any of the tourist offices June 15 through September 30, or year-round at the Assessorato alla Gioventù, Corte Contarina (off the Frezzeria) 1529 (☎ 041/27-07-646).

The 16,000L ($10.50) **biglietto cumulativo** ticket includes admission to nine museums and is valid for one year. But before purchasing your ticket at the box office of the Palazzo Ducale, determine how many of the other eight museums you realistically intend to visit.

Check with a tourist office for free tours being offered (erratically and usually during high season) in some of the churches, particularly the Basilica di San Marco and the Frari church.

1 Arriving

BY PLANE Flights land at the **Aeroporto Marco Polo,** due north of the city on the mainland (☎ 041/26-06-111). The most fashionable and traditional way to arrive in Piazza San Marco is by boat. The **Cooperative San Marco** (☎ 041/52-22-303) keeps that tradition alive, operating a *motoscafo* (shuttle-boat) service between the airport, with one stop at the Lido, and the Piazza San Marco; the cost is 15,000L ($9.85) each way. Call for the daily schedule of the dozen or so round-trips, which changes with the season and is coordinated with the arrival and departure schedules of principal airlines (most hotels will have the monthly schedule posted). A private water taxi into town is convenient but costly, about 110,000L ($72.35), and is worth considering if you have an exceptionally early flight, a lot of luggage, or are traveling with one or more people.

There are two bus alternatives: The airport shuttle bus, run by the **Azienda Trasporti Veneto Orientale (ATVO)** (☎ **041/52-05-530**), connects the airport with Piazzale Roma. Buses leave to and from the airport roughly every hour, cost 5,000L ($3.30), and make the trip in about 30 minutes. The slightly less expensive local **ACTV** bus no. 5 (☎ **041/78-01-11**) is cheaper still, at 1,500L ($1.00) per person. These buses leave to and from the airport and Piazzale Roma hourly and can take up to one hour. For either of the two bus alternatives, you will have to walk from the Piazzale Roma bus drop-off to the nearby vaporetto stop for your hotel or final destination.

BY TRAIN   Trains from all over Europe arrive at the **Stazione Venezia—Santa Lucia** (☎ **041/71-55-55**). To get there, all trains must pass through (though not necessarily stop at) a station marked VENEZIA-MESTRE. Don't be confused: Mestre is a charmless industrial city and the last stop on the mainland. Occasionally trains end at Mestre, in which case you'll have to catch any of the frequent 10-minute shuttle trains that connect Mestre with Venice; so when booking your ticket, confirm that the train's final destination is Stazione Santa Lucia.

At the far end as you come off the tracks at Santa Lucia is the luggage depot or deposito bagagli (near the head of track 7). You'll do well to pack a bag of essentials to take to Venice and leave your heavy gear here during your stay, especially if you're planning to look for accommodations. The depot charges 1,500L ($1.00) per piece per day and is open 24 hours daily. There's an Albergo Diurno (day hotel) at the far right side of the station as you face the tracks; it's open daily from 7am to 8pm and charges 5,500L ($3.60) for a shower. The WC is alongside track 14; an *Oggetti Rivenuti* (lost and found office), is also at track 14.

The official city tourist board, **Azienda Autonoma di Soggiorno e Turismo** (☎ **041/71-52-88**), operates an understaffed (and resultantly surly) information office between the station's large front doors. It's open daily from 8am to 7pm in the summer; closed Sunday in the winter.

The **train information** office (☎ **041/71-55-50**), marked with a lowercase "**i**," is also located in the station's main hall. It's staffed daily from 8am to 8pm. Two banks for **currency exchange** (cambio) keep long hours (usually until 9pm) and compete with each other for business. Compare their rates and commission charge (often in fine print) before exchanging money.

Finally, on exiting the station you'll find the Grand Canal immediately in front of you, making a heart-stopping first impression. The docks for vaporetto lines 82 and 52 are to your left; line 1 is to your right.

BY BUS   Although rail travel is more convenient and commonplace, Venice is serviced by long-distance buses from all over mainland Italy and some foreign cities. Final destination is the Piazzale Roma, where you'll need to pick up a vaporetto to connect you to stops in the heart of Venice.

BY CAR   The only wheels you'll see in Venice are those attached to luggage and the occasional skateboard. Arriving for a stay by car can be problematic and expensive—and downright exasperating if it's high season and the parking facilities are full, a not uncommon situation. There are three parking garages in Venice with differing rates, the two on the man-made island called the Tronchetto, Europe's largest parking lot, being the least expensive: **Garage Comunale,** on Piazzale Roma (☎ **041/ 52-22-308**) is the cheapest, charging 32,000L ($21.00) per day for an average-size car; and the **Venice Terminal** designated by a P (☎ **041/52-07-555**), charging 30,000L ($19.70) per day. If your hotel is a member of the Venetian Hoteliers Association, it may be able to supply you with a 40% discount voucher for one or both of these garages to submit upon departure; make sure you ask while making your reservation and before your arrival in Venice so you can pick your garage accordingly. From the Tronchetto Garage, take vaporetto 17 or 82, not the private boats that are notorious for cheating befuddled and tired tourists, and insisting they are the only way to get you to your destination (sometimes declaring that there is a daylong strike).

If these parking garages are full, your last choice would be **Garage San Marco,** on Piazzale Roma (☎ **041/523-22-13**); this privately-owned lot charges about 50,000L ($32.90) per day for an average-size car and offers no discounts. Vaporetto service lines 1, 82, or 52 are available. Leave your personal effects in your locked car or trunk at your own risk. If you're staying in Venice long, consider dropping your rental car off at the rental agency, and then rearranging for a new car upon your departure.

2 Orientation

VISITOR INFORMATION

In addition to the tourist office inside the train station (see above), there's a **tourist office** at the Palazzetto Selva (☎ **041/52-26-356**), located in between the Giardini (or Giardinetti) Reali, the small green park on the Grand Canal, and the famous Harry's Bar. This is a new location for the office; it used to be in a corner of Piazza San Marco. Hours are Monday through Saturday from 9:30am to 3:30pm in winter, daily 9:30am to 6:30pm in summer. The staff is as unwelcoming as their train station colleagues. Ubiquitous posters around town with exhibition and concert schedules are more helpful. Ask for a schedule of the month's special events and an updated listing of museum and church hours, as these can change erratically.

CITY LAYOUT

Keep in mind as you wander seemingly hopelessly among the calli (streets) and campi (squares) of Venice that the city was not built to make sense (or appear impressive) to those on foot but rather to those plying its myriad canals. No matter how good your map and sense of direction, time after time you'll get wonderfully lost and happen upon Venice's most intriguing corners and vignettes.

Venice lies $2^1/_2$ miles from terra firma, connected to mainland Mestre by the Ponte degli Liberta. Snaking through the city like an inverted S is the **Canal Grande (Grand Canal),** the wide main artery of aquatic Venice. The "streets filled with water" are in fact 177 narrow canals or *rios* that cut through the interior of the two halves of the city, flowing gently by the doorsteps of centuries-old palazzi. They would be endlessly frustrating to the landlubbing tourists trying to navigate the city on foot if not for the 400 small footbridges that cross them, connecting Venice's 118 islands.

Only three bridges (ponti) cross the Grand Canal: the **Ponte degli Scalzi,** just outside the train station; the elegant white marble **Ponte Rialto,** connecting the districts of San Marco and San Polo at the center of town and by far the most famous and recognizable; and the wooden **Ponte Accademia,** connecting the Campo Santo Stefano area of the San Marco district with the Accademia museum across the way in Dorsoduro.

Venice Orientation

Treviso

A4

Mestre

Fávaro
Veneto

14

**Marco Polo
Airport** ✈

Torcello

Burano

E13

Railway
Station **Murano**

Sant'Erasmo

Marghera

11

San Michele

CANNAREGIO
SAN
SANTA POLO SAN MARCO
CROCE
DORSODURO CASTELLO
LA GIUDECCA

Venice

**Ponte della
Libertà**

✈ **Airport on
the Lido**

Casino

Lido di Venezia

*Litorale
di Lido*

0 ⊢⊣⊢⊣⊢⊣ 100 m
160 km

| Airport | ✈ |
| Ferry Route | – – – |

NEIGHBORHOODS IN BRIEF

Since 1711, the city has been divided into six *sestieri* (literally "sixths," or wards).

San Marco The central sestiere is anchored by the magnificent Piazza San Marco and the Basilica San Marco to the south and the Rialto Bridge to the north. The most visited (and resultantly the most expensive) of the sestieri, it is the commercial, religious, and political heart of the city and has been for more than a millenium.

Cannaregio Sharing the same side of the Grand Canal with San Marco, Cannaregio stretches north and east from the train station to the Jewish Ghetto and into the vicinity of the Ca' d'Oro and the Rialto Bridge.

Castello This quarter, whose tony canalside "boulevard," Riva degli Schiavoni, is lined with first-class and deluxe hotels, is to the east, beyond Cannaregio and skirting the area around Piazza San Marco.

San Polo North of the Rialto Bridge, stretching west to just beyond the principal churches and *scuole* of Campo dei Frari and Campo San Rocco.

Santa Croce North and west, Santa Croce stretches all the way to Piazzale Roma and is the least visited section of Venice.

Dorsoduro You'll find the residential area of Dorsoduro on the opposite side of the Accademia Bridge from San Marco. Known for the Accademia and Peggy Guggenheim museums, it is the largest of the sestieri and is something of an artists' haven.

FINDING AN ADDRESS

Not confused enough yet? Each sestiere is divided further into an indeterminate number of small parrochie, literally parishes or neighborhoods. These indications don't
appear on maps and are of little or no use to the navigating tourist, although the
piazzas (called campi in Venice) within each parrochia are frequently reference points
and social hubs. There are hundreds of campi (or "fields"—they were unpaved for
centuries), but only one piazza: San Marco.

Within each sestiere is a most original system of numbering the palazzi, using one
continuous string of 6,000 or so building numbers, which wind their way among the
canals and calli in a fashion known to no living person except perhaps the postman.
When looking for an address, always find out first the name of the sestiere. The format for addresses in this chapter is the official mailing address: the name of the sestiere
followed by the building number within that district, followed by parenthesis with
the name of the street or campo on which you'll find that address: For example, San
Marco 1471 (Salizzada San Moisé), 30121 Venezia.

Venice shares its lagoon with several other islands. Opposite the Piazza San Marco
and Dorsoduro is **la Giudecca,** a tranquil working-class residential area where you'll
find the youth hostel and a handful of hotels (including the Cipriani, one of Europe's
finest). The slim, seven-mile-long **Lido di Venezia** is the city's beach; separating the
lagoon from the open sea and permitting car traffic, it is a popular summer destination because of its concentration of seasonal hotels but is also quite residential.
Murano, Burano, and **Torcello** are popular tourist destinations northeast of the city
and are easily accessible by boat. Since the 13th-century Murano has exported its glass
products worldwide; it's an interesting day trip, but shoppers can do just as well in
Venice's myriad glass stores. Burano was and still is famous for its lace, an art now
practiced by so few that prices are generally unaffordable. Torcello is the most remote
and the least populated. The 40-minute boat ride is worthwhile for history and art
buffs who will be awestruck by the incredible Byzantine mosaics of the cathedral. **San
Michele** is a cemetery island where such celebrities as Stravinsky and Diaghilev are
buried.

Finally, the industrial city of **Mestre,** on the mainland, is the gateway to Venice
and has nothing to explore. In a pinch, its host of inexpensive hotels are worth consideration when Venice's hotels are full.

Street Maps   The free map offered by the tourist office and most hotels has good
intentions, but it doesn't even show, much less name or index, all the pathways of
Venice. For that, pick up a more detailed map (ask for a *pianta della città*) for sale
in any of a number of bookstores or newsstands. Just how helpful the more elaborate maps can be is debatable—if you're lost, you're better off just asking a local
Venetian to point you in the right direction.

GETTING AROUND

To be a successful tourist in Venice, there are two rules of thumb: First, pack
light enough so you can get yourself and your luggage to your hotel door without
despairing at the absence of a (costly) porter just when you need him. Second, always
imagine yourself to be like a child's miniature battery-operated toy car that, when
driven into a wall or other obstacle, instantly turns and continues on its way. Time
and again, you'll think you know exactly where you're going, only to wind up at the
end of a dead-end street or at a canal with no bridge to the other side. Just remind
yourself that the city's physical complexity—that is, getting lost—is an integral part
of its charm and a memorable experience that Venice guarantees every visitor.

Venetian Dialect—What Would Dante Say?

If, after a few days in Rome and Florence, you were just getting the hang of corre-
lating your map to the reality of your new surroundings, you can put aside any
short-term success upon your arrival in Venezia. Even the Italians (non-Venetian
ones) look befuddled when trying to decipher street names and signs (given that
you can ever find any of the latter). Venice's colorful thousand-year history as a
once-powerful maritime republic has everything to do with its local dialect, which
absorbed nuances and vocabulary from the East and from the flourishing communities of foreign merchants who, for centuries, lived and traded in Venice. A lin-
guist could gleefully spend a lifetime trying to make some sense of it all. But for the
Venice-bound traveler just trying to make sense of Venetian addresses, the following should give you the basics. (And don't even try to follow a conversation
between two gondolieri!)

ca' The abbreviated use of the word "casa" is used for the noble palazzi, once
private residences and now museums, lining the Grand Canal: Ca' d'Oro, Ca'
Pesaro, and Ca' Rezzonico. There is only one palazzo, and it is the Palazzo Ducale,
the former doge's residence. However, as time went on some great houses gradually began to be called "palazzi," so today you'll encounter the Palazzo Grassi or
the Palazzo Labia.

calle Taken from the Spanish, this is the most commonplace word for street,
known as "via" or "strada" elsewhere in Italy. There are numerous variations.
"Ruga" from the French word "rue" once meant a calle flanked with stores, a
designation no longer valid. A "ramo" is the branch or offshoot of a street, and is
often used interchangeably with "calle." "Salizzada" once meant a paved street,
implying that all other less important "calles" were just dirt alleyways.

campo Elsewhere in Italy it's "piazza." In Venice the only piazza is the Piazza San
Marco (and its two bordering "piazzette"); all other squares are "campi" or the
diminutive, "campielli." Translated as "field" or "meadow," these were once small,
unpaved grazing spots for the odd chicken or cow. Almost every one of Venice's
campi carries the name of the church that dominates it (or once did).

canale There are three wide, principal canals: the Canal Grande, the Canale della
Giudecca, and the Canale di Cannaregio. Each of the other 160 smaller canals is
called a *rio*. A "rio terrà" is a filled-in canal—wide and straight—now used as a
street.

fondamenta Referring to the foundations of the houses lining a canal, this is
a walkway along the side of a rio. Promenades along the Grand Canal near the
Piazza San Marco and the Rialto are called "riva."

Note: With its countless stepped footbridges and with almost no elevators in any
of the buildings, Venice is one of the worst cities in the world for the physically
disabled.

BY BOAT A comprehensive vaporetto system of about a dozen lines is operated
by the **Azienda del Consorzio Trasporti Veneziano (ACTV),** C. Fuseri 1810, off
the Frezzeria in San Marco (☎ **041/52-87-886**). Transit maps are available at the
tourist office and at most ACTV stations (be aware that vaporetto stops and lines were
changed and renumbered in 1994—a number of the old maps are still in circulation).

Contrary to what you may think, it's easier to get around by foot; the vaporetti principally service the Grand Canal (and can be horribly crowded in the summer months), the outskirts, and outer islands. The crisscross network of small canals is the province of delivery vessels, gondolas, and private boats.

The average fare on most lines is 4,000L ($2.65); they run daily every 10 to 15 minutes from 7am to midnight, then hourly until morning; most ticket booths have timetables posted. Note, however, that not all stations sell tickets after dark; if you haven't purchased a block of tickets, you'll have to settle up with the conductor on board (you'll have to find him, he won't come looking for you), or gamble on a 40,000L ($26.30) fine, with no excuses accepted.

Although the city, no larger than New York's Central Park, is extremely easy to navigate on foot, boat lovers might want to consider the 15,000L ($9.85) **Biglietto 24 Ore** that entitles the bearer to 24 hours of unlimited travel on any ACTV vessel. The **Biglietto 3 Giorni,** covering three full days of unlimited travel, doesn't seem like much of a savings at 30,000L ($19.75), even less so for the **Biglietto 7 Giorni** for seven days at 55,000L ($36.15), unless you really intend to utilize the system. The **Biglietto Isole,** a ticket valid for unlimited one-day travel in one direction on line 12 (which services the islands of Murano, Mazzorbo, Burano, and Torcello) costs 5,000L ($3.30).

Line 1, ironically called the *accellerato* when it in fact is the slowest, is the most important for the average tourist, making all stops along the Grand Canal and continuing on to the Lido. **Line 82,** a *diretto,* also travels the Grand Canal, though it makes limited stops at Piazza San Marco, the Accademia Bridge, the Rialto Bridge, and the train station before circling Dorsoduro and crossing the lagoon to the Lido. **Line 52,** the *circolare,* is another major line, circling the perimeter of the city and crossing the lagoon to Murano on one side and the Lido on the other. **Line 12** also crosses the waves to Murano, continuing on to Burano and Torcello.

Since there are just three bridges spanning the Grand Canal, to fill in the gaps, *traghetti* gondolas cross the canal at seven or so intermediate points. You'll find a traghetto station at the end of any street named "Calle del Traghetto" on your map and indicated by a yellow sign with the black symbol of a gondola. The fare, regulated by the local government, is 1,000L (65¢) which you hand to the gondoliere when boarding. Most Venetians cross standing up, it's the foreigners who scramble for the few seats. For the experience, try the crossing that connects the Ca' d'Oro and the Pescheria fish market, opposite each other on the Grand Canal just north of the Rialto Bridge—the gondoliers expertly dodge water traffic at this point of the canal where it is the busiest.

BY WATER TAXI   Taxi acquei (water taxis) prices are high and not for the average tourist watching their lire. For journeys up to seven minutes, the rate is 27,000L ($17.75); click off 500L (30¢) for each additional 15 seconds. There's an 8,500L ($5.60) supplement for night service (10pm to 7am), and a 9,000L ($5.90) surcharge on Sunday and holidays; note that these two supplements cannot be applied simultaneously. If they have to come get you, tack on another 8,000L ($5.25).

There are six **water-taxi stations** serving various key points in the city: the Ferrovia or train station (☎ **041/71-62-86**), Piazzale Roma (☎ **041/71-69-22**), the Rialto Bridge (☎ **041/52-30-575**), Piazza San Marco (☎ **041/52-29-750**), the Lido (☎ **041/52-60-059**), and Marco Polo Airport (☎ **041/54-15-084**). **Radio Taxi** (☎ **041/522-23-03**) will come pick you up any place in the city, for a surcharge, of course.

ON FOOT   You can get a map and spend your day trying to make some sense out of it. Or then again, you can jettison the map and just wander. Look for the ubiquitous yellow signs that direct travelers toward five major landmarks: Ferrovia (the train station), Piazzale Roma, the Rialto Bridge, Piazza San Marco, and the Accademia Bridge. To truly experience the city, just walk and walk and walk. You'll be exhausted but elated at the end of the day.

BY GONDOLA   To come all the way to Venice and not indulge in a gondola ride could be one of your biggest regrets. Yes, it's touristy and yes, it's expensive (see "Special Interest Sightseeing: For the Romantic" for prices, details, etc.), but only those with a heart of stone will be unmoved by the experience. Do not initiate your trip, however, until you have agreed upon a price and synchronized watches. Oh, and don't ask them to sing.

FAST FACTS: Venice

Acqua Alta   The notorious acqua alta floods, a peculiarity related as much to the tides and winds as to rainfall, can start as early as October, usually taking place from November to March. If a flood is expected, a warning will be sounded one hour before its crest so people can get home, and the city puts out boardwalks (passarelle) along the major routes. Acqua alta generally lasts only about two or three hours at a time.

American Express   See "Currency Exchange," below.

Babysitters   There are no babysitting agencies in Venice per se. Your best bet is to make arrangements through the hotel, although this is a service usually not provided by the small hotels listed in this book. They may by able to help, however, but try to give them ample notice.

Banks   Banks are normally open Monday to Friday from 8:30am to 1:30pm and 2:35 to 3:35pm or 3 to 4pm; some banks are open on Saturday year-round (others in July or August only) and follow an 8:30 to 11:30am schedule. ATMs are relatively recent, though their numbers are rapidly growing.

Bookstores   Two centrally located bookstores that carry a line of soft- and hardcover books in English are the Libreria Sansovino in the Bacino Orseolo 84 immediately north of the Piazza San Marco (☎ 041/52-22-623) and the Libreria San Giorgio, C. Larga XXII Marzo 2087 (☎ 041/52-38-451), beyond the American Express Office. Both carry a selection of books about Venetian art, history, and literature.

Business Hours   Standard hours for shops are 9am to 12:30pm and 3 to 7:30pm Monday to Saturday. In winter shops are closed on Monday morning, while in summer it's usually Saturday afternoon. Most grocers are closed on Wednesday afternoon throughout the year. In Venice just about everything is closed on Sunday, though tourist shops in the San Marco area are permitted to stay open during high season. Restaurants are required to close at least one day per week (*il giorno di riposo*), though the particular day varies from one trattoria to another. Many are open for Sunday lunch but close for Sunday dinner and close Monday when the fish market is closed. Restaurants will close for holidays (*chiuso per ferie*) sometime in July or August, frequently over Christmas, and sometime in January before the Carnevale rush.

Climate   May, June, and September are the best months weatherwise to visit (and the most crowded). July and August are hot—at times unbearably so. April or late October are hit or miss; it can either be glorious, or cool, rainy, and damp (but far less crowded). Also see "Acqua Alta," above.

Consulates   The Consulate of the **United Kingdom** is at Dorsoduro 1051 (☎ **041/52-27-207**), at the foot of the Accademia Bridge; it's open Monday through Friday from 9am to noon and 2 to 4pm. The **United States** has a consulate in Milan (☎ **02/29-03-51**) as do **Canada** and **Australia.**

Crime   Be aware of petty crime such as pickpocketing on the crowded vaporetti, particularly the tourist routes where passengers are more intent on the passing scenery than watching their bags. Venice's deserted back streets were virtually crime-free; occasional tales of theft are beginning to circulate.

Currency Exchange   Both exchange offices (cambio) at the train station are open seven days a week. The **American Express** office, San Marco 1471, on Sz. San Moisé (☎ **041/52-00-844**) exchanges money commission-free. To find it: with your back to the Basilica di San Marco, exit the piazza by way of the arcade at the far left end; you'll see a mosaic sign in the pavement pointing the way straight ahead. The office is open in summer for banking Monday to Saturday from 8am to 8pm (all other services 9am to 5:30pm); in winter, Monday to Friday from 9am to 5:30pm and Saturday from 9am to 12:30pm . Be careful of the privately-owned cambio around town whose boards boast good rates but whose commonly high commissions appear at the bottom in small print. They follow the same schedule as retail shops, not banks, often staying open during lunch.

Dentists/Doctors   For a shortlist, check with the consulate of the United Kingdom or the American Express office.

Drugstores   Pharmacies take turns staying open all night. To find out which one is on call in your area, ask at your hotel or dial **041/52-30-573.**

Emergencies   Dial **113** to reach the police. Some Italians will recommend that you try the military-trained Carabinieri (phone **112**), in the opinion of some a better police force. For an ambulance, phone **041/52-30-000.** To report a fire, dial **041/52-00-222;** on the Lido, **041/52-60-222.**

Fax   From both the main post office and its Piazza San Marco branch (see "Mail," below) you can send faxes to almost any destination with the odd exception of the United States. For service to the United States, most hotels will agree to do it for either a per-page or estimated-per-minute cost. Or look for SERVIZIO FAX signs in the windows of cartolerie (stationery stores).

Holidays   Venice's patron saint, St. Mark, is honored on April 25.

Laundry   The self-service laundry most convenient to the train station is the Lavaget at Cannaregio 1269, to the left as you cross the Ponte alle Guglie from Lista di Spagna, open Monday to Friday from 8:30am to 12:30pm and 3 to 7pm; the rate is about 16,000L ($10.50) for up to 4.5 kilos (10 lbs.). At the Lavanderia a Gettone SS. Apostoli, at Cannaregio 4553a, on Salizzada d. Pistor just off Campo SS. Apostoli, you pay 12,000L ($7.90) for a load of 4.5 kilos (10 lbs.), or 20,000L ($13.15) for 8 kilos (17 lbs.); open Monday to Friday from 8:30am to 12:30pm and 3 to 7pm. It's (relatively) convenient to the Rialto Bridge area.

Lost & Found   The central Ufficio Oggetti Rinvenuti (☎ **041/78-82-25**) is in the annex to the City Hall (Municipio), at San Marco 4134, on Calle Piscopia o Loredan, just off riva del Carbon on the Grand Canal, near the Rialto Bridge (on the same side of the canal as the Rialto vaporetto station). Look for scala (stairway) C; the lost-and-found office is in the "Economato" section on the "mezzanino" level, one flight up. The office is ostensibly open only on Monday, Wednesday, and Friday from 9:30am to 12:30pm, but there's usually someone available weekdays from 9:30am until the building closes at 1:30pm.

There's also an Ufficio Oggetti Smarriti at the airport (☎ **041/26-06-436**), and an Ufficio Oggetti Rinvenuti at the train station (☎ **041/78-52-38**), right at the head of Track 14; open Monday to Friday from 8am to 4pm.

Luggage Storage   See above, "Arriving: By Train" for a safe place to check your luggage.

Mail   Venice's main Posta Centrale is at San Marco 5554, on Salizzada Fontego d. Tedeschi (☎ **041/522-06-06**), just off Campo San Bartolomeo, in the area of the Rialto Bridge on the San Marco side of the Grand Canal. This office is usually open Monday to Saturday from 8:15am to 7pm. Stamps are sold at Window 12.

If you're at Piazza San Marco and need postal services, walk through Sottoportego San Geminian, the center portal at the opposite end of the piazza from the basilica on Calle Larga dell'Ascensione. This branch is open Monday to Friday from 8:15am to 1:30pm and Saturday from 8:15am to 12:10pm.

Remember that you can buy stamps (*francobolli*) at any tabacchi with no additional service charge; postcards differ according to destination (to the United States 1,250L, or 80¢), letters according to weight. The limited mailboxes seen around town are red.

Rest Rooms   For the cost of an espresso or mineral water you can use the rest rooms in any bar (*signori* means men, *signore,* ladies). Museums and galleries will also have facilities. Public "WCs" can be found at the train station; near the Giardinetti Reali park next to the Tourist Information office (Palazzetto Selva); on the west side (Dorsoduro) of the Accademia Bridge; next to the post office branch just west of the Piazza San Marco on Calle Larga dell'Ascensione; and off Campo San Bartolomeo.

Shoe Repair   Try the one at Dorsoduro 871 on Calle Nuova Sant'Agnese, on the main route between the Accademia and the Peggy Guggenheim Collection.

Time   Dial **161** for exact time recorded in Italian only.

Weather   Dial **191** for weather forecast recorded in Italian only.

3 Accommodations

Hotels, like just about everything else in Venice, are more expensive than in any other city in Italy. Whatever you've been spending in other parts of the country, you can plan on spending a good deal more here with no apparent upgrade in amenities. At worst, inexpensive hotels are clean and functional; at best they are charming and thoroughly enjoyable. Some may even provide you with your best stay in Europe.

We strongly suggest that you book in advance once your itinerary is planned, regardless of the period. In June and September and during special events year-round, it can seem that there is not a budget lodging to be had in Venice, especially if you arrive after noon. If you haven't booked, arrive as early as you can, for time literally is money. The tourist office in the train station will book rooms for you, but the lines are long and (understandably) the staff's patience is sometimes thin. If you're holding a Rolling Venice card (see "Special Venice Discounts," above) the small office in the Santa Lucia train station will help with reservations free of charge.

The **Promove** organization is known for its wintertime hotel discounts (two-night minimum). All-inclusive packages for the period from November 1 to March 31 include hotel, a guided walking tour, and discounts at a number of museums and restaurants. Promove is represented by dozens of local travel agencies who, unfortunately, cannot except overseas credit card payments to hold reservations (you'll need

Venice Accommodations

Albergo Adua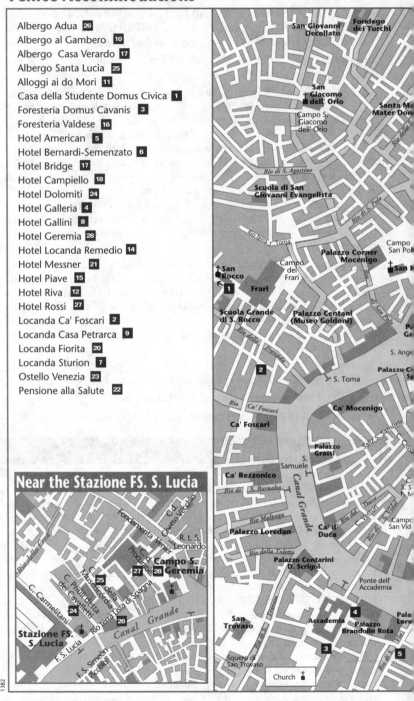

Albergo al Gambero

Albergo Casa Verardo

Albergo Santa Lucia

Alloggi ai do Mori

Casa della Studente Domus Civica

Foresteria Domus Cavanis

Foresteria Valdese

Hotel American

Hotel Bernardi-Semenzato

Hotel Bridge

Hotel Campiello

Hotel Dolomiti

Hotel Galleria

Hotel Gallini

Hotel Geremia

Hotel Locanda Remedio

Hotel Messner

Hotel Piave

Hotel Riva

Hotel Rossi

Locanda Ca' Foscari

Locanda Casa Petrarca

Locanda Fiorita

Locanda Sturion

Ostello Venezia

Pensione alla Salute

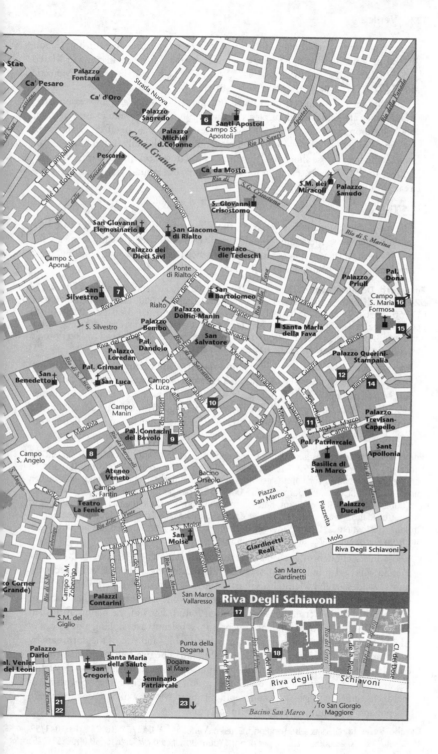

Stae

Ca' Pesaro

Palazzo
Fontana

Ca' d'Oro

Palazzo
Sagredo

Palazzo
Michiel
d.Colonne

Strada Nuova

6 Santi Apostoli
Campo SS
Apostoli

Canal Grande

Rio D. Santi

Pescaria

C. del Campanile

Calle D' Botteri

Ca' da Mosto

Rio di

S. Gi. Crisostomo

S.M. dei
Miracoli

Palazzo
Sanudo

San Giovanni
Elemosinario

S. Giacomo
di Rialto

S. Giovanni
Crisostomo

Rio di S. Marina

Palazzo dei
Dieci Savi

Fondaco
die Tedeschi

Campo S.
Aponal

Ponte
di Rialto

Pal.
Donà

Palazzo
Priuli

Campo
S. Maria **16**
Formosa

San
Silvestro **7**

Riva del Vin

Rialto

S. Silvestro

Palazzo
Bembo

Palazzo
Dolfin-Manin

San
Bartolomeo

Stagneri

Santa Maria
della Fava

15

Riva del Carbon

Pal.
Dandolo

San
Salvatore

Palazzo Querini-
Stampalia

Palazzo
Loredan

Merc S. Salvador

Pal. Grimari

12

14

Rimedio

San
Benedetto

San Luca

Campo
S. Luca

10

Palazzo
Trevisan-
Cappello

Campo
Manin

11

C. Larga S. Marco

Canonica

C. Mandola

Pal. Contarini
del Bovolo

9

Pal. Patriarcale

Sant
Apollonia

8

Campo
S. Angelo

Ateneo
Veneto

Campo
S. Fantin

Basilica di
San Marco

Teatro
La Fenice

Bacino
Orseolo

Piazza
San Marco

Palazzo
Ducale

Piazzetta

S.S. Moise
San
Moise

C. Largo XXII Marzo

Giardinetti
Reali

Molo

Riva Degli Schiavoni →

co Corner
Grande)

San Marco
Giardinetti

Campo S.M.
Zobenigo

Palazzi
Contarini

San Marco
Vallaresso

Riva Degli Schiavoni

S.M. del
Giglio

17

Palazzo
Dario

Punta della
Dogana

al. Venier
del Leoni

San
Gregorio

Santa Maria
della Salute

18

Dogana
al Mare

Seminario
Patriarcale

Riva degli

Schiavoni

21
22

23 ↓

To San Giorgio
Maggiore

Bacino San Marco

to send an international bank draft or money order, or arrange your hotel upon arrival in Venice): The most central agent is **Intras Travel** in Piazza San Marco 72/B (☎ **041/52-36-446** or fax 041/52-86-347); or **Kele e Teo** on the Mercerie 4930 (☎ **041/52-08-722** or fax 041/52-08-913).

Finally, keep in mind that most hotels usually observe high- and low-season rates, though they are gradually adopting a single year-round rate. Be sure to ask when you book, or upon arrival at a hotel, whether off-season prices are in effect. High season in Venice runs from March 15 through November 5, with a lull during July and August. Some hotels close altogether (sometimes without notice) from November or December until Carnevale, opening for about two weeks around Christmas and New Year's at high-season rates.

HOSTELS

The only accommodations to be had in this least-expensive price category are hostels and alternative operations, church- or university-affiliated. The following are the best in town. If they're full, the local tourist office has a more extensive listing, most of which operate in summer months only.

Foresteria Domus Cavanis. Dorsoduro 912a (Rio Antonio Foscarini), Venezia. ☎/fax **041/52-87-374.** 30 beds (in single and doubles), none with bath. 40,000L ($26.30) single; 60,000L ($39.50) double. Discount for students 15–25 years old. Continental breakfast 7,000L ($4.60) per person extra. Full board available. No credit cards. Open June–Sept only; closed Oct–May. Vaporetto: Accademia. Veer left around the museum, walk straight ahead on Rio Antonio Foscarini; the Domus Cavanis will be halfway down on your right.

The location is the draw here, just behind the city's important Accademia museum in the lovely Dorsoduro neighborhood, a recommended escape from the congested San Marco neighborhood. While the rooms in this converted dormitory are rather plain, beds are narrow, and the place is popular with groups, Padre Ferdinando Fietta runs a tip-top place with rock-bottom rates. The institutional-looking building surrounds a concrete playground but makes up in savings what it lacks in charm.

Foresteria Valdese. Castello 5170 (at the end of C. Lunga Santa Maria Formosa), 30122 Venezia. ☎ **041/52-860797.** Fax 041/52-39-745. 4 rms (2–3 beds), 3 dorms (8, 11, and 16 beds), none with bath. 2 mini-apts (sleeping 5 and 6, minimum stay often required) with kitchen and bath. 25,000L ($16.45) dorm bed; 35,000L ($23) per person double or triple; 140,000L–155,000L ($92.10–$102) mini-apt. Rates in rms and dorms include breakfast. No credit cards. Vaporetto: Rialto. Head southeast to the Campo Santa Maria Formosa; look for the Bar all' Orologio, just where C. Lunga Santa Maria Formosa begins. The campo is just about equidistant from Piazza San Marco and the Rialto Bridge.

Those lucky enough to get a place at this weathered, albeit elegant, 16th-century palazzo will find simple accommodations in a charming ambience. Affiliated with Italy's Waldesian and Methodist Church, the large dormitory-style rooms are often booked with visiting church groups, though everyone is warmly welcomed and an international and interreligious mix is often found. Each of the plainly furnished rooms in this once-noble residence opens onto a balcony overlooking a quiet canal. The frescoes that grace the high ceilings in the doubles and two of the dorms are by the same artist who decorated the Correr Museum. The two four-room apartments, complete with kitchen facilities, are the best budget choice in town for traveling families of five or six. A complete five-year renovation was launched in 1995 with minimal inconvenience to guests. The reception is open Monday to Saturday from 9am to 1pm and 6 to 8pm and Sunday 9am to 1pm.

Ostello Venezia. Giudecca 86 (on Fond. Zitelle), Venezia. ☎ **041/52-38-211.** Fax 041/52-35-689. 270 beds. 23,000L ($15.15) per person. Youth hostel card available for 30,000L ($19.75);

or on an installment basis for 5,000L ($3.30) per night for 6 nights. Rates include continental breakfast, sheets, and showers. V. Vaporetto: Zitelle. Just to the right of the vaporetto stop.

Modern and efficiently run by Claudio Camillo, this is Venice's largest dormitory. What's more, the view of the tip of Dorsoduro and Piazza San Marco in the distance makes commuting to the eastern end of La Giudecca island a pleasure. The three-night maximum stay is usually enforced only in summer. Arrive by midafternoon to guarantee yourself a bed in summer. From July to September registration opens at noon; the remainder of the year the check-in starts at 1pm. The rooms are closed until 5pm all year, and curfew is 1am. This youth hostel is open to budget travelers of all ages. Remember to add the 8,000L ($5.25) round-trip cost of the vaporetto to the net cost of staying at this hostel. The ample dinner, at 14,000L ($9.20) for three courses and fruit, is one of the best food values in town. Mealtimes are usually 6 to 9pm.

IN CANNAREGIO
DOUBLES FOR LESS THAN 100,000 LIRE ($65.80)

The Lista di Spagna, immediately to the left as you exit the train station, is full of trinket shops and budget hotels. This area is comparatively charmless (though safe), and in the high-season months is wall-to-wall with tourists who window-shop their way to Piazza San Marco, an easy half-hour to 45-minute stroll away. Vaporetto connections from the train station are convenient.

Albergo Adua. Cannaregio 233a (on Lista di Spagna), 30121 Venezia. ☎ **041/71-61-84.** 12 rms, 4 with bath. 52,000L ($34.20) single without bath; 77,000L ($50.65) double without bath, 115,000L ($75.65) double with bath; 90,000L ($59.20) triple without bath, 104,000L ($68.40) triple with bath; 150,000L ($98.70) quad without bath, 193,000L ($127.00) quad with bath. Low-season rates are approximately 10%–15% less. Breakfast 7,500L ($4.95) per person extra. MC, V. Vaporetto: Ferrovie. Exit the train station and turn left onto the Lista di Spagna. The hotel is relatively close by on your right.

The Adua family has been in business more than 30 years. Comfortable-size rooms appeal to all ages, but are particularly popular with students who don't mind the eclectic furnishings straight out of the 1970s or the rather creative pattern combinations. As many as four rooms may share a bath while en suite bathrooms are new and attractive. As a former pensione, this small hotel never had a breakfast room, so coffee and rolls are served in the kitchen or in your room.

✪ **Hotel Bernardi-Semenzato.** Cannaregio 4366 (on C. de l'Oca), 30121 Venezia. ☎ **041/52-22-257.** Fax 041/52-22-424. Main house: 18 rms, 10 with bath. Annex: 8 rms, 1 with bath. A/C TEL TV. 58,000L ($38.15) single without bath, 79,000L ($52.00) single with bath; 75,000L ($49.35) double without bath, 120,000L ($78.95) double with bath; 105,000L ($69.10) triple without bath, 130,000L ($85.50) triple with bath. Rates include continental breakfast. Inquire about off-season rates. MC, V. Closed Nov 20–Dec 10. Vaporetto: Ca D'Oro. From the vaporetto stop, walk a short distance straight ahead to S. Nova, turn right in the direction of Campo SS. Apostoli, and look for Cannaregio 4309, a stationery/toy store on your left; turn left on this narrow side street, the C. Duca, then take the first right onto C. de l'Oca.

From outside, this weather-worn palazzo doesn't begin to hint of the recent top-to-toe renovation completed in 1995, one that has left handhewn ceiling beams exposed, rooms outfitted with tastefully coordinated headboard/bedspread sets, and bathrooms newly modernized and brightly retiled. The young and enthusiastic English-speaking owners, Maria Teresa and Leonardo Pepoli, aspire to three-star style, and may eventually aim at a two-star category in 1997, but are content to offer one-star rates (prices get even more interesting when off-season rates apply). The recent addition of an annex three blocks away offers you the chance to feel like you've rented

🕐 Family-Friendly Hotels

Albergo Casa Verardo *(see p. 308)*   Two lovely connecting suites sleep families of four; one lucky family even gets a private terrace and view. But everyone gets to enjoy the attention and hospitality of the gracious Verardo family.

Foresteria Valdese *(see p. 302)*   Especially recommended for extended stays, there are just two mini-apartments here, sleeping five to six, with kitchenettes, located in a rambling historical palazzo in a residential neighborhood accessible to everything.

Hotel Bernardi-Semenzato *(see p. 303)*   A number of bright, redone rooms serve as triples, but it's really the family-run atmosphere, led by sympathetic Maria Teresa and Leonardo and their three children, that makes this a practical choice.

Locanda Sturion *(see p. 311)*   Scottish-born Helen or her daughter Nicolette will settle you into any of the spacious rooms, two of which will guarantee the special thrill of a Grand Canal view. From your window watch the action of Venice's aquatic Main Street within sight of the Rialto Bridge.

your own aristocratic apartment, with large rooms boasting intricate parquet floors, imposing 19th-century armoires, and Murano chandeliers—room no. 6 overlooks a narrow canal, no. 5 the lovely garden of a palazzo next door.

Hotel Dolomiti. Cannaregio 72–74 (on C. Priuli), 30121 Venezia. ☎ **041/71-51-13.** Fax 041/71-66-35. 50 rms, 20 with bath. TEL. 70,000L ($46.05) single without bath, 120,000L ($78.95) single with bath; 100,000L ($65.80) twin without bath, 145,000L ($95.40) twin with bath; 110,000L ($72.35) double without bath, 160,000L ($105.25) double with bath; 135,000L ($88.80) triple without bath, 198,000L ($130.25) triple with bath; 160,000L ($105.25) quad without bath, 240,000L ($157.90) quad with bath. Rates include breakfast. AE, MC, V. Closed Nov 15–Jan 31. Vaporetto: Ferrovie. As you exit train station turn left onto the Lista di Spagna and take the first left onto C. Priuli.

For those who prefer to stay in the vicinity of the train station, this is an old-fashioned, comfortable, and reliable choice. With 50 large, clean, but ordinary rooms spread over four floors, you have a better chance of finding available accommodations at this family-owned hotel than at some of the smaller ones we suggest. Sergio and Lorenzo, the efficient polylingual front-desk staff in the old-world lobby, supply weather forecasts, umbrellas, restaurant suggestions, and a big smile after your long day meandering about this remarkable city. *Warning:* There's no elevator, so ask about your room location.

✪ **Hotel Geremia.** Cannaregio 290/A (Campo San Geremia), 30121 Venezia. ☎ **041/71-62-45.** Fax 041/52-42-342. 20 rms, 14 with bath. TEL TV. 72,000L ($47.35) single without bath, 100,000L ($65.80) single with bath; 84,000L ($55.25) double without bath, 112,000L ($73.70) double with bath; 152,000L ($100.00) triple with bath; 192,000L ($126.30) quadruple with bath (rates reflect special discounts for readers of this book). Rates include continental breakfast. AE, MC, V. Vaporetto: Ferrovie. From the train station, turn left (east) onto Lista di Spagna and follow it until arriving in the Campo San Geremia. Hotel is on left.

If this gem of a one-star hotel had an elevator and was located in the high-rent San Marco neighborhood, it would cost three times what it does. Consider yourself lucky to settle into any one of these recently and tastefully renovated rooms—ideally one of the eight that overlook the small campo (better yet, one of two top-floor rooms with a small private terrace for guests who relish a Stairmaster-type workout). All rooms are outfitted with either blond wood paneling or deep green or burnished rattan headboards and matching chairs. Top-of-the-line bathrooms offer three-star amenities such as hair dryers and heated towel racks. A labor of love, this charming hotel is overseen by English-speaking owner/manager Claudio, who will regale you with helpful tips as well as free passes to the winter Casino, just 10 minutes by foot. It's also 5 to 10 minutes from the train station (pack light!) but is easy to find. Ask about rates for readers of this book, and inquire about off-season rates.

Hotel Rossi. Cannaregio 262 (on C. d. Procuratie), 30121 Venezia. ☎ **041/71-51-64.** Fax 041/71-77-84. 20 rms, 17 with bath. TEL. 60,000L ($39.50) single without bath; 70,000L ($46.05) single with bath; 90,000L ($59.20) double without bath; 120,000L ($78.95) double with bath; 145,000L ($95.40) triple with bath; 180,000L ($118.40) quad with bath. Rates include continental breakfast. AE, MC, V. Closed early Jan to mid-Feb. Vaporetto: Ferrovie. From the train station, turn left onto Lista di Spagna and take the fourth left onto the narrow C. d. Procuratie.

Located in a quiet cul-de-sac, this pleasant little place offers standard-style rooms and a lush green garden next door—it's an acceptable standby in this neighborhood, convenient to the train station. Stairs lead to rooms on three floors, so request a lower floor if you're not a climber. Rates are discounted during the low season.

DOUBLES FOR LESS THAN 130,000 LIRE ($85.50)

Albergo Santa Lucia. Cannaregio 358 (on C. d. Misercordia), 30121 Venezia. ☎/fax **041/71-51-80.** 18 rms, 7 with bath. 70,000L ($46.05) single without bath; 120,000L ($78.95) double without bath; 130,000L ($85.50) double with bath; 120,000L ($78.95) triple without bath, 160,000L ($105.25) triple with bath; 200,000L ($131.75) quad with bath. Rates include continental breakfast. AE, DC, V. Closed Jan 7–Feb 10. Vaporetto: Ferrovie. Turn left onto Lista di Spagna and take the 2nd left on C. d. Misercordia.

This rather contemporary building has a flower-decked flagstone terrace out front bordered by roses, oleander, and ivy. White patio furniture lures hotel guests to enjoy breakfast here, served in an old-fashioned way, with coffee and tea brought in sterling-silver pots (guests are also welcome to bring their own brown bag at lunch and enjoy it here). Friendly owner Emilia Gonzato oversees her operation with pride; the large rooms are simple but bright and clean. She doesn't speak English, but her son, Gianangelo, does.

IN SAN MARCO
DOUBLES FOR LESS THAN 100,000 LIRE ($65.80)

Albergo al Gambero. San Marco 4687 (on C. d. Fabbri), 30124 Venezia. ☎ **041/52-24-384** or 52-01-420. Fax 041/52-00-431. 30 rms: 1 with shower only, 3 with bath. 61,000L ($40.15) single without bath; 100,000L ($65.80) double without bath, 110,000L ($72.35) double with shower only, 125,000L ($82.25) double with bath; 135,000L ($88.80) triple without bath, 148,000L ($97.35) triple with shower only, 168,000L ($110.50) triple with bath; 170,000L ($111.85) quad without bath, 186,000L ($122.35) quad with shower only, 212,000L ($139.50) quad with bath. Rates are for Frommer's readers only. Rates include continental breakfast. MC, V. Vaporetto: Rialto. At the vaporetto stop, turn right along the canal, cross the small footbridge, turn left onto C. Bembo, which becomes C. d. Fabbri; the hotel is about 5 blocks ahead, on your left.

One of Venice's larger budget hotels occupies an enviable location midway between Piazza San Marco and the Rialto Bridge. The Gambero's basically furnished rooms are par for the course, though guests in any of the 18 canalside rooms will enjoy the serenades of the passing gondoliers. High ceilings (and no elevator) make rooms on the first two floors preferable. Breakfast is served in the lovely ground-floor Le Bistrot de Venise (see "Where to Dine," below), owned by the hotel.

✪ **Alloggi ai do Mori.** San Marco 658 (on C. larga San Marco), 30124 Venezia. ☎ **041/52-04-817** or 52-89-293. Fax 041/52-05-328. 11 rms, 7 with bath. TEL TV. 60,000L ($39.50) single without bath; 105,000L ($69.10) double without bath, 140,000L ($92.10) double with bath; 125,000L ($82.25) triple without bath, 160,000L ($105.25) triple with bath; 160,000L ($105.25) quad without bath, 220,000 ($144.75) quad with bath. Ask about off-season rates. MC, V. Vaporetto: San Marco. Exit the Piazza San Marco underneath the Torre d. l'Orologio

clock tower; turn right at the first opportunity (at the Max Mara store) and you'll find the hotel on the left, just before Burghy's.

Antonella, the young and *simpatica* owner of this super-central hotel, creates an
efficient yet comfortable ambience with special care given to Frommer's readers.
The more accessible lower floors (there is no elevator and the hotel begins on the
second floor) are slightly larger and offer interesting rooftop views, but the somewhat
smaller top-floor rooms boast views that embrace San Marco's many cupolas and the
nearby Torre d. l'Orologio whose two bronze Moors ring the bells every hour. All
rooms are sunny and pleasant, enhanced by the ambitious improvement-minded
owner/manager, who has recently added bright new wallpaper, large double-paned
windows to ensure quiet, and wonderfully firm mattresses for tourism-weary bodies.

Locanda Casa Petrarca. San Marco 4386 (on C. de le Schiavine), 30124 Venezia. ☎ **041/
52-00-430.** Fax 041/52-00-430. 7 rms, 3 with bath. 65,000L ($42.75) single without bath;
85,000L ($55.90) double without bath, 110,000L ($72.35) double with bath. Increase of 35%
of room rate for each additional bed. Breakfast 7,500L ($4.95) per person extra. No credit cards.
Vaporetto: Rialto. First you'll need to get to the Campo San Luca: from vaporetto stop, turn right
along the Grand Canal, then left on C. d. Carbon (just after San Marco 4176) which runs into
Campo San Luca. Cross the small campo and walk down C. d. Fuseri to no. 4337 (La Parigina
shoe store); take a left under a sottoportego arch and then a quick right onto C. de le Schiavine.
The Locanda will be on your left.

After living in London for 10 years, Nellie's English is more refined than that of most
of her guests. Her small inn has just six rooms, including one tiny single, so call to
reserve well in advance. Clean, unpretentious, simply decorated, and with nice bathrooms, this is a comfy, casual kind of place tucked away on a small canal near a popular store-lined street connecting the Rialto area with Piazza San Marco. It might be
a bit hard to find first time around, not unlike many other places—but that's part
of the Venice experience.

Locanda Fiorita. San Marco 3457 (Campiello Novo), 30124 Venezia. ☎ **041/52-34-754.**
Fax 041/52-28-043. 10 rms, 8 with bath. TEL. 70,000L ($46.05) single without bath, 100,000L
($65.80) single with bath; 100,000L ($65.80) double without bath, 140,000L ($92.10) double
with bath. 30% of room rate extra person. Rates include continental breakfast. AE, MC, V. Closed
Jan 8–Feb 8. Vaporetto: Accademia. Cross the Accademia Bridge and continue north to the large
Campo Santo Stefano. Cross the campo and at the far northern end after the church, take a
left at a flower stand. Go up three steps to reach the raised campiello, where you'll find the
villalike hotel.

Part of this *rosso veneziano* (Venetian red) hotel dates to the 1400s. The secular wisteria vine that partially covers its facade is at its glorious best in May or June. But this
small hotel is an excellent choice year-round, whether for its simply furnished rooms
with newly renovated bathrooms, or its enviable location on a tiny picture-perfect
campiello off the far grander Campo Santo Stefano, one of the city's most beloved.
Two lucky rooms (nos. 1 and 10) have their own little terraces beneath the lush wisteria pergola and overlook the campiello—although they can't be guaranteed upon
reserving, inquire upon arrival. Legend goes that the city's handful of small raised
campielli such as this one were once used as burial grounds (particularly during times
of pestilence), hence the elevated pavement. (For centuries, however, the city has used
the island of San Michele as the official cemetery.)

DOUBLES FOR LESS THAN 130,000 LIRE ($85.50)

✪ **Hotel Locanda Remedio.** San Marco 4412 (on C. d. Remedio), 30122 Venezia. ☎ **041/
52-06-232.** Fax 041/52-10-485. 13 rms with bath. A/C MINIBAR TV TEL. 120,000L ($78.95)
single with bath; 130,000L ($85.50) double with bath, 160,000L ($105.25) double with bath;
200,000L ($131.60) triple with bath. Rates include breakfast. Rates reflect special discounts for

readers of this book. MC, V. Vaporetto: San Marco. Exit Pz. San Marco under the Torre del'Orologio clock tower, turn right at the Max Mara store onto C. Larga San Marco; at the Ristorante All'Angelo turn left onto C. va al Ponte del'Angelo, and take the 1st right onto Ramo d. Anzolo. Cross the small footbridge onto the C. d. Remedio; the hotel will be on your right.

Renato is another of the new breed of Venice's young hotel owner/managers, striving to create quality and charming lodgings at inexpensive-to-moderate rates— something nonexistent in this tourist town until recently. By Venetian standards, the Remedio offers unusually large rooms in an ancient palazzo in a surprisingly quiet neighborhood just minutes from Piazza San Marco. Many of the larger rooms are located on the 2nd floor (one even has lovely ceiling frescoes) off a ballroom-size breakfast salon naturally lit by oversized leaded windows. Projected plans for 1996 include the addition of TV (with pay-per-view VCR), minibar, enlarged and modernized bathrooms, and optional air-conditioning—ambitious, hard-to-find amenities in this price bracket.

Hotel Gallini. San Marco 3673 (C. d. Verona), 30124 Venezia. ☎ **041/52-04-515.** Fax 041/ 52-09-103. A/C (upon request) TEL. 50 rms, 40 with bath (half with bathtub, half with shower). 85,000L ($55.90) single without bath, 130,000L ($85.50) single with bath; 120,000L ($78.95) double without bath, 180,000L ($118.40) double with bath; 240,000L ($157.90) triple with bath. Off-season rates are approximately 10% lower. Rates include continental breakfast. AE, MC, V. Closed Nov 15–Carnevale. Vaporetto: Sant'Angelo. Follow the zigzag road southward toward Campo Sant'Angelo. Exit the campo at northeast end by taking the store-lined C. de la Mandola. Take a right at the "Ottica" optometrist onto C. d. Assassini, which becomes C. d. Verona.

The amiable Ceciliati brothers, Adriano and Gabriele, have been at the helm of this large family operation since 1952, so you can be assured that things run without a glitch. Situated two minutes from La Fenice opera house and the nearby Campo Sant'Angelo, this conveniently located base offers four floors (but no elevator!) of bright, spacious rooms and big modern baths. A smiling housekeeping staff seems to be forever cleaning. Rich-looking marble floors in green, red, or speckled black alternate with intricate parquet floors to lend an old-world air of stateliness. Gondoliers' tunes waft up to the 10 rooms overlooking the narrow Rio d. Verona. A few rooms are equipped with air-conditioning for a daily supplement of 10,000L ($6.60).

Hotel Riva. San Marco 5310 (at Ponte dell'Angelo), 30122 Venezia. ☎ **041/52-27-034.** 19 double rms, 17 with bath. 100,000L ($65.80) double without bath; 130,000L ($85.50) double with bath; 180,000L ($118.40) triple with bath. Call for single rates. Rates include breakfast. No credit cards. Vaporetto: San Marco. Exit Piazza San Marco under the Torre del'Orologio clock tower; take the first right onto C. Larga (at the Max Mara store) and then left at C. va al Ponte de l'Anzolo (you'll find the Ristorante all'Angelo on the corner). Follow the street straight over two small bridges to the hotel with a weathered red facade.

This small hotel is in a quiet corner only marginally removed from the hub of St. Mark's Square. One of the three narrow canals that merge in front of it first passes under the Ponte dei Sospiri (Bridge of Sighs) before reaching here. A good-value choice for this high-rent neighborhood, all three floors of rooms have been gutted and redone, complete with new windows and reinforced walls and small, marble-tiled bathrooms. The top-floor rooms have original wood-beamed ceilings and lovely roofscape views; open your windows and listen to the gondoliers' serenades.

IN CASTELLO
DOUBLES FOR LESS THAN 100,000 LIRE ($65.80)

Hotel Piave. Castello 4838/40 (Ruga Giuffa), 30122 Venezia. ☎ **041/52-85-174.** Fax 041/ 52-38-512. 13 rms, 5 with bath. 65,000L ($42.75) single without bath; 98,000L ($64.50) double without bath, 138,000L ($90.80) double with bath; 135,000L ($88.80) triple without bath;

220,000L ($144.75) quadruple suite with adjoining bath. Rates include continental breakfast. AE, DC, MC, V. Vaporetto: San Zaccaria. Walk straight ahead on the C. d. Rasse to the small Campo SS. Filippo e Giacomo. Exit the campo right (east) and continue to the next small Campo San Provolo. Here take a left (north), cross the first small footbridge and follow the zigzag calle which becomes Ruga Giuffa, a popular store-lined strip.

The Puppin family's small and tasteful hotel is a steal at these prices: This level of graciousness coupled with the "buon gusto" in decor and ambience is a rare find in Venice's one-star price category (a request for a change of category is in effect; this could potentially increase prices for 1997). A discerning, savvy clientele seems to have ferreted out this pretty spot, so you'll need to reserve far in advance. Located on a busy store-lined calle a 10-minute walk northeast of Piazza San Marco, you may have a hard time finding it first time around, but it's well worth the search: The location is convenient and pleasant, the hotel cozy and lovely. So pack light and just ask any local to point you in the direction of the Ruga Giuffa.

DOUBLES FOR LESS THAN 130,000 LIRE ($85.50)

Albergo Casa Verardo. Castello 4765 (at the foot of Ponte Storto), 30122 Venezia. ☎ 041/52-86-127. Fax 041/52-32-765. 11 rms (all with bath). 120,000L ($78.95) double; 170,000L ($111.85) triple; 190,000L ($125.00) quad; 220,000L ($144.75) quad suite with private terrace. Breakfast 10,000L ($6.55) per person extra. MC, V. Vaporetto: San Zaccaria. From vaporetto stop, walk straight ahead on the C. d. Rasse to Campo SS. Filippo e Giacomo; cross the small campo to take the C. Rimpeto la Sacrestia, which begins at Bar Europa. Cross the first small bridge, the Ponte Storto, and you'll find the hotel immediately on your right.

Thought and care are evident in the decor of this bright, family-run place, from the copies of famous Renaissance masterpieces to the charming and eclectic array of collectibles and quasi-antiques throughout. With space in Venice a prized premium, these rooms could be considered oversize (while the bathrooms are typically tiny). Families will particularly appreciate the top-floor "suite" that sleeps four and boasts a small private terrace with a view of the city's rooftops. The accommodating Verardo family run their homey canalside hotel with pride; groups of party-inclined guests will fare better elsewhere.

A DOUBLE FOR LESS THAN 160,000 LIRE ($105.25)

Hotel Bridge. Castello 4498 (C. d. Sacrestia), 30122 Venezia. ☎ 041/52-05-287. Fax 041/52-05-287. 12 rms with bath. A/C MINIBAR TEL TV. 112,000L ($73.70) single with bath; 160,000L ($105.25) double with bath; 200,000L ($131.60) triple with bath. Rates include continental breakfast. Rates reflect special discounts for readers of this book. AE, DC, MC, V. Vaporetto: San Zaccaria. Walk straight ahead to the small campiello of SS. Filippo e Giacomo with a covered well and newsstand in the middle. At the campo's eastern end, exit by turning left (north) onto the C. d. Sacrestia. The hotel is on your right.

The fourth generation of the Rossi family has just brought their small hotel in a 15th-century palazzo from one- to two-star status after a laborious lobby-to-rooftop renovation completed in 1996. Pierluigi and Paola Rossi are justifiably proud of the lovely Venetian-style results: Rooms are decorated in handsome shades of blue and bordeaux, with light fixtures of Murano glass, hand-painted armoires, and freshly tiled bathrooms all with shower. Climbers to the top-floor guest rooms are compensated by exposed-beam ceilings and rooftop views. This is a surprisingly quiet street, since it's only a few buildings removed from the main strip connecting Piazza San Marco and Campo San Zaccaria.

WORTH A SPLURGE

Hotel Campiello. Castello 4647 (Campiello d. Vin), 30122 Venezia. ☎ 041/52-05-764. Fax 041/52-05-798. 16 rms with bath. A/C TEL TV. 130,000L ($85.50) single; 190,000L ($125.00) double; 235,000L ($154.60) triple. (Rates are about 30% lower in off-season.) Rates include continental breakfast. AE, MC, V. Closed Jan 7–27. Vaporetto: San Zaccaria. Facing the well-known waterfront Savoia e Jolanda Hotel, take the narrow alleyway on its left, which leads to the small Campiello d. Vin; the hotel is on your right.

Nestled on a tiny campiello just off the prestigious Riva degli Schiavoni (the canalfront location of the legendary Danieli Hotel and other pricey five-star contenders), is this gem of a family-run hotel within easy striking distance of the Piazza San Marco. The atmosphere here is airy and bright, largely due to the seamless and smiling management of the always-present Bianchini sisters, Monica and Nicoletta, who are as attractive and charming as they are efficient. A delightful blend of contemporary and traditional decor, the hotel offers comfortable hospitality and good-quality service that surpasses its two-star category. The hotel's original 15th-century marble-mosaic pavement is still evident in the lounge area which opens onto a pleasant breakfast room. Breakfast is an attractive and abundant buffet affair here.

IN DORSODURO

This residential neighborhood is generally less congested than the San Marco area.

DOUBLES FOR LESS THAN 100,000 LIRE ($65.80)

Hotel Galleria. Dorsoduro 878a (at the foot of the Accademia Bridge), 30123 Venezia. ☎ 041/52-04-172 or 52-85-814. Fax 041/52-04-172. 9 rms, 6 with bath. 75,000L ($49.35) single without bath; 100,000L ($65.80) double without bath, 130,000L ($85.50) double with bath; 169,000L ($111.20) triple with bath; 222,000L ($146.05) quad with bath. Rates include continental breakfast. No credit cards. Vaporetto: Accademia. With the Accademia Bridge behind you, the hotel is just to your left next to the Totem Il Canale art gallery.

Step through this 17th-century palazzo's leaded-glass doors and ascend the narrow spiral staircase to the reception area, complete with red velvet wallpaper and time-worn oriental carpets. English-speaking Wilma will settle you into one of the spacious rooms; some have carved or frescoed ceilings, others lean toward a more contemporary decor. But what puts this charming one-floor hotel on the map are the six rooms overlooking the Grand Canal—the same awesome view without the usual awesome rates of Venice's *grandes dames* hotels. Even the rooms not lucky enough to overlook Venice's aquatic main street will still provide you with a sense of the palazzo's history and a convenient base in the shadow of the city's most important museum.

Hotel Messner. Dorsoduro 216/237 (on Fond. Ca' Balà), 30123 Venezia. ☎ 041/52-27-443. Fax 041/52-27-266. Main House: 11 rms, all with bath. Annex: 20 rms, 15 with bath. A/C TEL (main house only). Main House: 110,000L ($72.35) single; 160,000L ($105.25) double; 210,000L ($138.15) triple; 230,000L ($151.30) quad. Room rates for Main House *only* reflect special discounts for readers of this book. Annex: 75,000L ($49.35) single without bath, 100,000L ($65.80) single with bath; 100,000L ($65.80) double without bath, 150,000L ($98.70) double with bath; 130,000L ($85.50) triple without bath, 200,000L ($131.60) triple with bath; 160,000L ($105.25) quad without bath, 220,000L ($144.75) quad with bath. Rates include continental breakfast. AE, DC, MC, V. Closed mid-Nov to mid-Dec. Vaporetto: Salute. Follow the small canal immediately to the right of La Salute Church. Turn right onto 3rd bridge and walk straight ahead until you see the white awning of the hotel just before reaching the Rio d. Fornace canal.

This two-part hotel consists of the Casa Principale (Main House), where you'll find a handsome beamed-ceiling lobby and 11 rooms in a stately 14th-century palazzo, and the quasi-adjacent 15th-century annex, with 20 rooms, just 20 meters away. With three rooms overlooking the picturesque Rio della Fornace, and the close attention to detail in decor, the Main House is usually preferred, but other guests opt for the independence and slightly lower rates of the Annex. The similarly-priced Pensione alla Salute next door (see below) is a convenient alternative when the Messner is full. Both are good canalside choices for this pleasant residential neighborhood close to La Salute Church and the Guggenheim Collection.

A DOUBLE FOR LESS THAN 130,000 LIRE ($85.50)

Pensione alla Salute (Da Cici). Dorsoduro 222 (on Fond. Ca' Balà), 30123 Venezia. ☎ **041/ 52-35-404** or 52-22-271. Fax 041/52-22-271. 58 rms, 30 with bath or shower only/no toilet. TEL. 90,000L ($59.20) single without bath; 120,000L ($78.95) single with shower only; 130,000L ($85.50) double without bath, 180,000L ($118.40) double with bath; 180,000L ($118.40) triple without bath, 220,000L ($144.75) triple with bath. Rates include continental breakfast. No credit cards. Vaporetto: Salute. Facing La Salute Church, turn right and head to the first small bridge. Cross it and walk as straight ahead as you can to the next narrow canal, where you'll turn left (before crossing the bridge) onto Fond. Ca' Balà.

An airy lobby with beamed ceilings and marble floors, a small but lovely terrace garden, and cozy cocktail bar occupy the ground level of this converted 17th-century private palazzo on the picturesque Rio della Fornace. Upstairs, the guest rooms have high ceilings and huge windows, many of them large enough to accommodate families of four or even five at 50,000L ($32.90) per person above the triple-room rates. The Salute is in a quiet residential neighborhood just off the main strip leading to the Guggenheim Collection, yet sees surprisingly few tourists. Breakfast is served outdoors in warm weather.

WORTH A SPLURGE

Hotel American. Dorsoduro 628 (on Fond. Bragadin), 30123 Venezia. ☎ **041/52-04-733.** Fax 041/52-04-048. 29 rms, all with bath. A/C MINIBAR TV TEL. 180,000L ($118.40) single; 270,000L ($177.65) double. Rates include continental breakfast. 60,000L ($39.50) extra person. AE, MC, V. Vaporetto: Accademia. Veer left around the Accademia museum, taking the first left turn and walk straight ahead until you cross the first small footbridge. Turn right to follow the Fondamenta Bragadin that runs alongside the Rio di San Vio canal. The hotel is on your left.

Despite its decidedly unromantic name, the Hotel American is my top splurge recommendation for both style and substance. The perfect combination of charm and utility, this three-story hotel located near the Peggy Guggenheim Collection offers a dignified lobby and breakfast room liberally dressed with lovely oriental carpets and marble flooring, polished woods, and leaded-glass windows and French doors. The best choices here are the larger corner rooms and the nine overlooking a quiet canal; some even have small terraces overlooking the canal. Every room is outfitted with traditional Venetian-style furnishings that usually include hand-painted furniture and Murano glass chandeliers. If it's late spring, don't miss a drink on the second-floor terrace beneath a wisteria arbor dripping with plump violet blossoms.

IN SAN POLO

A DOUBLE FOR LESS THAN 100,000 LIRE ($65.80)

Locanda Ca' Foscari. Dorsoduro 3887/B (on C. d. Frescada, at the foot of Crosera), 30123 Venezia. ☎ **041/71-08-17.** Fax 041/71-08-17. 11 rms, 3 with bath. 70,000L ($46.05) single with bath; 85,000L ($55.90) double without bath; 120,000L ($78.95) double with bath; 111,000L ($73.00) triple without bath; 137,000L ($90.15) quad without bath. Rates include breakfast. No credit cards (reservation will be held upon receipt of an international money order for equivalent of first night). Closed Nov 15–Jan 30. Vaporetto: San Tomà. Walk up C. Campaniel and turn left; once across the first small canal, turn immediately right onto the Fond. Frescada and then immediately left onto C. d. Frescada; hotel is on the left.

Though one of the more modestly priced hotels in Venice, this family-run "locanda" or inn in the university quarter is pleasantly bright and spacious, with big windows in most rooms, unusual (although soothing) pink and lavender ceilings, textured wallpaper, and burnished wall-paneling in the breakfast room—all the details that make a difference for the traveler used to accommodations where cheap equals bland. The patient and affable innkeepers, Giuliana and Walter Scarpa, explain that because of the overwhelming number of faxed requests for their few rooms, if you don't hear from them within 24 hours you should interpret this as a sorry-but-no-room-at-the-inn reply.

WORTH A SPLURGE

Locanda Sturion. San Polo 679 (on C. d. Sturion), 30125 Venezia. ☎ **041/52-36-243.** Fax 041/52-28-378. 11 rms, all with bath. A/C TV TEL. 140,000L ($92.10) single; 220,000L ($144.75) double, 260,000L ($171.05) double with Grand Canal view; 310,000L ($203.95) triple, 350,000 ($230.25) triple with Grand Canal view; 400,000L ($263) quadruple, 440,000L ($289) quadruple with Grand Canal view. Rates reflect discounts for bearers of this book. Rates include continental breakfast. AE, V. Vaporetto: Rialto. From the Rialto stop, cross the bridge, turn left at the other side, and walk along the Grand Canal; C. d. Sturion will be the 4th narrow alleyway on the right, just before San Polo 740.

Though there's been a pensione on this site since 1290, a recent gutting and rebuilding has made the Sturion into a lovely, moderately-priced hotel managed by the charming Scottish-born Helen and co-owner Flavia. The hotel is perched four flights (and 69 challenging steps) above the Grand Canal. Unfortunately, only two rooms offer canal views and command higher rates; the rest have a charming view over the Rialto area rooftops.

4 Where to Dine

Eating cheaply in Venice is not easy, so plan well and don't rely on the serendipity that may serve you in other cities. If you've qualified for a Rolling Venice card, ask for the discount guide listing dozens of restaurants offering 10% to 30% discounts for card-holders.

With the exception of the informal alternative spots, prices are for a meal consisting of a first course (primo) such as pasta and a main course (secondo) of fish or meat. If you order the fish, don't forget that the price indicated on the menu commonly refers to the *l'etto* (per 200 grams), a fraction of the full cost (have the waiter estimate the full cost before ordering). And don't forget to calculate in nominal charges for bread and cover (coperto), service (servizio), a salad or vegetable side dish (contorno) and drink (bevanda) when calculating the grand total. Venice dines early compared to Rome and other points south: you should be seated by 7:30 to 8:30pm. Most kitchens close at 10 or 10:30pm, even though the restaurant may stay open till 11:30pm or midnight.

Budget Dining: Pizza is the fuel of Naples and crostini (small, open-face sandwiches) the soul food of Florence. In Venice it's *tramezzini*—small, triangular white-bread sandwiches filled with thinly sliced meats, tuna, cheeses, and vegetables, and *cichetti* (tapaslike finger foods such as calamari rings, fried olives, or polenta squares), traditionally washed down with a small glass of wine called an ombra (shadow), a revered constitutional in Venice. Venice offers countless neighborhood bars and cafes where you can stand or sit with a tramezzino, a selection of cichetti, a panino (sandwich on a roll), or a toast (grilled ham and cheese sandwich). All of the above will cost approximately 1,500L to 2,500L ($1 to $1.65) if you stand at the bar, as much as double when seated. Bar food is displayed in glass counters and usually sells out by late afternoon, so don't rely on it for dinner. A concentration of popular, well-stocked bars can be found along the Mercerie shopping strip that connects Piazza San Marco with the Rialto Bridge, the always lively Campo San Luca (look for Bar Torino, Bar Black Jack, or the characterful Leon Bianco wine bar) and Campo Santa Margherita. Avoid the tired-looking pizza you'll find in most bars; neighborhood pizzerias everywhere offer savory and fresher renditions for a minimum of 6,000L ($3.95), plus your drink and cover charge—the perfect lunch.

Venice Dining

Church

312

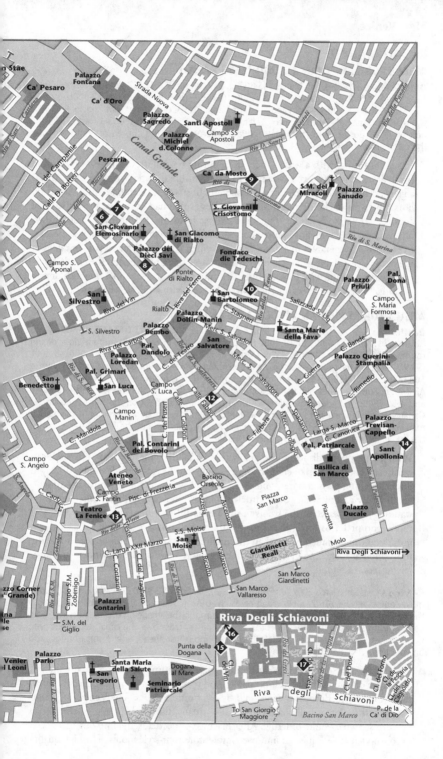

n Stae

Ca' Pesaro

**Palazzo
Fontana**

Ca' d'Oro

Strada Nuova

**Palazzo
Sagredo**

**Palazzo
Michiel
d.Colonne**

Santi Apostoli

Campo SS
Apostoli

Rio D. Santi

Apostoli

Canal Grande

Pescaria

C. del Campanile

Calle D. Botteri

Fond. delle Prigioni

Ca' da Mosto

Rio di

S. G. Crisostomo

9

**S.M. del
Miracoli**

**Palazzo
Sanudo**

6 **7**

**San Giovanni
Elemosinario**

**San Giacomo
di Rialto**

**S. Giovanni
Crisostomo**

Rio di S. Marina

**Palazzo dei
Dieci Savi**

8

**Fondaco
die Tedeschi**

Campo S.
Aponal

Ponte
di Rialto

Rio della Fava

**San
Silvestro**

Riva del Vin

Rialto

**Palazzo
Dolfin-Manin**

Riva del Ferro

**San
Bartolomeo**

10

C. Stagneri

Salizzada S. Lio

**Palazzo
Priuli**

**Pal.
Donà**

Campo
S. Maria
Formosa

S. Silvestro

**Palazzo
Bembo**

Merc. S. Salvador

**San
Salvatore**

**Santa Maria
della Fava**

C. Bande

Riva del Carbon

**Pal.
Dandolo**

C. del Teatro

**Palazzo
Loredan**

Pal. Grimari

**San
Benedetto**

Rio di S. Luca

San Luca

Campo
S. Luca

C. Fabbri

12

Merc. S. Salvadore

Campo
Manin

C. dei Fuseri

C. Goldoni

C. della Mandola

Rio di San Luca

C. Guerra

**Palazzo Querini-
Stampalia**

C. Rimedio

C. Specchieri

**Pal. Contarini
del Bovolo**

Campo
S. Angelo

Merc. S. Salvadore

Spadaria

Merc. Orologio

C. Larga S. Marco

C. Canonica

Pal. Patriarcale

**Palazzo
Trevisan-
Cappello**

**Sant
Apollonia**

14

C. Caotorta

**Ateneo
Veneto**

Campo
S. Fantin

Bacino
Orseolo

Pisc. di Frezzeria

C. Fighera

**Basilica di
San Marco**

Frezzeria

Piazza
San Marco

**Palazzo
Ducale**

Piazzetta

**Teatro
La Fenice**

13

Rio delle Veste

S.S. Moisè

**San
Moisè**

C. Vallaresso

C. Larga XXII Marzo

C. del Traghetto

Rio di S. Moisè

C. Contarini

**Giardinetti
Reali**

Molo

Riva Degli Schiavoni →

San Marco
Giardinetti

zzo Corner
' Grande)

Campo S.M.
Zobenigo

San Marco
Vallaresso

na
le
se

**Palazzi
Contarini**

S.M. del
Giglio

Punta della
Dogana

15

**Palazzo
Darìo**

**Venier
i Leoni**

**San
Gregorio**

**Santa Maria
della Salute**

Dogana
al Mare

**Seminario
Patriarcale**

Riva Degli Schiavoni

16

Rio di Cazie

17

Cl. della Pietà

Cl. del Dose

Cl. del Forno

Cl. de la Pescaria

Cl. del Vin

Riva degli Schiavoni

To San Giorgio
Maggiore

Bacino San Marco

P. de la
Ca' di Dio

IN SAN MARCO
MEALS FOR LESS THAN 12,000 LIRE ($7.90)

Osteria alle Botteghe. San Marco 3454 (C. d. Botteghe). ☎ **041/52-28-181.** Pizza 6,000L–12,000L ($3.95–$7.90); pasta courses 8,000L ($5.25); meat or fish dishes 12,000L ($7.90). DC, MC, V. Mon–Sat 11am–4pm and 7–10pm. Vaporetto: Accademia or Sant'Angelo. Find your way to the principal Campo Santo Stefano (follow the stream of people or ask), take the narrow C. d. Botteghe at the Gelateria Paolin across from the church of Santo Stefano; the osteria is on the right. PIZZA/ITALIAN.

Casual, informal with a wide variety of tempting possibilities and even easy to find (well, at least once you've located the bigger-than-life Campo Santo Stefano), this is a great, centrally-located choice for a pizza, light snack, or elaborate meal. Stand-up hors d'oeuvres (cichetti) and fresh sandwiches can be had at the bar or windowside counter, while more serious diners can choose from the dozen pizzas, pasta dishes, or tavola calda (a buffet of prepared dishes such as eggplant parmigiana, lasagne, and fresh, cooked vegetables in season, reheated when you order) and repair to tables in the back. Vegetarians will be happy with a simple pizza margherita, the classic can't-miss favorite, made with tomato sauce and mozzarella cheese, and a side dish or two of spinach, grilled peppers, or zucchini, enhanced with a drizzle of virgin olive oil.

MEALS FOR LESS THAN 20,000 LIRE ($13.15)

Rosticceria San Bartolomeo. San Marco 5424 (on C. d. Bissa). ☎ **041/52-23-569.** Menu turistico 11,000L, 15,000L, or 18,000L ($7.25, $9.85, or $11.85) in the ground-floor dining room, and 23,000L or 30,000L ($15.15 or $19.75) upstairs; pasta courses 6,000L–8,000L ($3.95–$5.25) in the ground-floor dining room, about 20% more upstairs; meat and fish courses 10,000L–14,000L ($6.55–$9.20) in the ground-floor dining room, about 20% more upstairs. AE, MC, V. Summer, Tues–Sun 9am–2:30pm and 4:30–9:30pm; winter, Tues–Sun 9am–2:30pm and 4:30–8:40pm. Vaporetto: Rialto. With the bridge at your back on the San Marco side of Canal, walk straight ahead to the Cam. San Bartolomeo. Take the underpass slightly to your left marked Sottoportego d. Bissa; you'll come across the rosticceria at the first corner. Look for GISLON, its old name, above the entrance. ITALIAN.

With a dozen pasta dishes, and as many fish, seafood, or meat entrees, this place can satisfy any combination of culinary desires. Since all the ready-made food is displayed under the long glass counter, you don't have to worry about any mistranslating—you'll know exactly what you're ordering. There's no *coperto* if you take your meal standing up or seated at the stools in the aroma-filled ground-floor eating area. For those who prefer to linger, head to the dining hall upstairs (though for a sit-down meal, you can do much better than this institutional setting). This appears to be the most popular rosticceria in Venice (and for good reason), so the continuous turnover guarantees fresh food.

✪ **Vino Vino.** San Marco 2007 (on Ponte d. Veste). ☎ **041/52-37-027.** Pasta 7,000L ($4.60), main courses 8,000L ($5.25). No credit cards. Wed–Mon 10am–midnight. With your back to the Basilica di San Marco, exit the Pz. San Marco through the arcade on the far left (west) side; keep walking straight, pass the American Express office, cross over the canal, turn right onto C. Veste just before the street jags left, and Vino Vino is just ahead, after a small bridge, and on your left. WINE BAR/ITALIAN.

Only a few years old, Vino Vino is already an institution, the informal wine-bar archetype offering simple, well-prepared food to accompany a very impressive selection of local and European wines sold by the bottle or glass. The Venetian specialties are written on a chalkboard but are also usually displayed at the glass counter so you can see what you're ordering. After placing your order, settle into one of a dozen or so wooden tables squeezed into two simple storefront-style rooms. The high quality of this ever popular locale is attributable to the owner—the eminent Antico Martini, a few doors down, with whom it shares a kitchen. It's also a great spot for a snack, or just a leisurely self-styled wine tasting (1,500L to 3,000L/$1 to $2 per glass). If you've come for dinner, the food often runs out around 10:30pm, so don't come too late.

MEALS FOR LESS THAN 30,000 LIRE ($19.75)

Le Bistrot de Venise. San Marco 4687 (on C. d. Fabbri). ☎ **041/52-24-384.** Appetizers and crepes 8,000L–14,000L ($5.25–$9.20); pasta courses 12,000L–15,000L ($7.90–$9.85); pizza 7,000L–12,000L ($4.60–$7.90) main courses 18,000L–24,000L ($11.85–$15.80). MC, V. Wed–Mon 9am–1am. Vaporetto: Rialto. From the Rialto Bridge vaporetto stop, turn right, walk along the Grand Canal, cross the small footbridge, then turn left onto C. Bembi, which becomes C. d. Fabbri; Le Bistrot is about 5 blocks ahead, on your left. VENETIAN/CONTINENTAL.

This is a comfortable, relaxed, visitor-friendly spot—and one that's open late—with indoor (there's a welcome No Smoking section!) and outdoor seating areas, young English-speaking waiters, and a varied, eclectic menu. You're welcome to sit and write postcards over a steaming cappuccino, enjoy a simple lunch such as risotto and salad, or dine when most of Venice is shutting down, lingering over an elaborate meal that might include dishes from 15th-century Venetian archival recipes, or simply opting for a large combination salad. Create your own pizza, mixing and matching more than 30 ingredients, or choose from a dozen entree or dessert crepes. The back room is the scene of both impromptu and scheduled cultural events—there are readings, live music, and a rotating display of paintings. Check the chalkboard for the current month's events.

✪ **Trattoria da Fiore.** San Marco 3561 (C. d. Botteghe). ☎ **041/52-35-310.** Pasta dishes 8,000L–20,000L ($5.25–$13.15); main course 16,000L–25,000L ($10.50–$16.50). AE, DC, V. Wed–Mon noon–3pm and 7–10pm. Vaporetto: Accademia. Cross bridge to the San Marco side and walk straight ahead to the wide expanse of the Cam. Santo Stefano. Exit the piazza at the northern end, taking a left at the Bar/Gelateria Paolin onto the C. d. Botteghe. The trattoria is on your right. VENETIAN/ITALIAN.

Don't confuse this trattoria with the well-known and very expensive Osteria da Fiore. You might not eat better here, but it will seem that way when your bill arrives. Start with the house specialty, penne alla Fiore (prepared with olive oil, garlic, and seven different in-season vegetables), and you may be happy to call it a night. Or skip right to another popular specialty, fritto misto, comprised of over a dozen different varieties of fresh fish and seafood. At 20,000L ($13.15), it's a bargain. The zuppa di pesce, a delicious bouillabaisse-like soup, is stocked with mussels, crab, clams, shrimp, and chunks of fresh tuna. At only 25,000L ($16.47), it doesn't get any better and is a meal in itself. This is a great place for an afternoon snack or light lunch at the Bar Fiore next door (10:30am to 10:30pm). Reservations suggested for the trattoria.

IN CASTELLO
MEALS FOR LESS THAN 20,000 LIRE ($13.15)

Alfredo Alfredo. Castello 4294 (C. SS. Filippo e Giacomo). ☎ **041/52-25-331.** Pasta dishes 6,000L–10,000L ($3.95–$6.60); main courses 8,000L–18,000L ($5.25–$11.85). No credit cards. Thurs–Tues 11am–2am. Vaporetto: San Zaccaria. From the Rv. degli Schiavoni waterfront, walk straight ahead on the C. d. Rasse to the Cam. SS. Filippo e Giacomo. ITALIAN/INTERNATIONAL.

Despite its modern fast-food appearance and multiple-translation menu, rest assured of the reliability (and resultant unwavering popularity) of this inexpensive spot with the local 20- and 30-something set. You'll get no disparaging looks for ordering just a pasta (and there are many: homemade lasagne al forno is a specialty), any of the variety of crepes, omelettes, or the unusual insalatoni (a number of large chef salad–type combinations with everything from olives and tuna to garbanzo or green beans and mozzarella). The menu goes on, but you're best off sticking to the simple and fresh stuff. Long hours make this place a rarity in town, but don't confuse it with the other Alfredo, notorious for fast food that could pass for airplane food.

Pizzeria/Trattoria al Vecio Canton. Castello 4738a (at the corner of R. Giuffa). ☎ **041/ 52-85-176.** Pizza 7,000L–10,000L ($4.60–$6.60); pasta courses 7,000L–12,000L ($4.60–$7.90); main courses 14,000L–22,000L ($9.20–$14.50). AE, CB, DC, MC. Wed 7–10:30pm, Thurs–Mon noon–2:30pm and 7–10:30pm. Vaporetto: San Zaccaria. From the Rv. degli Schiavoni water-front, walk straight ahead to Cam. SS. Filippo e Giacomo then turn right and continue east to Cam. San Provolo. Take a left heading north on the Sz. San Provolo, cross the first footbridge and you'll find the pizzeria on the first corner on the left. ITALIAN/PIZZA.

Good pizza is hard to find in Venice, and I mean that in the literal sense. Tucked away in a northeast corner behind Piazza San Marco on a well-trafficked route to Campo Santa Maria Formosa, the Canton's cozy tavernalike atmosphere and tasty fixings are worth the time you'll spend looking for the place. There is a full trattoria menu as well, with a number of pasta and side dishes (contorni) of vegetables suggesting a palatable alternative when you've looked one too many pizzas in the face.

MEALS FOR LESS THAN 30,000 LIRE ($19.75)

Trattoria alla Rivetta. Castello 4625 (on Sz. San Provolo). ☎ **041/52-87-302.** Pasta courses 8,000L–14,000L ($5.25–$9.20); fish courses 10,000L–18,000L ($6.60–$11.85); other main courses 10,000L–15,000L ($6.60–$9.85). AE, MC, V. Tues–Sun noon–2:30pm and 7–10pm. Vaporetto: San Zaccaria. With your back to the water and facing the Savoia e Jolanda Hotel, walk straight ahead (north) to the Cam. SS. Filippo e Giacomo; the canalside trattoria is literally tucked away next to a bridge just off the east (right) side of the campo. SEAFOOD/VENETIAN.

Lively, frequented by gondoliers, neighboring merchants, and tourists who are drawn to its bustling popularity, this is one of the safer bets for Venetian cuisine and com-pany in the San Marco area, an easy 10-minute walk east of the piazza. All sorts of fish—the specialty—decorate the window of this plain, brightly-lit place, where there's usually a short wait, even in the off-peak season. Not to worry, as the front part of the restaurant is a small bar area where a fresh array of delicious finger-foods and toothpicks are put out to keep you busy and happily sustained. Once seated, be sure to try the antipasto di pesce and whatever is penciled in as the daily special (often priced by the l'etto or per 200 grams).

WORTH A SPLURGE

Trattoria da Remigio. Castello 3416 (C. Bosello). ☎ **041/52-30-089.** Reservations recom-mended. Pasta courses 5,000L–8,000L ($3.28–$5.25); main courses 8,000L–18,000L ($5.25–$11.85). AE, DC, MC, V. Mon 1–3pm, Wed–Sun 1–3pm and 7–11pm. Vaporetto: San Zaccaria. Follow the Rv. degli Schiavoni east until you come to the white Chiesa d. Pieta. Turn left onto the C. d. Pietà, which jags left into C. Bosello. The restaurant is about 3 blocks ahead on your left. ITALIAN/VENETIAN.

Famous for its straightforward renditions of Adriatic classics, Remigio is the kind of place where you can order a simple plate of gnocchi alla pescatora (homemade gnocchi in a tomato-based sauce of seafood) and know it will be *buonissimo*. English-speaking head waiter Pino will talk you through the day's fresh fish dishes (John Dory, sole, monk fish, cuttlefish); sold by weight (l'etto); they are fresh and perfectly-prepared here, as is any antipasto. There are a dozen or so nice meat possi-bilities, quite a concession in this fish-crazed town. There are only two pleasant but smallish dining rooms here, so even late on a winter weekday you can expect a wait unless you've reserved. Remigio's is quite well known, although not easy to find, so just ask any local.

IN CANNAREGIO
MEALS FOR LESS THAN 30,000 LIRE ($19.75)

Ai Tre Spiedi. Cannaregio 5906 (Sz. San Cazian). ☎ **041/52-08-035.** Menu turistico: With choice of meat 22,000L ($14.50) or with fresh fish entree, 30,000L ($19.75). Pasta dishes 6,000L–8,000L ($3.95–$5.25); main courses 16,000L–26,000L ($10.50–$17.00). Expecting to accept credit cards in 1996. Tues–Sun 12:30–3:30 and 7–11:30pm. Vaporetto: Rialto. On the San Marco side of the bridge, walk straight ahead to the Cam. San Bartolomeo and take a left, following the stream of people past the post office, Coin department store, and Church of San Crisostomo on your right. Cross the first bridge after the church and turn right at the toy store onto Sz. S. Cazian. The restaurant is on your right. VENETIAN.

Venetians bring their visiting friends here to make a bella figura (good impression) without breaking the bank, then swear them to secrecy. Rarely will you find as pleasant a setting and as appetizing a meal as in this small, casually elegant trattoria with exposed beam ceilings and some of Venice's most reasonably-priced fresh-fish dining. If you order à la carte, ask the English-speaking waiters to estimate the cost of your fish entree, since it will appear priced by the l'etto (200 grams) on the menu. This restaurant, and the Trattoria da Fiore (see above), are two of our most reasonable choices for an authentic Venetian dinner. The more opportunities you have to eat around town, the more you'll understand what finds they indeed are.

IN SAN POLO
MEALS FOR LESS THAN 12,000 LIRE ($7.90)

Cantina do Mori. San Polo 401 (on C. Galiazza). ☎ **041/52-25-401.** Sandwiches and cichetti, each 1,500L–2,500L ($1–$1.65). No credit cards. Mon–Sat 8:30am–1:30pm and Mon, Tues, Thurs–Sat 5–8:30pm. Vaporetto: Rialto. Cross the Rialto Bridge to the San Polo side, walk to the end of the market stalls, turn left, then immediately right, and look for the small wooden CANTINA sign hanging on the left side of the street. WINE BAR/SANDWICHES.

Venetians stop to snack and socialize here before and after meals, but if you don't mind standing (there are no tables) and are in the market for a light lunch, this is one of the best and most famous spots in Venice to graze amid the variety of bar food. Do Mori, often associated with Le Do Spade, another venerable old-time bacaro nearby (see "Meals for Less than 20,000L," below), follows an odd schedule similar to retail store hours, so time your visit well.

Pizzeria da Sandro. San Polo 1473 (off the Cplo. d. Meloni). ☎ **041/52-34-894.** Pizza 7,000L–12,000L ($4.60–$7.90); pasta dishes 8,000L–12,000L ($5.25–$7.90); main courses 12,000L–18,000L ($7.90–$11.85). No credit cards. Sat–Thurs 12:30–3:30pm and 6:30–11:00pm. Vaporetto: San Silvestro. From the vaporetto stop, with your back to the Grand Canal, walk straight ahead to the store-lined R. Vecchia San Giovanni and take a left. Follow the stream of people heading towards the C. San Polo until you come upon the small Cplo d. Meloni; the pizzeria is just beyond on your right. ITALIAN/PIZZA.

Like most pizzerias/trattorias, Sandro offers a dozen varieties of pizza (his specialty) as well as a full trattoria menu of pastas and entrees. But if you're looking for a simple 10,000L ($6.60) pizza-and-beer meal, this is a reliably good spot on the main drag linking the Rialto to Campo San Polo (if you find yourself in Campo San Polo—and you should, but not right now—you've gone too far). There's communal seating at a few wooden picnic tables placed outdoors, with eight small tables inside. You'll be just as happy at the two pizzerias/trattorias we list in the 18,000L category if you're looking for a simple pizza-plus-drink combination.

MEALS FOR LESS THAN 20,000 LIRE ($13.15)

A Le Do Spade. San Polo 429 (Sottoportego Do Spade). ☎ **041/52-10-574.** Pasta dishes 7,000L–12,000L ($4.60–$7.90); main courses 8,000L–12,000L ($5.25–$7.90). No credit cards.

Mon–Wed, Fri and Sat 9am–3pm and 5–11pm, Thurs 9am–3pm. Vaporetto: Rialto or San Silvestro. At the San Polo side of the Rialto Bridge, walk away from the bridge and through the Rialto open-air market until you see the covered Pescheria (fish market) on your right. Take a left here and then take the second right onto the Sottoportego Do Spade. Walk 2 blocks; the wine bar is on your left. WINE BAR/VENETIAN.

Workers, fishmongers, and shoppers from the nearby Mercato d. Pescheria (fish market) flock to this historical *bacaro* wine bar (it was already 300 years old when Casanova was a regular). There's color and bonhomie galore amid the locals, here for their daily ombra. A large number of excellent Veneto and Friuli wines are available by the glass (1,500L to 3,000L/$1 to $2), accompanied by a counter full of cichetti. Unlike most bacari, and a great stroke of luck for the footsore, this quintessentially Venetian cantina has recently added a number of tables and introduced a sit-down menu to include a dozen daily changing pastas, soups, and seafood entrees, together with the ubiquitous local specialty of liver and onions. You won't be disappointed here.

Trattoria/Pizzeria San Tomà. San Polo 2864/A (C. San Tomà), ☎ **041/52-38-819.** Pizza 6,000L–12,000L ($3.95–$7.90); piatto unico (combination meal) 13,000L and 15,000L ($8.55 and $9.85). Menu turistico 20,000L ($13.15). Pasta 8,000L–16,000L ($5.20–$10.50); main courses 12,000L–22,000L ($7.90–$14.50). V, DC. Wed–Mon 12:30–3:30 and 6:30–11:30pm. Vaporetto: San Tomà. Walk straight on the C. d. Traghetto; turn right and you'll find yourself in the small Cam. San Tomà. Restaurant is on your left. ITALIAN/PIZZA.

Big appetites and big spenders can eat expensively here, but it's just as easy and enjoyable to spend surprisingly little. Piatto unico (single course) meals are unique to this place—the less expensive choice ($8.55) being home-baked lasagne and a house salad, the more expensive ($9.85) being roast chicken and baked potatoes. San Tomà is as popular as a pizzeria as a full-blown trattoria, and for a song you can enjoy the perfect pizza and glass of local Veneto wine al fresco in this charming neighborhood square.

WORTH A SPLURGE

✪ **Alla Madonna.** San Polo 594 (C. d. Madonna) ☎ **041/52-23-824.** Reservations recommended. Pasta 8,000L–14,000L ($5.25–$9.20); meat courses 12,000L–16,000L ($7.90–$10.50); fresh fish courses 8,000L–9,000L ($5.25–$5.90) per l'etto or 200 grams. AE, MC, V. Thurs–Tues noon–3pm and 7–10pm. Vaporetto: Rialto. From the foot of the Rialto Bridge on the San Polo side of the Grand Canal, turn left and follow the canal; C. d. Madonna (also called Sottoportego d. Madonna) will be the 2nd calle on your right (look for the big yellow sign). ITALIAN/VENETIAN.

This bright and busy trattoria, packing them in for over five years, has it all: a convenient location near the Rialto Bridge, five large dining rooms to accommodate the demand, an encouraging mix of local regulars and foreign patrons, a characteristic decor of high-beamed ceilings and walls frame-to-frame with local artists' work, and—most important—a competent and professional kitchen that prepares a menu of Venetian fish and seafood to perfection. With all of this, and (by Venetian standards) moderate prices to boot, it's no surprise this place is always jumping (don't forget to reserve). So don't expect the waiter to smile if you linger too long over dessert. Most of the first courses are prepared with seafood, such as the spaghetti or risotto with frutti di mare or pasta with sepie (cuttlefish), blackened from its own natural ink. Most of the day's special fish selections are best simply and deliciously prepared alla griglia (grilled).

IN DORSODURO
MEALS FOR LESS THAN 20,000 LIRE ($13.15)

Brasserie ai Pugni. Dorsoduro 2839 (at the foot of the Ponte d. Pugni). ☎ **041/52-39-831.** Menu turistico at 9,000L, 12,000L and 18,000L ($5.90, $7.90, and $11.85). No credit cards. Tues–Sun 12–3pm and 7–11:30pm. Vaporetto: Ca' Rezzonico. Walk due west towards the Cam.

San Barnaba. The restaurant is at the foot (south side) of the Ponte San Barnaba in front of the floating produce boat. ITALIAN/INTERNATIONAL.

Tourists seek out this no-frills canalside pub/bistro for the setting, the young local set for the unusual value-for-your-money. With no cover charge and tax included there are no hidden fees for simple meals even when you order à la carte. At 18,000L ($11.85), the most expensive menu turistico offers a daily-changing pasta, cotoletta alla milanese (the northern Italian version of Wiener schnitzel), and a house salad. As if that's not reason enough to make a return visit, you can't leave Venice without experiencing this residential corner nestled between two lovely piazzas, the colorful Cam. San Barnaba and the far more expansive Cam. Santa Margherita. The uncontested highlight is an old boat, moored just outside I Pugni—laden with fresh fruit and vegetables, it is the city's last remaining floating market.

MEALS FOR LESS THAN 30,000 LIRE ($19.75)

Taverna San Trovaso. Dorsoduro 1016 (on Fond. Friuli). ☎ **041/52-03-703.** Menu turistico 20,000L ($13.15); pizza and pasta courses 7,000L–14,000L ($4.60–$9.20); meat courses 10,000L–15,000L ($6.60–$9.85); fish courses 14,000L–22,000L ($9.29–$14.50). AE, DC, MC, V. Tues–Sun noon–2:30pm and 7–10:30pm. Vaporetto: Rialto. Walk to the right around the Accademia, taking an immediate right onto C. Gambara. When this street ends at a small canal, the Rio di San Trovaso, turn left onto the Fondamente Priuli; the taverna is on your left. ITALIAN/VENETIAN.

Wine bottles line wood-paneled walls, and vaulted ceilings augment the sense of character in this cozy neighborhood tavern, packed with locals and tourists alike. The menu turistico includes wine, an ample frittura mista, and dessert. Order à la carte from a wide variety of primi dishes (the gnocchi is great), or secondi (from a variety of pizzas to the local specialty of fegato alla veneziana) or simply grilled fish, the taverna's claim to fame. While in the neighborhood, stroll along the Rio San Trovaso towards the Canale della Giudecca: On your right you'll see the Squero di San Trovaso, one of the very few working boatyards in Venice that still makes and repairs the traditional gondolas.

5   Attractions

Venice is notorious for changing the opening hours of its museums and, to a lesser degree, its churches. Before you begin your exploration of Venice's sights, ask at the tourist office for the season's list of museum and church hours.

SUGGESTED ITINERARIES

If You Have 1 Day

I have a radical suggestion: If you have just one day in Venice, avoid the tourist-crowded sights: the Basilica di San Marco, Palazzo Ducale, Accademia, and the Peggy Guggenheim Collection. Instead, just wander among the labyrinth of streets and passageways, because this unique and ancient city "whose streets are filled with water" is its own most extraordinary attraction. For its weathered oriental beauty, its lifestyle, its East/West fusion of architecture and wealth of history, Venice has no match in Europe—or the world. Some of the quieter, residential neighborhoods off the beaten track include eastern Castello near the Arsenal, the Ghetto area (once the Jewish quarter) in northern Cannaregio, and the island of La Giudecca. At some point during the day, ride the no. 1 vaporetto line its full length from Piazza San Marco to the Ferrovia (train station), about 45 minutes each way. You'll cruise by the unbroken sequence of hundreds of proud palazzi that line Venice's principal aquatic boulevard,

Venice Attractions

 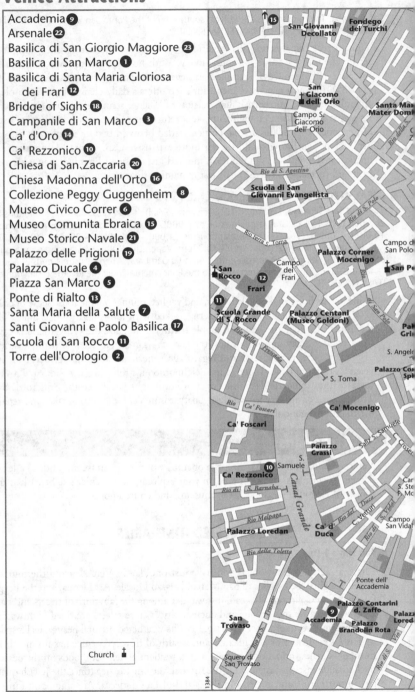
Church †

1384

320

Stae

Ca' Pesaro

Palazzo Fontana

Ca' d'Oro **14**

Palazzo Sagredo

16

Strada Nuova

Palazzo Michiel d.Colonne

Santi Apostoli

Campo SS Apostoli

Canal Grande

Pescaria

Ca' da Mosto

Rio di

Rio D. Santi

S.M. dei Miracoli

Palazzo Sanudo

17

S. Giovanni Crisostomo

San Giovanni Elemosinario

San Giacomo di Rialto

Rio di S. Marina

Palazzo dei Dieci Savi

Fondaco dei Tedeschi

13

Campo S. Aponal

Ponte di Rialto

San Silvestro

Riva del Vin

Rialto

San Bartolomeo

Pal. Dona

Palazzo Priuli

Campo S. Maria Formosa

S. Silvestro

Palazzo Dolfin-Manin

San Salvatore

Santa Maria della Fava

Palazzo Bembo

Merc. S. Salvador

Pal. Dandolo

Riva del Carbon

Palazzo Loredan

Palazzo Querini-Stampalia

Pal. Grimari

San Benedetto

San Luca

Campo S. Luca

Palazzo Trevisan-Cappello

Campo Manin

Sant Apollonia

Campo S. Angelo

Pal. Contarini del Bovolo

Pal. Patriarcale

1

18

19

Ateneo Veneto

Campo S. Fantin

2

Basilica di San Marco

5

3

Teatro La Fenice

Bacino Orseolo

Piazza San Marco

Palazzo Ducale

4

6

Piazzetta

C. Larga XXII Marzo

S.S. Moisè

San Moisè

Molo

Giardinetti Reali

Area of Inset →

zzo Corner Grande)

Palazzi Contarini

San Marco Vallaresso

San Marco Giardinetti

S.M. del Giglio

Riva Degli Schiavoni

Punta della Dogana

20

Cp. de l'Arsenal

Venier Leoni

Palazzo Dario

Santa Maria della Salute

22

8

San Gregorio

Dogana al Mare

Seminario Patriarcale

Riva   degli Schiavoni

P. de la Ca' di Dio

Riva de la Ca' di Dio

7

23 ↓

To San Giorgio Maggiore

Bacino San Marco

21

321

as picture-postcard perfect in the late afternoon light as at midnight; you might even do it again, after the city has gone to sleep and the quasi–traffic-free Grand Canal is illuminated by the moon.

If You Have 2 Days

Once you've thoroughly taken in the city's best sight—itself—move on to the host of monumental attractions. First among them has to be the magnificent **Basilica di San Marco** and its neighboring pink-and-white marble **Palazzo Ducale,** both on Piazza San Marco. While you're on the piazza, take in the **Museo Correr** and ride the elevator to the top of the **Campanile di San Marco** for a terrific view of the entire lagoon. If the warm weather has arrived, so have the outdoor orchestras, one for each of the historical cafes that line the magnificent Piazza San Marco.

If You Have 3 Days

Turn over your third day in Venice to art. In Dorsoduro, visit the **Accademia** for a look at the city's Renaissance heritage, and the nearby **Collezione Peggy Guggenheim,** one of Europe's best displays of 20th-century artworks. If you have time and energy after this, take in a third museum, the **Ca' Rezzonico** (also in Dorsoduro) or the **Ca' d'Oro** north of the Rialto Bridge—either provides you with a look at the interior of one of the great palazzi that grace the Grand Canal. In between, make sure you stop for sustenance at one of the city's myriad bacari wine bars for the cichetti hors d'oeuvres and the atmosphere.

If You Have 5 Days

For the sounds and smells of a Venice unchanged over the centuries, check out what's new at the **Rialto** by a stroll through the open-air produce market, the Erberia, winding up at the weird and wonderful Pescheria (fish market). In Castello, visit the cavernous **Church of Santi Giovanni e Paolo,** the Venetian Pantheon, then repair to one of the small outdoor cafes for some piazza life. Alternatively, visit the **Scuola Grande di San Rocco** in San Polo on the other side of town, whose interior is decorated with about 50 works by the local master Tintoretto. If by your fifth day you're ready to expand your horizons, explore the rest of the lagoon on islands such as **Murano (the glass island), Burano,** and **Torcello.**

THE TOP ATTRACTIONS

✪ **Basilica di San Marco.** San Marco, Pz. San Marco. ☎ **041/52-25-205.** Basilica, free; Museo Marciano (includes Loggia d. Cavalli), 3,000L ($2) adults, 2,000L ($1.30) students; Tesoro and Pala d'Oro, 3,000L ($2) adults, 2,000L ($1.30) students. Summer, Mon–Sat 9:00am–5:30pm, Sun 2–5:30pm; winter, Mon–Sat 9:30am–4:30pm, Sun 1:30–4:30pm. Last entrance 30 minutes before closing time. Vaporetto: San Marco.

Venice for centuries was Europe's principal gateway between the Orient and the West, so it should come as no surprise that the architectural style for the sumptuously Byzantine Basilica di San Marco, replete with five mosquelike bulbed domes, was borrowed from Constantinople. Legend has it that in 828 two enterprising merchants conspired to smuggle the remains of St. Mark the Evangelist from Alexandria in Egypt by packing them in pickled pork to bypass the scrutiny of Muslim guards. Thus St. Mark replaced the Greek St. Theodore as Venice's patron saint and a small chapel was built on this spot in his honor. Through the subsequent centuries (much of what you see was constructed in the 11th century), wealthy Venetian merchants and politicians alike vied with one another in donating gifts to expand and embellish this church, the saint's final resting place and, with the adjacent Palazzo Ducale, a symbol of Venetian wealth and power.

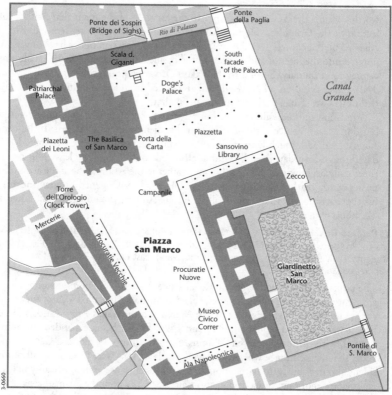

And so it is that San Marco earned its name as the Chiesa d'Oro (Golden Church), with a cavernous interior exquisitely gilded with Byzantine mosaics added over some seven centuries and covering every inch of both ceiling and pavements. For an up-close look at many of the most remarkable ceiling mosaics and for a better view of the oriental carpet–like patterns of the intricate pavement mosaics, pay the museum admission to go upstairs to the galleries (entrance to the Museo Marciano is in the atrium at the principal entrance). This is also the only way to the outside Loggia dei Cavalli, the open balcony that runs along the basilica's facade above the principle entrance, from which you can enjoy a closer look at the church's exterior. More important, it lets you mingle with the celebrated *quadriga* of four tethered, gilded bronze horses (dating from the 2nd or 3rd century A.D.) brought to Venice from Constantinople in 1204 together with the Lion of St. Mark (the patron saint's mascot) and other booty from the Crusades; they were a symbol of the unrivaled Serene Republic. The recently restored originals have been moved inside to the otherwise not terribly interesting museum. A visit to the Loggia is an unexpected highlight, providing an excellent view of the piazza and what Napoléon called "the most beautiful salon in the world." The 500-year-old Torre d. l'Orologio (Clock Tower) stands to your right, the Campanile (Bell Tower) to your left, and beyond, the glistening waters of the open lagoon. It's a photographer's dream.

The church's greatest treasure is the magnificent enamel- and jewel-encrusted golden altarpiece known as the Pala d'Oro, a gothic masterpiece created as early as the 10th century, and embellished by master artisans between the 12th and 14th centuries. It is located behind the main altar, which covers the tomb of St. Mark. Also worth a visit is the Tesoro (Treasury), to the far right of the main altar, with a collection of the Crusaders' plunder from Constantinople and other icons and relics amassed by the church over the years. Much of the Venetian booty has been incorporated into the interior and exterior of the basilica in the form of marble, columns, capitals, and statuary. Second to the Pala d'Oro in importance is the 10th-century *Madonna di Nicopeia,* a bejeweled icon absconded from Constantinople and exhibited in its own chapel to the left of the main altar.

Admission to the basilica is free but restricted and there is often a line to get in, but don't leave Venice without visiting its candlelit, glittering interior. In July and August (and with much less certainty the rest of the year) there are free tours Monday through Saturday given by church-affiliated volunteers. They leave four or five times daily beginning at 10:30am; groups gather in the atrium. Check the atrium for posters with yearly changing schedules. The basilica is opened Sunday morning for those wishing to attend mass; all others are strongly discouraged from entering (see hours above).

✪ **Palazzo Ducale and Ponte d. Sospiri (Ducal Palace and the Bridge of Sighs).** San Marco, Pz. San Marco. ☎ **041/52-24-951.** Admission 10,000L ($6.60) adults, 6,000L ($3.95) students. Daily 9:00am–7pm (winter hours may vary). Last entrance 1 hour before closing. Vaporetto: San Marco.

The pink-and-white marble gothic-Renaissance Palazzo Ducale, residence and government center of the doges ("dukes," elected for life) who ruled Venice for centuries, stands between the Basilica di San Marco and the water. After a succession of fires it was built and rebuilt in 1340 and 1424, forever being expanded and transformed, with intricately carved columns. A 15th-century Porta della Carta (Paper Gate, the main entrance where the doges' proclamations were posted) opens onto a splendid inner courtyard with a double row of Renaissance arches. Ahead you'll see Sansovino's enormous Scala dei Giganti staircase (Stairway of the Giants, scene of the doges' lavish inaugurations and never used by mere mortals), that leads to the wood-paneled courts and elaborate meeting rooms of the interior. The walls and ceilings of the principal rooms were richly decorated by the Venetian masters, including Veronese, Titian, Carpaccio, and Tintoretto, to illustrate the history of the puissant Venetian Republic while impressing visiting diplomats and emissaries from around the world with the uncontested prosperity and power it had attained.

If you want to understand something of this magnificent palace, the fascinating history of the 1,000-year-old Maritime Republic and the intrigue of the government that ruled it, search out the infrared audio tour (at entrance: 6,000L/$3.95). Unless you can tag along with an English-speaking tour group, you may otherwise miss out on the importance of much of what you're seeing.

The first room you'll come to is the spacious Sala delle Quattro Porte (Hall of the Four Doors), whose ceiling is by Tintoretto. The Sala del Collegio (College Chamber), the next main room, is where foreign ambassadors were received: It is richly decorated with Tintorettos and contains 11 pieces by Veronese. A right turn from this room leads into one of the most impressive of the spectacular interior rooms, the richly adorned Senato (Senate Chamber), with Tintoretto's ceiling painting, *The Triumph of Venice.* Here laws were passed by the Senate, a select group of 200 chosen from the Great Council. After passing again through the Sala delle Quattro Porte, you'll come to the Veronese-decorated Stanza del Consiglio dei Dieci (Room of the Council of Ten, the security police), which is of particular historical interest as in this room justice was dispensed. At times the Ten were considered more powerful than the Senate, and feared by all. Just outside the adjacent chamber, the Sala della Bussola (The Compass Chamber), notice the Bocca dei Leoni ("lion's mouth"), a slit in the wall into which secret denunciations of alleged enemies of the state were placed for quick action by the much feared Council.

The main sight on the next level down—indeed in the entire palace—is the Sala del Maggior Consiglio (Great Council Hall). This enormous space is made special by Tintoretto's huge *Paradiso* at the far end of the hall above the doge's seat. Measuring 23 by 75 feet, it is the world's largest oil painting; together with Veronese's gorgeous *Il Trionfo di Venezia (The Glorification of Venice)* in the oval panel on the ceiling, it affirms the power emanating from the Council sessions held here. Tintoretto also did the portraits of the 76 doges encircling the top of this chamber; note that the picture of the Doge Faliero, who was convicted of treason and beheaded in 1355, has been blacked out. Although elected for life since sometime in the 7th century, over time *il doge* became nothing but a figurehead; the power rested in the Great Council, comprised mostly of Venice's noble aristocracy and sometimes numbering well over 1,500 members. Exit the Great Council Hall via the tiny doorway on the opposite side of Tintoretto's *Paradiso* to find the enclosed Ponte dei Sospiri (Bridge of Sighs), which connects the palace with the grim Prigioni (Prisons). The bridge took its current name only in the 19th century, when visiting northern European poets romantically envisioned the prisoners' final breath of resignation upon viewing the outside world one last time before being locked in their fetid cells. Some attribute the name to Casanova who, following his arrest in 1755 (he was accused of spreading antireligious propaganda), crossed this very bridge. He was one of the rare few to escape alive, returning to Venice only 20 years later.

Readers who understand even a smattering of Italian should look into the Itinerari Segreti del Palazzo Ducal (Secret Itineraries of the Palazzo Ducale)—guided tours, in Italian only, of otherwise restricted quarters of this enormous, impressive palace, such as the doge's private chambers and the torture chambers. Make reservations for the tours, which cost 10,000L ($6.25) and begin at 10am and noon, at the "Direzione" at the Palazzo Ducale, or call **52-04-287**. It is possible that a tour in English will be made available beginning in 1997.

Campanile di San Marco (Bell Tower). San Marco, Piazza San Marco. ☎ **041/52-24-064.** Admission 5,000L ($3.30) adults, 2,500L ($1.65) students. June–Aug, daily 9am–7:30pm; Sept–May, daily 10am–4pm. Vaporetto: San Marco.

It's an easy elevator ride up to the top of this 324-foot bell tower for a breathtaking view of the lagoon, its neighboring islands, and the red rooftops and church domes of Venice. On a clear day you may even see the foot of the Alps. Originally built in the ninth century, then rebuilt in the 12th, 14th, and 16th centuries, it collapsed unexpectedly in 1902, miraculously hurting no one. It was rebuilt exactly as before, using the same materials, even rescuing one of the five historical bells that is still used today.

Torre dell'Orologio. San Marco, Pz. San Marco. No phone. Indefinitely closed for renovation. Vaporetto: San Marco.

Unfortunately the Clock Tower has been closed for a number of years and will most probably stay closed indefinitely. As you enter the magnificent Piazza San Marco, it is one of the first things you see, standing on the north side, next to the Procuratie Vecchie (the ancient administration buildings for the Republic). The Renaissance tower was built in 1496 and the clock mechanism of that same period still keeps perfect time. The two bronze figures, known as "Moors" because of the dark color of the bronze, pivot to strike the hour. The base of the tower has always been a favorite meeting place for Venetians, and is the entrance way to the Mercerie (from the word for merchandise), the principal retail street that zigzags its way to the Rialto Bridge.

○ Galleria dell'Accademia. Dorsoduro, at the foot of the Accademia Bridge. ☎ **041/ 52-22-247.** Admission 12,000L ($7.90). Daily 9am–7pm. Vaporetto: Accademia. Museum is directly in front of vaporetto stop.

The Accademia is the definitive treasure house of Venetian painting, which is exhibited chronologically from the 13th through the 18th centuries. There's no one hallmark masterpiece in this collection; rather, this is an outstanding and comprehensive showcase of works by all the great master painters of Venice, the largest such collection in the world. It includes the Bellini brothers and Carpaccio from the 15th century; Giorgione, Tintoretto, Veronese, and Titian from the 16th century; and from the 17th and 18th centuries, Canaletto, Piazzetta, Longhi, and Tiepolo, among others. Most of all, though, the works open a window onto the Venice of 500 years ago. Indeed, you'll see in the canvases how little Venice, perhaps least of any city in Europe, has changed over the centuries. Housed in a deconsecrated church and adjoining scuola, the church's confraternity hall, it is Venice's principal picture gallery, and one of the most important in Italy. Admission is limited, due to fire regulations, and lines can be daunting, but put up with the wait and don't miss it.

○ Collezione Peggy Guggenheim. Dorsoduro 701 (on C. San Cristoforo). ☎ **041/ 52-06-288.** Admission 10,000L ($6.60) adults, 5,000L ($3.30) students. Wed–Mon 11am–6pm (hours may vary yearly). Vaporetto: Accademia. Walk around the left side of the Accademia museum and take the first left. Walk straight, following the signs—you'll cross one canal, then walk alongside another, until turning left when necessary.

Considered to be one of the most important collections of modern art in the world and one of the most visited attractions in Venice, this collection of painting and sculpture was assembled by eccentric and eclectic American expatriate Peggy Guggenheim. She did a fine job of it, covering all the avant-garde movements in art—particularly the surrealists—from about 1910.

The 18th-century Palazzo Venier dei Leoni, never finished and thus its unusual one-story structure, was purchased by Peggy Guggenheim in 1949 and became her home in Venice until her death in 1979. The graves of her canine companions share the lovely interior garden with several of the collection's sculptures, while the patio at the side of the Grand Canal, watched over by Marino Marini's *Angel of the Citadel,* is one of the best spots to simply linger and watch the canal life. A new and interesting book and gift shop has opened in a separate building across the inside courtyard.

Check the tourist office for an update on museum hours; it is often open when many others are closed and sometimes offers a few hours a week of free admission. Don't be shy about speaking English with the young staff working here on internship; most of them are American.

○ Scuola Grande di San Rocco. San Polo 3058 (on Cam. San Rocco, adjacent to Cam. d. Frari and the Frari Church). ☎ **041/52-34-864.** Admission 8,000L ($5.25), students 6,000L ($3.95). Apr–Oct, daily 9am–5:30pm; Nov–Mar, daily 10am–4pm. Vaporetto: San Tomà. Walk straight ahead on C. d. Traghetto and turn right and then immediately left across campo San Tomà. Walk as straight ahead as you can, on Ramo Mandoler, C. Larga Prima, and finally Sz. San Rocco, which leads into the campo of the same name–look for the crimson sign behind the Frari Church.

This museum is a dazzling monument to the work of Tintoretto—the largest collection of his work anywhere. The series of the more than 50 dark and dramatic works took him 20 years to complete, making this the richest of the many confraternity guilds or *scuole* that once flourished in Venice.

Tintoretto, or Jacopo Robusti (1518–94), was a devout, unworldy man who only traveled once beyond Venice. His canvasses are filled with phantasmogoric light and intense, mystical spirituality.

⭐ Frommer's Favorite Venice Experiences

Basilica di San Marco. Don't let the line to get in deter you from visiting one of the most spectacular and unusual churches in the Roman Catholic world. You'll feel like you've been transported back to ancient Byzantium, or current-day Istanbul, in this 1,000-year-old dark and mystical space, whose vast vaulted ceilings, covered with glittering mosaics, will rivet your eye.

Piazza San Marco. If it's winter, splurge on the cozy warmth of Cafe Florian's theatrical warren of small sitting areas. But during warm weather, life spills outside, where the view of one of the world's greatest piazzas is yours for the price of a beverage. Each of the four historical cafes in the piazza (with Cafe Chioggia perhaps the best of the lot, just around the corner in front of the Palazzo Ducale) hires a small three- to five-piece *orchestrina* that plays into the late-night hours. A first-rate alternative to guarantee you the same sights and sounds: Secure a piece of the stone steps that line the Florian side of the piazza and sit for hours for free—and bring your postcards.

A Cruise down the Grand Canal. So you can't afford a gondola ride through the silent backwaters of Venice's myriad canals. The inexpensive alternative is, in many respects, just as romantic and far more enjoyable. The no. 1 vaporetto offers a ringside seat for the ride down Venice's aquatic main boulevard, offering a glimpse of daily life and the realization that things have changed preciously little.

Begin upstairs in the Sala dell'Albergo, where the most notable of the enormous, powerful canvases is the moving *La Crocifissione (The Crucifixion)*. In the center of the gilt ceiling of the Great Hall, also upstairs, is *Il Serpente di Bronzo (The Bronze Snake)*. Among the eight huge, sweeping paintings downstairs, each depicting a scene from the New Testament, *La Strage degli Innocenti (The Slaughter of the Innocents)* is the most noteworthy, so full of dramatic urgency and energy that the figures seem almost to tumble out of the frame. As you enter the room, it's on the opposite wall and at the far end of the room.

There's a guide to the paintings inside posted on the wall just before the entrance to the museum. There are a few Tiepolos among the paintings, as well as a solitary work by Titian. Note that the works on or near the staircase are not by Tintoretto.

Canal Grande (Grand Canal).

A leisurely cruise from Piazza San Marco to the Ferrovia (train station), or the reverse, is one of Venice's must-do experiences. Hop on the no. 1 vaporetto in the late afternoon (try to get one of the outdoor seats in the front of the boat), when the weather-worn colors of the former homes of Venice's merchant elite are warmed by the soft light and reflected in the canal's rippling waters, and the busy traffic of the city's main thoroughfare has eased somewhat. Some 200 palazzi, churches, and imposing republican buildings dating from the 14th to the 18th century (many of the largest now converted into banks, museums, and galleries) line this 2-mile ribbon of water that loops through the city like an inverted **S**, crossed by only three bridges. Some are condominiums whose lower floors are now deserted, but the higher floors are still the coveted domain of the city's titled families, who have inhabited these glorious residences for centuries; others have become the summertime dream-homes-with-a-view of today's expatriates, drawn here as irresistibly as the romantic Venetians-by-adoption who preceded them—Richard Wagner, Robert Browning, Lord Byron, and, more recently, Woody Allen.

CHURCHES & SCUOLE (GUILD HOUSES)

In addition to the churches and the scuole of the confraternities listed below, you may want to visit two churches in Cannaregio. **Santa Maria dei Miracoli** is an exquisite building of white marble by Pietro Lombardo from 1481–89, now under restoration. **Madonna Dell'Orto,** a gothic church, was the parish church of Tintoretto and is filled with his paintings.

Chiesa dei Frari. San Polo 3072 (Cam. d. Frari). ☎ **041/52-22-637.** Admission 1,000L ($.65), free on holidays. Mon–Sat 9am–noon and 2:30–6pm, Sun 3–6pm. Vaporetto: San Tomà. Walk straight ahead on C. d. Traghetto, turn right and then immediately left across Cam. San Tomà. Walk as straight ahead as you can, on Ramo Mandoler, then C. Larga Prima, and turn right when you reach the beginning of Sz. San Rocco.

Around the corner from the Scuola Grande di San Rocco, this immense 13th-century gothic church was built by the Franciscans ("frari" is a distortion of "frati" or brothers). Together with the Dominican Church of Santi Giovanni e Paolo in Castello, it is the largest church after the Basilica of San Marco and is something of a memorial to the ancient glories of Venice. Austere both inside and out, it houses two of Titian's masterpieces, the more striking being the *Assumption of the Virgin,* over the main altar. His *Virgin of the Pesaro Family* is in the left nave; Titian's wife posed for the figure of Mary, then died soon afterward in childbirth. The church's other masterwork is Bellini's important triptych *Madonna and Child,* displayed in the Sacristy (take the door on the right as you face the altar). The grandiose tombs of two famous Venetians are also here: Canova (d. 1822) and Titian (d. 1576).

At press time, a free tour was being offered in English every Thursday at 4pm, from August through September. Check at the church.

Chiesa dei SS. Giovanni e Paolo. Castello 6363, Campo Santi Giovanni e Paolo. ☎ **041/52-37-510.** Free admission. Mon–Sat 9am–12pm and 3–6pm. Open Sun for those attending services. Vaporetto: Rialto.

This massive gothic church was built by the Dominican order in the early 15th century and, together with the Frari Church in San Polo, is second in size only to the Basilica di San Marco. An unofficial Pantheon where 25 doges are buried (a number of tombs are part of the unfinished facade), the church, commonly known as Zanipolo in Venetian dialect, is also home to a number of artistic treasures. Visit the Cappella della Rosario off the left transept to see the recently restored ceiling canvases by Veronese. Also recently restored is the brilliantly colored *Polyptych of St. Vincent Ferrer* attributed to a young Bellini, in the right aisle. You'll also see the foot of St. Catherine of Siena encased in glass. Adjacent to the church is the old Scuola di San Marco, an old confraternity-like association now run as a civic hospital.

Anchoring the large campo, a popular crossroads for this area of Castello, is the ✪ **statue of Bartolomeo Colleoni,** the Renaissance *condottiere* who defended Venice's interests at the height of its power. The work is by the Florentine Andrea Verrocchio; it is considered one of the world's great equestrian monuments and Verrocchio's best.

Chiesa di San Giorgio Maggiore. San Giorgio Maggiore, across from Piazzetta San Marco. ☎ **041/52-89-900.** Free admission. June–Sept daily 9:30am–12:30pm and 2–6pm; Oct–May daily 10am–12:30pm and 2–4:30pm. Transportation: Take the Giudecca-bound vaporetto (no. 82) on Rv. degli Schiavoni and get off at the first stop, right in the courtyard of the church.

This church sits on the little island of San Giorgio Maggiore. It is the masterpiece of Andrea Palladio, designed in 1565 and completed in 1610. To impose a classical facade on the traditional church structure, Palladio designed two interlocking facades, with repeating triangles, rectangles, and columns that are carefully and harmoniously proportioned. The interior of the church, with its whitewashed surfaces, is a stark, unadorned space. The main altar is flanked by two epic paintings by Tintoretto, the *The Shower of Manna* to the left and the far more successful *Last Supper* to the right. Through the doorway to the right of the choir you will find Tintoretto's *Deposition*. To the left of the choir is an elevator that you can take to the top of the campanile, for a charge of 3,000L ($1.90), to experience an unforgettable view of the island itself, the lagoon, and the Doges' Palace across the way.

Chiesa di Santa Maria della Salute. Dorsoduro, Cam. d. Salute. ☎ **041/52-25-558.** Free admission to church; sacristy 1,000L (65¢). Daily 9am–noon and 3–6pm. Vaporetto: Salute.

Simply referred to as "La Salute," this crown jewel of 17th-century baroque architecture proudly reigns at a commercially and aesthetically important point, almost directly across from the Piazza San Marco, where the Grand Canal empties into the lagoon. The first stone was laid in 1631 after the Senate decided to honor the Virgin Mary of Good Health for delivering Venice from a plague. They accepted the revolutionary plans of a young, relatively unknown architect, Baldassare Longhena (who would go on to design, among other projects, the Ca' Rezzonico). He dedicated the next 50 years of his life overseeing its progress (he would die one year after its inauguration but five years before its completion). The only great baroque monument built in Italy outside of Rome, the octagonal Salute is recognized for its exuberant exterior of volutes, scrolls, and more than 125 statues and rather sober interior, though one highlighted by a number of works by Tintoretto and Titian.

Chiesa di San Zaccaria. Cam. San Zaccaria, Castello. ☎ **041/52-21-257.** Free admission. Daily 10am–noon and 4–6pm. Vaporetto: San Zaccaria.

Behind St. Mark's Basilica is a gothic church with a Renaissance facade, filled with works of art. The most important work is Giovanni Bellini's *Madonna Enthroned,* which has been recently restored, above the second altar in the left aisle. Apply to the sacristan to see the Sisters' Choir, with works by Tintoretto, Titian, Il Vecchio, Anthony van Dyck, and Bassano. The paintings aren't labeled, but the sacristan will point out the names of the artists. In the fan vaults of the St. Tarasius Chapel are the faded frescoes of Andrea del Castagno.

Scuola di San Giorgio degli Schiavoni. C. Furiani, Castello. ☎ **041/52-28-828.** Admission 5,000L ($3.20). Apr–Oct Tues–Sat 9:30am–12:30pm and 3:30–6:30pm, Sun 9:30am–12:30pm; Nov–Mar Tues–Sat 10am–12:30pm and 3–6pm, Sun 10am–12:30pm. Vaporetto: San Zaccaria.

At the St. Antonino Bridge (Fondamenta dei Furlani) is the second important guild house to visit in Venice. The Schiavoni were a trading colony of Dalmatian merchants who built their own confraternity. Between 1502 and 1509, Vittore Carpaccio painted a pictorial cycle of nine masterpieces illustrating episodes from the lives of St. George and St. Jerome. These appealing pictures freeze in time moments in the lives of the saints: St. George charges his ferocious dragon on a field littered with half-eaten bodies and skulls (a horror story with a happy ending); St. Jerome leads his lion into a monastery, frightening the friars; St. Augustine has just taken up his pen to reply to a letter from St. Jerome when he and his little dog are transfixed by a miraculous light, and a voice telling them of St. Jerome's death.

MUSEUMS & GALLERIES

Ca' d'Oro (Galleria Giorgio Franchetti). Cannaregio between 3931 and 3932 (on the narrow C. Ca' d'Oro). ☎ **041/52-38-790.** Admission 4,000L ($2.65). Daily 9am–2pm. Vaporetto Line: Ca' d'Oro. Museum entrance is 50 yards away.

The 15th-century Ca' d'Oro is one of the best-preserved and most impressive of the hundreds of patrician palazzi lining the Grand Canal. After the Palazzo Ducale, it is said to be the finest example of Venetian gothic architecture in the city. A laborious restoration of its pink-and-white facade (its name, the Golden Palace, refers to a gilt-covered facade that no longer exists) was only completed in 1995. Inside, the ornate beamed ceilings provide the setting for sculptures, furniture, tapestries, an impressive bronze and iron collection (12th to 16th centuries), and an art gallery whose two most important canvases include Mantegna's gripping and haunting *San Sebastiano*, immediately as you enter, and Titian's *Venus*, on the top floor, as well as lesser paintings by Tintoretto, Carpaccio, van Dyck, Giorgione, and others. For a delightful break, step out onto the palazzo's balcony, overlooking the Grand Canal.

Ca' Rezzomnico (Museo del 700 Veneziano). Dorsoduro (on Fond. Rezzonico). ☎ **041/ 52-24-543.** Admission 8,000L ($5.25) adults, 5,000L ($3.30) students. Summer: Daily 9am–7pm; winter Mon–Thurs and Sat 10am–4pm, Sun 9am–12:30pm. (Hours are irregular until 1997; call in advance.) Vaporetto: Ca' Rezzonico. Walk straight ahead to Cam. San Barnabà, turn right at the piazza and go over 1 bridge, then take an immediate right for the museum entrance.

This handsome 17th-century canalside palazzo offers an intriguing look into what living in a grand Venetian home was like in the last days of the Venetian Republic. Begun by Longhena, architect of La Salute Church, the Rezzonico home is a splendid backdrop for this collection of period paintings (most important, works by Tiepolo, Guardi, and Longhi), furniture, tapestries, and artifacts. This museum is one of the best windows into the sometimes frivolous life of Venice of 200 years ago, as seen through the tastes and fashions of the wealthy Rezzonico clan. The English poet Robert Browning, after the death of his wife Elizabeth Barrett Browning, made this his last home; he died here in 1889.

Museo Correr. San Marco, Pz. San Marco. ☎ **041/52-25-625.** Admission 8,000L ($5) adults, 5,000L ($3.15) students. Summer Wed–Mon 10am–5pm; winter Wed–Mon 10am–4pm. Last entrance is 45 minutes before closing time. Vaporetto: San Marco.

This museum, which you enter through an arcade at the end of Piazza San Marco opposite the Basilica, is no match for the Accademia but does include some interesting paintings of Venetian life, and a fine collection of artifacts, such as coins, costumes, the doges' ceremonial robes and hats, and an incredible pair of 15-inch platform shoes, that gives an interesting feel for aspects of the day-to-day life in La Serenissima in the heyday of its glory. Bequeathed to the city by the aristocratic Correr family in 1830, the museum is divided into three sections: the History Section, the Painting Section, and the Museum of the Risorgimento (1797–1866).

Of the painting collection from the 13th to 18th centuries, Carpaccio's *Le Cortigiane (The Courtesans)*, in room 15 on the upper floor, is notable, as are the paintings by the Bellini family, father Jacopo and sons Gentile and Giovanni. For a lesson in just how little this city has changed in the last several hundred years, head to room 22 and its anonymous 17th-century bird's-eye view of Venice. Most of the rooms have a sign with a few paragraphs in English explaining the significance of the contents.

Museo Storico Navale and Arsenale. Cam. San Biasio, Castello 2148. ☎ **041/52-00-276.** Admission 2,000L ($1.30). Mon–Sat 9am–1pm. Closed holidays. Vaporetto: Arsenale.

The Naval History Museum's most fascinating exhibit is its collection of model ships. It was once common practice for vessels to be built, not from blueprints, but from the precise scale models that you see here. The prize of the collection is a model of the legendary Bucentaur, the ceremonial barge of the doges. Another section of the museum contains an array of historic vessels. Walk along the canal as it branches off from the museum to the Ships' Pavilion, where the historic vessels are displayed.

From the museum, walk up the Arsenale Canal and cross the wooden bridge to the Campo del'Arsenale, where you will soon reach the land gate of the **Arsenale,** guarded by stone lions. The four marble columns of the gate, as well as the lions, are booty brought at various times from Greece. The Arsenale was founded in 1104, and at the height of Venice's power in the 15th century it employed 16,000 workers who turned out galley after galley on an early version of an assembly line at speeds and in volume unknown until modern times.

A HISTORIC DISTRICT

Il Ghetto (the Jewish Ghetto). Cannareggio, Cam. d. Ghetto Nuovo.

Venice's relationship with her longtime Jewish community fluctuated over time from acceptance to borderline tolerance, attitudes often influenced by the fear that Jewish moneylenders and merchants would infiltrate other sectors of the Republic's commerce under a government that thrived on secrecy and control. In 1516, 700 Jews were forced to move to the abandoned site of an old foundry (*ghetto* is old Venetian dialect for foundry, a word that would soon be used throughout Europe and the world) whose two access points were controlled at night and early morning, both protecting and segregating its inhabitants. Within one century, the community grew to 5,000. The Ghetto Nuovo (New Ghetto) annexed the Ghetto Vecchio, and later the Ghetto Nuovissimo (Newest Ghetto) was added. A very small, ever-diminishing community of Jewish families continues to live here today. The only way to visit any of the area's five historical synagogues is through one of the **Museo Ebraico**'s frequent organized tours conducted in English (the museum is at Campo d. Ghetto Nuovo 2902, ☎ **041/71-53-59;** summer hours are from 10am to 7pm, winter hours, 10am until 4:30pm; closed Saturday). Your guide will elaborate on the commercial and political climate of those times, the unique "skyscraper" architecture, and the daily lifestyle of the Jewish community until the arrival of Napoléon in 1797, who declared the Jews free citizens.

ESPECIALLY FOR KIDS

It goes without saying that a **gondola ride** will be a memorable experience of Venice for your child. If that's too expensive no one has complained about a tour on the convenient alternative, the no. 1 vaporetto.

Judging from the squeals of delight, **feeding the pigeons in Piazza San Marco** (purchase a bag of corn and you'll be draped in pigeons in seconds) could be the epitome of your child's visit to Venice, and it's the optimal photo op. Be sure your child won't be startled by the fluttering and flapping.

A jaunt to the neighboring island of **Murano** can be as educational as recreational—follow the signs to any *fornace* where a glass-blowing performance of the island's thousand-year-old art is free entertainment.

Before you leave town, take a ride to the top of the **Campanile di San Marco** for a bird's-eye view of Venice's rooftops and church cupolas, or get close up and personal to the four bronze horses on the facade of the **Basilica San Marco's outdoor loggia-with-a-view;** they're only copies (you can see the real ones in the Basilica's Museo Marciano), but the view from here is something hard for you or your children to forget.

Children enjoy the **Museo Navale & Arsenale** with its ship models and old vessels, and the many historic artifacts in the **Correr Museum.**

SPECIAL INTEREST SIGHTSEEING

VISITING A SQUERO (BOATYARD)   One of the most interesting (and photographed) sights you'll see in Venice is the **Squero San Trovaso** at Dorsoduro 1097 on the Rio San Trovaso southwest of the Accademia museum. This small boatyard, which first opened in the 17th century, is surrounded by Tyrolian-looking wooden structures that are home to the owners and hangars for the boats. Putting together one of the sleek black boats is a fascinatingly exact science that is still done in the traditional manner. The boats have been painted black since a 16th-century sumptuary law was passed to restrict the gaudy outlandishness that, at the time, was commonly used to out-do the Joneses. The boats have no modern equipment and rarely move at any great speed. The right side of the gondola is lower since the gondolier always stands in the back of the boat on the left. Although this squero, or boatyard, is the city's oldest and one of only three remaining, it works predominantly on maintenance and repair. Occasionally they build a new one (which takes some 40 to 45 working days), carefully crafting the gondola from the seven types of wood—mahogany, cherry, fir, walnut, oak, elm, and lime—necessary to give the shallow and asymmetrical boat its various characteristics. After they put all the pieces together, the painting, the *ferro* (the iron symbol of the city affixed to the bow), and the wood carving that secures the oar are commissioned out to various local artisans. Where there were once thousands of these elegant boats plying Venice's canals, today there are but 350.

Search out the squero, just north of the Zattere (the wide walkway that runs alongside the Giudecca Canal in Dorsoduro) next to the Church of San Trovaso. Aware they have become a tourist site, they don't mind if you watch them at work from across the narrow Rio di San Trovaso.

FOR THE ROMANTIC   A **gondola ride,** one of the great traditions, really is as romantic as it looks. Though higher prices are often quoted in peak season, the "official" rate is 80,000L ($52.65) for up to 50 minutes, for up to six passengers per vessel. It's the best $1-a-minute boat ride you'll ever experience. There's a 20,000L ($13.15) surcharge after dark, but aim for late afternoon before sundown when the light does its magic on the canal reflections. If the price is too high, ask around at your hotel or other tourists lingering about at the gondola stations if they'd like to share the cost. Establish cost, time, and route (any of the back canals are preferable to the trafficked and choppy waters of the Grand Canal) before setting off. And what of the accompanying musicians and serenading gondoliere immortalized in film? A musical ensemble of accordion-player-and-tenor is so expensive it is shared among several gondolas traveling together. A number of travel agents around town book the evening serenades for approximately 40,000L ($26.30) per person (ask at the American Express office).

There are 12 gondola stations spread throughout Venice, including Piazzale Roma, the train station, the Rialto Bridge, and Piazza San Marco. A number of smaller stations can be found about town, with gondoliers standing alongside their shiny black boats.

But before your dreams ebb away, read on: To tourists, gondolas mean romance, but to Venetians they're a basic form of transportation. With just three bridges that cross the Grand Canal, a number of two-manned "traghetto" gondolas ferry the general public back and forth at seven other points along the way, expertly dodging what at times can look like rush-hour traffic. You'll find on your map or during your meandering a traghetto gondola station at the end of any calle with the name "Traghetto." There's one, for instance, right alongside the San Tomà vaporetto station, or next to the Ca' Rezzonico museum. The ride is short and you must stand, but at only 1,000L (65¢) each way (handed directly to the gondolier; no tickets necessary), it's priced for the local citizenry, not the wealthy tourists.

ORGANIZED TOURS

Most of the centrally-located travel agencies will have posters in their windows advertising half- and full-day walking tours of the city's sites. Most of these tours are piggy-backed onto those organized by American Express (see "Fast Facts," above), known for the best value for the money. They should cost the same as the American Express tours, approximately 33,000L ($21.70) and 60,000L ($39.50) per person. The alternative of a personal guide (a list of qualified polylingual guides is available from the tourist office) is at least twice the above-mentioned rates. You can also cover most of the major sights of Venice by taking your own self-guided tours with the guide, *Frommer's Walking Tours: Venice.*

Free organized tours of the Basilica and some of the other principal churches can be erratic, as they are given by volunteers. Ask at the tourist board and check the monthly publication, *Ospite a Venezia (Guest in Venice)* for "Talks and Guided Tours." This can be one of many incidents that demonstrate how poorly organized the city's fractious agencies can be in these matters.

An organized tour visits **the Islands of the Venetian Lagoon,** including a brief visit to Murano, Burano, and Torcello for approximately 25,000L ($16.45), leaving from different booths on the Riva degli Schiavoni and from in front of La Zecca near the tourist office in Palazzetto Selva just west of the Palazzo Ducale. But buy a special one-day excursion ticket (round-trip) on the no. 12 vaporetto for 10,000L ($6.58) and you can do a tour yourself. The islands are small and easy to navigate. See "Exploring Venice's Islands," below.

6 Special & Free Events

During **Carnevale,** countless musical and cultural events (many of them outdoors and free of charge) fill the calendar for two or three weeks leading up to Ash Wednesday, the beginning of Lent. Things come to a climax the night of *martedì grasso,* "Fat Tuesday" or Mardi Gras (February 11 in 1997), with a grand finale fireworks display and some kind of big extravaganza in Piazza San Marco. Contact the tourist office for full details on the 1997 festivities. Good luck: they don't really get organized with printed material until a few weeks beforehand. Hotels should be booked months ahead, especially for the two weekends prior to Shrove Tuesday. Hotels will sometimes offer to fax you listings of events—if and when they receive them. You're better off just showing up, with a secure hotel reservation, and going with the flow. There's always something fun going on, much of it spontaneous. Since so much of Carnevale happens in the street, make sure to dress warmly; go to see and be seen and be ready for inclement weather, and don't forget your costume.

The **Voga Longa** (literally "long row"), a 30km (18-mile) rowing "race" from San Marco to Burano and back again, has been enthusiastically embraced since its inception in 1975, following the city's effort to keep alive the centuries-old heritage of the regatta. It takes place on a Sunday in mid-May; for exact dates in 1997, consult the tourist office. The event itself is colorful, and every local seems to have a relative or next-door neighbor competing; it's a great excuse for a party.

Stupendous fireworks fill the night sky during the **Festa del Redentore,** on the third Saturday night and Sunday in July. The celebration, which marks the July 1578 lifting of a plague that had gripped the city, is centered around the Palladio-designed

Carnevale á Venezia

Venetians once more are taking to the open piazzas and streets for the pre-Lenten holiday of Carnevale. The festival traditionally marked the unbridled celebration that preceded Lent, the period of penitence and abstinence prior to Easter, and its name is derived from the Latin *carnem lavare,* meaning "to take meat away."

Although lasting no more than 5 to 10 days today, in the 18th-century heyday of Carnevale in La Serenissima Republic well-heeled revelers came from all over Europe to take part in festivities that began months ahead, gaining crescendo until their culmination at midnight on Shrove Tuesday. As the Venetian economy declined, and its colonies and trading posts fell to other powers, the Republic of Venice in its swan song turned to fantasy and escapism. The faster its decline, the more raucous and unlicensed became its anything-goes merrymaking. Masks became ubiquitous—they afforded anonymity and pardoned a thousand sins, permitting the fishmonger to attend the ball and dance with the baroness, and the married to act as if they were free. The doges condemned it and the popes denounced it, but nothing could dampen the Venetian Carnevale spirit until Napoléon arrived in 1797 and put an end to the festivities.

Resuscitated in 1980 by local tourism powers to fill the empty winter months when tourism came to a screeching halt, Carnevale is calmer nowadays, though just barely. The born-again festival got off to a shaky start, met at first with indifference and skepticism, but in the years since then, it has grown from strength to strength. In the 1980s Carnevale attracted an onslaught of what was seemingly the entire student population of Europe, backpacking young people who slept in the piazzas and train station. Politicians and city officials adopted a middle-of-the-road policy that helped establish Carnevale's image as neither a free-for-all outdoor party nor a continuation of the exclusive private balls in the Grand Canal palazzi available to a very few.

Carnevale is at its dazzling best as it approaches its 20th anniversary, a harlequin patchwork of musical and cultural events, many of them free of charge, that

Chiesa del Redentore (Church of the Redeemer) on the island of Giudecca, which was built by way of thanksgiving. A bridge of boats across the Giudecca Canal links the church with the banks of le Zattere in Dorsoduro for the occasion, and hundreds of boats of every vintage and size fill the Giudecca Canal. It's one big floating feast until night descends and an awesome half-hour *spettacolo* of fireworks fills the sky.

The **Venice International Film Festival,** held in late August and early September, is considered the finest summer celebration of celluloid in Europe after Cannes. Films from all over the world are shown in the Palazzo del Cinema on the Lido as well as various venues across the city—and occasionally outside in some of the campi. Ticket prices vary but are usually modest; some outdoor screenings are free. Check with the tourist office for listings.

Venice hosts the latest in modern and contemporary painting and sculpture from dozens of countries during the prestigious **Biennale d'Arte,** an international modern-art show that fills the pavilions of the public gardens at the east end of Castello from late May through October of every uneven-numbered year (1995 marked its 100th anniversary). Many great modern artists have been "discovered" at this world-famous show. Note that the Giardini Pubblici gardens are marked "Esposizione appeal to all ages, tastes, nationalities, and budgets. At any given moment musical events are staged in any of the city's dozens of piazzas—from reggae and rave to jazz to baroque and chamber music—and special art exhibits are mounted at numerous museums and galleries. The recent involvement of commercial sponsors has met with a mixed reception, although it seems to be the direction of the future.

Carnevale is not for those who dislike crowds. The crowds are what it's all about. All of life becomes a stage, and everyone is on it. Whether you spend months creating an extravagant costume, or grab one ad hoc from the stands set up about the town, Carnevale is about giving in to the spontaneity of magic and surprise around every corner, the mystery behind every mask. Masks and costumes are everywhere, though you won't see much along the line of Batman or the Power Rangers. Emphasis is on the historical, for Venice's Carnevale is the chance to relive the glory days of the 1700s when Venetian life was at its most extravagant. Today's participants parade and pose in historic cafes and backdrop-perfect piazzas, dressed in elaborate re-creations of historical costumes or as characters from the commedia dell'arte, animating the masks that you see hanging year-round in gift shops all over town. Groups travel in coordinated getups that range from a contemporary passel of Felliniesque clowns to the court of the Sun King. There are the three musketeers riding the vaporetto; your waiter appears dressed as a nun; sitting alone on the church steps is a Romeo waiting for his Juliet; late at night crossing a small, deserted campo a young, laughing couple appear out of a gray mist in a cloud of crinoline and sparkles, and then disappear down a small alley.

The city is the quintessential set, the perfect backdrop; Hollywood could not create a more evocative venue. This is a celebration about history, art, theater, and drama, as one would expect to find in the land that gave us the Renaissance and Visconti. Venice and Carnevale were made for each other.

Internazionale d'Art Moderna" on most maps; take vaporetto Line 1 or 52 to the Giardini stop.

The **Regata Storica** (Historical Regatta), which takes place on the Grand Canal on the first Sunday in September, is first an extravagant seagoing parade in historical costume as well as a genuine regatta. Just about every seaworthy gondola in Venice, richly decorated for the occasion and piloted by gondolieri in colorful period livery that recall the halcyon days of the Serene Republic, participates in this maritime cavalcade. The aquatic parade is followed by three individual regattas that are wildly cheered on as they proceed along the Grand Canal. Grandstand tickets can be purchased through the tourist office; or come early and pull up a piece of embankment near the Rialto Bridge for the best seats in town.

Other notable events include November 21st's **Festa della Salute,** when a pontoon bridge is erected across the Grand Canal to connect the churches of La Salute and Santa Maria del Giglio, commemorating another delivery from plague in 1630 that wiped out a third of the lagoon's population; it is the only day the Salute Church opens its massive front doors (a secondary entrance is otherwise used). The **Festa d. Sensa,** on the Sunday following Ascension Day in May, reenacts the ancient ceremony when the doge would wed Venice to the sea. **April 25** is a local holiday, the feast day of Saint Mark, beloved patron saint of the Venice and of the ancient Republic. A special high mass is celebrated in the Basilica of San Marco.

Finally, the ultimate anomaly: Venice's annual **October Maratona (Marathon),** starting at Villa Pisani on the mainland and ending up along the Zattere for a finish at the Basilica di Santa Maria della Salute on the tip of Dorsoduro; it's usually held the last Sunday of October.

7 Shopping

Scores of trinket stores and middle-market to upscale boutiques line the narrow zigzagging Mercerie that runs north between the Piazza San Marco and the Rialto Bridge. More expensive clothing and gift boutiques make for great window-shopping on the Calle Larga XXII Marzo, the wide street that begins west of Piazza San Marco and wends its way to the expansive Campo Santo Stefano in the area of the Accademia museum. The narrow, crowded, store-lined Frezzeria, also west of Piazza San Marco, offers a grab-bag of bars, souvenir shops, and tony clothing stores.

In a city that for centuries has thrived almost exclusively on tourism, remember this: Where you buy cheap you get cheap. There are few bargains to be had and there is nothing to compare with Florence's outdoor San Lorenzo market; the Rialto Market is as good as it gets; you'll find cheap T-shirts, plastic gondolas that glow in the dark, and tawdry glass trinkets. Venetians, centuries-old merchants, are not known for bargaining. You'll stand a better chance for a discount when paying in cash, buying more than one, and when buying costly items.

There are two rules of thumb for shopping in Venice: If you have the good fortune of continuing on to Florence or Rome, then wait to shop for clothing, leather goods, or accessories when you get there. However, if you happen upon something that strikes you, consider it twice on the spot (and not back at your hotel), then buy it. Don't plan on returning: In this web of alleyways, you may never find that shop again.

Venice is famous for several centuries-old local crafts hard to come by elsewhere: **glass** from the island of Murano, delicate **lace** from Burano, and the **carta pesca** (papier-mâché) masks you find in endless botteghe or mask shops around town, where you can watch artisans paint amid their wares.

Now, here's the bad news regarding each of these local arts: There is such an overwhelming sea of cheap glass gewgaws, that it becomes something of a turn-off (shipping and insurance costs make most things unaffordable); there are so few women left in Burano willing to spend countless and tedious hours keeping alive the dying art of lace-making that the few pieces you'll see *not* produced by machine in Hong Kong are sold at stratospheric prices; masks are mass-produced with little attention to quality or finish.

Knowing this, if you would still like to bring a little bit of Venice back home with you—something we highly recommend—you need a shrewd eye to cut through all the dross and gloss. You'll be amazed at some of the lovely and authentic items you can find in even the most chock-a-block tourist traps. But for the occasional quality piece that you want at all costs, sidestep the mediocrity and head for the stand-out locations listed below.

CRAFTS

Murano Art Shop. San Marco 1232 (Frezzeria). ☎ **041/52-33-528.**

Come for the cultural experience if not a shopping spree in this small, precious shop where every inch of wall space is draped with the work of the city's most creative artisans. Fusing the timeless with the contemporary and whimsical—with a nod to

Shopping 337

the magic and romance of Venice past—the results are a dramatic and ever-evolving collection of masks, puppets, music boxes, marionettes, costume jewelry, and the like. It's all expensive, but this rivals a visit to the Doge's Palace.

DOLLS

Bambole di Trilly. Castello 4974 (Fond. d.l'Osmarin). ☎ **041/52-12-579.**

It seems every gift-store window is awash with collectible bisque-faced dolls in elaborate pinafores and headdresses. The hand-sewn wardrobes and painstakingly-painted faces are particularly exquisite here; the perfect souvenir starts at 29,000L ($19.10) and up in this well-stocked work space east of Piazza San Marco and north of Campo San Zaccaria.

EMBROIDERED LINENS

Jesurum. San Marco 4857 (Mercerie). ☎ **041/52-06-177.**

Since 1879, the tradition of hand-embroidery is showcased in Venice's premier (read: "very expensive") store of fine household linens. But some of the small items make gorgeous gifts for discerning friends: small, drawstring pouches for your baubles (18,000L/$11.85), hand-embroidered linen cocktail napkins in different colors (12,000L/$7.90), or hand-finished doilies and linen coasters (15,000L/$9.85).

GLASS

Marco Polo. San Marco 1644 (Frezzeria). ☎ **041/52-29-295.**

This spacious glass emporium just west of the Piazza San Marco stands out amid the plethora of cheap glass stops; the front half of the first floor offers a variety of small gift ideas (candy dishes, glass-topped medicine boxes, paperweights, etc.). Cheap they are not, but no one else has such a lovely representation of hand-blown Murano glassware. Consider a pair of lovely Murano drinking glasses or flutes—the back corner of the store has one of Venice's most impressive collections of glasses, from ultra-contemporary to historical reproductions. These are instant heirlooms.

GLASS BEADS

Anticlea. Castello 4719 (Campo San Provolo). ☎ **041/52-86-946.**

Exquisite antique and reproduced glass beads, once used for trading in Venice's far-flung colonies, now fill the coffers of this small shop east of Piazza San Marco, sold singly or already strung. Search for your "Venetian pearl" here or at the open-air stall below.

Susie and Andrea. Riva degli Schiavoni (near Pensione Wildner; just ask).

This open-air stall has hand-crafted beads that are new, well made and strung, and moderately priced. The stall operates from February through November.

MASKS

La Bottega dei Mascareri. San Polo 80 (at northern end of the Rialto Bridge). ☎ **041/52-42-887.**

A shortage of mask bottegas in Venice is not your problem; the challenge is ferreting out the few young and exceptionally talented artists producing one-of-a-kind theatrical pieces. Only the quality-conscious should shop here, where the charming Boldrin brothers' least elaborate masks begin under 18,000L ($18.40). Anyone who thinks a mask is a mask is a mask should come here first for a look-see.

T-SHIRTS

Voltolina, San Polo 4, on the Rialto Bridge (☎ **041/52-25-667**), is easy to find, selling everyone's favorite souvenir: T-shirts. A-lira-a-dozen elsewhere, these are made from good-quality cotton and are embroidered (with lots of the less expensive stamped variety) with clever scenarios of gondolas and Disney characters for kids, Commedia dell'Arte, and the likes for oldsters. **Venetee,** San Marco 4947, on the Mercerie (☎ 041/52-28-532), offers more unconventional, cutting-edge, and downright irreverent sayings and graphics on their T-shirts.

8　Venice After Dark

Whatever time of year you're visiting Venice, be sure to go to one of the tourist information centers for current English-language schedules of the month's special events (up-to-date entertainment listings are posted in the tourist offices and around town, but ask for a printed copy). The monthly tourist-oriented magazine *Ospite de Venezia* is distributed free of charge and is extremely helpful but is usually only available in the more expensive hotels.

If you're looking for nocturnal action, you're in the wrong town. You're best bet is to sit in the moonlit Piazza San Marco and listen to the cafes' outdoor orchestras, with the illuminated basilica before you—the perfect opera set.

THE PERFORMING ARTS

Venice has a long and rich tradition of classical music. Several Venetian churches regularly host classical-music concerts (with an emphasis on the baroque music that once flourished here) by local and international artists.

The city stood still in shock as the famous **Teatro la Fenice** went up in flames during a devastating fire in January 1996. For centuries it was the city's principal stage for world-class opera, music, theater, and ballet. A concert here was always a cultural experience, set in a gilt and red-velvet jewel box—nothing remained after the fire. While carpenters and artisans work around the clock to re-create a replica of the old Teatro Fenice of 1836 according to archival designs, the **Orchestra della Fenice** and **Coro della Fenice** intend to honor the scheduled performances for the 1997 season. The substitute venues around town have not yet been confirmed; neither has the proposal of creating a year-round tentlike structure in the unlikely area of the Tronchetto parking facilities near the Piazzale Roma.

Like the "phoenix" after which it was named, La Fenice itself will rise up out of the ashes—hopefully by mid-1998. Ticket costs should remain the same, starting at approximately 30,000L to 150,000L ($18.75 to $93.75). For information about a temporary box office and status of future performances, contact the tourist office. La Fenice is located at San Marco 1965, on Campo San Fantin (☎ 041/78-65-62 for information).

Chiesa di Vivaldi, known officially as the Chiesa della Pietà, is the most popular venue for the music of Vivaldi and his contemporaries. It was here that the "red priest" was choral director, and the church offers perhaps the highest quality ensembles. If you're lucky, they'll be performing *Le Quattro Staggioni (The Four Seasons)*. Tickets, sold at the church's box office in the church (☎ 041/91-72-47), on Riva degli Schiavoni, or at the front desk of the well-known Metropole Hotel just next door; they are usually priced at 30,000L ($19.75), students 25,000L ($16.45), should be a definite splurge for music lovers and one of the highlights of your stay. Information and schedules are available from the tourist office; tickets for most concerts can be bought at many of the principal hotels or travel agencies in town, including Agenzia Kele & Teo, Ponte d. Barretteri 4940, San Marco (☎ 041/520-87-22). A number of other churches such as Santo Stefano, San Stae, and the Scuola di San Giovanni also host concerts.

Close to the Rialto Bridge, the **Teatro Goldoni,** San Marco 4650/b, on Calle Goldoni near Campo San Luca (☎ **041/52-05-422**), is known for its theater season (January through May), which regularly features well-known international productions, though mostly in Italian. Tickets run 20,000L to 40,000L ($13.15 to $26.30). The box office is open Monday to Saturday from 10am to 1pm and 4:30 to 7pm.

Both contemporary and classic plays are staged in Italian at the **Ridotto Theater,** Calle Vallaresso, San Marco (☎ **041/52-22-939**), just a stone's throw from St. Marks Square. Recent productions have included works by Shakespeare, Molière, Alan Ayckbourn, and Neil Simon. Tickets range from 17,000L to 35,000L ($11.20 to $23.00). The box office is open Monday to Saturday from 10:30am to 12:30pm and 4:30 to 6:30pm.

CAFES

Venice is a quiet town in the evening and offers very little in the way of nightlife. Evenings are spent lingering over a late dinner, having a pint in one of the *birrerie* (see below) or nursing a slow glass of *prosecco* in one of the outdoor cafes in Piazza San Marco. For tourists and locals alike, Venetian nightlife mainly centers around the many cafe/bars in one of the world's most beautiful piazzas. It is also the most expensive and touristed place to linger over a Campari or cappuccino.

The nostalgic 18th-century **Caffè Florian,** at San Marco 56a–59a, on the side of the piazza nearest the water, is the most famous (closed Wednesday) and has the most theatrical interior. It's also extremely expensive—have a Bellini at the back bar and spend half what you'd pay at a table. It's said that when Casanova escaped from the prisons in the Doge's Palace, he stopped here for a coffee before fleeing Venice.

On the opposite side of the square at San Marco 133–34 are the old-world **Café Lavena** (closed Tuesday) and **Cafe Quadri** (closed Monday) at no. 120. At any of these spots, a cappuccino, tea, or Coca-Cola at a table will set you back about 9,000L ($5.95), but no one will rush you, and if the weather is good and the orchestras are playing, the outdoor tables are the best ticket in town. Around the corner (no. 11) and smack in front of the pink-and-white marble Palazzo Ducale with the lagoon on your right is the lesser known, slightly less expensive **Cafe Chioggia** (closed Sunday). Come here at midnight and watch the Moors strike the hour atop the Clock Tower from your outside table, while the quartet or pianist plays everything from jazz to pop till the wee hours.

CLUBS & BARS (BIRRERIE)

Although it boasts an old and prominent University, clubs and discos barely enjoy their 15 minutes of popularity before changing hands or closing down (some are only open in the summer months). Young Venetians tend to go to the Lido or mainland Mestre.

For just plain hanging out in the late afternoon and early evening, popular squares that serve as meeting points include **Campo San Bartolomeo,** at the foot of the Rialto Bridge, and nearby **Campo San Luca;** you'll see Venetians of all ages milling about engaged in animated conversation, particularly from 5pm till dinnertime. In late-night hours, for low prices and a low level of pretension, I'm fond of the **Campo Santa Margherita,** a huge open campo about halfway between the train station and Ca' Rezzonico. Look for the popular **Green Pub** (no. 3053, closed Thursday), **Bareto Rosso** (no. 2963, closed Sunday) and **Bar Salus** (no. 3112). Note that most bars are open Monday to Saturday from 8pm to midnight. **Campo Santo Stefano** is also worth a visit, namely to sit and sample the goods at the **Bar/Gelateria Paolin** (no. 2962, closed Friday) one of the city's best ice-cream sources.

Club El Souk. Dorsoduro 1056 (near Accademia). ☎ **041/52-00-371.** Winter Tues–Sun 10am–3pm, 5–8pm; Summer Tues–Sun 10pm–4am Vaporetto: Accademia. Follow the narrow C. Gambara to the right of the museum; the club is on your right before you reach the canal.

In order to survive (and it has, successfully), El Souk wears many hats. Self-billed as a "disco-pub," it serves sandwiches and pizzas during lunchtime to the tune of America's latest disco music, and offers a Happy Hour late afternoon. But the only reason you'd want to come is if you're in the market for a disco night (summer only). It's frequented mostly by curious foreigners and some young Venetians who seek them out.

Devil's Forest Pub. San Marco 5185 (C. Stagneri). ☎ **041/52-36-651.** C. Stagneri begins at the right (southeast) end of Cam. San Bartolomeo, which is at the foot of the Rialto Bridge on the San Marco side of the Grand Canal (with your back to the bridge, look for the Banca Commerciale Italiana on the corner).

The Devil's Forest and El Moro Pub (see below) are the latest in the city's trend to imitate British birrerie—something you wouldn't anticipate seeking out in Italy. But both pubs offer the outsider an authentic chance to take in the convivial atmosphere and find out just where the local Venetians hang out. The Devil's Forest has all the basic elements right: carved-wood bar, interior stained glass, and a good selection of draft beers, including Guinness Stout. A pint of beer costs 7,000L ($4.60), while a variety of simple pasta dishes and sandwiches run 6,000L to 8,000L ($3.95 to $5.25). Dart and backgammon boards are available to patrons. Open Tuesday to Friday from 8am to midnight and Saturday and Sunday from 8am to 1am.

El Moro Pub. Castello 4531 (C. d. Rasse). ☎ **041/52-82-573.** AE, V. Thurs–Tues 10am–1am. Vaporetto: San Zaccaria. Facing the Savoia e Jolanda Hotel, walk straight ahead on the C. d. Rasse. The pub is on your left. It's also an easy walk due east from Piazza San Marco.

This lively spot is the biggest draw in town for its half-dozen beers on tap (a pint will cost 8,000L/$5.25). A long list of pub-food has little to do with the expected British prototype: here instead you'll find a number of pizzas (6,000L to 12,000L/$3.95 to $7.90), grilled panini sandwiches (6,000L to 8,000L/$3.95 to $5.25) and, as a nod to American patrons, insalatoni (literally "big salads") that strive to resemble chef salads (9,000L to 10,000L/$5.90 to $6.60). The crowd can be a bit older here, where post-university types congregate at the bar. TVs sometimes transmit national soccer or tennis matches and the management welcomes those who linger, but sensitive nonsmokers won't want to.

Paradiso Perduto. Cannaregio 2540 (Fond. d. Misericordia). ☎ **041/72-05-81.** Thurs–Tues 7pm–1am. Vaporetto: Ferrovie. From the train station, walk along Lista di Spagna, past Cam. S. Geremia, and across the first bridge onto Rio Terrà San Leonardo; turn left onto Rio Terrà Farsetti, cross the bridge, turn right onto Fond. d. Misericordia, and the bar will be straight ahead on your left.

Good food at reasonable prices would be enough to regularly pack this restaurant, but its biggest draw is the live jazz performed on a small stage several nights a week. Extremely popular with American and other foreigners living in Venice, this bar was once devoid of tourists, primarily because it's hard to find and off the beaten path, but lately it looks like the word is out. If you feel like eating, you'll find a good selection of well-prepared pizzas and pastas for under 10,000L ($6.25); arrive early for a table. Beer runs 6,000L ($3.75). Open Thursday to Tuesday from 7pm to 1 or 2am.

THE CASINO

Casino Municipale di Venezia. Palazzo Vendramin Calergi, Cannaregio 2400 (Fond. Vendramin). ☎ **041/52-97-111.** Admission 18,000L ($11.85). Passport required. Nov–Apr (approximately), daily 3pm–3am. Vaporetto: Marcuola.

From May to October, the Casino moves to its nondescript summer location on the Lido, where a visit is not as strongly recommended as during the winter months when it is housed in this handsome 15th-century palazzo on the Grand Canal. Venice's tradition of gambling goes back to its glory days of the Republic, and they live on here in this august Renaissance palace built by Mauro Codussi. Though not of the caliber of Monte Carlo, and on a midweek winter's night, occasionally slow, this is one of only four casinos on Italian territory—and what a remarkable stage setting it is! Richard Wagner lived and died in a wing of this palazzo in 1883.

Check with your hotel before setting forth; some offer free passes for their guests. Otherwise it's may not be worth the admission cost if you're not a gambler or curiosity seeker.

FILMS

There are five cinemas in Venice, and two on the Lido, that often screen American, British, and Australian films. Call or check entertainment listings to see whether the movies are *versione originale* (in their original language, with Italian subtitles). On movie posters around town or in the local newspaper, *il Gazette,* it's usually abbreviated *"v.o."*

Both the **Accademia,** Dorsoduro 1019 (☎ **041/52-87-706**), on C. Corfu opposite El Souk disco near the Accademia, and the **Olimpia,** San Marco 1094, on Cam. San Gallo (☎ **041/52-05-439**) show relatively new American films every Wednesday and Thursday. Both are centrally located; tickets cost 10,000L ($6.55).

9 Exploring Venice's Islands

Venice shares its lagoon with three other principal islands, which you visit conveniently and easily. Vaporetto line 52 goes to all the islands; in addition, line 13 goes to Murano; line 12 services Murano, Burano, and Torcello; and lines 1, 6, and 82 make the journey to the Lido. Check the vaporetto schedules so you don't waste most of your day waiting.

Guided tours of Murano, Burano, and Torcello are operated by the **Serenissima Company,** with departures from a dock between Piazza San Marco and the Hotel Danieli, right next to the wharf for the *motonave* to the Lido (☎ **041/52-28-583** or 52-24-281). The four-hour, 40,000L ($26.30) tours leave daily at 9:30am and 2:30pm. See also "Organized Tours," above. whose foundation dates to the 7th-century, making this the oldest Venetian monument in existence.

MURANO

Murano is famous throughout the world for the products of its glass factories. Glass has been Venice's most important export since the early Middle Ages, when all glass furnaces were moved to the island of Murano both to protect the city from the possibility of mass conflagration and to make foreign industrial spying more difficult. Glass production virtually stopped after Napoléon's conquest in 1797, but was revived again in the 19th century and flourishes today.

As you stroll through Murano, you'll find the factory owners are only to glad to have you come in and watch their process. However, you'll have to be firm to resist the sales pitch that will go along with the demonstration.

The **Museo Vetrario (Museum of Glass Art),** Fond. 8, (☎ **041/73-95-86**), is housed in a Renaissance palazzo, and contains a spectacular collection of Roman, early Venetian, and 19th-century revival glass. The museum is open in summer from 9am to 7pm, in winter from 10am to 5pm; closed Wednesday. Admission is 8,000L ($5.25).

BURANO

Lace is the claim to fame of Burano, an art now practiced by so few island women that prices are generally exorbitant. However, it's still worth a trip if you have time to stroll in the island's opera-set of back streets, whose canals are lined with the simple, brightly-colored homes of the *buranesi* fisherman. Visit the school and lace museum, **Scuola di Merletti,** Piazza Galuppi (☎ **041/73-00-34**). If you go up to the second floor, you can see the lacemakers, mostly young women, at work. It's open Tuesday to Sunday from 9am to 6pm, closed Monday. Admission is 3,000L ($2.00).

TORCELLO

Nearby Torcello is perhaps the most charming of the islands. It's home to the oldest Venetian monument in existence, the **Cattedrale di Torcello (Santa Maria Assunta),** whose foundation dates to the 7th century. It is famous for its Byzantine mosaics, which rival those at Ravenna and in St. Mark's Basilica. The cathedral is open from 10:30am to 12:30pm and 2pm to 5pm. Admission is 1,500L, ($1).

Also of interest is the adjacent church dedicated to St. Fosca and a small archeo-logical museum, open from 10:30am to 12:30pm and 2 to 4pm; closed Monday. Admission is 3,000L ($2).

THE LIDO

Although a convenient 15-minute vaporetto ride away, Venice's Lido **beaches** are not much to write home about. The Adriatic waters have had pollution problems in re-cent years, and for bathing and sun-worshiping there are much nicer beaches in Italy. But the parade of wealthy Italian and foreign tourists (plus a few Venetians) who frequent this *litorale* throughout summer is an interesting sight indeed, though you'll find them at the elitist beaches affiliated with such deluxe hotels as the legend-ary Excelsior and the Des Bains.

There are two beach areas at the Lido. **Bucintoro** is at the opposite end of Gran Viale Santa Maria Elisabetta (referred to as the Gran Viale) from the vaporetto sta-tion Santa Elisabetta. It's a 10-minute walk; walk straight ahead along Gran Viale to reach the beach. **San Nicolò,** a mile away, can be reached by bus B. You'll have to pay 18,000L ($11.85) per person (standard procedure at Italy's beaches) for use of the amenities and umbrella rental. Alternatively, you can patronize the **public beach,** Zona A at the end of Gran Viale.

The Lido's limited sports amenities, such as golf and tennis, are affiliated with its deluxe five-star hotels. Although there is car traffic, the Lido's wide, shaded boule-vards are your best bet for jogging while you're visiting Venice. Vaporetto lines 1, 6, 52, and 82 cross the lagoon to the Lido from the San Zaccaria–Danieli stop near San Marco.

The Veneto

10

by Patricia Schultz

For centuries the Venetian Republic ruled most of the northeastern region called the Veneto, turning its attentions inland once its maritime power was well established throughout the Mediterranean and eastward. The inland cities of the Veneto had been around for centuries when the city of Venice was founded. As ancient Roman strongholds, these cities had already lived through a glorious period—Verona's wealth of Roman sites and its magnificent ancient amphitheater has garnered it the name "Little Rome." Columns topped by the winged-lion mascot of St. Mark and representing the Most Serene Republic still stand in the main squares of Padua, Vicenza, and Verona, symbol of those distant times. Venetian Renaissance palazzi and frescoed churches and basilicas still stand proudly today, making a tour through Veneto a rewarding and often fascinating trip.

Until the arrival of Napoléon in 1797, the Veneto built and embellished, sharing the bounty of the Serene Republic. Many of the Palladian villas that dot the hills of the Veneto were the extravagant summertime legacy of wealthy Venetian merchants whose urban palazzi-cum-warehouses lined Venice's Grand Canal. The Veneto would also boast churches and municipal buildings that showed the Byzantine-oriental influence so prominent in Venice's gothic architecture, buildings adorned with the frescoes of Giotto, and later of the Venetian artists Tiepolo, Veronese, and Tintoretto.

The Veneto is a region of great diversity. The northeastern boundaries of the region reach up to the pale, pink-tinged mountain range of the regal Dolomites that separate Italy from the Tyrol. Farther south, the alluvial plains surrounding the mighty Po River are unrelentingly flat, though punctuated with the Berici Mountains south of Vicenza and the Euganean Hills near Padua. In addition to the Po, the Adige, Brenta, Piave, and other rivers make fertile the hills that are rich with the vineyards, fruit orchards, and lucrative small-scale farms that together create the agricultural wealth that has been the Veneto's sustenance.

VENETO CUISINE & WINE   The Veneto's food products are as diverse as its geography. From the mountains and their foothills come a proliferation of mushrooms and game. Much of the cuisine is based on rice and corn; the appearance of polenta on most menus is frequent, sauced with a hearty game stew with hints of Austrian influence. Rice is commonly served as risotto, a first course along with the season's vegetables or, more characteristically, offerings from the Adriatic on the east. The ubiquitous olive oil of Tuscany's cuisine is here used only minimally—it is not unusual to sense the use of butter, so commonly associated with Emilian food. But above all it is the Adriatic that dictates even the landlocked cuisines of the Veneto. While some of the Mediterranean's best seafood also is a guaranteed price-jacker, ordering with your wallet and not your palate may serve you in good stead. The proliferation of desserts is a throwback to the two times in history that Veneto was ceded to Austria—sweet remnants are still evident in many pastry shops.

Verona and the Veneto play an all-important role in the production and exportation of wines: Soave, Bordolino, and Valpolicello are world-recognized labels that originate in these acclaimed vineyards. The rich volcanic earth of the Colli Euganei produces rich red wines while a light and *frizzante* Prosecco hales from the hills around Asolo. Wine is an integral element in any meal.

EXPLORING THE REGION

The order of this itinerary begins in Padova, the first principal stop west of Venice, continuing to Vicenza, and ending in Verona. Not only are the three cities we highlight here those that hold the most historical and artistic interest, but they are extremely accessible by public transportation. Trains between these cities are inexpensive, frequent, and user-friendly, all being major stops on the west/east Milano/Venice route. In fact, the distances between them are so small that you could very well stay put in Venice and tool into Verona—the most distant of the three—for an easy day trip. But this would be a great shame, indeed, as each of them (Verona, Padova, and Vicenza—in that order, in my opinion) warrants the time it takes to explore them slowly. Enjoy them in the late afternoon and early evening hours when the daytrippers have gone and the cities are left to their own—an aperitivo, a leisurely *passeggiata*, window-shopping along streets lined with tony boutiques, and a moderately priced meal of home-cooked regional specialties in a characteristic wine tavern amid much bonhomie and brio, followed by a good night's rest in a small and friendly hotel located just off the postcard-perfect main square. These three towns also offer a host of day excursions into the real countryside, where you'll need a car or the slightest sense of adventure to jump on a local bus and enjoy the back roads and backwaters of the Veneto.

1 Padova

42km (26 miles) W of Venice; 81km (50 miles) E of Verona; 32km (20 miles) E of Vicenza

The University of Bologna had already grown to 10,000 students by the time Padova founded its university in 1222. Padova was long the academic heartbeat of the powerful Venetian Republic and for this reason, one of the most important medieval and Renaissance cities in Italy. Dante and Copernicus studied here, Petrarch and Galileo taught here. And when you wander the narrow, cobbled, arcaded side streets in the timeless neighborhoods surrounding the "Bo" (named after a medieval inn that once stood on the present-day site of the university), you will be transported back to those earlier times.

Padova is a very vital city, with a young university population that gets about by bicycle and keeps the city's piazzas and cafes alive. The historical hub of town is still very evocative of the days when the city and its university flourished in the late Middle Ages and Renaissance as a center of learning and art.

Pilgrims of another ilk secure Padova's place on the map: For more than 700 years, the enormous Basilica di Sant'Antonio has drawn millions from around the world.

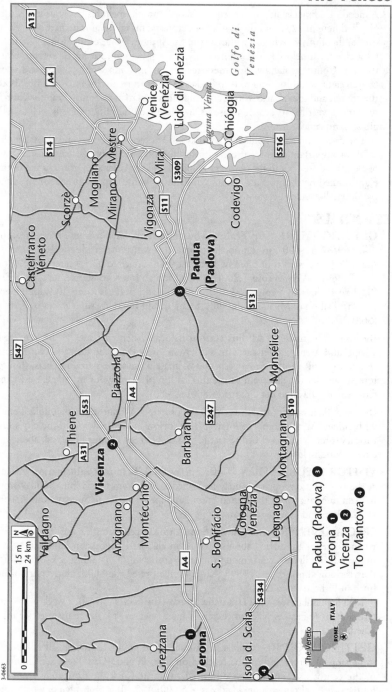

Padua (Padova) ❸
Verona ❶
Vicenza ❷
To Mantova ❹

A mendicant Franciscan monk born in Lisbon, Antonio spent his last years in Padova. He died here in 1231 and the basilica—a fantastic mingling of romanesque, Byzantine, and gothic—was begun within a year. St. Anthony is one of the Roman Catholic Church's most beloved saints, universally known, perhaps, for his powers to locate the lost. Countless handwritten messages left on his tomb within the great domed church call upon this power to help find everything from lost love to lost limbs. Both the church and the miracle worker are simply referred to as "il Santo," and the church warrants a visit for its artistic treasures and architectural importance as well as religious significance.

You can spend a few hours or a few days in Padova, depending on your schedule. Its most important sites for those with limited time are Giotto's magnificent, not-to-be-missed frescoes in the Scrovegni Chapel and the revered pilgrimage site of the eight-domed Basilica of Sant'Antonio di Padova, whose important equestrian statue by Donatello stands before it.

ESSENTIALS

GETTING THERE   By Train   The main train station is at Piazza Stazione (☎ 049/87-51-800), in the northern part of town, just outside the 16th-century walls. Padova is well connected by frequent train service to points directly west and east: Padova to Verona costs 7,200L ($4.75), add an InterCity supplement of 4,800L ($3.15); Padova to Venice is 3,500L ($2.30), add 3,400L InterCity supplement ($2.25); Padova to Milano is 19,000L ($12.50), add InterCity supplement of 9,200L ($6.05).

By Bus   The main **ATAP bus station** is located behind (east of) the Scrovegni Chapel and Arena Gardens area on Via Trieste (near Piazza Boschetti). Frequent bus service to Venice and Verona costs approximately the same as train tickets, though tourists and locals alike seem to use this station principally for the smaller outlying cities such as Bassono del Grappa (5,800L/$3.80).

By Car   Padova is located directly on the principal A4 autostrada that links Venice with Milan. All the points of interest listed below are located within the city's historical center, which is closed to traffic. When booking at your hotel, ask about the closest parking lot.

VISITOR INFORMATION   There are two **I.A.T. tourist information offices:** at the train station, open Monday to Saturday from 9am to 7:30pm, Sunday from 8:30am to noon; and at the Museo Eremitani, open Tuesday to Sunday from 9:30am to 12:30pm and 1:30 to 4:30pm.

SPECIAL EVENTS   The beloved **Sant'Antonio** celebrates his feast day June 13, when his relics are carried about town in an elaborate procession joined in by the thousands of pilgrims who come from all over the world. The dust has settled since the yearlong anniversary in 1995 that commemorated the 800th anniversary of his birth in Lisbon.

Mid-September sees the **Festa della Strada (Buskers' Festival),** a week of free entertainment that takes place in the city's main squares; ask the tourism office for a schedule.

GETTING AROUND   Hotels, restaurants, and points of interest all fall within the historical center and can be reached on foot. Public ACAP buses service much of the center's streets otherwise limited to traffic (pick up a bus map from the tourist office), although a one-day pass of 5,000L ($3.30) is probably not worth your while.

WHAT TO SEE & DO

Pick up a map from the tourist office and plan your attack. The **train station** marks the city's northernmost point, and the **Prato delle Valle** and **St. Anthony's Basilica** mark the southernmost.The following sites of interest can be organized into three clusters: the Cappella degli Scrovegni (also called the Arena Chapel) and the adjacent Museo Civico are across a small piazza from the Eremitani Church; the Caffe Pedrocchi can be found near the Palazzo della Raggione, where the Piazza della Frutta sits to the north and Piazza delle Erbe just to the south, with the Piazza degli Signori bringing up the west; and the Basilica of Sant'Antonio caps the southern end of town with the enormous Prato delle Valle piazza just beyond. Sites below are in geographical order.

✪ **Cappella degli Scrovegni (Arena Chapel).** Pz. Ermitani (off Cor. Garibaldi). ☎ **049/ 87-51-153.** Admission (joint ticket with the Museo Eremitani) 10,000L ($6.60). Feb–Oct, daily 9am–7pm; Nov–Jan, daily 9am–6pm. Entrance through the Museo Eremitani.

This is the one uncontested must-see during your stay in Padova, so be prepared for high-season lines, a wait made even longer by the small numbers of controlled groups allowed to enter the chapel at any one time (limits of 20-minute visits are often imposed during peak periods; check when buying your ticket). Once inside, art lovers armed with binoculars behold the scene in awe, so breathtaking is the recently renovated cycle of vibrant frescoes by Giotto that revolutionized 14th-century painting. A brilliant cobalt blue is the dominant color, in illustrations that are easy to understand in typical medieval comic-strip format; here they take on an unprecedented degree of realism and emotion. Together with the cycle of frescoes that Giotto would later paint in Assisi's St. Francis's Basilica, these are the largest and best preserved. Giotto worked from 1303 to 1306 to completely cover the ceiling and walls with 38 scenes illustrating the lives of Mary and Christ from floor to ceiling. With your back to the front door, the three bands that cover the walls are: top right, *Life of Joachim;* top left, *Life of the Virgin;* right center, *The Childhood of Christ;* left center, *Christ's Public Life;* right bottom, *The Passion of Christ* (the third panel of Judas kissing Christ is perhaps the best known of the entire cycle); left bottom, *Christ's Death and Resurrection.* Above the entrance is the fresco of the *Last Judgment:* Christ, as judge, sits in the center, surrounded by the angels and apostles. Below him, to the right, are the blessed, while to the left, Giotto created a terrible hell in which devils and humans are condemned to eternal punishment.

The area around the ancient Roman Arena where the chapel now stands was purchased in 1300 by a wealthy Paduan, Enrico Scrovegni. He built an extravagant palazzo (destroyed in 1820), and next to it the family chapel whose exterior remains simple and unadorned. Dedicated to his father, an unethical usurer notorious in his time, the son hoped to atone for his father's ways and commissioned Tuscan-born Giotto, whose work he had seen in the Basilica of Sant'Antonio. Giotto felt obligated to include the father in the portrait of the *Last Judgment*'s blessed souls.

Museo Civico Eremitani. Pz. Ermitani (off Cor. Garibaldi). ☎ **049/87-51-153.** Admission (joint ticket with the Cappella degli Scrovegni) 10,000L ($6.60). Feb–Oct, Tues–Sun 9am–7pm; Nov–Jan, Tues–Sun 9am–6pm.

The centuries-old cloisters that were once home to the monks (eremitani means hermits) who officiated in the adjacent Scrovegni Chapel (officially part of the museum complex) have been handsomely renovated to provide an airy display space as the city's new civic museum. Its prodigious collection begins on the ground floor with the Archeological Museum's division of Egyptian, Roman, and Etruscan artifacts and antiquities. The upstairs collection represents an impressive panorama of minor Venetian works from major Venetian artists from the early 15th century to the 19th century.

The entire collection has not yet been relocated from its previous home in the monastery of Sant'Antonio; it should feel at home in these new hallowed environs.

Chiesa degli Eremitani (Church of the Hermits). Pz. Eremitani (off Cor. Garibaldi). ☎ **049/87-56-410.** Free admission. Daily 7:30am–1pm and 3:30–7pm.

Padova's worst tragedy was the destruction of this church by Nazi bombings in 1944; some art historians consider it the country's greatest artistic loss. It has been remarkably restored to its original early 13th-century romanesque style, but the magnificent cycles of frescoes by Padova-born Andrea Mantegna could not be salvaged, except for a corner of the Ovetari Chapel on the right of the chancel. Here you'll find enough fragments of the late 15th-century frescoes to understand the loss of what was considered one of the great artistic treasures of Italy. Mantegna was born in Padova and studied under the Florentine master Donatello, who lived here while completing his commissions for the Basilica di Sant'Antonio as well as the famous equestrian statue that now stands in the piazza before it.

✪ **Caffè Pedrocchi.** V. VIII Febbraio 15 (at Pz. Cavour). ☎ **049/82-05-007.** Tues–Sun 9:30am–12:30pm and 3:30pm–8pm.

The Pedrocchi is a historic landmark, as beloved by the Paduans as "their" own St. Anthony. When it first opened in 1831 it was the largest cafe in Europe—who were they expecting? Famous are the literary and political characters and local luminaries who made this their command post—French-born Henri Beyle, a.k.a. Stendhal, had it in mind when he wrote: "The best Italian cafe is almost as good as the Parisian ones." Countless others were less reserved, calling it arguably the most beautiful coffeehouse in the world. Heavily damaged during World War II, it has been completely rebuilt in its original neoclassical 19th-century stage-set splendor and is again the social heartbeat for university students and ladies of a certain age alike (and take note: it has the nicest rest rooms in town, for the use of cafe patrons). In warm weather Pedrocchi opens wide its doors (and hence its curious description as a "doorless cafe") onto the pedestrian piazza; sit here for a while to absorb the Padovan spirit. As is always the case, drinks cost less standing at the bar, but then you will have missed the *dolce far niente* experience for which Pedrocchi has always been known. A cappuccino, tea, beer, or glass of white *prosecco* wine will cost 4,000L ($2.65) at your table, and hunger can be held at bay with a plate of dainty tea-time pastries or a grilled ham-and-cheese toast, each 4,000L ($2.65).

✪ **Palazzo della Ragione (Law Courts).** ☎ **049/82-05-006.** Admission 7,000L ($4.60). Feb–Oct, Tues–Sun 9am–7pm; Nov–Jan, Tues–Sun 9am–6pm.

Located just south of the historic Caffè Perocchi, and a necessary and inevitable destination for those meandering about the historic center of town, the expansive open-air markets of Piazza delle Erbe (Square of the Herbs) and Piazza della Frutta (Square of Fruit), and the 13th-century palazzo that surrounds them was the town's political and commercial nucleus for centuries. Before being distracted by the color and cacophony of the sprawling outdoor fruit and vegetable market stands, turn your attention to the magnificent Palazzo della Ragione, whose interior is as impressive as its exterior.

The two-story loggia-lined palazzo with street-level shops and cafes is topped with a distinctive sloped roof that resembles the inverted hull of a ship, the largest of its kind in the world. It was built in 1219 as the seat of Padova's parliament and was used as an assembly hall, courthouse, and administrative center to celebrate Padova's newly won independence as a republican city. Considered a masterpiece of civil medieval architecture, it was heavily damaged by a fire in 1420 that destroyed, among other things, an elaborate cycle of frescoes by Giotto that adorned the Salone (Great Hall). The Hall, 270 feet long, was almost immediately rebuilt and is today the prime draw, both for its floor-to-ceiling 15th-century frescoes, similar in astrological theme to those that had been painted by Giotto, and a large wooden sculpture of a horse attributed to Donatello (most art historians don't agree).

On the far side of the adjoining piazzas' canvas-topped stalls, flanking the Palazzo della Ragione, is the Piazza dei Signori, most noteworthy for the 15th-century clock tower that dominates it, the first of its kind in Italy.

☼ Basilica di Sant'Antonio. Pz.d. Santo (east of Prato d. Valle). Free admission. Summer, daily 7:30am–7:45pm; winter, daily 7:30am–7pm.

Standing out amid the cluster of stalls clogging the large piazza in front of the Basilica is Donatello's famous Gattamelata equestrian statue. The first of its size to be cast in Italy since Roman antiquity, it is important for its detail, proportion, and powerful contrast between rider (the inconsequential Venetian condottiere Erasmo da Narni, nicknamed the "Spotted Cat") and horse. It would have a seminal effect on Renaissance sculpture and casting and restore the lost art of the equestrian statue. The enormous Basilica houses the body of Padova's patron St. Anthony, simply and commonly referred to as "il Santo," who was born in Lisbon in 1195 (a worldwide yearlong festival commemorated his 800th anniversary in 1995) and died just outside of Padova in 1231. Work began on the church almost immediately but was not completed until 1307. Its eight domes bring to mind the Byzantine influence found in Venice's St. Mark's Basilica that predates Padova's romanesque-gothic construction by more than two centuries. A pair of octagonal, minaretlike bell towers enhance its Eastern appearance.

The imposing interior is richly frescoed and decorated, filled with a number of tombs, works of art, and elaborate inlaid marble flooring. Of most importance is the tomb holding the saint's body. In the direction of the main altar, it is found off the left aisle and is always covered with flowers, photographs, and handwritten personal petitions left by devout pilgrims whose numbers have remained constant over the centuries. The saint is the patron of lost or mislaid objects, and the faithful who flock here look for everything from lost love to lost health. The bronze bas-reliefs of scenes from the saint's life are the work of Donatello, as are the seven bronze statues and towering central *Crucifixion* that adorn the main altar (1444–48).

In his lifetime, St. Anthony was known for his eloquent preaching, so interpret as you will the saint's perfectly preserved tongue, vocal chords, and jawbone on display in a chapel in the back of the church. These treasured relics are carried through town in a traditional procession every June 13 to celebrate the feast day of "il Santo."

MARKETS

The third Sunday of every month sees the area of the Prato delle Valle inundated by over 200 antiques and collectibles dealers, one of the largest **antiques fairs** in the region. The quality of goods can be quite nice, but only early birds will beat the large number of local dealers to the worm. Antiques lovers with a car might want to visit Italy's second largest Mercato dell'Antiquariato at the Villa Contarini (in Piazzola sul Brenta, a lovely 30-minute drive), held the last Sunday of every month. An estimated 350 vendors hawk their wares; the villa is open for visits during those hours.

Less important, but far more frequent, is the weekly **Saturday outdoor market** also held in the Prato della Valle. Its large number of shoe stands is due to the many shoe factories for which the nearby Brenta Canal area has long been renowned; you might get lucky. At worst, both the monthly market listed above and this weekly market will give you a reason to visit the 18th-century Prato della Valle, said to be one of the largest piazzas in Europe. Located just southwest of St. Anthony's Basilica, it is ringed by a canal peopled with more than 80 statues.

WHERE TO STAY

Padova is convenient to both Venice and Verona. There isn't a wide choice of desirable hotels, but you'll pay close to half the rates of comparable accommodations in Venice and find the commute, just 19 miles, an easy and inexpensive one (and often a necessary one when Venice is booked full). The few good hotels here are often booked for local trade fairs or for religious- or commercial-tourism related reasons.

Low season is usually considered December and January, and July and August; both seasons you'd do well to inquire about discounts.

✪ **Hotel al Fagiano.** V. Locatelli 45 (west of Pz. d. Santo), ☎ **049/87-50-073.** Fax 049/87-53-396. 33 rms, 30 with bath. A/C TEL TV. 40,000L ($26.30) single without bath, 80,000L ($52.65) single with bath; 60,000L ($39.50) double without bath, 100,000L ($65.80) double with bath; 120,000L ($78.95) triple with bath. Breakfast 10,000L ($6.60) per person extra. Rates slightly discounted off-season. AE, DC, V.

Although small and family-run, don't expect much coziness and charm in this newly renovated and well-located hotel. But given the less than encouraging hotel situation in town, the Fagiano's bright, modern, and clean rooms are a standout choice that come highly recommended. Bathrooms have also been freshly redone and include niceties such as hair dryers and bright lighting. Located just a few steps off the expansive Piazza del Santo, don't confuse this Fagiano with the recently renamed Hotel Buenos Aires, formerly known as the Fagiano and just a block away.

Leon Bianco. Pzta. Pedrocchi 12 (at V. Cavour), 35122 Padova. ☎ **049/87-50-814.** Fax 049/87-56-184. 22 rms with bath. A/C MINIBAR TEL TV. 125,000L ($82.25) single; 156,000L ($102.65) double. Buffet breakfast 15,000L ($9.85) per person extra. AE, DC, MC, V. Parking available.

This is the three-star sister of the four-star Majestic listed below, and the most centrally located of its competitors. In fact, it's the best in terms of location regardless of category: The heartbeat of town—the landmark Caffè Pedrocchi and the open-air marketplace—is just outside your front door. The 100-year-old palazzo is done up in a contemporary theme and prides itself on its art collection, hung in the public areas. A top floor alfresco terrace is transformed into a breakfast area with the arrival of warm weather: Linger with your cappuccino under white canvas umbrellas with views over the city center's rooftops. An unusual hotel amenity is the extensive video library, of which a few dozen are in the original English version.

✪ **Hotel Majestic Toscanelli.** V. dell'Arco 2 (2 blocks west of V. Roma and south of the Pz. d. Erbe), 35122 Padova. ☎ **049/66-32-44.** Fax 049/87-60-025. 32 rms with bath. A/C MINIBAR TEL TV. 165,000L ($108.55) single; 215,000L ($141.45) double; 255,000L ($167.75) triple. Rates include buffet breakfast. Book 4 nights over a weekend in advance and pay for 3 (certain blackout dates). Rates discounted July 14–Aug 31. AE, DC, MC, V.

A four-star hotel this nice would cost twice these rates in Venice, which is why the Toscanelli often finds itself with guests who make this their home base while visiting the surrounding area. A 1992 refurbishment has kept the hotel's old-world charm fresh and handsome, from the lobby's Persian rugs and potted plants to the rooms redone in classic decor with coordinated pastel themes and burnished cherrywood furniture. Baths are big and done up in bright white marble tiles. This quiet, historic neighborhood is entirely closed to traffic, but it's an easy walk to the Via Roma and the Piazza delle Erbe. A brand-new restaurant in the secular cantina of the hotel opened in 1996. The Storico Toscanelli Pizzeria (☎ 049/87-52-845; closed Monday) specializes in pizzas (10,000L to 15,000L/$6.60 to $9.85) but offers a number of pasta dishes as well (7,000L to 10,000L/$4.60 to $6.60) and encourages you to eat as little or linger as long as you like.

WHERE TO DINE

Brek. Pz. Cavour 20. ☎ **049/87-53-788.** 1st courses 3,800L–6,000L ($2.50–$3.95); entrees 6,200L–8,000L $4.10–$5.25); vegetables 3,000L–5,000L ($2.00–$3.30). Sat–Thurs 11:30am–3pm and 6–10pm. No credit cards. ITALIAN.

I am both proud and embarrassed to admit that with the exception of a brief dalliance in Rome's McDonald's many years ago, I made my first acquaintance with Italian fast food only recently. It was in Padova's Brek (as in "Let's take a *brek* . . . ") self-service *all'italiana*. Put your language problems and calorie counting aside as you help yourself to pastas that are made up fresh while you wait and point to the sauce of your choice. There's a counter just for omelettes (and another for entrees) made express, and the dessert cart virtually groans with a copious array of cheeses, fresh fruits, fruit salads, and fruit-topped tarts and cobblers.

Enoteca L'Anfora. V. d. Soncin 13 (east of Pz. Duomo). ☎ **049/65-66-29.** Cichetti 500L–3,000L (35¢–$2.00), 7,000L–9,000L ($4.60–$5.90); main courses 12,000L–18,000L ($7.90–$11.85). Mon 5pm–midnight; Tues–Sat 9:30am–3:30pm and 5pm–midnight. No credit cards. PADOVAN.

Even the finest of the Veneto's wine labels cost less than 5,000L ($3.30) a glass—there are over 40 to choose from. This spot is a longtime favorite and a good choice for sampling typical pasta dishes like bigoli all'anitra (homemade pasta with a duck ragu) and spaghetti con gli scampi. A full meal (which, by the way, is not necessary) can be had by choosing from the limited but always fresh fish- and meat-based entrees. If you stop in for a glass of wine, I guarantee you'll either stay for a meal or make it a point to return for one.

✪ **Osteria Dei Fabbri.** V. d. Fabbri 13, ☎ **049/65-03-36.** First courses 8,000L–10,000L ($5.25–$6.60); main courses 15,000L–17,000L ($9.85–$11.20). Mon–Sat noon–3:30 and 5:30pm–1am. AE, DC, MC, V. PADOVAN.

Simple, well-prepared food is the great equalizer. This rustic old-fashioned tavern or osteria is a lively spot where intellectual types share tables with Zegna-suited bankers, and students stop by for a tipple or to find a quiet corner in which to pore over the newspaper (not encouraged during hours when meals are served). Some of the day's specials are displayed on the big oak bar—antipasti of grilled vegetables, rosemary potatoes, seafood salads—while hot dishes pour out of the kitchen. There's always at least one homemade pasta choice to start with, and osso buco, the specialty of the house, is especially memorable when accompanied by any of the local Venetian wines available by the bottle or glass.

✪ **Il Dotto.** V. Squarcione 23 (west of V. Roma). ☎ **049/87-51-490.** First courses 12,000L–15,000L ($7.90–$9.85); entrees 22,000L–25,000L ($14.50–$16.45). Tues–Sat 12:30–2pm and 7:30–10:30pm; Sun 12:30–2pm. Closed Sun dinner and Mon). AE, DC, MC, V. PADOVAN.

If you have the hankering and budget to experience an evening of fine yet inventive dining, something more discreet and less casual than the good straightforward meals reliably found in local trattorias and lively osterias, Il Dotto is your handsome and moderately priced choice. Located in the medieval section of town just south of the Piazza Erbe where antique stores abound, "Il Dotto" refers to the sage doctors of academia in the university's early days. But let the wisdom of the waiter walk you through a meal here; start with their famous pasta e fagioli or deservedly popular risotto, or ask about the changing selections featured in the mini-*degustazione* menu which, at 50,000L ($32.90), may well be the culinary climax of your stay in Padova.

PADOVA AFTER DARK

The classical music season usually runs from October to April at different venues around town. The historic **Teatro Verdi** is the most impressive venue. Programs are available at the tourist office. Look for posters advertising performances by the world-class **Solisti Veneti,** who are Padovans but spend most of the year, alas, traveling abroad.

DAY TRIPS FROM PADOVA

The **Euganean Hills (Colli Euganei)** are the center of the small but renowned wine industry of the Veneto, located southwest of Padova. A "Strada dei Vini" wine route map can be had from the tourist office (when in stock!). It also leads you to the small city of **Terme di Abano,** famous as a center for radioactive springs and mud treatments unique to this volcanic range.

The navigable Brenta Canal links Padova with Venice in the east. Ambitiously called **"The Forgotten Riviera,"** because of the 70-some-odd historic summertime villas built here by Venice's wealthy merchants, it can be visited on an organized bus tour (Reisen Tours, ☎ **049/79-35-44**) or by the Burchiello boat (New Siamic Express, ☎ **049/66-09-44**). Some of the villas are far more outstanding than others. A few are by Palladio. Some villas are open only to those arriving on organized tours. See the tourist office about a map if you want an independent do-it-yourself approach; but be careful about difficult, erratic visiting hours that differ from villa to villa.

An easy and enjoyable day trip can be made to the small city of **Bassano del Grappa,** 26 miles north of Padova. For information, see "Day Trips from Vicenza."

2 Vicenza

32km (20 miles) W of Padova; 74km (46 miles) W of Venice; 51km (32 miles) E of Verona

Vicenza pays heartfelt homage to Andrea di Pietro della Gondola (1508–80), born in nearby Padova, who lived out his life and dreams here under the name Palladio. He was the most important architect of the High Renaissance, one whose living monuments inspired and influenced architecture in the Western world over the centuries up to this very day. Vicenza is a mecca for the architecture lover. However, an evening stroll through illuminated piazzas and along boutique-lined streets is just as enjoyable for those of you who have never heard of Palladio—though you'll convert to a die-hard architecture buff once you do: A day here is worth a semester back in school.

Vicenza today is one of the wealthiest cities in Italy, thanks in part to a recent burgeoning of the local computer-component industry (Federico Faggin, inventor of the silicon chip, was born here) and traditional gold manufacturing.

ESSENTIALS

GETTING THERE   By Train   Most visitors arrive by train from Venice (50 minutes). The train station is in Piazza Stazione, also called Campo Marzio (☎ **0444/32-50-46**), at the southern end of Viale Roma. Expect to pay the following one-way fares: Vicenza/Venice 5,600L ($3.70), add 3,900L InterCity supplement ($2.55); Vicenza/Padova 3,500L ($2.30), add 3,000L InterCity supplement ($2.00); Vicenza/Verona, 5,000L ($3.30), add InterCity supplement of 3,600L ($2.35).

By Bus   The FTV bus station (the Stazione Pullman) is located on Viale Milano (☎ **0444/22-31-15**), just to the west (left) of the train station. Buses leave frequently for all the major cities in the Veneto and to Milano; prices are comparable to train travel.

By Car   Vicenza is on the A4 autostrada that links Venice to the east with Milano to the west. Coming from Venice, you'll bypass Padova before arriving in Vicenza.

VISITOR INFORMATION   The **tourist information office** is in the Piazza Matteotti 12 (☎ and fax: **0444/32-08-54**) next to the Teatro Olimpico. Hours are Monday to Saturday from 9am to 12:30pm and 2:30 to 6pm, Sunday from 9am to 12:30pm. In low season (mid-October through mid-March), closing time is 5:30pm.

CITY LAYOUT   The city's layout is quite straightforward and easy to navigate. The **train station** lies at its southernmost point. From here head straight ahead on **Viale Roma;** it ends at a turn-about with gardens beyond. Then head right (east) into the **centro storico,** marked by the Piazza Castello, from which the main thoroughfare starts, the **Corso Palladio.** The arrow-straight corso cuts through town, running southwest (from Piazza Castello) to northeast (Piazza Matteotti), site of the Teatro Olimpico. Along the corso you'll find urban palazzi by Palladio and his students; midway, the **Piazza dei Signori** will be found on your right (south) and perpendicular to the corso will be the **Contrà Porti,** a lovely palazzo-studded street, on your left (north).

GETTING AROUND   There is limited traffic (for taxis, buses, and residents) once you enter the Piazza del Castello and the centro storico. Everything of interest can be easily reached on foot; pick up a map at the tourist office. Even the two villas just outside town (see below) can be reached by foot or bike as well as by bus or car.

EXPLORING THE PALLADIAN HERITAGE

A biglietto cumulativo for joint entrances to the following four museums costs 9,000L ($5.90): the Museo Olimpico, Museo Civico, and the two less visited Museo Archeologico-Naturalistico and Museo del Risorgimento.

Piazza dei Signori

South of Corso Palladio, this is the site of the ancient Roman Forum and town hub still; this central square should be your first introduction to the city and its favored son, Palladio. The magnificent bigger-than-life ✪ **Basilica Palladiana** is not a church at all and was only partially designed by Palladio. Beneath it stood a gothic-style Palazzo della Ragione (Law Courts and Assembly Hall) that Palladio was commissioned to convert to a High Renaissance style befitting a flourishing late 16th-century city under Venice's patronage. He created two superimposed galleries, the lower with Doric pillars, the upper with Ionic. The roof was destroyed by World War II bombing, but has since been rebuilt in its original style. It's open Tuesday to Saturday from 9:30am to noon and from 1 to 7pm; Sunday from 9:30am until noon.

The towering 12th-century **Torre Bissara** (or Torre di Piazza) bell tower belonged to the original church and stands near two columns in the piazza's east end (the Piazza Blade), one topped by the winged lion of Venice's Serene Republic, the other by the Redentore (Redeemer). Of note elsewhere in the piazza are the Loggia del Capitanio (1570), begun but never finished by Palladio except for the four massive redbrick columns. Behind the Basilica is the Piazza delle Erbe, site of the daily produce market.

Corso Andrea Palladio

This is Vicenza's main street, and what a grand one it is, lined with the magnificent palazzi of Palladio and his students. The first one of note, starting from its southwest cap, is the Piazza Valamarana at no. 16, begun by Palladio in 1566. On the right, (behind which stands the Piazza dei Signori) is the Palazzo del Comunale, the Town Hall built in 1592 by Samozzi, Palladio's protégé and pupil. This is said to be Samozzi's greatest work.

From the Corso Palladio and heading northeast, take a left onto the Contrà Porti, the second most important street for its Palladian and gothic palazzi. The two designed by Palladio are the **Palazzo Barbarano Porto** at no. 11, and **Palazzo Thiene** at 12; gothic palazzi of note can be found at nos. 6 to 10, 14, 16, 17, and 19.

Returning to Corso Palladio, look for no. 145/147, the pre-Palladian **Ca d'Oro** (Golden Palace) for the gold leaf used in the frescoes that once covered its facade. It was bombed in 1944 and rebuilt in 1950. The simple palazzo at no. 163 was Palladio's home.

Before reaching the Piazza Matteotti and the end of the Corso Palladio you'll see signs for the **Church of Santa Corona,** set back on the left on the Via Santa Corona (open daily from 8:30am to noon and 2:30 to 6pm). An unremarkable 13th-century gothic church, it shelters two masterpieces that make this worth a visit: Giovanni Bellini's *Baptism of Christ* and Veronese's *Adoration of the Magi.* This is Vicenza's most interesting church, far more so than the cavernous Duomo southwest of the Piazza dei Signori, but worth seeking out only if you've got the extra time. At the end of the Corso Palladio at its northeastern end is Palladio's world-renowned Teatro Olimpico.

✪ **Teatro Olimpico and Museo Civico.** Pz. Matteotti (at Cor. Palladio), ☎ **0444/ 32-37-81.** Admission for each is 5,000L ($3.30); joint ticket for entrance to both is 9,000L ($5.90). Apr–Sept, 9am–12:30pm and 2:15–5pm; Sun 9am–12:30 and 2–7pm. Oct–Mar, 9am– 12:30pm and 2:30–5pm; Sun 9am–12:30pm.

The splendid Teatro Olimpico was Palladio's greatest work, begun in 1580, the year of his death and completed five years later by his student Vicenzo Scamozzi. It was the first covered theater in Europe, inspired by the theaters of antiquity. The seating area, in the shape of a half-moon as in the old arenas, seats 1,000. The stage seems profoundly deeper than its actual 14 feet, thanks to the permanent stage "curtain" and Scamozzi's clever use of trompe l'oeil. The stage scene represents the ancient streets of Thebes, while the faux clouds and sky covering the dome further the impression of being in an outdoor Roman amphitheater.

Across the Piazza Matteotti is another Palladian opus, the Palazzo Chiericati, which houses the Museo Civico (Municipal Museum). Looking more like one of the country villas for which Palladio was equally famous, this major work is considered one of his finest and is visited as much for its two-tiered, statue-topped facade as for the collection of Venetian paintings it houses on the first floor. Venetian masters you'll recognize include Tiepolo, Tintoretto, and Veronese, while the lesser known include works from the Vicenza or Bassano schools of painting.

VILLAS & THE BASILICA NEARBY

To reach the two villas in the immediate environs of Vicenza, southeast of the train station, you can walk, bike, or take the no. 8 bus. First stop by the tourist office for a map, and check on visiting hours, which tend to change from month to month and season to season.

The **Villa Rotonda** (☎ **0444/32-17-93**) alternatively referred to as Villa Capra Valmarana after its owners, is considered one of the most perfect buildings ever constructed and has been added to the World Heritage List by UNESCO; it is a particularly important excursion for students and lovers of architecture. Obviously inspired by ancient Greek and Roman designs, Palladio began this perfectly proportioned square building topped by a dome in 1567; it was completed by Scamozzi after Palladio's death, between 1580 and 1592. You will perhaps recognize it, for it is the model that inspired Jefferson's home in Monticello and the Chiswick House near London, and countless other noble homes and government buildings in the United States and Europe. It is worth a visit if only to view it from the outside. Admission for outside viewing is 5,000L ($3.30); admission for visits inside is 10,000L ($6.60).

From here it is only a 10-minute walk to the **Villa Valmarana** (☎ **0444/ 54-39-76**), also called "ai Nani" ("dwarves") after the statues that line the garden wall. Built in the 17th century by Mattoni, an admirer and follower of Palladio, it is a beautiful villa whose reason to visit is an interior covered with remarkable 18th-century frescoes by Giambattista Tiepolo and his son Giandomenico. Admission is 8,000L ($5.25); the villa is closed Monday.

Also in this area is the **Basilica di Monte Berico** built in 1668 by a Bolognese architect and, if you've already visited the Villa Rotonda, you will understand where he got his inspiration. The interior's most important work is in a chapel to the right of the main altar, a *Lamentation* by Bortolomeo Montagna (1500). The terrace in front of the church affords beautiful views of Vicenza, the Monti Berici, and the distinct outline of the nearby Alps. The basilica is open daily from 7am to 12:30pm and 2:30 to 7pm.

ORGANIZED TOURS

The success of a recent guided tour called "Vicenza per Mano" ensures that it will most probably run again in 1997, April through mid-October. Each of the two individual tours cost 20,000L ($13.15); both together cost 35,000L ($23.00). The morning tour leaves at 9:30am and includes a visit to the Basilica di Monte Berico, Villa la Rotonda (from the outside), and Villa Valmarana ai Nani (inside). The afternoon tour leaves at 3:30pm and visits all the sites within the historical center. Book through the tourist office, in advance if possible.

WHERE TO STAY

Unlike Padova, which gets the overflow from Venice, or the tourism-magnet Verona, Vicenza can be very quiet in August or in the winter months when trade fairs are not in town; some hotels close without notice for a few weeks. Make sure you call in advance.

A special weekend rate July to August became a year-long offer in 1996 for those visiting Vicenza Friday to Sunday. At least a dozen two- to four-star hotels participated by greatly reducing their rates; a number of other niceties were included, such as discounts at some museums and restaurants. For the 1997 status of this "Special Weekend," call the Vicenza È office (☎ **0444/32-08-54;** fax 0444/54-44-30) or ask at the tourist office.

Cristina. Cor. San Felice 32 (W of Salvi Gardens), 36100 Vicenza. ☎ **0444/32-37-51.** Fax 0444/54-36-56. A/C MINIBAR TEL TV. 33 rms with bath. 140,000L ($92.10); 190,000L ($125.00) double; 230,000L ($151.30). Rates include buffet breakfast. Discounts possible in low season. AE, DC, MC, V. Parking available.

Located west of the Piazza Castello and the green Giardino Salvi, this recently refurbished hotel is still within easy walking distance of the historic center's principal sites. A contemporary approach with occasional exposed beams and marble and parquet flooring results in a handsome lodging and makes this one of Vicenza's preferred three-star properties. An internal courtyard provides welcome parking space and guests have access to bicycles for touring the traffic-free center of town as well as the nearby villas just southeast of the train station. The bike-weary will delight at the recent addition of an in-house sauna.

Due Mori. V. Do Rode 26 (1 block west of Pz. d. Signori), 36100 Vicenza ☎ **0444/ 32-18-86.** Fax 0444/32-61-27. 26 rms, 23 with bath. TEL. 59,000L ($38.80) single with bath; 65,000L ($42.75) double without bath, 78,000L ($51.30) double with bath; 77,000L ($50.65) triple without bath, 91,000L ($59.85) triple with bath. Breakfast extra 9,000L ($5.90) per person. AE, MC, V.

The paint is barely dry from a renovation completed in January 1996. Add that to this family-run hotel's history as the oldest in Vicenza and its convenient location on a quiet side street just west of the sprawling Piazza Signoria, and you have the deservedly most popular spot in town at a price that can't be beat. All of this to say: Book early. If you prefer 19th-century decor, ask for one of the rooms with "arredamento antiquariato" when booking.

Palladio. V. Oratorio d. Servi 25 (E of the Pz. d. Signori), 36100 Vicenza ☎ **0444/32-10-72.** Fax 0444/54-73-28. 4 rms, 20 with bath. TEL TV. 255,000L ($36.20) single without bath, 85,000L ($55.90) single with bath; 105,000L ($69.10) double with bath; 135,000L ($88.80) triple with bath. Breakfast 10,000L ($6.60) per person extra. AE, MC, DC, V.

A popular two-star choice just a two-minute walk from the Piazza dei Signori (and equidistant from the Piazza Matteotti and the Teatro Olimpico), this family-run hotel offers small but efficient rooms in a quiet neighborhood. Parking can be arranged, as can daily bicycle rentals (10,000L/$6.60 per day)

San Raffaele. Vle. X Giugno 10 (SE of train station), 36100 Vicenza. ☎ **0444/32-36-63.** Fax 0444/54-22-59. 24 rms with bath. 55,000L ($36.20) single; 80,000L ($52.65) double; 100,000L ($65.80) triple. Breakfast extra 8,500L ($5.60) per person. AE, DC, MC, V.

As clean and simply furnished as you would expect an ex-convent to be (they've even kept a small chapel for the use of hotel guests), the San Raffaele is located up in the hills in the area of the Monte Berico Basilica and the Villa Rotonda. For those who arrive at the train station, it's a 1.5-mile bus ride from the station to Monte Berico; the tranquillity and views may be more than worth it for some. If you're interested, only two rooms have TVs, so ask in advance.

Vicenza. Stradella d. Nodari 5/7 (west of Pz. d. Signori), 36100 Vicenza. ☎ **0444/32-15-12.** 37 rms, 33 with bath. 45,000L ($29.60) single without bath, 60,000L ($39.50) single with bath; 65,000L ($42.75) double without bath, 85.000L ($55.90) double with bath. Breakfast extra at 5,000L ($3.30) per person. No credit cards accepted.

Forever popular with tourists as well as Italian businessmen without expense accounts, this well-known two-star hotel is recommended for its central location on a narrow street off the Piazza della Signoria. *Caveat:* No air-conditioning means open windows that let in the piazza's overflow of pedestrian noise. Occasional antiques and quasi-antiques fill the guest rooms and some of the bathrooms are almost new. This seems to be on everyone's shortlist, but I add—only if there's no availability at the Due Mori just around the corner that offers more and costs less.

WHERE TO DINE

Antica Casa Della Malvasia. Contrà d. Morette 5 (off Cor. Palladio). ☎ **0444/54-37-04.** Primi courses 5,500L ($3.60); entrees 8,000L–14,000L ($5.25–$9.20). No credit cards. Tues–Sun noon–3pm and 7pm–midnight. VICENTINO.

On a quiet, characteristic side street that links the principal Corso Palladio with the Piazza dei Signori is this ever lively, tavernalike osteria. Cooking is informal, homemade, and regional and there's usually one waiter or more whose English will help eliminate the guessing game. The food is reliably good, but it's just an excuse to accompany the selection of wines (70), whiskies (75), grappas (132), and teas (over 100). No wonder this place always buzzes. Even if you don't eat here, stop in for a late-night toddy, *Vicentino*-style.

Osteria al Campinile. V. Fontana 2 (1 block from Pz. Duomo). ☎ **0444/54-40-36.** Wines by the glass 1,500L–4,000L ($1.00–$2.65). No credit cards. Daily 9am–3pm and 5–9pm.

An authentic, warm and friendly wine bar, this osteria is the oldest in Vicenza, dating back more than 100 years. The discerning selection of Italian wines by the glass (predominantly from the Veneto) is limited but guaranteed to make you quite happy; if they don't, any one of the dozen grappas will. There are always a few cichetti finger foods to keep you standing till it's time to wander down the block to Righetti's to complete the *vicentino* experience.

Righetti. Pz. Duomo 3/4. ☎ **0444/54-31-35.** Primi 4,000L–5,000L ($2.60–$3.30); 8,000L–10,000L ($5.25–$6.60). No credit cards. Mon–Fri noon–2:30pm and 7–10pm. VICENTINO/ITALIAN.

For a self-service operation, this place is a triple surprise: The diners are all local (and loyal); the food is reliably good—of the home-cooked generous portions kind; and indoors is rustic, welcoming, and pleasant. But it's the opportunity to sit outdoors in the quiet, traffic-free Piazza Duomo that first drew me here. There are three or four first courses to choose from (Tuesday and Fridays are risotto days) and as many entrees. Evenings offer the added option of grilled meats (which makes eating indoors in the cold winter months so much more enjoyable), though this is the perfect relaxed place to revel in a simple meal of pasta and side vegetable.

WORTH A SPLURGE

✪ **Trattoria Tre Visi.** Contrà Port 6 (off Cor. Palladio). ☎ **0444/32-48-68.** Reservations suggested. Primi courses 10,000L ($6.60); entrees 20,000L–30,000L ($13.15–$19.75). Tues–Sun 12:30–2:30pm; Tues–Sat 7:30–100pm. AE, MC, DC, V. Closed Sun dinner and Mon. VICENTINO/ITALIAN.

Think of splurging nowhere else but in this most Vicentino of eateries. Located on this important palazzo-studded street perpendicular to the principal Corso Palladio, this rustic trattoria has been on these premises since the early 1600s in a landmark building that dates to 1470 (details such as the restaurant's fireplace are original features). Ignore the menu's items that concede to foreign requests and concentrate on the regional dishes they know how to prepare best. Almost all the pasta is made fresh daily, including the house specialty, bigoli con anitra, a fat spaghettilike pasta served with duck ragu. The region's signature dish, baccalà alla vicentina, is a tender salt codfish simmered in a stew of onions, herbs, anchovies, garlic, and parmigiano for eight hours before arriving at your table in perfection. Ask your kind waiter for help in selecting one of Veneto's fine wines: It will augment both the price of dinner as well as the memories you'll carry home with you.

CAFES

Gran Caffè Garibaldi. Pz. d. Signori 5. ☎ **0444/54-41-74.** No credit cards. Thurs–Tues 8am–midnight.

If it's a lovely day and you can't look another Palladian palazzo in the face, set up camp here in the shade of an umbrellaed table that overlooks the piazza. The most historically significant cafe in Palladio's city is as stage set–impressive inside as you would imagine. The upstairs restaurant is too expensive for what it offers, but the outside terrace and its smattering of tables gives you the chance to sit and gaze upon the wonders of the Basilica, yet another Palladian masterpiece. Choose from a glass case of tempting sandwiches and panini; each will cost you 4,000L ($2.65) and a cappuccino will cost 3,000L ($2.00) at your outside table; prices are slightly less at the bar, but go for the front-row seats in the theater-in-the-round that the city's beautiful Piazza dei Signori offers.

Offelleria Della Meneghina. V. Cavour 18 (between Cor. Palladio and Pz. d. Signori). ☎ **0444/54-36-87.** No credit cards. Tues–Sun 8am–1am and 3:30–8:30pm.

There are three much-coveted tiny tables here, but a visit to Vicenza's oldest pasticceria coffeehouse is all about standing at the small bar and taking in the early 19th-century fixtures (although the locale dates back to 1791) and ambience. Indulge in one, two, maybe three of their bite-size pastries made on the premises—Garibaldi loved them so much he used to send for them from Rome. This is the place to be for a Sunday noontime aperitivo before hurrying home for the traditional Sunday meal. Vicenza's second oldest pasticceria is Sorarù. A mere 100 years young, it's located just up the block in Piazzetta Palladio 17 (open Thursday to Tuesday from 8am to 1pm and 3 to 8pm); stop in to check out the competition. If you're more interested in a cafe-table-with-a-view, you needn't go far.

VICENZA AFTER DARK

Events take place pretty much year-round in the historical **Teatro Olimpico;** a good number of them are music concerts from jazz to chamber music, with tickets varying in cost according to event and seating arrangement. Contact the tourist office for a schedule, or contact **Agenzia Viaggi Palladio,** Contrà Cavour 18 (☎ **0444/54-61-11;** fax 0444/54-36-15) for tickets.

The well-established summertime series of **Concerti in Villa** takes place in June and July; some concerts are held in Vicenza's Villa la Rotonda, for others you will need a car. You're guaranteed first-class musical performances in historic and evocative settings. The tourist office will have the schedule and availability of seats; tickets cost 30,000L ($19.75).

DAY TRIPS FROM VICENZA

A tour of the **ville venete** is the most commonly preferred outing from Vicenza. Check at the tourist office to see availability of organized tours, something that has been on-again (and more frequently), off-again for the last few years. They help with the problem of erratic hours for visiting the villas, many of which are still privately owned and inhabited. At worst, the tourist office has realms of information, maps, and itineraries, and will help point you in the right direction to the most important villas (of which only a limited number are designed by Palladio). If you have access to a car, ask about the summer concert series, Concerti in Villa, which has drawn some first-class talent in the classical music world.

Bassano di Grappa, about 22 miles north of Vicenza, can be incorporated into a tour of the villas. Renowned for both its centuries-old ceramics and for grappa production, it is a picturesque town located on the Brenta River. Its covered bridge, arcaded homes painted in the traditional manner, and small squares make a lovely break from the art-laden larger towns in this chapter. Bassano's yearly Opera Estate festival takes place from mid-July through August, with alfresco performances of opera and concerts. For information, call **0424/52-18-50** or fax 0424/52-51-38.

The delightful town of **Marostica,** 17 miles from Vicenza, comes alive à la Brigadoon every other summer, in even years only, when the town commemorates a centuries-old chess game, reenacted with human figures in full Renaissance costume. Everyone in town takes part, and the setting is gorgeous. The next performance is in 1998, and tickets must be purchased months in advance; for information, call **0424/72-127** or fax 0424/72-800.

3 Verona

114km (71 miles) W of Venice; 80km (50 miles) W of Padova; 61km (38 miles) west of Vicenza

Suspend all disbelief regarding the real-life existence of Romeo and Juliet, and your stay in Verona will be extra-special, even magical. After Venice, this is the Veneto's most visited city. Verona reached a cultural and artistic peak under the puissant and often cruel della Scala or Scalageri dynasty that took up rule in the late 1200s. In 1405 it surrendered to Venice, who remained in charge until the invasion of Napoléon in 1797. During the time of Venetian rule, Verona became a prestigious urban capital and controlled much of the Veneto and as far south as Tuscany. You'll see the emblem of the scala (ladder) around town, heraldic symbol of Scaligeri dynasty. This was the city's golden heyday, and the magnificent palazzi, towers, churches, and piazzas you see today are picture-perfect testimony to its influence and wealth.

The presence of the monumental Arena amphitheater, a contemporary of the slightly larger Colosseum of Rome, is a clear sign of the prosperity Verona enjoyed in the days of the ancient Roman Empire, when it was a strategic military outpost, located on the major road from Germany to Rome. Seating over 20,000 people, the Arena was joined by the smaller Teatro Romano on the northern banks of the Adige River to entertain the local populace and visiting dignitaries with chariot races, circuses, and mock battles. Today the Arena is world known for its summer opera season (an extra-special program is already on the boards for its 75th anniversary, to be celebrated in 1998); the Teatro Romano is the evocative venue for the Shakespearean Festival, which usually features the aptly moving *Two Gentleman of Verona* or, better yet, *Romeo and Juliet*—who needs to follow what they're saying? We already know.

And what about Romeo and Juliet? Did they really exist? Originally a Sienese legend, first put into novella form in 1476, the story was subsequently retold in 1524 by Veneto-born Luigi da Porto. He chose Verona in the years 1302–4 during the reign of the della Scalas, and renamed the young couple Romeo and Juliet. The popular book was translated into English and became the source and inspiration of Shakespeare's tale. Translated into dozens of languages and performed endlessly around the world, this tale of pure love in the tempestuous days of a medieval city whose streets were stained with the blood and hatred between feuding families. . . . Well, maybe it wasn't really Verona, but it very well could have been.

ESSENTIALS

GETTING THERE **By Plane** Verona has a small, local airport 6 miles southwest of town in Villafranca (☎ **045/80-95-666**), but arriving there will almost certainly be an expensive alternative.

By Train Verona is easily accessed on the west-east Milan-Venice line as well as the north-south Brennero-Rome line. Departures for the following points east are frequent (costs quoted are one-way): Vicenza, 5,000L ($3.30), add InterCity supplement 3,600L ($2.35); Padova 7,200L ($4.75), add InterCity supplement 4,800L ($3.15); Venice 9,800L ($6.45), add InterCity supplement 6,200L ($4.10).

The Stazione Porta Nuova (☎ **045/59-06-88**) is located south of the Piazza Brà (and Arena) area and is serviced by at least half a dozen bus lines. The bus network within the historical center is limited, so if you have luggage you'll most probably want a taxi to get to your hotel.

By Bus The bus station, A.P.T. (Azienda Provinciale Trasporti) is at Piazza XXV Aprile (☎ **045/80-04-129**) directly across from the train station. Buses leave from here for all regional destinations, including Largo di Garda (9,000L/$5.90).

Although there is bus service to Vicenza, Padova, and Venice (only the summertime departures for Venice are direct; in other months there's a change), it is generally easier to travel by train.

By Car   The Serenissima autostrada (A4) links Venice and Milan; the exit for downtown Verona is Verona Sud. Coming from the north or south, use the A22 autostrada, taking exit Verona Nord.

VISITOR INFORMATION   The two most central tourist information offices are in Pz. Leoncini 61 (adjacent to the Arena, ☎ 045/59-28-28), summer hours Monday to Saturday 8am to 8pm daily, Sunday 9am to noon; winter hours Monday to Saturday 8am to 7pm, Sunday 9am to noon. Pz. d. Erbe 42 (☎ 045/80-30-086) summer months only 9am to 12:30pm and 2:30 to 7pm. There's also a small office at the train station (☎ 045/80-08-61) Monday to Saturday 8am to 7:30pm, Sunday 9am to noon.

A success in 1995 and 1996 and hopefully to become a permanent repeat performer in 1997, a tour bus departs thrice daily for a 1$^{1}/_{2}$-hour Giro Turistico tour of the city's historical center. The cost is 15,000L ($10.00) for an Italian guide, who will distribute headsets for English-speaking tourists. Check any of the tourist offices for specifics.

CITY LAYOUT   The city lies alongside the banks of the S-shaped Adige River. As far as the average visitor is considered, everything of interest—with the exception of the Teatro Romano—is found in the centro storico on the south side of the river's loop; there's no site that cannot be easily and enjoyably reached by foot. The massive and impressive ancient Roman amphitheater, the Arena, sits at the southern end of the city's hub in the airy cafe-ringed Piazza Brà. The piazza is linked by the popular Via Mazzini pedestrian thoroughfare to the Piazza delle Erbe and its adjacent Piazza dei Signori. The grid of pedestrian-only streets between are lined with handsome shops and cafes and make up the principal strolling and window-shopping destination in town. Slightly out of this loop (though still an easy walk) is the Church of San Zeno, west of the Arena, and Juliet's tomb, southeast of the Arena (only devout Juliet fans will appreciate the trek here). Both the train station and the Fiera di Verona conference center are located in the southern part of town beyond the Porta Nuova.

GETTING AROUND   Verona lends itself to walking and strolling and most sites are concentrated within a few history-steeped blocks of each other. Venture off the store-lined treadmill and seek out the narrow, cobblestoned side streets that are evocative of eras past. Little to no traffic is permitted in town, so upon arrival stash your car in a parking area suggested by your hotel, and let your feet do the transporting.

WHAT TO SEE & DO

If you're in town the first Sunday of any month, check if entrance is still free for the following sites (projected but not confirmed at time of printing): the Arena, Castelvecchio Museum, the Roman Theater, and Juliet's Tomb. Since there are so many churches in Verona, a recent admission charge has been imposed in an attempt to cover custodian charges and offer longer hours. An expensive biglietto cumulativo (inclusive ticket) is worthwhile only if you intend to visit all three churches involved: San Zeno, the Duomo, and Sant'Anastasia; this ticket is discounted in off-season months.

✪ **Arena Di Verona.** Pz. Braag. ☎ **045/80-30-204.** Admission 6,000L ($3.95). Tues–Sun 8am–7pm. During the July–August summer opera season 8am–1pm.

Italy's best known and best preserved Roman amphitheater after Rome's Colosseum, the elliptical Arena was built in a slightly pinkish marble around the year A.D. 100 and stands in the very middle of town with the Piazza Brà on its southern flank. Built to accommodate more than 20,000 people, it is in remarkable shape today (despite a 12th-century earthquake that left only four arches of the outer ring standing), beloved testimony to the pride and wealth of Verona and its populace. Its perfect acoustics have survived the millennia and make it one of the wonders of the ancient world and one of the most fascinating venues for live performances today (which are conducted without microphones). If you're in town during the summer opera performances in July and August, do everything possible to procure a ticket (see "Special Events," below) for any of the outdoor evening performances (for last-minute tickets, your hotel owner or manager will likely have his contacts and short-cuts for a nominal reward). Even opera-challenged audience members will take home the memory of a lifetime. The cluster of outdoor cafes and trattorias/pizzerias on the western side of the Piazza Brà line a wide marble esplanade called Il Liston; they stay open long after the opera performances end.

✪ **Piazza Delle Erbe.** Between V. Mazzini and Cor. Porta Borsari. Open-air produce and flower market Mon–Sat 8am to 7pm.

On the former site of the Roman Forum where chariot races once took place stands the bustling marketplace, the Square of the Herbs. The herbs, spices, coffee beans, and bolts of silks and damasks that came through Verona after landing in Venice from faraway Cathay have given way to the fresh and aromatic produce of one of Italy's wealthiest agricultural regions. The perfume of fennel and vegetables fresh from the earth assaults your senses, mixing with the cacophony of vendors touting their plump tomatoes, dozens of different variations of salad greens, and picture-perfect fruits that can't possibly taste as good as they look, but do. Add to this the canary lady, the farmer's son who has brought in a half a dozen puppies to unload, and the furtive pickpocket who can spot a tourist at 50 paces—and you have one of Italy's loveliest and most authentic outdoor markets.

✪ **Piazza Dei Signori or Piazza Dante.**

To reach the Piazza dei Signori from the Piazza delle Erbe, exit under the Arco della Costa (the Arch of the Rib), which you'll be able to spot by the enormous whalebone hanging overhead. It was placed here 1,000 years ago when it was said to have been unearthed during excavations on this spot, indicating this area was once underwater. Local legend goes that the rib will fall on the first person to pass beneath it who has never told a lie—thus explaining the nonchalance with which every Veronese passes under it. You'll leave behind the color and bustle of the marketplace and enter into a serene and elegant and slightly sober piazza, one of Verona's innermost chambers of calm. Its center is anchored by a large 19th-century statue of the "divine poet" Dante, who found political exile here as a guest of the Scaligeri family (in appreciation Dante wrote of the powerful Cangrande I in his poem "Paradiso"). If entering from the Archway, you'll be facing the Scaligeri's 13th-century crenellated residence before it was taken over by the governing Venetians. Left of that, behind Dante's back, is the Loggia del Consiglio (Portico of the Counsel), a 15th-century masterpiece of Venetian Renaissance style. Opposite that and facing Dante is the 12th-century romanesque Palazzo della Ragione, whose courtyard and fine gothic staircase should be visited. This piazza is Verona's finest microcosm, such a balanced and refined assemblage of historical architecture that you would do well to secure an outdoor table at the square's legendary command-post, the Antico Caffè Dante, and take it all in over a late-afternoon Campari and soda.

MORE ATTRACTIONS

Scaligeri Tombs. Corner of V. d. Arche Scaligeri, northeast of Pza. d. Signori. No entry; viewed from outside only.

Exit the Piazza dei Signori opposite the Arch of the Rib and immediately on your right, at the corner of Via delle Arche Scaligeri, are the elaborately decorated raised outdoor tombs of the della Scala or Scaligeri family. Two can be seen here behind the original decorative grillwork, those by the peculiar names of Mastino II (Mastiff the Second, d. 1351) and Cansignorio (Head Dog, d. 1375), while the most interesting is found over the side door of the family's private chapel Santa Maria Antica —the tomb of Cangrande I (Big Dog, d. 1329), with dogs (*cani*) holding up a ladder (*scale*), both elements that figure in the Scaligeri coat of arms. That's Cangrande I—patron of the arts and protector of Dante—and his steed you see above (the original can be seen in the Museo Castelvecchio). Recently restored, these tombs are considered one of the country's greatest medieval monuments.

Around the corner on V. d. Arche Scaligeri 2 is the alleged 13th-century home of Romeo Montecchi (of *Romeo and Juliet* fame), which incorporates the Osteria del Duca (See "Where to Dine," below).

✪ **Museo Castelvecchio.** Cor. Castelvecchio 2 (at V. Roma, on the Adige River). ☎ **045/ 59-47-34.** Admission 5,000L ($3.30). Tues–Sun 8am–7pm.

A five-minute walk west of the Arena amphitheater on the Via Roma and nestled on the banks of the swift-flowing Adige River, the "Old Castle" is a fairy-tale pile of brick towers and turrets, protecting the bridge behind it. It was commissioned in 1354 by the della Scala warlord Cangrande II to serve the dual role of residential palace and stronghold. It survived centuries of occupation by the Visconti family, the Serene Republic of Venice, and then Napoléon, only to be destroyed by the Germans during World War II bombing. Its painstaking restoration was initiated in 1958 by the acclaimed Venetian architect Carlos Scarpa and reopened in 1964, now a fascinating home to some 400 works of art. The ground-floor rooms, displaying statues and carvings of the Middle Ages, lead to alleyways, vaulted halls, multileveled floors, and stairs, all as architecturally arresting as the Venetian masterworks from the 14th to 18th centuries it offsets—notably those by Tintoretto, Tiepolo, Veronese, Bellini, and the Verona-born Pisanello—that you'll find throughout. Don't miss the large courtyard with the equestrian statue of the warlord Cangrande I (a copy can be seen at the family cemetery at the Arche Scaligeri) with a peculiar dragon's head affixed to his back. A stroll across the pedestrian bridge behind the castle affords you a fine view of the castle and the river's banks.

✪ **Casa di Giulietta.** V. Cappello 23 (SE of Pz. d. Erbe). ☎ **045/80-34-303.** Admission 5,000L ($3.30). Tues–Sun 8am–7pm.

There is no proof that a Capuleti (Capulets) family lived here, and it wasn't until 1905 that the city bought what was an abandoned, overgrown garden and decided its future. This doesn't seem to faze the millions of tourists who flock here every year to visit the simple courtyard and home (admission to latter only) that are considerably less affluent-looking than the Franco Zefferelli set as you may remember it. Myriad are those who leave behind graffiti such as "Gianni, ti amo, T" or who engage in the peculiar tradition (whose origin no one can seem to explain) of rubbing the right breast (now buffed to a bright gold) of the bronze statue of a forever nubile Juliet. It's not worth the entrance fee to see the virtually empty 13th-century home unless the current plans to set up some kind of museum by 1997 actually transpire. An adjoining upper terrace of a neighboring palazzo has recently been turned into an alfresco restaurant, **La Terrazza di Giulietta** which, considering the evocative nighttime setting and reasonable rates (40,000L to 50,000L/$26.30 to $32.90 per person) might just be the splurge required for newlyweds or newly unweds (☎ 045/80-03-900, closed Monday, AE, V).

La Tomba di Giulietta (Juliet's Tomb) is about a 15-minute walk south of here (near the Adige River on Via del Pontiere, admission 5,000L/$3.30; Tuesday to Sunday 8am to 7pm). The would-be site of the star-crossed lovers' suicide is found within the medieval cloisters of the Capuchin monastery of San Francesco al Corso; die-hard romantics may find it poignant and worth the trip. Others will find it a joke and shouldn't bother. The adjacent church is where their secret marriage was said to have taken place.

Basilica San Zeno Maggiore. Pz. San Zeno. ☎ **045/80-06-120.** Single admission 4,000L ($2.65); joint ticket admission Mar–Oct 9,000L ($5.90), Nov–Feb 6,000L ($3.95) for Duomo, San Zeno, and Sant'Anastasia. Mar–Oct, Mon–Sat 9am–6pm; Sun 1–6pm. Nov–Feb, Mon–Sat 10am–4pm; Sun 1:00–4pm.

This is one of the finest examples of romanesque architecture in Italy, built between the 9th and 12th centuries. Slightly out of the old city's hub but still easily reached by foot, San Zeno, dedicated to the city's patron saint, is Verona's most visited church. Spend a moment outside to appreciate the fine, sober facade, highlighted by the immense 12th-century rose window, the "Ruota della Fortuna" (the Wheel of Fortune!). This pales in importance compared to the entrance below, two pillars supported by marble lions and massive doors whose 48 bronze panels were sculpted from the 9th to the 11th century and are believed to have been the first casting in bronze since Roman antiquity. They are one of the city's most cherished artistic treasures and are worth the trip here even if the church is closed. Not yet as sophisticated as those that would adorn Florence's Baptistery doors in the centuries to come, these are like a naive illustration from a child's book and were meant to educate the illiterate masses with scenes from the Old and New Testaments. They are complemented by the stone bas-reliefs found on either side of the doors, the 12th-century work of Niccolo who was also responsible for the Duomo's portal. The 14th-century tower on the left belonged to the former abbey while the free-standing slender campanile on the right was begun in 1045. The massive interior is filled with 12th- to 14th-century frescoes and crowned by the nave's ceiling, designed as a wooden ship's keel. But the interior's singular highlight is the famous triptych of the *Madonna and Child Enthroned with Saints* by Andrea Mantegna (1459), behind the main altar. Absconded by Napoléon, the beautiful centerpiece—a showcase for the Padua-born Mantegna's sophisticated sense of perspective and architectural detail—was eventually returned to Verona, although two side panels stayed behind in the Louvre and in Tours. Look for the colored marble statue of a smiling San Zeno, much loved by the local Veronesi, in an act of blessing; it can be found in a small apse to the left of the altar.

Basilica di Sant'Anastasia. Pz. Anastasia at Cor. Anastasia. Single admission 4,000L ($2.65); joint ticket admission Mar–Oct 9,000L ($5.90), Nov–Feb 6,000L ($3.95) for Duomo, San Zeno, and Sant'Anastasia. Mar–Oct, Mon–Sat 9am–6pm; Sun 1–6pm. Nov–Feb, Mon–Sat 10am–4pm; Sun 1–4pm.

Built between 1290 and 1481, this is Verona's largest church, considered the city's finest example of gothic architecture, even though the facade remains unfinished. A lovely 14th-century campanile bell tower is adorned with frescoes and sculptures. The church's interior is typically gothic in design, highlighted by two famous *gobbi hunchback* who support the holy-water fonts, an impressive patterned pavement, and 16 side chapels containing a number of noteworthy paintings and frescoes from the 15th to the 16th century. Most important is Pisanello's *St. George Freeing the*

Princess of Trebisonda (1433) in the Giusti Chapel in the left transept; it is considered one of his best paintings and is of the armed-knight-and-damsel-in-distress genre—with the large white rump of St. George's steed as one of its focal points.

Teatro Romano (Roman Theater). V. Rigaste Redentore (over the Ponte Pietra bridge behind the Duomo, on the north banks of the river Adige). ☎ **045/80-00-360.** Admission 5,000L ($3.30). Tues–Sun 9am–3pm.

The oldest extant Roman monument in Verona dates back to the time of Augustus. There is something almost surreal about attending an open-air performance of Shakespeare's *Two Gentlemen of Verona* or *Romeo and Juliet* here—even if you can't understand a word. Concerts and dance performances are also given here.

The Duomo. Pz. Duomo (at V. d. Duomo). Single admission 4,000L ($2.65); joint ticket admission Mar–Oct 9,000L ($5.90), Nov–Feb 6,000L ($3.95) for Duomo, San Zeno, and Sant'Anastasia. Mar–Oct, Mon–Sat 9am–6pm; Sun 1–6pm. Nov–Feb, Mon–Sat 10am–4pm; Sun 1:30–4pm.

Begun in the 12th century and not finished until the 17th, the city's most important church still boasts its original main doors and portal, magnificently covered with low reliefs in the Lombard romanesque style that are attributed to Niccolo, whose work can be seen at the Basilica of San Zeno Maggiore. The church was built upon the ruins of an even more ancient paleochristian church dating to the late Roman Empire. Visit the Cappella Nichesola, the first chapel on the left, where Titian's serene but boldly colorful *Assumption of the Virgin* is the cathedral's principal treasure. Also of interest is the semicircular screen that separates the altar from the rest of the church, attributed to Sanmicheli. Don't leave the area without walking behind the Duomo to the river: Here you'll find the 13th-century Torre di Alberto della Scala tower and nearby Ponte della Pietra bridge. There has been a crossing at this point of the river since Verona's days as a 2nd-century Roman stronghold when the Teatro Romano was built on the river's northen banks.

VIEWS & GARDENS

The view of Verona from the Roman Theater is beautiful any time of day, but particularly during the evening performances—the ancient Romans knew a thing or two about drama. For other views, you can take an elevator to the 10th-century Church of Santa Libera above the theater, or to the former monastery and cloisters of San Girolamo, which now houses a small archeological museum. Above this is the Castel San Pietro, whose foundations go back to the times of the Romans and whose terraces offer the best view in town.

Nearby are the well-known, multitiered **Giardino Giusti,** gardens whose formal 16th-century layout and geometrical designs of terraces, fountains, statuary, and staircases inspired, among many, Mozart and Goethe. The gardens are open daily from 9am to dusk; admission is 5,000L ($3.30).

SPECIAL EVENTS

The well-known opera season that takes place every July and August in Verona's ancient amphitheater began in 1913 with a staging of *Aïda* to commemorate the 100th anniversary of Verdi's birth. Together with other operas, *Aïda* has been performed yearly ever since. Those seated on the least expensive, unreserved stone steps costing 35,000L ($23) enjoy fresh air, excellent acoustics, and a view over the Arena's top to the city and surrounding hills beyond. The rub is that Jose Carreras will only appear one inch high. Numbered seats just below cost from 135,000L ($88) to 230,000L ($151.30); all tickets are subject to an advance booking fee of 5,000L to 35,000L ($3.30 to $23). Opening night tickets are slightly higher. The box office is located in Via Dietro Anfiteatro

6/B; credit card purchase (AE, DC, V) accepted by phone (☎ **045/80-05-151;** fax 045/80-13-287); tickets are picked up the night of the performance. Bank drafts can be sent to the above address, but it's better to call or fax. If you hope to find tickets upon arrival, remember that *Aïda* is everyone's most requested performance; weekend performances are usually sold out. As a last-minute resort, be nice to your hotel manager or concierge—everyone has a connection, or a relative with a connection.

The setting is only a little less awesome at the Teatro Romano, and tickets are less expensive and easier to come by. Known for its Shakespeare Festival (mid-July to early September), it will be celebrating its 50th anniversary in 1998. Performances begin in June with jazz concerts while July hosts a number of ballet and modern dance performances. Check for schedule at **045/80-77-111;** box office is at Largo Divisione Pasubio 3 (☎ **045/59-00-89**). Last-minute tickets go on sale at the Teatro Romano box office at 8:15pm (most performances start at 9pm). Tickets range from 15,000L to 40,000L ($9.85 to $26.30).

Other important events are the famous four-day horse fair, *Fieracavalli,* in mid-November and the important five-day Vinitaly wine fair the first half of April. The Piazza San Zeno hosts a traveling antiques market the third Saturday of every month; come early.

WHERE TO STAY

Although the following prices reflect peak season rates, expect inflated prices during the July/August opera season or when one of the major trade fairs are in town. With these exceptions, low season is considered November through mid-March. The C.A.V. (Cooperativa Albergatori Veronesi) is an organization of dozens of two-to five-star hotels that will help you with bookings for a fee determined by your choice of hotel category, (☎ **045/80-09-844;** fax 80-09-372).

Hotel Armando. V. Dietro Pallone 1 (off V. Pallone, SE of the Arena), 37120 Verona. ☎ **045/80-00-206.** Fax 045/80-36-015. 20 rms, 15 with bath. TV TEL. 50,000L ($32.90) single without bath; 85,000L ($55.90) double without bath, 100,000L ($65.80) single or double with bath; 100,000L ($65.80) triple without bath, 120,000L ($78.95) triple with bath. Prices discounted 15% off-season. Breakfast is included, but can be optional at 8,000L ($5.25) per person. MC, V.

One block removed from the ancient town walls and an easy four-block stroll from the lovely Arena amphitheater, this small hotel recently underwent a complete renovation in 1996. An ambitious upgrading to two-star status resulted in improvements and amenities that approach three-star quality—and all for prices that resemble one-star hotels in Italy's larger cities. Only five rooms are without baths, so you'll pretty much have the communal bathrooms to yourself. New tiling throughout, elevator service, the eponymous restaurant next door, a quiet location, and frequent appearances by the concierge's friendly greyhound are all bonuses.

Hotel Aurora. Pz. Erbe 2 (southside of piazza), 37121 Verona. ☎ **045/59-47-17.** Fax 045/80-10-860. 19 rms, 17 with bath. A/C TEL TV. 80,000L ($52.65) single without bath; 150,000L ($98.70) double with bath. Prices discounted 10% off-season. Rates include breakfast. AE, DC, MC , V.

Until now it was location, location, location that had loyal guests return to the Aurora time and again. As of a 1996 refurbishing of all guest rooms and en suite baths, it will now be the updated decor as well. Eight doubles are blessed with the good fortune of overlooking one of the world's great squares, the Piazza delle Erbe, and its umbrellaed stalls that make up the daily marketplace. Consider yourself equally blessed if you snag the top-floor double with a small balcony, possibly more coveted than Juliet's itself!

✪ **Hotel Giulietta & Romeo.** Vc. Tre Marchetti 3 (south of V. Mazzini, 1 block E of the Arena), 37121 Verona ☎ **045/80-03-554.** Fax 045/80-10-862. 30 rms with bath. A/C MINIBAR TEL TV. 150,000L ($98.70) single; 200,000L ($131.60) double; 250,000L ($164.50). Rates include breakfast. Single and double rates in peak season reflect special rates for Frommer's readers. Add approximately 30% to all rates during the opera season and major trade fairs. AE, MC, DC, V.

In the shade of the Arena is this handsomely refurbished palazzo-hotel that is a recommended splurge for its upscale ambience, cordial and kindly staff, and its location in the very heart of the centro storico. Brightly lit guest rooms are warmed by burnished cherrywood furnishings, and large marble-tiled baths are those you imagine finding in tony first-class hotels at twice the price. The hotel takes its name seriously; sure enough, there are two small marble balconies à la Juliet, but their view is unremarkable. The hotel is located on a narrow side street that is quiet and convenient to everything, but you might want to just luxuriate in your room a little longer.

Locanda Catullo. V. Catullo 1 (just north of the Principle V. Mazzini; entrance from the alleyway Vc. Catullo), 37121 Verona. ☎ **045/80-02-786.** 21 rms, 4 with shower. 45,000L ($29.60) single without bath; 65,000L ($42.75) double without bath; 85,000L ($55.90) double with shower; 87,000L ($57.25) triple without bath; 115,000L ($75.65) triple with bath; 150,000L ($98.70) quad suite with bath. Slight discounts in off-season. No credit cards.

Up three flights of steps is this homey pensionelike place that has been run by the affable Mirella and Franco Pollini and their two young English-speaking daughters for more than 25 years. The location is convenient and central, the tasteful rooms are plain but spacious and clean, the bathrooms nice and bright—a hard-to-come-by combination that makes their prices all the more attractive if not rather rare. There are impressive details and touches everywhere such as hanging tapestries, decorative plaster molding, French doors, and marble or handsome parquet floors. Solo travelers will be happy in any of the six large single rooms that come equipped with a sink; they'll feel comfortable in the family atmosphere that prevails. Two bathless doubles have a small balcony for breakfast, though you'll have to bring your own: There's no breakfast service available, but the bar downstairs couldn't be more convenient.

Ostello Verona Villa Francescatti. Salita Fontana d. Ferro 15, 37129 Verona. ☎ **045/59-03-60.** Fax 045/80-09-127. 150 beds. 18,000L ($11.85) in dormitory rms; 22,000L ($14.50) in 4-bed rms. Breakfast and shower included. No minimum stay; maximum 5 nights. No credit cards. Rms closed 9am–5pm; 11:30pm curfew. From the train station take bus no. 72 to Piazza Isolo stop. Follow signs to hostel.

This rambling hilltop youth hostel is a busy meeting place for young people from all over the world, housed in a rather dignified villa whose origins reach back to the 15th century; it was a monastery and then a seigniorial residence. Sleeping arrangements these days are neither monastic nor regal: The smallest rooms sleep 4, the average 12, and the largest accommodate up to 30. Simple meals of limited choice (12,000L/$7.90) are served at 1pm and 7pm in a large room that has retained some of the original 16th-century frescoes. The villa is located just east of the ancient Teatro Romano, the oldest area of town, and can be reached on foot for the physically fit (usually a prerequisite for the youth hostel scene) from the center's main sites. Even here the local passion for opera reigns: The 11:30pm curfew is waived during the Arena's summer performances.

WHERE TO DINE

Osteria al Duomo. V. Duomo 7a (1 block southeast of the Duomo). ☎ **045/80-04-505.** 1st courses 7,000L ($4.60); 2nd courses 10,000L–15,000L ($6.60–$9.85). AE, MC, V.

Mon–Wed and Fri–Sun Noon–2:30 and 7–10pm. Wine tasting 11am–2:30pm and 5pm–1am. VERONESE.

You'll revel in both the city's history and the region's gastronomic importance during a meal at this small and welcoming inn: More than 100 years old, it is Verona's oldest osteria. Despite being busy during dining hours, a relaxed atmosphere encourages one to eat lightly (or not) and linger. Pray that the changing menu is offering plump, homemade gnocchi alla boscaiolo with mushrooms, diced bacon, and tomatoes in a light cream-based sauce, or the region's signature dish, *baccalà alla veneta*, codfish simmered in a sauce made of fresh tomatoes and onions. Some of the best wines from the renowned vineyards around Verona or the Veneto can be sampled by the glass (1,500L to 3,000L/$1 to $2). Live music Saturday night (9pm to midnight) livens things up considerably—there's even live mandolin music on Wednesday evenings!

✪ **Osteria dal Duca.** V. Arche Scaligeri 2 (east of Pz. d. Signori). ☎ **045/59-44-74.** 1st courses 6,000L–8,000L ($3.95–$5.25); 2nd courses 9,000L–14,000L ($5.90–$9.20). Menu turistico 20,000L ($13.15). AE. Mon–Sat 12:30–2:30pm and 7:00–10:30pm. VERONESE.

The constant flow of locals that makes up this trattoria's regular clientele are non-plused by the fact that they are eating in Romeo's house. There are no written records to confirm the historic ownership by the Montecchi (Montague) family and, thankfully, the discreet management never considered calling it "Ristorante Romeo" or illustrating placemats with his likeness. But here you are, nonetheless, dining in a characteristic palazzo dating to the Middle Ages and enjoying one of the nicest meals in town in a friendly neighborhood ambience. The menu is limited, ever changing, and recited for customers by the good-humored staff who seems used to foreigners pointing to what looks tempting at neighboring tables. You might find penne pasta with *pomodoro e melanzane* (fresh tomato sauce with eggplant) or a perfectly grilled chop or fillet with sautéed spinach or rosemary-roasted potatoes. It will be simple, it will be delicious, you'll probably make friends with the people sitting next to you, and you will always remember your meal at Romeo's Restaurant.

Pizzeria Impero. Pz. d. Signori 8. ☎ **045/80-30-160.** Pizzas 7000L–13,000L ($4.60–$8.55). Thurs–Tues noon–3:30pm and 7:00–midnight. PIZZERIA.

Location is not everything, but to sit with a pleasant lunch in this most sober but elegant of piazzas might just be one of those memories that stay with you for life. Impero's pizza is not going to win any culinary awards, but any of the dozen of so varieties will taste pretty heavenly if the sun is shining and you're sharing an outdoor table with your Romeo or Juliet. If Impero's is full and the Arena/Piazza Brà location is more convenient to your day's itinerary, try the well-known and always busy Pizzeria Liston, V. Dietro Listone 19 (closed Wednesday) that also serves a full trattoria menu as well (all credit cards accepted).

Trattoria alla Pergola. Pzta. Santa Maria in Solaro 10 (off V. Garibaldi near Ponte Garibaldi), Verona. ☎ **045/80-04-744.** 1st courses 8,000L–9,000L ($5.25–$5.90); 2nd courses 12,000L–20,000L ($7.90–$13.15). Thurs–Tues 12:30–2:30pm and 7:30–10pm. AE, DC, MC, V. VERONESE.

Family-run and proudly so, this is a favorite with the Veronesi who patronize it together with the occasional tourist whose hotel concierge is kind enough to share the information. This small restaurant offers a revolving roster of risottos and pastas—many of which are homemade. Look for the ravioli or gnocchi; their fillings and sauces may vary with the market's whims, but their deliciousness is a seasonless invariable.

CAFES, WINE BARS & PASTRY

Antico Caffè Dante. Pz. d. Signori. ☎ **045/59-52-49.**

Situated on the landmark Piazza dei Signori is Verona's oldest cafe. It's rather formal indoors (read: expensive) where meals are also served; it's most recommended for those who want to spend the extra lire for the million-dollar view of one of Verona's loveliest ancient squares from the outdoor tables smack in the midst of it all. Skipping a late-afternoon aperitivo here is as unforgivable as forgetting to take a look-see at Juliet's balcony. If you're lucky enough to attend a performance at the Arena, this is the traditional après-opera spot to complete—and contemplate—the evening's experience. It's open from 9am to 4am.

Caffè Filippini. Pz. Erbe 26. ☎ **045/80-04-549.**

This is the oldest of the cafe/bars lining Verona's awesome piazza, but repeated renovations have left little of yesteryear's character or charm. But centuries-old habits die hard: It's still the command-post of choice whether indoors or out (preferably out), a lovely spot to take in the cacophony and colorful chaos of the market. It's open daily in summer months; Thursday to Tuesday 8am to 1am in winter.

Caffè Tubino. Cor. Porta Borsari 15/d, Verona. ☎ **045/80-32-296.**

A block beyond Flego's on one of Verona's stylish pedestrian shopping streets is this venerable caffè/coffee bar that is an old-world temple of caffeine. Packaged blends of teas and coffees are displayed on racks lining parallel walls in a small space made even smaller by the imposing crystal chandelier. The Tubino brand is well-known, nicely packaged, and makes a great gift—and will have your clothes smelling like coffee if packed away in a suitcase corner. It's open daily from 7am to 11pm.

Carro Armato. Vc. Gatto at Vc. San Piero Martire (1 block S of Pz. Sant'Anastasia), Verona. ☎ **045/80-30-175.**

Here's a great choice for after-hours or any hour when you want to sit and sample some of the dozens of regional wines by the glass (1,500L to 3,000L/$1 to $2); you'll wind up making am informal meal out of fresh and inexpensive bar food. Oldsters linger during the day playing cards or reading the paper at long wooden tables, while a younger crowd fills the place in the evening. A small but good selection of cheeses and cold cuts or sausages might be enough to take the edge off, but there is always an entree or two and a fresh vegetable side dish that could pass as a meal, and a pretty tasty one at that. It's open Monday to Friday from 10am to 2pm and 5pm to 2am; Saturday and Sunday nonstop hours.

Da Aldo. Pz. d. Erbe 6, Verona. ☎ **045/80-00-894.**

Sicilian-born Aldo Napoli has been cranking out the best pizza-by-the-slice in Verona since 1967. As much a part of the Piazza Erbe as the Fountain of the Madonna, this hole-in-the-wall offers a dozen or so varieties sold by weight: Expect to pay an average of 2,500L ($1.65) per slice. Judging from its constant disappearing act, the onion/potato/peppers/olive variety is the best seller. No seats, but stand-up counters and soft drinks are available. Open Thursday to Tuesday 8am to 8pm.

Enoteca dal Zovo. Vc. San Marco in Foro 7/5 (off Cor. Porta Borsari), Verona. ☎ **045/80-34-369.**

Does Oreste, congenial owner of this wonderfully characteristic old wine bar just west of the Piazza Erbe, know everyone in town, or do they all stop by to imbibe because he has the best selection of Veneto wines in town? Averaging 1,500L ($1.00) a glass, you can go for broke and start with the very best at 3,500L ($2.30). Oreste's *simpatica*

American-born wife Beverly can give you a crash course. Salami, olives, and finger foods will help keep you vertical, since the few stools are always occupied by senior gentlemen who are as much a part of the fixtures as the hundreds of dusty bottles of wines and grappas that line the walls. Open Tuesday to Sunday from 8am to 1pm and 2 to 8pm.

Pasticceria Bar Flego. Cor. Porta Borsari 9, Verona. ☎ **045/80-32-471.**

There are eight tiny tables-for-two, but this small, beloved institution just one block west of the Piazza Erbe isn't conducive to spending a few hours writing postcards. It is conducive to savoring a frothy cappuccino accompanied by an unbridled sampling of their deservedly famous bite-size pastries you can point-and-order by the piece at 1,000L to 2,000L (65¢ to $1.30) each. Most of the selection leans towards the calorie-enriched dolci (sweets) though a fine sampling of salati ("salted," or anything not sweet) include minuscule pizzas and tiny sandwiches. A regional specialty are the zaletti, delicious cookies made with corn flour, raisins, and pine nuts—much better tried than described! It's closed on Monday.

Pasticceria Cordioli. V. Cappello 39, Verona ☎ **045/80-03-055.**

This is one of Verona's oldest pastry bars and lo! 'tis but a moment's stroll from Juliet's house on the same store-lined pedestrian street. There are no tables and it's often three-deep at the bar, but with coffee this good and pastries this fresh (made on the premises), it's obvious why. It's closed Sunday afternoon.

11

The Dolomites & South Tyrol

by Stephen Brewer

Mountains—the Alps and the Dolomites—dominate this region that stretches north from Lombardy and the Veneto. Here you'll discover a different Italy; in fact, you'll discover an Italy that doesn't seem very Italian at all. Most of the area—which encompasses the Trentino and Alto Adige regions—belonged to Austria until it was handed over to Italy at the end of World War I, and many residents (especially in and around Bolzano) still prefer the ways of the north to those of the south. They speak German, eat German food, and go about life with Teutonic crispness. And they have a lot to yodel about: The eastern Alps that cut into the region are gentle and beautiful; a little farther to the east arise the Dolomites, dramatically craggy peaks that are really coral formations that only relatively recently reared up from ancient seabeds. Throughout Trentino–Alto Adige, soaring peaks, highland meadows, and lush valleys provide a paradise for hikers, skiers, and rock climbers, and set amid these natural spectacles are pretty and interesting towns to explore.

EXPLORING THE REGION

While a car makes it possible to explore the remoter parts of the Dolomites and South Tyrol, you can see quite a bit of the region without one. You can reach all the major towns and even small villages by an excellent network of trains and buses. It would be possible to do most of the following tour, for instance, without a car.

Arrive in Trento and explore this lovely city at leisure, visiting the Duomo and Castello di Buonconsiglio and strolling along the pleasant streets lined with Renaissance palaces. Spend the night in Trento.

The next day, move on to Bolzano. If you are driving, make the short trip between the two cities on the Strada di Vino, stopping for wine tastings en route. Enjoy Bolzano in the early evening, when the old town is crowded with shoppers and workers.

After a morning exploring the Duomo and other sights in the old town, take the cable car up to Soprabolzano.

Move on to Merano, for a day of relaxation in this pleasant resort. You may want to spend part of the day exploring the Parco Nazionale della Stelvio or Parco Nazionale di Tessa.

Travel to Cortina d'Ampezzo via the Great Dolomite Road; while in Cortina, take the cable car up to the summit of Ra Valles for the spectacular views.

Trieste, The Dolomites & South Tyrol

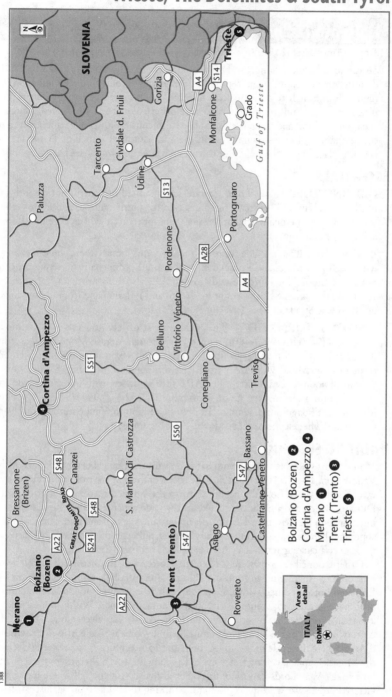

Bolzano (Bozen) 2
Cortina d'Ampezzo 4
Merano 1
Trent (Trento) 3
Trieste 5

371

1 Trento (Trent)

230km (143 miles) from Milan, 101km (63 miles) from Verona, 57km (35 miles) from Bolzano

Surrounded by mountains, this beautiful little city on the banks of the Adige River definitely has an Alpine flair. Yet unlike other towns up here in the far north, which tend to lean heavily to their Austrian heritage, Trento is still essentially Italian. The piazzi are broad and sunny, the palaces are ocher-colored and tile-roofed, Italian is the lingua franca, and pasta is still a staple on menus. With its pleasant streets and the remnants of its most famous event, the 16th-century Council of Trent, Trento is a nice place to stay for a night or to visit en route to Bolzano (see below).

ESSENTIALS

GETTING THERE   By Train   Strategically located on a main north-south rail line between Italy and Austria, Trento is served by hourly trains to and from Verona (one hour away; Verona is a major transfer point for trains to Milan, Florence, Rome, and other points south).

By Car   The A22 autostrada connects Trento with Verona (where you can connect with the A4 for Milan and Rome) and, farther south, Modena (where you can connect with the A1 for Florence and Rome); A22 also runs north to Bolzano and Innsbruck; the slower S12 also connects Trento and Bolzano, and from it you can get on the scenic Strada di Vino (see "En Route," below)

VISITOR INFORMATION   The **local tourist office,** near the train station at V. Alferi 4 (☎ **0461/98-38-80**), is open July through August, Monday to Saturday from 9am until noon and 3 to 6pm, Sunday from 10am until noon; September through June, Monday to Friday from 9am to noon and 3 to 6pm, Saturday from 9am until noon, closed Sunday. The **APT tourist office,** with information on the entire Trentino region, is at Corso Novembre III 132 (☎ **0461/91-44-44**), open Monday to Friday from 8:30am to 12:30pm and 2:30 to 6pm, Saturday from 9am until noon. The telephone area code for Trento is 0461.

WHAT TO SEE & DO

Most of what's notable about Trento has to do with the Council of Trent, called by the Vatican from 1545 to 1563 to counter the effects of the new wave of Protestantism that was sweeping down from the north. Many of the Council sessions took place in the **Duomo,** which is delightfully situated on the wide expanse of the cafe-filled Piazza Duomo; unfortunately, the wide expanses of the dark, gloomy, and plain interior are less appealing than the 13th-to-16th–century exterior, although the medieval crypt beneath the altar is fascinating (open daily from 6:30am to noon and 2:30 to 8pm).

Other Council sessions were held in the **Castello di Buonconsiglio,** which you can reach by walking north from the Duomo along Via Belenzani, then east on Via Roman—both are lined with the palaces built to house the not-so-ascetic church officials who came to Trento to attend the council sessions. Within the castello— a mazelike fortress that incorporates the 13th-century Castelvecchio and the 16th-century Magno Palazzo—you will eventually find your way to the **Museo Provinciale d'Arte,** where the pride of the collection is the 15th-century *Cico dei Mesi* (Cycle of the Months), an enchanting fresco cycle depicting life as it really was for peasant and lord alike (*Note:* Lords had more fun). You can also visit the cell where native son Cesare Battiste was held in 1916 after attempting to lead a revolt against Austrian rule; he was shot in the moat that surrounds the Castelvecchio. Admission to castello and museum is 6,000L ($3.95); hours are Tuesday to Sunday from 10am to 7pm.

WHERE TO STAY
DOUBLES FOR LESS THAN 65,000 LIRE ($42.75)
Al Cavallino Bianco. V. Cavour 29, 38100 Trento. ☎ **0461/23-15-42.** 24 rms, 3 with bath. 37,000L single without bath, 55,000L ($36.20) single with bath; 60,000L ($39.50) double without bath, 80,000L ($62.65) double with bath; 105,000L (69.05) triple with bath. AE, MC, V.

The surrounding neighborhood near the Duomo is charming, but that's not a word you would probably use to describe this Spartan hostelry, with its AstroTurf-covered atrium lobby and YMCA-like ambience. It is, however, spanking clean, and all of the really basic rooms, equipped with not much more than a bed and a chair, have a shower and a sink.

Hotel Venezia. V. Belenzani 70, 38100 Trento. ☎ **0461/34-111.** 47 rms, 20 with bath. 38,000L ($25) single without bath, 55,000L ($$36.20) single with bath; 60,000L ($39.45) double without bath, 80,000L ($62.65) double with bath; 100,000L ($65.80) triple with bath. MC, V.

With their 1950s-style furnishings, these simple, high-ceiling rooms are a bit dowdy but offer a lot of solid, old-fashioned comfort, and those in the front come with a big bonus—stunning views over the Piazza Duomo. Some of the younger members of the family who runs the place speak English and are more than happy to dispense advice on what to see and do in town and the surrounding area.

DOUBLES FOR LESS THAN 135,000 LIRE ($88.80)
Hotel Aquila D'Oro. V. Belenzani 76, 38100 Trento. ☎ **0461/98-62-82.** 20 rms, all with bath. MINIBAR TEL TV. 90,000L ($69.20) single, 130,000L ($85.55) double. AE, MC, V.

A recent renovation has created some of the nicest rooms in Trento, with a wonderful location right around the corner from the Piazza Duomo. Decor throughout is stylishly contemporary, with a nice smattering of oriental carpets, vaulted ceilings, and other interesting and cozy architectural touches in public rooms and guest rooms alike. In addition to such amenities as gleaming tile baths and minibars, there is free parking on the premises.

WHERE TO DINE
MEALS FOR LESS THAN 15,000 LIRE ($9.85)
Birreria Pedavena. Pz. Fera 13, 38100 Trento. ☎ **0461/98-62-55.** Wed–Mon, 8:30am–midnight. Antipasto and pasta, from 5,000L ($3.30); main courses 7,000L–15,000L ($4.60–$9.85); pizza from 6,000L (3.95). CAFETERIA/PIZZERIA.

It seems as if this dark cavernous beer hall–style cafeteria can feed all of Trento, and it just might. It draws a big crowd for coffee and pastries in the morning and keeps serving a huge mix of pastas, wurst, schnitzel, and pizza all day; in fact, it keeps some of the latest hours in town, making this something of a late evening hangout in a town where the nightlife is otherwise nil.

Pizzeria Duomo. Pz. Duomo 22. ☎ **0461/98-42-86.** Sun–Fri, noon–2pm and 6–10:30pm. Antipasto and pasta from 7,000L ($4.60); main courses 9,000L–16,000L ($5.90–$10.55); pizza from 6,000L ($3.95). MC, V. PIZZERIA/ITALIAN.

The most popular eatery around the Duomo has a no-frills, tile-floor and white-wall dining room, but offers much more romantic dining on its terrace overlooking the Duomo and the square. While it's possible to eat a full meal of the standard pasta and veal variety here, the pies are the big draw—in fact, they're so popular, topped with everything from tomatoes to wurst, you should be prepared to wait in line on Friday and Sunday nights.

MEALS FOR LESS THAN 20,000 LIRE ($13.15)

La Cantinota. V. San Marco 24. ☎ **0461/23-85-27.** Fri–Wed, noon–3pm and 7pm–11pm (piano bar, 7:30pm–2:30pm). Antipasto and pasta from 7,000L ($4.60); main courses 9,000L–25,000L ($5.90–$16.45). No credit cards. ITALIAN/TYROLEAN.

With its white tablecloths and fairly fancy yet reasonably priced menu, La Cantinota is probably the most popular restaurant in Trento. The fare includes Italian and Germanic-inspired dishes and is truly inspired, making use of fresh local ingredients: wonderful homemade gnocchi, rich risottos with wild mushrooms, grilled sausages with polenta and veal with a rich wine sauce. Be prepared: The adjoining piano bar is popular with local burghers who tend to intersperse Frank Sinatra renditions with yodeling.

EN ROUTE TO BOLZANO: THE STRADA DI VINO

Some of Italy's finest wines are produced on the vines that cloak the hillsides between Trento and Bolzano. (These local wines include many Pinot Grigios and Pinot Noirs among whites, and Vernatsch, the most common red of the region.) If you are traveling by car between the two cities you can make the trip on the well-marked Strada di Vino (Weinstrasse). Leave Trento on S12; 2km north (a little more than a mile) you will come to the village of Lavis, and from here easy-to-follow yellow signs will lead you along a series of twisting roads through seemingly endless vineyards and around Lago di Caldaro to Bolzano. Many of the vineyards have tasting rooms open to the public and sometimes offer cheese, sandwiches, and other refreshment as well. If you don't have your own wheels, the tourist offices in Trento and Bolzano can provide lists of local tour companies that lead wine tours.

2 Bolzano

154km (92 miles) from Verona, 118km (73 miles) from Innsbruck, 57km (35 miles) from Trento

Get out your lederhosen: Without even crossing a border, you're in a place that really doesn't resemble Italy at all. During its long history Bolzano has been ruled by the Hapsburgs, the Austrian Empire, and Bavaria. Though Bolzano has been part of Italy since the end of World War I, you get the sense here that, with its high gabled, Tyrolean-style houses, and preference for the German tongue, this pretty town at the confluence of the Talvera and Isarco Rivers is still Nordic at heart.

ESSENTIALS

GETTING THERE   By Train   Bolzano is about a half hour north of Trento and on the same north-south rail line; there is hourly service to and from Verona, even more frequent service to Trento. There is also hourly train service to and from Merano (45 minutes).

By Bus   Bolzano is the hub of the excellent SAD bus network, serving even the most remote mountain villages. There are four buses a day to and from Cortina (about 3¹/₂ hours, often with a change in Dobacchi) and almost hourly buses to and from Trento. The extremely helpful staff at the bus station, next to the train station, will help you make sense of the schedules.

By Car   The A22 autostrada connects Bolzano with Trento and Verona (where you can connect with the A4 for Milan and Rome) and, farther south, Modena (where you can connect with the A1 for Florence and Rome); A22 runs north to Innsbruck.

VISITOR INFORMATION   Two tourist offices, both near the Duomo, dispense a wealth of information on Bolzano and the South Tyrol. The **APT city tourist office,** Pz. Walther 8 (☎ **0471/97-56-56**), provides lists of accommodations, restaurants, and activities in and around Bolzano; it's open from Monday to Friday from 8:30am to 6pm and on Saturday from 9am to 12:30pm. The **APT provincial tourist office,** just off Piazza Walther at Pz. Parrochia 22 (☎ **0471/97-56-56**) provides information on hiking, skiing, sightseeing, and other activities throughout the region. The telephone area code for Bolzano is 0471.

WHAT TO SEE & DO

Pretty as Bolzano is, sights of great note are few and far between. Most visitors, tending to be Germans and Austrians who sweep down through the Alps for a few days of R&R, content themselves with exploring the narrow streets and broad piazzas and strolling through the parks that line the town's two rivers. The Piazza dell'Erbe, the sight of a lively morning market, is actually one long street that winds through the old town. At the center of town is Piazza Walther, dominated by the Duomo, with a jauntily colored-tile roof, but otherwise not much more than a glum hulk of an edifice (open Monday to Friday from 9:30am to noon and 2 to 6pm; Saturday from 9:30 to noon; Sunday for services only). A far more enticing church is the **Chiesa dei Domenicani,** just a few steps west of the Duomo, where you'll find two sets of frescoes; one from the 15th century, on the walls of the cloisters, depicts court life; the other, in the Capella di San Giovanni, is a 14th-century religious cycle that includes, among some other gruesome scenes, the *Martyrdom of Saint Matthew* (open daily from 9am to 6:30pm).

Of the many castles that surround Bolzano, the closest to the center is the **Castel Mareccio,** near the banks of the River Talvera just north of the center (follow the Lungo Talvera Bolzano north from the Ponte Talvera). Though it is now used as a convention center and its five towers rise from a residential neighborhood of recent vintage, this 13th-century fortress, surrounded by vineyards, is still a mightily romantic sight.

NEARBY EXCURSIONS

A nice walk of about 2km (a little over a mile) leads out of town north along Via Weggerstein to the 13th-century **Castello Roncolo,** beautifully ensconced high above the town and beneath a massive, foreboding cliff face; the interior is decorated with faded but fascinating frescoes. Admission is 1,000L (65¢); it's open March through November, Tuesday to Saturday from 10am to 5pm.

Several cable cars will whisk you right from the center of Bolzano into the surrounding mountains. The most dramatic ride takes you 3,000 feet up the slopes of **Monte Renon** to the village of Soprabolzano, where you can sip a beer and enjoy the view. The cable cars operate daily from 7am to 8pm, and the round-trip costs 7,500L ($4.95); the Bolzano terminus is a five-minute walk northwest from the train station on Via Renon).

WHERE TO STAY
DOUBLES FOR LESS THAN 85,000 LIRE ($55.90)

Hotel Feicher. V. Grappoli 15, 39100 Bolzano. ☎ **0471/97-87-68.** Fax 0471/97-48-03. 35 rms, 5 with bath. 38,000L ($25) single without bath; 58,000L ($38.15) double without bath; 75,000L ($49.35) double with bath; 90,000L ($69.20) triple with bath. MC, V.

The Tyrolean-style lobby is not without its charm, and there's a cozy, Heidi-like bar and self-service restaurant as well. Once upstairs you'll find perfectly serviceable, nononsense accommodations that, while a bit cramped, dark, and badly in need of some redecorating, are spotlessly clean, as are the shared facilities in the hallway. Many of the rooms without bath have sinks.

Hotel Regina A. V. Renon 1. 39100 Bolzano. ☎ **0471/97-21-95.** 30 rms, all with bath. TEL TV. 55,000L ($36.20) single; 80,000L ($52.65) double; 105,000L ($69.10) triple. Rates include breakfast. MC, V.

For pleasant and affordable lodgings in Bolzano, you need look no further than this modern hotel across the street from the train station. Though it's administered by the Catholic Church, the Regina is open to all and, except for a crucifix here and there, you won't many hints of its religious associations. The bright rooms are unusually large and, while quite plain, are very nicely decorated with streamlined Scandinavian furnishings, and all offer a level of comfort and have amenities you would expect in a much more expensive hotel.

A DOUBLE FOR LESS THAN 165,000 LIRE ($108.55)

Stadt Hotel Citta. Pz. Walther 21, 39100 Bolzano. ☎ **041/97-52-21.** Fax 0471/97-66-88. 100 rms, 88 with bath. TEL. 105,000L ($69.10) single; 160,000L ($105.25) double; 190,000L ($125) triple. Rates include breakfast. AE, MC, V.

This serviceable old-fashioned hotel commands pride of place on Bolzano's main piazza, with a handsome paneled and terracotta-tiled lobby. The large and sunny guest rooms, many with small terraces, retain the slightly frayed elegance of bygone eras, with comfy upholstered furniture, big bedsteads, and oriental carpets. The best rooms overlook the square and the Duomo. Mussolini stayed in one of them, no. 303, a suite with a corner balcony from which you, too, might be tempted to address the citizenry below.

WORTH A SPLURGE

Park Hotel Laurin. V. Laurin 4, 39100 Bolzano. ☎ **0471/31-10-00.** Fax 0471/31-11-48. 90 rms. MINIBAR TEL TV. 185,000L–250,000L ($121.70–$164.50) single; 275,000L–375,000L ($180.90–$246.70) double. Rates depend on style of accommodation, which vary from standard to deluxe, and include breakfast. AE, MC, V.

This extraordinarily stylish and gracious hotel, built in 1910 and recently and faithfully restored, is geared to business travelers, though it also provides a luxurious base for tourists who want to enjoy some of the region's most distinctive accommodations. Set in its own park between the train station and center of town, the Laurin has a swimming pool and shady terraces on which to relax in good weather. Many of the large, high-ceilinged guest rooms, handsomely decorated with art deco–style furnishings and with sitting areas equipped with settees and armchairs, face the garden from wide terraces. A lavish buffet breakfast is served in a sun-filled dining room that adjoins the hotel's elegant restaurant, the best in town; the grand lobby lounge doubles as a bar where live music is often performed on weekend evenings.

WHERE TO DINE

In Bolzano you'll encounter menus that seem altogether different from what you've seen in the south. That's because the fare up here in the Alto Adige is more or less Austrian, with a few Italianate touches. Canederli (dumplings) often replace pasta or polenta and are often found floating in rich broths infused with liver; speck (smoked ham) replaces prosciutto; and Wiener schnitzel grostl (a combo of potatoes, onions, and meat, the local version of corned beef hash) and pork roasts are among the preferred secondi.

Some of the cheapest eats in towns are supplied by the vendors who dispense a wide assortment of wurstel from carts all over town; the Kornplatz and Piazza dell'Erbe are especially good hunting grounds. To sample the local wines, step into **Etti's Theke** (get it, as in enoteca?) at Pz. d. Erbe, 11, a tiny little stand-up bar that in the early evening hours is crammed with white-collar workers throwing back a glass or two before heading home.

MEALS FOR LESS THAN 20,000 LIRE ($13.15)

Bassenhasuel. V. Andreas Hofer/Andreas Hoferstrasse 30. ☎ **0471/97-61-83.** Appetizers from 8,000L ($5.25); main courses 10,000L–25,000L ($6.60–$16.45). No credit cards. Wed–Mon 6:30pm–2am. AUSTRIAN.

The two floors of dining rooms are charming and cozy, with dark carved Tyrolean furniture, hardwood floors, and heavily beamed ceilings. The menu, like those in many other restaurants in town, is typically Tyrolean, which means mostly Austrian with some Italian touches. While an excellent minestrone is sometimes available, this is also the place to sample leberknodelsuppe, a thick broth with a liver dumpling floating in it. Pork loin, roast beef with potatoes, and other heavy northern fare dominate the entree choices.

Cavallino Bianco. V. d. Bottai/Bindergasse 6. ☎ **0471/97-32-67.** Appetizers from 7,000L ($4.60); main courses 9,000L–20,000L ($5.90–$13.15). No credit cards. Mon–Fri 7am–3pm and 7pm–midnight, Sat 7am–3pm. TYROLEAN.

This atmospheric stube (beer hall) is darkly paneled and decorated with carved wooden furniture to create a cozy, typically Tyrolean atmosphere. The restaurant opens early to operate as a cafe, dispensing coffee and pastry for breakfast, and remains opens well into the night, sending out hearty lunches and dinners of local fare with only a slight Italian influence. Fried Camembert, herrings, and assorted salamis are among the dozens of appetizers, while main courses of Wiener schnitzel or wurstel are accompanied by dumplings.

Free Flow. V. Renon 1. ☎ **0471/97-21-95.** Appetizers from 6,000L ($3.95); main courses, 8,000L–12,000L ($5.25–$7.90). Mon–Fri, 11:45am–2:15pm. CAFETERIA.

Don't look for a lot of atmosphere in this plain, brightly lit, tile-floored cafeteria adjacent to the Regina A Hotel. It dispenses hearty no-frills weekday lunches to a large crowd of laborers from the nearby railyards and office workers from the central city. The fare doesn't get any fancier than pasta topped with meat sauce, veal scallopine, or a platter of bratwurst with fries, but it's tasty and served in copious proportions.

3 Merano

86km (53 miles) from Trento, 28km (17 miles) from Bolzano

This well-heeled resort, tucked into a valley half an hour west of Bolzano, sports Europe's northernmost palm trees—the product of a mild microclimate that attracts a year-round crowd of mostly elderly, most Germanic vacationers. With its handsome, shop-lined streets, riverside promenades, and easy access to mountainous wilderness, Merano is the place to visit for a day or two of relaxation or hiking.

ESSENTIALS

GETTING THERE   By Train   Hourly train service links Merano with Bolzano (30 to 45 minutes, depending on number of local stops).

By Bus   SAD buses arrive and depart from the train station and stops in the center of town, connecting Merano with Bolzano hourly and with villages throughout the region. The staff at the SAD window in the train station is extremely helpful in helping nonlocals plan trips to the remoter parts of the region.

By Car   Route S 38, a pretty road that cuts through vineyards and mountain meadows, links Merano and Bolzano.

VISITOR INFORMATION   The tourist office, Freiheistrasse 45 (☎ **0473/ 35-223**), is open from Monday to Friday from 9am to 12:30pm and 4 to 7pm;

Saturday it opens an hour later, and is open Sunday from 10am to 12:30pm. The English-speaking staff can provide a list of accommodations and restaurants, help you with bus schedules, and equip you with maps and information on hiking and skiing in the area. The telephone area code for Merano is 0473.

WHAT TO SEE & DO

You can take the cure at the thermal establishment in the center of town, or just take a dip in the pool of mineral-rich water (a dip costs 15,000L/$9.85). But the preferred pastime in Merano is strolling. Prime itineraries are along promenades on the banks of the river Passer or up the delightful Passeggita Tappeiner, an easy upgrade that leads out of town into a very well-tended, parklike mountain wilderness.

THE NATIONAL PARKS

For more strenuous excursions, Merano is the gateway to two national parks. The tourist office in town provides information on them, as does the **Club Alpo Italiano,** Cor. Liberta 188, (☎ **0473/48-944;** open Monday to Friday from 6:30 to 8:30pm); both parks also have their own visitor centers within their boundaries.

Parco Nazionale della Stelvio

In this vast 1.3 million–acre wilderness east of Merano, elk and chamois roam the mountainsides and craggy snowcapped peaks pierce the sky. A network of trails criss-cross some almost virgin wilderness, and some of Europe's largest glaciers provide year-round skiing.

The park office is in Silandro, at V. d. Cappuccini 2 (☎ **0473/70-443**). It dispenses maps, lists of hiking trails, and *rifugi* (huts where hikers can overnight) within the park as well as other information; there are several buses a day from Merano to Silandro, which is about 30km (18 miles) east via route S38.

Parco Nazionale di Tessa

This Alpine wonderland surrounds Merano with a pleasant terrain of meadows and gentle, forest-clad slopes. A relatively easy path, the southern route of the Meraner Hohenweg, allows even the most inexperienced hikers to cross the park effortlessly in two days, and is conveniently interspersed with restaurants and farmhouses offering rooms to let. The northern route is much more isolated, difficult, and scenic.

The park office in Naturno, about 15km (9 miles) north on Route S44, provides a wealth of information on hiking trails, meals, and accommodations in the park.

WHERE TO STAY

April, August through October, and the Christmas holidays constitute high season in Merano, when rates are highest and rooms are scarce.

Hotel Europa Splendid. Cor. Liberta 178. 39012 Merano. ☎ **0473/23-23-76.** Fax 0473/ 23-02-21. 55 rms, all with bath. MINIBAR TEL TV. 78,000L–100,000L ($51.30–$65.80) single; 126,000L–160,000L ($82.90–$105.25) double. Rates vary with season and include breakfast. Half-board, 83,000L–108,000L ($54.60–$71.05) per person; full board, 99,000L–128,000L ($65.15–$84.20) per person, depending on season. AE, MC, V.

Conveniently located in the center of town a block off the river Passer, the Europa is an old-fashioned, family-run place that caters to guests who return year after year. The decor is charmingly faded, with an elegant, regency-style salon and Tyrolean-style bar downstairs. The large, bright guest rooms upstairs haven't been redecorated since the 1960s, but are homey and very comfortable. Many of the rooms have small, flower-filled balconies, and a large, sun-filled hotel terrace is on the first floor.

Hotel Meranerhof. V. Manzoni 1, 39012 Merano. ☎ **0473/23-02-30.** Fax, 0473/23-33-12. 70 rms, all with bath. MINIBAR TEL TV. Half-board, 120,000L–150,000L ($78.95–$98.70) per person, depending on season. Bed-and-breakfast–only rates are available on request, and the hotel also offers special weekend and weekly packages.

It's little wonder that this gracious hotel is so popular with Germans and Austrians who whisk down to Merano for a few days of relaxation. The large, high ceilinged guest rooms are very homey, with eiderdown quilts on the beds and armchairs for reading, and are nicely decorated with a pleasant mix of traditional pieces and contemporary, white-stained wood furnishings; they either face the town and river or have large balconies overlooking the garden and swimming pool. Downstairs, there is a series of elegant, ivory-colored salons, comfortably furnished with rose-colored couches and club chairs, and filled with rare Tyrolean antiques. A buffet breakfast, as well as lunch and dinner (accompanied by a lavish salad bar), are served in an elegant dining room.

WHERE TO DINE
Dolomiten. V. Haller 4. ☎ **0473/36-377.** Appetizers from 8,000L ($62.65), main courses 10,000L–25,000L ($5.80–$16.45). No credit cards. Thurs–Tues 6:30pm–2am. TYROLEAN.

It's pretty easy to forget you're in Italy in this friendly, vaulted-ceilinged, wood-paneled beer hall near the Duomo, where the decor and the food are strictly Tyrolean. Schlutzkrapfen (ravioli filled with sauerkraut), herrengrostl (a hearty stew of beef, potatoes, and herbs), and umpteen different kinds of wurstel are served family-style at long tables that you might find yourself sharing with a lederhosen-clad family.

Picnic-Grill. V. d. Corse/Rennweg 28. No phone. Appetizers from 5,000L ($3.30), main courses 6,000L–10,000L ($3.95–$6.60). No credit cards. Mon–Sat 9am–10pm. SANDWICHES/SNACKS.

If you've been yearning for the coffee shop back home, this brightly lit fast-food restaurant in the center of town is just the place for you. The menu seems to concentrate on anything that can be prepared quickly and nonfussily, including sandwiches and platters of ham and cheese, and there are many different kinds of wurstel and pasta as well.

EN ROUTE TO CORTINA: THE STRADA DI DOLIMITI
The Great Dolomite Road, the scenic route between Bolzano and Cortina going east, SS241 and SS48, is 110km (66 miles) of stunning views. The road curves around some of the highest peaks in the Dolomites, including 10,000-foot-tall Marmolda, and goes through a scattering of remote mountain villages and ski resorts before dropping out of a high pass into Cortina. Between June and August, some SAD buses follow this scenic route; at other times, during the winter months, the Strada di Dolomiti is often closed to all vehicles because of heavy snow.

4 Cortina d'Ampezzo
133km (82 miles) from Bolzano

Italy's glitziest mountain resort, put on the map when it hosted the 1956 Winter Olympics, is usually associated with the rich and the famous. True, Cortina can be expensive (especially in August and the high ski season months of January and February) and many Italian celebrities and business leaders do have houses here. What's often forgotten, though, is that Cortina is just plain beautiful. For all Cortina's fame, strict zoning has put the damper on development, and, as a result, this is still a mountain town of white timbered houses (old and new) and surrounded by meadows and the stunning Dolomite peaks.

ESSENTIALS

GETTING THERE   By Bus   Frequent **SAD bus service** provides the only public transportation in and out of Cortina. If you are coming from Bolzano on one of four daily buses, it is usually necessary to change at Dobbiaco, 32km (19¹/₂ miles) to the north. From June through August, though, some buses make a direct trip between Bolzano and Cortina and ply the incredibly scenic Strada di Dolimiti (be sure to ask what bus to take to follow this road). The bus station in Cortina is located in the former train station.

By Car   The spectacularly scenic S48 links Bolzano and Cortina, while S51 heads south toward Venice, connecting south of Belluno to Autostrada A27, for a total trip time of about three hours between Cortina and Venice.

VISITOR INFORMATION   The **APT tourist office,** Pzta. San Francesco 8 (☎ **0436/32-31**) is open Monday to Friday from 9am to 12:30pm and 4 to 7pm, Saturday from 10am to 12:30pm and 4 to 7pm, and Sunday from 10am to 12:30pm. In addition to a list of accommodations, the English-speaking staff will also provide information on ski slopes, hiking trails, and bus schedules. The telephone area code for Cortina is 0436.

WHAT TO SEE & DO

The main activity in Cortina appears to be prancing around town in the most fashionable skiwear money can buy. However, both skiers and nonskiers will enjoy the eye-popping scenery on a trip up the surrounding mountainsides on the funicular systems that leave right from town. The most spectacular trip is up to the ski station of Ra Valles (about 7,500 feet high) on a cable car that departs from a station near the Olympic Stadium (cost is 22,000L/$14.50 round-trip); from Ra Valles the views over glaciers and the hundreds of Dolomite peaks piercing the sky are stunning, and a handy bar serves sandwiches and other refreshments on an outdoor terrace.

You can visit the **Olympic stadium** for 2,000L ($1.30), and if you feel like taking a spin on the ice yourself, the cost is 12,000L ($7.90) for skate rental.

WHERE TO STAY

Cortina is booked solid during the high-season months of August and February. In those months rates shoot up astronomically, and they go up and down throughout the rest of the year, tending to be lowest in late spring. Keep in mind, too, that many innkeepers prefer to give rooms to guests who will stay several days or longer and who will take meals at the hotel. Given a lot of reasonably priced restaurants in town, you will probably be happy settling for a half- or full-board plan.

DOUBLES FOR LESS THAN 125,000 LIRE ($82.25)

Hotel Bellaria. Cor. Italia 266, 32043 Cortina d'Ampezzo. ☎ **0436/25-05.** Fax 0436/57-55. 22 rms, all with bath. TEL TV. 120,000L–240,000L ($78.95–$157.90) double. Rates include breakfast and vary with season. Weekly rates with half-board from 595,000L–650,000L ($427.65–$391.45) a person, depending on season. AC, MC, V.

When the Mujoni family who owns this pleasant hotel did a complete refurbishing recently, they decided to keep prices down for the benefit of the patrons who come here season after season. As a result, the handsome, sunny rooms, with alpine-style furnishings and shiny new baths, and overlooking the peaks, are really quite a bargain. Downstairs, there's a lovely paneled lounge, a dining room, and a pleasant terrace in front of the house.

Hotel Italia. V. Marconi 2, 32043 Cortina d'Ampezzo. ☎ **0436/56-46,** or 56-48. Fax 0436/57-57. 58 rms, 42 with bath. TEL TV. 105,000L ($69.08) double with bath. Rates include breakfast. Weekly rates with half-board from 600,000L–800,000L ($394.75–$626.30) per person, depending on season. AE, MC, V.

A friendly atmosphere prevails in this old hotel across from what once served as Cortina's train station and is now a hub for the buses that ply the mountain passes and shuttle skiers to nearby lifts. The ground floor lounges are equipped with tile stoves and fireplaces, and three meals a day are served in a cozy dining room. All of the guest rooms are different, furnished in styles that range from Alpine quaint to sixties modern; some of the coziest are tucked under the eaves on the top floor. Most rooms have private baths and many open onto terraces. The management prefers to rent rooms by the week on a meal plan, and it's possible to stay for shorter terms on a bed-and-breakfast arrangement at the rate above, but only when the hotel is not full.

Hotel Montana. Cor. Italia 94, 32043 Cortina d'Ampezzo. ☎ **0436/86-21-26.** Fax: 0436/86-82-11. 30 rms, all with bath. TEL TV. 70,000L–90,000L ($46.05–$59.20) single; 106,000L–168,000L ($69.70–$110.50) double. Rates include breakfast and vary with season. AE, MC, V.

Right in the center of town, this family-run hotel occupies a tall, pretty alpine-style house. Rooms are unusually cozy, with their old-style armoires, hardwood floors, and down quilts on the beds, and many open to little balconies overlooking the peaks. The best rooms in the house are the large, pine-paneled doubles. Half the rooms here are singles, making this an ideal spot for solo travelers or cranky twosomes who need to get away from each other for a spell. There is no restaurant, so guests fend for themselves come meal time.

A DOUBLE FOR LESS THAN 180,000 LIRE ($118.40)

Hotel Menardi. V. Majon 110, 32043 Cortina d'Ampezzo. ☎ **0436/24-00.** Fax 0436/86-21-83. 48 rms. 170,000L–330,000L ($111.85–$217.10) double. Rates vary with season and include breakfast. Half-board, 115,000L–200,000L ($75.65–$131.60) per person; full-board, 125,000L–215,000L ($82.25–$141.75) per person, depending on season. AE, MC, V.

One of the oldest and most charming hostelries in Cortina successfully combines the luxury and service of a fine hotel with the homelike comfort of a mountain inn. The Menardi family, who converted their farmhouse into a guest house in the 1920s, have over the years beautifully appointed their public rooms with antiques and comfortable furnishings, and done up their high-ceilinged, wood-floored guest rooms simply but tastefully with painted armoires and bedsteads, down quilts, and attractive floral fabrics. Rooms in the rear of the house are especially quiet and pleasant, looking across the hotel's spacious lawns to the forests and peaks; some newer rooms are located in an annex next door. Most guests take half-board to avail themselves of the excellent meals, but it is also possible to make bed-and-breakfast arrangements when the hotel is not fully booked.

WHERE TO DINE

Forget about finding inexpensive meals in Cortina—even pizzerias are few and far between. For a cheap meal, you might want to equip yourself for a picnic at **La Piazzetta,** Corso Italia 53, with a mouth-watering assortment of salamis, cheeses, breads, and other fare. Another source of supplies is **La Cooperativa,** Corso Italia 40, the largest, best-stocked supermarket for miles around.

MEALS FOR LESS THAN 20,000 LIRE ($13.15)

Al Camin. V. Alvera 90. ☎ **0436/20-10.** Appetizers from 8,000L ($5.25); main courses 10,000L–25,000L ($6.60–$16.45). MC, V. Tues–Sun, noon–3pm and 7–10:3pm. TYROLEAN.

If you follow the Via Alvera along the Ru Bigontina, a rushing mountain stream, about 10 minutes east from the center of town, you'll come to this charming, rustic restaurant. The tables in the wood-paneled dining room are grouped around a large stone fireplace, and the menu is appropriately homey and typical of the region; this is the place to try canederli (dumplings flavored with liver), and follow up with a plate of sausages and polenta.

La Tavernetta. V. d. Stadio 27 a/b. ☎ **0436/86-74-94.** Appetizers from 10,000L ($6.60); main courses 15,000L–30,000L ($9.85–$19.75). AE, MC, V. Daily, noon–2:30pm and 7:30pm–11pm. CONTINENTAL.

A former barn, just steps from the Olympic ice-skating stadium, has been delightfully converted to a very stylish yet reasonably priced restaurant, with handsome paneled walls, timbered ceilings, and tile floors. In fact, in a town where meals often seem to be overpriced, La Tavernetta is the best dining experience for the money. The menu relies on local ingredients and typical dishes of the Alto Adige, with some nice innovations to suit the tastes of Cortina's well-heeled tourists. You might, for instance, want to begin your meal here with a dish of polenta delicately infused with asparagus tips or gnocchi filled with spinach and topped with a rich wild game sauce, then move on to lamb chops grilled with herbs or a grilled saddle of venison.

Milan, Lombardy & the Lakes

by Stephen Brewer

There is a lot more to Italy's most prosperous province than the factories that fuel its economy. Many of the attractions here are urban—in addition to Milan, a string of Renaissance cities dots the Lombardian plains, from Pavia to Mantua. To the north the region bumps up against craggy mountains and romantic lakes (see our section on the lakes) and to the south Lombardy spreads out in fertile farmlands fed by the Po and other rivers. The Lombardians, who over the centuries have been ruled by feudal dynasties, the Spanish, the Austrians, and the French, are a little more continental than their neighbors to the south, faster talking, and a little more fast-paced as well. They even dine a little differently, tending to eschew olive oil for butter and often forgoing pasta for polenta and risotto. In short, what you'll encounter in Lombardy might not always be what you've come to expect of Italy, but the region is all the richer for the differences.

The Italian lakes have been admired over the centuries by poets and writers from Catullus to Ernest Hemingway. Backed by the Alps and ringed by lush gardens and verdant forests, each has its own charms and, accordingly, its own enthusiasts. Not least among these charms are their easy accessibility to many Italian cities, making them ideal for short retreats: Lago Maggiore and Lago di Como are both less than an hour distant from Milan, and Lago di Garda is tantalizingly close to Venice, Verona, and Mantua.

EXPLORING LOMBARDY

Since so many of the places of interest in Lombardy are easily accessible by train—and since driving is all but impossible in Milan and many of the smaller cities as well—you may want to save yourself the expense of a car while visiting the region. The ease of transportation also makes it possible to settle down in Milan or quieter Bergamo and visit other places on day trips.

Any tour of Milan begins in the Piazza del Duomo, which is within easy walking distance of the Galleria, La Scala, the Castello Sforzesco, and many of the major churches and museums.

If you are spending several days in Milan, after a morning of visiting Milan's art galleries and churches, make a trip to Pavia and the Certosa in the afternoon. Cremona, once Europe's premier center of violin-making, is an easy and interesting afternoon trip.

Next, make the short trip out to Bergamo and check into a hotel in the Citta Alta. Spend the day visiting the wonderful art gallery and other sights, and after dinner, enjoy an evening stroll through the narrow streets and piazzas.

Move on to Mantua, with a stop in Brescia to visit the sights of the centro storico. Arrive in Mantua in time to enjoy a stroll through its lovely piazzas and lakefront promenades. Spend the next day visiting the Palazzo Ducale, the Palazzo Te, and other sights.

1 Milan (Milano)

572km (343 miles) from Rome, 298km (179 miles) from Florence, 267km (160 miles) from Venice

Most visitors come to Milan well-equipped with preconceptions, not all of them flattering. True, Italy's financial center, business hub, fashion capital, and most industrialized city is crowded, noisy, hot in the summer and damp and foggy in the winter, less easy-going and more expensive than other Italian places—in short, not as immediately appealing a stopover as Venice, Florence, or Rome. Milan, though, reveals its long and event-filled history in a pride of monuments, museums, and churches, sets one of the finest tables in Italy, and supports a cultural scene that embraces La Scala, fashion shows, and nightlife. With its dazzling shop windows and sophisticated ways, Milan is a pleasure to get to know—and, despite all that's been said about the city's exorbitant prices, you needn't empty the bank account to do so.

ESSENTIALS

GETTING THERE By Train Milan is one of Europe's busiest rail hubs, with connections to all major cities on the Continent. There are 14 arrivals a day from Venice (4 hours), 10 from Rome (7 hours), and 8 from Florence (3 hours). Stazione Centrale, an amazing Fascist-era structure, is northeast of the center, with easy connections to Piazza del Duomo by metro, tram, and bus. Luggage storage is available.

By Car Milan is well served by Italy's superhighway (autostrada) system. The A1 links Milan with Florence and Rome, and the A4 connects Milan with Verona and Venice to the east and Turin to the west. Driving and parking in Milan are not experiences to be relished; however, if you do drive into Milan, park your car in a lot and leave it there for the duration of your stay.

By Plane Malpensa, 45km (27 miles) west of the center, is Milan's international airport. STAM buses run to Stazione Centrale hourly from 6:30am to 11pm and from Stazione Centrale to Malpensa half-hourly from 5am until noon and then hourly from noon to 9pm (schedules vary). Tickets (12,000L/$7.90) can be purchased at offices at the airport and bus station or on board the bus. Buses from Stazione Centrale leave from the east end of the building.

Linate, only 7km (4 miles) east of the center, handles domestic and some inter-European flights (if you're flying into Milan from another European city, try to book a flight that lands here; you'll save about 45 minutes to an hour getting into town). STAM buses run from Linate to Stazione Centrale every 20 minutes to half-hour from 7am to 11:30pm and from the bus station to Linate until 9pm; purchase tickets on the bus. You can also take a city bus, number 73, to and from Linate, from the southeast corner of Piazza San Babila.

VISITOR INFORMATION The main ATP tourist office is in Palazzo del Turismo on the Piazza del Duomo (☎ 02/80-96-62); hours are Monday to Friday from 8:30am to 8pm, Saturday from 9am to 1pm and 2pm to 7pm, Sunday from

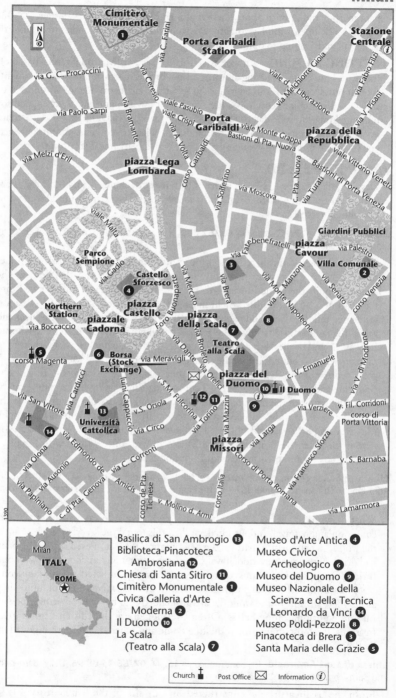

Basilica di San Ambrogio **13**
Biblioteca-Pinacoteca
    Ambrosiana **12**
Chiesa di Santa Sitiro **11**
Cimitèro Monumentale **1**
Civica Galleria d'Arte
    Moderna **2**
Il Duomo **10**
La Scala
    (Teatro alla Scala) **7**

Museo d'Arte Antica **4**
Museo Civico
    Archeologico **6**
Museo del Duomo **9**
Museo Nazionale della
    Scienza e della Tecnica
    Leonardo da Vinci **14**
Museo Poldi-Pezzoli **8**
Pinacoteca di Brera **3**
Santa Maria delle Grazie **5**

Church ✝   Post Office ✉   Information ⓘ

9am to 1pm and 2pm to 5pm. There is also an office in Stazione Centrale (☎ **02/ 66-90-532**), open Monday to Saturday from 9am to 6pm, Sunday from 9am to 12:30pm and 1:30pm to 6pm.

GETTING AROUND   An extensive subway system (Metropolitana Milanese), trams, and buses make moving around Milan a breeze. The metro closes at midnight, though buses and trams run later. Tickets good for one metro ride (or 75 minutes of surface transportation) cost 1,400 lire (90¢). You can also purchase a ticket good for unlimited travel for one day (4,800L/$3.15) or two days (8,000L/$5.25). Tickets are available at metro stations and at newsstands. It's obligatory to stamp your ticket when you board a bus or tram—you can be slapped with a hefty fine if you don't.

WHAT TO SEE & DO

Despite Milan's size and sprawl, many of its museums, churches, and other sights are within easy walking distance of one another in the vicinity of the Duomo and Castello Sforzesco.

Castello Sforzesco. Pz. Castello. ☎ **02/62-081.** Free admission. Tue–Sun, 9:30pm–5:30pm. Closed Mon. Metro: Cairoli.

Though it's been clumsily restored in this century, this fortresslike castle continues to evoke Milan's two most powerful families, the Viscontis and the Sforzas. The Viscontis built the castle in the 14th century and the Sforzas, who married into the Visconti clan and eclipsed them in power, reconstructed it in 1450. The most influential residents were Ludovico il Moro and Beatrice d'Este (he of the Sforzas and she of the famous Este family of Ferrara). After ill-advisedly calling the French into Italy at the end of the 15th century, Ludovico died in the dungeons of a chateau in the Loire valley—but not before the couple made the castello and Milan one of Italy's great centers of the Renaissance. It was they who commissioned the frescoes by Bramante and the rooms designed by Leonardo da Vinci, and these splendors can be viewed on a tour of the miles of salons that surround the castello's enormous courtyard. These salons also house a pinacoteca, with works by Bellini, Correggio, Magenta, and a 90-year-old Michelangelo, whose last, unfinished pietà is here. Also here is the extensive holdings of the Museo d'Arte Antica, filled with Egyptian funerary objects and prehistoric finds from Lombardy.

Chiesa di Santa Maria delle Grazie. Pz. Santa Maria delle Grazie. ☎ **02/49-87-588.** Admission to *Last Supper* 12,000L ($7.90). Tue–Sun 8:15am–1:45am, church only 3:30pm–7pm. Metro: Cadorna.

What draws most visitors here is the *Last Supper,* Leonardo's poignant portrayal of confusion and betrayal. Aldous Huxley called this mural the "saddest work of art in the world," a comment in part on the deterioration that set in even before the paint had dried on the moisture-ridden walls. A recent restoration has done away with centuries of overpainting, clumsy patching, and damage inflicted when Napoléon's troops used the wall for target practice. Even so, the *Last Supper* is still, quite literally, a mere shadow of the work the artist intended it to be—but amazingly powerful and emotional nonetheless. Often overlooked are the church's other great treasures, foremost among them the fine dome and other architectural innovations by Bramante.

Chiesa di Sant'Ambrogio. Pz. Sant'Ambrogio 15. ☎ **02/86-45-08-95.** Daily, 8am–noon and 3pm–7pm. Metro: Sant'Ambrogio.

From the basilica that he constructed on this site in the 4th century A.D.— when he was bishop of Milan and the city, in turn, was briefly capital of the Western

Empire—Saint Ambrose had a profound effect on the early church. Nothing is left of the structure in which Ambrose baptized Saint Augustine, but the 11th-century church built in its place is itself remarkable. It has a striking atrium, a portico by Bramante, a gold altar from Charlemagne's days in Milan, and the all-too-scant remains of a Tiepolo fresco cycle, most of it blown into oblivion by World War II bombs.

Chiesa di San Satiro. V. Torino. Daily, 9am–noon and 2:30pm–6pm. Metro: Duomo.

What makes this beautiful church so special is what it doesn't have—space. Stymied by not being able to expand the apse to classical Renaissance proportions, Bramante created a marvelous relief behind the high altar. The effect of the trompe-l'oeil columns and arches is not entirely convincing but nonetheless magical.

Duomo. Pz. d. Duomo. ☎ **02/86-46-34-56.** Admission to roof 4,000L ($2.65), 8,000L ($5.25) with elevator. Daily, 7am–7pm. Admission to Museo del Duomo, 7,000L ($4.60), 4,000L ($2.65) students. Tue–Sun, 9:30am–12:30pm and 3pm–6pm. Metro: Duomo.

When Milanese think something is taking too long, they refer to it as "la fabricca del duomo"—the making of the Duomo, a reference to the five centuries it took to complete the magnificent gothic cathedral that rises from the center of the city. The last of Italy's great gothic structures—begun by the ruling Visconti family in 1386—is the third largest church in the world, with its 135 marble spires, a stunning triangular facade, and 2,000-some statues flanking the massive but airy, almost fanciful exterior. The cavernous interior, lit by brilliant stained-glass windows, seats 40,000 but is unusually Spartan and serene. The poet Shelley used to sit and read Dante amid monuments that include a gruesomely graphic statue of *St. Bartholomew Flayed* and the tomb of Giacomo de Medici. Another British visitor, Alfred, Lord Tennyson, rhapsodized about the view of the Alps from the roof, and on a clear day you may well do the same. Across the piazza, the Palazzo Reale houses the treasure-filled Museo del Duomo (☎ **02/86-03-58**). Admission is 7,000L ($4.60), and it's open from Tuesday to Sunday from 9:30am to 12:30pm and 3pm to 6pm.

Galleria d'Arte Moderna. V. Palestro 16. ☎ **02/76-00-28-19.** Free admission. Tue–Sun, 9:30am–5:30pm. Closed Mon. Metro: Porta Venezia.

The villa where Napoléon and his stepson Eugene de Beauharnais lived, from which they ably administered their kingdom of Italy, houses a collection that is "modern" in the 19th-century sense. The salons are filled with works by Pellizza da Volpedo and other Italians who ushered in a new style of painting toward the end of the last century, as well as those by Cézanne, Gauguin, and other modernists.

Galleria Vittorio Emanuele II. Just off Pz. d. Duomo and Pz. d. Scala. Metro: Duomo.

Milan's late 19th-century version of a piazza is this wonderful steel-and-glass–covered, cross-shaped arcade. This shopping mall par excellence provides a lovely route between the Duomo and La Scala and is a fine locale for watching the flocks of well-dressed Milanese.

Museo Civico Archeologico. Cor. Magenta 15. ☎ **02/86-45-06-65.** Free admission. Tue–Sun, 9:30am–5:30pm, closed Mon. Metro: Cadorna.

The most fascinating finds in this sizable repository of civilizations past are the everyday items—tools, eating utensils, and jewelry from Roman Milan. The exhibits, which seem to fill every corner of the 16th-century monastery, also include Greek, Etruscan, and Roman pieces from throughout Italy.

Museo Civico d'Arte Contemporanea. Pz. d. Duomo 12. ☎ **02/62-08-39-14.** Free admission. Tue–Sun, 9:30am–5:30pm, closed Mon. Metro: Duomo.

While changing exhibits by works of living artists are often on display, contemporary here means anything 20th-century. The prize of the collection, hung in the regal salons of the Palazzo Reale across the piazza from the Duomo, are the works by De Chirico and Modigliani.

Museo Nazionale della Scienza e delle Tecnica Leonardo da Vinci. V. San Vittore 21. ☎ **02/48-01-00-40.** Admission 10,000L ($6.60). Tue–Sun, 9:30am–5:30pm, closed Mon. Metro: Sant'Ambrogio.

The heart and soul of this engaging museum are the reconstructions and models of Leonardo's submarines, airplanes, and other engineering feats. This former Benedictine monastery and its beautiful cloisters are also filled with planes, carriages, sewing machines, typewriters, optical devices, and other exhibits that comprise one of the world's leading collections of mechanical and scientific wizardry.

Museo Poldi-Pezzoli. V. Manzoni 12. ☎ **02/79-48-89.** Admission 10,000L ($6.60). Tue–Sun, 9:30am–12:30pm and 2:30–6pm; Sat until 7:30pm; closed Sun afternoons Apr–Sept. Metro: Duomo.

The pleasant effect of seeing the Bellinis, Bottecellis, Lippis, and Tiepolos amid these stuffily charming antique-filled salons is reminiscent of a visit to other private collections, such as the Frick Collection in New York City and the Isabella Stewart Gardner Museum in Boston. This stunning treasure trove, which leans heavily toward Venetian painters but also ventures widely throughout Italian painting and into the Flemish schools, was amassed by 19th-century collector Giacomo Poldi-Pezzoli, who donated his villa and its treasures to the city in 1881. The most reproduced work here, but by no means the finest, is Antonio Pollaiuolo's *Portrait of a Young Woman*, a haunting image you will recognize immediately upon seeing.

Pinacoteca Ambrosiana. Pz. Pio XI, 2. Admission 8,000L ($5.25). Sun–Fri, 9:30am–5pm, closed Sat. Hours are subject to change. Metro: Duomo.

Perhaps the most enchanting of Milan's many fine art galleries dates to 1609, and it is filled with treasures from the 15th through 17th centuries: An Adoration by Titian, Raphael's cartoon for his *School of Athens* in the Vatican, Caravaggio's *Basket of Fruit*, and 14 intimate rooms of other works. The adjoining Biblioteca Ambrosiana houses a wealth of Renaissance literaria, including the letters of Lucrezia Borgia and a strand of her hair.

Pinacoteca di Brera. V. Brea 28. ☎ **02/72-26-31.** Admission 8,000L ($5.25). Tue–Sat, 9am–5:30pm, Sun, 9am–12:30pm. Metro: Lanza.

This 17th-century palazzo houses three of Italy's greatest masterpieces: Andrea Mantegna's *Dead Christ*, Raphael's *Betrothal of the Virgin*, and Piero della Francesa's *Madonna with Saints (the Montefeltro Altarpiece)*. Of course, to limit your viewing to these works is like going to the Louvre and seeing only the *Mona Lisa*. Caravaggio's *Supper at Emmaus* is here, as are Bramante's frescoes from Casa dei Panigarola and a stunning collection of 20th-century works. The snack bar overlooking the courtyard is a fine place to slack your thirst and rest your tired feet.

Teatro alla Scala. Pz. d. Scala. ☎ **02/80-53-418.** Admission to Museo Teatrale 5,000L ($3.30), 4,000L ($2.65) students. Mon–Sat, 9am–noon and 2pm–6pm, Sun (May–Oct only), 9am–noon. Metro: Duomo.

Built in the late 18th century on the site of a church of the same name, La Scala is hallowed ground to lovers of Giuseppe Verdi, Maria Callas, and legions of other composers and singers who have hit the high notes of fame in the world's most revered opera house. It's been said that it is almost as hard to get a ticket to a performance here as it is to land a role on the stage of this acoustically perfect theater. Beautiful as the red and gold hall is, it is a reconstruction made necessary by a direct bomb hit during World War II. A whiff of nostalgia for days gone by pervades the Museo Teatrale alla Scala, where you'll find Toscanini's baton, a strand of Mozart's hair, and a fine array of Callas postcards.

SHOPPING IN MILAN

You can't come to Milan without doing it—or at least engaging in a little window-shopping. The best gazing is to be done along Via Monte Napoleone, lined with Milan's most expensive emporia. Thus inspired, you can scour the racks of Il Salvegente, V. Bronzetti 16, for designer clothing at wholesale prices. In a city that is this well dressed, it only stands to reason that some great-looking castoffs are bound to turn up at street markets: Check out Via Papinaio (Metro: Sant'Agostino) on Saturday mornings and the banks of the Naviglio Grande (Metro: Porta Genova) on the last Sunday of each month. There's an antiques market on Via Fiori Chiaria the third Saturday of each month.

WHERE TO STAY

While you can pay more for a hotel room in Milan than you would almost anywhere else in Europe, there are also some decent accommodations at reasonable prices in good locations (really). It's difficult to find rooms in any price category when fashion shows and trade fairs are in full swing (often in October and March). August is low season, and rooms stand empty—as does the rest of the city.

A HOSTEL

Piero Rotta Hostel. V. Martino Bassi 2, Milano. ☎ **02/39-26-70-95.** 348 beds. 20,000L ($13.15) per person. Rates include breakfast. IH card required (can be purchased at check-in for 30,000L/$19.75). No credit cards. 12:30am curfew; closed from 9am–5pm, but luggage storage available. Metro: Lotto.

Milan's hostel is in the outskirts near San Siro soccer stadium, in a leafy neighborhood that's safe and quiet but only a short metro ride from the center. Facilities are modern, spiffy clean, and run like boot camp—curfew and morning lockout hours are strictly enforced.

DOUBLES FOR LESS THAN 80,000 LIRE ($52.65)

America. Cor. XXII Marzo 32, Milano. ☎ **02/73-88-65.** Fax 02/73-81-490. 10 rms, 3 with bath. TEL TV. 45,000L ($29.69) single without bath; 65,000L ($42.75) double without bath, 80,000L ($52.65) double with bath; 110,000L ($72.35) triple with bath. Tram: 27 from the station; 12 from Duomo.

Though his establishment is a bit off the beaten track in a working-class neighborhood, the young owner works overtime to make his pensione one of the best in all Milan. The newly refurbished rooms occupy the fourth floor of an apartment house. Several have private baths, and all are nicely decorated with streamlined modern furnishings. For those interested in seeing flocks of young Milanese peacock around the dance floor, the Rolling Stone disco is on the ground floor; for more conventional sightseeing, the Duomo is about 20 minutes by foot or 10 minutes by tram.

Hotel Cesare Correnti. V. Cesare Correnti 14, 20123 Milano. ☎ **02/80-57-609.** Fax 02/72-01-07-15. 9 rms, none with bath. TV. 45,000L ($29.60) single; 65,000L ($42.75) double; 90,000L ($59.20) triple. Breakfast 5,000L ($3.30). No credit cards. Metro: Duomo. Tram: 8, 19.

You expect to find a sign saying ABANDON ALL HOPE YE WHO ENTER HERE on the dark stairway leading up to this third-floor pensione in an old building between the Duomo and the church of San Lorenzo. Press on, though, because the family-run establishment is clean and friendly. The basically furnished rooms, all with TV, share ample baths in the hallway, which also serves as a lounge. The family who runs the place will do a load of wash for you for 6,000L ($3.95).

Hotel Kennedy. Vle. Tunisia 6 (6th floor), 20124 Milano. ☎ **02/29-40-09-34.** Fax 02/29-40-12-53. 12 rms, 3 with shower, 2 with bath. 50,000L–60,000L ($32.90–$39.45) single without bath; 70,000L–85,000L ($46.05–$55.90) double without bath; 120,000L–140,000L ($78.95–$92.10) double with bath; 160,000L ($105.25) quadruple with bath. V. Metro: Porta Venezia.

The name reflects the management's fondness for the late president, and they're genuinely welcoming to the many, mostly young Americans who find their way to their family-run pensione about midway between the station and Corso Buenos Aires. Their homey establishment on the fifth floor of an office-and-apartment building (there's an elevator) is sparkling clean and offers basic accommodations, along with some nice amenities like a bar in the reception area and a 5,000L ($3.30) breakfast.

Hotel Paganini. V. Paganini 6, 20131 Milano. ☎ **02/20-47-443.** 8 rms, 1 with bath. 75,000L ($49.35) double without bath; 85,000L ($55.90) double with bath. Metro: Lima.

Occupying an old house on a quiet residential street off the Corso Buenos Aires, the Paganini has large, old-fashioned rooms that are eclectically furnished but not without charm, with parquet floors and high ceilings. The shared facilities are modern and kept spanking clean by the young, enthusiastic staff, who are happy to point their guests to restaurants and sights. The best rooms are in the rear, overlooking a private garden.

Hotel Ulrich. Cor. Italia 6, 21023 Milano. ☎ **02/86-45-01-56.** 7 rms, none with bath. 40,000L ($26.30) single; 70,000L ($46.05) double; 90,000L ($59.20) triple. No credit cards. Metro: Duomo. Tram: 12, 24.

A 10-minute walk from the Duomo, this pretty pensione offers a lot of comfort for the price. Each room has a TV and a tiny washroom with sink and bidet; large, spanking-clean bathrooms are in the hallway. Rooms on the street side open to small balconies. Given its amenities and central location, the Ulrich books up fast, so be sure to call ahead.

DOUBLES FOR LESS THAN 165,000 LIRE ($108.55)

Hotel Giulio Cesare. V. Rovello 10, 20121 Milano. ☎ **02/72-00-39-15.** Fax 02/72-00-21-79. 25 rms, all with bath. A/C TEL TV. 92,000L ($60.55) single; 152,000L ($100) double. AE, MC, V. Metro: Cordusio.

A recent renovation has brought this old establishment thoroughly up to date, with a grandiose marble lobby and sparkling modern baths. Rooms are rather antiseptic, with white tile floors and not much more furniture than a bed and desk, but the price is really quite remarkable given the central location and the modern comforts offered.

London Hotel. V. Rovello 3, 20121 Milano. ☎ **02/72-02-01-66.** Fax 02/80-57-037. 29 rms, 23 with bath. A/C TEL. 90,000L ($59.20) single without bath; 110,000L ($72.35) single with bath; 130,000L ($85.55) double without bath, 160,000L ($105.25) double with bath. MC, V. Metro: Cordusio.

The big fireplace and cozy green velvet furniture in the lobby say a lot about the comfort and friendly atmosphere that prevail at this old-fashioned hotel near the Duomo. Just beyond the lobby, there's a bar where beverages are available almost around the clock, and guests can purchase cappuccino in the morning. Upstairs, the rooms look like they haven't been redecorated since the 1950s, but they're roomy and bright. Guests receive a 10% discount at the trattoria next door, the Opera Prima.

Hotel Pavone. V. Dandolo 2, 20122 Milano. ☎ **02/55-19-21-33.** Fax 02/55-19-24-21. 24 rms, 21 with bath or shower. TV TEL. 90,000L ($59.20) single; 140,000L ($92.10) double; 189,000L ($124.35) triple. AE, MC, V. Tram: 12.

Just off the Corso Vittoria, about a 15-minute walk east of the Duomo, the Pavone is a no-frills establishment geared to business travelers (Linate, Milan's domestic airport, is only 10 minutes away by bus). Rooms are a bit Spartan, with gray tile floors and Scandinavian-style furniture, but perfectly adequate and quiet. Many are outfitted as triples and are large enough to accommodate an extra bed, making this a fine choice for families.

Hotel Rovello. V. Rovello 18, 20121 Milano. ☎ **02/86-46-46-54.** Fax 02/72-02-36-56. 10 rms, all with bath or shower. TV TEL. 160,000L ($105.25) single or double. AE, MC, V. Metro: Cordusio.

What was once a bare-bones budget hotel without much going for it except a great location near the Duomo has recently been beautifully refurbished. In the large guest rooms, handsome contemporary Italian furnishings are set off by gleaming hardwood floors and exposed timbers, and many have large dressing areas. Since the management has yet to raise prices commensurate with the level of comfort, this is really quite a bargain.

DOUBLES FOR LESS THAN 210,000 LIRE ($138.15)

Ariosto Hotel. V. Ariosto 22, 20145 Milano. ☎ **02/48-17-844.** Fax 02/49-80-516. 53 rms, all with bath. A/C MINIBAR TV TEL. 145,000L ($95.40) single; 208,000L ($136.85) double. Breakfast 14,000L ($9.20). AE, MC, V. Metro: Conciliazione.

Tucked away in a residential neighborhood of apartment houses and old villas near the Santa Maria della Grazie church, the Ariosto is a refreshingly quiet retreat—all the more so because many of the newly refurbished rooms, cheerfully decorated with blue fabrics and handsome white contemporary furnishings, face a private garden. Many of the doubles have separate dressing areas off the bathroom, and the best open onto balconies overlooking the garden.

Hotel Promessi Sposi. Pz. Oberdan 12, 20129 Milano. ☎ **02/29-51-36-61.** Fax 02/29-40-41-82. 40 rms, all with bath. TV. 120,000L–140,000L ($78.95–$92.10) single; 180,000L–220,000L ($118.45–$144.75) double; 222,000L–250,000L ($144.75–$164.50) triple. (Rates at the high end of the range reflect trade-fair periods). AE, MC, V. Metro: Porto Venezia.

Travelers often find their way to this rambling hotel, on a sunny corner across from the public gardens, on the recommendation of former guests who tend to crow about the friendly service and unusually pleasant accommodations. Downstairs, there's a cheerful lobby and bar area furnished with multicolored couches. Upstairs, the spacious rooms are airily decorated with rattan furniture and nicely equipped with amenities that include modern baths. The name, which translates as "the Fiancee," is a reference to the 19th-century masterpiece by the Lombardian novelist Manzoni.

Hotel Star. V. d. Bossi 5, 20121 Milano. ☎ **02/80-15-01.** Fax 02/86-17-87. 30 rms, all with bath or shower. A/C MINIBAR TV TEL. 135,000L ($88.80) single, 208,000L ($136.85) double. Rates include breakfast. AE, MC, V. Metro: Cordusio or Duomo.

These homey, old-fashioned lodgings near the Duomo couldn't be more conveniently located, but they are blessedly quiet—rooms face either an interior courtyard or a narrow street that's closed to through traffic. While decor's a bit dowdy, the rooms are unusually spacious and some have small balconies. The pleasant bar off the lobby is a fine place to put your feet up after a day of sightseeing, and a hearty buffet breakfast, included in the price of the room, is served in an adjoining lounge.

WORTH A SPLURGE

Doriagrande Hotel. Vle. Andrea Doria 22, 20124 Milano. ☎ **02/66-96-696.** Fax 02/
66-96-669. 112 rms, all with bath. A/C MINIBAR TV TEL. Special rate (see below) 240,000L
($157.90) single or double. Rates include breakfast. Metro: Loreto or Stazione Centrale.

This luxury hotel offers a special price that applies to weekends (Friday and Saturday nights), to most of August, and the Christmas/New Year holiday (check for exact dates before booking). For an especially comfortable stay in Milan, you may well
want to plan your visit to coincide with one of these periods when the hotel offers
the special rate above. The Doriagrande is one of the large newer hotels that cluster
around the station and is far more comfortable and stylish than most hotels in its
luxury class. The oversized guest rooms are exquisitely appointed with handsome
wood and marble furniture, fabric wall coverings, and beautiful marble baths, and
they come with such amenities as linen sheets, complimentary bedroom slippers and
bathrobes, and a sumptuous buffet breakfast.

WHERE TO DINE

Milan, of course, has its trademark dishes, most notable among them risotto alla
milanese, that wonderful rice dish with just a hint of saffron, and costoletta alla
milanese, the breaded veal chop that is Milan's answer to Wiener schnitzel and
began appearing on Milanese tables around the time of the Austrian occupation.
Kitchens in Milan also embrace the best of Italian regional cooking and make a generous nod to other European cuisines as well. In short, you can eat well and
adventurously in Milan, and while you can spend a lot dining here, you don't have
to. For one thing, geared to business as their city is, Milanese are more willing than
Italians elsewhere to break the sit-down-meal tradition and grab a sandwich or other
light fare on the run, and there are plenty of places where you can do so. And with
so many students and young professionals underfoot, Milan has no shortage of
pizzerias and other low-cost eateries.

MEALS FOR LESS THAN 15,000 LIRE ($9.85)

Brek. V. Lepetit, 20. ☎ **02/67-05-149.** Antipasto and pasta from 5,000L ($3.30), main
courses 7,000L–10,000L ($4.60–$6.60). Mon–Sat, 11:30am–3pm and 6:30pm–10:30pm.
Metro: Stazione Centrale. CAFETERIA.

This outlet of a popular cafeteria chain is not to be dismissed too quickly—the food
(of a straightforward pasta-and-tomato-sauce and veal-cutlet variety, with very good
roasted meats) is excellent, behind-the-counter service is friendly and helpful, and the
country-style decor is homey and pleasant.

Luini. V. Santa Radegonda 16. ☎ **02/80-69-18.** Panzerotto 4,000L ($2.65). Closed Sun and
Mon. Metro: Duomo. SNACKS.

At this stand-up counter near the Galleria, you'll have to elbow your way through a
throng of well-dressed people to purchase the specialite de la maison—panzerotto,
a pocket of pizza crust stuffed with cheese and tomato. You can also nab a panino
and other easily portable fare here.

Pizzeria Grand'Italia. V. Palermo 5. ☎ **02/87-77-59.** Pizza from 6,000L ($3.95). Wed–Mon,
12:15pm–2:45pm and 7pm–1:15am. Closed Tues (except in Aug). Metro: Cadorna. PIZZA/PASTA.

What seems like Milan's most popular restaurant serves a huge assortment of salads,
pizzas, pastas, and focaccia bread stuffed with cheese, mushrooms, and other fillings.
The late hours make this a prime night spot, and it's a heck of a lot of fun to watch
the chic young Milanese strutting their stuff.

Trattoria Sasa. V. Pergolesi 21. ☎ **02/66-92-674.** Pizza 7,000L–10,000L ($4.60–$6.60).
AE, MC, V. Daily, noon–3pm and 6pm–2am. Metro: Stazione Centrale. PIZZA.

This cozy family-run restaurant will go a long way toward convincing you that Milan
is really just a small town at heart. The pizza is superb, and it's accompanied by
carafes of a really decent house wine. Sasa is close enough to the train station to make
this a nice spot for a last meal before boarding a night train out of town.

Meals for Less than 20,000 Lire ($13.15)

Latteria Unione. V. Unione 6. ☎ **02/87-44-01.** Antipasto, pasta, and salads, from 5,000L
($3.30), main courses 7,000L–12,000L ($4.60–$7.90). No credit cards. Mon–Sat, 11:30am–
3:30pm. Metro: Missori. VEGETARIAN.

The main business here is dispensing milk and eggs to a press of neighborhood shoppers, but at lunchtime a crowd packs in for delicious, largely vegetarian fare. The
minestrone is delicious, as are the umpteen variations of risotto.

Rosticceria Peck. V. Cantu 3. ☎ **02/86-93-017.** Main courses from 7,000L–12,000L ($4.60–
$7.90). AE, MC, V. Tue–Fri, 8:45am–2:30pm and 4pm–7:30pm; Sat, 8am–1:15pm and 3:45pm–
7:30pm; Sun, 8am–1pm. DELI.

Milan's most famous food emporium offers a wonderful selection of roast veal,
porchetta, cheeses, pastries, and other fare from its exquisite larder in this natty
snack bar adjoining its collection of shops. Of course, you can also wander through
Peck's food halls to equip yourself amply for a picnic or hotel-room dinner. Metro:
Duomo.

Trattoria da Bruno. V. Bronzetti 1. ☎ **02/73-00-29.** Antipasto and pasta from 7,000L
($4.60), main courses from 9,000L–15,000L ($5.90–$9.85). No credit cards. Mon–Sat, noon–
2pm and 7pm–11pm. Tram: 60. MILANESE.

It's well worth the trek out to this attractive, family-run place, just off the Corso
Indipendenza about a 15-minute walk east of the Duomo. The soups here are delicious and fortifying and can be followed by costoletta Milanese and other straightforward main courses, which often include a selection of fresh fish. Bruno usually
offers a fixed-priced menu consisting of the freshest ingredients he has in the kitchen
that day, at a price that rarely edges over the 20,000L ($13.15) mark.

Meals for Less than 35,000 Lire ($23.05)

Ristorante Familiare della Cimbraccola. V. San Tomaso 8. ☎ **02/86-92-250.** Fixed menu,
wine included, 30,000L ($19.75). MC, V. Mon–Sat, 12:30pm–3pm and 7pm–10:30pm. Closed
Sun. Metro: Duomo. NORTHERN ITALIAN.

One of the best bargain meals in Milan is accompanied by vats of the house wine and
the antics of loquacious host Stefanini Arnaldo, who provides one of the best shows
in Milan as he scurries around the crowded, busy room and shouts back and forth
to the kitchen. The fare here doesn't get much fancier than pasta with meat sauce
and veal scaloppine, but it's good and served in copious portions.

Ristorante Versilia. Vle. Andrea Doria 44. ☎ **02/67-04-187.** Antipasto and pasta, from
8,000L ($5.25), main courses, 9,000L–16,000L ($5.90–$10.55). MC, V. Mon–Sat, noon–2:30pm
and 7–10pm. Closed Sat evening and Sun. Metro: Loreto. NORTHERN ITALIAN.

The white tiles and high-tech lighting suggest this single room between the station
and Corso Buenos Aires has more pretensions than it does. It's just a friendly,
family-run eatery that serves the surrounding neighborhood with excellent food
and attentive service. The risottos are superb, and daily specials often include a
wide selection of seafood.

PASTRY & GELATO

A chair can be a welcome sight after hours of walking in Milan, and the nicer the surroundings the better. **Pasticceria Marchesi,** V. Santa Maria alla Porta 13, is a distinguished tea shop only steps from the church of Santa Maria delle Grazie, making it a handy spot in which to dash off postcards of the *Last Supper.* The most elegant teashop in Milan is **Pasticceria Confetteria Cova,** nearing its 200th year in refined surroundings at V. Montenapoleone 8, near the similarly atmospheric Museo Poldi-Pezzoli. Enjoying a gelato on the steps of the Duomo seems to be Milan's favorite pastime. You can equip yourself for this activity at **Alemagna,** on the Piazza del Duomo, or the nearby **Passerini,** V. Hugo 4. **Zucca,** better known as the Camparino, is the most attractive of the many bars in the Galleria; the drink of choice here, of course, is Campari, to be enjoyed at your leisure while watching the crowds and soaking in the fin de siecle decor.

MILANO AFTER DARK

On Wednesdays and Thursdays Milan's newspapers tend to devote a lot of ink to club schedules and cultural events. If you don't trust your command of Italian to plan your nightlife, check out the tourist office in Piazza Duomo—there are usually piles of fliers announcing upcoming events lying about.

THE PERFORMING ARTS

In addition to opera and concerts, if you understand Italian you may want to go to a performance at the **Piccolo Teatro,** V. Rovello 2 (☎ **02/72-33-32-22**), known for its avant-garde productions.

Teatro alla Scala. Pz. d. Scala. ☎ **02/80-70-41** for information, 02/80-91-26 for reservations. Tickets 35,000L–270,000L ($23.10–$178.20).

La Scala's season opens December 7 and runs into July. Although it's very difficult to get tickets, a few seats, often in the gallery beneath the rafters, are sometimes available on the day of performance for those willing to wait in line at the box office. (See above also, under "What to See & Do.")

Conservatorio. V. d. Conservatoria 12. ☎ **02/76-00-17-55.** Tickets 25,000L–60,000L ($15.75–$39.60). Metro: San Babila.

This is Milan's major venue for classical music. A year-round schedule of classical concerts is presented here.

BARS & CLUBS

The Navigli and Ticinese neighborhoods are currently on the ascent, with many bars and cafes to serve a younger crowd.

Bar Magenta. V. Carducci 13. ☎ **02/80-53-808.** Tue–Sun, 7pm–3am. Metro: San Ambrogio.

The favorite haunt of models is busy from the moment the doors open well into the wee hours.

Capolinea. V. Lodovico il Moro 119. ☎ **02/89-12-20-24.** Cover 15,000L ($9.85) includes 1 drink. Tue–Sun, 8pm–2am. Metro: Porta Genova.

The best place in Milan to hear jazz attracts international performers and a heady mix of international clientele and students.

Nuovo Idea. V. de Castilla 30. ☎ **02/69-00-78-59.** Cover 20,000L ($13.15) includes 1 drink. Thur–Sun, evenings. Metro: Gioia.

Milan and Italy's largest gay club attracts a mostly male crowd of all ages and offers them everything from disco music to polkas.

Rolling Stone. Cor. XXII Marzo 32. No listed phone. Cover 12,000L–25,000L ($7.90–$16.44), depending on who's performing. Thur–Sun, until 3am. Tram: 12.

Milan's most popular club leans heavily toward rock, with an attendant crowd that is young, hip, and willing to wait outside to get in.

DAY TRIPS FROM MILAN
PAVIA & THE CERTOSA

At one time this quiet and remarkably well-preserved little city, 22 miles south of Milan, was more powerful than Milan. It was the capital of Lombardy in the 7th and 8th centuries, which explains why Charlemagne's coronation took place here. By the early Renaissance, the Viscontis and later the Sforzas, the two families who so influenced the history of Milan and all of Lombardy, were wielding their power here. It was they who made Pavia's university one of Europe's great centers of learning, and under them the Duomo (with the third largest dome in Italy) began to rise in 1488.

Essentials

GETTING THERE   By Train   Trains arrive every half hour from Milan (half an hour); most stop at the Certosa before reaching the main station in Pavia.

By Car   Via autostrada A7 or the slower S35.

VISITOR INFORMATION   The **APT tourist office** is near the train station at V. Fabio Filzi 2 (☎ **0382/22-156**); Monday to Saturday, 8:30am to 12:30pm and 2pm to 6pm.

What to See & Do

Leonardo and Bramante were among the many architects of the redbrick **Duomo,** which wasn't completed until the 1930s—just in time, relatively speaking, for the adjoining Torre Civica to collapse in 1989, taking part of the Duomo with it. The Duomo is open daily from 8am until noon and from 3 to 6pm.

The **Chiesa di San Michele** was the site of Charlemagne's coronation as emperor in 774, but the present, medieval-looking structure is a 12th-century reconstruction necessitated by an earthquake that leveled its predecessor. It's open daily from 8am until noon and from 3 to 6pm.

The **Castello Visconti,** entered from Piazza Castello, was one of the favorite haunts of Ludivico il Moro and Beatrice d'Este, Lombardy's giddily happy but ill-fated Renaissance couple (see Castello Sforzesco in Milan, above). The courtyards and salons where they played now house a fine collection of sculpture and painting. Admission is 5,000L ($3.29); open hours are Tuesday to Saturday from 9am to 1:30pm, Sunday from 9am to 12:30 pm; closed Monday.

The Certosa. Vle. Certosa. ☎ **0382/92-56-13.** Free admission. Tue–Sun, 9am–11:30pm and 2:30pm–6pm (until 4:30pm Nov–Feb and 5:30pm Sept, Oct, Mar, and Apr). Closed Mon. Trains from Milan usually stop at the station near the Certosa, just before the main Pavia station. From Pavia, buses from the Autocorriere station (next to the train station) make the 10-minute trip every half hour (there's a long walk up the Vle. Certosa from the bus stop).

One of the most grandiose buildings in Lombardy, if not in Italy, is this mausoleum of the Visconti family. The facade of colored marbles, the frescoed interior, and the riot of funerary sculpture provide yet more evidence that this brood of blockheaded tyrants were also dedicated builders with grand schemes and large coffers (they were also, remember, responsible for the Duomo and the castello in Milan). Among the finest and most acclaimed tombs is that of Ludivico il Moro and Beatrice d'Este, though their presence here is a twist of fate—the couple would lie together for eternity near the *Last Supper* in Milan's Chiesa di Santa Maria della Grazie if the monks there had not sold the tomb to the Certosa to raise funds.

The monks who inhabit the monastery adjoining the Certosa lead animated tours in Italian, and in other ways are much in evidence on the grounds. It is possible to visit their refectory and an adjoining shop, where they sell their Chartreuse liqueur and herbal soaps and scents.

En Route to Cremona—Lodi

A pleasant stop between Milan and Cremona is Lodi, about halfway between the two. (Depending on your route, you'll have to make a slight detour south from S415 or north from A1.) Just off the arcaded piazza is the **Church of the Incoronata,** with a delightful octagonal interior frescoed by Ambrogio Bergognone. The frescoes in another church, **San Bastiano** in the adjoining hamlet of Lodi Vecchio, are much less accomplished but enchanting nonetheless—they depict scenes from the farming lives of the 14th-century peasants the church was built to serve.

CREMONA

Violins have been drawing visitors to this little city on the river Po, 57 miles southeast of Milan, since the 17th century, when fine string instruments began emerging from the workshops of Nicolo Amati and his more-famous protégé, Antonio Stradivari. The tradition continues: Cremona's Scuola di Luteria (Violin School) is world renowned.

Essentials

GETTING THERE   By Train   Trains arrive almost hourly from Milan (1¼ hours). There are also 16 trains a day to Mantua (1 hour), so you can make a stop in Cremona enroute from Milan to Mantua. Hourly trains to Brescia (¾ hour) also make it possible to combine an excursion from Milan to Cremona and Brescia.

By Car   S415 is the most direct route, though A1 from Milan to Piacenza and A21 from Piacenza to Cremona is speedier.

VISITOR INFORMATION   The **APT tourist office** is near the Duomo at Pz. del Commune 5 (☎ **0372/23-233);** Monday to Saturday from 9:30am to 12:30pm and 3 to 6pm, Sunday from 10am until noon.

What to See & Do

The Museo Stradivariano, V. Palestro 17, displays the finest violins ever made. The admission of 5,000L ($3.29) includes entrance to the Palazzo Communale and other museums around town. Hours are Tuesday to Saturday from 8:30am to 5:45pm, Sunday from 9:15am to 12:15pm and 3 to 6pm.

Cremona's charms extend far beyond the musical. Its central Piazza del Commune is one of the largest and most beautiful town squares in Italy, fronted by remarkable structures. Among these is the 12th-century **Duomo,** clad in pink marble and overshadowed by Italy's tallest campanile; inside, it is covered with 16th-century frescoes. Admission is free and hours are Monday to Saturday from 7am until noon and 3 to 7pm, Sunday from 7am to 1pm and 3:30 to 7pm.

Nearby, the **Palazzo del Commune** rises gracefully above a gothic arcade and is embellished with terracotta panels. Its Saletta dei Violini displays another collection of violins. Admission, 5,000L ($3.29), includes admission to the Museo Stradivariano and other museums around town; hours are Tuesday to Saturday from 8:30am to 6pm, Sunday from 9am to 12:15pm and 3 to 6pm.

BRESCIA

Ringed by industrialized suburbs, Brescia does not readily beckon travelers to stop. Those who do, however, have the pleasure of wandering through a centuries-old town center where Roman ruins, not one but two duomos, and medieval palazzi line winding streets and gracious piazzas.

Essentials

GETTING THERE **By Train** Trains arrive from Milan about every half hour (1 hour). Brescia is on the main Milan-Verona-Venice route, so you can arrange a stopover en route from Milan to those places. You can also arrange a stopover in Brescia while en route from Milan to Mantua.

By Car Brescia is linked to Milan by the A4 autostrada, which continues east to Verona and Venice.

VISITOR INFORMATION The **APT tourist office** is at Cor. Zanardelli 34 (☎ 030/43-44-18); open Monday to Friday from 9am to 12:30pm and 3 to 6pm, Saturday from 9am to 12:30pm.

What to See & Do

The two duomos, the 17th- to 19th-century **Duomo Nuovo** and the much more charming 11th- to 12th-century **Duomo Vecchio** (also called Rotonda, for its shape), more or less fill the Piazza Duomo. The new duomo is open daily from 8am to 7:30pm; the old duomo April through September, Thursday to Tuesday from 9am to noon and 3 to 7pm. Brescia's Roman past emerges from the columns and other remains of the Capitolino, a temple erected in A.D. 73, and additional artifacts, including the famous first-century bronze Victory of Brescia, are on display at the adjoining **Museo Romano,** V. Musei 7 (☎ 030/46-031). Admission is 5,000L ($3.30); hours are Tuesday to Friday from 10am to 12:30pm and 3 to 5pm.

A few steps down the street and through the centuries bring you to the **Monasterio di San Salvatore e Santa Giulia,** where Charlemagne's ex-wife Ermengarde spent her last days. The museum is at V. Musei 81 (☎ 030/44-327); admission 5,000L ($3.30), hours Monday to Friday from 10am to 12:30pm and 3 to 6pm; on Saturday and Sunday the museum closes at 7pm.

Brescia's most enchanting building is its medieval town hall, the **Broletto,** Vc. Sant'Agostino 29. The city's prettiest square is the Piazza della Loggia, where the Torre dell'Orlogio, resembling the campanile on Piazza San Marco in Venice, bespeaks the days when Brescia was a Venetian stronghold. Brescia has a fine painting collection, the **Pinacoteca Tosio-Matinengo,** Pz. Moretto 4 (☎ 030/59-120), where works by Moretto, Foppa, and other painters of the school of Brescia hang alongside Raphaels and Tintorettos. Admission is 5,000L ($3.30), and it's open Tuesday to Friday from 9am to 12:30pm and 3 to 5pm; closed from Saturday to Monday.

2 Bergamo

47km (28 miles) from Milan, 52km (31 miles) from Brescia

Bergamo is two cities. Bergamo Basso, the lower, modern city, concerns itself with everyday business. Bergamo Alta, a beautiful Renaissance town perched on a green hill, concerns itself with entertaining the visitors who come to admire its piazzas and monuments and enjoy the lovely vistas from its belvederes.

ESSENTIALS

GETTING THERE **By Train** Trains from Milan arrive every hour (1 hour), from Brescia even more frequently (1 hour). The train station is in Citta Bassa; take bus nos. 1 or 3 to the funicular and make the free transfer for the ascent up the hill to the Citta Alta. Given the frequency of train service, you can easily make a daylong sightseeing loop from Milan, arriving in Bergamo in the morning, moving on to Brescia in the afternoon, and returning to Milan from there.

By Car   Bergamo is linked directly to Milan via the A4 autostrada, which continues east to Brescia, Verona, and Venice. Parking in or near the Citta Alta, most of which is closed to traffic, can be nightmarish. Try to leave your car down below and take the funicular up.

VISITOR INFORMATION   The **APT tourist office** is near the train station at Papa Giovanni XXIII 106 (☎ **035/24-22-26**), open Monday to Friday from 9am to 12:30pm and 3 to 6:30pm. There is a branch in the Citta Alta at Vc. Aquila Nera 2 (☎ **035/23-27-30**), open daily the same hours.

WHAT TO SEE & DO

Chiesa di Santa Maria Maggiore. Pz. d. Duomo. Free admission. 8am–noon and 3pm–6pm. Capella Colleoni: Free admission. Mar–Oct, Tue–Sun, 9am–noon and 2pm–6:30pm; Nov–Feb, Tue–Sun, 9am–noon and 2:30pm–4:30pm.

Behind the stunning marble facade lies an interior covered with frescoes and Renaissance tapestries. The finest works here are the choir stalls, designed by Lorenzo Lotto, a Venetian who worked in Bergamo during the 1520s. Another Venetian lies in the adjoining Cappella Colleoni, beneath frescoes by Tiepolo. You may have encountered Signore Colleoni before, astride the famous Verrocchio equestrian bronze in Venice; the much-honored soldier ruled Bergamo for the Venetian republic, and he rests here in an elaborate marble tomb near his daughter.

Galleria dell'Accademia Carrara. Pz. dell'Accademia. ☎ **035/39-96-43.** Admission 3,000L ($2), free on Sun. Wed–Mon, 9:30am–12:30pm and 2:30pm–5:30pm. Closed Tues.

A walk down the monumental staircase that links Bergamo Alta with Bergamo Bassa brings you to the city's exquisite art gallery, one of the finest in Italy. It is worth noting that a young Bernard Berenson, the 20th century's most noted connoisseur of art, wandered through these same galleries taking stock of what was here, and the inventory remains staggering: Bellini, Canaletto, Carpaccio, Guardi, Mantegna, and Tiepolo are all represented in the salons of a neoclassical palace.

Museo Donizettiano. V. Arena 4. ☎ **035/39-969.** Free admission. Mon–Fri, 9am–noon and 2:30pm–6pm. Closed Sat–Sun.

This charming little museum commemorates Gaetano Donizetti, who was born in Bergamo in 1797 and—little wonder given the romance of his boyhood surroundings—became one of Italy's most acclaimed composers of opera. Fans can swoon over his sheet music, piano, and other memorabilia, and thus inspired, make the pilgrimage to the humble house where he claimed to have been born in a cellar, the Casa Nateledi Gaetano Donizetti, at V. Borgo Canale 14.

Piazza Vecchia.

Life in Bergamo's Citta Alta revolves around this lovely piazza, considered to be one of the most beautiful squares in Italy with its 18th-century fountain and remarkable assemblage of medieval and Renaissance buildings. Many of the town's cafes and bars are here, as are many of its sights: the Chiesa di Santa Maria Maggiore and the Cappella Colleoni, the Duomo, the white-marble Biblioteca Civica, and the romantic-looking, 12th-century Palazzo della Ragione and its Torre del Commune.

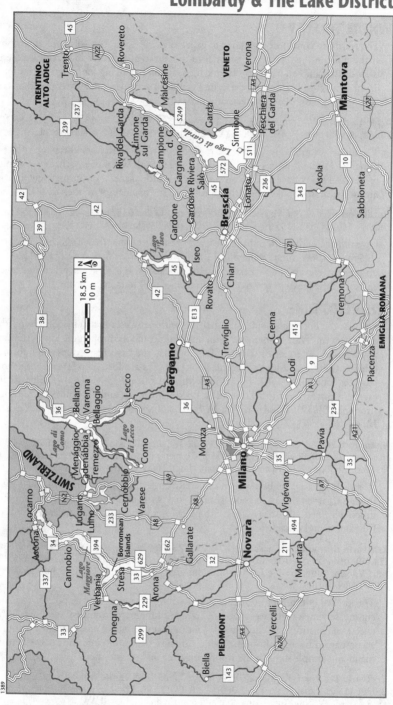

WHERE TO STAY

The reason to come to Bergamo is to experience the Citta Alta—if there's no room at the inns up there (and it's essential to call ahead and reserve to make sure there is), visit Bergamo on a day trip from Milan. If you're looking for budget accommodations, forget it. Fortunately, there are a couple of very nice, moderately priced places to stay amid the charming streets and piazzas.

Agnello d'Oro. V. Gombito 22, 24100 Bergamo. ☎ **035/24-98-83.** Fax 035/23-56-12. 20 rms, all with bath. TV TEL. 55,000L ($36.20) single; 95,000L ($62.50) double. AE, MC, V.

The inn of your dreams is in the heart of the old town. Perfectly in keeping with the romantic location, rooms are prettily decorated with warm color schemes and old prints, and many have balconies overlooking a little piazza. Not surprisingly, this is one of the most popular hostelries in town, so it's mandatory to reserve.

Hotel Gourmet. V. San Vigilio 1, 24129 Bergamo. ☎/fax **035/43-73-04.** 11 rms, all with bath. TV TEL. 85,000L ($55.90) single; 120,000L ($78.95) double. AE, MC, V.

Given their location just outside the walls of the Citta Alta, these large and comfortable rooms above a restaurant afford wonderful views over hills and valleys. They fill up quickly, especially on weekends with Milanese who bask in the peace and quiet and take their meals in the excellent (and expensive) restaurant downstairs.

WHERE TO DINE

Polenta, the flour-based side dish that vies with pasta as a first course in the north, appears in full force on Bergamo's menus. Your gambols through the Citta Alta can also be nicely interspersed with fortifying stops at the city's many cafes and informal eateries. Caffe del Tasso, Pz. Vecchia 3, began life as a tailor's shop 500 years ago and has been a bar since 1581. Forno Tresoldi, V. Colleoni 13, generously disperses its excellent pizzas and foccacia breads topped with meats and vegetables by the slice (from 3,000L/$2), Tuesday to Sunday from 8am to 1:30pm and 4 to 8pm; it's closed Monday.

Ristorante Sole. V. Colleoni 1. ☎ **035/21-82-38.** Antipasto and pasta, from 7,000L ($4.60); main courses 10,000L–20,000L ($6.60–$13.15); menu turistica 30,000L ($19.75). AE, MC, V. Fri–Wed, 12:30pm–2:30pm and 7pm–10pm, closed Thurs. NORTHERN ITALIAN.

It is difficult to dine better in more charming surroundings in Bergamo—on a romantic garden terrace in good weather, in a cozily decorated dining room at other times. The menu turistica comes with pasta (or a wonderful house polenta), meat or fish course, and dessert.

Trattoria Bernabo. V. Colleoni 31. ☎ **035/23-76-92.** Antipasto and pasta from 7,000L ($4.60), main courses 10,000L–20,000L ($6.60–$13.15); menu turistica 15,000L ($91.85). MC, V. Sept–June, Fri–Wed, noon–2:30pm and 7pm–midnight; closed July and Aug. NORTHERN ITALIAN.

The kitchen of this sophisticated, vaulted-ceiling restaurant elevates polenta to haute cuisine, serving it with hearty sausage, local mushrooms, or strands of creamy taleggio cheese to constitute an entire meal. You can sample one of these artistic creations, accompanied by a salad, on the menu turistica, or venture into the large à la carte menu and sample some of the wonderful pasta and meat dishes.

Trattoria Tre Torri. Pz. Mercato d. Fieno 7a. ☎ **035/24-43-66.** Antipasto and pasta from 8,000L ($5.25), main courses 12,000L–22,000L ($7.90–$14.45); menu turistica 30,000L ($19.75). MC, V. Thur–Tue, 10am–3pm and 6pm–midnight. Closed Wed.

The menu and service are more comforting than the somewhat stuffy and cramped surroundings would suggest; the best seats in the house are at the few tables brought out onto the street in good weather. While the ravioli and other stuffed pastas constitute a meal in themselves, the fixed menu may well tempt you to indulge.

3 Mantua (Mantova)

158km (95 miles) east of Milan, 62km (37 miles) north of Parma, 150km (90 miles) southwest of Venice

One of Lombardy's finest towns is in the farthest reaches of the region, making it a logical addition to a trip to Venice or Parma as well as to Milan. Like its neighboring cities in Emilia-Romagna, Mantua owes its past greatness and its beautiful Renaissance monuments to one family, in this case the Gonzagas. You'll encounter them in the massive Palazzo Ducale that dominates much of the town center, in their refreshing suburban retreat, the Palazzo Tei, and in the churches and piazzas that grew up around their court. One of Mantua's greatest charms is its location—on a meandering river, the Mincio, which widens here to envelop Mantua in a necklace of moodily romantic lakes.

ESSENTIALS

GETTING THERE   **By Train**   Trains arrive from Milan, via Brescia, nine times a day (2 hours) and from Verona (with connections to Venice) 11 times a day (40 minutes). There are also hourly trains from Cremona (1 hour), making it easy to visit that city en route to and from Milan.

By Car   The speediest connections from Milan are via the autostradas, the A4 to Verona and the A22 from Verona to Mantua. From Mantua it is also an easy drive south to Parma and other cities in Emilia-Romagna, on S420.

VISITOR INFORMATION   The **APT tourist office** is at Pz. Mantegna 6 (☎ **0376/32-82-54**); Monday to Saturday, 9am to noon and 3pm to 6pm, Sunday, 9am to noon.

WHAT TO SEE & DO

Chiesa Sant'Andrea. Pz. Mantegna. Daily 7:30am–noon and 3:30pm–7:30pm.

Mantegna, the Gonzaga court painter, is buried here and the crypt houses a reliquary containing the blood of Christ, but this 15th-century church is best known for its often-imitated facade. The architect, Leon Battista Alberti, fronted his cleanly classical building with what are considered to be the most graceful arches of the Renaissance, and they can be comfortably admired from a cafe in the Piazza Mantegna.

Palazzo Ducale. Pz. Sordello. ☎ **0376/32-02-83.** Admission 12,000L ($7.90), by guided tour (in Italian only). Daily 9am–1pm and 2:30pm–6pm; Mon 9am–1pm only.

Behind the walls of this massive, 500-room fortress-cum-palazzo lies the history of the Gonzagas, Mantua's most powerful family, and what remains of the treasure trove they amassed in a rule that began in 1328 and lasted well into the 17th century. Between their skills as warriors and their penchant for marrying into wealthier and more cultured houses, the Gonzagas managed to amass power, money, and an artistic following that included Pisanello, Titian, and most notably, Andrea Mantegna. The most fortunate of these unions was that of Francesco Gonzaga to Isabelle d'Este in 1490. This well-bred daughter of Ferrara's Este clan (and sister of Beatrice, who accomplished so much when she married into Milan's ruling dynasty) outfitted many of the frescoed and art-filled apartments you see today, including the Camera degli Sposi—the masterpiece, and only remaining fresco cycle, of Andrea Mantegna. More curious today, but less rewarding artistically, are the low-ceiling apartments of the dwarfs, who were part of Isabella's court.

Palazzo Te. Vle. Te. ☎ **0376/32-32-66.** Admission 12,000L ($7.90). Tue–Sun, 9am–6pm. Closed Mon.

Frederico Gonzaga, the refined and pleasure-loving son of Isabella D'Este, built this splendid Mannerist palace as a retreat from court life. Throughout the lovely, whimsical interior, sexually frank frescoes depicting Psyche and other erotically charged subject matter make unsubtle reference to one of Frederico's favorite pastimes. The greatest and most playful achievement here, though, has to do with power: In the Sala dei Giganti (Room of the Giants), Titan is overthrown by the gods in a dizzying play of architectural proportion that gives the illusion the ceiling is falling, along with the subject matter. The palazzo is a 20-minute walk from the center of town. En route, devotees of Mantua's most famous painter may choose to stop for a look at the Casa di Mantegna at V. Acerbi 47; admission is free and it's open daily from 10am to 12:30pm and 3 to 6pm (hours vary).

Piazza Broletto and Piazza delle Erbe

Mantua's squares open one into another, creating for walkers in the city the wonderful illusion that they are strolling through a series of opera sets. Aside from the Renaissance palazzi that surround these handsomely proportioned spaces, they are also graced with landmarks testifying to Mantua's long history: The **statue of Virgil** in the Piazza Broletto commemorates the poet, who was born near here in 70 B.C. and celebrated Mantua's river Mincio in his *Bucolics.* The Piazza delle Erbe opens on one end to the city's earliest church, the 11th-century **Rotonda di San Lorenzo.**

WHERE TO STAY

If you're interested in the lowest-priced accommodations, the tourist office can provide information and make reservations for rooms at five hostel-like farmhouses in the surrounding countryside. Rates are low, about 20,000L ($13.15) a person. Since several of the properties are within a few kilometers of town, you can reach them without too much trouble by bike or combination bus ride and trek.

A DOUBLE FOR LESS THAN 120,000 LIRE ($78.95)

Hotel ABC Moderno. Pz. Don Leoni 25, 46100 Mantova. ☎/fax **0376/32-50-02.** 31 rms, all with bath. 70,000L ($46.05) single, 115,000L ($75.65) double. MC, V.

A recent renovation has spruced up this hotel across from the train station considerably, but the prices are still remarkably low, considering such amenities as private baths and free breakfast. If the Moderno is full, bypass the other dumps nearby and check out the places below.

DOUBLES FOR LESS THAN 145,000 LIRE ($95.40)

Hotel Broletto. V. Accademia 1, 46100 Mantova. ☎ **0376/32-67-84.** Fax 0376/22-12-97. 16 rms, all with bath. A/C MINIBAR TEL TV. 90,000L ($59.20) single; 135,000L ($88.80) double. Breakfast 12,000L ($7.90). AE, MC, V.

Except for some beautiful wood-beamed ceilings, you won't find much evidence of the building's 16th-century origins in the tidy, tile-floored guest rooms here. But they are comfortably equipped and have new baths—and the wonderful location right in the center of town makes this a fine base for late-night strolls through the city's moonlit piazzas.

Hotel Mantegna. V. Fabio Filzi 10, 46100 Mantova. ☎ **0376/32-80-19.** Fax 0376/ 36-85-64. 39 rms, all with bath. A/C TEL TV. 95,000L ($62.50) single; 140,000L ($92.10) double. Breakfast 13,000L ($8.55). AE, MC, V.

On a quiet side street just a few steps south of the centro storico, the Mantegna offers solid comfort in surroundings that, despite associations the name of Mantua's most famous painter might summon, are thoroughly modern. The cozy narrow singles resemble ships' cabins, and the doubles are unusually roomy. All have been renovated within the past few years and have new baths, and many face a sunny and quiet courtyard. There's free parking behind the hotel.

WORTH A SPLURGE

Albergo San Lorenzo. Pz. Concordia 14, 46100 Mantova. ☎ **0376/22-05-00.** Fax 0376/ 32-71-94. 41 rms and suites, all with bath. A/C MINIBAR TEL TV. 215,000L ($141.45) single; 250,000L ($164.45) double. Breakfast included. AE, MC, V.

Mantua's best hotel has been fashioned out of a row of old houses and is every bit as charming and romantic as the piazzas and monuments that surround it. Oil paintings and oriental carpets grace the marble-floored salons, and the guest rooms, no two of which are alike, are furnished with exquisite 19th-century antiques and equipped with elegant baths and the other conveniences you would expect from a luxury hotel. A panoramic roof terrace overlooks the towers and rooftops of the centro storico.

WHERE TO DINE

Despite the fact that the most famous local dish is *stracotto di asino* (donkey stew), Mantovian cuisine can also be quite refined—exquisite risotto dishes, an array of pastas stuffed with pumpkin and squash, and given the proximity of lakes and rivers, a fine selection of fish appear on menus.

MEALS FOR LESS THAN 10,000 LIRE ($6.60)

Pescheria Lanfranchi. V. Pescherie. No listed phone. Main courses 4,000L ($2.65). Mon–Sat, 8:30am–1pm and 4:30pm–7:30pm. Closed Mon afternoons and Sun. SEAFOOD.

There's no end to the creatures, most of them deep-fried, you can purchase at this fish stall on wheels that's parked south of the centro storico near the banks of a scenic canal. A plate of squid, octopus, or lake fish makes a fine light meal or snack.

MEALS FOR LESS THAN 25,000 LIRE ($16.45)

Antica Osteria al Ranari. V. Trieste 11. ☎ **0376/32-84-31.** Antipasto and pasta, from 8,000L ($5.25), main courses 10,000L–20,000L ($6.60–$13.15). AE, MC, V. Tues–Sun, noon– 3pm and 7:15pm–11pm. REGIONAL MANTOVIAN.

Everyone, Mantovians and their visitors alike, love this rustic-looking osteria near the center of town. The menu is typically Mantovian, with such local dishes as an occasional donkey, lake fish, and ravioli stuffed with squash.

Al Garibaldini. V. San Longo 7. ☎ **0376/38-263.** Antipasto and pasta from 8,000L ($5.25), main courses 10,000L–18,000L ($6.60–$11.85). AE, MC, V. Thurs–Tues, noon–3:30pm and 7:30pm–10:30pm. NORTHERN ITALIAN.

If you're out for that special evening, this lovely spot in an old house near the Piazza delle Erbe probably qualifies as the most romantic restaurant in one of Italy's most romantic cities. There's even a garden for summer dining, and the kitchen prepares some wonderful risottos and pastas, roasted meats, and seafood.

Leoncino Rosso. V. Giustiziati 33. ☎ **0376/32-32-77.** Antipasto and pasta from 7,000L ($4.60), main courses 8,000L–15,000L ($5.25–$9.85). MC, V. Mon–Sat, noon–2:30pm and 7pm–2am. SEAFOOD/TRATTORIA.

This neighborhood establishment serves some of the best lake fish in town, though you can also eat very well here on a wide selection of pastas, veal dishes, and other trattoria fare. If you stick around after your meal, you can watch as Mom and Dad go home and a young crowd comes in to swill beer and enjoy one of Mantua's few late-night venues.

A DAY TRIP TO SABBIONETA

This tiny Renaissance jewel has been a backwater since 1591, when Vespasiano Gonzaga died and along with him faded his dreams of grandeur for Sabionetta, which he envisioned, à la Versailles, as the seat of his ducal court.

ESSENTIALS

GETTING THERE By Bus There are five buses a day from Mantua and several from Parma (about 45 minutes from both); make sure to check the time of the last return bus before setting out.

By Car Sabbioneta is on S420, the main Parma-Mantua road, about 20 miles southwest of Mantua, 17 miles north of Parma.

VISITOR INFORMATION The friendly **tourist office** is at V. Vespasiano Gonzaga 31 (☎ **0375/52-039**). It's open April through September, Monday to Friday from 9am until noon and 2:30 to 6pm, Saturday and Sunday from 1:30 to 7pm; October through March, daily from 9am until noon and 2:30 to 5pm (until 6pm Saturday and Sunday). The only way to visit the palaces and other buildings is on the guided tour (in Italian); the cost is 10,000L ($6.60).

STAYING IN A RENAISSANCE GHOST TOWN

A recent restoration has put some dazzle back into the Palazzo Ducale, the Teatro Olimpico, and the other structures that Gonzaga commissioned. They can be visited on a guided tour (see above), followed by a walk through Sabbioneta's quiet piazzas and dusty brick streets. The greatest pleasure, if you stay here overnight, is having the town to yourself when the last tourist buses pull out and only cats and ghosts seem to walk the streets.

WHERE TO STAY & DINE

Albergo Ristorante Al Duca. V. d. Stamperia 18. Sabbioneta. ☎ **0375/22-00-21.** 10 rms, all with bath. 55,000L ($36.20) single; 80,000L ($52.65) double. Rates include breakfast. V.

These charismatic lodgings would cost much more in Parma or Mantua, both of which are easily accessible by car and bus. The huge, high-ceilinged rooms are sparsely but comfortably furnished, and there is a homey trattoria downstairs.

4 Lago di Garda

Poets, composers, and mere mortals have been rhapsodizing about the Italian lakes for centuries—at least, ever since the 18th century, when it became de riguer for travelers on the Grand Tour to descend through the Alps and enjoy their first days on Italian soil on the shores of the lakes.

Lake Garda, the largest and easternmost of the lakes, laps against the flat plains of Lombardy and the Veneto at its southern extremes, and in the north becomes fjordlike and moody, its deep waters backed by Alpine peaks. All around the lake, Garda's shores are green and fragrant with flowery gardens, groves of olives and lemons, and forests of pines and cypress. This pleasing, vaguely exotic landscape has attracted the likes of poet Gabriele D'Annunzio, whose villa near Gardone is one of the lake's major attractions, and Benito Mussolini, whose Republic of Salo was headquartered here and who was captured and executed on these shores. Long before them, the Romans discovered the hot springs that still gush forth at Sirmione, the famed resort on a spit of land at the lake's southern reaches. Today's visitors come to swim (Garda is the cleanest of the major lakes), windsurf (Riva del Garda, at the northern end of the lake, is Europe's windsurfing capital) and enjoy the easy-going ambience of Garda's many pleasant lakeside resorts.

SIRMIONE

Garda's most popular resort juts several miles into the southern waters of the lake on a narrow, cypress- and olive-grove–clad peninsula. Despite an onslaught of visitors, pretty Sirmione manages to retain its charm. Vehicular traffic is kept to a minimum (the few motorists allowed onto the marble streets of the old town are required to switch off their cars' engines at traffic lights), and the emphasis is on strolling, swimming in waters that are warmed in places by underwater hot springs, and relaxing on the sunny terraces of pleasant lakeside hotels. One caveat, though: You might find Sirmione to be less than charming in July and August, when the crowds descend in full force.

ESSENTIALS

GETTING THERE   By Train   Connections are via nearby Desenzano, which is on the Milan-Venice rail lines, with trains almost every half hour in either direction, stopping in Verona, Brescia, and other towns on the busy corridor. If you are traveling from Bologna, Florence, Rome, and other cities to the south, change at Verona for Desenzano. From Desenzano, you can reach Sirmione in about half an hour by hourly bus or boat service.

By Bus   Frequent bus service links Sirmione with Riva del Garda, Gardone, and other towns on the lakeshore.

By Boat   Hydrofoils and ferries ply the waters between Sirmione and other towns on the lake; service is curtailed in the off-season months, October through April. Most boats are operated by Navigazione Lago di Garda (☎ **030/91-41-321**), head-quartered on the dock in Desenzano.

By Car   Sirmione is just off the A4 autostrada between Milan and Venice. From Bologna, Florence, Rome, and other points south, take the A22 autostrada north from Modena to Verona, and from there the A4 west to Sirmione. It's 89 miles) from Venice, 76 miles from Milan.

VISITOR INFORMATION   The **APT tourist office** is just outside the old town near the castle at Vle. Marconi 2 (☎ **030/91-61-14**). It is open April through October, daily from 9am to 10pm; November through March, Monday to Friday from 9am to 12:30pm and 3pm to 6pm, Saturday from 9am to 12:30pm and 3pm to 8pm, Sunday from 3pm to 8pm. The helpful, English-speaking staff dispenses a wealth of information about Sirmione and other sights on the lake and will reserve a room for you.

WHAT TO SEE & DO

In addition to its attractive though tourist-shop-ridden old town, Sirmione has many lakeside promenades, pleasant beaches, and even some open countryside where olive trees sway in the breeze. Anything you'll want to see can be reached easily on foot, though an open-air tram (2,000L/$1.30) makes the short run out to the Roman ruins.

Grotte di Catullo. ☎ **030/91-61-57.** Admission 8,000L ($5.25). Apr–Sept, Tue–Sun, 9am–6pm; Oct–Mar, until 4pm.

Whether or not these extensive ruins at the northern tip of the peninsula were really, as they are alleged to have been, the villa and baths of the pleasure-loving Roman poet Catullus is open to debate. Even so, their presence here, on a hilltop fragrant with wild rosemary and pines, demonstrates that Sirmione has been a deservedly popular retreat for millennia.

Castello Scaligero. ☎ **030/91-61-48.** Admission 8,000L ($5.25). Apr–Oct, Tue–Sun, 9am–6pm; Oct–Mar, until 4pm.

This moated and turreted castle at the southern and only land-side entrance to the old town was built in the 13th century by the della Scala family, who ruled Verona and much of the turf around the lake. The exterior is a lot showier than the gloomy interior, but the views over town and lake from the towers are stunning.

WHERE TO STAY

Sirmione has many pleasant, moderately priced hotels, all of which book up quickly in the high-season months of July and August, when they also charge higher rates (reflected in the high end of the rates below). You are not allowed to drive into the town until a guard at the entrance near the castle confirms that you have a hotel reservation.

A Double for Less than 100,000 Lire ($65.78)

Hotel Speranza. V. Castello 6, 25019 Sirmione. ☎ **030/91-61-16.** Fax 030/91-64-03. 13 rms, all with bath. 50,000L ($32.90) single; 90,000L ($59.20) double. MC, V.

The old crone at the desk can be a bit gruff, but this modest hotel on the upper floors of an old building that arches across Sirmione's main street near the castle can't be beat for the price and location. The bare-bones rooms are tidy and perfectly serviceable and actually look rather chic with their Spartan modern furnishings.

Doubles for Less than 150,000 Lire ($98.68)

Hotel Corte Regina. V. Antica Mura 11, 25019 Sirmione. ☎/fax **030/91-61-47.** 10 rms, all with bath. TEL TV. 90,000L–120,000L ($59.20–$78.95) single; 120,000L–150,000L ($78.95–$98.68) double. Rates include breakfast. AE, MC, V.

One of Sirmione's more moderately priced lodgings occupies a stone building on a narrow side street that leads to the lake and a beach. A recent renovation has brought the large, tile-floored rooms up to date with contemporary furnishings and new baths. A great deal of charm and friendly ambience remains, as does the pretty, quiet terrace in front of the hotel.

Hotel Eden. Pz. Carducci 17/18, 25019 Sirmione. ☎ **030/91-64-81.** Fax 030/91-64-83. 33 rms, all with bath. 105,000L–130,000L ($69.10–$85.50) single; 140,000L–180,000L ($92.10–$118.45) double. AE, MC, V.

Ezra Pound once lived in this pink-stucco lakeside hotel, which has recently been modernized with enormous taste and an eye to comfort. The lake can be seen from most of the bright, attractive rooms, which are decorated in handsome, contemporary furnishings and pastel shades and have large, gleaming baths. Downstairs, the marble lobby opens to a delightful, shaded terrace and a swimming pier that juts into the lake.

Hotel Olivi. V. San Pietro 5, 25019 Sirmione. ☎ **030/99-05-365.** Fax 030/91-64-72. 60 rms, all with bath. A/C MINIBAR TEL TV. 105,000L ($69.10) single; 130,000L ($85.85) double; 175,000L ($115.15) triple; 255,000L ($167.75) quad. AE, MC, V. Closed Dec 15–Jan 31.

This pleasant, modern hotel is not directly on the lake, which can be seen from most of the rooms and the sunny terrace, but commands a hilltop position near the Roman ruins in a countryside of pines and olive groves. Rooms are stunningly decorated in varying schemes of bold, handsome colors and have separate dressing areas off the baths, and most open to balconies. There is a swimming pool in the garden and a dining room where you can arrange to take meals on half- or full-board plan.

WHERE TO DINE

Ristorante Al Progresso. V. Vittorio Emanuele 18. ☎ **030/91-61-08.** Antipasto and pasta from 7,000L ($4.60), main courses 12,000L–18,000L ($7.90–$11.85). MC, V. Fri–Wed noon–2:30pm and 6:30pm–10:30pm. SEAFOOD/ITALIAN.

There's nothing fancy about this brightly lit room on the main street of the old town, but that's the Progresso's appeal. Many of the diners are repeat visitors who come to Sirmione for their annual vacations, and they rely on this old establishment to provide them with well-prepared, unfussy meals. Fresh grilled lake trout is often on the menu.

Ristorante Re Desiderio. V. Antica Mura 11. ☎ **030/91-61-47.** Antipasto and pasta from 7,000L ($4.60), main courses 10,000L–20,000L ($6.60–$13.15), pizza from 6,000L ($3.95). MC, V. Fri–Wed noon–2:30pm and 6:30pm–10:30pm.

The best place to dine here is on the terrace, which faces a quiet side street leading to a beach and where you'll probably be tempted to linger long after the last course. The menu, in several languages, tends to simple tourist basics of the penne with tomato sauce and veal with lemon sauce variety, but everything that comes out of the kitchen is well prepared and nicely served.

RIVA DEL GARDA

The northernmost town on the lake is not just a resort but a real place, too, with medieval towers, a nice smattering of Renaissance churches and palazzi, and narrow cobblestone streets where the everyday business of a prosperous Italian town proceeds in its alluring way.

Even so, the main attraction in Riva is its lakefront promenade, stretching for several miles past parks and beaches. The water is warm enough for swimming from May into October, and air currents fanned by the surrounding mountains make Garda a popular spot for windsurfing year-round.

ESSENTIALS

GETTING THERE   By Bus   Five buses a day link Riva and Desenzano (about a 2-hour trip).

By Boat   One boat (4 hours) and four hydrofoils (2 hours) run daily between Riva and Desenzano, making stops at major towns along the lake.

By Car   The fastest link between Riva and points north and south is via the A22 autostrada, which shoots up the east side of the lake (exit at Mori, 13km/9 miles, east of Riva). A far more scenic drive is along the western shore, on the beautiful corniche between Riva and Salo that hugs cliffs and passes through mile after mile of tunnel.

VISITOR INFORMATION   The tourist office, which supplies loads of information on hotels, restaurants, and activities in the area, is near the lakefront Giardini di Porta Orientale 8 (☎ **0464/55-44-44**). It is open April through October, Monday to Saturday from 9am to noon and 3pm to 6:30pm; November through March, Monday to Friday from 8:45am to noon and 2:15 to 5:30pm.

WHERE TO STAY

Albergo Vittoria. V. Dante 39, 38066 Riva del Garda. ☎ **0464/55-43-98.** Fax 0464/55-56-41. 15 rms, 14 with bath. 80,000L ($52.65) double. MC, V.

A short walk from the lake, this family-run hotel is one of the few low-cost places in the historic center of town. Downstairs there's a muraled dining room and a cozy, Tyrolean-looking bar with a vaulted stone ceiling. Upstairs, the guest rooms are nothing fancy but have streamlined modern furnishings and are kept in tiptop shape.

Hotel Sole. Pz. Novembre 23, 38066 Riva del Garda. ☎ **0464/55-26-86.** Fax 0464/ 55-28-11. 53 rms, all with bath. A/C MINIBAR TEL TV. 230,000L ($151.30) double. AE, MC, V. Closed Nov, Feb to mid-Mar.

One of the finest hotels in town enjoys a wonderful location right on the lake and main square. The attentive management lavishes a great deal of attention on the public rooms and guest rooms, and charges very fairly, given the amenities offered. The chicly contemporary lobby is filled with rare Persian carpets and abstract art, and the guest rooms, reached via a sweeping circular staircase, are warmly luxurious, with lush fabrics, tasteful blond furnishings, and marble baths; the best rooms have balconies that hang out over the lake. Amenities include a formal restaurant, a casual cafe/bar that extends onto a lakeside terrace, a rooftop solarium with sauna, and a garage.

WHERE TO DINE

Birreria Spaten. V. Mafferi 7. ☎ **0464/55-36-70.** Antipasto and pasta from 6,000L ($3.95), main courses from 7,000L ($4.60). MC, V. Daily, 10:30am–3pm and 5:30pm–midnight; closed Mon Oct–Apr. ITALIAN/TYROLEAN.

This large, noisy, indoor beer garden features a wide-ranging mix of food from both sides of the Alps, so you can dine here on the cuisine of Trento or Lombardy. The pizzas are great, and you may want to try some schnitzel, sauerkraut, or sauerbraten as well.

STAYING NEARBY IN LIMONE SUL GARDA

Limone sul Garda is a pretty resort wedged between the lake and mountains just 10km (6 miles) south of Riva. Despite an onslaught of tourists who come down through the mountains from Austria and Germany, it's a pleasant place to spend some time and has more moderately priced lakeside hotels than Riva does. The Romans planted lemon groves here and covered them with protective structures, the ruins of which are still visible on the hills around the town, and lemons continue to thrive on every available parcel of land.

Albergo Se. V. Nova 12, 25010 Limone sul Garda. ☎ **0365/95-41-82.** 12 rms, all with bath. 80,000L ($52.65) double, 96,000L ($63.15) double in July and August.

Delightfully situated on the lake amid vineyards and lemon groves just outside of town, this family-run pensione is one of the most relaxing places to stay in the area. Rooms are a bit small and basically furnished, but all open onto balconies overlooking the lake. A sunny terrace in front of the hotel has a pool to one side and overlooks a private beach.

Hotel Le Palme. V. Porto 30, 25010 Limone sul Garda. ☎ **0365/95-46-81.** Fax 0365/ 95-41-20. 28 rms, all with bath. TEL TV. Half-board: 65,000L–95,000L ($42.75–$62.50) per person, depending on the season. AE, MC, V. Closed Nov–Mar.

One of the most pleasant hotels on Garda is this gracious villa, wonderfully located on the lake at one end of Limone's narrow main street. Downstairs, a bar and restaurant flow onto a flowery lakeside terrace. Upstairs, the large, pleasant guest rooms are furnished in Venetian antiques, and all but a few face the lake; the best have small balconies. There's a small beach just a few steps down the road, and the hotel also has a small beach and a swimming pool nearby.

Where to Dine

Ristorante Gemma. Pz. Garibaldi 11. ☎ **365/94-01-45.** Thur–Tue, 11:30am–2:30pm and 6:30pm–10pm. Antipasto and pasta from 9,000L ($5.90), main courses from 12,000L ($7.90). MC, V. ITALIAN.

In a town where many eateries cater to tourists with fish and chips and bratwurst, Gemma remains an authentic, family-style trattoria. It also enjoys a pretty lakeside location, and the waves lap right against a dining terrace. Gemma is the best place in town for grilled lake trout, which, like all entries, can be accompanied by a fine spaghetti alla mare and other delicious pastas.

A DAY TRIP TO GARDONE

This little resort has two interesting attractions worthy of an excursion, including the home of Gabriele D'Anunzio, Italy's most noted modern poet.

The five daily boats and buses that travel between Riva and Desenzano also pull into Gardone, about halfway between the two.

The **tourist office,** V. Republica 35 (☎ **0365/21-551**), is open daily from 9am to 12:30pm and 3pm to 6pm.

Il Vittorale. Pzle. Vittoriale. ☎ **0365/20-130.** Admission 7,000L ($4.60) grounds only, 8,000L ($5.25) additional for villa. Daily 9am–12:30pm and 2pm–6:30 pm.

Gabriele D'Anunzio, once Italy's most famous soldier/poet, is nearly forgotten today by the younger generation. He bought this hillside estate in 1921 and died here in 1936. Aside from his verse, d'Annunzio left his mark as a sympathizer of Mussolini, an aesthete, and a Don Juan. The claustrophobic rooms of his ornately and bizarrely decorated villa are filled with bric-a-brac and artifacts from his colorful life, including many mementos of his long-running affair with the actress Eleanora Duse. Elsewhere on the grounds, which cascade down a hillside in a series of luxuriant gardens, are the patrol boat D'Annunzio commanded in World War I, a museum containing his biplane and photos, and his pompous hilltop tomb.

Giardino Botanica Hruska. V. Roma. Admission 6,000L ($3.95). Apr–Sept, daily 9am–6:30pm.

This small but delightful bower, planted a hundred years ago by the Swiss naturalist Arturo Hruska (a dentist whose clientele included European royalty), continues to bloom, with 2,000 species of exotic flora from around the world.

5 Lago di Como

The first sight of this dramatic expanse of azure-hued water, ringed by gardens and forests and backed by the snowcapped Alps, is likely to evoke strong emotions. Romance, soulfulness, even gentle melancholy—these are the stirrings that over the centuries Como has inspired in poets (Lord Byron), novelists (Stendhal), composers (Verdi and Rossini), and plenty of other visitors, too—be they deposed queens, such as Caroline of Brunswick, whom George IV of England exiled here for her adulterous ways, or well-heeled modern travelers who glide up and down these waters in the ubiquitous lake steamers. In addition to its emotional effects, Como is also just an enjoyable place to spend time. Less than an hour from Milan by train or car, its deep waters and verdant shores provide a wonderful respite from modern life.

COMO

The largest and southernmost town on the lake is not likely to charm you at first glance. Long a center of silk-making, this city that traces its roots to the Gauls, and after them, the Romans, bustles with commerce and industry. You'll probably want to stay in one of the more peaceful settings farther up the lake (see below), but Como amply rewards a day's visit with some fine Renaissance churches and palaces and a lovely lakefront promenade.

ESSENTIALS

GETTING THERE   By Train   Most trains, including 30 a day to and from Milan, arrive and depart from Stazione San Giovanni on Piazzale San Gottardo, about a 15-minute walk from the center of town. Luggage storage is available. Some trains arrive and depart from Stazione F.N.M, on Largo Leopardi.

By Boat   Ferries, many of which carry cars, are operated by Navigazione Lago di Como (☎ 031/30-40-60) and connect Como with most other towns on the lake; boats arrive and depart from the Lungo Lario Trieste, near Piazza Cavour.

By Car   The A9 autostrada links Como with Milan, where you can connect with the A1 for Florence and Rome and the A4 for Turin and Venice.

VISITOR INFORMATION   The **tourist office** dispenses a wealth of information on hotels, restaurants, and campgrounds around the lake from its offices at Pz. Cavour 17. It's open Monday to Saturday from 9am to 12:30pm and 2:30 to 6pm.

WHAT TO SEE

Part Renaissance and part gothic, Como's **Duomo** (in the center of town just off the lake) is festooned with the same sort of exuberant masonry that adorns the Duomo in Milan. Statues of two of the town's famous native sons, Pliny the Elder and Pliny the Younger, flank the main entrance. Inside, beneath an 18th-century dome by Juavara—whom you might remember as the architect who designed much of Turin—is a lavish interior hung with paintings and tapestries. The half-timbered, 13th-century **Broletto** (town hall) and adjoining Torre del Commune are on the other side of the Piazza del Duomo; and, as a study in contrasts, the starkly modernist and aptly named Casa del Fascio, built in 1936 as the seat of the region's fascist government, rises just behind the Duomo.

Como's main street, Corso Vittorio Emanuele II, cuts through the medieval quarter, where wood-beamed houses line narrow streets; and, just two blocks south of the duomo, the 12th-century, five-sided **Church of San Fedele** looms above a charming square of the same name. To see Como's most alluring church, though, it's necessary to venture into the dull, outlying neighborhood southwest of the center where, just off the Viale Roosevelt, you'll come to the five-aisle, heavily frescoed **Basilica of Sant'Abbondio.**

Lakeside life revolves around the Piazza Cavour and adjoining Giardini Publici, where the circular **Tempio Voltano** houses memorabilia that will enlighten you about the life and experiments of native son and electricity pioneer Alessandro Volta. It's open April through September, Tuesday to Sunday from 10am to noon and 3 to 6pm; October through March, from 10am to noon and 2 to 4pm; admission is 5,000L ($3.30). For a quick retreat and some stunning views, take the funicular up to the top of Brunate, the forested hill that looms over the town (from the Lungo Lario Trieste every half hour; 3,500L/$2.30 one-way, 6,100L/$4 round-trip).

WHERE TO STAY & DINE

Ostello Villa Olmo. V. Bellinzona 6. ☎ **031/57-38-00.** 13,000L ($8.55) per person. Open Mar–Nov, office open 7:30am–10am and 4pm–11pm.

Given Como's unrustic busyness and a decided lack of charming, reasonably priced accommodations, this well-managed, friendly hostel is all the more welcome. The location, in a charming old building near the lake, is great, and the multibed rooms are kept in tiptop shape. Other amenities include acceptable meals for 12,000L ($7.90), and laundry service.

Taverna Messicana. Pz. Mazzini 6. ☎ **031/26-24-63.** Antipasto and pasta from 7,000L ($4.60), main courses 9,000L ($5.90), pizza from 6,000L ($3.95). Tues–Sun, 11am–2pm and 7pm–midnight. PIZZA/ITALIAN.

Despite the name, this pleasant and popular trattoria serves some of the best pizza in Como, along with a wide range of delicious pasta and meat courses.

BELLAGIO

The loveliest town on the lake commands a picture-perfect location on a point of land that can only be described as Como's crotch—the lake forks into three distinct basins here, with one long leg sweeping north into the Alps; Como is at the southern end of the western leg, and Lecco is at the southern end of the eastern leg. Boats from Bellagio make it easy to visit most places on the lake, especially those on the nearby shores of what is known as the Centro Lago—not that you will be that willing to leave this pretty old town, with its steep narrow streets, lakeside piazza, and beautiful gardens.

ESSENTIALS

GETTING THERE   By Boat   Ferries, many of which carry cars, connect Bellagio with Como, Lecco, and more frequently, with towns on the Centro Lago: among them, Varenna on the eastern shore and Cadenabbia and Menaggio on the western shore. You can purchase a daily pass for 10,000L ($6.60) that is good for unlimited travel within the Centro Lago region.

By Car   Bellagio is connected to Como by a picturesque lakeshore road, S583, and to Lecco by a narrow, winding, and downright dangerous road.

VISITOR INFORMATION   The **tourist office,** which is unfortunately often closed, is at Pz. d. Chiesa 14 (☎ **031/95-02-04;** hours are Monday, Wednesday, and Thursday from 8:30am to 12:15pm and 2:30 to 6pm when it's open.

BELLAGIO'S GARDENS

One of Bellagio's famed gardens surrounds the **Villa Melzi,** built by Franceso Melzi, a friend of Napoléon and an official of his Italian Republic. The villa was later the retreat of Franz Liszt, and is now the home of a distinguished Lombardian family, who allows the public to stroll through their acres of manicured lawns and fountains and visit a pavilion where a collection of Egyptian sculpture is on display. It's open March to October, daily from 9am to 12:30pm and 2 to 4:30pm; admission is 5,000L ($3.30); phone **0344/95-03-18.** Bellagio's other famous gardens are those of the **Villa Serbelloni,** occupying land once owned by Pliny the Younger and now in the hands of the Rockefeller Foundation. The gardens can be visited on twice-daily guided tours, about two hours long, in Italian. From mid-April through mid-October, tours are Tuesday to Sunday at 10:30am and 4:30pm; the tour costs 5,000L ($3.30). Call **0344/95-02-04.**

VILLAS & GARDENS NEARBY

In Varenna

You can happily spend some time clamoring up and down the steep steps that substitute for streets in this charming village that until not too long ago made its living by fishing. The main attractions, though, are outside of town: the hilltop ruins of the **Castello di Vezio** and the more easily accessible gardens of the **Villa Monastero.** As you might guess from the name, this villa and the terraced gardens that rise up from the lakeshore were once a not-so-Spartan monastery—until it was dissolved in the late 17th century, when the nuns in residence began bearing living proof that they were on too friendly terms with the priests across the way. If you find it hard to tear your-self from the bowers of citrus trees and rhododendrons, you will find equally enchant-ing surroundings in the gardens of the Villa Cipressi next door.

Both gardens are open April through October, daily 9am to noon and 2 to 5pm and charge an admission of 4,000L ($2.65); call **0341/83-01-72** for more informa-tion. Ferries make the 20-minute run between Bellagio and Varenna about every half hour.

Villa Carlotta

Just outside Tremezzo, this is the most famous villa on the lake, a short boat ride from Bellagio. It was begun in 1643 for the Marquis Giorgio Clerici, who made his fortune supplying Napoléon's troops with uniforms; he spent much of it on his neoclassical villa and gardens. After a succession of owners, including Prussian royalty who lavished their funds and attention on the gardens, Villa Carlotta is now in the hands of the Italian government. The villa is filled with romantic paintings and Empire furnishings, but the gardens are the main attraction here: Azaleas, orchids, banana trees, cacti, and forests of ferns spread out in all directions.

The ferry landing is at Menaggio, about half a mile north of the gardens; call **0344/40-405** for more information. It's open April through September, daily from 9am to 6pm; March 15 to March 31 and October, daily from 9am to noon and 2 to 4:30pm. Closed November through mid-March. Admission is 8,000L ($5.25).

WHERE TO STAY

Giardinetto. Pz. d. Chiesa, 22021 Bellagio. ☎ **031/95-01-68.** 14 rms, all with bath. 80,000L ($52.65). MC, V.

The best lodging deal in town is to be found at this charming little hotel at the top of town, reached from the lakefront by Bellagio's narrow, stepped streets. A snug lobby, grouped around a big fireplace, opens to a vine-covered terrace, as do many of the rooms, which are comfortably furnished with old armoires and bedsteads.

Hotel du Lac. Pz. Mazzini 32, 22021 Bellagio. ☎ **031/95-03-20.** Fax 031/95-16-24. 48 rms, all with bath or shower. A/C MINIBAR TEL TV. 110,000L ($72.35) single; 175,000L ($115.15) double; rates include breakfast. Half-pension 125,000L ($82.25) per person; full-pension 140,000L ($92.10) per person. AE, MC, V. Closed Nov–Mar.

Old-fashioned comfort pervades this gracious, 150-year-old hotel overlooking the lake from Bellagio's main piazza. Cushy armchairs and a nice smattering of antiques and reproductions lend a great amount of charm to the guest rooms, and public areas include a rooftop sun terrace with sweeping lake views and a bar that spills onto the arcaded sidewalk. Meals are served in an airy first-floor dining room.

Apartments to Rent

Grand Hotel Villa Serbelloni. 22021 Bellagio. ☎ **031/95-02-16.** Fax 031/95-15-29. 13 apartments, all with bath. 700,000L–1,295,000L ($460–$852) a week, small apartment; 800,000L–1,540,000L ($526–$1,013) a week, medium apartment; 1,100,000L–2,275,000L ($724–$1,497) a week, large apartment. Rates are for 2 persons, and vary with season. AE, MC, V. Closed Nov–Mar.

Yes, this is the Serbelloni, the swank retreat of the titled and entitled. For those look-ing for less grandiose accommodations (while enjoying all the hotel's amenities), the hotel has recently added these stylish apartments in an outbuilding that also houses its fitness facilities. Terracotta floors and attractive rattan furniture create a casual, pleasing ambience in these units, all of which are equipped with kitchenettes and open onto terraces. While rentals are by the week, shorter stays can be arranged when space is available.

WHERE TO DINE

La Grotta. Salita Cernaia 14. ☎ **031/95-11-52.** Antipasto and pasta from 7,000L ($4.60), main courses 12,000L–18,000L ($7.90–$11.85), pizza, from 6,000L ($3.95). AE, MC, V. Tues–Fri (daily, Aug–Sept), noon–2:30pm and 6:30pm–10:30pm. ITALIAN/SEAFOOD/PIZZERIA.

Tucked away on a stepped street just off lakefront Piazza Manzini, this cozy, informal dining room has a wide-ranging menu that includes many pasta and meat dishes. Most of the regulars, though, come for the fish specials, including lake trout, or the delectable pizzas that are the best for miles around.

Trattoria Giacomo. V. Salita Serbelloni 45. ☎ **031/95-03-29.** Antipasto and pasta from 9,000L ($6.90), main courses 14,000L–25,000L ($9.20–$16.45). MC, V. Wed–Mon, noon–2:30pm and 6:30pm–9:30pm. LOMBARD.

What's sets this small, family-run restaurant apart from most moderately priced restaurants around the lakes is the breadth of its menu, which concentrates on typical Lombardian dishes rather than standard tourist fare. The risottos are delicious, and are often made with seafood. They can be followed with any number of veal dishes, including thick veal chops topped with mushrooms or cotoletta alla Milanese.

NEARBY PLACES TO STAY & DINE

In Mennagio

Ostello La Prinula. V. IV Novembre 86. ☎ **0344/32-356.** 13,000L ($8.55) per person. Open mid-Mar to mid-Nov, office open 7:30am–10am and 4pm–11pm.

This delightful hostel (really, it is) is easily accessible from Bellagio and other towns on the Centro Lago by boat. Family suites with private baths are available, and even the dorms are relatively cozy, with no more than six beds per room. The terrace has fine views of the lake, and the dining room serves a 13,000L ($8.55) dinner that's so good even locals come here to dine. You can explore the surrounding countryside on one of the bikes that are available for 15,000L ($9.87) a day.

In Varenna

Albergo Milano. V. XX Settembre 29, 22050 Varenna. ☎/Fax **0341/83-02-98.** 12 rms, all with bath. TEL. 144,000L ($94.75) double. Rates include breakfast. AE, MC. V.

You'd have to look hard to find a much more pleasant retreat by the lake. This family-run hotel occupies an old house hanging over Varenna's lakefront. Most of the simply furnished but comfortable rooms have views, though the two best in the house are the ones on the first floor that open onto a wide terrace. Breakfast is served in a charming, antiques-filled parlor on the main floor.

Villa Cipressi. V. IV Novembre 18, 22050 Varenna. ☎ **0341/83-01-13.** Fax 0341/83-04-01. All rms have bath. TEL TV. 97,000L ($63.80) single; 127,000L ($83.55) double; 10,000L–15,000L ($6.60–$9.90) extra for rms with lake view. Rates include breakfast. MC, V.

If you enjoyed your tour of Varenna's lush gardens (see above), there's no need to leave. The villa and several outbuildings have been converted to a hotel that's geared to conferences but takes other guests, space permitting. The large rooms are attractive, though they have been renovated without any attempt to retain the historic character of the building. Many take advantage of the high ceilings and contain loft bedrooms, with sitting areas below, and all enjoy marvelous views over the gardens.

6 Lago Maggiore

Anyone who reads Hemingway will know this lake and its forested shores from *A Farewell to Arms*. That's just the sort of place Maggiore is—a pleasure ground that's steeped in associations with famous figures (Flaubert, Wagner, Goethe, and Europe's other great minds seem to have been inspired by the deep, moody waters, backed by the Alps) and not-so-famous wealthy visitors. Fortunately, you need not be famous or wealthy to enjoy Maggiore, which is on the Swiss border just a short dash east and north of Milan.

STRESA

The major town on the lake is a pretty, festive little place, with a long lakefront prom-enade, a lively and attractive commercial center, and a bevy of restaurants and hotels that range from the expensively splendid to the affordably comfortable. Strolling and idling seem to be the main activities in town. Sooner or later, though, most visitors climb into a boat for the short ride to the famed Isole Borromee or board the *funivia* for the ascent to the hiking and biking trails in the mountains behind Stresa.

ESSENTIALS

GETTING THERE   By Train   Stresa is linked with Milan (1 hour) by 20 trains a day, and by several a day to and from Geneva ($2^{1}/_{2}$ hours)

By Boat   Boats arrive and depart from Piazza Marconi, connecting Stresa with the Isole Borromee and with many other lakeside spots; most boats on the lake are operated by Navigazione Sul Lago Maggiore (☎ **0322/10-87**).

By Car   Autosrada A8 runs between Milan and Sesto, near the southern end of the lake; from there Route S33 follows the western shore to Stresa; in Milan you can connect with the A1 for Florence and Rome and the A4 for Turin and Venice

VISITOR INFORMATION   The **tourist information office,** Principe Tomaso 70–72 (☎ **0323/32-405**), has information about hiking trails in the mountains. A cable car leaves from Pzle. Lido 8 every 20 minutes daily from 9:30am to noon and 1:40 to 5pm; it costs 8,000L/$5.25.

THE ISOLE BORROMEE

These three islands, named for the Borromeo family, who's owned them since the 12th century, float in the misty waters off Stresa and entice visitors with their stun-ning beauty. Public ferries leave for the islands every half hour from Piazza Marconi; a day pass (11,000L/$7.24) is the most economical way to visit all three. Private boats also make the trip out to the island; hucksters dressed as sailors will try to lure you aboard—especially for groups, the prices can be reasonable, but do your negotiating on the dock before you get on the boat.

Most of **Isola Superiore** (Isola Pescatore) is occupied by an not-so-quaint old fish-ing village—every one of the tall houses on this tiny strip of land seems to harbor a souvenir shop or pizza stand, and there are hordes of visitors to keep them busy.

Isola Bella remains true to its name, with splendid 17th-century gardens that ascend from the shore in 10 luxuriantly planted terraces. The **Borromeo palazzo** on the island can also be visited, providing a chance to tramp through room after opu-lently decorated room, including the one where Napoléon and Josephine once slept. It's open April through October, daily from 9am to noon and 1:30 to 5:30pm; ad-mission is 12,000L ($7.90); call **0323/30-556.**

The largest and most peaceful of the islands is Isola Madre, most of which is covered with the exquisite flora of the **Orto Botanico** (☎ **0323/31-261**). The botanical garden is open April through September, daily from 9am to noon and 1:30 to 5:30pm; admission is 12,000L ($7.90).

WHERE TO STAY

Hotel Meeting. V. Bonghi 9, 28049 Stresa. ☎ **0323/32-741.** Fax 0323/32-742. 24 rms, all with bath. MINIBAR TEL TV. 130,000L ($85.55) double, 100,000L ($65.80) single. Rates include breakfast.

The name comes from the proximity of Stresa's small conference setting, where a much-attended music festival in held in late August and early September. Although the lakefront is only a five-minute walk away, the setting is quiet and leafy, and the rooms, furnished in Scandinavian modern, are big and bright, and many have terraces. There's a cozy bar downstairs, as well as a casual dining room.

Hotel Mon Toc. V. Duchessa di Genova 67/69, 28049 Stresa. ☎ **0323/30-282.** Fax 0323/ 93-38-60. 18 rms, all with bath. 53,000L ($34.85) single; 81,000L ($53.30) double.

Just uphill from the train station, this family-run hotel surrounded by a big garden is convenient to the lake and town but far enough removed to provide an almost countrylike atmosphere. With oriental carpets and nice old furniture, the guest rooms are homey and much nicer than you would expect them to be at the price.

Hotel Primavera. V. Cavour 30, 28049 Stresa. ☎ **0323/31-286.** Fax 0323/33-458. 32 rms, all with bath. MINIBAR TEL TV. 130,000L ($85.55) double, 100,000L ($65.80) single. Rates include breakfast.

For much of the spring and summer, the street out front is closed to traffic and filled with flowering plants and cafe tables. This relaxed air prevails throughout this bright little hotel, just a block off the lake in the center of town. There's a lounge and bar downstairs, and the airy, tile-floored rooms upstairs are nicely furnished in walnut, and many have balconies overlooking the town or lake.

Hotel Verbano. Isola Pescatori, 28049 Stresa. ☎ **0323/30-408.** Fax 0323/33-129. 12 rms, all with bath. Half-board, 130,000L ($85.53) per person; full-board, 170,000L ($111.84) per person. Closed Nov–Mar.

This cozy little inn occupies one end of Isola Superiore, providing a wonderful lakeside retreat. The big old-fashioned rooms are charming, filled with a homey assortment of antiques and bright fabrics, and all look onto the lake. Meals are served in a bright dining room or on the lakeside terrace, where most guests prefer to spend their days. Evenings are especially pleasant, when the day-trippers have departed and the island is left to the families who live here, their cats, and the hotel guests (the Verbano is the island's only hotel). When the urge to explore the mainland strikes, the hotel's launch makes frequent runs into Stresa.

Worth a Splurge

Hotel la Palma. 28049 Stresa. ☎ **0323/93-39-06.** Fax 0323/93-39-30. 128 rms, all with bath. A/C MINIBAR TEL TV. From 140,000L ($92.10) single; from 230,000L ($151.30) double. Rates include a buffet breakfast; half-board and full-board rates also available. AE, MC, V. Closed Dec–Feb.

The Palma is one of the nicest of Stresa's luxury hotels and, given the high-level comfort and the amenities offered, one of the most reasonably priced. Most of the guest rooms, recently redone in rich floral fabrics and light woods, open to balconies overlooking the lake, and many of the marble baths are equipped with Jacuzzis. There is a rooftop sun terrace and fitness center, with steam room and sauna, but the most pleasant places to relax are in the flowery garden in front of the hotel and the terrace surrounding the lakeside swimming pool.

WHERE TO DINE

Hotel Ristorante Fiorentino. V. Bolongaro 9. ☎ **0323/30-254.** Antipasto and pasta from 6,000L ($3.95), main courses 8,000L–18,000L ($5.25). Fixed menu, 21,000L ($13.80). MC. V. Mar–Oct, daily, 11am–3pm and 6–10pm. Closed Nov to mid-Mar. ITALIAN.

It's hard to find friendlier service or homier trattoria type food in Stresa, especially at these prices. Everything that comes out of the family-run kitchen is made fresh that day, including canneloni and other pastas, and is served in a big, cozy room that's usually filled with locals. There's also dining on a patio out back in good weather. The hotel upstairs is currently closed for a total renovation (including the installation of private baths), but if the new rooms are as charming as the old ones, the Fiorentino will remain one of the best places in town to stay, as well as to dine.

Ristorante Pescatore. Vc. d. Poncivo. ☎ **0323/31-986.** Antipasto and pasta from 8,000L ($5.25), main courses 10,000L–25,000L ($6.60–$16.45). AE, MC. V. Fri–Wed, noon–3pm and 6–10pm. SEAFOOD.

Not too hard to figure out what dominates the menu here: In fact, this is where locals come for a fish meal, which can include a wonderful seafood salad, an appetizer of smoked salmon or tuna, any number of pasta dishes served with clams or squid, and fresh lake or ocean fish.

Taverna del Pappagallo. V. Principessa Margherita 46. ☎ **0323/30-411.** Antipasto and pasta from 7,000L ($4.60), main courses 12,000L–20,000L ($7.90–$13.15), pizza from 6,000L ($3.95). Thur–Mon, 11:30am–2:30pm and 6:30pm–10:30pm; daily during the summer. ITALIAN/PIZZERIA.

Most of Stresa seems to congregate here in the evenings for the most popular pizza in town. But just about all the down-home fare, including the delectable homemade gnocchi, that comes out of the family-run kitchen, is delicious. Weather permitting, try to nab one of the tables in the pleasant garden.

Piedmont (Piemonte) & the Valle d'Aosta

by Stephen Brewer

Loosely translated, Piedmont, or Piemonte in Italian, means "at the foot of the mountains." Those mountains, of course, are the Alps, defining the region and part of Italy's northern and western borders. These dramatic peaks are visible in much of the province, most of which rises and rolls over fertile foothills that produce a bounty that is as rich as the region is green. This is a land of cheeses, truffles, plump fruit and, of course, wines—among them some of Italy's most delicious reds, including Barbaresco and Barolo. Rising from the vineyards are medieval and Renaissance towns and villages, many of which are untrammeled by the 20th century.

Not that all of Piedmont is rural, of course. Turin, Italy's car town, is the region's capital, and within the ring of industrialized suburbs lies an elegant city of mannerly squares, baroque palaces, and stunning art collections. Turinese and their neighbors from other parts of Italy often retreat to the Valle d'Aosta, the smallest, northernmost, and most mountainous of Italian provinces.

EXPLORING PIEDMONT & VALLE d'AOSTA

While Turin is easily accessible by public transportation, much of the rest of Piedmont, and much of Valle d'Aosta, are not. This means that if you want to get off the beaten track and see the remoter parts of these regions, you may want to rent a car in Turin and set out to explore.

Arrive in Turin, and take a walk down the Via Roma, past the city's elegant cafes, chichi shops, and many of its most interesting sights as well.

On the second day, venture out from the city to the outlying sights of Stupingi, the Savoy's idea of a hunting lodge, and the hilltop basilica of Superga.

On day 3, for a taste of rural Piedmont, you can travel by train or bus—or better yet, by car—to the Renaissance wine towns of Asti and Alba. Quiet Alba and its outlying villages make a nice base from which to explore the countryside. On the fourth day, visit Barolo and other wine villages, tasting the local vintage at enotecas, and sleepy Renaissance towns, including Savigliano and Saluzzo.

On day 5, head north into the Valle d'Aosta, settling in Aosta or one of the valley's villages or resorts. Spend at least part of day 6 exploring Aosta's Roman ruins and medieval treasures. An exciting afternoon trip takes you up and over Mont Blanc via the Palud cable car.

On day 7, visit the Parco Nazionale del Gran Paradiso, one of Europe's most pristine natural wonderlands.

1 Turin (Torino)

669km (401 miles) NW from Rome, 140km (84 miles) E from Milan

It's often said that Turin is the most French city in Italy or the most Italian city in France. The reason is partly historical and partly architectural. From 1720 to 1861, Turin was the capital of the House of Savoy, whose royal members were as French as they were Italian and whose holdings extended well into the present-day French regions of Savoy and the Côte d'Azur. The city's francophile 17th- and 18th-century architects, inspired by the tastes of the French court, laid out broad avenues and airy piazzas and lined them with low-slung neoclassical buildings.

Most visitors come to Turin with business in mind (often at the Fiat and Pirelli works in the sprawling industrial suburbs). Those who take the time to look around the historic center, though, discover an elegant and sophisticated city that has changed little since more gracious centuries, with some stunning museum collections and the charm of a place that, for all its francophile leanings, is quintessentially Italian.

ESSENTIALS

GETTING THERE   By Plane   Caselle airport handles domestic and inter-European flights. Buses make the half-hour run to and from the airport and Porta Nuova station every 30 minutes (6,000L/$3.95).

By Train   From the main station, Porta Nuova, Turin is connected with Milan by 14 trains a day (a 1 1/2-hour trip) and with Rome by 10 trains a day (6 1/2-hour trip). Turin's Porta Susa train station is connected with Milan by 13 trains a day. There is also train service to Aosta and other major towns in Piedmont.

By Bus   The bus station is near the Porta Susa train station, in Piazza Susa. Buses are sometimes the only link between Turin and smaller Piedmont towns.

By Car   Turin is at the hub of an extensive network of autostradas. A4 connects Turin with Milan; A6 connects Turin with the Ligurian coast (and from there, with Genoa via A10); A5 connects Turin with Aosta; and A21 connects Turin with Asti and Piacenza, where you can connect with the A1 for Florence and Rome.

VISITOR INFORMATION   IAT tourist offices are located in the Porta Nuova train station (☎ **011/53-13-27**) and in the center of town at V. Roma 226, on Piazza San Carlo (☎ **011/53-51-81**). Both are open Monday to Saturday, 9am to 7pm. The regional tourist office is a good place to stop for info to help plan forays into other parts of Piedmont: Cor. Ferrucci 122 (☎ **0111/33-52-440**); Monday to Friday, 9am to 7pm and Saturday, 10am to 4pm.

GETTING AROUND   Central Turin is easily walkable, and there is a vast network of trams and buses. Tickets on public transportation are available at newsstands and cost 1,500L ($1). It's obligatory to validate your ticket when you board a bus or tram—you can be slapped with a hefty fine if you don't.

CITY LAYOUT   You will get a sense of Turin's refined air as soon as you step off a train into the mannerly 19th-century Stazione Porta Nuova. The stately arcaded **Via Roma,** lined with shops and cafes, proceeds from the front of the station through a series of piazzas toward the **Piazza Castello** and the center of the city, about a 15-minute walk. Directly in front of the station, the circular **Piazza Carlo Felice** is built around a garden surrounded by outdoor cafes that invite even business-minded Turinese to linger. A few steps farther along the street opens into the **Piazza San**

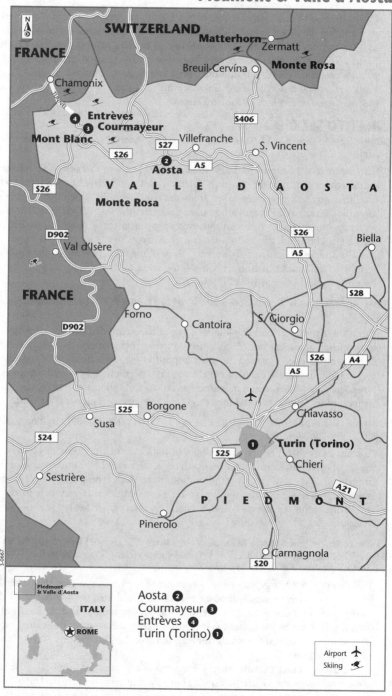

Piedmont & Valle d'Aosta

SWITZERLAND

FRANCE

Matterhorn
Zermatt
Breuil-Cervína
Monte Rosa

Chamonix

TUNNEL

Entrèves ④
③ Courmayeur
Mont Blanc

Villefranche
S. Vincent
S406

S27
S26
② Aosta
A5

VALLE D'AOSTA

Monte Rosa
S26

S26
A5
Biella

D902
Val d'Isère
S28

FRANCE

Forno
Cantoira
S. Giorgio
S26
A5
A4

D902

Borgone
S25
Susa
Chiavasso

S24
① Turin (Torino)

Sestrière
S25
Chieri

A21
PIEDMONT

Pinerolo

Carmagnola
S20

Piedmont
& Valle d'Aosta

ITALY

★ ROME

Aosta ②
Courmayeur ③
Entrèves ④
Turin (Torino) ①

Airport ✈
Skiing 🎿

Carlo, flanked by the twin churches of San Carlo and Santa Christina. At the end of Via Roma the Piazza Castello is dominated by the Palazzo Madama, so named for its 15th-century inhabitant, Marie-Christine of France. Just off the piazza is the Palazzo Reale, residence of the Savoys from 1646 to 1865, whose gardens now provide a pleasant respite from traffic and paving stones. A walk toward the river along **Via Po** takes you through Turin's university district to one of Italy's largest squares, the much-elongated **piazza Vittorio Veneto.**

WHAT TO SEE & DO
Duomo. Pz. San Giovanni. ☎ **011/43-66-101.** Free admission. Daily 7:30am–12:30pm and 3–7pm.

The controversial **Shroud of Turin** holds pride of place in this otherwise uninteresting, pompous 15th-century church. Allegedly, this is the shroud in which the body of Christ was wrapped when taken from the cross—and to which his image was miraculously affixed. Recent carbon dating suggests the shroud was manufactured sometime around the 14th century, but even naysayers might be moved by the haunting image. Unfortunately, the shroud is tucked away out of view and what you see today is a series of dramatically backlit photos of the relic. In front of the Duomo stand two landmarks of Roman Turin—the remains of a theater and the Porta Palatina, flanked by twin 16-sided towers.

Mole Antonelliana. V. Montebello 20. ☎ **011/81-70-49.** Free admission. Tues–Sun 9am–7pm.

Turin's most peculiar building—in fact, one of the weirdest structures anywhere—is comprised of a squat brick base, a steep conelike roof supporting several layers of Greek temples piled one atop the other, topped in turn by a needlelike spire, all of it rising 500 feet above the banks of the river Po. Begun in 1863 and designed as a synagogue, the Mole is now a monument to Italian unification and occasionally hosts temporary art exhibits. Ascend to the top for a fine view of Turin and the Alps.

Museo dell Automobile. Cor. Unita d'Italia 40. ☎ **011/67-76-66.** Admission 9,000L ($5.90). Tues–Sun 10am–6:30pm.

As befits a city that is responsible for 80% of Italian car manufacture, this shiny collection of mostly Italian automobiles draws car buffs from all over the world. Not too surprisingly, a century's worth of output from Fiat, which is headquartered in Turin, is well represented, and also on display are some oddities that include a roadster, emblazoned with the initials ND, that Gloria Swanson drove for her lead in *Sunset Boulevard.*

✪ **Museo Egizio and Galleria Sabauda.** V. Accademia d. Scienze 6. Museo Egizio: ☎ **011/ 56-17-776.** Admission 12,000L ($7.90). Tues–Sun 9am–7pm. Galleria Sabauda: ☎ 011/ 54-74-40. Admission 8,000L ($5.25). Tues–Sun 9am–2pm.

Turin's magnificent Egyptian collection is one of the world's largest, thanks to the fact that the Savoys ardently amassed artifacts through most of their reign. Of the 30,000 pieces on display, among the more captivating are the Temple of Ellessiya from the 15th century B.C. and the everyday paraphernalia—including eating utensils and much-shriveled foodstuffs from the tomb of the 14th-century B.C. architect Khaie and his wife.

The Savoy's other treasure trove, a magnificent collection of European painting, fills the salons of the Galleria Sabauda above the Egyptian collection. The Savoy's royal taste ran heavily to painters of the Flemish and Dutch schools, and the Van Dycks, Van Eycks, Rembrandts, and Van der Weydens, among others, comprise one of Italy's largest collections of northern European paintings. Italian artists, including those from the Piedmont, are also well represented.

Museo Nazionale del Risorgimento. V. Accademia d. Scienze 5. ☎ **011/56-21-147.** Admission 8,000L ($5.25). Tues–Sat 9am–6pm, Sun 9am–12:30pm.

Much of modern Italian history has been played out in Turin, and much of it, fittingly, in this palazzo that was home to the first king of a unified Italy, Vittorio Emanuele II, and the seat of its first parliament, in 1861. While any self-respecting town in Italy has a museum of the risorgimento, the movement that launched Italian unification, this one is the best. Documents, paintings, and other paraphernalia recount the heady days when Vittorio Emanuele banded with Garibaldi and his Red Shirts to oust the Bourbons from Sicily and the Austrians from the north to create a unified Italy.

PARKS & GARDENS

The **Parco del Valentino** (☎ **011/66-99-372**), a lush sweep of greenery along the Po south of Corso Vittorio Emanuele II, provides a wonderful retreat from Turin's well-mannered streets and piazzas. Inside the park, the **Borgo Medioevale,** built for Turin's 1884 world exposition, is a faithful reconstruction of a Piedmont village, while the **nearby Castello del Valentino** is the real thing—an 18th-century royal residence. The park is open daily from 8am to 8pm.

ATTRACTIONS NEARBY

Basilica di Superga. East side of the Po, north of the town center. ☎ **011/89-80-083.** Free admission. Daily 8:30am-12pm and 3pm-6pm. Reached by rack railway, with a terminus on Cor. Casale.

As thanksgiving to the Virgin Mary for Turin's deliverance from the French siege of 1706, Vittorio Amadeo II commissioned Juvan, the master Piedmontese architect, to build this baroque basilica on a hill high above the city. The exterior, with a beautiful neoclassic porch and lofty drum dome, is far more interesting than the gloomy interior, which serves as a mausoleum for the kings of Sardegna. There's a fine view of the Alps from the terrace, and getting up here, via a narrow railway through verdant countryside, is half the fun of a visit.

Palazzina di Caccia di Stupinigi. ☎ **011/35-81-220.** Admission 10,000L ($6.60). Tues–Sun 9:30am–12:30pm and 2–6pm. Bus: 63 from Porta Nouva train station to Pz. Caio Mario; change to bus 41.

Just about the only indications that this sumptuous, lavishly decorated palace was built as a hunting lodge are the frescoes of hunting scenes and a recurring deer motif—notice, for instance, the large, gold-plated buck on the roof. Much of the lodge, to which the members of the House of Savoy retired for hunts in the royal forests that still surround it, is given over to the decorative art and furniture collections of the Museo d'Arte e Ammobiliamento.

WHERE TO STAY
A HOSTEL

Ostello Torino. V. Alby 1, 10131 Torino. ☎ **011/66-02-939.** 97 beds. 17,000L ($11.20) per bed for IH members, 22,000L ($14.50) for nonmembers. Rates include breakfast. No credit cards. 11:30pm curfew. Check in from 7am–9pm and 3:30–11:30pm. Bus: 52 from Porta Nuova station.

It's modern, has a garden, and isn't too far from the center of town. Other pluses: there's a restaurant where you can get a complete meal for 12,000L ($7.90) and a laundry. One minus: Unless you're part of an authorized tour group, you can't stay here between December 22 and mid-February.

DOUBLES FOR LESS THAN 100,000 LIRE ($65.80)

Hotel Bellavista. V. B. Galliari 15, 10125 Torino. ☎ **011/66-98-139.** Fax 011/66-87-989. 18 rms, 7 with bath. TEL TV. 55,000L ($36.20) single; 90,000L ($59.20) double without bath, 110,000L ($72.35) double with bath; 140,000L ($92.10) triple with bath. AE, MC, V.

Step off the elevator on the sixth floor of this apartment house in a quiet residential neighborhood between the Porta Nuova railway station and the city center and you will find yourself in a sun-filled corridor that's a garden of houseplants and opens onto a wide terrace. Many of the simply furnished but comfortable rooms also have terraces, and most afford pleasant views over the surrounding rooftops—the best views in the house are across the river toward the hills.

Hotel Bologna. Cor. Vittorio Emanuele II 60, 10121 Torino. ☎ **011/56-20-290.** Fax 011/56-20-193. 50 rms, 45 with bath. TEL TV. 75,000L ($49.35) single; 100,000L ($65.80) double. Breakfast 6,000L ($3.95) for one, 10,000L ($6.60) for two. AE, MC, V.

You can't top this family-run hotel just across the street from the Porta Nuova train station for location and affordable comfort. Each of the 50 rooms, spread over several floors of a gracious 18th-century apartment house, is different. Some are quite grand, incorporating frescoes, fireplaces, and other original details (rooms 52 and 64 are the most elegant); others have recently been renovated in sleek modern style. All but a few have baths, and many have been outfitted with multiple beds for families.

Hotel Magenta. Cor. Emanuele II 67, 10121 Torino. ☎ **011/54-26-49.** Fax 011/54-47-55. 18 rms, 10 with bath. TV. 47,000L ($30.90) single without bath, 63,000L ($41.45) single with bath; 60,000L ($39.50) double without bath, 90,000L ($59.20) double with bath. AE, MC, V.

Just west of the Porta Nuova station, this homey pension occupies a wing of the second floor of an apartment house. A long central hallway, decked out with comfy couches, ornate moldings, and crystal chandeliers leads to rooms that are a bit less opulent but pleasant and spacious nonetheless, some with bath and TV. In the morning, you can grab an espresso and pastry at the little bar in the lobby.

WORTH A SPLURGE

Victoria Hotel. V. Nino Costa 4, 10123 Torino. ☎ **011/56-11-909.** Fax 011/56-11-806. 90 rms, all with bath. A/C TEL TV. 150,000L ($98.70) single, 180,000L ($118.40) deluxe single; 220,000L ($144.75) double, 250,000L ($164.50) deluxe double. Rates include breakfast. AE, MC, V.

Step through the doors of this somewhat plain-looking building and you'll think you're in an English country house. That's the whole idea, and the Anglophile decor works splendidly. The lobby is done up as a country house drawing room, with floral sofas, deep armchairs, and a view onto a garden, and the sunny breakfast room, where a sumptuous buffet is served, resembles a conservatory. Guest rooms, all with sleek Italian marble baths, are handsomely furnished with mahogany bedsteads, fabric wall-coverings, and writing desks; "deluxe" accommodations, each with its own distinctive look, are oversized and contain such flourishes as canopied beds and richly covered divans.

WHERE TO DINE
MEALS FOR LESS THAN 20,000 LIRE ($13.15)

Brek. Pz. Carlo Felice 22. ☎ **011/54-96-11.** Antipasto and pasta from 5,000L ($3.30), main courses 7,000L–12,000L ($4.60–$7.90). AE, MC, V. Mon–Sat 11:30am–3pm and 6:30–10:30pm. CAFETERIA.

This spiffy outlet of a chain of cafeterias, done up to look like a rustic trattoria, enjoys fashionable digs on the Piazza Carlo Felice. A lunchtime crowd lines up outside to enjoy the pleasing and affordable fare served up from the pasta and salad counters and a grill where meats are done to your taste as you watch. Sandwiches and the huge salads, washed down with wine by the glass, provide one of the most satisfying light meals to be had in Turin.

Da Mauro. V. Maria Vittoria 21. ☎ **011/83-97-811.** Antipasto and pasta from 8,000L ($5.25), main courses 10,000L–16,000L ($6.60–$10.50). MC, V. Tues–Sun 12:30–3pm and 7–10pm. Closed Mon and July. TUSCAN.

Tuscan dishes, including any number of spicy pastas, are the specialty in this pleasant trattoria, and they are deftly prepared. This is where Turinese come when they hanker for a grilled Florentine steak, and the scaloppine dishes, lamb, and roast game birds are always excellent as well.

Dai Saletta. V. Belfiore 37. ☎ **011/68-78-67.** Antipasto and pasta from 7,000L ($4.60), main courses 9,000L–15,000L ($5.90–$9.85). V. Mon–Sat 12:30–2:30pm and 7:30pm–1am. Closed Sun and Aug. PIEDMONTESE.

One of the few kitchens in Turin that remains open into the wee hours turns out a nice selection of homey trattoria fare, served in a tiny, cramped dining room near the train station. Homemade pasta dishes are delicious and constitute a meal in themselves, but it would be a shame not to try one of the delicious meat courses, which often include that Turinese favorite, bolito misto.

Porto di Savano. Pz. Vittorio Veneto 2. ☎ **011/81-73-500.** Antipasto and pasta from 7,000L ($4.60), main courses 9,000L–15,000L ($5.90–$9.85). MC, V. Tues 7:30–10:30pm, Wed–Sun 12:30–2:30pm and 7:30–10:30pm. Closed Mon–Tues lunch and July. PIEDMONTESE.

What is probably the most popular trattoria in Turin is tucked under the arcades along the city's largest piazza. Seating is family-style, at long tables that crowd a series of rooms beneath old photos and mementos, and the typically Piedmontese fare never fails to please. Several variations of gnocchi are usually made fresh daily, as is pasticcio, a pasta casserole, and these can nicely be followed with another house specialty, braised beef.

WORTH A SPLURGE

✪ **C'era una Volta.** Cor. Vittorio Emanuele II 42. ☎ **011/65-04-589.** Tasting menu, 45,000L ($29.60). AE, MC, V. Mon–Sat 7–10:30pm. Closed Sun and Aug. TURINESE.

To enter Once Upon a Time, you must ring a bell at street level, then climb the stairs to an large, old-fashioned dining room filled with dark credenzas. The food, delivered by a highly professional wait staff that has been here for years, is authentically Turinese and never seems to stop coming. A typical menu, which changes daily, might include crepes with ham and cheese, risotto with artichokes, a carrot flan, rabbit stew, a slice of beef with polenta, and any number of other homey, wonderfully prepared dishes.

CAFES

Cafe sitting is a centuries-old tradition in sophisticated Turin, and Via Roma and the piazzas it widens into are lined with gracious salons that have been serving coffee to Turinese for decades, even centuries. Auto executives and students alike frequent the city's two most famous, fin-de-siecle spots, **Baratti e Milano** and **Mulassano,** both on Piazza Castello. Some other places where you can stylishly sip an espresso and munch on a pastry beneath gilded mirrors and crystal chandeliers are **Casa del Caffè,** near the train station on Piazza Carlo Felice, and **Caffè San Carlo** and **Caffè Torino,** both on the Piazza San Carlo.

Turin has a sizable sweet tooth, satisfied by any number of pastry and candy shops. Perhaps the best chocolatier north of Perugia is **Pfatisch,** at Cor. Vittorio Emanuele II 76 (closed Sunday afternoon and Monday). A wider variety of sweets, including sumptuous meringues, is dispensed at **Fratelli Stratta,** Pz. San Carlo 191 (closed Sunday and Monday morning).

DAY TRIPS TO SAVIGLIANO & SALUZZO

Savigliano is one of those towns everyone dreams of stumbling upon in Italy—it's filled with Renaissance riches, but is still undiscovered. The town center is the broad expanse of the **Piazza Santa Rosa,** surrounded by arcades, overlooked by a medieval tower, and lined with many of the town's grand palaces, which once housed summering members of the Savoy clan. Unfortunately, these and another fine collection of palazzi along the **Via Jerusalem** are closed to the public, so you'll have to settle for a gander at their gorgeous facades.

The pride of Saluzzo is its sleepy upper town, huddled beneath its **Castello di Manta.** Along the warren of narrow lanes you'll find the 13th-century **Chiesa di San Giovanni** and the **Casa Cavassa,** which is worth a look, not for the musty civic museum it houses, but for its porticoed courtyard. Savigliano is 34 miles south of Turin, and is served by three trains a day from Turin (about a half-hour trip). From there, hourly trains make the 20-minute run to Saluzzo. Saluzzo is also connected with Turin by 15 buses a day.

The most direct driving route to Savigliano from Turin follows the A6 autostrada for 21 miles south to the exit near Brà; from the exit, follow S231 west for 6 miles. Saluzzo is another 8 miles west on S231. If you are making the sweep through the wine country via Asti and Alba (see below), you can continue west from Alba for 21 miles on S231 to Savigliano.

2 The Piedmont Wine Country

South of Turin, the Po valley rises into the rolling Langhe and Roero hills, flanked by orchards and vineyards. You'll recognize the region's place names from the labels of its excellent wines, among them Asti Spumante, Barbaresco, and Barolo. Tasting these vintages at the source is one reason to visit the wine country, of course; another is to stroll through the medieval and Renaissance towns that rise from the vineyards and the picturesque villages that crown many a hilltop. And vines are not all that flourish in the fertile soil—truffles top the list of the region's gastronomic delights, which also include down-home country fare like rabbit and game dishes, excellent cheeses, and plump fruit.

As you set out to explore the wine country, think of three words—*rent a car.* While it's quite easy to reach some of the major towns by train or bus from Turin, setting out from those centers for smaller places can be difficult (there are some buses, but they tend to be few and far between). The central road through the region is S231, a heavily trafficked and unattractive highway that links many of the region's towns and cities; turn off this road whenever possible to explore the region's more rustic backwaters. If you wish to spend a night or two in pleasant surroundings, head for Alba and the villages that surround it.

ESSENTIALS

GETTING THERE   By Train   Two trains an hour link Asti with Turin, only 45 minutes away; buses 2 and 4 connect the station with the center of town. There are

Horses & Donkeys

Asti and Alba, bitter rivals through much of the Middle Ages, each celebrate the autumnal harvest with equine celebrations that are horses of a very different color.

The **Palio,** Asti's annual horse race, is run the third Sunday of September. Like the similar but more famous horse race that the Tuscan city of Siena mounts, Asti's palio begins with a medieval pageant through the town and ends with a wild bareback ride around the Campo del Palio. The race coincides with Asti's other great revel, the **Douja d'Or,** a week-long fair-cum-bacchanal celebrating the grape.

On the first Sunday of October Alba pulls a spoof on Asti with the **Palio degli Asini** (Race of the Asses). The event, which coincides with Alba's annual truffle fair, is not as speedy as Asti's slicker, horseback palio, but it's a lot more fun. Good-natured as the event is, though, it is rooted in some of the darkest days of Alba's history. In the 13th century Asti, then one of the most powerful republics of northern Italy, besieged Alba and burned the surrounding vineyards. Then, to add insult to injury, the victors held their palio in Alba, just to put the humbled citizenry further in its place. Alba then staged a palio with asses, a not so subtle hint of what they thought of their victors and their pompous pageantry.

no direct trains between Turin and Alba; it's necessary to make the one-hour trip to Brà, nine-hour trip to Brà, 9 miles west of Alba, and connect there for the 15-minute ride to Alba via hourly train service.

By Car   Asti, 73km (44 miles) east of Turin, can be reached from Turin in less than an hour via the A21 autostrada. The most direct way to reach Alba from Turin is to follow the A6 autostrada for 35 km (21 miles) south to the exit near Brà, and from the autostrada exit S231 east for 24km (14^1/$_2$ miles) to Alba. If you want to work Alba into a trip to Asti—which you should—take A21 to Asti and from there follow S 231 southwest for 30km (18 miles) to Alba.

By Bus   Hourly buses make the trip between Alba and Turin in about 1^1/$_2$ hour.

VISITOR INFORMATION   In Asti, the **APT tourist office** is near the train station at Pz. Alfieri 34 (☎ **0141/53-03-57**), open Monday to Friday from 9am to 12:30pm and 3 to 6pm, and Saturday from 9am to 12:30pm. Among the office's offerings is a Carta del Vini, an annotated map that will point you to surrounding vineyards that provide wine tastings. In Alba, the **APT tourist office** is on Piazza Medford, across from the bus station (☎ **0173/35-833**), open Monday to Friday from 9am to 12:30pm and 2:30 to 6:30pm, and Saturday from 9am to 12:30pm.

ALBA

Lovely old Alba retains a medieval flavor that's as mellow as the wines it produces. Aside from the 14th-century Duomo—where the treasure is the choir, with inlaid stalls from 1500—there aren't too many sights to see. But it's a pleasure just to walk along the Via Vittorio Emanuele and narrow streets of the old town, checking out shop windows for a glimpse of Alba's other famous product, truffles.

On Saturday and Sunday mornings from October through December, Alba hosts a truffle market where you may well be tempted to part with your hard-earned cash for one of the fragrant specimens (which could cost as much as $1,000 a pound).

VISITING THE WINE VILLAGES

Just to the south of Alba lie some of the region's most enchanting wine villages. But before you set out on the labyrinth of small country roads, outfit yourself with a map and list of vineyards from the tourist office in Alba. **Grinzane di Cavour** is built around a castle housing an enoteca (open Wednesday to Monday from 9am to noon and from 2:30 to 6:30pm) where you can get enjoy a fine sampling of Barolo. Nearby is **Barolo** itself, a romantic-looking place with its own 12th-century castle and a number of shops selling the village's rich red wines. Tiny **Novello** crowns the adjoining hilltop, and just to the south, little **La Morra** affords stunning views over the rolling, vineyard-clad countryside and has a fascinating wine museum (open Monday to Friday from 8:30am to noon and 2:30 to 6pm).

ASTI

The Asti of sparkling-wine fame is a bustling modern city more concerned with everyday business than entertaining tourists, but there are many treasures to be found in the history-drenched old town—medieval towers (120 of them still stand), Renaissance palaces, and broad piazzas provide the perfect setting in which to sample the town's famous product.

For a look at the town's Renaissance palaces you need only to take a stroll along the **Corso Alfieri;** most of what's worth seeing in Asti is on or just off this main drag. This street and Asti's grandest piazza are named for the town's most famous native son, the 18th-century poet, Vittorio Alfieri. His home, on the corso at 375, houses a small, memento-filled museum.

Second to none in Asti is San Secondo, the town's patron saint. He was imprisoned in the Torre Rosse, one of many fine towers built by the town's powerful families, then beheaded on the spot where the church erected in his honor, the **Collegiata di San Secondo,** now stands (open daily from 7am to noon and from 3:30 to 7pm). Not only does this romanesque-gothic structure have the honor of housing the saint's remains in its eerie crypt, but it is also the permanent home of the coveted Palio Astigiano, the banner awarded to the horseman who wins the town's annual Palio (see below). The **Palazzo di Citta** (City Hall) is across the piazza.

Asti's "other" church is its 14th-century, redbrick **Duomo,** every inch of its cavernous interior festooned with frescoes by 16th- and 17th-century artists (open daily from 7:30am to noon and 3 to 7pm). The most notable feature of the church of **San Pietro in Consavia** is its round, 10th-century baptistery; the 15th-century interior and adjoining cloisters house a small archeological collection (open Tuesday to Saturday from 9am to noon and 3 to 7pm, Sunday from 3 to 7pm).

WHERE TO STAY
IN ALBA

Albergo Piemonte. Pz. Rossetti 6, 12051 Alba. ☎/fax **0173/44-13-54.** 12 rms. 50,000L ($32.90) single; 85,000L ($55.90) double without bath; 100,000L ($65.80) double with bath.

This homey old-fashioned hotel is nicely tucked away on a quiet piazza near the Duomo, making it a fine base for strolls through Alba's medieval streets. The pleasant rooms, reached through the family-run trattoria downstairs, face a quiet courtyard and are small but kept in sparkling, tiptop shape.

Hotel Savona. Pz. Savona 2, 12051 Alba. ☎ **0173/44-04-40.** Fax 0173/36-43-12. 98 rms, all with bath. A/C MINIBAR TEL TV. 85,000L ($55.90) single; 120,000L ($78.95) double; 200,000L ($131.60) triple suite. AE, MC, V.

While this fine old hotel facing a handsome brick piazza at the edge of the old town retains the charm of a solid, provincial hostelry, recent renovations have added a slick, modern look. Rooms are tastefully decorated in pastel shades with contemporary furnishings, shiny new baths (many with Jacuzzis), and minibars; many open to small terraces.

IN NOVELLO

The pretty hilltop village of Novello is about 15km (9 miles) south of Alba.

Albergo Al Castello da Diego. Pz. G. Marconi 4, 12060 Novello. ☎ **0173/73-11-44** or 73-12-50. Fax 0173/73-12-50. 10 rms, all with bath. TEL TV. 100,000L ($65.80) double, 150,000L ($98.70) suite. Rates include breakfast. MC, V.

You might expect the Addams family to greet you at the door of this spooky hilltop mansion, a brick Victorian pile built atop the ruins of a 12th-century castle. Not to worry: The welcome is friendly and the lodgings delightful. Rooms, reached by an endlessly winding staircase, are huge and filled with a pleasant mix of reproduction antiques; many of the baths are circular, tucked into turrets, and many rooms open to terraces. The enormous two-room suites occupy entire wings of the house, and are ornately furnished with draped beds and claw-footed divans. Breakfast is served in an intimate, paneled salon, while the cavernous dining room seats 1,000.

Hotel Barbabuc. V. Giordano 35, 12060 Novello. ☎/fax **0173/73-12-98.** 9 rms, all with bath. TEL TV. 140,000L ($92.10) double. MC, V.

Behind the centuries-old facade of a house near the village square lies this charming new hotel, airy and filled with light. Guest rooms, furnished with a tasteful mix of contemporary Italian furnishings and country antiques, wrap around a delightful garden. Downstairs, there's a handsome bar area, an enoteca where local wines can be tasted, and an intimate little dining room where family-style meals are served.

WHERE TO DINE
IN ALBA

Vineria dell'Umberto. Pz. Savona 4. ☎ **0173/44-13-97.** Antipasto and pasta from 9,000L ($5.90), main courses 10,000L–16,000L ($6.60–$10.55). No credit cards. Tues–Sun 8pm–midnight. Closed in Aug. PIEDMONTESE.

The main business here is dispensing wines by the glass, making this a fine place to sample the produce of the local vineyards. The simple fare that comes out of the kitchen, especially the selection of rich pasta dishes, is also very good.

IN ASTI

Trattoria del Mercato. Cor. Einaudi 50 (at Campo del Palio). ☎ **0141/59-21-42.** Antipasto and pasta from 5,000L ($3.30), main courses from 8,000L–15,000L ($5.25–$9.85). No credit cards. Mon–Sat, noon–3:30pm and 7:30–9:30pm. Closed Sun evenings. PIEDMONTESE.

There's plenty of atmosphere here, and it's just not of the romantic candlelight variety. Instead, this plain old room has the feel of an old-fashioned family sort of place, right down to the old crones who seem to pass the entire day over a glass of red wine. The food is old-fashioned, too, and excellent, including whatever pasta seems to be on the stove that day (often, there's an excellent risotto) and a rich rabbit stew.

IN BAROLO

✪ **La Cantinetta.** V. Roma 33. ☎ **0173/56-198.** Tasting menu, 40,000L ($26.30). AE, V. Tues–Sun, noon–3pm and 7–10:30pm. PIEDMONTESE.

Two brothers, Maurilo and Paolo Chiappetto, do a fine job of introducing guests to the pleasures of the Piedmontese table in their cozy dining room grouped around an open hearth. A seemingly endless stream of servings, which change daily, emerge from the kitchen: a wonderful country pâté, vegetables dipped in hot local olive oil, ravioli in a truffle sauce, risotto with wild mushrooms, a thick slab of roast veal, a tender cut of beef, and salad made with wild herbs. The wonderful house wines come from the vines that run right up to the door of this delightful restaurant.

IN LA MORRA

Ristorante Belvedere. Pz. Castello 5. ☎ **0173/50-190.** Antipasto and pasta from 10,000L ($6.60), main courses from 12,000L–20,000L ($7.90–$13.15). V. Tues–Sun, noon–3pm and 7–10pm. Closed Sun evenings and Jan–Feb. PIEDMONTESE.

Sitting in this rustic little restaurant, perched high above vineyards that roll away in all directions, is in itself a pleasure. The food arrives as one delight after another: A wonderful salad of truffles and Parmesan cheese, and homemade agnolotti in a mushroom sauce, are among the house specialties, which include many other homey pasta dishes and roast meats, all to be washed down, of course, with a bottle of the local Barolo.

3 Valle d'Aosta

Skiers, hikers, and fresh-air and scenery enthusiasts flock to this tiny, mountainous region north of Turin, eager to enjoy one of Italy's favorite Alpine playgrounds just a little more than an hour by train or car. Snowcapped peaks, among them the Matterhorn and Mont Blanc, rise above the valley's verdant pastures and forests; waterfalls cascade into mountain streams; small villages retain centuries-old Alpine traditions and romantic castles cling to the hillsides; there's even a fascinating little city lying at the heart of the region—Aosta, entrenched in its Roman and medieval past and a fine place to begin a tour of the surrounding mountains and valleys.

ESSENTIALS

GETTING THERE   By Train   Aosta is served by 10 trains a day to and from Turin (2-hour trip) and 10 a day to and from Milan (2½-hour trip).

By Bus   Aosta's bus station, directly across the piazza from the train station, handles 10 buses to and from Turin daily; buses also connect Aosta with other popular spots in the valley, among them Courmayeur, where you can connect with a shuttle bus to the Palud cable car (see below) and Cogne, a major gateway to the Parco Nazionale de Gran Paradiso (see below).

By Car   The A5 autostrada from Turin shoots up the length of the Valle d'Aosta en route to France and Switzerland via the Mont Blanc tunnel; there are numerous exits in the valley. Traffic can be very heavy in the busy tourist months, especially August and February, the height of the ski season.

VISITOR INFORMATION   The **tourist office** in Aosta, Pz. Chanoux 8 (☎ **0165/23-66-27**), dispenses a wealth of information on hotels, restaurants, and sights throughout the region, along with listings of campgrounds, maps of hiking trails, information about ski lift tickets and special discounted ski packages, outlets for bike rentals, and rafting trips. It's open Monday to Saturday from 9am to 1pm and 3 to 8pm, and Sunday from 9am to 1pm. The **office of the Club Alpino Italiano,** at the same address (☎ **0165/40-194**), can tell you about the best places to hike and climb. **Parco Nazionale del Gran Paradiso headquarters** are in Aosta at V. Losanna 5 (☎ **0165/44-26**).

AOSTA

This mountain town, surrounded by snow-capped peaks, is not only pleasant but it also has soul—the product of a history that goes back to Roman times. While you're not going to find much in the line of pristine Alpine quaintness here in the Valle d'Aosta's busy tourist and economic center, you can spend some enjoyable time strolling past Roman ruins and medieval bell towers while checking out the chic shops that sell everything from Armani suits to locally-made Fontina cheese. Aosta is also a fine base from which to make forays into less-trammeled parts of the region.

ROMAN AOSTA & OTHER SIGHTS

The Rome of the Alps sits majestically within its preserved walls, and the monuments of the Empire make it easy to envision the days when Aosta was one of Rome's most important trading and military outposts. Two Roman gates arch gracefully across the Via Anselmo, Aosta's main thoroughfare: The **Porta Pretoria,** the western entrance to the Roman town, and the **Arco di Augusto** (sometimes called Arco Romano), the eastern entrance built in A.D. 25 to commemorate a Roman victory of the Celts. A Roman bridge spans the river Buthier; just a few steps north of the Porta Pretoria you'll find the facade of the **Teatro Romano** and the ruins of the amphitheater, which once accommodated 20,000 spectators (open Monday to Friday from 9am to 6:30pm, Saturday and Sunday from 9am to 12pm and 2 to 5pm).

Behind the banal 19th-century facade of Aosta's **Duomo,** on Piazza Giovanni XXIII, lie two remarkable treasures: an ivory diptych from A.D. 406 that depicts the Roman emperor Honorius, and a 12th-century mosaic in the chapel.

The **Collegiata dei Santi Pietro e Orso** is a hodgepodge from the 11th through the 18th century. The 12th-century cloisters are a fascinating display of romanesque storytelling—40 columns are capped with carved capitals depicting scenes from the Bible and the life of Saint Orso. In a room above the main church, a haunting, 11th-century fresco cycle recounts the life of Christ and the Apostles. It's open from April through September, Tuesday to Sunday from 9am to 7pm; October through March from 9:30am to noon and 2:30 to 5:30pm.

NEARBY ATTRACTIONS

CASTLE OF FENIS This castle near the town of Fenis, built by the Challants, the viscounts of Aosta throughout much of the Middle Ages, is the most impressive and best preserved of the many castles perched on the hillsides above the Valle d'Aosta. You can scamper through ramparts, turrets, towers, and dungeons, and enjoy some fine views of the Alps and the valley below as well.

The castle (☎ **0165/76-42-63**) is 30km (18 miles) east of Aosta on route S26. Admission is 4,000L ($2.65), and hours are March through November, daily from 9am to 7pm, and December through February, daily from 10am to 5pm.

CERVINA-BREUIL & THE MATTERHORN You don't come to Cervina-Breuil to see the town, a banal collection of tourist facilities—the sight to see, and you can't miss it, is the Matterhorn. Its distinctive profile looms majestically above the valley, beckoning visitors to ascend to its glaciers via cable car to the Plateau Rossa (about 35,000L/$23 round-trip) or by an excellent trail past Lac du Goillet to the Colle Superiore delle Cime Bianche (about 3 hours). Cervina-Breuil is 30 miles northwest of Aosta via routes A5 and S406.

PILA It's well worth the trip up the winding road to this mile-high resort, 10 miles south of Aosta. The views are incredible. And aside from getting an eagle's-eye view of the valleys rolling away in all directions at your feet, you can also take a gander at Europe's two most spectacular peaks, Mont Blanc and the Matterhorn.

COURMAYEUR

This attractive hamlet is the Valle d'Aosta's resort extraordinaire, a pleasant collection of Alpine chalets catering to a well-heeled international crowd of skiers. Even if you don't ski, you can happily while away the time sipping a grog while regarding the craggy bulk of **Mont Blanc.** Thus fortified, you may want to board the cable car at outlying Palud for the heart-stopping ride over the summit all the way to Chamonix, in France (64,000L/$42.10 round-trip; 36,000L/$23.70 to the last aerie on the Italian side, Rifugio Turino). Be sure to bring your passport if you want to descend on French soil.

PARCO NAZIONALE DI GRAN PARADISO

The little town of Cogne is the most convenient gateway to one of Europe's finest parcels of unspoiled nature, the former hunting grounds of King Vittorio Emanuele that now comprise this vast and lovely national park. The park encompasses five valleys and a total of 1,400 square miles of forests and pastureland, where ibex, chamois, and many other Alpine beasts roam wild.

Humans, too, can roam these wilds via a vast network of well-marked trails. Cross-country skiing, kayaking, and horseback rides are other activities in this natural wonderland. Among the few places where the hand of man intrudes ever so gently on nature is in a few scattered hamlets within the park borders, and in the **Giardino Alpino Paradiso,** a stunning collection of rare Alpine fauna near the village of Valnontey, just a mile south of Cogne (open June 10 through September 10, daily 9:30am to 12:30pm and 2:30 to 6:30pm. Admission is 3,000L/$1.95).

Park headquarters are in Aosta, at V. Losanna 5 (☎ **0165/44-126**). Cogne is about 18 miles south of Aosta via S35 and S507; there is also frequent bus service to and from Aosta.

WHERE TO STAY

Many hotels in the Valle d'Aosta demand that guests take their meals on the premise and stay three nights or more. However, outside of busy tourist times, hotels often have rooms to spare and are willing to be a little more liberal in their policies. Rates vary with a confusing schedules of seasons; in general, expect to pay highest for a room in August, at Christmas and Easter, and the least for a room in the fall.

IN AOSTA

Belle Epoque. V. d'Avise 18, 11100 Aosta. ☎ **0165/26-22-76.** 12 rms. 40,000L ($26.30) single, 50,000L ($33) double. No credit cards.

Well, there's not too much belle about this little place, though the stuccoed old building has a cozy Alpine look to it. The same can't be said of the somewhat dank interior, but you can't beat the price for these spotless and Spartan rooms, which share similarly spotless baths.

Bus. V. Malherbes 18, 11100 Aosta. ☎ **0165/43-645,** Aosta. 40 rms, all with bath. TEL TV. 75,000L–85,000L ($49.35–$55.90) single, 100,000L–125,000L ($65.80–$82.25) double. Rates include breakfast. AE, MC, V.

One of the nicest things about this newer, family-run hotel is its location, on a pleasant side street just a short walk from the center of Aosta. Many of the rooms, which are large and comfortably furnished in a somewhat drab modern style, overlook meadows and the surrounding peaks.

Roma. V. Torino 7, 11100 Aosta. ☎ **0165/40-821.** Fax 0165/32-404. 33 rms, all with bath. TEL. 65,000L–88,000L ($42.75–$57.90) single; 114,000L–136,000L ($75–$89.50) double; 156,000L–186,000L ($102.65–$122.35) triple. Rates include breakfast. AE, DC, MC, V.

Tucked onto a side street near the center of town, the Roma is named for the monuments of the Empire that surround it. The paneled, plaid-decorated lobby and adjoining bar are pleasant places to relax, there's a covered terrace where breakfast is served in good weather, and the guest rooms are crisply modern and bright. Full board can be arranged.

IN COURMAYEUR

Eidelweiss. V. Marconi 42, 11013 Courmayeur. ☎ **0165/84-15-90.** Fax 0165/84-16-18. 30 rms, all with bath. TEL TV. 70,000L ($75.65) double. Rates include breakfast. MC, V.

In winter, the pine-paneled salons and cozy rooms of this chalet-style hotel near the center of town attract a friendly international set of skiers, and in summer many Italian families spend a month or two at a time. The Roveyaz family extends a hearty welcome to all and provides large, modern accommodations; many open onto terraces overlooking the mountains. The nicest rooms are those on the top floor, tucked under the eaves. Meals are provided in the cheerful main-floor dining room, and room and board rates are available.

IN COURMAYEUR-ENTREVES

La Grange. C.P. 75, 11013 Courmayeur-Entrèves. ☎ **0165/86-97-33.** Fax 0165/86-97-44. 23 rms. MINIBAR TEL TV. 150,000L–200,000L ($98.70–$131.60) double. Rates include breakfast. AE, DC, MC, V. Closed Oct–Nov.

What may well be the most charming hotel in the Valle d'Aosta occupies a converted barn in the bucolic village of Entrèves, only a few miles from Courmayeur. None of the rooms are the same, though all are decorated with a pleasing smattering of antiques and rustic furnishings. The stucco-walled, stone-floored lobby is a fine place to relax, with couches built around a corner hearth and a little bar area. A lavish, buffet breakfast is served in a prettily paneled room off the lobby.

WHERE TO DINE
IN AOSTA

Grotta Azzura. V. Croce di Citta 97. ☎ **0165/26-24-74.** Antipasto and pasta from 7,000L ($4.60), main courses 9,000L–15,000L ($5.90–$9.85), pizza from 6,000L ($3.95). MC, V. Thurs–Tues, noon–2:30pm and 6–10:30pm. PIZZA/SOUTHERN ITALIAN.

The best pizzeria in town also serves, as its name suggests, a bounty of fare from southern climes, along the lines of spaghetti with clam sauce and a wide selection of fresh fish. The pasta dishes are also good, and like the pizzas, are topped with rich local cheeses.

Trattoria Praetoria. V. San Anselmo 9. ☎ **0165/44-356.** Antipasto and pasta from 7,000L ($4.60), main courses 10,000L–16,000L ($6.60–$10.50). MC, V. Fri–Wed, 12:15pm–2:30pm and 7:15pm–9:30pm. NORTHERN ITALIAN.

This small trattoria, one of the friendliest in Aosta, takes its name from the nearby Roman gate and its menu from the surrounding countryside: rich polenta, hearty sausages, rich stews, fondues, and other mountain fare top a menu that is as popular with the locals as it is with tourists.

IN COURMAYEUR/ENTREVES

Maison de Filippo. Courmayeur-Entrèves. ☎ **0165/89-968.** Fixed-price menu 50,000L ($32.90). V. Wed–Mon, noon–2:30pm and 7–10pm. Closed Tues, June, part of July, and Nov. NORTHERN ITALIAN.

It would be a shame to come this far and not enjoy what is probably the valley's most famous restaurant, where the atmosphere is delightfully Alpine and the offerings so generous you may not want to eat again for a week. Daily menus vary, but often include a antipasto of mountain hams and salamis, a selection of pastas filled with wild mushrooms and topped with Fontina and other local cheeses, and a sampling of fresh trout and game in season. Service is casual and friendly, and in the summer you can choose between a table in the delightfully converted barn or on the flowery terrace.

Ristorante La Palud. S. la Palud, Courmayeur. ☎ **0165/89-169.** Antipasto and pasta from 9,000L ($5.90), main courses from 10,000L–18,000L ($6.60–$11.85). AE, MC, V. Thurs–Tues, noon–3pm and 7pm–10:30pm. Closed Wed. NORTHERN ITALIAN.

If you come to this cozy restaurant in the shadows of Mont Blanc on Friday, you are in for a surprise—a wide selection of fresh fish brought up from Liguria. At any time, though, a table in front of the hearth is just the place to enjoy the specialties of the Valle d'Aosta: creamy mountain hams, polenta with Fontina cheese folded into it, venison in season. There is a selection of mountain cheeses for dessert, and the wine list borrows heavily from neighboring Piedmont but also includes some local vintages.

CAFES

There are some excellent cafes in the valley where you can pleasantly while away the hours. The **Caffè Nazionale,** on Aosta's main square, Piazza Lamoux, dates from 1886, and little has changed since then; for an almost sacred experience, try taking your coffee and pastry in the frescoed room that was once a chapel of the dukes of Aosta. Up in Courmayeur, the "in" spot for an aprés ski grog is the **Caffè della Posta,** V. Roma 51, popular with a fashionable set since it opened 50 years ago.

Liguria & the Italian Riviera

by Stephen Brewer

From the top of Tuscany to the French border, Italy follows a crescent-shape strip of seacoast and mountains that comprise the region of Liguria. The pleasures of this region are no secret. Ever since the 19th century world-weary travelers have been heading for Liguria's resorts to enjoy balmy weather (ensured by the protective barrier of the Alps) and turquoise seas. Beyond the beach, the stones and tiles of proud old towns and cities bake in the sun, and hillsides are fragrant with the scent of bougainvillea and pines.

Liguria is really two coasts: the stretch east of Genoa is known as the Riviera di Levante (Rising Sun) and the stretch to the west of Genoa is known as the Riviera di Ponente (Setting Sun). Both are lined with fishing villages, including the remote hamlets of the Cinque Terre, and fashionable resorts, many of which, like San Remo, have seen their heydays fade but continue to entice visitors with palm-fringed promenades and gentle ways. Genoa itself, with its proud maritime history, is a world apart from the easygoing seaside places that surround it: brusque and clamorous, it is one of the most history filled, fascinating, and least visited cities in Italy.

EXPLORING THE REGION

Thanks to the trains speeding up and down the coast, it is a breeze to get around Liguria. If your time is limited, don't fail to include a stop in Genoa. Coming from Rome or Florence, you will probably want to approach the region from the south, in the Cinque Terre. If you're coming from France, the place to start is San Remo.

Settle into one of the Cinque Terre villages, and if possible, plan on spending at least two days so you will have time to partake of leisurely village life and to make the hike along the coast on the trails connecting the five villages. Then move on to one of the towns on the Monte Portofino promontory: Rapallo, Santa Margherita Ligure, or Camogli. Enjoy the easygoing ambience of these seaside towns, and make the trip out to picturesque Portofino.

Genoa should be explored on foot. You'll want to spend most of your time walking in the old town and visiting its museums and churches, but leave room for a port cruise and a refreshing trip up to one of the city's hilltop belvederes.

San Remo, the turn-of-the-century resort at the western end of Liguria, is a nice place to end your tour, relaxing while enjoying its seaside promenades and beaches.

1 Genoa (Genova)

With its dizzying mix of the old and the new, of sophistication and squalor, Genoa is as multilayered as the hills it clings to. It was and is, first and foremost a port city: an important maritime center for the Roman Empire, boyhood home of Christopher Columbus (whose much restored house still stands near a section of the medieval walls), and, fueled by seafaring commerce that stretched all the way to the Middle East, one of the largest and wealthiest cities of Renaissance Europe. It's easy to capture glimpses of these former glory days on the narrow lanes and dank alleyways of Genoa's portside old town, where treasure-filled palaces and fine marble churches stand next to laundry-draped tenements. In fact, life within the old medieval walls doesn't seem to have changed since the days when Genoese ships set sail to launch raids on the Venetians, crusaders embarked for the Holy Land, and Garibaldi shipped out to invade Sicily in the 19th-century struggle to unify Italy. The other Genoa, the modern city that stretches for miles along the coast and climbs the hills, is a city of international business, peaceful parks, and breezy belvederes from which you can enjoy fine views of this colorful metropolis and the sea that continues to define its identity.

ESSENTIALS

GETTING THERE   By Plane   Christofo Colombo is Genoa's international airport, handling domestic and inter-European flights. A bus connects the airport with Stazione Principe.

By Train   Genoa has two main stations, Principe, on Piazza Acquaverde near the old center, and Brignole, on Pizza Verde in the heart of the modern city. Many international trains and trains from other major Italian cities stop at both, but not always. The no. 33 bus connects the two, about 10 minutes apart, so all is not lost if you descend at the wrong one. There are hourly trains to and from Milan (about two hours), about eight trains a day to and from Rome (about six hours), and local trains every half-hour to Ventimiglia (three hours), with stops along the Riviera di Ponente.

By Car   The A10/A12 autostrada, linking France and Pisa, runs right through Genoa on an elevated motorway above the port; given heavy traffic and the difficulty of navigating Genoa's warren of streets, you will want to find a place to park your car the moment you get off the highway.

VISITOR INFORMATION   The main tourist office is at V. Roma 11/R. ☎ **010/54-15-41.** Monday to Friday, 8am to 1:15pm and 2pm to 6:30pm, Saturday, 8am to 1:30pm. There are also branches in the Principe train station (☎ **010/24-62-633**) and at the airport (☎ **010/24-15-247**); Monday to Friday, 8am to 8pm.

GETTING AROUND   Bus tickets (1,400L/90¢) are available at newsstands; you must stamp your ticket when you board a bus—you can be slapped with a hefty fine if you don't. Bus tickets can also be used on the funiculars and public elevators that climb the city's hills. You should be aware that Genoa's archaic street numbering system at times seems to have been designed to baffle tourists: Addresses in red (marked with an R) generally indicate a commercial establishment; those in black are offices or residences. So, two buildings on the same street can have the same number.

Warning: The old city can be dangerous after dark and even in mid-afternoons and Sundays, when shops are closed and streets tend to be deserted.

WHAT TO SEE & DO

Before setting out to see the palaces, churches, and art hordes that remain from Genoa's many centuries of splendor, equip yourself with a copy of "Genoa: The Old

City," distributed for free at tourist offices, museums, and many hotels. This indispensable booklet takes you on two extensive walking tours through the labyrinth of lanes and hidden piazzas of old Genoa, pointing out the many sights of architectural and historical interest along the way. An excellent starting point for a tour of the old city is Via Garibaldi (see below), which can be reached from other sections of the city on buses 18, 19, 10, 35, 39, or 40.

Cattedrale San Lorenzo. Pz. San Lorenzo. Treasury 2,000L (\$1.30). Cathedral Daily, 8am–noon and 4–7pm. Tues–Sat, 9:30am–11:45pm and 3pm–5:45pm; closed Sun–Mon.

The austerity of this 12th-century, black-and-white striped structure is enlivened ever so slightly by the fanciful French gothic carvings around the portal and the presence of two stone lions. In the frescoed interior, chapels house two of Genoa's most notable curiosities: In the first chapel on the right there is a shell fired through the roof from a ship offshore during World War II that (*mirabile dictum*) never exploded, and in the Capella di San Giovanni, a 13th-century crypt contains what Crusaders returning from the Holy Land claimed to be relics of John the Baptist. Fabled tableware appears to be the forte of the adjoining treasury: The plate upon which Saint John's head was supposedly served to Salome, a bowl allegedly used at the Last Supper, and a bowl thought at one time to be the Holy Grail.

Chiesa di Sant'Agostino. Pz. Sarzanno 35/R. ☎ **010/20-16-61.** Admission 8,000L (\$5.25). Tue–Sat, 9am–7pm, Sun, 9am–12:30. Closed Mon.

The ruined cloisters of this 13th-century church are the evocative setting for the eclectic holdings of the Museum of Ligurian Sculpture and Architecture. The collection, stunningly displayed, includes Roman columns, statuary and architectural fragments from Genoa's churches, and panels from Giovanni Pisano's crypt for Margherita of Brabant, wife of the German emperor Henry IV, who died in Genoa while en route to Rome for her husband's coronation as Holy Roman Emperor.

Civica Galleria di Palazzo Bianco. V. Garibaldi 11. ☎ **010/29-18-03.** Admission 4,000L (\$2.65). Tue–Sat, 9am–7pm, Sun, 9am–noon. Closed Mon.

One of Genoa's finest palaces, built by the powerful Grimaldi family, houses the city's most notable collection of art. The paintings here reflect the fine eye of the Duchess of Galleria, who donated the palace and her art to the city, and her preference for painters of the northern schools, most notably Van Dyck and Rubens. The collection also includes works by other European and Italian masters, including Caravaggio.

Galleria Nazionale di Palazzo Spinola. V. Pelocceria 1. ☎ **010/29-46-61.** Admission 8,000L (\$5.25). Tues–Sat 9am–7pm, Sun 2–7pm, Mon 9am–1pm.

Another prominent Genoese family, the Spinolas, donated their palace and magnificent art collection to the city two centuries ago. One of the pleasures of viewing these works is seeing them amid the splendor in which the merchant/banking family once lived. Among the treasures here are works by Van Dyck and other painters of the Dutch and Flemish schools, many of whom were brought to Genoa to paint portraits of the city's wealthy burghers. Italian masters are well represented here, too, Antonello da Messina and Guido Reni among them.

Palazzo Reale. V. Balbi 10. ☎ **010/247-0640.** Admission 8,000L (\$5.25). Mon, Tues, Sun 9am–1:30pm; Wed–Sat 9am–6:30pm.

The Royal Palace takes its name from its 19th-century tenants, the Royal House of Savoy. It was they who endowed the 17th-century palace with its ostentatious frippery, most in evidence in the hall of mirrors, the ballroom, and the throne room.

More aesthetically pleasing are the Van Dykes and other paintings gracing many of the salons.

Piazza San Matteo.

This beautiful little square is the domain of the city's most acclaimed family, the seagoing Dorias, who ruled Genoa until the end of the 18th century. The church they built on the piazza in the 12th century, San Matteo, contains the crypt of the Dorias' most illustrious son, Andrea, and the cloisters are lined with centuries-old plaques heralding the family's many accomplishments, which included drawing up Genoa's constitution in 1529. The Doria palaces surround the church in a stunning array of loggias and black-and-white-striped marble facades denoting the homes of honored citizens—Andrea's at no. 17, Branca's at no. 14.

Via Garibaldi.

Many of Genoa's museums and other sights are clustered on and around this street, one of the most beautiful in Italy, where Genoa's wealthy families built palaces in the 16th and 17th centuries. Aside from the art collections housed in the Palazzo Bianco and Palazzo Rosso (see above), the street contains a wealth of other treasures. The Palazzo Podesta, V. Garabaldi 7, hides one of the city's most beautiful fountains in its courtyard, and the Palazzo Turisi, at V. Garabaldi 9, now housing the municipal offices, proudly displays artifacts of famous Genoans: letters written by Christopher Columbus and the violin of Nicolo Paganini.

VIEWS & VISTAS

The no. 33 bus plies the scenic **Circonvallazione a Monte,** the corniche that hugs the hills and provides dizzying views over the city and the sea; you can board at Stazione Brignole. One of the best rides in town is the ascent on the Righi funicular (use a bus ticket), from Piazza Portello to a belvedere that offers stunning views and refreshing breezes. An elevator (4,000L/$2.65) lifts visitors to the observation platform atop the Gran Brigo, the modernistic tower that is the hallmark of the port, renovated for the Columbus celebrations in 1992; the observation platform provides an eagle's-eye view of one of Europe's busiest ports.

Hour-long harbor cruises provide a closer look at the bustle, along with closeup views of the Lanterna, the 360-foot-tall lighthouse built in 1544 at the height of Genoa's maritime might; Cooperativa Battellieri dei Porto di Genova ☎ **010/26-57-12;** daily from the aquarium at 11:30am and 3:15pm, 10,000L ($6.60).

WHERE TO STAY

Genoa is geared more to business than to tourism, and as a result decent, inexpensive rooms are scarce. On the other hand, just about the only time the town is booked solid is during its annual boat show, the world's largest, in October.

A HOSTEL

Ostello Per La Giovetti. V. Costanzi 10, 16136 Genova. ☎/fax **010/24-22-457.** 210 beds. 19,000L ($12.50) per person. IH card required, can be purchased at check-in for 30,000L ($19.75). Rates include breakfast. No credit cards. Midnight curfew. Closed from 9am–3:30pm, but luggage storage is available.

Not your typical hostel: it's new and attractive, and has great views over the city from its perch near the terminal of the Righi funicular. Families make out like bandits here, in four-bedded rooms with private baths; others sleep four to eight to a room. There's a big terrace, a bar, a cafeteria, and a Laundromat. It's only about 20 minutes to the center of town on the no. 40 bus, which makes the run to and from the Brignole station every 10 minutes.

Genoa

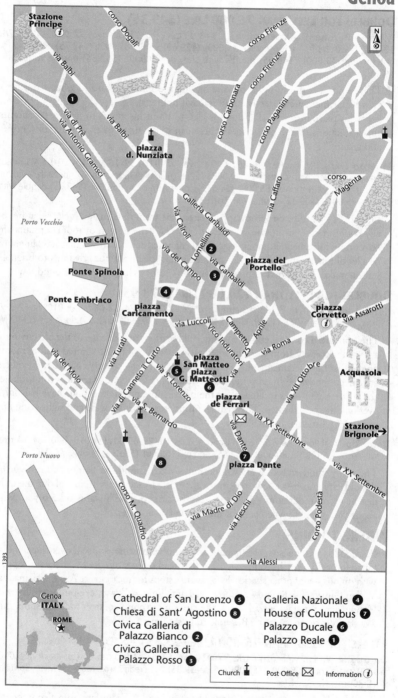

Stazione
Principe ⓘ

corso Dogali

corso Firenze

corso Firenze

via Balbi

via Balbi

via di Prè

via Antonio Gramsci

❶

corso Carbonara

corso Paganini

piazza
d. Nunziata †

corso
Magenta

Galleria Garibaldi

via Caffaro

Porto Vecchio

Ponte Calvi

Ponte Spinola

Ponte Embriaco

via Cairoli

Lomellini

via del Campo

❷

via Garibaldi

❸

piazza del
Portello

❹

piazza
Caricamento

via Luccoli

Vico Indratori

Campetto

Aprile

via Roma

piazza
Corvetto ⓘ

via Assarotti

via Turati

via del Molo

via di Canneto Il Curto

via S. Lorenzo

piazza
San Matteo †
❺ piazza
G. Matteotti
❻

via S. Bernardo

piazza
de Ferrari

via Dante

via XII Ottobre

Acquasola

via XX Settembre

Stazione
Brignole →

†

❽

Porto Nuovo

corso M. Quadrio

via Madre di Dio

❼
piazza Dante

via Fieschi

corso Podestà

via XX Settembre

1393

via Alessi

Genoa
○ ITALY

ROME ★

Cathedral of San Lorenzo ❺
Chiesa di Sant' Agostino ❽
Civica Galleria di
  Palazzo Bianco ❷
Civica Galleria di
  Palazzo Rosso ❸

Galleria Nazionale ❹
House of Columbus ❼
Palazzo Ducale ❻
Palazzo Reale ❶

Church †   Post Office ⊠   Information ⓘ

DOUBLES FOR LESS THAN 75,000 LIRE ($49.35)

Albergo Barone. V. XX Settembre 2/23 (3rd floor), 16121 Genova. ☎ **010/58-75-78.** 12 rms, 1 with bath, 1 with shower. 45,000L ($29.60) single; 65,000L ($42.75) double without shower; 70,000L ($46.05) double with shower; 80,000L ($52.65) double with bath. MC, V.

There's not a baron in sight, but the big, high-ceilinged rooms in what was once a grand apartment are perfectly comfortable if not regal. Marco, the young proprietor, keeps his place in tiptop shape and is glad to point his guests to nearby restaurants and attractions. Some of the rooms here can be set up with extra beds for families and groups.

Albergo Fiume. V. Fiume 9/R, 16121 Genova. ☎ **010/59-16-91;** Fax 010/57-05-460. 20 rms, some with bath or shower. 40,000L ($26.30) single without shower or bath, 45,000L ($29.60) single with shower, 65,000L ($42.75) single with bath; 65,000L ($42.75) double with shower, 75,000L ($49.35) double with bath. AE, MC, V.

Frankly, it's a little weird: the dapper gent at the front desk makes it clear that he really couldn't care less if you stay here or not, and the warren of rooms upstairs are eclectically furnished and pretty stark. But the international crowd that stays here can be a lot of fun, rooms and shared baths are squeaky clean, and the proximity to Brignole station makes this a good stopover if you don't want to lug your bags around town.

DOUBLES FOR LESS THAN 120,000 LIRE ($78.95)

Hotel Agnello D'Oro. V. Monachette 6, 16126. ☎ **010/24-62-084;** Fax 010/24-62-327. 35 rms, all with bath. TEL TV. 70,000L ($46.05) single; 110,000L ($72.35) double. AE, MC, V.

This converted convent enjoys a wonderful location, on the edge of the old city only a few blocks away from the Principe Station. While only the vaulted-ceiling rooms on the first floor retain any of the buildings original 16th-century character, the others have been renovated in crisp modern style and are quiet and extremely comfortable, about the nicest ones in Genoa for the price; some on the top floor have balconies overlooking the old town. The friendly proprietor dispenses wine and sightseeing tips in the cozy little bar off the lobby.

Hotel Rio. V. al Ponte Calvi 5, 16126 Genova. ☎ **010/29-05-51.** Fax 010/29-05-54. 47 rms, all with shower. TEL TV. 80,000L ($52.65) single; 115,000L ($75.65) double. AE, MC, V.

These airy, modern rooms are wonderfully located, amid the clamor and intrigue of the old city and just a few steps from the port. In fact, they're just about the only decent accommodations right in the centro storico. You'll want to keep your wits about you, though, when coming and going late at night.

WHERE TO DINE

Fast food is a Genoese specialty, and any number of storefronts all over the city disburse focaccio—the heavenly Ligurian flatbread often stuffed with cheese or topped with onions—and other snacks. Two favorite stops for focaccio are Antica Sciamadda, V. San Giorgio 14/R, and Poguotto, V. Lamellini 57. For an eye-popping survey of Genoese cuisine, take a walk along the city's most popular street for food shopping, Via San Vincenzo, near the Brignole train station.

MEALS FOR LESS THAN 15,000 LIRE ($9.85)

Da Guglie. V. San Vincenzo 64/R. ☎ **010/56-57-65.** Antipasto and pasta from 5,000L ($3.30), main courses 8,000L–15,000L ($5.30–$9.85). No credit cards. Mon–Sat noon–3pm and 7–10:30pm. LIGURIAN.

The busy kitchen here serves the neighborhood with takeout fare from a counter and accommodates diners in a bare-bones little room. Whether you want to stock up on provisions for a picnic or sit down to enjoy the friendly service, you can happily eat your way through Genoese cuisine: farinata, chick-pea crepes; focaccio bread; gnocchi with pesto; fried and boiled vegetables.

Trattoria da Maria. Vico Testadoro 14/R. ☎ **010/58-10-80.** Antipasto and pasta from 5,000L ($3.30), main courses 7,000L–12,000L ($4.60–$7.90); fixed-price menu 12,000L ($7.90). MC, V. Mon–Thur and Sun 10am–2:30pm and 7–9pm, Fri 10am–2:30pm. LIGURIAN.

Great homemade food at a great price is what draws the crowds of students and local business folks alike to the long communal tables of this boisterous little hole-in-the-wall in the old city. As befits a Genoese institution like this, the pasta with pesto sauce is especially delicious, as is pansotti, small ravioli covered with a walnut-cream sauce.

MEALS FOR LESS THAN 25,000 LIRE ($16.45)

Da Rivaro. V. d. Portello 16/R. ☎ **010/27-70-054.** Antipasto and pasta from 8,000L ($5.25), main courses 15,000L–25,000L ($9.90–$16.45). AE, MC, V. Mon–Sat noon–3pm and 7–10pm. ITALIAN.

Wonderfully located amid the Renaissance splendor of the nearby Via Garabaldi, this old institution does a brisk business with a loyal clientele from nearby banks and consulates. The decor is pleasantly reminiscent of a ship's cabin, with inlaid wood panels and long wooden tables lit by brass lanterns. The menu ventures far beyond Genoa to include a wide range of pastas (many with tomato and cream sauces) and grilled meat, though local seafood is always among the daily specials.

Trattoria Vegia Zena. Vico Serriglio 13–15/R. ☎ **010/29-98-91.** Antipasto and pasta from 8,000L ($5.25), main courses 10,000L–20,000L ($6.60–$13.15). Tues–Sat noon–2:30pm and 7:30–10pm, Mon noon–2:30pm. Closed Sun.

In the centro storico near the old port, this lively little place lives up to its name (which is dialect for Old Genoa) with expertly prepared Genoese dishes, with a bow now and then, thanks to the origins of the chef, to Sardegna. Pasta with pesto is excellent, followed by a fine selection of fresh seafood. The most popular dessert is seadas, fried, cheese-stuffed pasta topped with honey.

2 San Remo & the Riviera di Ponente

135km (81 miles) west of Genoa, 59km (35 miles) east of Nice

Gone are the days when Tchaikovsky and the Russian empress Maria Alexandranova joined a well-heeled mix of titled continentals and British gentry in strolling along San Remo's palm-lined avenues. They left behind an onion-domed Orthodox church, a few grand hotels, and a snooty casino, but San Remo is a different sort of town these days. It is still the most cosmopolitan stop on the Riviera di Ponente (Rising Sun), as the stretch of coast west of Genoa is called, catering mostly to sun-seeking Italian families in the summer and elderly Romans and Milanese who come to enjoy the balmy temperatures in the winter. In addition to the gentle ambience of days gone by, San Remo offers its visitors a long stretch of beach, a hilltop old town known as La Pigna, and a fine base from which to explore the rocky coast and Ligurian hills. For cosmopolitan pleasures, the casino continues to offer a well-attired clientele (jacket required in all but the slot machine rooms) the chance to try their luck.

ESSENTIALS

GETTING THERE   By Train   There are trains almost hourly to and from Genoa (about two hours).

By Car The fastest route in and out of San Remo is the A10 autostrada, though the slower coast road, S1, cuts right through the center of town

VISITOR INFORMATION The **tourist board** is at Largo Nuvolini 1 (☎ **0184/ 57-15-71**). It's open Monday to Saturday from 8am to 7pm, Sunday from 9am to 1pm. The telephone **area code** for San Remo is **0184**.

WHERE TO STAY
DOUBLES FOR LESS THAN 100,000 LIRE ($65.80)
Albergo Dom. Cor. Mombello 13, 18038 San Remo. ☎ **0184/50-14-60.** 10 rms, all with bath. 45,000L ($29.60) single; 80,000L ($52.65) double. No credit cards.

This rambling, dark, old-fashioned pensione near the casino and city center occupies the second floor of a 19th-century apartment house. The eclectically furnished rooms are carved out of former salons and tucked into the closed-off ends of ballroom-size hallways. So, be prepared for the unexpected: You may well find yourself staring up at an ornately plastered ceiling from a metal-frame bed crammed next to a marble fireplace.

Hotel Maristella. Cor. Imperatrice 77, 18038 San Remo. ☎ **0184/66-78-81.** Fax 0184/66-76-55. 33 rms, all with bath. TV. 65,000L ($42.75) single; 120,000L ($78.95) double. Half board, add 20,000L ($13.15) per person; full board, add 35,000L ($23) per person. MC, V.

If you follow the seaside promenade to its western end, you'll come to this creaky old villa surrounded by palm trees. What this family-oriented establishment lacks in luxury—guest rooms tend to be decorated with a hodgepodge of modern furnishings that clash with the parquet floors and fine old moldings—it makes up for with friendly service, a sunny garden, and proximity to the beach. Guests also have use of the gardens and swimming pool at the Hotel Miramare, a grander sister establishment just down the road.

Hotel Riviera. Cor. Inglesi 86, 18038 San Remo. ☎ **0184/50-22-15.** Fax 0184/50-22-16. 19 rms, 15 with bath. TEL TV. 55,000L ($36.20) single without bath, 65,000L ($42.75) single with bath; 75,000L ($49.35) double without bath, 95,000L ($62.50) double with bath. AE, MC, V.

While convenient to the beach and other attractions, this family-run pensione on one floor of a modern hillside apartment house is just far enough off the beaten path to enjoy peace and quiet, and it often has rooms when other places in town fill up. Oriental runners, crystal chandeliers, and attractively slip-covered furniture lend an air of elegance to the public areas, while the guest rooms, which overlook the sea and the old town, are modestly but attractively furnished in modern style.

Hotel Sole Mare. V. Carli 23, 18038 San Remo. ☎ **0184/57-71-05.** Fax 0184/53-27-78. 20 rms, all with bath. MINIBAR TEL TV. 60,000L ($39.50) single without bath; 65,000L ($42.75) single with bath; 90,000L ($59.20) double with bath. Breakfast 10,000L ($6.60). AE, MC, V.

Don't let the location on a drab side street near the train station put you off. This cheerful pensione on the upper floors of an apartment house is a delight and offers the best value in the resort. The bright, spiffy rooms are decked out with all the trappings of much more expensive hotels—such as pleasant modern furnishings, TVs, and minibars—and most open to a wide terrace that looks out to the sea.

DOUBLES FOR LESS THAN 165,000 LIRE ($108.55)
Hotel Paradiso. V. Roccasterone 12, 18038 San Remo. ☎ **0184/57-12-11.** Fax 0184/ 57-81-76. 41 rms, all with bath. MINIBAR TEL TV. 115,000L ($75.65) single; 150,000L ($98.70) double, depending on season. Half board, 100,000L ($65.75) to 130,000 ($85.55) per person. AE, MC, V.

A former villa, set in a pretty garden above the seaside promenade, has been topped off with several extra floors of very pleasant guest rooms, many of which have flower-filled balconies overlooking the sea. Furnishings are a homey collection of old armoires, armchairs, and upholstered headboards, the sort of old-fashioned comfort that brings a loyal clientele back year after year for their month by the sea. Cocktails are served in the grand salon in evenings, and guests can take meals in an airy dining room.

Hotel Villa Maria. Cor. Nuvoloni 30, 18038 San Remo. ☎ **0184/53-14-22.** 39 rms, all with bath. TEL. 100,000L ($65.80) single; 160,000L ($105.25) double. Rates include breakfast. AE, MC, V.

It's fairly easy to imagine San Remo's turn-of-the-century heydays in this charming hotel incorporating three villas on a flowery hillside above the casino. A series of elegant salons, with parquet floors, richly paneled ceilings, and crystal chandeliers spread across the ground floor, and the bedrooms, too, retain the grandeur of the original dwellings, with silk-covered armchairs and antique beds. All have modern baths and many have balconies facing the sea. Since rooms vary considerably in size and decor, ask to look around before you settle on one that strikes your fancy.

Long-Term Stays

Hotel Residence Garden Lido. V. Barabino 21, 18038 San Remo. ☎ **0184/66-77-66.** Fax 0184/66-63-30. 38 rms, all with bath. TEL TV. Apts, from 650,000L–1,300,000L ($427.65–$855.25) per week, depending on the number of people and season. Rooms, 70,000L ($46.05) single; 100,000L ($65.80) double; 130,000L ($85.50) triple; 160,000L ($105.25) quadruple. AE, MC, V.

These modern apartments overlooking the sea on the western edge of town are rented by the week and month. Studios and one-bedrooms, sleeping up to four people, are nattily done up in a nautical theme, with brass lamps and louvered cabinets. Most have well-equipped kitchens, sitting and dining areas, and balconies overlooking the beach. A few hotel-style rooms without kitchen are available by the night.

Staying in Nearby Bordighera

Sleepy Bordighera is only about 15 minutes west of San Remo via the trains that run every half hour or so. Don't come here for excitement: The town is known throughout Italy for its palm trees (it has the honor of supplying its ubiquitous fronds to the Vatican for Palm Sunday services) and its popularity with elderly pensioners.

Pensione Palme. V. Roma 5, 18012 Bordighera. ☎ **0184/26-12-73.** Fax 0184/25-19-77. 12 rms, 9 with bath. 35,000L ($23) single; 50,000L ($32.90) double without bath; 64,000L ($42.10) double with bath. No credit cards.

Atop an apartment house directly across the street from the train station, this simple pensione is sparkling clean and just steps from the beach. The friendly proprietor, who lived in New York for many years, charges very little for his really basic rooms, many of which contain enough beds to sleep a large family or traveling circus troupe.

Piccolo Lido. Lungomare Argentina 2, 18012 Bordighera. ☎ **0184/26-12-97.** Fax 0184/26-23-16. 30 rms, all with bath. MINIBAR TEL TV. 95,000L ($63) single; 130,000L ($85.50) double without sea view; 145,000L ($95.40) double with sea view. AE, MC, V.

This pink, sun-filled villa at the end of the seafront promenade is like a breath of fresh air. The newly renovated rooms, all with bath, are bright and attractive, with white tile floors, pastel area rugs, and bright contemporary furnishings. Many open onto terraces overlooking the sea.

WHERE TO DINE
Meals for Less Than 20,000 Lire ($13.15)

Ristorante Airone. Pz. Eroi Sanremesi 12. ☎ **184/53-14-69.** Antipasto and pasta from 7,000L ($4.60), main courses 10,000L–15,000L ($6.60–$9.90). MC, V. Tue–Sun, noon–2:30pm and 7:30pm–11:30pm. LIGURIAN.

With its pale gold walls and green-hued tables and chairs, this delightful restaurant looks like it's been transported over the border from Provence. The food, though, is definitely Ligurian, with a wide selection of fresh pastas, including gnocchi in pesto sauce, followed perhaps by a grigliata mista of fresh fish or braised veal with mushrooms, all of which can be nicely sampled on a 22,000L ($15.15) prix-fixe menu. For a more casual meal, light-crusted pizzas emerge from a tiled oven in the rear.

Trattoria Piccolo Mondo. V. Piave 7. ☎ **184/50-90-12.** Antipasto and pasta, from 8,000L ($5.25), main courses 10,000L–18,000L ($6.60–$11.85). No credit cards. Mon–Sat, noon–2:30pm and 7–10pm. Closed Wed evening. LIGURIAN.

You'll feel comfortably at home the moment you step into this decades-old trattoria on a narrow side street in the commercial district. The clientele is local, and they come here to enjoy the excellent risottos, pasta dishes, and veal topped with fungi porcini, as well as some distinctly Ligurian fare such as torte di verdura (succulent little pies made with fresh vegetables).

Meals for Less Than 30,000 Lire ($19.75)

Antica Trattoria La Pignese. Pz. Sardi 7/8. ☎ **0184/50-19-29.** Antipasto and pasta from 10,000L ($6.60), main courses 15,000L–25,000L ($9.90–$16.45). AE, MC, V. Tue–Sun, noon–2:30 and 7pm–10:30pm. SEAFOOD.

A San Remo institution since 1919, La Pignese occupies the bottom floor of an old house along the quay, with an elegant yet casual dining room, decorated with photos of soccer stars and turn-of-the-century street scenes, that opens onto a glass-covered terrace. A loyal clientele comes here to feast on a wide selection of seafood dishes, and you can get a nice sampling of the offerings with a gran digustazione de pesci, a multicourse appetizer of hot and cold dishes that might include smoked salmon, shrimp, dried cod, fresh sardines, and crepes stuffed with langoustine.

3 The Riviera Levante & Monte Portofino Promontory

The coast east of Genoa, the Riviera Levante (Rising Sun), is more ruggedly beautiful than the Riviera Ponente, less developed, and hugged by mountains that plunge into the sea. Four of the coast's most appealing towns are within a few miles of one another, clinging to the shores of the Monte Portofino Promontory just east of Genoa: Camogli, Santa Margherita Liguria, Rapallo, and little Portofino.

ESSENTIALS

GETTING THERE **By Train** Camogli, Santa Margherita, and Rapallo are about 10 minutes apart by trains that come through several times an hour. Each town is served by 8 to 10 trains a day to and from Genoa (30 to 45 minutes) and about 6 trains a day to and from Milan (2½ hours). To reach Portofino by land, it's necessary to take a taxi or bus (every 20 minutes) along the stunningly beautiful coast road from the train station in Santa Margherita.

By Boat From Santa Margherita, Tigullio ferries (V. Palestro 8/1b; ☎ **0185/28-46-70**) make hourly trips to Portofino and Rapallo from 10am to 4pm (hours of service varies considerably with season; schedules are posted on the dock).

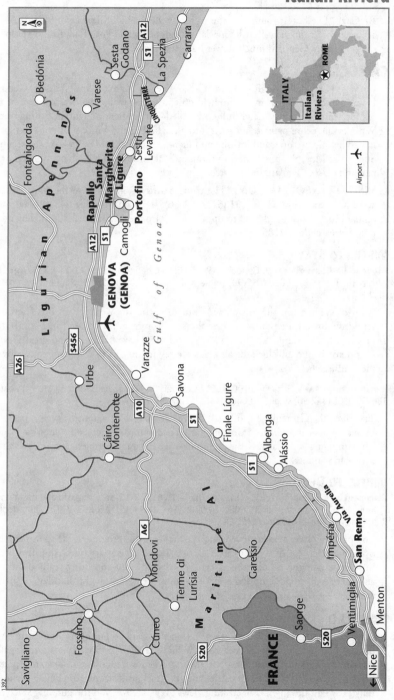

By Car   The fastest route into the region is the A12 autostrada from Genoa; exit at Recco for Camogli, at Rapallo for Santa Margherita and Portofino. Route S1 along the coast from Genoa is much slower but more scenic.

CAMOGLI

Camogli (Casa della Mogli—House of the Wives) is 26km (15 miles) east of Genoa. It was named for the women who held down the fort while their husbands went to sea for years on end, is delightfully unspoiled—an authentic Ligurian fishing port. With its tall, ochre-painted houses fronting the harbor and a nice swath of beach, it's incredibly picturesque, and it throws a much-attended annual party—on the second Sunday of May, the town fries up thousands of sardines in a 12-foot-round frying pan and passes them around for free.

VISITOR INFORMATION   The **tourist office** is across from the train station at V. XX Septembre 33 (☎ **0185/77-10-66**); it's open Monday to Saturday from 8:30am to 12:30pm and 3:30 to 6pm, Sunday from 8:30am to 12:30pm. The telephone **area code** is **0185**.

WHERE TO STAY

Albergo La Camogliese. V. Garibaldi 55, 16032 Camogli. ☎ **0185/77-14-02.** 17 rms, all with bath. TEL TV. 50,000L ($32.90) single with bath; 80,000L ($52.65) double with bath. AE, MC, V.

A lot of Genoese in the know come out to spend the weekend in this friendly, attractive little hotel hanging over the sea. Rooms are decorated in basic hotel modern, but are large, bright, and airy, and most have balconies and great views. Proprietor Bruno and his kids also run the restaurant of the same name just down the road (see below).

Pension Augusta. V. Schiaffino 100, 16032 Camogli. ☎ **0185/77-05-92.** All rms with bath. TEL. 50,000L ($32.90) single; 70,000L ($46.05) double. MC, V.

Try this if the Camogliese is full (see above). It's not as nice, but the plain, spacious rooms up a steep staircase from the harbor are perfectly adequate. One drawback: That rumbling you hear isn't the plumbing—it's the train roaring by just outside your bedroom window.

WHERE TO DINE

Ristorante La Comogliese. V. Garibaldi 78. ☎ **0185/77-10-86.** Antipasto and pasta from 7,000L ($4.60), main courses 10,000L–20,000L ($6.70–$13.15). AE, MC, V. Tue–Sun, noon–2:30 pm and 7pm–10:30pm. SEAFOOD.

You probably won't be surprised that the menu at this bright, seaside spot, perched over the beach on stilts, leans heavily to seafood. The hearty fish soup is a meal in itself, as are any number of pastas topped with clam and other seafood sauces, and there is always a tempting array of fresh fish entrees, caught that day, on hand as well.

RAPALLO

Stepping out of Rapallo's busy train station you may be put off by the traffic and blocks of banal apartment houses. Keep walking, though, because at its heart Rapallo remains a gracious old resort and port. Most of the town follows the sweep of a pretty harbor guarded by a medieval castle, and the gracious seafront promenade is cheerfully busy day and night. For striking views over the town and surrounding seacoast, hike or take the funicular up to the Sanctuary of Monteallegro.

VISITOR INFORMATION   The **tourist office** is at V. Diaz 9 (☎ **0185/54-573**). The telephone **area code** is **0185**.

WHERE TO STAY

Eurotel Rapallo. V. Aurelia Ponente 22, 16035 Rapallo. ☎ **0185/60-981.** Fax 0185/28-38-51. 65 rms, all with bath. A/C MINIBAR TEL TV. 115,000L–145,000L ($95.40–$75.65) single; 180,000L–210,000L ($118.45–$138.15) double. Rates include buffet breakfast. Half-board: add 30,000L ($19.75) per person; full-board: add 60,000L ($39.50) per person. Rates vary with season; are highest in July–Aug. AE, MC, V.

This ocher-colored hotel sprawling across a hillside above the town was built as a vacation-apartment house in the 1970s, and as a result the guest quarters are extremely large. Most are suitelike affairs with a living-room arrangement off to the side of the sleeping area. There is also a dining table in each, though no kitchen, and all open to large terraces overlooking the town and the sea. A pleasant garden is built around a large swimming pool.

Hotel La Vela. V. Milite Ignoto 21/7, 16035 Rapallo. ☎/fax **0185/50-551.** 10 rms, 4 with bath. TEL. 50,000L ($32.90) single without bath; 70,000L ($46.05) double with bath. MC, V.

There's nothing fancy about this friendly, family-run pensione near the seaside promenade and the center of town, but the old-fashioned rooms are spacious, sparkling clean, and all but a few of the singles have private baths. The best rooms are the ones with balconies overlooking the courtyard.

Hotel Paradiso. Cor. Colombo 72, 16035 Rapallo. ☎ **0185/54-088.** 8 rms, all with bath. 100,000L ($65.80) double.

All the rooms in this sun-filled, 100-year-old villa, just across from the marina, are doubles. They're quite charming, with bright floral bedspreads, big bay windows, and high ceilings, and all have baths with relatively modern plumbing. There's a lively and fun pizzeria on the ground floor, but the crowd thins out around 10 o'clock, so a quiet night's sleep is assured.

Camping

Campeggio Miraflores. V. Savagna 10, 16035 Rapallo. ☎ **0185/26-30-00.** 7,000L ($4.60) per person. No credit cards. Open Apr–mid-Oct.

Staying here in Rapallo's leafy hillside suburbs is not exactly roughing it. The campground has all the amenities (including hot showers) and is convenient to all the nearby sights via public transportation.

WHERE TO DINE

Ristorante Elite. V. Milite 19. ☎ **0185/50-551.** Antipasto and pasta, from 8,000L–25,000L ($5.25–$16.45), main courses 12,000L ($7.90). AE, MC, V. Fri–Wed, noon–2:30pm and 7:30–10pm. SEAFOOD.

The specialty at this popular restaurant in the center of Rapallo's commercial district is seafood, which the kitchen sends out in many different variations. The seafood salad and seafood risotto constitute light meals in themselves. Many locals come here for the fresh fish of the day, which can be enjoyed on the 35,000L ($23) prix-fixe menu and also includes hot and cold seafood appetizers and pasta topped with pesto or any number of other sauces.

SANTA MARGHERITA LIGURIA

Aside from its rococo basilica, this gentle seaside town boasts a palm-lined harbor, a nice beach, and a friendly ambience—all of which make it a fine place to settle down for a few days of sun and relaxation. Santa Margherita Liguria is 31km (19 miles) east of Genoa.

VISITOR INFORMATION The **tourist office** is near the harbor at V. XXV Aprile, 2b (☎ **0185/28-74-85**), open Monday to Saturday from 9am to 12:30pm and 3pm to 7pm, Sunday from 9am to 12:30pm. The telephone area code is 0185.

WHERE TO STAY

Albergo Annabella. V. Costasecca 10, 16038 Santa Margherita Ligure. ☎ **0185/28-65-31.** 11 rms, none with bath. 45,000L ($29.60) single without bath; 60,000L ($39.50) double without bath. No credit cards.

The nice proprietress manages to accommodate groups of just about any size in this old apartment, converted to an attractive pensione. Some of the rooms sleep up to four, and one family-style arrangement includes a double and a tiny room outfitted with bunk beds for the kids. None of the rooms have private baths, but shared facilities are ample and hot water is plentiful.

Hotel Europa. V. Trento 5, 16038 Santa Margherita Ligure. ☎ **0185/28-71-87.** Fax: 0185/ 28-01-54. 16 rms, all with bath. TEL. 75,000L ($49.35) double. AE, MC, V.

On a flowery side street below the Duomo, this newer hotel is quite pleasant and really quiet, even though it's just a few steps from the shops and restaurants along the harborfront. All of the very large rooms are doubles, plainly but comfortably furnished, and all have baths and pretty balconies.

Hotel Nuova Riviera. V. Belvedere 10–2, 16038 Santa Margherita Ligure. ☎ **0185/ 28-74-03.** 50,000L–65,000L ($32.90–$42.75) single without bath; 75,000L–90,000L ($49.35– $59.20) double without bath; 90,000L–105,000L ($59.20–$69.10) double with bath (some doubles with shower). Rates include breakfast. MC, V.

The Sabini family acts as if their sunny, turn-of-the-century villa was a private home and guests were old friends. Every room is different, and though modestly furnished, most retain the high-ceilinged elegance of days gone by. There's a pretty garden out front and a homey dining room where Signora Sabini serves breakfast with fresh-squeezed orange juice and a home-cooked, prix-fixe dinner for 30,000L ($19.75), 15,000L ($9.90) for homemade pasta and salad.

WHERE TO DINE

Trattoria Baicin. V. Algeria 9. ☎ **0185/28-67-63.** Antipasto and pasta, from 6,000L ($3.95), main courses 9,000L–18,000L ($5.90–$11.85). AE, MC, V. Tue–Sun, noon–3pm and 7–10:30pm, closed Mon and Nov 1–Dec 15. LIGURIAN.

In good weather, one of the best places near Santa Margherita's waterfront spills onto a sidewalk terrace. The husband-and-wife owners make everything fresh, from fish soup to gnocchi, that can be topped with their own pesto sauce. You can get a nice sampling of whatever happens to be on the stove that night on the tourist menu, about 25,000L ($16.45).

Trattoria da Prezzi. V. Cavour 21. ☎ **0185/28-53-03.** Antipasto and pasta from 5,000L ($3.30), main courses 7,000L–12,000L ($4.60–$7.90). No credit cards. Daily, noon–2:30 pm and 7pm–10pm.

The atmosphere in this cozy little restaurant, popular with local workmen and business folks at lunchtime, is of the tile-floored, whitewashed-walls variety. The food isn't fancy either, but lasagne, grilled swordfish, and other fare is always fresh and delicious; the menu depends entirely upon what the chef is making that day, so just ask what's available.

PORTOFINO

This little cluster of centuries-old houses surrounding a perfect slip of a natural harbor is almost too beautiful for its own good—unless you choose to sail in on your own yacht (and many do), you'll have to contend with day-tripping mobs. Portofino's few hotels are prohibitively expensive, making it difficult to enjoy the town in its quietest hours, but make an appearance in the late afternoon when the crowds have thinned out a bit to experience what remains so special about this enchanting place—its untouchable beauty.

VISITOR INFORMATION   The **tourist office** is at V. Roma 35 (☎ **0185/ 26-90-24**); it's open daily from 9:30am to 12:30pm and 1:30 to 6:30pm (shorter hours in the winter). The telephone area code is 0185.

4 Cinque Terre

Monterosso, the northernmost town of the Cinque Terre, is 93km (56 miles) east of Genoa

Olive groves and vineyards clinging to hillsides, proud villages perched above the sea, hidden coves nestled at the foot of dramatic cliffs—the Cinque Terre, named for five neighboring towns: Monterosso, Vernazza, Corniglia, Manarola, and Riomaggiore, is about as beautiful a coastline as you're likely to find in Europe, or anywhere. What's best about the Cinque is what's not here—cars, crowds, or much else by way of 20th-century interference. Actually, this can really only be said of the Quattro Terre—Monterosso, easily accessible by car, is more crowded, more expensive, and much less charming than its neighbors.

ESSENTIALS

GETTING THERE   By Train   You can take one of the hourly trains from Genoa to La Spezia (1½ hours), south of the Cinque Terre, then backtrack from there (about one an hour) on trains that stop at each of the five towns. Some of the Genoa–La Spezia trains stop at Levanto, on the northern end of the Cinque Terre; change there for local service into each of the five towns. Local trains make frequent runs between the five towns; you can buy a day ticket (4,500L/$2.95) good for unlimited trips.

By Car   The fastest route is via A12 autostrada from Genoa, exiting at Monterosso, where there is a huge car park. It's best to leave your car there and reach the other towns on foot or by train or boat. A narrow coast road hugs the mountainside above the towns, but all are closed to cars and, unless you're a resident, parking outside them is all but impossible.

By Boat   From the port in Monterosso, Navagazione Golfo dei Porto makes five trips a day to Manarola and Riomaggiore; Motobarca Vernazza makes hourly runs to Vernazza.

VISITOR INFORMATION   The only **tourist office** in the Cinque Terre is in Monterosso, at V. Fegina 38 (☎ **0185/81-75-06**). It's open April through October, Monday to Saturday, 10am to noon and 5pm to 7:30pm; Sunday from 10am to noon.

WHAT TO DO

Aside from swimming and soaking in the atmosphere of unspoiled fishing villages, the most popular activity in the Cinque Terre is hiking from one village to the next (each no more than a few miles apart) along centuries-old goat paths. Trails plunge through vineyards and hug seaside cliffs, affording heart-stopping views of the coast and the romantic little villages looming ahead in the distance. The well-signposted walks range in difficulty from the ridiculously easy (and paved) Strada del Amore, between Riomaggiore and Manarola, and the rocky, hilly climb between Vernazza and Corniglia. None of the trails seem to be too much for the well-dressed city slickers who come out from Genoa or La Spezia on Sundays, and a glass of wine and a gelato is only as far away as the next village.

WHERE TO STAY
A HOSTEL
Ostello Mama Rosa. P. Unita 2, 19017 Riomaggiore. ☎ **0185/92-00-50.** 20,000L ($13.15) per person. No credit cards.

Animal House, Italian-style! Mama or one of her minions hang out at Riomaggiore's train station to lure travelers into their barrackslike hostel just across the piazza. The price of a bed (in 10 windowless coed rooms, 4 to 10 bunks to a room) includes use of a communal kitchen, laundry facilities, and outdoor showers, and the chance to sit around the big commons room listening to an international mix of college kids discussing the meaning of life. It's probably a lot of fun if you're young—there's not even a curfew.

DOUBLES FOR LESS THAN 80,000 LIRE ($52.65)
Albergo Barbara. P. Marconi 21, 19018 Vernazza. ☎ **0185/81-22-01.** 9 rms, none with bath. 45,000L ($29.60) single; 70,000L ($46.05) double.

The rooms are really basic and none have private facilities, but they're big and right on Vernazza's pretty and lively harborfront. The guys downstairs in the Trattoria Capitano dispense the keys, and they also offer guests a discount on the superb and justifiably pricey meals they serve.

Albergo-Ristorante Da Cecio. 19010 Corniglia. ☎ **0187/81-21-38.** 4 rms, 6 others in the village. 70,000L ($46.05) double, all with bath. MC, V.

You'd have to look hard to do better than these rooms above a wonderful restaurant (see below) in the countryside just outside Corniglia. The four doubles are big and bright, with views over the sea, olive groves, and hilltop Corniglia, and they all have modern baths. The flowery terrace downstairs is a great place to dream an afternoon away. If they don't have room here, proprietors Elia and Nunzio will take you down to one of their six pleasant rooms in the village.

Marina Piccola. V. Discovolo 38, 19010 Manarola. ☎ **0185/92-01-03.** Fax 0185/92-09-66. 9 rms. TEL. 55,000L ($36.20) single without bath; 65,000L ($42.75) double without bath; 95,000L ($62.50) double with bath. AE, MC, V.

A cozy inn overlooking Manarola's little harbor—yep, it's mighty darned charming, all right, with a homey lobby built around a fireplace and tidy ocher-colored rooms, with pretty prints on the walls and brass beds, most with private bath. The same family runs a pleasant restaurant next door.

RENTAL APARTMENTS
Luciano e Roberto Fazioli. V. Colombo 94. 19017 Riomaggiore. ☎ **0187/92-05-87.** Rms and apts from 40,000L ($26.30). No credit cards.

The brothers rent rooms all over town out of a shopfront on the main drag. (Just head up the street with your bag; one of them will probably come out and nab you.) The guys aren't going to win an interior-decoration award, but their rooms and apartments are real homey, tucked away in ancient houses in the old town. They have cooking facilities and an acceptable variation of a bathroom, and some have wonderful views of the sea.

Villagio Marino Europa. 19010 Corniglia. ☎ **0187/81-22-79.** 300,000L ($197.35) 3 days, 400,000L ($263.15) 1 week, 800,000L ($526.30) 2 weeks, 1,700,000L ($1,118.45) 1 month. MC, V. Open June–Sept.

Accommodations here are in a long row of little bungalows, which look a lot like the changing huts at a beach, perched on a cliff between Manarola and Corniglia. They sleep four (in a double bed and bunk beds), have basic bathrooms and kitchens and open onto a terrace overlooking the sea. A lot of Italian families snap these units up for the whole summer, but depending on availability, they are also rented for short-term stays at the prices above.

WHERE TO DINE

Foccacerio II Frontoio. V. Gioberti 1, Monterosso. No phone. Foccacio 3,000L ($1.95). No credit cards. Fri–Wed 9am–1:30pm and 4pm–8pm. SNACKS.

If you stay in one of the four other Cinque Terre villages (which you should) and hike into Monterosso, the reward at the end of the trail will be a piece of the heavenly foccacio, reputedly the best in Liguria, that emerge from the ovens here. It comes topped with onions, herbs, and an incredible array of other ingredients, providing a great meal.

II Baretto. V. Roma 31, Vernazzia. ☎ **0187/81-23-81.** Antipasto and pasta, from 8,000L ($5.25), main courses 10,000L–20,000L ($6.60–$13.15); prix-fixe menu, 25,000L ($16.45). AE, MC, V. Daily noon–2pm and 7:30–9:30pm. SEAFOOD.

A table on the terrace of this lively trattoria affords a wonderful view down Vernazzia's main street, toward the little harbor and the fishing fleet that brings in the daily menu. Everything here is fresh: steamed mussels, squid (which appears in a number of pasta dishes), big slabs of grilled swordfish.

La Lanterna. Riomaggiore. Antipasto and pasta, from 7,000L ($4.60), main courses 9,000L–20,000L ($5.90–$13.15). MC, V. Daily in season noon–2:30pm and 7pm–10pm.

From a table on the terrace here, perched only a few feet above Riomaggiore's snug little harbor, you can hear the waves laps against the rocks and watch the local fishermen mend their nets. Not only is the setting romantic, but the food is great, too. The antipasto of shrimp, smoked tuna, and grilled swordfish is a meal in itself, but it would be a shame not to follow it with the house specialty, chiche—homemade gnocchi filled with seafood and topped with a spicy tomato sauce.

Ristorante Cecio. Corniglia. ☎ **0187/81-21-38.** Antipasto and pasta, from 7,000L ($4.60), main courses 9,000L–15,000L ($5.90–$9.85). Daily in season noon–2:30pm and 7pm–10pm. MC, V. LIGURIAN.

The stone-walled, wood-beamed dining room and flower-filled terrace overlooking olive groves, a five-minute walk from the center of the village, provide some of the most pleasant surroundings for a meal in the Cinque Terre. A nice selection of simple, homemade fare emerges from the family-run kitchen, including fresh pasta with a rich pesto sauce and grilled meats and fish, washed down with carafes of the house white. The rooms upstairs are unusually pleasant as well (see above).

Trattoria La Grotta. V. Colombo 123, Riomaggiore. ☎ **0187/92-01-87.** Antipasto and pasta, from 7,000L ($4.60), main courses 9,000L–18,000L ($5.90–$11.90). MC, V. Daily in season noon–2:30pm and 7–10pm. Closed Wed from Nov–Mar. SEAFOOD.

What was once the storage cellar of a centuries-old house is now an attractive dining room, with stone walls and a low, whitewashed ceiling. Most pasta dishes here are topped with morsels of fresh fish or shellfish, and the main course of choice—though the menu also includes a nice variety of grilled meats—is fish, caught only hours before.

15

The Bay of Naples & the Amalfi Coast

by Barbara Coeyman Hults

The Bay of Naples, where sea air, fragrant hills, mineral springs, and a stunning stretch of coastline out to the double-curve profile of Mt. Vesuvius, has been a favorite getaway spot for Romans since the days when emperors Augustus, Claudius, and especially Tiberius considered it a second home.

Today the beauty of this part of Italy is still unrivaled, despite the sometimes very aggressive onslaught of tourism. To travel through this area, you must first choose a base or two. My idea of the best location is to be as close as you can to what you came to see, not outside of town or on another island—even though prices are often better nearby, you'll spend precious time commuting. This philosophy leaves the ideal choices to be Capri or a town along the Amalfi Drive. Although Sorrento is wonderfully situated for touring in all directions, it is almost too tourist-oriented.

If you choose Capri, don't worry about its tourist masses. Although they do invade with each arriving ferry or hydrofoil, they can be ignored for the most part if you are spending the night—the majority leave by afternoon. At night the main piazza in the town of Capri does fill up, but much of the rest of the sweet-scented island is left to you. Few places in the world are as romantic, and the light here has a glow like no other.

Along the coast, the towns of Amalfi and Positano also have the downside of tourist buses, jamming the famously narrow cliffside Amalfi Drive with oversized traffic during the summer high season. Ravello sees fewer tourists, is often cooler than the coastal towns below, and has the advantage of an inland road, so that you can drive off to Pompeii or Naples at will, without traveling the cliffside road. Ravello's downside is its single long access road from the Amalfi Drive, which often leads to gridlock in season and on weekends.

Forget coming to the region in August, if possible. The weather is usually hot and humid, and less-expensive hotels can rarely afford air-conditioning (energy costs in Italy are about four times that of the United States). Spring and fall are the best times to travel, but June and July can be pleasant—and essential for the beaches. Winter is drizzly in general, and not all hotels that stay open are well-heated. You can live anywhere along the coastal route or on Capri without a car, because of the generally good and frequent bus, train, and boat service enjoyed by the region of Campania. Taxis are not

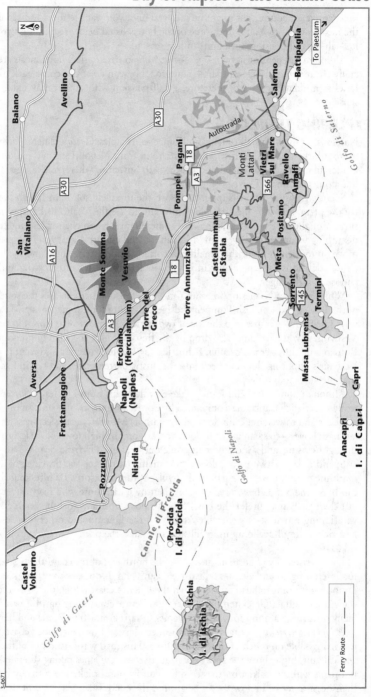

To Paestum

Battipaglia

Salerno

Golfo di Salerno

Avellino

Baiano

A30

Autostrada

Pagani

18

Pompei

A3

Monti Lattari

Vietri sul Mare

366

Ravello

Amalfi

Positano

San Vitalliano

A30

Monte Somma

Vesuvio

A16

Castellammare di Stabia

Meta

18

Torre Annunziata

Sorrento

145

Termini

A3

Torre del Greco

Ercolano (Herculaneum)

Aversa

Frattamaggiore

Napoli (Naples)

Massa Lubrense

Capri

Nisidia

Golfo di Napoli

Anacapri

I. di Capri

Pozzuoli

Prócida

I. di Prócida

Canale di Prócida

Castel Volturno

Golfo di Gaeta

Ischia

I. di Ischia

Ferry Route

3-0671

inexpensive, of course, but might be splurged on if you want to dine or disco late in the next town over. You'll find some of the hotels listed below require that you pay for half- or full-pension during the tourist season.

Although full pension saves money—prezzo fisso (fixed price) hotel meals are generally cheaper than restaurant fare—you probably won't want to come back to your hotel at midday for a meal; therefore, a half-pension with dinner may make more sense.

EXPLORING THE REGION

Naples is on the main rail route from Rome (see "Naples: Getting There," below for more information). The *Circumvesuviana* train from Napoli Centrale station stops at Herculaneum and Pompeii and proceeds to Sorrento, where you can get a local bus along the Amalfi Drive.

Spend at least a day in Naples, to absorb the uniquely southern Italian lifestyle, try the pizza, and visit the archeology museum to see the wealth of Pompeii's treasures brought here for safekeeping. For some, Naples is too chaotic and intense—a disturbingly concentrated version of Italian life and culture—and you may prefer to move on to the islands or the Amalfi coast after a brief taste. Others find the bright, almost delirious calliope of life in Naples invigorating and intoxicating and may choose to stay longer.

While based in Naples or Sorrento (on the peninsula that encloses the south end of the Bay of Naples), visit Pompeii and Herculaneum for a sometimes grisly yet always fascinating glimpse into the life of two ancient Roman towns frozen in time by Vesuvius. If you have time, also drop by the frescoed ruins at Villa Oplontis and the Roman amphitheater at Pozzuoli. Before leaving Naples, you may also want to climb Vesuvius's imposing slopes to peek into the dusty, barren crater and remind yourself that the volcano but sleeps.

Although both Capri and Ischia make easy day trips from Naples or Sorrento, to really experience Capri unaccompanied by hordes of tourists, stay at least one night on the island to watch it calm down and regain its Mediterranean sleepiness after the last ferry leaves—to swim in the rocky coves, explore the high town of Anacapri, enjoy the light cuisine, and watch the stars come out over the Thyrrean Sea.

Spend a day or two easing down the Amalfi coast, once the province of a great maritime power, now a string of fishing-villages-turned-resorts. (White-knuckle fans can brave the S163 *Amalfitana* drive in their own car; those who haven't yet made out their wills may prefer the bus.) Stop in posh Positano to rub shoulders with vacationing movie stars, venerable Amalfi for the Duomo and other legacies of its past riches, tiny Ravello up in its hillside aerie, and the pottery workshops of Vietri sul Mare.

Like its sister city of Sorrento anchoring the north end of the coast, there is nothing too interesting about Salerno at the drive's south end. It does, however, make a good jumping-off point to head farther down the Cliento coast (along the S18) and visit the virtually intact Greek temples at Paestum before continuing on to Calabria and Sicily or turning around to return to Naples or farther north to Rome and beyond.

A Note on Driving: A car is not only unnecessary in this treacherous coastal area, it is inadvisable on much of the Amalfi Drive. This road was carved out of the sheer vertical cliff, high above the rocky coast, its two narrow lanes taking (literally) hairpin turns with no barrier on the sea side. Tourist buses make the turns by beeping their horn to let you know they'll be around the bend. It's a magnificent drive, but you may want to leave driving to the locals.

The area around (or in) the city of Naples is not the most inviting place to drive. Cars are frequently robbed when entering or leaving Naples, and at many locations that attract tourists, parking on the street leaves you open to rampant theft (of the car itself or its contents). Besides, the traffic is not for anyone not seeking a chaos that defies description. Leave your car at your hotel if you have one and take the bus, train, or subway around the city and to nearby attractions.

EXPLORING BY BOAT   Albeit more expensive, boats make a sometimes more comfortable, and often more interesting, way to travel. They run all year round, but the best service is in high season (Easter through October). If you use Capri as a base, you can make day trips to Naples by boat and explore inland from there. You can be in Sorrento (from Capri) in only 20 minutes by hydrofoil. A longer boat trip will take you from Capri to Ischia (40 minutes). Positano and Amalfi (from which the bus climbs to clifftop Ravello) take about an hour by hydrofoil, and Salerno, anchoring the other end of the Amalfi coast, takes close to two hours. Note that ferries, where you can sit on deck and enjoy the incomparable view, take much longer, but can be worth it if you have the time—hydrofoils are for speed, and you sit below deck. See individual destinations below for more specific details.

1 Naples

219km (136 miles) SE of Rome

Naples, with its spectacular position by the bay, should be one of Italy's major tourist attractions. However, lack of success dealing with crime, traffic, and garbage had discouraged those most honest city officials who have tried to restore the city. Finally, there is now a mayor who seems to know how to do it, and the city has improved enormously in recent years. The mayor has made a serious effort to close off many of the streets—where you once had to scramble for your life in a snarl of traffic of epic proportions—to create pedestrian zones where people can stroll and see what a gorgeous city it actually is. Naples's many attractions are worth a few days' visit, but on a tighter time schedule, you definitely should at least spend a morning at the Archeology Museum prior to setting off for Pompeii. You'll either succumb to its charms and vitality, or run off to more peaceful spots.

ESSENTIALS

GETTING THERE   By Train   The ride from Rome is about three hours by the local (17,200L/$11.50; every two hours). For hydrofoils to Capri, get off at the first stop, Mergellina; if you're staying in town, stay on until the main station, Napoli Centrale. The station is in a not-very-nice section of town, so although it has been improving, try to arrive during daylight hours, so that you don't have to walk about this area by night—and watch out for pickpockets at any time of day. Bus service from in front of the station (Piazza Garibaldi) to all parts of the city and to the ferry port is rather frequent. There is also a Metro stop nearby.

By Car   If you're driving down from the north, the A2 (autostrata del Sole) connects Naples with Rome. If you're not in heavy traffic the trip will take about three hours. At Naples, A2 becomes I3, which continues south into Calabria. If you're bound for Herculaneum, Pompeii, Sorrento, or the Amalfi coast, switch to the S18 at Naples.

By Boat   If Capri is your base, a 70-minute ferry (*traghetto*) from the island lands you at the Molo Beverello dock in central Naples for 8,000L to 10,000L ($5.25 to

$6.60). If you don't mind the added expense and being stuck below deck, the hydrofoil (*aliscafo*) from Capri only takes 40 minutes, costs 18,000L ($11.85), and will drop you off at Naples' Mergellina dock. Naples also has direct boat connections to Ischia, Procida, Sorrento, and the Amalfi coast, as well as various ports in Sicily and Sardinia. Call Caremar in Naples (☎ **81/70-92-815**) for ferry schedules to Capri and Ischia. For Mergellina hydrofoils (*aliscafi*) call Aliscafi Mergellina (☎ **81/ 76-12-348**). If going to an island for the day, be sure to check the time of the last boat back to the mainland. It's usually about suppertime (no late boats). For very good, up-to-date timetables, buy the Naples daily paper, *Il Mattino*.

VISITOR INFORMATION   You will find **information booths** in the main train station (☎ **081/26-87-79**), at Mergellina station (☎ **081/76-12-102**), and in Spaccanapoli at Piazza Gesù Nuovo (☎ **081/55-23-328**), which is also open on Sunday from 9am to 2pm. The **main tourist office** is at Pz. Martiri 58, scala B (☎ **081/ 40-53-11**).

Qui Napoli is a handy publication for general tourist information and upcoming events. Pick up a free copy at the tourist offices or the new series of computerized information kiosks, part of the attempt to make Napoli more user-friendly.

CITY LAYOUT   From the massive **Piazza Garibaldi** in front of the main train station, **Corso Umberto I** stretches southwest toward the docks, ending just before them in Piazza Bovio. From here, **Via Agostino Depretis** continues on to **Piazza Municipio,** where the Castel Nuovo is located, just up the hill from the ferry dock at Molo Beverello. Just beyond the Castel Nuovo, **Piazza del Plebiscito,** near Santa Lucia, is one of the most important piazzas in town, home to the Palazzo Reale. Opening off it to the north (away from the water) is **Piazza Trieste e Trento,** where the Galleria Umberto I (Primo) is located. From there **Via Toledo** begins and leads to the Archeological Museum (changing its name to Via Roma after Piazza Carità, then to Via Pessina between Piazza Dante and the museum). This road almost bisects the city, running inland from the waterfront, and it continues through several more name changes up the hill to Capodimonte.

Most of the city's attractions are in Central Naples, which spreads up from the main docks toward the train station and **Capodimonte.** The most attractive neighborhoods stretch along the waterfront near the **Mergellina dock** (you'll need to take the bus or metro here). **Posillipo** is a cape on the far west of the promontory that makes up the north part of the Bay. **Chiaia** and **Santa Lucia,** where the Castel dell'Ovo is located, are the upscale areas. The most interesting neighborhood is Spaccanapoli, where splendid churches and palazzi with wash hanging in the courtyard share space with famous pizzerias and the university. Recent renovations have improved the area considerably and cleared some of the streets of traffic. On high, Capodimonte is the royal palace/museum that recently reopened in sparkling, restored condition. On the Vomero hill you'll find panoramas of the city, museums, and parks for a stroll.

GETTING AROUND   **By Bus or Tram**   Naples has a good bus service, but it's always packed like a Japanese subway, so I would suggest that you walk as much as possible. The bus ticket system has recently been simplified; 4,000L ($2.65) will buy you a ticket valid for a full day, while tickets valid for 90 minutes (you can transfer as often as you'd like) cost 1,200L (80¢). All tickets are good for the bus, metro, and funicular systems.

From the main train station take bus 106 or 150 to reach the Mergellina hydrofoil dock for Capri and Ischia. To reach the Molo Beverello and the dock for the Capri ferry (slower, but more scenic than the hydrofoil), take trams 1 or 4 from

Piazza Garibaldi. If arriving by hydrofoil from Capri to see the sights, take the 104 bus from the marina in Mergellina to Piazza del Gesù Nuovo, the beginning of Spaccanapoli.

By Metro   The metro is limited, but you can take it to Piazza Cavour to go to the Archeological Museum, Montesanto to visit Spaccanapoli, Piazza Amedeo to go to the pretty Chiaia area, or Mergellina, to enjoy the area or to take the hydrofoil (a 10-minute walk from the station). The metro also continues to Pozzuoli in the Campi Flegrei area. It uses the same tickets as the buses.

By Funiculare   Since you've no doubt heard the song that refrains "Funiculee, Funiculaa," you must take a funicular up the hill at least once. The funicolare at Montesanto (near the Metro stop) will take you up to the attractive and often cool Vomero hill, where the Certosa de San Martino and Castel Sant'Elmo await. The Chiaia funicular travels there from Piazza Amedeo. It also uses the same tickets as the buses.

FAST FACTS: Naples

Consulates   Most countries' embassies and consulates are in Rome, but the following countries have consulates in Naples as well: **United States** is at Piazza della Repubblica (☎ **081/58-38-111**), open July through mid-September, Monday to Friday 8am to 1:30pm; mid-September through June, Monday to Friday 9am to 12:30pm and 3 to 5:30pm. The **United Kingdom** is at V. Francesco Crispi 122 (☎ **081/66-35-11**), open in summer Monday to Friday 7 to 11am and 1 to 4pm; off-season 9am to 12:30pm and 3 to 5:30pm.

Crime   Yes, pickpockets are still prevalent, but not as numerous as they were a few years ago. Take precautions as you would in any major city.

Doctors & Dentists   You can get a current list of English-speaking doctors from the U.S. Consulate (☎ **81/58-38-111** or 761-4304).

Drugstores   There is a pharmacy in the Stazione Centrale that stays open late. In the "Agenda" section, the daily paper *Il Mattino* prints a list of those whose turn it is on the rotation to stay open overnight and on holidays.

Emergencies   Call **113** for police and general emergencies; for an ambulance, call **081/75-20-696.**

Police   Dial **113** for general emergencies. **081/77-94-11-11** is the central police station. Foreigners may have better luck calling the Ufficio Stranieri (☎ **081/ 79-41-435**).

Post Office   Piazza Matteotti station is off Via Diaz. It's open Monday to Friday from 8:15am to 7:15pm, and Saturday from 8:15am to noon.

WHAT TO SEE & DO
THE TOP ATTRACTIONS

✪ **Museo Archeologico Nazionale.** Pz. Museo. ☎ **081/44-01-66.** Admission 10,000L ($6.60). May–Sept, Mon–Sat 9am–7pm, Sun 9am–1pm; Sept–May, Tues–Sat 9am–2pm. Closed 1st and 3rd Mon of each month. Metro: Pz. Cavour.

Before you visit Pompeii, stop here to see a superb collection of paintings and sculpture from the site. Inside the museum, go to the top of the great staircase and turn left to see Pompeii's treasures: paintings, bronze statues, artifacts, and a scale model of the site. Europe's fascination with the neoclassical style arose from the excitement of the discovery of Pompeii. Pompeii's mosaics are one flight down on the mezzanine level, at the opposite side. These are some of Italy's finest artworks, brilliantly executed. The Nile scenes are enchanting and the *Battle of Issus* featuring Alexander the Great is dramatic. The *Farnese Bull* and the *Farnese Hercules* are two other luminaries, and they can be found on the ground floor, left as you leave the staircase.

✪ **Capodimonte Palace and Museum.** Parco di Capodimonte. ☎ **081/74-41-307.** Admission 12,000L ($7.90). Apr–Oct Tues–Sun 9am–7:30pm, Nov–Mar Tues–Sat 9am–2pm, Sun 9am–1pm. Bus: 22 or 23 from Pz. del Plebiscito; 160 or 161 from Pz. Dante.

The museum has recently been restored and the collections have been rearranged. This palace of the 18th-century Bourbon king Charles III is now being treated seriously as a tourist attraction and even the park area is scheduled for a remake—much overdue, but welcome. The rooms, in their delicate beauty, were designed to please Maria of Saxony, wife of Charles III. Start with the Porcelain Room on the first floor (room 94). Among the museum's portraits are some fine Renaissance works by Mantegna (*Crucifixion*), Bellini (*Transfiguration*), and a young Botticelli (*Virgin and Child with Angels*). Titian, Lorrain, Brueghel, and Caravaggio are also well represented. Artemisia Gentileschi, whose work was really only recently recognized because of a surge of interest in women painters from the late Renaissance, painted a striking *Judith.*

✪ **The Church and Cloisters of Santa Chiara.** V. Santa Chiara 49 (in Spaccanapoli). ☎ **081/55-26-209.** Free admission. Mon–Sat 8:30am–noon and 4:30–6:30pm; Sun 8:30am–noon (except for hours of Mass). Bus: 140. Metro: Montesanto.

The church was built for the 14th-century king Robert of Anjou—a patron of Petrarch and one of Naples' few good monarchs—and he was buried here in the robes of a Franciscan, the monastic order he joined late in life (the Clares are a sister Order). His wife, Queen Sancia de Mallorca, commissioned the cloisters as a votive offering. Her wish to enter the Order of the Clares had been denied by her father, who thought marriage to Robert a better idea. Robert's tomb stands behind the main altar, both solemn and stirring. The gothic-Provençal grandeur of the church, built between 1310 and 1328, is awe-inspiring. World War II bombs did heavy damage, and much has been restored during this century, fortunately with careful attention to historical accuracy. Queen Sancia's Cloisters are the merriest of their kind, decorated along the paths and under rose arbors with bright-colored majolica tiles; they were restored by Vaccaro in 1742. The scenes depicted the world that the sisters of the Order, usually nobles by birth, had left behind.

THE CHURCHES OF NAPLES

Duomo (Cathedral). V. Duomo 147 ☎ **081/44-90-97.** Free admission. Daily 8:30am–1pm and 5–7:30pm. Metro: Pz. Cavour.

The head and two vials of the blood of San Gennaro—of New York City festival fame—are conserved in an altar in the Duomo, and the blood obliges ecclesiastical fortune-tellers by liquefying from its dried state twice a year (September 19 and December 16). Fast liquefaction is good news for the whole community; if the miracle goes slowly, it means hard times. San Gennaro was beheaded in a nearby town and walked all the way here carrying his head, or so the legend goes. The church shows Naples' exuberance in swirls of marble and grillwork. Nothing is ever still in Naples: Statues seem to move about; even colored marble draperies seem caught in a breeze. The decoration in the Carafa Chapel, where the saint's body lies, shows more restraint. Its Renaissance altar with a statue of Cardinal Carafa (1497) is considered the finest work of the period in Naples.

Naples

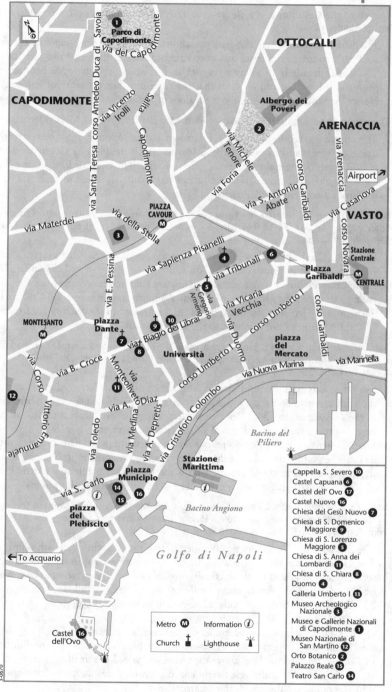

CAPODIMONTE

OTTOCALLI

ARENACCIA

Parco di Capodimonte ❶

via Santa Teresa

corso Amedeo Duca di Savoia

via del Capodimonte

via Vincenzo Irolli

Salita Capodimonte

Albergo dei Poveri ❷

via Michele Tenore

via Foria

VASTO

via Casanova

via Arenaccia

corso Novara

Airport ↗

Stazione Centrale

CENTRALE Ⓜ

via Materdei

via della Stella

PIAZZA CAVOUR Ⓜ

via Sapienza Pisanelli

via S. Antonio Abate

corso Garibaldi

❸

❹

❻

via Tribunali

Piazza Garibaldi

MONTESANTO Ⓜ

via E. Pessina

piazza Dante

❼

❽

❺ via S. Gregorio Armeno

via Vicaria Vecchia

via Duomo

corso Umberto I

corso Garibaldi

piazza del Mercato

via Marinella

❾ ❿ via Biagio dei Librai

Università

via B. Croce

❶❶ via Montoliveto

via A. Diaz

corso Umberto I

via Nuova Marina

via Cristoforo Colombo

❶❷

via Corso Vittorio Emanuele

via Toledo

via Medina

via A. Depretis

Stazione Marittima ⓘ

Bacino del Piliero ⌇

❶❸ piazza Municipio

❶❹ ❶❻

❶❺

piazza del Plebiscito

via S. Carlo

ⓘ

Bacino Angiono

← To Acquario

Golfo di Napoli

Castel dell'Ovo ❶❻ ⌇

Cappella S. Severo	❿
Castel Capuana	❻
Castel dell' Ovo	⓲
Castel Nuovo	❶❻
Chiesa del Gesù Nuovo	❼
Chiesa di S. Domenico Maggiore	❾
Chiesa di S. Lorenzo Maggiore	❺
Chiesa di S. Anna dei Lombardi	⓫
Chiesa di S. Chiara	❽
Duomo	❹
Galleria Umberto I	⓭
Museo Archeologico Nazionale	❸
Museo e Gallerie Nazionali di Capodimonte	❶
Museo Nazionale di San Martino	⓬
Orto Botanico	❷
Palazzo Reale	⓯
Teatro San Carlo	⓮

Metro Ⓜ	Information ⓘ
Church ✝	Lighthouse ⌇

3-0670

457

Church of the Gesù Nuovo. Pz. Gesù Nuovo. Daily 7:30am–1pm and 4–7:30pm. Bus: 140. Metro: Montesanto.

The plain front hides a very elaborate church inside, one which the Neapolitans prefer for their weddings. The Jesuit architect Valeriani built it between 1584 and 1601. The Gesù's facade is all solemn gray stone, but inside it's a baroque banquet, a profusion of marble and frescoes that manages to achieve a sense of harmony. Notice the fresco by Solimena above the door of *Heliodorus Driven from the Temple.*

✪ **Sant'Anna dei Lombardi.** Pz. Monteoliveto. Mon–Sat 7:30am–1pm. Metro: Montesanto.

This church is exceptional in Naples for its Renaissance sculpture. It has been severely damaged by war and by earthquakes. Most striking is the Pietà by Guido Mazzoni (1492) in which the eight figures are nearly life-size. The Correale Chapel, at right, has a fine altar in Tuscan style (four arches and a cupola), whose predella is a bas-relief by Tuscan sculptor Benedetto da Maiano.

Basilica of San Domenico Maggiore. Pz. San Domenico, off V. Benedetto Croce (in Spaccanapoli). ☎ **081/55-16-944.** Mon–Sat 8am–12:30pm and 4–7pm. Bus: 140 to Pz. Gesù. Metro: Montesanto.

Part of the Greek city walls were found below the guglia, or decorated steeple, which you'll see erected in front of the basilica, which was built between 1283 and 1324. Earthquakes and fires have necessitated significant renovations over the years. Cosimo Fanzago designed the high altar. St. Thomas Aquinas prayed before the Crucifix in the altar at the left near the entry, and it spoke to him. In the Sacristy are frescoes (1709) by Solimena and tombs of the Aragonese royals.

San Lorenzo Maggiore. Pz. San Gaetano, off V. d. Tribunali (in Spaccanapoli). Free admission. Church Mon–Sat 9am–12:30pm and 3:30–6pm; Excavations: Mon–Sat 9am–12:30pm. Metro: Pz. Cavour.

San Lorenzo is expansive and magnificent, a medieval church erected at the end of the 13th century. Boccaccio met his Fiametta here in 1334, and immortalized her in the *Decameron.* In 1345, Petrarch records being sheltered from a terrible storm here. Excavations underneath reveal a 6th-century church at its base, with a mosaic floor. Earlier Greek and Roman relics have also been unearthed here and are worth a visit. The gothic nave with its three arches has been restored to its original shape. In the first chapel to the left of the altar is the *Crucifixion* painted by Mattia Preti in 1666. Concerts are frequently given here, so be on the lookout for posters.

Certosa and Museum of San Martino. Lgo. San Martino 5 (in the Vomero section). ☎ **081/57-81-769.** Admission 8,000L ($5.25); under 18 and over 60 free. Tues–Sat 9am–2pm. Funicular: from Pz. Montesanto to Vomero.

The San Martino Monastery was founded during the Angevin rule (14th century). The Order became very rich and its art collections are extraordinary. The church seems in no way geared to the ascetic; its original gothic arches were remodeled with baroque swirls. The paintings here by Ribera, a court painter called Il Spagnoletto, are said to be his best, especially *Communion of the Apostles,* done in 1651. His *Deposition,* above the high altar, is another treasure.

The Grand Cloisters, off the former smaller ones, are expansive; on each side there are 17 columns with gray- and cream-colored marble decorations. The prolific artist Fanzago finished the level above the arches and added the small cemetery at one end, with 16 marble skulls. (He fought constantly with the monks, and one wonders if he was punishing them with this *memento mori.*)

You may enter the museum from the church cloisters. The museum is devoted to the daily life of Naples through the ages. If you're lucky, most of the rooms will be open. The presepio, or Christmas Crib, room holds a collection of Naples' famous craft.

Chapel of San Severo. V. d. Sanctis, off Pz. San Domenico (in Spaccanapoli). ☎ **081/55-18-470.** Admission 6,000L ($3.95) adults; 2,000L ($1.30) students. Mon and Wed–Sat 10am–5pm, Tues and Sun 10am–1:30pm. Bus 140 to Pz. Gesù. Metro: Cavour. Turn right at V. Nilo and left to 19 V. Francesco de Sanctis.

This memorial to the di Sangro family is one of Naples' many curiosities. Say hello to Cecco di Sangro, who's inside, over the door, bolting out of his coffin to greet you. The *Veiled Christ*, by Giuseppe Sammartino, is astonishing, carved from one block of marble, with a thin translucent shroud of marble covering the body of the Crucified Christ. A far more unusual sight is downstairs. Apparently these two corpses, masses of veins and arteries, were preserved by Raimondo di Sangro, a scientist/alchemist, in an embalming fluid. Unreliable gossip has it that the woman, who appears pregnant, was his mistress, caught with mummy number two, her lover. Sangro justice was swift.

MORE ATTRACTIONS

Castel Nuovo. Pz. Municipio. Admission 6,000L ($3.95). Mon–Sat 9am–7pm. Bus: 106, 150; Tram: 1, 4.

The massive castle's main attraction is its entrance, a marble arch that was entirely restored in 1988. A brilliant Renaissance monument, it was built to welcome Alphone of Aragon to Naples (1453–67), although the fortress dates back to 1279–82. How welcome Alphonse actually was to the Neapolitans we can only imagine; he may not have said, "Let them eat *sfogliatelle*," but he was of that temperament. The other great treasure is the Santa Barbara or Palatine Chapel, across the main courtyard, which is now part of a city museum. Inside is a lovely Madonna by Laurana, who, with the Gagini family of artists, was responsible for many of the great artworks of southern Italy.

Castel dell'Ovo. At the port of Santa Lucia. ☎ **081/76-45-688.** Free admission. Mon–Sat 9am–3pm. Bus: 104, 140, 150. Tram 1, 4.

Climbing around this massive structure is like having a real sandcastle to play in. It's the oldest fortress (1154) in Naples. It was along these shores of the Santa Lucia section that Naples began, once named Parthenope for the nymph washed ashore here after drowning herself—her siren song failed to lure Ulysses. This castle has its myth too: that Virgil built it (he's buried in Naples) on an enchanted egg submerged on the sea floor. If the egg breaks, the castle and all of Naples will fall. What we know for sure is that there was a Norman structure here that was enlarged by Frederick II, who held his parliament in the castle. In years to come his grandchildren were imprisoned here, as was Joanna I. Its parapet has a sweeping view of Naples' charming harbor and restaurants. Sometimes there are nighttime performances of Neapolitan songs and dances; check at the entrance.

Palazzo Reale. Pz. d. Plebiscito ☎ **081/41-38-88.** Admission 8,000L ($5.25). Tues–Sun 9am–1pm, Sat–Sun 9am–1pm and 4–7:30pm. Bus: 106, 150.

This royal palace (1600–02) gives an idea of the scale of noble life. Staircases were large enough for the entire court to enter and leave at once, it seems. There is a picture gallery and you can see the ornately baroque royal apartments, but if your time is limited, go to the newly reopened Capodimonte galleries instead.

San Carlo Opera House. Pz. Trieste e Trento ☎ **081/79-72-111.** Admission 5,000L ($3.30), free on Sunday. Daily 9am–noon. Bus: 106, 150.

San Carlo is now more than 250 years old, having been built in 1737; the interior was rebuilt in 1816 after a fire. Verdi, Donizetti, and all the greats of Italian opera hoped to hear their works performed here. During the winter months opera is staged and summer sees some concerts.

V. San Gregorio Armeno. In Spaccanapoli. Metro: Cavour.

This street is famous for its Christmas crèche (*presepio*) figures. If it's late fall, you will see the many sellers of beautifully hand-carved wooden—or hideous, mass-produced plastic—figures stocking up their wares. At its intersection with Via Tribunale (Via Porta Alba's extension), the church of San Gregorio Armeno is especially worth a visit now that the frescoes depicting the life of the saint have been restored.

WHERE TO STAY

The hotels along the harbor have the best views from the rooms (you often pay for seafront windows—however, it's usually worth it). The per-night rate is apt to be good if you book two or more nights. Otherwise, I recommend the waterfront area around Santa Lucia and Mergellina for hotels.

✪ **Le Fontane del Mare.** V. Niccolò Tommaseo 14, Naples 80121. ☎ **081/76-43-470.** 25 rms, 7 with bath. 110,000L ($72.35) doubles. AE. Bus: 140 or 150 from Napoli Centrale or Mergellina port.

Near the Villa Communale, which is in the Chiaia section near Santa Lucia, this hotel is clean and quiet, and some of the owner's antiques add charm. Fourteen of the rooms have views of the sea, but most of these are without bath. The neighborhood is pleasant, and the seaside has cafes and expensive restaurants for dining.

✪ **Hotel Belvedere.** V. Angelini 51. ☎ **081/57-88-169.** Fax 081/57-85-417. 27 rms, 25 with bath. A/C TV TEL. 90,000L–150,000L ($59.20–$98.70) single without bath, 150,000L ($98.70) single with bath; 180,000L ($118.40) double with bath. Funicular: from Pzta. Duca d'Aosta. AE, MC, V.

This hotel is just coming into its own as a good bet for those on a budget. It's not far from the center of town (just up the funicular on the Vomero), but its mood is far from the city. Rooms are nicely decorated with spreads and curtains in soft colors, and prints of local scenes or flowers are on the walls. The management is very helpful, and want to maintain a quiet, romantic spot. it is not for loud partying, but there is a pretty bar and restaurant with a view of the bay. There is sometimes a piano bar at night.

Hotel Casanova. V. Venezia 2. ☎ and fax **081/26-82-87.** 18 rms, 12 with bath. 25,000L ($17.35) single without bath, 30,000L ($19.75) single with bath; 42,000L ($27.80) doubles without bath, 55,000L ($36.20) doubles with bath; 75,000L ($49.35) triple with bath; 80,000L ($52.65) quad with bath. Breakfast 4,500L ($2.95). Metro: Stazione Centrale. AE, MC, V.

The great lover Casanova might not choose this spot for a romantic interlude, but if you want a clean, airy, plain inexpensive place near the station, go for it. Their rooftop terrace with bar service is a big plus, and a way to meet fellow travelers (mostly young ones). Some rooms have TV, fridge, and phone. The baths are clean, but need renovation with some pretty tiles. The management is friendly and helpful. Be aware of your surroundings in this area at night.

Hotel Pinto-Storey. V. Martucci 72. ☎ **081/68-12-60.** Fax 081/66-75-36. 25 rms, 19 with bath. AC TV TEL. 80,000L ($52.65) single without bath, 130,000L ($85.50) single with bath; 110,000L ($72.35) double without bath, 180,000L ($118.40) double with bath. AE, MC, V.

This hotel has a faithful clientele, and does try to upgrade its image with frequent renovation. The rooms are plain but equipped with the basic amenities. The bay is a short walk away (it's just below the Villa Floridiana). A small bar on the main floor is a way to relax after a hard day's touring for a coffee or an aperitivo.

Pensione Teresita. V. Santa Lucia 90. ☎ **081/76-40-105.** 13 rms, none with baths. TEL. 60,000L ($39.50). No credit cards. Tram: 1 or 4.

The rooms are clean, and the location—in Santa Lucia, near the Castel dell'Ovo—is good, but this spot requires a traveler who doesn't mind some dancers with bangles lounging about now and then. It's always full, mainly with tourists. It's not a good idea to wander about here at night alone, however, but it may make you feel somewhat safer to know you're in the same neighborhood as the Excelsior and other tony hotels.

WHERE TO DINE

The food many Americans think of as southern Italian does not exist here. Spaghetti and meatballs and heavy cheesecake are all often unfortunately thought of as Neapolitan. Pizza, on the other hand, is indeed Neapolitan, and is crisp and flavorful, never thick and soft. In addition to the recommendations below, head for **Pizzeria Port'Alba** at V. Port'Alba 18 (☎ **081/45-97-13**) for great pizza Margherita (with sauce, fresh mozzarella, and basil leaves).

True Neapolitan cooking is delicious, and sauces never drown the food. Pleasures await when you try the succulent *vongoli veraci* (clams) done *Posillipo*-style, with garlic, wine, and tomatoes. If you don't like garlic (*aglio*) or onions (*cipolle*), tell them when ordering. Among Neapolitan specialties is *panzarella alla napoletana*, a salad of crumbled bread, onions, tomatoes, anchovies, and basil. Mozzarella here is often made from the milk of the buffalo of nearby Avellino. Try it *in carrozza*, a Neapolitan French toast. *Braciole* is a tasty roll of pork with prosciutto, raisins, and hard-boiled eggs inside. This may be the place to try octopus (*polpo*), often made *alla Luciana* (stewed with tomatoes, olive oil, peppers, and garlic).

Ask for local wines from the slopes of Vesuvius. Lacryma Christi, or "Christ's Tears," is among the best-known and can be exceptional. Usually, when trattoria owners know that you want to try local dishes and wines they will want you to taste the best.

Brandi. Salita Santa Anna d. Palazzo 2, at the corner of V. Chiaia. ☎ **081/41-69-28.** Reservations required. Main courses 9,000L–20,000L ($5.90–$13.15). No credit cards. Tues–Sun noon–3pm and 6:30–midnight. PIZZA.

Many Neapolitan restaurants claim to be the oldest pizzeria in the world. This may indeed be *the* place—at any rate it has spent more than a century at its present location. It is said that the Margherita pizza, preferred by purists because the taste of the crust is best appreciated without too many distractions, was created here for Queen Margherita di Savoia, queen of Italy. Its patriotic tricolor—of red tomatoes, white, fresh mozzarella, and green basil leaves—is part of its fame. Even more minimal is the pizza bianca, just great crust with a splash of rich olive oil and some salt (some add rosemary leaves to it for a fresh taste).

Le Brace. V. Spaventa 14. ☎ **081/26-12-60.** Reservations not accepted. Main courses 7,000L–15,000L ($4.60–$6.60). Sat noon–midnight. PIZZA/SANDWICHES.

You can stop in here for a quick snack, although the crowds may make speed less likely. This well-known spot near the stations serves wood-fired pizza and sandwiches (*panini*) or pasta, plus omelettes and salads. The neighborhood isn't yet the best, but the clientele is—typical of Naples, it includes everyone from the bricklayer to the professor.

Dante e Beatrice. Pz. Dante 44–46 ☎ **081/54-99-438.** Reservations recommended. Main courses 10,000L–21,000L ($6.60–$14.80). No credit cards. Tues–Sun noon–4 and 8–midnight. Closed Aug 15–30. NEAPOLITAN.

A favorite among students (for its prices) and food lovers (for its quality) alike, this is not a spot for a romantic meal. However, it is just the place to watch Naples at its most voluble best. If you find that intimidating, go there at the opening hour in the evening, as Italians dine late, and Southern Italians even later. If *frittata di maccheroni* is on the menu, try it. It's crunchy outside and creamy within.

La Cantina di Triunfo. Riviera di Chiaia 34. ☎ **081/66-81-01.** Main courses 10,000L–25,000L ($6.55–$17.45). No credit cards. Mon–Sat 12:30–3pm and 7:30–11pm. Closed Aug. WINE BAR/NEAPOLITAN.

This little place is popular with locals—and has been for over a hundred years under the same family's reign—so you might want to go early (the afternoon hours are for wine and snacks only; full dinner menu is available from 7:30pm on). You might have tagliatelle with squid and artichokes before moving on to grilled fish. The menu varies according to what's fresh in the market, and take your food dictionary. *Crema fritta* for dessert is enriched with chocolate-nut cream. Rosolio after dinner or grappa will finish the evening languidly.

Mimi alla Ferrovia. V. Alfonso d'Aragona 21. ☎ **081/55-38-525.** Reservations advised. Main dishes 9,000L–25,000L ($5.90–$16.45). Mon–Sat 12:30–3 and 8–11pm. NEAPOLITAN.

Napoli is wonderful for dining, because not only are the trattorias excellent and full of local color, the prices are moderate at the better places, if you are careful what you order. As anywhere, fish is apt to be pricey. Don't go to Mimi's for a snack, but only if you want to splurge on the length of your meal and possibly also the cost. Ask for *assagi di paste povere* for a taste of several of the pastas of the day. The linguine alla Mimi is served in a spicy shrimp sauce. Try to get a table on the terrace (*terrazza*).

Vini e Cucina. Cor. Vittorio Emanuele 762 (across from Mergellina station). ☎ 081/66-03-02. No reservations. Main courses 6,000L–10,000L ($3.95–$6.60). No credit cards. Daily 12:30–3.00pm and 7–10pm. Closed Aug 20–30. NEAPOLITAN.

A dinner here is a good and very inexpensive way to celebrate home cooking Neapolitan-style. It fills up quickly with seekers of the famous *pasta e fagioli* (pasta with beans), pasta with cauliflower or pumpkin (*zucca*) sauce, grilled meat or fish, and pastries with chestnut puree. It is packed with Neapolitans, and therefore noisy and wild.

CAFES

Gambrinus. V. Chiaia 1. ☎ **081/41-75-82.** Drinks at table from 4,000L ($2.65). Wed–Fri til 11pm; Sat til 1am. Closed Aug 15–31.

Dating from the year of independence, 1860, Gambrinus's enormous salon is still very much in operation. Go into the inside room to see the frescoes and reliefs.

Scaturchio. Pz. San Domenico Maggiore. ☎ **081/55-16-944.** Pastries from 1,600L ($1.05) if you stand up; from 3,500L ($2.30) at a table. Tues–Sun 7:30am–8:30pm.

Since 1900, this has been the place to stop while wandering through Spaccanapoli to savor a cappuccino and *sfogliatelle*, light triangles of layered pastry with ricotta inside, flavored with bits of fruit or lemon. *Ministeriale* is a chocolate cake with liqueur and chocolate cream.

NAPLES AFTER DARK

Naples nightlife can be rough, and also expensive. It probably offers more sucker joints than any other port along the Mediterranean.

The **Teatro San Carlo,** V. San Carlo (☎ **081/79-72-331**), is one of Italy's largest opera houses, with one of the best acoustics. Built in 1737, it has been restored in a gilded neoclassical style. Grand-scale productions are presented here. The box office is open December through June, Tuesday to Sunday from 10am to 1pm and 4:30 to 6:30pm.

SIDE TRIPS FROM NAPLES
POMPEII

Besides the two major sites, you may want to take the *Circumvesuviana* train to Torre Annunciata to see the wonderful **Villa Oplontis** and its frescoes. The villa is open from 9am to one hour before sunset. You can also take a trip to the **Phlaegrean Fields (Campi Flegrei),** one of the bizarre attractions of southern Italy. The fiery fields, a land of myth and legend, contain a dormant volcano (Volcano Solfatara; ☎ **081/526-7413** for information) and the cave of the Cumaean Sibyl, Virgil's gateway to the Infernal Regions. The best center for exploring the area is **Pozzuoli,** reached by the Cumano Metro line from Piazza Montesanto.

Pompeii, near the sea and in fertile volcanic soil, has been inhabited since the 7th century B.C., when trading was already developed along this coast, with the Greek colonies in Italy of the time and with the Etruscans. But the Pompeii we know is the one the port town Rome founded in 80 B.C., which was devastated by an earthquake in A.D. 63 and was soon after lost forever in A.D. 79, when Vesuvius erupted and covered the area with ash and cinders. Much of our knowledge about the catastrophe comes from the letters of Pliny the Younger, who inherited and compiled the notes of his uncle (Pliny the Elder), who witnessed the devastation from a ship out on the bay before succumbing to its gases himself. Pompeii was forgotten for centuries, really until Charles III of Bourbon decided to see what lay beneath the soil (workmen had been turning up pieces of colored marble in the area that bespoke of greater riches underground).

The Roman city emerged from the rubble bit by bit, and is still emerging. Its contribution to history and art has been enormous—cold comfort to those who perished. About 20,000 people lived in Pompeii when it was destroyed, at a time when it was the most important city on the coast.

Pompeii is a tourist mecca, but the site is vast and you can always pull away from the multitudes of clicking cameras. It's spread out over more than ¹/₂ mile, mainly in the open air with little shade from the beating sun, so wear walking shoes and take sunblock.

Essentials

GETTING THERE   By Train   Pompeii is closer to Sorrento than to Naples, but it's only a pleasant (usually) 35-minute ride on the *Circumvesuviana* train from Napoli Centrale station. Round-trip fare is 2,500L ($1.65); get off at Pompeii Villa dei Misteri, *not* Pompeii Santuario. The same train also stops here coming from Sorrento.

By Car   Take the autostrada A3 toward Salerno for 13¹/₂ miles.

By Bus   Eurojet buses (☎ **06/47-44-521**) connect Rome with Pompeii, Sorrento, and Amalfi.

VISITOR INFORMATION   The **tourist office** is at V. Sacra 1 (☎ 081/ 85-07-255). Have a snack at the sandwich place opposite the entrance; it has out-side tables. Inside the ruins complex, the cafeteria is expensive, and you can't get back in, once out. Guides cost about 70,000L ($46.05) for a full morning, but off-season you might negotiate or try to assemble a group. Licensed guides (who must wear a badge) have keys to some of the more interesting sites, and if you can get a few people from your hotel together, you can hire one for two hours from **GATA Tours** (☎ 081/86-15-661; fax 081/53-68-577). Pompeii management is attempting to work out a less costly plan for visitors, which may be in place by the time you visit.

✪ Exploring the Ruins of Pompeii

Plan to spend at least four hours at the site (unless you have a full day) and also the Villa of the Mysteries, which is a short walk away. In general, a guide (who will approach you) is necessary to see many of the locked areas, which include some of the remains of residents (which look like plaster casts) and also the erotic art of the houses of pleasure, and some mosaics that are kept closed so tourists won't pick them apart for souvenirs (for more on guides, see "Visitor Information," above).

If the **museum** just inside the gates is open, go in. Plaster casts of some of the bodies found are exhibited there. The tightly-packed molten ash created sculptors' molds around the victims into which cement was injected to preserve them and make these casts. The gift shop near the entrance sells extensive reading material on Pompeii in English in case you want to delve deeper into Pompeian life. Check out the inexpensive prints as well.

Enter the site via the steep slope at the Porta Marina and you'll see to the right the ruins of **Tempio di Venere** or Temple of Venus, part of a fertility cult. Pass by the Basilica along the same road and cross to the **Tempio di Apollo,** where you'll see a copy of the beautiful statue of *Apollo the Archer* (the original is in the Naples Archeological Museum). The cult of Apollo goes back to the 6th century B.C., and the god was often appealed to for help in battle. The temple with its series of columns stood at the center of the site and was built during the 2nd century B.C. atop an earlier shrine. The **Forum's** massive rectangle stands in front, and was once filled with statues of local luminaries. On a clear day, Vesuvius is clearly outlined beyond it. Where today you see only two arches once stood the city's main temple, dedicated to Jupiter, Juno, and Minerva. The **Basilica** part (which you passed earlier) is partly intact at one end and you can see the row of columns where the tribunal stood. Column bases along the ground (broken in the earthquake some 16 years before the eruption of Vesuvius, but never repaired by the ancient city before it was buried in ash) show the division into aisles. Basilicas were not originally religious buildings, but places where law and business were transacted.

Past the Temple to Apollo to the left (which existed before the Forum) you'll notice a long table (from 20 B.C.) with semicircular holes of different sizes, like a long sink. This was the Control of Weights and Measures, which kept all the traders honest. The Forum also contained a Cereals Market to the left of the main altar. On its far side was the latrine, whose pipes are perfectly preserved to this day. The treasury was just beyond it. The provisions market stood to the temple's right, behind the three columns and pediment. Fish were cleaned at the center, where a masonry base remains.

Exiting past the temple, take the Via del Foro for one block and turn left into the **Terme del Foro,** a spa for the Romans with a dressing room and baths of graded temperatures (The *calderium,* or hot spa, has a large basin at one end); men and women were separated. Left of the baths is the pretty **House of the Tragic Poet,** which may

Pompeii

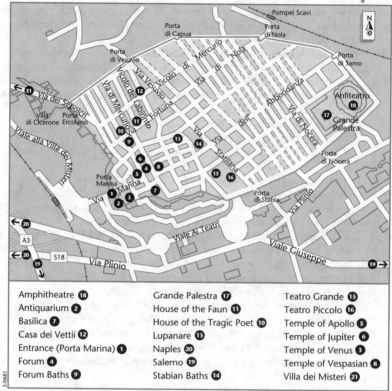

Amphitheatre **18**	Grande Palestra **17**	Teatro Grande **15**
Antiquarium **2**	House of the Faun **11**	Teatro Piccolo **16**
Basilica **7**	House of the Tragic Poet **10**	Temple of Apollo **5**
Casa dei Vettii **12**	Lupanare **13**	Temple of Jupiter **6**
Entrance (Porta Marina) **1**	Naples **20**	Temple of Venus **3**
Forum **4**	Salerno **19**	Temple of Vespasian **8**
Forum Baths **9**	Stabian Baths **14**	Villa dei Misteri **21**

3-0681

not be open, but you can see the famous CAVE CANEM (BEWARE OF THE DOG) sign in mosaic.

Retrace your steps past the baths and continue on for a block to Via della Fortuna and the **Casa del Fauno,** which covers an entire block. One of the earliest, largest, and finest houses in Pompeii, it was began in the 2nd century B.C. and has two atriums, or open courtyards. A copy of the *Dancing Faun* is set at the center rainwater pool. The gardens with oleanders and roses make this house a special treat.

Catercorner from the far corner of the baths, on Vicolo dei Vettii, the luxurious **Casa dei Vettii** was owned by the two Vettius brothers, who were merchants during the 1st century A.D. The entrance leads to an atrium, which is decorated with the beautiful mythological pictures of *Ariadne Abandoned* and *Hero and Leander*. The sculpture garden has been seeded with the same plants that originally grew here.

The atrium passes into the *peristyle* (column arrangement) where the wall decorations are exquisitely painted against a black background. The first room east of the peristyle contains wall paintings of dancing maenad and satyr couples. The central painting is of the goddess Hera and Ixion, who, as punishment for betraying Hera, was commanded by Zeus to be tied to a wheel that turned perpetually. The second painting explores a myth that only the Greeks could create: A wooden cow is being given by Daedalus to Pasiphae, who will be shut up inside it in order to consummate her love for a bull, from which union the Minotaur would spring. The third shows

Dionysus and a sleeping Ariadne. The second room contains another trilogy, this from Thebes. The paintings in these rooms are among the most important that survive from their time.

Nearby stands another peristyle, in which the exquisite wall paintings have a red background (the famous Pompeii red) and also depict mythological scenes. Look at the *dado,* or lower part of the wall painting, where cupids and psyches are busy gathering grapes, working gold, carrying flowers, and performing other activities—some think these 13 occupations had to do with the various business ventures of the wealthy yet still somewhat mysterious brothers Vettii.

To see a brick oven still intact in the local bakery, continue down Vicolo dei Vettii, cross Vicolo della Fortuna and enter Vicolo Storto. The **Pistrinum,** or bakery, is to the left.

To its left is the **House of the Wounded Bear,** where a mosaic indeed depicts a wounded bear. The word *have* that you see here and perhaps before in many houses means, loosely, "howdy," and was the equivalent of a welcome mat. A nymphaeum (shrine to the nymphs) of special delicacy sparkles in the garden.

The **Lupanare,** or bordello, lies beyond (Regio VII, Insula 12, 18 was the address that doubtless was whispered about town). There were quite a few brothels in Pompeii, but this one was two-story affair—for those who could pay more for privacy. The paintings are self-explanatory and definitely clarify the fantasies of Pompeian men about their anatomy. (Parents: These are definitely X-rated.)

Continue along the same street to another entertainment section. A Doric temple from the 6th century B.C. stands on one side. The rectangular **Palestra** was the site of an athletics club. The large theater or **Teatro Grande** had a section for an orchestra, but it was the nearby **Teatro Piccolo** that was used for musical performances, unless they were standing-room only. The two-story **Quadriportico** was the Gladiators' Barracks.

Back on Via Stabia, walk straight ahead; you'll find the Porta di Stabia. A left turn and a short nine-block walk will take you to the large palestra grounds and **Amphitheater,** the oldest known of its kind (built around 80 B.C.).

There is an exit here and you can walk around the outside of the site and far along the path to the **Villa of the Mysteries,** which was once a suburban house. The ten friezes here are extraordinary, and no one knows exactly what is going on in them. The rituals appear to be Dionysian, and in one a young woman seems being prepared for a sacrifice, in another a winged figure is about to whip a frightened woman. Guards will open some of the closed rooms for you, but will expect a tip of 1,000L to 2,000L (65¢ to $1.30).

Admission is 12,000L ($7.90); the ruins are open daily from 9:30am to 1 hour before sunset (about 4pm in mid-winter, 8pm in mid-summer). For information call **081/85-07-255.**

HERCULANEUM (ERCOLANO)

Much of Herculaneum (named after Hercules) is still underground, as it was when Vesuvius covered it in a river of mud on the same day as Pompeii's ruin (A.D. 79). This mud solidified to rock and preserved many of the kinds of objects—household goods, fabrics, and the second floor of many buildings—that were burned in Pompeii's cinders. A commuter city to Naples, weekend spot for rich Romans (whose villas occupied the high ground), and agricultural area, Herculaneum numbered about 5,000 people when it was destroyed. The J. Paul Getty Museum in Malibu was patterned after the Villa of the Papyri here, but this section is not open to the public.

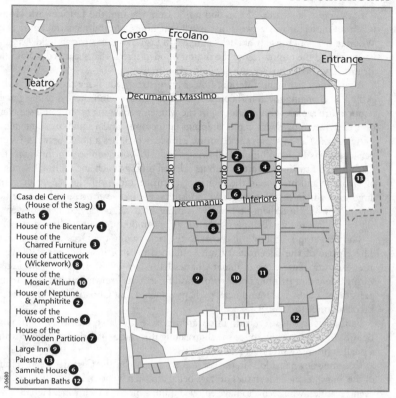

Herculaneum

Corso Ercolano

Entrance

Teatro

Decumanus Massimo

Cardo III

Cardo IV

Cardo V

Decumanus Inferiore

Casa dei Cervi
(House of the Stag) **11**
Baths **5**
House of the Bicentary **1**
House of the
   Charred Furniture **3**
House of Latticework
   (Wickerwork) **8**
House of the
   Mosaic Atrium **10**
House of Neptune
   & Amphitrite **2**
House of the
   Wooden Shrine **4**
House of the
   Wooden Partition **7**
Large Inn **9**
Palestra **13**
Samnite House **6**
Suburban Baths **12**

3-0680

Note: Although many plans are in store for this area, the area around Herculaneum is not always safe, and so take big-city precautions and stay where the people are.

Essentials

GETTING THERE   By Train   Herculaneum is closer (6 miles) to Naples than to Sorrento, and can be reached from either Napoli Centrale (15 minutes, 1,800L/ $1.20) or Pompeii via the *Circumvesuviana* train (stop: Ercolano). Walk down the hill to the entrance at Piazza Museo 1 (off Corso Ercolano.

By Car   Take the autostrada A3 toward Salerno for about 8 miles.

VISITOR INFORMATION   You can reach the ruins office at ☎ **81/73-90-963.**

Exploring the Ruins of Herculaneum

Left of the entrance you'll see excavations of the Sacred Area, where shrines have been uncovered. (Many of the surrounding covered buildings are greenhouses for flower cultivation.) The grid pattern and small size make the town easy to walk through. Many of the most interesting sights lie along Cardo IV, the street at the center, just after the Sacred Area.

At the start to the left, **the Inn** (Casa dell'Albergo) is among the largest of the structures. It was actually not an inn, but rather the home of a wealthy patrician with an orchard and garden. The **Mosaic Atrium House,** across the Cardo, once stood by the sea; its rippling tiles were caused by the waves of volcanic mud that ran below it during the destruction.

Back across the Cardo, the second house from the inn, the **Latticework House** (Casa a Graticcio) was a two-story apartment house around a central court. The **Wooden Screen House** (Casa del Tramezzo di Legno) was a patrician residence, and has preserved the impression of the sliding wooden screen that separated it from the atrium. Two bedrooms have their wooden bedframes.

Across the Decumano Inferiore (lower main street) you'll see the **Baths,** with a gym. The changing room had compartments for clothes, and this led to the graded temperature rooms, with tile floors. In the women's changing room you'll see Neptune carrying an oar, with cupid, dolphins, an octopus, and a squid for company.

Across the Cardo stands the **Samnite House,** which has a noble bearing. Its upper loggia has Ionic columns. Following Cardo IV you soon see, to the right, the **Carbonized Furniture House,** with its original dining couch and table. The mosaic of Neptune and his wife in the House of Neptune and Amphrite is a beauty. The large shop adjoining the house held foodstuffs, the best ever preserved from antiquity. You won't find them here today, as things that can be carried away are generally stored before they disappear—theft is an enormous problem at these sites.

The next stop is around the corner to the right, along the Decumano Massimo. The **House of the Bicentenary** was so named because it was opened 200 years after excavations were begun under Charles III (1738–1938). It's an elegant house, with gardens and paintings of mythological figures. Its known best because the impression of a cross was found here, perhaps evidence that Christianity had spread to Ercolano prior to A.D. 79.

Farther along this street, turn into Cardo V to see the large **Palestra** with its pool. Before you reach it, stop to see the shops along this cardo—a bakery with ovens and a phallus (to make sure the bread would rise).

Continue down Cardo V to the last house on the right, the **Casa dei Cervi** (House of the Stags), named for statues of stags being attacked by hounds, several satyrs, and even Hercules, who seems to have enjoyed quite a bit too much wine. Hercules was captured in a moment that few town founders would probably want publicized, much less sculpted.

The site is open daily from June to August, 9am to 8pm and from September to May from 9am to one hour before sunset. Admission is 12,000L ($7.90), and you can call **81/73-90-963** for more information.

A SIDE TRIP TO VESUVIUS   From Herculaneum you may want to take the bus up to the cause of all the damage—Vesuvius. At least the volcano has provided wonderful soil for vegetables and grapevines. If you want to ascend, there is a SITA bus (about every two hours; 2,000L/$1.30) that makes the climb daily from the train station in Ercolano until 4:30pm—unless you want to do it on foot (for those in shape only). You may have to pay 4,500L ($3.50) for a compulsory guide. Vesuvius's last eruption was in 1944, so keep in mind as you stare into the dull, bleak crater that doesn't look much more dangerous than your average large ditch that the mountain only sleeps. If the bus should not be running, a taxi is your costly, alternative. Take a sandwich and a drink.

POZZUOLI

Slow, magma-driven earthquakes have raised and lowered the ground level of this port town on a promontory west of Naples for centuries (an effect called bradyseism). Over the last few decades, these tortoise-paced tremors have shaken and cracked the town into a shabby, run-down look. There are, however, some striking ancient Roman ruins, and those earthquakes have recently had an interesting side-effect; an old

Roman market that was sunken for centuries offshore when the ground level subsided has been slowly raised out of the water for all to view.

Take the Cumano line from Piazza Montesanto. and follow the street down to the port. Remember that service stops at 11pm. The **tourist office,** at Pz. Matteoti 1A (☎ **081/52-66-639**) the intersection of Corso della Repubblica and Via Solfatara, provides maps and info on the local sights.

The Roman Amphitheater

The major tourist site in Pozzuoli is the well-preserved Roman Amphitheater (Anfiteatro Flavio) built around A.D. 79 (on Via Rosini; open daily 9am to 2 hours before sunset; admission 4,000L/$2.65). You can also walk up to the nearby, semi-dormant Solfatara crater, which occasionally emits jets of sulfurous steam that measure upwards of 140°F in temperature, and home to steaming pools of water and bubbling mud pits. It's about a 1 1/2-mile walk up Via Rossini, which becomes Via Solfatara; or jump on any city bus heading uphill.

2 Capri

Just 3.8 miles at its longest, this island three miles off Sorrento's peninsula has enchanted sailors, traders, mythmakers, emperors, and travelers for centuries. Capri is camera-ready, even on misty days. Rent the video of *It Happened in Naples* to whet your appetite (the port looks just the same), and be ready to shell out a scandalous amount for the quick and obligatory rowboat ride around the inside the luminous Blue Grotto—it's worth all those lire.

ESSENTIALS

GETTING THERE   By Boat   Capri is a 40-minute hydrofoil (*aliscafo*) ride (18,000L/$11.85) from Naples Mergellina dock or the Molo Beverello dock in central Naples. Or take a 70-minute ferry (*traghetto*) ride from Molo Beverello (8,000L to 10,000L/$5.25 to $6.60). From Sorrento, the hydrofoil takes 20 minutes, and costs 8,000L ($5.25), the ferry takes 40 minutes and costs 6,000L ($3.95). From Amalfi, the one-hour hydrofoil ride costs 15,000L ($7.95); the ferry takes three hours and costs 6,000L ($3.95).

The hydrofoil costs much more than the ferry but is faster. However, you are enclosed below for the ride, while by ferry you have the run of the decks and can enjoy the trip far more, including the spectacular approach to the Capri port of Marina Grande on the north side of the island (which means that most maps must be turned upside down to be intelligible). Both ferries and hydrofoils run about three times a day from Naples. For a current ferry schedule, buy a copy of Naples' daily paper, *Il Mattino,* which has a full lineup (it's available in major U.S. city newsstands as well). For ferry information in Naples, call **081/76-13-688.**

Visitors' cars are not permitted on the island.

Note: If coming by train from Rome through Naples straight to Capri, get off at the first stop in Naples, Mergellina station, if you want to take the hydrofoil, as the pretty dock is within walking distance of the station. (Check first that the train will stop there.) Napoli Centrale, the main station, is closer to the ferry dock (Molo Beverello); however, you don't want to be alone or late in that section.

GETTING AROUND   From Marina Grande, the funicolare (to the left across the piazza) rises to the town of Capri and charges 1,500L ($1). Buses from the town of Capri run to Anacapri or to Marina Piccola, and also costs 1,500L ($1) each way.

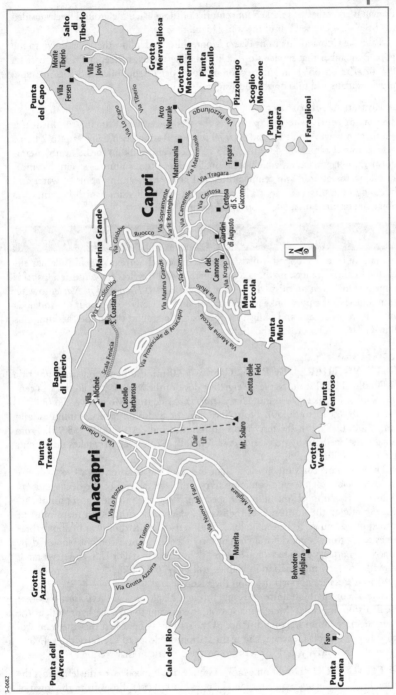

VISITOR INFORMATION   The **tourist office (AAST)** in Marina Grande is at the dock (☎ **081/83-70-634**). In Capri town, there is an office at Pz. Umberto I (☎ **081/83-70-686**). In Anacapri, head to Pz. Vittoria 5 (☎ **081/83-71-524**).

WHAT TO SEE & DO

Capri's principal sight is itself—a tall rock in the sea whose sides are strewn with pine and ilex, grapevines, lemon and olive trees, bougainvillea, roses, and jasmine. It's enchanting, flower-filled, and so sweet-smelling in late summer that Ulysses could never have sailed past without stopping, even if he was lashed to the mast to prevent his dallying. (Homer's *Odyssey* mentions several places along the coast from Salerno to Naples.) Its harbors and mountain (Monte Solaro rises to almost 2,000 feet), its triumphant offshore rocks (*I Faraglioni*) and sea grottoes, its Roman ruins, smart hotels, chic trattorias, and pricey boutiques have all made it the object of millions of visitors.

Avoid the main piazza and shopping streets during the day and you won't experience the tourist crush. Day-trippers from Naples stop briefly, shop, and head back to the mainland in late afternoon, leaving the island to its residents and the few visitors who choose to stay the night.

THE BLUE GROTTO

This large, partially undersea cave of several chambers draws tourists in long lines of boats because of the unearthly blue of its refracted light gleaming on the white sand bottom. Excavations have revealed objects that show this natural grotto was used as an ancient Roman nymphaeum—a shrine to the nymphs. Tiberius apparently came down here to enjoy the setting with his chosen ones of the moment, but his "secret underground staircase" your oarsman will probably point out to you has most recently been judged a natural cleft that leads nowhere. Sunny days are needed for the best light to filter through. You get the best light effects between 11am and 1pm.

Boats run in and out of the grotto daily from 9am to one hour before sunset, and there are a number of ways to get there. You can get a boat from the docks at Marina Grande for 10,000L ($6.60) that takes you to the entrance of the cave, then you must pay 15,000L ($9.90) for the second, tiny rowboat that actually enters. From Anacapri, you can either take the bus from Pz. Barile (every half hour in summer, hour in winter; 1,500L/$1) or walk down Via Tuoro and Via Grotta Azzurra and just pay the 15,000L ($9.90) for the second boat. Intrepid visitors can also swim in before or after the boats stop running, although be warned that the light isn't at its best for effect at these times and the strong currents warrant convincing a friend to join you for safety.

IN MARINA GRANDE & CAPRI

Augustus's Gardens (Giardini di Augusto). V. Matteotti. Free admission.

Follow Capri town's main street, Via Vittorio Emanuele, and continue along it when it turns into Via Serena, which leads to a left turn onto Via Matteotti, which passes the gardens. It's of interest not as a classical site but as a cool place to relax in summer and enjoy the view out toward the jagged sea rocks called *I Faraglioni*. Take your camera. Statues in the garden include one of Lenin, who fled to Capri—a most un-Communist refuge—when things were looking bad in St. Petersburg.

Villa Jovis. V. Tiberio. Admission 4,000L ($2.65). Daily 9am–1 hour before sunset.

The walk to the ruins is one of the island's most enchanting, especially when jasmine and honeysuckle are perfuming the soft air. These ruins of Tiberius's villa tell us a lot about the wily old emperor who moved the empire's capital to this little island

and communicated with the mainland by means of a light-code system. (The ruins of this lighthouse tower can be seen outside the villa's ground to the south.) The villa covered far more territory in those days and included gardens and ninfea (shrines to nymphs). The buildings were grouped near the cliff edge. The baths had the typical Roman plan of temperature-gradation rooms—the pools would go from hot through warm to frigid. If we're to believe Suetonius, the emperor's life here would have kept a *Hard Copy* reporter busy for years. His "nooks of lechery" to satisfy his appetite for boys and girls were part of his "criminal insanity." His cruelty rivals the worst tyrant's. On Capri, those the emperor was finished with or disliked were dispatched into the sea far below, where soldiers waited in boats to make sure they didn't swim off. A church marks the place (Salto di Tiberio) from which he is said to have thrown them.

Certosa di San Giacomo. V. Certosa. Free admission. Tues–Sun 9am–2pm. Take V. Camerelle to V. Cerio, and follow it down toward the sea.

Capri as a medieval island with a monastery is not its usual image. The 14th-century Certosa (Charterhouse of St. James) is worth a visit to view another aspect of the island's past. Much of present Caprese architecture can be seen in its lines.

IN ANACAPRI

Villa San Michele. V. Orlando. ☎ **081/83-71-401.** Summer daily 9am–6pm, winter daily 10:30am–3:30pm. Admission 5,000L ($3.30).

This beautiful villa was founded by Swedish physician Axel Munthe, who created a charming house and garden filled with the antiquities he loved. Many of the sculptures are Roman originals (look for the one of Medusa). His bust of Tiberius, with imperial bangs, shows a less-violent side of the emperor.

Church of San Michele. V. Sopramonte. Mon–Sat 9am–2pm, 3–5pm (except during Mass).

The simple church of St. Michael has a splendid floor of bright majolica (a type of ceramic) tile in which a bountiful Eden is the setting of Adam and Eve's expulsion. Those who ask "Why did Adam do it? He had *everything*." will find no answer in this lush paradise.

Mt. Solaro. Chairlift, Pz. Vittoria, Anacapri. Daily 9:30am–7pm. One-way 5,000L ($3.30), round-trip 7,000L ($4.60).

The chairlift (*segiovia*) will be familiar to skiers. It really is just a chair suspended well above the ground on a metal bar that carries it along a wire up the mountain. From it you'll see the island and its coasts, especially when you arrive (12 minutes) at the top, a height of 1,934 feet. There's a small cafe and souvenir stand at the summit. Walk back down for the wraparound scenery, if a path nearly 3,000 feet long doesn't faze you.

WALKS, BOAT TOURS & BEACHES

WALKS   Plan on a bit of hiking after all those lazy boat rides, or sitting on a terrace nursing a limoncello drink. To see how visitors fared before the funicular, take the lovely walk from the port of Marina Grande up to the town. It's best at dawn or dust. Follow the road to the right from the port, up Via Marina Grande to the Phoenician Steps that lead to Anacapri. You'll see the island's treasures close at hand as the panoramic road turns. There are 500 steep steps, which are a splendid way to go for hikers, but the funicular will suit less-willing tendons. You could always descend the path to the port and ride back up.

My favorite walk starts at the far side of the island and meanders along Via Tragara, from which you can see the Faraglioni, the two massive rocks that rise offshore. Very few walks on Capri are not beautiful.

Another wonderful road, the easiest walk if your time on Capri is short, runs from the town of Capri out to Tiberius's villa (see above) along Via Tiberio. Take the street that leads out of the main piazza to the left, away from the clock tower. You'll come to a fork: Follow the left side, Via Tiberio. If you can, return to the crossroads later to take the right-hand street, Via Matermania (which sounds to me like a Freudian condition). It leads to recklessly beautiful sights near the Arco Naturale. Don't blame me if you fall prey to the sirens or satyrs.

BOAT TOURS   Boats from the Marina Grande pier circle the island year-round, revealing many of Capri's 10,000 sea-level grottoes. Tours cost about 25,000L ($16.45) and last 1½ hours. You can also strike up independent deals with individual boatmen. If boatmen aren't busy they might do the same for 50,000L ($32.90) for a group of four. Your hotel can also help work out arrangements.

BEACHES   What is called **Tiberius's Baths** (Bagno di Tiberio) was apparently the bathing beach for Augustus's principal villa. You can see traces of the landing dock and swimming pool. Take the boat from Marina Grande to Bagni Tiberio (8,000L/ $5.25), or walk down (north) from Piazza Umberto. There's no charge to swim.

Anacapri's "beach" near the lighthouse (*Faro*) is usually less crowded, but be warned it is nothing more than a cove with a poured cement walkway, a roughly jagged lava ground (no sand) and plenty of spiny sea urchins. You can, however, rent fins and snorkeling equipment from the refreshments stand and swim out amid the schools of fish and the occasional solitary tiny island octopus. Local would-be Romeos might also be showing off their stuff by diving off the cliff on the far side of the cove to impress the crowd. Take the bus from Piazza Vittoria.

SHOPPING

Shopping on the island is highly developed and usually expensive. This is Krizia country. However, Capri's sandals—thin-strapped and chic—are lovely, not overly expensive, and not for walking tours. Lemons and their products, including perfume, are nicely packaged in Anacapri along the road near Villa San Michele, at **Limoncello,** V. Capodimonte 27 (☎ **081/83-72-927**). You might want to buy some lemon liqueur in a basket with a ceramic cup with a lemon pattern (about 15,000L/$9.85) as a gift for the neighbor who's taking in your mail while you're on vacation. *Limoncello* (which contains alcohol) is drunk after meals as a *digestivo,* or can be mixed with champagne or vodka. More elaborate ceramic gifts can be shipped home from this store.

WHERE TO STAY
CAPRI

In season (summer), reserve ahead. If you can't, check with the tourist office on the dock at Marina Grande, leave your luggage at the *deposito* across the landing dock, and go hunting. Ask for a list of alternatives to hotels—apartments and furnished rooms are also available now (see below). There is another luggage deposit at the top of the funicular's route. If you need a luggage carrier (for hotels on paths that taxis can't enter), they can be arranged for about 25,000L ($16.45) hotel-to-dock or vice versa (☎ **081/83-70-179**).

At last, **Rooms to Rent (*Affitacamere*)** have arrived (officially). At the tourist office, get a list of residents who rent rooms (*camere mobiliate*). They range from approximately 50,000L to 80,000L ($32.90 to $52.65) a night for a double, usually without a private bath. These rooms are regulated by the tourist office and are usually well-kept—it's a small island, and word travels fast if they're not.

Doubles for Less than 65,000 Lire ($42.75)

Belsito. V. Matermania, 80073 Capri. ☎ 081/83-78-750. Fax 081/83-76-622. 13 rooms, all with bath. TEL. 60,000L–80,000L ($39.50–$52.65) double with garden view; 100,000L–120,000L ($65.80–$78.95) double with seaview. Half- and full-pension plans available. Rates include breakfast. AE, MC, V. Open all year. From Pz. Umberto take V. Botteghe to V. Matermania, near Arco Naturale.

"Beautiful site" is what the name means and it is no exaggeration. Run by a friendly young couple from Capri, the hotel was once an 18th-century house , but now has a summer-camp feeling, rather laid-back. Rooms are simple, but the view from the terrace is spectacular. There is a bar on the premises, their restaurant-pizzeria is very good, and wood-fired pizza and focaccia are excellent.

Pensione Stella Maris. V. Roma, 80073 Capri. ☎ **081/83-70-452.** Fax 081/83-78-662. 10 rms, 6 with bath. TEL. Winter 50,000L–65,000L ($32.90–$42.75) double; summer (Easter to October) 90,000L–110,000L ($59.20–$65.80) double. Breakfast 15,000L ($9.85). No credit cards.

On the main street, across from the bus terminal, this hotel has simple rooms that are well cared for by a solicitous Caprese family. Some upper-floor rooms have sea views, and so reserve ahead. They are happy to guide you to good, inexpensive trattorias. The other guests might be Europeans on a thrifty holiday or college students seeking value and simple comfort. The rooms are bed-and-bureau affairs, but some bright tiles give the baths a bit of color.

Doubles for Less than 130,000 Lire ($85.50)

Aida. V. d. Birago, 80073 Capri. ☎ **081/83-70-366.** 9 rms, 8 with bath. 100,000L–140,000L ($65.80–$92.10) double. No credit cards. Open Apr 1–Oct 31. Walk up the stairs in the central piazza and pass the church. Turn left and then right at the next path and left on V. Birago.

Not far from Marina Piccola, Aida has a little garden and is beautifully cared for. The rooms are large, super-clean, and airy, and the staff is friendly. Flowers add charm to the rooms. The Aida has a romantic aura, and the clientele are apt to be having a quiet holiday away from it all. It's a short walk from the town center, along the Gardens of Augustus, a pleasant place for a walk after dinner.

La Prora. V. Castello. 80073 Capri. ☎ **081/83-70-281.** 7 rms, all with bath. 120,000L–140,000L ($78.95–$92.10) double. Breakfast 20,000L ($13.10). No credit cards. Open Apr 1–Oct 10. Just off V. Roma.

Room 11 has the balcony and the view. Otherwise stay here simply for the good value. The service is moderate but adequate and the rooms are kept very clean. Rooms without views are bright with tile floors and watercolor prints. It's centrally located, with restaurants and shopping just around the corner.

Quattro Stagioni. V. Marina Piccola, 80073 Capri. ☎ **081/83-70-041.** 12 rms, 8 with bath. 95,000L–105,000L ($62.50–$69.10) double without bath, 110,000L–120,000L ($72.35–$78.95) double with bath. Half-pension required in August of 100,000L ($65.80 per person). Rates include breakfast. MC, V. Open Mar 15–Oct 31. At the end of V. Roma, take a left; it's the 1st house on the left.

The owner loves flowers, and so guests can take advantage of his passion in the garden and in the rooms. Many have wonderful views. It's on the way (a lovely street) to Marina Piccola, and you can take the bus back. Simple but adequate meals are available.

La Tosca. V. d. Birago, 80073 Capri. ☎ **081/83-70-989.** 10 rms, 8 with bath. 90,000L–100,000L ($59.20–$65.80) double with bath. Breakfast 12,500L ($8.25). MC, V. Open all year.

Tosca has been one of my favorites, but management is currently changing, so who knows what the next two years will bring in terms of renovations or prices? In any case, it is wonderfully situated on the same path as Aida (of course), is quiet, and many rooms have small terraces that face the sea and the Faraglioni. It's set far back from the road, in a lovely garden of roses and jasmine. Rooms are basic; it's the location and the terraces that make it unusually attractive. Breakfast definitely needed improving last year.

Worth a Splurge

Villa Sarah. V. Tiberio 3/a, 80073 Capri. ☎ **081/83-77-817.** Fax 081/83-77-215. 20 rms, all with bath. TV, TEL. 145,000L ($95.40) single; 250,000L ($164.50) double. Rates include breakfast. AE, MC, V. Closed Oct 14–Easter.

The villa's flowery setting and panoramas have contributed to its standing as a top hotel in Capri. Ask for a room on the upper floor where sea views are best. Reserve well in advance as this simpatico place fills up quickly. The staff is generally friendly and the other guests are likely to be repeat customers.

ANACAPRI

Biancamaria. V. Orlandi 54, 80071 Anacapri. ☎ **081/83-71-463.** Fax 081/83-70-957. 14 rms, all with bath. June–Sept 100,000L–120,000L ($65.80–$78.95) single; 120,000L–180,000L ($78.95–$118.40) double. Apr, May, Oct 80,000L–100,000L ($52.60) single; 130,000L–150,000L ($85.50–$98.60) double. AE, MC, V. Closed Sept–Mar.

Next to the Caesar Augustus (see below), its views are similar, but the hotel is a simpler white building with bright tiles and terraces. Their garden is open for relaxing or sunbathing, and meals are available. Ask for a room on the sea side. The rooms are basic and comfortable, brightened by tiles and colorful spreads, and the management is helpful. It's well located, near the main piazza, for buses and trattorie.

Villa Eva. V. La Fabbriza 8, 80071 Anacapri. ☎ **081/83-72-040.** 15 rms, all with bath. 25,000L ($16.50) single; 50,000L–60,000L ($32.90–$39.50) double. No credit cards. Call from the port and they'll pick up.

Set off on its own, this attractive property has been popular with backpackers and other economizers for many years. The couple (Eva and Vincenzo) who run it understand hospitality. A swimming pool is a welcome addition, as is the bar, because Eva is out of the way. Camplike cabins are basic, as are the rooms in the main house. The atmosphere is casual, more like a camp than a hotel. The garden and terrace have sea views and the air is fresh up here, where Vespas usually fear to tread. Guests can make light meals in the kitchen.

Worth a Splurge

Caesar Augustus. V. Orlani 4, 80071 Anacapri. ☎ **081/83-73-395.** Fax 081/83-71-44. 58 rms with bath. 200,000L ($131.60) single or double, 250,000L ($164.50) suite. Breakfast 15,000L. AE, MC, V. Bus from Capri to center of town.

Rooms here vary from basic bed-and-bureau to deluxe, which may have a wraparound terrace over the sea and a luxurious tiled bath also with sea-facing windows. But most have an enchanting sea view from a cliff's edge (1,000 feet above sea level). On your terrace you can feel like Augustus, summoning a legion of mermaids below. On a clear day you can see Sorrento and Vesuvius. Bar and lounge rooms are huge, as is the long terrace above the garden and palm trees. Prices have gone up in recent years, but much-needed renovations to the public rooms and the baths have been performed. Some of the suites are fit for a honeymoon, with the bed in a curtained-off alcove, a chaise longue in the sitting room, and terrace. Prices are reduced off-season.

WHERE TO DINE
CAPRI

Aurora. V. Fuorlovado 18 ☎ **081/83-70-181.** Reservations critical. Main courses 9,000L–25,000L ($5.90–$16.45). AE, V. Daily noon–3pm and 7–11pm. Closed Nov–Apr. PIZZA/SEAFOOD.

A simple place with photos of the rich and famous on the wall, Aurora is considered by many to have the island's best pizza, which is their specialty. Local patrons are a sign of its quality. Lobster, stuffed squid, and scampi are the more expensive choices. Try a local wine from Campania. They recommend Greco di Tufo, from Vesuvius's volcanic soil.

Buca di Bacco. V. Longano 35. ☎ **081/83-70-723.** Reservations not necessary. Pizza 7,000L–12,000L. Main courses 9,000L–15,000L ($5.90–$9.98) AE, MC, V. Thurs–Tues noon–2:30 and 7–11pm. Closed Nov. PIZZA/CAPRESE.

This is a very charming spot, a bit cavelike, dug out of the walls, near the piazzetta, with a fresh, varied antipasto table. It's inexpensive, but they always seem to look as if they're waiting for someone special, and diners feel they're the one. Folk art adorns the walls and the food is wholesome, with pizza high on the list.

Al Grottino. V. Longano 27. ☎ **081/83-70-584.** Reservations required at dinner. Main courses 14,000L–24,000L ($9.20–$15.80). Wed–Mon noon–3pm and 7–11pm. AE, MC. V. Closed Nov 3–Mar 20. NEAPOLITAN.

I happened in here on a chilly October night and found a cheerful, cozy place where the English baby at the adjoining table was being adored by all the waiters. The diners are usually a mix of tourists and expatriates who have adopted Capri. They all come for the good food, such as linguini with shrimp and tomato sauce. The buffalo mozzarella from Caserta is a standard, and is presented in a variety of styles. To get here, walk left out of the piazzetta onto the narrow street on the way to the Villa Tiberio.

Le Grottelle. V. Arco Naturale 5. ☎ **081/83-75-719.** Main courses 9,000L–22,000L ($5.90–$14.50). AE, MC, V. Fri–Wed 12:30–3pm and 7:30–11pm. Closed Dec–Mar 31. PIZZERIA/CAPRESE.

A lovely walk from town along Via Matermania, and worth the effort—luckily, there are no high hills to climb. A grotto it is, where kitchen and dining terrace (with a spectacular view) are actual caves. This family-run spot presents a good pasta e fagioli (with beans) and fresh fish (crisply fried or otherwise). Ravioli alla caprese (with cheese, tomato, and basil) is a good opener. This is a good spot when the heat is mean.

Worth a Splurge

Luigi ai Faraglioni. S. d. Faraglioni, on the sea. ☎ **081/83-70-591.** Reserve table, and also boat (10,000L/$6.60) from Marina Piccola (unless you don't mind walking many stairs). Main courses 15,000L–30,000L ($9.85–$19.50). AE, MC, V. Daily noon–3pm and 7–11pm. Closed Oct–Easter. SEAFOOD.

Choose Luigi's not for its cuisine or service, which are both unexceptional, but for that ride out between the Faraglioni to their dock—it's worth the inflated prices. It's the place for a summer lunch with a view. Have tomato and mozzarella salad and a grilled fish. While I was there rock climbers were hang-gliding off the massive cliffs with ease. Surprise a friend with the boat ride and reserve some chilled wine on it. You'll pay a pretty lira, but what a sight. You might take the boat only one way (going is more dramatic) and then climb back up the cliff steps, which are not that steep and have flat walkways at intervals. The bar stays open between lunch and dinner for bathers, who pay for beach privileges and apparently must look like bikini models from *Sports Illustrated* or *GQ*.

ANACAPRI

Gelsomina. V. Migliara. ☎ **081/83-71-499.** Reserve on weekends. Main courses 9,000L–22,000L ($5.90–$14.50). AE, MC, V. Thurs–Tues 12:30–3pm and 7:30–11pm. Open Wed in summer. Closed Feb. CAPRESE.

In its own verdant world of grapevines and vegetable gardens, Gelsomina is quietly becoming a favorite on Capri among those in search of culinary treats (a food critic may be passing judgment at the next table). The emphasis on their own home-grown products has made dining here a treat. Roasted chicken and fish, rabbit caccia-tore, and gnocchi are but a few of its excellent choices. The walk is pleasant, but if you give them lead time they will come and pick you up in Anacapri (circumstances permitting).

Il Solitario. V. Orlando 54. ☎ **081/83-71-382.** Main courses 8,000L–18,000L ($5.25–$11.85). AE, MC, V. Tues–Sun 12:00–3pm and 7:30–11pm. Open Mondays in summer.

Simple and informal, this charming small spot occupies part of its owner's ivy-covered home. The pasta is wonderful, homemade and complemented with chickpeas or broccoli and sausages, among many other fresh sauces. Try the cannelloni alla caprese and finish your meal with a tartufo bianco ice-cream ball. Their house rosé is light and goes well with the simple, flavorful dishes.

CAPRI AFTER DARK

After dark is the time to find a seaside terrace and a cool summer drink (or a hot rum in the fall). You can go down to see Marina Grande after the day-trippers are safely gone, or check out the *piazzetta,* as Capri's main piazza (Umberto I) is called. Drinks tend to be expensive, from 8,000L ($5.25) up. Many hotels have terraces where you can have a cool white wine or a lemon liqueur. Anacapri has a large club called **Zeus** (V. Orlando 21, ☎ **081/83-71-169**). See if your hotel will provide a pass, making admission 10,000L ($6.60) instead of 30,000L ($19.75). Women sometimes are admitted free.

3 Sorrento

About 165 feet above the sea along the clifftop on the northern shore of a peninsula south of Naples, Sorrento is known for the siren songs that almost lured Ulysses to his doom in *The Odyssey.* The Roman emperors once used it as a place to relax.

Sorrento is consistently chosen by group tour operators a base for the entire Bay of Naples area because of its excellent location along the coast. Capri is a short hop across the bay, Pompeii is a short train ride, and Positano and Amalfi make a fine day trip by bus. Sorrento is a charming city, with major stores and supermarkets, but it does not have the outrageous charm of Capri or Positano. But you'll find pan-oramic views of the coast at many turns of the road and there are lovely gardens everywhere.

ESSENTIALS

GETTING THERE   By Train   From Naples' Stazione Centrale, the *Circum-vesuviana* train makes the one-hour trip (4,200L/$2.75). Trains run twice an hour from 4am to 11pm. (*Il Mattino,* Naples's daily paper, prints exact schedules.)

By Bus   From Rome, CIAT buses (☎ **06/47-42-801**) connect with Sorrento twice a day (23,000L/$15.15).

Other Islands in the Bay

Less glamorous than Capri, Ischia goes about its life quietly. Tourism is generally European, especially German, and is directed at its thermal spas. Its mountain (dormant volcano) roads are lovely, and there are many nice beaches, like the Spiaggia dei Maronti. You can stay at economical places near Ischia Porto such as the **Locanda sul Mare** (V. Iasolino 90, ☎ 081/98-14-70), where large doubles cost 50,000L ($32.90). Trattorias and pizzerias are plentiful in this area. Good bus service connects the principal cities. Ischia is linked by regular ferry service to Naples and Capri. The **tourist office** is at the hydrofoil dock (☎ 081/99-11-46).

Procida has preserved its fisherman's port–look to a remarkable degree and is the least touristy of the islands. There are a few hotels and trattorias, especially at the port, and good beaches. Buses travel to the Abbazia Archangelo Michele (Saint Michael the Archangel's Abbey) at the highest point. En route you can look down on a perfectly preserved fisherman's village. The **tourist office** on Via Roma at the right of the port (☎ 081/81-01-968) can help you to find rooms or apartments. Try also the **ETP Residence office,** V. Principe Umberto 1 (☎ 081/89-69-067) for apartment rental. Have lunch at **Crescenzo,** V. Marina Chiaiolella 33 (☎ 081/89-72-55), where the risotto alla marinara is delicious. At night the wood-fired pizza oven is lit. Procida is well linked by ferry to Naples, Ischia, and nearby Pozzuoli.

By Car   Sorrento is 30 miles from Naples on autostradas A3 and S145.

By Boat   From Capri, the cheapest way is via the Caremar ferry (☎ **081/80-73-077**), which makes the hour-long run about five times per day, less often in winter (5300L/$3.50). The hourly Alilauro hydrofoil (☎ **081/80-73-024**) takes only 15 minutes from Capri (8,000L/$5.25). Hydrofoils run from Naples and Ischia as well, for about double the ferry fare.

VISITOR INFORMATION   The **tourist office** on V. d. Maio 35 (☎ **081/80-74-033**) is very helpful once you get there. From Piazza Sant'Antonino bear right; it's within the Circolo del Forestiere complex (a club for foreigners that boasts a lovely terrace bar). The office is open Monday to Saturday from 8:30am to 2pm and 4 to 7pm (from October through March, they close at 6pm).

WHAT TO SEE & DO

The **Chiostro di San Francisco,** off Piazza Tasso next to the Villa Communale on the gulf, is a 14th-century cloister of lovely interlaced arches, flowers, and trees, and is often a quiet refuge. Its convent is now an art school and exhibits are sometimes hung in the adjoining areas. It is open from 9am to noon and 3 to 6pm, as well as on some evenings for jazz and classical music concerts in summer.

The **Museo Correale di Terranova** (on V. Correale, north of Piazza Tasso, ☎ 081/87-81-846) has an interesting collection of furnishings and paintings in the Neapolitan style enjoyed by local nobles. You can see good versions of Sorrento's famous *intarsia* work, in which paper-thin pieces of patterned wood are layered over each other in attractive patterns and then lacquered. It's open daily from 9am to 12:30pm and 3 to 5pm. You can also buy intarsia objects at **Gargiulo & Jannuzzi** on Piazza Tasso (☎ **081/87-81-041**), open daily from 8am to 10pm.

Punta del Capo is the nicest local beach. Continue along Corso Italia to Via del Capo and out to the end (or take the city bus—1,000L/65¢—from Piazza Tasso). Most of Sorrento's "beaches" are bathing piers, built out from the mainland and adorned with chairs and umbrellas as on a cruise ship. This is a rocky coast and there are no marvelous beaches here.

WHERE TO STAY

For those on a budget, Sorrento has several small, plain, but quite acceptable hotels. Unfortunately, singles will often have to pay for a double in season; few resort hotels have single rooms.

DOUBLES FOR LESS THAN 80,000 LIRE ($52.65)

Hotel City. Cor. Italia 221, 80067 Sorrento. ☎ and fax **081/87-72-210.** 13 rms, all with bath. 50,000L ($52.90) single; 80,000 double; 15,000L ($9.90) extra bed in room. MC, V.

Convenience is the thing here—the manager even sells ferry tickets from his lobby newsstand. The rooms are simple and have tiny balconies on the busy street, so nights can be noisy (Sorrento's flat streets lure the racing Vespas). Some doubles have garden patios.

Hotel del Corso. Cor. Italia 134, 80067 Sorrento. ☎ **081/87-81-299.** 20 rms, all with bath. 70,000L ($46.05) double. In Aug, half-pension (85,000L/$55.90) required. Breakfast 10,000L ($6.60). AE. Open Feb–Oct only.

On the main street, the building is lackluster, but it's pleasant enough inside. Rooms could also be a bit more attractive, but the price is right. It's well-located, near the station and everything else. The food is fairly good for a pensione, and the evening meal is complete, with soup, pasta, a meat entree, and dessert.

A DOUBLE FOR LESS THAN 110,000 LIRE ($72.35)

Loreley e Londres. V. Califano 2. ☎ **081/80-73-187.** 33 rms, all with bath. 100,000L ($65.80) double. AE, MC, V.

A longtime favorite because of its wonderful, flower-scented terraces, this hotel is an old Sorrentine villa filled with character. Seaside rooms (with balconies) are essential to avoid the noise. Rooms are rather large and are brightened with tiles and prints of old Sorrento. A terrace to relax in the sea air is a plus. The service is fine and the rooms are well maintained. There's an elevator down to a private beach.

SPLURGING JUST OUTSIDE OF TOWN

If you continue straight out the Corso Italia (take the orange bus 1,000L/65¢ or spend 15,000L/$9.85 for a taxi if you have luggage), you'll soon be on Via del Capo, which follows a cape that juts out north of Sorrento. Resort-style hotels here are more attractive and tranquil, and the prices are cheaper than the resorts in town (which are not included in this book because of their price). The one below is one of the best. You'll need a bus to get to the ferry or train station.

Pensione La Tonnarella. V. d. Capo 31, 80067 Sorrento. ☎ **081/87-81-153.** Fax 081/87-82-169. 23 rms, all with bath. TV TEL. 110,000L ($72.35) double with half pension, 170,000L ($111.85) double with full pension. Discounts in winter. AE, MC, V.

This lovely villa, set on terraces with flowers, eucalyptus and lemon trees, and bright tiles, is operated by the Gargiulo family with loving care. All but two rooms have sea views. An elevator connects with the private beach. Reserve as early as possible in summer. The food is excellent, so don't mind the meals requirement. Many come here from Sorrento to dine.

WHERE TO DINE

Sant'Antonino. Santa Maria d. Grazie 6 (off Pz. Sant'Antonino). ☎ **081/87-71-200.** Main courses 10,000L–22,000L ($6.60–$14.50). Tourist menu 18,000L ($11.80). AE, MC, V. Daily Feb–Nov noon–3pm and 7–midnight. SORRENTINE.

This is an easy spot to relax and start your Sorrento visit; it's located near the tourist office (if you can't find it, ask any local to point you the way). They serve good pasta with seasonal vegetable sauce and seafood. Locals and tourists are both found here, because of the central location and the low cost.

Il Giardiniello. V. Accademia 7. ☎ **081/87-84-616.** No reservations. Main courses 8,000L–18,000L ($5.25–$11.85). MC, V. Open Feb–Nov 10am–3pm and 7–midnight. ITALIAN/PIZZA.

This is a friendly, family-run spot where good pizza, or risotto with mushrooms, or gnocchi tempt an eager group of locals and tourists. Mamma cooks and seems to care about your pasta or pizza preference.

'O Parrucchiano. Cor. Italia 71. ☎ **081/87-81-321.** Reservations required. Main courses 10,000L–16,000L ($6.50–$10.50). V. Closed Wed Nov–May 12:30–3pm and 8–10:30pm. SORRENTINE.

Dine with most of Sorrento, it seems some days, in large, greenhouselike dining rooms amid plants and statues. This perennial favorite never changes, thanks to owner Enzo Manniello. It could do with a bit of sprucing up, but in the meantime enjoy the bean and escarole soup and other cucina povera dishes ("poor persons'" cooking—usually wonderful, with more vegetables than meat or fish as a base), or a mixed fry of fresh fish.

SORRENTO AFTER DARK

Get a copy of *Weekend* from the tourist office. It lists most local happenings as well as bars and clubs. In the tourist office building, the very well-run evening piano bar on a fine wide terrace is a good way to unwind. It's called the **Circolo dei Forestieri** (Foreigners' Club), on V. d. Maio 35 (☎ **081/87-73-012**). The cover charge is 15,000L ($9.90).

4 The Amalfi Coast

Positano is a tiny Christmas-tree-village sort of town that extends down to the sea from the main road—the Amalfi Drive (which, like everything here, was dug out of the cliffs). Priano, the next town, is losing its sleepy look as tourists overflow from the other towns. It's small and has fewer facilities, a plus or minus, and old-world charm that most resort towns have long ago lost. Gore Vidal's adopted home Ravello is lofty and elegant, reigning above the sea at the top of the cliffs. Positano is quiet and dreamy, more for the honeymooner than for the nightlife seeker. The sea-level towns of Cetara, Minori, and Maiori have wide attractive beaches and promenades along them, and farther along, Vietri-sul-Mare is world-famous as a ceramics center. Salerno on the south end of the drive is a big city, and where the coast goes to shop, full of large stores and restaurants. Little of the old city remains, unfortunately, because of World War II bombs.

GETTING AROUND   By Bus   Not only will taking the local **SITA** bus (☎ 081/87-82-708) that runs along the coast from Sorrento to Salerno be much less harrowing than driving yourself, but it will also give you a chance to sit back and enjoy the view—especially on the stretch from Positano to Amalfi where you'll follow the road's edge. Buses run about every hour from Sorrento or from Amalfi toward Sorrento. You buy a ticket for as far as you plan to go, and be sure to stamp it when you get on the bus. They have a loud and disagreeable inspector who likes to catch tourists who don't have their ticket stamped. These buses also pick up schoolchildren, so get on at the terminal (train station) for a seat. Sit on the right-hand, sea side unless vertigo is a problem—in places you'll look straight down to a rocky coast.

From Salerno, buses depart about every hour, connecting Sorrento with Positano (2,000L/$1.30), Amalfi (3,400L/$2.25), and Salerno (6,100L/$4). To go to Ravello, take the bus to Amalfi, where you'll connect with the Ravello bus, at the seafront piazza in Amalfi (every hour from 7am to 10pm; 1,500L/$1).

Traveling by bus, you could easily see Positano, Amalfi, and Ravello in a day, assuming you don't take a many-hour meal and siesta, Italian-style.

By Car   This drive is not for any but the most experienced drivers. There is nothing comparable to it in America. The stretch between Positano and Amalfi is all hairpin curves, very narrow, and full of huge tour buses barreling around curves. If you must, from Naples take autostrada A3 or S145 for 30 miles to Sorrento, then take the coastal route S145, which becomes S163 farther along for 10 miles to Positano, 11 miles more to Amalfi.

Note: If you're not comfortable with driving the coastal route the standard west-east direction, you can go overland from Naples or Sorrento to Salerno on route A30 and return back up the coast east-west, a method that many find easier on the nerves.

By Boat   **Alilauro hydrofoils** (☎ 81/80-73-024) are the easiest way to travel from town to town. There are several a day in summer, fewer in winter from Positano to Amalfi, at a cost of 7,000L ($4.50), or 13,000L ($8.55) to Salerno. In summer there are three a day to Capri at 13,000L ($8.55). It is thus easy to stay in one place and take the hydrofoil (or bus along the Drive) for the day to another, either returning to your original port for the evening or continuing on. Schedules change, so check at the port of each town when you know your plans. You might also want to be based in Capri, take the hydrofoil to Amalfi, then the bus to Ravello, returning to Capri from Amalfi. Another day trip from Capri: hydrofoil to Sorrento and then by another hydrofoil or bus to Positano, returning to Capri from Positano by hydrofoil. *Caveat:* Always find out the time of the last boat at night, if you plan to return.

POSITANO

Positano is closer to a watercolor painting than a picture postcard. Its color harmonies and splashy bougainvillea and geraniums lend enchantment. During the 10th century Positano was part of the Maritime Republic of Amalfi, which rivaled Pisa and Venice in importance. During the 16th and 17th centuries it was a major trading port for the Eastern Mediterranean. When the steamboat made its location less strategic to trade, the town suffered a decline that only recent tourism has helped to abate. In summer, however, tourism can be oppressive, as the town is small and tightly contained along the side of the cliff. There are few places to escape the multitudes. Still, you can sometimes catch Positano without a tour bus in sight (very early in the morning or on a November drizzly day). John Steinbeck perhaps summed it up best: "It is a dream that isn't quite real when you are there and becomes beckoningly real after you have gone."

ESSENTIALS

GETTING THERE   **By Bus**   The blue **SITA** bus (☎ 081/87-82-708) leaves from Sorrento, at the railroad station, about every hour from 6:30am to 9:30pm for Positano (35 minutes, 2,000L/$1.30). There's no direct route from Naples; you must go via Sorrento (see "Sorrento: Getting There," above).

By Car   Take S163 from Sorrento to Positano (35 minutes). From Naples, take route S18 south from Naples to Castellammare di Stabia, then follow the signs to Agerola and Amalfi, then double back up the coast to Positano. This is a faster route, bypassing the Sorrento tip of the peninsula. Parking in Positano is very scarce, limited to fancy hotels' lots or along the highway.

By Taxi A taxi from Naples costs about 130,000L ($85.50), which might make sense if you travel with a few people. Taxis take the route that runs across the peninsula, bypassing Sorrento. If you decide on a taxi, have your hotel on the Amalfi Drive send one to the Mergellina train station in Naples (first stop coming from Rome, where it's easier to find the driver and for him to park), or to the airport if flying in.

By Boat from Capri There are about five **ferries** (courtesy of Caremar ☎ 081/ 80-73-077) per day, taking 40 minutes and costing 10,000L ($6.60), as well as three Alilauro **hydrofoils** (☎ 81/80-73-024; 25 minutes, 13,000L/$8.55).

VISITOR INFORMATION Positano's very attractive **tourist office** at V. d. Saracino 4 (☎ 089/87-50-67) will give you *A Guest in Positano,* an information booklet, and maps. Check their bulletin boards for current events.

SPECIAL EVENTS Fireworks over the coast are Positano's way of celebrating the Feast of the Assumption on August 15 and also New Year's Eve, when the various coastal towns vie with each other for the most dazzling effects.

TOWN LAYOUT Positano's main road is the cliff road, which becomes route 145 (from route 163)—the beginning of the Amalfi Drive. From it the town spills down the cliff in gradations of bougainvillea terraces and winding streets and steps to the sea, where the pretty harbor of Marina Grande and a beach of sorts spread out. There is no town center as such. Beaches along this coast are for showing off the bikini or cooling off when the temperature rises, not really for lazing and swimming.

GETTING AROUND The town is built on a steep cliffside and levels are connected by ramps and steps. An orange bus makes its circle from the main street down to the port and back about every half hour (1,000L/65¢). Wear cork-soled shoes to avoid skidding on the steps or inclines on rainy days: This is the kind of town the espadrille was invented for. It's a town for walkers, as the bus covers only a limited area.

WHAT TO SEE & DO

Views from Positano, of the town itself or down the coast, are extraordinary. The city's Moorish architecture and bright fruit tones—raspberry, peach, and lemon, softened with evergreens—give it an allure that few spots have. Go to the Belvedere just outside town on the way to Sorrento for a panorama shot or walk up into the hills. Local buses connect with villages far up in the hills. Sod to plant the grapevines and lemon trees that flourish along this coast was often transported on mule- and human-back up the rocky cliffs.

Arrange to see Positano from the sea by night if possible, when it takes on its Christmas Village aspect. Ask at the port about night cruises or arranging with an individual boatman (prices vary widely depending on the season, number of passengers, and mood of the boatsmen). Most of the tourists who come through are day-trippers, and by night you can savor the romance without cameras clicking in your ear. A small boat to investigate the coast is a good way to spend the day too, if you can get a few people together to pay the boatman.

The **Church of Santa Maria Assunta,** named in honor of Positano's patron saint, has the bright tile cupola characteristic of this coast, where Eastern ideas were brought in by conquering armies and through trade. Above the central altar is a 13th-century Byzantine *Madonna and Child.* Legend has it that this Madonna spoke to the invading Turks, saying *posa* (rest), and that they did, sparing the town and naming it in the process. Other legends have the town named in honor of the Greek sea god Poseidon.

WHERE TO STAY

Rooms in Positano in a budget price range tend to be rather similar—simple bed-and-bureau affairs with whitewashed walls and tiles. The biggest difference for most is whether the room you're getting has sea views. The hotels are usually family-run, which means good service.

If you arrive without reservations, get a list of rooms to rent (*affittacamere*) from the tourist office—the Amalfi coast is finally realizing what a good source of income this is. Some of these accommodations are very well done, and others are just rooms, clean but without charm, but rarely are any unacceptable. Try **Pietro Pane's** at V. Canovaccio 5 (☎ **089/87-53-06**), for simple, clean rooms.

Doubles for Less than 85,000 Lire ($55.90)

Casa Guadagno. V. Fornillo 22, 84017 Positano. ☎ **089/87-50-42.** Fax 089/81-14-07. 15 rms, all with bath. Easter–October 100,000L ($65.80). 170,000L ($111.85) half pension. Rates include breakfast. No credit cards.

Pleasant and cheerful, this pensione is spread over three floors and an annex. The best rooms are in the main building on the higher floors. The ground-floor rooms are on the floor with the bar, although that is rarely noisy. Upper floors each have a wide communal terrace, and all pensione rooms have a view of the sea. From the annex the sea is visible at a side angle. Rooms are well kept and airy, and decorated with paintings of flowers or other scenes. It's down near the beach, a real plus.

✪ **Casa Celeste.** V. Fornillo 10, 84017 Positano. ☎ /fax **089/87-53-63.** 6 rms, 3 with shower. 55,000L ($36.20) per person all rms. Rates include breakfast. No credit cards. By bus, ask to be let off at the Chiesa Nuova, and walk about 15 minutes along the main road. If you have much luggage, call ahead and arrange for someone to pick you up.

A real family pensione, with some sea-view rooms and much hospitality. The Italian grandmother (nonna) we all want lives here, and her son Marco speaks English. The house is decorated wall-to-wall with art objects done by local students. Homemade jam is served for breakfast on the pretty terrace. The owner's husband has opened a snack bar (Da Ferdinando) just down the steps on the beach below. She will cook dinner if you wish or stop at her daughter's inexpensive Trattoria da Vincenza (see "Where to Dine," below). Reserve your room well in advance.

Villa Maria Luisa. V. Fornillo 40, 84017 Positano. ☎ **089/87-50-230.** 10 rms, all with bath. 45,000L ($29.60) single; 90,000L ($59.20) double. No credit cards.

This is a simply furnished place, with bright tiles and some good views. Rooms are brightened by sparkling ceramic tiles and colorful bedspreads. The owner is charming and tries to make your stay a happy one.

Doubles for Less than 150,000 Lire ($102)

California. V. Colombo 141, 84017 Positano. ☎ **089/87-53-82.** 10 rms, all with bath. 100,000L ($65.80) double. AE.

A terrace with greenery and flowers, that great sea view, and pleasant good-sized rooms with Mediterranean colors of blue, green, and white in the tiles have made California a good budget choice for many years.

Casa Cosenza. Scalinella staircase, 84017 Positano. ☎ **089/87-50-63.** 7 rms. 140,000L ($92) single without bath, 160,000L ($105.25) double with bath. No credit cards.

The address is a stairway here, about midway between the town and the sea. An enormous tiled terraced lets you dissolve into the gorgeous seascape and enjoy the merry tiled roofs of the town. Rooms 2 and 7 have little terraces, and cost more. Dating back 200 years, the house still has touches of the past in its architecture, but rooms are bright with tiles and simply decorated with family antiques.

WHERE TO DINE

Meals for Less than 25,000 Lire ($16.45)

Trattoria da Vincenzo. V. le Pasitea 172–78 . ☎ **089/87-51-28.** Main course 7,000L–20,000L ($4.60–$13.15). No credit cards. Open Apr–Oct daily 12–3pm and 7–11pm. NOUVELLE-NEAPOLITAN.

At Vincenzo, only the stone floor is cold. Your welcome is always warm and the dishes are nicely presented. The cooking is the thing, however, and Vito and his family are artists. Try the "Margaret," a ravioli version of the Margherita-style pizza of Napoli with ricotta, tomatoes, and basil. The place is casual, with both tourists and locals enjoying the vegetables of the season, given flair with Vincenzo style.

Il Grottina Azzurro. V. Marconi 158. ☎ **089/87-54-66.** Main courses 9,000L–15,000L ($5.90–$9.90). No credit cards. Daily 12:30–3pm and 7–11pm. Closed Wed in winter. NEAPOLITAN.

Up at the crossroads, where the road to Sorrento begins, this restaurant has been run for about 25 years by the Pollio family. Signora Concetta makes wonderful fresh pasta and gnocchi. Tables are set outdoors in summer, and summer renters mix with tourists and a few locals for an inexpensive meal.

Il Ritrovo. Localita Montepertuso, Pz. Cappella 77. ☎ **089/81-13-36.** Main courses 9,000L–25,000L ($5.90–$16.45). AE, MC, V. Daily noon–3pm and 7:30–11pm. Closed Tues and Jan in winter. NEAPOLITAN.

On the way up the hill toward Montepertuso, stop here for a simple meal made with local products. The outside terrace makes an attractive backdrop for your grilled meat and fresh fish. It's a bit off the regular tourist route, and attracts businesspeople from along the coast.

Worth a Splurge

Buca di Bacco. V. Rampa Teglia 8. ☎ **089/87-56-99.** Main courses 15,000L–35,000L ($9.80–$23). AE, MC, V. Closed Oct–Apr.

This place is a tradition in Positano, for tourists and the well-heeled summer people alike. You can enjoy a drink at the cafe overlooking the port, then dine on the terrace above the beach. Spaghetti with clams or shrimp might be followed by a mixed fish grill. Lemon cake or pie is usually on the menu, and an after-dinner *limoncello*, the lemon liqueur the coast is famous for, is tradition. The decor is mariner, and some people dress for dinner here.

A Nearby Place to Stay & Dine

Villaggio La Tranquillita. V. Roma 10, 84010 Priano. ☎ **089/87-40-84.** 20 bungalows, all with bath; campground. 50,000L ($32.90) single with bath; 80,000L ($52.65) double. Camping 30,000L ($19.75) per person. Breakfast included for all. AE, MC, V. Open Easter–Nov. 4 miles (25 minutes) down the coast road from Positano; the SITA bus stops at the door, ask the driver to let you off there.

The setting is one of the most beautiful along the coast. The view toward Amalfi requires too many superlatives for a shortlist, but don't forget your camera. The Maresca brothers have created a world that can be very simple for backpackers or very romantic for anyone. Their restaurant (the Continental) is excellent and this year has seen the addition of a brick, wood-fired pizza oven (8,000L/$5.25) per pizza. There is a stone dock at sea level, down a long stairway, for sunning or swimming.

POSITANO AFTER DARK

Africana (Marina di Praia, Priano ☎ **089/87-40-42**) offers disco by the sea in nearby Priano. The chic way to appear at this long-established club is by boat, if your hotel will arrange it or ask a local boatman. About 20,000L ($13.15) should do it, or 50,000L ($32.90) for a boatful. Otherwise, look for the prominent sign on the road.

EN ROUTE TO AMALFI

About 5 miles from Positano you'll see a sign to descend (by elevator or steps) to the **Emerald Grotto** (if you didn't go to Capri's Blue Grotto, don't miss this one). You can also see it via an excursion boat from Amalfi.

The next town along the coastal drive is **Priano,** about a mile beyond the Emerald Grotto. The majolica-tiled dome of its Church of San Gennaro is the town's landmark, and the town spreads out along the cliffs and down to the harbor. Less glamorous than Positano, Priano is also less pricey.

About two miles farther on, you come to Furore, where a mountain torrent cascades to an old fishing village, **Marina di Praia.** The village is now growing into a resort of its own. A walk across the Furore bridge and down the path to the sea is a wonderful way to spend the afternoon. The wine called *Furore* is made from grapes grown in these hills.

AMALFI

After the small places we've just visited, Amalfi seems like a big city. It occupies a valley along the coast and spreads up the hill.

Amalfi's history is impressive. Once a Maritime Republic (from about A.D. 850) that rivaled Pisa, Genoa, and Venice in power, doges ruled here, as they did in Venice. The *Tavole Amalfitane,* the first codified law of the sea, was adopted here and followed until 1500. Native son Flavio Gioia, inventor of the compass, is honored with a statue at the entrance to the town. Unfortunately the port is also the tour bus terminus and so much of its beauty has been lost. The town, however, is still enchanting once you enter the main piazza and see the cathedral.

ESSENTIALS

GETTING THERE   By Bus   SITA buses connect Amalfi with: Naples, three daily, (5,500L/$3.60), trip time is 2 hours; Sorrento, 14 daily (4,000L/$2.65), trip time is 1 1/2 hours; Positano (1,500L/$1), trip time ; and Ravello (1,500L/$1) every two hours, trip time is 30 minutes; and other towns along the coast. A once-daily bus connects with Rome as well. Amalfi is the major bus terminal on the coast; the main bus office (☎ **089/87-10-09**) is near the statue of Flavio Gioia at the port.

By Car   Amalfi is about 11 miles of hairpin turns down the Amalfi Drive (S163) from Positano.

By Boat   See the "Getting Around" section earlier in this chapter for specifics. In Amalfi, tickets are sold on the quay or in travel agencies near the port.

VISITOR INFORMATION   Amalfi's **tourist office** (V. Roma 19–21, at the back of the courtyard, (☎ **089/87-11-07;** fax 089/87-26-19) is about as unhelpful as possible. A machine that dispenses maps would be better. However, it's open Monday to Saturday from 8am to 1pm.

CITY LAYOUT   Amalfi rises up along a steep valley, in Christmas tree shape, until it disappears amid the torrents and grapevines of the cliff. Most important businesses are situated in the port area. Hotels and restaurants are found in the casbah labyrinths of tiny streets and archways that line the main street of the town, going up the hill.

WHAT TO SEE & DO

You can brush up on your local lore at the **Museo Civico** on Piazza del Municipio (☎ **089/87-10-66**). Admission is free, so definitely stop in on any day between 9am and 8pm to see the 11th-century *Tavole Amalfitane,* the ancient Law of the Sea.

One of Amalfi's most charming areas lies far up the hill along the town's main street, where ancient paper mills still produce richly textured paper with watermarks. It's available at the mills, or elsewhere in the town, as writing paper (see "Shopping," below). This part of town at the end of the 18th century had 16 paper mills and 15 pasta factories, both of which used the powerful torrent, the Canneto, that still can be seen rushing down the cliffs and heard rumbling its underground way to the sea beneath Amalfi. You can also still see a communal laundry, where gossip blended with soapsuds and washboards.

For the story of Amalfi's paper industry, with old manuscripts and paper presses, visit the **Museo della Carta** on Via Valle dei Mulini (☎ **089/87-26-15**), open Monday to Saturday from 9am to 1pm and 5 to 7pm. You may also be able to see paper made at one of the working mills. Make arrangements through your hotel.

✪ **Duomo (Cathedral of St. Andrew) and Cloisters of Paradise.** V.d. Duomo 147, ☎ **081/44-90-97.** Free admission. Daily 7:30am–1:30pm. The Cloisters are open the same hours, but require 5,000L ($3.30) admission.

Note: Appropriate dress is required to enter the church (no shorts, sleeveless shirts, or bathing suits). The long walk up the steps should not daunt you. It's worth the effort if only for the Cloisters (see below). The Duomo's brilliant, elaborate facade— with the look of a marble intaglia, opening in delicate arches and latticework—is enchanting and speaks of another Amalfi, one not crowded with tourist buses. It dates from the 9th century, but was reconstructed several times. The lovely campanile remains from the 1180 structure. The bronze door was once one of its prizes but has worn down (you can see a similar one in better shape if you visit Ravello). The interior mixes many styles, but not unhappily. The intricate mosaic style of the Cosmati gleams in the marble pulpit.

Descend the stairs into the *cripta* to see the happy arrangement of rich marble pilasters and the large statue of St. Andrew, whose bones are buried here at the altar. He must be pleased, because his bones oblige the town yearly the last week in November by giving off a fragrant perfume, called the manna of St. Andrew. The beautiful altar is the work of Domenico Fontana, and the large statue was given to Amalfi by Philip III of Spain.

From the porch of the Duomo, enter the Cloisters, where the art of Byzantium and that of the North Africa meet—there even a touch of the Norman architecture in the mullioned windows. The interlaced arches and palm trees also shelter some tomb art from the Roman and medieval periods. The mosaic work of the Cosmati is splendid.

A Side Trip to the Grotta Smeralda

Excursion boats to the Emerald Grotto in season charge about 10,000L/$6.60 per person and leave every few hours. Look for one at the pier. It's not as dazzling as Capri's grotto, but is definitely less crowded, and you can enjoy the coastline en route.

BEACHES & WATERSPORTS

Some hotels have private beaches and rent small boats and water gear. The small beaches at each side of Amalfi's harbor are public, but you might find more stretching room if you take the bus to Minori or Maiori, the next two towns down the coast.

For boat rental, try **Lido delle Sirene** at Piazzale dei Protontiini (☎ 089/ 87-21-47) or **Florio's** (☎ 089/87-21-47), both in Amalfi's harbor. Motorboat rental is usually about 25,000L ($16.45) per hour with reductions for longer periods. Boats are very comfortable and seat four.

SHOPPING

For *carta,* or handmade paper, go to **Antonio Cavaliere,** V. Fiume (☎ 089/ 87-19-54), one of the most respected of craftsmen. In addition to making paper in Amalfi's traditional fashion, he often adds dried flowers for romantic effects. If you stay in Amalfi at the Hotel Residence, you'll meet his son Franco, the manager.

Much of today's coral is mass-produced cheaply in Asia. Here, however is **Criscuolo,** Lgo. Scario 2 (☎ 089/87-10-89), a real, traditional Italian craftsman. Coral jewelry, cameos, and ceramics also grace the shop.

Near the Duomo at Piazza Duomo and at the piazza near the port you'll find more ceramics than the sea has squid. Most of it is not crafted in Amalfi, but if you ask questions and turn over enough plates, you'll find among the many Taiwanese imports some ceramics of the highest local caliber made in nearby Vietri sul Mare.

There are two attractive places in Piazza Duomo to enjoy or buy Amalfi's famous *limoncello* lemon liquor, and much more. The lemon trees of **Pasticceria Pansa,** founded in 1830, have long provided limoncello under the Villa Paradiso label. At **Antichi Sapori d'Amalfi,** near the cathedral steps, you'll also find a *digestivo* made from an ancient Cappuchin monk recipe. Farther up the street, near the paper mills at V. d. Cartiere 55, **La Valle dei Mulini** combines limoncello with extracts of laurel and fennel in a subtle mix to make another after-dinner digestivo.

WHERE TO STAY

If you arrive without a room and find that the hotels are full, ask the tourist office for a list of affitacamere (rooms to rent).

A Double for Less Than 80,000 Lire ($78.50)

Pensione Proto. Salita d. Curiali 4, 84011 Amalfi. ☎ **089/87-10-03.** 8 rms, 4 with bath. Summer, 60,000L ($39.50) single without bath; 75,000L ($49.35) double without bath, 90,000 ($59.20) double with bath; low season 50,000L ($32.90) single without bath; 60,000L ($39.50) double without bath, 65,000L ($43.75) double with bath. No credit cards. Follow signs from Pz. Duomo to church of Maria Addolorata.

Not for the light sleeper, the Proto is the last of the "cheap" hotels in Amalfi. There is a restaurant with piano bar on the premises, and so if you like evening entertainment under your roof, this may be the place. Rooms could use some new tiles and slipcovers, but the place is friendly. It's up several flights of stairs.

Doubles for Less Than 100,000 Lire ($65.80)

Hotel Lidomare. Lgo. Duchi Piccolomini, Amalfi. ☎ **089/87-13-32.** 20 rms, all with bath. TV TEL. Summer, 100,000L ($52.65) doubles; off-season 90,000L ($59.20) doubles. Rates include breakfast. AE, MC, V. Closed Nov–Mar. Take the stairway across from the Duomo to the next little piazza.

This 13th-century hotel has lots of family antiques to create a pleasant atmosphere, and it now has air-conditioning in some rooms. Much of the hotel is decorated with antique furnishings, but the bright tiles of the floors give them a modern air. Some rooms have little terraces, and baths have recently been added or renovated.

✪ **Hotel Marina Riviera.** V. P. Comite 9, 84011 Amalfi. ☎ **089/87-11-04.** Fax 089/ 87-13-51. 20 rms, all with bath. TEL. 80,000L–100,000L ($52.65–$98.70) singles, 100,000L– 150,000L ($65.80–$98.70) doubles. Rates include breakfast. AE, MC, V. Closed Nov–Mar. At east edge of town, near Atrani.

This place is a find, and one of the beauties of the coast. You get views of the sea and of Amalfi from most of the rooms and from the wide terrace. Recently completely redone, the hotel is dazzling with tile everywhere. Rooms have touches of antiques here and there, and some very attractive artwork. Proprietor Antonio Gargano's family has owned hotels through the ages in the Amalfi area, among them the glamorous and very expensive Hotel Santa Caterina up the coast.

Hotel Residence. V. Repubbliche Marinare 9, 84011 Amalfi (at the main port). ☎ **089/ 87-11-83.** Fax 089/873-070. 27 rms, all with bath. TEL. 100,000L–140,000L ($65.80–$92.10) doubles. Rates include breakfast. AE, MC, V. Closed Nov–Mar.

This is the best property in the town itself, located just to the right of the entrance to the main street from the port. All rooms have balconies that face the sea, which are lovely, but ask for a higher floor because the hotel faces the main piazza with all its action, including noisy Vespas. The hotel has a dramatic central staircase that climbs through landings decorated with antiques and flowers (or you can take the elevator).

A Double for Less than 150,000 Lire ($98.70)

Hotel Miramalfi. V. Quasimodo 3, 84011 Amalfi. ☎ and fax **089/87-15-88.** 48 rms, all with bath. TEL. Summer, 130,000L ($85.50) single; 195,000L ($128.30) double. Low season, 100,000L ($65.85) single with bath; 150,000L ($98.70) double with bath. Rates include breakfast. Half pension 100,000L ($65.80), full pension 150,000L ($98.70) per person. AE, MC, V. Open all year. Free parking.

On the road outside of town, but within walking distance of the town's center, the Miramalfi offers great views and a nice swimming pool and bathing area. Most rooms have sea-view balconies. Rooms here are the typical tile floor/stucco walls with watercolors and bougainvillea, but you may not notice with those seascapes outside. This easygoing place offers meals as well, in case it grows on you.

WHERE TO DINE

There is an excellent coffee bar/pastry shop across from the Duomo where you might want to indulge for a snack. For more substantial meals, try the following.

La Cantinella. V. Duca Mastalo (off Salita Truglio from the main piazza). ☎ **089/87-22-96.** Menu turistico 22,000L ($14.50). Main courses 7,000L–16,000L ($4.60–$10.50). AE, MC, V. Daily 12–3pm and 7:30–11pm (closed Mon in winter). SEAFOOD/PIZZERIA.

This cheerful-looking place is always filled with tourists. Fishing nets and mariner's gear comprise the decor, and the place is bright and well run. *Risotto alla pescatore* is excellent and usually on the menu. Apart from seafood you might want to try their vegetable dishes, eggplant parmigiana, grilled artichokes with lemon and olive oil, and escarole with garlic and lemon. The crowd is usually tourists from local hotels.

La Caravella. V. Camera 12 (near the tunnel). ☎ **089/87-10-29.** Reservations advised. Main courses 18,000L–25,000L ($11.85–$16.45). AE, V. Wed–Mon 12–3pm and 7–11pm. Closed Nov 10–30. CAMPANIA.

Under the arches, grottolike La Caravella continues to serve good food at a reasonable price. Try the fresh fish with Amalfi lemon sauce and a salad for a summer lunch. The walls are decorated with Amalfi prints. Tourists and summer renters make up the crowd.

A Splurge Lunch

Hotel Santa Caterina. S. Amalfitana (on the main road to Amalfi at the top of the hill). ☎ **089/87-10-12.** Main course 12,000L–30,000L ($7.90–$19.95). AE, MC, V. Daily 12:30–3pm and 8–10pm. CAMPANIA.

This glamorous hotel is one of the most enchanting anywhere, but it does cost even more than our usual splurge prices. However, lunch on the long arbor-lined terrace above the sea and their property filled with plants and flowers is something no one should miss. There's a good pizza oven (in a hollowed-out part of the cliff) and a daily buffet. Have a pasta with their lemon sauce—Amalfi lemons have a sweet and aromatic quality like no others—or ravioli with ricotta and lemon.

A SIDE TRIP TO ATRANI

Atrani is one of the most charming towns on the coast, partly because it is neglected by mass tourism. Its central piazza is down from the highway five minutes east of Amalfi (on foot); descend the stairs or road just before the tunnel to the sea level, walk under the arches, and you'll enter Atrani. White blocks of houses with blue doors and bougainvillea splashes wind their way up the hill in roads and steps, rather like North Africa. Budgeters will be soothed by the room rate at the quasi-hostel **A'Scalinatella,** in Piazza Umberto, the town's main piazza (☎ **089/87-19-30**). If you don't mind sharing a room you can do so for 20,000L ($13.15) and a laundry fee of 5,000L ($3.30). Rooms run from two to six beds. It's clean but can be noisy, since it's in the main piazza. Curfew is at midnight. Another cheapo is the **Pensione Chez Checco,** V. d. Dogi 9 (☎ **089/87-20-51**). The Greek-Hungarian-Italian couple who run it offer five double rooms with bath for 60,000L ($39.50) per person or 75,000L ($49.35) per person with half-pension in their nice restaurant. If you're staying here, take the pension option to save money on meals. Another good bet for dining, though more expensive, is the town's best restaurant, **'a Paranza,** V. Dragone 1–2 (☎ **089/87-18-40**). Ask for local specialties, which often include octopus, squid, or shrimp, but be sure to call first because they are closed Tuesdays from September to June, and for certain weeks in January and February. Prices run from 35,000L to 50,000L ($23 to $32.90) for a full meal, and they accept American Express, MasterCard, and Visa.

RAVELLO

Ravello occupies one of the most scenic spots in the world, high (over 1,100 feet) above the sea, and looking out along the coast to Sorrento and Capri and down toward Salerno from a bird's-nest perch above the cliffs.

Along with its stunning (inside that is) cathedral, there are two gardens that thrill the most jaded eyes. One of them, Villa Rufolo, inspired Wagner's Gardens of Klingsor scene in *Parsifal.* The other, Villa Cimbrone, is the fantasy of an eccentric English lord. The view is best in the afternoon during much of the year, but Ravello is splendid even without its panoramic distances. It has a sense of privacy that has lured Jackie Onassis, Richard Wagner, Greta Garbo, and other celebrities—D. H. Lawrence wrote much of *Lady Chatterley's Lover* while staying in Ravello, and Gore Vidal still keeps a villa here as a writing retreat. You can reach it on foot from Atrani if you're an avid climber, or at least in reasonably good condition. The road from Amalfi becomes traffic-clogged on weekends, so beware. It's quite a beautiful road, however, through the Valley of the Dragon River, and you'll see cliffside vineyards, lemon groves, and fig and olive trees. There is also a back road from Pompeii and Naples, which is much more direct (see below). Make sure you bring plenty of film.

ESSENTIALS

GETTING THERE   By Bus   The SITA bus runs hourly from Amalfi (1,500L/99¢).

By Car   From Amalfi, pass through the main square and follow signs to the left up the hill. It's a very circuitous route. From Naples, take the autostrada to one exit beyond Pompeii, heading toward Salerno by the inland route.

VISITOR INFORMATION   The tourist office is on Piazza Vescovado (☎ **089/ 85-70-96**, fax 089/85-79-77). It is open from May through September, Monday to Saturday from 8am to 8pm, and October through April, Monday to Saturday from 8am to 7pm.

SPECIAL EVENTS   Summer music festivals, including a Wagner festival, are held each year. Check with the tourist office for exact dates. San Pantaleone is feted on July 27 each year with a procession, feasting, and fireworks.

CITY LAYOUT   The Duomo occupies the main piazza (Piazza Vescovado) and the Villa Rufolo opens off it. A road from the Rufolo winds along to the Villa Cimbrone at the edge of the cliff above Amalfi. Roads are really for walkers—not cars—and are sometimes steep in Ravello. The main street (Via San Giovanni del Toro) begins at the Duomo's square and runs in the opposite direction.

WHAT TO SEE & DO

The Duomo (San Pantaleone). Pz. Vescovado. Admission to Duomo free, museum 2,000L ($1.30). Duomo daily 9am–1pm and 3–7pm. Museum May–Sept 9am–7:30pm, Oct 9am–5pm.

Ravello was once an important bishopric, and thus rated a fine cathedral. Panels on the bronze doors from the 12th century were brilliantly sculpted by Barisano of Trani (a town on Puglia's coast). The dramatic pulpit is a stunning work of art, in which twisted columns with mosaic patterns rest on the backs of lions. On the smaller pulpit in front, Jonah is disappearing into the mouth of a strange sea creature—more snail than whale—with a Chinese dragon–like head.

Adjoining the Duomo, there is a museum of Ravello treasures, such as the bust of one Signora da Ravello, and memorabilia of local Saint Pantaleone (a doctor) and a lovely reliquary containing part of the head of Santa Barbara.

Villa Rufolo. Entrance off Pz. Vescovado. ☎ **089/85-78-66.** Admission 4,000 ($2.65), discounts for children under 12. Jul–Aug daily 9:30am–1pm and 3–7pm; Sept–June daily 9:30–1pm and 2–4:30pm.

A fine Moorish tower, romantically crumbling, stands near the gate, beckoning you toward the elegant gardens. From the belvedere you'll see the famous postcard view of two Moorish cupolas beneath an umbrella pine framed by the sea. Prince Rufolo featured in Boccaccio's *Decameron,* suffering hard times (his own fault) before returning to the peace of Ravello. Pope Adrian IV, Charles of Anjou, and Robert the Wise have all been guests of the villa, but it is now the property of the state and therefore open to the public for all to enjoy.

Villa Cimbrone. Off Pz. Vescovado. ☎ **089/85-74-59.** Admission 5,000L ($3.30). June–Sept daily 9am–8pm; Oct–May daily 2–4:30pm. From outside the Villa Rufolo, follow the steep path down, watching for signs to the Villa Cimbrone.

This villa has a little bit for everyone. The cloisters near the entrance remain from the 12th century, a time when Ravello, as a bishop's see, had 13 churches and 4 convents. You can walk into the cloisters to see the Seven Deadly Sins, and walk out through the gardens, down into the Venus grotto, and out to one of the loveliest top-of-the-world belvederes in existence, complete with busts of Italy's famous emperors. As you wander about, look for the inscription from Lord Grimthorpe, the eccentric Englishman who created this villa and was also buried here: GLAD I CAME, NOT SORRY TO DEPART, says his enigmatic gravestone.

SHOPPING

Ravello is not a budget shopper's paradise, but still browse through the ceramics stores on and around the square and admire their very attractive wares. **Bric-a-Brac,** near the cathedral, has some pretty souvenirs in the form of small prints and paintings.

WHERE TO STAY

Ravello is rather expensive. Check with the tourist office when you arrive to see if there are any private rooms to let.

Doubles for Less than 100,000 Lire ($98.50)

✪ **Villa Amore.** V. del Fusco, 84010 Ravello. ☎ and fax **089/85-71-35.** 12 rms, all with bath. Summer, 55,000L ($36.20) single, 98,000L ($64.50) double; low season 65,000L ($42.75) single; 88,000L ($57.90) double. Half-pension required Jul–Aug at 80,000L per person. MC, V. Off V. Santa Chiara.

This place is well named—you'll find something to love here, starting with the owner, Ermalinda Schiavo. Furnishings are simple but sun terraces and gardens, exquisite panoramic views of the coast and sea make this a great choice. All rooms have a little balcony and are decorated with antique-style furnishings, smart tiles on the floor, and watercolors. Flowers abound, both outside and in the public rooms.

Hotel Toro. V.le Wagner 3, 84010 Ravello. ☎ and fax **089/85-72-11.** 9 rms, all with bath. Apr–June and Sept–Oct, 66,000L ($43.40) single, 95,000L (62.50) double; Jul–Aug 85,000L ($55.90) per person, with compulsory half-pension. AE, MC. Closed Nov–Mar. Just off the main piazza.

You enter a garden and then a villa with its own personality, long colonnades included. Rooms are simple but acceptable and meals are too. The owner takes good care of things.

Worth a Splurge

Hotel Caruso Belvedere. V. San Giovanni d. Toro, 84010 Ravello. ☎ **089/85-71-11.** Fax 089/85-73-72. 26 rms, all with bath. TEL. 175,000L–220,000L ($115.15–$144.75) double. Rates include breakfast. AE, MC, V. Free parking.

Guests are usually pleased with the relaxed atmosphere here. The Caruso rambles on and on, through arcaded paths, gardens flowing with bougainvillea, gothic arches, and views of the Mediterranean below. It's a place where you can spend time quietly. Rooms have paneled doors, antiques, and some have private terraces. All have good views as the gardens are extensive. The restaurant on the premises is quite good, serving fish done in several local styles, and some "international" dishes, such as veal chops and chicken, because of the tourist clientele. Meals cost about 50,000L ($32.90) and up, including the local wine, Grand Caruso, made from their own vines and processed in their vats on the premises. If you go in the fall you can watch the grape harvest.

WHERE TO DINE

In Ravello, the least expensive way to dine is to take half-pension at your hotel and to buy fruit and cheese or pizza for lunch.

Meals for Less than 40,000 Lire ($26.30)

Cumpa' Cosimo. V. Roma 42–44. ☎ **089/85-71-56.** Reservations recommended. Main courses 12,000L–25,000L ($7.90–$16.45). AE, MC, V. Closed Monday Nov–Mar 12:30–3pm and 8–10pm. CAMPANIA.

This is one of the best restaurants on the coast, fun and serious at the same time. Presiding over the three little rooms, Senora Netta, granddaughter of the original owners, makes pizza with lots of unusual vegetables, such as zucchini, but you might want to try a "variety of pasta" instead (*misto di pasta*) or her grilled sausages. Save room for the homemade ice cream. Everyone knows about this place, so be sure to reserve your table.

Villa Maria. V. d. Santa Chiara 2. ☎ **089/85-72-55.** Reservations recommended. Main courses 10,000L–25,000L ($6.60–$16.45). AE, MC, V. Daily 12:30–3pm and 7:30–10pm. Closed Tues in winter. CAMPANIA.

If for no other reasons, dine here especially for the view. The wide tree-shaded lawn set with tables is shaded by umbrellas during the day and lit by candlelight at night. Get there early for the tables that overlook those dramatic valleys. The cool shade on summer nights lures many local residents as well. They serve excellent grilled fish, or game birds and rabbits, whatever the local markets offer fresh. Be sure to order Ravello wine to go with your meal.

EN ROUTE TO PAESTUM

VIETRI SUL MARE   This little town, 20 miles past Amalfi near Salerno (SITA bus from Amalfi 2,700L/$4.10), is famous for its ceramics. Many of the dishes and plates you've seen in even the simplest hotels and longed for come from here. Just wandering around, after a stop at the tourist office in the central piazza, is fun, but look especially at two of the best known ceramics shops: **Solimene,** where the building itself is art, at V. Madonna degli Angeli 7 (☎ 089/21-02-43); and **Pinto,** at Cor. Umberto I 27 (☎ 089/21-02-71). You can get some good, reasonably-priced seafood at **La Sosta,** V. Costiera 6 (☎ 089/21-17-90). They're closed Wednesdays and in January. They accept American Express, MasterCard, and Visa. **La Taverna Paradiso,** on Via Diego Taiani (☎ 089/21-25-09), is another good bet, but they are closed Mondays and for a few weeks in mid-August (they accept American Express and Visa).

PAESTUM

Paestum and its museum are musts for anyone who loves antiquities. The temples are awe-inspiring, and well preserved because malaria and thieves long kept looters away.

If you want to have a swim after seeing the ruins, have someone point you toward the beach, which is a little more than a mile away.

ESSENTIALS

GETTING THERE   By Bus   Get the ATACS bus in Salerno at the Via Irno station (☎ **089/25-58-99**) direction: Agropoli. It costs 4,300L ($2.80) one-way and takes about an hour.

By Train   The train from Salerno leaves from Piazza Veneto (☎ **089/25-22-00**), takes 40 minutes and costs 3,900L ($2.55) one way

By Car   From Salerno, take route S18 south for 25 miles.

VISITOR INFORMATION   Paestum's **tourist office** is opposite the main site on Via Aquilia (☎ **0828/81-10-16**), open Monday to Saturday from 8am to 2pm.

THE GREEK TEMPLES

Paestum's three Greek Doric temples are from the 5th and 6th centuries B.C. Just past the main gates you'll see the ✪ **Temple of Neptune,** the largest and best preserved of the lot, built about 450 B.C. Its 36 columns are each almost 30 feet tall. The Basilica to the left was constructed about a century later. Both were probably dedicated to Hera, Queen of Heaven, and an earth goddess as well.

The **Forum,** to the right, dates from the later Roman era and was once filled with many of the kind of buildings that are seen in the ruins of the Forum in Rome: gymnasium, baths, curia, temple, and an amphitheater.

To the right of the Forum stands the **Temple of Ceres,** Goddess of Grain, built about 500 B.C. During the Middle Ages this was converted into a Christian church. Across the street form this temple is the 5th-century B.C. **Tomb of the Diver,** discovered in 1968, containing exceedingly rare Greek murals. The subject of the tomb dives serenely into the pool, an allegorical easy transition between worlds. It's thought to be one of the few ancient Greek paintings in existence.

The temples (☎ **0828/81-10-16**) are open from Monday to Saturday, 8am to; admission is 8,000L ($5.25). This admission charge also includes entrance to the museum at V. Magna Grecia 169 (☎ **0828/81-10-23**), which keeps the same hours and houses an astounding 33 of the original 36 meotopes from another ancient temple a few miles north of the main site, as well as various objects from the Paestum ruins.

WHERE TO DINE

Nettuno Ristorante. Zona Archeologica (☎ **0828/81-10-28**). Main courses 20,000L–25,000L ($13.15–$16.45). AE, MC, V. May–June and Sept–Oct daily 12:30–3pm; July–Aug daily 7:30–10pm. Closed Mon Nov–Feb. INTERNATIONALIZED ITALIAN.

The Nettuno resembles a country inn at the edge of the site, and has been a favorite spot for tourists for many years. The pinetree-shaded terrace faces the temples, so try to get a table alfresco. Their food is fairly basic and unsurprising—chicken and veal, spaghetti with clam sauce, salad, and crème caramel. They need to please a world of visitors.

LEAVING THE AMALFI COAST

The trains from Salerno that head to Naples and Rome are the most convenient way to return from the Ravello end of the Amalfi Drive. If you made the trip "backward" and ended up at the Positano end, you can take the bus or train from Sorrento to Naples. If continuing on to Sicily from Salerno, you can take the train from Piazza Veneto (☎ **089/25-22-80**) down the Calabrian coast to Villa San Giovanni, where, in summer, there is frequent ferry and hydrofoil service to Sicily and the Aeolian Islands, or continue to Reggio di Calabria, where ferries or hydrofoils will take you to Messina on Sicily's northeast coast.

16 Sicily

by Barbara Coeyman Hults

Although each year Sicily's economy and culture draws closer to Italy and even to Europe, the island is still very much its own, for better and for worse. Just across the Strait of Messina, in full sight of the Calabrian shore, Sicily maintains an aura redolent of its enclosed Arab past and its Greek pride. No matter how many boom boxes scream out Michael Jackson or Madonna, the present here is not Europe's present yet. Here you have entered another world entirely, where things are not always as they seem. For one thing, life is slower and more respectful of tradition. If you should have business with a local official, your meeting may well take place in an elaborate palace, uninteresting from the outside but dazzling within. You won't rush through your business, and he (yes, men are almost always in charge, but women are advancing in the professions) will probably send out for coffee and incredibly rich local sweets, or in summer, perhaps a fresh-fruit ice. You must both allow time to exchange pleasantries and flatter each other's country.

This is a land that has been inhabited since the Ice Age, at least 20,000 years ago, and early settlers left their mark in cave drawings near Palermo. By the time the ever-enterprising Phoenicians sailed into a Sicilian harbor (about the 8th century B.C.), Sicily's early tribes were already well established. Carthaginians preceded the Greek settlement, which was extraordinary in the 6th to 5th century B.C., when cities here rivaled those in Greece itself, attracting Plato, Archimedes, Pindar, and where native son Empedocles held forth on the elements of life. Romans built comfortable villas—their forte—and sent slaves into the fields to grow grain for their legions. Arabs created a fine civilization here in the 9th century, one perpetuated by the Normans after 1072. In the 13th century, the French Angevins and, later in that century, the Spanish Bourbons gained control. The Spanish ruled mainly by absentee viceroys who cared little about Sicily and a lot about their own bank accounts. When Garibaldi's Thousand landed at Marsala in 1860, Sicilians could finally say the land was theirs—but it still truly wasn't. Mafia control soon took up the power vacuum, and their own patronage system replaced Spain's, benefiting some, ruining many. Now, Sicilians, at least the thousands of well-to-do Sicilians, vacation in Europe and throughout the world and send their children to school in Paris and London. The result is a new Sicily, emerging now because only now

Men of Dishonor

Mafia lore remains attractive to movie audiences in America, and elsewhere in the world, but not in Italy, and certainly not in Sicily. Indeed, the Mafia has lost a degree of its famous respect and a bit of its foothold in Sicily in recent years, as their demands for protection payoffs crippled businesses, eliminated jobs needed by the young in Sicily, and caused prejudice against innocent Sicilians throughout the world.

The change has been gradual, but there was one dramatic moment, on May 24, 1992, a brutal watershed for Sicily, when the prosecutor beloved by most Sicilians and Italians in general, Giovanni Falcone, was murdered, with his wife and bodyguards, when a car bomb exploded while he was driving along the highway between Palermo's airport and the city. The reaction was a stunned horror, one of those national moments that burns itself into people's memory and causes everyone to recall exactly where they were when they heard the news. Two months later, Falcone's partner against crime, Borsellino, met a similar fate. This was too much even for Sicily, where a passive acceptance of endless murders had blocked hope of change (the newspaper *La Cronica di Sicilia* was popularly known as *La Cronica della Morte,* the Chronicle of Death).

Ruled through the centuries by foreign governments who rewarded sycophants and suppressed liberty, then controlled from behind the scenes by mafiosi who spread the expression "better a day as a lion than a hundred years as a sheep," Sicily had been forced to adopt the mentality that it was better to take Mafia money than side with a government that was probably just as corrupt. But in reaction to recent violence, the central government in Rome, where many politicians have been charged with Mafia affiliations, finally had to do something. Seven thousand troops were sent to Sicily in Operation Vespri Siciliani and the Palermo area became a fortress.

Now, just a few years after Falcone's murder, a new Palermo is emerging, one with restored spirit and hope. As an urban area, Palermo is starting to reclaim itself, to be able to live life without fear and walk outside at night to enjoy the city. In a way Sicily today is experiencing its best period in history.

has some headway been made against the Mafia (see box above). Italy's role in the world is at stake, and trying to forget or hide the issue is no longer possible.

Sicily is nicely laid out for the traveler, since the coast was where the greatest development occurred. The easiest way to see it is to move clockwise or counterclockwise around the coast, dipping into the often mountainous interior as your schedule permits. The western end of the island shows its Arabic temperament in everything from domes and fountains to sweet-and-sour mixtures on the menu. The echoes of the Greek heritage are still more prevalent to the East—even though the Greeks themselves haven't been here for millennia, they are recalled in Sicilian faces and Sicilian cooking. Spain culture shows its stripe in the shawls and fans of the women of Syracuse, to the southeast.

The traditional route for touring Sicily begins in Palermo on the northwest coast (or Messina, if you come by ferry from Calabria), makes its circle, and ends in Taormina, at the northeast. Without a car the best way to travel is by bus, as trains are unreliable and slow.

This is a good time to visit the island. Sicily, in fact, is one of the best regions in Italy to find good values. Avoid July and especially August, for the crowds and for the intense heat (the sirocco, a dry Sahara wind that flows across the sea, picking up moisture before hitting Sicily, can create a hot, humid climate that makes even walking an effort). Hotels and *trattorie* are relatively inexpensive and tour operator packages for round-the-island travel can be unbelievably inexpensive. A rail pass is often added by tour operators, such as Central Holidays (☎ 800/935-5000). Without a package, rail passes cost $168 for eight days in second class or $208 for 15 days per person, and are valid throughout Italy during that time. If you buy a package, which will include a few nights in a hotel, the cost is reduced, especially during the winter months. In the winter of 1996–97, Central Holidays land packages included a double room and car, with insurance and unlimited mileage, for seven nights in hotels throughout Sicily for $529 per person. Other tour operators offer similar deals—ask your travel agent. Off-season travelers, of course, should not expect beach weather in the winter. Although the island is not far from Africa, winter can be cool and drizzly.

ESSENTIALS

GETTING THERE   By Plane   Alitalia's inadequate service has opened the field to competitors, a great advantage to travelers. **Meridiana Airline,** once the Aga Khan's Alisarda line, is an excellent airline in the process of trying harder. Most of their flights are Rome to Palermo and return, but check with them for other inter-European flights, as their service expands. Ask your travel agent for information about them or call **091/32-31-41** in Sicily or 000/00-01-41 in Rome. But be aware that Alitalia often offers discounts for continuing flights within Italy to international travelers arriving in Italy on Alitalia. Check the price on the round-trip fare to Sicily when you book, not just to Rome. The flight from Rome to Palermo takes about an hour and costs about $100 each way, if booked from Rome.

By Ferry from Naples   The overnight ferry from Naples is one of the nicest ways to travel to Sicily, with or without a car. You leave Naples (Molo Beverello) at 8pm usually, and dine on board. Second-class in a four-bedded cabin (two double-deckers) costs 69,000L ($57.50) one-way per person, and first-class, for about double the price, has cabins with one double-decker. You arrive to see a very rosy dawn in Palermo. Call Tirrenia Lines in Naples, ☎ **081/72-01-111** (the large, overnight ships are called *navi*).

You can take a different ferry from an adjoining pier in Naples, the Molo Angioino, on Siremar's ships bound for the Eolie (or Aeolian Islands, sometimes called the Lipari Islands), and island-hop to Sicily. You leave at 8pm usually and arrive at Stromboli, the first stop in the Aeolian Islands, off Sicily, at first light (5am), in time to watch the volcano's constant fiery output of hot red rock rising up and down like juggler's balls against the sky (actually, you'll only be aware of red sparks, weather permitting). From Stromboli the ferry goes on to the next island, Panarea, and then Lipari (about 9am) and Vulcano (10am), before its final landing at Milazzo on Sicily's northeast coast before midday, sea permitting. Check the Neapolitan paper *Mattino* for daily information. Check with Siremar Ferries in Naples at ☎ **081/55-12-112.** The cost is 80,000L ($52.65) per person in tourist class, as far as Sicily. Once on the islands there is frequent hydrofoil and ferry service between them in summer. Off-season timetables are unreliable because of rough winter seas. Sometimes the islands are totally isolated because of weather. Hydrofoil service in summer also connects Palermo with the Aeolians.

By Ferry from Villa San Giovanni & Reggio di Calabria   Ferries (traghetti) link the Calabria mainland with Messina. There are about 52 ferries per day from Villa San Giovanni to Messina on the state railway line at a cost of 2,220L ($1.45) for the

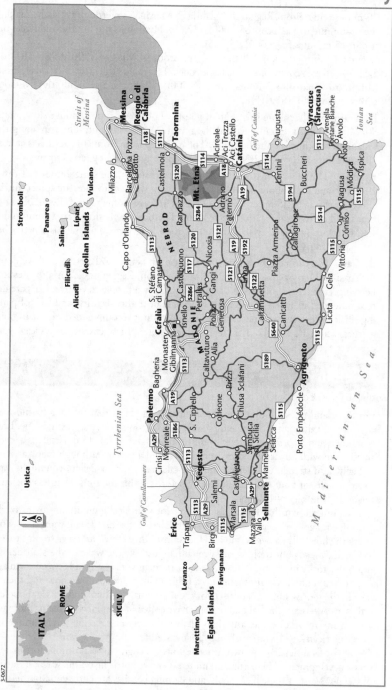

20-minute ride. From Reggio di Calabria to Messina, 15 ferries leave daily, making the 35-minute trip at a cost of 4,000L ($2.65). Hydrofoils run hourly, and make the trip in 15 minutes for 5,000L ($3.25).

For ferry information call the Siremar office in Milazzo **(090/92-86-381)** on Sicily's northeast coast, where the ferries dock. Ferries normally run once a day. From Milazzo to Panarea (3^1/$_2$ hours) costs 13,500L ($8.90); to Stromboli, the five-hour trip costs 18,500L ($12.15).

By Train   Only choose this route if you have plenty of time and love slow trains. Still, if you have a Eurail pass and the time to spare, why not? The trip along the Calabrian coastline is quite beautiful. The train trip from Rome to Messina is at least 10 hours long and costs 72,300L ($47.55) one-way, including ferry crossing.

By Bus   The bus from Rome to Messina takes about the same amount of time, 10 hours, and costs about 65,000L ($42.75) each way; youth fares are sometimes in effect, so check. SAIS buses (☎ **06/77-19-14**) leave Rome's Pz. d. Repubblica 46, near the Termini train station, at 9:30am. The bus means sitting in a comfortable seat, but with little ability to move about for a long time. The train is a better bet for that reason.

By Car   You can take a car ferry overnight from Naples to Palermo or drive down the coast and ferry across the Strait of Messina from Reggio di Calabria to Messina. Ferrying a car costs about 18,000L ($11.85) and two people travel free. Cars are not recommended in Palermo or Catania, because of traffic, security, and lack of parking. Pick up the car outside of town. Parking is not recommended except in hotel garages, which are found only in higher-priced hotels. In no circumstances leave your car on the street.

1 Cefalù

80km (50 miles) E of Palermo

On the island of Sicily there are three enchanting places that reflect a harmony of development through the ages and preserve an exceptional beauty. Cefalù is one, Erice is another, and Taormina, despite its tourist onslaughts, is the third. Cefalù is a lovely small town with a massive Norman cathedral and a beach. Although many arriving in Sicily head straight to Palermo and later take a day trip to Cefalù, you might want to stop there for your first taste of Sicily before you hit the somewhat less enchanting and idyllic city of Palermo.

It's a quiet town that makes a good base for visiting the mountain towns of the Madonie range—such as Castelbuono and Polizzi Generosa. If you want to stay on, check the hotels listed below and also the tourist office for *affitacamere* (rooms to let).

Cefalù spreads out under a massive cliff almost like the wake of the sea tide. Beneath this rocky promontory (called la Rocca), the town is wedged between earth and sea. Self-contained, Cefalù maintains a fishing village life, pausing now and then to take in the tourist stream. Tourists, for the most part, are there only to see the splendid twin-towered cathedral and perhaps have coffee in the piazza. It seems more like a town in Umbria or Tuscany than Sicily, all ocher and sienna tones, unlike the North-African–style whitewash of so many Mediterranean sea towns.

Tourist facilities have grown, but the town's geographical position, fortunately, limits development. The better and more expensive hotels lie on the seacoast outside of Cefalù. Most of these have pools, and bathing beaches are fairly good in this area.

Early Sicilian tribes, the Sicani and the Sikel, settled here during the 9th century B.C. The megalithic period can still be seen in the post-and-lintel gates of the Temple of Diana atop the cliff. Greeks, Romans, and Byzantines came in turn, then the

Muslims captured the town in A.D. 857, razed it to the ground, and settled their own community there. Normans put an end to that in the 11th century, and Cefalù grew to prominence under Roger II. Cefalù's massive cathedral was Roger's work. From the 15th century on, artists and tradesmen enlarged the town until in 1773 it became the seat of the Italian Parliament, summoned by King Ferdinand III after riots in Palermo.

ESSENTIALS

GETTING THERE   By Train   From Palermo, about 14 trains per day make the hour-long trip; 5,700L ($3.75) each way. Train service from Cefalù also continues to Milazzo, farther east along the coast (port for ferries to the Aeolian Islands). From Messina, six trains per day make the three-hour trip for 12,000L/$7.90.

By Bus   From Palermo, tickets are 7,600L ($5) one-way. The bus station is at Via Balsame, to the left of the train station, when facing the station. Forget the bus on weekends, as the single highway is bumper-to-bumper along the coast, especially in summer.

By Car   Route 113 connects Palermo with Cefalù, and continues on to Messina along the coast.

VISITOR INFORMATION   The **tourist office** is located on Cor. Ruggero 77 (☎ **0921/21-050;** fax 0921/22-386). It's open Monday to Friday from 8am to 2pm and 4 to 7pm, on Saturday from 8am to 2pm. You can find English-language newspapers at Muffoletto, Cor. Ruggero 98 and at Sutera, V. Vittorio Emanuele 16.

WHAT TO SEE & DO

The Duomo. Pz. Duomo off Cor. Ruggero. Daily 8am–12pm and 3:15–7:30pm, services permitting.

Finding it won't be a problem. Roger II was a religious man as well as a powerful king. Once shipwrecked offshore, he made a vow to the Virgin that he would build a mighty cathedral that could be seen from the sea by mariners if his life was spared. It was, and he built the Duomo. The city soon acquired a bishop, and became an important See of the bishopric and a center of learning where theological, humanistic, and juridical studies were pursued—the dream of ecumenical believers to this day.

Construction began in 1131 and was completed a hundred years later. Roger originally wanted it to be his tomb as well a pantheon of Normans, but his bones still lie in Palermo's cathedral. Bureaucracy thwarts even the mighty.

Inside, the 12th-century Byzantine-style mosaics are stunning. Christ as Pantocrator, or Almighty, looks down with gentleness, instead of the stern expression usually seen in this kind of mosaic, a lock of hair having dropped to his forehead, in a rare natural touch. Below him stands his mother and four archangels, and below them the 12 apostles. Notice also, in the transept, the marble statue of the Madonna.

The walls are plain for the most part, giving the cathedral a serene simplicity, and a cool place to relax when the sirocco blows. Appropriate dress is required: no bare shoulders or legs.

Museo Madralisco. V. Madralisco 13. ☎ **0921/21-547.** Admission 4,000L ($2.65). Daily 9am–12:30 and 4:30–7pm; Sun closed in afternoon.

A fine private collection, its best-known work is the *Portrait of an Unknown Man* (ca. 1460) by Antonello da Messina. This schemer is not someone you'd probably want to know anyway, but Antonello's character studies are at their best in this work. The other gem of the collection is an urn in crater form that dates from the 4th century B.C. in which a very realistic fish seller slices off a slab of fish the customer wants, as the latter gestures the amount. There are several other fine works of this era in the museum. A larger collection can be seen at the museum on the Aeolian island of Lipari, not far offshore,

From here walk to the far side of town where you'll see a breakwall. From here Cefalù's much-photographed fishermen's houses (the ones that appear in *Cinema Paradiso*) can be seen most effectively. Speaking of *Cinema,* its young director, Giuseppe Tornatore, who won an Oscar for the film, comes from nearby Bagheria. While you're wandering, near the beach on Via Vittorio Emanuele you'll see the lavatoio, a communal laundry of the 16th century.

OUTDOOR ACTIVITIES

Ascending the Rocca isn't for mountaineers only, although it is steep in places. Walk up the stairs near the bank in Piazza Garibaldi and follow the signs. Take a camera, sunshade, and water. Cefalù is even more beautiful from above. The megalithic structure called the Temple of Diana was built during the 5th century B.C.

The town beach is no treasure but it's nice for a quick dip. Water sports can be arranged; inquire at the tourist office.

WHERE TO STAY

Check with the tourist office for rooms to let and nearby camping, although most nearby campgrounds are noisy with a disco or a passing train, alas.

Pensione delle Rosa. V. Gibilmanna, 90015 Cefalù. ☎ **0921/21-885.** 10 rms, 7 with bath. A/C. 35,000L ($23) single without bath; 50,000L ($32.90) double without bath, 65,000L ($42.75) double with bath. Breakfast 8,000L ($5.25). Half pension 65,000L ($42.75), full pension 80,000L ($52.65) MC, V. Walk along V. Umberto, to the far right side of the cathedral, which becomes V. Gibilmanna, then follow the sign.

The best of the bargains, the delle Rosa may be worth the 20-minute trek. It is set amid olive trees, and views over the town and coast are smashing, especially in fall when the sea is bluest against the tannish town. Rooms are on the large side and some have little terraces and good views. Those that overlook the hillside are quieter, as unfortunately, the route to the highway is below the rooms with sea views. Tourists, especially Germans, have discovered it, making reservations difficult to come by in high season.

Riva del Sole. Vle. Lungomare 25, 90015 Cefalù. ☎ **0921/21-230.** Fax 0921/21-984. 28 rms, all with bath. A/C, TV, TEL. 110,000L ($72) doubles. Full pension 120,000L person ($80). AE, MC, V.

It isn't a beauty from the outside, but within it has charm. Rooms are large and often have wide balconies looking directly out to sea. It's in a good spot across from the beach and not far from the bus station, but these two features often equal noise, unless you come out of season.

WHERE TO DINE

A morning market near the harbor and several supermarkets can keep your costs very low. Otherwise, this is a resort town and few places are cheap if you want a full meal.

Arkade Grill. V. Vanni 9 (near the cathedral). ☎ **0921/92-19-50.** Reservations not accepted. Main courses 6,000L–15,000L ($3.95–$9.85). AE, MC, V. Fri–Wed noon–3pm, and 6–10pm. NORTH AFRICAN/SICILIAN.

This is modest place near the cathedral, run by Tunisians (so, of course, couscous is on the menu). They serve good Sicilian dishes as well, such as involtini (rolled beef stuffed with seasoned breadcrumbs and raisins). The atmosphere is relaxed with

Palermitani as well as tourists at the tables. The decor is basic, with some North African tiles and ceramic plates to enliven the walls.

L'Antica Corte. Cortile Pepe 7 (left off Cor. Ruggero). ☎ **0921/22-582.** Reservations not accepted. Main courses 9,000L–15,000L ($5.90–$9.85). AE, MC, V. Fri–Mon 12:00–3:00pm, 7–11pm. Closed Nov and Dec. SEAFOOD.

This is a good bet in hot weather. You can stay inside in air-conditioning or enjoy the arbor in the little courtyard. The catch of the day is plural here, for boats leave nightly for the open sea. They serve good grilled fish and shellfish. Palermitani often grace the courtyard.

Lo Scoglio Ubriaco. V. Carlo Ortolani d. Bordonare 2–4. ☎ **0921/23-370.** Reservations advisable on weekends. Main courses 9,000L–20,000L ($5.90–13.15). AE, MC, V. Daily, 12–3pm, 7–11pm. Closed Tues in winter and Nov. PIZZA/SEAFOOD.

This "drunken rock," as its name translates, has a lovely terrace out on the sea for pizza or full meals (of grilled fish or meat). Spaghetti al cartoccio has a good spicy tomato-and-seafood sauce. Everyone is there, from locals having a drink to visiting Italians and tourists. A bit off the usual tourist route, it sees fewer foreigners. It's at the far side of town from the train station. The food is not as great as the view, but the relaxed outdoor dining is a treat.

Da Nino. V. Lungomare 11. ☎ **0921/22-583.** Main courses 8,000L–18,000L ($5.25–$11.85). AE, MC, V. 12:30–3:30pm, 7–11pm. PIZZA/SEAFOOD.

Nino's is an outdoor restaurant with a seaside view; the interior was once a salt warehouse. There's a generous antipasto table, seafood, and pizza at noon, too. (Some pizzerias fire up the oven only at night, when it's cooler.) Penne all'arrabiata (with "angry" peppery tomato sauce) will fire up your blood. Try a sliced orange with olive oil and black olives to cool down (un arangia tagliata all'olio con olive). Two brothers run this usually merry, never tranquil place along the seaside promenade. It's a good value as they still seem to value tourists, a rarity in this area.

2 Palermo

233km (145 miles) W of Messina

Here is a city of Eastern charm and wiles with much bravado and garbage. Intellectuals and artists who disappear in its dark labyrinths rarely come up with a phrase that describes this port city. The port is its focal point, and it drew all the invasions mentioned in the introduction to this chapter. Norman and Swabian rulers succumbed to its languid charms and turned into Eastern potentates. (Frederick II traveled about the world with a retainer of elephants and a harem.) Palermo is filled with palm trees, flowers, red-domed roofs, and a purple mountain (Mt. Pellegrino), which keeps the distance in postcard perspective.

Although today it mixes grandeur and squalor, Palermo, from the 9th to the 11th century, was an Arab capital of luxurious design, filled with fountains, mosques (100 of them at one point), and minarets. Today, you can still see touches of this Palermo occasionally in a red-domed church or in the interlaced arches of a building. Sicily's cuisine at this western side of the island reflects the Arab preference for sweet-and-sour mixtures and very sweet desserts.

ESSENTIALS

GETTING THERE By Plane See "Getting There" under the Sicily introduction above for details. For Punta Raisi airport, call **091/59-16-91** (domestic), 091/ 59-12-95 (international). Buses from the airport to downtown cost 4,500L ($2.95) and run approximately every hour, stopping at the train station and at the Teatro Politeama.

By Train   Palermo is linked by train to Messina across the northern coast and from Messina to Rome. This 3½-hour ride from Messina costs 17,800L ($11.70) and is lovely if your time isn't limited. Trains arrive at the Stazione Centrale in Piazza Giulio Cesare (☎ **091/61-61-806**). See "Getting There" under the Sicily introduction above for details about train travel from the Italy mainland.

By Bus   The bus is Sicily's best transit bargain. The SAIS bus terminal (major) has its office near the train station at V. Balsamo 16 (☎ **091/61-66-028**). Most major cities are linked by good, regular service. Smaller towns have less frequent service. See "Getting There" under the Sicily introduction above for details about bus service from the Italy mainland.

The bus from Palermo to Catania is a wonderful idea until you reach Catania, where the bus depot is composed of several streets that muddy up when it rains. Drivers don't change the destination signs at the front of the bus until the last minute, and so foreigners and even Italians miss buses frequently because they simply can't find them in the brief seconds between the turning of the bus sign and the bus departure.

By Ferry   See "Getting There" under the Sicily introduction above for details. Ferries arrive at the Stazione Marittima, off Via Francesco Crispi (☎ **091/58-68-30**). Siremar line has an office at V. Francesco Crispi 118 (☎ **091/58-24-03**). S.N.A.V., a good hydrofoil service, has its office at V. Principe Belmonte 55, nearby (☎ **091/ 33-33-33**).

VISITOR INFORMATION   There is a **tourist office** at the airport counter, open Monday to Saturday from 8am to 8pm (☎ **091/59-16-98**). The one at the railroad station is open Monday to Friday from 8am to 8pm, Saturday from 8am to 2pm (☎ **091/61-65-914**); at the ferry station (in summer only) it is open Monday to Saturday from 9am to 1pm (☎ **091/58-68-30**). In the city itself, the main tourist office is at Pz. Castelnuovo 34, opposite the Politeama theater (☎ **091/58-38-47** or 60-38-351). They have a free booklet called *Palermo Flash Guide* that contains a map and useful addresses.

CITY LAYOUT   Palermo is a major port city that enjoys a wonderful geographical position, with Monte Pellegrino to the north providing a picturesque horizon. The tourist's city is easy to navigate, for the most part. There are three major arteries: Corso Vittorio Emanuele (the most important) runs almost at right angles to the harbor; Via Roma and Via Maqueda both run almost parallel to the harbor and both intersect with the corso. The intersection of Via Maqueda and Corso Vittorio Emanuele is called Quattro Canti, the site of four famous corner fountains that mark the division of four Palermitani neighborhoods.

The train station is about 10 blocks south of Corso Vittorio Emanuele on Via Maqueda. At the eastern end of Corso Vittorio Emanuele is the Palazzo dei Normanni and the Cathedral. Piazza Castelnuovo and the Politeama are at the northern end of the tourist city. Via Liberta, the chic fashionable street begins there. You'll see it if you arrive on the airport bus.

GETTING AROUND   Most of Palermo is flat, making walking the best way to get to most places. The grid pattern makes it even easier. However, city buses, crowded as they are, do a good job (AMAT ☎ **091/22-23-98**). You can pay a flat fare of 1,000L (65¢), or 1,300L (86¢) for a one-hour-on-all-the-lines ticket, or 4,000L ($2.65) for a full-day ticket. Cancel your ticket when you get on, or you could be fined 50,000L ($32.90). You can buy tickets at the AMAT kiosk opposite the Stazione Centrale (train station), in any tabacchi (tobacconist), or wherever you see the sign VENDITE BIGLIETTI AMAT.

From the train station, buses 5, 8, and 23 run along the Corso Vittorio Emanuele. Buses 14, 15, 16, and 19 go from the railroad station to the Politeama (Piazza Castelnuovo). No. 14 and 15 go to the seaside resort town of Mondello, where Palermitani sit at trattorias along the seaside and dine on seafood, or go to have an ice cream in the evening.

FAST FACTS: Palermo

American Express G. Ruggieri e Figli, V. E. Amari, 40 (☎ **091/58-71-44**) is near the port; open Monday to Friday from 9am to 1pm and 4 to 7:30pm, Saturday from 9am to 1pm. To report card theft, call Rome, **06/72-282.**

Bookstores Feltrinelli, V. Maqueda 459, opposite the Teatro Massimo (closed Monday morning), usually has a good selection of books in English. Libreria Flaccovio is at V. Ruggero Settimo 37.

Consulates The **United States** consulate is at V. G.B. Vaccarini 1, off Vle. d. Liberta (☎ **091/30-25-90**). The **United Kingdom** consulate is at V. Cavour 117 (☎ **091/58-25-33**).

Emergencies Call **113** for police; for the hospital, **091/60-61-111.** Road assistance is **116.**

Police Questura in Piazza Vittoria has an office for foreigners: ☎ **091/21-01-11.**

Post Office Main office is at V. Roma 322. Counter 15 has poste restante service Monday to Saturday from 8:15am to 7:30pm for letters; the package department closed at 1:15pm daily.

Safety Take normal big-city precautions. Keep money and valuables out of sight if you must carry them. Be sure you have a record of your credit card and passport numbers, and of your return ticket.

WHAT TO SEE & DO

✪ **Il Palazzo dei Normanni and Cappella Palatina.** Pz. Indipendenza. ☎ **091/65-61-111.** Free admission. Mon, Fri, and Sat 9am–noon unless Parliament is in session (it's the seat of the Sicilian Parliament). Chapel Mon–Fri 9am–noon and 3–5pm, Sat 9–noon, Sun and holidays 9–10am and noon–1pm. Bus: 104, 105, 108, 109, 110.

The Norman-Saracenic part of this palace is bathed in mosaics, mainly the work of Byzantine Greeks, whose work you'll see elsewhere in Palermo and in the cathedrals of Montreal and Cefalù nearby. See the Palatine Chapel with fresh eyes in the morning. It's one of the most beautiful of the world's jewel boxes. First, take the free tour of the palace and see the hunting scenes—more mythical than bloody—resembling Persian miniatures. The chapel is for adoration, rather than repose. Completed in 1140, its walls are aglow with scenes from the Old and New Testaments.

San Giovanni degli Eremiti. V. d. Benedettini 3. ☎ **091/65-15-019.** Daily 8am–1pm. Bus: 3, 24.

Just off the southeast flank of the royal palace (turn right when exiting) stands an exceptionally beautiful church (now deconsecrated) and cloisters that were built, it seems, with a mosque in mind—five exuberant red-orange domes grace the roof. The

charm is mainly in the exterior and in the palm trees and flowers of the elegant cloisters. It's one of those *Arabian Nights* dreams of Robert II's, combining east and west.
His reign was as close to Camelot as Sicily ever saw. Artists and poets were encouraged and his humanitarian nature allowed exceptional religious and racial tolerance.
Many of the Arabs that he conquered stayed on in Palermo when they could have
left, a tribute to the acceptance of the Norman king.

Il Duomo. Cor. Vittorio Emanuele at Pz. d. Cattedrale. ☎ **091/33-43-76.** Daily 7am–7pm,
holidays 4–6pm. Bus: 3, 24.

This cathedral is not one of the world's most beautiful. Too many styles are blended,
and the dome doesn't belong there. The basic church was built by William II's English archbishop, Walter of the Mill. However, six royal tombs inside do deserve your
attention. Among them are those of Roger II (very simple, near the entrance, at left)
and his daughter Constance (who married Emperor Henry VI). Emperor Frederick
II (Stupor Mundi) and his wife Constance of Aragon and son Duke William lead the
list of notable royals.

Quattro Canti. Intersection of V. Maqueda and Cor. Vittorio Emanuele. Bus: 3, 24.

These "Four Corners" are actually the concave corners of four 17th-century palaces
that were designed as a unit to form a piazza. Now this harmonious piazza is all but
forgotten in Palermo's clogging traffic, but the monuments are worth a look as you
pass. Each baroque arrangement begins with a fountain on the ground floor and rises
to the first-floor (second floor in America) statue of a king of Spain, with the patron
saint of one of the four sections of Palermo on the top floor. Recent cleaning has
made this corner more attractive, as Palermo commits to much-overdue renovation.

Piazza Pretoria. Off V. Maqueda just south of the Quattro Canti. Bus: 3, 24.

Piazza Pretoria is very attractive when not used as a car park. Strolling around the
fountain by night is a favorite pastime for Palermo's lovers or wanna-bes. Speculat-
ing on what's in the minds of the fountain's nude figures has occupied Palermitani
and tourists for centuries. Some are sea creatures from the knees down, some are
embarrassed, one graceful muse seems to have beheaded someone, another is talking
to the horse. In the piazza's nightlights it all comes together happily. Garibaldi apparently sat here to think things through during the 1870 revolution. Others were
simply scandalized by the nudity. The church at the intersection, San Giuseppi dei
Teatini, is a minimalist's nightmare, but lots of fun for those who enjoy angels by
the dozen. The damage done by a World War II bomb in 1943 has been rectified
well. To the north of the piazza, the yellow-and-green-tiled dome is the church of
St. Catherine, a baroque fantasy inside if you manage to catch it when it's open.

✪ La Martorana. V. Maqueda at Pz. Bellini. Mon–Sat 8:30am–1pm and 3:30–7pm,
Sun 8:30am–1pm.

Farther along Via Maqueda you'll come to the quintessential Palermo church, the
Church of San Cataldo, which is usually closed. You'll notice San Cataldo's red
domes, which give a hint of the East. The majestic bell tower and strong forms evoke
La Martorana's Norman past—the church was built in 1143 by Roger II's commander of the fleet. Inside the walls are covered with some of Sicily's oldest mosaics. The figure of Christ as Pantocrator (the Omnipotent) glows from the cupola,
while a more familiar note is struck below. We see Roger himself being crowned by
Christ, and the admiral benefactor, George of Antioch, at the foot of the Virgin. Services in the Greek rite are still conducted here. The name Martorana came from the
adjoining convent, where nuns developed the fine art of marzipan fantasies, called
frutti alla martorana in Sicily.

✪ **La Kalsa.** Bounded by Cor. Vittorio Emanuele and V. Lincoln N and S, the port and V. Garibaldi/V. Paternostro to the E and W. Bus: 3, 5, 23, 2, 25.

This is an interesting old part of Palermo, planned and built by Arabs, as a walled city for the emir and his ministers. Spanish viceroys later moved in, destroying much of the original city. Its name, *khalisa,* in Arabic means pure, but that is not what you'll think first on strolling through its labyrinthine streets. This can be a rough neighborhood, so watch your wallet and don't visit after dark. It bears bomb holes from World War II and crumbling buildings. Don't be discouraged. *Corraggio,* as the Italians say. You'll discover its hidden treasures soon enough.

From the harbor called "La Cala" (near Corso Vittorio Emanuele) go through the gate, and you'll be at Piazza Marina. Garibaldi's Gardens will be on your left (so named because the general planted a tree here). There is a touch of old Savannah (but with less moss), and many 100-year-old massive trees that tangle their wild roots here. Notice the wrought-iron rails by Basile, master of art nouveau. Turn right into Via Merlo until you see the Church of San Francesco d'Assisi, whose gothic doors date from 1302, not long after the saint's death. Inside you can admire the works of Serpotta and Laurana, two of the best sculptors who worked in Sicily. The church is normally open daily from 7 to 11am and 3 to 5:30pm, but there are plans to close it down for some much-needed restorations, so it may be locked up when you visit.

Head left at the Church of San Francesco into Via dell'Immacolatella and you'll see the gate to St. Lawrence's Oratory (Oratorio di San Lorenzo). It's well worth a peek if it's open because of its frescoes by the master Serpotta. Technically, it is never *really* open, but you should ring the bell, and if someone appears, he or she will show it to you and expect a tip of 2,000L ($1.30) or more (don't give more—the state pays them). Caravaggio's last known painting was stolen from here in 1969, so apparently someone knew how to get in.

Head back to Garibaldi's Garden, walk halfway along the side and follow signs to the right to Via Alloro and the Palazzo Abatellis.

✪ **Galleria Regionale della Sicilia.** Palazzo Abatellis, V. Alloro 4 (near the harbor). ☎ **091/61-64-317.** Admission 2,000L ($1.30). Mon and Wed 9am–1:30pm; Tues, Thurs, and Fri 9am–1:30pm and 3–6:30pm; Sun and holidays 9am–1pm. Bus: 3, 5, or 8.

This is a fine art gallery in a 15th-century palace. Have a look around, but be sure not to miss its treasure upstairs—Antonello da Messina's *Annunciation,* in which he captures the Virgin Mary a moment after the Annunciation, when she realizes what has happened. Her hand moves outward as if to shield herself from what is to come, but her eyes have already accepted it. His paintings are usually character studies, and, unfortunately, are usually in a poor state, and this is no exception.

Downstairs, Francesco Laurana's bust of Eleanor of Aragon (room 4) is a triumph, and so is the *Triumph of Death* by an unknown Flemish painter. Death comes to call, while some ignore him and some plead for mercy.

Museo delle Marionette. V. Butera 1. ☎ **091/32-89-60.** Admission 5,000L ($3.30), 3,000L ($1.95) students. Mon, Wed, Fri 9am–1pm and 4–7pm; Tues, Thurs, Sat 9am–1pm. Closed Sun and holidays. Call to see when shows are scheduled. Bus: 3, 5, 34, 35.

This museum is fun, with or without children, thanks to its more than 3,000 puppet exhibits. If you want to see a Sicilian puppet show, check with the tourist office first to be sure there'll be one. You might request one on arriving at the museum and hope a puppeteer is on the grounds.

Museo Archeologico Regionale. Pz. Olivella 4 (off V. Roma behind the main post office.). ☎ **091/66-20-220.** Admission 2,000L ($1.30). Mon, Wed, Thur, Sat 9am–1:30pm; Tues, Fri 9am–1:30pm and 3–5:30pm; Sun and holidays 9am–1pm. Bus: 101, 102, 103, 104, 122.

This museum, situated in a former convent, has collected some fascinating items from ancient Selinunte, especially the metopes taken from the temples. The Greek bronze called the *Ephebus of Selinus* is a fine example of 5th-century B.C. sculpture. Phoenician and Etruscan ware is well represented. Cave drawings are shown here in plaster casts—the originals are in the Addaura caves on Monte Pellegrino (inquire at the museum if you are interested in visiting them). Guided tours are usually in Italian.

✪ **Vucceria.** Off V. Roma, in back of the Church of San Domenico. Open Mon–Sat, early morning to early afternoon. Bus: 7, 34, 37.

The Vucceria is one of the most raucous and interesting street markets in the world—well, the Western Hemisphere anyway. Here you can buy any food you want and enjoy doing it. Mounds of cauliflower, olives, fish, sea urchins, pears, and soap bars are interspersed with street urchins, wide-eyed and vocal. Walk down the street behind San Domenico until you see the fish market, where tables under the trees are laden with oysters, eels, clams, calamari, and anything that swims and has gills. You can sample some of the wares at Shangai (see "Where to Dine," below).

Museo Etnografico Pitre. V. Duca degli Abruzzi, in Parco d. Favorita, at western end of Palermo. Admission 2,000L ($1.30). Sat–Thurs, 9am–1:30pm, closed Fri. Bus: 14 or 15 from Vle. Libertà.

If Sicilian culture is getting in your blood, you can go to this museum in the Parco della Favorita, about $1^3/_4$ mile north of the city. The famous Sicilian carts can be seen here in the original; there is a puppet theater, and hundreds of other items of folk craft.

Convento dei Cappuccini. Pz. Cappuccini 1 ☎ **091/21-21-17.** Donation 5,000L ($3.30) per couple would be well received. Mon–Sat 9am–noon and 3–5pm. Bus: 27 from Cor. Vittorio Emanuele.

Even Stephen King might shiver in the Cappuccini Convent. Originally a series of crypts for the Cappuccini monks, popular demand led to their opening the crypts for public use. Bodies (some 8,000) were preserved using various methods and placed here, dressed in their favorite clothes, for several hundred years, until 1881. Relatives used to come for a Sunday chat with the deceased. The baby Rosalia Lombardo was well preserved (d. 1920) and still looks as if she's sleeping. Signs will tell you where she is. This crypt is not for everyone.

WHERE TO STAY

Palermo is a good budget city. It's not a tourist mecca, so hotels can't charge high tourist prices. Summer is low season in prices, but Palermo can get very hot, and air-conditioning is nonexistent in the cheaper hotels. Ceiling fans and high ceilings are fine, except when the *afa* (hazy, hot, and humid weather) arrives. Check with a tour operator about independent packages at tourist-class hotels. The hotels that are chosen as bargains are in good condition and have friendly staffs, although English is rarely spoken beyond the very basics. The area around the railroad station has improved enormously in the last year, but you don't want to wander around at night, particularly alone.

DOUBLES FOR LESS THAN 45,000 LIRE ($29.60)

Hotel Liguria. V. Mariano Stabile 128, 90139 Palermo. ☎ **091/58-15-88.** 16 rms, 8 with bath. TEL. Summer 30,000L ($19.75) single without bath, 48,000L ($31.55) double with bath. Winter 54,000L ($35.50) double without bath, 64,000L ($42.10) double with bath. No credit cards.

This is a very friendly place with pleasant, airy, and cheerful rooms and tile floors. A clothes press is a thoughtful extra. Rooms on the street are noisy, however. It's near the famous (*Godfather III*) Hotel delle Palme. The tourist office has given owner Signora Lidia Grosso de Grana many awards for her hospitality. The neighborhood is central and safe, if you observe normal big-city precautions.

Hotel Petite. V. Principe d. Belmonte 84, 90139 Palermo. ☎ **091/32-36-16.** 6 rooms, all with bath. TEL. Summer 35,000L–42,000L ($23–$27.65) single; 55,000L–65,000L ($36.20–$42.75) double. Winter 38,000L–45,000L ($25–$29.60) single; 60,000L–70,000L ($39.45–$46.05) double. AE.

This hotel offers simple rooms on a cobblestone street near the harbor and the Politeama Theater in a recently renovated neighborhood. Rooms are clean and basic, with sparkling baths; and some have balconies. Colorful prints and fresh flowers add a bit of cheer. It's a pedestrian mall here, so you avoid car noise. However, you may have to contend with people noise on weekends, because there are outdoor cafes and bars nearby; but it's a safe, patrolled area of town. Like many hotels in town, it gets pretty hot in summer. They do not serve breakfast, but there are plenty of bars nearby.

Orientale. V. Maqueda 26, 90134 Palermo. ☎ **091/61-65-727.** 21 rms, 6 with bath. 24,000L ($15.80) single without bath; 34,000L ($22.35) double without bath, 49,000L ($32.20) double with bath. No credit cards.

Few courtyards compare with the one at this hotel. Writers and photographers could spend a lifetime exploring its enormous classical columns, palm tree, flowers, shoemaker in the portier's booth, washing hanging from the balconies, and the requisite cats. You'll ascend a vast worn pink marble staircase and meet the friendly owners, who don't speak English. Rooms are very clean and simple. Those facing the courtyard are the quietest. The neighborhood is near the train station, so you won't want to take an evening stroll. They do not serve breakfast.

Principe di Belmonte. V. Principe d. Belmonte 25, 90139 Palermo. ☎ **091/33-10-65.** Fax 61-13-424. 17 rms, 14 with bath. Summer 35,000L ($23) single without bath, 46,000L ($30.25) single with bath; 50,000L ($32.90) double without bath, 60,000L ($39.45) double with bath. Winter 49,000L ($32.25) single without bath, 74,000L ($48.70) single with bath; 92,000L ($60.50) double without bath, 96,000L ($63.15) double with bath. Breakfast 9,000L. AE, MC, V.

This is a bright, friendly place on a pedestrian mall that affords strolling after dark, which is not a given in most Palermo neighborhoods. Rooms are largish, simple, and attractive, with prints of Sicily on the walls. It's well maintained, and their bar is convenient for morning coffee and before-dinner drinks. The hotel seems to be on the way up, and the clientele is apt to be young and European.

DOUBLES FOR LESS THAN 65,000 LIRE ($42.75)

Alessandra. V. Divisi 99, 90133 Palermo. ☎ **091/61-67-009.** 24 rms, 22 with bath. TV TEL. Summer 34,000L ($22.35) single without bath, 44,000 ($28.95) single with bath; 60,000L ($39.45) double with bath. Winter 40,000L ($26.30) single without bath, 50,000L single with bath ($32.90); 70,000L ($46.05) double with bath. MC, V.

This hotel has recently renovated all the rooms, which are modern and clean. Some have a nice rooftop view. A pleasant sitting room has tables for takeout meals. The owner is eager to make this one of the best pensiones in the area, which is near the train station, and fine by day, but you need to exercise caution at night. An impressive long marble staircase rises through this old palazzo to the hotel, which is on the secondo piano (3rd floor). They only speak minimal English.

Ariston. V. Mariano Stabile 139, 90133 Palermo. ☎ **091/33-24-34.** 5 rms, 2 with bath. TV. Summer 34,000L ($22.35) single without bath, 38,000L ($25) single with bath; 55,000L ($36.20) double without bath, 65,000 ($42.75) double with bath. Winter 39,000L ($25.65) single without bath, 46,000L ($30.25) single with bath; 60,000L ($39.45) double without bath, 70,000L ($46.05) double with bath. No credit cards.

The modern rooms are plain, very clean, and not particularly atmospheric. The addition of TV helps, if only for the weather report. However, the management is friendly and the neighborhood is fine. Courtyard rooms are the quietest. The clientele in summer is apt to be young and international, in winter businessmen take advantage of its low rates and the washing machine (at a small fee).

Hotel Posta. V. Gagini 77, 90133 Palermo. ☎ **091/58-73-38.** 27 rms, 23 with bath. TV TEL. Summer 35,000L ($23) single without bath, 55,000L ($36.20) single with bath; 60,000L ($39.45) double without bath, 75,000L ($49.35) double with bath. Winter 40,000L ($26.30) single without bath, single with bath; 75,000L ($49.35) double without bath, 95,000L ($62.50) double with bath. AE, MC, V.

The bar helps the convivial spirit, and a bit of Italian helps too, as actors from a nearby theater often stay here. In the bar you'll see photos of Vittorio Gassman and other Italian luminary ex-clients. An easygoing family has run this hotel since 1921. It's in the center of Palermo, and thus a bit noisy; its name derives from the central post office, across the street. Rooms are attractive, with Sicilian crafts for decor. While you won't get CNN on TV you may get Telemontecarlo. Women traveling alone will be well taken care of.

WORTH A SPLURGE

✪ **Centrale Palace Hotel.** Cor. Vittorio Emanuele 327, 90139 Palermo. ☎ **091/58-84-09.** Fax 091/33-48-81. 90 rms, all with bath. A/C TV TEL. 150,000L ($98.70) single; 200,000L ($131.60) double. Breakfast 20,000L ($13.15). AE, MC, V.

Although the prices are excellent now, this hotel is aiming for the stars, and rates will probably be tripled before long. At last Palermo has a hotel that is both beautiful and well run. No rooms are duds here. Even the back rooms are tastefully furnished (many top-category hotels have dingy back rooms). Some rooms share the cheerful view that the rooftop restaurant has of Palermo rooftops and the distant mountain. The hotel is located just off Quattro Canti, in a restored palace. Guests dress up here, for there's a festive air. All is brand new, and flower arrangements, decor, and artwork are exceptional. The decor maintains an 18th-century palace ambience with a subdued elegance. It's set back in from the street, so noise is kept to a minimum. There is a restaurant, a bar, a piano bar, and even a garage. Stay here before new stars are added to its category and the prices explode.

WHERE TO DINE

Palermo has good trattorie at all prices, often with long strips of plastic at the door to keep the flies out; they are often very inexpensive, but check the posted menu outside first. But even when you dine at a ristorante you can splurge royally. Most of the best restaurants are located near the Politeama. Palermo has one of the world's best food markets, the Vucceria, where you can find all the things you've heard of and many that you haven't—picnics are as easy to arrange as walking through the streets in back of the Church of San Domenico on Via Roma.

Antica Focacceria San Francesco. V. A. Paternostro 58, catercorner to the church of San Francesco, ☎ **091/32-02-64.** Sandwiches, arancini (rice balls with meat and cheese centers), or pizza slices all about 2,000L ($1.30). No credit cards. Tues–Sun 9am–10pm. SICILIAN SNACKS.

You never thought you'd stop for a spleen sandwich, did you? Well, at least have a look. This focacceria has been serving U pane ca meusa (milza in Italian), which is very tasty spleen on focaccia dribbled with cacciacavallo cheese, for 162 years. They have pizza and lasagne, if courage dribbles out. This is Sicilian fast food, and it's very good here. Garibaldi stopped here, we are told, which may be true, but he is like an Italian George Washington, and has "slept here," "dined here," and "had temporary headquarters here" just about everywhere, it seems. The dark wood and mirrors maintain its antique atmosphere.

Shangai. Vc. Mezzani 34. ☎ **091/58-97-02.** Main courses 9,000L–25,000L ($5.90–$16.45). No credit cards. Mon–Sat 12–3pm and 7–11pm. Closed Sun.

It's Italian, not Chinese, and they'll be happy to cook whatever you see in the Vucceria market that surrounds it—how's that for ordering off the menu? All you need do is ask and a basket will be lowered to the fish stalls for your choices. A mixed fry (fritto misto) will let you taste several delicacies. The owner sometimes sings after lunch, when the mood strikes. The place is usually full; the decor is plain, and the clients noisy.

Da Toto. V. d. Coltellieri 5. No phone. Main courses 7,000L–19,000L ($4.60–$12.50). No credit cards. Lunch only. Mon–Sat 12–3pm. Closed evenings. SEAFOOD/SICILIAN SPECIALTIES.

Plainer than Shangai but equally good, Toto's is a place where locals run in with a fish wrapped in newspaper for the grill. The owner is sometimes moved to sing (*"M'ama"* is one of his favorite arias) and do magic tricks. You are apt to see the postman and the local lawyers feasting on vast plates of pasta with a simple tomato sauce, in order not to overload their palate for the fresh fish. Locals linger over strong after-dinner drinks and wonder aloud who you are, and what brought you Da Toto.

MEALS FOR LESS THAN 25,000 LIRE ($16.45)

Osteria Fratelli lo Bianco. V. Emerico Atari 104 (near the Politeama). ☎ **091/58-58-16.** Reservations not accepted. Main courses 8,000L–12,000L ($5.25–$7.90) No credit cards. Mon–Sat 12–3pm. 7–10:30pm. PALERMITANO.

With a clientele from dock workers (it's near the port) and professionals, this osteria is simple and good. Everyone eats together and the decor—tube lights and paper mats—is not what you come for. Tell Signor Berone to bring on some *piatti tipici*, such as involtini di pesce *spada* (stuffed swordfish).

Trattoria Paradiso. V. Serradifalco 23 (near the Politeama). No phone. Main courses 8,000L–22,000L ($5.25–$14.50). No credit cards. Mon–Sat lunch only 12–3pm. PALERMITANO.

The Paradiso serves a good pasta con le sarde, made with fresh sardines, sultana raisins, and wild fennel. You can't leave Palermo without a taste, at least. Mussels (*cozze*) mussels are served all tarantina, with anchovies, tomato paste, egg, and soaked bread. Octopus and shrimp and sea creatures are features, but watch the prices. The crowd could be performers at the Politeama or savvy Italian tourists or businessmen. Sicilian ceramics and polished kitchenware are the decor, but no one notices; the food's the thing.

MEALS FOR LESS THAN 35,000 LIRE ($23.05)

Al 59. Pz. Giuseppe Verdi 59 (opposite the Teatro Massimo, near the Politeama). ☎ **091/45-42-37.** Main dishes 9,000L–25,000L ($5.90–$16.45). Pizza 8,000L–10,000L ($5.25–$6.55). AE, MC, V. Dinner only, Thurs–Tues 7pm–1am. ITALIAN.

Al 59 is very popular for its cooking, more trendy Italian than strictly Sicilian, and its shaded terrace in the heart of town. Its very popular special is green ravioli with artichoke sauce. Otherwise any vegetable sauce will be interesting. The pizza is excellent.

Trattoria Primavera. Pz. Bologni 4 (near the Duomo). ☎ **091/32-94-08.** Reservations required, a few days in advance if possible. Main dishes 7,000L–25,000L ($4.60–$16.45). V. Wed–Mon 12:30–3:30pm and 7pm–midnight. SICILIAN.

If menus in Italian or Sicilian are confusing, here's a good alternative. Four-language menus are available, but the place maintains good local food despite the tourist influx. The *New York Times* liked it, assuring them a perpetual reservation list. The pasta with squid ink and pasta trapanese are good, the latter a cold sauce of tomatoes, basil, and garlic—just the ticket for Palermo's *afa*, when everyone melts. Tables on the piazza go quickly.

Trattoria Stella or Hotel Patria. V. Allora 104 (near the Regional Gallery in Palazzo Abatellis). ☎ **091/31-48-06** or 091/61-61-136. Reserve in advance, especially at night, for an outside table. Main dishes 8,000L–24,000L ($5.25–$15.80). MC, V. Mon–Sat 12:30–3pm and 7–10pm. SICILIAN.

In an open, somewhat dilapidated, once-hotel courtyard complete with palm tree, this is the place for summer nights. Fish and meats are grilled outside, a rare city treat. To keep in a tight budget range, you might try a grill and a salad. Try the fettuccine al macco, with cream of fava beans with wild fennel. The clientele will probably be interesting, made up mainly of Palermo's lawyers, writers, and artists. The neighborhood requires attention to your pocketbook, and you might want to go at midday first, although that caution still applies.

WORTH A SPLURGE

A Cuccagna. V. Principe Granatelli 21/a (near the Grand Hotel d. Palme and the Politeama). ☎ **091/58-72-67.** Reservations essential. Main courses 9,000L–25,000L ($5.90–$16.45). AE, MC, V. Oct–May Sat–Thurs 12:30–3:30pm and 7:30–11pm, June–Sept daily. Closed Aug. 14–31. ITALIAN.

Bright, crisp, and attractive Cuccagna is becoming Palermo's "in" favorite for seafood. Reasonably priced prix-fixe menus are sometimes available. Smoked swordfish, fish carpaccio, and such fare are elegantly served. The long antipasto table is always freshly prepared. Sicilian ceramics here and there make up the simple, comfortable, but sophisticated decor. The more expensive hotels often recommend this restaurant to guests in search of a good meal in a chic setting.

Charleston. Pz. Ungheria 30. ☎ **091/32-13-66.** Fax 091/32-13-47. Reservations essential. Jacket and tie required. Main courses 12,000L–35,000L ($7.90–$23.05). AE, MC, V. Mon–Sat. 1–3pm and 8–11pm. Closed Aug 5–25, when it opens at the beach in Mondello, a local beach (see below). Bus 3 or 24. SICILIAN.

Come here for the atmosphere of warm elegance. Upholstered chairs, banquettes, and large tables add to the gaslight comfort, which is not always a factor in good restaurants these days. Although the food is not the best in town anymore, the atmosphere and comfort are worth the extra cost. The same four people have managed the restaurant for about 25 years. If you're feeling adventurous, ask Maitre d' Hassan (one of the four) to order for you. Fresh fish, including lobster, is the thing to have. Also try their caponata (eggplant appetizer). Partake of the excellent wine list and desserts, since you've decided to splurge. Plan on spending 70,000L to 100,000L ($46.05 to $65.80) for a complete meal. In summer the restaurant moves to a seaside pavilion on Viale Regina Elena in nearby Mondello (☎ **091/45-01-71**).

PALERMO AFTER DARK

Palermo may seem wild, but after dark you have to make your own fun for the most part. The area around Via Principe di Belmonte near the Politeama is now a pedestrian mall with outdoor cafes and bars. Some Palermitani go to the lovely hotel

Villa Igiea, to the north of town, where a pretty terrace by the sea and an exotic tropical garden are conducive to late-night drinks. The **Jolly Hotel's bar** (Foro Italico 22) can be fun, and offers wide easy chairs to collapse in after the Sicilian sunset. Check the local papers and the tourist office for current musical events.

Mondello, $7^1/_2$ miles from Palermo to the east along the shore, is a favorite place for dinner in summer at one of the seafood trattorias or stalls along the beach. Late at night everyone has an ice cream in the main piazza at the Antico Chiosco, where there is a flavor for every mood, or you can have a drink outside. Bus 14 or 15 along Via Maqueda or Viale della Liberta, or bus 6 (summer only) are Mondello-bound.

If you've got disco in your soul, the **Villa Boscogrande,** where part of *The Leopard* was filmed, is the place (V. Tommaso Natale 91 ☎ **091/24-11-79**). Take bus 806.

If you decide to stay in Mondello, get a list of rooms to let from the tourist office in Palermo, or ask around, or ask at the newsstand in the square. Less-expensive beach communities stretch out along the coast at Sferracavallo and Isola delle Femmine, which also have campsites.

A SIDE TRIP TO MONREALE

The **Duomo** in Monreale is a popular day-trip attraction. During the 12th century a rivalry grew between King William II and his Palermo archbishop, an Englishman called Walter of the Mill. While William created Monreale, Walter added to Palermo's cathedral treasures.

The greatest part of the cathedral, the powerful mosaics, were executed by Greek and Byzantine craftsmen over a 10-year period. They are the most complete cycle of mosaics in the Byzantine tradition, and depict episodes from the Old and New Testaments. The majestic figure of Christ Pantocrator dominates the central apse. The lovely cloister is intact, and the capitals of its columns are finely carved, each different from the others. On one, near the southern corner, King William presents the cathedral to the Virgin Mary. It's open daily from 8am to 12:15pm and 3:30 to 6:15pm. Admission to the cloister is 2,000L ($1.30) and to the roof, for a panoramic view of Palermo, 2,000L ($1.30). Bus 389 from Palermo's Piazza Independenza will bring you here. The **tourist office** stands to the left of the church ☎ **091/65-64-270.** A number of fast-food places ring the cathedral's piazza.

ENROUTE FROM PALERMO TO ERICE
SEGESTA

Forty-one miles southwest of Palermo stands one of the most evocative of **Greek temples**. Its plain Doric form, on a hill amid fields of flowers and the 5th-century B.C. ruins of this ancient city give Segesta a special allure. Ancient Greece, of which Sicily was a part, is all around you in this lonely site, with the distant panorama of mountains and sea that Greeks always sought for their temples. It's a place to be in love or take a book and read the poets, or just be. In summer, classical plays are produced in the amphitheater. Check with the Palermo tourist office for dates and schedules. If you're driving, take autostrada A29 west from Palermo. There is also a daily train from Palermo that makes the $1^1/_2$-hour trip at a cost of 8,400L ($7).

SCOPELLO AND SAN VITO LO CAPO

The combination of mountains, grottoes, and seacoast make the peninsula west of Palermo one of Sicily's best and few remaining natural seacoast areas. If time permits, stop for a few days at Scopello, just northwest of Castellamare del Golfo (developed for Sicilian family holidays). Scopello is a good spot for entering the spectacular nature preserve called Lo Zingaro. Remember that this area is packed to overflowing with Sicilian and European tourists in August and many summer weekends. You can get there by bus from Palermo; **Companie Russo,** Cor. Garibaldi 55 (☎ 0924/31-364) runs three per day. The trip takes 3 hours and costs 11,400L ($7.50). Drivers can follow route A29 from Palermo to Castellamare del Golfo, then state road 113 north. From Segesta take E933 to Castellamare, and then north on state road 113 to the tip of the cape.

The **Tranchina** in Scopello (V. Armando Diaz 7, ☎ 0924/54-10-99) is an excellent place for rooms with private baths and for meals. The Sicilian-Japanese couple who run it have created a treasure, open all year. In summer, doubles run from 69,000L to 75,000L ($45.40 to $49.35) a night with breakfast or 90,000L to 95,000L ($59.20 to $62.50), including meals.

Seaside camping is worth investigating in the area. **Camping Ciauli** (☎ 0924/39-049) and Camping Baia di Guidaloca (☎ 0924/54-12-62) are good possibilities. The latter is more expensive but rates four stars in the camping listings. It's a mini-resort and fills up in season.

At San Vito lo Capo, beaches and beach life are pursued. If you'd like to stay, try the **Miraspiaggia** (V. Lungomare 40 ☎ 0924/97-23-55). Prices are similar to the Trancchina, above. The **Ocean View** (V. Arimondi 21 ☎ 0924/97-26-13) has very-basic rooms for singles only and charges about 40,000L ($26.30) per room with bath. San Vito is also ice-cream land where long seaside terraces let you enjoy a languid gelato.

3 Erice

93km (58 miles) from Palermo

Up above the clouds, literally, Erice is one of Sicily's most enchanting spots. It rises more than 2,300 feet at the summit, where the ancient cult of Astarte, also known as Aphrodite, or Venus (fertility and its spinoffs were the themes) had practices that would raise eyebrows even today. The ancients thought so, too, and if you could fly over the city you'd see that it was created in a triangle form, believed to be one of the most powerful forms for attracting mystic forces. Two sides of the triangle are walls, the other the cliff edge.

Carthaginians, Romans, and Arabs found the town's easy defenses worth fighting for, and then the Normans came and settled in during the late 11th century. Much of the present town was created during the 14th century, however, under the Spanish. The Spanish-style grillwork, interior courtyards, and tiles give the town its charm.

To walk these sometimes steep cobblestone streets, slippery when wet, you'll need nonskid soles. You can walk around town, with a break for coffee and Erice's famous almond pastry, in about half a day.

ESSENTIALS

GETTING THERE By Bus In Palermo, the Segesta line has frequent service (about every half hour) from its terminal near the train station, or its stop to the left of the Politeama theater, to the seedy but endearing port city of Trapani. Travel time is about 1³/₄ hours and the cost is 11,000L ($7.25). Call **091/62-15-250** for schedules. From Trapani, 12 buses a day leave for Erice from Piazza Montalto, a few blocks from where the Palermo bus lets you off. The trip takes about an hour and costs 2,500L ($20.85). If you go only for the day, remember that on Sunday the last bus to back Trapani leaves at 7:15pm and on weekdays at 10:15pm. Don't take the 1:30pm—it will be packed with schoolchildren and the very circuitous route up the mountain makes a seat necessary.

By Car   From Palermo, take the A29 to Trapani and backtrack out the S187 to the turn-off for Erice at Valderice, just before the mountain.

VISITOR INFORMATION   The **AAST office** is located at V. Popoli 11, near the bus stop (☎ **0923/86-93-88**). Posted hours are complicated and rarely accurate. Call or walk by mornings or after 4pm. They're open Sunday mornings only in summer.

WHAT TO SEE & DO

The Temple of Venus. Vle. Conte Pepoli (from the entrance, follow this viale along the wall to the western far corner). Free admission. Daily 8am–sunset.

Phoenician sailors knew the channel between Tunisia and Sicily well, and they use Mount Eryx as a landmark and also as an indication of what mood the channel's protectress goddess was in: blue was happy and mists meant trouble. The most ancient tribes fortified Erice during the seventh century, and they worshipped nature and the earth goddess.

A lonely altar stretching toward heaven was the way to worship this Venus, they decided. The rituals here became legendary; they soon became a magnet for international pilgrimages. Doves were sacred, and they were bred in the sanctuary and flew off to other Mediterranean posts and returned in nine days, a red dove (Astarte) leading the flock. The Greeks and then the Romans loved all this, and the cult grew into almost a state religion, attracting government officials, as the Delphi Sibyl did. After the Romans, however, little attention was paid to the goddess, and she was heard from no more. Only the base of the temple remains, at the northeast part of the site, which also includes the Norman castle.

The Norman Castle. Vle. Conte Pepoli (at the site of the Temple of Venus).

Ghibelline merlons stand like angel wings on top of the entrance. A moat outside and a trapdoor inside even today give the castle a fortress feeling. The Well of Venus, at the edge of the castle keep was, if you believe the guides, where the Astartean orgies reached their height; virgins were cast down, after losing that status. A feminist version says that sailors were cast down, when the goddess tired of them. Worship of the Venus Eryx, or Astarte, was common throughout the Mediterranean, and her festivals and orgies sometimes led to self-castration or prostitution. Take a stroll in the adjoining Balio Gardens and cool off afterward.

Museo Comunale Cordici. Pz. Umberto I. **0923/86-69-258.** Admission 2,000L ($1.30). Mon–Sat 8:30 am–1:30pm.

If you think that every sculptor in Sicily is named Gagini, you're partly right. It was quite a large, talented family. Here you'll find a superb *Annunciation* (1525) by Antonello Gagini who, along with Domenico Gagini, was one of the most prolific.

WHERE TO STAY

Enchantment is usually expensive in Erice. Except for those mentioned below, most accommodations are out of budget range. **Affitacamere Italia** (V. Palma 7, 91016 Erice, ☎ **0923/86-91-85**) or the tourist office may find you a room to rent, as an alternative.

You can always save money by visiting Erice on a day trip from Palermo, or by staying in Trapani, on the shore below, or in the pretty beach resort of San Vito lo Capo to the north.

✪ **Casa del Clero.** V. Nunzio Nasi, 91016 Erice (near the Church of San Giovanni). ☎ **0923/ 86-91-71.** 57 rms, 28 with bath. 60,000L ($39.50) per person; 85,000L ($55.90) half pension; 105,000L ($69.10) full pension. 10,000L ($6.60) per person extra for heat in winter. No credit cards.

For simplicity, tranquillity, and peace, this is the place. The rooms are simple, as befits the nuns who lived here, with an occasional Della Robbia ceramic Madonna to recall the convent past. All front rooms have small terraces and open to a sea view of the cape—one of the loveliest views in Italy. The other side of the hotel looks on a pretty garden. The public rooms are exquisite, decorated stylishly with antiques, a lemon tree, and large picture windows that look to the gardens and sea. A small pine forest out front freshens the air. Meals are simple and made with their home-grown products, including wine, as far as possible. The casa is under the auspices of the Catholic Church, but run by Mission X (no, called Mission X officially to indicate this unusual group, mainly ex-addicts, now essentially monastic), a group of mainly young people who have turned their lives around. Signor Paolo and Signora Elga, the managers, both speak English. Religious groups on pilgrimage are often here, so reserve well in advance. Let them know if you need help with luggage from the bus station or information about parking.

Casa San Cataldo. V. Sales 23, 91016 Erice. ☎ **0923/86-92-97.** 57 rms, 25 with bath. 60,000L ($39.50) per person; 85,000L ($55.90) half-pension; 105,000L ($69.10) full-pension. 10,000L ($6.60) per person extra for heat in winter. No credit cards.

Across the street and up the hill from the Casa Clero, the genial management is the same, and the rooms are similar. It lacks the spectacular view, but has good views of the garden and town. Museum-quality sculpture decorates some of the public spaces.

Ermione. V. Pintera Comunale 43. ☎ **0923/86-93-77.** Fax 86-92-42. 43 rms, all with bath. TEL. Doubles 95,000L–180,000L ($62.50–$118.40). AE, MC, V. Tell bus driver where you're going. He'll let you off along the road, before reaching the Erice gate. Call hotel for pickup, as it is quite a walk.

This hotel endeared itself to me when a young horse was attempting to enter through the main door as I was trying to exit. An employee ran to shoo him out saying, "Oh, people feed them sugar and they come all the time." Another horse, possibly the mother, was waiting outside. The Ermione is bizarre in appearance, multicolored and looking precarious, along a cliff edge at the end of a long road outside the town walls. Inside, rooms are simple and fairly large, many terraces are wide, with views of Erice, and the dining room is very good. Rooms facing away from the town often have terraces with fine views. Some front rooms however, look toward Erice's power antenna. Ask for a room at the back, to be sure. In a town of quaint hotels, this one is not quaint and still has some less expensive rooms. The clientele is often Italian and often groups attending a conference at the nuclear-energy institute in Erice. There is a shuttle bus to the town.

WHERE TO DINE

Inexpensive in Erice means a slice of pizza at a bar. Take a half-pension at a hotel or go to Trapani and have a good, inexpensive, air-conditioned meal there at the **Trattoria del Porto da Felice,** V. Ammiraglio Stati 45 (☎ **0923/54-78-22).** A full meal will cost about 25,000L ($16.45), and they're closed Mondays and Christmas week. You can also sit outside and watch the port life.

✪ Il Cortile di Venere. V. Sales 31 (near Pz. San Cataldo). ☎ **0923/86-93-62.** Reservations required. Main courses 18,000L–25,000L ($11.85–$16.45). Thurs–Tues 12:30–3pm and 7–10:30pm. AE, MC, V. TRAPANI REGIONAL.

This is probably Erice's most popular restaurant because of its romantic courtyard decor, good service, and carefully presented menu. The "courtyard of Venus" is tree-shaded and surrounded by 17th-century buildings; in winter the fireplace is cheerful. The food is equally suggestive: ravioli stuffed with lobster, bucatini with tuna bottarga (caviar), swordfish rolled and stuffed with spices, and steaks grilled over an open flame. Figs are the dessert, then indulge in some almond sweets. Go and fall in love.

La Pentolaccia. V. Guarnotti 17 (near bus stop). ☎ **0923/86-90-99.** Reservations suggested. Main courses 12,000L–16,000L ($8.55–$10.50). Sat–Thurs 12:30–3pm and 7–11pm. AE, MC, V. MEDITERRANEAN.

They offer couscous one night a week, but usually serve more traditional fare in this atmospheric former monastery, in keeping with Erice's past as a bishopric. It's cozy in winter and cool in summer. Locals come here for lunch in droves. Enjoying a meal of sausage and polenta or a grilled fish here in the medieval-inn atmosphere gives you energy to find your hotel again through Erice's almost-constant mists.

SIDE TRIPS TO THE ENGADI ISLANDS

Several ferries a day leave Trapani for all the islands (**Siremar** in Trapani ☎ **0923/ 54-05-15**). In summer the faster **hydrofoil** has frequent service (☎ **0923/27-780**) to Favignana. Schedules are not always reliable.

Favignana is the largest of the islands and local people often head out there for a swim, to stretch out uncomfortably on the rocks on summer weekends.

Levanzo is a green island of gentle slopes, few people, three restaurants at last count, and two cafes. The man to know on the island is one Signore Giuseppe Castiglione (V. Calvario 11, above the marina; ☎ **0923/92-17-04**). He will meet your boat and take you to the cave (on his property) where 6,000-year-old Paleolithic drawings of animals and abstract designs have been discovered. He charges 15,000L ($9.85) per person, less at group rate, to drive there (several hours) and then walk to the cave. The trip from Trapani takes 20 minutes and costs 9,200L ($6.05).

Take your hiking shoes to **Marettimo.** Its mountains (Monte Falcone reaches almost 2,100 feet), pines, and rocky coves, with some Roman ruins and a castle thrown in, will speak to the nature lover.

EN ROUTE TO AGRIGENTO
SELINUTE

The Greek city of **Selinus,** founded in the 7th century B.C., reached its peak in the 5th century B.C. Its enemies were Segesta to the north and the Carthaginians to the south. Strife and earthquakes repeatedly destroyed the city, with the final calamity hitting the city in about the 13th century—the exact date of the final quake is unknown.

Selinute is 55 miles southeast of Trapani. If you're driving, take route 115 from Trapani to Castelvetrano, then follow signs to Selinute or Marinella. If you are not easily discouraged, you may want to go there by bus. There are many buses each hour from Trapani to Castelvetrano, costing about 4,000L ($2.65). When you arrive, ask when the next bus is leaving for Selinute; there are about five a day, but the schedules in this part of Sicily are not reliable. The trip should cost about 1,700L ($1.10) for a 20-minute ride.

Maps available at the entrance gate will lead you about the site. The **Acropolis** was restored to its present condition by archaeologists. **Temple G,** one of the largest in Greek Sicily, was left half-finished when the slaves erecting it sighted Carthaginian ships approaching. In the nearby **quarry of Cusa** you can see the beginnings of columns that were in the process of being hollowed out from the stone and now lie in the disarray in which they were left when the war alert began. Just across the river to the west, you can see a sanctuary devoted to Demeter (Malophoros) where more than 12,000 votive objects have been recovered.

Selinunte's fishing village/beach resort, Marinella, is a good place to relax after temple-hopping. It's about a mile from the site. Restaurants are plentiful. The **Lido Azurro,** V. Marco Polo 98, at its salty spot has windows overlooking the sea. Good grilled fish will cost about 35,000L ($23) for a full meal. Bars at the harbor have panini (sandwiches). In the morning fishermen eat Sicilian cornetti (croissants) and brioche, warm and stuffed with lemon cream to keep the sea chills away.

4 Agrigento

129km (80 miles) S of Palermo

Agrigento was once one of Greece's fairest cities. The temple area will give you a taste of it, but tourism and manufacturing in the area (cement mixers own the southern coast) along the roads detract a bit. By night the temples are spectacularly floodlit, so plan to stay over at least one night.

In 581 B.C. colonists from nearby Gela and from Rhodes and Crete began not only to set up a trading port, but also to make plans for a major Greek capital. Tyrannical rulers made sure of it and roasted the opposition (literally). Several prominent Greek scientists and philosophers, such as Empedocles, were born in Agrigento, and contributed basic knowledge to their fields. Sanctuaries to Greek Chthonic (Underworld) deities, and to Demeter and Persephone were built to encourage underwater streams for irrigation and healthy crops. Then wars and earthquakes took their toll. Fortunately many temples were left in good condition and their position on the hill is superb.

ESSENTIALS

GETTING THERE   By Train   There is frequent service from Palermo, seven trains a day; the two-hour trip costs 11,000L ($7.25). If you are coming from Messina, connect through Enna in central Sicily, but it is more convenient to take the bus.

By Bus   There is good bus service from Sciacca, Palermo, and Trapani. From Palermo, Autoservizi Cuffaro (☎ **091/91-63-49**) sends six buses a day from Piazza Balsama near the train station, a 2¼-hour ride for 10,200L ($6.70).

From Trapani, Autoservizi Lumia (☎ **0922/20-414**) runs four buses a day from Piazza Garibaldi, a four-hour ride costing 15,200L ($10).

By Car   From Sciacca, take the E931. From Palermo, take the S121 to the S189.

VISITOR INFORMATION   The **AAST office** is at V. Empedocle 73 (☎ **0922/ 20-391**). They don't speak English very well, but they do have maps and brochures.

WHAT TO SEE & DO

✪ **The Valley of the Temples.** V. d. Templi (entrance on S. Panoramica). Free admission. Bus: 1, 2, 3, or 4 from the train station.

The site is usually open, and the temples are illuminated at night, but since this is Sicily, check with the tourist office first if you are going especially to see them lighted. Early morning and dusk are the most attractive daytimes, out of the strongest sun (photographers prefer dusk). From the entrance on the Strada Panoramica, you might cross the street to view the temples on the hill first. Get a map or study the diagram at the entrance. The Temple of Hercules (Ercole), reached through a garde, is the oldest temple of the Greek era here. Built about 520 B.C., it still shows searing from fires set by Carthaginian invaders.

The ✪ **Temple of Concordia,** about halfway up the hill, is exquisite in its simple Doric form, softened in early spring when the almond trees are in flower. This is one of the world's best-preserved Greek temples, a state owed to its having been converted into a Christian church during the 6th century. At that time the columns were walled in and the cella (altar) was removed for a Christian one. Behind the temple stands the remains of the sacrificial altar. In early spring, a dance festival is held on these grounds, attracting an international cast.

The view from the **Temple of Juno** (Giunone) makes the climb, past Byzantine tomb recesses, worth it. The columns originally numbered 34, and about 25 still stand after the last (ancient) earthquake. Carthaginian fires turned part of the walls a rosy red.

Retracing your steps and crossing the street, you'll come to the **Temple of Jupiter** (Giove Olimpico). Here the Sleeping Giant lies. He's a copy of the 38 telemones, decorative columns that once held up this massive structure (one of the largest in the world) dedicated to the Olympian Zeus. The National Museum down the road has the real thing (see below).

The round altars in this area were used for Chthonic rituals, about which little is known.

Museo Nazionale Archeologico. Contrada San Nicola. ☎ **0922/49-726.** Free admission. Tues–Sat 9am–1:30pm and 3–5pm, Sun 9am–12:30pm.

Near the road that leads up to the main city, in an area called the Quartiere Ellenistico-Romano near the church of San Nicola, you'll find a well-ordered museum, whose star, of course, is the Telemone (Gigante) from the Temple of Jupiter and a model of the temple with these massive columns in place. Look also for the child's sarcophagus that shows his transit in stages into the next world.

Casa di Pirandello. Frazione Kaos. ☎ **0922/48-326.** Free admission. Open Mon–Fri 9am–1 hour before sunset. Sat–Sun 9am–1pm. Bus: 11 from Pz. Marconi in Agrigento.

Pirandello, like many writers, was loathed by his neighbors because of the mean face he gave his homeland in his short stories. But then came a Nobel Prize in Literature in 1934, and all was forgiven. You can visit his nicely placed house, full of interesting photographs and memorabilia, and even the tree he wrote about: "One night in June I dropped down like a firefly beneath a huge pine tree in the garden . . ." He died in 1936, and is best known in the United States for his play, *Six Characters in Search of an Author.*

WHERE TO STAY

Note: Take only rooms with bath at the first two hotels. Shared bathrooms are inadequate or worse.

Bella Napoli. Pz. Lena 6, 92100 Agrigento (off V. Bac Bac). ☎/fax **0922/20-435.** 41 rms, 25 with bath. TEL. 25,000L ($16.45) single without bath, 40,000L ($26.30) single with bath; 55,000L ($36.20) double without bath, 70,000L ($46.05) double with bath. AE.

A friendly owner, Mario, and a rooftop terrace make this a pleasant place. Rooms are adequate to very nice and bright. Of the two hotels, the Napoli is the more personal and they try harder to please the public.

Concordia. Pz. San Francesco 13, 92100 Agrigento (off V. Atenea, the main street). ☎ **0922/59-62-66.** 20 rms, 22 with bath. TV, TEL. 33,000L ($21.70) single without bath, 47,000L ($30.92) single with bath; 52,000L ($34.20) double without bath, 82,000L ($53.95) double with bath. Rates include breakfast. No credit cards.

Reserve early for there are very few hotels at these prices here, and so the Concordia is usually full (it wouldn't be in a less desperate setting). The rooms are simple, and the management is friendly. An advantage is that you can have meals on a half-pension basis in the adjoining trattoria La Forchetta (see below). Avoid the basement rooms, and ask for a view (a bit of distant sea). Rooms with bath are the only way to go. Or you'll end up taking a less-than-happy shower in the dingy basement.

WORTH A SPLURGE

Villa Athena. V. d. Templi, 92100 Agrigento. ☎ **0922/59-62-88.** Fax 0922/40-21-80. 40 rms, all with bath. A/C TV TEL. 170,000L single ($111.85); 250,000 double ($164.45). AE, MC, V.

This 18th-century villa is set in the Valley of the Temples and has most of the luxuries, including a swimming pool and bar. It's comfortable and relaxed, and most rooms are modern. More expensive rooms have wonderful terraces that look over the gardens toward the temples. The restaurant is also quite good. The hotel's restaurant, in its own building, serves some Sicilian food (swordfish is ubiquitous in Sicily) and a more international menu because of the vast numbers of tourists who pass through. It is quite good, although not the most inventive. Service is generally friendly, with generations of local people working here.

WHERE TO DINE

The site of Agrigento has a built-in tourist lure, and prices show it. You might try the self-service food at the Tavola Calda, at V. Pirandello 1, near Pz. Aldo Moro. The kitchen opens early, and the Sicilian food here is very good, and so is the pizza. Sicilian workers come for lunch and finish up everything, so don't be tardy.

La Forchetta. Pz. San Francesco 11. ☎ **0922/59-62-66.** Reservations not required. Main courses 8,000L–15,000L ($5.25–$9.85). Menu turistico 20,000L ($13.10). Mon–Sat 12:30–3pm and 8–11pm. No credit cards. AGRIGENTO REGIONAL.

A family operation, and usually busy, thanks to the Concordia hotel next door (if you're staying there for more than a night, you can work out a half-pension plan). It's small and wood-paneled, and the diners often compare travel mishaps. There's always a special of the day, such as a mixed fry of fish or spaghetti alla Norma (in an eggplant and cheese sauce).

Le Caprice. S. Panoramica d. Templi 51. ☎ **0922/26-469.** Main courses 11,000L–20,000L ($7.25–$13.16). Sat–Thurs 12:30–3pm and 8–11pm. Closed July 1–15. Bus 9. SICILIAN.

Seafood again? Yes, but you haven't tried theirs. The menu includes other good things as well. Stuffed swordfish and stuffed veal rolls are both good. Sicilians come up with interesting mixtures for their breadcrumb stuffings. This is a popular place, and one of the best in Agrigento. Watch what you're ordering, as the bill can mount up quickly.

EN ROUTE TO SIRACUSA

The Roman villa at Piazza Armerina is a beauty, or at least the oceans of mosaics are. Romans really enjoyed their baths, and decorated them with provocative women and wild beasts very often. This is not exactly on the main route from Agrigento to Siracusa, but makes an interesting and worthwhile detour. If driving, continue eastward along S115 (E931) to Gela, and turn up S117 to Piazza Armerina. Then take S124 to Siracusa. By bus you'll have to go to Caltagirone (a ceramics capital with a long ceramic stairway) and change for Casale. Three buses a day make the hour-long trip, costing 7,200L ($4.75) each way, to Caltagirone. Casale is about a half-hour beyond; from Piazza Municipio it costs 3,000L ($1.95).

5 Siracusa

56km (35 miles) SE of Catania

Siracusa (Syracuse) was once a thriving metropolis of ancient Greece. Its naturally protected harbor and adjoining hills made it easy to defend, and it occupied an ideal area for trade between the eastern and western Mediterranean. But the Greeks weren't the first to realize this. Traces of human life in this part of southeast Sicily have been recorded as far back as the upper Paleolithic, about 18,000 B.C.

In 734 B.C. settlers from Corinth arrived to create a new western Greece. Always sensitive to natural beauty, the Greeks found that here in abundance, especially in the harbor setting and the island of Ortygia, across a narrow canal. In the Archeological Park, the Greek (and Roman) amphitheaters, altars, and even the caves where slaves (war prisoners) quarried building stone, have all been preserved. Siracusa's fine museum records the city's history during much of this time.

About 415 B.C. the city's quarrels with Athens, where an overseas rival to its glory was not appreciated, led to war. Under the Tyrant Dionysius (tyrant was a political term close to "czar," and only later generalized to mean political bully"), the city grew and developed a powerful navy. Read Thucydides's accounts of these times in *The Peloponnesian War.*

The city's history is similar to that of the island as a whole: Carthaginians from present-day Tunisia, not far offshore, were the next enemy, and after the Punic Wars, Rome arrived. Later, during the 9th century A.D., Arabs sacked the city, then the Normans came on the scene under Roger II, attempting to "unify" Sicily. The last rulers were the Spanish Bourbons. Initially, their rule was enlightened, but during the 19th century it became abusive; the absentee-viceroy system produced gross inequalities here as it did in South America. Finally, Garibaldi and his troops made Sicily part of the new Italian nation.

ESSENTIALS

GETTING THERE   By Train   Usually you must change trains in Catania for Siracusa. To Catania from Messina, trains run every hour (eight per day); fare is 7,500L ($4.95). From Palermo five trains per day make the four-hour trip, which costs 17,800L ($11.70). From Agrigento, change trains for Catania at Caltanisetta or Enna; there are four trains per day, and the trip takes about three hours in all; the fare is 9,400L ($6.20). Catania's train station is at Via Papa Giovanni XXIII (☎ 095/53-16-25). There are about 18 trains a day to Siracusa, a 1³/₄-hour trip, costing 6,700L ($4.40) one-way.

By Bus   Buses from Palermo are frequent: Autoservizi Cuffaro (☎ 091/91-63-49) has six buses a day; the trip takes 2¹/₄ hours, and the cost is 10,200L ($6.75). From Messina SAIS runs eight buses per day (this is also the Taormina bus, although no one will tell you), taking 1¹/₂ hours, and costing 9,500L ($6.25). SAIS also has five buses per day) from Agrigento, a 2¹/₂-hour trip for 16,000L ($10.55). From Piazza Armerina take the bus to Caltagirone, where buses run five times per day, a one-hour trip costing 7,000L ($4.50).

Catania's SAIS bus station, when it rains, is two long marshy streets where buses line up, and drivers turn their direction card at the last minute, leaving travelers (including Catanese) to guess which one they want. AST buses (☎ 095/28-12-80) make the 1¹/₂-hour trip from Catania 13 times a day, fewer on Sunday, from V. Luigi Sturzo 220, left of the train station. Tickets cost 6,100L ($4). SAIS is to the right of the station on V. d'Amico 181 (☎ 095/53-61-68). Tickets are 6,000L ($4).

By Car   From Agrigento, state road 115 leads to Siracusa, as does highway E45. From Piazza Armerina take state road 124 all the way east. From Palermo state road 121 east to Enna, then 192 to Catania, and south on 114. From Messina, highway E45 south leads to Catania and continues to Siracusa. *Note:* Do not drive into Catania; stay on the highway outside, even though it's a sea of oil refineries and other industry.

VISITOR INFORMATION The main **tourist office** on the mainland is at V. San Sebastiano 43 (☎ **0931/67-710**). On Ortigia, it's on Via Maestranza (☎ **0931/ 65-201**), near Piazza Archimede.

WHAT TO SEE & DO

Archeological Park. Vle. Augusto. ☎ **0931/66-206.** Admission 2,000L ($1.35). June–Sept daily 9am–6pm, Oct–May daily 9am–4pm. Bus: 1, 4, 5, 8, or 10, or walk to the end of Cor. Gelone.

The Teatro Greco, or Greek Theater, is a site where playwrights such as Aeschylus and Euripides endured opening-night jitters during the 5th century B.C. It's beautifully situated amid wildflowers and olive trees, although the fine sea view is no more, thanks to the Romans, who obstructed it with a backdrop. The theater we see today is an expansion of an earlier one; it was completed between 238 and 215 B.C. and is one of the finest and largest preserved theaters in the world. Theater was extremely important to the ancient world, where the plays provided catharsis as well as entertainment. When the Romans came they added gladiatorial combat and killing wild beasts, changing the culture from Aeschylus to Rambo. Greek plays are performed here in early summer in even-numbered years; check with the tourist office.

The **Latomie del Paradiso** ("Caves of Paradise") are not quite what these actually were. They were really quarries where slaves spent much of their time extracting stone with rather primitive tools. The paradise is on the outside, where lush tropical vegetation—lemon and orange trees, oleanders, and palms—create an oasis. The enormous cavern called the **Orecchio di Dionisio** (Ear of Dionysius) was so named because the Tyrant Dionysius supposedly listened from above to slave conversations, transmitted perfectly because of the excellent acoustics. Call out or clap your hands and listen to the sound reverberate through the caverns. Other tales have Dionysius enjoying the acoustical qualities of the screams his tortured slaves emitted. Farther inside the cave you'll see the grotto where cordmakers plied their trade for centuries. Mary Renault's *The Mask of Apollo* will get you ready for this era.

The **Anfiteatro Romano,** or Roman amphitheater, is predictably large (154 yards at its widest), surpassed only by the Colosseum in Rome and the Arena of Verona. On the parapet on top you can still see the engraved names of box-seat holders. The large basin at the center is too small for aquatic sports and may have been used to drain the blood and gore from Rome's popular blood sports.

Catacombe di San Giovanni. Pz. San Giovanni (just off Vle. Teocriti heading east from the Archeological Park). ☎ **0931/67-955.** Admission 2,000L ($1.35). June–Sept daily 10am–noon and 3–6pm. Oct–May Thurs–Tues 10–noon. Bus: 1.

Saint Paul stopped on his way to Rome from Malta and delivered a sermon on a spot that is now in the catacombs of this church, where a modern altar marks the exact site (in the Cripta di San Marziano). Some early markings on stone, faded frescoes, and Latin inscriptions give a feel for the early church. The Byzantine church above was built during the 6th century and was once Siracusa's cathedral.

Museo Archeologico. Vle. Teocrito 66. ☎ **0931/46-40-22.** Admission 2,000 ($1.35). Tues–Sat 9am–1pm, Sun 9–12:30. Bus: 4, 5, and 12 from Ortygia.

Local history from neolithic pottery and Sikel jewelry through the Greek and Roman periods are carefully laid out here, and paths are color-coded throughout the museum. The most celebrated object is the sensual *Landolina Venus*, who is rising from the sea clutching her robe that covers very little. It's a Roman copy of a Greek original. Among the Hellenistic pieces, look for the *kouroi*—athletic young men—and some theatrical masks.

EXPLORING ORTYGIA

Ortygia is an island just offshore across a bridge—a place to wander through shadowy streets of Sicilian baroque palaces and to relax in an outdoor cafe near the waterfront or at the Piazza del Duomo. To get there, head down Corso Umberto and cross the bridge, or take bus no. 1, and get off at the bridge (ask for Or-*tee*-ja). The southeast of Sicily was almost flattened by an earthquake in 1693, and the rebuilding campaign attracted the finest architects and city planners to the area.

The excavation you see as you cross the bridge into Ortygia is the **Temple of Apollo** (6th century B.C.), which was once a great Doric temple. The window belonged to a Norman church that was erected on this spot.

Pass through Piazza Archimede, where a fountain depicts the nymph Arethusa as she is transformed into a spring (that spring can be seen at the Fonte Aretusa along the waterfront).

The Piazza del Duomo is beautiful at most hours, but baroque shadows are the most seductive in late afternoon or in night light. This site has been sacred since Sicily's first human settlements, and each new religion built its own shrine over that of the former. Columns from the Greek shrine to Athena have been incorporated into the present 17th-century **Duomo,** and a Norman font stands in the Baptistery. Noteworthy statuary of the saints by the Gagini clan, including Antonello Gagini's *Madonna of the Snow,* are worth investigating.

In the right corner of the piazza stands the 18th-century **Palazzo Benevantano del Bosco** that still houses the noble family. At the southern end of the piazza, the church of **Santa Lucia** (a Sicilian saint) is the focus of a procession in December, when the festival of light is celebrated. Santa Lucia's martyrdom took place in Siracusa near the Church of San Giovanni. Her eyes were put out; and she is often depicted carrying them on a plate. Beneath the church are 2nd-century catacombs, which may be inaccessible owing to a restoration project.

The piazza fills with Siracusans and tourists regularly. Lovers and artists, families with children, and cafe sitters make up the usual scene. Come back after supper for a coffee or drink.

Ortygia's **Museo Regionale d'Arte Mediovale e Moderna** is located in the Palazzo Bellomo at V. Capodieci 14 (☎ **0931/65-343**), and here you'll find a restored painting of the *Annunciation* by Antonello da Messina and Caravaggio's *Burial of Saint Lucy.* Admission is 2,000L ($1.35), and they're open Tuesday to Saturday from 9am to 1pm.

BEACHES

When the summer heat is on, go south to the sea beaches. The beach at Fontane Bianche, about 11 miles away, is one of the best, but nearby Arenella, about 5 miles off, attracts the locals. Buses service both beaches. Take bus 21 or 22 from the post office (cost is 700L/45¢).

WHERE TO STAY

Bellavista. V. Diodoro Sicolo 4, 96100 Siracusa. ☎ **0931/41-13-55.** Fax 00931/37-927. 49 rms, 37 with bath. A/C TV TEL. 54,000L ($35.50) single without bath, 85,000L ($55.90) single with bath; 78,000L ($51.30) double without bath, 140,000L ($92.10) double with bath. Rates include breakfast. AE, MC, V.

Because there are still some rooms without bath here it falls into the budget range. Try for a room with a sea-view balcony. This family-run place near the Archeological Park is by far the best of the budget group. A sun terrace lets you worship that Siracusa *sole.*

Bel Sit. V. Oglio 5, 96100 Siracusa. ☎ **0931/60-245.** 10 rms, 6 with bath. 35,000L ($23) single without bath, 40,000L ($26.30) single with bath; 45,000L ($29.60) double without bath, 55,000L ($36.20) double with bath. No credit cards.

La famiglia in Italian means "the family," and you're apt to meet many of them here, watching TV, playing games, and having coffee. Rooms are basic and okay, with simple furnishings and clean baths, and the neighborhood is fairly quiet even though it's near the station. The elevator is essential—the hotel's on the fifth floor.

Centrale. Cor. Umberto 141, 96100 Siracusa. ☎ **0931/60-528.** 14 rms, none with bath. 25,000L ($16.45) single; 40,000L double. No credit cards.

Modern and clean, this is a good-enough choice. Siracusa is in need of cheaper, attractive housing, but in the meantime, this will do. It's clean—no fancy fixtures, but at least the baths are kept clean. Not all rooms have luxuries—like windows. You won't want to move in permanently, but it'll do for a night.

Gran Bretagna. V. Savoia 21, 96100 Siracusa. ☎ **0931/68-765.** 12 rms, 6 with bath. 50,000L ($32.90) single without bath, 56,000L ($36.85) single with bath; 80,000L ($52.65) double without bath, 94,000L ($61.85) double with bath. Rates include breakfast. AE, MC, V.

The location, on the southern esplanade along the sea in Ortygia, is great. Many of the very simple rooms face the sea, and the restaurant is fairly good, but not particularly inexpensive. Management has had its ups and downs here, so rooms are sometimes well cared for, sometimes not. Art nouveau touches and green plants enliven the interior. Reservations are essential all summer. Only a few rooms have a private shower, and the hall showers are only passable. If you can reserve room 8 you'll get a terrific terrace, and room 7 has a frescoed ceiling.

HOSTELS & CAMPING

Ostello della Gioventu. V. Epipoli 45, 96100 Siracusa. ☎ **0931/71-11-18.** 18 rms. 20,000L ($13.10) per person. Rates include breakfast. Bus: 9, 10, and 11 from Pz. Pancali. Usually you need to be a member, but they are not always all that strict.

The hostel is located just outside of town (six miles), up on a ridge above the city near the Castle Euralio, from which weapons were lobbed in ancient times against invaders. The breezes are better here than in town and management is friendly. It's clean, easygoing, and there's a maximum of four beds per room. There's also a good pizzeria nearby.

Camping Fontane Bianche. Fontane Bianche. Vle. d. Lidi, 476 96100 Siracusa ☎ **0931/79-03-33** or 356. 6,500L ($4.25) per person; 10,000L ($6.60) tent rental; 5,000L ($3.30) sleeping bag rental. Bus: 21 or 22 from the post office in Siracusa (1/2 hour), or drive.

This is the best campground in the area, 13 miles from Siracusa, near the best beach. A grocery and restaurants are nearby, but for a better choice of foods, buy some groceries in Syracuse before you go.

WHERE TO DINE

If you want some great *gelato*, head for **Corrado Costanzo,** V. Silvio Spaventa 7–0 (☎ **0931/83-52-43**). His ice cream made from jasmine, rose, and tangerine is a Sicilian wonder. For more complete meals, here are a few suggestions.

Darsena. Rv. Garibaldi 6. ☎ **0931/66-104.** Reservations required. Main courses 12,000L–25,000L ($7.90–$16.45). AE, MC, V. Thurs–Tues 12:30–3pm and 7:30–11pm. SEAFOOD.

Another good Ortygia spot, the Darsena ("dock" in Arabic) is a large, many-windowed place that isn't quaint, but the food is good, and it's air-conditioned. Just the latter can be enough of a reason to come here on some summer days. As for their food, if it swims, scuttles, or just buries itself in the deep, the Darsena is apt to serve it. If you've never had ricci (sea urchins) try them here. You're in for a pleasant surprise. But watch for that *conto* mounting up.

Nonna Margherita. V. Cavour 12, Ortygia. No phone. Pizza from 6,000L ($3.95). No credit cards. Tues–Sun noon–3pm and 7:30–11pm. Often closed July and Aug. PIZZERIA.

One of the best pizzerias in these parts, this place is usually filled up. The wood-fired oven is certainly never quiet. Locals and tourists are elbow to elbow, while sizzling cheese dribbles and conversation flows with the beer or wine.

Spaghetteria do Scogghiu. V. Scina 11 (downhill from Pz. Archimede). No phone. Spaghetti courses from 6,000L ($3.95). No credit cards. Tues–Sat noon–3:30pm and 7:30–11pm. PASTA.

This is Ortygia's answer to inflation. They sport a full antipasto table and 20 varieties of pasta, from aglio e olio (garlic and oil) to tutto mare ("all the sea," with mussels, shrimp, and squid). The Russo brothers know how to make diners happy, and you get to watch them flip their pans.

WORTH A SPLURGE

Archimede. V. Gemmellaro 8, Ortygia. ☎ 0931/69-701. Reservations advised in summer and on weekends. Main courses 14,000L–25,000L ($9.20–$16.45). Mon–Sat 7:30–11pm and Sun 12:30–3:30pm. AE, MC, V. SEAFOOD.

Three large, attractive rooms with a somewhat formal touch (waiters in professional attire, flowers) make this a place for special evenings. Here you can have ricci (sea urchin) or lobster as a sauce with pasta. Cassata, that exotic blend of sweetened ricotta, delicately flavored with candied pumpkin, and enclosed in alternating squares of sponge cake and green-colored almond paste (to resemble the pistachio cream from which it was originally made) is a must for a sweet finale, and easy to share. Candied orange, cherries, and other flavors may be added.

SIDE TRIPS FROM SIRACUSA

If you're intrigued by baroque architecture, take a trip to **Noto,** 19 miles to the southwest. Here the art of the baroque is at its finest hour in Sicily. You may have to hurry to see it before its gone—the cathedral dome recently collapsed because money for restoration was tied up elsewhere. Perhaps the scandal that ensued (this was a page-one story throughout Italy) will have jolted the powers that be out of their *riposo.* To the west of the Duomo, a palazzo with wonderfully sculpted balconies will require your camera. (Unfortunately for visitors, much of Noto will soon be scaffolded as repairs are supposedly being made.)

In any case, have lunch at the **Trattoria del Carmine,** V. Ducezio 9 (☎ 0931/83-87-05), a tiny spot that sports a *New York Times* review. They have good pastas and rabbit in a lively vegetable sauce, sausage, and other good meat dishes. Nettini (Noto folk) and tourists blend comfortably here. Afterward the **Caffe Sicilia,** where Sicily's nobles once enjoyed their sweets, Cor. Vittorio Emanuele 125, will lure you with a cassata.

AST runs 13 buses per day from Siracusa's terminal, a 45-minute ride, costing 3,700L ($2.45).

6 Taormina

53km (33 miles) N of Catania, 250km (155 miles) E of Palermo

Sprawled languidly across the top of a cliff above the sea, this town of small palazzi with grillwork balconies dripping with flowers, massive clouds of purple bougainvillea, the coast below, and the snowy peak of Mt. Etna in the distance has been adored through the ages. The list of celebrities who have come here would keep a gossip columnist busy for years. Its position, far above the sea and reached by circuitous mountain roads, is about perfect, and the cars and buses that chug that road all summer and on spring and fall weekends know it. Unfortunately tourism has taken its toll, but has not completely spoiled the town. You simply have to work around it.

One magnificent Greek theater is the only place of historical interest. Apart from that, there is the beach down below, or you can take a day trip to Etna, hike in the hills, or make a stop at Castelmola and Forza d'Agro. If you feel ambitious, you can take a day trip to Messina, and even across the strait to Reggio di Calabria. Two statues of Greek warriors (*I Bronzi*) can be seen in Reggio's museum. On the other hand, you could just sit in the town's tropical garden and listen to the birdsongs half the afternoon.

ESSENTIALS

GETTING THERE   By Bus   Taormina can be reached by bus from Catania or Messina. SAIS buses leave from Catania at V. D'Amico 181 (☎ **095/53-61-68**), near the railroad station. There are 11 buses per day, and tickets cost 5,100L ($3.35). SAIS also maintains service from Messina at the train station, Pz. d. Repubblica 46 (☎ **090/77-19-14**). There are 13 per day, and the trip takes 1¹/₂ hours; tickets cost 5,100L ($3.35).

By Train   Trains stop at Naxos, at the foot of the Taormina "mountain." Unless you're going to stay in Naxos the bus from Catania or Messina is a better choice; by train you have to change to the bus in Naxos. From Messina there are 30 trains to Naxos daily; the trip takes 50 minutes and costs 4,200L ($2.75). From Catania there are 29 trains daily; the trip takes 45 minutes and costs 4,200L ($2.75). A stop on trains from Siracusa (13 trains daily, taking two hours, costing 13,499L/$8.90) can be arranged.

By Car   Autostrada A18 runs along the coast, passing Catania, Taormina (Naxos), and Messina.

VISITOR INFORMATION   There are **tourist information offices** on Largo Santa Caterina (☎ **0942/23-243**), Largo Corvaia (☎ **0942/23-243**), and Corso Umberto 144 (☎ **0942/23-751**).

WHAT TO SEE & DO

Taormina's major attraction is the **Greco-Roman amphitheater** on Via Teatro Greco (☎ **0942/23-220**). Sit at the center of the cavea for a perfect panorama where the theater walls part to a vision of the sea and Mt. Etna in the distance. Greeks knew where to place theaters. Built during the 3rd century B.C., it was rebuilt by the Romans about five centuries later. Because of exceptional acoustics it is often used for musical performances and during the film festival in late summer, so check with the tourist office. Admission is 2,000L ($1.30), but free for those under 18 or over 60. It's open daily from 9am to two hours before sunset.

You'll find yourself on the main street (Corso Umberto) much of the time. At one end, the tourist office is lodged in the lovely 11th- to 14th-century **Palazzo Corvaia.** In its main hall the Sicilian Parliament met in 1410 to choose a successor to the Aragonese king. The 17th-century **Church of Santa Caterina** is often open for quiet reflection, just down the corso. It contains several interesting works of art. In back of it are the remains of the Roman Odeon (theater). Apart from that, stroll through the town's streets, ending up at the exquisite Villa Comunale, a lovely and welltended (rare in Sicily) public garden.

Outdoor Activities

The beach at **Mazzaro** can be reached by funicular (tickets are 2,000L/$1.35 during the day; 2,500L/$1.70 after 7:30pm). You can also try the beaches at Naxos, 20 minutes downhill by bus (fare is 1,500L/$1). If you are a serious hiker, spend a day hiking in the **Alcantara Gorge** or on Mt. Etna (see below).

WHERE TO STAY

Taormina's hotels fill up rapidly in season. Check with your travel agent about independent packages in the larger tourist hotels in Naxos. However, Mazzaro and Naxos are both at sea level and have less exciting views than Taormina, a major reason for being in this area. Easter through mid-October is high season here.

Adele. V. Apollo Arcageta 16, 98039 Taormina. V. Off Pz. Sant Antonio at south end of town. ☎ **0942/23-352.** 16 rms, 9 with bath. 40,000L ($26.30) single without bath; 60,000 ($39.50) double without bath, 80,000L ($52.65) double with bath. Rates include breakfast.

At one end of town near restaurants, nightlife, and a supermarket, this pensione is clean but can be noisy. Guests are often the international young, going one better than backpacking. It's perfectly acceptable to drop your suitcase here, but there is little to charm you into sleeping late, or coming home early.

Columbia. V. Iallia Bassia 11, 98039 Taormina. ☎ **0942/53-287.** 10 rms, 2 with bath. 30,000L ($19.75) single without bath; 42,000 double ($27.65) without bath, 50,000L ($32.90) double with bath. Rates include breakfast. No credit cards.

Being near the public gardens is a plus here. You can hear the birdcalls and the air is apt to be cooler. The rooms are clean and average. The management is friendly and accommodating. Fresh flowers are often arranged in the halls. Many guests are repeat birdwatchers who like the location.

Cuscona. Cor. Umberto 238, 98039 Taormina. ☎ **0942/23-270.** 18 rms, 8 with bath. Summer 60,000L ($39.40) double without bath, 70,000L ($46.05) double with bath. Low season 50,000L ($32.90) double without bath, 60,000L ($39.40) double with bath. Rates include breakfast. No credit cards.

At the southern end of the corso (where the best views of Mt. Etna are), this hotel has the advantage of being in the middle of everything, but also has a downside, noise. Rooms are nothing special, but some have balconies opening on the garden of the Palazzo Duca San Stefano. The clientele is international and often young, and they are merry or noisy, depending on your viewpoint.

Grazia. V. Iallia Bassia 20, 98039 Taormina. ☎ **0942/24-776.** 8 rms, 4 with bath. 30,000L ($19.75) per person without bath, 35,000L ($23) per person with bath. No breakfast. No credit cards.

Here there's a terrace on the top floor, and guests can use the TV room. It's set on high, dramatically, in keeping with the Palermitano owner's passion for the opera—you may hear bits of arias now and then. A television room is provided for guests. It's very well cared for, and was completely remodeled a few years ago. The rooms are bright thanks to largish windows. It's near the steps to the Greek theater, not far from Piazza Vittorio Emanuele. Many French visitors seem to favor this pensione.

Pensione Diana. V. di Giovanni 6, 98039 Taormina (near Pz. Vittorio Emanuele). ☎ **0942/23-898.** 4 rms. 30,000L ($19.75) singles 40,000L ($26.30) double without bath. No credit cards.

The tiny Diana is run by Signora Diana, who makes sure that the very basic but comfortable rooms are in good condition. Ask for a sea view (over the rooftops). The pensione is located near Porta Messina, it's convenient, and you'll feel as if you have Sicilian relatives. Guests are usually young and international.

Villa Astoria. V. Luigi Pirandello 38, 98039 Taormina. ☎ **0942/23-943.** 8 rms, 3 with bath. Summer 54,000L ($35.50) doubles without bath, 65,000L ($42.75) doubles with bath. Low season 45,000L ($29.60) doubles without bath, 54,000L ($35.50) doubles with bath. Rates include breakfast. MC, V.

Trees shade the facade and keep the rooms fairly cool in summer. Rooms facing the sea have small balconies. Those on the street are very noisy. A tavola calda (hot-foods deli) with a terrace is on the ground floor. It's near the funicular to the beach and bus terminal. This part of town is getting very lively as new trattorie and pizzerie seem to be opening each year.

WORTH A SPLURGE

✪ **Villa Belvedere.** V Bagnoli Croce 79, 98039 Taormina. ☎ **0942/23-791.** Fax 0942/62-58-30. 47 rms, all with bath. A/C TEL. Summer: 144,000L ($94.75) single; 225,000L ($148) double. Low season: 80,000L ($52.65) single; 90,000L ($59.20) double. Rates include breakfast. MC, V. Closed Jan 10–Feb 20 and Nov 11–Dec 14.

This is one of the best choices in Taormina. Located near the public garden, the Belvedere is situated in its own terraced garden, often jasmine-scented. Many rooms have views of Etna; all have sea view. Some rooms come with TV and a minibar. Guests can enjoy the large sitting rooms, decorated with antiques and ship paintings, and also the lounge chairs and umbrellas on the wide terrace. The swimming pool, on one level of the garden, has a bar and serves snacks. Prices are the same with or without view; reserve well in advance.

✪ **Villa Fiorita.** V. Pirandello 39, 98039 Taormina. ☎ **0942/24-122.** Fax 0942/62-59-67. 25 rms, all with bath. A/C TV TEL. 140,000L–150,000L ($92.10–$98.70) doubles with bath. AE, MC, V.

The Fiorita always seems to be full of flowers, as the name suggests. It stretches up the hill from its entrance near the funicular stop in town almost all the way to the Greek theater. Very well appointed rooms are decorated with antique reproductions. Some rooms have terraces and sea views; others look out on the gardens. Stained-glass windows enliven the halls. Exposed rock from the cliffside, long corridors, and stairways give the building a castle feeling. Although there are many stairs inside, the steps are wide and graded; climbing them should not be a problem for most people (except the *portiere* who has to carry your bags). An interior garden shelters an ancient Greek tomb. A pretty breakfast room also serves snacks. The garden swimming pool on an upper level makes summer heat almost enjoyable.

WHERE TO DINE

Taormina is expensive, but there are a few places whose prices are in line with a budget, and groceries and pizzerias abound. **Mamma Mia,** V. Bagnoli Croce 57, has been satisfying American appetites for many years, and she has walls filled with photos and postcards from patrons to prove it. She'll make up sandwiches "that thick" with whatever you want and then send you to son **Roberto,** nearby at V. Cala Pitrulli 9, (☎ **0942/62-62-63**), for some delicious fresh nougat in a variety of flavors. There's also a supermarket at V. Apollo Arcajeta 49, at the Etna (west) end of Corso Umberto. The far ends of town (east and west) are where the less-expensive restaurants are located.

✪ **Il Ciclope.** Cor. Umberto. ☎ **0942/23-263.** Fax 0942/62-59-10. Reservations recommended. Main courses 8,000L–20,000L ($5.25–$13.15). AE, MC, V. Thurs–Tues 12:30–3pm and 7:30–10pm. Closed Jan 7–Feb 6. SICILIAN/MEDITERRANEAN.

An old, established trattoria presided over by Salvatore Sturiale, with a terrace on the main street and a very attractive dining room inside. Sicilians come from nearby cities to dine here, where good quality products are combined with inspired preparation. A selection of seafood antipasto is a good beginning. Here fettuccine with vongole veraci (those tiny, tasty clams) is prepared well and all kinds of swordfish, even carpaccio, and gnocchi with eggplant and basil should keep you happy. Try the cassata for dessert if it's on the menu. A version of this rich but light cake and almond cream confection was presnted to the noble table with fanfare in *The Leopard*, Lampedusa's brilliant book (later a movie) about Sicily on the eve of the revolution in 1870.

Trattoria da Nino. V. Pirandello 37. ☎ **0942/21-265.** Main courses 7,000L–14,000L ($5.90–$9.20). AE, MC, V. Daily 12–3:30 and 8:30–11pm. Closed Fri in winter. PIZZA.

Inexpensive and basic, Nino is a good modern place for a homemade pasta, especially with mushrooms or seafood sauce, or salad or a grilled chicken or veal dish. Tourists and young locals are apt to be there.

Trattoria La Botte Giara. Pz. Santa Domenica 4. ☎ **0942/24-198.** Main courses 8,000L–15,000L ($5.25–$9.85). MC, V. Daily 12–3:30 and 8–10:30. Closed Mon in low season. PIZZA/SICILIAN.

One of the town's nicest terraces is the plus here. A wood-fired pizza oven is another happy feature. Italian families often come for dinner. Antipasto table treats could make up a full meal, or their eggplant parmigiana pizza would do for a meal. Sicilian ceramics and flowers add color to the decor, and signed Italian celebrity photographs adorn the walls.

Trattoria U Lantimaru. V. Apollo Arcageta 14. ☎ **0942/24-565.** Main dishes 8,000L–12,000L ($5.25–$7.90). AE, MC, V. Wed–Mon 12:30–3pm and 7–11pm. Closed Sun night in low season. SICILIAN.

How this trattoria keeps to its old ways, one can only marvel at. It looks like a real osteria, about as plain as you'll find. It's spacious and serves hearty dishes; their roast chicken is very tasty. In warm weather, a few tables are placed outside, near the entrance to the Pensione Adele.

U Bossu. V. Bagnoli Croce 50. ☎ **0942/23-311.** Reservations suggested. Main courses 8,000L–16,000L ($5.25–$10.50). MC, V. Tues–Sun. 12:30–3pm and 7–10:30pm. SICILIAN.

Under new management, which happily means keeping the old tradition of good food at reasonable prices, U Bossu's one room is delightfully decorated with Sicilian folk art, including a scene from *Cavalleria Rusticana*. The main character of the opera, Turiddu, is also honored with a dish called *Casareccia al Turiddu,* with eggplant, olives, capers, tomatoes, and ricotta. Soups such as pasta e fagioli or lentil are excellent. The very fresh antipasto table and the Sicilian menu will keep U Bossu among the best in town. Their bruschetta (tomato on garlic toast) is peppery, so tell them you don't like spices if pepper is a problem. The crowd here is apt to be savvy about Sicilian food. Homemade cannoli for dessert are tiny and crisp.

WORTH A SPLURGE

Luraleo. V. Bagnoli Croce 31. ☎ **0942/24-279.** Reservations recommended. Main courses 15,000L–22,000 ($9.85–$14.50). AE, MC, V. Wed–Mon 12:30–3pm and 8–11pm. INTERNATIONAL.

A wide garden terrace with a vine-covered arbor or a country-style room within, with tiles and dark wood are your choices. Diners are often in love, or look that way in their Armani and Krizia silks. Grills of all sorts are brought sizzling to the table, from agnello (lamb) to vitello (veal), and an alphabet of fish as well.

A' Zammara. V. Fratelli Bandiera 15. ☎ **0942/24-408.** Fax 0942/24-08. Reservations required on weekends. Main courses 15,000L–28,000L ($9.85–18.45). AE, MC, V. Summer, daily 12:30–3pm and 8–11pm; Low-season: Thurs–Tues same hours. SICILIAN.

Another shaded terrace, perhaps the most intimate and romantic. You're apt to linger over coffee and try an after-dinner drink. Fish with or without pasta is the star, but the daily choices are varied. But if you haven't tried pasta con le sarde (with fresh sardines, wild fennel, and sultana raisins), this might be the time. If it's not on the menu, have the host choose a pasta dish for you. Evenings are apt to be crowded.

TAORMINA AFTER DARK

On the main street near the clock tower, **Caffe Wunderbar,** Pz. IX Aprile, mixes cool icy drinks in summer and warms up the rum for winter grog. It's the most comfortable bar east of England, with easy chairs to unwind in. In summer their wide outdoor terrace is merry and moves well over to the cliff-edge side of the street. Watch those mimosas. The lire add up quickly, so keep a clear head. A smarter bar is the **Mokambo,** also on the piazza. Armchairs and sofas make this teashop/ice-cream bar a treasure.

If you're looking for a disco try **Bella Blu** on Via Guardiola Vecchia, which has been going on forever, with a slightly older crowd. **Settimo,** San Pancrazio 50, is the younger crowd's disco of choice at the moment, with strobe lights and marble columns. You can also try **Tiffany Club,** V. San Pancrazio 5 (☎ 0942/62-54-30), or **Tout Va,** V. Pirandello 70 (☎ 0942/23-82). The latter tends to draw a local crowd, since a car is needed to get there; taxis are available, but inquire how late the taxi will be willing to pick you up for the return trip.

A bit more private is the **Bar Marrakesh,** which looks like a direct import from Morocco (down the stairs near the Duomo at Piazza Garibaldi). The gay spot is nearby, **Le Perroquet,** Piazza San Domenico (☎ 0942/24-462).

SIDE TRIPS FROM TAORMINA
A LUNCH EXCURSION TO CASTELMOLA

Three miles northwest of Taormina, Castelmola is a great place to go for lunch, and Il Faro is the favorite spot, where you'll be treated like the owners' family.

To reach the restaurant, follow the signs from Taormina up the mountainside (landslides in 1996 closed some of the roads, but most are now open) and take Via Rotabile Castelmola. The restaurant is beyond the town of Castelmola, continuing on the road to the right. (You might have your hotel call for exact directions from where you are, and the family will be on the lookout for you.) Or take the bus from the Taormina bus station (costing 5,000L/$3.30) to Castelmola, then walk along Rotabile Castelmola to the restaurant—you can call or have your hotel call Il Faro to have someone meet the bus from Taormina if possible. A taxi to Castelmola will cost 10,000L/$6.60.

✪ **Il Faro.** Contrada Petralia (V. Rotabile Castel Mola). ☎ **0942/28-91-93.** Reservations advised. Main courses 8,000L–20,000L ($5.25–$13.15) No credit cards. Thur–Tues 12:20–3pm and 7:30–10pm. Closed Wed.

All is homemade or home-grown by Piero and Francesca and you can watch it grow from the arbor terrace. Start with bruschetta al ortolana (garlic toast with their own olive oil and bits of tomato), then have homemade pasta and the fish, or meat (rabbit and game may be on the menu) if you prefer, followed by a homemade dessert. It's a place to celebrate. If you linger over a grappa or some of Castelmola's almond wine you can watch the cloud shadows pass over the steep valleys to the sea. Take your camera.

MT. ETNA

Mt. Etna (over 9,000 feet) is more beautiful from afar, but to climb its sides, some-times lonely as a moonscape, sometimes lush with fruit trees and grape vines, is some-thing you may want to do.

CIT Tours (Corso Umberto) runs trips to the top (twice a week in season) for about 65,000L ($42.75) per person. It's worth it if you don't have much time to spare. Otherwise, take the train to Giarre-Riposto south along the coast and connect with the Circumetnea train. Pack a lunch and water. Do not go anywhere near the top without checking with the guards—tourists have been killed by unexpected explosions.

MESSINA

On your way from or to the ferry to Calabria, or as a day trip from Taormina, be sure to stop at the **Regional Museum** to see more of the great Antonello da Messina's work (take bus 8, 27, or 28 from the train station). Have lunch (delicious *arancini* oranges) at famous **Pippo Nunnari,** V. Ugo Bassi 157 (☎ 090/29-38-584; closed Monday). The snack bar is inexpensive (no credit cards), but the adjoining restau-rant is pricey. But you should have pasta alla Norma (with eggplant), named for Bellini's opera, while you are in Sicily, and this is a good place.

Trains and buses leave Taormina frequently for Messina, a 40-minute trip. If there's time, take the hydrofoil across the Strait of Messina to Reggio di Calabria. The museum there has two wonderful Greek bronze warriors (*I Bronzi*) found in the sea by a fisherman.

THE AEOLIAN ISLANDS

GETTING THERE   The Aeolian islands of **Lipari, Stromboli,** and **Panarea** can be reached from Milazzo on the northeast coast of Sicily, where ferry and hydrofoil service is available. In summer the islands are booked to the shoreline, so plan ahead. There is much less frequent service in winter, and sometimes high seas make the islands inaccessible. Although the ferries (*traghetti*) are about half the price of the hydrofoil (*aliscafo*), the trip will be much longer. From Milazzo there are 14 hydro-foils daily to Lipari; the trip takes an hour and costs 16,500L ($10.85); to Panarea, the trip takes two hours and costs 42,800L ($28.15); and to Stromboli, 1 1/2 hours, the trip costs 45,600L ($30). By ferry it takes two hours to reach Lipari and costs 9,800L ($6.45); Panarea requires five hours and costs 23,500L ($15.45); and the trip to Stromboli takes seven hours and costs 34,000L ($22.35).

STAYING ON THE ISLANDS   Do not arrive at night on gorgeous Panarea or volcanic Stromboli as there are no street lights (the locals like it that way).

You might want to splurge in Stromboli at **La Sirenetta** (☎ 090/98-60-25). The hotel is air-conditioned, and has a swimming pool. A double with bath costs 140,000L to 260,000L ($92 to $171.05). To really get away from it all, **Mario lo Schivo** (☎ 090/98-12-880) has five well-recommended rooms on the far side of the island at Ginostra. A double with bath costs 50,000L ($32.90); no credit cards are accepted. The ferry and hydrofoil stop there, but check with Mario and again at the port before you leave.

On wealthy Panarea, **Da Francesco,** V. san Pietro (☎ 090/98-30-23), at the port, has doubles for 60,000L to 90,000L ($39.50 to $59). Lipari, the capital of the islands, has far more hotels, and many stores and cafes, but the island is less exotic. It has a Michelin star restaurant called ✪ **Filippino** (☎ 090/98-11-002), where you might expect to spend 50,000L ($32.90) for a fine meal, Sicilian-style.

Index

Savings are subject to certain restrictions and availability. Good for domestic and international travel that originates in the U.S. Valid for flights on most airlines worldwide.

Minimum Ticket Price	Save
$200.00	$25.00
$250.00	$50.00
$350.00	$75.00
$450.00	$100.00

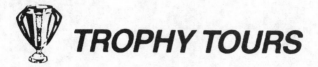

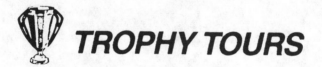